LAWRENCE OF ARABIA

WRITINGS BY JEREMY WILSON ON T. E. LAWRENCE

Lawrence of Arabia: The Authorized Biography of T. E. Lawrence
T. E. Lawrence: A Guide to Printed and Manuscript Materials

WORKS EDITED

T. E. Lawrence, *Wartime Letters and Diaries: A Companion to "Seven
Pillars of Wisdom"*
T. E. Lawrence, *Letters to E. T. Leeds*
T. E. Lawrence, *Minorities*

INTRODUCTIONS

T. E. Lawrence, *The Mint*
T. E. Lawrence, translator, *The Odyssey of Homer*
T. E. Lawrence, compiler, *Military Report on the Sinai Peninsula*

LAWRENCE
OF ARABIA

The Authorized Biography
of T. E. Lawrence

Jeremy Wilson

Atheneum

NEW YORK

1990

First published in Great Britain in 1989
by William Heinemann Ltd., London

Atheneum
Macmillan Publishing Company
866 Third Avenue, New York, NY 10022

Library of Congress Cataloging-in-Publication Data
Wilson, Jeremy.
Lawrence of Arabia : the authorized biography of T.E. Lawrence
/ Jeremy Wilson.
p.   cm.
Includes bibliographical references.
ISBN 0-689-11934-8
1. Lawrence, T.E. (Thomas Edward) 1888–1935.
2. Soldiers—Great Britain—Biography.   3. Great Britain.
Army—Biography.   4. World War, 1914–1918—Campaigns—
Middle East.   5. Middle East—History—20th
century.   I. Title.
D568.4.L45W55   1990
940.4′15′092—dc20
[B]   89-49008   CIP

Macmillan books are available at special discounts for bulk
purchases for sales promotions, premiums, fund-raising, or
educational use. For details, contact:

Special Sales Director
Macmillan Publishing Company
866 Third Avenue
New York, N.Y. 10022

10   9   8   7   6   5   4   3

PRINTED IN THE UNITED STATES OF AMERICA

To my wife Nicole
and our children
Peter, Emily, and Edward

Contents

List of Maps

Note

*Those who like to keep an appropriate map open while
reading will find that most of the places referred to in the
war chapters appear on the maps printed in editions of
Seven Pillars of Wisdom.*

Note on the Transcription of Quoted Material

Letters, reports, memoranda, and printed material

The wording of quoted text has been transcribed exactly as in the original except that the following conventions have been silently applied, in order to make quoted passages more readable.

In general, the original spelling and punctuation have been reproduced, but obvious errors such as unclosed parentheses have been corrected. In a few cases passages have been lightly re-punctuated in order to make their meaning clear at first reading.

Contractions which might be unfamiliar to general readers have usually been written out in full.

Ampersands have generally been transcribed as 'and'.

The use of capital letters has been brought into line with modern practice (e.g. 'north' rather than 'North'). This kind of capitalisation was often inconsistent, even within a single document, and it would have been a needless source of distraction to some readers.

The fully capitalised form used in military documents for place-names (e.g. DAMASCUS) has not been reproduced.

Numbers lower than 100 have been written as words except where numerals were required by the context. The same rule has been applied to most round numbers over 100.

The use of italics and quotation marks has been standardised throughout the text. For example, book titles which were originally underlined or placed in quotation marks have been printed in italics.

Lawrence frequently wrote rows of dots (typically between five and thirteen) as punctuation. He did this both in the middle of sentences and at the ends. The number of dots has been standardised: three are used... in the middle of sentences, and four at the end....

Telegrams

Cipher telegrams were used by the army and diplomatic service as a day-to-day method of communication. To reduce the time taken encoding, transmitting and decoding these messages, words which could be left out without ambiguity (typically 'the') were frequently omitted.

Anyone reading a large number of these telegrams becomes completely unaware of such omissions, since the missing words are unconsciously supplied. However, in a book addressed to general readers it seemed best to reinstate the missing words in the text. My object in doing so has been to prevent readers from being distracted by an irrelevant telegraphic practice, and this purpose would have been defeated by printing the inserted words within square brackets. These insertions are not, therefore, indicated. The references state clearly which documents are telegrams, and in every case give a source for the text as transmitted.

Arabic words and names

During Lawrence's lifetime it was usual to render Arabic words into English by approximate phonetic spellings. As a result there were widely varying forms. Lawrence deliberately reproduced this inconsistency in *Seven Pillars*, where he wrote: 'Arabic names are spelt anyhow, to prevent my appearing an adherent of one of the existing "systems of transliteration".'

Even today there is no universally accepted method of transliteration from Arabic to Roman script, and it would be difficult to justify altered spellings when quoting from *Seven Pillars* and contemporary documents. I have therefore left Arabic words and place-names as they stand.

I felt that to introduce modern academic spellings such as 'Hijaz' and 'Sharif' into my own text would only add further variants. Instead, I opted in each case for one of the versions used in the documents. In the same way, I have given personal names in one of the forms commonly used by British officials at the time, rather than the fuller form which would be technically correct.

Omissions and insertions

Omissions have been shown thus . . .

Words inserted in quoted text (other than those inferred in telegrams, see above) are printed within square brackets.

Sense and Nonsense
in the Biography of T. E. Lawrence

ROMANCE and enigma seem to have become an inseparable part of T. E. Lawrence's reputation. When I began research specifically for this book, in the mid-1970s, I was often told that my task was hopeless. At this distance in time no one could solve the biographical riddles.

This had indeed been the case as long as the official archives relating to Lawrence's military and political career remained under embargo, and biographers were denied access to essential material for the period between 1914 and 1922. While this was so, no final judgment of his role during the Arab Revolt was possible, and very little information at all was available concerning either his work in Cairo during 1915-16 or his involvement in British diplomacy after the war.

In 1968, however, the great majority of these Government papers suddenly became available. At any time thereafter, an authoritative reassessment of this much-debated figure should have been possible – but for various reasons none was forthcoming. Biographers dipped into the official archives in search of previously unpublished material, but none of them attempted a systematic investigation. One scholar did carry out a serious study of Lawrence's part in the Arab Revolt, but his book was published only in German, and has been ignored by British biographers.[1] Twenty years later, in Lawrence's centenary year, his reputation in the English-speaking world seemed little affected by the release of the archives. This was regrettable, since a proper assessment of his career was long overdue.

In the mind of the general public, both in Britain and abroad, he remains one of the most famous Englishmen of his generation. Yet ever since the 1950s, doubts have been expressed about his real achievement, and some writers have challenged the whole basis of his reputation. In 1962 the popular image of Lawrence was radically changed by David Lean's film *Lawrence of Arabia*, and the process has since been continued by a number of sensational biographies. Many of these have been highly speculative, yet subsequent writers have treated unproven suggestion as historical fact, and added further speculation of their own. In this way layer upon layer of invention has accumulated, leaving a grotesque impression of Lawrence's career. Its outline (with variants) runs something like this:

> Illegitimate son of a religious maniac mother who dominates her children by flogging them – is taken up in early childhood by an unscrupulous 'mentor', D. G. Hogarth, and indoctrinated with imperialist views – is sent to Carchemish for training as a spy while pretending to be an archaeologist – goes to Cairo at the outbreak of war as a spy-master – gets involved in the Arab Revolt – is motivated by virulent imperialist (or perhaps pro-Arab, or pro-Zionist) feelings – is sodomised at Deraa (or invents the whole story) – is carried away by blood-lust at Tafas – is involved in treacherous diplomacy at the Peace Conference and under Churchill at the Colonial Office, during which he deceives everyone (or perhaps is manipulated by everyone) – enlists to get away from it all – indulges in masochistic floggings – has debatable sexual inclinations – seeks a substitute mother in Mrs Bernard Shaw – and is finally murdered by the secret service for reasons that can only be hinted at.

The errors of fact and interpretation in these accounts ought to have been plain to anyone familiar with the source materials available in print; but apart from a handful of protests by specialist reviewers, the sensational fictions have rarely been challenged. It seems that ordinary human scepticism has been numbed by the sheer quantity of bizarre claims. The public no longer knows what should be believed and what should be denied and, as a result, many serious-minded people have come to regard the subject of T. E. Lawrence with caution, if not distaste.

Such a state of affairs might be tolerable if Lawrence had accomplished nothing and if his career had lacked any lasting historical significance. But despite his detractors' claims, this is not the case: even at their irreducible minimum, Lawrence's achievements cannot lightly be dismissed. His most severe critics have to admit that he played a role of some importance while serving as a British liaison officer during the Arab Revolt. After the war, fellow-officers who had seen his work at first-hand said that his contribution had been outstanding. Although some of these witnesses may have exaggerated, others were men of high integrity. Their testimony cannot be entirely groundless. He was also involved in diplomatic negotiations which reshaped the Middle East, first during the war itself, then at the Paris Peace Conference, and finally while working in the Colonial Office. There is ample evidence that he played an influential role, particularly in the Cairo Conference settlement of March 1921.

Next, his literary achievement: Lawrence had hoped since childhood to become a writer, and according to his own statements this remained his strongest ambition. Three of his works have been very successful. *Seven Pillars of Wisdom* has sold more than a million copies and has been widely translated. The continuing popularity of this long and relatively expensive book about a First World War campaign is surely remarkable. Barrack-room life in the RAF, the subject matter of his second book, *The Mint*, might seem to have still less appeal. Yet this work too has been translated into several languages, and since 1978 it has been reprinted regularly in *Penguin Modern Classics*. Lawrence's translation of the *Odyssey* has also earned a place in English literature, as one of the most successful renderings addressed to the general public. It has run through many editions, and is still available in bookshops after more than fifty years. Finally, Lawrence was a prolific letter-writer, and editions of his correspondence have been widely read.

Even on this minimal reckoning, Lawrence's military, diplomatic and literary achievements merit biographical investigation. But his life is interesting for another reason as well. He knew and corresponded with many of the leading figures of his time. These included archaeologists such as D. G. Hogarth and Leonard Woolley; military leaders such as Allenby, Trenchard and Wavell; diplomats and politicians such as Nancy Astor, Gertrude Bell, Churchill, Curzon, and Lloyd George; and writers such as Buchan, Conrad, Doughty, Flecker, Forster, Graves, Hardy, Sassoon, and Shaw, to name only a selection. Then there were friends in the world of art: Eric Kennington, Augustus John, Paul Nash, William Roberts, and William Rothenstein; the architect Sir Herbert Baker, and H. S. Ede of the Tate Gallery. As long as historians are interested in figures such as these, they will also seek information about Lawrence.

One reason for this curiosity will be that Lawrence's personality and career provoked extreme reactions among his contemporaries, often of passionate loyalty, occasionally of bitter antagonism. Few were able to write about him without revealing something of their own values and prejudices. Yet it is impossible to make sense of these attitudes while the truth about Lawrence is obscured by sensational claim and counter-claim.

In the future, the 'Lawrence of Arabia' legend will itself interest social historians. Public enthusiasm for media idols is usually short-lived, but in Lawrence's case it has endured for more than sixty-five years. Instead of fading, the legend has evolved, keeping pace with changing popular interests. In 1919, Lowell Thomas gave Britain a romantic military hero unsullied by the horrors of the Western Front. Afterwards, when Lawrence wrote *Seven Pillars*, he was thought to exemplify the 'intellectual man of action'. During the Second World War his reputation as a leader again came to the fore, and *Seven Pillars* was included in the standard library issued to British fighting units. By the 1950s, the intense patriotism of the war period was fading, and attacks on conventional values became commonplace (Lord Altrincham, for example, made social history by daring to criticise the Queen's speeches). Predictably, the accumulated Lawrence legend came under attack. Then, in the early 1960s, Lawrence became fair game for amateur psychologists, and when the 'permissive society' focused public attention on private lives there was a glut of salacious allegations. During the 1970s and 1980s the vogue has been for espionage, and it has been claimed that Lawrence became a clandestine 'intelligence operative' before the First World War.

The development of this Lawrence legend shows how a popular topic can take on a life of its own as a result of continuing exposure. Successive accounts alter, as writers vie with one another to say something new. In this process, however, stories are not necessarily improved. It is not just the truth which suffers: often the ingredients which originally made an event worth reporting are sacrificed as well. The improbable figure presented in some recent biographies lacks almost all the qualities that made Lawrence fascinating to his contemporaries.

In reality, his biography has no need of such embellishments. His experiences in the Arab Revolt contained an extraordinary degree of drama: as he said himself, the story he had to tell in *Seven Pillars* was 'one of the most splendid ever given a man for writing.'[2] The renunciations of his later career are hardly less intriguing. In Churchill's words: 'The world looks with some awe upon a man who appears unconcernedly indifferent to home, money, comfort, rank, or even power and fame. The world feels not without a certain apprehension, that here is some one outside its jurisdiction; some one before whom its allurements may be spread in vain; some one strangely enfranchised, untamed, untrammelled by convention, moving independently of the ordinary currents of human action'.[3]

The sensational treatment of Lawrence's life, however entertaining, has helped to conceal his true development and motivation. For example, writers seeking an excuse to dwell on his maltreatment by the Turks at Deraa in November 1917 have suggested that this experience was responsible for the profound depression he felt during the later stages of the war. It would have been more rewarding to admit that this depression was evident several months *before* the Deraa incident. By placing such emphasis on the events at Deraa, even at the expense of chronology, these writers have been led to discount early evidence of the central dilemma in his wartime career.

Likewise, the claim that Lawrence began working for British Intelligence at Carchemish before the First World War provided biographers with a dramatic new angle on the early years of his adult life. It also supplied an explanation, *deus ex machina*, for his elevation by October 1916 to an influential position in the Cairo Intelligence Department. The result, however, is that attention has been distracted both from his achievements as an archaeologist at Carchemish and from the merit of two years' hard work in Cairo Intelligence during 1915 and 1916. Thus a single biographical fiction makes a nonsense of Lawrence's development during six important years.

No serious historical study of Lawrence could have been attempted before the embargo on Government papers began to expire. The idea of taking on the official biography was first put to me by a publisher three years later, in 1971. Having already edited Lawrence's commonplace-book *Minorities*, I could foresee the time and very costly research that would be needed. For this reason, I turned the proposal down. During the next three years, however, no other strongly qualified biographer came forward, and finally, in the autumn of 1974, I decided to accept the commission.[4]

This dearth of candidates illustrates another of the central problems in tackling Lawrence's life. As he warned Robert Graves in 1927, 'I'm rather a complicated person, and that's bad for a simple biography.'[5] Obvious among these complications is the sheer diversity of his career. Normally a figure of such stature would be subject to exhaustive study in university departments, but Lawrence's life was too varied to fit in neatly with modern academic demarcations. As a result, no faculty is really interested in more than a small fraction of his life. Holders of university posts are obliged to work mainly in their own fields, and are naturally unwilling to trespass widely into other academic provinces. Thus while individual scholars may be expert in one aspect of Lawrence's career, they are likely to know little about large parts of his life. A specialist in medieval military architecture would not normally want to pass judgment on twentieth-century diplomatic history. Likewise, there are few archaeologists with knowledge of the Hittite period who could write with any proficiency about the development of high-speed motorboats. How many guerilla leaders have successfully translated the *Odyssey*, or set up a private printing press? The diversity of Lawrence's activities and interests has prevented anything but piecemeal academic research. It has also presented a special challenge to his official biographer: the need to meet high standards of historical scholarship in many different fields.

While this problem has discouraged academic attention, it cannot, on its own, account for the wary attitude towards Lawrence found in British universities. The situation abroad is different: major historical theses have been published in France and Germany, and there have been several American studies of Lawrence's writing.[6] Caution about him in Britain seems to stem from two causes. First, all scholars prefer to deal with evidence and reasoning, while the Lawrence literature in this country has been saturated with myth and enigma. The view elsewhere has been more sober.[7] Secondly, attacks on his integrity have raised far stronger passions in Britain than abroad. British scholars, bombarded by allegations that he was a dishonest eccentric, cannot be blamed for choosing some other subject for research.

Much of this hostility towards Lawrence is rooted in aspects of British culture and history. At different times, his reputation has been savagely attacked by well-defined interest groups in Britain. The first of these to speak out was one associated with the Anglo-Indian administration in Mesopotamia. In 1921, Churchill adopted Lawrence's policy for this region and swept away years of painstaking effort by ambitious imperialists. Lawrence's responsibility for this public humiliation was never forgiven. As a result, thousands of Englishmen regarded him with a deep antagonism (passed down, in some families, to the present generation).

Lawrence also offended a second group. At a time when society was far more rigid than it is today, he rejected his 'proper' place in the social order and chose to enlist. Military rank was then a potent sign of social status, and after the First World War a great many ex-officers continued to use their military titles in civilian life. They were bitterly angry when it was revealed that the famous Colonel Lawrence had joined the ranks of the RAF as A/c Ross. His action seemed to undermine the respect which they considered due to the officer class. The depth of feeling on this issue is difficult to understand today, and has surprised me more than once when talking about Lawrence to people of that generation. Naturally, those who felt threatened by his unconventional attitude took action to defend themselves: in no time, uncomplimentary gossip began to circulate about his social eccentricity. The stories usually included some incident in which, while attempting to be 'clever,' he had behaved with appalling rudeness. I have never been able to substantiate any of these tales: no one seems actually to have witnessed an incident of this kind. Yet the gossip is often repeated, sometimes by biographers who do not realise that its original purpose was derogatory. There is a flagrant example in Henry Williamson's book *Genius of Friendship*,[8] describing how Lawrence had snubbed a social-climbing hostess. The story is told as though Williamson had heard it from the victim. Years later, when I asked him for his source, he admitted that it had come from an Air Force officer who did not like Lawrence.

More recently, there has been vociferous criticism of Lawrence from British pressure groups associated with the Middle East. Although his true role has been little understood, he clearly occupied a position of some influence in Britain's policy towards the Arabs between 1914 and 1922. This episode in British diplomacy has proved to be extremely contentious, and Lawrence's reputation has been attacked virulently by some pro-Arab and some pro-Zionist writers. In many cases, polemicists have used his name simply to attract attention to their views about much wider issues. As the debate is directly related to the modern conflict over Palestine, there has been far too little disinterested scholarship. Historical interpretations are sharply divided, and Lawrence's biographers have been faced with opposing and incompatible statements by writers whose expertise in these questions is widely acknowledged. In order to resolve this problem I was obliged to go back to the contemporary documents. In the process, a fresh view has emerged, not only of Lawrence, but of the events themselves.

Much of the controversy about Lawrence in Britain can be traced to these differing viewpoints, and it is essential to be aware of them. In almost every case the hostility stems from an emotional allegiance rather than research and analysis. As a result the criticism has often taken the form of abuse or innuendo instead of reasoned argument.

It has also been claimed that veterans of the Western Front felt slighted by the blaze of publicity given to Lawrence (and to Allenby's Palestine campaigns). Individuals may have had such feelings, but the records suggest no general resentment: the fault clearly lay with the publicists and not with those who had fought in the Middle East. A grudge of this kind may nevertheless have prompted Richard Aldington's vehement attack on the popular Lawrence legend. Aldington was a passionately embittered writer who had suffered deeply as a result of war service on the Western Front. By the 1950s he was living abroad, in self-imposed exile, and he had come to see Lawrence as the hero of a decadent society which he detested. He seems to have believed that if he could destroy Lawrence's reputation, this would in some way deeply wound the British establishment.[9]

In his researches, Aldington compared statements made by Lawrence at different times and to different people with those made by three contemporary biographers. He found many discrepancies between these sources, and presented the variants as evidence that Lawrence had told vainglorious lies. The obvious flaw in this argument was the assumption that Lawrence, rather than his three biographers, was responsible for the anomalies. This was extremely naïve. The earliest biographer, Lowell Thomas, was a popular journalist whose work brimmed over with romantic exaggerations. Lawrence was able to influence the text very little, but thought he could safely assume that intelligent readers would recognise it for what it was; his policy was therefore to refrain from comment. The second biographer, Robert Graves, was a poet and novelist whose book was written very hurriedly under pressure from his publishers. Although Lawrence saw the draft, he warned Graves that he had not had the time to correct all the mistakes. Only the third biographer, Liddell Hart, made any attempt at a scholarly treatment, and it was his project which received the greatest help from Lawrence. Given the differing qualities and aims of these authors, it would be amazing if their accounts agreed in every detail.

Conflicting evidence, as Aldington must have known, is a common problem for historians. Even after a short time-span, remembered versions of an incident hardly ever correspond exactly. Moreover, retrospective accounts are often coloured by self-justification and by wisdom after the event. Material gathered from autobiographies or interviews rarely turns out to be wholly consistent with contemporary sources.[10]

In Lawrence's case, special factors have helped to generate conflicting evidence. First, those who knew him were inevitably exposed to the popular legend; many found it impossible to distinguish this from their own recollections. Interviews and published reminiscences often contain inaccuracies which are difficult to explain in any other way.

Secondly, Lawrence's career brought him into contact with people from all ranks of society. To the public at large, the only remarkable thing about some of his acquaintances was the fact that they had known him. Most of his close friends, particularly those in the RAF and Tank Corps, refused to capitalise on this public interest; but there were a few who traded on it and fabricated incidents and anecdotes to bolster their apparent importance in his life.

Thirdly, even greater distortions occur when people are encouraged to recall something 'new' about Lawrence. No interviewee likes to be found wanting, and wholesale fiction is amazingly common. Sometimes, the details have been very ingeniously worked out to tie in with known events. Fortunately, however, these yarn-spinners have rarely had access to Lawrence's vast unpublished correspondence. While their statements may tally with readily available sources, lesser-known material will usually expose enough invention to cast doubt on everything they have said.

It is curious that while such people will take immense care over a central fiction, they often give themselves away in minor details. This is the case with the much-publicised reminiscences of John Bruce. In pursuit of cash rewards for his story, Bruce embroidered it considerably. Thus in 1938 he sold an article to the *Scottish Field* [11] in which he claimed to have been in India on spying expeditions with Lawrence, who dressed like a native and spoke the local language. The story was a complete falsehood, but Bruce thought it safe because ten years earlier there had been press reports that Lawrence was spying in India. As Bruce had not actually been in India with Lawrence, he had no idea that the press rumours were untrue. He said many other things about his relationship with Lawrence, and could have been an important biographical witness. As it is, however, his testimony can be faulted on so many points that every uncorroborated statement must be regarded with extreme caution.

Bruce's Indian spy 'revelations' also demonstrate how a popular myth can inspire what appears to be substantiating evidence. If there were no reliable contemporary documents to show that the 1928 press stories were false, Bruce's account might be accepted as proof that they were true.

Lastly, accounts of Lawrence's life have often been distorted in order to fit a preconceived theory (for instance that he exemplified some archetype such as the 'romantic hero who rejected worldly rewards').

These oversimplified interpretations rarely stand up to close examination, and usually obscure more than they illuminate.

I have tried very hard to avoid such pitfalls. The surest way to do so was to base my account of Lawrence's career on contemporary documents, using later statements only when they were consistent with these sources. Fortunately, an enormous amount of contemporary evidence has survived, relating to every stage in his life. The documents now available in public and private archives fully justify the claim made some years ago by Paul Adam, one of several French intellectuals who have written on Lawrence: 'By a paradox which is not without logic, the very mystery of Lawrence's case has provoked both research and testimony. As a result we know far more about him than we do about people who were never thought to be mysterious.'[12]

The extent of this source material is so great that it is impossible to include a satisfactory account of it in this book. I have therefore compiled a separate annotated reference work: *T. E. Lawrence: a Guide to Printed and Manuscript Materials*.[13]

The first object of my research was to collect as much of this contemporary information as possible. I soon found that it was better to copy entire documents than to work from notes. Very often a statement which seemed insignificant on its own turned out to be important when set alongside other material from the same period. Relevant documents are scattered throughout the world and, unless transcripts are brought together in one place, all but the most obvious interrelated statements will be overlooked. Even where a single institution holds many documents, it can be impossible to examine them in the proper sequence. For example, there is a great deal of transcribed correspondence among the T. E. Lawrence papers at the Bodleian Library, but the letters to each recipient are grouped separately and bound in a series of alphabetical volumes. Library rules and practical considerations make it impossible to use all these volumes at once, yet that would be the only way to read the letters in chronological order.

This is a minor problem compared with the situation at the Public Record Office, where information is scattered through countless files. It can be extremely difficult to locate specific documents in the maze of departmental records. Thousands of hours were spent working through these official papers; the time involved probably explains why biographers have hitherto made so little use of this material.

The task of gathering photocopies and transcripts of contemporary documents continued during ten years. At the core of the chronological archive thus formed was Lawrence's own correspondence. He once wrote: 'of course somebody will want to write a life of me some day, and his only source will be such letters as chance has preserved. Had they been all kept, there would be a pretty complete history of events since 1910: volumes of stuff enough to discourage any historian: but chance will narrow his pile down.'[14] Lawrence was wrong in thinking that his letters would be discarded. At that time many people retained correspondence as a matter of course, and in his case the letters had a financial value. Comparing his address book with groups of surviving letters, it seems unlikely that much has been lost. More than four thousand letters, telegrams, official memoranda, and minutes written by Lawrence, and about twelve hundred letters and telegrams addressed to him, are now preserved in libraries or private collections. I was able to copy the vast majority of these documents, thanks to their owners and to a request for such co-operation made on my behalf by Lawrence's youngest brother and literary executor, A. W. Lawrence.

Copies of many other relevant documents have been added to the archive, especially for the war and diplomatic periods. This material was essential if Lawrence's contribution was to be seen in its proper context. I particularly wanted to discover contemporary opinions about him exchanged between third parties who were in a position to judge his work.

By the time the biography had been completed, the archive formed a sequence of day-to-day records running to about four million words (more than twelve times the length of the book). Some of the material it contains had not been available to other biographers; a great deal more, though available, seems not to have been consulted. While many of the documents were individually informative, the most valuable conclusions often came through juxtaposition. Even the most familiar letters have taken on a new significance when put alongside other material from the same period. For example, the letters Bernard Shaw wrote to Lawrence during the winter of 1922-3 are well known and often admiringly quoted. However, when read in sequence with other documents in the archive, their advice appears to be very ill-considered, and Shaw's motives seem questionable. His irresponsible counsel was to have a far-reaching effect on Lawrence's life.

The archive records in minute detail Lawrence's military activities, diplomatic negotiations, service work, and writing. This incontestable

primary evidence made it possible to write the biography with little
recourse to later reminiscences. One important result is that the account
of his role in the Arab Revolt no longer relies on *Seven Pillars*. I have
quoted contemporary documents in preference to Lawrence's book, even
though that has proved to be remarkably accurate on questions of fact. In
some instances, however, passages from *Seven Pillars* have been included
because they have assumed a new significance in the light of
contemporary materials. I have also quoted Lawrence's explanations of
his own thinking and, less frequently, descriptions which help to convey
the atmosphere of the Revolt.

Research established the factual record, but the content, approach, and
style of this biography remained to be decided when I began writing in
the autumn of 1986.

The term 'biography' covers two very different types of work, both
equally legitimate. The first seeks primarily to give a factual narrative,
together with the most objective account possible of the subject's
personality and opinions. One might call this 'historical biography'. The
second type also includes a biographical narrative, but makes this the
basis for subjective interpretation. The very *raison d'être* of such works
lies in the author's analysis and value judgments, and it is this subjective
content, rather than the historical record, which gives these studies their
novelty and interest. One might call them 'critical biographies'.

A critical biography written with intelligence and perception can be
extremely rewarding. I myself have enjoyed the studies of Lawrence by
Paul Adam, André Malraux and Victoria Ocampo.[15] It has to be said,
however, that the knowledge, calibre and diligence of a critical biographer are all-important. In my judgment, the great majority of Lawrence
biographies belonging to this genre are of mediocre quality.

In many cases their argument is invalid because of factual errors or
premature conclusions. For example, it is often claimed that because
Lawrence posed for so many portraits, he must have been exceedingly
vain. Deeper investigation does not support this conclusion. There is no
record that Lawrence ever actually asked anyone to paint his portrait or to
photograph him, and in the overwhelming majority of cases there is
positive evidence that the request came from the artist or photographer.[16]
On reflection, this does not seem very surprising, since portraits of
Lawrence were extremely saleable. However, this entirely changes the
inference that can be drawn from the number of portraits. The biographer

must now ask whether or not it was reasonable for Lawrence to agree to be painted, free of charge, by some of the most talented artists of the day. The answer is so obvious that the question is not even interesting: indeed, the position would only have been intriguing if Lawrence had refused.

In other cases, critical biographers have presented highly tendentious interpretations of Lawrence's life without any supporting analysis whatsoever. This is impossible to justify, but it seems that the controversy over his career has left the truth in so much doubt that writers have felt free to indulge in pure speculation. In a similar fashion, psychological comment has been flawed by dramatic and grossly over-simplified statements about motivation, ignoring the elementary principle that human decisions are almost always influenced by a complex range of factors. Moreover, few of these 'critical' studies display any depth of research. At best, the results have been misleading because they focus too narrowly on Lawrence's life with disregard for the historical context; at worst, these authors have ignored, distorted, or suppressed large parts of the evidence in order to give their preconceived theories an illusion of credibility.

One difficulty with such books is that the abuse of evidence is rarely obvious except to someone with a detailed and comprehensive knowledge of the subject. A biography which is readable and superficially plausible may, unknown to the critic, be more a work of fiction than a historical study. Worthless and untenable theories, like some of those put forward in *T. E. Lawrence* by Desmond Stewart,[17] have often been praised by non-specialist reviewers.

Although I know that many people would have preferred my own biography to be an 'interpretation', there was an overwhelming case for a carefully researched historical study, and that is the approach I decided to take. As a general principle, I have restricted critical judgments to straightforward issues where the comment is unquestionably valid. For example, in April 1929, Lawrence made a great fuss about newspaper revelations that he was anonymously translating the *Odyssey*. His astonished indignation was clearly absurd, since for several months previously he himself had been telling friends and acquaintances about his work on this project.

There were several instances, however, in which I thought it necessary to state my personal conclusions even though the issues were much more complex. Where the subject (e.g. Lawrence's sexuality) was of great biographical significance, the discussion has been placed in the main text. In less important cases (e.g. Lawrence's reaction to RAF discipline) my own conclusions have been placed in the endnotes. I have used these notes extensively to deal with matters that are not central to the narrative.

A biography such as this must not merely be accurate; it must be seen to be accurate. At the end of my research I could have written a narrative of Lawrence's life in which my conclusions were expressed entirely in my own words. This, however, would have required the reader to place total trust in my reliability, and it would have been only too easy for future writers to challenge my account in order to suggest alternatives. I have therefore adopted the principles set out in Winston Churchill's biography of his father. In the introduction he wrote: 'The style and ideas of the writer must throughout be subordinated to the necessity of embracing in the text those documentary proofs upon which the story depends. Letters, memoranda, and extracts from speeches, which inevitably and rightly interrupt the sequence of his narrative, must be pieced together upon some consistent and harmonious plan. It is not by the soft touches of a picture, but in hard mosaic or tessellated pavement, that a man's life and fortunes must be presented in all their reality and romance. I have thought it my duty, so far as possible, to assemble once and for all the whole body of historical evidence required for the understanding of Lord Randolph Churchill's career . . . Scarcely any statement of importance lacks documentary proof'.[18]

I too have used extensive quotation, and the essential points can be seen to rest everywhere on contemporary evidence rather than on some theory of my own. Individual extracts were chosen for a number of different reasons. The first was to give authority to the factual record: in many important instances the truth about events was not clear from evidence commonly available, and this had led some biographers to false conclusions. I thought it necessary to set out the new information which lay behind my own deductions. Secondly, I used quotation to illustrate Lawrence's values, aims, motivation and critical judgment, and to show how he was assessed by his contemporaries. Lastly, there can be more subtle benefits in the use of quotation. Those who have never carried out research in historical archives can have little idea of the human interest to be found in letters, telegrams, and notes written down while the events were still unfolding. There is often a fascinating interplay of personalities, and the documents can be alive with ambition and jealousy, generosity and humour. It is virtually impossible to retain these qualities in paraphrase: however brilliant the historian, accounts which summarise the documents almost invariably make duller reading than the documents themselves. In many cases, therefore, I have used quotation simply to preserve the drama that was so vividly present in the source materials; and also on occasion to illustrate attitudes which are very distant from those held today. Examples are the messages which passed back and forth during the siege at Kut, and the kind of statements made by the French and Anglo-Indian imperialists.

Most of the passages quoted contain a narrative element, but they have not been selected for that reason. I have in no sense attempted to 'tell Lawrence's story in his own words.'

In a work which had to deal with complex historical events, studious attention to chronology was essential. But there are at least three circum-stances in which non-chronological presentation can seem useful in a biography. First, it is often necessary to explain the background to some new field of the subject's activity. In such cases historical recapitulation is usually unavoidable. Secondly, events which form part of the story may have occurred simultaneously in different places. A rigorously chrono-logical treatment, even if possible, would be very confusing, but it is important not to let the time-sequence get too far out of phase. Related to this is a third problem: it can be difficult to keep track of the subject's involvement in different spheres of activity over a long period. The temptation is to describe these independently – in Lawrence's case, for example, dealing separately with his service life and his work on the subscribers' edition of *Seven Pillars*. It is without question easier to give the reader a clear understanding of individual topics in this way; but the logical outcome of such a treatment would be a series of essays, not a biography. Even where spheres of activity seem completely unconnected, they are related, from a biographer's point of view, because the subject divided his time between them and they had a simultaneous influence on his life. The danger of non-chronological treatment in such cases is that influences which cross over from one sphere into another are overlooked. How many biographers, for example, have realised that Lawrence's state of depression while serving in the Tank Corps during the summer of 1925 corresponds exactly with a period of anxiety arising from financial and technical difficulties in the production of *Seven Pillars*?

Incomplete treatment can be equally damaging. Lawrence's develop-ment has rarely been very clear in biographies. Many have concentrated almost entirely on the Arab Revolt, saying little to explain how this man came to find himself in Arabia in October 1916, endowed with a most unusual combination of personality and accomplishments. Others have focused on certain topics and periods without providing an adequate linking account. This means that there is little sense of continuity: Lawrence's moods and ambitions seem to change abruptly and without explanation. The source materials, unlike these biographies, show his career to have been a sequence of natural and considered steps. I have tried to bring out this continuity while treating each period in a manner which reflects its historical and biographical interest.

Another aim has been to place Lawrence's public career in its political and military setting. His activities during and after the First World War formed part of important, complex, and much-debated historical events. In many instances it is impossible to understand his motivation and achievements without a knowledge of their wider context, and I have therefore included much background information. Priority has been given to material which sheds light on Lawrence's career. Thus I have given far more space to the McMahon-Hussein and Sykes-Picot negotiations of 1915-16 than to the post-war conferences in Paris and in Cairo, even though Lawrence was more deeply involved in the latter than in the former. The reason is that the earlier negotiations set up a framework of diplomatic commitments which deeply influenced his decisions for several years. By contrast, it is not necessary to know about the post-war conferences in great detail in order to understand their effect on his life. To cite another example, his observations in Mesopotamia in 1916 influenced his later thinking on several issues, notably on the merits of the Anglo-Indian administration there. For this reason I have given space to the 1916 mission, even though it had no great importance in the short term.

The style of the book had to be appropriate to its aims. The emphasis in a historical (as opposed to a critical) biography should be on the story, rather than on the manner in which it is told. In 1928, commenting on D. G. Hogarth's *Life of Charles M. Doughty*, Lawrence wrote: 'Hogarth's style is that perfection of English – an invisible garment for his ideas. It would be the despair and ambition of everyone who had anything to say, if they were wise. Do you see, how there isn't a "fine line" in the book? If I had done it there would have been many: and people would have liked them: and it would have done Doughty wrong.'[19] A conspicuous prose style would also be a handicap in a work which seeks to blend extracts from documents by many different hands into a readable narrative.

A further cause of distraction can be the excessive use of endnote references. It was necessary to give sources for quoted material, and in order to reduce the number of notes I have tried, where possible, to attach any comment to the same references. It would be impractical to give a source for every statement of incidental fact, and for the benefit of future researchers I intend to put a marked-up copy of the text with the T. E. Lawrence papers in the Bodleian Library.

Finally, I would like to say something about the status of an 'official biographer'. The expression is commonly used in publishing circles, but to me it has the aura of an 'official version', inspired and possibly censored by the subject's loving relatives. I greatly prefer the term 'authorised biography', which, for me at least, lacks this unfortunate connotation.

I would not have accepted the role of Lawrence's official biographer if there had been any hint of future censorship, and A. W. Lawrence, as literary executor, insisted from the outset that I should publish whatever conclusions I reached. We agreed that it would be best if my work was totally independent, and I avoided troubling him with questions about his brother's life except as a last resort when the information seemed unavailable elsewhere. When the book was in draft I sent parts of it for comment to several well-qualified critics. I was glad when he agreed to read the chapters describing Lawrence's childhood and work as an archaeologist, and I was grateful for the notes that he and other readers sent me. But the responsibility for the content of this biography is mine and mine alone.

Part I

Archaeology and Travel

1888-1914

As a boy T.E. always thought he was going to do great things, both 'active and reflective' – 'I hadn't learnt you can't do both' – and determined to achieve both.

Note by B. H. Liddell Hart on a conversation with Lawrence, 1st August 1933

*Thomas Edward Lawrence, known to his family as
'Ned', was born in the early hours of 16th August
1888 at a house rented by his parents on the outskirts of Tremadoc in Caernarvonshire. He would
remember nothing of this Welsh birthplace
since the family moved north to Kirkcudbright in
Scotland when he was only thirteen months old. A
brother, Montagu Robert ('Bob'), was three years
older than Ned. Another boy, William George, was
born soon after the family had settled in Scotland.*

*Before Ned was three years old the house in
Kirkcudbright was put up for sale by its owners
and the Lawrences had to move again. After a brief
stay in the Isle of Man they travelled to Jersey
and set about finding a new home on the nearby
coast of Brittany. In December 1891 they rented
a secluded house called the Chalet du Vallon in
Dinard. It was here that T. E. Lawrence first began
to explore the world outside his home.*

CHAPTER 1

Childhood

December 1891 – October 1907

DURING the closing decades of the nineteenth century Dinard grew from
a small fishing village to a substantial town. The 1894 *Baedeker* described
it as 'a modern village, picturesquely situated on a rocky promontory on
the left bank of the estuary of the Rance, opposite St. Malo and St. Servan.
It has two beaches, with sea-baths, the chief of which, with the Casino, is
on the small bay nearest the sea . . . The neighbouring heights, sprinkled
with villas, command a pleasing view of the bay of St. Malo, with its islets
and reefs . . . Dinard is a more agreeable residence than St. Malo, as it
offers various sheltered promenades.'[1]

At that time British travellers found the cost of living in France very
low, and many English people settled in Brittany where they could live
comfortably on a modest income. By the 1890s there were several large
British communities near St Malo, for example at Dinan ten miles up the
Rance and at St Servan. The school in Dinan had accepted English pupils
since 1820 and published an English-language prospectus.

Dinard, however, had grown primarily as a fashionable resort, popular
with wealthy visitors who spent the summer in its villas and first-class
hotels. Only a few British families lived there all the year round, but those
who did had no need to learn French, since English was generally understood by the local tradespeople.

The Chalet du Vallon was a comfortable house built in 1885. Although
near to the town centre, it stood in a secluded garden approached by a
long walled path. There were few immediate neighbours, but a school,
the Ecole Sainte-Marie, was conveniently close. The Lawrence family
seemed to prefer this seclusion to the social life of Dinard. Although the
mother, Sarah Lawrence, rarely left the house, neighbours found her a
pleasant acquaintance. The father, Thomas Lawrence, was more often to
be seen. He was a quiet, reserved man who enjoyed walking and cycling,
and probably sailing too, since Lawrence later recalled that 'my father had
yachts and used to take me with him from my fourth year'.[2] Children of
English and French families in Dinard mixed freely together and were

welcomed in each others' homes. The daughter of a neighbouring English family, the Herberts, often played with the Lawrence brothers. The Lawrences met one French family, their landlords the Chaignons, very frequently. Here a lasting friendship gradually developed, which would later prove valuable to the English boys.

Ned and Bob Lawrence had an English governess who gave them elementary schooling, which was taken very seriously in the household. These lessons were supplemented when Lawrence was five by an hour's schooling each morning at the Ecole Sainte-Marie. Physical education was also considered important, and Lawrence with three other English boys took the steam ferry twice a week across the Rance to St Malo where they attended a private gymnastics class.

At the end of the nineteenth century St Malo was still an ancient fortified town (much of it had to be rebuilt after the Second World War). Lawrence can scarcely have forgotten the view from Dinard of its imposing ramparts – defences which had successfully resisted an assault by Marlborough's army. Its narrow streets and ancient buildings had changed little since the time when it had been a flourishing port, the home of Jacques Cartier and of the famous *corsaire* Surcouf. Memories of this fairy-tale stronghold may well have kindled his later interest in history and military architecture.

When Mrs Lawrence was expecting a fourth child, in 1893, the family travelled to Jersey for the birth. There was concern that a son born in Dinard might eventually be called up for French military service. The child was a boy and was christened Frank Helier, the second name marking his birthplace.

In the spring of 1894, when Bob was eight and Ned nearly six, the family moved to England. Their new home, Langley Lodge, was set in a private estate near the edge of the New Forest, just over a mile south-east of the main Totton to Lyndhurst road. The surroundings were no less beautiful than at Dinard, and the house was even more isolated. To the north and west lay forest, Southampton Water was a short distance away to the east, and to the south there was sparsely populated countryside as far as the Solent shore nine miles away. The Lawrences were very remote from the mainstream of English life. Southampton, the closest large town, was more than an hour's journey distant.[3]

While the children were now to grow up in English surroundings, Lawrence's years in France would have a great influence upon his attitude towards foreign travel. It was in France that he had begun to form ideas about the world beyond his family. His experience had not been that of a tourist, screened from the French in English-speaking hotels; nor had he been like the children of diplomats and colonial administrators, generally proud of their isolation in a British compound. He had lived in France on equal terms with a foreign people; he had spoken their language and had sensed no barrier. Before he was old enough to become mistrustful, he knew that he was welcomed by both French and English families. As a result he never felt the apprehension about living in foreign countries that was so common among the British. In the late Victorian era the English overseas were generally insular, class-conscious and nationalist. Lawrence himself would later write that they reinforced their national character 'by memories of the life they have left. In reaction against their foreign surroundings they take refuge in the England that was theirs. They assert their aloofness, their immunity, the more vividly for their loneliness and weakness. They impress the peoples among whom they live by reaction, by giving them an ensample of the complete Englishman, the foreigner intact.'[4]

Integration while overseas was rare, and those who sought the company of foreigners rather than their British peers risked denunciation for 'going native'. Lawrence was to become one of those Englishmen who, in his own words, 'feel deeply the influence of the native people, and try to adjust themselves to its atmosphere and spirit. To fit themselves modestly into the picture they suppress all in them that would be discordant with local habits and colours. They imitate the native as far as possible, and so avoid friction in their daily life . . . They are like the people but not of the people'.[5]

It was in this latter spirit that Lawrence would return during his student years to visit French families, and would tour on his bicycle in France as confidently as in England. The series of journeys which thus began would eventually take him to Palestine and Syria; yet the style of his travelling would remain the same. Before going to the Middle East he would learn Arabic, and he would accept enthusiastically the village hospitality offered to Arab travellers. As a result he was to gain a better knowledge of Arab ways than most British visitors. This in turn would help him to share the life of the bedouin tribesmen while working as a British liaison officer with the Arab forces during the First World War.

The move from Dinard to the New Forest was a happy one for the Lawrence children. Encouraged by their father, they spent three summers in open-air pursuits. From the shore of Southampton Water they could look across at the commercial shipping in Southampton and the many passenger liners which linked this great port to every part of the globe. Sometimes the boys were taken to Lepe where they could see the yachts racing off Cowes. As in France, they made friends with local children, notably the Lauries, whose father was agent of a neighbouring estate.

A governess was again employed to give lessons to the boys, but by the autumn of 1896 when Bob was nearly eleven, there was a need for more conventional schooling. The family could not afford boarding-school fees for four sons, and there were no good schools within easy reach so, in the summer of 1896, the Lawrences moved to Oxford where the boys could receive an excellent education at little cost.

Ned Lawrence was just eight when he left the New Forest. By then he had developed a liking for the countryside and outdoor activities. As an adult he would often say that his favourite place was London, yet many years later when he bought a house of his own it was to be almost as isolated as Langley Lodge.

The Lawrences' new home in Oxford, 2 Polstead Road, was a large semi-detached red-brick house built about six years previously. Unlike Langley Lodge it was surrounded by streets of suburban houses, all dating from the great expansion of north Oxford during the last years of the nineteenth century. Bob and Ned Lawrence were enrolled at the City of Oxford High School for Boys in the autumn of 1896. The school had been founded fifteen years earlier by the City Corporation and the University, with the 'hope that the best education may be provided . . . both for those who will leave for business or the English Civil Service, at about the age of fifteen, and those who will stay on till it is time and enter the University.'[6] Although the Oxford Corporation had originally proposed to offer fifty scholarships, few were awarded. As a result, the great majority of the 150 pupils at the school in Lawrence's time were fee-paying and came from middle-class families.[7] The headmaster, A. W. Cave, had built up a considerable academic reputation for the school, and of the fourteen boys in Lawrence's year, seven would go on to the University.

Despite its success the school suffered from constant financial dif-ficulties. As a result science teaching was seriously weakened by a lack of facilities, and there was no formal science specialisation in the upper forms. The school's great strength was in classics, taught on traditional lines. A Board of Education report in 1906 stated that 'in languages they might be described as old fashioned . . . The grammar, which is systematically taught from text-books, is regarded as of more importance in itself than is consistent with the ideas of modern educational theorists.'[8]

Recollections of Lawrence during this period must be treated with caution. All were written at least thirty years later when he had become famous. One impression, however, by the teacher who had been his form master in the Upper IVth in 1901, reads so like a school report that it may even have been based on contemporary notes:

'I found him quiet, very able at Form work, but lacking the enthusiasm which one generally associates with clever boys. The ordinary Form work was no trouble to him. The work of the Form in my day was mapped out for the special behoof of the under-dog. Lawrence did not come into this category and escaped any special direction or correction that might have been required.

'His mind was not always on Form work, although he gave no trouble. He was evidently forming resolutions as to the conduct of life, for he had already begun to criticise his elders, an awkward and hindering habit in any youth . . . He detested "side" and was severe in his looks on any boy who gave way to "swank".

'He had a strong sense of humour, which must have saved him many times in troublesome boyish days. He knew no fear and we all wondered why he did not play games . . . When the free-wheel bicycle came into use, he was the first boy in the School to have one and to have the first three-speed gear. He was anxious too, so I have been informed, to see whether a combination of a two-speed arrangement in the gear-wheel was possible if there could be at the same time a three-speed in the hub. It shews his interest in mechanical things . . .

'He was an enthusiast on physical excellence in human beings, although his own build was not as handsome as that of his brother Will, or as upright, tall and straight as that of his elder brother M.R.

'He was unlike the boys of his age and time, for even in his schooldays he had a strong leaning towards the Stoics, an apparent indifference towards pleasure or pain.'[9]

Lawrence disliked organised games. He later wrote: 'You know, I've never, since I was able to think, played any game through to the end. At school they used to stick me into football or cricket teams, and always I would trickle away from the field before the match ended.'[10] Many years afterwards, when Robert Graves wrote in the draft of his biography of Lawrence that organised games were 'too tame for him', Lawrence emended the passage to read: 'He took no interest in organised games because they were organised, because they had rules, because they had results. He will never compete – in anything.'[11] It is clear that the objection was to competition rather than to physical exertion; Lawrence was good at gymnastics and an accomplished cyclist. His fitness showed when he was made to take part in school athletics. In 1904 he was third (of fifteen) in the two-mile cycle race.[12] His attitude towards games is shown in articles which appeared in the school magazine in the spring of 1904. The first, signed 'Goalpost', is titled 'Playground Football' (it is almost certainly by Lawrence since a very similar article called 'Playground Cricket' in the next issue is signed by him): 'we do not score by goals. As a matter of fact there seems to be only one goal in the place where we play the game, so that it would be rather difficult to know whose goal it was. The chief way to score is to kick the ball against a window; this scores the price of the window. It is rather expensive to be a good player. The method of play is entirely different from ordinary football, although that may seem a trivial matter to some. It is not necessary to kick the ball; you can kick any one else; it will do just as well, unless they are bigger than you, but there you have to take your chance.'[13]

The second article, 'Playground Cricket', is more moderate: 'The stumps deserve mention. A wooden wall was improvised for wicket-keeper, and three stumps were chalked upon it, in white and blue. These having slightly faded a second pair in white was applied to the first, coinciding in width but not in height; consequently six inches of blue overtop the white bails. The profound wisdom which dictated this may not appear at first sight, but the fact is that when big boys are bowling the blue is counted as the top; when big boys are batting the stumps do not extend beyond the white. That shows our wisdom. Unfortunately some facetious individual (we would duck him if we could find him) has added four more white stumps, and four more bails, which slightly disconcert the batsmen, but greatly improve the chances of the bowler.'[14]

Evidently he was well-liked, and despite his eccentric attitude to games no one could regard him as a weakling. A classmate later wrote: 'How often a group of us, absorbed in some discussion of cricket or football, would gradually become conscious of a silent addition to our number, contemplating us with that provocative smile of his, till one of us would seize him and close in friendly wrestling, to feel even then the strength of those iron wrists.'[15]

In addition to their academic education, the Lawrence boys received a strongly religious upbringing. Both parents were convinced Christians, though their faith had a different emphasis. Lawrence's youngest brother (Arnold Walter, a fifth son who was born in 1900) has written: 'My mother . . . held religious convictions profoundly. She totally accepted the tenets of her brand of Christianity and had no doubt they constituted a complete code of binding rules for conduct; but she could only in small part share in my father's emotional, almost mystical, religious feeling'.[16] She was 'religious by upbringing (a fundamentalist) not by temperament. She went to church only at 11 a.m. on Sundays, with the rest of the family, after "morning prayers" by my father, who was more religious-minded.'[17]

Since moving to Oxford the family had worshipped at St Aldate's, opposite Christ Church, even though several other churches were closer to their home in Polstead Road. The rector of St Aldate's, Canon A. M. W. Christopher, was a prominent evangelical, whereas many other Oxford priests supported the High Church movement.

Most children received a religious upbringing at that time, but Lawrence was an unusually receptive pupil. Religious instruction gave him ethical values and a thorough knowledge of the Scriptures. He also began during childhood to study the geography and history of the Bible lands.

In the summer of 1904, at the end of his sixteenth year, he sat the Junior Oxford Local Examinations. The mark-sheets survive, providing an interesting record of Lawrence's ability (the first of the two marks given below shows his performance; the second is the mark awarded to the top candidate in that subject). He gained a distinction in Religious Knowledge (162:188), and passed in Arithmetic (77:100), History (112:156), English language and literature (210:269), Geography (93:140), Latin (204:341), Greek (186:353), French (205:293), and Mathematics, i.e. algebra and geometry, (122:321). His overall total was excellent, and he was placed in the First Class. Of the 6,720 candidates that year, only seventy-nine obtained a higher total.[18]

Despite this achievement, his contemporaries did not see him as a committed intellectual. According to 'Scroggs' Beeson, his closest schoolfriend, Lawrence 'left no impression of unusual erudition. A happy faculty of perceiving and ingenuously acclaiming new features in the already familiar made him appear rather as novice than mentor.'[19]

It was probably in the autumn of 1904 that Lawrence hurt his leg in a playground scuffle. At first he did not think the injury serious and continued the day's lessons despite considerable pain. His brothers wheeled him home on a bicycle and when the doctor was called, the leg was found to be broken just above the ankle. It took a long time to mend and as a result he missed the rest of term.

During his convalescence he amused himself by extensive reading, and also by copying medieval designs in poker work (then a popular technique: patterns were burned on wood using specially shaped 'points' heated by a 'poker machine'). The works he read were probably on history and archaeology. According to his mother he had bought two second-hand books on Layard's excavations at Nineveh, and knew them almost by heart. It may have been these which first attracted him to archaeology, although he had begun to collect rubbings from medieval church brasses a year or two earlier. By the age of fifteen he was 'best known, almost to notoriety, for his archaeological rummagings (with C. F. C. Beeson) in and about Oxford.'[20] Beeson records that their friendship centred on a shared interest in archaeological research, 'undertaken by Lawrence with a passionate absorption beside which my urge was more akin to the curiosity of a magpie in a Baghdad bazaar.'[21] During their later years at school the two friends cycled over a wide area in search of brass rubbings.

This interest in medieval artefacts took them to Oxford's Ashmolean Museum, where they met the Assistant Keeper, C. F. Bell. He saw them as an inseparable pair, devoting themselves to the kind of antiquarian pursuits recorded in the Annual Report of the Museum for 1906: 'During the past year the considerable disturbance of the ground for the foundations of new buildings in the city, at Hertford College, Jesus College, St. John's College, in High Street and in the Cornmarket on the sites of the Civet Cat and Leopold Arms, has produced many remains of pottery and glass of the 16th and 17th centuries. Owing to the generosity of Mr. E. Lawrence and also C. F. C. Beeson, who have by incessant watchfulness secured everything of antiquarian value which has been found, the most interesting finds have been added to the local antiquities in the Museum.'[22] It is not unusual for teenagers to take up archaeology with a passionate interest; many people who later become professional archaeologists are first drawn to the subject when fifteen or sixteen. Mindful of this, museum staff welcome young enthusiasts, who are often willing to approach the dullest task with dedication. Given sympathetic guidance, their contributions to museum work can be extremely helpful. This was certainly true in Lawrence's case.

During Lawrence's later years at school other factors began to shape his personality. The first was physical: unlike his four brothers he stopped growing when he reached 5ft 5ins. This shortness in stature was probably inherited from his mother, although she liked to claim that it had been caused in some way when he broke his leg. Short stature can have an influence on personality, and it is true that Lawrence was apt to behave in an unconventional fashion, perhaps in order to be noticed. This characteristic would persist in one form or another throughout his life. He also developed an almost obsessive will-power, and while still at school began to experiment with self-imposed tests of physical endurance, going for long walks and cycle rides, and spending periods without food and sleep. These activities set him apart from other boys.

There was another factor which now led him to distance himself from his contemporaries. During early childhood he had become aware that there was something irregular about the circumstances of his birth. It has been suggested that his suspicions were first roused when he overheard part of a conversation between his father and a solicitor.[23] He probably added gradually to this knowledge over several years, and by his own account he had concluded, before he was ten, that he must be illegitimate. At that age, however, he could not possibly have understood the full implications.[24]

Lawrence was the only one of the brothers who discovered this secret, and as he passed through adolescence he must have become increasingly aware of the social rejection that would follow if the truth were revealed. He was surrounded by the high-minded morality of Victorian Oxford, where bastardy would have been an unthinkable disgrace. His knowledge made him a party to his parents' deception, yet he said nothing to them or to his brothers about what he suspected.

All Lawrence's written statements about his illegitimacy were made much later, after he had heard his mother's version of the facts.* There is therefore nothing to justify the common assumption that since childhood he had known the full story. On the contrary, such evidence as there is suggests that he did not. Notes written by C. F. Bell indicate that while Lawrence knew before the First World War that he was illegitimate, he had completely misconstrued his parents' situation.

Bell's notes are in general accurate apart from some trivial errors in dates, yet they contain an account of Lawrence's family background,

* Following his father's death in 1919. As it is uncertain how much Lawrence discovered about his ancestry during his childhood, the essential facts are set out in Appendix I.

apparently derived from Lawrence himself, that is wholly incorrect. Bell wrote: 'the details . . . imparted by T. E. Lawrence to Hogarth [Keeper of the Ashmolean 1908-27] and repeated by him to me . . . amounted to this: that the "father", Mr. Lawrence, who was known in Oxford, was *not* the boys' father at all, but that Mrs. Lawrence, whom we all knew . . . *was* their mother . . . Mrs. Lawrence had been governess in the house of a man of some position who was the father of the boys – or at least of the elder ones. Mr. Lawrence married her later and adopted the children.'[25]

Since Lawrence's parents had told him nothing directly, and behaved as a normal married couple, this might have seemed the most obvious explanation of the scattered allusions he had heard. Indeed the true facts, which his mother told him in 1919, would have seemed far less probable given the *mores* of the time.

Whatever the extent of his knowledge, it is clear that during adolescence he knew that he was illegitimate. This deprived him of the sense of status and security which most children of his social class would have drawn from their family background and ancestry. As a result he would have to build up his own identity and self-esteem through personal achievement and moral integrity. When considering other ways in which knowledge of his illegitimacy may have influenced his development, it is important to bear in mind that he might not have believed, before 1919, that Mr Lawrence was actually his father. This could help to explain why Lawrence's remarks about his parents suggest that he had felt much stronger emotional ties with his mother than with his father.

The detachment shown in references to his father is all the more surprising since Mr Lawrence lived on private means and was therefore usually at home. While the boys' mother was busy running a large household, their father spent a good deal of time with them and was responsible for many of the interests they developed. In Arnold Lawrence's words: 'his influence can scarcely be overestimated. He was a skilled photographer – his camera is in the Oxford Museum of the History of Science; a handyman – and taught his children carpentry; he regularly bought the best bicycle of next year's model and liked riding 100 miles a day. He knew French grammatically, and in old age quoted Horace to express his own sentiments, and a line of Homer for its metrical felicity. He was interested in current affairs and church architecture; his best friend, H. T. Inman, was author of *Near Oxford* – an excellent guidebook to churches'.[26] From his father Lawrence gained skills and enthusiasms which were later to be very important in his life.

This parental influence extended much further. During his childhood Lawrence acquired certain attitudes towards life which belied the family's income of £300-£400 a year (then equivalent to a middle-rank professional salary). Mr Lawrence himself had been brought up in a wealthy landowning family where he had acquired an aristocratic disdain towards money and the necessity of working for a living. By practising a good deal of financial restraint, he was able to retain these attitudes in later life, and he passed them on, perhaps unconsciously, to his sons. Lawrence wrote home in 1911: 'I fear Father is right about us and our careers: but this idealist disregard for the good things of the world has its bright side. And to say that he had five sons, none making money, would be a glorious boast – from my point of view at least.'[27]

In the tradition of the leisured classes, Mr Lawrence had learned to fill his days with absorbing pastimes. This attitude affected his sons, and Lawrence would always retain an aristocratic habit of seeking fulfilment chiefly in his own pursuits. The lives of all five brothers show an indifference towards the kind of career ambition that would normally motivate men in their social and financial position. Although Lawrence said little about his father, the values he inherited from this tall, gentle, unobtrusive figure were to influence him greatly.[28]

The contrast between Lawrence's father and mother was considerable. Mrs Lawrence's sons knew little about her background, but Lawrence himself later found out that she too had been an illegitimate child. She had been brought up in Perthshire and on the Isle of Skye by her uncle, a minister of the Episcopal Church of Scotland. Able and intelligent, she had been taught to value education highly. Despite her origins she acquired sufficient qualifications to seek work as a governess. This profession offered many openings to girls from Scotland, since the renowned qualities of the Scottish nanny were much appreciated by aristocratic families both in Britain and abroad. It was doubtless her constant encouragement which spurred her five sons to seek academic success.

She worked long hours to maintain the standards she felt proper for their household, and in his letters, Lawrence often showed concern for her, urging her to take more rest. The sacrifice she made for the needs of her family reflected an indomitable willpower, which she applied no less to herself than to those around her. This dominant personality brought her directly into conflict with Lawrence as he grew towards adulthood. He increasingly resented her intrusions into his private affairs, and, as he himself had a strong character, their relationship worsened. In 1927, when he had lived apart from her for many years, he wrote a letter which shows how deeply he was scarred by this adolescent conflict: 'Mother is rather wonderful: but very exciting. She is so set, so assured in mind. I think she "set" many years ago: perhaps before I was born. I have a terror of her knowing anything about my feelings, or convictions, or way of life. If she knew they would be damaged: violated: no longer mine. You see, she would not hesitate to understand them: and I do not understand them, and do not want to. Nor has she ever seen any of us growing: because I think she has not grown since we began . . . She has given me a terror of families and inquisitions. And yet you'll understand she is my mother, and an extraordinary person. Knowledge of her will prevent my ever making any woman a mother, and the cause of children . . . the inner conflict, which makes me a standing civil war, is the inevitable issue of the discordant natures of herself and my father, and the inflammation of strength and weakness which followed the uprooting of their lives and principles. They should not have borne children.'[29] The bitterness expressed in this letter can only reflect the feelings of his youth, since afterwards he had lived away from home.

At one point, probably in the autumn of 1905, tension reached such a pitch that Lawrence ran away. On at least two occasions he stated that this was 'because of trouble at home'.[30] The incident undoubtedly marked the end of his childhood dependence on his mother. Once, writing to a friend, he remarked that seventeen was 'the age at which I suddenly found myself. You may have begun a little earlier, since the being torn out of home is an education in itself.'[31]

When he ran away there were no relatives to stay with and enlistment was one of the few courses open to him. A local recruiting office placed him in the Royal Garrison Artillery (part of the Royal Artillery) as a boy soldier and he was posted to the Falmouth Garrison. He served for a time in the small sub-section which manned the fort situated on the opposite side of the River Fal between St Just-in-Roseland and St Mawes. At that date boy soldiers between fourteen and eighteen were specifically recruited by the Royal Artillery to serve as trumpeters. They were taught both trumpet and bugle and when proficient, blew the various bugle calls that regulated military life.

Lawrence was shocked by the brutality of the men in the RGA: 'every incident ended in dispute and every dispute either in the ordeal of fists (a forgotten art, today) or in a barrack-court-martial whose sentences were too often mass-bullying of anyone unlike the mass . . . I cannot remember a parade during three months without a discoloured eye. Usually five or six men bore fighting damages.'[32]

This experience must have seemed considerably worse than the problems he had run away from: 'the other fellows fought all Friday and Saturday nights and frightened me with their roughness.'[33] It seems that he appealed to his father for help and as a result was bought out.[34]

Many children rebel against their parents and run away from home in their teens; but the incident is testimony to Lawrence's self-confidence, and to the conflict of strong personalities which blocked an easier solution to this adolescent tension between mother and son. Knowledge of his illegitimacy may also have played a part in his decision to run away. He later wrote: 'My mind was not so peaceful then, for I had not tried everything, and made a final choice of the least ill.'[35]

After he had become famous, his mother liked to stress the harmony of their family life during his childhood; she and her eldest son therefore denied that Lawrence had ever run away from home. Lawrence himself evidently knew that it had hurt her, for he regretted mentioning it to one of his biographers, to whom he wrote: 'This is hush-hush. I should not have told you . . . I'd rather keep this out of print, please: the whole episode.'[36]

It was at about this time that the emphasis of Lawrence's schooling changed. In the Junior Locals two years before, he had gained barely a third of the marks of the top candidate in mathematics. As the marks were not disclosed, his school did not know this and had decided to put him up for a mathematics scholarship at the University. However when he was nearly eighteen he abruptly switched from mathematics to history. Later references in his letters show that this change was his own decision, and the matter may have been contentious. His comments about mathematics suggest that he had no liking for the subject: 'the average intelligence in a month could learn all the arithmetic that he or she will ever need thereafter, till dying day. About one person in a thousand wants to know more. I should isolate these repulsive cases and protect all other children from their contact. Mathematics are well enough for a mathematician, but for me addition, subtraction, and division, with multiplication are enough. Since I dropped maths I've never needed a log. or done an equation, or used a trig. formula'.[37] This dislike of mathematics may have been partly due to missing a school term when his leg was broken. The gap in his knowledge caused by such a long absence would have been a continuing handicap, since the study of maths is cumulative. But the change also reflected something in Lawrence's intellectual make-up. He would never be attracted to pure theory, whether in mathematics, philosophy, economics or politics. In the same way, though he would learn to read and speak a foreign language, he felt no need to acquire a deep knowledge of its grammar.

Another motive for the change in subject must have been the interest in medieval history which had developed through his enthusiasm for brass-rubbing and archaeology. During his last year at school he read history books borrowed for him by his father from the library of the Oxford Union, and took private coaching from L. C. Jane, a historian whose slightly unconventional approach suited Lawrence well.

In the summer of 1906 he sat the Senior Oxford Local Examinations, a necessary step towards university entrance. While waiting for the results he set out on a bicycle tour of Brittany to visit castles and historic churches. This was the first time he had left England on his own, but he had few anxieties since his base would be the Chaignons' house in Dinard. His elder brother Bob had visited them as a paying guest two summers previously, and Lawrence was to stay with them on the same basis. He intended to spend two weeks travelling with his schoolfriend Beeson, returning to England in mid-August. In the event, however, his visit was to be extended, and he stayed on for nearly a fortnight after Beeson left.

During this holiday he wrote to his family at regular intervals, and the dozen letters which survive total more than twenty thousand words. These contemporary documents provide a much more reliable picture of Lawrence at the close of his eighteenth year than the later reminiscences of family and friends. There are remarks which bear on his relationship with members of his family; there are comments which illustrate different facets of his developing personality; and there is a good deal of material that displays his various abilities, interests and opinions.

At first sight, the letters seem curiously impersonal, and this itself must be a reflection of Lawrence's relationship with his family. He told his mother: 'you want more details of myself; I really have none to give',[38] and again, 'there will be no private or family messages in [this letter], although there have not been anything of the sort in any letters of mine up to the present.'[39] When addressing a letter to his father he wrote:

'it does not make the least difference in style, since all my letters are equally bare of personal information. The buildings I try to describe will last longer than we will, so it is only fitting that they should have the greater space.'[40]

Despite this reserve he shows a good deal of filial affection and much concern for his mother's health: 'Give my love to Florence [Messham, who had been his nanny and was now accompanying his mother on a holiday], and tell her to keep you strictly idle and quiet: no work. I am glad to hear that you are feeling better: by all means become quite well before you return: this trip is intended to set you up.'[41]

There are also messages for his parents from people they had known when they lived in Dinard twelve years before: 'Everyone over here wants you to come back. Mr. Fécélier was speaking so nicely of you yesterday: you were "*capable*", "*aimable*", etc.';[42] 'Frère Fabel . . . asked dozens of questions about all of you . . . he also said that you were the best neighbour he ever had. He would be quite intoxicated with joy if he could see you again';[43] Mr. Lewis . . . enquired after you, and your bicycle, with great affection.'[44]

Other passages in these letters reflect Lawrence's upbringing. His parents were staunchly Protestant so not surprisingly he found the Bretons 'ignorant and priest-ridden'.[45] His mother's influence is clear in other ways. Years later he wrote that she had been 'brought up as a child of sin in the Island of Skye by a bible-thinking Presbyterian . . . she remodelled my father, making him a teetotaller, a domestic man, a careful spender of pence.'[46] The young Lawrence therefore disapproved of alcohol, remarking, for instance, on the drunkenness in Dinard: 'Everyone mixes raw brandy with their cider, and they get fearfully mad with drink.'[47] His expenditure is frequently and carefully accounted for: 'I fear I will be sixpence short in England; I had forgotten the sum charged for bringing the luggage to the Docks Station, when I kept some English money unchanged . . . I am one half-penny short deducting bicycle fare. I shall have to change that sovereign for the half-penny, unless I carry my own luggage to the station, which might perhaps be the easier course.'[48]

Lawrence's father had encouraged his sons to take an interest in current affairs, and several comments reveal the family's Tory opinions, for example: 'The Whites were interested in the Unemployed so I gave them a history of the movement, for it is undoubtedly engineered. Mr. White has no sympathy with them.'[49] References to his elder brother in the letters are less than respectful: 'The people here say that I am much thinner than Bob, but stronger, and have a better accent. Still Bob's fatness is much better than my muscle in their eyes'.[50] Bob had embraced his mother's form of religion and hoped to become a medical missionary. He was at that time an undergraduate at St John's College, Oxford, struggling through the pre-clinical syllabus for a medical degree. He was probably the least academic of the brothers: 'he's queer company', Lawrence later wrote, 'you will not persuade him of anything . . . He is illuminated from inside, not from out. His face, very often, shines like a lamp.'[51] Bob was therefore an easy target. When visiting a castle which had well-preserved latrines, Lawrence teased: 'By the way, did not Bob . . . go and see this castle? What could he have been thinking about not to mention these most attractive domestic conveniences?'[52]

The third brother, Will, was only sixteen months younger than Lawrence and the two were very close. While on holiday that summer, Will came across a mound which appeared to be a barrow, and wrote to Lawrence asking how to excavate it. The reply was helpful though filled with bantering admonitions. It ended encouragingly: 'Let me know how the matter progresses . . . keep an accurate account . . . and mark on a plan where each important article is found. You have my best wishes for success . . . Don't give up at once, if you do not find anything. Digging is an excellent exercise.'[53] Frank, the fourth brother, was now thirteen, and the five-year age gap seems to have prevented the development of a close relationship. Arnold, however, was still a small child, and Lawrence's almost fatherly affection towards him is often reflected in these letters.

Lawrence clearly also revelled in gossip, some of which seems to have been reported home for his mother's benefit: 'The servant question is very acute over here: they take percentages of everything bought and this raises the prices. Mrs. Purvis says that if she buys a franc's worth of vegetables from a woman at the door, on going she will slip a *sou* into the hand of the cook. If she orders anything in the shops the servant goes on her next opportunity and demands her commission which is always given.'[54] This willingness to listen to local chatter seems to have been a feature of Lawrence's personality; it would continue throughout his life and it was to help him in a curious way when he began to travel further afield. Any outsider who wants to be accepted in a foreign community must enter into the spirit of its gossip. A few years later, while overseeing Arab workmen, his knowledge of their family scandals would help to make him popular,[55] and during the First World War he would advise British officers serving with the Arab armies to learn 'all you can about your Ashraf and Bedu. Get to know their families, clans, and tribes, friends and enemies, wells, hills, and roads. Do all this by listening and by indirect enquiry. Do not ask questions. Get to speak their dialect of Arabic, not yours. Until you can understand their allusions avoid getting deep into conversation, or you will drop bricks.'[56]

The 1906 letters also show that he already enjoyed making provocative remarks about people. This would be another lifelong trait. He liked resounding statements and he also liked to shock (when he meant to be malicious the tone was much quieter). He wrote home on August 24th that one Toby Purvis had told him that 'a cousin wrote Lady Brassey's books. General Buller he says drinks terribly: it was the cause of his Colenso failure. General Baden-Powell he regards as possessed of little ability: he seems rather of the Winston Churchill type. Toby heard from an officer that the King was very annoyed when Baden-Powell placed his own head on the Mafeking stamps: he does not think that we will hear much more of him. He said that when the uncles Moulton died, Dardie would have nearly £7,000 a year: her eldest boy is four, and the youngest eighteen months. The "Adonis" of Dinard still lives here, but he is Adonis no longer: he has got very fat and drunken looking, and seldom appears in public.'[57]

At this time, as later, Lawrence's letters contain some biting personal assessments: 'I forgot to mention that, owing to paralysis of his eye, [Toby Purvis] squints terribly. He is certainly very clever at making himself pleasant, and has good manners, joined to good powers of observation; but much of his pleasantness lies, I expect, on the surface, and is only shown to strangers. He will be entertaining enough for one drive I hope.'[58] The style of these judgments in letters home displays a degree of youthful arrogance and may also reflect his upbringing. Yet Lawrence's ability to assess character quickly and accurately would later be crucial to his role in the Arab Revolt.

Though constantly aware of his short stature, he took pride in his strength and was pleased when this was admired: 'when he heard of my Fougères ride [Mr Lewis] declared I was very strong and that I had inherited Father's talent . . . I am beginning to be proud of myself.'[59] Mme Chaignon 'got a shock when she saw my "biceps" while bathing. She thinks I'm Hercules'[60]. Again: 'My leg muscles are like steel now. I expect I'll delight Mother when I return. I'm as brown as a berry.'[61]

He was now beginning to find vegetarianism attractive: 'our *déjeuner* was an innocent one; nothing had to be killed to feed us. Milk, bread, butter, was our total. Price 4d.'[62] This attitude was not however encouraged by his hosts: 'The Chaignons declare I will kill myself if I don't eat more meat; they say all vegetarians fill an early grave, although I'm not a veg. out here, no Frenchman has any opportunity to be.'[63] During the next three years he adopted vegetarianism seriously; it formed one aspect of the idealism which began to mark much of his thinking.

His letters occasionally reveal a strongly romantic side to his nature. One of the set texts in the English Literature paper for the Senior Locals had been Tennyson's poetry. On August 26th he sent home a string of descriptive passages, mainly from Tennyson and Shelley, to illustrate the evening seascape at Dinard. The letter continued: 'You really must excuse this battery of quotations, but I have got into the habit of quoting any appropriate lines to myself, and this time I thought I would put them on record . . . The sea was of the wondrous blue met with sometimes here, and all was perfect; *there was no-one else there*. This last makes such an addition to one's enjoyment of nature and her prodigal loveliness; all this scene was reserved for me alone: it is a wonderful surpassing thought on which to reflect, I can only wish my mind was more receptive and my emotions more deeply affected. Nature contains that spirit and power which we can witness but not weigh, inwardly conceive but not comprehend, love but not limit, imagine, but neither define nor describe. Nature is incomprehensible, fleeting, and yet immortal, and a love for it and its impressions are both ineradicable.'[64] Such passages seem very strange when set alongside the arid descriptions of castles and churches which make up the bulk of the 1906 letters. At this time, however, Lawrence was reading Ruskin's *Stones of Venice*, and the content of his letters may be an unconscious imitation of this book (in which eloquence alternates with technical accounts of Venetian architecture).

Lawrence's enthusiasm for history was now leading him in new directions. His starting-point had been the intriguing medieval figures to be found on monumental brasses. From these he had passed quite naturally to details of costume, heraldry and armour, and to three-dimensional effigies on tombs. By 1906, however, he was interested in every trace of the medieval world. Through extensive reading he learned the relationships between churches, ceramic fragments, costume, and military architecture. As Beeson noted: 'Brasses and the bypaths they opened into mediæval history confirmed the gradual concentration of Lawrence's interest in the development of Gothic architecture and the design of military buildings in particular.'[65] His main preoccupation was now with 'the minds of the designers of these defensive works and the extent to which history had tested their intentions.'[66]

This was no casual interest. The 1906 letters show the discipline of his detailed observation and the knowledge that lay behind it. An example is his description of tombs in Lehon Abbey: 'The effigy [of Tiphaine du Guesclin] lay on the north side of the presbytery, and was most remarkable . . . She was dressed in a jupon, which buttoned down the front with twenty-two circular buttons; the button-holes were yet quite clear, slightly puckered round her waist, which was exceedingly small, and tightly drawn. The front of the jupon terminated in a tassel, with large bow. The jupon closed quite close round her neck, forming a low collar like the modern military tunic. The sleeves (no man's jupon ever had sleeves), were fairly full and descended to the wrist; underneath it was seen the edge of the vambrace. She wore genouillères, with square plates beneath them, jambs and sollerets, of three large and heavy laminated plates. She also had rowell spurs, and her feet rested on an eagle expansed bearing a shield (billets or) on the front, held in its beak . . . Her hands were bare, and finely shaped. Her head was resting on a cushion, with a corded tassel at each corner; her hair, confined by a narrow fillet alone, flowed in two curls one outside each ear, while the rest was cut short, and parted regularly down the centre. Her face was perfect, without any mutilation, and exhibited the calm repose and angelic purity which the mediæval sculptor knew so well to blend, with a certain martial simplicity and haughtiness. The figure . . . in its combination of female dress and armour, is so far as I know unique.'[67]

It is clear that Lawrence was combining two purposes in these letters home. The first was to give his parents regular news of his activities, the second to provide notes for his own future use; the following year, when sending home one such description, he wrote: 'This is not for you to read, it is only a note to refresh my memory'.[68] These descriptions were intended to supplement the information given in guidebooks, so they were longest when he found the guides unhelpful. A curious result is that his letters say very little about some of the best-known monuments he visited.

Though Lawrence was now a competent photographer he had not taken a camera on this 1906 tour, thinking that it would be difficult to carry one on his bicycle with all his other baggage. As it turned out, he realised that other things were more dispensable and regretted that he had to rely on commercial picture postcards of places like Fougères: 'I shall certainly return there next year for another examination, and I shall bring a camera with me: Father's one if possible: it is a paradise for a photographer.'[69]

As his schoolmaster had noted two years earlier, Lawrence had a technical interest in bicycles: 'Is Father going to have wood rims and constrictors on his new one? Fixed gear and fixed wheel, north road bar etc? It would be best.'[70] That summer he rode considerable distances on his own machine and felt fit enough to cycle a hundred miles each day (on one outing, from Dinard to Fougères and back, he covered 114 miles). But cycling was a means to an end, and he remarked that: 'A motor bicycle would be very useful for getting away to the antiquities round about.'[71]

He received his Senior Locals results while still at Dinard. The published lists showed that he had been placed in the First Class, as in the Junior Locals two years before. The marks gained were not disclosed at the time, but the mark-sheets survive and show that of 4,645 candidates, only twelve had achieved a higher total. In several subjects he had done well compared with the candidates who took first place (whose marks are also given here). In English Language and Literature he shared first place (439 marks) and he had also gained a distinction with equal third place in Religious Knowledge (183:216). Other good results were Arithmetic (84:100), History (193:262), and French (214:278). In Political Economy (171:194) he was in fact second, but all the candidates did badly and no distinctions were awarded. His results in Latin (191:459) and Greek (193:430) probably reflect his attitude towards grammar. His total in mathematics (algebra and geometry) was very poor: (79:239).[72]

When Lawrence learned of his passes and distinctions he wrote home: 'The result is on the whole not as good as I had hoped, although I am quite satisfied with the English. I wonder whether there is any profession in which a knowledge of one's tongue is of the slightest use . . . In the Divinity I had hoped for more. Polit. Econ. is not surprising; I expect we both made asses of ourselves [he was referring to Beeson, who scored 90 in this paper] . . . in the English my essay on Physical Culture in 2000 A.D. evidently went down'.[73]

That autumn was mainly taken up with work for Oxford entrance, although he won a school essay prize on the subject of 'Our Colonies'. He tried for a scholarship at St John's College, but early in December he learned that he had not been successful. In January 1907 he sat the examination for Jesus College where, by virtue of his birth at Tremadoc, he would be eligible for a Welsh award. Lawrence was a strong candidate and showed in the interviews that he could speak with authority about medieval pottery and brass rubbings. He won a Meyricke Exhibition, worth £50 a year, in Modern History.

His result in Senior Locals had not been quite good enough to qualify him for exemption from Responsions, an examination normally taken before entering the University. In March, while still at school, he had to take papers on Xenophon's *Anabasis*, Caesar's *De Bello Gallico*, and in algebra. During the Easter holidays, perhaps mindful that he was going to a college with a large Welsh membership, he went on a cycling tour of the Welsh castles, visiting Dinas Bran (Crow Castle), Caernarvon, Harlech, Chepstow, Caerphilly, Tintern Abbey and Raglan. He wrote of the Welsh: 'After ten days in Wales I ought to be able to sum up all the character, habits, peculiarities, virtues, vices, and other points of the Welsh people. I am sorry I cannot do this yet. They seem to me to be rather inquisitive, more dirty, and exceedingly ugly. I am at last discovering where I got my large mouth from, it's a national peculiarity. At the same time they appear honest; I have had no extortionate bills'.[74]

After taking his additional Responsions subject (a paper on de Tocqueville) during the summer term, Lawrence left the Oxford High School at the end of July 1907; he was nearly nineteen. Many years later he remarked that he had been educated there 'very little, very reluctantly, very badly',[75] and he told his biographer Liddell Hart that he had found school 'an irrelevant and time-wasting nuisance, which I hated and contemned.'[76] There seems to be a contradiction between these statements and his achievements, explained perhaps by another retrospective comment: 'They drag those "boy" years out too much. In my case they were miserable sweated years of unwilling work: and when after them I suddenly went to Oxford, the new freedom felt like Heaven. I don't think men ever work as hard as boys are made to work (unless they are working for themselves, when it isn't work at all) nor do I think the miseries of grown-up feelings are as bad as those of boys.'[77]

CHAPTER 2

Oxford University
October 1907 – June 1909

LAWRENCE entered Oxford University on 12th October 1907 as an exhibitioner at Jesus College. Since he had lived in the city for eleven years it may have been a less momentous step for him than for most of his fellow students. His elder brother Bob was already at St John's College, and Will would go up, also to St John's, in 1909.

The expense of maintaining and educating three fully grown children (with two younger boys following on) placed an increasing strain on the family budget. As Lawrence's Exhibition would not cover the full cost of residence in college he continued to live at home. In one way this decision would greatly diminish the effect of being at university. Normally students learn about living with their peers by being thrown together in an enclosed college environment, but Lawrence was never to participate fully in this life. Moreover, during his three undergraduate years he would take no part in sport or other college activities.

Like many of the most talented undergraduates, he concentrated on his subject and tended not to be gregarious. He belonged to the intellectual élite of scholars and exhibitioners which, in 1907, had less in common with the mass of students than would be the case today. Many of his contemporaries who came from wealthy families did not see academic achievement as the main purpose of attending university. Of the twenty-eight freshmen at Jesus that autumn, four won First Class Honours in Finals. But only seven of the remainder attained Seconds, whereas eleven were awarded Thirds, two received Fourths, and four failed to get an Honours degree.[1]

From the start Lawrence's main academic contacts were outside the college. His principal tutor, Reginald Lane Poole, was a Fellow of St John's. Lawrence also continued to see a good deal of L. C. Jane, although he did not resume regular coaching with him until the last few terms before Finals. Through his archaeological activities he had long-standing friends at the Ashmolean, notably C. F. Bell and, from March 1908 onwards, E. T. Leeds, a new assistant keeper. Several schoolfriends, such as Beeson, were also up at Oxford, though only E. F. Hall was at Jesus. There was moreover a strong contingent of Welsh students in the college, among whom Lawrence may have felt something of an outsider.

For all these reasons it is unlikely that he spent much time in college during his first two terms, particularly as he was busy with university examinations. Yet it was probably quite difficult to concentrate on academic work at home, since the house was also occupied by three younger brothers. In the summer term of 1908, therefore, he moved into rooms at Jesus. It was only then that he made friends among his fellow undergraduates.

Student behaviour is traditionally unconventional and, taking this into consideration, not many of the exploits credited to Lawrence deserve special mention.[2] During the summer that he spent in college in 1908 his most notable prank was canoeing along the Trill Mill Stream, which runs under the streets of Oxford.[3] Like many undergraduates before and since, Lawrence posed deliberately as an eccentric. One remarkable scholar, A. T. P. Williams, who later became Bishop of Winchester, recalled meeting Lawrence 'almost always late at night, walking in the quadrangle at Jesus. I do not know when he went to bed; some nights, I am pretty sure, not at all, certainly seldom till well on in the small hours.'[4] Another contemporary, A. G. Prys-Jones, wrote that Lawrence 'sat cross-legged on the floor quietly explaining that he never sat on chairs if he could help it, that he never indulged in the meals known as breakfast, lunch, tea and dinner, nor smoked nor took drinks; in fact he did nothing which qualified him to be an ordinary member of society. But he added, drolly, that he had no objection whatsoever to my doing any of these things'.[5]

One aspect of university life has changed beyond recognition since Lawrence's day: the nature of relationships permitted between the sexes. Although there was a small number of women's colleges at both Oxford and Cambridge, the two sexes had few opportunities to mix freely, and emotional friendships during the undergraduate years were strongly discouraged. These constraints formed part of a wider attitude towards relationships between men and women which was generally accepted, and which could easily be justified as a rational response to progress in medicine. Infant mortality had fallen greatly, notably in the middle and upper classes; yet there was still no sure method of contraception except sexual abstinence. As a result, the emphasis in marital life was on the virtues of companionship rather than on sex. Young men were taught that women were a fit subject for romantic admiration, but that a desire for sexual gratification was sinful. Lawrence would recall how, 'at Oxford the select preacher, one evening service, speaking of venery, said, "And let me implore you, my young friends, not to imperil your immortal souls upon a pleasure which, *so I am credibly informed*, lasts less than one and three-quarter minutes." '[6] Lawrence was echoing views held sincerely by many Englishmen of his generation when he later wrote scathingly of those 'who regarded our comic reproductive processes not as an unhygienic pleasure, but as a main business of life.'[7]

Young men of the ruling classes were taught that abstinence in general would prepare them for their duties; moral leadership would fall to those who could resist the temptations to which others succumbed. The basis for this view came directly from the Protestant Christianity which Lawrence so wholeheartedly accepted. Before going to university he had taught at St Aldate's Sunday school and served as an officer in the Church Lads' Brigade. Canon Christopher had retired from St Aldate's in 1905, but the Lawrence brothers continued to attend weekly Bible classes which he gave at his home.

During Lawrence's three years as an undergraduate he increasingly practised self-denial, exploring and stretching the limits of his physical capability. He tried staying awake for long periods and, in addition to vegetarianism, experimented with fasting. While he took no part in formal sport, he built up his strength and stamina by arduous cycling over long distances. He made no secret of his desire to subjugate his body to his will. E. F. Hall, whose rooms at Jesus Lawrence often used, recalled that: 'He came one evening into my rooms . . . and began to fire a revolver, blank cartridge fortunately, out of the windows . . . one glance at his eyes left no doubt at all that he told the truth when he said that he had been working for forty-five hours at a stretch without food, to test his powers of endurance.'[8]

By June 1908, the end of his first year at Oxford, Lawrence's tutors had formed a good idea of his academic potential. For his final history examinations he would have to sit various set papers, and also to select one of ten alternative special subjects. This choice would not have to be made until mid-November 1909, but Lawrence began to explore the topics long before then. It seems likely that he was at first attracted by the paper on Military History and Strategy. This would have been a natural extension of his enthusiasm for military architecture; he later told Liddell Hart that he had become interested in the subject while still at school.[9] At Oxford he 'read some French study of Napoleon's Italian campaign, and then browsed in his despatches, a series of about twenty-five vols. These interested me in his text-books, and so they got me to Bourcet (?), Guibert, and Saxe, in that order. Then I read other "manuals of arms" of the 18th century . . . I made a series of maps of, and visited, Rocroi, Crécy, Agincourt, Malplaquet, Sedan and two other Franco-German War places whose names I forget. But my interests were mainly mediaeval, and in pursuit of them I . . . went elaborately into siege-manoeuvres ·. . . I also tried to get an idea of the bigger movements, and saw Valmy and its neighbourhood, and tried to refight the whole of Marlborough's wars.'[10]

When a subject attracted him he would study it with immense energy; but otherwise his work was sound rather than exceptional. L. C. Jane, who probably knew Lawrence's academic abilities as well as any of his university tutors, later wrote: 'I found out in the first week or two that the thing was to suggest rather out-of-the-way books – he could be relied on to get more out of a suggestive sentence in a book than an ordinary man would get from a volume . . . He had the most diverse interests histori-cally, though mainly mediaeval. For a long while I could not get him to take any interest in later European history – was very startled to find that he was absorbed by R. M. Johnston's *French Revolution* . . . Lawrence was not a bookworm, though he read very fast and a great deal: I should not call him a scholar by temperament and the main characteristic of his work was always that it was unusual without the effort to be unusual.'[11]

In 1908 the examiners in Modern History introduced a new option allowing candidates to present a thesis 'on some question within any special subject offered by them in the Examination.'[12] If Lawrence chose 'Military History and Strategy' as his special subject, he would be able to display his knowledge of medieval military architecture in depth, both in a thesis and in the ensuing viva.

Accordingly, in the summer of 1908 he went on the longest of his French cycling tours, to examine medieval castles and fortifications. Bicycles (which could be taken to a distant starting-point by train) had revolutionised European tourism, and Lawrence's 2,400-mile journey was not exceptional. He crossed to Le Havre in mid-July, having worked out a route which would take him to see the most important castles he had not already visited. First he cycled eastwards via Château Gaillard, Gisors and Pierrefonds to Coucy. Then, turning southwards and avoiding Paris, he made for Provins, the third city of medieval France. It had 'a most puzzling twelfth century keep [the Tour César], and remains of town walls. I was in and around them for hours, and came to the conclusion that the architect was making experiments when he built them . . . the keep would have been almost incapable of defence, and yet in spirit it is half a century ahead of its time. It ranks with Château Gaillard in importance for my thesis.'[13] He continued southwards along the level roads of the Seine Valley as far as Châtillon, and then turned west to see Montbard and the cathedral at Vézelay. He had taken a camera with him, and managed to take photographs of the interior of this great medieval church, built to serve the needs of pilgrims eight hundred years before.

Letters home show that he found the journey very enjoyable, despite the fact that he was cycling long distances every day in the summer heat: 'I'm riding very strongly, and feel very fit, on my diet of bread, milk and fruit . . . I begin on two pints of milk and bread, and supplement with fruit to taste till evening, when more solid stuff is consumed: one eats a lot when riding for a week on end at any pace. My day begins early ('tis fearfully hot at mid-day), there is usually a château to work at from 12-2, and then hotel at seven or eight. I have no time for sight-seeing: indeed sometimes I wonder if my thesis is to be written this November or next, I find myself composing pages and phrases as I ride. The roads have been almost uniformly bad, but the hills all rideable.'[14]

From Vézelay he continued south to Nevers and thence onwards up the valley of the River Allier. After Thiers his route was hilly, with a very long climb up through pine forests to La Chaise Dieu. At Le Puy he had to turn eastwards across very difficult country to reach Tournon in the Rhône valley. The hilly country was sometimes spectacular: 'Part of my ride was up a superb gorge, with river foaming in the bottom, and rock and hill on each side: it was the finest scenery I have ever come across: truly the Auvergne is a wondrous district: but *not* one for a cycle: I'll take a walking tour there some day I hope . . . From Le Puy I rode up for ten miles more (oh dear 'twas hot!) consoling myself with the idea that my sufferings were beyond the conception of antiquity, since they were a combination (in a similar climate) of those of Sisyphus who pushed a great weight up hill, of Tantalus who couldn't get anything to drink, or any fruit, and of Theseus who was doomed ever to remain sitting:– I got to the top at last, had fifteen miles of up and down to St. Somebody-I-don't-want-to-meet-again [St Agrève], and then a rush down 4,000 feet to the Rhône.'[15]

Next he visited Crussol, 'a fine xii century castle on a 500 feet precipice over the Rhône.'[16] He wrote home that he had spent the night there, without mentioning that the castle was a roofless ruin. Then in one day he cycled down the flat roads of the Rhône valley from Valence to Avignon, 'glorious with its town walls and papal palace'.[17]

At Arles it was the medieval rather than the massive Roman buildings which impressed him: '*The* thing in Arles is the cloister of St Trophimus: it is absolutely unimaginably fine with its sculptures and its proportion: all other architecture is very nearly *dirt* beside this Provençal Romanesque, when the scale is small (Provence has never done anything big in anything at all) . . . The amphitheatre (Roman) at Arles is magnificently and gigantically ugly, as everything of that sort must be.'[18]

At Les Baux de Provence, a ruined medieval hill-top town, he thought he caught his first glimpse of the Mediterranean, 'a grey line far away on the horizon'.[19] Since leaving Southampton he had travelled more than five hundred miles south, and he was experiencing a truly hot climate for the first time. He now did some of his cycling after sundown, and saved money from time to time by sleeping rough.

Lawrence reached the coast at Aigues-Mortes in the Camargue: 'It is a lovely little place, an old, old town huddled along its old streets, with hardly a house outside its old walls, still absolutely unbroken, and hardly at all restored or in need of it. From it St. Louis started for his crusades, and it has seen innumerable events since. Today it is deserted by the world, and is decaying fast: its drawbacks are mosquitoes (a new experience for me, curtains on all the beds) . . . It is however almost on the sea, and exceedingly pleasant (above all, if one could get acclimatised quickly to these brutes, I'm all one huge bite).

'I bathed today in the sea, the great sea, the greatest in the world . . . I felt that at last I had reached the way to the South, and all the glorious East; Greece, Carthage, Egypt, Tyre, Syria, Italy, Spain, Sicily, Crete... they were all there, and all within reach... of me. I fancy I know now better than Keats what Cortes felt like, silent upon a peak in Darien. Oh I must get down here – farther out – again! Really this getting to the sea has almost overturned my mental balance: I would accept a passage for Greece tomorrow'.[20]

However, he turned westwards to continue his tour. The Roman amphitheatre at Nîmes, the best-preserved in France, 'proved fair, no more'.[21] He was more interested in the Maison Carrée, a rectangular building nearly two thousand years old in the style of a Greek temple: 'I never saw a handsomer little place; it makes one marvel what the Parthenon must be.'[22] The fortified medieval church at Agde was more relevant to his purpose: 'It has a front seat in my thesis.'[23]

The walled city of Carcassonne exceeded all his expectations: 'It is of all dates: much Roman work: much Visigothic, a splendid Saracenic tower, some Carlovingian work, and mediæval of all sorts to the end of the fourteenth century: *nothing later* except a very little modern restoration. This makes it the most interesting and most valuable object-lesson in military architecture (for at all periods it was a first-class fortress) and it happens also to be wonderfully picturesque . . . Also I have a superb plan, showing the different periods of the buildings . . . there is much of the twelfth [century] for me; so much that I cannot satisfy myself upon it: in fact could only do so by carting it back to Oxford and fixing it on Brill hill.'[24] This letter, written after an afternoon's exploration of the city, suggests that Lawrence underestimated the extent to which Carcassonne had been restored by Viollet-le-Duc in the second half of the nineteenth century. It is now recognised that some of these restorations, while scholarly in concept, were almost certainly inauthentic. Lawrence's comment about 'very little modern restoration' seems to disregard a great deal of obviously new stonework in the upper levels of the fortifications. Perhaps he thought this unimportant, as his prime interest was in the layout and main structure of the defences which in most places were clearly original. Moreover Viollet-le-Duc was regarded at that time as the greatest authority on French medieval architecture, and Lawrence had already studied his lavishly illustrated accounts of Carcassonne. Without the preconceptions derived from this reading, Lawrence might have looked at some of the restorations with a more critical eye.

From Carcassonne Lawrence turned north and rode via Toulouse to Albi, 'where the Cathedral disappointed me, inside: the sculptures of which I had heard so much were Renaissance, and certainly second class: there were however yards and yards of them; 'tis wonderful they managed to do so many . . . Outside it is marvellous, and reminded me much of a beer-barrel, or a huge series of beer-barrels, piled round a blanc-mange mould. It is all of rose-coloured brick, and one of the most strikingly original buildings extant.'[25]

He continued northwards through the Tarn. When he reached Cordes he sent his family a long description of this, 'the most picturesque town I have come across in my travels.' The letter shows that he already possessed the powers of observation and description which would be so evident in his later writing.

'Imagine a valley, formed by the space between four ranges of hills: in the middle of this place a hill, about as steep as Mont St. Michel, and a matter of 400 feet high. Cover this with houses, all over, and you have a fair idea of the general view. The house-roofs are almost flat, and of red semicircular tiles:–

'Inside, the streets (two streets paved) are so steep that one can only maintain one's balance with great difficulty, and a strange horse cannot mount. Join these streets by narrow alleys of flights of broken, irregular stairs alternating with tiny squares of gravel about one house (say twenty feet long) each way. In places throw archways over the streets, or make them run under tunnels for fifty yards. Put in eight or ten fortified gates of the fifteenth and sixteenth centuries and fairly complete town walls, built over and round with a tangled ramshackle mass of hovels and ruined cottages. Let every other house be of stone, and of the fourteenth century, with charming Flamboyant windows of two lights, divided by exquisitely carved pillars and shapely capitals of a bunch of vine leaves or other naturalistic foliage. Half these windows are blocked up with a mass of broken tiles and mortar; over the others are worm-eaten shutters with splendid iron-work, and hinges of the Renaissance time. Between the windows are string courses, often carved with grotesques, of animals with human heads, hunting scenes etc. The roofs project a couple of feet, with gargoyles grinning down into the middle of the tiny streets, only a matter of two yards wide. These houses are usually of three storeys, and are mixed up with modern houses (modern for Cordes that is), perhaps of the sixteenth century with transomed and mullioned windows, and square-headed or ogee doorways. The market hall is fourteenth, the church fifteenth century. Some of the houses are in ruins, others tottering. There are only three straight ones in the town (these are now the *Mairie*), all the rest lean backwards and forwards, or are shored up by a stable, or a buttress thrown across the streets to a similarly affected house: and so two sick men support each other. Some are of brick, plastered, or have been plastered, for it has usually fallen away, revealing blocked doors and windows, niches, and sculptured blocks built into the later work. All the wood-work is old and weather-warped, much of it quaintly carved, with all sorts of dilapidations.

'The streets are all grass-grown, and full of piles of dirt and rubbish: there are no drains, hardly even surface ones, but the sun quickly dries a little damp, and in winter the rains will carry all down to the bottom of the hill. Every wall is hung with grass and creepers, all the house windows are full of flowers, growing in rusty tin cans or earthenware jugs, broken and worn with use, and with half their brilliant glaze worn off. Each house has its little trellis of vines, and each is a subject or half a dozen for a painter. The colouring is simply unequalled. One could stay here for months, painting every day, supposing one escaped fevers or other trifles of that sort. A visit here is a glimpse back three centuries'.[26]

From Cordes Lawrence rode north-west, visiting Najac ('a splendid thirteenth-century castle entirely unrestored');[27] Cahors, where he found the fortified Pont Valentré 'curious rather than beautiful';[28] Bonaguil ('a castle of the middle fifteenth century, most interesting')[29] and Pujols, another twelfth-century castle. Then on via Montaigne and Hautefort to Chalusset where he spent his twentieth birthday. The castle here was 'a *most wonderful* thing of the thirteenth century . . . with *donjon* of the twelfth century *and a large beak on the front of it.* "Eureka" I've got it at last for the thesis: the transition from the square keep form: really it is too great for words'.[30] After this he went to Montbrun, 'a most charming little castle with twelfth-century keep: it is really, architecturally a most important place.'[31] Then to Niort 'which was magnificent; nothing could possibly have been more opportune or more interesting for my thesis,'[32] and on to Montreuil-Bellay and Loches. By this time he was six days ahead of his original timetable. He zig-zagged on, visiting Lavardin, Mondoubleau, Vendôme, Fréteval, and Orléans: 'all monuments and picture postcards of Joan of Arc, the cathedral is however good in spite of it.'[33]

On August 28th he went to see Chartres, expecting it to be 'like most French cathedrals spoilt by restoration, so I slipped out before breakfast to "do" it.'[34] The letter he wrote home that evening is one of the most interesting to have survived from this period; its uninhibited expression of religious feeling contrasts sharply with the reserved tone of other letters to his mother.

'What I found I cannot describe – it is absolutely untouched and unspoilt, in superb preservation, and the noblest building (for Beauvais is only half a one) that I have ever seen, or expect to see. If only you could get an idea of its beauty, of its perfection, without going to look at it! Its date is late twelfth and early thirteenth century. It is not enormous; but the carvings on its three portals are as fine as the best of all Greek work. Till yesterday I would put no sculptors near the Greeks of the fifth century. Today the French of the early middle ages *may* be inferior, but I do not think so: nothing in imagination could be grander than that arrangement of three huge cavernous portals, (thirty-odd feet deep), of gigantic height, with statues everywhere for pillars, bas-reliefs for plain surfaces, statuettes and canopies for mouldings. The whole west wall of the cathedral is chased and wrought like a Florentine plaque, and by master hands! You may think the individual figures stiff – the details coarse – everything is hard and narrow I admit, but when you see the whole – when you can conceive at once the frame *and* the picture, then you must admit that nothing could be greater, except it were the Parthenon as it left the hands of Pheidias: it must be one of the noblest works of man, as it is the finest of the middle ages. One cannot describe it in anything but superlatives, and these seem so wretchedly formal that I am half tempted to scratch out everything that I have written: Chartres is Chartres: – that is, a gallery built by the sculptors to enclose a finer collection than the Elgin Marbles. I went in, as I said, before breakfast, and I left when dark: – all the day I was running from one door to another, finding in each something I thought finer than the one I had just left, and then returning to find that the finest was that in front of me – for it is a place absolutely impossible to imagine, or to recollect, at any rate for me: it is over-whelming, and when night came I was absolutely exhausted, drenched to the skin (it had poured all day) and yet with a feeling I had never had before in the same degree – as though I had found a path (a hard one) as far as the gates of Heaven, and had caught a glimpse of the inside, the gate being ajar. You will understand how I felt though I cannot express myself. Certainly Chartres is the sight of a lifetime, a place truly in which to worship God. The middle ages were truer that way than ourselves, in spite of their narrowness and hardness and ignorance of the truth as we complacently put it: the truth doesn't matter a straw, if men only believe what they say or are willing to show that they do believe something. Chartres besides has the finest late xvi and early xvii [century] bas-reliefs in the world, and is beautiful in its design and its proportions. I have bought all the picture postcards, but they are of course hardly a ghost of the reality, nothing ever could be, though photography is best for such works. I took a photo myself of Philosophus, a most delightful little statuette, about eighteen inches high . . . it may give one an idea of how the smallest parts of the building are finished with as much care as the centre-posts of the main doorways, and if Philosophus were of Greek marble there would be photographs of him in every album, between the Hermes of Praxiteles and the Sophocles of the Lateran. He is great work. I also tried to take a photo of the masterpiece, the Christ of the south portal, but that cannot be worth looking at. I expect I will burn my photos of Chartres as soon as they are visible. Yet perhaps with care and time, one would get something worthy from a photograph. We must return there (I would want assistants) and spend a fortnight in pure happiness.'[35]

From Chartres Lawrence cycled to Brittany, where he spent a few days before returning to England on September 8th. His tour had been very successful and he brought back a large number of picture postcards, photographs, notes, sketches and plans for his thesis.

In the autumn of 1908 the Oxford University Officers' Training Corps was formed. This was one of many such units advocated by the Secretary of State for War, Lord Haldane, as part of a programme of army reforms. By the following summer 626 members of the University had volunteered; Lawrence had been among the first to do so. His decision came as a complete surprise to many of his friends, though possibly not to those who knew that he had already been an officer in the St Aldate's Church Lads' Brigade. After the lessons of the Boer War, there were many in Britain who preached the need for renewed national commitment to combat a growing threat from overseas. Lawrence, like most other young men of his social background, felt deeply patriotic.

Although he joined this military scheme, there are few signs elsewhere that he took any greater part in undergraduate life during his second year at Oxford. He did not take rooms in Jesus College when he came back from France, preferring to live at home. Yet there were no spare rooms available in the house at Polstead Road, and he had now reached the stage where he needed a separate study. His parents knew that this problem of space would continue, since there were three younger brothers to follow. They therefore decided during the autumn to build a two-room bungalow for Lawrence at the bottom of the garden. When this was completed it had a grate, electricity, water, and a telephone to the house.

To make his new study quiet, Lawrence hung the walls with green cloth. He slept and worked in this bungalow for the next two years, gaining not only a degree of independence, but also the habit of isolation. During this time he read voraciously; like many other students he stayed awake late into the night and often slept through the morning. His choice of books went well beyond the scholarly works required for the history course. He studied medieval writings such as the *chansons de geste*, and also enjoyed historical romances about the Middle Ages, reading Maurice Hewlett's *Richard Yea and Nay* over and over again.

That autumn he discussed his survey of French castles with C. F. Bell at the Ashmolean. Bell later wrote: 'We were talking one day about what his next step should be and I said "Why don't you go to the Holy

Land and try to settle once and for all the long contested question as to whether the pointed arch and vault were copied or developed from Eastern sources by the Crusaders, or whether it was they who taught their use to the Arabs?" . . . The suggestion was the origin of Lawrence's first visit to the Levant.'[36]

The idea of travelling to the Holy Land appealed greatly to Lawrence. In writing a thesis along the lines Bell had suggested he could incorporate all the research he had already done in France. Moreover, he could change his chosen special paper from 'Military History and Strategy' (which, in 1910, was to include a paper he found of little interest, about the Waterloo Campaign) to 'The First Three Crusades, 1095-1193', a medieval subject already close to his heart.

Before the end of the year he had made up his mind to go to the East if possible. By good fortune, an archaeologist and traveller with personal knowledge of the areas he would need to visit had just been appointed Keeper of the Ashmolean. This was D. G. Hogarth, to whom Lawrence was introduced at the beginning of January 1909. The following account of their first conversation was given by Hogarth to Robert Graves some years later: 'Hogarth . . . said, "This is the wrong season to visit Syria: it is too hot there now." "I'm going", said Lawrence. "Well, have you got the money? You'll want a guide and servants to carry your tent and baggage." "I'm going to walk", Lawrence said. "Europeans don't walk in Syria," said Hogarth, "it isn't safe or pleasant." "Well, I do", said Lawrence.'[37]

Nonplussed, Hogarth suggested writing to C. M. Doughty, one of the most distinguished Arabian travellers then living, for advice about the practicality of the journey. Doughty's reply was hardly encouraging: 'I have not been further North in Syria than latitude 34°. In July and August the heat is very severe by day and night, even at the altitude of Damascus, (over 2,000 ft). It is a land of squalor, where a European can find little refreshment. Long daily marches on foot a prudent man who knows the country would I think consider out of the question. The populations only know their own wretched life, and look upon any European wandering in their country with at best a veiled ill-will.

'The distances to be traversed are very great. You would have nothing to draw upon but the slight margin of strength which you bring with you from Europe. Insufficient food, rest and sleep would soon begin to tell . . .

'I should dissuade a friend from such a voyage, which is too likely to be most wearisome, hazardous to health and even disappointing.

'A mule or horse, with its owner should, at least in my opinion, be hired to accompany you.

'Some Arabic is of course necessary . . .'[38]

It is known that Lawrence originally intended to take someone with him on this journey. The most likely person would have been Beeson, who had taken part in many of his expeditions and was good at drawing buildings. However the proposed companion, whoever it was, now backed out of the project. Lawrence replied to Doughty on February 8th: 'My little pleasure trip appears to be more interesting than I had bargained for: I have fortunately a few months to think about it in.'[39]

Lawrence began preparing himself for the journey by reading Doughty's *Travels in Arabia Deserta* in the Bodleian. Since he would need some spoken Arabic he consulted David Margoliouth, Laudian Professor of Arabic at Oxford, and was recommended to a Syrian Protestant clergyman, the Rev. Nasar Odeh, from whom he took lessons. Lawrence also took lessons in drawing from E. H. New, a well-known architectural illustrator. Lawrence had found that it was not always easy to photograph the features of castles he wished to illustrate, and this problem had been a handicap during the 1908 French tour. For example, he had written to Beeson about Chalusset: 'it was impossible to photo: but I can plan, and have a *sketch* which it shall be your duty to render presentable.'[40] New was an ideal drawing teacher and Lawrence surely found him excellent company. According to Gilbert Murray, New 'was well read, especially in poetry, and talked about art and literature with a sincerity that was very charming.'[41] He had recently illustrated a biography of William Morris and was beginning his 'New Loggan' drawings of Oxford colleges. These were bird's-eye views, and it was said that no one knew better than he did where to find good vantage points for such work. It was probably with his encouragement that Lawrence took to climbing Oxford buildings: 'I used to go up all the towers and roofs, to get new angles of photography for architectural reasons.'[42]

It may also have been through New's influence that Lawrence now began to take an enthusiastic interest in the work of William Morris. His letters show that he read works by Morris extensively during the next four years and was strongly attracted by the ideals of neo-medievalism and craftsmanship they advocated, though he seems to have been less affected by their utopian socialism, which was quite alien to his own upbringing.

The notion of running a printing press after Morris's example appealed to Lawrence's romantic nature. Commercial printing had long since abandoned the standards of the early craftsmen who had tried to make their printed books as beautiful as medieval manuscripts. Morris had revived hand-printing and had aimed to 'produce books which would be a pleasure to look upon as pieces of printing and arrangement of type.'[43] Lawrence had no experience of printing, but discussed the idea of setting up a press with several friends, one of whom was Leonard Green: 'We decided that we would buy a windmill on a headland that was washed by sea. We would set up a printing press in the lowest storey and live over our shop. We would print only rather "precious" books . . . they would not be bound except to suit the temperament of the possible purchaser, and then only in vellum stained with Tyrian dye'.[44] When Lawrence heard of a private collection of Kelmscott Press books in a house near Broad Campden, he cycled to see it with another friend, Vyvyan Richards, who later recalled: 'Above all, on a special oak lectern, lay open the great Morris / Burne-Jones *Chaucer*, the book we had come specially to see, a feast to us then in itself.'[45]

As the date of his departure for Syria approached, Lawrence worked through useful books such as *Practical Hints for Travellers in the Near East* by E. A. Reynolds-Ball.[46] In May, Hogarth provided an introduction to H. Pirie-Gordon, who had toured Syria the previous year on horseback; Pirie-Gordon lent Lawrence an annotated map. In the meantime Sir John Rhys, Principal of Jesus College, had asked Lord Curzon to arrange with the Turkish authorities for *irades*, or letters of safe conduct, to facilitate Lawrence's journey.

Map 1: *Lawrence's 1909 walking tour of Crusader Castles*

CHAPTER 3

First Steps in the East
June 1909 – December 1910

LAWRENCE left England on 18th June 1909 on board the SS *Mongolia*. He spent the voyage working at his Arabic and, after a delay changing ships at Port Said, finally reached Beirut on July 7th. There he made contact with tutors at the American University who assured him that they had been 'taking walking tours in their summer holidays for years, exactly as I proposed to do . . . everybody, from the Consul downwards, tells me that travelling is as ordinary as in Europe. [Thomas] Cook has a permanent camp at Petra, the brute!'[1]

He began the first stage of his tour on July 8th, walking thirty miles down the coast road to Sidon on the first day. His itinerary then took him to Nabatiyeh, where he hired a guide to reach the fortress of Beaufort and thence Banias, 'whose people have the finest castle, and the worst reputation, in S. Lebanon.'[2] After this he went on to Hunin ('The castle there was trifling in strength but as for fleas!')[3] There he parted company with his guide, continuing alone to Tibnin and to Safed, which stands on a hill 2,700 feet high: 'In the day's march I went up and down the height of Mt. Blanc – and Palestine is all like that: a collection of small, irritating, hills crushed together pell-mell, and the roads either go up and down all the time, or wind in and about the rocks of the valleys, and never reach anywhere at all.'[4] From Safed he went eastward to Chastellet, an ancient ford across the Jordan, and then down the Jordan valley to the Sea of Galilee, which he skirted on the western shore. Continuing southward he visited Belvoir, then walked via Endor to Nazareth and eventually Athlit before returning up the coast road to Haifa, Acre, Tyre, Sidon, and Beirut. He completed this section of his programme in three weeks.

In one way he found this journey through the Bible lands disappointing, since the arid landscape bore so little resemblance to the scenery he had somehow expected: 'it is such a comfort to *know* that the country was not a bit like this in the time of Our Lord. The Renaissance painters were right, who drew him and his disciples feasting in a pillared hall, or sunning themselves on marble staircases: everywhere one finds remains of splendid Roman roads and houses and public buildings, and Galilee was the most Romanised province of Palestine. Also the country was well-peopled, and well watered artificially: there were not twenty miles of thistles behind Capernaum! and on the way round the lake they did not come upon dirty, dilapidated Bedouin tents, with the people calling to them to come in and talk, while miserable curs came snapping at their heels: Palestine was a decent country then, and could so easily be made so again. The sooner the Jews farm it all the better: their colonies are bright spots in a desert.'[5]

He got back to Beirut from this first part of his tour on August 2nd and wrote a 5,000-word letter to his family, to give them 'an idea of Northern Palestine in summer.'[6] They must have been delighted to receive it, not least because of its many Biblical allusions.

The account of his contacts with the local people reveals a good deal about his willingness to adopt the ways of the country: 'In the evening I get, either bread or *leben*, or more rarely *haleeb*. Sometimes I have to join in the native *burghul*, which is wheat, boiled in some way I fancy, but very greasy. One could not eat much of it, without a river near at hand to help it down. There are I believe other native dishes, but not among the peasant class at this time of year: I at least have found none, though the priests (native Arabs) give me stews and meat-messes of divers sorts.

'Nobody drinks anything but water, except coffee, for visitors. When I go into a native house the owner salutes me, and I return it and then he says something to one of his women, and they bring out a thick quilt, which, doubled, is laid on the rush mat over the floor as a chair: on that I squat down, and then the host asks me four or five times how my health is; and each time I tell him it is good. Then comes sometimes coffee, and after that a variety of questions, as to whether my tripod is a revolver, and what I am, and where I come from, and where I'm going, and why I'm on foot, and am I alone, and every other thing conceivable: and when I set up my tripod (sometimes, as a great treat) there are cries of astonishment and "*Mashallah*"s, "by the life of the Prophet", "Heavens", "Give God the glory" etc. etc. Such a curiosity has never been seen and all the village is summoned to look at it. Then I am asked about my wife and children, how many I have etc. I really feel a little ashamed of my youth out here. The Syrian of sixteen is full grown, with moustache and beard, married, with children, and has perhaps spent two or three years in New York, getting together enough capital to start him in business at home. They mostly put my age as fifteen, and are amazed at my travelling on foot and alone.

Riding is the only honourable way of going, and everyone is dreadfully afraid of thieves: they travel very little.

'However meanwhile the women have been getting my evening meal, served up on one of those large straw dishes I mentioned: (the "charger" for John the Baptist's head is translated by this in the Arabic version) then they pour water on my hands from a pitcher . . . and if very polite, will offer to wash my feet. The next thing is bed, which is the same quilt as that on which I am sitting, laid either in the house, or outside, on the roof of an outbuilding or verandah. Another quilt on top acts as blanket, and also there are pillows. These quilts are of course far too hot for a European to stand, since they are stuffed with wool, and feathers and fleas (in about equal quantities I fancy), so usually I lie on both mine, and hope for the best. One goes to bed soon after nine, and gets up at sunrise (about 4.30). Dressing consists of smoothing one's hair, and moistening one's hands and face in the stream from the pitcher: then on the road after bread and *leben*. Sometimes the people of the house will take money for one's lodging, sometimes not.'[7]

During this first part of his tour Lawrence had averaged twenty-two miles a day, and on one occasion walked thirty-six. He left Beirut for the next stage of his journey on August 6th and reached Tripoli a week later, having spent three or four days at the American Mission School in Jebail where he was welcomed by the principal, Miss Holmes, and her staff: 'She was most exceedingly kind in feeding me up, and as she had plenty of books and a marble-paved hall, with water ad lib and trees (real green ones) in her garden I was very happy.'[8] Lawrence's opinion of the American Mission's activities in Syria was to change over the coming years, but in 1909 it was favourable: 'it is doing much the most wonderful work of all in Palestine. It is Presbyterian, and has most brilliant men at the head of it. They recognised that at present conversion of Muslim in Syria was impossible . . . they have opened schools for both parties all over the country. In these the instruction is given in English, and includes many very important matters . . . Thus English is a common language in Syria, and in ten years no other will be needed. The influence . . . has promoted emigration to America, and I don't think there is a village in north Syria where one of the people has not been to America (they never stay more than a few years). These men are all eager for reforms in Syria, and dissatisfied with the government, so that the secretary of the government of the Lebanon (a high Turk) said to me – "the recent reform of the constitution in Constantinople (i.e. the revolution) is entirely due to the American mission." They have so educated the country (without touching on politics) that public opinion rejoiced in reform. They have colleges all over Syria, and Asia Minor, and in Constantinople (mostly self-supporting) and in all of them the religious side is emphasised: also every school is a mission station'.[9]

On his way north to Tripoli he had visited castles at Batrun, Mseilha, Enfeh and Tripoli. Then, on August 14th, he set off into the interior: 'It will take me at least three weeks to get to Aleppo (there are fifteen castles in the first 125 miles) and from there to Edessa another week. Then to return will take ten days, to Damascus. Altogether it will take till the end of September to do this piece.'[10]

On August 16th, his twenty-first birthday, he reached the magnificent Crac des Chevaliers, 'which is I think the finest castle in the world: certainly the most picturesque I have seen – quite marvellous: I stayed three days there'. Thence on to Safita and beyond: 'I will have such difficulty in becoming English again, here I am Arab in habits and slip in talking from English to French and Arabic unnoticing'.[11]

Venturing into the interior to see the castle at Masyad he was shot at, from about two hundred yards, by 'an ass with an old gun,'[12] but managed to scare off his attacker by firing back (at extreme range) with his pistol: 'I'm rather glad that my perseverance in carrying the Mauser has been rewarded . . . the man simply wanted to frighten me into money-payment'.[13] At the end of the month, when he had reached Latakia, he wrote home reassuringly: 'you may be happy now all my rough work is finished successfully: and my Thesis is I *think assured.*'[14] But from Latakia he struck inland once again to Sahyun: 'perhaps the finest castle I have seen in Syria: a splendid keep, of Semi-Norman style, perfect in all respects: towers galore'.[15] He stayed there two days, then walked on to Aleppo 'by forced marches, 120 miles in five days, which no doubt Bob or Will will laugh at, but not if they had to do it stumbling and staggering over these ghastly roads: it took me thirteen hours of marching per day, and I had an escort with me (mounted) so I lost no time. By the way it is rather amusing to contemplate a pedestrian guarded carefully by a troop of light horse: of course everybody thinks I am mad to walk, and the escort offered me a mount on the average once a half-hour: they couldn't understand my prejudice against everything with four legs.'[16] The escort was a precaution taken after the shooting incident near Masyad.

Lawrence realised when he reached Aleppo that he was running short of time, and he decided to hire a carriage there with two men and two horses to take him inland to Urfa and back. This final stretch of the journey, which lasted only ten days, took him through an area rich in Hittite remains. D. G. Hogarth, who had visited this region the previous spring, was one of the pioneer authorities on Hittite seal stones. He had presented a collection of these seals to the Ashmolean fifteen years earlier and was now keen to increase it; consequently he had asked Lawrence to look out for seals during this section of the castle tour. All kinds of ancient objects could be bought quite readily from villagers, who augmented their meagre incomes by robbing graves and selling their finds to itinerant *antika* dealers based in Aleppo.

On the way back from Urfa, at Seruj, Lawrence's camera was stolen from the carriage while the coachman he had left on watch slept. This was a serious loss, since no picture postcards of these Crusader castles were available and photographs were essential for his thesis. Worse was to come: a few days later while touring villages near the Euphrates in search of Hittite seals he was attacked. 'I meant to buy more, and found some rather jolly ones in a Turkish village one hour north of Tell Bashar; – but a beggar followed me from Meyra and bagged all my money and valuables (not content with pounding me behind the ear with a stone and biting open the back of my hand). I recovered most; but with such work that I was too sick of the district, and had (after due baksheeshing) too little cash to spare to search further.'[17]

He was back in Aleppo by September 19th, making strenuous efforts through the local authorities to recover his lost camera, but with no success. By the 22nd he had decided to abandon his further plans. He wrote to his family: 'After all I'm coming home at once, for lack of money. Of course you could send me more but I'd want new clothes, those I wear at present shall be left in Beyrout, I'd never get them past the sanitary inspection at Port Said:– new boots, the present being "porous", I've walked them to bits at any rate, and my feet lately have responded to it. They are all over cuts and chafes and blisters, and the smallest hole in this horrid climate rubs up in no time into a horrible sore. I can't imagine how many times I would have had blood poisoning already if it hadn't been for my boracic: but I want to rest the feet now or there will be something of the sort. To undertake further long walks would be imprudent, for even in new boots these holes would take long to heal.'[18] Before leaving Aleppo he also wrote to Sir John Rhys at Jesus College to excuse himself for arriving in Oxford late for the beginning of term: 'I have had a most delightful tour . . . on foot and alone all the time, so that

I have perhaps, living as an Arab with the Arabs, got a better insight into the daily life of the people than those who travel with caravan and dragomen. Some thirty-seven out of the fifty-odd castles were on my proposed route and I have seen all but one of them: many are quite unpublished, so of course I have had to make many plans, drawings and photographs . . . I am exceedingly sorry to leave the two castles in the Moabite deserts unvisited. I would go to them certainly, only that last week I was robbed and rather smashed up. Before I could be fit for walking again (and it is very hard physically in this country) the season of rains would have begun. It is most unfortunate, for the getting here is expensive: the actual travelling, my beggar-fashion, costs practically nothing of course.'[19]

Lawrence took the railway south from Aleppo to Damascus, where he spent three days before returning by train to Beirut. He had spent nearly three months in Syria and already hoped to return there after Finals: 'this is a glorious country for wandering in, for hospitality is something more than a name: setting aside the American and English missionaries, who take care of me in the most fatherly (or motherly) way . . . there are the common people each one ready to receive one for a night, and allow one to share in their meals: and without a thought of payment from a traveller on foot. It is so pleasant, for they have a very attractive kind of native dignity'.[20]

He travelled the whole way to England on the RMS *Ottoway* rather than taking the quicker route across France from Marseilles by train. This gave him the chance to recover his strength before reaching Oxford in mid-October: 'It will be pleasant to have fourteen days with no sight-seeing to do; nothing to do but eat.'[21] During the voyage home he drew up a detailed statement of his expenses on the tour, which amounted to £71 8s. 6d.[22]

The ship called in at Naples, and Lawrence had time to visit the National Museum. He found its collection of bronzes 'beyond words'.[23] He also went to a local bronze foundry, hoping to get a reproduction of a statue (which he referred to humorously as the 'footballer') for his brother Will. There was 'none to be got worthy under £2', and instead he bought 'a Hypnos head, very good work, but a bad cast, modern naturally. I asked the price and tumbled down with it to eight francs, little more than the value of the metal. You will admire it immensely; and I'll give you five minutes to find out the fault in the casting'.[24] He brought the Hypnos back to Oxford and found a place for it on a seat in the bay window of his study in the garden bungalow, where it became his most cherished ornament. It was a free-hand copy of the well-known Hypnos in the British Museum bronze room (itself a Roman copy of a Greek work dating from the fourth century BC). According to Vyvyan Richards, Lawrence would lie on the floor and contemplate it.[25]

Lawrence's letters show that his interest in medieval sculpture had led him to study the Greek masters. Now that he had learned to draw, he began to try three-dimensional work, and this became an occasional hobby. Much later he wrote that he had 'modelled and carved with some hope and vigour, for nearly four years: and did slowly gain the power to express something of my meaning in clay or stone. And I did thereby come to understand a little the limitations and triumphs of a sculptor's aim.'[26] When his youngest brother Arnold was sixteen, Lawrence would advise him to 'keep up an interest in sculpture. It is finer far than flat work, much more difficult to do and to appreciate, and gives one complete satisfaction where it is well done. I would rather possess a fine piece of sculpture than anything in the world.'[27]

Lawrence was now twenty-one, and entering his last year at university. He had far more freedom than most undergraduates, since by using the side-gate of his parents' house he could come and go at any hour he pleased. With Finals approaching, he decided to take regular private tutorials from L. C. Jane, who later wrote: 'Midnight to 4 a.m. was a favourite time (living at home, he had not to bother about college regulations).'[28] The bungalow also gave him the liberty to work or read late into the night without disturbing his family. 'You know, I think, the joy of getting into a strange country in a book: at home when I have shut my door and the town is in bed – and I know that nothing, not even the dawn – can disturb me in my curtains: only the slow crumbling of the coals in the fire: they get so red, and throw such splendid glimmerings on the Hypnos and the brass-work. And it is lovely too, after you have been wandering for hours in the forest with Percivale or Sagramors le desirous, to open the door, and from over the Cherwell to look at the sun glowering through the valley-mists. Why does one not like things if there are other people about? Why cannot one make one's books live except in the night, after hours of straining? . . . if you can get the right book at the right time you taste joys – not only bodily, physical, but spiritual also, which pass one out above and beyond one's miserable self, as it were through a huge air, following the light of another man's thought. And you can never be quite the old self again. You have forgotten a little bit: or rather pushed it out with a little of the inspiration of what is immortal in someone who has gone before you.'[29]

During the winter of 1909-10 Lawrence completed his thesis, calling it *The Influence of the Crusades on European Military Architecture – to the End of the XIIth Century*. The maximum length allowed was 12,000 words, and the thesis had to be submitted before the Easter vacation began on 19th March 1910. He had the final draft typed, although this was not a requirement. It contained numerous illustrations, including his own plans, sketches and photographs, as well as drawings copied by Beeson from published sources,[30] and picture postcards.

Lawrence hoped that his result in Finals would be good enough for him to pursue an academic career; the next step would be to prepare for a B.Litt. He had spent a good deal of time during his undergraduate years working with E. T. Leeds on various archaeological projects. That spring, for example, he had helped Leeds rearrange the Medieval Room at the Ashmolean. During the autumn they did their best to collect and record pottery fragments which came to light during excavations for a new book stack at the Radcliffe Camera. If Lawrence chose a research topic that combined his academic knowledge of the Middle Ages with this private interest in medieval pottery, the way might be open to a career in archaeology.[31] Like other undergraduates, however, he felt unwilling to commit himself; indeed he took a certain pride in neglecting plans for a career. He later wrote: 'I fought very hard, at Oxford and after going down, to avoid being labelled'.[32]

The idea of revisiting Syria appealed to him strongly. On November 30th he wrote to Doughty: 'the Crusading Fortresses I found are so intensely interesting that I hope to return to the East for some little time. It struck me that I ought to see you first . . . and so I asked Mr. Hogarth if it were possible.'[33] Hogarth had written a letter of introduction and as a result it was arranged that Lawrence should meet Doughty in mid-December.

Lawrence's scheme for setting up a private press was also taking shape. He had passed on his enthusiasm for fine printing to Vyvyan Richards and the two were thinking of forming a partnership. The project clearly owed more to the ideals preached by William Morris than to any first-hand knowledge of the tasks involved. A letter written by Lawrence to his father some months later describes the basis for their plans: 'If we are to preserve the utmost elasticity in our relations, we cannot be bound by a written agreement. We must (if such agreement exists) inevitably go outside and beyond it whenever we feel inclined: so that there will always be a contradiction between our theory and our practice . . . There cannot be any fixed hours of work. We both feel (at present) that printing is the best thing we can do, if we do it the best we can. That means, though, (as it is an art), that it will be done only when we feel inclined. Very likely sometimes for long periods I will not touch a press at all. Richards, whose other interests are less militant, will probably do the bulk of the work. The losses (if any) will be borne by us both, according as we are in funds (we will approximate to a common purse): the profits will be seized upon as a glorious opportunity to reduce prices.

'You will see, I think, that printing is not a business but a craft. We cannot sit down to it for so many hours a day, any more than one could paint a picture on that system.'[34]

Lawrence's parents did not approve. Richards was two years older than their son, and they could see no natural basis for this friendship. 'It would be hard to imagine two more diverse minds than his and mine', Richards later wrote. 'I had spent all my boyhood since the age of ten getting classics, with scholarships and distaste, in the orthodox public school way. My father was an inventor and a man absorbed altogether in business; my mother, an American . . . Archaeology, architecture, art – all such matters I scorned. I was one of the leaders in the college games with a proper sense of their importance.'[35]

Towards the end of his life Richards confessed the true basis for his friendship with Lawrence: 'Quite frankly for me it was love at first sight. He had neither flesh nor carnality of any kind; he just did not understand. He received my affection, my sacrifice, in fact, eventually my total subservience, as though it was his due. He never gave the slightest sign that he understood my motives or fathomed my desires.'[36]

Though Lawrence hid the fact from Richards, he can hardly have been unaware of this difficulty in their relationship. He chose to be tolerant; moreover he had a gift for persuading people to do what he wanted, and skilfully diverted Richards' infatuation into an enthusiasm for printing. Although Richards had previously known nothing whatsoever about this craft he soon found himself the instrument of Lawrence's ambition to set up a private press.

The difference in their attitudes towards one another is clear from their own statements. Richards wrote: 'The rest of my life at Oxford was spent in almost daily companionship with my new exciting friend.'[37] Lawrence, on the other hand, while prepared to defend what he saw as Richards' good points, also had many reservations. Writing to his brother Will about Richards, he said: 'Your character of him seems to me very apt and fairly complete: though I must say I think some of the "snobbery" which gives such an unpleasant conceit to his judgments comes rather from lack of understanding, than intentionally. Richards is exceedingly narrow in his outlook and interests, and is too apt to condemn generally where he does not find the particular colour and cast of thought that appeals to him. He is not at all intellectual, but an artist to the finger-tips . . . As soon as you get him on what he thinks really good he loses entirely his critical sense, and becomes a most fiery prophet. He has said things to me of an intimacy and directness which are beyond anyone else I have met. Altogether though he is a most complex and difficult personality, and I do not think he will get any better on acquaintance. He is quite in earnest about the printing: just as I am. I fancy we each of us trust the other entirely in that, without any great love, personally. But he will do his best for the press, and I also, so that only a little *savoir vivre* is necessary to make a very satisfactory partnership. I am most fortunate to have found a man of tremendous gifts, to whom craftsmanship is at once a dream and an inspiration . . . I think even Mr. Jane would be satisfied if our association produced the best book of modern times . . . To do the best of anything (or to try to do it) is not waste of opportunity:– and to be keeper of a museum would not be my best, any more than to teach history: I want something in which I can use all these things instead of being used by one of them.'[38]

Richards' homosexual feelings had no place in Lawrence's emotional life; while still an undergraduate he had fallen in love with a girl he had known since childhood. His affection for her was noted by close friends such as E. F. Hall, who often saw them together.

Lawrence and Janet Laurie had played together at Langley Lodge when he was six or seven. The two families had become close friends and after 1899, when Janet went to boarding school in Oxford, she had been a regular visitor to the house in Polstead Road. In 1901 her father had died, and she had been obliged to return home, but she was always welcomed by the Lawrences in Oxford and continued to see the boys quite often.

These visits were encouraged; Janet was much the same age as Bob, and Mrs Lawrence hoped that they would marry.[39] Janet liked all the boys but had no strong feelings for Bob, who was 'so terribly good'.[40] However, her company had always been enjoyable and she laughed readily; now she had grown into a good-looking if slightly tomboyish young lady. Both Lawrence and his brother Will found her very attractive. She visited Lawrence at Jesus College, and he often saw her at his home.

According to her own account, one evening after dinner when the two had remained behind at table, he bolted the dining room door and asked her quite unexpectedly if she would marry him. Like many of his contemporaries he was deeply secretive about his personal feelings and had an extremely inhibited attitude towards courtship. The depth of his affection now came as a complete surprise to her; she had never thought of him as a husband, and moreover was attracted to his tall and handsome brother Will. She realised that Lawrence was perfectly serious, but in her embarrassment laughed off the proposal. Although he often saw her afterwards he never mentioned the incident again. Some years later however he would prove the strength of his loyalty to her by an act of extraordinary generosity.

On 28th July 1910 the results of the Honour School of Modern History were published in Oxford. Lawrence and nine other candidates had been awarded First Class Honours. As his tutors had hoped, the thesis had been a remarkable success. The research in Syria had made an original contribution to knowledge. He later wrote to his brother Will that, in future, 'I fully expect Theses will be frowned upon: partly my fault, in straining the statute far beyond what ever was intended. Simple pieces of secondary work were supposed. Yet there will always be room for a good Thesis: though they will be less essential to a good degree than was prophesied my year.'[41]

L. C. Jane later told Robert Graves that Lawrence 'took a most brilliant First Class, so much so that Mr R. L. Poole (his tutor at Jesus) gave a dinner to the examiners to celebrate it.'[42] C. T. Atkinson, one of the examiners, was probably more objective than Jane: 'The thesis was an excellent piece of work and just "made" what was otherwise a not very exciting First: "safe but rather slight".'[43] Another of the examiners, W. H. Hutton, wrote to Robert Graves in 1927: 'I have just looked up his marks. There were ten papers, and a translation paper, and a thesis. His thesis was marked "most excellent", but it was not that which won him his first class, but the other papers which were all good and some very good.'[44] Ernest Barker, a Fellow of St John's who had given Lawrence tutorials on the Crusades, concluded: 'I should doubt if Lawrence ever was, or ever wished to be, an "historical scholar" in the ordinary sense of the word. He was not interested in historic fact just for its own sake. He took the Oxford

History School because it came in his way, and because it was a hurdle to be jumped . . . he made it interesting to himself by doing something of his own free choice, and by doing it on the spot: but when the History School was past – well, it was past, and history had served its turn.'[45]

The result was very satisfactory, especially since the thesis had shown that Lawrence had an aptitude for research. Before he could begin post-graduate work, however, he needed finance. This problem would have to be resolved before the next academic year began in October, but first he took a well-earned holiday, cycling for a month in France, accompanied for part of the time by his younger brother Frank.[46]

Frank, then seventeen, did not entirely share Lawrence's enthusiasm for castles and literature ('Ned is rejoicing over some books he has discovered at the price of a franc. Each time I have a bath he goes and buys a book instead.'[47]) But Frank enjoyed adventurous exploration, for instance at Coucy, where 'Ned and I, evading the *gardien*, went over the rest of the castle by ourselves, and by dint of forcing locks and climbing over doors and up walls succeeded in getting into every part of it. There are some very fine cellars under parts of the castle . . . When we had got to one end Ned felt himself slipping down into a pit, and got rather a shock as we could not see in the least how deep it was. However he saved himself, and, coming back later with a few matches, we found it was only six feet deep. We went quite a long way in the cellars . . . though until you got used to the light (it was almost pitch dark) it was very hard to see where you were going. Several times I walked straight into pillars . . . We went round the bottom of the moat (which is nearly thirty feet deep, now quite dry), wading waist deep through a fertile crop of nettles . . . When we at last came out we had to climb over the entrance gate to get out, as it was locked.'[48]

Lawrence's hope of returning to Syria to study Crusader castles was evidently still alive. In late August he told his parents: 'I have met a man who has told me how to get the Syrian camera I may want half price or so, secondhand. Which is useful.'[49] When Frank bought a traditional flint and steel ('not a curiosity, it is meant for work'), Lawrence learned how to use it 'for his next Syrian trip. He lit a person's cigarette with it this evening, but failed to get the candle to light.'[50]

During this holiday Lawrence bought *Petit Jehan de Saintré*, a fifteenth-century novel of knightly manners, and other French works including two volumes of Montaigne, de Nerval, a version of *Tristan and Iseult* and a French anthology. But he also wrote asking Vyvyan Richards to find out how much a copy of Doughty's *Travels in Arabia Deserta* would cost in London, and if possible to obtain Hogarth's *Wandering Scholar in the Levant*, 'one of the best travel books ever written.'[51]

Lawrence was back in England by the middle of September and found that Jesus College was willing to give him money for postgraduate work. The College Minute Book records, under an entry dated 15th October: 'Mr Lawrence's exhibition for the current academical year is made into a grant of £50 to help him pursue his studies abroad (if necessary) with a view to the degree of B. Litt.'[52] On 19th October a further entry records that 'Mr Lawrence who took a first class in the History School last summer is granted the privileges of a Scholar and his exhibition for the present academical year is converted into a grant of £50 with a view to his being free to study his research subject in continental museums.'[53] Lawrence also tried for one of the two research fellowships offered by All Souls College to the best candidates in a competitive examination, which took place on October 25th-27th, but he was not successful.

The subject of his B. Litt. research was to be 'Mediaeval Lead-Glazed Pottery from the 11th to the 16th Centuries.'[54] C. F. Bell of the Ashmolean later wrote: 'I certainly must have had something to do with the choice of this theme, as it had long been one of my favourite problems'.[55] The project was formally accepted by the University on November 1st. Lawrence travelled that night to Rouen and from there wrote to Leeds: 'I hope . . . that you are aware of your new dignities. You are appointed (with the Regius Professor of Modern History, who was once Mr Oman) to supervise my researches into the origin and intentions of Mediæval Pottery of the XIth – XVth [*sic*] Cents: (especially grotesque): and if you get back to Oxford by when I return, I must call on you in cap and gown and receive instruction . . . The greatest and purest joy will be if you are set up at a huge table to *viva* me solemnly on what we have discussed and discovered together.

'It should create a good impression on your mind to know that I am in Rouen looking at medieval pots: Mr Bell got me letters from Mr Salomon Reinach [Keeper of National Museums in France] that make me out to be a sort of god: and they all rush about the museum here offering me keys and cupboards and cups of coffee: the last rather a bore.'[56]

Lawrence's letter from Rouen contains the earliest known reference to a dramatic change in his plans (though the news will have come as no surprise to Leeds): 'Mr Hogarth is going digging', Lawrence wrote, 'and I am going out to Syria in a fortnight to make plain the valleys and level the mountains for his feet:– also to learn Arabic. The two occupations fit into one another splendidly.'[57]

The sudden decision to join Hogarth's excavations at Carchemish in Syria was a turning-point in Lawrence's life.[58] On October 23rd Hogarth had returned to Oxford from Turkey, where he had finalised official arrangements for the new dig. It is unlikely that Lawrence had known very much about Carchemish before this, although he had passed close to it during his 1909 walking tour. He would now have learned that the significance of the site had long been recognised by archaeologists. As the excavations were to be an important stage in Lawrence's career something must be said about the background to this expedition.

English scholars had known of an ancient site at Jerablus on the Euphrates since the early eighteenth century, when Henry Maundrell, in his book *Journey from Aleppo to Jerusalem*,[59] described a visit he had made there in April 1699.

By 1872 the ruins at Jerablus had been identified as Carchemish, capital city of the Syrian Hittites. Four years later George Smith, a British Museum Assyriologist, visited the site. He was impressed by what he found and made detailed notes and sketches; but he fell ill and died on the journey back to England. Eventually his papers reached the Museum, which could scarcely ignore his summary of Jerablus: 'Grand site: vast walls and palace mounds: 8,000 feet round: many sculptures and monoliths with inscriptions: site of Karchemish.'[60]

The following year the archaeologist Sir Henry Layard became British Minister at Constantinople, and he applied for a *firman* [permit] to excavate at the site. In December 1878, therefore, the British Consul at Aleppo, Patrick Henderson, began the first investigation of Carchemish on the British Museum's behalf. In the spring of 1879 the ruins were visited and surveyed by Lieutenant Herbert Chermside, who was instructed to estimate the cost of thorough excavations. Meanwhile Henderson started negotiations to buy an interest in the site.

In the first year Henderson's work showed great promise. Part of a great stairway bordered with carved reliefs was uncovered, and investigation confirmed that the mound was not a natural feature. Despite great difficulties, seven large stones and some smaller fragments were shipped back to London. There, the carvings and hieroglyphics were conclusively identified as Hittite.

This early fieldwork was not properly supervised, and the excavations were carried out unscientifically without adequate records. Henderson himself was not free to spend much time at the dig, where work was directed by one of his employees. Thus in September 1880 he wrote to the Museum: 'I regret exceedingly that the great pressure of my other duties at present is such as to preclude my giving the time and attention to the excavation I would wish. I am obliged to trust a great deal to a native overseer as I can only spare a few days now and then to ride out to the excavations, which are at a distance of about ninety miles from Aleppo, over a dreary and desolate waste.'[61] This arrangement was so unsatisfactory that in 1881 the work was abandoned.

Twenty-six years elapsed before the British Museum found itself in a position to undertake proper excavations at Carchemish; but it did not lose interest in the site, of which it remained part-owner. In the autumn of 1907 Sir Edward Maunde Thompson, then Director and Principal Librarian of the British Museum, invited Dr E. Wallis Budge, Keeper of the Department of Babylonian and Assyrian Antiquities, to put forward proposals for some Hittite excavations. It was felt that the Museum should 'contribute to the solution of the Hittite problem, which had recently been illuminated by Dr Hugo Winckler's discoveries at Boghaz Keui.'[62]

D. G. Hogarth was asked to visit northern Syria in 1908 and inspect alternative sites. Even before he left, Budge thought that Carchemish would be the best choice. An internal memorandum dated 1st February 1908 states: 'There are certainly antiquities to be found at Jerablus, for Dr Budge himself saw several reliefs projecting from the smaller mound in 1888, and Henderson, Smith, Hanbury, Wright and others have obtained antiquities – both Hittite and Assyrian – from that site. The larger mound Dr Budge believes to have remained untouched, and he thinks it most important that Mr Hogarth should make maps and plans of it, and of all the portions of the smaller mound which await excavation . . . It is of importance to obtain permission to excavate at Jerablus, for whether it be the site of the ancient city of Carkemish or not, the small mound has yielded many monuments. Moreover the Americans are anxious for a *firman* to excavate it'.[63]

Hogarth had travelled for more than two months in Syria in the spring of 1908 making a long circuit during which he visited alternative Hittite sites such as Tell Basher and Tell Ahmar. He concluded that Carchemish, despite the earlier excavations and some damage done at various times to its visible monuments, still probably 'contained more than the other sites and represented a more important Hittite centre.'[64] One of the chief inducements to dig there was the hope of finding a bilingual text, equivalent to the Rosetta Stone, which would enable scholars to decipher Hittite script and understand the Hittite language. The Euphrates at Carchemish had been the boundary between the Hittite and Assyrian empires, and therefore between the unknown Hittite language and Assyrian (written in cuneiform) which archaeologists could understand. 'Where more likely', Hogarth asked, 'to find monuments set up in two systems of writing for the edification of two neighbouring races?'[65]

Accordingly, on 18th June 1908 the British Museum had applied for permission to dig at Jerablus. The Imperial Ottoman Museum at Constantinople, which controlled such permissions, had acknowledged the request; but that month had seen the first of a series of rebellions in the Turkish empire which culminated in the overthrow of Sultan Abdul-Hamid in 1909. The British Museum had heard nothing more of its request for two years, but it had not pressed the matter. At the best of times anti-Christian sentiment could lead to violence in the Syrian provinces, and it would have been foolish to risk excavations there during such a period of unrest.

By the spring of 1910 the situation was much calmer and the Museum had decided that it would probably be safe to begin work at Carchemish in January or February 1911. There was no commitment at this stage to a long-term excavation. The Museum was planning a single trial season, in the hope that this would establish whether the site was worthy of more extensive works. In March 1910, therefore, Frederic Kenyon, who had taken over as the Museum's Director and Principal Librarian, had written to the British Ambassador in Constantinople asking him to raise the matter of the permit. This move had produced the desired result and in May the Museum had learned that permission for a two-year excavation would be given to Hogarth, who had been nominated by the Museum to direct the work.

There were several conditions attached to this permit, which had finally been issued on 13th September 1910. All antiquities discovered were to be the property of the Imperial Ottoman Museum (although these objects could be photographed and casts taken). All objects found had to be deposited in a store controlled by the Turkish authorities, and the expedition had to pay the salary of a Turkish Commissaire who would oversee the dig on behalf of the Imperial Ottoman Museum. The administrative clauses stated that the permit was valid for two years, that it was not transferable, and that it would be void unless excavations began within three months of the date of issue.

Since Hogarth was not planning to begin work until February 1911 he could not comply with the last of these requirements. To avoid difficulties, therefore, he had gone to Constantinople in October 1910 and arranged for the starting date to be deferred until February. While there he had raised the problem of safety at Jerablus with the Embassy staff. They were rather pessimistic about the region and had recommended applying for a temporary police post at the site.

Lawrence seems to have heard about the purpose of this visit to Constantinople while Hogarth was still away. Seeing an enviable opportunity to return to Syria, Lawrence went to see E. T. Leeds at the Ashmolean, who later recalled that Lawrence had unexpectedly asked him whether there were any digs in prospect 'in the Near East or elsewhere' which he might join. Leeds knew a good deal about Hogarth's Carchemish plans and had replied, 'Why on earth didn't you speak sooner?'[66] He thought the arrangements were probably too far advanced, as R. Campbell Thompson had already been nominated as Hogarth's assistant. It also seemed unlikely that the British Museum would pay the cost of sending an inexperienced archaeologist to the site. When Hogarth returned to England, however, he was asked whether Lawrence could join the dig. Hogarth did not know Lawrence well at this time, but he had been impressed a year earlier by the Syrian walking tour. Bell and Leeds were confident that Lawrence would make a good archaeologist, and his personality must have seemed to Hogarth well fitted for this career. 'Your true antiquary', Hogarth had written not long before, 'is born, not made. Sometimes an infirmity or awkwardness of body, which has disposed a boy to shun the pursuits of his fellows, may help to detach the man for the study of forgotten far off things; but it is essential that there be inborn in him the type of mind which is more curious of the past than the present, loves detail for its own sake, and cares less for ends than means.'[67]

Hogarth agreed to take Lawrence, but the British Museum could hardly be asked to finance this addition to the party, and absence abroad on work which had nothing to do with the proposed B.Litt. would disqualify Lawrence from the Jesus College scholarship. So Lawrence was now awarded, 'entirely through Hogarth's initiative and whole-hearted advocacy,'[68] a Senior Demyship at Magdalen College, Oxford. The award, in effect a junior research fellowship, was announced on 14th December 1910. It could run until the summer of 1914 and was worth £100 a year. This meant that if Lawrence went to Carchemish the Museum would not need to pay more than his on-site living expenses.

The dig, however, might not last more than four months, while the award was for four years. To qualify for it Lawrence gave as a research subject 'Norman Castles in the Levant'; additional fieldwork in Syria and Palestine would enable him to expand his B.A. thesis into a book. Most of his time would nevertheless be spent in Oxford, and the project could run in parallel with his B.Litt. research on medieval pottery.

Lawrence now had two reasons for returning to Syria and for both of them he would need to improve his Arabic. He therefore arranged to spend the first two months of 1911 at the American Mission School in Jebail which he had visited during his 1909 walking tour. He also began to study Assyrian grammar and cuneiform, which would prove useful if Assyrian inscriptions were found at Carchemish.

He had more distant projects as well. One was for an academic book (or possibly two) which he sometimes referred to as 'my monumental work on the Crusades',[69] and elsewhere as *Richard*.[70] There are also references (in letters written many years later) to his having considered writing an account of the background of Christ: 'Galilee and Syria, social, intellectual and artistic, of 40 B.C. It would make an interesting book.'[71] As a diversion from these serious plans he thought of writing a travel book which would recount 'adventures in seven type-cities of the East (Cairo, Jerusalem, Baghdad, Damascus etc.)' and arrange 'their characters into a descending cadence: a moral symphony.'[72] Even before starting to write the book he had decided on a title. It was derived from *Proverbs* (ix.1): 'Wisdom hath builded a house: she hath hewn out her seven pillars'.[73] But 'Seven Pillars of Wisdom' was also a deliberate echo of Ruskin's *Seven Lamps of Architecture,* and there was a clear analogy between the structure of Ruskin's book and the idea behind Lawrence's project. This analogy was of course lost when he later used the title for his book about the Arab Revolt.

The money from Magdalen would allow Lawrence to advance another of his plans. Before leaving England he talked to Vyvyan Richards, who had now taken a teaching post at Chingford on the border of Epping Forest. They agreed to form a loose business partnership and began to make plans for setting up the press. Before anything could be printed, Richards was to design a new typeface based on the rounded script of the *Book of Kells*, and also to build a neo-medieval hall to house the press machinery. This hall would incorporate roof-beams from an old building in Oxford to be demolished by Jesus College. Lawrence's contribution would be to finance the scheme, but he had no means to do this without help. He hoped that his father would buy a site for the press and lease it to Richards, and would also provide a loan to pay for the building. In the early stages at least, both the partners would earn their livings in other ways: 'Richards and I decided . . . that he would continue teaching for the present . . . we thought it would be wiser, since my power of earning the demyship depends on my health, and my ability to spend it on the press depends on my getting a salary, digging, next year and the year after . . . It is a great battle of the wits, creative, on his side, for he is doing the work, and utilitarian on mine, for I am to provide the materials beyond his keep. It will be a comfort when we get through into smoother water with the whole thing.'[74]

Lawrence left for Syria expecting his father to settle the financial arrangements with Richards, who could then put the building work in hand. He seems not to have foreseen his father's lack of enthusiasm for helping Vyvyan Richards, especially in a scheme which owed so much to romantic idealism and so little to commercial sense.

CHAPTER 4

Beginnings at Carchemish

December 1910 – June 1911

ON 10th December 1910 Lawrence sailed for Beirut on board the Messageries Maritimes steamship *Saghalien* which was scheduled to call at Naples, Athens, Smyrna and Constantinople. On the way, the ship developed engine trouble and as a result he had much more time ashore at these ports than he had expected. He seized the chance to visit Athens and explored the Acropolis with the enthusiasm born of a classical education: 'There were no porters, no guides, no visitors. And so I walked through the doorway of the Parthenon, and on into the inner part of it, without really remembering where or who I was. A heaviness in the air made my eyes swim, and wrapped up my senses: I only knew that I, a stranger, was walking on the floor of the place I had most desired to see, the greatest temple of Athene, the palace of art, and that I was counting her columns and finding there only what I already knew. The building was familiar, not cold as in the drawings, but complex, irregular, alive with curve and subtlety, and perfectly preserved. Every line of the mouldings, every minutest refinement in the sculptures were evident in that light, and inevitable in their place. The Parthenon is the protocathedral of the Hellenes. I believe I saw the Erectheum, and I remember coming back to look again at the Propylea, and to stand again beside the Niké Apteros: but then I came down again into the town, and found it modern and a little different . . . and so only this about Athens, that there is an intoxication, a power of possession in its ruins, and the memories that inhabit them, which entirely prevents anyone attempting to describe or to estimate them'.[1]

At Constantinople the *Saghalien* was delayed for several days, and Lawrence used the time to see the city and its museums. He did not reach Beirut until December 21st and arrived at Jebail, his final destination, on Christmas Eve.

In London Frederic Kenyon, Director of the British Museum, was taking the final administrative steps needed before Hogarth could begin work at Carchemish. On December 13th the Lords Commissioners of the

Treasury were notified of the plans and requested to allocate £2,000, to be drawn as usual in such cases from the Museum's Grant-in-Aid for Purchases. It was not until the end of the month that Kenyon agreed formally to take Lawrence, and he then wrote a further letter to the Treasury seeking approval for the additional cost: 'an offer has been received from Mr. T. E. Lawrence (an Arabic scholar, acquainted with the country, and an expert in the subject of pottery) to join the expedition at Jerablus and to take part in the excavations. Mr. Lawrence is willing to give his services (which will be of very material value) without salary, but I would ask your Lordships to sanction the payment of his actual living expenses while engaged on the excavations, and of his travelling expenses from Beyrout to Jerablus and back'.[2]

Lawrence's knowledge of Arabic was somewhat generously described in this letter, but he was now at Jebail working hard on the north Syrian dialect that would be spoken in the neighbourhood of Jerablus. During this stay at the American Mission School he made friends with two of the teachers: Miss Fareedeh el Akle, who taught him Arabic, and Mrs Rieder, who encouraged him to improve his French. He made good progress in Arabic and even learned to read and write very simple phrases, though he was suffering from eye-strain which hampered his studies.

Hogarth intended to start work at Carchemish on about February 20th, a week before the deadline imposed by the digging permit. He left England at the beginning of the month, travelling out via Turkey. When he arrived at Constantinople, however, he found the city deep in snow and his journey onwards hindered by quarantines. As a result, by February 20th he had only reached Beirut. The following day he wrote to Kenyon that 'all direct communications with Aleppo are cut by snow. The railway over the Lebanon has been blocked for more than a month and at the best no hope is held out of it being opened again for a week. If any more snow falls it will be longer . . . As the road from Alexandretta is also impassable, there is only one possible way – to go down the coast to Haifa, from there to Damascus by train and thence via Rayak to Aleppo – an affair of three or four days . . . [Campbell] Thompson left here some days ago by that route, but it is not known if he succeeded, for no telegraph is working in the interior and no post comes down'. Two days later he added a postscript: 'A wild fall got up yesterday and still blowing. Much fresh snow on the mountains. Impossible to land at Haifa, so even that way is closed for the moment. Can't say when we can get on. If possible, I shall try crossing Lebanon on foot.'[3]

At Beirut he was joined by an experienced archaeological overseer who had worked with him on several previous excavations. This was Gregorios Antoniou (generally known as Gregori), a Cypriot from Larnaca. Lawrence came down from Jebail to join them, and they made their way to Aleppo via Damascus. The train journey from Haifa to Damascus gave Lawrence his first close acquaintance with Hogarth, whom he had previously seen as an eminent and distant figure: 'He has been very interesting indeed so far, especially on Arabian geography . . . We had a carriage to ourselves, and were otherwise most comfortable . . . Mr. Hogarth of course knew all the country by repute, and by books, and we identified all the mountain peaks and wadies and main roads . . . at Dera'at all was sunny, and we had a French *déjeuner* in the Buffet, where Mr Hogarth spoke Turkish & Greek, & French, & German, & Italian & English all about the same, so far as I could judge: it was a most weird feeling to be actually so far out of Europe'.[4]

At Damascus they were again delayed by the appalling weather (this was the worst winter in northern Syria for many years) and, as Hogarth reported sourly to Kenyon, the last stage of their journey was less enjoyable: 'Finally we got a train on the night of the 27th and in the company of time-expired soldiers from the Hauran and of returned Mecca pilgrims who stormed the train irrespective of class, came up here uncomfortably enough.'[5] Hogarth, Thompson and Lawrence at last reached Jerablus on March 11th, more than a week after the digging permit had expired. In view of the weather the Turkish authorities made no difficulties.

The ruins of Carchemish covered ten acres and had lain untouched for thirty years. Lawrence must have been excited by the prospect of finding out what lay beneath the surface. Hogarth later wrote this description of the city as they found it: 'The site . . . is a large oval surrounded by high embankments except on the north-east where the Euphrates flows past it. These embankments, in places as much as twenty-five feet high, conceal city fortifications of crude brick, and are pierced with two gates, one on the south and one on the west. On the north-east by the river but within the enceinte, rises a much higher and more important mound. Its summit is about 130ft above the mean level of the river, and it has evidently served as an acropolis. It is about 320 metres long from NW-SE and falls with a very steep slope to the river and a gentler one towards the town. The top is flattened and shows signs of having carried important Romano-Syrian structures, huge fragments of which have fallen down, and lie on the landward slope. The oval below this mound (i.e. the main area of the enclosed site) presented . . . different aspects in its eastern and western halves. The eastern, entirely uncultivated, was occupied in parts by hummocks and in part by superficial remains of structures of two epochs. The earlier are those of a Romano-Syrian town, largely built of earlier materials: the later are those of Arab houses, made of old blocks re-used. The hummocks appear to consist entirely of chips and stone-refuse thrown up by searchers for squared stone, and testify to the fact that the early structures on this part of the site have been very systematically destroyed by later builders. The western half of the city area is free of such refuse heaps and of structural remains later than Romano-Syrian: and less even of the latter show above the ground there than on the eastern half. A small tract near the circuit wall on the south-west has been brought under cultivation. One would expect to find the Romano-Syrian structures at any rate less disturbed on this half of the site.'[6]

Hogarth's object in this exploratory season was to find out enough about the site to judge whether the Hittite remains were worth more thorough excavation. He could not attempt any systematic digging in a single season and had not brought the equipment that would be necessary for such work. He knew that Henderson had discovered Hittite remains at the foot of the mound, including part of a large staircase. The position of this earlier digging was clear from the spoil heaps left behind and from a large stone relief still partly visible above ground. Hogarth decided to begin work in the same place since it seemed likely that there would have been buildings in the vicinity of a stairway. Also he knew that Henderson's men had reburied in their trenches some finds that could not be transported to England.

Excavation began on March 13th and soon more than a hundred men were employed. Hogarth found this workforce 'good of its kind though wholly unskilled. Since there are neither roads nor towns of any size in the district, the natives had never done navvy work and had no idea how to handle any tools but the simplest, or to deal with large stones. In training them Gregorios soon proved his value, and without him we should not have done in the following six weeks half the work that was actually done.'[7]

The expedition took over a stone-built house in Jerablus belonging to the local liquorice company. This provided little shelter from the cold weather and their first impressions of life in the village were very bleak. 'It is fortunate I brought a month's complete supplies out,' Hogarth reported, 'for there is almost nothing to be got here yet, not even bread. I have never been in so poor a country.'[8]

In 1908, when the excavations had first been planned, the Museum had expected Hogarth to run them himself. Now that he was Keeper of the Ashmolean, however, long absences abroad were no longer possible. He would soon have to return to Oxford, and since the dig had started late he could spend only five weeks on the site. It had been arranged that Campbell Thompson, the second-in-command, would take over when Hogarth left. Thompson, however, was a cuneiformist with little experience relevant to these excavations, and Hogarth had some doubts about his capability. After watching him at work for a few days Hogarth wrote to Kenyon: 'Thompson ought really to have a second helper besides Lawrence. The latter will second him admirably in observing and recording – in fact he is a far better *archaeologist* properly speaking than Thompson – but not in driving'.[9]

Another preoccupation was the Berlin–Baghdad Railway, which was being built by German construction companies. The route had not been fixed when the British Museum applied to excavate at Jerablus in 1908. Now, however, the railway had become a threat. Hogarth told Kenyon: 'It seems certain that the Baghdad Railway is going via Jerablus. Could you speak to Sir E. Grey [the Foreign Secretary] about the latter in view of possible future complications with the Railway? If the Company gets (as usual) a wide strip (10 kilometres or so) on either side of their line, it will include our site. But your rights to excavate it ought to be reserved . . . Of course I cannot be quite sure of the exact point chosen for the bridge-head. I doubt if it has been decided yet.'[10]

The choice of route was probably no accident since Hogarth later heard that the scheme to go via Carchemish had been favoured by Meissner Pasha, director of the railway project, 'simply in the hope of getting loot for himself out of the site. He is a collector of antiques and art objects!'[11] The railway bridge across the Euphrates at Jerablus would take several years to build, and there was already a construction camp there with a team of German engineers. Since the railway company also employed local labour, there was competition between the German and English expeditions.

Lawrence's first duties at Carchemish were a natural continuation of his work on medieval pottery in Oxford: 'It seems likely that I will take particular charge of the pottery found: that would be a business very much to my taste.'[12] Very little pottery came to light during the first few weeks, but Lawrence was kept busy and his Arabic was constantly in demand on the site. After a few days he wrote about the dig to his parents: 'Work begins at sunrise (6.0 a.m.), we breakfast first and walk down a little later. Thompson is surveying the site, and will be to the end of the week. Mr. Hogarth does the writing up of the results: I do the squeezing* and drawing the inscriptions and sculptures, and (with the great Gregori . . .) direct the men. Work goes on (with an hour for lunch) till sunset. Then home: write up journals: and catalogues: feed, and go to bed. This week has been extra busy putting up shelves, and fitting doors, windows etc. This I have done mostly, being handiest . . . We uncovered a great entrance staircase with some Hittite slabs on each side . . . there is no doubt of the great richness of the site . . . many of the slabs found have been too defaced for photography. These I have been trying to draw on a large scale for reproduction: this has been a big business. One lion's head is very fine work, artistically: also a god or king . . . The district is exceedingly pretty, from the model-village with its spring to the Euphrates, and the plain of Tell Ahmar, and the Taurus, snow-covered, to the north. The whole affair till now has been ideal, or would be if one had time to think about it.'[13]

The digs were yielding many fragments of stone bearing Hittite inscriptions, and Carchemish soon proved extremely rich in these texts. Many years later the distinguished Assyriologist R. D. Barnett would write: 'The collection of inscriptions from Carchemish has proved of the greatest importance in the study and decipherment of this script. Whatever the reasons may be, the Carchemish texts equal or exceed both in number and importance those from all other sites. It certainly seems that at least in the first millennium BC the metropolis of the hieroglyphs was Carchemish.'[14]

The discovery of these indecipherable texts was a continuing source of frustration, especially to Thompson. Despite their hopes of a bilingual inscription, none was found and the site yielded almost nothing in cuneiform. Lawrence, however, was enjoying himself greatly and his letters to England were filled with accounts of entertaining incidents. He was more used to rough living than his companions and watched their discomfort with amusement. On March 27th, for instance, he wrote to Leeds about their living accommodation: 'the house . . . is of stone, with mud floors and roof, and from the roof little bits drop all day and all night:

---

* i.e. making a copy of an inscription or design by applying wet paper over it.

and it is full of birds that baptize the bald-heads at their leisure . . . Then there are the cats: Father (who is only suffered, not encouraged) . . . comes in at the holes in the roof and walls by night, and offends lewdly in our beds. Then D.G.H[ogarth] throws a boot towards it and hits Thompson, and plants it in the bath, or knocks the light down: and when he has got out and repaired damages he finds the cat in his bed when he lies down again. So much for Father. Mother is plaintive, and rather a bore: she wails aloud for food, usually about 2 a.m: then she gets it, but in a tin: of late she receives sympathy, in spite of one very irregular night, when she woke me up with her claws over the face, and [roused] the rest of the expedition (who sleep together, with piled revolvers) by trying to escape my yells by jumping off the jam-tins through the window. She only knocked the tins down of course, and fell short in the wash-basin. Of late Mother has been in the family way, with Thompson a very gallant midwife. Her four kittens . . . make a ghastly noise in the Expeditionary bedroom half the night: I am a tolerable sleeper, but the others get up two or three times each, and draw beads on each other with revolvers.'[15]

The lack of a light railway or lifting tackle imposed a considerable restriction on the digging. Some parts of the site were totally inaccessible beneath Roman cement foundations. Elsewhere, the Hittite remains lay under tons of shattered Roman masonry: 'Whenever we break fresh ground dozens of these huge blocks have to be moved. Some of them weigh tons, and we have no blasting powder or stone-hammers with us. As a result they have to be hauled, prehistoric fashion, by brute force of men on ropes, helped to a small extent by crowbars. At this moment something over sixty men are tugging away above, each man yelling *Yallah* as he pulls: the row is tremendous, but the stones usually come away. Two men out of three presume to direct operations, and no one listens to any of them, they just obey Gregori's orders, and their shouting is only to employ their spare breath.'[16] One of the three Englishmen had to be on the site whenever work was going on, and Lawrence spent a great deal of his time there. This gave him the opportunity to learn much more about the local people.

By the end of March, Hogarth had cleared as much of the stairway as he could. The upper part seemed to have been destroyed; in any case it gave out beneath huge stones and earlier spoil heaps that could not be moved. Lower down, however, it was well preserved and he decided to dig at its foot, hoping to find buildings. Into this area, which Henderson had not disturbed, he cut a trench leading out from the staircase and roughly equal to it in width. This eventually revealed a low wall about one and a half metres high which continued the line of the stair. Beside the wall were carved slabs, some very broken, which had evidently stood on top of it. In front was a surface paved with round cobblestones from the Euphrates, and it seemed that the wall had formed one side of a roadway approaching the staircase. Since the wall suggested a substantial building, this part of the site was later christened 'the Lower Palace'.

Unfortunately the Hittite level was nearly seven metres underground and it was therefore impossible to excavate a large area without a light railway to carry away spoil. There were also obstacles such as Roman remains and some of Henderson's earlier spoil heaps on the surface. As a result, Hogarth's trench could only extend twenty metres or so and although the carved reliefs he had found were very interesting, the rest of the Lower Palace had to remain unexplored. The reliefs evidently formed a narrative series and showed Hittite warriors in full panoply; these were of great interest since no such pictures had previously been discovered. Among them was a great slab, almost complete, which carried the longest Hittite hieroglyphic text ever found. It seemed, however, that the Hittite city had been very thoroughly ransacked and destroyed, and Hogarth feared that this did not augur well for the excavations.

Since further work near the staircase was blocked in almost every direction, he began trial diggings on the mound itself in an attempt to find out what lay within it. Pits were dug in the top and headings driven into the sides, but again the diggers faced daunting obstacles. Hogarth could not hope to do more than find out whether there were any remains of early buildings on the mound.

After only two and a half weeks' work he wrote to Kenyon: 'It is too early, of course, to prophesy: but I begin to foresee or suspect two things: (1) that there is no important *primitive* stratum here, except, perhaps, inside the big mound (2) that the earliest and most important building is in the Acropolis mound under at least 20ft. of debris and silt, and probably under much more. To get down to this, or to get into it from the sides of the mound, will be a very heavy task owing to the size and weight of the fallen blocks.' He already had doubts about re-commending future seasons: 'I should not advise you to go on here in order to get only Hittite inscriptions of a comparatively late period and Hittite-Assyrian reliefs. You want cuneiform records, and early and fairly well-preserved buildings with their decoration and furniture. These we have not yet got.'[17]

By now Hogarth was more confident about Thompson's ability to take over the dig. Furthermore, 'in certain archaeological points on which he is weak, Lawrence is strong . . . I have found Lawrence an admirable adjutant, and you will be wise to make all the use of him you can. He gets on excellently with Thompson.'[18]

Though Lawrence found digging 'tremendous fun, and most exciting and interesting',[19] his letters reflect the growing doubt about a second season. Indeed, Hogarth was now considering the alternative sites he had visited in 1908, notably Tell Ahmar, which he thought might repay two seasons' work in 1913–14 if Carchemish came to nothing. Lawrence was enthusiastic about this prospect, especially since Hogarth would not be free to work there, 'and the place would be left to Thompson and myself. Thompson is not a digger, so the direction of that part would be my share . . . Mr. Hogarth suggested that a season or half a season with Petrie in Egypt might be valuable experience: and of course it would be. Digging in any case would be always a thing I would try to do, and the more I know of it the better.'[20]

While Lawrence worked at Carchemish, his father was still trying to reach some kind of arrangement with Vyvyan Richards about financing the projected printing venture. Neither of Lawrence's parents liked Richards, and they would have been happy to see the scheme abandoned. Lawrence, however, stuck to it tenaciously, urging his father on: 'I do not much concern myself about the exact arrangements (one cannot at this distance) but I would prefer one on which Richards . . . agreed: if not, let it be . . . [father's] arrangement, since it is he who provides the money. Only it is not a gift or loan to Richards, as a person merely. It is an attempt to get started the press we both desire so much: the mere question of whether Richards himself is approved or not does not enter the question hardly at all. I gathered that Florence [Messham] does not like him: his assumption of intellectual conceit tired her: but remember that people do not usually wear their inside skin out. I think myself that he is quite a heaven-sent partner.'[21]

He returned to the subject in another letter: 'Richards has been a little remiss in the business line I expect: of course he has no time to spare for it, with all the interest of type-designing, and the annoyance of his school-work. I do not think a lease of less than twenty years would be sufficient: my own wishes would put it at thirty or forty to be altogether on the safe side. But I fear very much he will never get it done: in which case I fear my opportunities of doing something good that will count will be very small: at least I am not going to put all my energies into rubbish like writing history, or becoming an archaeologist. I would much rather write a novel even, or become a newspaper correspondent:– however there is still hope that Richards may pull the thing through: I am doing nothing to help out here, while he is going steadily ahead through twice as much mess as we have any conception of, with no side interests whatever. There is something really great – and fine – about the man. One feels so selfish enjoying oneself out here when one might be in the fight. It is no laughing matter to be working against the twentieth century.'[22]

Despite this passionate outburst, Lawrence was progressing steadily towards an archaeological career. In due course Hogarth wrote to Flinders Petrie, head of the British School of Archaeology in Egypt: 'Can you make room on your excavations next winter for a young Oxford graduate, T. Lawrence, who has been with me at Carchemish? He is a very unusual type, and a man whom I feel quite sure you would approve of and like. He has very wide and exact archaeological knowledge, though not of Egyptian things, and, in view of his being employed in the future by the British Museum or others, I should very much like him to get some experience of your School, particularly in tomb digging. I think if you put him to help, for example, on a prehistoric tomb site you would not repent it. If he goes to you he would probably come on foot from north Syria. I may add that he is extremely indifferent to what he eats or how he lives. He knows a good deal of Arabic, though it is of the northern Syrian variety. I hope very much that you will be able to make room for him, for about a month at least, for I can assure you that he is really worth while.'[23]

Hogarth and Gregori left Carchemish on April 20th, having given Thompson careful instructions about work to be attempted during the rest of the season. In practice, the amount that could be undertaken was limited by the number of workmen that could be properly supervised. Thompson and Lawrence, together with Sheikh Hamoudi, a local man trained as an overseer by Gregori, could not handle more than eighty men. Hogarth felt that the season had already produced a number of worthwhile finds, as he told Kenyon: 'You have got and will continue to get quite enough Hittite sculpture and inscriptions . . . to justify the dig. Small things are still very few. I regard the result so far as adequate, but not brilliant, and unless the yield of the Palace increases or the western part of the site proves better preserved, I should probably not advise a second season. But a full first season must be done.'[24]

After Hogarth left, Lawrence sent home a fuller account of life on the dig: 'After breakfast we go down to the site, at which the men have been under their overseers since about 5.30 . . . The men dig till 8.30, have a half hour's rest, and then go on till twelve, when they knock off for an hour and a half: after that they work till five. We have dinner about seven or half-past, according to the mercy of Haj Wahid, the cook-cavass.

'While the men dig we loaf: which resolves itself into copying inscriptions, measuring depths and levels, and photographing. For the last I have five cameras, none much good but my own. Thompson is only a button-pusher. While we are at work on the top of the hill there is very little to do, as at present; so Thompson and I have divided the day, working each a morning or an afternoon at the house on our finds, or at the digs, alternately. I have control over the pottery . . .

'The most pleasing part of the day is when the breakfast-hour gets near: from all the villages below us on the plain there come long lines of red and blue women and children, carrying bread in red-check handkerchiefs, and wooden measures full of *leben* on their heads. The men are not tired then, and the heat is just pleasant, and they chatter about and jest and sing in very delightful style. A few of them bring shepherd's pipes, and make music of their sort. As a rule, they are not talkative: they will sit for minutes together at the house-door without a word . . . Some of the workmen are rather fine-looking fellows: all of course as thin as sticks: and the majority small: there was no one within an inch of Mr. Hogarth's height: indeed the majority are hardly more than mine. Many shave their heads, others let their hair grow in long plaits, like Hittites.

'Today, Saturday, is pay day . . . Each man, or nearly each man, gets an extra every week, according to the value of his finds. This little gamble appeals to them immensely.'[25]

Lawrence's plans for the future were now gradually changing. When he came to Carchemish he had had three firm projects. The first was to prepare an Oxford B.Litt. on medieval pottery; the second, to set up a printing press with Vyvyan Richards; and the third to develop his thesis on Crusader castles into a book.

Now, however, he was strongly attracted by the life he was leading at Carchemish. Outdoor work on the dig was balanced by intellectual luxuries in the evenings, such as talking to Hogarth and Thompson or reading. The idea of combining field archaeology with travel and writing, as Hogarth had done, appealed to Lawrence greatly. He was thinking increasingly of Doughty's example and began to find himself more interested in the people of Syria than in its ancient buildings. Before leaving England he had thought of travelling among the itinerant Soleyb, a people in whose company he might pass unobtrusively among the Arabs. In May, as the prospects for a second season at Carchemish faded, he wrote earnestly about the idea to his parents: 'The Soleyb . . . are not gypsies . . . and deny all connection with them. They are pagan, and by common consent the original, pre-Arab, inhabitants of Arabia. They go on foot, often, by preference, since some have wealth and baggage-camels: are great hunters of gazelles, hospitable simple folk, in no way fanatical. They are much despised by the Arabs, who as you will see in Doughty are feather-brained and rampol-witted. He always has a good word for the Soleyb, but told me he thought their mode of life would be very primitive . . . I am not trying to rival Doughty. You remember that passage that he who has once seen palm-trees and the goat-hair tents is never the same as he had been: that I feel very strongly, and I feel also that Doughty's two year wandering in untainted places made him the man he is, more than all his careful preparation before and since. My books would be the better, if I had been for a time in open country: and the Arab life is the only one that still holds the early poetry which is the easiest to read . . . the Soleyb . . . never touch Egypt or Sinai; but wander among the Aneyza, as far as Resafeh: sometimes a few will come into Damascus: more to Baghdad (from which I would start): usually they will only trade with towns like Resafeh, through the agency of half-nomadic Arabs. A spring and summer with them (which is what I was thinking of) would be a fresh experience: but I have no intention of making a book of it. I would not even go down in Arabia proper . . . I do not like the modern habit of wrenching all legends into the purpose of anthropology.'[26] Lawrence discussed the idea with Hogarth, who reminded him that the Soleyb were reputed to eat the gazelle they hunted raw. Hogarth later recalled that this 'seemed to give him pause!'[27]

On his return to England, Hogarth drafted a long report for the British Museum, setting out the conclusions he had been able to reach about the digs. He ended: 'I venture to recommend that the work be allowed to continue under Mr. Campbell Thompson's direction . . . throughout the coming summer, so long as he is able to keep it going economically, or until he has proved that neither the Acropolis nor the ground near its landward foot and on the West of the site is likely to yield adequate return to your expenditure . . . If in the course of May and June, he hits on a favourable spot or on spots where the Hittite stratum can be explored, without too great expenditure, he might well be allowed to continue as long as funds are available . . . even six months more work at present rates would leave a balance on the total credit probably sufficient for winding up the excavation . . . A site, so extensive and so notorious as Jerablus, demands, I think, a very full trial, which can hardly last for less than a full season.'[28]

Hogarth must already have known that a satisfactory exploration was impossible, given the scale of the site, the small workforce that remained, and the obstacles presented by post-Hittite debris. In these circumstances a first season could show that further digs were warranted, but could not definitely prove the contrary. Thompson was now to test a large area by digging pits at intervals in the hope of chancing on something that would justify more thorough excavation, although as Hogarth said, 'pitting over a site, which carried no superficial indication of what its lower stratum contains, is haphazard work at best'.[29]

On May 14th the site was visited by Gertrude Bell, already a traveller and archaeologist of some distinction. Hogarth's two young assistants did their utmost to conceal their inexperience and the season's disappointing results. Lawrence wrote home: 'she told Thompson his ideas of digging were prehistoric: and so we had to squash her with a display of erudition. She was taken (in five minutes) over Byzantine, Crusader, Roman, Hittite, and French architecture (my part) and over Greek folk-lore, Assyrian architecture, and Mesopotamian ethnology (by Thompson); prehistoric pottery and telephoto lenses, Bronze Age metal technique, Meredith, Anatole France and the Octobrists (by me): the Young Turk movement, the construct state in Arabic, the price of riding camels, Assyrian burial-customs, and German methods of excavation with the Baghdad railway (by Thompson). This was a kind of hors d'oeuvre: and when it was over (she was getting more respectful) we settled down each to seven or eight subjects and questioned her upon them. She was quite glad to have tea after an hour and a half, and on going told Thompson that he had done wonders in his digging in the time, and that she thought *we* had got everything out of the place that could possibly have been got: she particularly admired the completeness of our note-books.

'So we did for her . . . It would have been most annoying if she had denounced our methods in print. I don't think she will.'[30]

Gertrude too wrote home about the meeting, but if their efforts had impressed her, she did not comment on the fact: 'I . . . found Mr.

Thompson and a young man called Lawrence (he is going to make a traveller) who had for some time been expecting that I would appear. They showed me their diggings and their finds and I spent a pleasant day with them.'[31]

Thompson was planning to finish work at the end of June; without cuneiform inscriptions the dig held little interest for him and he was to get married as soon as the season was over. Early that month Lawrence wrote to Leeds that 'the site looks as though it has small-pox with complications, pits and eruptions everywhere . . . and Thompson is packing with a sort of ghoulish joy . . . the course of true love.'[32] Hogarth, however, was in less of a hurry. The dig could be continued cheaply for some time, and the cost so far was barely more than half the budget. He therefore wrote telling Thompson to stay on as long as there was worthwhile work, perhaps even into August. Lawrence was delighted, although an extension to the season would interfere with the plans he had made to visit Syrian castles. He wrote to Hogarth: 'the idea of digging on is glorious, for there is really hope of several parts of the digs.'[33] Thompson's dismay can be imagined, but he wrote loyally to Kenyon: 'Both Lawrence and I are delighted at the prospect of continuing, however long . . . Lawrence tells me that he is in no wise troubled by the heat of this country, as he walked continually throughout last summer through Syria . . . I spent a year at Mosul, six months in the Sudan and two summers at Chicago'.[34]

Towards the end of June their luck began to turn, and they made a series of interesting finds. Earlier, they had extended Hogarth's trench at the foot of the staircase a few metres and discovered that the 'Lower Palace' wall turned back at right angles. By excavating inside this corner they had hoped to reveal the interior of a palace room; but to their disappointment the back of the wall was only rough stonework and this had cast doubt on the whole 'Lower Palace' theory. Now, however, they discovered rooms behind the wall in another place; the truth was that their first pit had struck some kind of courtyard. They also found two Hittite houses with walls standing to a good height and interesting pottery including a great many model horses made from terracotta.

Lawrence's delight over these finds was shortlived. On June 24th they received a cable from Kenyon which contradicted Hogarth's instructions: 'Thompson care of British Consul Alep. When Palace with north acropolis and houses and tombs well tested stop work Kenyon.' Thompson replied at once: 'Closing fortnight'[35] and Lawrence wrote to his family dejectedly: 'Have had orders to clear out as soon as possible: so in a fortnight we will shut down the digs. By the terms of the telegram from the British Museum they are so disappointed at our results that there will be no second season. It is a great pity for we had on the strength of our former orders, just begun important clearances. We will leave the site like a warren, all disfigured with rubbish heaps and with all the work only half done: altogether about the most unsatisfactory job that one can imagine.'[36]

CHAPTER 5

An Undecided Future

June 1911 – June 1912

IN London, Kenyon reported to the Standing Committee of the British Museum Trustees that 'after consultation with Mr. Hogarth, he had come to the conclusion that enough had been done to show the general character of the Jerablus site, and that a discussion of the results was necessary before carrying the work further. He had accordingly instructed Mr. Thompson to wind up operations'.[1] In reality, Hogarth had not agreed to this, and he was very disappointed when Thompson closed down the dig so quickly. Later, he criticised Thompson for the decision, not least because the recent finds had been so interesting. They included 'limestone lined graves with bronze axeheads and scores of "champagne" cups.'[2]

On July 8th Thompson and Lawrence left Jerablus to spend a few days, on Hogarth's suggestion, at Tell Ahmar, a few hours' journey from Carchemish. Thompson later explained the purpose of this visit: 'Here, abutting on the river, was a mound a hundred yards long, running steeply down to the water, where an ancient ramp, cut into the conglomerate, marked the old Hittite staithe. Round this citadel, on the landward side, was an earth wall enclosing an area half a mile long by a quarter wide, and close outside this lay the pieces of the great basalt obelisk, inscribed in Hittite pictographs . . . This had been first noted by Hogarth . . . Miss Gertrude Bell later took a squeeze of it, from which a great cast was made for the Ashmolean Museum. In the north-east Gate lie the broken pieces of two Assyrian lions; Hogarth and Norton had taken squeezes of the cuneiform inscriptions on these, but the characters were so worn by the weather that Mr. L. W. King of the British Museum . . . could only make out the opening invocation to the gods. As everyone knows, it is far easier to read cuneiform from the original stone than from a squeeze; and as the two lions were inscribed in duplicate, I was able to make out most of the text'.[3]

Lawrence parted company with Thompson on July 12th, and was free to go looking for Crusader castles. He began a fortnight's tramp during which he examined the fortifications at Urfa, Harran, Biridjik, and Rum

Kalaat. During the journey he kept a diary in which he wrote technical notes on their architecture.[4] In the notebook which contains this diary there is the draft of a letter which he now sent anonymously to *The Times*. He had realised how successfully Hogarth was using that paper to promote interest in Carchemish,[5] but it is hard to believe that Hogarth would have approved of this undiplomatic outburst:

Sir, Everyone who has watched the wonderful strides that civilisation is making in the hands of the Young Turks will know of their continued efforts to clear from the country all signs of the evil of the past. They may not know, however, that this spirit is gaining ground in the provinces. All visitors to Aleppo will have seen the great castle that rules it from every part, with its ring of battlements and its memories of prehistoric, Hittite, Assyrian, and Roman dominion. This great mass is now to be cleared away and levelled, and one of the prominent Levantine financiers of the town has the project of constructing there a new quarter for the poorest of the inhabitants on the lines of the London East End. The property will soon be put up to auction, and there are strong hopes that the end will be achieved.

The sister town of Urfa (Edessa) is not lagging behind. It also intends to sell its castle; but, as owing to its inaccessibility the site is useless, the stones will have to be sold for building material. A beginning has been made by the clearance of the old Greek town walls: as these were one of the largest as well as one of the most complete circuits in the Turkish Empire, there can be no two opinions as to the improvement effected.

The little town of Biredjik in the same province is faced with a difficulty. Its own great castle it is clearing away, and building a gaol with the proceeds, but there is a second of these monuments of oppression, Rum Kaleh, a day's journey up the river, with which it is beyond the present strength of the town to grapple. It is hoped that the coming of the Baghdad Railway may mean its final conversion to modern uses. If so, this will be the second benefit of the sort conferred by the railway, since the ruins of Carchemish are to provide materials for the approaches to the new iron girder bridge over the Euphrates.

Everybody will sympathise with these latest and most worthy efforts of the Constitutional Government to let a little light into its darker provinces. Yours, &c., Traveller'.[6]

The Times published the letter on August 9th, under the headline 'Vandalism in Upper Syria and Mesopotamia'. One reaction was a strong protest by the German Consul in Aleppo to his British counterpart about the reference to the Baghdad Railway Company.

This was the first time anything written by Lawrence had been published, apart from the contributions to his school magazine; but he had ambitions to write, and an essay from this period surviving in manuscript may also have been drafted with the idea of publication. Titled 'Mores Romanorum', it describes an event which had occurred at Jerablus in the middle of May. It is the earliest example of a 'literary' essay by Lawrence that has survived:

"Hoja [overseer], that man there with the shovel does no work."

"No Sir."

"We will send him off tonight."

The Hoja's hand doubtfully touched his lips and forehead, "Yes sir, but... he is a son of Ibrahim Mul'Ali... the Moghreby (magician)...?"

"No matter, Hoja."

Late in the afternoon we lay limply on our beds, listening gratefully for the dying away of the two-hour tumult always born of pay day, when on a sudden a new voice, surcharged with anger, took shrill mastery of the babble. It rose till it compelled all to a hush that stayed unbroken after itself had ceased. A minute later the Hoja intruded, white and trembling, crying out, "The Moghreby has cursed the digging: we must not go on till you have taken back his son or death will come of it. O Sir what are we to do?"

"No matter, Hoja: do you not know we are greater magicians than he?"

The Hoja went out half-comforted, but we turned to one another and consulted what we might do. The crisis was grave, for if unallayed, fear of the magician would rob us of half our men next week. At last, "Haj Wahid", called my friend to our servant, a Kurd, proud of his fighting ancestry, "go out and bring us a hair of this fellow." "From his clothes, sir?" "No, from his head." In a few minutes a cry and a burst of excited query proclaimed the insult achieved. Haj Wahid returned in triumph with a short grey hair.

"From his beard, Khawaja", said he, expectantly. "Good: Haj Wahid, tell the people we are making a wax image, and in it we are putting this hair. Then when we drive a pin into the heart, the Moghreby will straightway drop dead. But if we melt it before your fire, his life will run away from him to Gehanum, even as the drops of hot wax fall into the fire and are consumed." Haj Wahid's eyes sparkled, and in a few minutes his kitchen was busy with the hum of voices, and loud expressive "*wallahs*" of amazement and delightful expectation.

To watch the triumphal dying of the sun – radiating surges of unimaginable rose, blush-like, to the heart of the dust-clouds which ever in the evening whirl over those desolate plains of the upper Euphrates – I stood that evening in the door of the house, when a figure in dusky white rushed from behind a wall, and almost threw itself at my feet.

"Effendi, Effendi," gasped Mul'Ali, "they lied to you, indeed they did lie: I am a poor man, I said no harm of you: Effendi, dismiss all my sons if you will, only in the Name of Allah the Merciful, the Compassionate, give me back that hair!'

X[7]

On July 28th Lawrence returned to Jerablus, meaning to finish off one or two small jobs on the site. The next day however he became very ill with dysentery and noted in his diary: 'Cannot possibly continue tramp in this condition.'[8] He was unable to look after himself and was taken in by Sheikh Hamoudi. Weakened by the privations of his walking tour, Lawrence remained in a serious condition for several days. He cannot have been comforted to know that Hamoudi was advised not to help such a sick man, for fear of blame if things turned out for the worst. Lawrence had to give Hamoudi a note absolving him from any responsibility.

Lawrence continued his diary throughout this illness, noting, for instance, on July 31st: 'The Hoja awfully good all these days, with me making quite unprecedented demands on his time and patience. But poor man, a most dreadful bore as well, does his best by five or six repeats to get every idea of his into my thick head, which usually understands before he speaks. In the evening tried a little *burghul* well-boiled in milk. Dahoum came to see me'.[9]

Dahoum had worked during the digging season as one of the ex-pedition's donkey boys. He carried water and ran general errands for Thompson and Lawrence. In late June, Lawrence had described him in a letter home as 'an interesting character: he can read a few words (the only man in the district except the liquorice-king) of Arabic, and altogether has more intelligence than the rank and file. He talks of going into Aleppo to school with the money he has made out of us. I will try and keep an eye on him, to see what happens. He would be better in the country, only for the hideous grind of the continual forced labour, and the low level of the village minds.

'Fortunately there is no foreign influence as yet in the district: if only you had seen the ruination caused by the French influence, and to a lesser degree by the American, you would never wish it extended. The perfectly hopeless vulgarity of the half-Europeanised Arab is appalling. Better a thousand times the Arab untouched. The foreigners come out here always to teach, whereas they had much better learn, for in everything but wits and knowledge the Arab is generally the better man of the two.'[10]

Lawrence's views were changing radically: just two years earlier he had sung the praises of the work being done by the American Mission Schools. It seems that Dahoum, a young Arab of fourteen or fifteen, personified all that Lawrence now admired in the native population. The romanticism in his outlook was common enough among Englishmen of that generation. Critics of Victorian achievement pointed out that the Industrial Revolution had been accompanied by a decline in social morality. It is clear from Lawrence's letters that he shared this view; for example he found Blackwood's *Centaur* 'very good, though not "all the way" enough for me: but at the same time more reasoned and definite as an attack on the modern world than anything I've read – bar Morris.'[11] Such attitudes had breathed new life into the philosophical concept of the 'noble savage', and it is clear that Lawrence thought the simple agricultural peasantry in Syria in some way untainted by the vices that had debased the poor in Britain.

Lawrence nonetheless encouraged Dahoum's efforts to educate himself, and wrote to the American Mission School at Jebail for help: 'He is beginning to use his reason as well as his instinct. He taught himself to read a little, so I had very exceptional material to work on but I made him read and write more than he ever did before. You know you cannot do much with a piece of stick and a scrap of dusty ground as materials. I am going to ask Miss Fareedeh for a few simple books, amusing, for him to begin on. Remember he is to be left a Moslem.'[12] A month later he amplified this request: 'What I wanted for the donkey boy was a history book or a geography which should be readable and yet Arab . . . nothing with a taste of "Frangi" shall enter Jerablus by my means. I have no wish to do more for the boy than give him a chance to help himself: "education" I have had so much of, and it is such rot: saving your presence! The only stuff worth having is what you work out yourself.'[13] While helping Dahoum, Lawrence was able to improve his own knowledge of Arabic, and he was now planning to return to Jerablus in the winter, with the idea that while travelling 'the strongly-dialectical Arabic of the villages would be good as a disguise'.[14]

It is most unlikely that Dahoum shared Lawrence's romanticism. He saw education as a means to escape from the miserable poverty of the village peasantry, and Lawrence's interest in him must have seemed a miraculous opportunity. He would not have understood his benefactor's strange Victorian ideals. During the days Lawrence spent at Hamoudi's house, when it was feared that he would die, Dahoum came to see him every evening. The care Lawrence received from these two villagers probably saved his life and he did not forget it. Two years later he would take them both to England as a reward and, from this time on, the references to Dahoum in Lawrence's letters show an almost fatherly concern.

On August 3rd, still very weak, Lawrence abandoned any plans for further tramping that summer and decided to return to England. He had found at Jerablus a letter from Hogarth sent on by Thompson which raised strong hopes of a second season. On the way home, therefore, Lawrence was already planning his return: 'I am coming out I hope again for the winter in Jerablus: not for the joy of fragments of antiquity (mostly reburied by us) but for the buying of the stolen ones, and the controlling the stone-loving instincts of the railway builders. If I can manage it not a cut stone of Carchemish shall decorate their embankments.'[15]

He also wrote enthusiastically from Aleppo to Hogarth: 'You emphasise the importance of the palace:– most certainly that is the place . . . we have there a great palace, most likely of Sangara [a king of Carchemish in the ninth century BC] for it is the last Hittite building in Carchemish (cp. pottery) not extending over much ground . . . not at all deep (about a 3m. max.) fairly well preserved, for there is a good height of wall . . . and with very interesting pottery. Try and get a look at the rough notes I made on the "Palace" pottery, the two or three photographs of it, and the coloured drawings Thompson made of some pieces . . . A second season would clear all the palace, and be a fairly satisfactory wind up to the digs. If they are left as at present it will only mean someone going on in a few years' time: and now I know three fifths of the pottery, and the men know their job and the railway has not come. Surely the ground plan of the palace of Sangara would be a tolerable result?'[16]

When Lawrence reached Beirut in early August he was delighted to find that the poet James Elroy Flecker had been appointed to the British consulate. Flecker and his wife Hellé had just arrived, and on August 8th Lawrence wrote: 'I have been doing little but talk to them. I had to wait an extra day here because of things for me in the P.O. which was shut when I got there.'[17] After a brief visit to Damascus, Lawrence sailed from Beirut on August 12th, travelling by sea to Marseilles and thence overland to England.

He spent the summer recuperating; it was to be several months before his strength fully returned. However, he had plenty to do. On the journey home he had told a friend: 'I have to write a specimen chapter of a book at Oxford if the publishers will accept my terms: so that I will be held there till mid-October.'[18] This project was almost certainly *Crusader Castles*, the book he planned to make from an enlarged revision of the successful thesis. He now worked critically through its text. The special terms referred to, which seem to have prevented the scheme getting any further, related to the inclusion of a great many plans and photographs.[19]

Since the finds during the final month at Carchemish had been so encouraging, Hogarth wanted to resume the work for a short season. In terms of scholarship the excavations were clearly incomplete, and due to Thompson's hurried departure, a third of the £2,000 allocated remained unspent. The most compelling argument, however, was that Turkish law would allow the British Museum to excavate only one site at a time. The Imperial Ottoman Museum, represented at the site by its Commissaire, wrote to Kenyon on August 2nd expressing its hope that there would be a second season. Clearly Hogarth would not be given permission to work at Tell Ahmar or anywhere else in the Turkish Empire without a more satisfactory ending at Carchemish. It was therefore decided to reopen the excavations for two months in the spring of 1912.[20]

Lawrence's letters suggest that he was told little of these deliberations, though he knew that Hogarth felt that more work should be done. In late August he told Vyvyan Richards with a certain pride that 'Hogarth is pressing the British Museum for a second season at Carchemish as a result of the wonderful pottery discoveries of the last two months . . . my star is in the ascendant you may imagine. If he can overcome the reluctance of the officials it will mean four months more joy next spring. We will see: he vows to raise Hell if his wishes are not conceded: a very good man,

Hogarth.'[21] At the end of September, when the decision had been made, Lawrence wrote to a friend: 'Doctors dispute over my carcase: they seem to agree that I mustn't go to [the] east again for three months: as a matter of fact I am very busy, for it is the *pottery* (O the despised pottery!) which is the reason of our second year's dig. I am in the seventh heaven or thereabouts as a result.'[22]

At this stage the British Museum's plans suffered a setback. Campbell Thompson, now married, did not wish to return to Carchemish unless he could be accompanied by his wife, and Kenyon refused to allow this. On October 4th, however, Hogarth reported that Leonard Woolley had agreed to take over. Woolley, then aged thirty-one, had worked as an Assistant Keeper at the Ashmolean. He was about to take part in the University's excavations in Nubia, but he would be free to go to Carchemish at the end of February 1912. Hogarth had not been very impressed with Thompson and felt that the change was no loss: 'we have Lawrence, who knows place and people as well as Thompson.'[23] In the meantime Petrie had agreed to take Lawrence at one of his Egyptian sites during January.

In the autumn of 1911, though he was still unfit, Lawrence decided that he should return to Jerablus and work on his Arabic. Also, Hogarth had recommended building a house for the archaeologists near the site and Lawrence was to supervise its construction before Woolley arrived. His journey took on an additional urgency when Sir Louis Mallet at the Foreign Office warned Kenyon that the Baghdad Railway, according to rumours in Aleppo, 'was likely to traverse the precise spot at Jerablus (Carchemish) where Dr Hogarth had lately been excavating, and . . . the site itself was threatened with destruction.' Mallet recommended that Hogarth should send someone out 'to protect any property from injury by natives or other untoward incident.'[24]

Lawrence left England at the end of November (he had chosen to attend the Oxford degree-giving ceremony held on 11.11.'11, a unique date which no doubt appealed to him). On his way to the coast he called on Doughty to discuss the idea of travelling with the Soleyb. Doughty, however, was critical of the scheme. Passing through Damascus not long afterwards, Lawrence visited Haji Mohammed el Bessam, whose father had known Doughty years before. Bessam too advised against the Soleyb scheme and 'said that they did not go far enough into Arabia to please me. Still he will be charmed to send me amongst his own people for a time, so there is still hope! He said that the danger was nothing like as great as it was thirty years ago. In fact with a good servant, almost nothing at all.'[25]

When Lawrence reached Aleppo he found that the German plans had been changed and there was no immediate danger to the site. In the near future the engineers would be busy building store-sheds, repair shops and accommodation. He learned that two bridges would be built, since a temporary structure would be necessary before the main work could begin. The only immediate concern was that the railway's projects would lead to a shortage of men and an increase in local wage levels.

Another pressing matter was the uncertainty as to who owned the Carchemish site. With the likelihood of continuing excavations and the possibility that part of the site might be bought for the railway, several local landowners were advancing claims to title. R. A. Fontana, the British Consul at Aleppo, suggested that Lawrence should go to Biridjik with the Consular dragoman to examine official records and find out who the owners really were. By the time Lawrence had done this and reported his findings to Hogarth, he had only been able to spend a few days studying Arabic at Jerablus.

He took a steamer to Egypt on 2nd January 1912, to join Petrie at Kafr Ammar some fifty miles up the Nile from Cairo. The site was a graveyard and Lawrence found the work repulsive: 'It is a strange sight to see the men forcing open a square wooden coffin, and taking out the painted anthropoid envelope within, and splitting this up also to drag out a mummy, not glorious in bright wrappings, but dark brown, fibrous, visibly rotting – and then the thing begins to come to pieces, and the men tear off its head, and bare the skull, and the vertebrae drop out, and the ribs, and legs, and perhaps only one poor amulet is the result: the smell and sights are horrible. Digging here is very unlike our Carchemish work – and very much easier. They have nothing of our complications of depth, or of levels, and fragmentary rests of cities or civilisations. I shall be glad to be back in Syria . . . Mr Hogarth was quite right in arranging for no longer: I'm no body snatcher, and we have a pile of skulls that would do credit to a follower of Jenghis Khan. These men are less squeamish than our fellows.'[26]

After a week Lawrence had taken a dislike to both Egypt and the Egyptians, although happily the dig moved to earlier graves in which the bodies had not been mummified. He was nevertheless glad to work under Petrie: 'I like him exceedingly, but rather as one thinks of a cathedral or something immovable but by earthquake. He is a quite inspired archaeologist – and I am picking up hints of sorts all day long.'[27] Petrie was sufficiently impressed by Lawrence to offer him £700 towards the cost of two seasons' excavation in Bahrain and Lawrence later consulted Hogarth about this proposal: 'Prof. Petrie spoke to me two or three times in Egypt about the Persian gulf and south Arabia . . . he declared that he believed the early dynasties came round by sea from Elam or thereabout to Egypt: and that Bahrein was a stage of their going. Finally in my last week with him he suggested my going down there to dig, say next year, as a preliminary season, to be followed by a second on a larger scale, if it seemed promising. He said he could provide the funds.

'I told him I'd ask you about it: and that I'd rather you got what profits were going: he didn't seem to think the ideas were incompatible . . . Of course it could only be if Hittite were not going:– and on account of the railway works I think you will certainly interrupt the Jerablus digs for a little: they must go on some day though. At the same time I would like to dig in the Persian gulf, and as Bahrein is nominally British, I suppose we might carry off the stuff.'[28]

Lawrence left Kafr Ammar on January 30th and sailed for Beirut on February 2nd. On the way he sent home a diatribe comparing the Egyptians very unfavourably with the men of Jerablus: 'The Egyptian people are horribly ugly, very dirty, dull, low-spirited, without any of the vigour or the self-confident independence of our men. Besides, the fanaticism of the country is deplorable, and the treatment of the women most un-European: most of the Petrie workmen have several wives, and have had many more, and one could not stand or work close to them for a few minutes without catching fleas or lice. Nor could one talk to them with the delicious free intimacy of the men of Carchemish. They either got surly, or took liberties. They were frenetic, and querulous, foul-mouthed, and fawning.'[29]

Unknown to Lawrence, events were taking place in England which would greatly prolong the excavations at Carchemish. After giving a lecture about the site, Hogarth had quite unexpectedly received a cheque for £5,000 towards the cost of continuing work there. This had been sent by Walter Morrison, a wealthy businessman who practised philanthropy on a remarkable scale (for example, he made one of the largest single gifts ever received by the Bodleian Library). Morrison was deeply interested in archaeology; he had been a founder and the chief benefactor of the Palestine Exploration Fund. He met Hogarth regularly since they both served on the PEF committee.

The extent of Morrison's generosity never became public in his lifetime because most of his gifts were made under strict conditions of anonymity. He applied these conditions to the Carchemish donation and Hogarth was obliged to warn Kenyon: 'You may have guessed who he is. If so don't, please, communicate your guess to anyone at present.'[30] With funding assured, work would continue at Jerablus for several seasons, during which the British Museum would contribute a further £2,000, making £7,000 available in all.

Although Lawrence was working for the British Museum at Carchemish he felt a personal loyalty to the Ashmolean. He often bought Hittite seals from dealers and villagers to add to Hogarth's collection in Oxford. On the way back from Egypt he called at Damascus to visit the dealers and bought a rare cylinder seal: 'The man came down gloriously from a lira to ten francs, in less than three hours:– and eventually (late this afternoon) I condescended to take it at that, with a little Hittite gable seal (not novel – two four-legged beasts) thrown in.'[31]

He reached Aleppo on February 8th expecting to find money there for building the expedition's house – but as the funds had not yet arrived he had to borrow from Fontana at the Consulate. A few days later he wrote to Flecker: 'Of course when I got to Aleppo I found that the British Museum idiots had sent me orders to buy the site and build the house, and had forgotten to provide the funds . . . Am sniffing at another glorious Cappadocian-Hittite cylinder, aspersing its rarity: have been doing this for a week with a 50% effect so far: if the funds hold off much longer, I'll be begged to take it *belash* [for nothing]. On the whole, to buy *antikas* is a sport, not commerce'.[32] At last, on February 20th, £50 arrived from the Museum, and Lawrence started for Jerablus the following day. Woolley, who was expected soon, had decided to bring two Egyptians with him to help with photography and making squeezes, 'leaving myself and Mr. Lawrence far more free for less mechanical work.'[33] When he heard this, Lawrence was disgusted: 'they will be rather a blot on the landscape,' he wrote to Hogarth, 'but I don't care, for the railway has brought a horrible crew – the sweepings of Aleppo – already . . . Woolley talked of bringing a gang another year!'[34]

Lawrence and Woolley already knew each other slightly, having met at the Ashmolean some years before; but the circumstances of this new contact clearly gave scope for tension. Woolley, eight years older than Lawrence, was coming to take charge, and had greater experience of archaeological field-work. Lawrence, on the other hand, was already familiar with Carchemish and its workforce, and at that point knew much more about Hittite archaeology than Woolley.

When Lawrence reached Jerablus on February 24th he found that the Kaimmakam (Governor) of Biridjik would not give permission for their house to be built. Lawrence could do nothing except wait until the Turks received instructions from Constantinople. In the meantime, he made friends with the German railway engineers and agreed to let them clear away the heaps of stone spoil left on the site after the 1911 season. Since the Germans needed stone for buildings and embankments, and the spoil-heaps hampered the excavations, this arrangement suited both parties.

Woolley arrived on March 13th, but the Turkish guard on the site refused to let him begin work. Woolley sent an urgent message to the Kaimmakam asking for permission to proceed, but this met with a curt refusal. It turned out that the Kaimmakam wanted a bribe, thinly disguised as salary for an unofficial Commissaire. To Lawrence's delight, Woolley took the law into his own hands and told the Kaimmakam that he intended to begin work: anyone who obstructed him would, if necessary, be shot. The Kaimmakam gave in, but other difficulties were quickly raised and Lawrence found himself being prosecuted for trespass by one of the people who claimed to own part of the site. The case went before a local Islamic court (which had in fact no jurisdiction over foreigners) and the digging permit was impounded. Woolley's high-handed methods secured its return, and earned Lawrence's admiration.

Lawrence recorded these incidents in letters to England, and they lost nothing in the telling. Woolley had become 'a most excellent person' in his eyes.[35] The Kaimmakam received an official rebuke from Constantinople and there were no further bureaucratic problems.

Woolley began the season with about a hundred men. His first objective was the long task of excavating the north end of the mound, where Thompson had made some promising finds. In the middle of April, however, strong winds made it impossible to work there, so Woolley looked for a more sheltered part of the site. He chose a place on the river bank where superficial ruins suggested that there might have been a water gate, and his hopes were quickly rewarded when the workmen uncovered a pair of finely carved lions, each more than three metres long, and the remains of a grand Hittite stairway which had once led to a landing place.

By the end of April the expedition house was finished and provided not merely accommodation but a photographic darkroom and archaeological store as well. The living quarters were soon decorated lavishly with objects from the site and with a Roman mosaic floor rescued from a nearby field. Lawrence would now be able to live at Jerablus between digging seasons. However, lacking a publisher for his book, he seems to have lost interest in visiting castles in the area and instead planned to return with Woolley to England in mid-June. 'The only pity is my Arabic, which is going forward painfully . . . The break from season to season spells ruination to it, and it is a thing which I value as much as anything I'm doing. I manage an hour every day at it in the early morning with Dahoum and a dictionary.'[36]

At the beginning of May Hogarth spent nine days at the dig, having travelled out via Constantinople. Soon after he arrived he wrote back to Kenyon that: 'Lawrence is even more useful this year than last, as he has now quite mastered the local Arabic and through his residence here after the dig last year has come to know all the villagers intimately.'[37]

On the way out Hogarth had met the Kaiser, 'and got his explicit promise to make all right for us with the *Baghdadbahn* people, if there is any trouble. I showed him a few of the photos and he was immensely interested.'[38] As it happened, the railway company was giving valuable assistance. It had cleared away much of the first year's spoil, enabling Woolley to cut a wide trench from the staircase towards the newly found water gate, to see if there was a road connecting them. On May 9th, Hogarth reported, there 'appeared the finest Hittite inscription yet found, a sort of obelisk very finely engraved on two faces in relief. Also the upper part of a life-size head almost in the round.'[39] The work carried out by the railway to remove spoil had saved the expedition hundreds of pounds, and Hogarth told Kenyon with relief: 'The workshops, houses, hospital etc have greatly changed the place, but, as wages do not appear to have risen, the railway has so far been an unmixed benefit.'[40]

He had now concluded that 'the lower levels of the citadel . . . and the "Lower Palace" contain the most important secrets of the site and no effort should be spared to explore them thoroughly. In both these regions the excavators will be working in the *interior* of Hittite buildings, instead of outside them as heretofore, and if they are ever to find archives, will find them . . . If the co-operation of the Baghdad Railway Engineers could be secured for removing the uppermost (mediaeval and Roman) layers of the citadel without expense to us, it would be a very good thing.'[41] He commended Woolley for his work, and also Lawrence, 'who now knows the local people and their speech very well, and having had a longer training in Hittite things than Woolley, is an invaluable adjutant to the latter. Both ought, I think, to be secured for the remainder of the excavation.' He recommended that Woolley should be offered thirty shillings a day, and that Lawrence, having 'done an immense amount of work for you in these two seasons, ought also to begin to receive a salary.'[42] He had evidently discussed this with Lawrence, and suggested the rate of fifteen shillings a day which was paid in subsequent seasons.

Lawrence's knowledge of Arabic was increasingly important. There was ample funding for the dig, but, if they were to continue on a larger scale, it would be necessary to supervise more men. His responsibility in this area was increasing: 'Woolley gets on well with the men, but so far as possible I take what I can of that from him and he runs the actual dig.'[43] For this, Lawrence needed to speak the local dialect fluently with a wide vocabulary, and Hogarth asked him to work at it. Lawrence wrote to his friends at Jebail: 'Mr. Hogarth is very anxious to make me learn Arabic; and so I am going to stay here July and August alone.' He planned nevertheless to go home at Christmas 'and to carry Miss Fareedah [el Akle, who had taught him Arabic at the Jebail Mission School] away with me for six weeks in England. There will be more digs in February but all through January Miss Holmes [Principal of the School] will be bereft (*inshallah!*).'[44]

Since Lawrence was staying on, Woolley asked him to spend some time working over the season's results and sorting pottery. More than a thousand fragments of carved and incised basalt had been recovered from the area at the foot of the stairway, and the task of fitting them together was very time-consuming. Lawrence was also to visit several villages where Hittite remains had been reported. 'From outside we hear of many carved and inscribed stones. After the digs I will load up a donkey with a squeeze-paper and camera and go and copy them. In my three months here I will have a good deal of leisure, though I have to cement the floors of two rooms, and repair the mosaic pavement, and tile the bathroom, and glaze and waterproof the roof of the dining room: not to mention fitting up pottery and stones.'[45] Woolley's two Egyptian boys had run away late in the season, so Lawrence was again responsible for photography. 'We have decided that we cannot do it all ourselves next year, and so I have the training of a boy – Dahoum of course – as well to see to. You have no idea how hard it is to instil elementary optics into his head in imperfect Arabic. He will put plates the wrong side out. However all these are little worries, which are working towards my improvement in Arabic: I hope to be fluent – though still incorrect – by Xmas.'[46]

Woolley closed down the dig early in June. When the men had been paid off, he spent a few days with Lawrence excavating a Hittite cemetery five miles away. Later, having worked for another week clearing up loose ends at Jerablus, the two went to Alexandretta to arrange shipment of their various purchases. Woolley sailed for England on June 20th, confident after this first season together that he and Lawrence had formed a successful partnership.

CHAPTER 6

Learning from the Arabs
June 1912 – June 1913

WITH a sense of relief, Lawrence set off back to Carchemish, stopping at Aleppo on the way: 'There is a sort of feeling of blessed peace in the air at the ending of my immediate digging work. Woolley is off and I am my own master again, which is a position that speaks for itself and its goodness . . . I seem to have been months away from Jerablus, and am longing for its peace. You know there one says "I don't want to talk" and there is silence till you break it, or "I want to be alone" and twenty men post themselves around you out of sight that not even a hoopoe or an ant may cry out and break your rest . . . Really this country, for the foreigner, is too glorious for words: one is the baron of the feudal system.'[1]

Lawrence planned to travel during the summer, taking Dahoum as a servant and companion. He had obtained official letters of introduction to the Governors of the towns he hoped to visit: 'the Vali [of Aleppo] described me as a Professor of the University of Oxford, who had made excavations at Jerablus, and was now travelling for pleasure: that I was an inestimable person, whose worth archaeologically and intellectually they (the Government) were quite unable to express in words . . . *Therefore* all Kaimmakams, Mutessarifs, Mirdirs and government officials are to see that I am well lodged, well fed, provided with transport, with guides, interpreters, and escorts, if I express a wish. If I desire to travel without these accompaniments I am to be permitted: and tidings are to be sent to Aleppo that I have arrived, that I am being entertained, and that I have departed satisfied.

'I cannot use these beautiful letters except upon need. I don't want to make a progress, but a tour. However I have also got the ordinary official recommendations, which all important travellers carry: and these I will present first and watch their operations. It is rather quaint that a person of my superlative attainments should travel with a donkey and a boy to push it.'[2]

During this holiday between digging seasons Lawrence occasionally wore Arab dress.[3] His knowledge of the local dialect was strengthening daily: 'it is almost fluent when I am on ordinary ground: my grammar is atrocious (Arabic is exceeding difficult there) and I slur over all my inflections of necessity: with a larger vocabulary and a simpler grammatical scheme (i.e. a nearer approach toward the Bedouin Arabic) I'll get on easily in two years' time. And as Mr Hogarth said "One who knows Arabic is never at a loss".'[4]

These plans were threatened, however, by an epidemic of cholera in the villages around Aleppo. Lawrence feared that the Baghdad railway workers, who travelled frequently between Aleppo and Jerablus, would bring the disease to the village. He wrote to a doctor in England for medical advice, and prepared for the worst as the hot summer weather arrived. During the first half of July he was occupied making improvements to the house and finishing off some minor archaeological tasks. By the middle of the month he was ready to visit Seruj and Urfa where there were reports of inscribed stones; but then several people fell ill at the same time, and the journey had to be postponed: 'First of all I had malaria – a short spell of the usual two-day sort. Mrs Haj Wahid got a new baby, and turned very ill. Haj's boy fell down and broke his head to pieces and had to be tied up; Haj himself went drinking and collapsed with internal troubles of sorts. So I brought in Dahoum to help Haj's mother in the kitchen, and he ungratefully produced malignant malaria . . . and raved his head off for three days until he nearly died. I had to sit on his chest half one night to keep him in bed. The little Armenian doctor did the main part of the work (he's our consulting physician) and now Haj and Dahoum are convalescent, and more trouble than ever. This morning, when I woke up, Dahoum (who can just stand) was trying to sweep out the big room . . . and Haj Wahid was feeding his donkey. I have to watch them all day to keep them in bed.'[5]

When these patients had recovered, Lawrence went across to Biridjik, but there he felt feverish again. On his return to Jerablus he had a third attack of fever and 'judged it prudent, in view of the excavations to follow so close, if I rested a bit in the cool'.[6] He had learned that construction work on the railway was going to halt for a month or two, so there seemed to be no threat of interference with the excavations. Therefore, at the beginning of August, he abandoned his plans to go on a trek and instead left with Dahoum for Beirut and Jebail, where he stayed at the American Mission School working on his Arabic. Both he and Dahoum were making some progress with writing the language, which was to prove very useful when Dahoum was sent to report on finds in the villages.

While staying in the Lebanon, Lawrence occasionally visited the Fleckers at their summer home in Areya. Hellé Flecker later recalled: 'my husband bore the heat very well, what he again missed was . . . intelligent society . . . [He] was delighted to be able to talk literature and Oxford again, and to hear of the "amazing boy's" astonishing adventures in Asia Minor'.[7]

As always, Lawrence's letters referred to the books he was reading. Apart from the works he had brought from England, he had access to the Mission School library at Jebail, and well-read friends such as Flecker and Fontana helped to broaden his literary taste. That summer, as well as a Hewlett novel, he read Spenser, Catullus, Marot, the *Koran*, Simonides and Meleager. 'Parts of Simonides are very splendid: also Antipater of Sidon, Tyrtaeus, and Hipponax: all in Bergk and the *Anthology*. I got a Greek dictionary . . . in Beyrout, and have made great play with it.'[8]

Lawrence decided to return to Carchemish at the end of August, when he expected Woolley to arrive. Dahoum, who had now mastered simple photographic work, would henceforward rank with the expedition's Arab headmen. He had become 'very useful now, though a savage: however we are here in the feudal system, which gives the overlord great claims: so that I have no trouble with him'.[9] As a field archaeologist, Lawrence would need a reliable assistant like Hogarth's Gregori. Dahoum was growing into this role, as was Hamoudi, who now worked increasingly with Woolley (he continued to do so for many years afterwards). Although Lawrence took a fatherly interest in Dahoum, the relationship was that between teacher and pupil, or master and trusted assistant. The notions which made Lawrence respect the young Arab's simplicity would also mean that he could never treat Dahoum as an equal.

Just as Lawrence was about to leave Jebail, he received a telegram from Haj Wahid, the expedition's cook and general factotum who was guarding the house at Carchemish. Instead of suspending operations, the railway engineers had tried to take advantage of Lawrence's absence by demolishing part of the ancient city wall of Carchemish, meaning to use the stone for a nearby embankment. Woolley had told their chief, Herr Contzen, that the railway could only take stone from the excavation spoil-heaps, but the nearby city wall had seemed to the engineers a much more convenient source.

Lawrence travelled as quickly as possible to Aleppo and telegraphed the authorities while Haj Wahid kept armed guard over the disputed wall. Finally, to Contzen's dismay, Lawrence arrived with the Commissaire and the local Minister for Public Instruction, armed with orders from Constantinople forbidding the Germans to proceed.[10] For a while after this the relationship between the English and German camps at Jerablus was very cool.

There was now an outbreak of smallpox in the village. Lawrence must have sought medical advice about this unexpected threat because he gave all the children a crude form of inoculation. Most of the adults were resistant to the disease, having had it already. As a result, of two hundred people in the village, only two died. Lawrence was especially pleased that 'of the thirty to forty children down at once (!) not one is marked on the face. It would have made a row if anything had gone wrong: but it didn't, and a lot of people died in the district, which makes our record more creditable . . . Tell no one that I practise medicine without a licence!'[11] His letters home mentioned the smallpox, against which he had presumably been vaccinated, but he did not say that cholera had also reached Jerablus. Luckily, there were few cases among the men who worked on the digs; the two that Lawrence looked after recovered.

Reading between the lines of his letters home, it is clear that Lawrence's parents would have liked him to return to work in Oxford. When they forwarded details of a vacant academic post, his reply was revealing: 'I am afraid no "open fellowship" for me: I don't think anyone who had tasted the East as I have would give it up half-way, for a seat at high table and a chair in the Bodleian. At any rate I won't . . . This summer has been one of the pleasantest I have ever had.'[12] The previous day he had written to his brother Bob: 'you know after all, I feel very little lack of English scenery: we have too much greenery there, and one never feels the joy of a fertile place, as one does here when one finds a thorn-bush and green thistle. Here one learns an economy of beauty which is wonderful. England is fat – obese.'[13]

Woolley was now on his way back from England. Before he arrived, Lawrence amused himself decorating the lintel of the main doorway into the house: 'I have carved a great sun disk, with crescent moon, and wings, on our stone door-lintel – the dining room door that is. As I had no chisels I carved with a screw-driver and a knife. It is a Hittite design and use, and looks very fitting.'[14] His delight with this joke would be renewed each time a visitor to the excavations paused to admire the forged Hittite relic.

By September 28th, when Woolley reached Aleppo, there was still no sign of the season's stores although they had been dispatched many weeks before. The cause of this delay was the disruption to shipping in the months leading up to the Balkan War, which finally broke out on October 18th. For the next year communications between Carchemish and England were erratic, and since letters frequently went astray there were many problems. On this occasion Woolley and Lawrence had to spend three days in Aleppo buying sufficient stores to tide them over. There was, however, no longer any difficulty getting them to Jerablus, a journey which had hitherto involved a two-day carriage drive. The railway was running a goods train which took only seven hours, and passenger services between Aleppo and Jerablus were to begin on November 1st.

In addition to buying stores, Woolley and Lawrence spent nearly £200 on antiquities: 'Aleppo is very full of things:– and we are the first buyers for nearly six months. Woolley has brought out a deal of money to speculate in antiquities: and he is in a fair way of making about 300%. I am more modest, because I have still scruples about engaging in trade! Also I have little money to spend: somehow, the temptation to make money is so very nauseous! . . . now I am making fifteen shillings a day: a very curious feeling: I don't like that also, but I felt incapable of refusing what will make me semi-independent.'[15]

Woolley's recruiting for the season completed the humiliation of the German engineers. Lawrence wrote: 'The man in charge of the bridge works had assured me of the utter impossibility of our finding more than fifty local men (and those the wasters)'.[16] But as Lawrence expected, the railway workforce applied *en masse* for jobs on the excavations, and Woolley recruited two hundred men without difficulty. The railway works had to be suspended while arrangements were made to bring labourers from Aleppo. Lawrence wrote home: 'I told you of my row with the chief engineer when he began to take away the walls of the *Kala'at*. Well, to return that compliment we took all his workmen, down to his grooms, his night-watchers and his carriage drivers and masons. Then we sent back those we found unsuitable. He was rather crushed.'[17]

Woolley had two main objectives in this third season. One was to excavate the north end of the acropolis and expose the foundations of an early building there, tentatively named 'Sargon's Fort'. The other was to dig trenches in the area still unexcavated at the foot of the Lower Palace stairway, in order to find out whether it would be worthwhile digging there in future.

Funds were to be a constant problem during the autumn. Because of the postal disruption no money had arrived when the excavations began, and Woolley was obliged to borrow large sums in Aleppo. Worse still,

Kenyon in London had calculated the budget for the season's work on a completely different basis from that used by Woolley, who was expecting a much higher figure. As a result, Woolley would in due course find that he had insufficient funds. Lawrence once remarked with some justification in a letter to Hogarth: 'It's very unsatisfactory doing things by letter: you never seem to understand us – or the reverse'.[18] The difficulty was exacerbated when letters went astray.

In the first fortnight of the dig there was a very satisfactory find when work on a room in the Lower Palace, only partly opened up by Hogarth the previous year, revealed a doorway with long and perfect Hittite inscriptions. 'After our great stone of the Hogarth period this is the best inscription yet discovered here, and we are correspondingly glad. Also to find them in place as door jambs is an important piece of evidence architecturally.'[19]

The light railways which Woolley had ordered from Europe were still held up in transit and he had, therefore, to modify his goals for the season. Big labour gangs were essential if much was to be achieved; yet for a time the workforce seemed to be under threat because the Turkish authorities were travelling through the countryside levying able-bodied men for the war. 'They visited the Euphrates bridge works and decimated the workmen, and entirely broke up the construction of the station: they have only old men and boys left. Thereupon we ventured a risk and forbade the police and soldiers to set foot in the *Kala'at*, offering our house as a temporary refuge for runaways among our men. So far we have not lost one, but it is not quite a secure game to play. We also recovered the village donkeys which had been impressed.'[20] Hogarth, viewing the worsening situation from England, was concerned that the season might have to be abandoned: 'I hope to goodness all this trouble in the Balkans is not making trouble for you,' he wrote to Woolley, 'but I greatly fear that labour, at any rate, will run short if there is conscription going on pretty generally.'[21] In these disturbed times Lawrence learned a good deal more about the aspirations of the local people. He told his parents, 'I am gathering a store of Arab news and notions which some day will help me in giving vividness to what I write'.[22]

In the autumn he did write, for the new *Jesus College Magazine*, an article describing his visit with Dahoum that summer to the ruined palace of Ibn Wardani. They had been shown the building by an old guide and his son, who had told them of the different scents in each room. The truth was probably more prosaic, for Lawrence told his parents that 'the palace of Ibn Wardani has many strange scents about it, as I wrote: it is famous all over north Syria, and my description is more like the rumour than the reality'.[23]

Towards the end of this essay Lawrence wrote with evident approval about Arab asceticism, describing for the first time an outlook which he would later refer to as 'the gospel of bareness in materials'.[24] This barren creed appealed to some fundamental element in his own nature, and it often recurs in his later writings: 'At last we came into a great hall, whose walls, pierced with many narrow windows, still stood to more than half their height. "This," said he, "is the *liwan of silence*: it has no taste," and by some crowning art it was as he had said. The mingled scents of all the palace here combined to slay each other, and all that one felt was the desert sharpness of the air as it swept off the huge uncontaminated plains. "Among us," said Dahoum, "we call this room the sweetest of them all," therein half-consciously sounding the ideal of the Arab creed, for generations stripping itself of all furniture in the working out of a gospel of simplicity.'[25]

Apart from archaeological work, Lawrence occupied himself with furnishing the expedition house. 'I bought in Aleppo a very handsome beaten bronze plate in the manner of the Italian-Arab platters in the Fortnum room in the Ashmolean:– very good work, though worn. We are pleased with this in our living room: it, with the mosaic peacocks and gazelles, the Bokhara rugs, and a strange cement-and-Roman-pillar table that I made (and the copper-hooded fire) make a good beginning in the furnishment of our room: we hope to line it with Hittite bas-reliefs (trial casts!) and are buying any cheap (and pretty) Damascus tiles we find . . . we are building a store room, two stables, and a huge warehouse of antiquities: so that before we leave here we will have a large colony of buildings under our care. We of course are architects and head masons: no one can complain of the monotony of our daily occupations: if only our stores had come and our light railway!'[26]

Lawrence's earlier comment about 'gathering a store of Arab news and notions' was a veiled allusion to something which he did his best to conceal from his parents. The Milli-Kurds, a nomadic people who roamed a large tract of land on the far side of the Euphrates (i.e. in Mesopotamia), had a long-standing feud with the Turkish Government. The distraction of the Balkan War seemed to offer them the chance to strike at their Turkish overlords, and Lawrence heard that they intended to sack Aleppo. As Woolley wrote later: 'The plan affected me closely, for the line of march proposed by the Kurds was through Jerablus, and as they had promised openly to cut the throats of all the Germans on the Baghdad line between Aleppo and the river, I felt that my own position might be none too secure.'[27] The two archaeologists did their best to cultivate the friendship of the local Kurdish leaders, which was not difficult because many Kurds were working on the dig. On November 1st, Woolley wrote to Kenyon: 'Here we are much in the dark as to what is going on in Turkey, but tonight news reaches us that the Bulgarians have advanced victoriously south of Adrianople. If Stamboul falls, it may be the signal for serious events out here – here perhaps more than in most parts of the Empire. Should a row come, we shall stop at Jerablus, as being the safest place; possibly we should be all right, but communication would be difficult and you must not, in that case, expect to hear from me.'[28]

A week later he suddenly discovered how little money Kenyon intended to provide that season. The situation was extremely embarrassing, since Woolley had decided to concentrate on expensive heavy work (despite their disagreements, the Germans helped throughout this season by removing spoil-heaps). With all this well in hand, Woolley now found that he was virtually bankrupt: 'The statement of my real allowance for the season comes at such a time that if I stop work altogether at the end of this week I shall not have quite sufficient in hand for travelling and salaries.'[29] For every reason, this was no moment to run out of funds. The war news was bad and there now seemed a real risk that Constantinople would fall. If the Kurds then advanced on Aleppo there might be a general massacre of foreigners. Woolley reported that Fontana was 'doubtful . . . whether either the travelling money or the salaries of Mr Lawrence and myself need be taken into serious consideration. Personally, I am more optimistic, and think that though the probable raid by the Hamdieh Kurds on Aleppo via Jerablus would mean a lot of damage, we shall ourselves be sheltered by the Arabs. But I must keep a good supply of cash in hand, as if trouble comes we shall depend largely on that.'[30] Without the assurance of further money, Woolley had no alternative but to reduce the scale of work much earlier than planned. Progress on the main site was halted, and with only a handful of men he excavated a nearby cemetery. Meanwhile he paid some of the season's expenses with a large cheque overdrawn on his personal account in England, appealing to Kenyon to arrange for it to be covered. Ironically, the season's stores arrived just as the main dig was closed down. Lawrence wrote: 'we have loganberry jam and wheatmeal biscuits and linen sheets and shortbread: and everything possible photographic and chocolate and asparagus and medicines to stock a ship: not to mention the eleven pound tins of curry-powder in stock, which we feel to be a great stand-by.'[31]

Woolley and Lawrence planned to work in the cemetery until late December and then return to England. The archaeologists' pay continued during the time they spent travelling to and from the site, but stopped between seasons. The journey to England and back was therefore worth making, even though Lawrence did not mean to stay there for more than a fortnight or so: 'Then out here again as quick as possible: you have no idea of how much there is to do here, with tombs being plundered and buildings destroyed every day in the districts round about.'[32]

By mid-November work on the graveyard was finished, and so for the final week the remaining workmen were transferred to the North Gate of Carchemish. The existence of this gate had not previously been suspected, but indications on the surface suggested to Woolley that there might be something interesting underneath. When digging began it was soon obvious that the task would be a big one: 'even so,' Woolley reported, 'this season has given us the lie and to some extent the character of a whole range of masonry fortifications with gateway and projecting towers, resembling the defences of Sinjirli . . . certainly much work should yet be done on a part of the site where we had not expected to dig at all.'[33]

The dig closed down at the Islamic festival of Bairam, and Woolley and Lawrence went to visit Busrawi Agha, an influential Kurdish chief, to plead for protection of their belongings if there was a revolt while they were away. The expedition house was to be kept under guard and, as an additional precaution, all the monuments that could not be removed from the site had been reburied. They returned to Carchemish for a final week to photograph objects and copy inscriptions, then left together at the end of November, arriving in England on December 17th. Lawrence had hoped to bring Fareedeh el Akle home that Christmas, but now had too little money to do so: 'it is no use to take her unless one can show her about.'[34]

Kenyon had been increasingly concerned about the political situation and the lack of news. Before they reached England he had decided to send a cable to Jerablus instructing them to leave at once. Hogarth agreed, but was 'more inclined to expect serious trouble next spring than now. Kurds and Bedouin won't know the truth for some months. *Then* they'll move. And the Armenians will await the spring. Before that the Yemen will probably kick out the Turks, and so all too probably will the Hejaz.'[35]

On their way home, Woolley and Lawrence had called as usual on F. Willoughby Smith, the American Vice-Consul at Beirut. Lawrence had come to know him through the American Mission School at Jebail and thought that he was very ill-informed about the local situation; he and Woolley now told him of their fears about the Kurds.

Willoughby Smith wrote up their news in a long report which his superior eventually transmitted to Washington. It gives a very detailed account of the history of Kurdish unrest and the nature of the threat to Aleppo, showing that Lawrence and Woolley, concerned primarily for their own safety, had learned a good deal about the Kurdish and Arab independence movements in the Turkish Empire. Within two years this knowledge would become a valuable asset to Lawrence and would influence his thinking during the early stages of the war. The report (printed in Appendix II), bears out Lawrence's later claim that: 'The Armenian revolutionaries had come to [me] for help and advice, and [I] had dipped far into their councils. The opposition party of the Kurdish reactionaries against the Young Turks had encouraged [me] to ride in their ranks and seek opportunity in the Balkan crisis.'[36] But his motive for these contacts was self-preservation and not, as some biographers have claimed, work for British Intelligence.

The British Museum was unwilling to let the digs resume unless the situation became more stable and, before allowing Lawrence and Woolley to return to Syria in January 1913, Hogarth discussed the outlook with them. Afterwards he wrote to Kenyon: 'They are so anxious to go on that they (especially Woolley) minimise risks of interruption. I told them that you will not let them start and incur the expense of journeys etc. in February unless there is a pretty clear prospect of their being able to do a decent spell of work. Lawrence says he is returning to Syria in January and on his report early in February and perhaps on one from Fontana, you must act.'[37] Kenyon also saw them, and noted that Lawrence seemed 'very confident that, if trouble came, they would, at the worst, be able to get away to the coast; and I have tried to impress on him that it is very desirable to avoid serious risk, not merely for their own sakes, but in the interest of the Museum, and indeed of the political situation generally. What I am most afraid of is an attack on the Germans which would give an excuse for German intervention, or compel the Turks to come down in force in order to meet such intervention. However, we can only wait and see what the next six weeks produce, before it is time for Woolley to start.'[38]

During his meeting with Kenyon, Lawrence raised another matter: the principle originally suggested by Hogarth that the British Museum should have rights to any purchases made by the excavators within ten miles of Carchemish. The previous July, during the interval between digging seasons, Lawrence had bought a small tomb group from the railway workmen which he hoped might go to the Ashmolean. It had come from the British Museum's reserved area, but Lawrence argued that the ten-mile limit should only apply while the digs were in progress. Kenyon's position in the matter was very reasonable; he wrote to Hogarth: 'it seems to me that it is only fair to the Museum that it shall apply at all times. Otherwise, the area from which the Museum is entitled to draw would be liable to be milked dry between the seasons, when Lawrence is there with no excavations to occupy his time. And as the whole opportunity, both inside the limit and without, arises from the Museum excavations, I don't think the Museum can be called grasping if we adhere to the under-standing as originally suggested by you. What do you think?'[39]

Hogarth's reply was equally reasonable, and is interesting for its comments on Lawrence: 'To avoid possible misconception I had better say at once that the question is entirely of his raising not mine. Until the matter of the tomb group from the Railway cutting came up, no difficulty occurred . . . From what he tells me its component parts are very ordinary objects . . . quite plain vases and terracotta of the ordinary types: and I feel no burning desire for them. But (chiefly, I believe, because Lawrence carried out an elaborate scheme of deception with the co-operation of one of his dearest Jerablus boys, in order to get them) Lawrence has got the lot near his heart and makes this fuss about them being deposited at his own local museum with which he has been concerned since boyhood.' Among the arguments for enforcing the limit at all times, Hogarth noted: 'Lawrence might "corner" things and have them kept for vacation, more especially since the natives deal more readily with him than with Woolley'. Also, 'Woolley has Lawrence buying [for the British Museum] while Woolley is there and [Lawrence's] only chance is vacation (This, by the way, is important, since Lawrence is the cheaper and better buyer).' Finally: 'There is, however, this on the other side, which is worth serious attention. Buying in this way is a matter of trouble, anxiety and some risk. Lawrence won't take nearly so much trouble if not buying *con amore ed entusiasmo*, and it will probably pay *you* best in the long run to let it be worth his while, even if you don't get *all* his spoil. As I have said, he is much the best buyer and the most likely to get at secrets.'[40]

Kenyon discussed the question with Hogarth when they next met, and later sent a résumé of their decision for the record: 'considering the amount of money which the Museum is spending on the work at Jerablus, it is fair that it should receive the finds proceeding from what may be called the sphere of influence of those diggings. Of course this would not preclude an amicable arrangement if more things of certain types appear than we require, but it would give us the first call within that area. The working of the alternative arrangement would be very precarious . . . I hope Lawrence has not found his employment under the Trustees so unsatisfactory as to make him unwilling to get things for the British Museum as well as for the Ashmolean.'[41]

Lawrence left England on 9th January 1913 and travelled out to Syria via Calais, Marseilles and Port Said, where he broke the journey to revisit Petrie at Kafr Ammar. There was still a prospect of digging in Bahrain, and Lawrence reported to Hogarth that Petrie had agreed to let the Ashmolean have half the proceeds. Lawrence then went to Jerablus and found everything calm there; afterwards he returned to Aleppo to await political developments. He wrote to Woolley: 'The Kurds here are quiet, with no intention of doing anything unless matters get bad in Stamboul. They are then going all out, and the Arabs have promised to move with them (our men as well!). The richer Armenians in Aintab, Aleppo, etc. are leaving: some are in Beyrout, more in Egypt . . . Digging is quite possible if *Constantinople holds straight*. So it is your business to settle, upon what happens before this letter arrives. At present, latest news here is of the fall of the cabinet: how or why is not known: it sounds to me like war and the Young Turk party on top again: if so matters will hum. I am going to stay a few days in Aleppo, to learn what has happened.'[42]

A week later Lawrence was still there, though he wanted to go up to Alexandretta and see to the shipment of some antiquities. He was still very apprehensive about the situation: 'Aleppo quiet politically, but as pessimistic as it can be: what a fortune one would make with a cargo of cheap rifles now! Armenians are arming frantically'.[43]

He wrote to Hogarth: 'I rather hope you will decide to postpone digging till the Autumn: but really you will know what chance there is of a renewal of the war... One hears nothing in Aleppo.'[44] In England, however, Woolley was very keen to resume the digs. Eventually, as it seemed that the Turkish Government would hold out in Constantinople, Kenyon agreed to let work begin. Lawrence had returned to Carchemish, where he passed the time in various ways. Apart from working on his Arabic, he had made some repairs to the house. A Canadian canoe he had ordered from an Oxford boatyard arrived in February. It had a small motor and henceforward provided a lot of amusement.

The risk of a Kurdish rebellion gave Lawrence good reason to improve his skill with a rifle during these weeks. On February 22nd he wrote: 'this afternoon I put four shots out of five with a Mannlicher-Schönauer carbine into a six-gallon petrol tin at 400 yards... very good that.'[45] He had probably been given this rifle by Fontana, as thanks for helping the Royal Navy to smuggle firearms to the Aleppo consulate.[46]

Shortly before Woolley arrived, Lawrence heard that natives had discovered an ancient cemetery at Deve Huyuk, a village on the railway between Aleppo and Jerablus. He first sent Dahoum across to find out what was happening, and then went himself. 'I spent about £10 there before Woolley came: though the people were only plundering, with no idea of what to keep or look for. So that my work there was educational for the more part.'[47] After his visit he wrote excitedly to Hogarth: 'The Hittite graves were full of great bronze spears and axes and swords, that the wretches have broken up and thrown away, because Madame Koch [an Aleppo dealer] . . . didn't buy such things. I got some good fibulae which are yours, and not Kenyon's this time at all events... (eighteen miles away) much better than the British Museum ones, some bracelets and ear-rings of bronze, a curious pot or two... and as a sideline, some Roman glazed bottles, with associated Greek pottery, and a pleasant little lot of miscellanea... tomorrow I return there to gather up, I hope, Hittite bronze weapons in sheaves:– unless the police get there first. It is exciting digging:– a plunge down a shaft at night, the smashing of a stone door, and the hasty shovelling of all objects into a bag by lamp-light. One has to pay tolerably highly for glazed pottery, so I will probably buy no more... glass is found, but very dear... bronze is thought nothing of'.[48] It turned out later that the weapons discarded by the villagers were made of iron not bronze.

When Woolley reached Aleppo on February 27th, Lawrence showed him samples of the finds. Woolley was impressed, and later reported to Kenyon that he had sent Hamoudi, the Carchemish foreman, 'to supervise the work, to preserve tomb-groups, and to keep off Aleppo dealers. On our way here we visited the village and spent a day and a night there, looking after the digging, taking proper notes and buying everything of value . . . We have secured a number of intact tomb-groups and a collection of picked specimens from the other graves. These include bronze bowls of various shapes, either plain or with repoussé and chased decoration in Phoenician style, iron spears and daggers, bronze arrowheads and a bronze sword-shape finely decorated; glazed faience vessels of Graeco-Phoenician types resembling specimens from Cyprus, and glazed beads and amulets imitating the Egyptian; Greek black-figured vases, and plain pottery closely preserving middle-Hittite traditions; alabasters, fibulae and ear-rings; bronze horns from a head-dress of Hittite character, a few Phoenician seals and scarabs, and other small loot . . . Our visit was opportune, for on the same day three men had been sent out to the place by the agent for the Berlin museum in Aleppo; they were however intercepted by our cook [Haj Wahid] who by the use of his revolver persuaded them to take the next train home. We have arranged for any further objects of interest to be reserved for us.'[49] Phoenician materials such as those found at Deve Huyuk are relatively rare, so Lawrence and Woolley were delighted.

The fourth Carchemish season began on March 21st. Lawrence, with seventy men, started to clear the South Gate, and Woolley, with 130 men, tackled the Lower Palace area. The light railways had at last arrived, but Gregori was inexplicably absent (it turned out that the letter telling him of the new season had gone astray). Without him Woolley and Lawrence were kept extremely busy. Since the Baghdad Railway was now running a three-and-a-half-hour passenger service to Jerablus, they were constantly distracted. Lawrence wrote home: 'we dig furiously, and are inundated by visitors: it makes our day very difficult: we start in the morning early as usual, when it is too cold to do any writing of notes or planning or photography: and then about 10am. comes one batch of visitors, and about 3pm. a second. They are usually foreigners or distinguished people, or people with introductions:– and we have to show them all over: such a dull set!'[50]

The problems of supervising two hundred men on such a large site were now considerable, and Woolley asked Kenyon to think of sending out a third Englishman in future seasons. An architect, skilled at making plans of buildings, would be ideal. Also, 'it would be a good thing if one or other of us were able to leave the site occasionally for a day or so at a time; a great deal of surreptitious digging is going on throughout the country and reports are constantly reaching us of finds which it would be worth while our going to see; but at present this is impossible, and a good many opportunities of securing objects for the Museum have to be passed over.'[51]

The first month's work was very satisfactory, both at the South Gate and the Lower Palace. The digging provided a great deal of information about the Hittite buildings, and also some new sculptures. Woolley next decided to clear more ground at the sides of the great staircase, hoping to find the remains of Hittite buildings there. He set a second group to follow up a line of small carved reliefs uncovered in the course of work on the Lower Palace during March.

The political situation had calmed, almost to Lawrence's regret. He wrote to a friend at Jebail: 'down with the Turks! But I am afraid there is, not life, but stickiness in them yet. Their disappearance would mean a chance for the Arabs, who were at any rate once not incapable of good government.'[52]

By the middle of April, the new wall of carved reliefs had proved to be a major discovery. Unlike the original Lower Palace wall, this series was in excellent condition. 'We have found more this year', Lawrence wrote, 'than we have ever found before.'[53]

Elsewhere on the dig they were using dynamite to break up massive Roman concrete foundations. By the time he was twenty-five, Lawrence had learned a good deal about ways to demolish masonry with explosives. On April 26th he wrote home that fifteen new carved reliefs had been found during the month: 'Not bad that, especially as they seem to be working up to a great gate, and that the inner part of the palace is well preserved. Our digs are the richest British Museum dig since Layard's now....'[54]

By the end of that month it was clear that the staircase work would yield little more than a plan, though Woolley reported that 'at the top the numerous slabs and beams of polished basalt gave promise of a building of fine character lying outside the limit of this season's work.'[55] But any disappointment with the staircase dig was outweighed by the new sculptured wall, which showed a parade of soldiers and was now christened the 'Herald's Wall'. Even more important was the structure it led to, where the reliefs represented a royal family. This was dubbed the 'King's Gate': 'We called it the King's Gate (and it is apparently only a one-sided gate after all!) because it had to have a name, and we already have about four "palaces" running.'[56] Woolley noted that it was 'by far the finest monument yet discovered' at Carchemish. 'It is difficult to overestimate the importance of this gateway in its bearing upon our future work. We now know that outside the ruined area of the Lower Palace, in a part of the *Kalaat* where we had hardly expected to dig, there are buildings of the best period, rich in sculpture, and standing six feet high. Nothing before has promised so well for the site. Clearly our work will have to be extended in this direction'.[57]

Lawrence had an excellent visual memory. Woolley later recalled: 'He would look at a small fragment of a Hittite inscription which had just come to light and remark that it fitted on to an equally small piece found twelve months before, and although there were many hundreds of such in our store-room he was always right'.[58] In this way he had now succeeded in building up the longest linear inscription yet discovered. A piece of this had been found during March: 'Mr. Lawrence, who was copying this large fragment, was able to join it up with another large (but worn) fragment recovered by Mr. Thompson from a flourmill outside the *Kalaat*, and with smaller fragments found scattered over a wide area in 1911, in the spring and in the autumn seasons of 1912 and during the present season.'[59]

When the harvest began in early May, many of the men left to work in their fields. Woolley gave up major excavations on the site and instead turned his attention to an area just north of Carchemish near the village of Yunus, which had been the ancient city's main graveyard. By excavating this cemetery he hoped to find Hittite and other artefacts in a historical sequence which would make it easier to date the various monuments at Carchemish. He wrote: 'now, when the success of our town digging is assured, seems the right moment for securing such information. The cemetery has probably been, to a large extent at least, plundered in antiquity, but I hope to secure inscribed grave stelae, pottery and bronzes covering a period from at least as early as Late Hittite I to the Babylonian conquest.'[60]

The week before starting on the Yunus cemetery, Woolley cleared away a mound of earth that had been left between two excavated areas near the Lower Palace and discovered fragments of a great statue. Lawrence wrote: 'we have found a colossal face, which was hideous: the mouth was a pout with a cicatrice across the top:... the nose was gone (the only bright spot) the eyes were like a codfish's, the hair was like a braid. The ensemble we have called Hadad [a Hittite god] and feel revenged upon him: Woolley slept near it one night by accident in the court yard, and started up three times with evil dreams.'[61]

Lawrence was having equal success outside the dig. Quite apart from the important Deve Huyuk finds, he had bought a good collection of seals and other Hittite objects for the Ashmolean. Indeed, he had been so successful that he had outstripped Hogarth's purchasing grant, even though he often sold *antikas* to the Ashmolean for less than they had cost. His dedication to Hogarth's collection was not shared by Woolley, and they disagreed over the disposal of seals found in a second cemetery at Deve Huyuk. Lawrence wrote to Leeds: 'Woolley wants the whole Deve Huyuk collection to be *offered* to the British Museum and the Ashmolean to have the rest – the leavings, so to speak. That is all very well for the bronze bowl groups, where there are many duplicates of each thing, but it won't do for the cremation cemetery, since spheroids don't duplicate each other:– besides the only possible place for decent seals is in the Ashmolean. Therefore I have told Woolley, that I have given the seals to you, and have no intention of asking them back. He talked of writing to Hogarth on the matter, suggesting that the seals be kept neutral for the moment, and of course if Hogarth agreed to that I couldn't very well present them to you by force. Only I should be rather annoyed, because I want the Ashmolean to be the best collection of that sort in the running, and the seals are not part of any tomb-group, and don't help to date anything: each was found by itself in an urn of burnt bones. Therefore there can be no sort of objection to divorcing them from the London half of the collection, and I'll be glad if you will lump them into the register at once as purchased.'[62]

The number of Hittite seals at Oxford was substantially increased by Lawrence's contributions. Ashmolean records show that between a third and a half of the remarkable collection assembled under Hogarth's direction before the First World War was purchased in the field by Lawrence. He also bought other kinds of *antikas* for the museum, often refusing payment.

Just as the spring 1913 season was ending, the Turkish Government asked whether Lawrence or Woolley would run a small excavation at Rakka, a medieval site a hundred miles down the Euphrates. At this stage it was not certain whether the necessary funding could be raised, and Lawrence told Leeds: 'I said that I would, but that to pay the salary which I at present enjoyed would double the cost of the dig: and they don't want to spend more than they can help. I suggested a gratification in a part-share of the objects found, which they accepted, and we are now discussing the amount of my share. If the thing comes off, it will be this summer, either July, or August. If I could get a decent collection of that Rakka ware (say a case) in the Ashmolean for no more expense than at present appears probable, I think both D.G.H. and Bell would be pleased.'[63]

Lawrence was planning only a short stay in England during the summer. When the graveyard digs were finished he would be busy for a while cataloguing and photographing the many objects found, and there were also the ancient sites at Abu Galgal and elsewhere that he had not been able to visit the previous year. His workload of pottery fragments was enormously increased during the last week of the digs when Woolley and Gregori 'wandered . . . almost to Yunus village, looking for something new, when all of a sudden we found that the surface pottery took a new aspect: we put twelve men on and have had two days' work as yet . . . we have got a pottery factory, with furnaces and wasters, of the latest neolithic period'.[64] Lawrence reported that: 'There are about 11,000 fragments, and there must be about twenty complete pots amongst that lot: we collected together three or four such ourselves. It has, as you may imagine, kept us busy.'[65]

Woolley left Jerablus to return to England on June 14th, very happy with his season's work. Hogarth, who had seen the photographs of the Herald's Wall and King's Gate, had written that they were the best things found archaeologically for many years: 'Kenyon is lyrical'.[66] Lawrence stayed on at Carchemish for a while; he had thought of travelling in Asia Minor, but there was now too little time if he was to get back to England: 'next year we hope to make some arrangement with the British Museum about our travelling money. It is absurd that one should have to come home, to draw one's salary and keep for that fortnight.'[67] As it was, he had now cut his planned visit to England to ten days or so, having spent less than three weeks at home during the previous eighteen months. His parents must have feared that such a long period in Syria was beginning to affect his values. For example, in the first season Lawrence had told them that the men had chosen Sunday for their day of rest, 'though they are nominal Mahommedans'.[68] In March 1913, however, he had begun a letter home with the casual remark: 'Today is Friday, which is our Sunday'.[69] This comment (which reached his parents in Oxford a few days after Canon Christopher's death) drew a protest. Lawrence replied: 'You complain of our keeping Friday – but would it be quite considerate to make two hundred workmen miss their day for the sake of the two of us?'[70]

It seems probable that he was already beginning to lose the evangelical fervour that he had learned at St Aldate's. Under the influence of the bedouin culture, his Christianity would be replaced during the next few years by something approaching agnosticism. There is evidence that by 1913 he had already begun to favour some bedouin attitudes. For example on June 15th he wrote home: 'As for a poor appetite, which in Arnie Father deplores, it is a thing to be above all thankful for. If it were himself who felt no desire to eat, would he not rejoice aloud. To escape the humiliation of loading in food, would bring one very near the angels. Why not let him copy that very sensible Arab habit, of putting off the chewing of bread till the moment that instinct makes it desirable. If we had no fixed meal-hours, and unprepared food, we would not fall into middle-age.'[71]

CHAPTER 7

Achievement at Carchemish

June – December 1913

LAWRENCE left Jerablus at the end of June and arrived in England a fortnight later. The visit was to be a very short one, and he took with him Hamoudi and Dahoum, the villagers who had looked after him during his illness two years before. They lived in his garden bungalow at Polstead Road and created a good deal of amusement by cycling round Oxford in their Arab clothes. Hamoudi spent part of the time with Woolley, and Dahoum made himself useful unpacking materials at the Ashmolean. Bell arranged for Dahoum to be sketched by Francis Dodd, and Lawrence was present during the session. This was probably the first time Lawrence had seen anyone sit to a professional artist, and it left him with a lifelong fascination for portraiture. He wrote to Bell with immense gratitude: 'Dodd turned up smiling in the morning and got to work like a steam engine:– black and white, with little faint lines of colour running up and down in it. Number 1 was finished by midday, and was splendid: Dahoum sitting down, with his most-interested-possible expression... he thought it great sport – said he never knew he was so good-looking – and I think he was about right. He had dropped his sulkiness for a patch.

'No 2 was almost a failure. Dodd gave it up half-finished.

'No 3. standing, was glorious. My brother came to the door with some people, and Dahoum, just at the critical moment looked round a little bit annoyed, to see what the dickens the matter was. Dodd got him on the instant, and promptly stopped work in the funk of hurting it. It is an absolute inspiration: no colour, 'cause it was perfect as it was, unfinished.'[1]

By August 25th Lawrence was back in Aleppo, having travelled overland with Hamoudi and Dahoum to Italy and then by boat to Alexandria. A few days later he reported to his family from Carchemish: 'The Hoja and Dahoum entertain large houses nightly with tales of snakes as long as houses, underground railways, elephants, flying-machines, and cold in July. I have not yet had the chance of hearing anything ludicrous.'[2]

Before the fifth season began Lawrence had time to visit several villages where local people had reported finding antiquities. The trip was disappointing. At Hammam, the presence of a government tax official made it impossible to excavate some Hittite graves, and then: 'I saw one rather melancholy thing on my trip down the river. The Arabs of Kala'at en Nejm, a very large and splendid Arab mediaeval castle on the Euphrates, had dug out a pit in the old fourteenth century town'.[3] They had found 'great masses of glazed pottery, with Arab inscriptions in green-gold on white, and about forty jugs and cups, and lamps in glass, with applied ornaments in red, blue and green... fishes, snakes, birds, and conventional flowers: some they said, inscribed. Unfortunately, they had hopes that there was gold at the bottom of the pit, and had smashed to atoms all the glass and pottery. One could pick up all over their dumps little scraps of mosaic glass with fish and birds, but no hope remained of patching anything together. The stuff was too hopelessly scattered.

'The work was done about a month ago. I think it was jolly hard luck that I didn't happen to be there at the moment. I was in Kala'at en Nejm two months ago, and two days ago... and this happened in between. A little of that mosaic glass would have gone down very well, with my penury!'[4] He wrote home: 'Each of these glass vessels would have been worth from £500 to £1,000 if brought complete to Europe. If I had gone to Kala'at en Nejm two weeks earlier we would have all been very well off for a little time! I don't suppose such another store house of Arab glass has ever been discovered in history.'[5]

In mid-September, before Woolley arrived for the beginning of this fifth season, Lawrence went down to Aleppo to meet his younger brother Will who had now graduated from Oxford and was on his way to a teaching post in India. Will spent several days at Jerablus and was feasted by the Kurdish chief Busrawi. He much enjoyed his visit to Carchemish and referred to Lawrence as his 'Bedawi brother',[6] and 'a great lord in this place.'[7] After leaving he wrote reassuringly to his parents: 'You must not think of Ned as leading an uncivilised existence. When I saw him last as the train left the station he was wearing white flannels, socks and red slippers, with a white Magdalen blazer, and was talking to the Governor of Biredjik in a lordly fashion.'[8]

There were other visitors at this time, including Hubert Young, a lieutenant in the Indian Army who stayed on a few days after Will had left. Since the dig was still closed, Lawrence had to devise ways of passing the time. Young recalled going out on the Euphrates in the canoe, competing with Lawrence at target shooting, and carving gargoyles.[9] Lawrence wrote to C. F. Bell on October 1st: 'Carchemish has been dreadful of late. I got intermittent fever, and to console me a huge number of visitors turned up. In the East one has quite a lot of work to keep them fed and amused... I couldn't burke the feeding, but I gave each a lump of soft limestone and set them in competition to carve gargoyles for the roof... it really is a tip worth trying, since it kept them hard at work for three days.'[10] The carvings were made between September 25th and 28th, and were also referred to in a letter from Lawrence to Will: 'I persuaded Young . . . to spend his spare time carving gargoyles for the better adornment of the house. He managed in limestone an ideal head of a woman; I did a squatting demon of the Notre-Dame style, also in limestone, and we have now built them into the walls and roof, and the house is become remarkable in north Syria. The local people come up in crowds to look at them.'[11]

The model for Lawrence's own carving was Dahoum and when Woolley arrived a few days later he was shocked by it. Writing to Hogarth about the house (which had just been enlarged) he said: 'Lawrence spent his holidays carving improper gargoyles for it, faintly reminiscent of Dahoum, so it is in every sense of the word monstrous.'[12]

Woolley seems to have jumped to the conclusion that Lawrence had carved the figure while living alone with Dahoum. Many years later, when writing an essay for *T. E. Lawrence by his Friends*, Woolley gave an account of the carvings which is incorrect, and salacious in its insinuation: 'Dahoum . . . was then a boy of about fifteen, not particularly intelligent (though Lawrence taught him to take photographs quite well) but beautifully built and remarkably handsome. Lawrence was devoted to him. The Arabs were tolerantly scandalised by the friendship, especially when in 1913 Lawrence, stopping in the house after the dig was over, had Dahoum to live with him and got him to pose as model for a queer crouching figure which he carved in the soft local limestone and set up on the edge of the house roof; to make an image was bad enough in its way, but to portray a naked figure was proof to them of evil of another sort. The scandal about Lawrence was widely spread and firmly believed.'[13]

This account is factually misleading: it is clear from the contemporary documents that Lawrence spent almost no time on his own at the Carchemish house, either in June or September 1913, since there was a stream of visitors. Even without visitors, he would not have been alone there since Haj Wahid and his family lived in the house permanently.

Moreover, we know that the figure was carved when Young and other visitors were present in September, not in June as Woolley states. Finally, the 'queer crouching figure' was intended to look like a gargoyle, and Lawrence was not trying to make an accurate portrayal of a human form. Taking this into account, and given the fact that other people were present, it seems most unlikely that Dahoum posed in the nude, although this is what Woolley implies. Woolley evidently did not know the truth about the carvings.

This passage in Woolley's essay is followed, somewhat incongruously, by a statement that in his opinion Lawrence was not homosexual: 'The charge was quite unfounded. Lawrence had in his make-up a very strong vein of sentiment, but he was in no sense a pervert; in fact, he had a remarkably clean mind. He was tolerant, thanks to his classical reading, and Greek homosexuality interested him, but in a detached way, and the interest was not morbid but perfectly serious; I never heard him make a smutty remark and am sure that he would have objected to one if it had been made for his benefit; but he would describe Arab abnormalities baldly and with a certain sardonic humour. He knew quite well what the Arabs said about himself and Dahoum, and so far from resenting it was amused, and I think that he courted misunderstanding rather than tried to avoid it; it appealed to his sense of humour, which was broad and school-boyish. He liked to shock.'[14] Lawrence's letters from this period bear out this opinion entirely, and it is legitimate to ask why Woolley should have included the allegations in his essay. Gossip of this kind is common enough but would not normally appear in a serious memoir, especially when it was known to be unjustified. Woolley must have realised that this disingenuous combination of allegation and 'loyal disclaimer' would cause many readers to believe the worst.

The confident manner in which Woolley published his libellously inaccurate account of the carving episode must raise doubts about his other testimony regarding Lawrence. This is a matter of some importance since Woolley is the only qualified person to have written about Lawrence's work as an archaeologist at Carchemish on the basis of personal knowledge. Woolley's essay in *Friends*, though interesting, has a slightly hostile ring throughout; it gives the strong impression that Lawrence was dilettante in his attitude towards archaeology.

A great many documents concerning the Carchemish excavations have survived and from these it is possible to form an independent view of Lawrence's contribution to the dig. When Woolley's essay in *Friends* is compared with these contemporary sources it becomes clear that he was biased. For whatever reason, the essay deliberately slights Lawrence: it passes lightly over the very large amount of work he did at Carchemish, where he shared the daily tasks almost equally with Woolley; it states that Woolley rather than Lawrence took field notes, without mentioning that it was Lawrence who maintained the detailed catalogues of pottery and sculpture finds; it gives no credit to Lawrence for his extensive buying of *antikas* on behalf of the Ashmolean and the British Museums, though this was an important activity in which Lawrence was evidently much more able than Woolley. While Lawrence is credited with an ability to recognise different fragments of a sculpture or inscription, the essay does not indicate the special value of this ability at Carchemish, where very many of the monuments and inscriptions had been smashed and dispersed when the city was destroyed.[15]

Distorted testimony is a problem faced by all historians, and it is particularly common in statements about Lawrence. When a witness is found to display bias one does not usually have to look very far to find a motive. Woolley may have been influenced by several factors. First, he was an inveterate raconteur who thought nothing of improving his yarns. In Lawrence's words, he was 'a curious person . . . he tells the wildest stories as a habit'.[16] A memoir by E. T. Leeds points to other difficulties as well: 'Woolley . . . was a source of mirth and lent himself to some delightful descriptions [in Lawrence's letters to Leeds and Hogarth]. These caused great enjoyment to the Ashmolean. We all knew our Woolley. Kindly, earnest, extremely hard-working, but one of the ablest drawers of the long bow it has ever been my fortune to meet. Imbued with a passionate belief in his own connoisseurship, resulting in more than one disastrous break in his purchases, he could with difficulty see that tactful disagreement with his diagnoses and downright condemnation were synonymous among friends. If Woolley had only avoided encroachment into the deeper recesses of historical and archaeological research, his fame in the future would be greater even than that he has deservedly won as the best of contemporary excavators abroad. A desire to transform geese into swans has always been his serious failing.'[17] Lawrence later made a similar criticism when discouraging a publisher from asking Woolley to edit Herodotus: 'A good fellow, witty, sociable, experienced; an admirable digger, who from two broken bricks will deduce a palace. Only your Herodotus would be too complete under Woolley's hands: the next generation would find it out. That would be a pity. Notes should be accurate, if possible.'[18] Woolley's monthly reports from Carchemish were studded with superlatives: finds were often described as 'the most important', 'the finest', 'the largest'. It is clear from Kenyon's Carchemish papers that these judgments were not always shared by Hogarth, and that Hogarth discussed the finds independently with Lawrence. Woolley read through these files in the 1920s when he was writing the second volume of the Carchemish report. He must have discovered and bitterly resented the implied criticisms.

There was also some coolness, after the war, on Lawrence's side. In 1920 Woolley published an entertaining account of events at Carchemish in his book *Dead Towns and Living Men*. Lawrence made no secret of his dislike of the book, saying it was 'very untruthful, which is not a deadly sin: but a very vulgar book too. Carchemish was a miracle, and he turns it into a play.'[19] Woolley almost certainly heard about Lawrence's reaction and cannot have been pleased to have his work condemned by a colleague who had since become so famous.

The tone of Lawrence's post-war remarks and of Woolley's essay in *Friends* has led many people to conclude that they had never got on together; but contemporary records show that they worked alongside one another very happily at Carchemish, and that Lawrence enjoyed Woolley's company. There is no note of personal hostility in the surviving documents prior to 1920, and the occasional disagreements caused by Lawrence's excessive loyalty to the Ashmolean were successfully smoothed over by Hogarth.

The brief season of autumn 1913 was extraordinarily fruitful; there were important finds even before the digging began. Lawrence wrote: 'We . . . had to cut away a little earth to bank up our railway line, and found out a new line of sculptures in basalt, running in two directions. We have come upon the point of the right angle of the corner, about six inches away from the end of our work last spring! It will make our season a burning success if we find nothing else'.[20] As before, Woolley divided his labour force into two. One group worked in the King's Gate area; the other on the top of the mound, where he hoped to explore levels on the south end beneath the foundations of a later Roman Temple.

At the end of October he wrote to the British Museum: 'I have much pleasure in laying before you my report on the most successful month's work that has yet been done upon this site.'[21] So far, work on top of the mound had proved disappointing, but he enthused over the discoveries at its foot: 'altogether we have found during the past month, on this lower site, seventeen reliefs, one of our best inscriptions, the double lion base and broken statue that stood over it, besides many fragments of sculpture.'[22]

By now Woolley was convinced that there was much more to be discovered. Hogarth had written on October 9th urging him to excavate some complete buildings so that their plans could be published. This was especially important because there would only be money for one further season. Woolley replied on November 3rd pointing out the difficulties: 'Our new building lying behind the Herald's wall etc. is probably, at least for a good part of its area, better preserved [than the Lower Palace]; but it is going to be a huge place and whether we get it cleared by next autumn is quite doubtful. Of course I'll do my best; I quite realise the importance of getting the plans; but we can't force the pace beyond a certain point. I can without any difficulty get next spring a complete plan of the city walls, and should like to have the South Gate finished and the West Gate dug: but the wall and its towers can be traced all along the North side of the Euphrates bank, with towers and postern gates. The Water Gate plan is practically complete . . . Really we must assure a continuation of the dig beyond next summer; it would be ludicrous and shameful to stop with our present prospects, and the thing couldn't anyhow be wound up decently by the end of next season . . . The top of the *Kala' at* is nearly finished: I feel that we ought to do any amount more work up there, but that must wait until our future is more assured.'[23]

He wrote to Kenyon in the same vein three days later: 'Things have gone very well indeed, and I think that the promise for the future is excellent . . . It would be heartbreaking to chuck up this work at the present stage. We need at least as much money again before we can begin to think that we have made an impression on the site . . . Moreover I am now convinced that the whole *Kala' at* is not the whole of Carchemish, but the royal city, outside which lay the bulk of the town; for the greater part of our *Kala' at* must have been given over to great public or royal buildings and as such would repay excavation. Of course one must go at it by degrees; but there is an awful lot to be done, and we can't stop short at this initial stage.'[24] In the hope of attracting further funds, it was decided that Woolley should put a report about the site in *The Times*, and Hogarth would also write an article for the *Illustrated London News*.

Work stopped for the winter on December 4th. When the planned excavation on the acropolis had finished, the men had been put on to a small postern in the north wall but: 'As is usually the case at Carchemish, what seemed to be but a small piece of work proved on trial to be a considerable excavation, and the main part of it has to be left over till next season.'[25] Yet the season had been extraordinarily successful, with buildings, reliefs, inscriptions, and many other finds of importance.

Lawrence and Woolley had suggested to the Museum that they should not go back to England for the three winter months, since the cost of the return voyage was far higher than that of keeping them at Jerablus on half pay. Moreover, there was a great deal of work for them to do at Jerablus. Woolley wrote to Kenyon that: 'We have got all fragments of stone inscriptions into our new museum, for working on; there are I fancy about 2,000; having done that we ought to start on the sculpture fragments. Copying inscriptions will also take some time.'[26] Kenyon accepted the idea, and agreed to pay them full pay for one month while they worked on the finds, and half pay for two months' holiday. They decided to spend December at Jerablus and then to travel in January and February. Lawrence planned to go down towards Antioch, looking for *antikas*, while Woolley intended to visit Egypt.

A few days later Lawrence wrote to Vyvyan Richards, confessing at last that he could not join in the printing scheme he had persuaded Richards to embark on: 'The fault was in ever coming out to this place, I think, because really ever since knowing it I have felt that (at least for the near future) to talk of settling down to live in a small way anywhere else was beating the air: and so gradually I slipped down, until a few months ago when I found myself an ordinary archaeologist. I fought very hard, at Oxford and after going down, to avoid being labelled: but the insurance people have nailed me down, now.

'All this preface is leading up to the main issue – that I cannot print with you when you want me. I have felt it coming for a long time, and have funked it. You know I was in England for a fortnight this summer, and actually found myself one afternoon in Liverpool Street coming up to you . . . and then went back again. I have got to like this place very much: and the people here – five or six of them – and the whole manner of living pleases me. We have 200 men to play with, anyhow we like so long as the excavations go on, and they are splendid fellows many of them . . . and it is great fun with them. Then there are the digs, with dozens of wonderful things to find – it is like a great sport with tangible results at the end of things – Do you know I am keen now on an inscription or a new type of pottery? and hosts of beautiful things in the villages and towns to fill one's house with. Not to mention seal-hunting in the country round about, and the Euphrates to rest in when one is over-hot. It is a place where one eats *lotos* nearly every day, and you know that feeling is bad for one's desires to do something worth looking at, oneself.

'Which is the end, I think, of the apologia... do write and tell me if there is any hope of your pulling it off on your own? Carchemish will not be finished for another four or five years: and I'm afraid that after that I'll probably go after another and another nice thing: it is rather a miserable come down'.[27]

Although Lawrence had abandoned the printing scheme, he does seem to have been working on one of his other personal projects during 1913. This was the proposed travel book about seven cities of the East (the original 'Seven Pillars of Wisdom'). He later wrote that it was 'a queer book, upon whose difficulties I look back with a not ungrateful wryness'.[28] It was probably never completed, though he had now visited all of the seven cities it was to describe (he once listed these as Constantinople, Cairo, Smyrna, Aleppo, Jerusalem, Urfa and Damascus:[29] on other occasions, however, he included Baghdad,[30] which in 1913 he had not visited).

On about December 10th a letter arrived from Kenyon which changed Lawrence's and Woolley's winter travel plans. Kenyon asked them whether they would be prepared to accompany a survey party making maps in the Sinai Desert south of Beersheba. Woolley replied by cable: 'Both ready survey work January 1st'[31] and sent a letter of confirmation on the same day. Shortly afterwards he wrote: 'We should both greatly like to do the work, but I have some misgivings about this place: really we ought to be working on into January . . . though your letter took so long in reaching us that we may well be too late for the job, I hope they will still want us; it would be a splendid trip.'[32]

The task in hand was in truth very demanding. Lawrence wrote: 'We are working over our many thousand fragments of carving, trying to make out which is which, and to group them again into sculptures fit to photograph. It is a most awful job. It took four men just three hours to carry the fragments of a lion about fifty yards – from one store room to another – and there over a thirty-five foot room the pieces were lying three and four deep over the floor and the three shelves that run round the room. You will appreciate the difficulty of picking out of this pile (which takes half a day to turn over) the particular claw or ear or scrap of jaw required to complete a broken lion in the excavations. And it would require a genius to tell which is lion hair, and which human hair, in the tangle of tiny fragments, many of them no bigger than a penny: some of them weighing three or four tons. We have got together the figure of a charioteer in magnificent style:– as good as fine Greek work – about two feet high, and we only need the chest and beard to complete a colossal statue of a standing god in the round about seven feet high.'[33] At the end of December they were working late into the night, trying to achieve as much as possible before leaving for Sinai. The weather had turned so cold that outdoor photography was very unpleasant; but they carried on, knowing that Hogarth wanted to include a good many photographs in the first volume of the British Museum's official report on the Carchemish excavations, which was to be published in 1914.

Woolley and Lawrence were looking forward to the journey south: 'It will be warm down there, and sunny: which will be pleasant after our snow and frost up here.'[34] But they had little idea what was required of them. Lawrence wrote home: 'we got a wire from the British Museum [a confirmation that they were to go to Sinai] asking us to do the archaeological part of a survey of Arabia Petraea (Gaza-Petra) under-taken by the Palestine Exploration Fund. So we go off in two days . . . not knowing in any respect more than I have told you . . . we are taking down the necessaries and Dahoum with us to make arrangements locally.'[35]

Before leaving they spent a solitary Christmas together at the ex-pedition house: 'Woolley went out into the outer quad (outer at my request) and sang two short carols, and "Auld Lang Syne". The effect was really beautiful, from a little distance'.[36] There would not be another peacetime Christmas for five years.

CHAPTER 8

The Wilderness of Zin
January – August 1914

LAWRENCE and Woolley set off to join the Sinai expedition on 29th December 1913. At Aleppo, Woolley received a letter from Sir Charles Watson, Chairman of the Executive Committee of the Palestine Exploration Fund, giving them detailed instructions: 'You are no doubt acquainted with the Survey of Western Palestine on the scale of one inch to the mile, which was carried out by the Society in 1872-77, and which has been the basis of exploration in Palestine since it was published. The southern limit of that survey was a line running approximately from west to east, through Gaza and Beersheba, to Masada on the western shore of the Dead Sea.

'The country, of which the survey is now to be taken in hand, is that south of the previous survey, up to the line of the Egyptian frontier, which extends from Rafah, on the Mediterranean coast about 20 miles south west of Gaza, in a S.S.E. direction, to the head of the Gulf of Akabah. The eastern limit of the new survey will be a line running north through the [Wadi] Arabah, from the Gulf of Akabah to the southern end of the Dead Sea.

'This country, notwithstanding its proximity to Palestine and Egypt, is but little known, and, though it has been crossed by travellers in certain parts, is to a great extent unexplored. A favourable opportunity has now presented itself, and Captain Newcombe R.E., with a party of the Royal Engineers, has obtained permission to make a survey of the district. The topographical work will be carried out by Captain Newcombe, but it is of great importance that an examination of the country should be made from the archaeological point of view, as there are many remains of great interest to the Bible student, and it is for this part of the work that the Committee are desirous of enlisting the services of yourself and Mr. Lawrence . . .

'Speaking generally, the objects of the expedition are as follows:–

1. To produce an accurate map of the country on the scale of half an inch to the mile.

2. To make special plans of important localities, ruins, and other archaeological remains.

3. To take photographs of buildings and other points of interest.

4. To take squeezes and photographs of any inscriptions that may be found.

5. To collect geological specimens, and ancient stone and flint implements.

6. To record carefully all names now in use . . .

'On the conclusion of your work a complete report should be furnished, giving all the information that has been obtained, and including lists in Arabic of all places.'[1]

Woolley replied at once, noting, however, that: 'Two months is a very short time wherein to tackle so big a piece of work as seems to lie before us'. He also mentioned the possibility of taking Dahoum, 'one of our Jerablus men, who is a good photographer and excellent at squeeze-work; his wages would be only twelve piastres (about 1/9d) *per diem*, and he is a very useful fellow'.[2]

They joined Captain Newcombe on January 10th. He later recalled: 'I rode northwards to Beersheba from my Survey camp, to meet the two eminent scientists, who had left their studies of Hittite remains at Carchemish. I . . . expected to meet two somewhat elderly people; I found C. L. Woolley and T. E. Lawrence, who looked about twenty-four years of age and eighteen respectively . . . My letters to them arranging for their reception had clearly been too polite. Undue deference ceased forthwith.'[3]

From Newcombe they learned a good deal more about the survey project, although they had already guessed (as Lawrence remarked in a letter to his parents) that: 'We are obviously only meant as red herrings, to give an archaeological colour to a political job.'[4]

To understand the background of this Sinai expedition, and the reasons why Woolley and Lawrence had been asked to join it, it is necessary to go back to events which began in the spring of 1913. As Sir Charles Watson's letter to Woolley makes clear, a triangle of uncharted land remained between the PEF maps of Western Palestine and the Egyptian Survey Department's maps of Sinai. Egypt was at that date effectively controlled by Britain, and Kitchener was the British Agent. Kitchener had himself worked on the PEF Survey of Western Palestine in the 1880s and he now saw good military reasons for wanting a map of the missing area. In April 1913, a request had been sent via the Director of Military Operations in London to the Foreign Office, asking whether it might be possible to obtain permission for the work from the Turkish Government. Sir Arthur Nicolson at the Foreign Office replied to the DMO on May 2nd that such an approach would probably not succeed. On September 19th, however, the DMO tried again: 'The fact that the Balkan War is over has so modified the situation, as it stood last May, that Brigadier General Wilson hopes that the objections, which were then held to make it undesirable to approach the Ottoman Government on this subject, may no longer hold good.

'The proposed Survey is very desirable from a military point of view, and is essential for the proper study of the problem presented by the defence of the north-eastern frontier of Egypt.'[5]

Sir Eyre Crowe of the Foreign Office contacted the British Embassy in Constantinople, putting forward the DMO's suggestion that the request for the survey should be made in the name of the PEF. It was thought more likely that the Turks would agree if the expedition were presented as a scientific exploration. On 29th October 1913, the Embassy cabled that: 'Turkish Government have decided to allow "Survey of Palestine Exploration Committee" to be completed up to the Egyptian frontier'.[6] The following day, therefore, Colonel Hedley (head of the Geographical Section of the War Office in London, and a recently elected member of the Executive Committee of the PEF) wrote to Sir Charles Watson and explained the proposal.

The PEF committee discussed this project at their meeting on November 4th, and decided to send an archaeologist with the survey party: 'It is a part of Palestine which has not been properly examined hitherto, and a careful investigation will probably lead to interesting results.'[7] The Committee's first choice for this work was T. E. Peet, an experienced Egyptologist. Later, when it learned that Peet was not available, the Committee decided to approach Kenyon, no doubt with a view to securing Leonard Woolley's services. This choice was not surprising since both Hogarth and Walter Morrison were members of the PEF committee, and Hogarth at least knew that Woolley meant to spend the winter in the East.

Kenyon had a particular reason to be interested in this proposal. The Museum had already calculated that it would save a useful sum by keeping Woolley and Lawrence on half-pay during January and February rather than paying their return voyage to England. However, if the PEF were to employ them during this period their half-pay could be stopped altogether and the saving would be even greater. Accordingly, he replied to Watson: 'Hogarth concurs in the idea of lending our men from Jerablus to the P.E.F. survey for about two months from the latter part of December, and suggests that, as the time is short, *both* should go. Their names are C. L. Woolley and T. E. Lawrence. The former is the senior man, with rather wider experience; the latter is the better at colloquial Arabic, and gets on very well with natives. He has, I think, more of the instincts of an explorer, but is very shy.

'Time being short, I have written already to Jerablus, to ask them if either or both care to entertain the idea, and to cable their answer . . . Both are good men: Hogarth can tell you more about them, if you wish.'[8]

Some days later this was followed by a letter from L. W. King of the British Museum, suggesting a rate of pay: 'In view of Lawrence's knowledge of Arabic, Sir Frederic agrees with me in thinking he and Woolley might be paid at the same rate, say £1 a day each, in addition to their travelling expenses and maintenance.'[9] It is interesting that Kenyon should now feel that Woolley's and Lawrence's services were of equal value. For their work on the excavations at Carchemish Woolley received twice as much as Lawrence. This large difference no longer reflected their respective worth to the Museum, but it was maintained because Lawrence was still receiving £100 a year as a Senior Demy of Magdalen College.

When Woolley and Lawrence reached Beersheba in January 1914 they discovered that no equipment or stores had been provided, so they had to buy what they could for the journey. Fortunately Lawrence had brought his own camera and some squeeze paper from Carchemish. They went first to map the town of Sabaita, 'in some ways the most desert place we have seen: since there was no water and no soil for miles round: only a ruined town of white limestone in a gently rolling upland of red flints'.[10] From there they worked slowly southwards. Lawrence did not find the journey comfortable: 'over the consequences of much riding of camels I draw thick veils: but take it as a summing up that we are very unhappy: Woolley is the more uncomfortable, since he is a flesh-potter: I can travel on a thistle, and sleep in a cloak on the ground. Woolley can't, or at least, is only learning to, quite slowly.'[11]

On the way to Ain Kadeis something happened which Lawrence would have reason to recall. He, Woolley and Dahoum had sent their baggage caravan on ahead to make camp, while they continued more slowly, examining ruins. They were delayed by this work and so failed to reach the camp that night. When they arrived at the proposed campsite the following morning, they found no one there: the baggage camels had taken a different route in the featureless desert. When Lawrence and Woolley failed to rejoin the baggage convoy there was some alarm and a wide area was searched. Not knowing this, they had waited at the campsite until midday. Since no one appeared, they travelled on until they reached the Egyptian border post at Kuseime, where they were received with enormous relief. Lawrence wrote to his family: 'They were just going to report our strange disappearance to Cairo!' He noted: 'It shows how easy it is in an absolutely deserted country to defy a government.'[12]

Early in February, the survey party split. Newcombe had intended from the outset to cover the southernmost section himself (from latitude 30°15′ down to Akaba): 'it is a very rugged bit, but I ought to see it myself and can probably go as quickly as anyone else: also being so far from one's base will add to the difficulty.'[13] Lawrence and Dahoum were to go with him, working down to Akaba and then returning via the Wadi Arabah. Woolley, with another party, went north-east.

The hardships they had encountered in the first part of the journey were not made more palatable by the knowledge that Kenyon had sent them to Sinai as an economy measure. They wrote bitterly to Hogarth, who passed the complaint back to Kenyon: 'Both grumble very much about their half-pay having been cancelled, their view being that the PEF allowance barely remunerates for a hard extra job imposed on them: and that our Fund, which stood to gain anyhow by the saving of their travelling expenses home, is now standing to gain more than is fair to them. They say that they had made various plans for the two months (bits of exploration at Hammam and in Mesopotamia) which they much wished to realise but had to forego: and now all they get is this thankless job and bare expenses. They say they are both hard up and needed the cash'.[14]

To make matters worse, Woolley and Lawrence were able to find almost nothing that related to the Biblical period in which the PEF was interested. The Jews may have spent forty years in this wilderness during the Exodus, but their passage had left no recognisable signs. Woolley wrote to Sir Charles Watson from Tell Kurnub on February 17th: 'I know of course that Byzantine sites are late for the interests of the Society, but the fact is that there are very few places where traces of earlier occupation exist; the country, at all other points, has been inhabited by nomads only; south of Beersheba there are hardly any old town remains, and the cities of Joshua xv etc either lay north of our boundary or were largely mythical; they may have been small collections of tents such as exist today, but just as today there are only three built houses between Beersheba and Akabah, so it was throughout history, with the single exception of the Byzantine period, and of a few early forts, of which we have found three dating back to the second Millennium B.C. and one (at Abde) of the second century B.C. Much of the country is so bad that even the Bedouins move out of it in the summer and come north of Beersheba and its district. You cannot find many traces of nomads, for they leave but few that will last. Indeed I fear that the results of the Survey as a whole can hardly but be a disappointment to the Society at least so far as biblical research is concerned.

'In the time at our disposal the only possible course has been to visit the most promising sites and to omit altogether such parts of the country as are reported by the surveyors to present on the surface little or nothing of interest . . . A great deal of our work is concerned with Byzantine things simply because they exist, and as we are to examine the archaeology of the country they cannot be omitted'.[15] Commenting on an earlier account of Ain Kadeis given by H. C. Trumbull, which misdescribed it as an 'oasis of verdure and beauty',[16] Woolley added: 'It speaks wonders for the Children of Israel that they left Moses alive after he brought them to a place like that.'[17]

Lawrence learned a great deal from this six-week journey with Newcombe's survey parties. 'Living with him we got a clear insight into his methods. He had five parties under him, and yet in this unmapped wilderness always knew exactly where each party was, and how its work was going on . . . This labour of organisation would have been enough for most men, living as roughly and uncomfortably as Newcombe did: yet in addition he contrived to map a larger district than any of his assistants. Off by dawn with guides and instruments, he would return to camp at dark, and work perhaps till midnight, arranging and calculating and recording for the benefit of the other parties. He was the prime begetter of the Survey'.[18] Through observing and occasionally helping in this work, Lawrence acquired a grasp of surveying techniques which he would later put to good use.

The map-makers also taught him a great deal about the geology of different landscapes, and he used this knowledge to enrich his writing. Passages in the report of his journey down to Akaba foreshadow the magnificent landscape descriptions of *Seven Pillars*. For example: 'The way down is very splendid. In the hill-sides all sorts of rocks are mingled in confusion; grey-green limestone cliffs run down sheer for hundreds of feet, in tremendous ravines whose faces are a medley of colours wherever crags of black porphyry and diorite jut out, or where soft sandstone, washed down, has left long pink and red smudges on the lighter colours. The confusion of materials makes the road-laying curiously uneven. The surface is in very few cases made up; wherever possible the road was cut to rock, with little labour, since the stone is always brittle and in thin, flat layers. So the masons had at once ready to their hand masses of squared blocks for parapets or retaining walls. Yet this same facility of the stone has been disastrous to the abandoned road, since the rains of a few seasons chisel the softer parts into an irregular giant staircase; while in the limestone the torrent has taken the road-cutting as a convenient course, and left it deep buried under a sliding mass of water-worn pebbles.'[19]

When Newcombe and Lawrence reached Akaba, the Kaimmakam forbade them to work in his area, and though this did not hinder Newcombe a great deal (maps of the locality already existed), it provided Lawrence with a number of adventures. On one occasion he wanted to examine the extensive ruined fortifications on Geziret Faraun, a small island known to the Crusaders as Graye, about four hundred yards offshore near Akaba. The Turkish police prevented him taking a boat but he managed to reach the island on a makeshift raft.

After this episode, to his disgust, he was escorted on the return journey northwards by a lieutenant and a squad of soldiers. Lawrence and Dahoum regarded this as a challenge and shook the soldiers off by making forced marches over appalling terrain: 'It is a country of awful crags and valleys, impassable for camels, and very difficult on foot. The lieutenant has gone home.'[20] There was some point to this expedition, however, and they found what Newcombe was looking for: 'the two great cross-roads through the hills of the Arabah that serve modern raiding parties entering Sinai, and which served the Israelites a bit earlier. Nobody would show them us, of the Arabs, which accounts for our rather insane wanderings without a guide...'[21] This journey also gave Lawrence his first chance to visit Petra. It was the place, rather than the monuments, which impressed him, but he wrote little about it, saying: 'you will never know what Petra is like, unless you come out here... Only be assured that till you have seen it you have not had the glimmering of an idea how beautiful a place can be.'[22]

By the time he reached Petra, Lawrence was running very short of money and had too little left to pay off his guides and get back to Carchemish. Luckily he met 'two English ladies . . . curious people. At first they were dull, but later one of them, Lady Evelyn Cobbold, improved vastly . . . I borrowed a lot of money from her, since our post arrangements broke down'.[23] From Petra he travelled eastwards to Maan, where, after another minor conflict with the Turkish authorities, he took the railway northwards to Damascus, some 230 miles distant. He would revisit this railway in very different circumstances three years later.

While Woolley and Lawrence were in Sinai, the British Museum had been fortunate in its quest for funds. Without waiting to be prompted by the articles which appeared simultaneously in the *Illustrated London News* and *The Times* on January 24th, Walter Morrison offered a further £10,000 for the work, and the full excavation of Carchemish seemed assured. Hogarth planned to visit Jerablus and agree a plan of campaign to last for several years ahead. He also wanted to talk seriously to Lawrence: 'His Magdalen Senior Demyship is running out. Is he to go on at Jerablus? If so, he will need a higher salary after this year. But does he want to go on with what leads nowhere in particular, and is it right that he should? This must be discussed with him. If he does not wish to go on, *someone else must be found this summer.*'[24]

Hogarth was doubtless questioning whether Lawrence should continue in a subordinate position at Carchemish, where most of the credit for successful results would go to Woolley. Lawrence, now twenty-five, might better advance his career by conducting a dig of his own, as Petrie had suggested, or by returning to Oxford and completing his B.Litt. on medieval pottery.

Woolley and Lawrence were back in Jerablus at the beginning of March. To their surprise, they learned that the British Museum had forgotten to renew their digging permit, which had therefore expired. As a result they had to delay starting work. While waiting for a new permit, they spent some time putting up the fallen sculptures on the wall at the foot of the great staircase which Hogarth had excavated in 1911: 'The effect will be very fine when the wall is finished.'[25]

On March 22nd it was at last possible to begin the season's excavation, but this was interrupted almost immediately by a fracas between the German railway engineers and their men. According to a report by Fontana, who went to Jerablus immediately afterwards: 'The affray seems to have arisen from the fact that the Kurdish workmen on the line at Jerablus are paid monthly, and that the wages they actually receive are much less than those promised and agreed upon . . . Thus a Kurd having received wages less than those promised loudly protested, and tried to force his way into the German Bureau, but was ejected by a Circassian who, in the struggle, fired his revolver. The other Kurds near him, to the number of fifteen or twenty, then began to stone the engineers, who took refuge in the Bureau. The Circassians fired on the Kurds who withdrew to the railway embankment, and from there fired their revolvers at the Bureau, the Germans firing from one of the windows. A large crowd of about 250 Kurds and Arabs then collected on the steep *Kalaat* mound, at a distance of about 100 yards from and above the embankment and Bureau, and to this mound Mr. Woolley and Lawrence also hurried as soon as the firing began. It was there that the Englishmen were twice deliberately fired at, from below, by the Circassian Zacharia, at a distance of about 100 paces, a boy standing by Mr. Lawrence's side being wounded by the second shot. From the enquiry I made it is evident that no shot was fired from the mound, in spite of the fact that the arrival of a wounded Kurd, believed to be dead, caused the greatest excitement, and the beginning of a rush was made down the hill. Mr. Woolley himself pursued and disarmed the foremost man, Mr. Lawrence also seizing another, and by superhuman efforts and good humour the Englishmen, aided by their head-men Hadg Wahid, Hamoudi, and two others, managed to stop the rush and calm the crowd. Had they failed, the six Germans in the Bureau, which is a mere hut, would undoubtedly have been slaughtered . . . I propose suggesting to the Vali that distinguished Ottoman Decorations conferred upon both Mr. Woolley and Lawrence, who saved the situation at Jerablus and who have, besides, rendered such signal services to the Ottoman Museum, would serve to materially demonstrate the well-earned gratitude of the Ottoman Government. Distinguished German Decorations might also be conferred upon them with equal reason.'[26] Woolley and Lawrence lost a good deal of time making statements to the Turkish authorities who came to investigate the affair, a further irritation since the season was already late getting under way.

The site had now become famous and eminent visitors arrived by the trainload. By recompense, the German railway engineers, who had continued to remove spoil from the digs during the winter, now lent some extra wagons for the light railway, which enabled clearing work to proceed more quickly. In the evenings Woolley and Lawrence worked at their report for the PEF, which was to be published as a monograph. Lawrence planned to spend about six weeks completing it during the summer in England, where he could consult historical source materials.

Although he described the Kurdish incident in letters to Leeds and other friends, Lawrence said nothing about it at first to his parents. They were therefore very alarmed to read an exaggerated report in *The Times* on March 25th, headed 'Riot on the Bagdad Railway': 'According to a telegram received at the offices of the Anatolian Railway Company, in the course of the disturbance the Kurds destroyed some sheds belonging to the works, and attacked the German engineers, eight of whom were wounded. One Austrian and one British subject were also wounded. The nature of their wounds is not stated. A telegram from the British Consul at Aleppo does not mention any British wounded, but adds that two British subjects, Messrs Woolley and Lawrence, engaged in excavations on behalf of the British Museum, exerted themselves to restrain their own Kurds from joining the other Kurdish labourers in an attack upon the Germans, and that one of them was fired upon by the Circassian guard belonging to the Germans, but was not hurt.'[27]

Hogarth, who arrived at Jerablus a few days after this incident, reported to Kenyon that it was no more than 'the long expected row between the German engineers and their men, with whom relations had always been bad.' He recognised, however, that Woolley and Lawrence 'did splendid service to the Germans by preventing their own 300 men (who mostly had their arms with them) from joining in. This they did at much risk to themselves simply by the great influence they have with the men of the locality. I hear nothing but praise of them and they have been publicly thanked by the Governor General'.[28]

As the season's work got under way, Woolley as usual split the labour force into two groups which he and Lawrence could supervise. One worked clearing the area between the West Gate and the building they supposed to lie behind the Herald's Wall, while the other worked on a postern gate in the North Wall. Much of the clearing work involved breaking up Roman concrete foundations using explosives, and in late March one of the workmen was killed when a mass of concrete fell on him. It was the only fatality at Carchemish in six seasons of digs. Hogarth wrote to Kenyon that the expedition was conspicuously short of supervisors, considering the scale of the work. Woolley agreed: 'Hogarth wants to promise me two assistants (besides Lawrence) for next year: it would be an enormous blessing, as the dig is too big to be properly run by two people.'[29] Hogarth's presence for three weeks helped a good deal, but he had to leave on April 19th, having written to Leeds:

'I'll tell Mrs. Lawrence about all the fighting and the fuss when I get back. Meanwhile reassure her.'[30]

Lawrence had decided to stay on at Carchemish and was even planning to learn Kurdish. He wrote home: 'I don't think that I will ever travel in the West again: one cannot tell, of course, but this part out here is worth a million of the rest. The Arabs are so different from ourselves.'[31]

At first, the 1914 season produced few interesting objects. Woolley was concentrating on heavy clearance work, exposing the town's fortifications and clearing out more of the buildings around the Lower Palace to establish their ground plans. Lawrence wrote: 'we have found nothing this year, and don't expect to find anything . . . next year perhaps. It makes a difference in one's working as to whether one has obtained a new grant . . . or is in want of one.'[32] At the beginning of May, however, they found some seals and a bronze greave from the armour of a Hittite soldier. Lawrence was delighted: 'I think this is one of the most interesting things of all found in Carchemish. It came out in the West town gate, which seems well preserved.'[33]

The flow of visitors continued throughout the season. On May 4th Lawrence told his family: 'In the last two months we have been alone to dinner just four times.'[34] Guests were received in the expedition house, which through successive enlargements had become a sizeable building. The interior was also impressive; that spring Lawrence took photographs of the living room and sent them to his family with a note on the antiquities used as furnishing. Since there were to be more Europeans in future seasons, a second sitting room was built, as well as a new *antika* store, stable, charcoal store and wash house.

With all this going on, Lawrence's occupations were varied, especially on Fridays when the digs were shut down: 'in the morning we slept later than usual, and then I riveted up a set of points on our light railway till midday. In the afternoon read a little, measured up a building, worked at the plastering of a broken relief, bathed, and shot a little at 200 yds. Now I ought to be reading, but am not.'[35]

Around May 19th the expedition was visited by Stewart Newcombe and his assistant Lieutenant Greig, the two RE officers who had been in charge of the Sinai Survey. Woolley and Lawrence had done their best to interest the surveyors in archaeology and had invited them to visit Carchemish on their way back to England. To provide Newcombe with an excuse for this detour Woolley had suggested that the region might yield information of military interest (for example about the engineering of the

Baghdad Railway). Newcombe had put this to Kitchener, and had accordingly been given specific instructions. After a brief visit to Carchemish,
the two officers travelled 150 miles westward to the Taurus mountains,
hoping to find out about the exact route and construction of the railway
through this most difficult terrain.

Lawrence was planning to leave Jerablus on about June 10th. The
season had been quietly satisfactory, with interesting excavations at the
West Gate and progress at the foot of the mound. In the last week of May,
Woolley wrote to Hogarth: 'The awful mess on the river side of the
cement mass is also clearing up as we see what is beyond it: now that the
plan works out we must retrace our steps a little bit and we shall have an
intelligible line of buildings right along from the Water Gate to the
Herald's wall and also, I hope, a continuous wall-front on the other side
from the Water Gate to the stairs i.e. a walled passage or roadway between
the two.'[36] There were several points at which major new discoveries
seemed likely, and an architect was to be recruited for the autumn to make
plans of the buildings and fortifications. 'Both of us', Woolley told
Kenyon, 'are glad to have reached the end of the season, being pretty tired
and considerably slack in consequence. I want a summer in England to
buck me up again'.[37]

On June 2nd Lawrence wrote to his family saying that he intended to
take about a fortnight extra on his way home in order to visit Baghdad.
Immediately after this, however, a letter arrived at Carchemish from
Newcombe, who had reached Constantinople. He had found the railway
construction road through the Taurus mountains and with some minor
difficulties had been able to travel along it. But it had proved difficult to
obtain much information about the railway itself. He therefore asked
Woolley and Lawrence to try and take the same route on their way home.
This was clearly a request for information which could be of military
significance, but they accepted the challenge, delighted at this opportunity
to score off the German railway engineers and the Turkish authorities.

Early in June, therefore, they took leave of the men at Jerablus and set
out via the Taurus mountains for their summer holiday in England.
Lawrence was planning to return before the end of August, and the new
season would begin in September. Woolley later wrote: 'in June 1914 the
catalogue had been brought up to date and of inscribed stone fragments
alone more than two thousand had been recorded, and complete type-lists
of all Early Bronze Age pottery had been drawn up'.[38] Lawrence left these
precious notes behind, but took his camera for the Taurus journey.

By a mixture of bluff and good luck, he and Woolley got on to the railway construction road where they chanced on a senior Italian engineer who had just been sacked by the Germans. Woolley loved Italy and spoke the language fluently. He made friends with the disgruntled engineer who gave him all the information Newcombe wanted. Woolley later wrote: 'It is the only piece of spying that I ever did before the War.'[39]

Woolley and Lawrence had to spend the next two months in England working on their archaeological report for the PEF. About half the text had been written during the last season at Carchemish, but there was still a good deal of work to do, especially on the plans and illustrations.

Lawrence returned to his bungalow at Polstead Road, but spent much of his time working in the Bodleian and the Ashmolean. On July 5th he visited the Hogarths, with whom Gertrude Bell was staying for the weekend. She had returned to England from the greatest of her Arabian journeys, made during the preceding winter. It was, as Hogarth later said, 'a pioneer venture', and perhaps the most valuable result was the 'mass of information that she accumulated about the tribal elements ranging between the Hejaz Railway on the one flank and the Sirhan and Nefûd on the other, particularly about the Howaitât group, of which Lawrence, relying on her reports, made signal use in the Arab campaigns of 1917 and 1918.'[40] After this meeting in July 1914, Hogarth wrote to Woolley: 'I have now heard all her adventures which seem to have been dramatic. She and Lawrence traversed most of Arabia yesterday morning.'[41]

There was sad news from another friend. Flecker, who had contracted tuberculosis, had left Beirut in the summer of 1913. He was now dying in a sanatorium in Switzerland. To cheer him, Lawrence had sent a long and entertaining description of the battle between the Kurds and Germans at Jerablus. Flecker replied in late July: 'I am sorry if you really can't come and see me as – well I won't be macabre. Should like to see you again so much. I am miserable. Many thanks for the jovial account of the Row. You promised me some toys from Carchemish – you horror and never have sent none. Too weary for more.'[42]

At 11 p.m. on 4th August 1914, twelve days before Lawrence's twenty-sixth birthday, Britain entered the Great War. He would never see Carchemish again. Later, he wrote with nostalgia of his early adult life: 'The first time I left England [in 1906] was a dream of delight . . . I began my own, independent, voluntary travels. France, mainly: then further afield, by slow degrees, until the War cut short that development of me into a sort of Hogarth: a travelled, archaeological sort of man, with geography and a pen as his two standbys.'[43] Yet Lawrence's very words point to the underlying continuity between his pre-war and wartime careers. Geography and writing were to be his principal activities for the next two years, and throughout the war he would draw on his earlier knowledge and experience. There would also be continuity in Lawrence's development as a person. While some people respond to the challenge of war with hitherto unsuspected ability, this was not so in his case. By August 1914 the personal qualities which would bring him fame were already evident.

Part II

The Years of Conflict

Reshaping the Middle East 1914-22

Do make clear . . . that my objects were to save England,
and France too, from the follies of the imperialists, who
would have us, in 1920, repeat the exploits of Clive or
Rhodes. The world has passed by that point. I think,
though, there's a great future for the British Empire as a
voluntary association.

T. E. Lawrence to D. G. Pearman 16th February 1928.
Pearman was preparing lectures on the Arab Revolt

CHAPTER 9

London and Cairo
August – December 1914

WHEN war broke out in August 1914 most young men of Lawrence's background immediately volunteered for service. His brothers were all affected in one way or another, except for the youngest, who was still at school. Bob had chosen a career in medicine; as soon as he completed his training, he would go to the front. Will, then teaching in India, felt it his duty to return to England as soon as he could and join up. Frank, though still an Oxford undergraduate, had planned a career in the army; he was given a commission straight away. Lawrence also intended to volunteer. First, however, he had to finish work on the Sinai archaeological report.

That summer Turkey held back from the conflict, and some members of the Cabinet hoped that the Sultan might be dissuaded from taking sides with Germany. Lord Kitchener, now Secretary of State for War, asked that the PEF Sinai Survey report should be published as rapidly as possible. It might help to persuade the Turks that the survey had been purely archaeological. Lawrence therefore spent the summer in Oxford, living in his garden bungalow at Polstead Road and researching the history of Sinai in the Bodleian Library. Woolley, as the principal author, was also prevented from enlisting, and the chapters went back and forth between them.

During these weeks Lawrence had second thoughts about his 'youthful indiscretion-book'[1] on seven eastern cities, much of which was now in draft. He decided that it was immature and burned it.

It seemed unlikely that there would be further seasons at Carchemish until the war was over, and he planned to enlist in September when the Sinai text was completed. By that time, however, the glut of volunteers had become so great that men under six feet tall were being refused. He and Woolley wrote to Newcombe asking whether they might be able to get work in Military Intelligence. They were told to wait, since their specialist knowledge of the Middle East would become useful if Turkey entered the war. Lawrence wrote: 'the Egyptian people say they want me but not yet, and the War Office won't accept me till the Egyptian W.O.

has finished with me. I have a horrible fear that the Turks do not intend to go to war'.[2] Eventually Woolley lost patience and joined the Artillery for service in France.

Lawrence, however, was occupied with illustrations and maps for the Sinai report and this kept him busy until mid-October. He also spent a good deal of time in the Ashmolean, where Hogarth was drafting a catalogue of the Hittite seal collection. Kenyon, thinking that Lawrence might be available for some time, recommended to the British Museum Trustees on October 10th that he should be employed 'in arranging Hittite antiquities in the new rooms of the Egyptian and Assyrian Department, and be paid for that work and as a retaining fee, £4 a week from the Carchemish Excavation Fund.'[3]

By the third week in October, however, Lawrence had found a war job in London. For the time being he had given up hope of an Intelligence post in Egypt, writing on October 19th: 'Turkey seems at last to have made up its mind to lie down and be at peace with all the world. I'm sorry, because I wanted to root them out of Syria, and now their blight will be more enduring than ever.'[4] Two days later he began work, as a civilian, in the Geographical Section of the General Staff (GSGS). Hogarth knew the head of the department, Colonel Hedley, and was probably responsible for finding Lawrence this post. Hogarth and Hedley were both on the Council of the Royal Geographical Society and on the Committee of the PEF. Hedley had overseen the Fund's involvement with the Sinai Survey, and for this reason already knew a certain amount about Lawrence.

Experienced map officers were in great demand at the front, and ten days after Lawrence joined the Geographical Section only he and Hedley remained there. He found himself working from nine in the morning until seven or eight at night, and often later. Although the GSGS was busy with maps of France, some of his work was concerned with Newcombe's Sinai Survey. He was well qualified for this, having a knowledge of the area and an ability to work with Arabic place-names. When civilian clothes proved an embarrassment in dealings with other War Office staff, he was commissioned as a Temporary 2nd Lieutenant-Interpreter.[5]

Turkey finally entered the war at the end of October, and map-making of enemy-held territory in Sinai, Syria and western Arabia was then transferred to Egypt. Lawrence expected to leave for Cairo almost at once. He had few regrets; he had written to Dr Cowley at the Bodleian not long before: 'I disapprove of London on eighteen counts . . . London seems curiously unmoved.'[6]

He had not lost touch with his archaeological work during this period at the War Office. The PEF Sinai report, to be titled *The Wilderness of Zin*, was passing through its proofs.[7] He was also concerned about the fate of the Carchemish site and the Arabs who had worked there. When Fontana suggested that the British Museum continue employing the headmen as site guards, Lawrence agreed, telling Kenyon: 'I expect that the issue of the fight with Turkey will transfer all the antiquities at Carchemish to your account... that would be only a little item in the peace-bargain... and on this presumption it would be worth your while to continue paying the guards; Mr. Fontana's wire means that they have not been pressed for military service: the expense of them will come to about £12 a month.'[8] The Museum therefore made arrangements to pay Hamoudi, Haj Wahid, Dahoum and others through Alexander Akras, an Aleppo businessman who, though a Turkish citizen, had strong Anglophile sentiments. Before the war he had worked as dragoman at the Aleppo Consulate.[9]

In mid-November Lawrence's departure for Cairo was postponed when he was given an urgent job to do: 'I was to have gone to Egypt on Sat last: only the G.O.C. there wired to the W.O. and asked for a road-report on Sinai that they were supposed to have.

'Well, of course they hadn't got it – not a bit of it. So they came to me, and said "write it."

'I thought to kill two or three birds with my stone, so I offered 'em *The Wilderness of Zin*... they took it and asked for more.'[10] The report was to cover the whole of northern Sinai, as far west as the Suez Canal. Lawrence had only visited a small part of this area during his work with the Sinai Survey: 'So I'm writing a report from the military point of view of a country I don't know, and haven't visited yet. One of the minor terrors is, that later on I'm to get my own book, and guide myself over the country with it. It will be a lesson in humility, I hope.

'It's rather hard luck though, to have devilled my way all over Sinai, and then to have to write two books about it, gratis. And this second one is an awful sweat, for it has to be done against time, and the maps are not yet drawn. So I have to oversee them also, and try and correlate the two. It will not astonish you to hear that I have found a grey hair on my pillow this morning. The W.O. people are very easily to be deceived into a respect for special knowledge loudly declared aren't they?

'I'm to go out on Saturday next, I am told. I don't care, but I'm sure somebody will ask the W.O. for an epic poem on Sinai about next Friday, and I'll be turned on to that, gratis.'[11] It took Lawrence nearly a month to compile the *Military Report on the Sinai Peninsula*. The information it contained was all to be found in the Department's files, but the task of collating and editing it into a 190-page book often meant working far into the night; on November 21st he wrote to the PEF, 'I am to stay here another week... there is so much Sinai stuff in hand that I am quite glad.'[12]

On Turkey's entry into the war the British consulate in Aleppo had been closed down, but Lawrence heard that Fontana had arranged beforehand to remove the more valuable personal possessions from the Expedition's house. Lawrence was hoping for news of Dahoum and the other men, and wrote to Mrs Fontana: 'early in October Mr. Fontana was making efforts to have the military service of our head men carried out on the dig, as guards. I wonder if he got this through, before he left. I hope the men will carry off everything from the house before any Turk can sack it. It would grieve me if any Turk shot me with my own revolver. However I asked Haj Wahid and Dahoum to see to them. Between them they can dispose of all things cunningly in the village.'[13] Lawrence shared the popular feeling that the war would soon be over, and he ended his letter optimistically: 'All goes well, except among the Turks. Are there any commissions I can do for you in Aleppo next spring?'[14]

He finally left for Intelligence work in Egypt on 9th December 1914, travelling with Newcombe overland through France to Marseilles and thence by Messageries Maritimes steamer to Port Said. Major-General Callwell, the Director of Military Operations in London, had written to Sir John Maxwell, General Officer Commanding in Egypt: 'I am sending you out this week . . . a youngster, 2nd Lt. Lawrence who has wandered about in the Sinai Peninsula, and who came in here to help in the Map branch.'[15]

The British authorities in Egypt had already been engaged in military planning for some time, and many discreet preparations had been made during the months of uncertainty about Turkish intentions. When Lawrence reached Cairo, he would need to familiarise himself with the current military and political situation, and to learn about the various projects in hand.

Although Egypt was nominally under Turkish suzerainty, the country was already in effect controlled by Britain, and its security would be of vital interest because of the Suez Canal. On November 2nd the British Cabinet had formally abandoned the pre-war policy of maintaining the Turkish Empire in its existing form, and on December 17th Egypt was declared a British protectorate. Sir Henry McMahon, whose previous posts had included that of Foreign Secretary to the Government of India, was nominated High Commissioner.

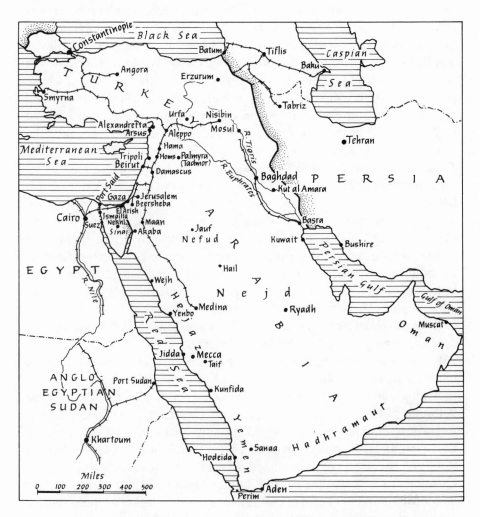

Map 2: *The Turkish Empire in January 1915*

The main objective of British policy in Egypt was to defend the Suez Canal, but there were two schools of thought as to how this might best be done. One believed that every means should be used to defeat Turkey, and that some kind of pre-emptive attack would be the most effective way to defend British interests. The leading advocate of this policy was Lord Kitchener, who had served as British Agent in Egypt until August 1914 and was now one of the most influential members of the Cabinet. The other school argued for a passive garrison strategy, whereby the British presence in Egypt would be used only to restrain local pro-Turkish movements and to fend off any attack on the Canal. This strategy was supported by three powerful interest groups. First, there were many who believed that Britain's effort should be concentrated on the Western Front, and that 'sideshows' should be avoided. Secondly, there were the French, whose policy towards the Middle East was influenced by fears that Britain would use the war as an excuse to annex regions where France had colonial ambitions (the French were also convinced 'Westerners', because the European war was being fought on their territory). Finally, there was the Government of India, which had long regarded the Middle East as its own sphere of interest and resented the prospect of initiatives from Cairo in the region.

It is significant that none of those arguing for a passive garrison on the Canal had any direct responsibility for defending Egypt. The authorities on the spot, however, knew that if the Turks mounted a serious offensive, it would be necessary to hold a very long front in a desert region which lacked natural defensive positions. A successful Turkish thrust at any point might easily interrupt traffic through the Canal.

If passive defence was undesirable, there remained the question of deciding how best to disable the Turks. This would not necessarily involve an advance across Sinai; a more damaging and economical attack might be made elsewhere. The Turkish front in Sinai was supplied by a very long line of communication. This stretched northwards through the Palestine railway system, then inland to Damascus, and finally northwestwards through the Taurus and Amanus mountains before reaching Constantinople. It seemed that the best plan might be to land a British force and attack one of the vulnerable sections of this line.

Another factor was the possibility that Arabs in enemy territory might be induced to rebel. The Turkish line of communication to Sinai ran for nearly a thousand miles through Arab provinces. At the outbreak of war these areas were not strongly held by Turkish troops, and in the more remote parts of the Empire local leaders often exercised a good deal of political power.

Revolutionary Arab nationalist movements had existed for some time before the war, and their aspirations were widely known. A number of schemes for winning independence had been envisaged, but none had been practicable. Such an attempt could only be sustained if there were an external source of arms and ammunition. The most promising course would be a mutiny of Arab troops supported by the general populace; an Arab nationalist rising on these lines would mimic the successful Young Turk revolution of 1908. Such plans seemed feasible because the Turkish army was made up of conscript units, and the Arab provinces were therefore largely garrisoned with local troops.

As long as British policy had been to maintain the Turkish Empire in its pre-war form, no encouragement had been offered to the Arab nationalists. When Turkey took sides with Germany, however, the official British attitude changed. It seemed likely that the Turkish Empire would be dismantled if the Allies won the war, and the Cabinet had therefore to consider what kind of future for the region would be most beneficial to British imperial interests. Until the war, Turkey had presented no threat to British maritime traffic through the Suez Canal. A new settlement would have to prevent any potentially unfriendly power from gaining a dominant position in the eastern Mediterranean. One solution would have been for Britain to annex a major portion of the Ottoman Empire, but influential members of the Cabinet argued that there was nothing to gain by taking on the cost of further responsibilities in this region.

The Government looked for advice to its chief specialist on the Middle East, Lord Kitchener, whose knowledge of Arab affairs had been gained during long service in Egypt and the Sudan. For some years he had been anxious about German influence in Turkey, and even before the war he had thought that Turkish rule in the Arab provinces might one day be replaced by some form of self-government under British tutelage.

During 1914, as it became clear that there was a possibility of war between Britain and Turkey, Arab nationalists had tried to establish a dialogue with British officials in Cairo and elsewhere. In retrospect, two sets of these secret conversations appear particularly significant. One set related chiefly to the eastern Arab provinces known as Mesopotamia; the other to a Red Sea province known as the Hejaz, where Mecca and Medina, the two most holy cities of the Islamic world, are situated.

In August 1914 an approach had been made to the British in Cairo by Abdul Aziz al Masri, a figure of such stature in the Arab world that his statements could not lightly be dismissed. Al Masri had been one of the leading figures in the Young Turk revolution and had served with distinction as an officer in the Turkish Army. He was also a convinced Arab nationalist. Early in 1914 he had founded al Ahd, a secret society dedicated to the cause of Arab independence whose membership was confined almost entirely to Iraqi officers in the Turkish Army. Neither the British nor the Turks knew about al Ahd. In February that year, however, the Turkish Government, suspicious of his activities, had arrested him. In April it was learned that a secret court had condemned him to death, even though it had uncovered no firm evidence against him. Since he came from an Egyptian family, his case had been taken up forcefully by the British authorities in Cairo, supported by the Foreign Office and the British press. As a result he had been pardoned by the Turks on April 21st. On his release he had travelled to Egypt, virtually an exile.

In mid-August, without giving specific details of al Ahd, he had revealed the scope of its ambitions to the British authorities in Egypt. The official who interviewed him reported: 'Abdul Aziz is deputed by a Central Committee at Baghdad to ascertain the attitude of the British government towards their propaganda for forming a united Arabian state, independent of Turkey and every other Power except England, whose tutelage and control of foreign affairs they invite.

'Arabia is defined as the land of Arabic-speaking people, bounded on the north by the line Alexandretta – Mosul – Persian Frontier . . . The movers regard the strength of the movement to lie in Bagdad, Nejd, and Syria. Southern Arabia is admittedly too broken up by internal dissension to be a source of immediate support. No leader is named.

'Abdul Aziz is quite carried away with enthusiasm for the project, and believes the Arabs to be ripe for revolt. He believes the majority of Syrian Christians and Druses to be on his side, but probably considerably over-estimates their worth and enthusiasm.

'He stated frankly that a statement of English goodwill or neutrality was not sufficient, but asked for tangible assistance in the shape of money and armaments . . . handed over secretly in Mesopotamia or elsewhere.

'In return, England would be assured for ever against a movement through Persia on India, and would receive preferential mercantile treatment throughout a rapidly developing Arabia (including Syria).'[16]

At that moment there was still some hope that Turkey would stay out of the war, and al Masri had received no encouragement; but his approach was not forgotten either in Cairo or London.

Towards the end of October, as Turkish intentions became clear, al Masri asked for a private interview with Captain Gilbert Clayton, the principal British Intelligence officer in Cairo. Clayton's report on this meeting states that, after some general discussion, he asked al Masri 'whether he thought the Arabs . . . would make common cause with the Turks. I added that such an event would be deeply regretted by Great Britain, whose friendly attitude towards the Arabs need be in no way changed by any hostile policy which Turkey might embark upon . . . I further sounded him as to the best means of making the Arab chiefs aware of Great Britain's attitude towards them.

'Aziz Bey was not hopeful of any great assistance being afforded by the Arabs unaided. He said that they were not organised and that, in the absence of any definite lead, they would almost certainly go in with the strongest present power, in this case the Turks. Further, the Turks of late had been assiduous in their efforts to win over the Arabs by giving presents to Chiefs and making every kind of promise, and there were indications that they had achieved some success in this direction.

'Colonel Aziz Bey then came to the real matter on which he wished to speak. He began by saying that the only way in which the Pan-Arabian programme could be carried out successfully and the country freed from Turkish domination was an organized revolution backed by a comparatively small but well equipped force. The nucleus of this force could be obtained from the [Turkish] Mesopotamian Army, in which the seeds of disloyalty had been sown for some time past and in which were large numbers of officers, N.C.Os, and men who were only waiting for the word . . . With these men as a nucleus, a military force of some 15,000 men could be formed in some suitable locality on which a Turkish advance would be slow and difficult, and this would serve as a centre round which the forces of the Arab Chieftains would rally.

'Funds, rifles and ammunition, artillery and all the material required to equip this nucleus force would have to be guaranteed by Great Britain, but Aziz Bey deprecated strongly the dispatch of Imperial Troops of any kind as likely to create an impression that annexation of territory was contemplated.

'In short, Great Britain would supply the sinews of war and the Arabs would supply the fighting element. In this way a close alliance would be cemented between Great Britain and the newly-formed Mohammedan Power, to the mutual advantage of both.

'Aziz Bey concluded by saying that, although the success of the undertaking depended largely on commencing preparations before war actually broke out, he was at the moment somewhat out of touch with the actual situation in Mesopotamia and . . . it would be necessary for him to communicate with his friends there before taking any active measures.'[17]

Clayton had argued that it would be impossible for Britain to take the steps al Masri proposed while still at peace with Turkey, and also gave it as his personal opinion that the British Government would be unlikely to consider such a scheme. He wrote: 'The scheme appears, as presented to me, vague, and the details do not seem to have been thought out. To carry it through successfully would necessitate a more favourable com-bination of circumstances than appears probable, and to promise to support it would be to give pledges the extent of which it would be difficult to estimate.'[18]

Although Clayton refused to contemplate any hostile act by the Arabs until Turkey declared war, the British Government had already decided to take action of its own in Mesopotamia. On October 16th the first units of an Indian Army Expeditionary Force (known as IEF 'D') had sailed from Bombay. Their objective was to secure the British oil installations at the head of the Persian Gulf which were vital to the Royal Navy. Britain formally declared war on Turkey on November 5th, and on the following day the first Indian troops went ashore. Within three weeks the lower reaches of the Shatt al Arab (the river formed by the confluence of the Tigris and Euphrates) were under Indian Army control as far north as Basra. The IEF had been ordered to assure the local Arabs of British support against Turkey, but the terms of a proclamation issued by the Chief Political Officer, Sir Percy Cox, gave little encouragement to Arab nationalists: 'The British Government has now occupied Basra . . . yet we have no emnity or ill-will against the populace, to whom we hope to prove good friends and protectors. No remnant of Turkish Administration now remains on this region. In place thereof the British flag has been established – under which you will enjoy the benefits of liberty and justice'.[19]

Imperial rule was the very *raison d'être* of the Anglo-Indian community, and the Government of India was intensely hostile to native independence movements. The Arab secret societies had counterparts in India, where nationalist fervour had led to a spate of 'anarchical crimes' between 1907 and 1909. Strong measures had been taken: seditious meetings, publications and associations were banned, and special tribunals had been set up to deal with native unrest. Trouble had broken out again, however, at the end of 1912. During an official procession a bomb had been thrown at the elephant bearing the Viceroy, Lord

Hardinge. He had been seriously injured and only narrowly escaped with his life. During 1914 native revolutionary activities in India had once again increased.

The attitude of the Government of India towards schemes for Arab independence was wholly coloured by these domestic problems. It was impossible for colonial administrators to support nationalists in the Turkish Empire while suppressing identical movements elsewhere. If Arab nationalism were successful, the example would have an incalculable effect on native attitudes in India.

In any case, the Indian administration had imperial ambitions of its own in Mesopotamia. The fertile plains between the Tigris and Euphrates only needed efficient irrigation to yield an immense surplus of grain which might greatly relieve the dangers of famine in India. In sending Sir Percy Cox as Chief Political Officer to Basra, Lord Hardinge had envisaged nothing other than an Indian imperial administration.

The strength of Anglo-Indian opposition to Arab nationalism was not yet appreciated, either by the Foreign Office or by the British staff in Egypt. Thus on November 13th the High Commission in Cairo had cabled to the Foreign Office about the potential value of encouraging nationalist feeling, both in the Arabian Peninsula and in Mesopotamia: 'Leaders of the Arab movement here suggest that the Arabs may be suspicious of the intentions of Great Britain to annex territory, and more especially to occupy the Red Sea ports . . . An excellent effect would be produced by a definite statement on the part of the British Government that there was no intention to undertake any military or naval operations in Arabia, except for the protection of Arab interests against Turkish or other aggression, or in support of an attempt by Arabs to free themselves from Turkish rule.

'Is any further action now desirable here in connection with the Arab movement as a whole?

'Aziz Bey el-Masri is an important factor . . . but is prevented by lack of means from prosecuting his schemes. His idea is to start a revolution in Mesopotamia . . . Funds, arms, and warlike material would have to be guaranteed before he could take any further steps.'[20]

Sir Edward Grey, the Foreign Secretary, replied: 'You can give the assurance you suggest in the name of the British Government.

'The Arab movement should be encouraged in every way possible.

'Aziz Bey might be sent to organise with a sum of £2,000, or thereabouts, if you think it would be useful. He can report results to the

[British] Agency [in Cairo], and then further support might be given to any movement he was able to initiate among the Arabs.'[21]

When al Masri was told that the British attitude towards his plans was now favourable, he asked the Cairo officials to help him get in touch with various Arab officers in Mesopotamia, among whom 'by far the most important' was a young Iraqi called Nuri as-Said.[22]

Cairo also hoped to draw Sayid Taleb into this plan. Taleb was a prominent Iraqi civilian who had acquired considerable political power in the province of Basra during the years leading up to the war. In the summer of 1914 he had become, for a short while, *de facto* ruler of the *vilayet,* in open defiance of the Turkish Government. That autumn, however, the Turks had acted, and he had been obliged to take refuge in Kuwait. There he had offered his services to the British.

Taleb's rise to power had been achieved by unscrupulous methods, and the Indian Government's political staff in Mesopotamia considered him untrustworthy. In Cairo, however, it was believed that Taleb might be useful to al Masri's scheme. A memorandum argued that he could have been 'induced to use his very considerable influence both within and without Basra in our favour and to our great advantage. He is very corrupt and mainly influenced by the prospects of pecuniary advantage. But amongst the party of Aziz el Masri . . . he has friends and relatives capable of exercising great influence upon him'.[23]

Contact between al Masri and the Iraqi nationalists could only be established with the co-operation of Indian Government officials now in Basra; but since his scheme had political implications, no action could be taken without clearance from the Viceroy. He in turn consulted Sir Percy Cox in Basra.

On December 3rd Cox, having interviewed Nuri as-Said, set out his objections to these proposals. He wrote: 'Nouri Saeed, who appears to me to be primarily a visionary socialist, is a delicate Arab youth of about twenty-five years of age, suffering from some affection of the chest, and is highly Europeanised. The scheme of himself and his associates seems to be mainly to raise to better things the Arab nation generally, and at our having occupied Basrah he expressed delight on the ground that the Arabs would achieve their ideals more easily under liberal British rule than any other. Nouri Saeed said that it was in the hope of inspiring the Arabs of Irak with the national ambitions of his party that he had come to Basrah, and they had entered into relations with Sayyid Talib . . . and were of the opinion that he would be able to put them in touch with tribal notables. In reply to a question as to what his present plans were, and if and how he wished to co-operate with us, he stated that he thought that if we intended to advance farther in the course of time he might be able to help by converting and detaching from the army some of Djavid Pasha's officers [Djavid was Vali of Baghdad], also that if he travelled in the Euphrates valley he might . . . be able to win over some of the tribal sheikhs to his ideals, and persuade them that under British rule they were more likely to achieve them, and should accept it accordingly. I regard the scheme as visionary and impracticable. I am sure that, [given] the backward condition of the tribes and Sheikhs with whom they would have to deal, the "young Arabs" and their propaganda would not have the slightest effect on them. In any case they might do more harm than good and would be of no immediate use to us. I recommend that, until the situation has cleared, Aziz el Masri be overawed from leaving Egypt.'[24]

Cox's telegram made it clear that the IEF command was already thinking in terms of a military conquest of Mesopotamia including Baghdad: 'We have nothing to fear from the populace of Baghdad and there is good reason to hope that once we are in control over Baghdad and the river and telegraph to Basrah, the tribes in the Euphrates valley . . . will accept our régime automatically.'[25]

In short, the Anglo-Indian leadership believed that it could achieve total mastery of Iraq and establish colonial government without active resistance from the inhabitants. They thought it both unnecessary and undesirable to make any political concessions to Arab nationalists. This convenient assumption was to prove very wrong, as the events of the next five years would show.

The gulf between this Anglo-Indian viewpoint and al Masri's is clear from an interview he gave at almost the same date to the *Times* correspondent in Cairo, Philip Graves. Al Masri declared that 'for reasons of conscience and the fact that he had been identified with the Arab movement he could not serve us in Irak if we proposed to annex that country. It was a matter of honour.'[26] Instead of direct annexation, al Masri recommended that Iraq should be turned into a 'buffer state' with an Arab government. 'He quite realised that . . . a military occupation . . . would long be necessary and that the new Government would have to depend entirely, both economically and financially, pending the development of its resources, upon British India.'[27]

Al Masri also gave a clear warning of the difficulties which the IEF might face without active support from local Arab leaders. Graves noted that al Masri 'supposed that the Anglo-Indian forces would eventually push forward towards Baghdad. There, however, there would be stronger opposition to face than at Basra: Kurd and perhaps Arab levies with regulars from Mosul and Kerkuk would by that time be in line. He remarked that though Basra and the Fao region which were in constant touch with India . . . had apparently accepted the invasion with calm and indeed with satisfaction, yet it was not certain that the Arabs and especially the Arab officers farther north would do the like. An invading army was sometimes an irritant however well it behaved and however great were the grievances of those whose country it invaded against their Government. Should some of the Arab officers in Baghdad take a mistaken view of the situation, they might stir up trouble in the line of communications of the Anglo-Indian Army in consequence of their relationship with many of the tribal chiefs of Irak. Some of these chiefs . . . could put a considerable number of guerillas into the field'.[28]

The Government of India, however, had endorsed Cox's views, and in due course a brief summary was transmitted to Cairo with instructions from the Foreign Office to 'refrain for the present from giving any definite encouragement to Aziz Ali'.[29] This message brought the al Masri scheme to a standstill. The authorities in Basra subsequently deported Sayid Taleb and Nuri as-Said to India, where they were kept under close surveillance. Al Masri remained at liberty in Cairo.

The al Masri episode demonstrated to British officials in Cairo that they were powerless to influence events in Mesopotamia, but it also provided a valuable insight into the politics of Arab nationalism. Files preserved by the Cairo High Commission and the Foreign Office in London show that Britain knew of similar movements in Syria and in the Arabian Peninsula. Indeed there had been promising contacts between Cairo and the Hejaz nationalists for some time.

Although there was a Turkish governor and a local military garrison in the Hejaz, there was also an extremely influential Arab leader. This was Sherif Hussein, the Emir of Mecca. As guardian of the Holy Places, Hussein was a religious leader revered not only in the Hejaz but throughout the Moslem world. He held a degree of temporal power in and around Mecca, and he had succeeded in whittling away the influence of the Turkish provincial governor. He had been secretly involved in schemes for Arab independence since the early years of the century, and was seen as a potential figurehead by many Arab nationalists. The Turks were aware of these sympathies, but attempts to neutralise his influence had been unsuccessful.

Early in 1914 one of his sons, the Emir Abdullah, had visited Cairo. In private meetings with Lord Kitchener and Ronald Storrs, the Oriental Secretary, Abdullah had asked what the British attitude would be if the Turks attempted to depose his father. He had been offered no British support, but these discussions paved the way for more fruitful contacts after the outbreak of war.

In September, Storrs had suggested opening a correspondence with Abdullah. This was authorised by London, and Kitchener sent a message for transmission to Abdullah, which asked whether, in the event of war with Turkey, 'he and his father and the Arabs of the Hedjaz would be with us or against us.'[30] Cairo's secret messenger was well received in Mecca, and returned with a reply which, while non-committal, was also encouraging. Abdullah had asked for 'a written promise that Great Britain will abstain from internal intervention in Arabia and guarantee the Emir against foreign and Ottoman aggression.'[31] The messenger had been told that Hussein would undertake not to support the Turkish war effort if Britain made this guarantee.

By the time this reply was reported to London, Turkey had entered the war. Kitchener therefore offered the assurance Hussein wanted, should 'the Arab nation assist England in this war'.[32] This phrase, approved by the Prime Minister and Sir Edward Grey, was a broad hint that if Hussein's Arab nationalist movement went beyond the Hejaz, Britain would support it. The encouragement of a wider Arab movement was fully intended. In London, Kitchener was now advocating his scheme for setting up an independent Arab state, and he believed that secular unity might be achieved over a wide area by transferring the spiritual leadership of Islam from Constantinople to Mecca. His message encouraged Hussein to cherish such ambitions: 'It may be that an Arab of the true race will assume the Caliphate at Mecca or Medina, and so good may come by the help of God out of all the evil which is now occurring.'[33]

The reply to this second letter reached Egypt on December 8th. The messenger from Cairo had been received secretly by Sherif Hussein, and brought back notes of their conversation. The Sherif had indicated his general intention of breaking with Turkey, but had also said that this would have to be delayed, possibly for several months. In the meantime he would avoid as far as possible taking any action which might damage British interests.

The delicacy of the Sherif's position was well understood in Cairo. The Hejaz had never been self-sufficient economically, and it depended on outside sources for food supplies. For centuries it had relied on support from Egypt, and before the war, its food had come mainly from Egypt and India. Much of the pilgrim traffic had now been interrupted. This had been an important source of income, and Hussein was therefore in considerable financial difficulties. For the present he depended very heavily on Turkey.

The staff in Cairo saw that even if there were no final break between Sherif Hussein and Constantinople, his attitude towards Britain would be extremely important. The reason was that an Islamic jihad against the Allies had been proclaimed on November 14th by the Sultan of Turkey in his role as Caliph. The Turks believed that a Holy War would create a conflict of loyalties among the millions of Islamic subjects in Russia and in French and British colonies. Moslem troops in the Allied armies might refuse to fight against fellow-Moslems on the Turkish side.

The authorities in Constantinople had confidently expected that their call for a jihad would be echoed by the Sherif, whose endorsement, as guardian of the Holy Places, was essential. During the weeks that followed, however, Hussein managed to avoid lending his support, offering a succession of adroit excuses. Britain was very grateful for the Sherif's inaction. Although the full effect of a jihad could not be estimated, the potential danger seemed considerable, especially in Egypt, where pro- Turkish loyalties were widespread and the Canal installations offered a vulnerable target.

By December 15th, when Lawrence reached Cairo, co-operation with the Arabs seemed to offer one of the most promising openings for British policy in the Middle East. Al Masri's scheme had not yet been halted, and the Sherif's friendship was already yielding valuable results. The efforts of British officials in Cairo to foster Arab nationalism had been not merely sanctioned but encouraged by Kitchener and Grey in London. Although the Anglo-Indian authorities in Mesopotamia now put an end to the al Masri project, there was no doubt in Cairo that London would welcome some kind of understanding with Hussein.

CHAPTER 10

Intelligence Duties

Cairo: December 1914 – August 1915

LAWRENCE and Newcombe were joined in Cairo after a few days by Leonard Woolley, and also by two young Members of Parliament, George Lloyd and Aubrey Herbert. These last were both very knowledgeable about the Turkish Empire; each had served for a time as an honorary attaché at the British Embassy in Constantinople. Lawrence wrote cheerfully to Hogarth: 'There wasn't an Intelligence department it seemed, and they thought all was well without it:– till it dawned on them that nobody in Egypt knew about Syria. This was the day we got there, so they changed their minds about sending us flying as a good riddance – and set us to collect intelligence instead.'[1] This frivolity should not be taken literally; a note in the Cairo GHQ War Diary for December 22nd reads: 'Organisation [of] Military Intelligence Department proceeding under Captain Newcombe R.E. with five other officers sent from home. Badly needed.'[2]

Lawrence was pleased with both the posting and his colleagues. It was a youthful team: Newcombe, the senior in rank, was only thirty-four. Lloyd was a year younger, while Herbert and Woolley were thirty-two. After a few days Lawrence wrote in high spirits to Leeds: 'today we got the Office, and we all have the Intelligence: it is only a simple process of combining the two. However we have to complicate it by wireless and paid agents (beautiful words) and air reconnaissance and light of nature . . . Newcombe is Director... a magnificent but unpaid position . . . Woolley looks after personnel... is sweet to callers in many tongues, and keeps lists of persons useful or objectionable. One Lloyd who is an M.P. of sorts and otherwise not bad looks after Mesopotamia... and Aubrey Herbert who is a quaint person looks after Turkish politics: between them in their spare time they locate the Turkish army, which is a job calling for magnifiers . . . I am bottle-washer and office boy pencil-sharpener and pen wiper... and I think I have more to do than others of the faculty.'[3]

The Intelligence Department was soon extremely busy. Lawrence wrote that he was in the office from morning till night, interpreting information and writing 'little geographical essays. It doesn't sound exciting, but it has been far and away the best job going in Egypt these few weeks. The people at the Pyramids or on the Canal have had a very dull time.'[4] Since he had worked on maps for two months at the War Office he was given the task of liaising between Military Intelligence and the Survey of Egypt, a civilian department of the Egyptian Government which was responsible for producing maps. Much of the information needed for revisions had to be collected from Intelligence sources, and these liaison duties soon became important.

The work of the Intelligence Department was not restricted to gathering information. From the outset it examined broader questions of strategy. Within days of their arrival, a friend of George Lloyd's visiting Cairo set down opinions which can only have been gleaned from Lloyd himself: 'The Intelligence Department . . . have done invaluable work already collecting and tabulating information and initiating ideas which never could have dawned in the heads of the General or his surroundings . . . A well-run Intelligence Department will really run him as regards policy, and this is what will shortly happen I think.'[5]

Although it was new, the Department had replaced an earlier Intelligence office, which had long been advising the British authorities in Cairo. The continuity with previous work was provided by Gilbert Clayton, Newcombe's chief, who had worked in Cairo Intelligence before the war and had now been promoted Lieutenant-Colonel.

Clayton also controlled a separate Egyptian civil Intelligence service. Through his military and civil responsibilities he was in close contact with both Major-General Maxwell (the GOC) and the High Commissioner. In addition to these duties, Clayton was the Cairo representative of Sir Reginald Wingate, Governor-General of the Sudan (generally referred to by his Egyptian Army rank of 'Sirdar', i.e. C-in-C). Thus Clayton was personally responsible to the three most senior British officials in the Middle East. This multiple role demanded unusual ability and a good deal of tact in dealing with superiors and staff. Lawrence would later write: 'Clayton made the perfect leader for such a band of wild men as we were. He was calm, detached, clear-sighted, of unconscious courage in assuming responsibility. He gave an open run to his subordinates . . . and he worked by influence rather than by loud direction. It was not easy to descry his influence. He was like water, or permeating oil, creeping silently and insistently through everything. It was not possible to say where Clayton was and was not, and how much really belonged to him.

He never visibly led; but his ideas were abreast of those who did'.[6] Through Clayton, the enthusiastic specialists recruited to the new Intelligence Department soon found themselves involved in the largest questions of future policy, both military and political.

Lawrence shared fully in this political work. As Newcombe later wrote: 'We worked in the same room together. Lawrence, Woolley and I had breakfast, lunch, and dinner together daily at the Continental Hotel for nine months. So Lawrence knew all that any other of us did and of course read all reports which we all discussed together . . . "maps" was only a nominal part of his job: and he was in fact as much in the picture as any of us . . . Lawrence, Woolley, and I rode daily on push bikes from the Continental Hotel to the Intelligence Office (in the Egyptian Army office, next to Clayton)'.[7]

One of the Department's first tasks was to study schemes for a British landing somewhere on the Syrian coast. The most vulnerable point in Turkish communications with Sinai (and also with Mesopotamia) was clearly Alexandretta. On December 4th, before Lawrence and Newcombe arrived, Maxwell had written to Kitchener: 'If any diversion is contemplated, I think the easiest, safest, and most fruitful in results would be one at Alexandretta. There . . . we strike a vital blow at the railways and also hit German interests very hard . . . Alexandretta would not want a very large force. All other places – Rafah, Jaffa, Acre, Beirut – are too far from the Turkish lines of communications.'[8] On his fifth day in Cairo Lawrence wrote to Hogarth: 'The interest may shift violently to the north almost any day:– so far as we are concerned it has shifted already'.[9]

The scheme for taking Alexandretta was envisaged purely as a British operation, but it seemed possible that the effect of a landing there might be greatly increased by Arab nationalist action. Information now reaching Cairo suggested that if Turkish military communications were cut by British intervention, the Syrian Arabs would seize the opportunity to declare a general revolt.

There was, however, a difficulty in giving direct encouragement to Syrian nationalists. Just as India saw Mesopotamia as a potential colony, France had long-standing imperial ambitions in Syria. The French regarded themselves as protectors of the Maronite Christian community in the Lebanon, where there were substantial French commercial interests, and vociferous French pressure groups were making no secret of their hope to colonise a much wider area.

For several years before the war there had been tension between pro-French elements and the Syrian nationalists, who had no wish to exchange their Islamic Turkish masters for the infidel French. A telegram from Cairo to London early in December reported the opinion of an important Damascus sheikh, recently arrived in Egypt, that 'the majority of Mahometans are anxious to come to an understanding with Great Britain and throw off the Turkish yoke but are deterred from taking action by their fear of France. If given any guarantee that the French would not occupy Syria they would side whole-heartedly with Great Britain.'[10]

Politicians in London tended to accept that much of northern Syria would become a French colony after the war, but in Cairo it was now apparent that such a policy would lead to difficulties between Britain and the Arab nationalists. At the very least, it was necessary to clarify the British position. Maxwell therefore asked Kitchener 'what the ultimate policy of England regarding Palestine and Syria in connection with the Arab movement will be? . . . It is necessary to know what line will be taken, as there is a good deal of nibbling even among officers of the Turkish Army, but I do not want anything said or done which may afterwards prove to have been a breach of faith.'[11] Kitchener replied that no policy had yet been defined, 'but if our troops arrive in Syria we hope they would be well received by the population.'[12] Both Kitchener and Maxwell knew that a British landing might encourage Syrian nationalists to revolt, and that the result could be a new Arab government utterly opposed to French colonisation. If the military arguments for such a landing prevailed, France might have to scale down her ambitions.

Syria was the Arab province Lawrence himself found most interesting, and he was deeply absorbed in this debate about its future. Before the war he had seen for himself how ruthlessly the native villagers were exploited by corrupt Turkish officials, and he had learned a certain amount about nationalist aspirations. His commitment to the ideal of Arab self-rule had already made him an opponent of French ambition. He knew that French colonial administration, unlike British, would tend to destroy Arab culture, language and social structure. Others in the Intelligence Department shared this opposition to France, though possibly not for the same reasons. Aubrey Herbert, for example, wrote: 'This is a war for liberty and small peoples, not for French financiers.'[13]

From the outset, therefore, Lawrence was one of the most enthusiastic advocates of Arab self-government in Clayton's Intelligence Department. When he saw that the Alexandretta scheme might lead to an Arab revolt in Syria, he enthusiastically provided information and arguments that might persuade his seniors to act.

The case for a British landing was set out in two memoranda prepared by the Cairo Intelligence Department at the beginning of January. The first reviewed Intelligence about Turkish military intentions, and concluded that there was an imminent risk of attack on the Canal by a force of up to 100,000 men. Three British 'diversions' were considered, a landing at Alexandretta being by far the most attractive.[14] A more detailed argument in favour of this operation was set out in a memorandum dated January 5th. This pointed out that Alexandretta possessed the only natural harbour on the Syrian coast and had potential as a major port. The town itself had great strategic importance from both a naval and military standpoint. The memorandum quoted a Turkish naval officer's opinion that: 'the Power that held Alexandretta would control Cyprus . . . and be virtual master of the Eastern Mediterranean and of the Suez Canal'.[15] More important still, Turkish supplies to Syria, Sinai and Mesopotamia had to pass through Alexandretta, because the Baghdad railway tunnel through the Amanus mountains inland had not yet been completed.

Although this memorandum is unsigned, Lawrence must have had a hand in it. At the time the department was very small, and parts of the document are suggestive of his style. As Syria was his area of special interest it is not surprising that he took a lead in advocating the project. He later said that 'the Alexandretta scheme . . . was, from beginning to end, my invention, put forward necessarily through my chiefs (I was a 2nd. Lieut. of three months' seniority!)'[16] In reality, however, it is clear that he did not initiate the project in Cairo, since Maxwell had advocated a landing at Alexandretta a month before these memoranda and the idea was already under consideration in London.

The second memorandum also shows that the Alexandretta proposal was seen in Cairo as a way to make use of Syrian nationalism: 'We have been informed from two good sources that the Germans in command in Syria dread nothing so much as a landing by us in the north of Syria – they say themselves that this would be followed by a general defection of their Arab troops. There is no doubt that this fear is well founded, and that a general Arab revolt, directed by the Pan-Arab military league, would be the immediate result of our occupation of Alexandretta following on a defeat of the Turkish forces in the south . . . Within the last few years the Arab National feeling has developed in an astonishing degree, and while European [assistance] is a general demand, the partition of the Arab country between different European powers would be deeply resented. The Germans had already before the war made themselves hated; the popularity of the French even amongst the Maronites has greatly diminished, and any operations by them would be disliked by the Greek Christians and forcibly opposed by the Mohammedans. On the other hand there is amongst all classes and religions a very widespread desire for interference by Great Britain.'[17] As Lawrence later wrote: 'A landing at Alexandretta in February 1915 would have handed over Syria and Mesopotamia to their native (Arab) troops then all in their home stations, and complete, and automatically established local governments there'.[18]

The Intelligence Department memorandum of January 5th formed the basis of a telegram from Cairo to the Foreign Office urging action at Alexandretta.[19] It was probably this sequence of events which prompted Lawrence to believe that the initiative for the scheme had been his own. During January and February 1915 the War Office and Admiralty studied the project in considerable detail. The potential benefits of a successful landing, as far as British efforts in Egypt and Mesopotamia were concerned, were not seriously disputed; but it was argued that the operation would require a much larger force than the two to three thousand men envisaged in the Cairo memorandum. A War Office paper dated January 11th estimated that a force of twenty-one thousand would be needed.[20] In Cairo the Intelligence Department worked on the project for some time, gathering additional geographical and military information. Their reports contained much propaganda for the scheme. For example, a paper dated January 19th states: 'A defeat of the Turkish forces at Alexandretta, i.e. on the borders of the real Turk country of Asia Minor, would do far more to bring about the collapse of Turkey than a similar defeat either in south Palestine or in the Caucasus.'[21]

During January the scheme met with general approval. It was discussed in Cabinet on the 13th, and planning went ahead on the basis that the action would be carried out in parallel with naval bombardment of the Dardanelles.

Wartime censorship prevented Lawrence from giving details of these military questions in his letters to England, but he now wrote triumphantly to Hogarth: 'Our particular job goes well. We all pulled together hard for a month to twist "them" from what we thought was a wrong line they were taking – and we seem to have succeeded completely: so that we today have got all we want for the moment, and therefore feel absolutely bored.'[22]

As anticipated, early in February the Turks mounted an attack on the Canal. It was beaten off with surprising ease, and the enemy force retired so unexpectedly that the British failed to mount a crushing counter-attack. It was later realised that the Turkish commander had expected that the Canal defences would be crippled by a general Moslem rising in Egypt as soon as his force approached. Since no such rebellion took place he had no alternative but to retire. Afterwards the Turks put out face-saving statements that the attack had merely been a 'reconnaissance'.

The British authorities were well aware of Egyptian antagonism, but knew in advance that there was little to fear. On the eve of the Turkish attack Lawrence had written: 'Aubrey Herbert unearths futile conspiracies. The ten principals of the last conspiracy were sold by their underlings, and then came each one independently and secretly by night to the General, and gave away his fellows. It was so hard to keep them from meeting on the doorstep... and when the plot matured it was like the Man who was Friday. Nonetheless the Egyptian townsmen do hate us so. I thought it was only a coldness... but it is a most burning dislike. They are also very much afraid.'[23]

During the first weeks of 1915 the Department had expanded, and by the beginning of February it contained a remarkable diversity of talent and specialist knowledge. There were, however, tensions: Aubrey Herbert and George Lloyd were both Etonians from upper-class families, and they objected strongly to Newcombe. Lloyd's views can be judged from comments by a friend: 'Newcombe is a surveyor by profession . . . He is an intelligent, narrow minded and jealous man, extremely hard working and underbred, a horrid man to work under and George finds him so.'[24] Lloyd decided to leave Cairo as quickly as possible, and vented his feelings by drafting a very critical memorandum on what he saw as Newcombe's shortcomings. When, by accident, this came into Newcombe's hands, Lloyd's departure was assured. Herbert, who described Newcombe as 'a vain ambitious inarticulate man',[25] made himself equally insufferable. Within a few weeks they had both gone.

Those who remained became a tight-knit group. Lawrence wrote: 'We meet very few other people, except officers on business... see a good deal of them, from General Maxwell downwards. He is a very queer person: almost weirdly good-natured, very cheerful, with a mysterious gift of prophesying what will happen, and a marvellous carelessness about what might happen. There couldn't be a better person to command in Egypt. He takes the whole job as a splendid joke.'[26]

The Intelligence Department had now taken over production of the *Turkish Army Handbook*,[27] a secret reference work which had to be revised very frequently. The principal expert on the Turkish Army was Philip Graves, who joined the Department in January, but everyone in Intelligence contributed information and Lawrence organised the printing. In addition to regular duties, there were numerous specific requests: 'we advise all sorts of people in power on geographical points. The ignorance of these people would give them impossible-ever-to-sit-down-again experiences in a preparatory school. "Who does Crete belong to?" "Where is Piraeus?" '[28]

The atmosphere in the office was in some ways more reminiscent of a university department than a military unit, and professional soldiers often felt uneasy with members of this very intellectual group. This feeling was exacerbated by Lawrence, who abhorred pomposity and inefficiency, and found plenty of both in the military bureaucracy. He was working under considerable pressure and had no time for lengthy regulation procedures. Worse still, regular officers would sometimes find themselves a target for his mischievous humour. At Oxford he had often drawn attention to himself by unconventional behaviour. This quirk had now become habitual, and could offend. In his own words: 'When in fresh company, I would embark on little wanton problems of conduct, observing the impact of this or that approach on my hearers, treating fellow-men as so many targets for intellectual ingenuity: until I could hardly tell my own self where the leg-pulling began or ended. This pettiness helped to make me uncomfortable with other men, lest my whim drive me suddenly to collect them as trophies of marksmanship'.[29] Aubrey Herbert's first impression (which doubtless had a social bias) was of 'an odd gnome, half cad – with a touch of genius'.[30]

Those who worked alongside Lawrence learned to tolerate his eccentricities; most of them knew him well enough to like the personality beneath, and they had a healthy regard for the ability and dedication he brought to his work. Others, outside his immediate circle, were often resentful. Ernest Dowson, who as Director of the Survey of Egypt was in almost daily contact with Lawrence at this period, later wrote: 'for truthful balance it has of course to be recognized . . . that it was not only the pompous, the inefficient and the pretentious whose co-operation Lawrence's ways tended to alienate. Many men of sense and ability were repelled by the impudence, freakishness and frivolity he trailed so provocatively.'[31] These difficulties were aggravated still further by his appearance. He seemed an 'extremely youthful and, to our unseeing eyes, insignificant figure with well-ruffled light hair, solitary pip on sleeve, minus belt and with peaked cap askew'.[32] Such indifference to dress was general in the Intelligence office during 1915. Herbert was described as 'being, after Lawrence, the untidiest officer in Egypt',[33] and Newcombe said that he himself, though 'a Regular of sixteen years' service . . . also wore slacks without a belt (and I believe General Maxwell, G.O.C. did the same).'[34]

While the Department continued to advocate the Alexandretta project, it was also working on schemes to encourage Arab unrest elsewhere. One of these concerned the south-west Arabian Peninsula, much of which was controlled by rival sheikhs whose allegiance to Constantinople was purely nominal. A few were definitely hostile to Britain, but others remained undecided. For some time before the war Clayton had been courting an enigmatic and influential leader in the province of Asir, north of the Yemen. This was Sayid Mohammed ibn Ali, more commonly known as the Idrisi. Messengers from Pan-Arab nationalist leaders based in Egypt had been allowed to visit him, with discreet encouragement from Cairo, since the Idrisi was known to be anti-Turk.

Clayton's efforts had been complicated, however, by the influence traditionally wielded in the region by the Government of India. The eastern shore of the Arabian Peninsula was seen by India as neighbouring territory, and through a series of separate treaties individual chieftains had been brought under British tutelage. This treaty policy was still being pursued, for example with the young Wahhabi chieftain ibn Saud. The Government of India also controlled a small area on the south-western tip of the peninsula, at Aden. This had been annexed in 1839 as a refuelling station on the sea-route from Britain. The resident British administrator, who reported to Bombay, had established a degree of British influence extending northwards up the Red Sea coast. In January the Government of India had protested strongly about Cairo's diplomatic initiatives in this region, and negotiations therefore took place to define respective spheres of activity. Sir Henry McMahon, who had now taken up his post as High Commissioner, pointed out that the Idrisi had much closer links with Egypt than with Aden. Delhi, however, argued forcefully that the British Resident in Aden should control negotiations with the Idrisi, and even attempted to extend Aden's authority to the Hejaz. It was to be some weeks before the question was resolved.

The future of the Arabian provinces, and of Syria in particular, was widely debated in Cairo during the first weeks of 1915. There were vociferous political factions in the city representing pro-French Maronites and various types of Arab nationalist. As McMahon noted: 'The majority of Syrians inhabiting Egypt, many of whom are in Government employ, are . . . strongly British in their leanings, and they have for many years looked to His Majesty's Government to release them from the disabilities which their mother-country has suffered under Turkish rule. It was, therefore, only to be anticipated that the outbreak of war with Turkey should raise their hopes and lead to the formulation of definite projects. The small number of Syrians who looked to the French for deliverance were in a similar case. There has consequently been much animated talk and bitter expression of partisan sentiment.'[35]

To British irritation, the pro-French lobby in Cairo was being actively encouraged by French diplomats. McMahon wrote: 'The French Government have, of course, for long been aware of the advantages to be obtained from a control of Syrian opinion in Egypt. The appointment of Monsieur Albert Defrance as the Representative of the Republic in Cairo was no doubt due to a desire to improve their position in this respect . . . his wife, a Levantine and sister-in-law of an ex-Governor of the Lebanon, would be thought well fitted to cultivate intimate relations with the Syrian residents, especially through the medium of the French colony, not a few of whom have married Syrians.'[36]

Defrance had been joined by François Georges-Picot, a highly capable career diplomat who had served for ten months as French Consul-General in Beirut before the war and was now working as Secretary at the French Agency. Clayton afterwards described Picot as 'an enthusiast in the cause of French expansion in the Eastern Mediterranean and . . . one of the Anglophobe school of 1898 and previous.'[37] According to McMahon: 'it is fairly clear that his main duty was to mobilize Syrian opinion in favour of French pretensions. Almost immediately after his arrival rumours were spread of a French expedition to Syria and Monsieur Picot . . . energetically recruited volunteers to accompany the invading forces. The movement caused some excitement which was most undesirable at that moment'.[38] At the request of the British authorities the project was halted, but 'Monsieur Picot's activities, however, did not cease here. A project for a Syrian *corps d'éclaireurs* [scout corps] followed, but came to nothing without any intervention whatever on our part . . . Considerable efforts were also directed to obtaining from the club *L'Union Syrienne* a public manifestation of sympathy for France and an expression of confidence in Monsieur Picot's championship of Syrian interests. These manoeuvres were equally unsuccessful.'[39]

The publicity given to French aims was causing deepening anxiety in the minds of most Syrian nationalists. Early in February Clayton drew up a briefing document on the future of Syria, attaching a statement of non-Maronite Syrian Christian views on the one hand, and the opinion of a well-known Pan-Arab spokesman, Rashid Rida, on the other. The non-Maronite Christian argument was for a British protectorate on the Egyptian model, which would unite Egypt and Syria (including Palestine and Sinai) under one titular Sultan. By contrast, Rashid Rida sought British support for independence in all the Arab provinces of the Turkish Empire, without any form of protectorate. Both, however, were totally opposed to any form of French colonisation; it was suggested that France should be bought off by compensation elsewhere.

Clayton pointed out that a decision on future policy was urgently needed, since otherwise Britain might find that commitments had been given which would later prove embarrassing. He argued that there was nothing to be gained from British involvement in the internal affairs of Syria. A fortnight later McMahon sent a paraphrase of Clayton's paper to the Foreign Office, together with the two Arab statements. He added: 'The Syrian question in this country is entering upon an acute phase under the impulsion of increasing propaganda in the Press, the various organs of which, in accordance with their origin and complexion, support respectively the rival interests of France and England. The polemical nature of these publications has become so marked in the last few days that orders have had to be given to the censorship to suppress them indiscriminately on both sides.'[40] He suggested that the proposal for an expanded Egyptian Sultanate might be the basis for a solution, which he summarised as: 'the extension of the dominion of the Sultan of Egypt over Syria, under our Protectorate with one or more local governments adapted to the needs of the various sections of the country. This would render unnecessary the acquisition of any portion of Syria by either France or ourselves, or its exclusion from Mahomedan dominion. It would, as in Egypt, ensure to various conflicting interests, national or religious, a settled administration with all due regard to their individual sentiment.'[41]

Lawrence was fully aware of these issues, and it seems that at this time he himself favoured such an arrangement. The British, as protectors, would rule indirectly, working through the existing political system on the

Egyptian model. This was quite unlike French colonial practice, which sought to reorganise every overseas territory on French lines. He wrote home on February 20th: 'So far as Syria is concerned it is France and not Turkey that is the enemy.'[42]

At about this time it became apparent to the British staff in Cairo that the Alexandretta scheme was being quietly shelved. They did not know the full reasons, which included a serious shortage of naval transport. As a result they placed the entire blame on France. This seemed a reasonable conclusion, since on February 17th Grey telegraphed to McMahon: 'The French Ambassador has spoken to me about agitation in Egypt for the [British] annexation of Syria. It is a point on which French opinion is most sensitive and you should do all you can to discourage any movement of the kind even as regards Alexandretta or places near Syria.

'We have promised to associate the French with us if we undertake any serious military operations in that region.'[43]

This telegram crossed with McMahon's earlier dispatch suggesting a Syrian-Egyptian Sultanate. The Foreign Office reaction was unequivocal: there was no obvious territory to offer France in compensation for Syria, and any negotiations on the issue would be better postponed until after a British victory in the Dardanelles. Grey cabled to McMahon: 'Your memorandum about Syria is being considered, but it is perhaps well to say at once that it would mean a breach with France if we put forward any claims in Syria, and to claim it for Egypt would be equivalent to claiming it for ourselves. You must be careful therefore not to arouse the susceptibilities of France about Syria; if this were done our relations with France would be impaired in a way that would be most unfortunate while we are prosecuting war in common.'[44]

Hopes had been running high in Cairo for action at Alexandretta and a non-French solution to the Syrian question. These telegrams were therefore extremely disappointing. Lawrence wrote bitterly to Leeds: 'everything has been left undone, that we ought to have done, and we have done nothing at all. So I'm as sick as might be, and yet not so sick as the rest of us. Some day I shall tell you all about it – but not now. Only for your present guidance do curse and spit at and abominate the F.O. and all its desolations. It has cogged all our dice against us.

'So you see I'm bored, and Woolley's bored and Woolley wants to go home, and I want to go somewhere where there are no politics'.[45]

While British officials in Cairo dealt with day-to-day diplomacy, wider policy was settled by the Foreign Office in London, and ultimately by the Cabinet. During the spring of 1915 the Government began to formulate its general policy towards the Middle East, and this would ultimately have a profound effect on activity in Cairo.

The Foreign Office did not at this time want to hold detailed discussions with France about future claims in the Middle East, but the question came up again almost immediately. The prospect of a Dardanelles victory prompted Russia to ask for Allied recognition of her claims to Constantinople. On March 10th the War Council decided that Britain should accept the Russian request, but only if there were a reciprocal agreement to British and French claims in the region. Since the British desiderata had yet to be formulated, papers representing the views of different departments were circulated before the next War Council meeting.

Kitchener's memorandum argued forcefully for British control of both Mesopotamia and Alexandretta. He accepted that France would take Syria, and that Russia, as now agreed, would be established at the Dardanelles. But as a result, 'the position of Egypt will be considerably affected. It must not be forgotten that, after the conclusion of peace, old enmities and jealousies . . . may revive. We have, in fact, to assume that, at some future date, we may find ourselves at enmity with Russia, or with France, or with both in combination . . . should we at any time find ourselves in opposition to either or both of these two Great Powers, our communications with India by the Suez Canal might be seriously endangered and Egypt itself might be placed in considerable jeopardy.'[46]

Kitchener therefore urged that France should be restricted to 'Syria proper'. This would allow the fulfilment of his scheme for a new Arab state: 'it is to our interests to see an Arab kingdom established in Arabia under the auspices of England, bounded on the north by the valley of the Tigris and Euphrates, and containing within it the chief Mahommedan Holy Places, Mecca, Medina, and Kerbela. In this eventuality the possession of Mesopotamia – as we already hold the Persian Gulf, the Red Sea, and Egypt – would secure all the approaches to the Mahommedan Holy Places. This, in [the British Empire's] position as the greatest of Moslem States, would greatly enhance our prestige amongst the many millions of our Mahommedan subjects.'[47]

The War Council met on March 19th, the day after the navy had attacked the Dardanelles forts with heavy loss. The Prime Minister reported that he had already heard indirectly about French claims in the Middle East. The scale of these demands, which included Cilicia, Syria and Palestine, was much larger than expected. Sir Edward Grey began a discussion of the British desiderata by posing two fundamental questions: '1. If we acquire fresh territory shall we make ourselves weaker or stronger? 2. Ought we not to take into account the very strong feeling in the Moslem world that Mohammedanism ought to have a political as well as a religious existence?' He continued: 'If the latter question were answered in the affirmative, Arabia, Syria, and Mesopotamia were the only possible territories for an Arab Empire. If we took this standpoint we could say to our Moslem subjects that, as Turkey had handed itself over to the Germans, we had set up a new and independent Moslem State.'[48]

After some inconclusive discussion Grey observed that Britain's first requirement was 'the preservation of a Moslem political entity,' and further, 'that we are pledged to the maintenance of the Moslem Holy Places.'[49] As a first step, it would be necessary to decide what the boundaries of the Moslem state should be. The Council agreed to this proposal, and decided that Russia should be told that the new state 'would have to include Arabia, and the question would arise as to what was to go with it. In the meantime, it would be premature to discuss the partition of Turkey.'[50] A few days later the French Ambassador in London informed Grey that his Government would like to discuss their claims in the Middle East. Grey agreed to this in principle, but explained that the British position was as yet undecided. However, he repeated the substance of the British message to Russia about a future Islamic state, adding: 'Its centre would naturally be the Moslem Holy Places . . . We, ourselves, had not yet come to a definite opinion whether Mesopotamia should be included . . . or whether we should put forward a claim for ourselves in that region.'[51]

Although there was clearly a case for reaching an agreement with France about the future of the Middle East, some members of the Cabinet saw advantages in delaying these negotiations until victory had been won in the Dardanelles. The question of British desiderata was passed some weeks later to an *ad hoc* inter-departmental committee chaired by an experienced senior diplomat, Sir Maurice de Bunsen.

While these issues could conveniently be shelved in London, it was impossible to set them aside in Cairo, where the future of Turkey's Arab provinces was a burning question. For the time being, Grey's directive had ruled out any action which might be seen by France as provocation, but Lawrence, and probably others, still hoped to find some way of triggering a nationalist revolt in Syria. Towards the end of March he had an opportunity to send two uncensored letters to Hogarth who, though still a civilian in Oxford, had influential friends in Whitehall. The content of these letters is unusually interesting, since Lawrence was able to discuss freely the topics which are so noticeably absent from his correspondence with family and friends in England.

In the first he urged Hogarth to help revive the Alexandretta scheme, suggesting arguments which might influence the Admiralty and Foreign Office. He argued (as did many others) that Alexandretta itself lay outside the area France could legitimately claim, writing: 'The French insist upon Syria – which we are conceding to them: there remains Alexandretta, which is the key of the whole place as you know. It's going to be the head of the Baghdad line, and therefore the natural outlet for north Syria and north Mesopotamia: it's the only easy road from Cilicia and Asia Minor into Asia etc. etc. Also it's a wonderful harbour, and thanks to Ras Khanyir on the south can be made impregnable. It is cut off from Syria, and is neither Syria nor Asia Minor. In the hands of France it will provide a sure base for naval attacks on Egypt – and remember with her in Syria, and compulsory service there, she will be able any time to fling 100,000 men against the canal in twelve days from declaration of war . . . The only place from which a fleet can operate against Egypt is Alexandretta, because there is no English port from which one can blockade it. Smyrna and Constantinople are shut in by islands: whereas Alexandretta has only Cyprus in front of it, and the water round that is too deep for a large naval harbour to be built.

'If Russia has Alexandretta it's all up with us in the Near East. And in any case in the next war the French will probably be under Russia's finger in Syria. Therefore I think it absolutely necessary that we hold Alexandretta... and thanks to the Amanus [mountains] we needn't hold anything else, either in Syria or in Asia Minor. The High Commissioner is strongly of the same opinion, and General Maxwell also, when he is awake and sober. Kitchener has pressed it on us: Winston seems un-certain, and someone . . . in the F.O. is blocking it entirely. I think that perhaps you can get a move on'. Lawrence suggested tempting Churchill, then First Lord of the Admiralty, with the prospect of mineral wealth in the Alexandretta region: 'If Winston settles on a thing he gets it, I fancy: especially with K's help.

'Then go to the F.O. if possible. Point out that in Baghdad [Railway] Convention France gave up Alexandretta, to Germans, and agreed that it formed no part of Syria. Swear that it doesn't form part of Syria – and you know it speaks Turkish: and also tell F.O. . . . that it is vitally important we hold it. One cannot go on betting that France will always be our friend. If France has all Syria south of Alexandretta, she ought to be content'.[52]

Lawrence's apparent acceptance of a French Syria was purely tactical, since he fully expected a large-scale nationalist revolt in the region if British forces occupied Alexandretta. This is hinted at earlier in his letter, where he noted that Turkey had 'only 50,000 disaffected troops in Syria . . . and the whole country is mad against them'.[53] Indeed there were several places where the conditions for an Arab uprising seemed to be ripening. He wrote: 'Idrisi is at open war with the Turks in Asir: Sherif has almost declared himself, and the Vali and staff of Hedjaz have taken refuge in Damascus'.[54] This last remark suggests that Cairo Intelligence had picked up some news of the latest dispute between Hussein and the Vali, which had flared during February when a secret Turkish plot to depose (and possibly assassinate) the Sherif had come to light.

Lawrence's second letter, on March 22nd, was more explicit about his ideas for a widespread Arab movement. His hopes were now pinned on the Idrisi, who was fighting a neighbouring Turkish-controlled chieftain, the Imam of the Yemen. Lawrence's letters suggest that this was seen in Cairo as a starting-point for wider action. However, Clayton could not intervene directly, because it had been agreed that British relations with Arab chieftains on the Red Sea littoral south of Kunfida would be handled by the Government of India through its representative in Aden. Kunfida, a port on the Red Sea, was the most northerly town controlled by the Idrisi, and Cairo was not therefore empowered to negotiate with him.

Clayton knew there was little chance that this local action would spread northwards and become a general anti-Turk movement as long as the Idrisi was subject to India's divide-and-rule policy, which did little to ease frictions between neighbouring chieftains. A much more constructive and enthusiastic British attitude was required. He wrote: 'I have suggested to the High Commissioner the advisability of offering two or three officers from here to go to the Idrisi as advisers and channels of communication between him and the British authorities. I am so afraid that [India] will enter into an agreement with the Idrisi and encourage him and then not support him well enough. If we support him he must be successful and any check will mean great loss of British prestige – we know that his opponents will be assisted by expert German advice and he ought to be given similar advantages . . . In any case if we support the Idrisi in any way, our prestige is pledged and we have to see him through.

Personally, I think it will very probably result in bringing over all the waverers to us, and it will undoubtedly have an effect in Egypt where the Idrisi is so well known.'[55]

Lawrence told Hogarth: 'You know India used to be in control of Arabia – and used to do it pretty badly, for they hadn't a man who knew Syria or Turkey, and they used to consider only the Gulf, and the preservation of peace in the Aden Hinterland . . . Egypt (which is one Clayton, a very good man) got hold of the Idrisi family . . . and for some years we had a little agreement together. Then this war started, and India went on the old game of balancing the little powers there. I want to pull them all together, and to roll up Syria by way of the Hedjaz in the name of the Sherif. You know how big his repute is in Syria. This could be done by Idrisi only, so we drew out a beautiful alliance, giving him all he wanted: and India refused to sign. So we cursed them, and I think that Newcombe and myself are going down to Kunfida as his advisors. If Idrisi is anything like as good as we hope we can rush right up to Damascus, and biff the French out of all hope of Syria. It's a big game, and at last one worth playing. Of course India has no idea what we are playing at: if we can only get to Assyr we can do the rest – or have a try at it . . . If only India will let us go. Won't the French be mad if we win through?'[56]

Others were cautious about the proposal. Kitchener's scheme for a new Arab Caliphate would depend on co-operation from the Sherif of Mecca, who was in dispute with the Idrisi about possession of Kunfida. This difficulty stood in the way of the common action Lawrence had envisaged. Through support for the Idrisi Britain might well alienate Hussein. Eventually, to Lawrence's disappointment, the plan to send him to Kunfida was abandoned. He wrote to Leeds at the Ashmolean: 'The only branch I want, Arabian politics, they won't give us, but leave in the hands of a juggins in Delhi, whose efforts are to maintain the Aden Hinterland – a cesspit – in its status quo.'[57] Two days later, in a letter to Hogarth, he added: 'There aren't going to be any nice schemes anytime, I believe: at least everything boils up gloriously, and one is told to be ready to start by the Thursday in next week – and then it never becomes the Thursday of this week'.[58]

At about this time Lawrence wrote a long analysis of the internal factors which would have to be taken into account when the future of Syria was decided. He gave a great deal of thought to this paper: its conclusions were based on his own knowledge of the country and on a vast amount of diverse information which had accumulated in Intelligence Department files. He was Clayton's specialist on Syria, and the views he now expressed were destined to have far-reaching influence.

His account began with a long description which emphasised the geographical, cultural, racial, linguistic and religious diversity of Syria. After this he turned his attention to the six major cities. He argued that two of these, Jerusalem and Beirut, should be set apart because they were too cosmopolitan to be considered essentially Arab. The people of Jerusalem, he wrote, 'with the rarest exceptions, are characterless as hotel servants, living on the crowd of visitors passing through. Questions of Arabs and their nationality are as far from them as bimetallism from the life of Texas'.[59] Beirut, on the other hand, 'would be all bastard French in feeling, as in language, but for its Greek harbour and its American College. Public opinion in it is that of the Christian merchants, all fat men . . . Beyrout is the door of Syria, with a Levantine screen through which shop-soiled foreign influences flow into Syria. It is as representative of Syria as Soho of the Home Counties'.[60]

There remained: 'Damascus, Homs, Hamah, and Aleppo . . . the four ancient cities in which Syria takes pride. They are stretched like a chain along the fertile valleys of the interior, between the desert and the hills; because of their setting they turn their backs upon the sea and look eastward. They are Arab and know themselves such.

'Damascus is the old inevitable head of Syria. It is the seat of lay government and the religious centre, three days only from the Holy City by its railway. Its sheikhs are leaders of opinion, and more "Meccan" than others elsewhere. Its people are fresh and turbulent, always willing to strike, as extreme in their words and acts as in their pleasures. Damascus will move before any part of Syria. The Turks made it their military centre, just as naturally as the Arab Opposition . . . Damascus is a lode star to which Arabs are naturally drawn, and a city which will not easily be convinced that it is subject to any alien race.

'Hamah and Homs are towns which dislike one another. Everyone in them manufactures things . . . Their industries were prosperous and increasing; their merchants were quick to take advantage of new outlets, or to meet new tastes . . . They demonstrated the productive ability of Syria, unguided by foreigners . . . Yet, while the prosperity of Beyrout has made it Levantine, the prosperity of Homs and Hamah has reinforced their localism, made them more entirely native, and more jealously native than any other Syrian towns. It almost seems as though familiarity with plant and power had shown the people there that the manners of their fathers were the best.

'Aleppo is the largest city in Syria, but not of it, nor of Turkey, nor of Mesopotamia. Rather it is a point where all the races, creeds and tongues of the Ottoman Empire meet and know one another in a spirit of compromise . . . Aleppo would stand aside from political action altogether but for the influence of the great unmixed Arab quarters which lie on its outskirts like overgrown, half-nomad villages. These are, after the *Maidan* of Damascus, the most national of any parts of towns, and the intensity of their Arab feeling tinges the rest of the citizens with a colour of nationalism, which is by so much less vivid than the unanimous opinion of Damascus.'[61]

Lawrence next turned his attention to Syrian politicians, but found little to admire: 'All of them want something new, for with their superficiality and their lawlessness is combined a passion for politics, the science of which it is fatally easy for the Syrian to gain a smattering, and too difficult to gain a mastery. They are all discontented with the government they have, but few of them honestly combine their ideas of what they want. Some (mostly Mohammedans) cry for an Arab kingdom, some (mostly Christians) for a foreign protection of an altruistic thelemic order, conferring privileges without obligation. Others cry for autonomy for Syria.'[62] He saw 'no national feeling' in Syria: 'Between town and town, village and village, family and family, creed and creed, exist intimate jealousies, sedulously fostered by the Turks to render a spontaneous union impossible. The largest indigenous political entity in settled Syria is only the village under its sheikh, and in patriarchal Syria the tribe under its chief . . . All the constitution above them is the artificial bureaucracy of the Turk . . . By accident and time the Arabic language has gradually permeated the country, until it is now almost the only one in use; but this does not mean that Syria – any more than Egypt – is an Arabian country. On the sea coast there is little, if any, Arabic feeling or tradition: on the desert edge there is much. Indeed, racially, there is perhaps something to be said for the suggestion – thrown in the teeth of geography and economics – of putting the littoral under one government, and the interior under another.'[63]

Looking ahead, Lawrence argued that 'an Arab Government in Syria, today or tomorrow, would be an imposed one, as the former Arab Governments were.' However, there were two factors which might help to provide a basis for political cohesion. First, a kind of patriotism based on common language rather than racial or territorial boundaries: 'The heritage of the Koran and the classical poets holds the Arabic-speaking peoples together.'[64] Secondly, there was the Arab consciousness of a shared history, 'the dim distortion of the old glories and conquests of the Arabian Khalifate, which has persisted in the popular memory through centuries of Turkish misgovernment.'[65] Lawrence concluded that these factors would be insufficient in themselves, and sketched out the kind of additional bond he thought necessary: 'only by the intrusion of a new factor, founded on some outward power or non-Syrian basis, can the dissident tendencies of the sects and peoples of Syria be reined in sufficiently to prevent destructive anarchy. The more loose, informal, inchoate this new government, the less will be the inevitable dis-illusionment following on its institution; for the true ideal of Syria, apart from the minute but vociferous Christian element, is not an efficient administration, but the minimum of central power to ensure peace, and permit the unchecked development of customary law.'[66]

Lawrence's proposed solution does not appear until the final sentence of his paper: 'the only imposed government that will find, in Moslem Syria, any really prepared groundwork or large body of adherents is a Sunni one, speaking Arabic, and pretending to revive the Abbassides or Ayubides.'[67] An educated reader such as Clayton would immediately have grasped the meaning of this allusion to the Abbasid Caliphate of Baghdad and the Ayyubid Sultanate established at Damascus after Saladin's conquest of Syria. Indeed, Lawrence had set out the analysis in such a way that it could lead to only one conclusion: that the Arab Caliphate advocated by Kitchener should include inland Syria and its four principal cities, Damascus, Homs, Hama and Aleppo. He had also suggested that the Arab peoples of the interior need not come under the same government as the cosmopolitan regions on the coast. Seven months later these two principles were to be adopted as key elements in British policy towards the future of Syria.

As the spring of 1915 progressed, it became evident that Lawrence's hopes for an Arab rebellion had been premature. Although the conditions seemed to be right, some essential factor was still missing, and Britain had failed to take any action that might tip the balance. The Alexandretta scheme had been set aside, Hussein was inexplicably silent, and support for the Idrisi had been left to India. In this last connection Lawrence wrote to Hogarth on April 26th: 'Arabian affairs have all gone to pot. I've never seen a more despicable mess made of a show. It makes one howl with fury – for we had a ripping chance there.'[68] He asked Hogarth to keep pressing for a landing at Alexandretta: 'it seems to me the only thing left to us'.[69]

This sense of frustration persisted throughout the summer. Hussein, the central figure in plans for a new Caliphate, showed little sign that he was ready to break with the Turks. No further message from him was received in Cairo, although the means for communication existed. Native trading vessels were still able to cross the Red Sea between Arabia and the Sudan. By this route letters occasionally passed between the Sherif and the Grand Cadi, leader of the Sudanese Moslems.

Sir Reginald Wingate, Governor-General of the Sudan, strongly supported the idea of Arab independence. In the late spring he persuaded the Grand Cadi to write to Hussein, encouraging thoughts of a new Caliphate. To support this initiative, Grey telegraphed McMahon authorising publication, if desirable, of a statement 'that His Majesty's Government will make it an essential condition in any terms of peace that the Arabian Peninsula and its Moslem Holy Places should remain in the hands of an independent Sovereign Moslem State.'[70] Since British policy regarding Syria and Mesopotamia was still undecided, Grey added: 'Exactly how much territory should be included in this State it is not possible to define at this stage.'[71] As regards the Caliphate issue, he stressed the diplomatic point that this 'must be decided by Moslems without interference from non-Moslem Powers. Should Moslems decide for an Arab Khalifate, that decision would naturally . . . be respected by His Majesty's Government'.[72]

In Cairo it was felt that Grey's expression 'independent Sovereign Moslem State' was too far in advance of political reality. Hussein might have ambitions towards some form of overall leadership, but at this stage other Arab chieftains were unlikely to recognise him as a temporal rather than a religious authority. McMahon wrote: 'the idea of an Arabian unity under one ruler recognised as supreme by other Arab chiefs is as yet inconceivable to the Arab mind'.[73] No public statement was issued, but the gist of Grey's message was given to the Cadi and to other prominent Arabs in Egypt and the Sudan. There could be little doubt that it would reach Hussein.

By this time the Dardanelles campaign had grown into a large-scale commitment. The naval defeat in March had been followed by a decision to land an army on the Gallipoli Peninsula, and during the late spring a Mediterranean Expeditionary Force was assembled for this purpose in Egypt. This gave extra work to the Cairo Intelligence Department. Lawrence wrote: 'the Med-Ex. came out, beastly ill-prepared, with no knowledge of where it was going, or what it would meet, or what it was going to do. So we took pity on it, and said that we would be its Intelligence Base, and its map base . . . It's very dull: but of course I haven't any training as a field officer'.[74]

During April his own job had become more demanding when the Department had started issuing daily Intelligence Bulletins. The task of putting these together became one of his principal activities. Issues varied in length between one and eleven pages, and totalled about 150 pages a month. They carried miscellaneous information of military or political interest relating to every part of the Turkish Empire. There was a very wide variety of sources: information was obtained from agents, neutral travellers, air reconnaissance, prisoners, captured documents, and Intelligence reports from other commands.

Lawrence described these bulletins in a letter to C. F. Bell: 'We edit a daily newspaper, absolutely uncensored, for the edification of twenty-eight generals: the circulation increases automatically as they invent new generals. This paper is my only joy: one can give the Turkish point of view (in imaginary conversations with prisoners) of the proceedings of admirals and generals one dislikes: and I rub it in, in my capacity as editor-in-chief. There is also a weekly letter to "Mother" (the London W.O.) in which one japes on a grander scale yet. Last week I sent them an extract from a Greek paper of Smyrna, freely translated, which compared our fleet at Smyrna, in its efforts at blocking the harbour, to an excited gentleman – but I don't think this is quite fit for your ears. It was elaborate, and very long.'[75]

On the same day he wrote to Leeds that he was working in the office from 9 am to 7 pm, 'with one's work carrying over into the hotel in the evening, and bothering one all night with speculations as to where that [Turkish] Army Corps II has gone. Athens swears it's in the Caucasus, who think it's in Syria: an Italian has talked to it near Adana, Basra claim it on their front: it is certainly at Scutari on the Bosphorus, and what are these other things: has it split up into pieces, and how is it each piece is bigger than the whole used to be? There are forty divisions in the Turkish Army, in peace time, and that is doubled now that it is war, and the only one really settled, the one we "defeat" from time to time on the Canal, is located in the Caucasus by the Russians, at Pardirma by the Athens people, in Adrianople by Bulgaria, at Midia by Roumania, and in Bagdad by India. The locations of the other thirty-nine regular, and forty reserve divisions are less certain.'[76]

Another project which interested him at this time was pioneering work on the use of aerial photography for making maps. If the technical problems could be solved, this would be extremely valuable for mapping areas behind enemy lines. Experiments were carried out during the spring of 1915 under the supervision of the Survey of Egypt, and the principles learned were put to the test during the operations in Gallipoli. Newcombe and Lawrence supported the trials with enthusiasm. Both were well qualified for the work, Newcombe as a survey officer, and Lawrence through his map liaison duties and personal knowledge of photography. The experiments were successful, and as a result aerial surveying was used extensively in the Middle East during the First World War.[77]

Lawrence also spent part of his time interviewing prisoners, many of whom were Arabs recruited by the Turks in Syria. He later wrote: 'I always knew their districts, and asked about my friends in them. Then they told me everything!'[78] In this way he occasionally heard about events at Carchemish. For example, he had told Hogarth in January: 'News has come through that the Germans have laid a light line through the South Gate, and are taking stone from the *Kalaat* at Jerablus . . . I don't suppose that they will do serious harm merely to spite us: brutes they are.'[79] But the information was fragmentary and he heard nothing of Dahoum or the other headmen.[80] In May the Intelligence Bulletin noted that the German railway bridge at Carchemish had at last been opened. Lawrence added an editorial comment: 'The temporary bridge has enabled through communication across the Euphrates for about the last two years; hence the completion of the bridge is of little military importance.'[81]

All these activities left him with little leisure time, but in any case he found almost nothing to interest him in Cairo: 'Anything fouler than the town buildings, or its beastly people, can't be'.[82] By comparison, he recalled Jerablus as 'a village inhabited by the cleanest and most intelligent angels.'[83] He had, however, made friends with Ronald Storrs, Oriental Secretary to the High Commissioner. Storrs, who had gained a first in Classics at Cambridge, was a highly cultured person, and Lawrence found his company congenial. They were both widely read, and Storrs later recalled: 'I would come upon him in my flat, reading always Latin or Greek, with corresponding gaps in my shelves. But he put back in their proper places the books he did not take away; of those he took he left a list, and never failed to return them reasonably soon, in perfect condition.'[84] Storrs was a fluent Arabist and had met many Arab leaders during his work for Gorst and Kitchener at the British Agency before the war. He had been the intermediary in Kitchener's dealings with Hussein, and was likely to play a central role in any further contacts. This may also have drawn Lawrence to him.

On May 9th Lawrence's brother Frank was killed in action at Richebourg l'Avoué on the Western Front. Lawrence wrote to his father: 'to die for one's country is a sort of privilege: Mother and you will find it more painful and harder to live for it, than he did to die: but I think that at this time it is one's duty to show no signs that would distress others: and to appear bereaved is surely under this condemnation.'[85] Frank had been his mother's favourite, and she was deeply distressed. Lawrence was evidently hurt by a letter she wrote to him, to which he replied:

> Poor dear Mother
>
> I got your letter this morning, and it has grieved me very much. You *will* never never understand any of us after we are grown up a little. *Don't* you ever feel that we love you without our telling you so? – I feel such a contemptible worm for having to write this way about things. If you only knew that if one thinks deeply about anything one would rather die than say anything about it. You know men do nearly all die laughing, because they know death is very terrible, and a thing to be forgotten till after it has come.
>
> There, put that aside, and bear a brave face to the world about Frank. In a time of such fearful stress in our country it is one's duty to watch very carefully lest one of the weaker ones be offended: and you know we were always the stronger, and if they see you broken down they will all grow fearful about their ones in the front . . .
>
> I didn't go to say good-bye to Frank because he would rather I didn't, and I knew there was little chance of my seeing him again; in which case we were better without a parting.'[86]

He rarely expressed such personal feelings in his letters home, especially as he knew that the mail to England was read for censorship by a fellow-officer. In the same way, he was unable to tell his parents about the more interesting aspects of his secret political and military work in Cairo.[87]

They had, at best, a partial view of his activities and can have had little idea of the value and importance of his role. This, for example, was the general account of his office duties he sent home on June 23rd: 'I got a letter yesterday asking for more details of what I am doing. Well, drawing, and overseeing the drawing of maps: overseeing printing and packing of same: sitting in an office coding and decoding telegrams, interviewing prisoners, writing reports, and giving information from 9 a.m. till 7 p.m. After that feed and read, and then go to bed. I'm sick of pens, ink and paper: and have no wish ever to send off another telegram. We do daily wires to Athens, Gallipoli, and Petrograd: and receive five times what we send, all in cypher, which is slow work, though we have a good staff dealing with them . . . We have only war work:– European Turkey, Asia Minor, Syria, Mesopotamia, Arabia, Sinai, and Tripoli:– we all dabble in them all. One learns a lot of geography, some people's names, and little else.'[88]

Although much of this was routine, he enjoyed working on maps, and the Intelligence Bulletins sometimes provided an opportunity for comic relief. In the issue of July 1st, for example, he mischievously printed a message from Haifa in imperfect English: 'A man who shot at the seaplane flying over Haifa received a bomb on his head until he was utterly destroyed. The Christian priests were compelled to attend the funeral of his remains'.[89] In another issue he published scandalous allegations about Madame Koch, whose pre-war dealings in antiquities had so often been an irritation. He now described her as: 'about fifty-five years old, very clever, very charming, good looking, artistic, well-educated, with a distinguished *grande dame* air, great humour, a love for political work, and a capacity for running a salon. Her husband is alive, and lives somewhere in the house, but is not allowed to come upstairs. She holds a reception every evening for the German employees of the Bagdad Company, who have the edifying spectacle of seeing their chief, Foellner, sitting at a low chair at her feet, in silent admiration of her, and being noticed by her occasionally. He does all she asks of him, so her favour is important to any rising man in the company. She and Foellner went once on holiday to Jerusalem together, and went home to Germany at the same time, and returned together. He is a little pale, fish-like man, very timid, and crooked in his ways.'[90]

By the middle of June there had still been no news from Hussein and, as further encouragement, propaganda leaflets were dropped by air over areas in the Hejaz. These incorporated a version of the message Grey had authorised some weeks before. An English translation was sent back to London, and read in part: 'The Government of His Majesty the King of England and Emperor of India has declared that when this war ends it shall be laid down in the terms of peace as a necessary condition, that the Arabian peninsula and its Mahommetan holy places shall remain independent. We shall not annex one foot of land in it, nor suffer any other Power to do so. Your independence of all foreign control is thus assured, and with such guarantees the lands of Arabia will, please God, return along the paths of freedom to their ancient prosperity.'[91]

Although the terms of Grey's message had been approved by the India Office in London, the Government of India in Delhi took exception to this new public assurance. Lord Hardinge disliked any encouragement of Arab nationalism, and objected strongly to a statement from Cairo which would affect India's diplomatic freedom. He complained that the proclamation went 'much further than was ever intended. The expression "Arabian Peninsula" is open to serious misinterpretation and might be held to tie our hands in Oman and even to indicate an intention to withdraw from Aden.'[92]

During the second week in July a visitor to Cairo brought news from the de Bunsen Committee, set up by the War Council in April to consider British desiderata in Asiatic Turkey. The Committee had achieved little more than a preliminary investigation of the problem, sketching out several alternative proposals. All of these envisaged an independent state in the Arabian Peninsula, but they suggested differing regions of direct rule or zones of influence in Syria and Mesopotamia. A member of the Committee, Sir Mark Sykes, had set out on a tour of the Middle East and India to sound out the reactions of British officials.

The British staff in Cairo welcomed any opportunity to put their views to those working on Middle East policy in London. Sykes was therefore well received at GHQ and in the Residency, where his charm and sense of humour were an immediate success. Now thirty-six, he had been born into a Yorkshire landowning family and had inherited his father's estates and baronetcy in 1913. Before the war he had spent some time in the Middle East where he had travelled widely. Also, like Herbert and Lloyd, he had worked for a while as an honorary attaché at the Constantinople Embassy. Since 1911 he had been a Member of Parliament, popular for his wit and eloquence. He had a forceful personality and tremendous energy. It seemed to the Cairo staff that Sykes might become a powerful advocate in London for their point of view, and detailed arguments were put to him demonstrating that none of the de Bunsen proposals was entirely satisfactory. McMahon and Maxwell expressed agreement with Kitchener's scheme for a non-Ottoman Caliphate based on Mecca, and they suggested that its influence might extend well beyond the Arabian Peninsula. Unlike the de Bunsen Committee, both advocated exclusive British suzerainty over Palestine, since otherwise France might share control of territory very close to the Suez Canal. They also proposed that the Damascus region of Syria should be included in the British sphere, at the expense of French claims. In putting the case for this, they cited Islamic links between Damascus and Mecca, as well as the 'geographical and religious isolation of Damascus from Beirut and the Lebanon'.[93] This reasoning is distinctly reminiscent of the argument Lawrence had used some months earlier in his paper on Syria.

Sykes was also introduced to a selection of Christian and Moslem Syrians including the Pan-Arab spokesman, Rashid Rida. Despite the divergent opinions they represented, their views would help in one way or another to reinforce the arguments of the Cairo staff. A report by Sykes to the War Office on July 14th shows that he had been persuaded.[94]

On this brief visit to Cairo he also found time to visit French diplomats (he was a Francophile and a devout Roman Catholic). They doubtless assured him, since this was central to French propaganda at the time, that Britain and France were in perfect agreement over Syria. Moreover, they seem to have succeeded in convincing him that any tension over the question was purely the result of agitation by enemy agents. This opinion was repeated uncritically in his report to London, and he went on to urge that a formal agreement with France over the future of Syria should be reached at the first opportunity.

A note surviving in French archives shows that Sykes also took it upon himself to discuss with them the details of British desiderata in the Arab provinces.[95] This private initiative, in advance of any agreed British Government policy, was a culpable indiscretion and he made no mention of it in his report. It would have caused much irritation had it been discovered by the Foreign Office.

Sykes left Cairo in mid-July to consult the British Resident in Aden. A few days later another welcome visitor, D. G. Hogarth, arrived from London. Hogarth, then in his early fifties, was an acknowledged authority on the geography and history of the Middle East, but he had been unable to find a useful war job. He had come to Cairo hoping to be given an

Intelligence post with the Gallipoli expedition. No request came; instead he stayed in Egypt for several weeks working on a project for Clayton.[96]

While he was there, Lawrence was sent on a brief visit to Athens to improve liaison with the Levant branch of British Intelligence run by Major Samson (known by his pseudonym 'R'). By this time Lawrence was highly regarded by his superiors. Samson had written to Newcombe shortly before: 'It is very kind of you to offer to send us Lawrence for a few days to help us to get our dislocation in order. The man who has taken charge of it says he would like a little time longer to get it into shape as he feels that at present he would hardly sufficiently benefit by Lawrence's visit. May I telegraph when he is ready and ask you to send Lawrence to us for a few days? We would gladly pay the cost of his journey and of course we should hope he would consider himself our guest during his stay here.'[97]

Lawrence spent about a week in Greece, leaving again on August 14th. Afterwards he wrote home: 'Athens was very hot, and glare of sun very bad. Otherwise not dull. I was in office there from 9 a.m. (when shops opened) till 7 p.m. (when shops shut): so I bought nothing, and saw nothing:– except the Acropolis from the window.'[98] For some time after this, 'till the work grew important',[99] he was Samson's representative in Cairo. The journey to Athens was Lawrence's only break from office work during 1915, except for a brief visit to the Western Desert, where the Senussi, still loyal to Turkey, was a constant problem.[100]

On his return to Cairo he found that messages had arrived from the Sherif of Mecca, ending a silence which had lasted for eight months.

CHAPTER 11

The McMahon Pledge
August – October 1915

LAWRENCE later wrote that Hussein's messages received in August 1915 'came as a bombshell'.[1] The Sherif was offering an alliance, but as a condition he made territorial demands which seemed little short of outrageous. Previous correspondence had referred to Arab independence in the Hejaz and the Arabian Peninsula. Now, however, Hussein was asking for a vast area, including the whole of Syria and Mesopotamia. He set out the precise boundaries of this region which was, it seemed, to form the territory of a new Arab Caliphate.

Storrs, who was the first to read the messages, was inclined to dismiss their content as a bargaining posture. He advised McMahon: 'it may be regarded as certain that [Hussein] has received no sort of mandate from other potentates. He knows he is demanding, possibly as a basis of negotiation, far more than he has the right, the hope, or the power to expect.'[2] Storrs also noted that: 'There is a curiously exact resemblance between the terms herein proposed, and the views frequently expressed by Shaykh Rashid Rida, especially in regard to frontiers. This tends to confirm what has been already suspected, that the Shaykh is in communication with the Sherif.'[3]

The officials in Cairo concluded that Hussein was asking Britain to create an enormous Arab kingdom with himself at its head. Such an idea would not have appealed to the many local chieftains whose territory was involved. Moreover it would be condemned outright by the Governments of India and France. McMahon telegraphed a précis of Hussein's letter to the Foreign Office, with the comment: 'His pretensions are in every way exaggerated, no doubt considerably beyond his hope of acceptance, but it seems very difficult to treat with them in detail without seriously discouraging him.' He proposed sending a courteous but evasive reply, little more than a restatement of Kitchener's earlier message. It would suggest that 'the discussion of boundary details is . . . premature during the war'.[4]

Despite the extent of the Sherif's demands, Britain still wished, in principle, to reach an agreement with him. Even the India Office had accepted the idea of an independent Arab state based on the Moslem Holy Places. Austen Chamberlain, the new Secretary of State for India, agreed that the Sherif's territorial demands were exorbitant, but wrote: 'at the present point in the negotiations, a communication which is limited to generalities in reply to such definite proposals as those made by the Sheriff will not only not engage him for our cause, but may lead him to think that we were not serious in our overtures.'[5] Chamberlain recommended inviting an Arab negotiator to Cairo so that it might be 'possible to come to close quarters with [Hussein's] proposals, and to reduce them to reasonable dimensions.'[6]

The Foreign Office mentioned this possibility to McMahon, but approved his earlier draft reply. George Clerk, head of the War Department, minuted: 'My own feeling is that Sir H. McMahon and his advisers are in a better position than anyone else to gauge the Sherif's sentiments'.[7] Clerk argued, moreover, that there was a strong objection to opening territorial negotiations with Hussein. Such a move would inevitably lead to a conflict of interests with France: 'we must be very careful to do nothing which will look like stealing a march on our Allies.'[8] McMahon too rejected the India Office suggestion. He felt that it was too early to 'discuss even a preliminary agreement, and it might at this stage injure the Sherif's chances of the Khalifate to advertise his dealings with us by sending a son or other notable to treat with us.'[9]

The Sherif had insisted on a positive or negative response to his grandiose proposals within thirty days. On August 30th his messenger, Sheikh Oreifan, set out from Cairo with a reply which politely ignored them.[10] Years later, Storrs recalled: 'we could not conceal from ourselves (and with difficulty from him) that his pretensions bordered upon the tragi-comic.'[11]

At the beginning of September Newcombe was posted to the Dardanelles. His place at the Intelligence Department was taken for some weeks by Colonel A. C. Parker, a nephew of Lord Kitchener's who had been Governor of Sinai before the war. Lawrence was probably repeating the general opinion when he wrote to his parents that Parker was 'an authority on Sinai and not much else'.[12]

Newcombe's departure meant that Lawrence was now one of the most experienced and knowledgeable officers remaining in Cairo Intelligence. He had been there longer than anyone except Clayton (Leonard Woolley, although still in Egypt, had been detailed to handle liaison with the French Navy and rarely visited Cairo). Lawrence's work on the Intelligence Bulletin had given him an encyclopaedic knowledge of the Ottoman Empire, and also of the Turkish Army and its dispositions. Each day an immense amount of military and political information passed through his hands.

Lawrence and other members of the Intelligence staff spent a good deal of time listening to Arab nationalists, an occupation which was viewed with disfavour by French representatives in Cairo. Eventually a formal protest was made by the French Embassy in London, noting the unhelpful activities 'of certain British officials of secondary rank'. Britain, the Ambassador claimed, had already recognised that 'Syria with Cilicia constitute, for France, a reserved zone where no sharing of her interests can be tolerated. If the attitude of General Maxwell and certain of his immediate colleagues conforms scrupulously to this, there are, under their orders and sometimes quite close to them, some members of the staff who do not seem to accept it very deeply. The very day that an agitator is officially sent packing by the Residency, he often receives a messenger from somebody of this kind who assures him of the authorities' sympathy, questions him about his projects and encourages him to pursue his propaganda. Under the pretext of gathering information, the Intelligence Department in particular has opened its doors to every champion of the Arab movement who shows himself hostile to our influence. It could be regarded as excessive that most of them are subsequently retained as helpers . . .

'In bringing [these facts] to the notice of the Foreign Office, the Embassy only wishes to permit it to put a stop to an agitation which could end up by disquieting French opinion, particularly sensitive to anything which concerns Syria, with a risk of damaging the perfectly harmonious relationship between the two Allied Governments.'[13]

This complaint met with very little sympathy in Cairo, and in reply McMahon sent the Foreign Office a scathing commentary on French diplomatic intrigues. He pointed out that the Intelligence Department was 'responsible among its other duties for keeping in touch with the general political situation and it is obviously impossible to do this without a full acquaintance with the views and aspirations of . . . the various parties and schools of thought which are represented in the country . . . The practice has been therefore to listen to and treat all parties alike. At the same time great care has been taken . . . to give no indication of what form the future settlement might take. Whether junior officers or officials have occasionally given vent to personal views in favour of one scheme or another, it is perhaps impossible to say, but, if this has been the case, it is obvious that such opinions can have no official weight, though in a country like Egypt more importance may be attached to them than they deserve.'[14]

Early in September the Cairo Intelligence Department received new and very important information about Arab nationalist activities in Syria and other parts of the Turkish Empire. This came from a young Arab officer, Sherif Mohammed al Faroki, who had crossed to British lines at Gallipoli under a white flag, ostensibly to arrange for burial of the dead. Once safely in Allied territory, he had explained that he was a member of an Arab secret society headed by Abdul Aziz al Masri, and that he wished to place himself in British hands, on condition that he was not treated as a prisoner. Faroki had claimed that there were many other Arab officers in the Ottoman Army who would be ready to desert if Britain undertook to help them organise an Arab revolt. As a first step he had asked to be sent to Egypt (where al Masri was living) and later to the Sherif of Mecca.

Although Faroki was young, he was clearly a person of some stature. He came from a prominent family in Mosul, the principal city of northern Mesopotamia. The family claimed descent from the Caliph Omar ibn El Khattab. He was well educated and spoke French, Turkish, and a little Russian in addition to Arabic.

Sir Ian Hamilton, GOC at Gallipoli, had consulted the War Office, asking what action should be taken. In London it was decided that Faroki should be to sent to Egypt as he had requested, so that he could be interviewed more carefully: 'Clayton at Cairo will be able to ascertain from Aziz Ali what credence is to be given to this proposal'.[15] Faroki had therefore been escorted from Gallipoli by an Arab member of the British Intelligence staff, who translated a long 'statement' into English and made additional notes on their conversations. Once in Cairo, Faroki was questioned in detail by Intelligence officers with a wide knowledge of Arab nationalism and events in Syria. Lawrence, a specialist in these regions, was strongly placed for this work. Moreover, he was fluent in French and Arabic, two of Faroki's languages.

Faroki must have come through the questioning very well. Furthermore, his credentials were accepted by al Masri. Since he had served as a staff officer he was able to provide a great deal of military information, many details of which could be verified from other Intelligence sources.

His statements about Arab affairs made sense in themselves and helped to explain fragmentary rumours which had reached the Intelligence Department over a long period.[16]

It was important to know whether Faroki could be believed, because his testimony completely altered the perception of Arab nationalist activity held by British officials in Cairo. He claimed to belong to a powerful and very widespread Pan-Arab organisation, not previously identified by British Intelligence. This underground society, he explained, was active in both Syria and Mesopotamia and was in direct contact with the Sherif of Mecca. The claim was borne out by Faroki's considerable knowledge of the secret correspondence which had passed between Cairo and Sherif Hussein.

Faroki gave the history of his involvement with these secret societies. He had served before the war in Mesopotamia, where he had joined al Ahd, the military society committed to Arab nationalism. Subsequently he had been moved to Aleppo, where he had served as ADC to the local commander, Fakhri Pasha. While in Syria Faroki had learned of al Fatat, a secret civilian organisation with similar aims to al Ahd. It too was totally dedicated to independence throughout the Arab provinces. He claimed to have been instrumental in establishing close collaboration between the two societies, which had begun early in 1915. While both societies were willing to offer Britain certain privileges in exchange for material help, they were wholly opposed to any form of colonial annexation. For this reason al Fatat in particular was implacably anti-French.[17]

If Faroki was right, these secret societies had created much better co-ordination in the Arab nationalist movement than the Cairo staff had suspected. The societies had infiltrated Arab units of the Ottoman army throughout Syria and Mesopotamia and had also won support among civilian leaders in both the settled and nomadic regions.

In due course there had been contacts between al Fatat and Sherif Hussein, and the society had learned of his correspondence with Egypt. In the spring of 1915 the secret co-ordinating committee of al Fatat and al Ahd had been given details of British offers to the Arabs in the event of a rebellion.

The Damascus nationalists were intensely suspicious of Allied intentions, but had nevertheless agreed to support a rebellion if Britain would make specific guarantees about Arab independence in Syria and Mesopotamia. The boundaries they had set out were those which Hussein had subsequently asked for in his message to Cairo.[18]

If this new information was correct, the British reply to Hussein's territorial requests had been badly misjudged. It now seemed possible that the Sherif had indeed been speaking on behalf of Arab nationalist leaders throughout Syria and Mesopotamia, and that far more hung on the negotiations than anyone in Cairo had suspected. Through Hussein, Britain might win Arab support in a large area behind enemy lines: but if the negotiations failed, Arab disillusion would be equally widespread. Those who had recently dismissed Hussein's 'pretensions' now feared that the evasive reply McMahon had sent might have an unfortunate outcome. They must have noted with anxiety Faroki's statement that: 'About three months ago representatives [of the secret societies] were sent to Jedda [a Red Sea port close to Mecca] with instructions that if England agreed to these [territorial] limits they were to discuss and modify with them other articles of the agreement, otherwise they were to come back without discussing the other points'.[19]

Although Faroki had not come as a negotiator, he offered to serve as an intermediary in Britain's dealings with the Arab nationalists. The role he envisaged is clear from a statement made to British Intelligence: 'I am not authorised to discuss with you officially our political programme, but if no agreement between you and our representatives who came to Jedda has yet been made I can, for the sake of shortening negotiations . . . give answers to any questions you wish to make *re* the agreement and if necessary make modifications in its articles . . . I promise to try my utmost to convince my comrades of their advisability, and I am confident I can convince most of them to go by my agreement.'[20]

To the chagrin of the Intelligence Department, Faroki also gave details of an Arab rebellion which had been planned some months earlier in the expectation of a British landing at Alexandretta. He claimed that the nationalists had even managed to ensure that Alexandretta was badly fortified: the defences had been designed by an Arab officer in the Turkish army who had 'arranged his trenches and batteries where they could be of no possible use to anyone.'[21] In several towns, anti-Turkish feeling among Arab troops had been brought to the point of mutiny.

Faroki's news about recent anti-nationalist repression in Syria was already known, in general terms, to the Intelligence Department. Jemal Pasha, the Turkish commander in Syria, had long been aware of Arab unrest. In the early months of the war he had chosen to ignore it, despite incriminating documents about Arab nationalists left behind in the French

Consulate at Beirut. Jemal's attitude had changed, however, after his unsuccessful attack on the Suez Canal in February 1915. When he heard rumours of British plans for a landing at Alexandretta, he had rightly connected them with Arab demonstrations such as a mutiny of troops at Homs. As a result Faroki and other Arab officers had been arrested on suspicion of treachery. No firm evidence could be found against them, and they had eventually been released; but the suspicion remained, and they had been posted to front-line regiments outside Syria.

Jemal took other steps to eliminate the danger of an Arab nationalist rising. In June, the 25th Division had been sent to Gallipoli; it was entirely Arab, and had been crucial to schemes for a revolt. At every opportunity thereafter Jemal posted experienced Arab divisions away from Syria, replacing them with untrained recruits. Although this reduced the effective garrison there, it removed the risk of a well organised and heavily armed rebellion. In addition, he had begun to prosecute civilians compromised by the French Consulate documents. On August 28th eleven Arabs were publicly hanged in Beirut, and a further forty-five were condemned to death *in absentia*. Other sentences included imprisonment and exile, and more executions were to follow. Among the first to die was one of the founders of al Fatat. Nobody could tell where this campaign against Arab nationalists would end. The British staff in Cairo recognised that if Jemal continued as he had begun, the secret societies would be rendered powerless.

Much of the information Faroki brought was processed by Lawrence, whose concern about developments in Syria is expressed in a contemporary letter to George Lloyd (then working for Military Intelligence in Gallipoli). Lawrence complained: 'Our stout men didn't "see any advantage" in stirring up north Syria – and so four [Arab] divisions have been added thence to the [Turkish] Dardanelles army. The other three or four will follow, as soon as they raise scallywags to replace 'em, unless we some day do something.'[22]

The action Lawrence had in mind was a British landing at Alexandretta. His letters during the summer of 1915 show that he had never relinquished this scheme, and as early as August he had foreseen that there was 'an off chance of it. Only the big show [Gallipoli] must go wrong or go right first.'[23] In mid-September Intelligence sources showed that Alexandretta and its neighbourhood were lightly garrisoned and that there was little to fear from the second-class Turkish forces in Cilicia and North Syria. Both McMahon and Maxwell looked favourably on the idea of landings at Ayas Bay which the Intelligence Department were again promoting.[24]

There was a new reason for considering the scheme at this particular time. During the spring and early summer Turkey had displaced entire Armenian populations from their homelands, committing terrible mass-acres and leaving thousands to die of starvation in the desert. Lawrence wrote to Lloyd: 'The women and children of Armenian villages have all been expelled from Cilicia to Mesopotamia and Syria, but the men of fit age all sent into labour battalions. So north Syria is full of unarmed battalions of Armenians and Christians, fit men, with no relations or home ties. In addition there are many outlaws, Mohammedan and Christian, in the hills:– all of it good material for a rising backed by us: a few hundred men, a company or two of machine guns, 10,000 rifles, and acceptance of the Armenian offers of volunteers arriving daily from America, and we'll have all the Armenias and Cilicia in a horrible tangle. The G.O.C. [Maxwell] is willing, and if you'll back up we can carry over the French and have a huge loot. Sherif in rear and Armenians in front'.[25]

If Turkish communications could be cut at Alexandretta, Lawrence hoped that there would be a simultaneous rising in the Hejaz. This might be triggered by a nucleus of Arab nationalist deserters. He wrote to Lloyd of Faroki's plans 'to slip into the Hedjaz, have a chat about tactics with the Sherif, slip out again, raise the ten Syrian officers and the 600 rank and file we took on the Canal, add to them fifty officers and 2,000 men now in India, and drop into the Hedjaz heavily this time. Nuri Shaalan [chief of the Rualla, an important nomad tribe based far inland at Jauf, beyond control of the Turks] has promised to help him, and can cut telegraph wires, tear up the Hedjaz line, and provide transport, which will enable them to proclaim the Sherif Khalifa, and roll up Syria (with the help of Syrians) from the tail end. It will come off, if the first landing and attack on Medina succeeds. The G.O.C. is shy of it, Clayton is for it: I – but you will guess what I'm at'.[26]

The British staff in Cairo knew, however, that any proposal to land at Alexandretta would meet with strong French opposition. To have any chance of adoption, the scheme would have to be put forward at a very well-chosen moment.

Lawrence's letters home occasionally contain faint hints of these secret preoccupations, buried in the descriptions of his routine activity. For example, on September 29th he wrote: 'I go to the office every morning, run out to Giza to the Survey Department usually for an hour or so before mid-day, and go back to the office again after lunch till about 6. I knock off then, because it is almost dark, and I want to ride home without lighting up. There is usually a little to do there before dinner, and after dinner telegrams in cypher come in from Medforce or Athens, or Russia or London or India at any hour of the night. Then at 6 a.m. the messenger from Alexandria turns up, with papers from the Residency:– and that's the next day's work . . . The work consists in finding out where the Turkish army is: that is, to know at any moment where each of the 136 regiments is:– how many men are in each, who commands it, and what artillery is round about it. Then we have to tell anybody who wants to know what any place in Turkey is like: what the landing places are, what the roads are like, if the people are friendly or not, and how long it would take to get reinforcements there. Then we have to try and find out what is happening politically in the interior of the country, and how the harvests are, and who are the local governors, and things like that.

'There are other things also. At present I'm making a directory . . . of the tribes of northern Arabia: and publish a little daily paper for the knowledge [of] Generals, India, Medforce, Aden and the Home Government . . . In addition I have maps to settle: not the actual drawing, of course, but the style of it, the colours to be used, and what is to be put in or left out. That is the most interesting part of the work, though I am very fond of my army. Following it about is like making a map of the movements of a fly before breakfast.'[27]

While Faroki's information was being digested in Cairo, a sequence of events began which not only diminished the prospects for a revolt in Syria but also considerably weakened Britain's position in the Middle East. For some time the Allies had been hoping to prevent Bulgaria from siding with the Central Powers. On September 22nd, however, Bulgaria announced a treaty with Turkey and decreed general mobilisation. It was clear that within days there would be an invasion of Serbia, and with German support, victory seemed inevitable. This would open up a continuous railway link from Berlin to Constantinople, allowing German arms to pour into Turkey.

The Allies could do little to prevent this outcome, but it was decided that a force should be landed in Salonica (a Greek seaport at the northern end of the Aegean) with the object of stiffening Serbian resistance. At the beginning of October, therefore, two divisions were hurriedly dispatched from the Dardanelles, where the unsuccessful summer offensive had been followed by a dangerous stalemate. This transfer so weakened the Allied forces in Gallipoli that any thoughts of further offensive action had to be set aside.

Although few people yet spoke of it openly, the future of the Gallipoli enterprise was already being questioned in Intelligence circles. If the Allies had to withdraw, a large Turkish army would be released for action elsewhere. Those responsible for defending Egypt were very concerned about this possibility. For some months the Cairo Intelligence Department had been monitoring improvements to the Turkish railways in Syria and Palestine.[28] By the end of September an extension to the Palestine railway system was complete almost as far as Beersheba, and from there a metalled road had been constructed as far as El Auja on the pre-war Egyptian frontier. A new attack on Egypt seemed imminent, and Turkey might soon be in a position to mount and sustain a major offensive against the Canal.

In this threatening situation the attitude of Arab nationalists towards Britain suddenly became very important. Hussein's pro-British stance had already done much to neutralise the Turkish call for a jihad, and a rebellion in any part of the Ottoman Empire would have tremendous propaganda value for the Allies. Even a small amount of unrest in Syria and Palestine would force the Turks to police thousands of square miles of territory and take costly precautions to protect the railway and other installations against sabotage. A more serious revolt would divert enemy forces on a large scale, and ease the threat to Egypt.

However, what would happen if the Arabs now decided that there were few advantages to be gained from alliance with Britain? A truly neutral attitude was improbable. The Turks were prepared to pay a high price for co-operation in the war effort, and many Arab leaders had already accepted their offers. A more general switch in Arab loyalties would relieve the Turks of many problems and greatly increase the danger to Egypt. It would also probably result in an effective jihad.

It seemed to the Cairo staff that the risk of such a change in Arab attitudes was growing. Despite early confidence, the war was not going well for Britain, and the Arabs could be forgiven for thinking it wiser to side with Turkey. Any admission of military failure at Gallipoli would deal a severe blow to British prestige, and this would be exploited ruthlessly by enemy propaganda. The Arabs could have little doubt that if Britain were finally to lose the war, Turkish reprisals in rebel areas would be terrible.[29]

On October 5th news from the Sudan seemed to confirm that the Arabs were wavering. In a long letter to the Sudanese Grand Cadi, Sherif Hussein had remarked: 'The country suffers much by drifting . . . because we are afraid that Islam will condemn us as revolting against its [Turkish] rulers and tearing asunder its unity. We stand at this critical point, until we are able to find out which is the lesser of the two evils.'[30] The letter had been passed on to Wingate, who cabled to Clayton: 'It would appear that the Sherif is in great perplexity regarding the course he should pursue . . . The impressions I have received from this document are that the Sherif is increasingly apprehensive for his own position and in absence of news of our success in Gallipoli, is probably inclined to turn a more willing ear to overtures from Constantinople than formerly.'[31]

The Intelligence Department sounded out Faroki on the likelihood of such a change, and his replies gave little reassurance. He told Clayton: 'We would sooner have a promise from England of half what we want than a promise from Germany and Turkey of the whole, but if England refuses us we must turn to Germany and Turkey.'[32]

Faroki's threat that the secret Committee in Damascus might make an accord with Turkey could not readily be dismissed as bluff. Hussein's future in the Hejaz was now guaranteed, but nationalists elsewhere had good reason to doubt that the Allies would support their ambitions. Pre-war contacts between members of al Fatat and French diplomats in Syria had forewarned them of French opposition to any form of Arab independence. Al Ahd had similar misgivings about British intentions in Mesopotamia, and these doubts had been greatly reinforced by the imperialist attitude of the Anglo-Indian forces now advancing towards Baghdad. If the Allies would not support Arab independence in Syria and Mesopotamia, there was nothing to be gained from siding with them. The Turks, for their part, were now prepared to offer a degree of future Arab autonomy in exchange for co-operation, while at the same time Jemal's repression was a calculated deterrent to thoughts of rebellion. Faroki had been shocked to hear that well-known Arab nationalists were being executed in Syria. He must have realised that the bargaining position of the Damascus Committee *vis-à-vis* either Britain or Turkey was rapidly weakening. Unless a deal with one or the other was reached very soon there would be little hope of achieving any of the nationalists' objectives.

It was clear to the Cairo staff that Britain's position in the Middle East was now at risk. On October 9th Clayton sent Wingate a long letter about the threatening situation. He foresaw that the Central Powers would soon capture the railway link through Serbia 'and then come, with Bulgarian assistance, to the relief of the Turks in the Dardanelles and – in my opinion – eventually . . . make another determined attack on Egypt which, after all, is striking at England in one of the vital spots of the Empire. I have thought for some time that they had this object in view, and I told the G.O.C. so two or three months ago when he asked me why I thought they were so pertinaciously continuing the railway in Palestine and road-digging in Sinai. One cannot help feeling an uneasy instinct that our whole Balkan, Near Eastern and Arabian policy since the outbreak of war has been merely opportunist and without any directing spirit. Recommendations from those who are qualified to speak on various subjects seem to have not been called for and, even when volunteered, do not appear to have led to any result . . . I may be wrong but it looks to me that if things go at all against us, we may find ourselves up against some pretty big things. The Germans have not failed to see what is our most vulnerable spot and are making for it.

'In this connection, I have had some extremely interesting discussions with . . . a leading spirit in the Pan-Arab party [Faroki] . . . Their aims are . . . very much more moderate and practical [than Rashid Rida's] and do not appear to be tinged to the same extent by Moslem fanaticism . . . [They] are not carried away by the dream of an Arab Empire but appear to be reasonable men, quite prepared to give and take and fully aware of the fact that the elements of such an Empire do not exist among the Arabs. They ask for a general recognition of their aspirations by England and the promise of a fair measure of self-government in the various countries concerned under the guidance and with the help and support of England – *but of no other power*. (This is of course the crux, owing to French claims in Syria).'[33] Maxwell had asked for a report on Faroki's views, and Clayton assured Wingate that he would 'take the opportunity of rubbing in the fact that if we definitely refuse to consider the aspirations of the Arabs we are running a grave risk of throwing them into the arms of our enemies'.[34]

While Clayton was working on this memorandum, he received the first news, from Port Sudan, of Hussein's reply to the stalling letter Cairo had sent in August. The initial telegraphed summary contained little to suggest that Hussein had reacted strongly. Later that day, however, a further cable arrived warning Clayton of the 'paramount importance the Sherif attaches to an immediate understanding on the boundaries question in a manner satisfactory to Pan Arabic aspirations.'[35]

The full text of Hussein's letter would not reach Cairo for a week, but these intimations of its content were enough to cause disquiet. It seemed that a positive reply would have to be sent almost at once if Arab good-will was to be retained, even though the British Cabinet had still not announced a policy towards Syria and Mesopotamia.

Maxwell and McMahon had repeatedly asked London for guidance about these regions, with no result. It seemed to the officials in Cairo that further indecision would probably sacrifice everything that had so far been achieved through Hussein. They therefore decided to apply pressure on the Cabinet through every available channel. At best the result would be a decision that satisfied the Arabs. At worst, the responsibility for a rupture with the Sherif would rest squarely in London and not in Egypt.

Clayton knew that his memorandum to Maxwell would be transmitted to the War Office. He therefore wrote it with a view to its effect on Kitchener. He underlined the Arab predicament, writing: '[Faroki] states that the party have now come to the conclusion that the moment is approaching when action is imperative . . . they are convinced that they can no longer remain neutral and, unless they receive a favourable reply from England within a few weeks, they have decided to throw in their lot with Turkey and Germany and to secure the best terms they can . . . A very thorough discussion on the subject with Mahommed Sherif el Farugi, [Faroki] together with the experience of the past year, during which there have been considerable opportunities of studying the Pan-Arab Movement, lead to the conviction that the proposals now put forward are of very grave and urgent importance . . . Up to the present our policy with Arabs, notably with the Idrisi and the Sherif of Mecca, has been in the main successful, but there are indications that, as the successful resistance of Turkey continues, a feeling of doubt and uneasiness is spreading. The Sherif of Mecca recently approached His Majesty's Government with proposals very similar to those put forward by el Farugi, and defined the boundaries of the territories to which the Arabs lay claim. A somewhat evasive reply was sent to him which evidently raised doubts in his mind as he replied with unusual celerity . . . That the attitude of the Sherif is that of the majority of the Arab peoples there can be little doubt . . .

'A favourable reply to the Arab proposals, even though it did not satisfy their aspirations entirely, would probably put the seal on their friendship . . . On the other hand to reject the Arab proposals entirely, or even to seek to evade the issues, will be to throw the Young Arab party definitely into the arms of the enemy. Their machinery will at once be employed against us throughout the Arab countries, and the various Arab chiefs, who are almost to a man members of, or connected with, the Young Arab party, will be undoubtedly won over. Moreover, the religious element will come into play and the *Jehad*, so far a failure, may become a very grim reality, the effects of which would certainly be far-reaching and at the present crisis might well be disastrous.'[36]

To avoid such an outcome Britain would have to negotiate a settlement of the Arab territorial claims. The Cairo Intelligence staff had already discussed a possible scaling-down of these demands with Faroki, hinting that Syria might be divided along lines reflecting geographical, religious and ethnic differences. It seems that Faroki did not reject the idea completely, and the approach therefore looked promising. Lawrence was almost certainly involved in these discussions. Months before, he had set out detailed arguments for such a solution in his paper 'Syria, the raw materials', and his superiors were now thinking on similar lines. The principle of splitting off the multi-racial coastal region from the Arab interior was gathering momentum in Cairo. From now on the idea of giving the Arabs Damascus, Hama, Homs and Aleppo, the four Arab cities of inland Syria, was frequently voiced.

In his memorandum Clayton stated that Faroki's party 'realize that to carry out the idea of an Arab Empire in its entirety is probably outside the region of practical politics at present, and he at any rate appreciates the fact that England is bound by obligations to her Allies in this war . . . El Farugi states that a guarantee of the independence of the Arabian Peninsula would not satisfy them, but this together with the institution of an increasing measure of autonomous government, under British guidance and control, in Palestine and Mesopotamia, would probably secure their friendship. Syria is of course included in their programme but they must realize that France has aspirations in this region, though el Farugi declares that a French occupation of Syria would be strenuously resisted by the Mohammedan population. They would however no doubt seek England's good offices towards obtaining a settlement of the Syrian question in a manner as favourable as possible to their views, and would almost certainly press for the inclusion of Damascus, Aleppo, Hama and Homs in the Arab Confederation. In el Farugi's own words "our scheme embraces all the Arab countries including Syria and Mesopotamia, but if we cannot have all, we want as much as we can get".'[37]

Clayton gave copies of this memorandum both to Maxwell and to McMahon, and each forwarded it to London. Other copies went to

Wingate in the Sudan and to Sir Ian Hamilton in Gallipoli. To increase the effect in London, Storrs wrote to Kitchener's private secretary: 'The Arab question is reaching an acute stage. I gather from the Sherif, as does Clayton from Faroki, that they feel, rightly or wrongly, that their time has come to choose between us and Germany . . . I have thrashed the thing out at great length with Clayton, and beg you to give all possible prominence to the note being sent home by G.O.C. in this week's bag.'[38]

Knowing that it would be several days before Clayton's memorandum reached England, Maxwell cabled a summary to Kitchener on October 12th. He stressed the danger of a revitalised jihad, adding: 'the active co-operation which the Arabs would be prepared to give in return for our support would be of the greatest value in Arabia, Mesopotamia, Syria and Palestine. The question is important and requires an early decision.'[39]

The force of this concerted effort by Cairo officials reflects their previous failures to get a hearing in London. Although they were in much closer touch with the Arab world than any other branch of British Government, their advice and requests had repeatedly been ignored or shelved. Al Masri's proposals for action in Mesopotamia, and Clayton's negotiations with the Idrisi, had been blocked by the Government of India from its seat more than two thousand miles away. The Alexandretta scheme, despite widespread approval, had thus far been successfully obstructed by France. Clayton knew that these opponents, who were well-represented in London, would do their best in the present instance to whittle down any territorial concessions to the Arabs.

Moreover the Cairo argument was very strong. Were it not for French and Anglo-Indian opposition, Britain would sacrifice little by accepting the kind of arrangement now proposed. In Aubrey Herbert's words: 'We, if we were concerned alone, could settle with the Arabs tomorrow to our mutual satisfaction. We do not lose by our concessions [in Mesopotamia], for in some respects we actually gain by what we give up. In the immediate future we may hope largely to turn our enemies into our friends in Mesopotamia and Sinai, and in the more distant future we can look forward to the advantages without the disadvantages of annexation; since, in spite of a commercial, financial and political monopoly of Mesopotamia, we shall not be called upon to bear the burden of the administration of that country beyond the limits of our own interests.'[40]

As it happened, these messages from Cairo reached London at an extremely sensitive moment, for it was at this point that the War Office was at last obliged to consider an Allied withdrawal from the Dardanelles. On October 11th, the day before receiving Maxwell's telegram, Kitchener had asked the British commander in Gallipoli to estimate probable losses during an evacuation. He knew that if such a step were taken a Turkish attack on Egypt would become very probable. In reply to Maxwell's telegram he therefore cabled: 'The Government are most anxious to deal with the Arab question in a manner that would be satisfactory to the Arabs . . . You must do your best to prevent any alienation of the traditional loyalty of the Arabs to England.'[41]

Two telegrams sent to Cairo the following day show that the War Office was now alarmed about the developing threat to Egypt. One, from Kitchener to Maxwell, read: 'Please reply urgently, giving any information that you may have on the progress that the Turkish railway across the desert has made towards Egypt. The German invasion [of Serbia] will very probably lead to their being able to send troops and guns to Constantinople and from there organize an attack on Egypt. You should send as soon as possible your full plans for meeting such a contingency.'[42] The other cable, addressed to Clayton, asked whether there was any recent information on the unfinished Baghdad Railway tunnels through the Amanus and Taurus mountains north-west of Aleppo. A day later Cairo received still another query: 'Please ascertain from Turkish prisoners . . . the time taken in the journey from Syria to Constantinople and what parts of it were covered by rail route and march respectively. If sufficient coal can be provided by the Central Powers, how many trains per day could be run on the various sections in each direction? With regard to the number of engines and the amount of rolling stock available, can you obtain any details?'[43]

Lawrence was asked to deal with these urgent questions. He had helped Newcombe to obtain information about the Taurus section of the line just before the war, and more recently he had contributed reports on both the Baghdad and the Syria-Palestine railways to the Intelligence Bulletin.[44] The information he now provided was far from reassuring. According to the latest reports, the Turkish railway works had reached Beersheba. While the Taurus railway tunnels were still some way from completion, alternative routes by road had been improved. He calculated that under existing conditions between twenty and thirty days would be needed to move a battalion from Constantinople to Beersheba: 'the railways seem to take about 1,000 to 1,500 men daily. If the railways were properly organized this capacity could probably be doubled.'[45]

Nor was Maxwell very optimistic about the defensive capacity of the Force in Egypt. His manpower had repeatedly been reduced by transfer of troops to Gallipoli, and as things stood he would need considerable reinforcements if he were to fend off a serious attack. He would also need warships to counter any heavy guns brought by the Turks to threaten traffic in the Canal. In a supplementary telegram he added: 'As all the great camel-raising tribes are pan-Arab, a satisfactory settlement of the Arab question would go far to make a serious invasion of Egypt impossible.'[46]

The next day he replied to a request from Kitchener for more information about Arab demands. Once again he stressed that matters had reached a critical stage: 'it is necessary and urgent to waste no time, otherwise [the Arab secret societies] and the potentates will throw in their lot with the Turks . . . which will increase very materially our difficulties in Mesopotamia and Arabia, also with the Senoussi, and make very much easier the invasion of Egypt . . . The time is past in my opinion for vague generalities, and our best course seems to me to be to eliminate [from Arab demands] what we cannot and will not allow, and to treat the rest as a basis for negotiation. But we must bear in mind in so doing that, even if we insist on retaining the *Villayet* of Basra as British, the rest of Mesopotamia must be included in the negotiation; likewise, on the west, the Arab party will, I think, insist on Homs, Aleppo, Hama, and Damascus being in their sphere . . . I feel certain that time is of the greatest importance, and that, unless we make a definite and agreeable proposal to the Shereef at once, we may have a united Islam against us.'[47]

The full text of Hussein's letter reached Cairo on October 18th. In places it was couched in language so obscure as to defy meaningful translation. However, the content bore out Faroki's claims about contacts between Hussein and the secret nationalist societies in Damascus. The Sherif protested at McMahon's attitude towards the Arab territorial demands: 'your Excellency will pardon me and permit me to say clearly that the coolness and hesitation which you have displayed in the question of the limits and boundaries . . . might be taken to infer an estrangement or something of the sort . . . I am confident that your Excellency will not doubt that it is not I personally who am demanding of these limits which include only our race, but that they are all proposals of the people, who, in short, believe that they are necessary for economic life.'[48] Worse still, there were passages which could be read as veiled threats that Hussein would ally himself with Turkey unless the British attitude improved. He said that the Arabs' motive for seeking agreement with Britain was 'so [as] not to meet her or any of her Allies in opposition to their resolution, which would produce a contrary issue, which God forbid . . . In order to reassure your Excellency I can declare that the whole country, together with those who you say are submitting themselves to Turko-German orders, are all waiting the result of these negotiations, which are dependent only on your refusal or acceptance of the question of the limits and on your declaration of safeguarding their religion first and then the rest of rights from any harm or danger.'[49]

McMahon telegraphed a résumé of the letter to the Foreign Office that evening, and the full text was sent off by courier. An outline draft reply was already being prepared by Clayton, in consultation with Ronald Storrs. As the text took shape Clayton discussed it with Faroki in order to get some idea of Syrian nationalist reaction. Later that night, McMahon sent a second cable to London containing the response which Clayton had worked out. This was prefaced with the comment: 'I understand that Faroki, in the course of further conversations, expresses the opinion that the Arab party would accept an assurance on the following lines'.[50]

Some kind of territorial commitment could no longer be avoided. McMahon therefore proposed that Britain should accept the principle of Arab independence over a large area, while making carefully worded reservations to cater for French and Anglo-Indian interests. Lawrence's idea of Arab autonomy in inland Syria was an integral part of the scheme: at the western boundary the independent area would include 'the purely Arab districts of Aleppo, Damascus, Hama and Homs'.[51]

While Clayton, Storrs and McMahon were ultimately responsible for letters to Hussein, it is clear from surviving documents that their content was discussed by leading members of the Intelligence staff, including Lawrence. A letter sent to his family the following day shows that he knew and approved of the latest development: 'There is going to be rather a busy winter in the Levant. I am pleased on the whole with things. They have gone against us so far that our Government has become more reasonable, and the final settlement out here, though it will take long, will I think, be very satisfactory. We have to thank our failures for that: and to me, they are worth it.'[52] He had good reason to be happy: a scheme which had grown from one of his own ideas now seemed on the brink of success. Months of argument about the future of the Arab provinces had left him single-minded in his opposition to French ambitions in inland Syria, and his case had now been taken up by the highest British officials in Cairo.

Contemporary evidence lends substance to a statement by Hogarth, who had firsthand knowledge of Clayton's staff at this period. He later wrote: 'T. E. Lawrence, whose power of initiative, reasoned audacity, compelling personality, and singular persuasiveness I had often had reason to confess in past years, was still a second lieutenant in the Cairo military intelligence, but with a purpose more clearly foreseen than perhaps that of anyone else, he was already pulling the wires.'[53] Hogarth listed Lawrence alongside McMahon, Clayton, Storrs and Wingate when discussing the key figures in British dealings with Hussein. Elsewhere, he wrote that Lawrence had been 'a moving spirit in the negotiations leading to an Arab revolt.'[54]

In London, having consulted his department about the news from Cairo, Grey now agreed with Kitchener that substantial assurances would have to be given to the Arabs. He cabled to McMahon on October 20th: 'You can give cordial assurances on the lines, and with the reserve about our Allies, proposed by you.' While emphasising the need for caution over the north-western area claimed by France, and reminding McMahon of Anglo-Indian interests, Grey stated: 'the important thing is to give our assurances that will prevent the Arabs from being alienated, and I must leave you discretion in the matter as it is urgent and there is not time to discuss an exact formula.'[55]

The final wording of the reply had therefore to be decided in Cairo, and the task was extremely difficult. By the Declaration of London, made in September 1914, the Allies had pledged themselves to reach prior agreement on every aspect of the peace terms. This tied McMahon's hands: he had no knowledge of any Anglo-French accord over the future of the Turkish Empire (in reality negotiations had not even begun), and he could not pre-empt such an agreement by making any firm commitment to Hussein of a kind which the French might reject.

The Cairo staff knew that both France and the Government of India had ambitions to control as much as possible of the Arab areas. If the scale of these colonial aims were spelled out in the reply to Hussein, the negotiations would end. On the other hand an obviously vague formula would also run the risk of rejection.

In reality, a genuine agreement would be impossible without a compromise between French and Arab demands, involving major concessions on one side or both. This would require lengthy negotiations, which were out of the question in the present crisis. Therefore the only way forward was to send a message which contained such subtle reservations that the document could be interpreted differently by each party. A reply in this time-honoured diplomatic style might save the immediate situation, and allow breathing-space to discuss a full settlement.

The text eventually agreed upon appeared at first sight to offer British support for Arab independence in most of the area demanded. There were, however, exceptions and reservations. Hussein, on behalf of the Damascus Committee, had asked for the districts of Mersina and Alexandretta, but these areas were clearly non-Arab and were immediately excluded. In order to appease the Government of India the reply also drew attention to its existing treaties with certain Arab chiefs, and suggested that 'special administrative arrangements' would be needed to protect British interests in the provinces of Basra and Baghdad.

It had been more difficult to arrive at a formula dealing with the Mediterranean coast of Syria. France would surely insist on taking the Lebanon, but how much else besides? Moreover the question of Palestine had to be left open. France had ambitions there too, but the Cairo staff believed that for strategic reasons some form of British control was essential. They also knew that London regarded proposals relating to the future of the Holy Land with caution. Like Cairo, the de Bunsen Committee had set aside French aspirations; however, it had also recognised that the Holy Places were important to all the Christian Churches and to Jews and Moslems. Russia in particular would be unlikely to accept a French administration. The Committee had therefore recommended that the future of Palestine should 'be the subject of special negotiations, in which both belligerents and neutrals are alike interested.'[56]

Those passages in McMahon's letter which related to Palestine were destined to rank among the most controversial statements in British diplomatic history. As Lawrence was later to be involved in the Palestine question it is useful to understand the thinking that lay behind Cairo policy at this stage.

Only two parts of the reply actually named any area of the Mediterranean coastal region. The first, as already noted, set aside the districts of Mersina and Alexandretta. In the second, the text stated that 'portions of Syria lying to the west of the districts of Damascus, Homs, Hama and Aleppo cannot be said to be purely Arab, and should be excluded from the limits demanded.'[57] Lawrence's earlier memorandum supplies the rationale behind this much-disputed formula. Of the six Syrian cities, Hussein was to be offered only four: those that Lawrence had characterised as essentially Arab. He had argued that neither Beirut in the Lebanon nor Jerusalem in Palestine met this test, and that for ethnic and geographical reasons these northern and southern coastal areas could be split off from the purely Arab interior. Although Beirut and the Lebanon were not actually named in the reply, they were clearly excluded from the area of Arab self-government because they lie to the west of Homs and Damascus. The last of the six cities, Jerusalem, was not named either, yet it was not immediately obvious from the text whether Palestine was to be in or out of the Arab area. The letter did not stipulate any kind of arrangement for the coastal area south of Damascus.[58]

At first sight this silence over Palestine seems illogical. The argument used for excluding the Lebanon (i.e. that the area was not 'purely Arab') applied at least as strongly there. The explanation must be that while McMahon and his advisers had no intention of offering complete Arab independence in Palestine, they knew it would be highly impolitic to make a specific reservation. Jerusalem was one of the holiest cities of Islam, and Hussein, himself a religious leader, could not be expected to agree to its exclusion from the future Arab state. It was for this reason that McMahon's letter left this section of the western border undefined.

Despite this, Palestine was still excluded by the terms of the McMahon reply as it was covered by a 'catch all' reservation inserted primarily to allow for French interests elsewhere. As McMahon explained in a dispatch to the Foreign Office, he had left a large loophole to accommodate any solution reached with France: 'I am not aware of the extent of French claims in Syria, nor of how far His Majesty's Government have agreed to recognize them. Hence, while recognizing the towns of Damascus, Hama, Homs and Aleppo as being within the circle of Arab countries, I have endeavoured to provide for possible French pretensions to those places by a general modification to the effect that His Majesty's Government can only give assurances in regard to those territories "in which she can act without detriment to the interests of her ally France".'[59]

The reservation applied as much to Palestine as to other parts of Syria. Although Britain intended to resist French colonial ambitions in this region, it was impossible to deny the strong historical and religious links between France and the Holy Land. These interests had in some degree a legally defined status, since Turkey had for centuries recognised France as sole protector of the Latin Church and its clergy in Palestine. The

French Government could claim a duty to ensure that any successor to the Turkish administration respected the position of the Roman Catholic Church. Many Arab Moslems held extreme anti-Christian views, and French opinion would have condemned placing the Christian Holy Places under a totally independent Arab government.

It has been argued that, in excluding Palestine from the area conceded to the Arabs without specifically saying so, the British staff in Cairo were guilty of a wholly cynical deception. This charge loses most of its force, however, when the McMahon letter is taken in the context of the policy towards Palestine advocated in Cairo at that time. Only three months earlier, when Maxwell and McMahon had been consulted by Sir Mark Sykes, both had advocated an Arab domestic administration for Palestine supervised by Britain under arrangements similar to those in Egypt. Sykes had reported McMahon's proposal that 'the Palestine portion of British territory should be included in the Dominions of the Sultan of Egypt. Jerusalem would thus nominally remain under a Moslem ruler, while the nature of its local self-administration could be adapted to meet international interests under British protection.'[60] When McMahon's letter to Hussein was drafted, the Cairo staff still saw this as the most desirable and probable solution. It was expected, moreover, that Hussein would be nominated Caliph, and that he would therefore have influence throughout the Middle East including Palestine. Thus in October 1915 the Cairo staff believed with good reason that an exclusion of Palestine from the area of total self-government would have little practical effect on its Arab inhabitants. They could not possibly have foreseen that this reasoning would be overturned by the Balfour Declaration two years later; by the large-scale Jewish immigration which followed; and finally by the partition of Palestine in 1948.[61]

Despite the exceptions and reservations included in McMahon's letter, the staff in Cairo did their best to impress upon London the need for a settlement which went as far as possible to meet Arab hopes. The letter left the way open for a very generous solution, giving the Arabs a large area of independence, and excluding all but British advisers. It was up to London, however, to persuade France that these provisions should apply in inland Syria. In explanatory notes for the Foreign Office, McMahon urged that French influence be kept to a minimum: 'I venture to emphasize the fact that the eventual arrangement would be very greatly facilitated if France would consent to forego any territorial claims she may have to purely Arab territories, such as Damascus, Hama, Homs and

Aleppo. The inclusion of such districts in Arabia will be insisted on by the Arabs, and although they might possibly agree in regard to them to accept from France a similar arrangement to that which we are proposing elsewhere, it is obvious that this will give rise to trouble . . . In the face of the vital importance to the Allied cause of the present issues involved, France could hardly be unreasonable on this point and the question of compensation elsewhere if necessary is well worthy of serious consideration.'[62]

The letter to Hussein was finally completed on October 24th and dispatched by messenger the following day. Looking back on the whole episode Clayton wrote: 'The speed with which H.M. Government acted – or rather allowed action to be taken – at the last moment is somewhat surprising. The High Commissioner came out of it very well, I think, in taking the responsibility upon himself of replying to the Sherif without further reference. The F.O. telegram certainly gave him a free hand but, in their usual way, they left several openings for making a scapegoat in the event of necessity, and there is many a man who would have funked it, and referred his proposed reply for approval.'[63]

McMahon's self-confidence can be explained by the provisional nature of this reply. He had indicated that the frontiers of Arab independence could not finally be settled without French concurrence, and further negotiations with Hussein to this end seemed inevitable. At some later stage the exact status of Syria and Palestine would have to be defined and agreed. For the moment, however, it was hoped that enough had been said to retain Arab goodwill. Discussion of these territorial questions would be easier when the military situation was less critical.

CHAPTER 12

Tackling the French
October 1915 – March 1916

ONCE McMahon had replied to Hussein, the diplomatic initiative passed to London. The very existence of these negotiations about Ottoman territory placed Britain under an obligation to consult her Allies, and as the future of Syria was affected, immediate discussions with France were essential. In the stress of war conditions Anglo-French jealousies had flourished, and the Foreign Office was anxious to avoid any further cause of friction.

An agreement with France seemed equally necessary if Britain's position *vis-à-vis* Hussein was to be secured. McMahon's carefully worded letter might not buy a great deal of time; if Hussein and his advisers took offence at its reservations there might be another crisis, and the threat of a Turkish attack on Egypt was still very real. At best, McMahon's offer would be treated by the Arabs as a bargaining position in the usual oriental fashion: further demands would certainly follow, with requests for clarification. Yet it would be impossible to define the area of Arab independence more precisely without French agreement.

The difficult task of persuading France to accept a territorial compromise would fall to the Foreign Office; and the British staff in Egypt could only await developments. Aubrey Herbert, who passed through Cairo in October, wrote a long memorandum about the situation. As he saw it, the case was straightforward: 'No one who knows Syria can fail to realise the bitter disappointment to French aspirations involved in the loss of Damascus and those terrains. The connection between France and parts of Syria has been very close, and the ambition to make that connection closer still is ages old. But this is not a time when dreams can outweigh strategy. It is after all only the partial sacrifice of a territory that is not yet hers, that is asked of France . . . If the Arabs are united against us, France is no nearer to obtaining Syria, and she must look forward to trouble in Morocco and Tunis. It is unfortunate that it is we who should have to ask her to face this unpalatable necessity, but it is clear that we cannot support her in the West, the Serbians in Serbia, and gratuitously create a new war theatre in the East [i.e. in defending the Canal] without straining our resources to the breaking point.'[1]

On October 28th McMahon cabled to the Foreign Office that French diplomats in Cairo seemed to have heard about the exchange of messages with Hussein. The following day he wired again to say that they were making contact with Faroki and al Masri. He asked for advice and suggested that the French Government should be dissuaded from opening parallel negotiations with the Arabs. It was clear that if France weighed in at this delicate moment with a blunt assertion of her territorial claims, the consequences might be serious.

The Foreign Office, however, had already taken action. Even before the full text of McMahon's letter reached London, Grey had spoken to the French Ambassador, Paul Cambon, inviting his government to send a representative for discussions. The choice fell on François Georges-Picot. Although he had spent a relatively short period in the Middle East, he was deeply committed to French aspirations there. Since August 1915 he had been serving at the Embassy in London.

On the British side, it was decided that the negotiations should be entrusted to a senior inter-departmental committee. This was to be chaired by Sir Arthur Nicolson, the Under-Secretary of State for Foreign Affairs, and would meet for the first time in mid-November.

The other problem faced by the Foreign Office was a predictably hostile reaction to the McMahon commitments from the Government of India. When the question of his reply to the Sherif had been considered in London there was not time to consult Lord Hardinge. Sir Austen Chamberlain at the India Office had accepted the decision to give McMahon a free hand, and afterwards had sent an apologetic telegram to Hardinge. It said: 'the matter was represented to me as extremely urgent, and both Lord Kitchener and Sir E. Grey attached the utmost importance to returning an immediate and favourable reply to the Arab overtures.'[2]

When copies of the various telegrams between London and Cairo finally reached Delhi, Hardinge was furious. The Indian Expeditionary Force in Mesopotamia was advancing victoriously towards Baghdad, and plans were taking shape for administering the new Anglo-Indian colony. The Government of India now saw its prize slipping away. Hardinge cabled to London: 'We think we should not have been committed to such a policy and that we should have been consulted before a pledge of such vital importance to the future of India was given. We have always regarded . . . the creation of a strong Arab state lying astride our interests in the East and in the Gulf as a not unlikely source of ultimate trouble . . . We have always contemplated as a minimum the eventual annexation of Bussorah [Basra] *vilayat* and some form of native administration in Baghdad *vilayat* under our close political control. The McMahon guarantees apparently [put] annexation out of the question. By surrendering Bussorah *vilayat* to an Arab Government of any kind, we shall not only be preparing trouble for ourselves at the head of and along the southern littoral of the Gulf, but shall be giving up the main fruits of hard-won victories in Mesopotamia. This will not only be abandoning enormous potential sources of revenue, but will also be resented by the Indian people, and the European commercial community, who look to Mesopotamia as a field for commercial expansion and emigration in return for the blood of their countrymen there shed. We sincerely trust that the formula may be amended so as to admit of H. M. Government having a free hand in the eventual disposal of Bussorah and Baghdad *vilayats*, which have been won at such a cost.'[3]

Adding insult to injury, McMahon had suggested that the terms of his pledge to the Arabs should be incorporated in a proclamation to the Mesopotamian people. When this was put to the IEF commander, General Sir John Nixon, he cabled a reply which typified the Anglo-Indian attitude towards Arab nationalism: 'the formation of an autonomous state in Iraq appears to be impossible and unnecessary. Here in Iraq there is no sign of the slightest ambition of the kind among the people, who expect and seem to be quite ready to accept our administration . . . we are of the opinion that from the point of view of Iraq it is highly inexpedient and unnecessary to put into the heads of the backward people of the country what seem to us the visionary and premature notions of the creation of an Arab state – notions which will only tend to make endless difficulties for Great Britain here and serve no present purpose but to stimulate a small section of ambitious men to turn their activities to a direction from which it is highly desirable to keep them for many years to come.'[4]

During the next few months the Government of India tried very hard indeed to overturn the McMahon commitments, at any rate as far as Mesopotamia was concerned. The language of its statements was often emotive. Sir Arthur Hirtzel, Secretary of the Political Department at the India Office, spoke for example of 'the security of India and (I believe) the peace of the world'.[5]

Grey, Kitchener and McMahon all recognised that the concessions to Hussein had been made in order to prevent the Arabs siding with Turkey.

Hardinge and the India Office, however, urged that the McMahon pledge should be void unless the Arabs immediately rose against the Turks. This was a deliberate misrepresentation of the undertakings, which contained no such condition, but it seemed to offer the best hope of overturning them. Thus Chamberlain wrote: 'we must of course abide by Sir H. McMahon's promises if the Arabs do their part . . . but my information is that the Sherif is a nonentity without power to carry out his proposals, that the Arabs are without unity or the possibility of uniting, and I disbelieve in the reality and efficacy of the suggested Arab revolt in the army and elsewhere . . . The next step should be to make clear to them that the promises made by McMahon are dependent on the immediate action by them in the sense of their offers and will not be binding on us unless they do their part at once.'[6] When Wingate saw this, he wrote in the margin 'Rot'.[7] Nevertheless the Anglo-Indian interpretation was pressed at every opportunity, and found some sympathy among Foreign Office officials concerned by French reaction to the Arab claims.

In preparation for the discussions with Georges-Picot, the Foreign Office looked for ways in which it might be possible to reconcile the French and Arab positions. The de Bunsen Committee had already suggested a hypothetical division of Asiatic Turkey into different spheres of European control or influence. McMahon's proposals had introduced a new factor, namely the principle that any direct colonial administration would be restricted to regions near the sea, while inland there would be Arab self-government under British guidance. There was only one respect in which the de Bunsen suggestions and McMahon's proposals were really incompatible: it had never been envisaged in London that France would be asked to give up the inland area of northern Syria now conceded to the Arabs.

There seemed to be an obvious practical compromise: French guidance should be substituted for British in this northern area. Such a possibility had already been mentioned by McMahon himself, although he had advised against it. On November 6th Grey raised the point again in a telegram to Cairo: 'I propose to concentrate on getting French consent to the inclusion of Damascus, Hama, Homs, and Aleppo in Arab boundaries. But to do that we must be prepared to sacrifice the provision that the Arabs are to seek the advice and guidance of Great Britain only and that all European advisers and officials are to be British.

'Was this inserted to secure our interests or to please the Arabs? If the former only, I shall regard myself as free to drop it . . . if we can thereby secure French agreement to promise the four cities to the Arabs. Our primary and vital object is not to secure a new sphere of British influence, but to get the Arabs on our side against the Turks.'[8]

McMahon replied the following day, stressing that the Arabs would not concede the four inland towns. They had, in fact, 'repeatedly expressed the determination to fight for those territories if necessary.'[9] He confirmed that the clause about British advisers had been 'inserted at the express request of the Arabs, who were anxious that the same provision should apply to all Arabia and especially in the territories above mentioned where they do not welcome the idea of French influence.'[10] However, he was obliged to admit that a substitution of French for British advisers in northern Syria would be covered, as far as his pledge was concerned, by the reservation he had made in favour of French interests.

On November 4th Maxwell received a telegram from Kitchener which gave the first intimation that a withdrawal from the Dardanelles was being seriously considered in London. The message stated that Kitchener would shortly visit Gallipoli in order to assess the prospects for himself. As the potential threat to Egypt was obvious, he asked Maxwell and McMahon to join him for a secret conference at Alexandria on November 8th or 9th.

The staff in Cairo were fully prepared for this eventuality. A decision as far-reaching as withdrawal from Gallipoli would create the kind of military situation in which French objections to the Alexandretta scheme might be overruled. Maxwell therefore immediately cabled to London: 'If there is any question of a decision of ours whereby the Turks would be released from Gallipoli, I consider that before this is done, or at least simultaneously, we should occupy Alexandretta in force, thus preventing any reinforcements to Syria or Mesopotamia by destroying the railway towards Adana, and also assisting the Arab movement and preventing it being blocked; the effect would be also to prevent any invasion of Egypt. If the coup were a surprise, a force of one division, supported by the French fleet, could easily take and hold Alexandretta, and it would be easy to reinforce it if necessary.'[11]

The prospects for a landing still seemed very good, and it would probably lead to nationalist rebellion in a large area of the hinterland. Although many of the disaffected Arab units had now been removed from Syria, this had been offset to some extent by the influx of Armenians. Moreover, Cairo Intelligence had been informed by Faroki that the political and military leadership for a northern revolt was already in place.

A landing now would serve its original aims and help greatly to prevent a major Turkish offensive on the Canal. It would also repair the damage which an admission of failure at Gallipoli would inflict on British prestige in the East.

Maxwell's telegram to Kitchener about the Alexandretta scheme also mentioned the possibility of action in the Hejaz, which Faroki had been planning for two months: 'I propose to select a small force from Arab Turk prisoners of war and to send them via Akaba to cut the Hedjaz railway at Maan, after which they could join the Sherif of Mecca.'[12]

The Intelligence Department had only a few days to prepare a detailed brief for the meeting between Maxwell, McMahon, and Kitchener. On the same day as this telegram to London, Lawrence wrote: 'things are boiling over this weekend, and we have never been so busy before! This is a good omen, and a thing to make one very content.'[13]

Kitchener's first response to the Alexandretta proposal, on November 5th, was negative. He cited the increased danger from submarines, and argued that a much larger force would be needed in order to secure the whole Ayas Bay area. Maxwell passed these comments to the Intelligence Department, and on the following day he cabled again: 'The disadvantages of the Alexandretta scheme . . . are in my opinion so entirely outweighed by the advantages both from a military and political point of view that I urge and recommend it . . . I suggested one division as a sufficient force to take and hold Alexandretta as a surprise coup, but I fully realised that perhaps a force of 100,000 men would be required to consolidate and hold the position permanently . . . I understand that the passes can be held with comparatively few men.

'In any case, supposing 100,000 men are required, the effective occupation of Alexandretta and the destruction of the railway in the vicinity would enable us to hold Mesopotamia and the Suez Canal with considerably less forces.'[14] When the military historian Liddell Hart later enquired into this episode, he found that Lawrence had been largely responsible for the detail of Maxwell's reply.[15]

The meeting with Kitchener finally began on November 10th, not at Alexandria as first planned, but on board HMS *Nelson* off Mudros on the island of Lemnos. By the end of the first day Kitchener was totally converted to the Alexandretta proposal, and cabled to the Prime Minister recommending it. However, the War Office was now dominated by 'Westerners' who opposed any deployment of troops away from the Western Front. The General Staff argued strongly for passive defence of

Egypt, and raised a string of technical and strategic objections to the Alexandretta scheme. Their criticisms, which anticipated the worst possible eventuality of every kind, were telegraphed back to Kitchener on November 12th. In his reply he took an equally pessimistic view of the prospects if British strategy in the Middle East were to be limited to a garrison on the Canal. He remarked pointedly: 'McMahon, Maxwell and myself must be admitted to know the difficulties of defence in Egypt'.[16] The objections raised in London, he argued, had already been considered, but: 'The political situation in the East in our opinion so seriously affects the purely military situations as to outweigh those military disadvantages which might otherwise be weighty.'[17] Moreover, he had asked another senior officer at the Mudros conference, General Sir Charles Monro, to assess the Alexandretta scheme, and although Monro was a convinced 'Westerner' he too had dismissed the General Staff objections.[18]

Kitchener's support for the Alexandretta scheme would prove counterproductive. He had delayed far too long before facing up to the difficulties in Gallipoli and, despite his popularity in the country, Government colleagues saw that he could not cope with the great responsibilities now resting on his shoulders. During the preceding weeks he had become an isolated figure, guilty of ill-considered judgments and stubborn indecision on important issues. It was too easy for opponents to represent his renewed enthusiasm for Alexandretta as a quixotic gesture which would commit Britain to another catastrophic intervention in the East.

There was some relief, therefore, when France took a hand in the Alexandretta debate. A French officer who had accompanied Kitchener to Mudros had alerted Paris to the proposal. On the very day that Kitchener cabled Monro's favourable conclusions to London, an uncompromising note from the French Embassy was passed to the War Office. A translation telegraphed to Kitchener read: 'Should the British Government be considering a disembarkation of troops in the Gulf of Alexandretta, in order to cut off the railway line that leads to Palestine, [the French] Government would have to take into consideration not only the economical interests but also the moral and political situation held by France in these countries.

'French public opinion could not be indifferent to anything that would be attempted in a country that they consider already as being intended to become a part of the future Syria; and they would require of the French Government that not only could no military operation be undertaken in this particular country before it has been concerted between the Allies, but even that, should such an action be taken, the greater part of the task should be entrusted to the French troops and the Generals commanding them.'[19] The French military attaché in London insisted that such an operation could only take place if it was jointly planned and executed. On the following day the French Government delivered its *coup de grâce*, by informing London that on military and strategic grounds its advisers were unanimously opposed to an Allied landing at Alexandretta.[20]

As far as the Cabinet was concerned, this ended the affair. Although two Anglo-French meetings were arranged to discuss Alexandretta, the outcome was a foregone conclusion.[21] Maxwell and McMahon, however, remained at Mudros for a few days, supporting Kitchener in his fight to keep the project alive.

While the Cairo staff waited for a decision, a letter arrived from Sherif Hussein in reply to McMahon's territorial offer. The message was long and, as usual, obscurely worded. Its main points, however, were clear enough. The Sherif agreed to give up the *vilayets* of Mersina and Adana, but refused any compromise over the Lebanon, arguing that the population was Arab, whether Christian or Moslem. He was prepared to contemplate a British administration of the areas already occupied by the IEF in Mesopotamia, but only for a short time and in exchange for financial compensation. Hussein expressed two fears in the letter. The first was that by declaring a revolt against Turkey he would incur the wrath of Islam. The second was that the Allies might at some future date be forced to sue for peace, and in so doing would abandon the Arabs to their fate at the hands of Turkey and her German allies. Hussein asked for a guarantee that this would not happen.

In one sense his message seemed to be satisfactory: there were no longer any veiled threats that the Arabs might go over to the Turks. On the other hand the Sherif's intransigence about the Lebanon showed how difficult it would be to reconcile Arab and French ambitions. Unless Hussein's Syrian advisers relented on this point, a compromise would be impossible.

No reply could be sent until McMahon returned from Mudros. In the meantime Clayton was concerned about developments in London, and particularly the continuing opposition from the Government of India, whose purpose was clearly to weaken Cabinet support for McMahon. He wrote to Wingate: 'India are furious and making every difficulty . . . However, I do not give up the hope that the High Commissioner will be able to steer a middle course – and at any rate the Government seem to have decided that they must back him up and fulfil the pledges he has given, which is satisfactory'.[22]

Ironically, while Anglo-Indian officials derided Hussein as a political weakling, they were also trying to raise the spectre of a strong Arab kingdom which would pose a threat to British interests. Clayton wrote: 'India seem obsessed with the fear of a powerful and united Arab state, which can never exist unless we are fools enough to create it. On the other hand they talk of the lack of unity among the Arabs as a grave objection, whereas this is the main safeguard against the powerful state which they say they dread . . . I shouldn't have thought that anyone could consider it within the bounds of practical politics and it will have to be our business to see that it does not ever become a possibility, owing to our backing one horse to the exclusion of the others. Such are my views for what they are worth, but we shall see what happens.'[23]

During this period of uncertainty in Cairo, Lawrence received news that his brother Will had been reported missing. Will, who had returned from India that spring in order to join up, had been serving in France as a Royal Flying Corps observer for less than a week. It was to be some time before his death was confirmed, but there could be little hope that he was alive. The loss affected Lawrence deeply; the two brothers had been very close, and he recalled sadly how they had missed meeting one another in March when the liner that took Will to England had passed through the Suez Canal. Lawrence had gone to Port Said hoping to meet it, but there had been a scare on the Sinai front and the ship had been delayed. They had only managed to speak to one another by telephone.

Before going on active service Will had asked Lawrence to be his executor, a request which would have had little significance, except that an uncle had died early in May leaving their father £25,000 (at that date a very large sum indeed). Mr Lawrence had decided to divide £15,000 of this between his sons. Although Will had spent the two preceding years in India, he had been deeply in love with Janet Laurie, the girl for whom Lawrence also had shown a strong affection in 1910. When Will wrote that he wished to bequeath his money to her, if he died, Lawrence had replied: 'I . . . was going to agree, for such a time as Janet remained unmarried. Today I hear from Father that it's likely to remain so only a very short time, so that my trust would automatically expire. I don't know what your feelings in this matter will be: you will however understand that you cannot well leave anything in such a manner to another man's wife.'[24] In the event, Will had died before the inheritance was distributed, and his estate was negligible. Lawrence wrote sadly to Leeds: 'first one and now another of my brothers has been killed. Of course, I've been away a lot from them, and so it doesn't come on one like a shock at all... but I rather dread Oxford and what it may be like if one comes back. Also they were both younger than I am, and it doesn't seem right, somehow, that I should go on living peacefully in Cairo.'[25]

On November 17th Sir Mark Sykes returned to Egypt after visiting India and Mesopotamia on his mission to discuss the de Bunsen Committee proposals. Like other observers, he had recognised the extraordinary lack of co-ordination in British policy towards the Middle East. Decisions were taken in London, Cairo, Aden, Basra and New Delhi, yet there were few direct contacts between the individuals concerned. Much work was being needlessly duplicated, while broader questions which could not be tackled from one place alone were ignored. Thus no effective measures were being taken to counter the Islamic propaganda put out by Turkey, which was causing trouble for the Allies in India and elsewhere. Sykes himself was fascinated by publicity and subversion, and during his tour he had devised a scheme for an Islamic Bureau which would co-ordinate British policy in the Middle East and also specialise in propaganda. He was an ambitious young politician and dreamed that he would be allowed to take charge of this organisation, an activity for which some people might think him well qualified.

He discussed the idea in Cairo, where the need for better co-ordination was well understood. In Clayton's view, however, the chief value of such an organisation would be as an extended Intelligence Department, acting as a clearing-house for information and helping to formulate and harmonise policy. To maintain contact with the various factions in Middle Eastern politics, the new Bureau should be based in Cairo.

During the ten days Sykes spent in Egypt he was brought up to date on the correspondence with Hussein; he also had several conversations with Faroki. The conclusion Sykes drew from these talks was shortly to assume great significance, and it is therefore important to understand the original context.

Although Faroki was in touch with al Masri and other Arab nationalists in Cairo, he still had no formal status and could speak neither for Hussein nor for the Damascus Committee.[26] He had been used by the

Cairo staff as a sounding-board to assess Arab reaction to different proposals but, as he had said at the outset, his opinion could only be a personal one and he was powerless to give any firm commitment.

His position was by no means easy. Hussein and his Syrian advisers were not dealing with the British face-to-face, and it was a simple matter for them to adopt an uncompromising stance. Faroki, on the other hand, was exposed to persuasive argument and leading questions from his British hosts. He understood that the French difficulty was a real one, and that it would not be resolved by Arab intransigence. Contemporary reports show that he admitted the need for concessions, however unwelcome these might be to Arabs from Syria. It is also possible that, as a native of Mosul, he may not have harboured such vehement anti-French feelings as did the Syrian nationalists.

When he met Sykes, in late November 1915, the Arab question seemed to be at a turning-point. Although the Alexandretta scheme was virtually dead, this was not known in Cairo. Faroki therefore believed that the Allies might shortly take action to block the principal line of communication from Turkey to Syria and Mesopotamia. This would give his fellow-nationalists the opportunity to start a revolution which might eventually spread throughout the Arab provinces. As long as the Allies remained at Alexandretta it would be impossible for the Turks to bring in adequate supplies and reinforcements, and many of their garrisons would be at the mercy of the local populace. The goal that al Ahd and al Fatat had dreamed of might at last be within their grasp.

After meeting Faroki, Sykes cabled a report to London which shows that the two men went into the discussions with quite different objectives. Faroki's priority was an Allied landing at Alexandretta, while Sykes was looking for Arab concessions to France. As no action could be taken at Alexandretta without French agreement, Faroki was under very great pressure to suggest ways in which a compromise with France might be reached.

The task was a difficult one: in October he had been willing to contemplate French rule in the Lebanon, but Hussein's most recent letter had rejected this course. Faroki had therefore to find an alternative. Sykes reported on November 20th that in Faroki's opinion the Arabs would accept no French colonial administration in the areas south of a line from Alexandretta through Urfa to the Persian frontier. However, he had persuaded Faroki to accept the idea of 'a convention with France to allow her a monopoly of all concessionary enterprise in Palestine and Syria . . .

the Arabs further agreeing to employ in this area European *employés* and none but Frenchmen as advisers'.[27] Faroki stressed, as a point of honour, that these advisers would only be sent on request. In addition there would be special recognition of French educational establishments. A corresponding treaty could be made with Britain as regards other self-governing Arab regions, and in Mesopotamia Britain would have direct rule over Basra and areas to the south.

Faroki's concessions were, however, strictly conditional. Sykes wrote that Faroki had 'insisted' that his agreement 'was dependent on the Entente landing between Mersina and Alexandretta and making good the Cilician Gates or the Amanus Pass; stipulating further that, until this had been done, the Sherif should take no action.'[28]

It is unlikely that anyone in London attached great importance to this report at the time. It was one of a series of telegrams Sykes sent to the War Office that week dealing with Arab policy, and his opinions changed from day to day. In any case both the War Office and the Foreign Office knew that there would be no landing at Alexandretta.

There were copies of these telegrams in the Cairo files, and also of several longer reports by Sykes on the Arab question. When the Cairo staff read them, they must have realised that his ebullient self-confidence disguised a very indifferent intellect, for these documents reveal an extraordinary lack of organised thought and logical deduction. In political questions Sykes showed a taste for bold, all-embracing solutions and dealt in an impressive manner with grand schemes and vital issues; but he clearly lacked the ability or self-discipline to undertake any systematic examination of detail. As a result much of what he wrote was little more than political rhetoric. Worse still, he was inconsistent: he would advocate contradictory policies on successive days with equal enthusiasm, apparently without realising that such changes involved rethinking his entire position. This trait was combined with a boundless optimism which led him to discount the obstacles in his path.

These shortcomings may have owed something to a very fragmented education. During his childhood he had travelled constantly, attending a succession of schools in England, Belgium and Monaco, or being taught by private tutors. He had developed no taste for study and had abandoned his Cambridge degree course.

Sykes tackled problems in the manner of a politician rather than a public servant, looking for rapid, visible solutions without troubling himself deeply over finer points. Like many politicans, he was keen to

identify himself with laudable causes, and he was seen as a deeply
religious and honourable man. Yet he was also ambitious and, as events
would show, was capable of wholly cynical manoeuvring when this
would achieve some short-term goal.

He had reached his present position through a combination of personality, social standing and good luck. As a Member of Parliament he
had many acquaintances in Whitehall, and he had managed to get into the
War Office with the help of a friend, Kitchener's private secretary. His
views on the Middle East owed more to an amateur enthusiasm for the
subject than to any depth of knowledge, but fellow-politicians were
impressed by his charm, energy and self-confidence. His opportunity had
come when he was asked to serve on the de Bunsen Committee as an
observer for Kitchener. Most members of the Committee had been senior
civil servants with heavy departmental responsibilities. By contrast Sykes
had been able to devote almost all his time to its work. He had seized the
chance, and although he was the Committee's most junior member his
inventive mind had been largely responsible for the alternative geographical and political proposals it considered. His subsequent tour to
Egypt and India had probably been made at his own suggestion.[29]

In normal circumstances Sykes could not have risen to a position of
influence in the formulation of British policy towards the Middle East;
specialist experts in Whitehall would have recognised that his views
were superficial and often eccentric. However, few people remaining in
London in 1915 were qualified to make such a judgment. The exception
would have been Kitchener himself, to whom Sykes was nominally
responsible; but Kitchener was extremely busy, and for whatever reason
he preferred to deal with Sykes through his secretary.[30]

In Cairo there was no shortage of expertise on the Arab question,
and as the Intelligence staff began to know Sykes better they became
increasingly aware of his failings. Lawrence would later describe him as
'the imaginative advocate of unconvincing world movements . . . a bundle
of prejudices, intuitions, half-sciences. His ideas were of the outside; and
he lacked patience to test his materials before choosing his style of
building. He would take an aspect of the truth, detach it from its circumstances, inflate it, twist and model it, until its old likeness and its new
unlikeness together drew a laugh; and laughs were his triumphs . . . He
would sketch out in a few dashes a new world, all out of scale, but vivid
as a vision of some sides of the thing we hoped.'[31] Following this visit by
Sykes to Cairo, Clayton too viewed him with some caution.

In London, the inter-departmental committee chaired by Sir Arthur Nicolson had met for the first time on November 13th to consider how best to approach negotiations with the French. It decided to tell Georges-Picot formally about the present state of negotiations with the Sherif, and to stress the need to avoid an Arab alliance with Turkey. The committee hoped that France would be more ready to make concessions in Syria when it was realised that Britain was prepared to give up territory already conquered by the IEF in Mesopotamia.

On November 23rd, however, when Georges-Picot joined the second meeting, he was adamant; indeed the scale of French demands was staggering. He insisted 'that the French must of course have the whole of Syria and Palestine, and that their southern boundary must be the present Egypto-Turkish frontier'.[32] France also claimed Cilicia and the Mosul district of northern Mesopotamia.

As regards the Arab question, 'M. Picot was asked . . . whether the French, in view of Arab feeling and the possibility of bringing them in with us instead of against us, would not be willing to offer the Arabs their independence.'[33] He replied that 'Syria was very near the heart of the French and that now, after the expenditure of so many lives, France would never consent to offer independence to the Arabs, though at the beginning of the war she might have done so.'[34] To justify this position, Georges-Picot argued that the Arab movement had no potential value: 'He thought that it had been much exaggerated by the Cairo authorities, and that, in reality, it had little or no strength or following.'[35]

In this manner, the initial discussions reached what the minutes describe as an 'impasse'. After the meeting Georges-Picot went to Paris for consultations with his Government.

McMahon and Maxwell returned to Cairo from Mudros in late November, knowing that the Alexandretta scheme was strongly opposed in London. Kitchener, however, was going to London and they must have hoped that he could persuade the Cabinet to change its mind before a final decision was taken.

The news about Alexandretta was a great disappointment to the Cairo Intelligence Department, and to Lawrence in particular. As it was now virtually certain that Gallipoli would be abandoned, an attack on Egypt seemed very probable. The British staff in Egypt took every opportunity to present the case for landings. When Gertrude Bell arrived on November 26th[36] to join the Intelligence Department her support was immediately enlisted. She wrote home: 'Mr. Hogarth and Mr. Lawrence (you don't know him, he is also of Carchemish, exceedingly intelligent) met me and brought me to this hotel where they are both staying. Mr. Hogarth, Mr. Lawrence and I all dined together'.[37] Within three days she had written a long letter about the Alexandretta scheme to Lord Cromer, the distinguished elder statesman of Britain's relations with the Middle East, in which she set out the Cairo arguments very forcefully. Her reputation as an expert on Arab affairs was already considerable, and the Cairo staff must have hoped that this support would carry some weight in London.[38]

Gertrude Bell had come to Cairo at the suggestion of Captain Hall, head of Intelligence at the Admiralty. Her firsthand knowledge of the Arabian tribes was invaluable. She wrote: 'I am helping Mr. Hogarth to fill in the Intelligence files with information as to the tribes and sheikhs. It's great fun and delightful to be working with him. Our chief is Col. Clayton whom I like very much.'[39]

The Cabinet's final decision about Alexandretta would affect Britain's relationship with Hussein. For the present, therefore, his comments on McMahon's territorial proposals remained unanswered. On November 30th McMahon cabled to London, discussing the question of a reply: 'I am faced with the great difficulty which besets our treatment of the Arab question if the policy of awaiting in Egypt the threatened Turko-German advance is adhered to. This policy will jeopardise any attempt to secure Arab co-operation and it would appear unwise urging the Arabs into premature activity which through want of our support and fear of Turkish retaliation might hasten their abandonment of our cause.'[40]

To add to McMahon's difficulties, British prestige in the Middle East had now suffered a further blow at Turkish hands. The confident Anglo-Indian advance in Mesopotamia had run into difficulties, and by late November a retreat had begun. McMahon wrote: 'The serious situation . . . now facing us in Egypt and Mesopotamia renders the alienation of Arab assistance from the Turks a matter of great importance, and we must make every effort to enlist the sympathy and assistance, even though passive, of the Arab people.'[41]

He recommended sending a reply to Hussein which restated Britain's inability to make commitments about areas where French interests would be affected, while expressing the hope that a satisfactory agreement might be reached. In Mesopotamia, however, there seemed few real obstacles to a formula which would satisfy British and Arab aspirations. Equally, there seemed little objection to a guarantee that the Allies would not conclude a separate peace with Turkey without securing Arab freedom. McMahon recommended a grant to the Sherif of fifty thousand sovereigns, payable in instalments. This had become essential to the finances of the Hejaz, since the Turks had ceased to pay any subsidy. He also pointed out that it would be very helpful if he could have a definite statement of French policy.

His outline reply was put to the French Government via Georges-Picot, but the Foreign Office was not optimistic about the reaction. While McMahon waited for news, Clayton received from London a detailed account of the confrontation between Georges-Picot and the Nicolson Committee. This was the first Cairo knew of what had taken place. Colonel Parker, who had been present, reported that George Clerk of the Foreign Office had come to him after the meeting 'and suggested that I should get General Callwell [Director of Military Operations and Intelligence at the War Office] to put forward the view strongly that on military grounds it was essential that the French should do all they could to assist [on the Arab question], pointing out that if they did not it might mean that we should have to withdraw all our troops from France to face Mohammedan risings in all our possessions.'[42]

Having observed Georges-Picot's earlier activities in Cairo, Clayton could well imagine the scale of the difficulty. He sent a copy of Parker's letter to Wingate, writing: 'As you will see things did not start propitiously which is not surprising with Picot as French representative . . . Picot's claims are preposterous and his arguments practically "NIL". However Lord K. is at home now and also Sykes . . . so things may have gone better recently.'[43] McMahon's views were no less definite. On December 10th he cabled to the Foreign Office: 'The selection of Picot as their representative . . . is a discouraging indication of the French attitude. Picot is a notorious fanatic on the Syrian question and quite incapable of assisting any mutual settlement on the reasonable commonsense grounds which the present situation requires.' He added: 'It is unfortunate that the adviser of the French Government here, Defrance, is a man of similar type . . . I am informed that he sent a few days ago for a leading Arab notable of Damascus now in Egypt, and told him as follows: "You can tell all your friends here from me, and I tell you this in my capacity as representative of the French Government, that Syria shall never be part of an Arab Empire. Syria will be under the protection of France and we shall shortly send an army to occupy it . . ."

'This is not helpful but while the present attitude of the French Government continues it appears useless for me to remonstrate with him.

'In the meantime both the desirability and the difficulty of detaching the Arabs from our enemy are daily increasing. The conditions of Arabia never justified an expectation of active or organised assistance such as some people think is the object of our proposed mutual under-standing. What we want is the material advantage of even passive Arab sympathy and assistance on our side instead of their active co-operation with the enemy.

'This advantage will become of still more vital importance to us if, as now seems probable, time does not longer permit of action elsewhere and we have to await the enemy's advance on Egypt.'[44]

This telegram from McMahon crossed with the Foreign Office com-ments on his proposed letter to Hussein. It confirmed that no action would be taken at Alexandretta, and continued: 'we have little hope of obtaining from the French Government, whose attitude with regard to Syria is also very difficult, any assurance that will really satisfy the Arabs. On the other hand we must try and keep the negotiations with the Sherif in being'.[45] McMahon was asked to tell Hussein that the question of Syria was still under consideration, and that a further communication on the subject would follow. Likewise, more time would be needed to negotiate a precise agreement which would safeguard British interests in Meso-potamia. A reply to the Sherif on these lines was sent on December 14th.

Now that the Alexandretta scheme was dead, the Cairo staff must have feared that Hussein would do nothing, and that after the war neither France nor the Government of India would be willing to give up any territory to an independent Arab state. McMahon therefore included a caution in his letter, clearly designed to forewarn the Sherif about the consequences of inaction: 'it is most essential that you should spare no effort to attach all the Arab peoples to our united cause and urge them to afford no assistance to our enemies. It is on the success of these efforts and on the more active measures which the Arabs may hereafter take in support of our cause, when the time for action comes, that the permanence and strength of our agreement must depend.'[46]

In London, the Foreign Office was still trying to find some means of bringing the French round to a more constructive attitude. George Clerk minuted against McMahon's telegram of December 10th, 'I quite agree with this estimate of M. Defrance and M. Picot, but the latter has been particularly chosen, for his very fanaticism, by his Government and M. Cambon is more *intransigeant* even than M. Picot.

'Moreover, the urgency of the Arab question gives the French a lever for forcing us to recognise their preposterous claims, of which they are taking every advantage, and I am convinced that we shall have to come to an agreement with France before we can say anything, I won't say definite, but even plausible, to the Sherif of Mecca.

'M. Picot is now in Paris, nominally trying to get his Government to agree to the very anodyne reply to the Sherif which Sir H. McMahon proposed about Syria, and the most favourable issue I expect is that the French Government will make us the "great concession" of agreeing, if we will definitely recognise the French claim to the whole coast from Egypt to Mersina.'[47]

Clerk gave it as his opinion that the matter had become too serious for negotiations between Georges-Picot and Foreign Office civil servants: 'I think it must be treated between Government and Government . . . This is a matter for consideration by the War Committee and I would venture to urge that that body should hear the views of Sir Mark Sykes, who is not only highly qualified to speak from the point of view of our interests, but who understands the French position in Syria today – and in a sense sympathises with it – better probably than anyone.'[48]

Sykes, who had just returned from Egypt, was only too keen to give his opinion. Kitchener's diminishing credibility within the Cabinet, little understood in Cairo, had created an opening for some other expert on Middle East affairs. It was a golden opportunity for Sykes, who had spent the previous three months discussing every aspect of the Arab question with leading authorities in Egypt, India and elsewhere. On December 16th he put on a bravura performance in front of the War Committee. Though some may have cavilled at his rhetorical exaggerations, there was no disputing the range of Sykes's knowledge. He was better informed about the state of Middle East politics than anyone else in London.

As a result he was invited to attend the third meeting of the Nicolson Committee, at which Georges-Picot would be present, on December 21st. In response to British pressure there had been a very considerable moderation in the French position, and when the meeting took place Georges-Picot was prepared to accept a much reduced area of direct administration. There would be an enlarged Lebanon, its constitution modelled as far as possible on existing arrangements, under a governor appointed by France. Inland, the new Arab state would have to be divided into two spheres of influence: France would enjoy exclusive commercial and administrative rights in one, Britain in the other.

This was the kind of arrangement previously discussed by the Foreign Office, and there seemed therefore to be a basis for agreement. As the members of the Committee could not possibly spare the time needed to work out all the ramifications, Nicolson suggested that Sykes and Georges-Picot should 'examine the whole question so as to clear the ground of details and collaborate . . . in drawing up a memorandum which would co-relate the various factors of the general problem.'[49]

A week later Sykes wrote to Clayton: 'I have been given the Picot negotiations. I have proposed to concede Mosul and the land north of the Lesser Zab if Haifa and Acre are conceded to us – Picot seems to waver on this and I have good hopes of getting the essential.'[50] This news, together with a one-page summary of discussions at the third Nicolson Committee meeting, was the last Cairo would hear of Anglo-French negotiations for nearly four months.

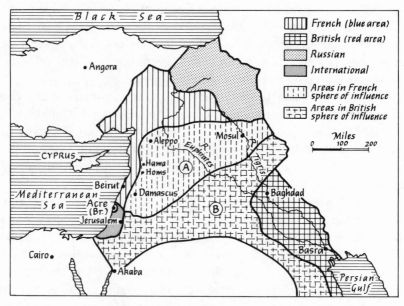

Map 3: *The Sykes-Picot Agreement*

During three days at the beginning of January 1916 Sykes and Georges-Picot hammered out the draft memorandum which would ultimately be the basis of an Anglo-French understanding, generally referred to as the Sykes-Picot Agreement.

The memorandum began with a summary of French, Arab and British desiderata, and a note on religious interests affecting Palestine. This part of the document was remarkable in one respect only: the account of Arab wishes differed markedly from the statements repeatedly made by Hussein and by the Syrians in Cairo. It stated: 'The ideal of the Arab leaders would be to establish a confederation of states under the aegis of an Arabian prince, roughly approximating to the Arabian Peninsula plus the Ottoman provinces of Basra, Bagdad, Jerusalem, Damascus, Aleppo, Mosul, Adana, and Diarbekir, with its littoral under the protection of Great Britain and France. That such a state should agree to select its administrative advisers from subjects of the two protecting Powers, and that it should accord especial facilities to both Powers in matters of enterprise and industrial development.'[51]

The references to France, French advisers and French protection as part of an Arab 'ideal' doubtless smoothed the passage for the Sykes-Picot proposals, but they were wishful thinking. The blame for this must lie with Sykes, now posing as the ultimate expert on Arab matters. His only possible justification lay in the remarks made by Faroki during their conversation in Cairo some weeks earlier. But Faroki's concessions at this meeting had been conditional on an Allied landing at Alexandretta, which was now out of the question; therefore nothing he had said could now be considered binding. Far from representing the Arab ideal, the concessions had been wrung from him with difficulty, and had been described by Sykes immediately afterwards as 'the best I could get'.[52] They had never been endorsed by Faroki in writing, still less by Hussein. Moreover, as Sykes knew, Faroki had no authority to commit the Arabs to anything.

Having set aside Syrian objections to French involvement, Sykes and Georges-Picot drew up a map which gave the Arabs considerably less than this falsified 'ideal'. The memorandum specified areas of direct French administration on the north Syrian littoral (the 'blue' area) and direct British administration in the regions of Basra and Baghdad (the 'red' area). The interior of Syria and northern Mesopotamia was divided up into zones of French influence ('Area A') and British influence ('Area B'). Jerusalem and the Holy Places were to be governed under an international administration. The arrangement was less generous to the Arabs than anything hitherto envisaged in Cairo, and could not possibly have been accepted by Hussein. It gave France a vast area of influence in Syria and northern Mesopotamia, and allowed for substantial Anglo-Indian colonisation in Iraq.

The Sykes-Picot memorandum and map of January 5th were widely circulated in Whitehall, but they were not sent to Egypt for comment. This was extraordinary, not least because one of the experts who saw the document in London pointed out the need to consult McMahon. Brigadier-General Macdonogh, head of Intelligence at the War Office, wrote: 'If . . . we are to go on with the discussion I think that it would be desirable to have Sir H. McMahon's opinion on the Memorandum before ascertaining the views of the French Government. To me it appears that the one point of importance is to get the Arabs in on our side as early as possible. I would therefore suggest that all that is necessary at the moment is that we should be in a position to inform the Sherif what are the approximate limits of the country which we and the French propose to let him rule over.'[53]

It is clear that someone in a position of authority took a deliberate decision not to consult McMahon. In this way the Sykes-Picot proposals were shielded from rejection by Hussein or by representative Arab opinion in Cairo. The 'further communication' McMahon had been promised about French ambitions in Syria for transmission to Hussein was to be news of an Anglo-French *fait accompli* rather than a basis for negotiation.

This decision might have been excusable if the Sykes-Picot memorandum had received universal approval in London, but the reverse was true. The comments which survive in official files are almost all hostile. Captain W. R. Hall, head of Intelligence at the Admiralty, pointed out that the memorandum made no attempt to meet Hussein's wishes. The Sherif had asked for an assurance, Hall wrote, that 'all territories properly considered as inhabited by Arabs shall (with certain exceptions) be part of an independent Arab state, guaranteed by the Allies. He does not appear ever to have been willing to exclude Syria, and more especially the Arab centre of Beirout, from the Arab state.

'Further, he and other Arab leaders in touch with the British have . . . expressed themselves very emphatically against their being placed under any obligation to accept French advisers locally, whereas they stated that they were prepared to welcome British'.[54] Hall concluded that an agreement on these lines would do nothing to advance Britain's relations with Hussein: 'From the strategical point of view . . . the only advantage which would at present be gained seems to be the possibility of giving definiteness to the assurances [offered to Hussein] which would in themselves be unsatisfactory.'[55]

Quite apart from the possible effect on Britain's relationship with the Arabs, the failure to consult McMahon was to cause deep resentment among British officials in Cairo. The Sykes-Picot proposals differed substantially from anything previously agreed between them and the Foreign Office. Such an unexpected course of action by the Foreign Office therefore requires explanation.

At first the decision not to consult Cairo seems to have been only tacit. Sykes may not have been responsible, but he had good personal reasons for going along with it. Unlike McMahon, he had no previous experience of diplomatic negotiation. Nevertheless, he had now been asked to represent Britain in what he saw as an important international discussion. The outcome would affect the lives of millions and shape the whole future of the Middle East. Such a task appealed strongly to his political ambition. He aimed to play an increasingly influential role in Arab affairs, and a solution which pleased the Cabinet would be of great benefit to his own career. To consult Cairo would be to admit that there were greater experts than himself on the Arab question. This was hardly an admission that Sykes wanted to make, since he also hoped that he, rather than any of the Cairo officials, would ultimately be chosen to head the proposed Arabian Bureau. Worse still, he must surely have realised that the British staff in Cairo would protest at the distorted account of Arab aims which seemed to legitimise the Sykes-Picot memorandum.

It was probably this last consideration, rather than any other, which influenced Sir Arthur Nicolson, who must also have played an important part in the decision not to consult McMahon. Nicolson was responsible for the negotiations, and Sykes could certainly not have excluded Cairo without his agreement.

The overriding need, as Nicolson saw it, was to reach an accommodation with France which would reduce Anglo-French tension and remove the grounds for any future French suspicion of British intentions in the Middle East. This last consideration might soon become important. A limited advance across Sinai to positions which would assure a more economical defence of Egypt was already under discussion, and the ultimate defeat of Turkey might well involve a major British thrust into Palestine and Syria. The fate of the Alexandretta scheme had demonstrated that the French would try to veto such moves unless their colonial desiderata in Syria had previously been secured.

Hussein and the Syrian Arabs had no such motive for seeking agreement with France. McMahon's reports showed that their stance was, and always had been, extremely hostile to French ambitions. Judging by Hussein's most recent statements, there was little likelihood that he could be persuaded to accept the Sykes-Picot proposals; and as long as the tedious process of negotiating with him continued, French suspicions would be a running sore in the vital partnership between London and Paris.

If the Foreign Office had seen the Syrian Arabs as committed allies in the war against Turkey their interests might well have been respected. The reality was different: Syrian representatives had done nothing except make noisy political and military demands. Their position was not comparable to Hussein's: he had already helped Britain by refusing to endorse the jihad, and it was now unlikely that he could recover his position with the Turks. He would have his Arabian kingdom as a reward. The Syrians, on the other hand, could offer no practical help to the Allies now that the Alexandretta scheme was dead. There was a growing belief in London that neither Hussein nor the Syrians had anything new to contribute. Naturally this view was strongly promoted by the India Office, represented on the Nicolson Committee by Sir Arthur Hirtzel.

Nicolson's thinking at this time is clear from a letter to Lord Hardinge: 'We are making a certain progress in respect of the Arab negotiations. I do not myself believe that they will ever fructify into anything really definite . . . I do not think that we can possibly expect the Arabs to come over to our side unless we are in a position to furnish a considerable British force to give them some stiffening. People talk of the Arabs as if they were some cohesive body, well armed and equipped, instead of a heap of scattered tribes with no cohesion and no organisation. I think myself that we are trying to treat with a shadow, and it would be a delusion to imagine that we should be able to detach a really powerful Arab force from Turkey.'[56]

By the beginning of 1916 the Cabinet had accepted that the war would be won or lost in Europe; plans were in hand for a concerted Allied offensive that summer. The Suez Canal was now adequately garrisoned, and nothing the Arabs could do would affect the coming battle in the West. The future of Syria was of little concern to Britain, and the result of a rebellion there no longer seemed important. Was it worth disrupting the entente, just to placate a group of Syrian politicians?

Doubts about any future Arab action were reflected in the deliberations of the Nicolson Committee when it met to discuss the Sykes-Picot memorandum on January 21st. An important qualification was approved, which read: 'If the Arab scheme fails the whole scheme will also fail and the French and British Governments would then be free to make any new claims.'[57] A clause to this effect was incorporated in a preamble to the Sykes-Picot text which survives in various drafts. In later versions it read: 'It is understood that the putting into effect of these proposals is contingent on the successful assistance of the Arabs and their leaders in the establishment of an Arab State or Confederation of Arab States under the protection of France and Great Britain; and on their active co-operation with the Allies'.[58]

This clause, which probably reflects the influence of the India Office, clearly contradicted the essence of McMahon's pledge to Hussein three months before. Without decisive action on their part, the Syrian and Mesopotamian Arabs would not have any claim to self-determination. However, the new formula had considerable attractions in British eyes. For the duration of the war the Sykes-Picot Agreement would eliminate Anglo-French tension over Syria; but afterwards, if the Arabs had taken no substantial military action, it would be void. The Ottoman Empire could then be divided up between the Allies on whatever lines seemed appropriate.

Further protests or demands from Hussein would only interfere with such a felicitous arrangement. This was doubtless a further reason for saying nothing to Cairo. From now on McMahon's role should be to placate the Arabs without making embarrassing concessions. McMahon would be able to do this more gracefully while he remained unaware of the Sykes-Picot terms. It would therefore be advantageous to delay telling him for as long as possible.

The Cairo Intelligence Department had many other preoccupations at this time. In January 1916 the last of the Mediterranean Expeditionary Force was evacuated from Gallipoli, and as a result there were two separate armies with their staffs in Egypt. Their combined strength, some 275,000 men, formed the largest Allied army outside France at any time during the war. Medforce was now commanded by Lieut.-General Sir Archibald Murray, while the Force in Egypt remained for the present under Sir John Maxwell. Lawrence commented wryly: 'One could hardly move about for generals! We had 108'.[59] Cairo Intelligence, which had hitherto carried out some tasks for both forces, was likely to face drastic reorganisation. In mid-December it had been transferred from the Cairo War Office to GHQ at the Savoy. For the time being, however, its structure remained intact, and the threat seemed to diminish in late January when Medforce headquarters were moved away to Ismailia.

Lawrence was now working three sessions every day: from 9 am until 1.30 pm, 2.15 pm until 8.30 pm, and again from 10 pm until midnight. He wrote to Leeds: 'the fact is I am written out and worked out: an absolute mechanical toy now, who does a daily round, and goes to bed at odd hours . . . thirteen hours a day in an office, seven days a week, is too good for one's nerves: especially when one is a miserable grain of faith trying to move mountains. Mountains is a polite term for the F.O.'[60]

Few working papers from the Cairo Intelligence Department are now available, but the daily Intelligence Bulletins survive. They show that from the autumn of 1915 onwards Lawrence was handling a growing amount of information about defences on the north-eastern frontier of Turkey (referred to as the Caucasus Front). The Grand Duke Nicholas had taken over command of the Russian forces there in September 1915. On being told of Allied plans to withdraw from the Dardanelles he had decided to launch a big offensive before the Turkish forces opposing him were reinforced by troops released from Gallipoli.

The Russian advance began early in January 1916, and was extremely welcome to British commanders in Egypt. They saw that it might have the effect of stalling Turkish preparations for a large-scale attack on the Canal. This was the background to one of the more obscure incidents in Lawrence's Intelligence career.

Some of the Arab troops sent away from their home areas in Syria and Mesopotamia had been posted to the Caucasus Front, and among them were units and commanders listed by Faroki as secret enemies of the Ottoman Government. One of Lawrence's tasks was to follow the movements of every Turkish unit, which he did by collating information gathered by Intelligence from prisoners captured on the various fronts. As the Russian plans took shape, he evidently realised that some practical benefit might be gained from the information Faroki had provided. In his own words: 'I . . . put the Grand Duke Nicholas in touch with certain disaffected Arab officers in Erzeroum. Did it through the War Office and our military attaché in Russia.'[61] Erzurum, the principal fortress town of eastern Turkey, was not originally among the Russian objectives. Despite its immensely strong fortifications, it was to be captured by the Grand Duke in mid-February.[62]

Lawrence referred to this incident on several occasions after the war, and it is alluded to in *Seven Pillars*.[63] Fuller details may one day be disclosed if the relevant secret service papers are released. However, the documents already available leave no doubt that he was in a position to provide the Russians with valuable information. Many years later Liddell Hart noted after a talk with Lawrence in which Erzurum was mentioned: 'He put Russian General in touch with Arab on staff.'[64] Lawrence asked Liddell Hart not to publish a full account of the incident as this might endanger relatives of the Arab concerned who were still living in Turkey. (It is for such reasons that secret service papers, when they survive at all, are embargoed for a hundred years).

There can be little doubt that the Caucasus campaign diverted Turkish attention from Egypt during the winter of 1915-16. Moreover, the Canal garrison had been strengthened by divisions from Gallipoli. These factors meant that a successful attack on Egypt would require a larger Turkish force than could now be assembled in Sinai. Lawrence wrote home in late January: 'There is no real sign of the Turks' coming on. Of course they can see that it would be lunacy now we are so well prepared: just in the first moments of joy, when the Germans joined hands with the Bulgars, and the blockade of Turkey was ended, they thought about conquering Egypt. Now they have got sensible again. It is very difficult for them (for lack of camels) to bring more than a small force down.'[65]

This informed comment contrasts with the grossly inflated estimates of Turkish numbers put out by Colonel Holdich, a senior member of Murray's Intelligence staff at Ismailia. In mid-February Holdich set aside Lawrence's figures and confidently predicted an attack on the Canal by 250,000 men. As Lawrence later remarked: 'My estimates of enemy strengths always were issued to the nearest hundred: he suppressed them and put forward his own, which seemed to me to be only in the farthest ten thousands. Holdich was excellent in Operations, and fatal in Intelligence.'[66] The Ismailia figure was greeted with derision in the War Office.

It was late January before a further message from the Sherif of Mecca arrived in Cairo. Even by Hussein's standards, the language of the new letter was obscure and contradictory. Conciliatory phrases suggested that he was willing to set aside the question of French ambitions in Syria, at any rate for the duration of the war. But elsewhere he firmly rejected conceding any 'span of land' to France, and affirmed that 'at the first opportunity after this war is finished, we shall ask you (what we avert our eyes from today) for what we now leave to France in Beirut and its coasts.'[67] Most important of all, however, in the closing paragraphs Hussein spoke of 'that action, the time of which has now come near, and which destiny drives towards us with great haste and clearness'.[68] He went on to indicate that he would soon need arms and ammunition.

This message was extremely welcome in Egypt. Wyndham Deedes, an expert on Turkey who had come to Cairo from Gallipoli Intelligence, noted in his diary after dining with Lawrence and others: 'The letter from the Shereef was very satisfactory . . . If now the French *intransigeance* can be overcome there is every reason to hope that things will run quietly and smoothly.'[69]

The letter did not ask for further concessions, and McMahon therefore replied immediately, noting the Sherif's constructive attitude and encouraging him to make further efforts in the Allied cause. As regards the future of northern Syria, McMahon stated plainly that Britain set a high value on the alliance with France, and that this relationship would remain in place after the war.

On January 25th he sent a copy of the letter to London, and cabled briefly the following day: 'The Sherif's messenger has lately returned with a letter and messages . . . these are of a friendly and satisfactory nature.'[70] The reaction in London was considerably less enthusiastic; by this time the Anglo-French negotiations had reached an advanced stage. Sykes had written to Nicolson on January 24th urging that it would be in everyone's best interest to finalise the agreement as soon as possible. His remarks about the Arabs show that he had again succumbed uncritically to French propaganda: 'until the Arabs know where we stand as regards the French, they will continue to set us by the ears whenever they can. This is natural to them and they endeavour to flatter the English by constantly harping on their dislike of the French and French methods – as a matter of fact I do not believe their dislike of the French is as great as they pretend even among the Moslems. Once the situation is clear, we can go forward with a real Arab policy and without fear of getting into trouble'.[71] Georges-Picot would certainly have approved of these sentiments.

The full text of Hussein's message reached the Foreign Office on February 2nd. In a covering letter McMahon expressed warnings which entirely contradicted the advice Nicolson was receiving from Sykes. 'One aspect of the Sherif's letter must not be overlooked,' McMahon wrote. 'Satisfactory as it may be to note his general acceptance for the time being of the proposed relations of France with Arabia, his reference to the future of those relations adumbrates a source of trouble which it will be wise not to ignore.

'I have on more than one occasion brought to the notice of His Majesty's Government the deep antipathy with which the Arabs regard the prospect of French administration of any portion of Arab territory.

'This has been continuously and persistently impressed upon me by everyone who knows the Arab mind, and this without any wish to flatter British sentiment.

'The Sherif . . . voices what I have every reason to believe to be the real feeling of the Arab party. The French are much mistaken in thinking that their advent into Arab territory will be welcomed by the Arabs; as the exact opposite will be the case.

'In this lies considerable danger to our future relations with France, because difficult and even impossible though it may be to convince France of her mistake, if we do not now endeavour to do so by warning her of the real state of Arab feeling, we may hereafter be accused of instigating or encouraging the opposition to the French, which the Arabs now threaten and will assuredly give.'[72]

Unlike other documents reaching the Foreign Office, this important dispatch seems to have been totally disregarded for two days. It was received on Wednesday February 2nd, but the first minute on its contents is dated February 4th, and Nicolson did not comment on it until Saturday February 5th. During this interval crucial events were taking place, to which the dispatch was directly relevant.

It was on February 2nd that Nicolson submitted the Sykes-Picot draft to Grey for consideration by the Government. He noted: 'The four towns of Homs, Hama, Aleppo, and Damascus will be included in the Arab State or Confederation, though in the area where the French will have priority of enterprise etc. You will see from Sir H. McMahon's telegram No. 707 of the 20th November, 1915, annexed herewith, that it had been contemplated that this sphere would be reserved for the development of special French interests.'[73] The telegram Nicolson attached had not been written by McMahon. It merely forwarded from Cairo the report by Sykes of concessions he had wrung from Faroki, all of which had been explicitly conditional on an Allied landing at Alexandretta.

The object in drawing attention to this questionable document was doubtless to suggest that the Arabs, and McMahon himself, were fully reconciled to the idea of a substantial French presence in inland Syria. It seems a curious coincidence that the telegram should have been produced on the very day that a dispatch arrived from McMahon which stated exactly the opposite.

While McMahon's dispatch languished somewhere in the Foreign Office, apparently unread, the Sykes-Picot text received British approval at a meeting on February 4th. It was decided that the draft agreement should be submitted in this form to Russia. The only change was that the existing preamble was scrapped. However, the condition requiring Arab action was retained in another form, in which it was even more precise and stringent. The meeting agreed that Georges-Picot should be authorised to 'inform his Government that the acceptance of the whole project would entail the abdication of considerable British interests, but provided that the co-operation of the Arabs is secured, and that the Arabs fulfil the conditions and obtain the towns of Homs, Hama, Damascus and Aleppo, the British Government would not object to the arrangement.'[74] From this point on, the condition that would decide whether Sykes- Picot was valid or not was rarely included in working versions of the text (although it was to be reiterated in the final exchange of notes). Later, when Lawrence learned of it, he realised that the Syrians would gain nothing unless Hussein's rebellion reached northern Syria. Knowledge of this proviso was to have a great influence over his actions during the Arab Revolt.

It was only when the Sykes-Picot draft had been approved that Nicolson found time to comment on the message from Hussein enclosed with McMahon's dispatch. He minuted: 'I do not consider this letter at all satisfactory as regards the Shereef's remarks respecting the French. I wish in his telegram No. 70 [reporting the arrival of Hussein's letter] Sir H. McMahon had given us some indication of this. He made no mention of the northern parts in this telegram – and we were led to believe that the Shereef had not taken any serious notice of them – while on the contrary he employs rather ominous language in regard to them.'[75] Nicolson must have known, however, that there were a great many statements in Foreign Office files about Arab hostility to French ambitions in Syria. Moreover, the new letter from Hussein, together with McMahon's specific warning, had been at the Foreign Office throughout the last stages of the Sykes-Picot negotiations. Nicolson's remark therefore seems particularly specious. Grey noted: 'This Arab question is a regular quicksand.'[76]

If Nicolson had wanted, he could easily have reopened the Anglo-French discussions in the light of Hussein's letter and McMahon's warning. The Sykes-Picot Agreement had not at this point been formally ratified by either Britain or France. This could not be done without Russian approval, and as it happened there were to be substantial modifications during the Franco-Russian talks (these affected non-Arab areas in the extreme north-east). On February 16th, however, Nicolson wrote to McMahon: 'I think it will be some little time before we are able to communicate with you in respect of the Arab negotiations. We have come to a certain accord with France as to her limits, and we now have to obtain the concurrence of Russia. When this has been secured we shall then have to come to some decision as to what we should say further to the Shereef of Mecca. For the moment he seems to be in a fairly good disposition towards us, so there is no immediate hurry to decide . . . how we shall present the French case and desiderata to him. I dare say the discussions at Petrograd will take some little time. In the meantime I am . . . sure you will be able to keep the Grand Shereef friendly disposed towards us.'[77]

Thus Nicolson rejected McMahon's advice in favour of that from Sykes, who could flatter himself that his influence in London was now greater than McMahon's. The truth was quite different. Nicolson must have known that McMahon's judgments were correct, but in the wider context of British foreign policy he found it more convenient to accept the opinion so confidently offered by Sykes. His justification was the belief that there would be no Arab Revolt, and that the Sykes-Picot arrangement would never be implemented. He was an experienced and responsible diplomat, and if he had foreseen the outcome of Hussein's rebellion he would surely not have committed Britain to an accord with France which could only lead to embarrassment after the war.

As for Sykes, he seems not to have understood the caution with which career civil servants view an ambitious politician. He now saw himself as a leading figure in Middle East affairs, but few others shared this view. As comments in Foreign Office files show, his activities were regarded with a certain apprehension.

Contrary to his hopes, his success in reaching an accord with Picot did not lead to immediate promotion. Soon after returning from Cairo he had circulated a grandiose scheme for an Arabian Bureau, with himself at its head. By now, however, control of the project had quietly passed into other hands. An inter-departmental committee had considered the matter and decided that the Bureau should be under Clayton, who had written to Captain Hall at the Admiralty: 'My ideas are somewhat different from those of Sykes, in that what I want to start is a Bureau here which will be a centre to which all information on the various questions connected with the Near East will gravitate. My idea is to have here a staff of men who are competent to sift and catalogue this information and to bring it into a form in which it is easily digested by those who may not be experts in the various questions . . . if you can let Hogarth come later on, he will be of the greatest value . . . if Mark Sykes can come out too, all the better, but I do not think it necessary to tie him down as a permanent member of the Bureau; he would be more useful as a freelance, available to go wherever it was necessary to obtain information.'[78]

This arrangement was finally confirmed on February 4th, the day that the Sykes-Picot text was approved in London. Clayton's appointment must have been a great blow to Sykes, who was instructed to accompany Georges-Picot to Russia and help explain the Anglo-French agreement. It would be April before he returned to London, and he would then look for another way to carve out an influential role for himself.

Even before the structure of the Arab Bureau had been settled Clayton began to choose a team of specialists for its work. It was inevitable that Lawrence would be among them. Ever since coming to Cairo he had been actively involved in Arab affairs. Clayton, Maxwell and McMahon all had great confidence in his reports.

An example of Lawrence's work for Clayton at this time was a long unsigned memorandum called 'The Politics of Mecca', sent to McMahon on February 1st for transmission to the Foreign Office. The paper was clearly written at Clayton's request to counteract Anglo-Indian propaganda in London. It argued that Hussein was a significant leader with valuable contacts throughout the Arab provinces. On the other hand it showed that he could not possibly create the kind of powerful Arab state feared by India. For consumption in London, Lawrence wrote: 'his activity seems beneficial to us, because it marches with our immediate aims, the break up of the Islamic "block" and the defeat and disruption of the Ottoman Empire, and because the states he would set up to succeed the Turks would be as harmless to ourselves as Turkey was before she became a tool in German hands. The Arabs are even less stable than the Turks. If properly handled they would remain in a state of political mosaic, a tissue of small jealous principalities, incapable of cohesion, and yet always ready to combine against an outside force.'[79]

The paper reached London not long after the Sykes-Picot text had been approved, and provoked very different reactions at the Foreign Office. One minute read: 'This able memorandum, the work presumably of Miss Bell, would be valuable to the War Office and the India Office.'[80] Below this, however, another official wrote: 'I am inclined to think that this account is somewhat partial and highly coloured.'[81]

Lawrence pursued this attack on the Anglo-Indian viewpoint in an article for the Intelligence Bulletin on February 10th. The Government of India had recently released the text of an interview with their protégé ibn Saud, in which the Wahhabi leader had described Hussein as 'essentially a trivial and unstable character', who 'could never be depended upon'. Ibn Saud had made it clear that he would never accept Hussein's leadership. Even if the Sherif proclaimed himself Caliph, this 'would not make any difference to his status among other Chiefs and there would be no question of their accepting any control from him, any more than they do now. Each individual Chief would continue . . . to control his own affairs and his own tribes as hitherto, with this exception, please God, that they would in future be immune from Turkish oppression.'[82] Lawrence commented: 'The Wahabis, who pose as the reformers of Islam, with all the narrow minded bigotry of the puritan, and Ibn Saoud as their chief, cannot express an opinion which is representative of the rest of Islam. In the Sherif of Mecca's scheme of expansion, all that is desired of Ibn Saoud and Ibn Rashid is neutrality towards him, and towards each other . . .

'It is to the more civilised centres of Islam, in Syria and Western Arabia, that the Sherif must look for the driving power which will carry his venture to success. It is his aim to reconcile the different warring elements – to prevent, for instance, the Idrisi and the Imam Yahya from dissipating their strength through personal jealousy – and though up to the present he has not done more than persuade the Imam to refrain from giving active assistance to the Turks, a study of his methods and past career by no means bears out the estimate of him expressed by Ibn Saoud.

'It is no doubt his aim to set up an Arab Empire, which will unite in himself the spiritual and temporal power at present exercised by the Sultan of Turkey, and present an undivided front to the rest of the civilised world. Such a scheme is impossible of realisation. The Arabs, it is true, are not indifferent to the question of the Caliphate, and they are at one in their common dislike of the Turks. The Sherif, by taking advantage of this, may unite them in one supreme effort, which will result in the disappearance of Ottoman rule from Arabia, and the assumption by himself of the Caliphate, but he will never succeed in exacting more than a religious allegiance from the great Chiefs. Leaving out of account the great distances, and the lack of effective communication, long years spent in the struggle for bare existence have engendered in the Arabs a distrust of their neighbours, and a passion for independence which put any permanent union, or submission to one single authority, out of the question.

'Their main desire is to be rid of the Turks, and to be allowed to live their lives as they please.'[83]

During the first months of 1916 the British staff in Cairo could only guess at events in London. Nicolson's telegram of February 10th withholding details of the Anglo-French agreement fuelled a growing pessimism about the kind of deal that Sykes and Georges-Picot might have put together. Rumours put about by pro-French elements did not ease the situation.

Clayton had recruited Wyndham Deedes to Cairo Intelligence, for the time being as his second-in-command, but ultimately to serve as an expert on Turkish affairs for the Arab Bureau. Lawrence wrote on February 21st that Deedes was 'a very excellent man. I like him best of the bunch'.[84] They discussed the Arab situation together, and the comments Deedes wrote in his diary probably reflect Lawrence's views as well as his own. Later that month he noted the acute anxiety of Syrian Arabs in Cairo: 'their general concern in the matter is that the French should not be allowed to go to Syria, that they should have no more at the very outside than economic and financial concessions . . . It is difficult rather to account for this extraordinary dislike and, if asked, they quote Tunis and other places where the French have colonies of Moslems . . . How difficult this makes our position at the present moment is quite obvious, because we ourselves know that our F.O. have made some sort of arrangement with the French by which we believe they are to have some territorial aggrandisement . . . News of this is only [now] reaching our friends who are continually coming to us and asking whether it is true we have sold them to the French.'[85]

At the end of February a further letter from Hussein reached Cairo. It contained no reference whatsoever to territorial questions, but set out details of the military steps his sons would shortly take in Syria and the Hejaz. He reported that the prospects for a rising in Syria had greatly worsened, owing to the drastic measures the Turks had been taking against Arab nationalists. Nevertheless he still hoped that something might be achieved. His son Feisal would try to detach any Arab units included in the large force Turkey was planning to send to the Canal. The principal movement, however, would take place further south, where

Hussein's Hejaz levies would be used in an attack on Medina. The letter closed with a list of weapons, ammunition, foodstuffs and funds that would be required. Hussein asked for these stores to be stockpiled at Port Sudan until he was ready to use them. His secret representative would collect the money, 50,000 sovereigns, in three weeks' time.

McMahon wrote optimistically to London that the Arab movement seemed to have reached an important stage; but the Foreign Office was no longer enthusiastic, and minutes on Hussein's letter reflect a prevailing confidence that the Arabs would not actually commit themselves to action. The Sherif's Syrian proposals seemed potentially embarrassing to Anglo-French relations, and Nicolson mentioned them cautiously to the French Ambassador, who dismissed them as wholly improbable. For his part, Cambon reiterated the charge that British officials in Cairo were acting against French interests. Nicolson wrote about this privately to McMahon on March 8th giving the French view that rumours of a British disagreement with France over the future of Syria 'would lead the Syrian Arabs to believe that we were opposed at any possible future period to the realisation of French aims in Syria. This, you know, is directly contrary to the fact.'[86]

The War Office, still under Kitchener, took a more positive view of the Arab Revolt, and by March 7th Maxwell had already set about obtaining weapons for Hussein in the Far East and elsewhere. There were also rifles and ammunition in Egypt which had been returned from Gallipoli. Much of this *matériel* was technically condemned, and needed skilled attention before it could be made serviceable; it was, however, immediately available. Stockpiles soon began to accumulate in Port Sudan.

On March 9th the Foreign Office, still maintaining silence on the Anglo-French agreement, sent a two-line reply to McMahon's telegrams about the Arab plans: 'You may pay the money and inform the Sherif that his proposed help is accepted.'[87] McMahon did so on the following day, writing: 'We are grateful to note the active measures which you propose to take. We consider them the most suitable in the existing circumstances, and they have the approval of His Majesty's Government'.[88]

In mid-March 1916 the Mediterranean Expeditionary Force was at last amalgamated with the Force in Egypt. Sir Archibald Murray took command and Maxwell returned home. Both Lawrence and Woolley were mentioned in his valedictory dispatch of March 16th. Lawrence's name was also included in a list for the distribution of Allied honours, and by a supreme irony he was awarded the French Légion d'Honneur in a citation dated March 18th.

The majority of Intelligence work was henceforth to be concentrated at Murray's Ismailia headquarters. Lawrence was one of only seven to remain under Clayton's direct supervision at the Savoy Hotel office in Cairo. From now on he would divide his time between Arab affairs and maps. He told his parents that the reorganisation 'makes no difference so far as I am concerned'.[89]

Not long after reaching Egypt, Murray had decided to advance across northern Sinai, recognising that fewer troops would be required to hold a line at El Arish than to garrison the whole Canal. Preparations were soon in hand, and morale improved considerably. This, together with the Sherif's news, led Lawrence to write: 'Things in the Near East are going better than they have been since we came out, I think. There is some faint prospect of the result of the war being good, when it does come.'[90]

A few days later he received a letter from his father, who was about to distribute the legacy inherited some months previously. Mr Lawrence now transferred investments worth £5,000 to each of the three surviving sons. Lawrence's income thereafter was to be about £270 per annum, sufficient to give him financial independence on a modest scale if he survived the war.

CHAPTER 13

Witness to Tragedy

Mesopotamia: April – May 1916

DURING the first fifteen months of the war against Turkey, the campaign in Mesopotamia had been conducted quite separately from Britain's military operations in Europe and the Mediterranean. The landing by the IEF 'Force D', in November 1914 had been undertaken by the Government of India; its political objectives were theoretically controlled from London by the India Office, but Indian Army headquarters in Simla were responsible for command and logistical support. This arrangement had proved to be unworkable.

Mesopotamia (now known as Iraq, although historically this name applied only to lower Mesopotamia) formed the north-eastern corner of Turkey's Arab empire. It was bordered to the east by Persia, and to the south by the Arabian Gulf; westwards the frontier was defined approximately by the River Euphrates. Between Baghdad and the Syrian city of Damascus, 450 miles to the west, lay desert. The IEF therefore saw little relationship between its activities in Mesopotamia and Arab aspirations in Syria. However, nomadic tribes and trading caravans travelled freely across the central region, and the attitudes of their principal chiefs were affected both by the Arab nationalist movement in the west and by the conduct of the Anglo-Indian invaders in the east.

During 1915 the IEF had been enlarged, and had occupied most of the southern part of Mesopotamia. It had then been decided that a division commanded by General Townshend should advance up the Tigris to the strategically important town of Kut al Amara, deep inside Turkish-held territory. The advance had seemed feasible because the River Tigris would serve as a line of communication. This objective was ambitious in itself, but it had then been superseded by a still more daring plan, to advance further upstream and take Baghdad.

At first Townshend's move had been remarkably successful. Kut had been occupied in September 1915, and he had then continued northwards, fighting a major action at Ctesiphon, some twenty miles short of Baghdad, on November 22nd. After this, however, the forces opposing him had been heavily reinforced. Well-trained Turkish troops replaced the half-hearted Arabs he had previously encountered.[1] Townshend had been obliged to retreat to Kut where his force of 17,000 men was quickly surrounded. During the months that followed, the rest of the Anglo-Indian Army, still nearly 200 miles further south, had been unable to relieve him.

The decision to advance on Baghdad had been approved by the War Council in London without serious investigation. Since the campaign was in the hands of the Indian Government, it had received little attention at the War Office. This attitude had changed, however, when the siege of Kut began. The Turks soon made it impossible for river steamers to reach the town, and by the end of 1915 it was clear that Britain faced a débâcle hardly less damaging to her prestige than the withdrawal from Gallipoli. Reinforcements could only be sent at the expense of other theatres, and this was of direct concern to Sir William Robertson, Chief of Imperial General Staff. Early in February 1916, at Robertson's instigation, responsibility for the campaign in Mesopotamia was taken over by the War Office. It was to be some months, however, before Whitehall was fully in control. Meanwhile there were rumours that the IEF was severely handicapped by inadequate support.

The extent of these problems was unclear in London, and Robertson sent General Webb Gillman to Mesopotamia to find out the truth of the situation. He would discover that the commanders in Mesopotamia were faced with inexcusable shortages of transport, equipment and supplies, owing to consistent penny-pinching by the Government of India.

By the end of February 1916 the siege of Kut had lasted for three months. On March 8th the second major attempt to relieve the town failed. Turkish positions were now very strong, and it was evident that saving Townshend's force would be very costly in men and materials. The besieged garrison was running short of food and would not be able to hold out for many more weeks. Khalil Pasha, the Turkish commander, therefore proposed that Townshend should negotiate a surrender, pointing out that the British force could achieve nothing further: 'you have heroically accomplished your military duty.'[2]

Townshend urged the GOC in Mesopotamia, General Sir Percy Lake, to permit talks with Khalil: 'If he is willing to give me reasonable and honourable terms I should agree to give up to him, i.e., to say my force must be allowed to march out through the Turkish lines with its arms, artillery and pouch ammunition and join you, and I must also be allowed to evacuate my sick and wounded and baggage by steamer and barges.

These in other words, are the terms granted to Massena by the Austrians after the defence of Genoa . . .[also] what the British force granted to the French at Lisbon by the Convention of Cintra in 1808.

'These terms would not only be honourable to myself and my troops, but also I see no disadvantage to the Government in abandoning this battered village . . . nothing like as large as Douaumont or other villages in France, taken and retaken daily in the great battle now raging . . .

'Holding [the opinion that he does] the Turkish commander will, I believe, grant me honourable and reasonable terms, though of course I have only done my duty like all officers and men here.

'Should these terms be refused, I would neither make nor receive further overtures and would hold on as long as my food and ammunition lasted, but he would be wise to accept my terms. There is now roughly one month's food possibly on starvation diet. I might possibly hold out till April 17th . . . This proposition might be put before the Government to learn their wishes on the subject . . . if there is any doubt in your minds as to the certainty of early relief.

'Negotiations, to be successful, should be begun soon while I have food to bargain with.

'Lastly, I would emphasise the fact that you have had great losses, and a third effort, even a successful one, will undoubtedly entail heavy losses bearing in mind the great strength of the Turkish field defences and the fact that you are not yet concentrated in full strength '.[3]

Lake, who had taken over command in Mesopotamia only a few weeks earlier, was loath to think of surrender; but he agreed to pass the message on to London. His own objections were meanwhile sent to Townshend: 'It does not appear that even taking the most gloomy view of your prospects of relief any advantage would be gained by entering into negotiations at this stage. Any terms offered by Khalil Pasha while our preparations for your relief are going forward would inevitably be cancelled if our next attempt were not successful. Moreover, the mere fact of your asking for terms would at once be published abroad, and would produce evil effects as regards loss of prestige scarcely less than those involved by the enforced surrender of Kut . . .

'The mere fact of Khalil proposing to offer terms is indication of a desire on his part to set free his force for operations elsewhere.'[4]

This optimistic talk of enemy weakness was echoed in Simla and London. The C-in-C India cabled to Robertson: 'Khalil Bey's readiness to negotiate . . . seems to me to disclose apprehension of the floods or of the Russians or both on the part of the Turks, as well as a design to proclaim us as the negotiating party for the surrender.'[5] Robertson, pointing to Turkish difficulties on the Caucasus front, replied: 'At present . . . Turkish railways and communications are much congested, and the supply of munitions, reinforcements, stores, etc. to Baghdad is bound to suffer greatly in consequence. My general information is to the effect that the difficulties of the Turks are serious. I regard Khalil Bey's overtures as a confirmation of this and as an indication that, given determined action on our part, success is assured.'[6]

Events were to prove that neither Robertson nor the Indian Army headquarters in Simla had any idea how serious the situation in Mesopotamia was. All other considerations apart, the advance up the Tigris had been started without adequate provision for river transport. A later parliamentary enquiry, the Mesopotamia Commission, would conclude that this 'shortage of transport was fatal to the operations undertaken for the relief of Kut. Large reinforcements could not be moved to the front in time to take part in critical battles . . . Looking at the facts, which from the first must have been apparent to any administrator, military or civilian, who gave a few minutes' consideration to the map and to the conditions in Mesopotamia, the want of foresight and provision for the most fundamental needs of the expedition reflects discredit upon the organising aptitude of all the authorities concerned.'[7] This crippling deficiency meant that Townshend's surrender was in reality unavoidable.

In March 1916, however, the War Office was still confident that the situation could be saved. Kitchener thought it would be useful if disruption were created behind Turkish lines, and accordingly he decided to implement a plan whose very nature demanded the greatest secrecy. He knew that the Turkish élite was not united behind the war effort, and having spent many years in the East he also knew that corruption was endemic in the Turkish Empire. It therefore seemed possible that a large well-placed bribe might in some way relax the Turkish Army's grip on Kut.

There were few Englishmen qualified to carry out such a delicate mission. Kitchener settled on Wyndham Deedes, who had worked for three years with the Turkish Gendarmerie in North Africa and had also spent several months in Constantinople attached to the Turkish Ministry of the Interior. At the beginning of the war Deedes had worked for a time in the Turkish section of Military Intelligence in London, where

Kitchener had been impressed by the range of his knowledge and Turkish contacts. Deedes was now in Cairo, but Kitchener had not lost sight of him. In mid-March, therefore, a secret telegram was sent proposing that Deedes should go to Basra and make suitable overtures.

Deedes was most unwilling to take on such a mission, but Kitchener insisted. On March 18th Deedes noted in his diary: 'Very trying day indeed. Never likely to forget it. Telegrams kept passing between ourselves and London with reference to the question of I going to Basra. If it was a question of buying a Turkish general at Basra, that is a thing they can do on the spot and would not require the assistance of anyone from here.'[8]

As an alternative, Cairo suggested that Kitchener revive Abdul Aziz al Masri's plan for an Arab insurrection in Mesopotamia. This now seemed a natural extension of British policy towards Hussein. Abdul Aziz had attracted a group of Iraqi nationalists to Cairo, including Nuri as-Said, and there was enthusiastic talk of Mesopotamian independence. Deedes's diary noted that if the War Office was 'now prepared to consider the whole question of putting into operation Arab co-operation such as has been proposed to us very often by the Aziz party, and such as we have been trying for months to get the War Office to accept . . . we would get to work so as to see what mutual arrangements could be made.'[9] There would, however, be a price for Arab co-operation. The War Office would have to authorise 'certain concessions *now* to the Arab party, and make certain promises for the future'.[10]

Kitchener decided to follow up this suggestion as well as his own scheme, and McMahon was authorised to approach Abdul Aziz al Masri. Deedes must have been considerably relieved by the decision, since it would excuse him from undertaking the mission. Although he was well qualified for dealing with Turks, others were much better informed about the Arab question. At first Clayton suggested that George Lloyd might be sent, but Kitchener rejected the idea, feeling perhaps that a serving Member of Parliament ought not to be mixed up in such a dubious affair. Instead the choice fell on Lawrence (who later said that he had been chosen because the War Office hoped that Arab co-operation could help at Kut as it had at Erzurum).[11]

There were, moreover, other reasons why it was convenient to send Lawrence to Mesopotamia. A few weeks previously Gertrude Bell had visited India. The Viceroy had suggested that on her way back to Egypt she should call in at Basra, as her specialist knowledge of the Arabs might be of help to the IEF Intelligence Department. Such a visit might also help to establish co-operation in Intelligence work between Mesopotamia and Egypt, under the aegis of the new Arab Bureau. She had therefore arrived in Basra on March 3rd, and after a fortnight wrote: 'other things being equal . . . I think for the moment I had better stay here. I am very busy with the tribal stuff to which otherwise no one would be paying attention . . . If we go forward, as it is possible we may before long – we must go forward or let Kut surrender – we shall get almost immediately into relations with these tribes, and it might be well that I should be on the spot.'[12]

During the two months she had spent in Cairo during the autumn of 1915 she had observed how the Intelligence Department was using aerial photographs as a basis for maps. She must have mentioned this to the Intelligence staff in Mesopotamia, since the authorities in Basra now asked Cairo to send an officer who could give instruction in the new technique. Lawrence, who had been providing liaison between Royal Flying Corps photographers and the Survey of Egypt, was without doubt the best qualified person. At the same time he was given a brief by Clayton to discuss the Arab Bureau and future Intelligence co-operation, matters which Gertrude Bell was pursuing largely on her own initiative. By coincidence she wrote to Lawrence on March 18th: 'I have always thought an exchange of people in the various Intelligence Departments would be an immense advantage and I should think yet more favourably of the scheme if it involved your coming out here.'[13] Before this letter could reach Cairo he had joined her in Basra.

The potential for an Arab insurrection in Mesopotamia had often been discussed in the Cairo Intelligence office, and Gertrude Bell's letters to Lawrence from Basra refer to attempted contacts with Arab leaders behind Turkish lines. In some areas Arab unrest was already a handicap to the Turkish forces. Lawrence later wrote: 'The conditions were ideal for an Arab movement. The people of Nejef and Kerbela, far in the rear of Halil Pasha's army, were in revolt against him. The surviving Arabs in Halil's army were, on his own confession, openly disloyal to Turkey. The tribes of the Hai and Euphrates would have turned our way, had they seen signs of grace in the British. Had we published the promises made to the Sherif . . . and followed it up, enough local fighting men would have joined us to harry the Turkish line of communication between Bagdad and Kut. A few weeks of that, and the enemy would either have been forced to raise the siege and retire, or have themselves suffered investment, outside Kut, nearly as stringent as the investment of

Townshend within it.'[14] This was the kind of situation that Deedes and Clayton thought it might be possible to bring about.

Lawrence had to leave for Mesopotamia before their consultations with Iraqi nationalists in Cairo had been completed. He wrote home: 'I am going away, for a month or six weeks, to consult with some people and suggest certain things. Is this vague enough? I hope to meet Miss Bell shortly, since we are much on the same tack.'[15] However, there was still a good deal of uncertainty about the precise nature of his mission. The al Masri scheme, which appealed to him strongly, would take some time to arrange, since it would involve sending a nationalist political mission to Basra. Lawrence was also charged with Kitchener's secret bribery project, for which £1,000,000 would be available. He left Cairo on March 20th and sailed from Suez two days later on the SS *Royal George*, carrying a letter of introduction from McMahon to Sir Percy Cox:

20.3.1916

My dear Cox,

I send these few lines to introduce Captain Lawrence who is starting today for Mesopotamia under orders from the W.O. to give his services in regard to Arab matters.

He is one of the best of our very able intelligence staff here and has a thorough knowledge of the Arab question in all its bearings.

I feel sure that you will find him of great use. We are very sorry to lose so valuable a man from our staff here.

I hope things are going well on your side. We are anxiously awaiting news of Townshend's relief but have heard nothing for ages.

All is going well here. Please forgive haste.

With best wishes,
Yours ever sincerely,
A. H. McMahon.[16]

By coincidence Aubrey Herbert had recently been put in charge of naval Intelligence in Mesopotamia and the Persian Gulf, and was also in Cairo, on his way to Basra. He wrote to a friend: 'Lawrence has gone down . . . he will get there a week ahead of me. He thinks that he is likely to be out of favour coming from Egypt, which is quite likely. In which case he will do nothing about speaking to P. Z. Cox. But I don't think anything much can be done except from home'.[17]

Everyone in Cairo anticipated Indian objections to the al Masri scheme. After all, in December 1914 Cox had rejected a very similar proposal. On March 21st, therefore, McMahon tried to present the scheme in a form that would be acceptable to the India Office: 'A general movement throughout Arabia must always suffer from lack of organisation and cohesion which, although temporarily inconvenient to us now, renders an Arab union less likely to be a future embarrassment to us, which it might otherwise possibly become . . .

'It remains to enlist the active support of another section – that of the Arab element in the Turkish army . . . It can be best approached through the Arab Society in that army, of which Aziz el Masri and Faruki are influential members and which has already done much work . . . It would now seem wise to send Masri and Faruki to Mesopotamia to get into touch with the army and I would recommend this.

'They however demand for themselves and the Arab military element whom they have to approach some definite assurance of British policy towards Arabia. They consider this essential to the success of any effort to win over the Arab element in the army.

'They would be tolerably content with the assurances already given to the Sherif.'[18]

Clayton and Deedes were already trying to assemble a party of Arabs who could be sent to Mesopotamia. But the task was difficult because Arab nationalists were viewed with extreme suspicion by the Government of India. Specific objections had been raised to al Masri in 1914. On March 22nd, however, after discussions with Lord Kitchener, Grey cabled a guarded approval for sending al Masri and Faroki, adding: 'You can give assurances, if necessary, but you should be very careful not to exceed in any way the limits of the assurances already given to the Shereef.'[19]

On March 24th, two days after learning of the Cairo scheme, the India Office cabled to the Government of India: 'In view of the intention of the Shereef to attempt at once to detach the Arab element from the Turkish army in Arabia and Syria, a corresponding movement is thought desirable in Mesopotamia, and McMahon has been authorised to send Faruki and possibly also el Masri to get into touch with the Turkish army there with this object . . . if you see any objection in the existing circumstances to the despatch of these two persons and especially of the latter telegraph as soon as possible repeating to Sir H. McMahon.'[20] The telegram was copied to Sir Percy Lake at Basra.

In the meantime Deedes and Clayton had been working hard in Cairo. Their progress is indicated by instructions for Lawrence sent on to Basra by Deedes: 'Without going into the details of the various telegrams which have passed between here and the War Office . . . they (W.O.) are apparently quite convinced that the time has come to put the whole scheme into operation . . . I have within the last two or three days had interviews with Azziz, Nuri [as-Said], Faroki, Hassan Khaled and Dr. Shahbander, and, without referring to the particular case now under review, with Sheikh Reshid Riza. In my first interview with Azziz I found him just a little bit difficult. I said that we were not prepared today to do more than give general assurances concerning Arab independence. Azziz then tried to go into details and wished to pin me down to some detailed convention. The following day I saw the Colonel [Clayton] who said "you had better put the matter plainly before them and say that we do not intend to tie ourselves down to any details as to our future relations with such Arab government as is brought into existence in Irak until we have had an opportunity of seeing what the nature of that government is and how far it is in a position to carry out such assurances as it may give us." In a word for your own information please note that we refuse to discuss with this party today any other consideration but a simple *promise* to do all we can to help Arab *independence*. As a result of various meetings it was finally agreed that the party should go off at first available opportunity to join you at Basrah. Such party will probably consist of the following:– Azziz (the War Office were against Azziz going as they are a little bit afraid of him, but we wired back saying that he was essential owing to his influence with Turkish and Arab officers; and please note that Faroki tells me that you need not be afraid of Azziz or of his going to extremes, he is sound enough at the bottom but wants a little checking). 2. will be Nouri. Nouri should help you considerably for as you know he is very moderate; but please note in this connection that he has not got the complete confidence of Azziz. I do not mean to say that Azziz mistrusts him, but . . . he thinks he is rather young and not quite big enough to be fully trusted with a matter of this sort. 3. will be Dr. Shahbander whom the Colonel looks on as our sheet anchor. Hang onto him for all you are worth and work the others as far as possible through him. At least that is my opinion and I am sure you won't mind my giving you this advice.'[21]

Faroki was to remain in Cairo: 'It will be essential to have somebody here to write to your party at Basrah, and as you know Faroki is essential for the correspondence with the Sherif.'[22] Clayton and Deedes also hoped to involve Sayid Taleb, the Iraqi politician who had effectively ruled Basra before the war. With help from Arabs now resident in Egypt he might be put into a co-operative frame of mind.

Lawrence was instructed to contact a number of Arabs in Basra who had been associated with Sayid Taleb. Deedes wrote: 'As regards actually what you can do both now and when the Mission comes, I have no doubt that we or the War Office will be able to give you fuller instructions, but broadly speaking, as far as I can see, it will be a matter of seeing how far such military *co-operation* as the Mission can put at our disposal can be made use of, and (when their proposals have received the approval of the G.O.C.) to do all you can to get the Arab and our own forces to co-operate. We have promised them every possible assistance.

'The most important thing of all (at all events when we are getting into touch and buying people and so on) will be cash. As to arms and so on instructions will no doubt be sent you. Finally the War Office have asked us for the names of, and given permission for the going to Basrah of, any Turkish, Arab and Kurd officers at present in India who we wish to co-operate with us. I am getting a list from our friends and these individuals will I think shortly be joining you at Basrah.'[23]

There had been no immediate response either from Delhi or Basra to the India Office cable about sending al Masri and Faroki to Mesopotamia. Then, on March 30th, General Lake sent an uncompromising refusal to countenance the scheme, evidently after consultations with Sir Percy Cox: 'we feel unable to concur in the deputation either of Farokhi or el Masri to Mesopotamia now.

'The Turks maintain to the fullest extent vigilance in the search for spies, and it is not considered possible that either of the above individuals could themselves pass over from occupied territory to the sphere of the Turkish troops opposed to us on the Tigris or Euphrates, or could be of any practical use to us if they did. From the political standpoint it appears to us that their political views and schemes are much too advanced to be safe pabula for the communities of occupied territories, and their presence in any of the towns of Irak would be in our opinion undesirable and inconvenient. Should it be possible for them to reach by other routes than via the Persian Gulf or Irak the districts in the rear of the Turkish forces now operating against us, there would appear to be no military objection to their attempting such measures as they may think feasible for detaching the Arab element in the Turkish army.

'But in previous attempts made from here to utilise captured Arab officers professing to be able to influence their compatriots in the Turkish ranks they have always eventually been found unwilling or unable to face the practical difficulties and risks involved.'[24] This telegram, addressed to the India Office, was copied to Robertson and to McMahon, and was immediately supported by similar messages from Hardinge and the Secretary of State for India.

In the light of this opposition McMahon had no choice but to abandon the al Masri plan. Deedes noted in his diary: 'it is so obvious that the atmosphere of Basra is *invincible* to anything of this nature that no matter whom we send there, I don't see how they could agree'.[25] McMahon cabled to the Foreign Office about the possible adverse effect of this disappointing outcome on the Arab nationalists in Cairo, and added: 'In point of fact it was not intended that al Masri and others should pass over to Turkish lines.

'It was thought that the presence of one or two prominent and carefully selected members of the Arab party in our ranks would afford the Arab element in the Turkish army a much required guarantee of our unity of interest and good faith, and materially assist in establishing good local relations, the absence of which have been recently complained of by Sir P. Lake.

'At the same time it was fully recognised that once we were agreed as to the end, our agents would have to be given free scope in their choice of means.'[26]

As nobody in Cairo placed much hope in Kitchener's bribery scheme, Clayton, doubtless very irritated by the Anglo-Indian attitude, cabled to London asking that Lawrence should not be retained at Basra any longer than necessary.

In this way the most promising part of Lawrence's mission was abandoned before he set foot in Basra. He remarked obliquely in *Seven Pillars* that co-operation with the Arabs 'was not the way of the directing parties there . . . and till the end of the war the British in Mesopotamia remained substantially an alien force invading enemy territory, with the local people passively neutral or sullenly against them.'[27]

Lake's rejection of the Cairo scheme crossed with a telegram to Basra from Robertson explaining the secret aspects of Lawrence's visit. This contained the first intimation Lake had been given of Kitchener's bribery proposal: 'Most secret and for yourself personally. Captain Lawrence is due at Basra about the 30th March from Egypt to consult with you and if possible purchase one of the Turkish leaders of the Mesopotamian Army, such as Khalil or Negib [Ali Nejib, Khalil's subordinate, was commander of the Turkish forces besieging Kut] so as to facilitate the relief of Townshend. You are authorised to expend for this purpose any sum not exceeding one million pounds. As no suitable native was immediately available Lawrence proceeds alone, but perhaps a suitable go-between can be found in Basra. Subsequently and independently the High Commissioner, Egypt, has suggested to the Foreign Office the utility of negotiating with Arab elements in the Turkish Army with a view to detaching them from the Turks and making them side with the Arab movement. Masri, Dr. Shahbander and another Arab officer will probably be sent to Mesopotamia for this purpose, but may arrive too late to affect Townshend's position. If the opportunity offers you should co-ordinate and make the fullest use of the two efforts. High Commissioner, Egypt, will have informed Masri, or will inform him through you, of the political promises he is authorised to make to the Arab elements in the Turkish Army.'[28]

This telegram was slightly corrupted in transmission: although the words 'million pounds' were discernible, the figure before them was not. Lake immediately cabled back for clarification. As to the secret proposals, he had already rejected the al Masri scheme, and was not optimistic about the prospects for bribery. He wired: 'I will of course give Lawrence every assistance in his task but fear that the limits of Townshend's powers of resistance leave us too little time to get Lawrence in touch with Turkish leaders. Since however Khalil Bey has himself made overtures to Townshend it is possible the latter might be able to square him. Would there be any objection to this course?'[29]

At this time Lake was travelling up the Tigris to the front, and he therefore cabled instructions about Lawrence to Basra. When Lawrence arrived he was first to be introduced to Cox and then sent up river as quickly as possible to the advance headquarters. Lake also instructed Colonel Beach, the head of his Intelligence staff, to radio Townshend about the bribery idea: 'Although the Army Commander sees no reason whatever to doubt the ultimate success of operations for the relief of your force, he wishes to foresee every possible eventuality. Please therefore consider the following matter. Should the Army Commander obtain sanction to expend, say, half a million pounds sterling on purchasing the relief of Kut, could you arrange the matter in personal communication with Khalil Bey?'[30]

Townshend replied: 'Were such a course to become expedient I think negotiations ought to be carried out with Khalil by the Commander of the relieving force and not by me. He is directly in touch with London etc. A Brigadier General should be deputed under flag of truce to meet Khalil. He should know French. He would act for G.O.C. Relief Force who would have to furnish him with a signed guarantee for Khalil's perusal. As Commander of the besieged force I cannot deal satisfactorily with such a matter . . . Nor would it enter my mind to negotiate unless the Army Commander himself were to give me a formal and personal order so to do, when I should assume the Army Commander too had the order direct from the Secretary of State to enter into such *pourparlers*. In the event of another failure of the relief force I do not believe that half a million pounds would be all the Government would have to pay.'[31] By the time this message arrived, the War Office had repeated the defective phrase in Robertson's telegram, authorising any payment up to £1,000,000.

Lawrence did not reach Basra until the evening of April 5th (for three days every ship arriving there had been boarded in search of him). At British headquarters he found Gertrude Bell and also Campbell Thompson, who had been his companion at Jerablus in 1911.[32] He spent three days in Basra, working with Gertrude Bell for part of the time. It is unlikely, however, that she knew of his secret instructions. She wrote to her family on April 9th: 'This week has been greatly enlivened by the appearance of Mr. Lawrence, sent out as liaison officer from Egypt. We have had great talks and made vast schemes for the government of the universe.'[33]

Lawrence's chief priority in Basra was to see Sir Percy Cox. He was immediately told that the al Masri scheme was dead, but he found Cox rather more receptive to his ideas than had been feared. In particular, Cox shared the view that more co-operation was needed in British policy towards the Arabs. He suggested a conference between representatives from Egypt, Mesopotamia, India, and Aden, with the purpose of harmonising the principles of action in the Middle East, and evolving a uniform policy. Lawrence reported: 'Cox disassociates himself from India very clearly; he does not know how Cairene he is. He favours the hoisting at Bagdad of the British flag and Arab flag together, but until peace is declared is against a definite declaration that we will not annex Bagdad for fear of tying our hands. He can be brought round on this point as the [local] people at Basra are getting tired of us, and the anticipation of something better when peace comes would prevent Bagdad going the same way, should the army perhaps want formal annexation of all conquests.

'Cox is entirely ignorant of the Arab Societies and of Turkish politics . . . He does not understand our ideas but is very open and will change his mind as required.

'His complaint of Cairo is that Mesopotamia was mentioned to the Sherif. I think that I have put this right.

'He is against the introduction of Arab officers as he thinks that we wish to rid Egypt of some gas-bags who are impatient there. I tried to explain, but I feel sure he will not take any step involving a policy without a lead from England.'[34]

Lawrence had not yet received the letter written by Deedes on March 26th, and at first he was uncertain what to do. As Cox wrote to Beach a few days later: 'The only instructions he had were to report himself to Headquarters here and he brought a demi-official introduction to me from Sir Henry McMahon . . . He himself understood that he had been sent here in order to give assistance . . . in the carrying out of a certain project which, I understand, was recently suggested to the Army Commander in a telegram from the War Office. I have not actually seen this telegram but have been told roughly the purport of it . . . As Lawrence had no definite instructions and I had had no communication with you on the subject, and as no one at General Headquarters had any authority to give him detailed instructions, I telegraphed to you . . . Your reply only directed him, after seeing myself and More [a member of the Military Intelligence Staff in Basra], and obtaining from him an Arab prisoner officer on parole, to join H.Q. at once.'[35]

Cox was extremely perturbed by the bribery proposal, and wished to dissociate himself from it: 'The project in view is pretty sure to become known sooner or later especially if it proves unsuccessful and I cannot afford as a Political Officer of the Government of India to be identified with it.

'I explained the above point of view to Captain Lawrence and informed him that I was ready to give to Captain More the names of the individuals who might be ready to co-operate, and that Captain More could send for them to his private house where Lawrence could interview them. The latter is of opinion, and I think he is probably right, that to expect to bring off the coup by sending an Arab prisoner on parole across to the Turkish lines . . . is out of the question. His idea when coming here was to utilise Seyyid Talib (which is out of the question as he is in Madras), or one of his former confederates of whom there are two or three in Basrah. He has seen them at More's house . . . and without telling them precisely what they were wanted for he has had long talks with both of them and invited them to co-operate by getting into touch with certain of the Turkish commanders; but both of them . . . have failed to come to the scratch on the ground that the risks are too great. There is no one else now here . . . whom it would be in the least possible to induce to take on the business. Had either . . . agreed . . . to co-operate it was Lawrence's intention to take him up with him to [advance] H.Q. and not discuss the specific project until he reached there. As things are, however, he proposes to go up without anyone just to see you in accordance with instructions.

'From Sir Henry McMahon's letter attached it would appear that Lawrence is intended to remain here, and if he did I should think he would be a very valuable addition to the Intelligence Staff; but he did not understand this at all and came under the impression that he was intended simply to undertake this business if necessary and see us all here from the liaison point of view, and then return.'[36]

Lawrence was not at all impressed by the Arabs he had met, and cabled to Clayton: 'I have been looking up the pan-Arab party . . . It is about twelve strong. Formerly consisted of Sayed Taleb and some jackals.

'The other Basra people are either from Nejd, interested in Central Arabia only and to be classed with Arabia politically, or peasants who are interested in date palms or Persians. There is no Arab sentiment and for us the place is negligible. This partly explains Cox's limitations. He, however, admits that Bagdad stands on a different footing and should not be entered until policy has been determined on.'[37]

Lawrence must have been in considerable doubt about the value of remaining in Mesopotamia when he left Basra on April 9th to meet General Lake. The journey by river steamer up the Tigris took six days. When he arrived he found the headquarters staff 'living in a steamer with good awnings and a saloon!'[38] Senior officers who already knew the nature of his mission made no secret of their disgust. Lake himself saw little hope of relieving Kut in time to save Townshend's force, but was not yet reconciled to the idea of negotiating with the Turks. He had ordered a final relief attempt.

The circumstances of Lake's first meeting with Lawrence could hardly have been worse, but after their discussions he sent Robertson a résumé

of the position which showed an awakening interest in the Arabs behind
Turkish lines. In the immediate future, however, there seemed little
prospect of carrying out the bribery scheme, nor even a means to attempt
it: 'The only channel which has appeared to give any prospect of being
found practicable is the employment of Sayid Talib, late Nakib of Basra.
Lawrence on his way here through Basra discreetly sounded Suleiman
Feizi, who is a former confidential agent of Talib's, and also sounded
another of Talib's old entourage, but found that both were too nervous to
give any prospect of their acting by themselves. Neither they nor any of
the prisoners of war or deserters who are now in our charge are suitable
for employment as intermediaries, for they are not men of sufficient
standing, and no Turkish general would dare entertain such an offer if it
reached him through an unsubstantial individual . . . Finally neither
Khalil's personality nor Ali Nejib's opportunities at this late hour in my
opinion give the slightest hope of the success of the overtures suggested,
and their failure would be calamitous to our prestige.

'I propose nevertheless to avail myself of the services of Captain
Lawrence for a short time for liaison purposes as affecting Egypt and
Mesopotamia, and for work in connection with any opportunity that may
arise for alienating from the Turks any likely Arab elements in the
Turkish Army. In this latter connection, please instruct me definitely as to
the political promises which Masri was to be authorised to make to the
Arab soldiery . . . and inform me as to whether such promises are still
permissible.'[39]

There was too little time for any such initiative to help Townshend,
and during the ensuing days all thoughts were concentrated on the last
attempts at relief. The period of waiting was miserable, not least for
Lawrence who had caught a fever. The marshy region beside the Tigris
was very unhealthy in the sweltering heat and the air was alive with
disease-carrying insects.

On April 22nd the relieving force under General Gorringe was heavily
defeated. Lake cabled despondently to London: 'Gorringe considers that
the troops have, for the present, reached the limit of their offensive
powers, and that they are not capable of further effort without two or three
days' rest. They have been engaged continuously since 5th April, fighting
the enemy and floods, and have in this period incurred 9,700 casualties,
which represents 25 per cent of his effective fighting force. We are still
twelve miles from Kut on the right bank and fifteen miles on the left bank.
Floods on either flank limit our power of manoeuvre, and each attack,

without several days of artillery preparation which our time limit precludes, is costly. The enemy's losses are estimated since the 5th as approximately equal to our own, but he continues to retrench each position taken.'[40]

Lake promised that Gorringe would make one further effort before Townshend's food ran out, but hardly anyone still thought that a relief was possible. Townshend himself radioed to Lake: 'The news . . . is very bad and the facts must be faced . . . Gorringe . . . has now been repulsed a second time, I suppose with heavy losses . . . the 29th is my extreme limit of resistance . . . therefore, short of a miracle, he will not be able to relieve me, and there are no miracles in war. Therefore, I think that you should see if Khalil will not allow my garrison to go down and join your force . . . Kut being given up to the Turks. These would be perfectly honourable terms . . . I expect that to get Khalil to agree will cost some money, but it would be well worth it; besides, the Turks cannot feed my force . . . They have not enough ships to take it to Bagdad, and if it had to march, the force would all die, both from weakness and Arab bullets . . . In three or four days the men will be so weak as to be incapable of all exertion, and such are the stenches in Kut that I fear pestilence at any time.'[41]

Lake forwarded this message to London, with the comment: 'Neither Gorringe nor his senior divisional commander are sanguine of success, owing to the physical and moral condition of the troops . . . and owing to the undoubtedly fine fighting qualities of the troops who are now opposed to us.'[42] Gorringe was planning a last attack, but 'if this effort fails I request that I may be authorised to open up negotiations on the lines suggested'.[43]

On the evening of the 24th a river steamer, the *Julnar*, was sent up river towards Kut laden with 270 tons of supplies. The risks of this desperate attempt to run the Turkish blockade were all too obvious, and every man in the crew was a volunteer. If the boat got through, Townshend's force would be able to hold out for another month. The following morning, however, a reconnaissance plane sighted the *Julnar* aground just eight miles short of the beleaguered town.

With this loss, all hopes of saving Kut were at an end. Colonel Beach asked Lawrence to be ready if needed to assist in Townshend's surrender negotiations. He would be joined by Aubrey Herbert, who was now also at Lake's advance headquarters. Herbert was fluent in Turkish and Arabic as well as French, the language of international diplomacy. He had met Khalil and many other Turkish leaders in Constantinople before the war.

At about midnight on April 25th a message came from Kitchener himself, discouraging any further attempt to relieve Kut; the previous efforts had already cost 23,000 casualties. He was, however, optimistic about the prospects for bargaining with the Turks: 'You will not forget in negotiating that the enemy has suffered heavy punishment . . . he has probably very small supplies of food and ammunition, and that the Russians are pressing east of Baghdad and in the Caucasus. As you are aware ample funds are at your disposal for the purpose of negotiations. These and other factors should greatly assist in getting the terms we want.'[44]

In the early hours of the morning Lake transmitted Kitchener's instructions to Townshend, authorising him to start negotiations and to offer up to £1,000,000 if necessary. Lake said that Lawrence and Herbert, who were specially qualified for such diplomacy, would be available if required. Accordingly, on the morning of April 26th, Townshend sent messages to both Khalil and Ali Nejib, asking for an armistice and ten days' food to keep those in the town alive while arangements for surrender were made. He also asked permission for Lawrence and Herbert to join him. In his letter to Khalil, Townshend set out his hopes for an honourable release, citing the same historical precedents he had given Lake on March 10th. He asked that his men might be allowed to withdraw with their arms to Amara and then leave for India, pointing out that the Turks had neither food for his troops nor transport to take them to Baghdad. The men would be unable to march there in their present weakened state.

Khalil replied that evening, and it was agreed that he would meet Townshend on the river the following day. Before setting out, Townshend radioed to Lake: 'I am to meet Khalil about 10 a.m. I hope to arrange satisfactory preliminaries i.e. six days' armistice – you to send up food at once – and I hope to arrive at a rough understanding that we are to go free. I shall also propose that Khalil negotiates with your headquarters for regulating details etc. It is impossible to do so here. Had this begun at your headquarters yesterday food would have been arriving by now. I am ill in body and in mind which is not to be surprised at . . . I have had my share of responsibility and I consider that you should conduct these negotiations.'[45]

This was followed three hours later by an account of Townshend's meeting with Khalil: 'At first although extremely nice he declined to hold out hopes of anything but unconditional surrender followed by captivity.

After I had talked with him for about half an hour and talked of money he promised me that I could certainly have some grounds for hope of better terms, but that he must communicate with Enver [one of the ruling triumvirate in Constantinople].'[46] As a condition for any further negotiation, however, Khalil had demanded that Townshend's force should move out of Kut into a camp, for which tents would be provided. Only afterwards would the cargo of food from the *Julnar* be released. Townshend had replied that he could not leave Kut without consulting Lake. His report continued: 'You see how all these details keep arising to delay matters, and I suggested to him that negotiations should be entered upon by you down there. He is willing to send a deputy if you ask him, so I think you should start at once, especially as I have no knowledge of international law . . . I can see no use in moving out into camp from any point of view, even that of enabling the Turks to proclaim success.

'My sick and wounded certainly cannot be moved except in a steamer. My guns it seems to me should be destroyed before I move, and I can take no baggage or kit, surrounded as we are by water. Khalil should be asked to wire Enver at once to ask if, in the event of his getting our forty guns and £1,000,000, he can let us go free to India, for he refuses to consider our remaining in Mesopotamia.

'We could there liberate an equal number of combatants in India and Egypt.

'Please wire back . . . at once so that I can answer Khalil this afternoon. I shall have no food in two days.'[47]

Lake replied that unless Khalil's attitude changed there seemed little hope of reaching any terms other than unconditional surrender. If the Turks could be persuaded to allow Townshend's garrison to leave for India on parole, he could offer them his guns, the money, and possibly an exchange of prisoners. However, if Khalil insisted that the force should move out of Kut into a camp, Townshend must destroy his guns and useful stores, and also try to block the river by sinking vessels in it. Protection should be sought for the Arab civilian population in the town.

Lake argued that transferring the negotiations to his headquarters would cause further delay, and it would therefore be better for Townshend to complete the preliminaries at any rate. He again offered to send Herbert, Lawrence, and Colonel Beach.

That evening Townshend radioed again, telling Lake that a Turkish ceasefire was now in force. He concluded: 'I do not see how I could possibly shift all my troops out of the town quarters and the dug-outs in the defences with their accumulated baggage. The men cannot carry it and cannot march, and to turn them on to necessary works in a camp would be cruel. Besides Khalil cannot possibly have enough tents, and the sick and wounded could not possibly be moved. Then, supposing he had enough steamers to take these troops to Baghdad, you can imagine the arrival there – no proper quarters – the condition of the sick and wounded. It would be a real drama and I hope in the cause of humanity you will be firm to let us come away in our own ships to India, paroled if necessary. If we have to go up river instead seventy-five per cent at least would die.'[48]

Aubrey Herbert, who kept a diary throughout his stay at advance headquarters, noted the general despondency. On April 28th he wrote: 'For the last two days I have been standing by to go to Kut, constantly dressing in hot puttees and then undressing. A wave of heat has come and the air is black with flies . . . These are the things that we have to bargain with, Townshend's guns, exchange of Turkish prisoners, and another thing [the money]. Home orders are that the operations of this [relief] force are not to be reckoned as a bargaining asset. We are not to retire because of Kut, or to save Townshend . . . Yesterday morning I talked to Lake . . . I said it was quite clear to me that the Turks would procrastinate, if it was only from force of habit, and that the end of that meant un-conditional surrender . . . Townshend is very anxious that we should negotiate from this side. I think it ought to come from him. He has made a desperately gallant fight of it, and his position has not been taken. Lack of food makes him surrender, not force of arms. This [relief] force has been defeated by the Turks. But he evidently fears that he is going to be blamed whatever happens and wants us to do it from here'.[49]

Townshend again wrote to Khalil appealing for something better than unconditional surrender; otherwise he would destroy his guns, and there would be no further offer of payment. If Khalil would guarantee his force release on parole and send food from the *Julnar*, Townshend would move the fit men into a camp, leaving only the sick and wounded in Kut. He ended: 'If you give me the guarantee I ask details could be arranged later between your delegates and my own. That they may be settled as speedily as possible I would ask you to be so good as to give a safe conduct for three officers of Sir Percy Lake's Headquarter Staff, namely, Colonel Beach, Captain Herbert and Captain Lawrence to come up here by steamer and act as my delegates.'[50]

Khalil himself might have been willing to accept the broad lines of Townshend's offer, but Enver, the ultimate authority, refused to countenance it. Enver's reply, which Khalil passed to Townshend, read: 'Upon one single condition, namely, that he will hand over to us everything in Kut . . . His Excellency General Townshend himself, only with his personal effects and his sword, may go whither he will, but on condition that he gives his word of honour never during the whole continuance of this war to fight against Turkey and her Allies. Should he refuse this offer, which is final, break off negotiations and carry out your military duty'.[51] Thus the offer of money was haughtily disdained: Enver, whose corruption was infamous, knew well enough the propaganda value of refusing it. Stories about the bribery attempt were now circulated by Turkey to the world's press, and only the strictest censorship prevented their appearing in Britain.

This reply was transmitted to Lake during the evening of April 28th; Townshend stated that his duty was clearly to reject the offer of personal freedom. Later, he sent a second message: 'I would suggest as a last resource, if the Government wish to save the lives of quite forty or fifty per cent of my force, to offer Khalil two millions and an equal number of Turkish combatants to let us be sent to India . . . Khalil is at his headquarters near you. Why not let Beach and Aubrey Herbert negotiate this? Enver probably wants to announce a big victory that Kut has fallen. He may well be open to reason afterwards. This comes of negotiating with starvation at the gate, *vide* my [message] of March 10th' (see pp. 254-5 above).[52]

Lake telegraphed to London asking for permission to offer as much as £2,000,000. He told Townshend he had passed on the request, but stressed that there seemed few grounds for hope. Beach, Herbert and Lawrence would try to reach Khalil's headquarters on the following day in order to negotiate. However, if the Turks remained obdurate, Townshend should destroy his guns, stores and wireless, attempt to block the river, and then surrender.

That night Townshend recognised that his troops had passed their limit of endurance. At 6 a.m. on April 29th he sent a letter telling Khalil that the condition of his men now obliged him to surrender. He pointed out once again that it would be best for the Turks not to encumber themselves with the sick and wounded. He then destroyed his guns. Just before midday he telegraphed news of the surrender arrangements to Lake, and not long afterwards his radio operator reported that a Turkish force was seen to be approaching Kut. Shortly after 1 p.m. there was a last message: 'To all ships and stations from Kut. Good-bye and good luck to all.'[53]

In ignorance of these developments, Beach, Herbert and Lawrence had prepared themselves early that morning to cross into Turkish lines. Herbert recorded in his diary: 'Beach, Lawrence and I went out of the trenches with a white flag and walked a couple of hundred yards or so ahead, where we waited, with an unpleasant battlefield smell round us. It was all a plain, with the river to the north, and the place crawling with huge black beetles and singing flies, that had both been feeding on the dead.'[54] After a while the Turks sent a party to find out what was wanted, and Herbert explained that Beach had a letter for Khalil that must be delivered personally. This information was passed back to the Turkish lines, and the group remained in no-man's-land for several hours waiting for a decision. Finally Beach agreed to hand over the letter provided his party was taken to see Khalil. They were then led blindfold through the enemy lines, first on foot and later on horseback. Lawrence had hurt his knee and had to walk the whole way. The discussions with Khalil began before he arrived.

Lawrence's role was now a minor one; the senior officer present was Colonel Beach, who alone could take responsibility for any terms that were put forward on the British side. Lawrence and Aubrey Herbert were of equal rank, but Herbert was much better qualified for these negotiations. The talks were held largely in French, which Beach could not easily follow. Herbert did most of the talking, and Beach later wrote that 'any success we had is all due to him.'[55]

Now that Townshend had surrendered, both the secret missions for which Lawrence had been sent to Mesopotamia were pointless. No authorisation to increase the British financial offer to £2,000,000 had been received from London by the time Beach's party had set out for the Turkish lines, but in any case it would have made no difference given Enver's definite refusal. (Permission had in fact been given, but the telegram from London did not reach Lake's headquarters until 5.50 p.m. that afternoon, and there was no means of passing the message to Beach.)

Khalil had already accepted the principle of exchanging Townshend's sick and injured for healthy Turks in British prison camps. When Beach tried to obtain an agreement covering all the men, Khalil said he would again refer the matter to Enver, but offered little hope. As Townshend had now destroyed the artillery at Kut, Herbert's negotiating position was considerably weakened, but the question of money was delicately raised: 'I said that the third condition we had offered was financial support for the civilians of Kut. I said we had offered one or two millions, purposely adding on one million on my own. This he brushed aside'.[56] Khalil asked for river steamers to transport the healthy men from Kut up to Baghdad, promising to return the boats afterwards. Beach had to refuse this request, even though he knew that a march to Baghdad would be fatal to many of Townshend's men. Lake had too few river craft for his own supplies, and had already lost the *Julnar*. Khalil for his part refused to give any guarantees concerning the fate of the Arab population in Kut. After a time, according to Herbert's diary, Khalil 'yawned, I thought more rudely than negligently, and I said the heat made us all sleepy. He apologised and said he had had much work to do . . . We ended. I told him that we admired his name as a soldier and his chivalry, and that we thought the Turks clean and splendid fighters. He answered with appropriate compliments, and we said goodbye to him'.[57]

Khalil offered hospitality for the night since it was too late to go back to the British lines. Lawrence noted: 'they gave us a most excellent dinner in Turkish style – which was a novelty to Colonel Beach, but pleased Aubrey and myself.'[58] Beach enjoyed the food, but was disconcerted by Turkish customs. He wrote home: 'Dinner – jolly good – Turk of course. Only snag is you've a spoon and fork but no plate. So you have to dive your spoon into a dish for *each mouthful*, which is embarrassing and I didn't like it. But the food was good.'[59]

During the evening Beach decided to ask whether Herbert could stay behind and act as a liaison officer in Kut. He also hoped that Lawrence and himself would be allowed to come up with the steamers sent to fetch the wounded. If so, it might be possible to get a larger number of men counted among the sick. Herbert 'dictated a letter in French to Lawrence, asking [Khalil] for permission for me to stay . . . How Lawrence wrote the letter I can't think. The whole place was one smother of small flies, attracted by the candle. They put it out three times. Beach and I kept them off Lawrence while he wrote. We got an answer at about two in the morning. Khalil said that it was not necessary.'[60]

In the early dawn the British party set off back to their own lines. For much of the way they were not blindfolded, and afterwards Beach wrote: 'One melancholy satisfaction I had out of it was that what I saw of the Turkish force from inside convinced me of their wellbeing, and of the hopeless task it would have been for us to have another try at barging through with our present force. Of course one's always taught that when you've had the worst knock yourself is the time to keep on, because the enemy is probably in as bad or worse case. So one had visions of having given it up when just one more push would have got us in! But those visions, as I say, were quite swept away, which is in its way satisfactory.'[61] His letter home probably summarised all their thoughts: 'It was a mighty interesting business . . . but a very sad one, and of course anxious too. A sad bit of history to have been mixed up with – I suppose the biggest British surrender there's ever been. But what can we do? There was nothing else for it.'[62]

Beach and Lawrence returned to Lake's headquarters. Later that day Beach tried to go up to Kut on one of the boats sent to collect the sick, but the Turks refused to let him. Finally, on May 2nd, Lake's headquarters steamer set off down-river for Basra, with Lawrence and Beach on board.

Lawrence stayed in Basra for several days, discussing Intelligence matters in considerable detail with both Beach and More. He also visited the various departments involved with map production, and advised them on the use of aerial photography.

It was agreed that Gertrude Bell would stay on, at any rate for the time being, as Mesopotamian correspondent of the Arab Bureau. This was confirmed a few days later in a telegram from General Lake to the Government of India: 'You are, I think, aware that Captain Lawrence was recently deputed here temporarily from Egypt in connection with certain projects of which the Arab Bureau was one . . . In view of the modified aspect in which the institution is presented to us by Lawrence, I propose that Miss Gertrude Bell . . . should act as corresponding officer for Mesopotamia . . . Cox and Lawrence who discussed the suggestion are of opinion that Miss Bell is well qualified for the task and her assumption of duties would be agreeable to Cairo and ourselves.'[63] Thus Gertrude Bell's temporary visit to Mesopotamia became permanent. She was destined to achieve great distinction there, both during and after the war.

Lawrence left Basra on board the troopship *Nitonian* on May 11th, and during the voyage back to Egypt he wrote a long report about the situation in Mesopotamia. By chance Webb Gillman, the general sent out by the War Office to investigate the IEF difficulties, was travelling on the same ship. The two had also been at Lake's advance headquarters together and despite the difference in rank they got on well. Lawrence wrote: 'He is from near Cork and excellent company but we sit on the deck and write reports and notes all day'.[64] During the two weeks they spent together Gillman discussed 'every page' of Lawrence's report, while drafting his own submission to the War Office.[65]

Lawrence reached Suez at midnight on May 25th and the following afternoon he was back at the Intelligence Office in Cairo. His comments on the Anglo-Indian performance in Mesopotamia were very critical. Clayton wrote: 'Lawrence's account of Kut is sad hearing. Mismanagement on all sides and muddle of the worst – the Indian Government seem to have come out of it very badly. One gathers from him that (1) Townshend should never have been placed in such a position (2) that he should have been extricated with reasonable ease. However I suppose that the real truth will appear some day.'[66]

Lawrence's written report to Clayton about the state of affairs in Mesopotamia contained many constructive recommendations; but while it spoke highly of some officers it was in parts very damning. It was never circulated in its original form. Colonel Stirling, one of his seniors in Military Intelligence, recalled the unease when General Murray asked to see it. Lawrence had 'spared no one in his criticisms. He criticised the quality of the stones used for lithographing, the system of berthing barges alongside the quays, the inefficiency of the cranes for handling stores, the want of adequate medical stores, the blindness of the medical authorities and their want of imagination as to their probable ultimate requirements. And, horror of horrors, he criticised the Higher Command and the conduct of the campaign in general!

'The Commander-in-Chief, General Sir Archibald Murray, who was a distinguished soldier of the old school, expressed a desire to see the report. There was consternation that night in the General Staff, for we were convinced that, if he were to read it, apoplexy would be the result and we should lose our C-in-C. Hurriedly therefore, we sat down and bowdlerised the report until we considered it fit to be put before his professional eye! Lawrence, however, was abundantly right in most of his criticisms'.[67] There has been a good deal of speculation about the content of this document, and since it contains evidence of Lawrence's competence in Intelligence and mapping, sections dealing with these topics are reproduced in Appendix III.

At the drama of Kut, Lawrence was a helpless spectator, sharing in the despondency at Lake's headquarters as Townshend's messages charted each step towards the inevitable surrender. It has been suggested that he was universally disliked by the Anglo-Indian officials he met. The records show, however, that both Cox and Lake recognised his ability. Colonel Beach, writing home about the mission to Khalil, wrote: 'My other pal was a little man called Lawrence – archaeologist. Captain General Staff "for the war" – from Egypt Intelligence. Knows Turkey and Asia well. Jolly good fellow.'[68] For his part, Lawrence observed and was shocked by the attitude of Indian Army officers towards their native Indian troops and the indigenous Arabs of Iraq. The visit to Mesopotamia left him with a strong distaste for the Anglo-Indian style of administration. The spectacle of European imperialism at work strengthened his conviction that the Arabs should be given self-determination. He would later oppose sending European troops to the Hejaz, and would do his utmost to keep British officers with strongly imperialist views away from the Arab Revolt.

He rejected not merely the philosophy of imperialism, but also its cost. After the war, looking back on his experiences in Mesopotamia, he was to write: 'We pay for these things too much in honour and in innocent lives. I went up the Tigris with one hundred Devon Territorials, young, clean, delightful fellows, full of the power of happiness and of making women and children glad. By them one saw vividly how great it was to be their kin, and English. And we were casting them by thousands into the fire to the worst of deaths, not to win the war but that the corn and rice and oil of Mesopotamia might be ours. The only need was to defeat our enemies (Turkey among them) . . . All our subject provinces to me were not worth one dead Englishman.'[69]

In all, 1,136 sick and wounded men from the Kut garrison were exchanged in May 1916, and a further 345 three months later. Nearly twelve thousand soldiers and non-combatants passed into captivity. The great majority of these men were Indian. As Townshend had foretold, barely a quarter ever returned.

CHAPTER 14

The Revolt Begins
May – September 1916

SHORTLY before arriving back in Egypt, Lawrence had written to his family: 'I expect to find letters and papers knee-deep in Cairo when I return. The accumulation of two months' business and pleasure will be awful to see'.[1] He quickly discovered that a great deal had taken place during his ten-week absence.

For one thing, there had been a major change in organisation. On March 21st it had been agreed that the small branch of Military Intelligence remaining in Cairo under Clayton's supervision would specialise in political work relating to the Near East. Four days later Hogarth had returned to Egypt, temporarily seconded to Clayton's staff to help set up the new Arab Bureau. For this purpose he took three rooms in the Savoy Hotel no longer required by Military Intelligence.

The Bureau was not yet properly funded and there was no money to pay for the staff it needed. Fortunately much of its work was indistinguishable from that carried out by the specialist Intelligence officers remaining with Clayton, and the Bureau began to function with their help. While the arrangement was satisfactory at this early stage, there was scope for contention as the Arab Bureau workload increased. Although Clayton was in charge of both the Bureau and Cairo Military Intelligence, the former was controlled by the Foreign Office and answerable to McMahon, while the latter was part of the Egyptian Expeditionary Force headquarters staff. It would eventually dawn on GHQ that Intelligence officers were spending a large part of their time working for the High Commission. Lawrence, however, was delighted with a situation which allowed him to give much of his time to Arab affairs.

Hogarth had also brought news of the Anglo-French negotiations. Unlike anyone in Egypt, he had seen the Sykes-Picot memorandum of January 5th. He was concerned about a possible conflict in British commitments and set about drawing up a memorandum which gave the history of correspondence between Hussein and the British officials in Cairo, spelling out precisely what had been promised, and what had not.

On April 14th the long silence from London over Syria was finally broken. Clayton received an extraordinary telegram from Sykes, discussing isolated details of the Anglo-French agreement in terms which meant little to anyone ignorant of the full text. It was not even clear what status the proposals had, although Sykes spoke of the agreement being 'finally made about the 24th' of April.[2] The telegram said enough, however, to suggest that the terms fell far short of Arab hopes. Worse still, Sykes mentioned that Picot might shortly arrive in Cairo for direct talks with the nationalists and warned that: 'The French attitude in regard to the Arabs at present is not sufficiently conciliatory for Picot to go to Egypt without danger. If he gets there with matters in the present posture, Arab Anglophiles and Maronites will begin to quarrel and gossip, and you will have a cloud of intrigue confusing your dealings with the Sherif.'[3]

Sykes argued that this situation could be avoided by further diplomacy in London. He suggested that a sufficient basis for Franco-Arab agreement could be established if France would give to the independent Arab state (whose nature was not defined in the telegram) a port on the Syrian coast. Sykes wanted to forestall direct negotiations on this point in Cairo: 'In my mind it is essential that the French should have become practical before Picot goes to Egypt. I advise therefore the following procedure which I have got Picot's approval of i.e. that you send here to London two Arab officers representative of the intellectual Syrian Moslem Arab mind, that when I have got their point of view . . . I compare it with Picot's, that when Picot has been got into the right frame of mind I bring them together and they have an informal talk, Picot then gets Paris to make a concession of the principle of an Arab state outlet on the Syrian littoral . . . The position is then clear, Picot can proceed to Egypt to act as an adviser to Defrance, Sir Henry conducting negotiations with the Sherif. The fundamental danger will then be removed of an absolute split on principle. Bargaining on details is natural to Arabs and French.'[4]

It is clear from other documents that Sykes had no intention of revealing the Anglo-French proposals to the Arabs.[5] However, this was not the impression given by his inept telegram to Cairo. Assisted by Hogarth, the British staff there were able to grasp the essentials of the deal that was now being reached, and they were extremely worried.

In the autumn of 1915 it had seemed to the Cairo staff that an agreement with France over Syria would be necessary in order to proceed with Anglo-Arab negotiations. Then, however, the Sherif had unexpectedly set aside the territorial issue for the duration of the war. It seemed pointless to raise the question of Syria now, because successive Turkish measures against the nationalists had made a northern rising most improbable. Hussein, for his part, was on the point of declaring a revolt in the Hejaz, and the immediate effect of reopening territorial discussions would be to postpone this action. The wisest course was surely to drop the question of Syria for the time being.

In a series of telegrams to London, McMahon and Clayton asked for clarification and argued that there was no longer need for a precise formulation. Clayton cabled to Sykes on April 20th: 'Any agreement on main principles between the Allies is all to the good, but to divulge it at present and to insist on any particular programme would I am convinced be to raise considerable feeling, to strengthen Arab-Turkish *rapprochement*, and possibly to affect injuriously the political and military situation of the Allies in Turkey at a moment when the true attitude of the Arabs is not quite clear.

'In view of the hoped-for development of war on the part of the Shereef as a result of our past negotiations with him, I feel it would be most impolitic to raise now with the Arabs the Syrian question which is quiescent for the moment.'[6]

As to the scheme for sending two representative Syrians to London, Clayton merely remarked: 'I do not consider the presence in London of any Arab officers with whom we are at present in touch would in any way assist you.'[7] His contemporary notes show that he saw no possibility of agreement between Picot and Syrian representatives, and felt that a confrontation was to be avoided, whether in Cairo or in London. He agreed wholeheartedly with Sykes that it would be undesirable for Picot to come to Egypt.

Two days later McMahon cabled the Foreign Office, asking for more information: 'I confess to being somewhat in the dark as to how matters stand, and I am unaware whether the proposals outlined by Sir M. Sykes have received the approval of the three Governments concerned, or whether they are merely suggestions as a result of his and Picot's conversations in Petrograd'.[8] McMahon advised against raising the question of Syria with the Arabs at this moment, but added: 'a satisfactory understanding on the subject between the Allies would be all to the good, and facilitate subsequent negotiations, and I trust I may be kept informed of the various stages to which that understanding may arrive.'[9] In a dispatch which reached London on April 28th, McMahon again stressed the advantage of holding back: 'Realising that the present stage of military operations in the Ottoman Empire is transitional, but daily declaring itself more and more in our favour, we have made every attempt to avoid definite commitments for the future . . . the longer a final pro-gramme is postponed the stronger becomes our position as negotiators, and the more reasonable will the [Arabs] be likely to show themselves towards our views.'[10]

These messages met with a cool reception in London, not least because they also referred to efforts made in Cairo by Wyndham Deedes to negotiate with opposition parties in Turkey. The Sykes-Picot Agreement gave Constantinople and the Dardanelles to Russia, and therefore ruled out any hope of co-operation between Britain and disaffected Turks.[11] Although McMahon's position was blameless he became the subject of irritated minutes in Foreign Office files. Launcelot Oliphant, for example, noted against one of his telegrams: 'I venture to think that this . . . is by no means satisfactory. It shows that there is considerable confusion in Sir H. McMahon's mind, and that matters are merely drifting.'[12]

Sykes was now back in London and trying to establish a new position of influence for himself in Middle Eastern affairs. He urged that to clarify the situation he should meet Picot and Clayton at the earliest opportunity somewhere in Europe. It is perhaps significant that he did not suggest a meeting with McMahon. Several of McMahon's telegrams had been an embarrassment to his Anglo-French negotiations, and from this time on Sykes took every opportunity to criticise the High Commissioner. He seems to have assumed that Clayton and McMahon were not in agreement (whereas in reality the content of McMahon's messages closely followed Clayton's memoranda). Some weeks later Sykes would vehemently denounce McMahon in front of the War Committee and urge his re-placement.[13]

It was not until April 24th that Sir Arthur Nicolson decided to send the Sykes-Picot text to Cairo. His intention was evidently to put a stop to any further protests or diplomatic initiatives. He minuted: 'I am afraid that the whole subject is becoming entangled. We, Russia and France are now quite clear and in accord as to our interests and aspirations in the Ottoman Empire . . . I think that we should let Sir H. McMahon fully know the present position of our arrangements . . . as regards Asiatic Turkey'.[14] The Sykes-Picot Agreement was finally transmitted to Egypt on April 27th, but Cairo was not at this stage told that the concessions to Arab nationalism would lapse unless Hussein's forces took the northern cities of Damascus, Homs, Hama and Aleppo.

Private reactions in Cairo to news of Sykes-Picot can be judged from Deedes's diary: 'Yesterday a reply came . . . setting out in the full glare of day the Franco-Russian agreement with ourselves . . . These arrangements of course definitely lose our adherence from the Arab, Syrian and other Turkish opposition parties . . . So much, therefore, for all my attempts to collect and blend the various movements here in Cairo. At the same time, never having been given a lead as to what the Home Government wished, it has been difficult to know how to act.'[15]

Hogarth sent a long commentary on the terms to Captain Hall, noting that 'the conclusion of this Agreement is of no immediate service to our Arab policy as pursued here, and will only not be a grave disadvantage if, for some time to come, it is kept strictly secret.'[16] He expressed the hope, no doubt general in Cairo, that Sykes-Picot would be 'regarded by our Government now as a purely opportunist measure, with the mental reservation that it cannot but need considerable revision sooner or later. For it contains several features which do not promise any final solution of the Near Eastern Question.'[17]

All that the Cairo staff could do now was to plead that the Sykes-Picot terms should remain secret. On May 3rd Clayton telegraphed defensively to the Director of Military Intelligence at the War Office: 'If our views have hitherto mainly reflected the Turkish and Arab side of the question, it is because these aspects alone were especially accessible to us.

'We have suffered some disadvantage by not knowing the general policy of H.M. Government . . . but we have confined our attention to the acquisition of information and carefully steered clear of all engagements.

'The present arrangement seems the best possible. It does not clash with any engagements which have been given to the Sherif and has the advantage of clearly defining our position *vis-à-vis* other parties.

'At the same time, I feel that divulgence of the agreement at the present time might be detrimental to our good relations with all parties and possibly create a change of attitude in some of them which would be undesirable just at present and would certainly handicap our Intelligence work. It might also prejudice the hoped-for action of the Sherif who views French penetration with suspicion . . . it is difficult to foresee the interpretation he might place on the two spheres of influence.

'Lapse of time, accompanied by favourable change in the situation, will probably render acceptable in the future what is unpalatable today.'[18]

In reality, the British and French Governments had other compelling reasons for keeping the Sykes-Picot terms secret. The Agreement would have been interpreted by Ottoman propagandists as evidence of Christian ambitions, and would have inflamed opinion against the Allies throughout the Islamic world. By the time Lawrence returned to Cairo, Sykes-Picot had been ratified.

As the implications of the Agreement were absorbed in Cairo, McMahon saw that it would be necessary to adjust policy towards the Sherif's revolt. In March he had indicated the British Government's general approval for the Arab plans, which at that time included a revolt in Syria. Hussein seems meanwhile to have heard (almost certainly from Faroki) of the earlier British proposals for a landing at Alexandretta; he cannot, however, have been told of their rejection. He therefore began to include British intervention at Alexandretta in his overall plan. Arab nationalist forces in Syria were now very weak; it would only be possible to risk a northern rebellion if Turkish communications had been cut.

Although the Alexandretta scheme had been widely mooted in Cairo, it had never been mentioned in the correspondence with Hussein. When the Sherif raised the idea (in a letter which reached Cairo on March 20th), McMahon thought it best to wait for instructions from London before sending a reply. As soon as news of the Sykes-Picot terms began to reach Cairo, McMahon realised that a British landing at Alexandretta was out of the question. He also concluded that Britain could not support an Arab nationalist campaign in the areas allocated to France.

A telegram from Wingate on April 16th suggested that the Arabs were now totally committed to action in Syria. After talking about Arab plans to Hussein's messenger, Sheikh Oreifan, Wingate cabled: 'The first step will be taken by Ali, the Sherif's son, who will cut the railway communication between Medina and the Syrian frontier. Feisal will simultaneously raise the standard of revolt against the Turks in Syria, irrespective of whether or no the British troops co-operate by landing on the Syrian coast.'[19] In order to carry out this programme there were further requests to Britain for rifles and money, needed 'to feed and equip the Arab levies who will join the Sherif's army, and to subsidise Chiefs of tribes who will be required to cut the Turkish lines of communication in Syria and on the line to Baghdad.'[20]

McMahon knew that a revolt in Syria would be impossible without decisive British help. His reaction was passed on to Wingate by Clayton: 'Feisal proposes to operate in a sphere which we have definitely left to France. In view of the avowed hostility of the Sherif to French influence how can we justify to the French our action in assisting to place in their sphere a force which will inevitably be violently opposed to their aims? . . .

'The Sherif allows that Syria is useless for revolutionary purposes. Can we expect that the Hedjaz Arabs with their proverbial lack of organisation, and far from their base, can do more than waste our money and supplies in a series of aimless and indecisive raids in a country which they are too uncivilised ever to rule as it should be ruled? . . . the Sherif has always his eyes towards the northern Syrian coast, and Feisal's action is likely to be as much directed against France and Russia as against the Turks. France at least will not fail to think this.

'The High Commissioner feels very strongly that at present the Sherif should be advised to confine himself to securing the Railway, and clearing the Turks out of the Hedjaz, and, in conjunction with the Idrisi, out of the Yemen.

'We can safely back this for all we are worth with further funds and material as required in proportion to the results obtained. It is a definite plan which has a good chance of succeeding and we shall gain what we want in the shape of a public demonstration to the Moslem world that the Sherif is against the Turks. All chance of a genuine jihad is then gone. We do not want to create a powerful and united Arab Kingdom either under the Sherif or anyone else, even were such a thing practicable. It would be a danger and a cause of future embarrassment in view of our arrangements with France and Russia. We merely wish to keep the various Arab races and factions on our side and deny them to the enemy, which we have succeeded in doing so far without giving any embarrassing guarantees.'[21]

A few days later a new letter arrived from Hussein which brought matters to a head. He wrote: 'It will be absolutely necessary . . . that a sufficient number of British troops should land at a convenient point [on the Mediterranean coast of Syria] . . . and occupy the railway line connecting Syria with Anatolia so as to make it easy for our friends in Syria to rise up with their followers . . . Were it not for the eight divisions of Turkish troops in those districts, they would have risen and done their duties long ago. They are then unable to be the first to rise, and the rising must start from here first, and as soon as we rise up we will lay hold on the railway line from Medina, and then advance gradually upon Syria. Then they will be able to rise up.'[22]

McMahon knew that it would be impossible to meet Hussein's request, but he had no wish to explain his reasons for rejecting it. On May 8th he wrote diplomatically: 'It is always wise to concentrate rather than divide one's forces; and for this reason we strongly advise Your Highness to recall your son from Syria and to take the action which you propose in Hejaz and the south alone for the present.'[23]

The contrasting statements about Arab strength in Syria made by Hussein and Oreifan were a foretaste of the widely differing military claims that would shortly begin to emerge from the Hejaz. After talking to Oreifan, Wingate had written: 'It is considered certain that the Turkish troops in the Hejaz and other Arabian provinces are incapable of resistance and will be faced with the alternative of surrender or extermination.'[24] British officials in Cairo were unimpressed, and doubted Hussein's ability to achieve anything more than local success. Experience at Gallipoli and in Mesopotamia had shown that the Turks were a formidable enemy. Although there was less British enthusiasm for an Arab revolt than there had been some months previously, it was agreed that the Hejaz rebellion should not be allowed to fail. An independent administration in Mecca opposed to Turkey would have propaganda value throughout the Moslem world. On May 22nd Clayton wrote to Wingate: 'I hope we shall soon hear of the Sherif making a definite move – once he has openly and definitely declared himself against the Turks we shall have scored an enormous asset, even though his operation may not have any very great actual military effect.'[25]

On May 24th news came that Hussein's revolt was at last about to begin. This was welcomed in Cairo, where it had been feared that the surrender at Kut and British opposition to a rising in Syria might have persuaded Hussein to postpone action once again. Hussein now asked for an additional 60,000 sovereigns, and requested that Storrs should bring this money secretly to a point on the Arabian coast where he could meet Sherif Abdullah. Since the precise details of Hussein's plans were still unknown in Cairo it was felt that this would be very useful. Clayton wrote to Wingate that the proposal was 'a great chance as Abdulla is the mainspring of action, I think, and clever and judicious pumping should result in much very useful information. For this reason I insisted on strengthening Storrs by sending Hogarth and Cornwallis'.[26] (Kinahan Cornwallis was the only full-time member of the Arab Bureau apart from Hogarth.) The British party left Cairo at the end of May, but carried only 10,000 sovereigns; the balance had been reserved until there was proof that the revolt had really begun. According to a summary prepared for the Committee of Imperial Defence, the mission's objectives were 'to give

Abdullah a true conception of the military situation, to discover the exact intentions and position of the Sherif, and explain away any suspicions that may exist as to the future of Syria.'[27]

In reality the Sherif's hand had been forced by Turkish moves. He had learned in April that a force of 3,500 Turkish soldiers would shortly pass through the Hejaz on their way to the Yemen and he naturally suspected that this expedition was being sent to nip his revolt in the bud. In early May, while Feisal was in Damascus considering whether it was possible to start a rising, the Turks had without warning executed twenty-one leading Syrian nationalists there. A further message from Hussein reached Port Sudan on May 27th, explaining that Feisal had been recalled from Syria because the Turks had discovered his plans. The revolt would have to begin at once.

This was the position when Lawrence returned to Cairo from Meso-potamia at the end of May. He at once took up his previous work on the daily Military Intelligence Bulletins and suggested that a supplementary 'Arab Bureau Summary' could be produced from time to time, covering the areas now dealt with by the Bureau. The first of these supplements was issued on June 6th, a week after his return. Not long afterwards the new periodical was given its own name, the *Arab Bulletin*. Hogarth, as acting head of the Bureau, was to take overall responsibility for the journal; but he was on his way to the Hejaz when the first issue was assembled. It was signed by Lawrence, who remained closely involved with the *Bulletin* for the next five months. He soon felt 'written out, for now I have two newspapers (both secret!) to edit, for the information of Governors and Governments, and besides heaps of writing to do:– and it is enough.'[28]

The Storrs mission arrived at a prearranged rendezvous in the Hejaz on June 6th and was surprised to learn that action against the Turks had begun on the previous day. Abdullah was supervising operations in the field; as a result they were only able to meet Zeid, Hussein's youngest son, and Sherif Shakir, one of Abdullah's senior officers. The British delegation learned that Feisal and Ali had already attacked Medina and the railway to its north; Hussein would shortly act in Mecca while Abdullah moved on Taif. Another force was to attack the Red Sea port of Jidda.

Even at this stage Hogarth could see that the Sherif knew little about military practicalities. He reported: 'The general impression which I . . .

derived from the interview was this – That the Revolt was genuine and inevitable, but about to be undertaken upon inadequate preparation, in ignorance of modern warfare, and with little idea of the obligations which its success would impose on the Sherifial family. In both the organisation of the tribal forces and the provision of armament far too much has been left to the last moment and to luck. If the Arabs succeed, it will be by their overwhelming numbers and by the isolation of the Turkish garrisons'.[29]

Zeid brought a letter from Hussein to the meeting, asking for a great deal more money: not merely the 60,000 sovereigns already requested but a further 20,000 for Ali and Feisal, as well as funds for running the new Sherifian administration. In addition Hussein needed six machine guns, six mountain guns with Moslem gunners, ten thousand more rifles, ammunition, and many tons of food. Once again he asked for a British landing on the Syrian coast: 'It is inevitable that upon our rising the Turks will send all forces possible . . . against us: so, as we are inadequately supplied, we draw your attention to something that will relieve this thrust, to wit operations either cutting their lines of retreat as previously suggested or something similar. This is exceedingly urgent: our trust is in God.'[30] Zeid too raised the question of a British landing but was told that no such action could be taken without a decision by the Council of Allies, and that British forces were heavily committed on other fronts. However, Storrs suggested that the Royal Navy might help in the forthcoming attack on Jidda by a bombardment, and after some hesitation Zeid agreed. The British party returned to Cairo, arriving in mid-June. During their journey back they heard that Kitchener had lost his life in the sinking of HMS *Hampshire*. But for his initiative and support the Arab Revolt would have remained a dream; he had died on the day that it began.

During the first weeks of the Revolt the Arabs were fairly successful. Mecca was cleared of Turks within a few days, although the outlying barracks held out until July 4th. Jidda was attacked on June 9th, with help from the British Navy, and fell a week later. Abdullah's force quickly captured Taif but the Turkish fort there was strongly held, and showed no willingness to surrender. The only large setback was at Medina, where Feisal's tribesmen found themselves outnumbered and outclassed. The Turkish garrison had now been reinforced, and was under the command of Fakhri en din Pasha, an officer noted for his ruthlessness. It emerged during the attack that Arab tribesmen were terrified of artillery, which they had never experienced before, and the attempt to take Medina failed. An effort to blockade the town was equally unsuccessful. Although Ali's force had torn up long stretches of the Hejaz Railway to the north, the Turks were soon able to repair it.

The 'Arab Bureau Summary' for June 23rd recognised that there would probably be a long siege at Medina, although little reliable news had reached Cairo about events there. That day McMahon sent a message to Hussein, congratulating him on 'the strategy and the bravery by which your Highness and the noble Arab nation have been able to achieve the first decisive victory whose results, diligently pursued, should deliver you from the oppression under which you have so long suffered, and restore to you the land which was your birthright since the beginning . . . We are awaiting with deep interest news regarding the success of your operations at Medina, and in the matter of the destruction of the railway line northwards. In them and all your other operations I wish you complete success.'[31]

The telegram went on to detail the supplies sent in response to Hussein's latest request: 3,000 rifles with ammunition; machine guns with ammunition; guns and their equipment, with Egyptian crews; six tons of coffee; 210 tons of barley; six tons of sugar; 102 tons of rice; and 233 tons of flour. The message was passed to the cipher office by Lawrence. In addition to its other duties, the Arab Bureau had now taken over all the administration connected with shipment of British supplies to Hussein.

The start of Arab operations quickly led to tensions between the various British authorities involved in support and liaison work. On June 15th General Murray cabled the War Office to raise the question of control: 'The time now seems to have arrived when operations should come under military supervision. I am supplying, as you know, all possible assistance in supplies and munitions, but I am aware that military assistance cannot be given beyond this. I am prepared, if you wish, to assume such military supervision as it is possible to exercise from here'.[32] Robertson's reply was firmly negative: 'There are many interests involved in the Arab Movement. The Foreign Office, India Office, and the French and Russian Governments are all interested and there are many ramifications of the question. As you say military assistance must for the present be confined to provision of munitions and supplies, and while I should be glad of all possible assistance you can give in this I do not think the time has yet come to make a change as to the general control and supervision of the Sherif's operations.'[33]

Murray's reaction to this decision was unfortunate. As Lawrence subsequently wrote: 'Sir Archibald Murray . . . wanted, naturally enough, no competitor and competing campaigns in his area. He disliked the civil power [in Egypt] . . . which might yet be a sprag on his rolling wheel. He could not be entrusted with the Arabian affair, for neither he nor his Staff had the necessary competence to deal with so curious a problem. On the other hand, he could make the spectacle of the High Commission running a private war sufficiently ridiculous. His was a very nervous mind, fanciful and even ungenerous. When he found the opportunity he bent his considerable powers to crab what he called the rival show.

'He found help in his Chief of Staff . . . General Lynden Bell'. Other influential officers at GHQ followed this lead, 'and so the unfortunate McMahon found himself . . . reduced to waging his war in Arabia with the assistance of his Foreign Office attachés.'[34]

When Murray discovered the extent to which his Intelligence Staff in Cairo were involved with the administration of supplies to the Revolt, he wrote to McMahon: 'I do not know who is supervising this campaign of the Sherif's against the Turks. It is evident I can do nothing except to give such assistance in material as I am asked for. It is also quite obvious that the branch of my Intelligence Department at Cairo can only be used for purposes of Intelligence, not operations . . . I should be very glad if you will send me a line to tell me who is supervising, or controlling, the action of the Sherif, if anyone.'[35]

There was no accident about the moment Murray chose to make an issue of the role played by Cairo Intelligence. On the morning of June 20th, the day McMahon received this letter, Clayton had left Egypt for a month, on a working visit to England. He would discuss the present state of Arab affairs with the War Committee and take part in detailed exchanges of information at the Foreign Office.[36]

Murray was now determined to have a clear demarcation between his own operations and those of the Sherif, and Clayton's ambiguous position could no longer be tolerated. A note in the Ismailia Intelligence Diary for June 24th sets out the General Staff complaint: 'Great confusion arises over the Sherif of Mecca's rebellion. It is in no way under Egyptforce. Yet demands for material are made on us by the High Commissioner and Sirdar independently.

'It is complicated by the fact that the Arab Bureau is under the High Commissioner: and that Clayton is the Sudan Agent of the Sirdar and is, further, liaison between Egyptforce and the Government of Egypt and therefore under us. The Arab Bureau works in the same office as Clayton in his dual regime at Cairo and it is difficult therefore for Egyptforce to know where it stands.'[37]

The Ismailia staff had been particularly irritated by Clayton's role as Cairo Agent for the Sudan. Although the EEF was providing military supplies for Hussein, the telegraphed requests for these, as well as for money and provisions, were going to Clayton's office rather than GHQ. Murray now sent a message asking Wingate to route *all* future telegrams for Clayton via EEF Headquarters.

Murray's anger against Clayton was nurtured by Colonel Holdich, chief of the Ismailia Intelligence Department, who had become increasingly hostile to the Cairo Intelligence branch. In practice, Clayton's arrangements with Intelligence and the Arab Bureau were working very successfully. Holdich had been piqued, however, by the independent line taken in Cairo. Worse still, he had been proved wrong some weeks earlier when he had suppressed the Cairo assessment of the Turkish threat in favour of his own alarmist appreciation. He now wanted control of both organisations.

As one of the Intelligence officers most prominently involved in work on Arab affairs, Lawrence found himself caught up in this power game. The Arab Bureau report for May and June 1916 noted: 'The return of Captain T. E. Lawrence from Mesopotamia late in May greatly strengthened us since, though not definitely attached to the Bureau, he works continually in co-operation with it.'[38] His relations with Ismailia Headquarters became strained, and he began to fear that he would shortly have to choose between the Arab Bureau and Intelligence. On July 1st he wrote home: 'The Reuter telegram on the revolt of the Sherif of Mecca I hope interested you. It has taken a year and a half to do, but now is going very well. It is so good to have helped a bit in making a new nation – and I hate the Turks so much that to see their own people turning on them is very grateful. I hope the movement increases, as it promises to do . . . This revolt, if it succeeds, will be the biggest thing in the Near East since 1550 . . . the army here are very savage at being left out of the Arabia business, and I may have to cut adrift of them, which would reduce my pay a good deal . . . It is curious though how the jealousies and interferences of people on your own side give you far more work and anxiety than the enemy do.'[39]

During the summer, while Clayton was away, these internal politics became an increasing hindrance to liaison work with Hussein. Murray issued orders that Hogarth alone should deal with communications from the Sherif of Mecca, and that no one else should pass on requests for *matériel* to GHQ. The order continued: 'The Commander-in-Chief is particularly anxious that no Officer of the Cairo branch of G.H.Q. Intelligence shall attempt to deal . . . with any communication from the Sherif which may come into his hands.'[40]

Colonel Parker, who had again taken charge of the Cairo Intelligence Department in Clayton's absence, wrote on July 6th: 'G.H.Q. are inclined to take the line that it was foolish to get the Sherif to come in now, when assistance is not possible – and rather look upon it as a mess they do not wish to be mixed up in – I was warned officially that no officer in this office was to assist Hogarth in any way – I managed to get this somewhat modified so that Lawrence assists in all but where action is necessary, and Hogarth is permitted to consult me. Also Cornwallis is being definitely allowed to do Arab Bureau work, so we go on as before'.[41]

To make matters even worse, another intense rivalry was growing between McMahon in Cairo and Wingate in the Sudan, whose staff was daily involved in the shipping of supplies to Hussein. All these tensions continued throughout the summer and early autumn of 1916 and were well known to members of the Cairo Intelligence Department. Despite a veil of formal courtesy, the animosity between Murray, McMahon and Wingate was blatantly obvious in the communications which passed between them.

These difficulties hampered the efficiency of British material support for the Revolt, which failed to keep up with Hussein's urgent requests. There were, however, other problems. Early in July one of Wingate's officers, Lieut-Colonel C. E. Wilson, visited Jidda and reported that the Sherif 'appears to have started his revolt without sufficient preparation and somewhat prematurely'.[42] Wilson argued that if there were a serious reverse at Medina the Sherif would 'more than probably try to put the blame on the British Government owing to supplies not being available when he expected them.

'The seriousness of the consequences to the British Government should the present Hedjaz revolt fail is too patent to call for remark.'[43]

His conclusion was that a British officer should be sent to Jidda permanently, to ensure better liaison with Hussein; a few days later he himself was posted there. Since Hussein thought it extremely important that the rebellion should not appear to be orchestrated by infidels, Wilson was given the official title of 'Pilgrimage Officer'.

In late July, following the initial Arab success around Mecca, the Red Sea ports of Rabegh and Yenbo were taken (in the latter case through action by the Royal Navy). Around Medina, however, the Arab Revolt had settled down to a precarious stalemate. The British were confidently landing supplies at Rabegh for the Arab forces outside Medina and hoped that all was going well; but news from the interior was vague and often conflicting, as successive issues of the *Arab Bulletin* show.

In reality, though Cairo did not know it yet, the arms, ammunition, and other supplies landed at Rabegh were not being sent inland. Feisal and Ali therefore soon found themselves in a difficult position, unable to fight effectively or even to feed and pay their forces. As rumours of these problems reached Cairo there seemed an increasing danger of a strong counter-attack by the Turkish Army in Medina, which had now been substantially reinforced from the north.

Although Murray was not responsible for directing Hussein's military actions, the EEF stood to benefit from a successful revolt in the Hejaz, which would reduce the Turkish forces available for defending Sinai. At the beginning of July, Robertson asked the War Committee to consider whether Murray might not undertake operations across Sinai to Akaba on the Red Sea and El Arish in the north. Murray found Akaba of considerable interest, since Turkish units based there would present a very real threat to the right flank of any British force advancing across northern Sinai. Akaba was only seventy miles from the Hejaz Railway, and a British force there might also be of some value to the Sherif. A War Office memorandum of July 1st concluded that British forces established at El Arish and Akaba 'would directly threaten the Turkish communication between Syria and the Hejaz, and would encourage the Syrian Arabs, while at the same time effectively defending the eastern frontier of Egypt.'[44] However, it was thought that for climatic reasons these operations could not be undertaken before October.

On July 6th the War Committee approved the Akaba and El Arish schemes in principle, and instructions were issued to Murray and the naval authorities to concert their plans for the occupation of Akaba.[45] A week later Murray wrote to Robertson: 'I am making a study of the Akaba problem and am in touch with the Navy on the subject. I am surprisingly short of topographical information and have telegraphed to the War Office to send what the Intelligence there has, and I am arranging for Naval reconnaissance . . . I would like to undertake a raid against the

Hedjaz railway to destroy a vulnerable part of the line I have within striking distance. I am working out plans and details for this. Of course I shall not act without letting you know first, especially as the Sherif appears touchy about destroying the railway, which is surprising, considering the success of his own operations at Mecca and Medina depends to a large extent on cutting the Turkish communications.'[46]

In Egypt, Murray's request for information was passed to the Cairo Intelligence branch. There it was dealt with by Lawrence, who had first considered a landing at Akaba, among other places, in the spring of 1915. Now, as before, he rejected the scheme, for reasons which are evident from an account written shortly after the war: 'To take Akaba meant a naval expedition and a landing. The landing would not be difficult, but afterwards there was no logical objective. There was no covering position to the beach, which could be shelled always from the hills. The enemy garrison was posted in these hills, in elaborate prepared positions, constructed one behind the other in a series, as far as the mouth of Wadi Itm. If the British advanced to this point they would have effected nothing material, and would be exposed to continual flank attack from the hills. The Turks would be quite secure, for their line of communications with their railway base, seventy miles away, was up this very Wadi Itm, and so they would be able to increase their defending force or to change its disposition at their will.

'The British would be able to deliver themselves from these attacks only by forcing the twenty-five miles of the gorge in the teeth of the enemy, to deny them access to the coastal range. Now the Wadi Itm was from 2,000 to 5,000 feet in depth, and often less than 100 yards in width, and ran between fretted hills of granite and diorite whose sides were precipices hundreds of feet in height. The hundred-yard width of the bed was so encumbered by rocks that in places camels could pass only two abreast. It was winding and blind, afforded innumerable natural positions for defence, and hiding places not merely in the cliffs, but in the boulder-masses on the floor. The many side-ravines allowed easy retirement to forces knowing the country. There was water in these side-ravines, but none in the main valley; another advantage to the defence.

'The Turks had organised the valley in position after position, prepared to cover every foot of these twenty-five magnificently defensible miles. Then the granite valley ended in a sandstone plain, which was open and not difficult to cross, but dry. Beyond the plain was another range of heights, the tilted edge of the limestone plateau of Syria, rising 2,000 feet in a single heave up a twisting hill road to a crest over 4,000 feet in height. On the head of this lay great springs enough to supply some thousands of men. From them the land ran down gently, across involved valleys separated by rolling wormwood covered slopes, for twenty more miles into Maan, a main station on the Hedjaz Railway, 400 km from Damascus, and 800 from Medina.

'The approach Akaba-Maan thus formed a natural defensive position of almost unequalled strength, and the Staff in Egypt estimated that to carry it against a weak enemy might take three Divisions, almost the complete strength of Sir Archibald Murray's army: but success would depend on the speed of the operation, and the Turks might be able to reinforce by rail and route march faster than we could disembark, for the Akaba water-supply was inconvenient, and to land so great an expedition in a harbourless Gulf would not be easy. In fact a British landing there was out of the question'.[47]

Lawrence reported that the Akaba plan would be a folly, and although the proposed operation was not immediately abandoned, Murray's interest evaporated during September when he realised how large a force would be required. This would be embarrassing, because Hussein had meanwhile become very enthusiastic about the scheme. He was ignorant of the terrain, and imagined that a landing would involve little cost to the British while greatly assisting the Hejaz rebellion.

At the end of August Colonel Wilson visited Yenbo to meet Sherif Feisal, who had not previously been in direct contact with any British representative. Wilson reported that Feisal 'struck me as being an exceedingly nice man, well educated, and altogether impressing me very favourably. Though he may at times, perhaps, be inclined to exaggerate matters it is clear he regards his position as very critical, and I think there is no doubt that it is so.'[48] Feisal spoke bitterly about the lack of supplies from Britain and of ammunition shortages during a month's continuous fighting. As a result his forces had been obliged to retire gradually towards the coast at Rabegh. Wilson countered these complaints by explaining that 'trained men for blowing up the railway had been sent to Port Sudan but were stopped from coming across by the Sherif; that dynamite for them to use had been sent back from Jeddah by the Sherif; that sixty-odd boxes of bombs had been on board a warship for weeks as the Sherif said he did not want them landed. I told him all this, thinking it as well for Feisal to know that all the blame for the shortage of munitions did not lie at the door of the British Government. Feisal went as near cursing his saintly father as I suppose a son of a Grand Sherif could and added "My father tries to do everything but is not a soldier". Having had a month's experience of the old gentleman I was able to agree cordially.'[49]

Feisal, who had already been forced back to Kheif, warned Wilson that the Turks would try to break through to Mecca in time for the annual Muslim pilgrimage. They had nominated a new Emir of Mecca, Sherif Haidar, and their propagandists had issued a proclamation in his name. It condemned Hussein for 'trying to place the House of God, the *Kibla* of Islam, and the tomb of the prophet, under the protection of a Christian Government . . . He who sees what has befallen others should beware, lest the same misfortune befall him also. The Sherif . . . should have considered the fact that England would not help him unless she was afterwards to govern him, and that the moment she stretches her finger to Hejaz she will not relax her efforts until, by degrees, she annexes it to the other countries which she has already fraudulently occupied.'[50]

Wilson reported Feisal's view that it was 'now impossible for him to push the Turks back . . . if the latter make a really strong and sustained attack he states they will succeed in breaking through in which case he fears most of his Arabs will disperse'.[51] This danger would be greatly reduced, however, if the tribesmen were confident that the revolt would be successful. Feisal would have liked a substantial European contingent landed at Rabegh, to convince his forces that Britain was really committed to supporting them. However, he asked for three hundred men only, this being the most that his father would sanction.

In the matter of European troops Hussein had to balance the potential military value of British help against the damage it might do to his position as a religious leader. If Christian soldiers were sent to the Hejaz the fact would be used by Turkey as proof that the Emir of Mecca had abandoned religious principle in the pursuit of temporal power. Hussein's status as a spiritual figurehead was one of his strongest assets, and his ability to recruit support might be severely undermined by any further Christian involvement. The risk was clear from Sherif Haidar's proclamation, which had attempted to extend the religious objection even to Muslim troops fighting for the Allies: 'No matter how much the Sherif Hussein contradicts our belief that the Hejaz will be a field for Christian troops, and thinks that England will send him Moslem troops, the fact is that the troops whom England will send him, whether Moslem or Christian, are but servants of England, fighters in the army of a Christian

Government, wearing her arms and obeying her orders, and thus there is really no difference in them . . . There is no one who denies that if those Moslem troops . . . conquer the Ottoman troops, the result will be a victory for Christian England over Moslem Turkey. In other words, the result will be (God forbid it), that Christianity will have the upper hand over Islam, in the cradle of Islam and the house of Mahommed (Prayers of God on him).'[52]

Feisal was less concerned with this religious issue than with the practical business of holding up the Turkish Army. He gave Wilson a long list of requests: not only for British troops at Rabegh, but also for aeroplanes, mountain guns, machine guns and rifles. He pleaded for a British expedition against the railway farther north, and Wilson's report warmly advocated a landing at Akaba.

If the Turks were to attack Mecca they would have to advance to Rabegh along the Sultani Road, and then move southwards down the coast to Mecca. The alternative routes, though shorter, were too mountainous for a substantial force. Feisal's ill-equipped and demoralised army seemed no great obstacle to the coming Turkish thrust.

His complaints about the shortage of British supplies raised suspicions about the Sheikh of Rabegh, Hussein ibn Mubeirik, who had been put in charge of distributing British shipments there. The Sheikh had been recommended by Oreifan, even though he had a blood feud against the Sherif's family. It was now feared that he might after all be working for the Turks. Sherif Zeid was sent to investigate, but Hussein ibn Mubeirik protested his innocence and his loyalty to the Arab cause. Zeid was not entirely convinced, and decided to stay in Rabegh himself.

On his return to Jidda Wilson learned that Ali had sent for Sherif Hussein's permission to move to Rabegh. This request had been prompted by Nuri as-Said, who had now volunteered for service with the Sherifian forces. On joining Ali, he had rapidly concluded that this force was serving no useful purpose near Medina and would be better placed at Rabegh. The possibility of such a move came as a relief to Wilson, since it would help to strengthen Feisal's position.

Wilson met Feisal again on September 9th, and this time Colonel Parker was also present. Parker had been posted from Cairo to help with Intelligence and liaison work in the Hejaz. Feisal repeated all his previous requests and voiced his fear of treachery at Rabegh. Both Englishmen came away from the meeting convinced that a British force was needed to hold Rabegh until the Arabs could strengthen it from their own resources, perhaps after the capture of Taif. Neither of them was very sensitive to the religious issue. Parker wrote: 'The political arguments against such a landing are unconvincing. The Sherif has accepted Christian help, and that cannot be denied in any case. Moreover the fact of withdrawing such a force would be an ample refutation of the suggestion that the British wish to establish themselves and finally to take possession of the Arab holy countries.'[53] Wilson left for Cairo on HMS *Dufferin* convinced that the Revolt was in danger of collapse, and that the only way to save it would be to land a British force in the Hejaz.

On September 12th, he attended a conference at Ismailia with Murray, McMahon, Clayton, and others to discuss the question of sending British troops to Rabegh. McMahon supported Wilson strongly; but while Feisal had asked for only three hundred regular troops and two aeroplanes, Murray pointed out that the British force must be sufficient to defend itself if deserted by the Arabs. He set out the minimum size of a viable expedition as follows: 'We will put down a brigade of infantry. Then you must have a field ambulance, because I do not think I could send an infantry brigade down there without sending a field ambulance. Then we could send one or two batteries, immobile eighteen-pounders, or perhaps a howitzer brigade; say two batteries of howitzers. I think at least one company of engineers must go; you must fortify the place . . . half a wing of Royal Flying Corps, A.S.C., details, and of course the usual landing officers to put the thing ashore.'[54] This was a much larger force than Feisal had proposed, but Wilson raised no objection; indeed he expressed a preference for sending a brigade.

However, the scale of the contingent would increase the difficulty of sending Christian troops. Clayton told the meeting that Wingate had suggested sending British troops from Egypt to the Sudan, thereby releasing Sudanese Moslem units for the Hejaz. Wilson, while recognising this possibility, knew that Feisal had asked specifically for British troops. He said that there would be 'no comparison between the moral effect of British troops and troops from the Sudan'.[55]

No one at the conference disputed that the presence of a British expeditionary force at Rabegh might save the Revolt. Serious objections were raised, however, by Murray, who pointed out that no such military commitment had been foreseen when Hussein had been encouraged to rebel. The EEF had no men to spare: the loss of so many troops would not only rule out an action at Akaba, but would handicap the forthcoming campaign across northern Sinai to El Arish. His statement to the conference on this point spelled out a factor which would dominate British attitudes towards the Revolt: 'This war', Murray said, 'is a war which covers the whole Empire, more or less. We are absolutely clear at the War Office as to our line of policy, as are all the Allied nations. We have made up our minds that we will concentrate in the West every single man we possibly can, and that we shall allow the secondary theatres of war to struggle on with the minimum of troops, and that we will on no consideration undertake fresh campaigns or fresh liabilities . . . I was sent here for three purposes: I was sent out to reorganize the Gallipoli Army when it came off the Peninsula; I was sent out to despatch every single available man to the main theatre of war in France; and I was sent out here with the balance (and that balance I was asked to keep as small as possible) to protect Egypt'.[56]

He went on to list the increasing demands on the modest force left at his disposal, then continued: 'On the top of that I am asked now to begin the conduct of another campaign. There is no good telling me that you only want this and that. From the experience of war, and experience of recent campaigns, it is absolutely clear that you start and you grow. You start with a brigade, that brigade wants some artillery, then aeroplanes and camels. Then comes a request that the force may be moved to another point, about ten miles, which it is absolutely essential to hold. So the campaign grows'.[57] He agreed to put the matter to the War Office, but warned that he would not send troops unless positively ordered to do so from London. McMahon was asked to draft a formal request, and Murray cabled it in full to London that evening. It appealed for the forces that Murray had outlined, with the comment: 'I fully appreciate the political and religious objections of landing British Government troops in the Hijaz and the capital which hostile propagandists will make of such action, especially in India, but it is a matter for H.M. Government to decide whether this would not be preferable to the very serious situation which might result from the total collapse of the Arab movement . . . Mahommedan troops would be preferable to British if available but the presence of European officers and technical troops necessary for any such force makes the distinction of less value and importance.'[58] If the War Office agreed to send British troops, McMahon promised 'that no advance will be made beyond Rabegh in any circumstances, that a brigade is the absolute maximum, and that it will be withdrawn immediately the present crisis is over.'[59]

Murray was not at all surprised by the War Office response. He had been Robertson's predecessor as CIGS and knew that the 'Westerners' in London were utterly opposed to any new sideshows outside Europe. Predictably, Robertson refused to countenance a British intervention at Rabegh: 'it is futile sending a Brigade to give moral support and equally futile to lay down that the Brigade would not go beyond Rabegh and would be the absolute maximum. Gallipoli and Mesopotamia should have given quite sufficient proof of such futility.'[60] Murray must have hoped that this decision would bring the 'Rabegh question' to a close, but Wilson and Parker could not ignore Hussein's difficulties in the Hejaz, and continued to argue for direct British action.

As Feisal had anticipated, the Turks now sent out a strong expedition in an attempt to force the Sultani Road. Their progress, however, was hampered both by Feisal's tribesmen and by difficulties in the mountainous section of the route. Arab morale rose, and was further boosted when the fort at Taif surrendered to Abdullah's army on September 22nd. At much the same time Ali arrived at Rabegh with a thousand men. Hussein ibn Mubeirik fled into the hills, and it was found that he had been hiding stockpiles of British supplies in the village.[61] These were now distributed.

It was decided that Ali should remain in Rabegh and build a defensive position there. He was encouraged to recruit and train a force of Arab regulars under Abdul Aziz al Masri, who had joined him from Egypt. Al Masri took Nuri as-Said as his second-in-command. The aim was to recruit five thousand men for these new units, which were referred to as the 'Arab trained bands'. Their discipline and loyalty would help to stiffen the tribesmen, who tended to scatter in the face of a determined attack. In the absence of a British brigade, it was hoped that these Arab regulars would provide a rallying-point for the defence of Rabegh.

Throughout the summer Lawrence had collected news about the Revolt, writing brief reports for the *Arab Bulletin*. He also helped to arrange the shipment of British supplies. One of his more entertaining projects was to create a set of Hejaz postage stamps which would proclaim Hussein's independence throughout the world. Lawrence had proposed this scheme in mid-July, and not long afterwards had told his family about it: 'It's rather amusing, because one has long had ideas as to what a stamp should look like, and now one can put them roughly into practice. The worst is they can only be little designs, not engraved, so that the finer detail is not possible.'[62] At first he had hoped to use flavoured gum on the stamps 'so that one may lick without unpleasantness',[63] but in the end the only suitable paper available in Egypt was a pre-gummed stock used for the labels that re-sealed censored correspondence. The taste of its gum is not recorded. Lawrence and Ronald Storrs enjoyed themselves thinking of suitable illustrations for the stamps. Their objectives were firstly, 'to make it self-evident to the world that the series was not a survival or copy of the Ottoman postage stamps in any form whatsoever, but an entirely new and independent national issue which had not moulded itself on that of any other Government, least of all on that of the Ottoman Empire,' and secondly, 'that the design should in wording, spirit, and ornament be, as far as possible, representative and reminiscent of a purely Arab source and inspiration . . . To achieve these two purposes all existing designs of postage stamps were swept aside, and designs never adopted before for stamps were drawn from beautiful existing specimens of Arabesque ornament.'[64] The first stamps were produced during September 1916 and were put into use by Hussein during October.

Clayton had come back from London with a much clearer idea of the way in which Foreign Office policy had evolved during the preceding months. While reading through the relevant files there, he had seen the successive revisions of the preamble to the Sykes-Picot text. The Cairo staff, who may have been entirely ignorant of the secret proviso up to this point, now knew that Hussein's forces would have to capture Damascus, Homs, Hama, and Aleppo if there were to be even the limited independence in Syria and Mesopotamia granted under Sykes-Picot. From this time on, Lawrence was aware that the Arabs would gain little or nothing if the Revolt failed to spread into Syria. The Sherif's progress thus far held little promise of such an outcome.

In late September 1916 the General Staff took decisive action to prevent Cairo Intelligence working on McMahon's projects. Clayton was stripped of his Military Intelligence duties, and left only with the Arab Bureau, which would henceforth be an entirely separate organisation.

Lawrence was keen to remain with Clayton, and wrote home on September 24th: 'If I leave G.H.Q. Egypt, which I have hinted several times lately, it will be to join the Arab Bureau, which is doing all the work of the Sherif's revolt'.[65] He was alarmed, however, to learn that Holdich, now in control of all Intelligence, would not allow him to transfer to the Bureau. This meant that he would in future be completely cut off from Arab affairs. His disappointment was not merely personal: he knew that

Hussein's rising was fragile and feared that if deprived of effective staff support in Cairo it might eventually collapse. As he later wrote: 'I was confident in the final success of the Arab Revolt if it was properly advised. I had been a mover in its beginning, and my hopes lay in it, and I was not strong enough to watch it being wrecked by the jealousies of little-spirited intriguers in Egypt, for their own satisfaction.'[66]

In an attempt to make Holdich change his mind, Lawrence began to behave intolerably towards the Ismailia Intelligence Department: 'I took every opportunity to rub into them their comparative ignorance and inefficiency (not difficult) and irritated them yet further by literary airs, correcting split infinitives and tautologies in their reports.'[67] Clayton had meanwhile put in a request for Lawrence's transfer to the Arab Bureau, routing it through official channels in London in order to circumvent Murray's staff. He badly needed Lawrence for the Bureau.

While this move was still being arranged, Clayton determined to make use of Lawrence on Arab work. On October 9th he wrote to Wingate that Storrs was about to visit the Hejaz again, hoping to see Abdullah and possibly Hussein: 'I propose to send Lawrence with him, if G.H.Q. will let him go. They ought to be of use and, between them, to bring back a good appreciation of the situation'.[68] Storrs was a civil servant with no training in the kind of specialised observation that Clayton needed; this was why Clayton had sent Hogarth and Cornwallis to accompany him on a similar journey in May. Hogarth had left for England in early August, however, and would not return in time to join this new expedition. Cornwallis had lately been appointed Director of the Arab Bureau, and could not possibly be spared. Lawrence therefore seemed the best choice, and the quality of his earlier report from Mesopotamia suggested that he would be an excellent observer.

To avoid difficulties with GHQ, Lawrence applied for leave (this seems to have been the first he had taken since arriving in Egypt nineteen months previously). 'I took this strategic moment to ask for ten days' leave, saying that Storrs was going down to Jidda on business . . . and that I would like a holiday and joy-ride in the Red Sea with him. They hated Storrs, and were glad to get rid of me for the moment. So they agreed at once, and began to prepare against my return some rare place to which I could be banished to rust out in idleness hereafter. Needless to say, I had no intention of giving them such a chance . . . It was a crooked way to get free . . . but we were dealing with queer company, who could only be combated in their own manner'.[69] By the time Lawrence returned, his transfer to the Arab Bureau would have come through. Meanwhile, Holdich had no idea that he was about to go on an Intelligence mission to the Hejaz.

Storrs and Lawrence left Cairo on October 12th, travelling to Suez by train. There they boarded the *Lama* for the three-day voyage down the Red Sea to Jidda and the pitiless heat of Arabia.

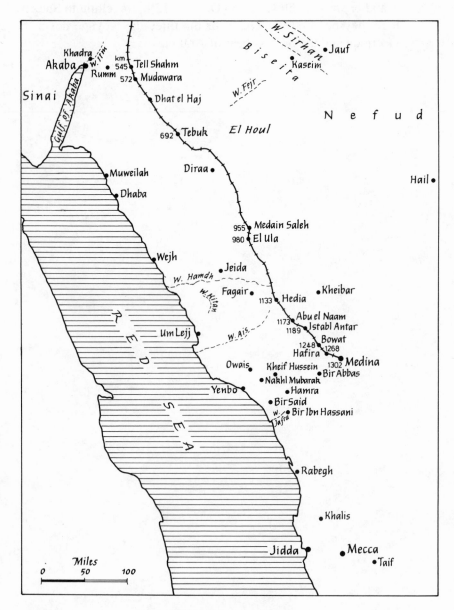

Map 4: *The Red Sea Campaign*

CHAPTER 15

Intelligence Mission to the Hejaz
October – November 1916

DURING the early autumn of 1916 messages from the Hejaz had alternated between exultation and despondency, and it had gradually become clear that Hussein himself did not know the true state of affairs. From his vantage point in Jidda, Colonel Wilson had reported that the Arab armies under Ali, Abdullah and Feisal were operating more or less independently of one another. He had found, moreover, that there was a considerable divergence between Hussein's ideas and those held by each of his sons. Clayton hoped that Lawrence, with his fluent Arabic and sympathy for the Arab cause, would bring back a useful assessment of the position.

As it happened, the Sherifian military position had unexpectedly improved at the beginning of October. As the Turkish advance along the Sultani Road went farther into the hills, its supply caravans were attacked by raiding parties from the hostile tribes on either side. This helped Feisal's army to gain the upper hand in a series of engagements which began on October 6th around Bir Abbas, some thirty miles south-west of Medina. Despite the threat of a new advance, the annual pilgrimage to Mecca had taken place without interference.

Although the future of the Revolt seemed uncertain, the Arab Bureau was delighted with the achievement thus far. There could be no doubt that the rebellion in the Hejaz had materially weakened the potential strength of the enemy facing Murray's army in Sinai. A summary pointed out that: 'The equivalent of a Turkish division has been eliminated, all its effectives having been either killed or captured. Turkish rule and control has been replaced in the greater part of the Hedjaz by free Arab rule under the chief of the Descendants of the Prophet. The pilgrim roads from Jeddah, central and southern Arabia have been reopened and for the first time for many years satisfactory and more enlightened government established in the country.

'The Arabs, without the assistance of any non-Arab troops, have secured their independence in the part of Arabia where lies the very heart and centre of their national and religious sentiment'.[1]

Feisal's success at Bir Abbas suggested that additional troops might not be needed to defend Rabegh after all. Hussein, however, was urging that a brigade should be held in readiness, and that any available Muslim troops should be sent to garrison the town at once so that Ali's units could be used for an assault on Medina.

This proposal met with no sympathy in London, but was warmly supported by Wingate, who had just been put in charge of British military liaison with the Sherif. The control of political negotiations remained with McMahon, a division of responsibility which did nothing to ease tension between the various British authorities. Matters were made worse because McMahon now opposed Wingate over the Rabegh question. On October 13th he wrote: 'The Sirdar . . . is already agitating for the despatch of aeroplanes with their British escort, and I fear he will soon discover pressing need for a brigade to follow. I will do my best to prevent it'.[2]

This letter was addressed to Lord Hardinge, the former Viceroy of India, who had now taken over Nicolson's post at the Foreign Office. McMahon went on to question whether Wingate's location and personality fitted him for his new responsibilities: 'No one appreciates the Sirdar's ability and high qualifications for this control [of military liaison] better than myself, but owing to his geographical position in Khartoum and the total dearth of military resources or supplies at his disposal in the Sudan, I cannot see how he can control things from there without throwing all the work of it upon Murray and myself.

'There is also another aspect of his control which I naturally could not refer to in official correspondence, and would not even do so here but for the necessity of giving words of warning, and that is that the Sirdar has lived so long in the limelight that it may prove physically impossible for him to conduct Hedjaz operations without attracting to them a stronger blaze of limelight than is good for the Arab cause!'[3]

By this time, however, McMahon was fighting a lost cause. Tensions in Cairo had produced a good deal of adverse comment about the handling of the Revolt, not only from Murray but even from some of his own subordinates. In London, his diplomatic record had been attacked by Sykes, while Hardinge, now in a very influential position, had lost none of his hostility. Mounting criticism had put McMahon in a vulnerable position and this latest squabble proved to be the last straw. The disadvantage of Wingate's location was obvious from London too, and on October 12th he received a telegram offering him McMahon's post in Cairo.[4] Before Lawrence returned from the Hejaz, Grey would write to a Cabinet colleague: 'I have decided, in consultation with the Prime Minister, that the Sirdar shall be appointed High Commissioner of Egypt to replace McMahon. The appointment will be announced on November 6th and will take effect at the end of the year.'[5]

Lawrence arrived in Jidda on October 16th for the meetings with Sherif Abdullah. The principal British representatives were Storrs and Colonel Wilson. On the second day they were joined by Abdul Aziz al Masri, now Hussein's acting Chief of Staff. Lawrence took only a minor part in the discussions, but he observed the participants closely. He drafted 'personality' notes for the Arab Bureau, reporting that Abdullah was: 'Aged thirty-five, but looks younger. Short and thick-built, apparently as strong as a horse, with merry dark brown eyes, a round smooth face, full but short lips, straight nose, brown beard. In manner affectedly open and very charming, not standing at all on ceremony, but jesting with the tribesmen like one of their own sheikhs. On serious occasions he judges his words carefully, and shows himself a keen dialectician. Is probably not so much the brains as the spur of his father: he is obviously working to establish the greatness of the family, and has large ideas, which no doubt include his own particular advancement . . . The Arabs consider him a most astute politician, and a far-seeing statesman: but he has possibly more of the former than of the latter in his composition.'[6]

This meeting took place in very embarrassing circumstances for the British party. Abdullah had repeatedly asked for an Allied brigade at Rabegh and for a flight of British aeroplanes. The second request had been agreed to by the RFC while discussions were still continuing about the dispatch of a brigade. Eventually a ship carrying the flight had left for Rabegh, but by this time Colonel Parker had stressed the dangers of sending an RFC unit without defensive troops. As a result Wingate had changed his mind, and just as the ship transporting the flight reached Rabegh it had been ordered back. Storrs noted in his diary: 'I found, to my astonishment, that Wilson had only just been informed of H. M. Government's final decision to send no British troops to the Hijaz. Collectively therefore it was our business to announce to Abdullah that the brigade on which the Sherif had set so much store would not be sent, and that the flight of aeroplanes promised and actually dispatched to Rabegh was being withdrawn on the very day that the appearance of Turkish planes had been reported . . . The moment when we had to explain that the decision for the brigade included the aeroplanes also was not pleasant, and I do not wish to have to appear before an Arab a second time in this light.'[7] Lawrence reported to Clayton that 'Abdulla . . . is very quiet in manner: all the same one could see that the decision against a brigade was a heavy blow (mostly, I think, to his ambitions). He was very cut up at first, and tried to get the order changed, as he was afraid to inform his father of it'.[8]

Lawrence was determined, if possible, to see all of Hussein's sons. After this meeting with Abdullah in Jidda, he would go north up the coast and see Ali at Rabegh. It would be very difficult, however, to visit Feisal, whose forces were operating inland. Until now, the few British officers who had visited the Hejaz had not been allowed to leave the Red Sea ports. The negotiations which made his visit to Feisal possible are described in *Seven Pillars*. Lawrence had told Abdullah: 'I thought that I might perhaps urge his opinions more powerfully if I was able to report on the Rabegh question in the light of my own knowledge of the position and local feeling. I would also like to see Feisal, and talk over with him his needs and the prospects of a prolonged defence of his hills by the tribesmen if we strengthened him materially. I would like to ride from Rabegh up the Sultani road towards Medina as far as Feisal's camp.

'Storrs then came in and supported me with all his might, urging the vital importance of full and early information from a trained observer for the British Commander-in-Chief in Egypt'.[9] While Storrs and Lawrence were present, Abdullah spoke to Hussein by telephone and tried to obtain his consent: 'The Sherif viewed the proposal with grave distrust. Abdulla argued the point, made some advantage, and transferred the mouthpiece to Storrs, who turned all his diplomacy on the old man. Storrs in full blast was a delight to listen to in the mere matter of Arabic speech, and also a lesson to every Englishman alive of how to deal with suspicious or unwilling Orientals. It was nearly impossible to resist him for more than a few minutes, and in this case also he had his way.'[10]

Before leaving Jidda Lawrence sent a telegram to Clayton about the meeting with Abdullah: 'Nobody knew the real situation in Rabegh, so much time was wasted. Aziz el Masri is going to Rabegh with me tomorrow.

'Sherif Abdullah apparently wanted a foreign force at Rabegh as a rallying point if the combined attack on Medina ended badly. Aziz el Masri hopes to prevent any decisive risk now and thinks an English Brigade neither necessary nor prudent. He says the only way to bring sense and continuity into the operations is to have English staff at Rabegh

Sarah Lawrence with her four eldest sons at Langley Lodge, *c.* 1894
(l–r Ned, Will, Sarah Lawrence holding Frank, Bob)

The five Lawrence boys in the garden at Polstead Road, 1902
(l–r Frank, Will, Ned holding Arnold, Bob)

left: Portrait of C.M. Doughty by Eric Kennington, commissioned by Lawrence in 1921 and later presented to the National Portrait Gallery

above: Crac des Chevaliers, the west face of the inner ward sketched by Lawrence in August 1909. He called it 'the finest castle in the world' and spent three days examining it, one of which was his twenty-first birthday

Oxford University Officers Training Corps, signals section, *c.* 1910. Lawrence is seated front row left. The semaphore signal in the back row reads 'O[xford] U[niversity] A[rmy] V[olunteers]'

above: Hypnos, the Greek god of sleep. Lawrence bought a cast of this head from a foundry in Naples in 1909, writing later: 'I would rather possess a fine piece of sculpture than anything in the world'

above right: Janet Laurie, a friend since Lawrence's childhood. She claimed that he had proposed to her in 1910

below: The last known photograph of all five Lawrence brothers, 1910 (l–r Ned, Frank, Arnold, Bob, Will)

below right: D.G. Hogarth by Augustus John, a portrait commissioned by Lawrence for *Seven Pillars of Wisdom* and later presented to the Ashmolean Museum

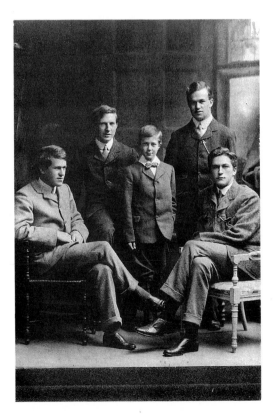

above: Dahoum, Lawrence's future assistant at Carchemish, photographed by Lawrence during the first season in 1911. *above right*: Sheikh Hamoudi, who became Leonard Woolley's assistant at Carchemish and Ur, photographed by Lawrence, 1911

below: Gregori, D.G. Hogarth's assistant in several previous excavations, photographed at Carchemish by Lawrence. *below right*: Two sketches drawn by Lawrence to illustrate the fortnightly report from Carchemish to the British Museum, 12 May 1911

Lawrence and Woolley photographed at Carchemish
by a visitor, Dr Heinrich Franke, in 1913

The Lower Palace wall at Carchemish
reconstructed while waiting for a new digging permit, 1914

above: Doorway to the expedition house, showing the lintel carved by Lawrence in 1912. To his amusement visitors often admired it as a genuine Hittite carving *above right*: Pick men and basket men digging a trench on the summit of the Carchemish mound, 1911. Photograph by Lawrence

below: Lawrence in Arab clothes, including some of Dahoum's, photographed by Dahoum *c.* 1912. *below right*: Dahoum photographed by Lawrence on the same occasion

Exterior of the expedition house at Carchemish, *c.* 1913

Living room of the expedition house, 1913–14,
furnished by Lawrence and Woolley with Eastern antiquities

Dahoum sketched by Francis Dodd at the Ashmolean Museum,
July 1913, while he and Sheikh Hamoudi
were on a brief visit to England as Lawrence's guests

dealing direct with Sherif Ali and Sherif Feisal without referring detail to the Sherif of Mecca of whom they are all respectfully afraid.'[11]

While in Jidda, Storrs and Lawrence dined with Colonel Brémond, head of the French Military Mission which had arrived there at the end of September. What Lawrence heard about Brémond's attitude to the Revolt was not reassuring. Shortly afterwards he wrote: 'The French military mission . . . say "Above all things the Arabs must not take Medina. This can be assured if an Allied force lands at Rabegh. The tribal contingents will go home, and we will be the sole bulwark of the Sherif in Mecca. At the end of the war we give him Medina as his reward".

'This is of course a definite policy, agreeable to their larger schemes. It breaks down, I think, in the assumption that an Allied force at Rabegh would defend Mecca for good and all. Once the Turks are able to dispense with the tribal resistance, they will be able to advance along any of the central or eastern roads to Mecca, leaving the Franco-British force a disconsolate monument on the dusty beach at Rabegh.'[12]

This summary of Brémond's policy was perfectly correct. On the very day he met Lawrence, he cabled to Paris: 'If the Arabs took Medina they would immediately try to go into Syria. It is therefore in our interests that Medina does not fall into the hands of the Sherif of Mecca before the end of the war.'[13] Brémond's orders from Paris had not been revised after the Sykes-Picot Agreement, of which he had not been informed. Lawrence, however, realised how much the Arabs stood to lose if their rebellion never reached Damascus. From this time on he was determined that Brémond's policies should not succeed, and he urged that the French Military Mission should be withdrawn from Jidda.

During this visit to the Hejaz, Lawrence concluded that the real argument against sending in a European brigade had little to do with religion. He reported: 'I do not think that there is really much religious antipathy to Christians landing in the Hejaz. On the Turkish side the religious cry would be used as a stick with which to beat the Sherif... and on the Arab side it is used as an excuse to hide the really political objections to our coming. The beduin cannot realise how unattractive we find the Hejaz, and believe that an armed landing by us is the prelude of eventual occupation.

'As however their objection is political it does not in the least apply to the landing of technical units.'[14] He rejected the GHQ argument that such units would be dangerously exposed without the protection of a large force, and he wrote to Clayton: 'it was pushing the principle [of not sending Christian troops] a little too far, when they counter-ordered the aeroplanes. After all, I am going to land at Rabegh, and am just as much "British troops" as they are . . . The actual moment when the planes were called back was a particularly unfortunate one.'[15]

He had also listened attentively to everything said by Abdullah and al Masri which bore on the internal politics of the Hejaz. His conclusion was that Hussein 'seems to be getting a little old, and [looks] upon his sons as boys not quite fit to act independently. Abdullah humours him, and tries to wheedle him round by diplomacy. Feisal is a little impatient sometimes . . .

'There is great need of some Intelligence work being done at Jidda. The opportunities are quite good, and at present there is no one to do this... If one stayed there, and worked, one would be able to appreciate the Hejaz situation quite well . . . The tone of public opinion at Jidda is rollicking good-humour towards foreigners. It will however be quite a good thing when the French Political Mission goes.'[16]

Storrs, Lawrence and al Masri travelled by sea to Rabegh on October 19th; there they met Sherif Ali and Colonel Parker. Storrs was treated to a long exposition of Arab difficulties, used as justification for various requests. He noted in his diary: 'While thoroughly agreeing with the necessity for these and other requirements, I disincline to attach too much importance to these alternations of depression and exultation, or indeed to any item of news proceeding from the north-east, until such time as Aly and Feisal have evolved some system of Intelligence, with means of conveying it daily to Rabegh.'[17]

Lawrence was not impressed by Sherif Ali's qualities as a war leader. He described him as: 'Short and slim, looking a little old already, though only thirty-seven. Slightly bent. Skin rather sallow, large deep brown eyes, nose thin and a little hooked, face somewhat worn and full of lines and hollows, mouth drooping. Beard spare and black. Has very delicate hands. His manners are perfectly simple, and he is obviously a very conscientious, careful, pleasant, gentleman, without force of character, nervous and rather tired. His physical weakness makes him subject to quick fits of shaking passion with more frequent moods of infirm obstinacy. Apparently not ambitious for himself, but is swayed somewhat too easily by the wishes of others. Bookish, and learned in law and religion. Shows his Arab blood more than his brothers.'[18]

Lawrence spent only three days in Rabegh before setting out on the hundred-mile journey inland to meet Feisal. Ali had considerable misgivings about this expedition and would have refused to let Lawrence go but for the written request Abdullah had sent in Hussein's name. Afterwards Colonel Parker wrote to Clayton: 'Before Lawrence arrived I had been pushing the idea of going up country and had hoped to go up. Don't think I grudge him, especially as he will do it as well or better than anyone. Since he has been gone, Ali has had a reaction on the subject and is not inclined to agree to other trips, also most necessary. Even Aziz is not allowed to go north to look round.'[19]

During the first day's journey, Lawrence with his Arab guides rode from 3 a.m. until midnight, with two three-hour breaks at midday and in the early evening. He later wrote in *Seven Pillars*: 'the long ride that day had tired my unaccustomed muscles, and the heat of the plain had been painful. My skin was blistered by it, and my eyes ached with the glare of light striking up at a sharp angle from the silver sand, and from the shining pebbles. The last two years I had spent in Cairo, at a desk all day or thinking hard in a little overcrowded office full of distracting noises, with a hundred rushing things to say, but no bodily need except to come and go each day between office and hotel. In consequence the novelty of this change was severe, since time had not been given me gradually to accustom myself to the pestilent beating of the Arabian sun and the long monotony of camel pacing.'[20] He was extremely tired by the time he reached Feisal's camp in the mid-afternoon of October 23rd.

He found the Arab leader in a despondent mood. The Turks had recovered from their defeat at Bir Abbas, and had already succeeded in driving Feisal's army back about thirty miles to Hamra. The principal difficulty was still a lack of supplies. Hussein, who had no knowledge of military affairs, had not thought it necessary to make proper arrangements for logistical support before the Revolt began and, as a result the distribution of British arms and ammunition was extremely haphazard. Feisal found himself once again without the materials he needed to resist a Turkish attack; he felt bitterly let down. Lawrence reported that he had met Feisal 'in a little mud house built on a twenty foot knoll of earth, busied with many visitors. Had a short and rather lively talk, and then excused myself, and went off to the Egyptian artillery; who were very comfortably encamped in a palm grove. Zeki Bey [commander of the Egyptian detachment sent by Wingate] received me warmly, and pitched me a tent in a grassy glade, where I had a bath and slept really well, after dining and arguing with Feisul (who was most unreasonable) for hours and hours.'[21]

Feisal made a strong impression on Lawrence, as he had earlier done on Wilson. After these first meetings Lawrence described him as: 'tall, graceful, vigorous, almost regal in appearance. Aged thirty-one. Very quick and restless in movement. Far more imposing personally than any of his brothers, knows it and trades on it. Is as clear skinned as a pure Circassian, with dark hair, vivid black eyes set a little sloping in his face, strong nose, short chin. Looks like a European, and very like the monument of Richard I at Fontevrault. He is hot tempered, proud and impatient, sometimes unreasonable and runs off easily at tangents. Possesses far more personal magnetism and life than his brothers, but less prudence. Obviously very clever, perhaps not over scrupulous. Rather narrow-minded, and rash when he acts on impulse, but usually with enough strength to reflect, and then exact in judgement. Had he been brought up the wrong way might have become a barrack-yard officer. A popular idol, and ambitious; full of dreams, and the capacity to realise them, with keen personal insight, and very efficient.'[22]

It was evident that of all Hussein's sons, only Feisal had the extraordinary mixture of qualities needed to lead the Arab Revolt. Days before, Lawrence had listened despondently while Brémond spoke of French plans to prevent Arab insurrection from spreading into Syria. It seemed that Hussein, Ali and Abdullah would be little match for Brémond's skilful manipulation. Feisal, however, was altogether more formidable, and Lawrence did not hesitate to stress the importance of Syria. Their first conversation is described as follows in a draft of *Seven Pillars*: 'As my eyes grew accustomed to the shade, I saw that the little room held many silent figures, all looking at me and at Feisal steadily . . . he inquired how I had found the journey. I spoke of the heat, and he asked how long from Rabegh, commenting that I had ridden fast for the season. "And do you like our place here in Wadi Safra?" "Well; but it is far from Damascus." There was a quiver, and everybody present stiffened where he sat, and held his breath for a silent minute. Some, perhaps, were dreaming of how far off success seemed to be, others thought my word a reflection on their late defeat. It had fallen like a sword into their midst, but Feisal at length lifted his eyes and smiled at me and said, "Praise be to God, there are Turks nearer us than that." We all smiled with him, and then I got up and excused myself for the moment.'[23]

This exchange is not included in Lawrence's reports to Cairo: at the time the question of Arab action in Syria was still extremely sensitive. There can be little doubt, however, that he was anxious to dispel any

feeling of complacency among the Arabs about their limited achievements in the Hejaz. Unlike Feisal, he knew of Sykes-Picot and of the need
to take Damascus, Homs, Hama and Aleppo.[24] He later wrote: 'In my
view, if they did not reach the main battlefield against Turkey, they would
have to confess failure, to remain a side-show of a side-show . . . I had
preached this to Feisal from our first meeting in Wadi Safra.'[25]

At 6.30 am the following day, Lawrence saw Feisal again, 'and we had
another hot discussion, which ended amicably.'[26] Afterwards he wrote to
Parker: 'Feisal is a very impatient general, who is very intelligent, and
understands things well. Only I'm afraid that some day he will get wild,
and spoil the whole show, by trying to go too fast. It's a pity as he is a very
nice fellow . . . For news: not much. Feisal's main force is at Khaif . . .
sitting still. He himself proposes to go to Yanbo al Nakhl [about thirty
miles inland from Yenbo] and thence to the Railway. The danger is that
the Turks have now got their whole force on the Sultani road, and might
be let through to Rabegh. By going off towards Hafira he may draw off a
third of the force towards the north, and Abdullah may get as much
towards the east. The Arabs will only serve in their districts, so to
distribute their forces strengthens them. The Turks on the other hand
follow a more normal law! If Feisal will only go slow for two months, till
Aziz is ready, he may make himself as big as he desires.'[27]

Later that day Lawrence walked round the Arab camp talking 'to all of
Feisul's men I could . . . They seemed a very tough lot, and were most
amusing, also in the best of spirits imaginable for a defeated army.'[28] His
reports gave a vivid picture of the difference between Hussein's rising and
a European campaign: 'The forces actually mobilised are continually
shifting. A family will have a gun, and its sons will serve in turn, perhaps
week by week, and go home for a change as often as replaced. Married
men drop off occasionally to see their wives, or a whole clan gets tired,
and takes a rest. For these reasons the paid forces are more than those
serving, and this is necessary, since by tribal habit wars are always very
brief, and the retention in the field of such numbers as the Sherif has
actually kept together is unprecedented. Policy further often involves the
payment to sheikhs of the wages of their contingent, and many such
payments are little more than disguised bribes to important individuals.'[29]

'With the exception of the Bishawi retainers, and the "soldiers" at
Rabegh, these forces are entirely tribal. About 10% are camel-corps, and
the rest infantry, some of whom are desert tribes, and some hill tribes. I
did not see much (or think much) of the desert tribes, but the hill men

struck me as good material for guerilla warfare. They are hard and fit, very active; independent, cheerful snipers. They will serve only under their tribal sheikhs, and only in their home district or near it. They have suspended their blood feuds for the period of the war, and will fight side by side with their old blood enemies, if they have a Sherif in supreme command: except in exceptional circumstances they would not, I think, obey the orders of a man belonging to any other tribe . . .

'The tribal armies are aggregations of snipers only. Before this war they had slow old muskets, and they have not yet appreciated fully the uses of a magazine rifle. They would not use bayonets, but enjoy cutting with swords. No man quite trusts his neighbour, though each is usually quite wholehearted in his opposition to the Turks. This would not prevent him working off a family grudge by letting down his private enemy. In consequence they are not to be relied on for attack in mass. They are extremely mobile, and will climb or run a great distance to be in a safe place for a shot, preferably at not more than three hundred yards range, though they are beginning to use their sights empirically. They shoot well at short ranges, and do not expend much ammunition when in contact with the enemy, though there is any amount of joy-firing at home. Feisal gives them fifty cartridges each, keeps a tight hold of his reserves, and prevents waste as far as possible.

'The Arabs have a living terror of the unknown. This includes at present aeroplanes and artillery. The sound of the discharge of a cannon sends every man within earshot to cover. They are not afraid of bullets, or of being killed: it is just the manner of death by artillery that they cannot stand. They think guns much more destructive than they really are, but their confidence is as easily restored, morally, as it is easily shaken. A few guns – useful or useless – on their side would encourage them to endure the Turkish artillery, and once they get to know it, most of their terror will pass. At present they fight only at night, so that the Turkish guns shall be blind . . .

'I think one company of Turks, properly entrenched in open country, would defeat the Sherif's armies. The value of the tribes is defensive only, and their real sphere is guerilla warfare. They are intelligent, and very cheerful, almost reckless, but too individualistic to endure commands; or fight in line, or help each other. It would, I think, be impossible to make an organised force out of them. Their initiative, great knowledge of the country, and mobility, make them formidable in the hills, and their penchant is all for taking booty. They would dynamite a railway, plunder a caravan, steal camels, better than anyone, while fed and paid by an Arabic authority. It is customary to sneer at their love of pay: but it is noteworthy that in spite of bribes the Hejaz tribes are not helping the Turks, and that the Sherif's supply columns are everywhere going without escort in perfect safety.'[30]

'Feisul has made arrangements for rewards for booty taken; thus he pays £1 per Turkish rifle, and gives it back to the taker, and pays liberally for captured mules, or camels, or Turks . . . His cause has for the moment reconciled the inter-tribal feuds, and Feisul had Billi, Juheina, and Harb, blood enemies, fighting and living side by side in his army. The Sherif is feeding not only his fighting men but their families, and this is the fattest time the tribes have ever known: nothing else would have maintained a nomad force for five months in the field. The fighting men in the Hejaz include anyone strong enough to hold a gun, between the ages apparently of twelve and sixty. Most of the men I saw were young. They are a tough looking crowd, all very dark coloured, and some negroid: as thin as possible, wearing only a loose shirt, short drawers, and a headcloth which serves for every purpose. They go about bristling with cartridge belts . . . As for their physical condition, I doubt whether men were ever harder. Feisul rode twelve days' journey in six with 800 of them, along the Eastern Road, and I have had them running and walking with me in the sun through sand and over rocks for hour after hour without their turning a hair. Those I saw were in wild spirits, as quick as hawks, keen and intelligent, shouting that the war may last for ten years'.[31]

Lawrence spent twenty-four hours at Hamra discussing the military situation and future strategy. Afterwards he returned directly to Yenbo, intending to meet HMS *Lama* which was due to pass there. He arrived on the morning of October 26th, but the *Lama* did not appear on October 29th as expected. Lawrence spent five days waiting in Yenbo, using the time to write a series of detailed reports which finally totalled some seventeen thousand words.

No other reports from British officers in the Hejaz compare with Lawrence's, either for detailed observation or quality of writing. His talent for description had been refined by the discipline of making notes about architecture and archaeological finds, and he now had a remarkable ability to portray what he saw. Work on maps had taught him to record the shape of the landscape through which he travelled, and he kept a detailed log of travelling times and compass bearings throughout his journeys. Later these were used, together with his sketches of hill contours, as a basis for map revisions in Cairo. The route reports included valuable military information such as the location of wells and the suitability of terrain for wheeled vehicles. Although it was normal practice to write notes on 'personalities', his comments were particularly impressive, both for their physical descriptions and their shrewd evaluation of character.

Lawrence's comments on the political and military situation were influenced by his personal sympathies, as was the case with every other British officer in the Hejaz. His reports display a strong enthusiasm for the Arab cause he had tried for two years to promote from Cairo. One passage in particular shows how deeply he had been impressed by his firsthand contact with the Revolt, and by the rhetoric of Arab nationalism which Feisal was using to unite the tribes: 'A thing which has struck me rather forcibly while in the Hejaz is the bigness of the Revolt. Looked at from Egypt it loses some of its proportion, in our engrossment in the office telephones, and Canal defence, and the communiqués. Yet we have here a well-peopled province, extending from Um Lejj to Kunfida, more than a fortnight long in camel journeys, whose whole nomad and semi-nomad population have been suddenly changed from casual pilferers to deadly enemies of the Turks, fighting them, not perhaps in our manner, but effectively enough in their own way, in the name of the religion which so lately preached a Holy War against us, and fighting them with the full and friendly consciousness that we are with them and on their side. This has now been going on for five months during which time they have created out of nothing a sort of constitution and scheme of government, for the areas behind the firing line.

'The Beduin of the Hejaz is not, outwardly, a probable vehicle for abstract or altruistic ideas. Yet again and again I have heard from them about acts of the early Arabs, or things that the Sherif and his sons have said, which contain nearly all that the exalted Arab patriot would wish. They intend to restore the *Sheria* [Islamic law], to revive the Arabic language, and to rebuild the prosperity of the country. They believe that by liberating the Hejaz they are vindicating the rights of all Arabs to a national political existence, and without envisaging one state, or even a federation, they are definitely looking north, towards Syria and Baghdad. They do not question the independence of the Imam, or Ibn Saoud: they wish to confirm them... but they want to add an autonomous Syria to the Arab estate.

'Above and beyond everything we have let loose a wave of anti-Turkish feeling which, embittered as it has been by some generations of subjection, may die very hard. There is among the tribes in the firing line a nervous enthusiasm, common I suppose to all national risings. A rebellion on such a scale as this does more to weaken a country than unsuccessful foreign wars, and I suspect that Turkey has been harmed here more than it will be harmed elsewhere till Constantinople is captured, and the Sultan made the puppet of European advisers.'[32]

On October 31st HMS *Suva* put in to Yenbo. Colonel Parker, knowing Lawrence's intended route, had come up with her to learn about conditions inland. Afterwards he noted in his diary: 'It appears most important that His Excellency the Sirdar should have first hand information of the nature of the country and the situation and I have therefore advised Lawrence if he can spare the time to proceed to Jiddah and endeavour to obtain a passage, possibly in the [Admiral] C.-in-C.'s ship . . . to Port Sudan, proceeding thence to His Excellency. This he is doing, Captain Boyle having been so kind as to offer to take him to Jiddah.'[33]

Lawrence left Jidda on board HMS *Euryalus*, the flagship of Admiral Wemyss, who had since June been one of the mainstays and best-informed observers of the Revolt. Having crossed the Red Sea they arrived in Port Sudan on November 5th. Here they encountered two other British officers, Major Joyce and Captain Davenport, who were travelling in the opposite direction. The British Government had again authorised the dispatch of a flight of aeroplanes to Rabegh, and since no military escort was available from the EEF, Wingate was sending two companies of Egyptian Moslem troops from the Sudan. Joyce and Davenport were in charge of this contingent, and they would also help train the regular Arab units al Masri was trying to form.

From Port Sudan Lawrence travelled inland with Wemyss to see Wingate at Khartoum. They arrived to find that there had just been a further crisis over Rabegh: at the end of October reports had reached the town that a Turkish column was at Bir ibn Hassani, only three days' march away. Wingate had cabled to London on November 2nd stressing the danger of the situation. He had explained that the Sherif was asking repeatedly for guns and technical personnel to stiffen the Arab forces. However, no further men or weapons could be spared from the Sudan. A French contingent of about a thousand Moslem troops from North Africa was due to arrive in Egypt in mid-November, but Brémond was insisting that it should not proceed to Rabegh except as part of 'an Anglo-French force, minimum strength six battalions, with two mountain batteries and four field batteries.'[34] As a temporary expedient Wingate had asked the

Navy to assemble as many ships at possible at Rabegh, both to protect the town with gunfire and to help with an evacuation if the Turks broke through. He could 'take no further action pending a decision by H.M.'s Government and the French Government'.[35]

The War Committee had reconsidered the position that same day, partly on the strength of Wingate's telegram, and partly at the instigation of the French. A note had been delivered to the Foreign Office by the French Embassy on November 1st, reporting Brémond's view that 'it would be highly imprudent to land the guns and *mitrailleuses* sent from Algiers unless they could be protected by a sufficient escort to secure their not falling into enemy hands . . . the Chargé d'Affaires has been instructed by his Government to request in the most pressing manner His Majesty's Government to examine afresh the question of sending a sufficient force to Rabegh to constitute a base'.[36] Brémond was an experienced professional soldier, and his arguments against landing a small force at Rabegh were exactly those Murray had used at the Ismailia conference on September 12th.

Despite this plea, the War Committee meeting on November 2nd had reaffirmed its previous decision not to dispatch a brigade. If the naval presence at Rabegh seemed insufficient to defend the town, Wingate was authorised to send 'whatever French, British and Sudanese military assistance is immediately available'.[37] In communicating this decision to Murray, however, Robertson had warned against releasing any men from the EEF: 'You should understand these instructions are not intended to extend to the despatch of any troops from your command to Rabegh . . . I do not know if [Wingate] will ask you for assistance but in any case there is no question of sending anything of the nature of an expeditionary force or such other force as may involve us in still another campaign'.[38] As Wingate had no further troops available in the Sudan, this restriction left him with nothing to offer.

At the same meeting the War Committee had agreed that the French should be asked 'to send whatever troops they have immediately available, irrespective of whether they are Christian or Mahommedan'.[39] Wingate had been informed.

Ironically, on the day that these decisions were taken in London, news had reached Khartoum that the rumour of a Turkish column at Bir ibn Hassani was false. Nevertheless, Parker telegraphed that the scare had 'destroyed all morale at Rabegh which proves that the Rabegh force could not stand for a moment if threatened . . . I consider the best solution would be for the British Government to reconsider their decision and land a brigade at Rabegh.'[40] Wingate was considering his next move when Lawrence and Wemyss reached Khartoum.

By chance, their arrival also coincided with the announcement that Wingate was to replace McMahon as British High Commissioner in Cairo in December. McMahon had been identified with the pro-Arab policy conducted from Cairo during the preceding months, and to Lawrence his unexplained removal seemed a victory for French and Anglo-Indian interests in London. The news seemed ominous, and Lawrence was uneasy about the future of Britain's promises to Hussein. He later wrote: 'The dismissal of Sir Henry McMahon confirmed my belief in our essential insincerity'.[41]

Nevertheless, McMahon's departure would end the absurd division of military and political responsibility for dealings with the Revolt. From Khartoum, Wingate had been unable to stay in close contact with the latest thinking in Cairo.[42] Wingate and Wemyss were therefore now the two most senior British officers directly involved with the Arab campaign, while Lawrence had just returned from the most extensive Intelligence-gathering mission yet undertaken in the Hejaz. Their meeting was an occasion for far-reaching discussions about the present difficulties and future potential of the Sherifian forces.

By this time Lawrence had strong opinions on these subjects. In particular he argued that the hill passes between Medina and Rabegh gave Feisal's Arab tribesmen a great natural advantage, enabling them to block a much larger conventional force. If properly equipped and advised, the local tribes could make these hills into an impregnable shield and the question of defending Rabegh itself would never arise. He had arrived at Khartoum in an optimistic frame of mind.

The War Committee's refusal to send a brigade to Rabegh seemed conclusive; it had considered the question three times during the previous month, reaching the same decision on each occasion. As a result, the discussions at Khartoum concentrated on alternative measures. This shift in emphasis seems to have concealed the extent to which those taking part disagreed about the Rabegh question. Wemyss and Lawrence were both totally opposed to any large-scale Allied landing, thinking that it would weaken the Revolt. In their view, the Arabs would tolerate a small number of advisers and technicians, and would willingly accept a flight of British aircraft, but the arrival of a largely Christian brigade would be a different matter. At best, there was a risk that the Arab tribesmen would leave all the fighting to these Allied regulars. At worst, they might see the landing as an invasion, and go over to the Turks.

Wingate, however, had been greatly disappointed by the War Committee's decision. He felt that the opinion of professional soldiers such as Wilson, Parker and Brémond should carry more weight. In the extreme case, difficulties over Christians and Moslems would surely vanish. He later wrote: 'When I put to [Lawrence] the contingency of an advance in force on Rabegh by the Turks, and the possibility of arresting this advance by a brigade of British or French troops summoned there on the urgent appeal of the Sherif, I understood him to agree that in such an emergency the Arabs would welcome this help, and, in spite of their religious objections, would cling to this hope of success rather than acquiesce in the certain defeat that failure to hold Rabegh would mean.'[43] It is clear, however, from later documents that both Wemyss and Lawrence must have thought this argument purely academic.

At the end of their discussions Wingate drafted a telegram to the Foreign Office which appeared to accept the War Committee decision. Since no British troops were available, he would again ask Colonel Brémond to send the Moslem contingent arriving shortly from North Africa.[44] He showed the text of this telegram to both Wemyss and Lawrence, and Wemyss at least left Khartoum under the impression that they were all agreed. Lawrence cannot have been pleased at the idea of inviting such a large French presence to the Hejaz but, having spoken to Brémond, he knew that it was unlikely to be sent as long as British troops were withheld.

For the present, Wingate accepted that Feisal's army was the sole obstacle to the Turks, and he promised to do what he could to strengthen it with guns, machine guns and air support. The Arab trained bands scheme, though promising, was still in embryo.

In the event that the Turks did not now take Rabegh and advance on Mecca, there remained the long-term question of an Arab offensive. The principal objective would be to capture Medina, the last Turkish stronghold in the Hejaz. This, however, would be a major operation, and every British officer visiting the Hejaz had concluded that it should not be attempted until the Sherifian forces had resolved their problems of communication, organisation and fighting strength. For example, Captain Bray, an Indian Army officer who had recently visited the three Red Sea ports in Arab hands, had concluded: 'The military situation is one most difficult to define owing . . . to the lack of reliable information and the constantly changing opinions and demands of the Arab leaders . . . The Arab plan is for all three brothers to concentrate on Medina and take the offensive. Their concentration on Medina appears to me an excellent plan and the only one possible. But I submit that they should be advised firstly to make no serious attack till all three are concentrated there, and when so concentrated, that they should commit themselves to no *general* action in which a defeat would have serious consequences for the whole Arab cause. By constantly cutting the railway they will keep the Turks tied down to Medina and short of supplies etc.; by making rapid attacks and withdrawals they will gradually wear him down and they are experts at this kind of warfare.'[45] At the Khartoum meeting Lawrence expressed very similar conclusions: a direct attack on Medina would be unlikely to succeed until the Sherifian forces were more efficiently organised and better trained. As things stood, the only hope was to cut the Hejaz line permanently, leaving the Turks in Medina without supplies. If this could be achieved, Fakhri's garrison would eventually have to surrender.

In the meantime there seemed to be two areas in which British help to the Arabs could be made more effective. First, there was an urgent need for military training and technical advice. Wingate had already decided to increase the number of Arabic-speaking British officers in the Hejaz. Apart from Joyce and Davenport, whom Lawrence had already met, there was Major Garland, an engineer officer from Egypt who was training the Arabs to use explosives. A still larger staff of advisers seemed to be needed, and Wingate told the War Office: 'The necessity for the presence at Rabegh of a small expert military staff to superintend the organisation of Arab trained bands and to advise on and appreciate the military situation is very urgent. Colonel Newcombe, an artillery officer and an engineer officer should be sent as soon as possible . . . If possible Colonel Newcombe's assistants should have previous experience of Arabs.'[46] The group Newcombe would command was to leave for the Hejaz within a few weeks. It would be known as the British Military Mission.

The other area for improvement was liaison and Intelligence. Britain would not be able to give the Arabs effective support unless Wingate was much better informed about the military situation and the true capability of Hussein's forces. He needed frequent and accurate reports on all aspects of the campaign, but information obtained from Arab sources was notoriously unreliable. For example, while the Khartoum discussions were taking place Parker discovered that Ali's force defending Rabegh amounted to less than four thousand men. He wrote: 'Considering that the numbers have been considerably increased since the date of the Admiral C.-in-C.'s visit and that there were [then] said to be 5,000 men at Rabegh, it shows what reliance can be placed on the ordinary statement of fact made by Arab leaders.'[47] It was clear that a British Intelligence organisation would be much more satisfactory. Bray had reached similar conclusions, but he had also stressed the difficulties which faced British officers in the Hejaz. While visiting Rabegh he had tried to help Parker advise on the defences. Afterwards he had written: 'The position properly organised would be a strong one, unprepared it is extremely weak. Everything pointed to the fact that [the Arabs] wished to do just enough to please us and that they never seriously considered the possibility of having to defend it. Great difficulties were put in our way both as regards our examining the ground and assisting them in training their men. We offered to hold machine gun courses daily from 6 to 9 a.m. on the beach and though they got into difficulties with the guns at once they refused our assistance; it was the same with every offer of assistance of this description we made. Nuri [as-Said] Bey was in my opinion too young and inexperienced to be in command of serious military operations and he and Hilmi were obviously jealous of any action on our part that would bring us in contact with the Arabs. His plans for the defence of Rabegh were childish in the extreme and either he was convinced that no occasion would arise for the defence of the locality or else he was totally incapable.

'[Ali] confessed to Colonel Parker that he was entirely ignorant of military affairs. The sole direction was left to Nuri Bey assisted by Hilmi as artillery officer. The latter was absolutely ignorant as to the handling of machine-guns. I fear these guns will soon be out of order.'[48] Bray's suggestion was to send an experienced Moslem officer from the Allied armies to perform liaison and Intelligence duties on Feisal's staff.

This question was not resolved at the Khartoum meeting, but on November 11th, just after Lawrence had left for Cairo, Wingate received a cable from Robertson at the War Office: 'In view of the importance of establishing at Rabegh a Military Intelligence system it is suggested that an officer should be specially detailed to undertake as soon as possible the work of organising such a system on the spot. Bray [who had returned to London] thinks that Feisal would welcome the proposal, if judiciously approached, and it is possible that an organisation of this description might lead to our obtaining valuable military information about Turks generally. Bray will probably be sent out to you shortly, but as you may need him to train Arab bands, it is suggested that unless you have someone available in Sudan you could obtain an officer from G.O.C. Egypt. The names Lawrence or George Lloyd occur to me as suitable.'[49]

There were, however, other plans for Lawrence's future when he got back to Cairo. Clayton had gone to some trouble to secure his services, and the Arab Bureau report of October 31st had noted that: '2/Lieut. Lawrence, who has since the inception of the Bureau given much unofficial assistance, has been on a mission to the Hejaz . . . On his return he will become a regular member of the staff with propaganda as his special domain. This important subject, which was one of the original objects for which the Bureau was formed, has hitherto been dealt with by Capt. P. Graves of the Military Intelligence, in addition to his ordinary duties. By transferring it to the Bureau and putting it in the hands of an officer who will devote all his time to it, it is hoped that the scope may be considerably enlarged.'[50]

On receiving Robertson's cable about Hejaz Intelligence, Wingate immediately dispatched a copy to Clayton, adding: 'I propose sending Newcombe to Yenbo but in view of the possible delay of his arrival I think Lawrence would do this work excellently as a temporary arrangement. George Lloyd might do well for Rabegh.'[51] Wingate suspected that Clayton would oppose this plan, as is clear from a message he sent to Wilson on the same day: 'I telegraphed to you to ask who you would like to send [to Yenbo] – my own idea is that pending Newcombe's arrival (and he is undoubtedly just the man for that place) Lawrence, who knows Feisal well, would be most suitable, but I can imagine Clayton crying out against it, as I am afraid the Arab Bureau is rather hard put to it.'[52] He was right about Clayton's reaction, and shortly afterwards he received a strong protest: 'The importance of an Intelligence system as suggested is obvious and the establishment of such a system was one of the subjects of Parker's mission. Lawrence was sent there with much the same object. The difficulties at present are apparently the impossibility of getting British officers into the interior and the inaccuracy and unreliability of Arab agents . . . G.H.Q. are prepared to hand Lawrence over to the Arab Bureau and I think his great knowledge and experience of far greater value at headquarters where he will be almost indispensable. The same applies to Lloyd, whose strong points are politics, economics and commerce, and who in addition does not I believe know Arabic.

'I strongly deprecate therefore sending either of these two officers, especially Lawrence.'[53]

There was also opposition to the proposal from Wilson, to whom Lawrence would report if he returned to the Hejaz. Wilson's relationship with Lawrence had got off to a bad start when they had met in Cairo some weeks before. Lawrence had disagreed with Wilson's view that it was undignified for Europeans to wear Arab clothes (Lawrence later wrote, 'I had called them uncomfortable merely. To him they were wrong.')[54] There had also been some coolness between them when Lawrence visited Jidda, and he had later sent veiled personal criticisms of Wilson to Cairo, suggesting that Storrs should be asked 'a few leading questions'.[55]

Wilson now argued that if Lawrence returned to the Hejaz it should be to Rabegh rather than Yenbo. Doubtless he preferred to keep this untried newcomer under the scrutiny of a senior officer such as Parker. Wingate, however, insisted that Lawrence should go to Yenbo in order to report on the situation and to arrange supplies. He used the same argument to persuade Clayton: 'It is vitally important to have an officer of his exceptional knowledge of Arabs in close touch with Feisal at this critical juncture; but, as soon as Newcombe arrives, Lawrence will return to the Arab Bureau where I consider his services would be most valuable. G. Lloyd will . . . make a tour to Jidda and Rabegh. With Parker, Joyce and others at Rabegh it is quite possible his services will not be required there permanently'.[56]

Thus when Lawrence reached Cairo in mid-November, his future was uncertain. A few days passed before he was told about the plan to send him to Yenbo; in the meantime he was thoroughly preoccupied with the Rabegh question.

Although the Cabinet had believed that its decision about Rabegh was final, it had underestimated French persistence. On November 8th Paris had responded to the War Committee's request (of November 2nd) that France should send any contingents available without waiting for British participation. The reply alleged that Murray was now facing a much reduced number of Turks in Sinai, and that: 'It cannot be held at present that the absence of a brigade would endanger the defence of Egypt, whereas its presence [at Rabegh] seems necessary and sufficient to block a Turkish advance. The mere news of a Turkish offensive has already demoralised the Sherifian tribes. Colonel Brémond, Colonel Wilson, and all other well-wishing people who have observed the Arab enterprise close to, have been struck by the many kinds of rivalry that divide the sheikhs, and the inability of the rebel army to stand up to regular troops.

The arrival of a few French technical detachments will not instil courage into the bedouin. These units would be a valuable addition, but they cannot provide the kind of field force that British infantry would form. Sending these French units to Rabegh on their own would mean unnecessarily risking their sacrifice, thereby handing to the Turks the guns and machine guns intended for the Sherif's army . . .

'The French Government has asked its Ambassador to request H. M. Government again to give its full attention to this question, stressing . . . that any decision by the War Committee would have to be carried out in full before it is too late'.[57]

As a result of this letter a meeting had been held at the Foreign Office on November 10th. Grey, Curzon and Austen Chamberlain had agreed that 'it is of the highest importance to deny Rabegh to the enemy'.[58] Robertson had been asked to examine the question again and let the War Committee know what force would be necessary to block the Turks. On the following day Robertson consulted Murray, who argued that diverting troops to Rabegh would eliminate his offensive capability in Sinai.[59] The French had, of course, no sympathy with Murray's plans for an offensive that would take British forces into Palestine; this was a further reason for wishing to transfer part of his army to the Hejaz.

None of the authorities in Egypt wanted to send troops to Rabegh. Clayton was therefore pleased to find that Lawrence had returned from the Hejaz strongly opposed to the scheme. He asked Lawrence to write a memorandum on the subject, and the result was 'a short and very pungent note',[60] part of which read: 'All the forces fighting for the Sherif are made up of tribesmen, and it is the tribal army 3,000 to 4,000 strong under Sidi Feisal . . . that has held up the advance on Mecca or Rabegh of Fakhri Pasha's army for five months. Rabegh is not, and never has been, defensible with Arab forces, and the Turks have not got there because these hill tribes under Feisal bar their way. If the hill tribes yield the Turks need not look to any further opposition to their advance until near Mecca itself. This situation affects our consideration of the scheme to land an Allied force at Rabegh; so long as the tribes hold out such a force is not necessary. If the tribes give way the Turks will reach Rabegh in about four days. This does not give time for the collection, embarcation, transport, disembarcation, and preparation of a position for a British force to hold the front of 6,000 yards of the palm grove at Rabegh. The British force therefore must arrive at Rabegh while the tribes are still resisting the Turks if it is to get there in time. At present the tribes' opinion is chauvinistic. They are our very good friends while we respect their independence. They are deeply grateful for the help we have given them, but they fear lest we may make it a claim upon them afterwards. We have appropriated too many Moslem countries for them to have any real trust in our disinterestedness, and they are terribly afraid of an English occupation of Hejaz. If the British with or without the Sherif's approval landed at Rabegh an armed force strong enough to take possession of the groves and organise a position there, they would, I am convinced, say "We are betrayed", and scatter to their tents.'[61]

The memorandum also stated Lawrence's suspicion of Brémond's aims. It ended: 'The policy of not landing a British force at Rabegh should not be made an excuse for doing nothing in the Hejaz. If we spare ourselves this expense and trouble, it is all the more incumbent upon us to stiffen the tribal army, on which we are going to rely for the defence of Mecca. This stiffening is (by request) not to consist of personnel, but of materials. Sherif Feisal asked nearly four months ago for three batteries of quick firing mountain guns, and not only have none been sent, but he has not been given any written or verbal answer to his demand . . . the British Government can certainly supply them if it wishes, and if it does not it must take the responsibility if the tribes' resistance fails, and they will certainly not carry on for an indefinite time in the present circumstances. On the other hand, if they are given these guns (whose value will be mainly moral) they will, in my opinion, be able to hold up the present Turkish force as long as they require. Their morale is excellent, their tactics and manner of fighting admirably adapted to the very difficult country they are defending, and their leaders fully understand that to provoke a definite issue now is to lose the war. To continue the present *guerre de course* is sooner or later to wear out the Turks completely, and force them back on a passive defence of Medina and its railway communications.'[62]

Clayton circulated extracts from this memorandum, with a covering note which read: 'The following observations by Lieut. Lawrence, an officer of great experience and knowledge of Arabs, who has just returned from a visit to Feisal's camp and also Rabegh, are very pertinent to the question of the despatch of a brigade to Rabegh, which seems again to be under consideration by H. M. Government.'[63]

Murray was delighted by Lawrence's forthright condemnation of the Rabegh scheme, and without reference to Wingate cabled the entire document to London, sending a parallel wire to Robertson suggesting that he read it.[64] As a result, Lawrence's counterblast to the arguments put forward by Wilson, Parker and Brémond was before the Cabinet within days. While Lawrence had hoped that his memorandum would undermine support for the Rabegh scheme, he cannot have imagined that it would receive such attention.

Lawrence was not alone in his protest. Admiral Wemyss wrote to Wingate on November 19th: 'As a general principle both McMahon and Murray are thoroughly in accord with your policy. Imagine therefore all our feelings when the telegram was received saying that the War Council were reconsidering the question of sending troops to Rabegh! – I waited for nothing, and telegraphed to the Admiralty . . . telling them that I considered it would be most dangerous to the success of the Sherif's cause; and I found that Murray had done the same to the War Office. It is really heartbreaking to think that at last, when everybody principally concerned has arrived at the same conclusion, the War Council should be induced to consider other steps through the machinations of the French diplomats.'[65]

However, these statements by Wemyss and Lawrence ran counter to the response from Wingate, who had already sent London 'a guarded despatch, half-tending towards direct interference'[66] (as Lawrence later put it). Wingate had argued in favour of sending a brigade, but had suggested that 'from the political and religious standpoint, it would be desirable to delay to the last moment the despatch of such troops. They should . . . be held in readiness at Suez [rather than being sent immediately], as it is just possible the measures now being taken by Feisal may so threaten the advance as to cause the enemy to pause'.[67]

The net effect of these contradictory messages on the War Committee was to suggest that the advice Wingate had received from Colonel Wilson was fallible, and that the French position owed more to political considerations than to the specific needs at Rabegh. As a result no immediate decision was taken. While Wingate continued to argue for intervention, every message from Cairo opposed it. Most of the telegrams were copied to the Arab Bureau where they were seen by Lawrence. He made it his business to see that French motives were well understood. For example, McMahon wrote to the Foreign Office: 'I have always feared that whatever the Sherif and his sons may say our occupation of Rabegh would, for one reason or another, have a disintegrating effect on the Arab tribal forces now in the field. Lawrence, who has just returned from the Arab camp, and whom I know to be a very shrewd observer, has confirmed my opinion on this point. He has moreover told me, as doubtless you will have heard from the Sirdar, that the French hold the same view, and it is with this very object that they are magnifying the dangers of the present situation and advocating action at Rabegh. Colonel Brémond even went so far in a moment of confidence as to tell Lawrence that the French object was to thus disintegrate Arab effort, as they by no means wished to see them turn the Turks out of Medina any sooner than could be avoided. France would prefer to assist in handing over Medina to the Arabs at the end of the war, and make as much political capital as possible with the Arabs by her assistance in this matter.

'It is as well to remember this in any proposals that the French may now or hereafter make in regard to our joint assistance to the Sherif.

'It is of course always the old question of Syria and unless we keep our eyes upon them, the French in the furtherance of their Syrian policy will create unnecessary obstacles in the way of our policy within our own Arab sphere. I already see signs that we will not be allowed to conduct even the local operations at present contemplated [by Murray] after the capture of El Arish, against Beer Saba and the Hedjaz Railway, without embarrassing offers of French co-operation.'[68]

On November 19th Lawrence was told of the decision to send him back to Yenbo on a temporary liaison posting. The idea of returning did not appeal to him. In *Seven Pillars* he wrote: 'I urged my complete unfitness for the job.'[69] There is evidence of this protest in a telegram from Clayton to Wingate, in which he passed on Lawrence's comments on the proposed Intelligence operation in the Hejaz: 'Yenbo depends on Feisal. Without his permission no one can do anything. Feisal is most unlikely to permit a non-Arab authority to run an Intelligence section in his territory.

'He has his own agents and would probably impart their information if Lawrence was sitting in his own camp. He might take advice as to their direction but he is *very* difficult to advise.

'If his confidence were won he might give a freer hand than Lawrence now expects, but the facilities in any case would be personal and would take time to arrange.'[70] Wingate replied: 'I fully appreciate the force of Lawrence's remarks but his own influence with Feisal will, I am confident, result in the establishment of a good Intelligence system when he gets to Yenbo.'[71] (At this point Wingate had still not seen Lawrence's memorandum on the Rabegh question, which would later be the cause of some irritation.)

The following day Clayton sent Wingate a letter about the Arab Revolt based in part on discussions with al Masri, whose efforts to form regular Arab units at Rabegh had been systematically balked by Sherif Ali. Al Masri was now totally disillusioned with both Ali and Hussein.[72] He had therefore asked for his regular force to be brought under direct British control or, alternatively, transferred to Feisal's command at Yenbo. Having read Lawrence's reports, Clayton already believed that Feisal was the best hope for Arab leadership in the field. This meant that he too favoured a greater effort at Yenbo: 'I feel that, for strategical and political reasons, Yanbo stands out as far better than Rabegh as the future base of our military activity in the Hejaz. The outstanding advantage which Yanbo possesses is the fact that it is an admirable base for offensive operations . . . To my mind it is absolutely vital that we should assist the Arabs to prosecute an offensive as soon as possible. They could doubtless keep up the present state of affairs for some considerable time but, in view of the Arab nature, as time goes on we are running an increasing danger of finding that the Arabs get sick of the show and begin to melt away. It is only by an offensive that they can be kept together and in the field. The immediate threat on Mecca having died away somewhat, it seems to me that, while keeping Rabegh as it is, our future efforts should be based on Yanbo.

'The Hejaz railway is the key of the whole problem and it is the permanent cutting of that railway, or at least the dislocation of its running, which is the most important point to aim at.

'The Turkish force at Medina can stay there as long as it likes, provided it is rendered incapable of a serious offensive and when eventually the railway is cut permanently, as a result of our activities further north, the Medina Division is lost.'[73] The proposition that it would do little harm if a Turkish garrison remained at Medina reversed one of the key assumptions behind Arab plans and Wingate's own thinking. Four months later, however, Lawrence would argue on the same lines when propounding a new strategy for the Revolt.

The differences of opinion between Clayton and Wingate at this point were caused in part by their geographical separation. Wingate's chief responsibilities were in the Sudan, and he had little concern for Murray's difficulties. Clayton, on the other hand, had daily contacts with the EEF, and had hitherto played an important role in Murray's Intelligence Department. Even after the separation of the Arab Bureau, he had access to much wider Intelligence resources than Wingate. From his base in

Khartoum, Wingate was obliged to rely heavily on information about the Hejaz sent by Wilson, who had been his own nominee. Wilson, however, was confined almost entirely to Jidda, where he dealt mainly with Hussein, Abdullah, and Brémond. He left Parker to keep an eye on the situation at Rabegh, and his contacts with Feisal had been minimal.

Wingate almost always adhered to Wilson's views, but these were less highly regarded in Cairo. Many EEF staff officers would have agreed with Murray that: 'Men like Wilson and Parker, now with the Sherif, are good Arabic scholars, know the habits and customs of the country, but their recommendations as to military actions are often futile and impossible of execution.'[74] Clayton for his part placed greater trust in Lawrence, whom he himself had sent to the Hejaz. Lawrence now dis-agreed with Wilson on many issues and regarded Brémond's influence as pernicious.

These difficulties would be greatly reduced at the end of the year when Wingate moved to Cairo. In the meantime there was tension, and this was exacerbated by the memorandum Lawrence had written on the Rabegh question. Once Wingate had seen it he did everything possible to counter-act Lawrence's arguments. Later he wrote to Wilson: 'The whole point of this little "storm in a teacup" was evidently an attempt [by Murray] to get out of any responsibility for sending troops to the Hedjaz . . . basing it on Lawrence's views that the landing of Christian troops in any numbers at Rabegh would at once cause Feisal's Arabs to throw in their hands and return to their homes.

'There may be something in what Lawrence says, but he appears to me to have omitted the one and important essential, and that is that the Arabs have no more desire to come under the heel of the Turks again than has the Sherif himself, and when it comes to a matter of almost certain defeat, the Arabs will, in my opinion, welcome any steps taken to save them . . .

'I have no doubt that Lawrence has done all this in perfectly good faith, but he appears to me to be a visionary and his amateur soldiering has evidently given him an exaggerated idea of the soundness of his views on purely military matters.

'However, as you will see from my two replies to the Foreign Office, I am quite prepared to stake my military reputation on the views expressed by yourself and Parker, who are good soldiers and experienced in Arab ways . . . I think there is a great deal to be said for Lawrence's view of the French policy in the matter and as far as I can recollect you are also not entirely happy about French disinterestedness . . .

'I am principally annoyed in all this matter, not so much on account of the apparent want of straightness on the part of certain people who should be above that sort of thing, but on account of the huge loss of time when I am working at very high pressure, morning, noon and night . . .

'It seems to me strategically absolutely unsound to abandon Rabegh for Yenbo, although I quite agree that Yenbo may be made quite a useful subsidiary base for helping Faisal and perhaps training some contingents there if the personnel is available.

'I am rather disappointed at the Arab Bureau being drifted about by any wind that blows.'[75]

That same day Clayton wrote to Wingate in conciliatory terms, placing the entire blame for the memorandum affair on Murray. He even went so far as to claim that Murray had asked Lawrence to write it! No doubt he felt that this diplomatic lie would be helpful, both to himself and Lawrence, since Wingate was about to take over as their superior in Cairo.[76]

News of Lawrence's memorandum had been particularly unwelcome to Colonel Wilson at Jidda, who was not pleased to have his judgment challenged by this junior from Cairo. His critical attitude owed much to Lawrence's demeanour, which fell so far short of accepted military standards. As Dowson had already noted, Lawrence often antagonised very able regular officers, and Wilson was a case in point. Lawrence's conduct in the Hejaz can be judged by the later comments of Captain Boyle, whose ship had collected him from Yenbo some weeks previously. Boyle wrote of Lawrence's 'off-hand and somewhat rude manner', saying that he had been 'a little astonished when a small, untidily dressed and most unmilitary figure strolled up to me on board the ship I was temporarily commanding and said, hands in pockets and so without a salute: "I am going over to Port Sudan . . . "

'Looking at him I saw three stars on one shoulder strap, the other was blank, so I pointed out the first lieutenant . . . and told Lawrence to report himself to that officer, which he did. The first lieutenant, who had witnessed this meeting, subsequently speaking of it, said he had "properly told off Captain Lawrence" for his lack of manners.'[77]

On closer acquaintance Wilson would see Lawrence in a different light, but for the present he was furious. He wrote to Clayton: 'Lawrence wants kicking and kicking *hard* at that, then he would improve. At present I look upon him as a bumptious young ass who spoils his undoubted knowledge of Syrian Arabs etc. by making himself out to be the only authority on war, engineering, running H.M.'s ships and everything else. He put every single person's back up I've met, from the Admiral down to the most junior fellow on the Red Sea.'[78]

Such was the atmosphere when Lawrence set out on his second mission to the Hejaz, this time as Wilson's subordinate.

CHAPTER 16

Temporary Posting with Feisal
December 1916 – January 1917

LAWRENCE left Cairo on November 25th, and was in Yenbo by the beginning of December. From the outset his role was uncertain, and soon after arriving he wrote to Wilson that: 'General Clayton's orders to me were to go ashore and do what seemed best, and it would be hard to be more definite.'[1] As he found that Wilson had already sent a senior officer, Major Garland, to advise and help train the Arabs based in Yenbo itself, he decided to join Feisal inland as soon as possible.

The military position had changed since Lawrence's first visit to the Hejaz. By November Feisal had concluded that his tribesmen would block any Turkish advance through the hills south-west of Medina. The Sherifian leaders had begun to think of an extension northwards to Wejh, a small Turkish-held port two hundred miles up the coast from Yenbo. Possession of this northern base would allow them to attack the Hejaz Railway around El Ula, so far north of Medina that the line could not be protected by Fakhri Pasha's garrison. At the very least this thrust would extend the front and reduce the number of Turkish troops available for action against Rabegh. Feisal hoped, however, to keep the line cut permanently, thereby forcing the Medina garrison to surrender.

Details of this plan had been worked out at a meeting between Feisal, Ali and others held on November 16th at Rabegh. The first priority was to consolidate the Arab front in the hills west of Medina, and various steps had been decided upon to this end. Ali was to advance from Rabegh to Bir ibn Hassani in Wadi Safra. Feisal, with a large part of his army, would move northwards from Wadi Safra to Wadi Yenbo where he would establish a new position at Kheif Hussein. The remainder of his force would be placed under Hussein's youngest son, the Emir Zeid, who was to hold Bir Said and protect the route from Wadi Safra to Yenbo. These moves would prevent any Turkish advance from Medina towards Yenbo, Wejh or Rabegh. Meanwhile Abdullah, with a large force, had set off from Mecca to the region east of Medina. His role was to attack the railway and to prevent supply caravans sent by pro-Turkish tribes farther east from reaching the town. The Arabs hoped that these measures would contain the Turks in Medina while Sherif Nasir moved on Wejh with a two-thousand-strong force which he had already raised in the area north of Yenbo. Nasir, who came from one of the most influential families in the Hejaz, had already proved himself an extremely capable leader.

Once at Kheif Hussein, Feisal would build up his army by new recruitment. If Nasir's force proved insufficient to capture Wejh, Feisal would then be in a position to send reinforcements. Once the Arab position south-west of Medina had been secured, Feisal would move his operational base from Yenbo to Wejh.

At the end of November Feisal began to carry out his part of the scheme, moving north into Wadi Yenbo. He believed that the natural strength of Zeid's position at Bir Said would allow the force remaining there to keep the Turks in check. Lawrence, who had been told of these plans, rode inland on December 2nd expecting to meet Feisal's army at Kheif Hussein. He was astonished, therefore, to find the Arab force much closer to Yenbo at Nakhl Mubarak, one of the date plantations of Yenbo al Nakhl. It was apparent that something had gone badly wrong.

Lawrence explained the débâcle in a report to the Arab Bureau: 'While [Feisal] was in Wadi Yambo in early December the unexpected happened. The Arabs under Sidi Zeid became slack and left a by-road near Khalis unguarded. A Turkish mounted infantry patrol pushed up along it into Wadi Safra . . . The front line of Arabs, hearing news of this enemy six miles in their rear, broke with a rush to rescue their families and property in the threatened villages. Zeid's main body followed suit. Zeid himself fled at top pace to Yambo; and the astonished Turks occupied Hamra and Bir Said unopposed.'[2] As a result of this collapse there was no obstacle to a direct Turkish advance from Wadi Safra to Yenbo, and Feisal had no option but to withdraw almost to the coast.

He must have been pleased, at this difficult moment, to be joined by a liaison officer bringing the promise of more effective British support. Lawrence would be the first British officer to spend time with a Sherifian army inland, and Feisal asked him to wear Arab dress. This was, Lawrence wrote in *Seven Pillars*, so that 'the tribesmen would . . . understand how to take me. The only wearers of khaki in their experience had been Turkish officers, before whom they took up an instinctive defence. If I wore Meccan clothes, they would behave to me as though I were really one of the leaders; and I might slip in and out of Feisal's tent without making a sensation which he had to explain away each time to strangers.'[3] Feisal also pointed out that Arab dress would be more comfortable for desert living than uniform. Lawrence, who was already accustomed to wearing Arab clothes, agreed readily and was kitted out with fine white robes indicative of high rank. He later advised other British liaison officers: 'If you wear Arab things, wear the best. Clothes are significant among the tribes, and you must wear the appropriate, and appear at ease in them. Dress like a Sherif, if they agree to it.'[4]

After only two days with Feisal, Lawrence realised that there was little hope that the Arabs would hold the position at Nakhl Mubarak; their morale was gone, and a retreat to the coast seemed inevitable. He therefore returned hastily to Yenbo so that he could warn Garland. It seemed unlikely that the town could be held by Feisal's defeated army alone and Lawrence therefore arranged for an urgent message to be sent out to HMS *Suva*, which by good fortune had arrived a few days earlier with stores. On board was Captain Boyle, the Commander of the Red Sea Patrol Squadron. Lawrence hoped that more warships could be brought in to add their firepower to the town's defences. Within a short time Boyle was able to assemble five ships at Yenbo, including the monitor *M.31*, a vessel specially designed for coastal bombardment.[5] Lawrence also requested an air reconnaissance of the area round Wadi Safra and Bir Said.

Lawrence's earlier optimism about the role of Feisal's army had evaporated. He wrote despondently to the Arab Bureau: 'I had better preface by saying that I rode all Saturday night, had alarms and excursions all Sunday night, and rode again all last night, so my total of sleep is only three hours in the last three nights and I feel rather pessimistic. All the same, things are bad.'[6] He explained that support for Feisal among the hill tribes had disintegrated and that the prospects seemed grim. Lawrence knew that once the Arabs left the hills they would be no match for regular Turkish forces: 'In fact, the shield of Rabegh [i.e. the hill tribes] on which . . . I relied for all the defensive work is now gone. There is nothing now to prevent the Turks going south except Ali's anaemic force at Rabegh itself, the possibility of a recrudescence of the warlike spirit of the Harb [tribe] in their rear, or the fear of Feisal behind them all. Feisal's position becomes difficult. He is cut off by the Wadi Safra from the Hejaz proper, and his power of cutting the Sultani Road becomes remote. He is left with the Juheina only and they are a tribe with the seeds of trouble all present in them, in the jealousy of the Ibn Bedawi family of the hold Feisal is getting over their tribesmen . . . He has had a nasty knock in Zeid's retreat, and he realised perfectly well that it was the ruin of all his six months' work here up in the hills tying tribe to tribe and fixing each in its proper area. Yet he took it all in public as a joke, chaffing people on the way they had run away, jeering at them like children, but without in the least hurting their feelings, and making the others feel that nothing much had happened that could not be put right. He is magnificent, for to me privately he was most horribly cut up.'[7] In this new situation, Lawrence noted, Feisal 'becomes a tribal leader, not a leader of tribes.'[8]

Another difficulty was that Feisal's local knowledge was poor this far from Mecca. Lawrence wrote: 'He knows little more about Wadi Yenbo than we do. The names of places, sorts of roads and water supply are strange to him. He could still strike north, raise the Billi and Hueitat tribes and develop into South Syria, only he cannot do this while the Turkish force is free to attack Mecca in his absence.

'I asked him about the effect on the tribes of the fall of Rabegh and Mecca. It seems both have a great name among the tribes and he was not sure that the warlike feelings of the Juheina would survive the recovery of them by the Turks . . . Anyway he himself would not stick in the north and see Mecca fall . . .

'Feisal received me most cordially and I lived all the time with him in his tent or camp, so I had a very great insight into what he could do at a pinch. If I was not such a physical rag I would tell you all about it.

'P.S. Don't use any of above in *Bulletin* or elsewhere, it is not just – because I am done up.'[9]

A Turkish advance on Rabegh now seemed imminent. Parker, who handed over British liaison duties there to Major Joyce on December 5th, wrote a gloomy analysis of the position. As before, he recommended that an Allied force should be landed: 'the more so since the Trained Bands scheme has failed. [This] was perhaps a somewhat desperate expedient, since it depended on the caprice of a most changeable man. Had the Sherif given at the first full trust and authority to Aziz el Masri I believe that a force of some value would have been in existence now.'[10]

This Turkish threat to Rabegh was exactly what Wingate had feared, and he asked the Foreign Office to reopen the question of a landing. His anxiety increased when, on December 7th, Wilson cabled: 'The emergency period does appear imminent, though the lack of accuracy of Intelligence makes it extremely difficult to estimate the degree of the emergency. I telegraphed Lawrence this morning urgently for information and his views, but have no answer yet. I certainly think at least a brigade of troops . . . should be held ready for immediate embarcation at Suez, or as I have previously proposed at Port Sudan.'[11] Wilson reported that he had now asked the Sherif whether Christian rather than Moslem troops could be sent if necessary.

Feisal too recognised that the latest reverse endangered not merely his own position but the Revolt itself. On December 7th Lawrence forwarded a message from him to General Murray, asking the British to mount a diversion. Feisal drew attention to the Turkish forces which the Arab insurrection had drawn off from Sinai: 'The relief to you should be great, but the strain upon us is too great to endure. I hope your situation will permit you to press sharply on towards Beersheba, or feign a landing in Syria, as seems best, for I think the Turks hope to crush us soon and then return against you.'[12]

As Lawrence had feared, the Turks attacked the position at Nakhl Mubarak, and by the morning of December 9th the relics of Feisal's army, some fifteen hundred men, had arrived in Yenbo; the rest of the Arab forces had melted away to their villages. With Zeid's men this gave a total of around two thousand to defend the town. While Garland organised some rudimentary defences Lawrence arranged liaison with Boyle's warships. He noted: 'The place is in a plain, and naval gunnery would be very effective. At present there is a monitor, besides patrol ships. Garland has sited trenches round the perimeter of the town, to be held by such troops as will hold a trench; and the fifteen or twenty machine guns available with the ships' landing parties are to do the rest. The place would not stand a regular attack, but should be proof against a raid. If we had some armoured cars we could keep the Turkish patrols fifteen or twenty miles back in the plain.'[13]

It seemed that Yenbo would be secure as long as the British Navy could keep warships there. Boyle went ashore and looked over the approaches, concluding that the Turks would have to cross several miles of very flat open sand, some of it soft, before reaching the town. While doing so they would be exposed to ships' guns firing at close range. Although a night raid seemed possible, it would hardly be worth the risk since the naval guns would force a retreat at daybreak.[14] After talking to Feisal and the Egyptian gunners he cabled to Wemyss: 'The Arabs now admit their retirement was not necessary, and evidently they put up no fight. The Egyptian officers say the Turks were in no great strength but had three mountain guns and four machine guns. Feisal is undecided as to his future plans.'[15] Boyle arranged for seaplanes from HMS *Raven* to bomb the Turkish positions inland, and Lawrence drew a rough map of the area for the pilots.

For the moment, Feisal and Zeid were trapped in Yenbo, and Abdullah's army east of Medina was too far away to help if the Turks decided to advance. On its own, Ali's force at Rabegh could present little opposition. The crisis was so grave that on December 9th the War Office instructed Murray to hold a brigade in readiness, in case the Government should now decide in favour of a landing at Rabegh.[16]

On December 10th Wilson, Brémond, and George Lloyd discussed the emergency at a meeting with Hussein in Jidda. The Sherif now requested Allied troops to hold Rabegh; he was asked to put this in writing, and afterwards sent Wilson a note stating that three thousand men were required. Moslem troops would be preferable, but Christians could be sent if necessary.

The following morning Hussein informed Wilson that he had changed his mind. Later in the day, however, a cable arrived from Lawrence headed: 'British troops for Rabegh'. This underlined the pessimism at Yenbo: 'Sherif Feisal points out that the situation is entirely changed with the loss of Wadi Safra . . . the obstacle of public opinion amongst Harb and Juheina has disappeared with the dispersal of these tribes and everybody sees how serious the Arab position is . . . Without such a force at Rabegh, first, he will not be free to develop an attack on the railway . . . and, secondly, he thinks that the revolution may collapse in about three weeks' time.'[17] Lawrence also wrote to Clayton: 'Feisul has now swung round to the belief in a British force at Rabegh. I have wired this to you, and I see myself that his arguments have force. If Zeid had not been so slack things would never have got to this pass. The Arabs, outside their hills, are worthless.'[18] Lawrence's endorsement of the Rabegh scheme, which until now he had opposed so strongly, must have carried some weight.

In the light of Feisal's appeal, Wilson went to see Hussein again on the evening of December 11th, accompanied this time by Storrs. Hussein begged for Moslems to be sent, saying that he could not sanction the landing of Christian troops. However, he also asked for a Christian force to be held in readiness in case the situation deteriorated further.

Afterwards Storrs wrote in his diary: 'It has been my good or bad fortune on three separate voyages to Jedda to happen each time upon a

Rabegh crisis; and though the present circumstances were doubtless graver than upon other occasions, the chief interest was to see whether, in the place of the usual demands for brigades and batteries, anything in the nature of concerted Arab action would be proposed. No such scheme was forthcoming, but the request for fifteen hundred Moslem troops (to hold Rabegh) was explained, justified, and repeated although they were "Now almost certainly too late to prevent the Turkish advance".[19] During the three-hour meeting Hussein 'hinted his disappointment at our not having designated some able Moslem general to the conduct of his military operations. I replied that we had never dreamed of so marked and direct interference in his internal affairs'.[20] Storrs took this opportunity to point out that al Masri's advice had been almost entirely ignored. After further discussion Hussein agreed to appoint al Masri Minister of War. This was to prove no more meaningful, however, than the previous appointment as Chief of Staff .

At this time al Masri was in Rabegh helping Ali to organise a large-scale advance towards Wadi Safra. The intention was to draw off some of the Turkish pressure on Feisal's defeated army at Yenbo; but Joyce for one had little faith in the ability of Ali's force to withstand regular troops.

Although the danger to Rabegh was apparent to everyone, it was difficult for the British to decide how best to act. The problems were aggravated by Hussein's enigmatic personality. Envoys were charmed by his apparent sincerity and gracious manners, but they knew that he had little grasp of military affairs, and his behaviour was notoriously unpredictable. For example, at the end of October he had suddenly proclaimed himself 'King of the Arab nation' without consulting his European allies. This had created diplomatic problems for both Britain and France. He was prone to reversing his position on important issues, and often put a highly eccentric interpretation on written documents. Before landing Christian troops in the Hejaz, Wilson thought it essential to obtain an unambiguous written request. But Hussein was now procrastinating, and there seemed little chance that he would sign such a document in time to save Rabegh.

The atmosphere was not helped by Hussein's attempts to blame Britain for the military fiasco. On December 12th Wilson wired: 'In view of the Sherif's strong objection to landing Christian troops immediately I hesitate to recommend it being done, in spite of the risk which has been explained to him. Both yesterday morning and evening the Sherif stated that the Arabs' plan was based on our promise of cutting the Hejaz railway. If he had known we were not going to do so other plans of action would have had to be made. He ascribes the position of affairs to the fact that it was not done.'[21]

The truth, as Wilson strongly suspected, was quite different. At no point had McMahon offered to cut the Hejaz Railway, and the issue was now being raised to conceal Sherifian failures. Neither Hussein nor his sons had sufficient military expertise to defeat the Turkish Army, and the Revolt had depended from the outset on untrained Arab tribesmen. These difficulties had been compounded by inadequate military Intelligence and a total lack of forethought as to supply and communications. By mid-December the Revolt had almost collapsed on the battlefield, the one area outside Britain's control. From the start Hussein had been dependent on British help in money, food and arms. His rebellion was now surviving only through the presence of the Royal Navy's Red Sea Patrol, which formed the one serious obstacle to a Turkish advance on Yenbo, Rabegh, or indeed Mecca.

In the event, the naval presence was sufficient, and the Turks did not follow up their success. The closest they came to a decisive action was on the night of December 11th, when they seemed poised to attack Yenbo. Storrs (who arrived there not long afterwards) reported: 'the Turks were within fifteen miles of the town, and might have attacked that very night. Monitor *M.31* . . . was standing close in to bombard them in case of necessity. The aircraft vessel *Raven* was at Sherm Yenbo and the sea-planes had been quite recently bombing the Turks. I gather that the single trench, though technically an indifferent achievement, yet covered the plain across which the Turks must advance. By the 12th there was a regular panic ashore, and many notables including Feisal had boarded HMS *Hardinge*. The Turks moreover were reported closer still, some said within six miles, and in greater numbers than hitherto suspected.'[22] In reality, however, the danger had abated during the night. Lawrence wrote in *Seven Pillars*: 'Afterwards, old Dakhil Allah told me that he had guided the Turks down to rush Yenbo in the dark that they might stamp out Feisal's army once for all; but their hearts had failed them at the silence and the blaze of lighted ships from end to end of the harbour, with the eerie beams of the searchlights revealing the bleakness of the glacis they would have to cross. So they turned back: and that night, I believe, the Turks lost their war.'[23]

When this took place Lawrence was no longer at Yenbo; it was only later that he heard about what had happened on shore. He had gone on board HMS *Suva* on the afternoon of December 11th, and at 4 pm the ship had sailed for Rabegh. He was going there urgently in order to see Major Ross, commander of the RFC flight operating in the Hejaz. Feisal badly needed information about the strength of Turkish forces inland, but up to this point the results of reconnaissance flights near Yenbo had been useless. While in Rabegh Lawrence also wanted to discuss various matters with Joyce.

During the voyage he wrote despondently to Clayton about the value of his own role: 'My position at Yenbo is a little odd. I wire to Colonel Wilson only, and got a letter from him to say that I was in charge of supplies at Yenbo. That is not possible, for Abd el Kader, as agent of Sherif Feisul, runs the supply question ashore, and our interference would not be welcomed – and is not necessary. Whatever may be the position at Rabegh and Jidda, I can vouch that Yenbo is a most efficiently run show. All that a "supply officer" has to do is to hand over the way-bills or whatever you call them, to Abd el Kader.

'I regard myself as primarily Intelligence Officer, or liaison with Feisul. This was all right while Feisul was in the interior, as they seem settled to have no one but myself in there. Only he is now in Yenbo, half-besieged, and in these circumstances Garland is much more use than I could be. For one thing, he is senior to me, and he is an expert on explosives and machinery. He digs their trenches, repairs their guns, teaches them musketry, machine gun work, signalling: gets on with them exceedingly well, always makes the best of things, and they all like him too. He is quite alive to Intelligence work also, though he has not been in contact enough with things or documents to know much outside the immediate area here. Anyway he is the best man for Yenbo, and while he is here, I am wasting my time walking about with him. That is really why I am going down to Joyce, to see if he can suggest anything worth doing.'[24]

There is a hint in the final paragraph of this letter that Lawrence was trying to evade Wilson's supervision. He enclosed reports for the Arab Bureau, remarking that they 'have not been sent (except in very brief précis) to Colonel Wilson. If they are to be any good at all they should reach you within a reasonable period of despatch – and to send them to Jidda is only waste of a week or ten days. They would not add to Colonel Wilson's information: and I have no means of duplicating them.'[25]

Between December 11th and 16th Lawrence visited both Rabegh and Jidda. He had a disagreeable encounter with Brémond who was on the point of crossing the Red Sea for talks with Wingate about the Rabegh question. Brémond argued that Hussein should now be put under pressure to accept an Allied force. This reminder of French scheming seems to have renewed Lawrence's hostility towards a Rabegh landing.

Lawrence was away on this journey when Storrs arrived in Yenbo on December 13th and met Feisal for the first time. Storrs was impressed, as other British observers had been, by Feisal's appearance and personality, but a sense of dejection was also evident. 'I visited Sherif Feisal about 9.15', Storrs wrote. 'The notice I had given him had apparently enabled him to crowd on every inch of silk in Yenbo, but I was immensely struck with his personal appearance which in fact realises that of the legendary noble Arab. He was slightly thinner than I had been led to suppose and I am informed that the anxieties of the last two months have really worn him down considerably . . . After coffee and interchange of compliments Sherif Feisal, whose mien generally is that of one chastened by failure, reiterated, but always in a minor key, the complaints he had made to Captain Lawrence as to our delay in supplying the artillery requested four months ago. He admitted that nothing was to be now gained by enlarging upon this grievance and I took the opportunity of pointing out to him that, after the recent retreats, the courage of his Arab tribesmen stood in some need of vindication in the eyes of the world; even if they were for the moment unable to face their foes in the open field, their intimate knowledge of their own mountainous country would surely render them more redoubtable enemies in guerilla warfare. Sherif Feisal's first and last request, to which he several times reverted, was that the British should guarantee him the possession of Rabegh and Yenbo; with these two as bases upon which to fall back he would not hesitate to advance again upon the Turks and to take Wejh; it was the dread of being cut off that paralysed his strength.'[26]

On December 14th Brémond and George Lloyd, who had taken part in some of the recent discussions with Hussein, arrived in Khartoum to consult Wingate. The Revolt now seemed to be so near collapse that it was necessary to reconsider British policy towards it. After these talks Wingate cabled to the Foreign Office: 'Our efforts to train and organise an Arab force capable of meeting the Turks in the field have been unsuccessful, mainly owing to the inertness and ignorance of the Arab leaders: and the conduct of Arab levies in recent skirmishes affords little or no grounds for believing that they will be able to withstand a sustained advance by the Turks.'[27] He had concluded, with Brémond's encouragement, that the only hope was to send British troops as soon as possible: 'The immediate question for decision by H. M. Government is whether we shall make a last attempt to save the Sherif and his Arabs in spite of themselves.'[28] Lawrence would later write: '[Brémond's] specious appreciation of the danger of the existing state of affairs made a real dupe of Sir Reginald Wingate, who was constitutionally inclined to [the French] remedy. He was a British general, commander of a nominal expeditionary force . . . which in reality comprised a few liaison officers and a handful of storemen and instructors. If Brémond got his way, he would be G.O.C. of a genuine brigade of mixed British and French troops, with all its pleasant machinery of responsibility and despatches.'[29]

Wingate allowed himself to be persuaded that Hussein would accept Christian troops if put under pressure to do so. He sent Wilson a telegram for transmission to the Sherif: 'I fear in view of the doubts expressed by your Highness regarding the political wisdom of sending Christian troops, that H. M. Government will refuse to send them. If however the urgent necessity of preventing the failure of your Highness's and the Arab cause induces H. M. Government to accept the inevitable risk and to send these troops, I am confident that your Highness will accept them, and will try everything possible to prevent any misunderstanding, or false suspicions on the part of your Highness's military commanders and Arabs generally.'[30] In a covering message Wingate instructed Wilson to 'induce the Sherif to send me a satisfactory reply.'[31]

This message arrived in Jidda just as Hussein was leaving for Mecca and there was not time to decode the whole of it. However, Wilson spoke to the Sherif when he had seen enough to grasp the essentials. He cabled back on December 15th: 'there is no doubt that the Sherif really believes that the landing of Christian troops in the Hedjaz would very dangerously imperil his cause.'[32] Wilson was unwilling to press as hard as Wingate would have liked. His own attitude towards the Rabegh question was changing because he had learned from other Arab sources that the Sherif's anxieties about a British landing were probably well founded. He now told Wingate that the Grand Cadi at Mecca, known to be a moderate, had warned that the day Christian troops landed in the Hejaz the Sherif's power and influence would be broken.

Wilson had become increasingly wary of Brémond's scheming and doubtless recognised the influence behind this new approach. He now knew that Lawrence's contentious Rabegh memorandum had been well founded, and from this time his attitude was much less hostile. It was now Wingate's turn to come up against his sense of straight dealing. He insisted that unless the Sherif specifically asked for Christian troops they should not be sent. Instead he recommended that two Moslem battalions should go to Rabegh, together with Brémond's North African contingent at Suez, 'if he really means to assist'.[33]

Wingate thought this response completely unsatisfactory and decided to increase the pressure on Hussein. On December 16th he telegraphed to the Foreign Office that he would send the Sherif an ultimatum. Since no Moslem troops were available, and since it would be impossible to hold Christian troops indefinitely on standby, Hussein 'must therefore decide . . . whether or not he requires a European Force to be landed at Rabegh in the course of the next fortnight. If his reply is in the negative he must understand we shall regard his refusal as final, and that our present offer will not be repeated.

'There is always a chance that Turkish lack of initiative, coupled with nervousness regarding their communications, might still deter them from undertaking an offensive of sufficient force to overwhelm native Arab levies; but this chance seems to me a very small one.'[34]

This ultimatum was approved, and Murray was authorised to send the troops held on standby if Hussein could be brought to agree. Otherwise, as the Foreign Office pointed out, 'the responsibility for the collapse of the Sherif's movement . . . will rest with him, owing to his final refusal of British military assistance for which he had asked and which we were prepared to send.'[35]

While these exchanges were taking place there were unexpected military developments in the Hejaz. On December 16th, aerial reconnaissance observed what seemed to be a Turkish withdrawal from the approaches to Yenbo, and this was confirmed two days later by the news that Nakhl Mubarak had been evacuated. At first it seemed that this might be a local measure to avoid further bombing raids from HMS *Raven*'s two sea-planes. However, the withdrawal proved to be more general. It was now feared that the Turks might be concentrating their resources against Ali's makeshift force advancing from Rabegh, which had met little opposition thus far. Feisal re-occupied Nakhl Mubarak and almost immediately began a further advance inland, even though his forces were ill-prepared. His hope was to trap the Turkish Army in the hills, between his own force and Ali's.

Once the pressure on Yenbo had eased, Lawrence's thoughts turned to longer-term problems. On December 19th he wrote to Wilson, taking up once again the question of sending modern artillery to Feisal: 'I personally feel strongly that the inferior quality of these troops demands a superfine technical equipment. They have not the tactical skill to make an inferior gun, by superior handling, equal to the better gun of their enemies. Unless we can give them weapons in which they have confidence they will not be capable of meeting the Turkish artillery. When with Feisul in November, I wrote down to Colonel Parker, and asked for a battery of British field guns, latest pattern, with telescopic sights. The guns supplied to Feisul are two German-made fifteen-pounder guns, very much worn, without telescopic sights or range-tables, with defective fuses and ammunition, and lacking essential parts of elevating gear, etc. I think that a battery of used 18-pounders, with complete equipment, should be supplied to replace them.'[36] The request was futile: modern artillery was in heavy demand on every front and nothing could be spared to help the Arabs.

During these last weeks at Yenbo Lawrence had learnt a good deal from watching Garland teach the Arabs how to use explosives. He wrote in *Seven Pillars* that Garland 'had his own devices for mining trains and felling telegraphs and cutting metals; and his knowledge of Arabic and freedom from the theories of the ordinary sapper-school enabled him to teach the art of demolition to unlettered Beduin in a quick and ready way . . . Incidentally he taught me to be familiar with high explosive. Sappers handled it like a sacrament, but Garland would shovel a handful of detonators into his pocket, with a string of primers, fuse, and fusees, and jump gaily on his camel for a week's ride.'[37]

Garland's health was poor, and in mid-December he went to Cairo on leave. He could ill be spared, and Lawrence wrote to Wilson: 'I hope it will be arranged that he returns here when his leave expires; his knowledge of tools and arms has been invaluable, and when Feisul is able to restore communication with the Hejaz Railway, it will be possible for him to go up there and direct his explosive parties personally. Everybody ashore likes him.'[38] Ignorance of explosives had been a great handicap to the Revolt. The Arabs had torn up great stretches of line by hand, but this left the rails undamaged and repairs were easy. In the summer of 1916 Hussein had ordered that explosive supplied by Britain should be returned, because no one in the Sherifian armies knew how to use it. It was for this reason that Garland had been sent to teach basic demolition techniques. Much more damage would be done, however, if he could go inland himself and decide where to lay the dynamite charges. He was also designing special mines with automatic trigger mechanisms, which could be used to blow up trains; but trials were required to perfect them and they needed expert handling. Lawrence hoped that Feisal would eventually see the strength of these arguments. It seemed unlikely, however, that the Arabs would allow Christian officers to take part in attacks on the railway close to the holy city of Medina.

As Feisal began to push forward towards Wadi Safra in the hope of trapping the Turks, news came that Ali's force had taken fright on the strength of a false rumour and had retreated headlong to Rabegh. By December 22nd, therefore, Feisal was back in Nakhl Mubarak, very angry that the opportunity to catch the Turks had been missed. Fakhri's army seemed to be regrouping for some purpose, and if he decided to advance on Rabegh now, there was little to stop him. Rumours and counter-rumours came in from the hill tribesmen, and in Rabegh emergency plans were drawn up for an evacuation.[39]

During the last days of 1916 it became imperative for Feisal to take some kind of aggressive action. Since there was no hope of defeating the Turks around Medina, the only feasible course was to attack their lines of communication. The best scheme seemed to be for Feisal to advance on Wejh as quickly as possible with most of his army, and from there to mount a large-scale offensive against the railway. This would certainly divert Turkish attention from Rabegh.

The scheme was quite unlike the plans for Wejh that had been dis-cussed in mid-November. Feisal had never envisaged taking his main force to Wejh until strong defensive positions had been created in the hills south-west of Medina. As it was, the armies commanded by Ali and Zeid had proved completely ineffective. The risk of moving now seemed very great. Lawrence later wrote: 'Our fear was not of what lay before us, but of what lay behind. We were proposing the evacuation of Wadi Yenbo, our only defensive line against the Turkish division in Wadi Safra, only fifteen miles away. We were going to strip the Juheina country of its fighting men, and to leave Yenbo, till then our indispensable base, and the second sea-port of the Hejaz, in charge of the few men unfit for the march north, and therefore unfit for anything at all dangerous. We were going to march nearly two hundred miles up the coast, with no base behind and only hostile territory in front . . . If the Turks cut in behind us we would be neatly in the void.'[40] However, a move to Wejh 'now appeared not merely the convincing means of securing a siege of Medina, but an urgent necessity if a Turkish advance on Mecca was to be prevented.'[41]

While Lawrence was discussing the Wejh scheme with Feisal, he thought of another way to menace the Hejaz line. Abdullah's army, far inland, was supposed to be interrupting traffic but was not doing so. After the war, Lawrence would write: 'If only Abdulla had been threatening Medina properly at this time, the Turkish expedition against Rabegh would have been prevented, but his men had run short of water and food in their attempted blockade of the town on the east, and he had recalled the bulk of them to his own distant base of Henakiyeh.'[42] This base, well to the north-east of Medina, was a long way from the railway. Lawrence therefore suggested to Feisal that Abdullah should move west to Khaibar, no closer to Medina but much better placed for operations against the line. Then, however, Lawrence had second thoughts, and said that Abdullah might not be able to maintain himself at Khaibar. Feisal, who seems not to have understood him, interjected: 'You mean Wadi Ais...'[43]

This was not the first time Wadi Ais had been mentioned: it ran slightly north-of-east from the coast near Yenbo towards the Hejaz Railway, and three weeks previously there had been some talk of sending Nuri as-Said there. No one had thought of it, however, as a base for Abdullah's force; yet the valley was well-watered and accessible from the coast and it would be easy to keep a large army there supplied with food and arms. Lawrence urged Feisal to send a message asking Abdullah to go there, explaining that the move would have great strategic advantages. As he wrote in the *Arab Bulletin*, Wadi Ais was 'a natural fortress about 100 kilometres above Medina on the railway line. [Abdullah] would there be astride the Medina lines of communication, and no Turkish advance towards Mecca, Yambo, or even Rabugh would be possible till he had been dislodged'.[44] If at the same time Feisal moved to Wejh, the two Arab armies would dominate a two-hundred-mile stretch of the railway and the Medina garrison would be at their mercy. Feisal was convinced by these arguments, and a messenger was dispatched to Abdullah.

With Abdullah in this new position, the risk of leaving Yenbo so lightly defended would be much smaller, but Feisal was still uneasy. On December 27th Wilson arrived to urge him on. Feisal agreed with the need for action, but pointed out, as Lawrence wrote shortly afterwards, 'that the Rabugh force had proved hollow, and that the Turks in Hamra were open to strike at Rabugh and Yambo as they pleased. Now that Zeid was discredited, and Ali shown a broken reed, he could not risk leaving the area himself. In the circumstances Colonel Wilson gave Feisal his personal assurance that the Rabugh garrison (with British naval help) would be capable of resisting any Turkish attack until Feisal had occupied Wejh. There was no means of giving force to this assurance, but it seemed a reasonable and necessary risk to take, since without it Feisal would not have moved north.'[45]

That day Lawrence wrote to the Arab Bureau enquiring about the British Military Mission; he knew that Newcombe's arrival in the Hejaz would bring his liaison posting with Feisal to an end. However, it would be useful for Intelligence reasons if he visited the little-known Wadi Ais, and he hoped that this would prolong his stay. He asked: 'Have you any news of Newcombe? The situation is so interesting that I think I will fail to come back. I want to rub off my British habits and go off with Feisul for a bit. Amusing job, and all new country. When I have someone to take over here from me I'll go off . . . I wonder what the next week will bring forth, here and there. Somehow I do not believe in a Turkish advance on Mecca, though they could, if they wished.'[46] Newcombe, however, was not yet ready to leave Cairo. The Military Mission would be composed of four officers: Newcombe, an Engineer; two artillery officers, Majors Vickery and Cox; and a medical officer, Major Marshall. Newcombe was to go to Yenbo while the others would be stationed at Rabegh; they would all report to Wilson. In addition, Captain Bray had recently been sent back to the Hejaz, reaching Jidda on Christmas Day.

In Yenbo the Turkish threat seemed to be receding all the time and on 2nd January 1917 Lawrence reported: 'The Turks were getting rather nervous in Wadi Safra, I think, as their main force seems to have moved towards Ghayir or Gaha. So we pushed out a strong reconnaissance at midnight towards Wadi Safra. We will hear tonight of the evacuation of the Wadi by the Turks, I expect, and that means the end of the threat on Rabegh probably . . . The Wejh scheme is going strong. Feisal may start tomorrow, if Wadi Safra news tonight is good . . . If Hamra is re-taken and Feisal moves northward, the trick is played!'[47] On the night of January 3rd Lawrence went out with a small raiding party to attack a Turkish post in the hills. There was no engagement at close quarters, but this marked his first personal involvement in the fighting.

Feisal's army finally left Nakhl Mubarak the following day and moved a short distance to Owais. Lawrence returned from his night raid just as it was leaving and he accompanied it for part of the way. Afterwards he wrote: 'The order of march was rather splendid and barbaric. Feisal in front in white. Sharaf on his right, in red headcloth and henna-dyed tunic and cloak, myself on his left in white and red. Behind us three banners of purple silk, with gold spikes, behind them three drummers playing a march, and behind them a wild bouncing mass of 1,200 camels of the bodyguard, all packed as closely as they could move, the men in every variety of coloured clothes, and the camels nearly as brilliant in their trappings – and the whole crowd singing at the tops of their voices a war song in honour of Feisal and his family! It looked like a river of camels, for we filled up the Wadi to the tops of its banks, and poured along in a quarter-of-a-mile-long stream.'[48]

Naval support would be crucial during Feisal's northward advance along the level strip of land beside the Red Sea. There was a shortage of transport camels and the Arab army could not carry the provisions it would need. Feisal waited at Owais while Lawrence arranged with Boyle for the necessary supplies to be put ashore. By January 9th all was ready, and on the same day a message came from Abdullah that he was moving to Wadi Ais.[49]

Lawrence also heard that he was definitely to be relieved. Three days earlier Wilson had cabled to the Arab Bureau: 'I consider the Wejh operations offer a good opportunity to Newcombe and the other two to know Feisal and the various sheikhs . . . I wish him to proceed to Yenbo where Lawrence, who has received instructions from me to hand over to him, will meet him.'[50]

Lawrence therefore stayed behind in Yenbo to wait for Newcombe while Feisal marched north. He was not the only person who now felt that the initiative was passing to the Arabs. In a report to the Admiralty of January 10th, Admiral Wemyss wrote: 'As time goes on, I am strengthened in my opinion that the Turks find it beyond their power to move on Mecca. The latest trustworthy report is that an epidemic of some sort exists amongst the Turks at Medina . . . and although the Arabs have proved themselves to be most indifferent fighters in the open, I am still of opinion that if properly guided and led they should be able to seriously hamper any movement on the part of the enemy, by guerrilla warfare.'[51]

The improving position may have been one of the factors behind Hussein's final refusal of Allied troops for Rabegh, reported by Colonel Wilson on January 11th. Wilson commented: 'It is quite understood by the Sherif that . . . most probably no troops will be available should he ask for them at a later date.'[52]

During the first stages of its march, Feisal's army passed through friendly country. Um Lejj, the half-way point, had already been taken, and he set up camp some miles inland where there was adequate water. Meanwhile Lawrence heard that Newcombe would go straight to Um Lejj rather than to Yenbo, and went there himself on board HMS *Suva*. He wrote home with obvious regret that his liaison job with Feisal was about to end: 'My Arabic is getting quite fluent again! I nearly forgot it in Egypt, where I never spoke for fear of picking up the awful Egyptian accent and vocabulary. A few months more of this, and I'll be a qualified Arabian. I wish I had not to go back to Egypt. Anyway I have had a change.'[53] He must have expressed similar regrets to Hogarth, who wrote to E. T. Leeds a few days later: 'T.E.L. is still away and writes from time to time that he wishes to stay away from Europe and all things European for ever and ever, and get thoroughly Arabized. Things are going pretty well in his part of the world – a great deal better than at one time I suspected: but we've been through more rough water than has appeared. Early mistakes coming home to roost and all that sort of thing! However I think I see the way out now.'[54]

On January 16th Major Vickery of the British Military Mission arrived at Um Lejj. Lawrence took him inland with Captain Boyle to see Feisal. Later remarks by Boyle about this meeting have a different emphasis from the brief account in *Seven Pillars*: 'On arrival', Boyle wrote, 'we found a great encampment of camel-skin tents in the centre of which stood Feisal's. It was a striking scene, but the absence of any sanitary precautions made it an unpleasant place on a hot day. Feisal gave us luncheon, at which we sat on the ground and ate out of a large bowl, which was stood on ammunition boxes in front of him.

'In it was a greasy stew out of which we helped ourselves to pieces of meat with our fingers. Feisal handed me choice morsels and I understood that this was a special mark of favour to his principal guest, so I felt obliged to eat them. Vickery saved the situation by producing a large flask of whisky, a proceeding frowned on by Lawrence, but laughed at by Feisal, and the contents were very welcome.'[55]

This was Lawrence's first contact with Vickery, who spoke excellent Arabic and had seemed an ideal choice for the Military Mission. Lawrence must have been astonished to see him drink whisky in Feisal's presence. Since alcohol is forbidden to Moslems the action could only serve to distance Vickery from those he had come to advise. It was soon apparent that Vickery's attitude towards the Arabs was very different from Lawrence's, and the tension between the two men was exacerbated by other factors. Vickery was older, of higher rank, and had greater military experience. Before the day was out, each had formed a low opinion of the other.

During the meeting with Feisal, plans were made for a joint attack on Wejh. Five hundred and fifty Arabs judged to be of indifferent fighting quality were to be put on board HMS *Hardinge* and landed on the far side of the town. Their role would be to prevent the Turks escaping northwards while Feisal's main army, now strengthened by men from Sherif Nasir's force, attacked from the south. Arrangements were made for a final rendezvous between the Navy and Feisal's army shortly before the attack.

Although Newcombe was expected at Um Lejj, he had not arrived by the evening of January 17th, and the Arab army was due to set out on the following day. Vickery was going up to Wejh by sea and Lawrence felt that his own duty was to remain ashore with Feisal. He left behind a cheerful letter for Newcombe: 'So I miss you by a day! I'm very sick, but it was either that or miss Wadi Hamdh [which Feisal's army would cross on its way north], with the foreknowledge that I may never see Wadi Hamdh again, and that I will certainly see you at Wejh.

'I prepared Feisul (who is an absolute ripper) carefully for you . . . This show is splendid: you cannot imagine greater fun for us, greater vexation and fury for the Turks. We win hands down if we keep the Arabs simple... to add to them heavy luxuries will only wreck their show, and guerilla does it. It's a sort of *guerre de course*, with the courses all reversed. But the life and fun and movement of it are extreme.

'Vickery had a funny idea that nothing had yet been done out here. It's not true: may I suggest that by effacing yourself for the first part, and making friends with the head men before you start pulling them about, you will find your way much easier? They tried the forceful game at Rabegh – and have spoiled all the show. After all, it's an Arab war, and we are only contributing materials – and the Arabs have the right to go their own way and run things as they please. We are only guests.'[56]

Newcombe reached Um Lejj during the morning of January 18th. When he heard that the Arab army was striking camp a few miles inland he immediately commandeered a horse and set off to join it. Lawrence's diary records that the army set off at about 1 pm, and that 'Newcombe turned up 1.15.'[57] Thus his temporary duties with Feisal ended earlier than he had hoped. Newcombe, who enjoyed Lawrence's company, asked him to stay on as far as Wejh; the week-long march would provide a useful handing-over period.

Feisal's army of ten thousand Arabs, half of them mounted on camels, formed a magnificent spectacle. The mood of exultation increased when a messenger brought news that Abdullah's force, while moving to Wadi Ais, had surprised and captured an important member of the Turkish élite together with a valuable baggage caravan. This good fortune called for celebration and for a time Feisal's progress northwards halted.[58]

This unplanned delay must have given Newcombe an early insight into the peculiar nature of Arab operations. As a result, Feisal missed the rendezvous before Wejh previously agreed with Boyle, leaving Admiral Wemyss in an unexpected quandary: 'The non-appearance of Faisal made it incumbent on me to decide whether I should attack without him or await his arrival. I finally decided on the former step, the principal argument in favour of this being the presence of the five hundred Arabs on board the *Hardinge*. It would have been impossible to keep these men any longer on board, owing to the difficulties of feeding them, and also for sanitary reasons.'[59] On January 23rd, therefore, the Arab landing party, accompanied by Vickery and Bray, was put ashore north of Wejh. These were not Feisal's best troops, but they were able to advance on the town under cover of the ships' gunfire. Although the attack was undisciplined by European standards, the Turkish garrison was eventually defeated. The victory was consolidated by a naval landing party and Wejh was in Allied hands by the time Feisal's main army arrived.

Afterwards there was looting. Lawrence noted in his diary: 'At Wejh the people of the town are all Egyptian . . . and strongly anti-Sherif. So the Bisha men robbed them, and sacked the town: they broke every box and cupboard, tore down all fittings, cut open every mattress and cushion for gold . . . Feisal had sent word to Wejh a week before, that if they stayed in the town, and let the Turks stay, the resulting damage would be on their own heads. So he made no effort to recover their goods.'[60]

Despite the success, both Vickery and Bray were deeply shocked by the style of Arab warfare they had witnessed. Both were to write bitterly of the lack of discipline and planning. For example, Vickery noted that although Feisal's army 'only embarked on a four days' march, due north, parallel to the coast line, and within twenty miles of it, a great part . . . lost its way and arrived at the rendezvous two days late.'[61]

The British Military Mission now lacked a clear role. Its original purpose had been to help train Arab regulars in Rabegh; but that scheme had come to nothing, and after the capture of Wejh the greatest need for military expertise was farther north. In the short term the most useful thing it could do would be to help with attacks on the railway. Feisal had intended to move against the line as soon as possible after reaching Wejh. When he arrived there, however, it was clear that Abdullah's presence in Wadi Ais had reduced the need for immediate large-scale action. Feisal therefore planned a series of smaller raids, while taking steps to con-solidate his new position and recruit men from the local tribes. Since the raids from Wejh would reach the line a long way north of Medina, there was increasing pressure on Feisal to allow Newcombe and Garland, the two British officers expert in demolition, to go inland.

It was soon to become evident that the campaign in the Hejaz had been won before the Military Mission arrived. Following weeks of crisis during which it had seemed that the Turks might march to victory at any time, the repositioning of Abdullah's and Feisal's armies in January had shifted the military balance in favour of the Arabs. The Turks would now be obliged to place troops along hundreds of miles of railway, their only line of communication to Medina. This would leave Fakhri with too few men to conduct an offensive. They were also experiencing difficulties maintaining their advanced positions in the hills south-west of Medina. Sporadic raiding by the hill tribes on Turkish supply columns during January demonstrated that the whole area was hostile, and that a much larger Turkish force would be required if such an extended front was to be secure. An Intelligence summary in the *Arab Bulletin* of January 29th noted that there had now been 'a very considerable measure of [Turkish] withdrawal on all the Rabugh roads, as well as from the Yambo direction. All advanced posts at and about Hamra, at Khafia and Bir Zeid, and at Hafah have been called in, and Bir el-Raha and Ghayir . . . are the southernmost positions. We have learned in various ways that much material of all kinds has been or is about to be retired to Medina, and there remains little doubt that Turkish offensive movements towards Yambo and Rabugh are abandoned for the present.

'If this is so, Sidi Abdullah's stroke, which preceded by two or three days our first inkling of Turkish withdrawal in the south-west, probably had something to do with it. Added to uneasiness about communications and shortage of supplies, there is also probably serious sickness in Medina. Considering his small strength, one wonders why the Tur-kish Commanding Officer ever undertook these fruitless and abortive offensives. It is just possible they were intended only as demonstrations, to create panic, and induce us to land troops in the [Moslem] Holy Land, to the advantage of the Turkish Sinai operations, and of Pan-Islamic propaganda directed from Medina. If so, we have avoided a very pretty trap.'[62] From now on the presence of Arab armies at Wejh and Wadi Ais would preclude any further Turkish offensive in the Hejaz. This position could only be reversed by massive reinforcements to the Medina garrison, which Turkey could ill afford.

The British authorities were greatly encouraged. Wingate wrote to Robertson: 'The Arab leaders have always beautiful plans and describe them most plausibly, but – and this is a new and encouraging feature – some of them of late have actually matured.'[63] He felt that the time was ripe to attempt co-ordinated action by all the Sherifian forces against Medina, and Newcombe's staff began to make detailed plans.

Other observers were not quite so optimistic, for while the Turkish position in the Hejaz had deteriorated, this had not been due to any improvement in Arab fighting capability. The projected operation would involve not merely Feisal's army, but the forces commanded by Ali, Abdullah, and Zeid. On January 25th Wemyss wrote a gloomy account of a conversation with al Masri, who had been the disgusted witness of Ali's brief sortie from Rabegh: 'I think that he is dissatisfied and disappointed. He spoke of the impossibility of doing anything serious with the Shereef and his sons, whom he described as being ignorant, medievally monarchical and of opinion that nothing could or should be done except under the direct guidance of one of the Shereefian family – in fact, a sort of Arabian Hapsburg . . . he is so evidently disappointed at his position and so bored with the whole thing that I suspect his one idea is to get out of it all'.[64] Vickery noted other difficulties: 'The value of the Sheref's Armies as a military force is nil', he wrote, 'if they are exploited on wrong principles and if they are asked to undertake tasks which would tax trained troops . . . As irregular armies confining themselves to guerilla operations, they are a force of some potential value. The question as to how far they are to be equipped with modern arms and instruments requires immediate decision. It is not known how far other Sherefial leaders interest themselves in the training of their troops but certainly Sheref Feisal ignores it and relies entirely on a few [ex-]Turkish Officers and Arab leaders . . . The Arab camel troops, infantry and horsemen are good. The weak points are the artillery and machine gun sections. They are weak points because they are untrained and because all think the simple possession of these troops and guns is in itself a guarantee of victory.'[65]

With hindsight, such criticisms seem to throw considerable doubt on the wisdom of attempting operations against Medina *en masse*, yet this remained the official scheme. Despite his own observations, Vickery maintained that: 'The maximum amount of success can only be obtained when all armies work on some concerted plan, controlled and advised from some central channel. Spasmodic operations undertaken by one army not in conjunction with the others cannot give the best results.'[66] It would be some time before the British military hierarchy accepted that Hussein's armies were incapable of such concerted action.

Lawrence could not feel deeply involved in the immediate military activities being planned at Wejh, since he was now preparing with some regret to go back to his office in Cairo. Feisal, however, was unwilling to see him go. Lawrence had shown a remarkable grasp of the political and military situation; but for him, Abdullah would not have moved to Wadi Ais and the future of the Revolt would still have been precarious. No other British adviser in the Hejaz had the encyclopaedic knowledge Lawrence had gained during two years in the Cairo Intelligence Department. Storrs's autobiography recounts how, during their visit to the Hejaz three months previously, Lawrence had displayed this knowledge to great effect: 'As Syrian, Circassian, Anatolian, Mesopotamian names came up, Lawrence at once stated exactly which [Turkish] unit was in which position, until Abdallah turned to me in amazement: "Is this man God, to know everything?" '[67]

Feisal must also have sensed that Lawrence's commitment to the Arab cause was quite unlike the attitude of other British officers in the Hejaz. The lack of sympathy with the Revolt so often evident in their reports must have been reflected in their behaviour. In many instances condemnation of the Revolt was wholesale. One RFC officer, for example, wrote: 'So far as I have been able to judge we have not here a budding Arab nation struggling to be free of Turkish dominance. If the Turk is disliked it is only because all authority is disliked, even the most rudimentary law and order. The rebellion is an attempt on the part of the Shereefian family to secure for themselves a greater position and power in Hejaz.

'I have gained no impression of their being leaders of a popular movement towards freedom nor of a religious movement . . . In fact, apart from a small number of men, whose loyalty is personal, the Shereef's army in this part of the Hejaz is kept in being by largesses of food, clothing, blankets, tents, waterproof sheets – all the paraphernalia of a civilised army, which are undreamt of wealth to the Arab tribes.

'In addition they secure, by adherence to the Shereefian side, short Lee-Enfield rifles or Turkish Mauser rifles, which weapons they invariably carry fully charged and cocked – a cause of frequent accidents.

'These forces diminish seriously when any advance is proposed . . . Serious contact with Turkish troops would mean wholesale desertion by men who are with the Shereef only because of what they can get.'[68]

Lawrence' s reports were much more constructive, drawing attention to successful aspects of Feisal's campaign. He did not seek to deny Arab shortcomings, but he tried to analyse their causes, and constantly looked for ways to develop the military potential which he sensed was there. This was partly a deliberate policy. If the only reports reaching London were hostile, lasting damage would be done to Hussein's cause. French and Anglo-Indian interests would cite these criticisms as proof that the Arab Revolt did not deserve support. Lawrence tried in some measure to redress the balance.

The discrepancies between his portrayal of the Revolt and reports by other British observers must sometimes have puzzled readers in the Arab Bureau. Take, for example, these differing comments on the Yenbo crisis of December 11th-12th. The same RFC officer wrote: 'It was reported by a scout – falsely – that the Turks were within three miles of Yenbo. There was a general cry raised all over the town "everyone must be awake" but there were no orderly movements or arrangements made, apart from the taking up of prearranged positions by the small Egyptian force to meet the supposed attack. To lessen their night fright the guardship . . . played the searchlight on the supposed line of Turkish advance. The alarm died with dawn.'[69] Lawrence's comment had a quite different emphasis: 'I think the Arabs have made a fair show. The night that Turks were rumoured to be within a few miles the garrison was called out about 10 p.m. by means of criers sent round the streets. The men all turned out without visible excitement, and proceeded to their posts round the town wall without making a noise, or firing a shot. This is in contrast to their usual waste of ammunition without excuse, and shows an intention of rising to an emergency. The sentries have also kept a fairly good watch, and the outpost lines have been maintained steadily by day and night, at considerable distances outside the walls.'[70]

Lawrence realised that much of the irritation was caused by cultural differences, such as the Arab indifference towards formal discipline and British Army procedures. Regular army training was not the best preparation for working with bedouin tribesmen. Moreover, the Arabic-speaking British officers sent to the Hejaz had all spent their earlier careers in colonial service, mainly in India, Egypt, or the Sudan. The attitude towards natives prevalent in these places was inappropriate for work in Arabia, where the British were acting as advisers, not masters. Lawrence saw this clearly, and later wrote of Vickery: 'To this society of Sheikhs and Sherifs with their sense of personal dignity he came fresh from years in Government circles, where he had experienced servility and rebellious insolence, but never friendship. His examples of native authority had been clerks or officials, not men born to power, and the veil of office . . . lay between him and the people.'[71]

Lawrence, on the other hand, had spent his pre-war years as a civilian employer at Carchemish. Although he had not treated the villagers there as equals, neither had he hidden behind his privileged status as an Englishman. He had mixed freely and had sought to build up a relationship of mutual respect. In Carchemish, as in the Hejaz, there was no tradition of discipline in the European sense, and the tribesmen would ignore direct orders. Nevertheless, as Lawrence had discovered, an Arab labour gang could achieve remarkable results if given the right kind of encouragement. This was the lesson he was to apply during the Revolt.

When he had been told to return to the Hejaz two months earlier, he had protested that there was more useful work for him in Cairo. Now, however, he had seen how much depended on the attitude of British liaison officers in the field. There were many things he could do to advance the Arab cause if he remained in the Hejaz, and it was clear that this would be worthwhile, since the Revolt was taking pressure off the EEF. In addition, he had discovered a personal affinity with Feisal, even in matters such as their sense of humour. In background and ability they were very different, yet they complemented one another in many ways. Lawrence's knowledge of the workings in Cairo and ability to get things done there were matched by Feisal's rank and persuasive power among the Arabs. They each had a romantic vision of the Arab national movement, strong enough to transcend everyday setbacks, and they both knew that they were helping to shape momentous historical events. If the Revolt succeeded it would be the most important event in Arab history since the Crusades. Feisal had been born into this role, and alone among his brothers had the qualities needed to perform it. Lawrence was a fascinated outsider who had steeped himself in Middle Eastern history since studying the Bible as a child. In the epilogue of *Seven Pillars* he was to rank historical ambition among his principal motives during the Revolt: 'I had dreamed, at the City School in Oxford, of hustling into form, while I lived, the new Asia which time was inexorably bringing upon us.'[72]

Both Feisal and Lawrence wanted their partnership to continue. On January 25th a cable from Jidda informed the Arab Bureau that: 'Feisal writes to the Sherif asking him to wire you that he is most anxious that Lawrence should not return to Cairo as he has given such very great assistance.'[73] Since this request came from Feisal himself, Clayton had little choice but to accede. Lawrence left for Cairo on January 27th, but he was to return almost immediately to the Hejaz on an indefinite liaison posting.

CHAPTER 17

Looking Northwards
January – March 1917

LAWRENCE was delighted to learn that he would be rejoining Feisal, even though he knew that the work would be demanding. He wrote home on January 31st: 'Things in Arabia are very pleasant, though the job I have is rather a responsible one, and sometimes it is a little heavy to see which way one ought to act. I am getting rather old with it all, I think! However it is very nice to be out of the office, with some field work in hand, and the position I have is such a queer one – I do not suppose that any Englishman before ever had such a place.

'All of which is rather tantalising reading to you, because I cannot enter into details. I act as a sort of adviser to Sherif Feisul, and as we are on the best of terms, the job is a wide and pleasant one. I live with him in his tent, so our food and things (if you will continue to be keen on such rubbish!) are as good as the Hejaz can afford.'[1]

His new role would require, among other things, great sensitivity in political questions. Arab aspirations and Anglo-French policy were as far apart as ever, and this chasm, so often papered over in the past, would become increasingly obvious as the Revolt moved northwards. Whatever the difficulties, Lawrence's superiors would expect him to keep Feisal enthusiastically on Britain's side.

Lawrence knew far too much of the real situation to underestimate the dangers. To succeed, he must turn his friendship with Feisal into a relationship of deep and unshakeable trust. Until now, his principal task had been to provide effective communication with Cairo; in the future, he would need to do much more than this.

The main threat to Anglo-Arab relations was France. Brémond and other members of his Military Mission had already shown that they would seek to advance French interests by every means possible, even at the expense of British military objectives.[2] There was a constant danger that French propaganda would cause an irreparable rift with Hussein.

By chance, however, a French initiative now gave Lawrence the opportunity to strengthen his influence over Feisal. Earlier that month it had been suggested in Paris that if Hussein did not want Christian troops at Rabegh, an expeditionary force might be sent to Akaba instead. This would advance against the Hejaz Railway, cut off supplies to Medina, and thereby eliminate the Turkish threat to Mecca. The religious difficulty could not possibly apply at such a great distance from the holy cities. Accordingly, French representatives in London and Cairo were instructed to put forward the case for landing an Allied force at Akaba. To make the proposal more attractive, Paris offered to contribute two Senegalese battalions from Djibouti, as well as Brémond's units camped at Suez.[3]

Both the War Office in London and Murray in Cairo rejected the proposal out of hand. Brémond was informed on January 24th that no such landing could be undertaken in the existing circumstances. He was not, however, convinced: he had always favoured a landing at Akaba, both for military and political reasons, and he was particularly keen at this moment to find a useful role for his Suez contingent. Unless he did so, the French War Office would soon redeploy it elsewhere, and he would be left with neither a force to command nor any means to exert real influence in the Hejaz.[4]

At the end of January, therefore, Brémond left Jidda for Egypt, determined to get the French plan accepted. In his view, if men could be spared from the EEF for Rabegh, they could be spared for Akaba. He knew that both Wingate and Clayton saw this as the best point from which to attack the Turkish supply line to Medina. Murray would surely give way, particularly as France had offered substantial help.

On the way north, Brémond's ship called briefly at Wejh, where he put the scheme to Feisal and Newcombe. Feisal said that, according to the latest Arab intelligence, there were only 150 gendarmes at Akaba, and that he himself intended to capture the town. Newcombe, who had visited Akaba during the Sinai Survey, agreed wholeheartedly that it would be a good location for a new base.[5]

Later, after visiting his contingent at Suez, Brémond travelled up to Cairo, and on February 3rd he found time to call on Lawrence, who knew that Murray had opposed a landing at Akaba, but was hardly surprised at the Frenchman's persistence. One of Brémond's principal aims was to prevent an Arab nationalist rebellion spreading into Syria. He was therefore deeply anxious about Feisal's move northwards, even as far as Wejh. Until very recently, he had been hoping to impede the Arab movement by introducing Christian troops at Rabegh. The new Akaba plan might prove a more effective method of obtaining the same result.

An Anglo-French force advancing inland would very soon convince local tribes that Hussein's European allies were bent on imperial conquest. French propaganda would reinforce this view, and the Revolt would gain no adherents in the critical region between the Hejaz and Syria. In effect, an Allied landing at Akaba would contain the Arab rebellion inside the Hejaz.

As things stood, Lawrence saw little likelihood that Murray would drop his resistance to the scheme. GHQ knew that the terrain between Akaba and the railway seventy miles inland was extremely difficult. Unless a very large force were sent, there would be no chance of stopping Turkish supplies to Medina. However, Lawrence was alarmed to learn that Brémond intended to revisit Wejh and press the plan on Feisal and Newcombe (it is most unlikely that Brémond had told him of Feisal's unpromising reaction three days earlier). He therefore decided to return to the Hejaz at once. In *Seven Pillars* he wrote: 'I had not warned Feisal that Brémond was a politician [in an earlier draft he wrote 'a crook']. Newcombe was in Wejh, with his friendly desire to get moves on. We had not talked over the problem of Akaba. Feisal knew neither its terrain nor its tribes. Keenness and ignorance would lend an ear favourable to the proposal. It seemed best for me to hurry down there and put my side on its guard.'[6]

Lawrence was determined to expose Brémond's true intentions. The French Military Mission had already given Wilson countless problems at Jidda, since it had deliberately encouraged an attitude of mistrust towards Britain in Arab minds. Now that Brémond's attention was focused on the northern operations, he would certainly try the same tactics with Feisal.

When Lawrence reached Wejh on February 6th he was relieved to find that Feisal had no intention of agreeing to Brémond's proposals. Nevertheless, he took the opportunity to deal with the French question once and for all. He therefore explained that Brémond wanted an Anglo-French force at Akaba in order to contain the Arab movement in the Hejaz, and that such an outcome would mean the ruin of Arab hopes in Syria. It might conceivably have been possible to warn Feisal of the danger without disclosing the truth about the Sykes-Picot Agreement, but it would have been very difficult. Lawrence decided to take Feisal into his confidence. He was to be attached to Feisal's staff for the foreseeable future, and it would be better to establish mutual trust at the outset. Sooner or later the truth would emerge, and if he lied now, his relationship with Feisal would be constantly at risk. Moreover, it would be particularly difficult to deceive a man such as Feisal. As Lawrence later wrote: 'lying . . . was the worst gambit against players whose whole life had passed in a mist of deceits, and whose perceptions were of the finest. The Arab leaders showed a completeness of instinct, a reliance upon intuition . . . they understood and judged quickly, effortlessly'.[7]

He therefore told Feisal plainly that the McMahon-Hussein correspondence offered no certainty of Arab independence in Syria and that there was a secret treaty on this matter between France and Britain. France was certain to gain Lebanon, and would rule the interior of Syria as well unless the Arabs captured Damascus, Homs, Hama and Aleppo, the four cities named in the Sykes-Picot proviso.[8] The decision to disclose this secret information to Feisal cannot have been easy, as the consequences might have been very serious indeed. Lawrence was no doubt influenced by his conviction that Feisal would become the Arab leader most closely involved with Syria. Frankness was the only practical course, and in the long run it would surely serve Britain's interests best. Moreover, he sensed instinctively that his trust would not be betrayed. The nature of his work during the Arab Revolt demanded many such judgments of character, and from the success he achieved it is clear that he was rarely wrong.

Knowledge of the Sykes-Picot proviso brought about a fundamental change in Feisal's plans. From now on, he knew that it was vital for the Arabs to take Damascus and the other inland cities before the end of the war. When the northern campaign began, his forces must give priority to regions east of the Jordan designated by Britain and France as a potential area of Arab self-government. An attempt to seize areas such as the Lebanon might only serve to undermine Allied sympathy for other Arab claims. That would be undesirable, since the Arabs would need Britain's support in order to hold French ambitions in check. Lawrence argued that Feisal would, in any case, be best advised to leave the Mediterranean littoral to the EEF. The coastal regions would be inaccessible to bedouin raiding parties, which could not operate very far from the inland desert. It would be extremely difficult for Arab irregulars to work in harmony with a European army, and the most useful thing Feisal could do would be to secure the right flank of the British advance. This would ensure continuing supplies of money and *matériel* during the campaign, as well as political support after the war. France could make no valid protest as long as the Arab campaign was seen to focus on objectives defined in the McMahon-Hussein correspondence and the Sykes-Picot proviso.

Lawrence believed, however, that the Arabs might win two major improvements on the Sykes-Picot terms. The first related to frontiers: it was already recognised in some quarters that the boundaries hurriedly drawn up during the Anglo-French negotiations were unworkable. In particular, the Arab state in Syria would need a port on the Mediterranean coast, since otherwise its external trade would be entirely under French control. Lawrence suggested to Feisal that, if the occasion presented itself, the Arabs should try to occupy a strip of the littoral north of the Lebanon. French claims were not very strong in that region, and the British Government might be prepared to support this territorial gain.

Secondly, there was the vexed question of advisers to the future Arab government in Syria. Under Sykes-Picot, these were to be exclusively French. McMahon's staff, however, had never favoured this provision, and Lawrence hoped that it might become unenforceable. If the British had their way, no French troops would be involved in the advance through Palestine. At the end of the war, therefore, France would be in no position to impose advisers on the Arab forces holding Syria.

These would appear to be the main factors in Lawrence's analysis of the situation in February 1917. If the Arabs succeeded they would secure the territory allocated to them under the Sykes-Picot Agreement, and would be strongly placed to challenge its least acceptable provisions. At best, there was a real chance that Britain would help the Arabs create a viable and truly independent state in Syria. Lawrence later wrote: 'I had early divulged the existence of this thing [Sykes-Picot] to Feisal, and had convinced him that it was only to be set aside if the Arabs redoubled their efforts against the Turks . . . His only escape was to do so much to help the British that after peace they would not be able for very shame, to shoot such allies down in fulfilment of a secret treaty.

'Then, at least, there would be a modification, in which he would secure something: while, if the Arabs did as well as I intended, there would be no one-sided talk of shooting, for they would be in place to return shot for shot, and as armed men in their own houses to get their won freedom recognised by their victorious allies. I begged him not, like his father, to trust our promises – though one could not know if Hussein trusted us out of stupidity or craft – but to trust in his own performance and strength . . . Feisal, a reasonable and clear-eyed statesman, accepted my point of view as the normal between nations, and his conviction of the hollowness of promises and gratitude did not sap his energy. Yet I did not dare to take so frankly into confidence the other men in our movement'.[9]

It was against this background that Lawrence tackled the more immediate question of Akaba. He was relieved to hear that Feisal had offered no encouragement to Brémond, but he now learned with some concern that the Arabs had made plans of their own for capturing the town. The Arab leadership had envisaged an operation very similar to the one that had succeeded at Wejh. In Lawrence's view, however, this scheme was open to the same military objections as the one that had been proposed by Brémond.

Details of the Arab scheme were set out in a report by Newcombe written just before Lawrence returned to Wejh. The first step would be the capture of Dhaba and Muweilah, two villages on the Red Sea coast which would serve as intermediate bases. Muweilah, the farthest north, was almost 120 miles from Wejh, about half-way to Akaba. These operations, involving Arab troops put ashore by the Royal Navy, were already in hand.[10]

Newcombe, who was now planning to take part in Arab raids on the Hejaz line, was enthusiastic about anything that would distract Turkish attention. He wrote: 'The sooner Akaba is attacked after Dhaba, the easier will operations be for me on the railway towards Tebuk, especially should I be lucky enough to get at Tebuk or north of it . . . this chance will be greatly increased directly Akaba is taken.

'The Turks will have their attention attracted to Akaba and be less concerned with the southern part of the railway. The whole movement to Akaba depends on ships: movement by land will be too slow and laborious.

'Feisal has not yet made up his mind *when* to go to Akaba, hence no definite programme can be given from here beyond asking that plans be prepared and matured.'[11]

Lawrence's first task was to deter Feisal from carrying out this scheme. Possession of Akaba itself was immaterial. What mattered was the track leading eastwards from the town through Wadi Itm and up onto the Maan plateau. If, as Feisal hoped, the Arabs were soon to operate in the northern deserts, they would need this line of communication. It was the only practical route for sending British arms, ammunition, and other supplies inland.[12] Lawrence therefore argued that no action should be undertaken at Akaba unless it was certain to give Feisal possession of Wadi Itm as well.

Unlike Feisal, Newcombe, or indeed Brémond, Lawrence had seen air reconnaissance reports about this mountainous track. These had been prepared on Murray's instructions during the summer of 1916. At that time Lawrence had been specifically asked to consider whether the defences there could be overcome (see pp. 293-5). He now explained that the natural strength of Turkish positions in Wadi Itm was so great that a force trying to advance from the coast would face almost insuperable difficulties. There was no need for the Turks to keep these defences manned or to maintain a large garrison at Akaba (the town itself was in any case undefendable). There would be ample warning of any enemy approaching from the west, and this would leave more than enough time to send a defending force from Maan. The landing Feisal proposed at Akaba would not merely fail to take Wadi Itm; it would bring the whole Turkish scheme of defence into operation. As a result, the inland route so essential to future Arab campaigns would be lost indefinitely.

Lawrence's rejection of the Arab scheme would have carried little weight if he had been unable to propose anything better. However, he was ready with a tentative suggestion which held out a much better promise of success. He had studied military strategy sufficiently to look at such problems from more than one angle, and he saw that in the case of the Wadi Itm there was indeed an alternative option. Assault on the Turkish defences by a force landed at Akaba would be futile, but the Wadi Itm track might well be captured through a surprise attack at the *inland* end. Given a sufficient force of local tribesmen, the Akaba road could be seized near Maan itself. This would prevent Turkish troops going out to man the Wadi Itm defences. If this blocking action could be maintained, even for a relatively short time, it would be a small matter to pick off the few permanent Turkish posts down to Akaba. Thus the prepared defences in Wadi Itm would fall into Arab hands without a fight.[13] No European invader could carry out such a coup; but in the extraordinary circumstances of the Arab Revolt, Lawrence's scheme might well be possible. The area around Maan was so thinly populated that a mounted Arab force could reach its objective without detection, striking quickly and with devastating effect.

Two things, however, would be necessary. First, before the attack, utmost secrecy, since if rumours reached the Turks, they would garrison the Wadi Itm without waiting for an attack. Secondly, after the Wadi Itm had been taken, a large Arab force would have to be brought to Akaba as soon as possible. This would be needed to hold the Maan road against the inevitable Turkish counter-offensive. The only way to get such a force to Akaba in time would be by sea.

At this stage neither Lawrence nor Feisal could be certain that the scheme was really feasible. The idea was simple, but its implementation would call for a great deal of local knowledge and co-operation. Fortunately, they would soon have direct contacts with tribal leaders from areas farther north, and these questions could then be answered. In the meantime, the project must remain secret. Such secrecy was not easy to achieve in the Arab army. The nomadic tribesmen moved freely between areas controlled by Feisal and those controlled by the Turks. Both Feisal and Lawrence knew of this, and from time to time they profited from it in order to send the Turks misleading information. However, it often meant concealing their real intentions from Feisal's entourage until disclosure was absolutely necessary.[14] Lawrence was equally cautious about reporting these Akaba plans to Cairo. Akaba was strategically a key point, and he knew that the prospect of Arab control there might be opposed in some quarters. During the months ahead there were to be several occasions when the subject of Akaba had every reason to appear in Lawrence's reports, but he would find it politic to remain silent.[15]

The earlier Arab scheme for a landing at Akaba was now dropped and further local action there discouraged. Lawrence's plan would take some time to arrange, but he did not see this as a disadvantage, since he thought that the capture of Akaba should be part of a much larger general movement northwards which could not yet begin. First, the Arabs must carry out the concerted operation against Medina that had been planned for so long. Feisal's role in this would be to cut the Hejaz line permanently at El Ula, 100 miles east of Wejh. The armies of Ali and Abdullah would then close in on Medina and isolate the city. Once Fakhri Pasha was cut off from all hope of rescue, he would surely surrender. Only after the fall of Medina should the Revolt move northwards, driving the Turks back up the railway, first to Maan, and later to Damascus and Aleppo. It was at this later stage that a supply base at Akaba would become necessary.

Feisal seemed to accept the change of plan, as is clear from a naval telegram of February 11th: 'Feisal proposes concentrating his efforts against the railway in the vicinity of El Ula and does not contemplate further operations on the sea coast at present.'[16] A few days later, when coastal tribes offered to take Akaba in the name of the Sherif, Lawrence advised against such premature action.[17]

His discussions with Feisal about the strategy of the Revolt are reflected in a letter home written a few days later: 'There is a bunch of about twelve thousand Turks in Medina and the neighbourhood, clinging to certain important water-supplies and roads south and west of Medina, and surrounded, on all sides except the Railway, by Arabs. The Turks are also holding the Hejaz Railway, which we now threaten from Tebuk downwards, but not as yet in any force. The Arabs proved incapable of taking Medina, held by its present garrison, and the Medina garrison proved unable to advance through the Arabs against Mecca. So now we have shifted part of our forces north to this place, and the struggle for the Railway will probably be the feature of this second phase of the Hejaz Campaign.

'The Arab Movement is a curious thing. It is really very small and weak in its beginning, and anybody who had command of the sea could put an end to it in three or four days. It has however capacity for expansion – in the same degree – over a very wide area . . . On the other hand the Arab Movement is shallow, not because the Arabs do not care, but because they are few – and in their smallness of number (which is imposed by their poverty of country) lies a good deal of their strength, for they are perhaps the most elusive enemy an army ever had, and inhabit one of the most trying countries in the world for civilised warfare.'[18]

The letter also contains a passage which reflects his awareness of the Sykes-Picot proviso and the need for the Revolt to spread northwards: 'I hope that the show may go as we wish, and that the Turkish flag may disappear from Arabia. It is indiscreet only to ask what Arabia is. It has an east and a west and a south border – but where or what it is on the top no man knoweth. I fancy myself it is up to the Arabs to find out! Talk about Palestine or Syria or Mesopotamia is not opportune, when these three countries – with every chance – have made no effort towards freedom for themselves.'[19]

The task of mounting an attack on the railway at El Ula proved to be less straightforward than expected. It had been assumed that the principal local tribe, the Billi, would rally to Feisal's cause. In the event, however, the Billi leaders proved difficult, and their attitude hindered recruiting. This was a serious blow, because the personnel of Feisal's army had to change as it moved into each new tribal area. Lawrence's notebook records that 'Feisul . . . said that the Juheina were gradually slipping home from Wejh, as they hated being in a strange country. He intends shortly to send off all except the Merawin and half the Rifaa, whom he must keep, as the attitude of the Billi is not as enthusiastic as one could wish.'[20]

There were also problems within the Sherifian army. On February 10th a section of the Ageyl mutinied against their commander, Abdullah

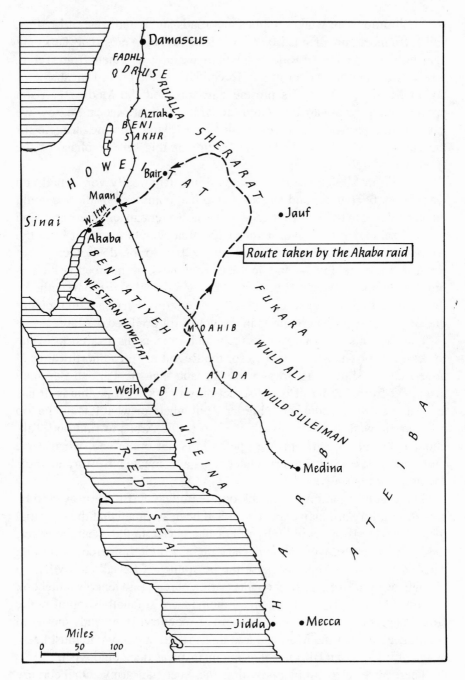

Map 5: *Tribes of the Hejaz and southern Syria*

ibn Dakhil, whose discipline had been severe. Two men were killed and many wounded before the affair ended. Lawrence wrote home: 'As a matter of fact progress is difficult. The Arabs of the Hejaz are all for the Sherif, some keenly enough to volunteer, others less keen, but all well-wishers. Only, they are tribesmen, and as such are rebellious by instinct. They hate the Turks, but they don't want to obey anyone's orders, and in consequence they turn out only as a mob of snipers or guerilla-fighters. They are wonderfully active, quite intelligent, and do what they do do fairly well. They are however not fit to meet disciplined troops in the open, and it will be a long time before they are.'[21]

Other difficulties arose because of traditional enmities. Lawrence noted: 'Feisul has been spending the last few days bringing together the Sheikhs of the different tribes under him, and making them swear to preserve peace between their men. If men of the same tribe fall out, the case is settled by their sheikh. If men of different tribes fall out, it is referred to Feisul. If men of different tribes come to blows, both are to be arrested, and brought to Feisul for judgment. This is an effort to prevent blood feuds being exercised within the army. Our present move into Billi, Beni Atiyeh, Howeitat, and Moahib country makes the situation much more complicated.'[22]

Despite the initial hesitancy, tribal leaders from a wide area were soon declaring for Feisal, and by mid-February he was effectively in control of all the land between Wejh and the railway. He was also, with encouragement from Lawrence, seeking support farther north in the regions towards Maan.[23] As a result, a continuous stream of visitors arrived. Lawrence wrote that on February 17th: 'There came in to Feisul . . . five chief men of the Sherarat [a tribe from the area north-east of Tebuk], with a present of ostrich eggs; the nephew of Ibn Jazi [chief of the central Howeitat living around Maan] with his felicitations on the capture of Wejh; a cousin of Nawaf's [the son of Nuri Shalaan, chief of the Rualla] with a horse as a gift from him to Feisul; Ahmed abu Tageiga with the respectful homage of the Western Howeitat [from the Red Sea coast below Akaba]; the cousin and ten principal sub-chiefs of Auda abu Tayi [chief of the eastern Howeitat, based around Maan], to present his compliments to Feisul, and consult with him what they could best do to further his plans . . . and some more men of the Billi and Wuld Ali. The whole country is full of envoys and volunteers, and great sheikhs coming in to swear allegiance, and the contagion of their example is chasing away the last hesitations of the Billi . . .

'Feisul swore the Abu Tayi sheikhs on the Koran to wait while he waited, march when he marched, to show mercy to no Turk, but to everyone who spoke Arabic, whether Baghdadi or Aleppine, or Syrian, and to put the needs of Arab Independence above their lives, their goods, or their families. He also began to confront them with their tribal enemies, and force them to swear internal peace for the duration of the war. The use we hope to make of these distant tribes is the traditional one. When we determine the day of our attack on the Railway, news will be sent up and down the line. The Howeitat say they will stop every trolley, cut the wires, besiege every station, arrest every patrol – and Feisul will send them his new ally, dynamite, and men to use it, to interrupt the line as far as possible north and south and in as many places as possible'.[24] Auda abu Tayi had sent a message offering to attack the line around Maan. Lawrence noted: 'Feisul will consent, as he regards action against Maan as morally useful. He does not think Auda can do much there.'[25]

The support of these northern and eastern tribes was extremely important. In the short term, it would broaden the impact of the forthcoming offensive and help to prevent the Turks from mounting a crushing counter-attack at any one point. In the long term, it would be essential for the campaign northwards up the railway as well as the eventual capture of the Wadi Itm road. Lawrence later wrote: 'If we wanted to get beyond Tebuk towards Maan or Akaba (and we did badly), it was clear that we must find a way round by the east, and for this we should require the favour of the nomads there. Our route would run first through the Billi and Moahib country so far as the railway, and would then cross part of the district of the Fejr. We had the Fejr. Beyond them lay the various tribes owning obedience to Nuri Shalaan, the great Emir of the Ruwalla, who, after the Sherif and ibn Saud and ibn Rashid was the fourth figure in the desert . . . His favour would open to us Wadi Sirhan, the famous roadway, camping ground, and chain of water holes, which in a series of linked depressions extended from Jauf, Nuri's capital, in the south-east, northwards to Azrak . . . near Jebel Druse, in Syria. It was the freedom of this Wadi Sirhan we needed, to get from our Fejr friends to the tents of the Eastern Howeitat, the famous abu Tayi, of whom Auda, the greatest fighting man in all Arabia, was chief. Only by means of Auda abu Tayi could we swing the tribes from Maan to Akaba so violently in our favour that they would help us take Akaba and its hills from their Turkish garrisons; only with his active support could we come from Wejh to Maan. Since our Yenbo days we had been longing for him and trying to win him . . . Auda was an immense chivalrous name, but an unknown quantity to us, and in so vital a matter . . . we could not afford a mistake. He must come down and see us, so that we might weigh him and frame our future plans actually in his presence.'[26] The scheme to take Wadi Itm from the east was too secret to be entrusted to messengers, and Auda was therefore sent an invitation to come to Wejh.

The northern chiefs were more than ready to join the Revolt. Lawrence began to fear that some of them might act before the railway had been cut at El Ula and proper plans made for a further advance. If this happened, there might be a repeat of the chaos in supply and communication that had crippled Sherifian strategy in the early days of the Hejaz revolt. Premature action would also bring Turkish reinforcements to the region, making a subsequent Arab advance more difficult. He asked Feisal 'to get Nuri [Shalaan] to postpone any action by the northern Rualla, Kerak men, or Druses till . . . the attack on the Railway is over.'[27] Activity in the region of Maan would be particularly damaging. When rumours came in that the Turkish garrison at Akaba had been withdrawn from the town, Lawrence noted: 'Feisal will not occupy it officially in any case, since the news of the taking of Akaba might arouse undesirable excitement in Syria.'[28]

Although no major operation against the line had begun, preparations were in hand for several small expeditions. Feisal had given permission for Garland and Newcombe to accompany raiding parties. Through their expert knowledge of explosives, they would greatly increase the damage done to the railway and to rolling-stock. This was the first time the Arabs had allowed any British officer other than Lawrence to go inland.

Despite these plans, there was disappointment in some quarters that the Arabs had not done more to exploit their new military advantage. Britain had been pouring money and supplies into the Hejaz campaign for months, and it seemed extraordinary that so much time was needed to mount conclusive operations against Medina. The delay in attacking El Ula seemed particularly regrettable because very little had been done farther south. To Feisal's irritation, neither Ali nor Zeid showed any inclination to leave Rabegh. In mid-February Lawrence wrote: 'Feisul rather angry, as he wanted pressure put on the Sultani Road. He wired and told them so.'[29] Abdullah, for his part, was 'sitting quietly in Wadi Ais, and watching loaded trains go northward. We have sent him a letter telling him to get a move on. It is really rather stupid of him to have made that very decent march to Wadi Ais, to be in a position to cut the railway, and then leave it alone.'[30]

It was not until February 18th that Brémond arrived, on board the *Saint-Brieuc*. He had had little success promoting his Akaba landing scheme in Cairo, and the main purpose of this new visit to Wejh was to improve his position with Feisal. He brought six French machine guns as a gift.

He seems not to have pressed the matter of Akaba, although he still hoped that Feisal would come round to the idea of an Anglo-French landing. On the way from Suez his ship had stood close inshore there, and the town had seemed to be totally deserted. According to Lawrence's contemporary notes: 'Feisul told him he disapproved of the Akaba push, and painted the difficulties he had had with the Billi . . . he was sorry to have had to come to Wejh – it was lack of artillery which drove him to broaden his front, and lengthen his threat against the Railway. Had he had French guns to reply to the guns which the French had supplied [before the war] to the Turks, he would have gone straight for Medina. As it was he had to use his mobility and his superior numbers – and there was really no saying where this protraction of his front would end!'[31]

Brémond was very anxious to find a way of influencing Feisal's planning, and at the very least he wanted full reports on the activities of this northern Arab army. It was also necessary to find a useful role for some of the technical experts now at Suez. He tried to persuade Feisal to accept an officer as adviser, and various other personnel. Lawrence wrote: 'About the Staff Officer Feisal said he had none with him, and the attitude of the tribes – and conditions of tribal warfare – made scientific military knowledge unprofitable. He had with him two demolition officers [i.e. Newcombe and Garland] and one officer as adviser in matters of finance, supplies, and geography. Brémond therefore offered a demolition officer, and tried to attach a Syrian doctor to Newcombe as part of his staff. An "interpreter" and three men had been landed to teach the Arabs the use of the new automatic rifle.'[32] Only the machine-gun instructors were accepted. As these were not acting in a staff role they were ill-placed to influence or report upon Feisal's plans.

When Brémond's visit was over, Lawrence returned briefly to Cairo: he needed wireless equipment and other materials at Wejh, and also wanted to finish clearing up his affairs in the Arab Bureau. He wrote home: 'It is of course by far the most wonderful time I have had . . . I have now been made a Captain and Staff Captain again, which is amusing. It doesn't make any difference of course really, as I am never in uniform in Arabia, and nobody cares a straw what rank I hold, except that I am of Sherif Feisul's household.

'Can't think of anything else to say, as have become a monomaniac about the job in hand, and have no interest or recollections except Arabian politics just now! It's amusing to think that this will suddenly come to an end one day, and I take up other work.'[33]

He arrived in Egypt to find that the General Staff had just reached an agreement with Wingate that would greatly affect the future of the Arab Revolt. The background to this decision was Murray's advance across northern Sinai during December 1916. The EEF was now preparing for a major offensive against the Gaza-Beersheba line. If this succeeded, the road would be open for a British advance into Palestine in the autumn and Murray's forces would soon be in direct contact with the Arabs of Palestine and Syria. For this reason it was agreed on February 21st, the day before Lawrence reached Cairo, that any action by the Arabs in Akaba, Maan, and areas to the north would be controlled by Murray. Wingate would be responsible only for Sherifian operations in the Hejaz, to the south of the Akaba-Maan line.

From Lawrence's point of view this change was extremely important. Feisal would not be able to carry out a campaign in Syria without British money and supplies, yet when the Arab campaign reached Akaba it would suddenly lose the benefit of Wingate's wholehearted enthusiasm. Murray's attitude was less certain: the Revolt had never been very popular at EEF headquarters, and if Feisal were to gain the support he needed, the Arabs would have to prove that they could make a worthwhile contribution to Murray's success.

While in Cairo, Lawrence wrote Clayton an account of the contacts which Feisal had been making with tribes to the north. The note reflects the advice he had given and the policy he believed Feisal had accepted. All immediate action should be confined to attacks on the railway, since these would help in the scheme to take El Ula and Medina. Elsewhere, however, nothing should be done to excite the Syrian tribesmen before the time was ripe for a more general northern campaign.

'i. Sherif Feisul's present intention is to raise all the nomad tribes from the Howeitat at Jauf el Derwish, north of Maan, to Medina. This involves combining the Auda Abu Tayi, Ibn Jad, Ibn Jazi, and Abu Togeiga, Howeitat; the Beni Atiyeh; the Billi; the Moahib; the Fukara; the Aida; the Wuld Suleiman; and the Juheina. He has written to all these tribes, and most of them have come in to him.

'ii. Other [more northerly] tribes have sent in, without being applied to. They include the Rualla, Beni Sakhr, Sherarat, and some Kerak, Hauran, and El Husn (Yarmuk) Arabs. With the exception of the Sherarat and Rualla these peoples all own land, and are open to reprisals on the part of the Turkish government. Sherif Feisal has therefore decided not to use them. Letters have been sent begging them to remain quiet till called upon for service. They have been informed that the Arab Forces are concentrating on the desert sections of the Railway, and that their help would be useless in the case.

'iii. Feisal was also approached by Hebron and Nablus peoples, who saw in him an alternative to conquest by the British. He sent the same reply as to (ii) asking them to keep quiet. His own idea is that Arabs should not operate west of the River Jordan and the Dead Sea – Wadi Araba line.'[34] It was in fact Lawrence who had recommended to Feisal that the Arabs should remain east of the Jordan.

Clayton repeated the gist of this memorandum to the War Office, noting: 'Four British Officers are stationed in the area in which Feisal is operating, and are aiding him in every possible way with advice and assistance. Captain Lawrence, who has completely gained Feisal's confidence, will probably proceed [to El Ula] with him.'[35] Others too understood the growing importance of Lawrence's role. After long discussions with Vickery (one of the other British officers now based at Wejh), Wilson's deputy at Jidda wrote: 'Lawrence with Feisal is of inestimable value'.[36]

Before Lawrence left Cairo, news came that Garland, with a party of Arabs, had succeeded in derailing a train during a night raid on the Hejaz line. Although in the darkness Garland had been unable to assess the damage, the engine had overturned and fallen down a small embankment. The value of this operation was readily understood in the Arab Bureau. A few months earlier it had been estimated that there were only about 40 locomotives, 700 box wagons and 600 trucks on the entire thousand-mile narrow-gauge railway system south of Damascus. This rolling stock was used to supply not merely the force in Medina, but the Turkish Army in Palestine and Sinai. According to Arab Bureau calculations, 'about ten locomotives will be engaged in the Damascus-Beyrout sector. The remaining thirty will have to work [from Damascus] to Beersheba and Medina. To run one train a day to each place would take about twenty engines (running time to Beersheba about forty hours, and to Medina about 100 hours). In addition a certain number of engines will be under repair, and engaged in local construction, breakdown, or armoured-train work.'[37] Turkish locomotives were therefore important targets: each engine put out of action would significantly reduce the enemy's ability to move men and supplies.

Garland's report once again drew attention to the difficulties experienced by British regular officers when working with bedouin tribesmen. 'The wearing of Arab dress', Garland wrote, 'was most annoying and encumbering, in fact I regarded it as one of my chief troubles. I realised, too, that the time of the year is approaching when a white man will be unable to wear the Arab head-dress in the Hejaz sun.'[38] He criticised the state of the camels, the slow progress, and the tribesmen themselves: 'It is of course obvious to anyone knowing Arabs at all, that military work of any kind is difficult with the best of them. The majority of them show no respect, tending rather to insolence, and, I suppose from their traditional weakness for looting, seem to regard the stranger as legitimate plunder. In military operations they continually incur unnecessary risks by their stupid conduct, such as singing and shouting within hearing of the enemy, approaching enemy positions (as we did the railway line) up the middle of broad wadis that could be seen for miles by any outpost on the top of any of the small *jebels* [hills] adjoining the line . . . And of course it is quite useless for the Britisher to endeavour to introduce military ideas, or in any way to command; he can only make tactful suggestions, and hope by example to get them to do as he wants. It requires much patience and perseverance, and a lot of fraternization, for they strongly resent the application of the term "soldier" to themselves.'[39] Despite his value as an explosives expert, Garland's difficulty in coming to terms with Arab ways was to prove a continuing handicap, and he was later withdrawn from the Hejaz. Lawrence once remarked that he was 'a sick man, an ex-Sergeant, not very good, apt to stand on his dignity at the wrong moment. Not the type for the job.'[40]

As Lawrence travelled back to Wejh, at the end of February, he was unaware of the new problem that awaited him. It seems that Feisal had been very perturbed to learn about the Sykes-Picot proviso, and he had become anxious to move as soon as possible against Damascus, Homs, Hama and Aleppo. He was also under intense pressure from Syrians on his staff who wanted to spread the campaign northwards. As a result, the question of Syria now occupied his entire attention, and he had begun to abandon the cautious step-by-step policy Lawrence had advocated.

Reports confirmed that the Akaba region was almost free from Turkish troops, and this seemed to present a golden opportunity.

Within a few days of Lawrence's departure, Feisal had set aside warnings about the Wadi Itm defences, and had raised the subject of Akaba with Vickery, then the only British officer remaining at Wejh. Vickery, like Newcombe, felt that action at Akaba would help the Arabs to tackle the railway. He wrote to Clayton: 'I should be very glad of instructions on the question of taking Akaba with troops from Sherif Feisal's army.

'Sherif Feisal is very anxious to occupy the town as he thinks – with some reason too – that its capture and occupation by him would have an excellent political effect on the Syrians. He has also been asked to take the town by the Howeitat.

'He further considers, and I agree with him, that the farther north he proceeds, the farther north on their line of communication must the Turks go. [If] Sherif Feisal threatens [the Hejaz Railway] from Wejh, Dhabba and (when taken) Akaba . . . the Turks must defend their line, and without reinforcements they can only do this by withdrawing from their posts south of Medina, and by weakening their garrison at Medina. The longer the line which they have to guard against raids, the more scattered will be their troops, and they will be weak everywhere and strong nowhere.

'Sherif Feisal asked for a seaplane reconnaissance of Akaba and ships to transport his troops. His information was that there were only twenty-five men (Turks) in the town, and the rest of the Turkish force was camped at El Beira ten hours – presumably thirty-five miles – east of Akaba.

'I pointed out to Sherif Feisal that the taking of the town was very easy, but the nature of the surrounding country was such that its retention was impossible unless one was prepared to hold the hills which command the town. For this a considerable force would be necessary. He seemed to think that he could spare this force when he got the rifles which have been asked for.

'I told the Sherif that I could give no promise or undertaking for any assistance . . . without referring the matter to you. I told him this as I understand there are some difficulties in the question of an attack or occupation of Akaba.

'The Sherif said there was no urgent hurry in the matter, and requested me to let him know if I could arrange a reconnaissance etc. as above, at my convenience.'[41]

Although Feisal had stated that there was no urgency, this report shows that he did not think it necessary to wait for the fall of Medina before going north. In talking to Vickery, he had presented the taking of Akaba as a helpful step in the campaign against Medina, even though it was in reality a move in the opposite direction. This impatience exactly reflected the mood of Syrians in his entourage such as Nesib el Bekri, a Damascus landowner who had been deeply involved in secret Arab in-dependence movements before the war. For Nesib, the revolt in the Hejaz was almost irrelevant, and its outcome was in any case assured. The real prize would be Syria, his own country. He saw that a northern rebellion at that moment would catch the Turks unprepared, but he knew too little about military affairs to realise how quickly a revolt would die unless it could be supplied with money, arms, ammunition, and other necessities.

Since the outset, inattention to such matters by the Arab political leadership had crippled operations in the field. In June 1916 Hussein had made exactly the same kind of blunder that Nesib and others were now advocating. Feisal himself had little grounding in military strategy, and in reply to Nesib he could only cite the opinions of advisers such as Lawrence, which were inevitably regarded as suspect.[42]

When Lawrence reached Wejh on March 3rd, he must have realised how greatly Feisal had been swayed. The situation was easily rectified, but the incident served as a warning for the future. Many years later he remarked that Feisal 'always listened to his momentary adviser, despite his own better judgment.'[43] Lawrence's reports contain no allusion to this wavering over Akaba, or anything further about Feisal's northern plans. In view of the reports by Vickery, Newcombe, and others during the same period, this silence can only have been a deliberate policy. He must nevertheless have been very anxious to know how Cairo would respond to Vickery's request for guidance.

A few days after this, Vickery left Wejh for service in France. He was one of two artillery officers who had been attached to the British Military Mission when it was thought that gunnery would play a major role in the Revolt. As things had turned out, their expertise had hardly been called upon, and it was wholly irrelevant to the campaign against the railway. Artillery officers were in great demand elsewhere, and Wingate felt that he could no longer justify retaining them. Lawrence had mixed feelings about the decision. 'In one way, it was a pity, for he was a soldier to his finger-tips, with great irregular experience, and knew Arabic through and through in the way we all should have known it, but we got on better without him for he had never accepted our conditions. He was too worldly to like the Arab revolt . . . Then he was ambitious. His mind ran on decoration and promotion, and, as he saw no public for the Arab campaign, he called service in it professional suicide.'[44]

Operations against the railway were now gathering pace. In early March it was learned that demolition parties from Abdullah's force in Wadi Ais had destroyed a bridge and several sections of line north of Medina. Lawrence wrote: 'This news, following on Garland's feat, is most satisfactory.'[45] A few days later he heard that Newcombe had destroyed 2,500 metres of line. The *Arab Bulletin* of March 12th noted that there had been at least seven recent attacks at widely spaced points along the railway.

Lawrence's main task at this time was to help establish Feisal's base at Wejh. In particular, he was involved in setting up an administrative system to cope with supplies arriving by sea, and installing the new wireless station. There were now also two armoured cars at the base, lent, together with their British crews, by the EEF. In the morning of March 8th, while he was busy with these arrangements, an urgent message arrived from Cairo. A few days earlier, British Intelligence had learned that orders had been issued for the evacuation of Medina. The Turks had realised that it might soon be impractical to defend the whole length of the railway to Medina, now that it was threatened by Arab armies from both Wejh and Wadi Ais. Instead, they were planning a staged withdrawal five hundred miles northwards to a new defensive position south of Maan.[46]

This should have been excellent news: when the Turks left, Hussein's armies would have achieved every objective they had been fighting for in the Hejaz. However, the proposed withdrawal was extremely unwelcome to General Murray, who was on the point of launching his attack on Gaza. Although his army was superior to the Turkish force on the Gaza-Beersheba line, this advantage might easily be lost. He had little reserve strength because many of his troops had been transferred to the Western Front during the preceding months. If the Turks now gave up Medina and the southern half of the Hejaz Railway, they would be able to transfer a large number of experienced and well-armed men to the Sinai front. This would radically change the balance of forces there.

Clayton had therefore sent orders to Wejh that every effort must be made to prevent the Medina garrison from going north. If the city could not be captured, the Turkish force must be kept where it was or destroyed as it attempted to withdraw.

When the message arrived, Lawrence was the senior British officer present in Wejh. Newcombe and Garland had not yet returned from their raids on the railway, and Vickery had left. The task of persuading Feisal to take urgent action was made more difficult because Clayton did not wish the Arabs to be informed of the intended Turkish withdrawal. They had been hoping that Medina would be abandoned, and Clayton must have feared that if the news leaked out nothing would be done to stop Fakhri leaving. Compliance with the order from Cairo would, however, prolong the status quo in the Hejaz, perhaps for a considerable time, and this would be a great sacrifice for Feisal. The continued Turkish occupation of Medina, the second most holy city of Islam, had become a symbol of Arab weakness. Moreover, if existing plans were followed, a delay in ending the Hejaz campaign would put off the moment when Feisal could advance into Syria.

The instructions placed Lawrence in a very awkward predicament, since all Feisal's thoughts were now directed towards the north. He realised that it would be impossible to persuade Feisal to take effective action against the line unless the true situation was explained. It seemed safe to do so because there had now been a great increase in trust between them. According to *Seven Pillars*, Lawrence appealed to Feisal's sense of honour, arguing that while Britain had done many things to assist the Arab Revolt, it was now Murray's turn to ask for assistance.[47] While Lawrence may well have pitched his request in these terms, he doubtless dropped hints of another, much stronger, argument. He now knew that the whole future of the Arab campaign in Syria would depend on Murray's good-will. If Feisal could hold the Medina garrison, Murray would be under a deep obligation.

Feisal agreed to do everything possible. Detailed plans were hurriedly drawn up, and messages sent out to Sherifs Ali and Abdullah, as well as to tribal leaders, asking them to attack the railway above Medina and to destroy any Turkish force that left the town. If the line could be kept out of action, it would be almost impossible for the Turks to move. There was no British liaison officer with Abdullah, whose military performance during the past few weeks had been very disappointing. Lawrence therefore decided to go up to Wadi Ais himself.

He wrote to Colonel Wilson explaining that the urgency of the order had left little time to make all the necessary arrangements: 'I hoped to get it up to Newcombe, but cannot, as he is coming in, without saying by what road . . . In the circumstances . . . I got Feisul to take action. In spite of

General Clayton's orders I told him something of the situation. It would have been impossible for me to have done anything myself on the necessary scale. One must inform one's G.O.C.!

'He has written to Sherif Ali to send the eastern Juheina and Harb direct to Bowat-Muheit as soon as possible . . . Feisul says nothing in his letter to give away [his] own knowledge, but the note was urgent enough to impel Ali to action I think.

'A messenger has left for Abdulla telling him, at the risk of losing three quarters of his force, to smash and cut and attack everything animate or material from Bowat up to Hedia.

'Saad el Ghoneim [a renowned fighting chief from the Juheina tribe] has left for Fagair in Wadi Hamdh, to attack the line temporarily till we reach him. I am off tomorrow with a 2.95 gun [and] a machine-gun company . . . to try and hold up one of the water reservoirs and smash it.

'The Mule Mounted Infantry [one of Feisal's units of Arab regulars] is being sent, probably to Abdulla, to make way against the new Turkish Camel Corps. They are 160 strong, with two machine-guns, and are good. They proceed forth to Fagair, and if in time, will join Abdulla. If not, they will go for the Turks wherever they are.'

After giving details of the action to be taken by several other Arab groups, Lawrence concluded: 'The plan (spur of the moment, I wish one had had more notice) is to get something going at once against the water arrangements, to give time for concentration. For this purpose these light advance parties are going up, to risk anything to gain time. Then when the camels [requested for the El Ula operation] come, and Ali has moved, the main forces of the three brothers will be from Medina to El Ula along the line, and the Turks will find movement most difficult. That will, I think, take ten days . . . I think the weak point of the Turk plans lies in the trains of water and food. If we can cut the line on such a scale that they cannot repair it, or smash their locomotives, the force will come to a standstill. They must have little repair material in Medina – and will not be able to transport that much besides food and water. If only we can hold them up for ten days. I'm afraid it will be touch and go. I am taking some Garland mines with me, if I can find instantaneous fuse, and if there is time, I will set them, as near Medina as possible: it is partly for this reason that I am going up myself, and partly with a view to smashing Hedia [the only station with a water supply for two hundred kilometres south of El Ula], if it can anyhow be done. Feisul will do anything he can. Only it's fearfully short notice.'[48]

Although he had no experience as an officer in the field, he was now preparing to take an active part in operations against the line. The mines Garland had invented for blowing up trains were still at an experimental stage, and no Arab had been trained to use them. Lawrence wrote in his notebook: 'I am to start for [Abdullah] tonight, to explain, reconnoitre, and if possible mine the railway or take a station.'[49] In this role it might even become necessary for him to assume command. An additional note reads: 'Feisul has authorised me to bring down the Fagair troops to Abdulla, use them myself, or send them north as I think best.'[50]

On March 10th Lawrence with a small escort set out for Wadi Ais.

CHAPTER 18

Wadi Ais
March – April 1917

THE long ride inland to Abdullah's camp was particularly unwelcome to Lawrence. He had a severe outbreak of boils on his back, the result of unfamiliar diet and spartan living conditions. Not long after setting out he went down with dysentery and began to suffer bouts of high fever. Some of the notes he made on this journey are barely legible.

On the second evening, while camped in the Wadi Kitan, he found himself in one of the most unpleasant predicaments that he would face during the whole war. The small party which accompanied him had been assembled in haste, and it contained a motley selection of Arabs from different regions. Tensions between them were inevitable and, following a quarrel, one of the Ageyl was murdered by a Moroccan. Lawrence realised that justice would have to be done quickly before the other men took matters into their own hands. He described his feelings in *Seven Pillars*: 'Then rose up the horror which would make civilized man shun justice like a plague if he had not the needy to serve him as hangmen for wages. There were other Moroccans in our army; and to let the Ageyl kill one in feud meant reprisals by which our unity would have been endangered. It must be a formal execution, and at last, desperately, I told Hamed that he must die for punishment, and laid the burden of his killing on myself. Perhaps they would count me not qualified for feud. At least no revenge could lie against my followers; for I was a stranger and kinless.'[1] Lawrence was appalled by the gruesome task, but there was no alternative. He was now very feverish, and his hand was so unsteady that it took three shots to carry out the execution. The memory of it would remain with him for the rest of his life. Had the incident occurred later in the campaign, when he had been hardened by the experience of fighting, it might have been easier; but this was the first man he had killed in the Arab cause.

The shock of the experience heightened his sickness. His log of the journey contains a note in shaky writing beside a sketch map of the Wadi Kitan: 'Camped here. Awful night. Shot.'[2] He later wrote that he had roused the men before dawn 'in my longing to be out of Wadi Kitan. They had to lift me into the saddle.'[3]

He reached Abdullah's camp four days later and handed over letters from Feisal. After explaining the plans for urgent action against the railway, his strength gave out completely. Dysentery was followed by a heavy bout of malaria, and it would be a few days before he recovered sufficiently to do anything further. During this period of enforced idleness his mind distanced itself from day-to-day preoccupations, and he began to see the Arab Revolt in a broader perspective.

There had been a fundamental change since he had last thought deeply about Arab strategy in the Hejaz. Until now, every long-term plan had centred on the need to drive the Turks from Medina. Yet just when this objective was within reach, Murray had ruled against it. The new aim was to keep as many Turks as possible away from the Palestine front. As Lawrence pondered this, he began to see wider implications. Why should the Arabs take Medina at all? The Turkish garrison no longer presented any threat to the rest of the Hejaz, and as long as it remained where it was, it could not be used against the British in Sinai. The Turks had also to hold the Hejaz Railway, and this would mean constant patrolling against Arab attacks. The five-hundred-mile track south of Maan ran through desert where bedouin raiding parties could come and go as they pleased. As raids increased in frequency, thousands more Turkish soldiers would be needed to defend the line. The immobilisation of so many men and weapons would be a positive handicap to the Turks. It would therefore be in Britain's interests to keep Fakhri Pasha's garrison in Medina: not only at this time, but as long as the war continued.

Lawrence summarised this conclusion in *Seven Pillars*: 'We must not take Medina. The Turk was harmless there. In prison in Egypt he would cost us food and guards. We wanted him to stay at Medina, and every other distant place, in the largest numbers. Our ideal was to keep his railway just working but only just, with the maximum of loss and discomfort. The factor of food would confine him to the railways, but he was welcome to the Hejaz Railway, and the Trans-Jordan railway, and the Palestine and Syrian railways for the duration of the war, so long as he gave us the other nine hundred and ninety-nine thousandths of the Arab world. If he tended to evacuate too soon, as a step to concentrating in the small area which his numbers could dominate effectually, then we should have to restore his confidence by reducing our enterprises against him.

His stupidity would be our ally, for he would like to hold, or to think he held, as much of his old provinces as possible. This pride in his imperial heritage would keep him in his present absurd position – all flanks and no front.'[4]

Such tactics would also help to minimise Arab losses; British advisers in the Hejaz had noted how badly Arab morale suffered when casualties were heavy, and had argued in favour of guerilla action rather than conventional engagements. Lawrence now believed that, given time, Arab guerilla raids could actually win the war: 'The death of a Turkish bridge or rail, machine or gun or charge of high explosive, was more profitable to us than the death of a Turk . . . Most wars were wars of contact, both forces striving into touch to avoid tactical surprise. Ours should be a war of detachment. We were to contain the enemy by the silent threat of a vast unknown desert, not disclosing ourselves till we attacked. The attack might be nominal, directed not against him, but against his stuff; so it would not seek either his strength or his weakness, but his most accessible material.'[5]

According to this strategy, the Revolt should be extended as widely as possible: there was no longer any virtue in postponing a campaign in Syria until Medina fell. Indeed, if the Hejaz campaign were to be prolonged indefinitely, simultaneous action in the north would be essential. Otherwise, the Arabs might not have a chance to occupy Damascus before the end of the war. A change in British policy along these lines would accommodate Feisal's growing impatience to take action in the north. Nevertheless, the rebellion in Syria must be properly planned.

Lawrence would be unable to begin work on this new strategy until he got back to the coast. For the moment, his priority was to see that sufficient action was taken to prevent the Turks leaving Medina. On March 22nd he was well enough to write to Wejh: as illness had prevented him from attacking the line, it was all the more important that some kind of action was being taken at El Ula. Without continuous prompting, Feisal might well lose interest in the railway. Indeed, the Arab leader could be forgiven for hoping privately that the Turks would manage to leave Medina. Lawrence therefore addressed an urgent letter to whichever British officer was now with Feisal: 'Please beg him not to remain in Wejh unless it is absolutely necessary. The effect both on Arabs and Turks of knowing him to be near the line would be very great: and if he left his heavy baggage in Wejh he could fall back on it in case of need, quickly. He has aeroplanes now, and Wejh is very easy to defend. Also if the Turks pushed west from El Ula I would get Sidi Abdullah to march up the line towards El Ula – which would have the effect of bringing the Turks back. In fact I hope most strongly to find him at [Wadi] Jayadah or Ainsheifa [on the western approach to the railway] soon.'[6]

The tone of these remarks seems to hint at another aspect of Feisal's character. Years afterwards Lawrence admitted that 'Feisal was a timid man who hated running into danger, yet would do anything for Arab freedom – his one passion, purely unselfish . . . it made him face things and risks he hated. At the original attack on Medina he had nerved himself to put on a bold front, and the effort had shaken him so that he never courted danger in battle again.'[7] In his wartime reports Lawrence did his best to conceal this timidity, knowing that the British military establishment would despise a leader with any taint of cowardice. But others had already noted the weakness. For example, before the move to Wejh an RFC officer had written: 'Sherif Feisal has greater breadth of character [than Ali] and no more strength. He is easily frightened and lives in constant dread of a Turkish advance though he seems to conceal that fear from his army.'[8]

As regards his own plans, Lawrence wrote in a second note on March 22nd: 'I hope to go down to the railway tomorrow for a preliminary reconnaissance, and after that will be able to say what can be done: but in any case I will stay here a bit, as it is most important that the Turks should not be able to concentrate much of their Medina force at El Ula against [Feisal], and I am afraid if I do not stay here not much will be done.'[9]

This visit to Wadi Ais had confirmed Lawrence in his earlier impression that Abdullah would be more useful to the Arab cause as a politician and diplomat than as a military leader. Later, in a detailed report to Colonel Wilson, he wrote: 'The conditions in his camp were, I thought, unsatisfactory. He had a force of about 3,000 men, mostly Ateiba. They seem to me very inferior as fighting men, to the Harb and Juheina. They are of course altogether Bedouin, and their Sheikhs are ignorant, lacking in influence and character, and apparently, without any interest in the war.

'Sidi Abdulla himself gave me rather the same impression . . . [he] spends his time in reading the Arabic newspapers, in eating, and sleeping, and especially in jesting with one Mohamed Hassan, an old Yemeni from Taif . . . Abdulla and his friends spend much of the day and all the evening in playing practical jokes on Mohamed Hassan. These take the form usually of stabbing him with thorns, stoning him, or setting him on fire . . .

Sidi Abdulla is fond of rifle practice, and also of Arabic poetry. Reciters from the camp while away much of his time with songs and dances.

'He takes great interest in the war in Europe, and follows the operations on the Somme, and the general course of European politics most closely. I was surprised to find that he knew the family relationships of the Royal Houses of Europe and the names and characters of their ministers. He takes little interest in the war in the Hedjaz. He considers the Arab position as assured, with Syria and Iraq irrevocably pledged to the Arabs by Great Britain's signed agreements, and for himself looks particularly to the Yemen. He regards this, rather than Syria, as the future basis of strength of the Arab movement, and intends, as soon as set free from the boredom of these . . . operations, to chase Muhieddin out of Abha, Idrissi out of Arabia and compel the Imam to the position of a feudatory. This sounds a large operation but Abdulla is convinced of its practicability, and has even worked out the details of his actions.'[10] Lawrence thought Abdullah unwise to put so much faith in the vague McMahon-Hussein commitments over Syria and Iraq, but refrained from telling him so. However, the scheme to take over the southern regions sounded intriguing, and in his report to Wilson, Lawrence suggested that it might be given serious consideration, as it would 'transform the Sherif's state from a loose hegemony of Bedouin tribes into a populous, wealthy and vigorous kingdom of villagers and townspeople.'[11]

As regards operations against the railway, Abdullah's attitude was 'hardly favourable. His Ateiba knew nothing of the country in which they were, and their Sheikhs are nonentities . . . Of his five machine guns only two were effective for lack of armourers or spares . . . His regular troops (seventy Syrian deserters, the gunners, and machinegunners) lack nearly all equipment, and he had taken no steps to help them. His Ateiba were two months in arrears of pay, simply through *laissez faire*, for the gold was present in the camp to pay them up in full. He understands very little about military operations and the only officer in the camp, Sidi Raho, the Algerian Captain [sent by Brémond], is either unable, or unwilling to persuade him to move. Since his arrival in Wadi Ais, Sidi Abdulla had not ordered any attack on the railway. The destruction of the bridge over Wadi Hamdh near Abu el Naam was the work of Dakhilallah el Gadir, permitted certainly by Abdulla but not suggested or encouraged in any way by him.'[12] Fortunately, Lawrence had been able to work up some enthusiasm among Abdullah's retainers, notably Dakhilallah el Gadir and Sherif Shakir. He described these two as the 'outstanding personalities of Abdulla's camp . . . thanks to their help I was able to influence him to take rather more interest, and feel rather more responsible in Hedjaz affairs than formerly.'[13] When Lawrence explained to them what ought to be done to the railway, they persuaded Abdullah to authorise more frequent action.

Lawrence could not safely write this kind of critical report while he was still at Abdullah's camp. Instead he sent a cryptic message to Wejh: 'I cannot explain on paper why so little has been done hitherto. Do you remember what Nero did when Rome was burning? Am making headway steadily and hope to have a force of my own shortly.'[14]

From what he had seen at Wadi Ais, Lawrence must have been increasingly doubtful that any operation against Medina could succeed if it depended on large-scale action by Abdullah. This conclusion only served to strengthen the case for his new strategy of leaving the Turks in Medina indefinitely.

However, while his later report contained severe military criticisms, Lawrence also stressed his regard for Abdullah's talent in other fields: 'I hope that in making . . . strictures on Sidi Abdulla's behaviour, I have not given the impression that there is anything between us, he treated me like a prince and we parted most excellent friends in spite of my having said some rather strong things about the tone of his camp. I had come straight from Feisal's headquarters where one lives in a continual atmosphere of effort and high thinking towards the better conduct of the war – and the contrast with this of Abdulla's pleasure-loving laughing entourage was too great to be pleasant. One must remember however, that Abdulla is the head and cause of the Hedjaz revolt and neither his sincerity nor his earnestness can be called in question. I do think however that he is incapable as a military commander and unfit to be trusted alone with important commissions of an active sort.'[15]

Lawrence noted with satisfaction that suspicions of France had led Abdullah to dismiss Brémond's latest ploy: 'Sergeant Claude Proste, of the French Army, now with Sidi Abdulla, brought him a letter from Colonel Brémond, pointing out that the English were surrounding the new Arabic Kingdom on all sides (quoting Aden, Baghdad [recently captured from the Turks], and Gaza as instances) and hoping that Sidi Abdulla realized the situation. I asked him for his opinion on the point, and he spoke very strongly against Colonel Brémond, and Berchet, French interpreter at Jiddah. He said they were everlastingly trying to sow discord between the Sherif and the British, and that he was

much afraid they might influence English opinion. He said that his
father always believed Colonel Brémond's reports at first, but cooled
off a few days later'.[16]

Towards the end of March, Lawrence was fit enough to set out on the first
of two expeditions against the railway. Hedia and its water supply were
too strongly held to attack with the resources Abdullah offered, and it was
decided instead to raid the station at Abu el Naam. After observing the
Turkish garrison there for a day and a half, Lawrence realised that even
here the Arab force led by Sherif Shakir was insufficient to attempt
capture, so a different plan was adopted. Under cover of darkness,
Lawrence laid one of the Garland mines and cut the telegraph wires. Early
the following morning, while a train was in the station, the Arabs attacked
with a mountain gun and a howitzer. Lawrence reported afterwards: 'The
results of the bombardment were to throw the upper storeys of the large
stone buildings into the ground floors, which were reported to contain
stores and water-cisterns. We could not demolish the ground floors. The
water-tank (metal) was pierced and knocked out of shape, and three shells
exploded in the pumping room and brought down much of the wall. We
demolished the well-house, over the well, burned the tents and the
wood-pile and obtained a hit on the first wagon of the train in the station.
This set it on fire, and the flames spread to the remaining six wagons,
which must have contained inflammable stores, since they burned
furiously. The locomotive was behind the northern building, and got
steam up, and went off (reversed) towards Medina. When it passed over
the mine it exploded it, under the front bogies (i.e. too late). It was
however derailed . . . [but] the seven men on the engine were able to
"jack" it on the line again in about half an hour (only the front wheels
derailed) and it went off towards Istabl Antar, at foot pace, clanking
horribly.'[17] Part of the station surrendered, and the Arabs were able to take
twenty-four prisoners. Lawrence concluded: 'I think that the attack – as
an experiment – justified itself. It had the effect in the next three days, of
persuading the Turks to evacuate every out-post and blockhouse on the
line, and concentrate the garrison in the various railway stations, which
facilitated the work of the dynamite parties.'[18]

On the second raid the Arab party was led by Dakhilallah el Gadir. The
line was again blown up at several points, and Lawrence laid a second
Garland mine. By mistake he buried the trigger mechanism a fraction of
an inch too deeply, and a train passed without setting it off. After dark he

dug it up: 'a most unpleasant proceeding: laying a Garland mine is shaky work, but scrabbling along a line for 100 yards in the ballast looking for a trigger that is connected with two powerful charges must be a quite uninsurable occupation.'[19] He relaid the mine, and its charges later isolated a Turkish repair train.

Although he had failed to destroy a locomotive, his two expeditions did a good deal of damage, and he had been able to show the Arabs the type of operation that would cause most disruption. He arranged with Shakir and Dakhilallah that the line would be raided frequently, causing the maximum dislocation to the Turks: 'Dynamiters have been ordered to blow up not more than five rails per night, and so something every night . . . I think a constant series of petty destructions of rails is the most efficient means of keeping the line out of order. Large demolitions are no more difficult to repair and the blowing up of culverts is a waste of time and explosives.'[20]

When Lawrence returned to Wadi Ais from his second expedition, he found an urgent handwritten message from Feisal (the original is in imperfect French): 'I was very sorry to learn that you were ill', Feisal wrote, 'I hope that you are already better and that you would like to come back to us in a short time, as soon as possible. Your presence with me is very indispensable, in view of urgency of questions and the pace of affairs. It was not at all your promise to stay there so long. So I hope that you will return here as soon as you receive this letter.'[21]

Lawrence decided to go back to Wejh as quickly as possible. Before leaving, he secured Abdullah's promise that demolition parties would be sent regularly to the line, and also that there would be an artillery attack on Hedia. However, he wrote some days later: 'I am doubtful whether [Abdullah] will keep either promise, unless urged on by someone in his camp. He is too lazy and luxurious to inconvenience himself.'[22]

Feisal had good reason to wish that Lawrence was back in Wejh. During the preceding three weeks he had faced mounting difficulties in several areas. As Lawrence had feared, his attention had again turned towards the north, and he had shown little interest in operations on the railway. This had soon brought him into conflict with a new British arrival, Major Joyce.

Joyce had reached Wejh on March 17th. He was to act as Senior British Officer, responsible for the armoured cars and the RFC flight that would shortly move up from Rabegh, where he too had been based during the previous four months. His dealings with the Arab leadership there had been so frustrating that he had written on one occasion: 'Privately I think Sherif Ali a little s**t, though very pleasant and nice to talk to. He is getting no moves on at all. He can't organise and won't let anybody else even try and the days pass by and the time wasted makes me mad.'[23] This experience evidently coloured Joyce's attitude towards Feisal, and his early reports from Wejh express considerable irritation at the unending delays.

Joyce was annoyed to discover how much time Feisal was giving to delegations from tribes far outside the present theatre of operations. After a few days he reported sourly: 'Feisal is quite happy about things and assures me that nothing now passes north along the line . . . [his] whole attention is now turned northwards and he considers the actual taking of Medina the work of Abdalla, Ali and Zeid.'[24]

Feisal continued to promote operations farther north, despite Joyce's efforts to focus attention on El Ula. In late March he cabled the following devious message to Wilson: 'The northern tribes are coming in steadily, but I have no rifles to give them as I promised. I am asked by you all to cut the railway quickly, but my force would consist of these tribes who require rifles. I beg you to help.'[25] Both Joyce and Wilson knew that the rifles were not required for action at El Ula.

On April 1st, Joyce was finally able to report that 'Sherif Sheraf and the majority of Feisal's army left Wejh yesterday. Their destination is Abu-Raka and from there to attack some portion of the railway line and occupy it . . . Faisal at last realises the necessity of this move and is determined to accomplish it.' He added, however: 'I cannot press him further about his own departure and the good effect it would likely have if he went to Abu-Raka himself. He insists that his presence in Wedj is absolutely essential at present, meeting the deputations from northern and eastern tribes which arrive nearly every day, and he considers it most important that he should be here to receive them'.[26] Joyce evidently hoped to curb these activities, because he continued: 'The whole of Sherif Faisal's endeavours, with the exception of the actual occupying of a portion of the line, are now concentrated on the north with the idea of getting the tribes in this region to co-operate and make a general attack on the line between Derra and Tabuk. His ambitions probably go even further and aim at getting the whole line south of Damascus.

'I feel sure it would be advantageous if the limits of the Hedjaz operations could be defined as soon as possible. The further north they extend entails more money and more rifles . . . in order to save disappointment and possible friction later, I feel certain that something definite should be laid down.

'I have endeavoured to confine Faisal to local ambitions and military operations, but from somewhere he has developed very wide ideas and I would like to feel certain they are in accordance with the general plan.'[27]

One of the reasons for Feisal's concern about the north was growing alarm about French activities. The machine-gun instructors left at Wejh by Brémond had been a source of irritation from the start. This is evident from a letter Colonel Wilson had written during a visit some weeks earlier: 'Feisal came on board to see me last evening and was very agitated about the French here. I rubbed it in to him that he must not kick them out "*sans cérémonie*" and again recommended that he should wait and see what [the] Sherif wished.

'He wanted me to tell the French they were not wanted and if I did not that he would, hence my lecture. Damn Brémond and his nasty ways, he creates more beastly situations for me than one would have thought possible.'[28]

Syrians in Feisal's entourage were increasingly worried by rumours that France intended to invade Syria and take control there (such thoughts had doubtless occurred to Feisal when Brémond offered to send French colonial troops to Akaba). There now seemed to be evidence of definite preparations, and in reality the authorities in Paris were seriously considering such a project. A French officer, charged with preparing a feasibility study for landings on the Syrian coast, had recently been interviewing Arab representatives in Alexandria, Cairo and Port Said. He had wished to assess potential Arab reaction, and the motive for his questions must have been obvious.[29] Moreover, there were firm plans to send a contingent of French support troops to join the EEF. Its role would be to ensure that the tricolour was present during any advance through Palestine, and the first units were about to arrive in Egypt.[30] Feisal had undoubtedly heard something of these new initiatives, possibly from Arab contacts in Egypt, but more probably from the French contingent at Wejh.

Arab anxiety increased when Brémond visited Wejh on April 1st. He was determined to place some more of his men there if at all possible. The tone of his discussions with Feisal can be judged from his later report: '[Feisal's] attitude was very firm. I asked him to take some Muslim soldiers with him, so that they would have the honour of taking part in the capture of Medina. He replied that he was not going to Medina, but further north, and that the soldiers would not, therefore, derive any satisfaction from coming with him. He asked again, emphatically, for some 75mm Schneider mountain guns. Can I have a reply about this, so that I can promise him a definite number ... and, if possible, can they be sent to me? In this way I will have a reason to increase the [French] detachment at Wejh and to place NCOs around Feisal; this is important at a time when he is committing himself to the north in a very decided state of mind about us, and with a purely Syrian entourage.

'He imagines, obviously wrongly, that France alone will oppose his Syrian projects, Britain being only concerned with the question of Mesopotamia.'[31]

The effect of Brémond's visit can be judged by a report from Wejh written a few days later. It said that Feisal had 'expressed considerable alarm at a rumour which had reached him to the effect that the French were about to land sixty thousand men in Syria. He feared that if this were true England would cease to supply him with arms and munitions, and that the French would take Syria without the assistance of the Arabs.

'He expressed the utmost apprehension of such a contingency and went so far as to say that, if it should come to pass, he would first fight the Turks, and then the French.'[32]

Feisal must have feared that the Arabs would lose Syria altogether unless they acted quickly to secure the northern cities. According to this report, he had now 'told the ... Sheiks of the northern tribes that he hopes to move north in about two months' time and that they must all be ready to rise against the Turks, each in his pre-arranged place, on a date to be decided upon later. All they need do at present is to get their people ready and wait. Meanwhile, he would have the necessary arms ready and would arrange with the Druses and also with the Arabs north near Aleppo, Hama, and Homs.'[33]

There was still another factor which caused Feisal to recall Lawrence. By March 23rd he knew that Auda abu Tayi would shortly arrive in Wejh. Auda was the Howeitat chief who would say whether or not Lawrence's scheme for taking Akaba was feasible, and whose co-operation would be essential if the plan were to be put into action. It was therefore important that Lawrence should be at Wejh.

Auda arrived at Wejh in early April, and on the 5th Feisal held a meeting at which leaders from the Howeitat, Beni Sakhr, Rualla and other northern tribes were present. Newcombe reported that two alternative plans for extending the Revolt were discussed. The first was the scheme Feisal had worked out with Lawrence two months earlier: 'to move along the railway clearing up the Turkish posts . . . and eventually taking Maan. Then to move north again, using Akaba as a base.'[34] The second was more precipitate: 'to proceed direct with a small force to the Druse mountains [east of Deraa] and from there to descend on the railway between Damascus and Maan and from Deraa to Afuleh, using the Druse, Beni Sakhr, Huitat, and Anazeh.'[35] To make either campaign possible, Feisal asked for twenty thousand British rifles, ammunition, and explosives.

Newcombe and Joyce told Feisal that they thought the second proposal better than the first, on the grounds that it was 'more economical, more rapid, and, if successful, obtaining the same results'.[36] Needless to say, however, they also 'urged on Faisal that his future plan must not be allowed to interfere with the business which is already in hand, viz. the defeat of the Turks at Medina, El Ula, and Medain Salih, which should be cleared up in order to make the northern move fully effective.'[37]

It seems curious that two officers so experienced in the vicissitudes of Arab warfare should have urged Feisal to adopt the more daring and risky of the alternative plans. The scheme for a step-by-step advance via Maan was much more likely to succeed, and only two months previously Newcombe himself had recommended that the Arabs should set up a base at Akaba.

One factor was probably ignorance. Neither Joyce nor Newcombe had any detailed knowledge of the terrain east of the Jordan. They had therefore to rely on Arab judgments about such matters as the feasibility of transporting supplies to a large raiding force that would be based nearly six hundred miles north of Wejh. These Arab estimates were almost certainly optimistic.

Another factor may have been the most recent orders from Cairo on the subject of Akaba. Five weeks previously Vickery had written requesting guidance about Feisal's enthusiasm for capturing the town. Clayton's comments, which had taken a little while to reach Wejh, had been wholly negative. This could be explained in part by the crisis that had meanwhile arisen over Medina; but those familiar with British policy in Egypt may have suspected other motives behind Clayton's emphatic rejection. The note, addressed to Lawrence, read: 'With reference to the attached letter from Major Vickery, the situation has changed somewhat since it was written and the move to Akaba on the part of Feisal is not at present desirable.

'It is essential that he should concentrate his energies on immediate operations against the Railway, and a move on Akaba as is proposed, might distract him from this objective . . . the sea-planes and ships for transport which are asked for are not available, so that in any case, the operation cannot be carried out at present.

'I appreciate Major Vickery's arguments in favour of the occupation of Akaba, but, on the other hand, his arguments to Feisal, as to the difficulty of retaining Akaba against hostile attack are equally convincing.

'It is questionable whether, in the present circumstances, the presence of an Arab force at Akaba would be desirable, as it would unsettle tribes which are better left quiet until the time is more ripe.'[38]

At the very least, it would have been unwise to encourage Feisal to think of taking Akaba without new instructions from Cairo. Newcombe, who had known Clayton for several years, could probably guess at the unspoken objection behind this message. The truth was that Clayton, like many others concerned about the future defence of Egypt, wanted to see Akaba in British, not Arab, hands.[39]

Lawrence travelled back to Wejh hoping that everyone would see the wisdom of his new strategy, and that the emphasis of Feisal's campaign could now be switched away from Medina towards the north. However, these views were shortly to put him at cross purposes, both with his British colleagues in the Hejaz, and with his superiors in Cairo.

CHAPTER 19

'A Useful Diversion'
April – July 1917

WHEN Lawrence reached Wejh on the afternoon of April 14th, he found Feisal 'in a nervous and exhausted state'.[1] The chief cause is evident from a report written by Joyce on the following day: '[Feisal] is still very much upset and disturbed by the rumour, which I believe emanates from the French, that about sixty thousand French troops have either actually landed or were about to land in Syria.'[2] Over the past weeks, Joyce had displayed such opposition to Arab action in the north that Feisal must have begun to suspect British collusion with French schemes to deprive the Arabs of Syria. At all events, Joyce's contemporary reports show that Feisal was now trying to convince him that Arab independence in Syria was essential to the future of the Hejaz.[3]

In these circumstances, Lawrence's return had been keenly awaited, and he reported that Feisal was 'very annoyed with me for staying [away] so long'.[4] Despite this, Feisal must have been pleased by Lawrence's sudden enthusiasm for action in Syria, which corresponded exactly with his own feelings. Lawrence no longer insisted on carrying out the El Ula scheme: he saw no need to capture Medina or even to block the railway before extending the Revolt.

The other British officers at Wejh were much less receptive to these new ideas. As Newcombe was away, Lawrence had to put his case to Joyce and Bray – the Indian Army officer who had been so critical of the Arabs at the capture of Wejh. Both men were certain that if the Arabs occupied El Ula and Medain Saleh, Medina would fall. In their view, Hussein's three armies now held decisive advantages: of superiority in numbers, of geography, and of reliable supplies. The situation seemed particularly favourable because it was believed (in fact wrongly) that the Turks had succeeded in evacuating a substantial part of their forces from Medina. From the standpoint of western military thinking, therefore, the Arab position seemed so strong that the surrender of Fakhri's garrison was a foregone conclusion.[5] All that remained was to work out the final details for co-operation between the various Arab forces. For this purpose it had been arranged that Feisal, accompanied by Colonel Wilson, would shortly go to meet Abdullah at Fagair in Wadi Hamdh.

In this atmosphere of high expectation, Lawrence's new ideas were dismissed. The El Ula attack was scheduled for mid-May, and neither Joyce nor Bray had time to think deeply about the possible benefits of his strategy. In any case, British policy on such issues was determined in Cairo, and there could be no radical change of course without approval from Clayton and Wingate, four hundred miles away. Lawrence argued in vain that Feisal's army could not occupy the line at El Ula for very long, since it would be vulnerable to attack from both north and south.

There was, however, limited agreement when he suggested that some-one might be sent north to raise a tribal force and attack the railway near Maan. Such raiding, if successful, would hamper any movement of Turkish reinforcements down from Maan to El Ula. As Lawrence wrote in *Seven Pillars*: 'Neither my general reasoning . . . nor my particular objections had much weight. The plans were made, and the preparations advanced. Everyone was too busy with his own work to give me specific authority to launch out on mine. All I gained was a hearing, and a qualified admission that my . . . offensive might be a useful diversion.'[6]

Privately, Lawrence was now convinced that Feisal's immediate objective should be the Akaba-Maan supply route which would open the door to operations further north. As the Howeitat leader Auda abu Tayi was now at Wejh, it was at last possible to assess the scheme for approaching Akaba from inland.

Lawrence quickly saw that Auda was as remarkable as his reputation, and that he had the personality, tribal strength, and local knowledge needed to carry out the Akaba scheme. The vivid description of him in *Seven Pillars* is closely based on Lawrence's contemporary reports: 'He must be nearly fifty now (he admits forty) and his black beard is tinged with white, but he is still tall and straight, loosely built, spare and powerful, and as active as a much younger man. His lined and haggard face is pure bedouin: broad low forehead, high sharp hooked nose, brown-green eyes, slanting outward, large mouth . . . pointed beard and moustache, with the lower jaw shaven clean in the Howeitat style. The Howeitat pride themselves on being altogether bedu, and Auda is the essence of the Abu Tayi [tribe]. His hospitality is sweeping . . . his generosity has reduced him to poverty, and devoured the profits of a hundred successful raids. He has married twenty-eight times, has been wounded thirteen times, and in his battles has seen all his tribesmen hurt, and most of his relations killed. He has only reported his "kill" since 1900, and they now stand at seventy-five Arabs; Turks are not counted by Auda when they are dead. Under his handling the Toweihah [tribesmen] have become the finest fighting force in western Arabia. He raids as often as he can each year . . . and has seen Aleppo, Basra, Taif, Wejh, and Wadi Dawasir in his armed expeditions.

'In his way, Auda is as hard-headed as he is hot-headed. His patience is extreme, and he receives (and ignores) advice, criticism, or abuse with a smile as constant as it is very charming. Nothing on earth would make him change his mind or obey an order or follow a course he disapproved. He sees life as a saga, and all events in it are significant, and all personages heroic. His mind is packed (and generally overflows) with stories of old raids and epic poems of fights. When he cannot secure a listener he sings to himself in his tremendous voice, which is also deep and musical . . . He speaks of himself in the third person, and he is so sure of his fame that he delights to roar out stories against himself. At times he seems seized with a demon of mischief and in large gatherings shouts appalling stories of the private matters of his hosts or guests: with all this he is modest, simple as a child, direct, honest, kind-hearted, affectionate, and warmly loved even by those to whom he is most trying – his friends.'[7] When the Akaba scheme was explained to him, Auda pronounced that it was feasible, and in discussions during the third week in April he and Lawrence began to work out detailed plans.

Lawrence gave only the broadest hints about the nature of this project to his British colleagues, and maintained a complete silence about the proposed operation in his reports to Cairo. His reason for doing so can only have been Clayton's letter about Akaba, which he had now seen for the first time; he was well qualified to read between the lines of this forthright opposition to an Arab attack on the town. During the preceding months the two of them must have discussed Akaba on many occasions, and he surely knew about the strategic considerations on which Clayton's attitude was based. They were spelled out in an internal memorandum written by Clayton at about this time: 'the occupation of Akaba by Arab troops might well result in the Arabs claiming that place hereafter, and it is by no means improbable that after the war Akaba may be of considerable importance to the future defence scheme of Egypt. It is thus essential that Akaba should remain in British hands after the war.'[8]

In the light of Clayton's letter, Lawrence must have suspected that if he told Cairo of his plan, he would receive an unequivocal order to abandon it. Failing that, there would probably be a lengthy debate, and the French might be consulted. He can have had no illusions about their reaction: if Brémond got wind of an Arab move on Akaba, he would urge the French Government to use every possible channel of influence to block it. In this process the scheme would inevitably be publicised. Once the Turks had been forewarned, the inland approach to Akaba would become impossible, now or in the future.

Lawrence had now reached a point of no return. In *Seven Pillars* he wrote: 'I decided to go my own way, with or without orders.'[9] Having seen Clayton's letter, he could not encourage Feisal to take Akaba without being guilty of acting against orders from a superior officer. Yet he was sure that the capture of Akaba was in the best interests of both the Arabs and the British. Everything in Syria would be lost to the Arabs unless Feisal managed to carry the campaign northwards out of the Hejaz. Likewise, if the Arab Revolt never spread to Syria, the EEF would have to fight its way northwards without the benefit of Arab assistance.

His decision had not been taken lightly. He had given much thought to the scope for future co-operation between Murray and Feisal. The EEF attack on Gaza at the end of March had failed to break through, and he knew that Murray was preparing for a new assault. The Turkish lines of communication into Palestine would be threatened by an extension of Arab activity northwards, and Murray would also have reason to be pleased if the Arabs could deprive the enemy of Akaba. Lawrence later wrote that Akaba's 'special value to the Turks was that, in their hands, it might, when they pleased, be constituted a threat on the right flank of the British army . . . it now lay behind the British right, and a small force operating from it would threaten either El Arish or Suez effectually. The British staff felt the inconvenience of this uncontained enemy base in all their efforts to prolong their right wing against Beersheba . . . So we wanted to get to Akaba at once, while it was yet lightly held. Early in the war there had been a big force there: but they had been drawn off for Palestine and Hejaz, and the new troops who would be sent there when the Turkish Staff decided to perturb Murray by threatening his right, had not yet begun to arrive. Murray himself (and before him Maxwell) had wished to take the place, but had not dared.'[10] Sensitive to this threat, Murray had sent a force in February to occupy Nekhl, half-way along the road from Akaba to Suez. The destruction of the well at Nekhl had denied one possible line of attack to an advancing Turkish force, but there were other routes across Sinai. Knowing this, Lawrence could imagine how grateful the British Headquarters would be to see the threat removed. A direct link between the Arabs at Akaba and the British forces in Sinai would also bring great benefits to Feisal. Lawrence had not forgotten that Wingate's sphere of command stopped short of Akaba, and that Feisal's campaign in Syria would depend entirely on Murray's support. If the Arabs succeeded in as big a venture as Akaba, Murray would realise how valuable they could be. Lawrence later wrote: 'The Arabs needed Akaba . . . to link up with the British. If they took it the act gave them Sinai, and made positive junction between them and Sir Archibald Murray. Thus having become really useful, they would obtain material help. The human frailty of Murray's staff was such that nothing but physical contact with our success could persuade them of our importance. Murray was friendly to us: but if we became his right wing he would equip us properly, almost without the asking . . . Accordingly, for the Arabs, Akaba spelt plenty in food, money, guns, advisers.'[11]

In summary, Lawrence felt that he could see the justification of his proposed action better than those in Cairo. Clayton's letter about Akaba was five weeks old, and it could be argued that the objections actually stated there did not apply to the inland scheme. Once Feisal had taken Akaba, the immediate military benefits would outweigh considerations about the future defence of Egypt. Above all, Akaba was vital to the progress of Feisal's campaign: without it, the Arab Revolt might be confined to the Hejaz for the duration of the war. Lawrence concluded that it must be taken as soon as possible, without warning, and without British help.

Details of the Akaba plan were settled within days of Lawrence's return to Wejh.[12] He had originally imagined that it would follow a general Arab advance up the railway towards Maan. Now, however, Akaba would have to be captured in a separate operation, long before Faisal's main force moved northward. The venture would therefore be more difficult and more risky. He and Auda worked out a scheme to travel north-east with a small party, joining the Howeitat in their spring pastures near Maan. A fresh tribal force would be raised there, which would first create a noisy diversion around Maan itself, and then take control of the route down to Akaba. In *Seven Pillars* Lawrence described this trek as 'an extreme example of a turning movement, since it involved a desert journey of six hundred miles to capture a trench within gunfire of our ships: but there was no practicable alternative . . . Auda thought all things possible with dynamite and money, and that the smaller clans about

Akaba would join us. Feisal, who was already in touch with them, also believed that they would help if we won a preliminary success up by Maan and then moved in force against the port.'[13]

By chance, while these deliberations were taking place, Lawrence obtained valuable Intelligence about the state of the Wadi Itm defences. On April 20th the Royal Navy had put a landing party ashore at Akaba, in order to investigate rumours that a German officer had arrived and was engaged in laying a minefield offshore. The naval party overpowered the local defences and took eleven prisoners. It also located the minefield, which was subsequently destroyed.

Later on the same day, Captain Boyle brought the prisoners to Wejh, and Lawrence was able to interrogate them. Six were Syrian Arabs, who immediately volunteered for service with the Sherif. They gave Lawrence exact information about the disposition and strength of Turkish forces in the area. It transpired that the permanent garrison based in Akaba totalled only 330 men from the Turkish Gendarmerie, and that the great majority of these were Arabs. Better still, the posts along the track to Maan were very lightly held. This news confirmed Lawrence's hopes: as long as the Turks could be prevented from sending in reinforcements, the defences of Akaba and Wadi Itm against an attack from inland were negligible.[14]

This was excellent news, and Lawrence felt that the expedition should set out as soon as possible. He had already concluded that his own presence would be indispensable, as this was the surest way to see that the party held to its objective. The bedouin were notoriously rapacious, and neither Akaba itself nor the barren track that led there offered much prospect of loot. Around Maan, however, there were richer targets, and the tribesmen might well be tempted by them.

On his own, Lawrence could not guarantee that the expedition stayed on course. He could not reveal to the Howeitat the full reasoning behind the Akaba plan, and Auda might choose to ignore him. This problem was diminished, however, when Feisal appointed Sherif Nasir as overall leader of the expedition. Nasir was widely respected, and had earned his place as one of the most trusted leaders in the Arab army. He was well aware of Lawrence's special status with Feisal, and he knew how greatly the Revolt depended on British help. It was most unlikely that he would ignore Lawrence's advice.

There was another very important reason for Lawrence to accompany the expedition. If Akaba were captured, supplies and reinforcements would be needed urgently, and these could only be brought in by British ships. Somehow, news of the successful coup would have to be taken to Egypt. If one of Boyle's patrol vessels passed Akaba at the right moment, something might be done to attract its attention.[15] However, this was uncertain, and the alternatives had therefore to be considered. Akaba was several days' journey from Wejh, even by the shortest route, and it seems likely that Lawrence realised at the outset how much quicker it would be to ride directly across Sinai to Suez. If he went himself, he would be able to state exactly what was needed, and use his influence to see that it was sent quickly. The reaction would be much slower if such startling news were brought in by an Arab tribesman.

Only Feisal and a handful of the Arab leaders knew what was being planned. As far as the British were concerned, Lawrence's northern expedition was a purely Arab affair, directed primarily against Maan. It was tolerated because few men would be withdrawn from Joyce's railway enterprise. Lawrence later wrote: 'the venture was a private one. I had no orders to do it, and took nothing British with me. Feisal provided money, camels, stores, and explosives.'[16]

Such was the lack of interest in Lawrence's activities that his British colleagues failed to grasp the implications of the plan, even when they learned its essential details. In late April, Wilson accompanied Feisal to the meeting with Abdullah at Fagair. Lawrence, who would not be involved in the railway operations, remained behind, but Auda went, probably to speak on behalf of the northern tribes in any wider discussions. During the journey to Fagair, Wilson travelled in the same armoured car as Auda, who told him a certain amount about the northern scheme. Wilson's subsequent report, which was mainly about the forthcoming railway operations, contained almost casual statements about the expedition: Auda was to travel north, 'probably' accompanied by Lawrence; the first aim would be to disrupt the railway around Maan, which would then be captured; if this succeeded, the force could clear out the Turkish posts down to Akaba. Neither Wilson, nor Clayton when he read the report, seems to have realised at the time what the true objective was, although all the elements of the Akaba plan were there. Doubtless they assumed that, like many other ambitious Arab schemes, it would come to nothing.[17]

While Feisal and Auda were away, Lawrence took an armoured car and spent several days locating the wreck of an RFC plane that had crash-landed in Wadi Hamdh.[18] He did not get back to Wejh until May 3rd, by which time the Fagair party had also returned.

To his complete surprise, he learned that Sir Mark Sykes had spent a few hours there on the previous day, and had talked at length with Feisal. During these conversations, Sykes had tried to obtain Feisal's consent to various propositions related, as Feisal must instantly have recognised, to the secret Anglo-French agreement over Syria. Sykes had then left for Jidda, where he was to meet Sherif Hussein.

Lawrence probably knew something of the background to this visit. Five months earlier, in late December 1916, Britain and France had agreed that when the EEF advanced into Palestine, a French political officer would be appointed to Murray's staff. More recently, when the French Government had learned of the planned assault on Gaza, they had nominated François Georges-Picot to this post.

The prospect of having to deal with Georges-Picot was most unwelcome to Murray's staff, and it had been decided that a British political officer should be appointed to work alongside Georges-Picot. This official would be the Frenchman's only channel of communication with GHQ. In due course Sykes had been nominated for this delicate liaison job, although a replacement was to be found as quickly as possible.

From the British side, the whole arrangement was little more than a nuisance. However, the Foreign Office was keen to forestall any dispute with France. The two political officers would advise Murray on any aspect of the military administration affected by the Anglo-French agreement. They hoped also to develop political relationships with Arab leaders, and to pave the way for implementation of the Sykes-Picot terms.

Ironically, when Sykes and Georges-Picot arrived in Egypt on April 22nd, the EEF was still blocked outside Gaza, with no immediate prospect of advancing into Palestine.[19] However, before setting out from England, Sykes had made arrangements to meet a small number of (carefully selected) Syrian Arabs. In Cairo, he and Georges-Picot began a series of talks with these representatives. Their aim was to bring the Arabs to a point at which the content of the Anglo-French agreement would seem acceptable.

At these meetings, the Arabs were presented with the idea that, after the war, Britain and France would help them to create an independent inland state or confederation. This would depend on its two European allies for protection, and would give in return financial and other concessions – in practice, those embodied in the Sykes-Picot Agreement. However, Sykes and Georges-Picot took care not to reveal that Britain and France had already divided the proposed autonomous area into two distinct spheres of influence. As Sykes put it, the task was 'to manoeuvre the delegates, without showing them a map or letting them know that there was an actual geographical or detailed agreement, into asking for what we are ready to give them.'[20]

Sherif Hussein, who had earlier been informed that a French political officer would join Murray's army, had found out that certain discussions were to take place in Egypt. He soon became alarmed, and asked for explanations. Accordingly, after hurried consultations with the Foreign Office, it had been agreed that Sykes should go down to Jidda for talks. He would reveal certain aspects of Anglo-French policy, in much the same way as he had done in Cairo. He would also, if possible, secure the Sherif's agreement to a further meeting, at which Georges-Picot would be present. Sykes had therefore left Egypt on April 30th, and on the way south had called at Wejh to see Feisal.[21]

As previously agreed with Georges-Picot, Sykes had explained the position to Feisal in very general terms, stressing that the Arabs would 'have to deal with an indivisible Entente; that, under whatever overlord, an enlightened progressive régime must be established in Syria; and that certain districts of the latter, which present peculiar difficulties, must remain under special tutelage in any event.'[22]

Sykes probably found these discussions quite uncomfortable: Feisal, an acute politician, already knew more about the Anglo-French agreement than Sykes meant to divulge, and his questions were doubtless very penetrating. Sykes, who tended to report such meetings in the best possible light, wrote afterwards that he had 'explained to [Feisal] the principle of the Anglo-French Agreement in regard to Arab Confederation. After much argument, he accepted the principle and seemed satisfied'.[23] Following his subsequent meeting with Hussein, Sykes cabled Georges-Picot: 'I am satisfied with my interviews with Sherif Feisul and the King of the Hejaz, as they both now stand at the same point as was reached at our last joint meeting with the three Syrian delegates in Cairo.'[24]

Lawrence left no record of the conversation he had with Feisal on his return to Wejh. Nor is there any account in his notebooks of the discussions which took place on the morning of May 7th, when Sykes made a second brief visit on his way back from the meeting with Hussein in Jidda. Lawrence's pocket diary merely notes that he saw Sykes and Wilson that day. Despite this silence (which is maintained in *Seven*

Pillars), there is contemporary evidence that he was extremely alarmed by the way Sykes was handling the discussions with the Arab leaders, and later comments by Sykes suggest that, during this meeting at Wejh, Lawrence disagreed with him openly .

By this time several of the British officials in the Hejaz either knew or suspected that some kind of Anglo-French agreement had been reached. Those who were dealing directly with the Arabs had been expressing their concern about the situation for some months. Now that the Arabs were taking serious steps towards a campaign in Syria, the need to settle the question of future French involvement was becoming increasingly urgent. Lawrence had solved his own dilemma by telling Feisal the essentials of the Sykes-Picot Agreement. In March, Wilson had urged that the position should be made as clear as possible to the Sherif, writing: 'I feel very strongly that the settlement of Syria etc., should not be arranged behind his back, so to speak: he is, in my opinion, well deserving of the trust of the British Government and I feel sure we will greatly regret it in the future if we are not quite open and frank with him now over the whole matter.'[25] Like Lawrence, Wilson believed that a policy of deception was morally indefensible and that it would almost certainly be counter-productive.

Joyce too saw dangers ahead and argued that if Britain did not intend to support Arab claims in Syria, Feisal should be told at once. On April 15th he had written to the Arab Bureau that Feisal had 'announced to Colonel Newcombe and myself that the Hejaz could never be an independent country owing to its more or less barren soil, and only by having Syria could it possibly be maintained. I feel confident that it is essential that the limits of the Arab movement be defined as soon as possible. They will not seriously tackle the work in hand [i.e. the operation at El Ula] owing to their enemies being constantly on the north . . . furthermore it should be defined to what extent we intend to support their schemes. Otherwise the trust they have hitherto placed in us and all the assistance that has been rendered will be practically nullified. I merely state these opinions for the local situation here. We are essential to the success of their movement and they count on our backing for all their ultimate aims, and the position is not a satisfactory one.'[26]

Despite all these warnings, Sykes had not come to the Hejaz with any intention of clearing up Arab misunderstandings. It was obvious, more-over, that he felt no obligation to do so. He remained sublimely confident that the present policy of vagueness and deceit could be continued. In his reports and in conversation with British and French officers, he made no attempt to disguise his cynicism about Allied commitments to the Arabs. Thus Brémond heard from Lieutenant Millet, an English-speaking officer of the French Military Mission at Jidda, that Sykes had 'received him in a most friendly manner, giving an impromptu briefing. Sir Mark was of the opinion that if the Hejaz bedouin were fighting poorly, it was because they were undernourished. He claimed that all the tribes in the Damascus-Aleppo-Baghdad triangle would prove very good in combat, and were merely waiting for weapons to attack the Turks; naturally, one would allow them to continue in the belief that they were fighting for their independence.' To Millet's objection that this would raise difficulties in the future, Sykes had replied: 'I am not looking so far ahead; to do a good job, one must seek the immediate benefit; part of France is occupied by the Germans, as is Poland, and yet we have no doubt that these territories will be handed back after the war. For the moment, our task is to beat the Germans wherever we can. As for dividing territories, we will always be able to make arrangements when the war is over.'[27] Millet noted that Sykes seemed to regard as unimportant any concessions made at this moment to the Sherif and the Arabs in general. His conclusion about Sykes was damning: 'no subtlety, crude common sense, simplistic politics, scant knowledge of the people and places involved, great self-satisfaction.'[28]

Within a month of this visit to the Hejaz (and after further experience of Sykes's opportunist diplomacy), both Wilson and Newcombe were to protest in very strong terms. Newcombe would write that Sykes's policy 'entails throwing great responsibility on our government to see the . . . Arab cause through to the end: otherwise we are hoodwinking the Sherif and his people and playing a very false game in which officers attached to the Sherif's army are inevitably committed and which I know causes anxiety in several officers' minds: in case we let them down.'[29]

The disingenuous attitude displayed by Sykes made these British officers deeply aware of their own moral responsibility. They would be expected to give whatever assurances were needed to keep the Arabs fighting on Britain's side; but while doing so they would know that their Government did not intend to keep its promises. Lawrence was more deeply troubled than his colleagues, as he was about to set out on an expedition that he himself had advocated, whose sole aim was to take the Revolt out of the Hejaz and into Syria. As a result, Arab tribesmen would soon begin to sacrifice their lives for the disputed territory.

He had little time to think over this problem, however, as the Akaba expedition was on the point of leaving. On May 9th, two days after meeting Sykes, he set off north-east with Sherif Nasir, Auda abu Tayi, and a party of about forty-five Arabs. They took 20,000 sovereigns with them to finance recruiting, and a large quantity of explosive.

It was only when the long camel ride began that Lawrence had time to reflect, and he was soon tormented by doubts. These were aggravated by the cheerful presence of Nesib el Bekri, a passionate believer in Syrian independence, who was to accompany the expedition on its first stage. He was travelling north to carry out a mission of his own, aiming to strengthen support for Feisal among the leaders there.

Four days into the journey, Lawrence suffered an outbreak of boils and high fever, similar to the one he had experienced two months earlier during the ride to Wadi Ais. The illness did nothing to improve his troubled state of mind. On May 13th he noted cryptically in his diary: 'The weight is bearing me down now . . . pain and agony today'.[30] In this mood, the trust and comradeship of his companions became a burden rather than a solace, and he felt increasingly isolated. His sense of guilt and depression seems to have been accentuated by illness and by the desolate landscapes through which the expedition was passing.

After riding for ten days, they reached the Hejaz Railway near Diraa, and blew up a section of the line before passing on into the desert beyond. Then, on May 20th, they began to cross a barren plain known as El Houl. Lawrence wrote in *Seven Pillars*: 'We, ourselves, felt tiny in it, and our urgent progress across its immensity was a stillness or immobility of futile effort. The only sounds were the hollow echoes, like the shutting down of pavements over vaulted places, of rotten stone slab on stone slab when they tilted under our camels' feet, and the low but piercing rustle of the sand, as it crept slowly westward before the hot wind along the worn sandstone, under the harder overhanging caps which gave each reef its eroded, rind-like shape.

'It was a breathless wind, with the furnace taste sometimes known in Egypt when a khamsin came; and, as the day went on and the sun rose in the sky it grew stronger, more filled with the dust of the Nefudh, the great sand desert of Northern Arabia, close by us over there, but invisible through the haze. By noon it blew a half-gale, so dry that our shrivelled lips cracked open, and the skin of our faces chapped; while our eyelids, gone granular, seemed to creep back and bare our shrinking eyes. The Arabs drew their head-cloths tightly across their noses, and pulled the brow-folds forward like vizors with only a narrow, loose-flapping slit of vision.

'At this stifling price they kept their flesh unbroken, for they feared the sand particles which would wear open the chaps into a painful wound: but, for my own part, I always rather liked a khamsin, since its torment seemed to fight against mankind with ordered conscious malevolence, and it was pleasant to outface it so directly, challenging its strength, and conquering its extremity. There was pleasure also in the salt sweat-drops which ran singly down the long hair over my forehead, and dripped like ice-water on my cheek. At first, I played at catching them in my mouth; but, as we rode further into the desert and the hours passed, the wind became stronger, thicker in dust, more terrible in heat. All semblance of friendly contest passed. My camel's pace became sufficient increase to the irritation of the choking waves, whose dryness broke my skin and made my throat so painful that for three days afterwards I could eat little of our stodgy bread. When evening at last came to us I was content that my burned face still felt the other and milder air of darkness.'[31]

In the late morning of May 24th, while crossing a desert of dried mud flats called the Biseita, they realised that one of the party had gone missing. His loaded camel was still following on, but the saddle was empty, and no one had seen him dismount. It seemed that the man, whose name was Gasim, must have dozed off and fallen to the ground. He would be unable to rejoin the caravan because it left no trace on the hard ground, and mirages made it impossible to see very far in the desert. Unless someone went back to look for him, he would certainly die. Lawrence felt he had to take upon himself the responsibility of finding Gasim, who was one of his own men. He decided to turn back, telling no one and hoping that an exact compass course would bring him to the expedition at its next camp. In *Seven Pillars* he wrote: 'I looked weakly at my trudging men, and wondered for a moment if I could change with one, sending him back on my camel to the rescue. My shirking the duty would be understood, because I was a foreigner: but that was precisely the plea I did not dare set up, while I yet presumed to help these Arabs in their own revolt. It was hard, anyway, for a stranger to influence another people's national movement, and doubly hard for a Christian and a sedentary person to sway Moslem nomads. I should make it impossible for myself if I claimed, simultaneously, the privileges of both societies . . . My temper was very unheroic, for I was furious with my other servants, with my own play acting as a Beduin, and most of all with Gasim'.[32] After riding for a time Lawrence found Gasim, half-maddened by the desert sun. However, they regained the expedition safely.

Entries written in Lawrence's notebook during those days convey the horror of this desert: '*Giaan* [mud flats] are purgatory. Sun reflects from them like a mirror – flame-yellow, cutting into our eyes, like glare burning glass on closed lids. Head if veiled too hot: besides camel might stray. Ride eyes shut [two words unclear] it sees steer. Heat in waves and eyes often going black. μετακυμιων. Camels exhausted and foot-burnt.'

'The heat on Bisaita and on last stretch into Kaseim deadly. Air streaming past as thick smoke with dust sun-blinking in it. Iridescent dusk. Nasir beat Ali and Othman [Lawrence's servants], for letting me go back alone. Not their fault. I didn't tell. Think tonight worst yet my experience.'[33]

By this time, however, the most difficult part of their journey was over: they had reached the Wadi Sirhan, a long series of depressions with occasional wells and vegetation. Auda knew that they would find the Howeitat there, and three days later they reached the first encampment. Here Auda left them for a few days, while he went to explain their purpose to Nuri Shalaan, paramount chief of this whole region.

During Auda's absence, Nasir and the remainder of the party moved northwards from camp to camp, recruiting men for the operations at Maan and Akaba. At each place there were tribal feasts, which Lawrence described in his notebook with increasing revulsion. On May 28th he wrote: 'We sat on the tribal lurid and worn red rugs each side of the tent, with a dusty space in the middle, leaning our elbows on camel saddles covered with felt rugs. White and brown coffee were brought round in drinking cups not rinsed and so [a] round flavour and then two men came in carrying a copper butt, sixty inches across and perhaps five inches deep brimful of white rice topped with legs of sheep and ribs with in the middle the boiled head, afterward the neck buried in the rice to the ears, which stuck up like withered leaves, the jaws opened to cracking point and yawning upwards showing the open throat, the tongue sticking to the teeth, and the gristling hair of the nostrils and jaws round the incisors, lips left full. This was set down on the earth between us, steaming hot, and then more men carried in a black cauldron, eighteen inches deep, from which with a blistered enamelled iron bowl and tin . . . they ladled out in small pieces all the rest of the inside and underside of the sheep, little bits of yellow intestine, the white cushion of the tail and white tail fat and brown muscle and skin and meat floating in steaming fat and *semn*, the liquid cooking sheep's butter of the Beduin. These bowls full of scraps they poured over the larger pieces in the bath till there was a pyramid of flesh, and till the rice around its base rose and floated in the oil. The host, groping in the cauldron, had proudly found and placed on the apex, the liver of the sheep. He urges us, seeming unwilling, to sit in the dust, then with a *bismullah al Rahman el Rahim* [In the name of God, the Beneficent, the Merciful] we plunged our hands into the pile, and kneaded neat little balls of rice and liver and fat and flesh and swallowed them, and sucked our fingers to make easier the rolling of the next, while the host with a foot-long dagger with a silver hilt cut, off the larger bones, strips of meat easily torn by the fingers to mouth size – for the sheep had been boiled in milk, and then seethed in butter, and was tender.'[34] Two days later he noted: 'Have feasted noon and sunset since evening of May 27, and am very tired of it. All of us too. When we have eaten our fill we stop, a few moments, crouching round the dish, with our right wrists resting on our knees, and our right hands hanging over the dish, with the fat and oil and rice cooling and congealing onto them in a thick swab, till the others are finished, and then with an explosive *Maazibna Gauwak Allah* [host, may God strengthen thee] all the circle breaks up suddenly, and we group ourselves outside the rugs while a man with a coffee cup ladles water from a wooden bowl over our fingers and the tribal cake of soap goes round. Then a cup of coffee'[35]

The succession of feasts was something of an ordeal, especially to Nesib el Bekri, a sophisticated northerner, who managed to excuse himself. Lawrence felt unable to do so, and wrote: 'I had been twenty-eight years well fed and had no right to despise these fellows for loving their mutton. Nesib was of their race, and brothers and sisters may tell the truth, where we cannot. But I wish to God I was quit of it.'[36]

It was not just the feasting that Lawrence resented. The work of recruiting involved constant affirmation that the Arabs were fighting for their independence. As British liaison officer with Feisal, he was asked again and again to give assurances on this point. On June 2nd he noted: 'All day deputations, fusillades [of welcome], coffee, ostrich eggs. Dined with Auda. Lies.'[37] He found his position impossibly difficult, not least because he feared the outcome of the planned meeting between Sykes, Picot and Hussein. He could not be sure what would happen, but there seemed little likelihood that Sykes would put Britain's relationship with Hussein on a more straightforward footing. His clearest statement of the dilemma is in *Seven Pillars*, where he wrote: 'Arabs believe in persons, not in institutions. They saw in me a free agent of the British Government, and demanded from me an endorsement of its written promises. So I had to join the conspiracy, and, for what my word was worth, assured the men of their reward . . . In this hope they performed some fine things, but, of course, instead of being proud of what we did together, I was continually and bitterly ashamed.

'It was evident from the beginning that if we won the war these promises would be dead paper, and had I been an honest adviser of the Arabs I would have advised them to go home and not risk their lives fighting for such stuff'.[38]

Lawrence's contemporary notes show that he soon found his role in the recruiting process intolerable. His jottings about the Wadi Sirhan were bitter and disjointed: 'hopeless and sad beyond all the rest of the desert. Hideously green, unbearable, sour, putrid smelling. Salt and snakes of evil doing. Leprosy of the world! Evil not [?truth]'.[39] Then, on June 5th, he wrote in his diary: 'Can't stand another day here. Will ride north and chuck it.'[40] The significance of this entry is clarified by a message scribbled in the notebook he was to leave behind: 'Clayton. I've decided to go off alone to Damascus, hoping to get killed on the way: for all sakes try and clear this show up before it goes further. We are calling them to fight for us on a lie, and I can't stand it.'[41]

In full knowledge of the risks involved, he now planned to make a secret journey: he would go north, still deeper into enemy territory, travelling among tribesmen whose loyalty to the Sherif was questionable, and who knew that the Turks had put a price on his head. If he failed to return, the notebook containing his message to Clayton would probably find its way back to Cairo.

Unlike Newcombe and Wilson, he was not a professional soldier. He had no habit of unquestioning obedience to help him cope with his predicament. Instead, he had been brought up to believe in un-compromising standards of personal conduct, and these now conflicted with a patriotism he felt no less deeply. The manner in which Britain was prepared to treat the Arabs bore no relation to the chivalrous kind of warfare Lawrence had imagined and admired during his childhood. He was being forced to play a role which undermined the whole basis of his self-esteem. As an illegitimate child, he had inherited no sense of security or social position from his family. His future public status, no less than his self-respect, would depend on what he made of himself. Although he despised conventional careers, he had hoped for honourable distinction, and the war had seemed to offer such an opportunity. He later wrote that in August 1914 he 'had meant to be a general and knighted, when thirty'.[42] Now, however, it was unthinkable that he should accept honours earned in such a manner.

In the published text of *Seven Pillars* this acute personal crisis is given little prominence. The Akaba campaign is described in a succession of triumphal chapters so enriched by lavish descriptions of the desert landscape that the journey takes on an epic quality. After writing the book, Lawrence explained to a friend that he had felt it 'a fault in scale to represent the Arab Revolt mainly as a personal tragedy to me.'[43] An early draft, however, deals much more openly than the final text with the reasons for his northern journey: 'I wanted an excuse to get away from the long guiding of people's minds and convictions which had been my part since Yenbo six months before. It should have been happiness, this lying out, free as air, with life about me striving its uttermost whither my own spirit led: but its unconscious serving of my purpose poisoned everything for me. A man might clearly destroy himself: but it was repugnant that the innocence and the ideals of the Arabs should enlist in my sordid service for me to destroy. We needed to win the war, and their inspiration had proved the best tool out here. The effort should have been its own reward:– might yet be, for the deceived – but we the masters had promised them results in our false contract, and that was bargaining with life, a bluff in which we had nothing wherewith to meet our stake. Inevitably we would reap bitterness, a sorry fruit of heroic endeavour.

'My ride was long and dangerous, no part of the machinery of the revolt, as barren of consequence as it was unworthy of motive . . . At the time I was in reckless mood, not caring very much what I did, for in the journey up from Wejh I had convinced myself that I was the only person engaged in the field of the Arab adventure who could dispose it to be at once a handmaid to the British army of Egypt, and also at the same time the author of its own success . . . I knew that when we had taken Akaba I would have to lead the movement, either directly or indirectly . . . Accordingly on this march I took risks with the set hope of proving myself unworthy to be the Arab assurance of final victory. A bodily wound would have been a grateful vent for my internal perplexities, a mouth through which my troubles might have found relief.'[44]

Despite these confused and self-destructive motives, he also knew that his journey might serve a useful purpose. He wanted to assess for himself the spirit and resources of the leaders who had sent messages of support to Feisal. He later wrote: 'while I still saw the liberation of Syria happening in steps, of which Akaba was the indispensable first, I now saw the steps coming very close together, and . . . planned to go off myself . . . on a long tour of the north country to sound its opinion and learn enough to lay definite plans. My general knowledge of Syria was fairly good, and some parts I knew exactly: but I felt that one more sight of it would put straight the ideas of strategic geography given me by the Crusades and the first Arab conquest, and enable me to adjust them to the two new factors in my problem, the railways in Syria, and the allied army of Murray in Sinai.'[45]

Lawrence also intended to recommend a policy of restraint to the northern leaders. In the Hejaz, the Revolt had begun without adequate preparation, and Hussein had only been saved by the Royal Navy. In Syria, no such help would be at hand. If the northern tribes rebelled too soon they would be defeated, and there would be terrible reprisals. Lawrence knew that Nesib el Bekri would go north to these same leaders, telling them how successful Feisal had been and holding out the promise of rapid victory. During an argument with Lawrence on June 3rd, Nesib had turned against the Akaba plan, proposing instead to raise a rebellion around Damascus. He lacked funds and arms, but anti-Turkish feeling in Syria was very strong, and Lawrence feared what might happen.[46]

The military aspects of Lawrence's extraordinary journey were later summarised in a report to Clayton. From this source, as well as his pocket diary and later statements, it appears that his total itinerary was rather more than three hundred miles. Starting from Nebk, he rode north via Burga (east of Jebel Druse) and reached Ain El Barida near Tadmor about June 9th. There he enrolled a small group of Arabs under Sheikh Dhami of the Kawakiba Aneza, and rode with them to Ras Baalbek, fifty miles north of Damascus, arriving on June 11th. They damaged a small plate-girder bridge there near the station, using about 4lb of explosive: 'The effect on the traffic was of course very slight, but the Metowila of Baalbek were most excited, and it was to arouse them that I did it. The noise of dynamite explosions we find everywhere the most effective propagandist measure possible.'[47] A month later British Intelligence in Switzerland obtained information about these events from a Turkish officer who had left Damascus on June 19th and passed through Constantinople ten days later. According to his account, which was clearly exaggerated: 'The whole province of Baalbek is in a state of revolt and Baalbek itself has been occupied by the Turkish troops from Gaza. Six battalions of the third division have been withdrawn from that front for the purpose of quelling the insurrection in this province. The station at Ras Baalbek has been burned. The Vali of Damascus has been sent to enquire into the trouble there. Nedjib Bey, son of Mahommet Said, chief of the Metuali tribe at Hermel, was responsible for the revolt and attack on Baalbek.'[48]

Turning southwards, Lawrence travelled to the outskirts of Damascus. There, on about June 13th, he met Ali Riza Pasha Rikabi, a high official in the city who was also a secret Arab nationalist, and warned him against the kind of premature rising that Nesib el Bekri might advocate. After this, he continued south, visiting Druse leaders. As he passed through each tribal territory, he was provided with a new escort.

His final call was at Azrak, a desert oasis about fifty miles east of Amman, where he saw Nuri Shalaan. Nuri's influence was so great that his co-operation, whether open or covert, would be essential to Feisal's northern campaigns. Although he was sympathetic to the Arab cause, the economic welfare of his tribes depended on Turkish goodwill, and at this stage he could not have openly declared for Feisal even if he had wanted to. Moreover, like many Arab nationalists in the north, he was deeply mistrustful of British and French intentions. These doubts were continually fuelled by Turkish propaganda.

Nuri was, by any standards, a grim figure. Lawrence wrote in *Seven Pillars*: 'he was very old; livid, and worn, with a grey sorrow and remorse upon him and a bitter smile the only mobility of his face. Upon his coarse eyelashes the eyelids sagged down in tired folds, through which, from the overhead sun, a red light glittered into his eye sockets and made them look like fiery pits in which the man was slowly burning. Only the dead black of his dyed hair, only the dead skin of the face, with its net of lines, betrayed his seventy years.'[49] Nuri's rule was absolute, and he had killed two of his brothers in his rise to power: 'he had none of the wheedling diplomacy of the ordinary sheikh; a word, and there was an end of opposition, or of his opponent.'[50]

Lawrence found this visit to Azrak very distressing. He later wrote: 'The abyss opened before me suddenly . . . when in his tent old Nuri Shaalan bringing out his documents asked me bluntly which of the British promises were to be believed. I saw that with my answer I would gain or lose him: and in him the fortune of the Arab movement: and by my advice, that he should trust the latest in date of contradictory pledges, I passed definitely into the class of principal. In the Hedjaz the Sherifs were everything, and ourselves accessory: but in this distant north the repute of Mecca was low, and that of England very great. Our importance grew: our words were more weighty: indeed a year later I was almost the chief crook of our gang.'[51]

It seems that Nuri extracted some kind of personal pledge from him: if Britain failed the Arabs, Lawrence would submit himself to dreadful retribution, perhaps even death. When asked, years later, what the pledge had been, he replied: 'Prefer not to reveal'.[52] Whatever it was, the bargain was to cause him a great deal of anguish later in the war. At the time, however, it may have seemed a way out of the moral dilemma that had spurred him to make this northern journey.

Lawrence returned safely to Nebk on June 18th, and took up the responsibilities he had been unable to evade. From now on, he would do everything in his power to see that Britain honoured her commitments: 'I salved myself with the hope that, by leading these Arabs madly in the final victory I would establish them, with arms in their hands, in a position so assured (if not dominant) that expediency would counsel to the Great Powers a fair settlement of their claims. In other words, I presumed (seeing no other leader with the will and power) that I would survive the campaigns, and be able to defeat not merely the Turks on the battlefield, but my own country and its allies in the council-chamber. It was an immodest presumption . . . it is clear that I had no shadow of leave to engage the Arabs, unknowing, in such hazard. I risked the fraud, on my conviction that Arab help was necessary to our cheap and speedy victory in the East, and that better we win and break our word than lose.'[53]

With this principle to sustain him, he would continue to do what his superiors demanded; but he could never forget the immoral role he was being forced to play. During the remainder of the war he would often choose to place himself in extreme danger. He was wounded several times, and on many occasions was lucky to survive where others, close to him, were killed.

By the time he reached Nebk, the recruitment had been completed. The expedition, now a substantial force, moved to Bair. From there, Nasir began to make contact with tribesmen to the west of Maan. Their help would be needed in the operation to take control of the road towards Akaba. While this was going on, Lawrence took a small raiding party to blow up the railway much farther north. His aim was to give the impression that Nasir's force, whose presence near Maan had been reported to the Turks, would shortly move up into the Hauran. He set out from Bair on June 20th.

After three days he left the main group, making a detour which was scarcely less hazardous than his earlier journey. Taking only one or two companions, he visited the Yarmuk valley, in the hope of damaging an important bridge carrying the railway which branched west from Deraa into Palestine. He had no success, but the reconnaissance was useful.[54]

After this he visited more tribal leaders, and while doing so he had at least one narrow escape. A secret meeting took place near Ziza with Fawaz el Faiz, the principal Beni Sakhr leader, who had assured Feisal of his loyalty. In the draft *Seven Pillars* Lawrence described how 'three of us had crept in after sunset to their rich family tents . . . with letters to them from their fellow-conspirators of the Fetah. Fawaz, their senior, was a notable Arab, a committee-man of the Damascus group, prominent in the party of progress and independence. True to profession he had received me with fair words and hospitality, fed us with a rich supper, and brought out for us, in the night after we had talked, his richest quilts.

'I had slept an hour or two when a charged voice, whispering through a smoke-smelling beard into my ear, roused me. It was Nawaf, the brother, to say that under the friendly seeming, Fawaz had sent word by horsemen to Ziza, and soon the troops would be here to take me. I whispered back for his counsel, and he told me to follow and crawled away through the tent-wall. I drew with me my few things in their light saddle-bags and found my camel knee-haltered behind Nawaf's tent, which was the next.

'With her were my two men, waiting, and Nawaf's mare, held ready. We mounted together, and Nawaf, his rifle loaded across his thigh, led us to the railway, and beyond it into the desert . . . I asked him what return I could make, but in reply he asked only for silence, saying that the honour of his family was not yet repaired. A few days later Fawaz was dead, and though there was no evidence, yet my fears always bound it up with that clash between the brothers.'[55]

Lawrence returned to Bair on June 28th, to find that Nasir was ready to carry out the first stage of the Akaba plan. The main force moved to Jefer, some thirty miles east of Maan, where it was to wait in readiness. Meanwhile, the tribesmen Nasir had previously contacted to the west attacked and captured Fuweila, a Turkish post which covered the head of the pass between Maan and the descent towards Akaba. This was where the track leading down towards Wadi Itm was to be blocked.

As soon as news came that this had been done, other parties began raiding north of Maan and attacking the railway to the south. It was hoped that these operations would distract Turkish attention from the Akaba road, but they failed to do so. The Turks in Maan learned very quickly about the trouble at Fuweila and, by coincidence, were in a position to do something about it. They had just been reinforced by a fresh battalion, and this was immediately sent out. It drove the tribesmen out of Fuweila and occupied the important springs at Aba el Lissan nearby.

When Nasir, Auda, and Lawrence heard the news, they realised that they must defeat or at least contain this unwelcome force. As long as it was free to move, the Akaba plan would be hopeless. By dawn on July 2nd, their forces had surrounded the Turkish battalion at Aba el Lissan, and all day long Arab snipers harrassed it from hiding places on higher ground. Finally, at dusk, the position was charged, and the terrified defenders scattered. Three hundred Turks were killed and 160 taken prisoner, while the Arabs lost only two men. Lawrence himself had intended to take part in this last stage of the battle, but during the charge he accidentally shot his camel in the head and was thrown to the ground.

The success of this attack on a trained and slightly larger force seemed astonishing, as did the small number of Arab casualties. Later, however, it was realised that the Turkish infantry was easily shaken by cavalry action. An EEF report written the following year observed that the efficiency of the Turkish rifleman was 'seriously impaired by his indifferent marksmanship. He rarely hits anything that he aims at, even at close ranges . . . and since fire effect is the only effect which the mounted attack has to fear, we are able to gallop the Turkish infantry with a light heart on occasions when we might hesitate in the face of a better shooting enemy.'[56]

When Lawrence interrogated some of the prisoners he learned that Maan itself was very lightly defended. It seemed that the Arabs'might easily capture the town, and some of their leaders were keen to try, as they had little food and Maan offered rich prospects of loot. Lawrence, however, resisted this temptation. Once taken, Maan would be impossible to hold. He wrote in *Seven Pillars*: 'We had no support, no regulars, no guns, no base nearer than Wejh, no communications, no money even, for our gold was exhausted, and we were issuing our own notes, promises to pay "when Akaba is taken", for daily expenses. Besides, one did not change a strategic scheme to follow up a tactical success. We must push to the coast, and reopen sea-contact with Suez.'[57]

The decision to leave Maan alone marked, in effect, the end of the adventure, since the fall of Akaba was now a foregone conclusion. Having set up a garrison at Aba el Lissan, the victorious Arab force made its way downwards, across the Guweira plain and into the Wadi Itm, where many of the Turkish posts proved to be empty. The only real opposition was at Khadra, the main fortified position at the mouth of the wadi. However, the defences there had been designed to resist an attack from the sea, not from inland, and the outnumbered Turks found themselves in a hopeless situation. After some negotiation they surrendered, and on July 6th, eight weeks after leaving Wejh, the Arabs entered Akaba.

They found little food in the town for their own needs, let alone those of their 650 Turkish prisoners. Apart from the ruins of a sixteenth- century stone fort, the place was merely a village of mud and rubble houses; its population before the war had been about a thousand. Supplies were required very urgently, and as soon as the necessary defensive posts had been established, Lawrence set out with a small party along the old pilgrimage road across Sinai to Suez. They completed the 160-mile journey from Akaba almost without stopping, in forty-nine hours.

He was not expected. Only four days earlier, Clayton had written: 'It is not known what are the present whereabouts of Captain Lawrence, who left for the Maan area or Jebel Druse area some time ago, accompanied by Auda abu Tayi, sheikh of the Howeitat, but lately an Arab rumour came into Wejh to the effect that he and the small party with him had blown up a large iron bridge south of Maan. These Arab activities in the Maan area are probably the outcome of Captain Lawrence's arrival in this neighbourhood.'[58]

Lawrence travelled up from Suez to Cairo by rail. At Ismailia station, where he had to change trains, he noticed a party of high-ranking officers, one of whom was Admiral Wemyss. Although Lawrence was haggard and virtually unrecognisable in Arab dress, he managed to catch the eye of Wemyss's Flag Captain, Burmester. Within hours a storeship was on its way to Akaba.

CHAPTER 20

The Consequences of Akaba
July – August 1917

BY July 9th, when Lawrence reached Suez, he had been out of touch with events in Egypt and the Hejaz for two months. During this period, the earlier hopes of military success on both these fronts had been dashed.

In Sinai, Murray's army had been rebuffed a second time at Gaza, with very heavy losses. When the scale of this defeat had become known in London, Murray had been recalled, and on June 28th General Sir Edmund Allenby arrived in Cairo to take his place.

In the Hejaz, the promised operations against Medina had failed to materialise. During the spring and summer of 1917 a succession of bitterly pessimistic assessments came in from Newcombe, Garland, Hornby, and other British officers in the field. The general tenor of their comments can be summed up by quoting Newcombe. First, there was a lack of discipline among the tribal forces: 'The fault is at the top. No one is punished. A man has but to refuse to do a thing and he is petted and patted and given backshish. I am not allowed to punish anyone and cannot send a man back or take away his rifle. Everyone knows this: hence the trouble.'[1] Secondly, there was the question of pay: 'Bedouins . . . are useful and will fight now-and-then, but not risk being hurt. The great trouble with them is that they can always get paid by going back from the Railway to the Sherif behind, so after one day's fight, they go. They always get higher pay by refusing to do anything till they get enough.'[2] The effect of these two factors was crippling, and Newcombe asserted 'the impossibility of doing anything serious with a gang of untrained, undisciplined men, half of whom are frightened and have no intention of doing anything except for money . . . All the difficulties of cutting the line are from our side. The Turks put very few in our way . . . the opportunities missed are too sad to write about'.[3]

As early as May, Newcombe had reached the conclusion that, of the forces at his disposal, only seven people (including himself) were actually doing any harm to the Turk, 'and our feeble efforts only annoy him slightly. Meanwhile I am asked to be patient with the bedouin, and not to punish or be severe . . . I have no hope of doing anything of material damage to the Turk . . . It is obvious from this and former reports, that either all of us are wasting our time here, instead of getting on with the war, or an entirely new line must be taken.'[4] In this report he demanded that a particular Arab should be punished. If this could not be done, Newcombe asked to be relieved of his duties in the Hejaz immediately.

The general despondency among British officers in the Hejaz must have led the Cairo staff to doubt that Hussein's armies were capable of achieving very much more. Nonetheless, it had now been agreed in principle that Feisal should be allowed to raid the northern railways if he could find a way of doing so. These were the main Turkish lines of communication to Palestine and the Hejaz, and Arab action against them would be useful to the British army blocked outside Gaza. The Arab Bureau recognised, however, that it would be very difficult to get adequate supplies to raiding parties working so far to the north.[5]

Lawrence reached Cairo at midday on July 10th and immediately called on Clayton, who was astonished to see him. Their first discussion was taken up with the question of sending supplies and money to Nasir, and other steps necessary to consolidate the Arab position at Akaba. Lawrence spent little time explaining how the town had been captured. Instead, he handed Clayton a brief written report on the expedition and his secret journeys farther north.

Within hours, the Arab victory was the talk of GHQ. Such news was especially welcome after the failure at Gaza. When his success was set alongside the dismal results from the Hejaz, it was obvious that Lawrence had a special talent for leading bedouin tribesmen. Recognition of this fact gave new authority to his ideas about future action. According to *Seven Pillars*, he told Clayton that 'Akaba had been taken on my plan by my effort. The cost of it had fallen on my brains and nerves. There was much more I felt inclined to do, and capable of doing:– if he thought I had earned the right to be my own master.'[6]

In his report, Lawrence set out a scheme of operations which the Arabs of Syria might be able to undertake in conjunction with an advance by the British Army in Palestine. Basing his conclusions on the discussions he had held with northern leaders, he wrote: 'I am of opinion that given the necessary material assistance Arab forces can be arranged about the end of August as in the sketch map attached. These levies will not (any more than the Hedjaz Beduin) be capable of fighting a pitched battle, but forces 1, 2, 4 and 5 [see opposite] may be able to ensure a cessation of traffic on the railways in their areas, and forces 6 and 7 should suffice for the expulsion of all Turkish posts in their districts, and the occupation of all ways of communication. Force 3 is our striking force (of perhaps six thousand not bad men) and may be able to rush Deraat [where the line to Palestine joined the Hejaz Railway], or at least should cut off the garrison there and hold up the line in the neighbourhood. I would propose to cut the bridge at Hemmah [carrying the Palestine railway across the Yarmuk valley] from Um Keis by force 2, if possible, as a preliminary . . . and if Damascus could be taken over by a part of force 3 it would mean a great accession of strength to the Arab cause.

'These various operations fortunately need not be accurately concerted. If they took place in numerical order (as in the map) it would be easiest – but there is little hope of things working out just as planned. If they come off, the line of communication of the Turkish force in the Jerusalem area would appear threatened – but I do not think the Arabs can be advised to take action unless the Egyptian Expeditionary Force can retain the Turks in front of them by a holding attack, to prevent large drafts being sent up to the Hauran [south of Damascus]. Force 3 is capable of only one effort (lasting perhaps 2 months) and if it is crushed Arab hopes in Syria will depend on the yet untried possibility of action between Homs and Aleppo – on which it is too soon to speak.'[7]

Clayton was naturally impressed that a force of Arab tribesmen had been able to take Akaba without British foreknowledge or support. He therefore considered Lawrence's proposals very carefully. It had already been agreed that Arab raiding against Turkish lines of communication behind the Palestine front would be desirable; but Lawrence was suggesting much more than this. In due course General Allenby sent for him, partly to congratulate him on the Akaba victory, and partly to question him about these new and interesting projects.

Despite his recent achievements, Lawrence must have been extremely anxious about the meeting, since the future of Feisal's northern campaign was in the hands of the EEF. If Allenby were unsympathetic, the Revolt might yet be confined to the Hejaz. Lawrence therefore sketched the future military value of Arab co-operation in generous terms. There were rumours that the Cabinet wanted Jerusalem captured by Christmas,[8] and he stressed the contribution that the Arabs could make to such a victory by cutting Turkish lines of communication at Deraa.

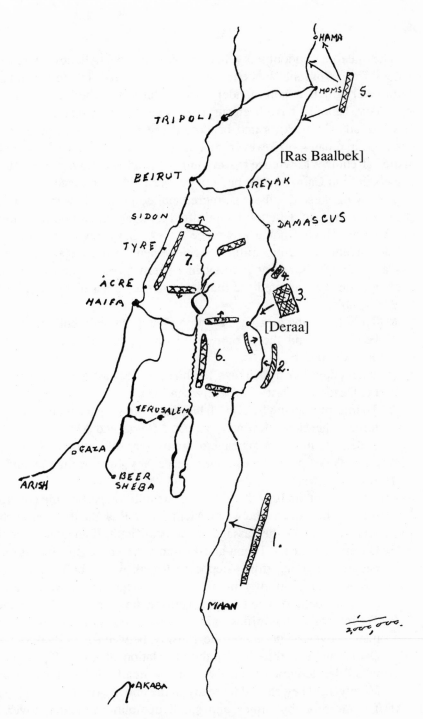

Map 6: *Lawrence's proposals for Arab action in Syria, July 1917*

The meeting undoubtedly had its comic side. Allenby, a cavalry general fresh from the Western Front, was then fifty-six. He was a large man, every inch a commander, whose ferocity when angered was legendary. He must have been surprised when Lawrence arrived dressed in white silk Arab skirts and head-cloth, resplendent with gold-bound headrope and dagger. However, this unconventional garb had not been a matter of choice: Lawrence's army uniform had been ravaged by moths while stored in Cairo, and he had not yet been able to replace it.

Following these discussions, more detailed proposals were drawn up at the Arab Bureau. Clayton then drafted a memorandum on the subject for Allenby. Having noted Lawrence's view that a revolt in Syria was not dependent on further military achievement in the Hejaz, he wrote: 'As a result of his recent journey in eastern Syria Captain Lawrence is of opinion that, granted the material assistance asked for, the Arabs should be able:–

(a) To hold Akaba as a base of supply, and maintain communication between it and the Syrian desert, in the direction of Damascus and Aleppo.

(b) To occupy, during August, the hill country east and south-east of the Dead Sea, west of the Hejaz Railway.

(c) To interrupt, in daylight, with large demolition parties and covering forces, the Hejaz Railway between Deraa and Maan, on such a scale as to make the passage of trains very difficult and dangerous . . . This operation can take place any time from the end of August onwards.

(d) To interrupt, in daylight, with large demolition parties and covering forces, the railway between Aleppo and Ras Baalbek on such a scale as to make the passage of trains difficult. If an attempt on the Orontes bridges at Hama and Restan were successful the through passage of trains from Aleppo to Reyak would be rendered impossible for about two months. These bridges are now unguarded . . . This operation can take place during the first half of September.

(e) To interrupt, by mines laid secretly and small demolitions, under cover of darkness, the railway between Ras Baalbek and Damascus, and thus hinder the circulation of trains. These raids would be delivered from the east, by small parties of Arabs and Metowala. They should be ready in the end of August.

(f) To interrupt, by mines and small demolitions, under cover of darkness, the railway between Kiswe [21km south of Damascus] and Khirbet el Ghazale [17km north of Deraa] on such a scale as to disorganize traffic. These raids would be carried out by small parties from the Leja. They can take place any time in September.

(g) To attempt the demolition of one (or some) of the railway bridges in the Yarmuk valley, between the sea of Tiberias and Deraa. This would be attempted by a raiding party of Howeitat, Sherarat, and Kawarna from Azrak.'[9]

Lawrence thought that if Akaba could be held, and one of the larger Yarmuk bridges demolished, it would be possible to launch 'a general attack on Deraa and the three railways running north, south, and west from it, from the Gebel Hauran, by a force of probably 8,000 Arabs and Druses. These, while not "storm-troops," are respectable fighting men, and should be able to occupy most of the area and the approaches to it. Their success would lead to risings of a local character in the hills between the Jordan and the Hejaz Railway, from Deraa to opposite Jericho, and to similar risings in the hills along the Nazareth – Damascus roads.'[10]

There were, however, two very important conditions which would have to be met if these plans were to be implemented. First, Allenby must provide the necessary material and financial support. Second: 'The above operations are entirely contingent on a decision to undertake major operations in Palestine with which the movement of the Arabs must synchronise. If minor operations only are intended in Palestine, the Arab operations as suggested above would probably lead to the destruction of many of the Arab elements, and most certainly to that of the Druses, were they to take action. Unless operations of such magnitude as to occupy the whole of the Turkish Army in Palestine were undertaken the proposed Arab operations must be abandoned.'[11] In other words, the British must not trigger an Arab revolt in Syria and then allow it to fail.

Neither Clayton nor Allenby believed that all the actions Lawrence proposed would take place, but even a few of them would be useful. Allenby telegraphed details to the War Office, noting: 'Captain Lawrence . . . is quite confident that provided the necessary measure of material assistance is afforded by us, this could be successfully carried out.'[12] The possible benefits to British efforts in Sinai and Palestine were obvious, and here Allenby repeated Clayton's memorandum almost word for word: 'There is no doubt that Turkish railway communications south of Aleppo would be seriously disorganised even by the partial success of Lawrence's scheme, whilst its complete success would effectively destroy [the Turks'] only main artery of communication between the north Syria and Palestine and Hedjaz fronts, and possibly extensive local risings throughout the Jordan Valley might be produced.'[13]

The capture of Akaba brought Lawrence high commendations, not least from officers who had personal experience of working with the Arabs. Wilson, who only seven months earlier had described him as a 'bumptious young ass,'[14] now cabled to Wingate: 'I recommend strongly that Lawrence be granted a DSO immediately for his recent work. He went off with a Sheikh and a Sherif and I am confident that the . . . successes gained against trained troops, which should have excellent results on general operations, are due to his personality, gallantry, and grit.'[15]

The achievement which most impressed the staff in Cairo, however, was his journey into Syria. When Wingate sent news of the fall of Akaba to the War Office he described this secret reconnaissance as 'little short of marvellous.'[16] Lawrence's feats were admired in London, and three days later Wingate informed him that, 'The Chief of the Imperial General Staff has requested me to convey his congratulations on your recent exploit and I do so with the liveliest satisfaction. It was a very gallant and successful adventure which it has been my pleasant duty to bring to the notice of the higher authority for special recognition, and I sincerely trust this latter will not be long delayed. I hope you are taking a rest and making up some of the arrears of sleep which you must be badly in need of.'[17]

The 'special recognition' Wingate had recommended was a Victoria Cross. In a telegram to the War Office he pointed out that the Turks had put a £5,000 reward on Lawrence's head. Knowledge of this had 'considerably enhanced the gallantry of his exploit. He was moving among a highly venal population, of whom some at least were definitely hostile. In spite of this, he seized every opportunity of damaging the railway, interviewing tribesmen and obtaining information regarding the country and its inhabitants, and finally successfully directed the operation in the Maan region, the result of which was that 700 Turks were destroyed and 500 captured.

'I strongly recommend him for an immediate award of the Victoria Cross, and submit that this recommendation is amply justified by his skill, pluck and endurance.'[18]

The irony of this praise was completely lost on Lawrence's superiors. They would have been shocked to know that he had made the northern journey hoping that it would bring his involvement in the Arab war to an end. He was relieved, therefore, when a technicality prevented the award of a VC (the journey had not been witnessed by another British officer). Instead, he was shortly afterwards appointed a Companion of the Order of the Bath and promoted to the rank of major. Although the medal was primarily intended for the northern ride, this could not be publicised. Wingate wrote: 'For obvious reasons I have of course been obliged to curtail the official communiqué and have confined the scope of his reconnaissance – in public – to the Maan-Akaba neighbourhood.'[19] This need for secrecy was stressed in a telegram to London: 'it is very important for political reasons that nothing should be known publicly of Lawrence's Syrian reconnaissance beyond the official communiqué which we are publishing here.'[20] Significantly, however, the CB was backdated to the day in early June when Lawrence had set out on the northern ride. His letters home show total rejection of this decoration, which he refused to acknowledge.[21]

The essential next steps in Lawrence's scheme were to move Feisal's headquarters up to Akaba and make sufficient defensive arrangements to hold the track through Wadi Itm against recapture. This would provide access to the Syrian interior, enabling raiding parties to harass the Turkish lines of communication. In the longer term, the settled peoples south of Damascus could be prepared for the Revolt. Lawrence later wrote: 'When the Hauran joined us our campaign would be well ended.

'The process should be to set up another ladder of tribes, comparable to that by which we had climbed from Wejh to Akaba: only this time our ladder would be made of steps of Howeitat, Beni Sakhr, Sherarat, Rualla, and Serahin, to raise us to Azrak, the desert oasis nearest Hauran or Jebel Druse. We needed to reach more than three hundred miles – a long stride without railways or roads, but one which would be made safe and comfortable for us by an assiduous cultivation of desert power, the control by camel-parties of the desolated and unmapped wilderness of mid-Arabia from Mecca to Aleppo and Bagdad.

'In character our operations . . . should be like naval war, in their mobility, their ubiquity, their independence of bases and lack of communications . . . Camel raiding-parties, self-contained like ships, might cruise without danger along the enemy's cultivation frontier, and tap or raid into his lines where it seemed easiest or fittest or most profitable, with always a sure retreat behind them into the desert-element which the Turks could not explore . . . Our fighting tactics should be always tip and run: not pushes, but strokes. We should never try to maintain or improve an advantage, but should move off to strike again somewhere else. We should use the smallest force in the quickest time at the farthest place . . .

'The necessary speed and range at which to strike, if we were to make war in this distant fashion, would be attained through the extreme frugality of the desert men, and their high efficiency when mounted on their female riding camels . . . We had found that on camels we were independent of supply for six weeks . . . Our six weeks' food would give us capacity for a thousand miles out and home.'[22]

The transfer of Feisal's base from Wejh to Akaba would mean the end of the El Ula scheme. After some debate, however, Lawrence gained his point. Doubtless the advantages to Allenby of a northern campaign outweighed the irritation of a continuing stalemate in the Hejaz. It was therefore agreed that Wejh would be closed down, and that Joyce should move up to Akaba as senior British officer.

Another major change proposed by Lawrence was that in future Allenby should take direct responsibility for Feisal and his army. In the north, Feisal would have to co-operate with the EEF rather than the forces of Ali or Abdullah. Moreover, Akaba was seven hundred miles from Mecca, but only one hundred miles from Allenby's advance headquarters. It was logical to place the Arab northern army under Allenby's overall command, if Hussein would accept this arrangement. Lawrence therefore set off for Jidda on July 17th, to seek Hussein's agreement and to talk with Wilson about plans for the move to Akaba.

On the following day, a cable was received in Cairo from the War Office approving Lawrence's northern proposals. Allenby's reply, on July 19th, shows that Arab action now played a significant part in his plans for a September offensive: 'The advantages offered by Arab co-operation on the lines proposed by Captain Lawrence are, in my opinion, of such importance that no effort should be spared to reap full benefit therefrom.

'The co-operation offered by Captain Lawrence comprises the effect-ive interruption at widely separated points of the enemy's sole main artery of communication between his forces operating in this theatre and in the Hedjaz and his base at Aleppo, whilst simultaneously raising against him a series of widely spread risings among the disaffected populations of Syria and northern Palestine, which would be backed by a considerable force of armed Arabs from tribes East of the Jordan.

'If successfully carried out, such a movement, in conjunction with offensive operations in Palestine, may cause a collapse of the Turkish campaigns in the Hedjaz and in Syria and produce far-reaching results, both political as well as military . . .

'As stated in [Allenby's telegram of July 16th] the majority of Arabs upon whose support Captain Lawrence relies are of camel-breeding tribes, whose custom it is to migrate eastwards after the October rains to graze their herds in the Central Syrian desert, and whose active support it would be impossible to rely upon during the grazing period (November to March). Captain Lawrence is therefore anxious not to defer commencement of his operations against the railway later than mid-September.

'As it is desirable that the utmost advantage should be derived from the Arab movement (and, furthermore, as there are indications that offensive operations on a large scale may be undertaken by the Turkish command at an early date on the Mesopotamian front, in which case . . . an offensive in Palestine may become imperative) [I] ought to be prepared to undertake such operations as may be possible with the force at my disposal by the middle of September.

'Whilst realising that the transport situation, and the necessity of meeting essential demands of other theatres, make it impossible to supply immediately in full the requirements of my force, I would urge that every effort be made to hasten the dispatch of reinforcements (including artillery and aeroplanes) to this theatre, in order to enable me to adopt a policy of active offensive within two months from now, should such action be rendered necessary by the situation at that time.'[23]

Although Robertson, the CIGS, was vehemently opposed to 'side-shows', these arguments seem to have impressed him. A few days later he wrote to the C.-in-C. in India, indicating his qualified support for the scheme: 'Allenby gives us a promising prospect of what he can do if only we can give him another division and a certain amount of heavy artillery, and we have got on foot a good Arab scheme for disturbing the Turks. We are inclined to think that the Turk is heartily sick of the war and if he can be beaten in Mesopotamia and given a good blow in Southern Palestine he may throw his hand in. I am a bit doubtful about this but am inclined to think it is worth trying, provided it does not make too big a demand upon us . . . Allenby only requires a little more help, which I can give him. On the other hand some of our politicians here are dying to go to Jerusalem and Damascus, and other places. This I am dead against. The further we go north from Southern Palestine the greater is the strain upon our resources and the stronger the enemy becomes.'[24]

While Allenby pressed for action, the British political staff in Cairo reflected uneasily on possible French reactions to Lawrence's new venture. What effect would a successful Arab rebellion in Syria have on the final political settlement there? Clayton wrote at length about this question to Sykes, who had now returned to England: 'The future prospects of the Arab movement have assumed rather a different aspect in the light of the information gained by Lawrence during his recent trip. There seems little doubt that the northern tribes are really ready for business, and every reason to hope that they are effective. Faisal's name is one to conjure with, and, if the general rising of these tribes is attended with the success which Lawrence seems to think quite possible, Faisal will be regarded as the saviour of Syria. Already he is accepted in practically all the districts through which Lawrence passed and by the Arab Committee of Damascus. It is, therefore, not improbable that Faisal may make good before the French can get to work and it will then be with him that they will have to deal. Frenchmen of the [imperialist] school such as Brémond and Co., will be quick to see this and may try to counter it in either of two ways, viz:

1. By putting obstacles in Faisal's way and trying to prevent our supporting the movement of the northern Arabs on the score that it is in their sphere and that we must therefore keep "hands off".

2. By maintaining that it is they who must run the whole movement and not us, and that it is from them that all advice and material support must come.

'As regards (1), I would emphasise that at present the movement of the northern tribes is a military operation and, as such, an integral part of the Allied operations in Palestine. It is not our fault that the Allied effort in Palestine is at present a purely British one and we should not allow questions of "after the war" politics to rob us of an invaluable ally in our Palestine campaign.

'As regards (2), the Arab movement will be largely independent and run by the Arabs themselves and a measure of *material* assistance is all that they require. This can be shared between us and the French, if necessary, or even all come from the French, but in any case, for the present, can only reach the Arabs through British sources. As regards European personnel, none is advisable or necessary at present in the north beyond Lawrence, who is of course essential and unique. In short it is Faisal who will run the show and, if it succeeds to any really considerable extent (not a contingency that is out of the question), it is Faisal with whom the French must deal. My own advice to the French would be to encourage and back Faisal and the northern Arab movement as much as possible.'[25]

Lawrence called in at Wejh on his way south to Jidda, hoping to see Feisal. He was taken by air to the inland headquarters set up by Newcombe and Joyce near the railway. Feisal was delighted to learn that there was now approval for large-scale northern operations, and at Lawrence's request wrote letters to Hussein urging the transfer of his army to Allenby's command. He also took steps to send Arab reinforcements to Akaba straight away.[26]

On July 22nd Lawrence reached Jidda where he discussed with Wilson personnel and other requirements for the new base at Akaba. Wilson was more than ready to agree to this move, having always favoured the idea of a Syrian campaign. He knew that action against the railway in the north would directly affect Turkish supplies to Medina, and for the present he was thoroughly disillusioned about the chances of further success in the Hejaz. The conclusions reached during these talks are set out in a memorandum he wrote on July 28th: 'I am prepared, subject to the approval of the G.O.C., Hedjaz [Wingate], to place the services of the following officers of the Hedjaz Mission at the disposal of the General Officer Commanding in Chief, E.E.F., for the proposed Syrian-Arab operations:

Lieutenant Colonel P.C. Joyce, G.S.O.
Captain W. E. Marshall, M.C., R.A.M.C., Medical Officer
Captain T. E. Lawrence, Staff Captain
Captain R. Goslett, Army Service Corps, Supply Officer
Captain H. S. Hornby, Royal Engineers.'[27]

Goslett and Marshall had gained experience of Arab operations in the Hejaz, and their presence at Akaba would ensure that the northern Arab forces were provided with adequate base support. By now it had been realised that British supervision of supplies and communications was essential, since few of the Arabs had the training needed to handle base administration efficiently.

Wilson had originally intended to send Newcombe to Akaba as well, but after discussing the matter with Lawrence he wrote: 'I understand that his services will not be required for the Emir Feisal's operations'.[28]

Newcombe's recent reports, seen by Lawrence in Cairo, suggested that his period of usefulness with the Arabs was at an end. Not long after this he left the Hejaz for service with the EEF.

The British officers transferred to Akaba would come under Allenby's command. Their duties were set out by Clayton as follows: 'Captain Lawrence – to serve with Beduin troops and to advise and, as far as possible, direct their operations.

'Lieut. Col. Joyce – to advise and control the trained Arab troops under Jaafar Pasha. These troops will be concentrated at Akaba and will form the garrison of that place. Should future developments require it they will be available for service in the Hauran as support to the Druses.

'Capt. Goslett, A.S.C. – to be supply officer at Akaba and in charge of all consignments sent from Egypt or the Hejaz.'[29]

Arrangements had already been made to transport part of Feisal's regular army to Akaba. The remainder, under Jaafar Pasha, would be taken there in late August with Feisal himself.

A few days earlier, Wilson had written to Hussein, asking for a meeting: 'Captain Lawrence, of whom your Highness has heard, has arrived here today; he was with Sherif Nasir, and has himself been north of Damascus and seen various Sheikhs. He saw Emir Faisal at Wedj and has seen His Excellency the High Commissioner and His Excellency the General Officer Commanding in Chief in Egypt . . . Captain Lawrence and I go to Cairo in four days' time and I would much like to have the honour of meeting your Highness with Captain Lawrence before we go, as there are matters for which your Highness's approval is necessary.'[30] Thus it came about that on July 28th Lawrence met the Sherif of Mecca for the first time.

Both Lawrence and Wilson had expected Hussein to make difficulties over the transfer of Feisal's army to Allenby's command. In the event, however, Hussein did not oppose the idea, and signed a letter confirming Feisal's appointment as Supreme Commander of all Arab forces operating northwards from Akaba: 'The Emir Faisal will have a free hand to deal direct with the British General Commander-in-Chief in all military matters, which will facilitate the co-operation between my army and that of Great Britain.'[31] This diplomatic formula maintained the fiction that the Arab forces were operating as an independent command, while ensuring that in future the British would be able to direct Feisal's operations without needing to secure Hussein's approval.

Characteristically, Hussein took up the rest of this meeting with a lengthy and none-too-lucid exposition of his religious views. Although he claimed to have renounced any ambition for the Caliphate, it was clear that he was still hoping for some position of greater spiritual authority in the Arab world. Lawrence found this unexpected topic of considerable interest, and wrote a detailed account of the conversation.[32]

On the following day Hussein asked to see Lawrence again, and used the meeting to give his version of the discussions with Sykes and Georges-Picot in May. Lawrence had doubtless heard from Wilson and others that the talks had been singularly unsatisfactory. Far from setting out the true political situation in clear, unambiguous terms, Sykes and Georges-Picot had left the matter more confused than ever. The only agreement to emerge had been a vague understanding that France would act in Syria on the same basis as Britain in Baghdad. Both Georges-Picot and Hussein had been delighted with this formula, but only because each put a completely different construction upon it. Georges-Picot, familiar with the Sykes-Picot terms, thought that Britain intended to impose direct rule in Baghdad: he could therefore claim that Hussein had agreed to direct French rule throughout Syria. Hussein, on the other hand, was working on the basis of his correspondence with McMahon. He believed that permanent British rule of Baghdad was not intended, and that by this new understanding France had relinquished her claims in both Syria and Lebanon. This absurd formula had been knowingly suggested by Sykes, who doubtless regarded the 'agreement' as a personal triumph. When Wilson discovered the role that Sykes had played, he was disgusted.[33]

Lawrence reported Hussein's views to Cairo as follows: 'The main points were that he had altogether refused to permit any French annexation of Beyrout and the Lebanon. "They are Arab countries but I will neither take them myself nor permit anyone else to take them. They have deserved independence and it is my duty to see they get it."

'He said that he refused a detailed discussion of boundaries, on the grounds that hostilities between Turkey and the Allies still continue and all decisions taken now would necessarily have to be modified in accordance with the actual results of military operations, for which he must have an absolutely free hand. "If advisable we will pursue the Turks to Constantinople and Erzeroum – so why talk about Beyrout, Aleppo and Hail?"

'He is extremely pleased to have trapped M. Picot into the admission that France will be satisfied in Syria with the position Great Britain desires in Iraq. That, he says, means a temporary occupation of the country for strategical and political reasons (with probably an annual grant to the Sherif in compensation and recognition) and concessions in the way of public works. "I was ready without being asked to guard their interests in the existing railways, and assist their schools: but the Hedjaz and Syria are like the palm and fingers of one hand, and I could not have consented to the amputation of any finger or part of a finger without leaving myself a cripple."

'In conclusion the Sherif remarked on the shortness and informality of conversations, the absence of written documents, and the fact that the only change in the situation caused by the meeting was the French renunciation of the ideas of annexation, permanent occupation or suzerainty of any part of Syria – "but this we did not embody in a formal treaty, as the war is not finished. I merely read out my acceptance of the formula 'as the British in Iraq' proposed to me by M. Picot, since Sir Mark Sykes assured me that it would put a satisfactory conclusion to the discussion." '[34]

Not long afterwards, Lawrence wrote home about the meeting, giving his impressions of Hussein: 'I had never met the Sherif himself before, and liked him exceedingly: a very simple straightforward old man, clever enough too, but knowing so little. Upon us as a people is the responsibility of having made him a ruling power, and he is pitifully unfit for the rough and tumble of forming a new administration out of the ruins of the Turkish system. We will have to help him and his sons, and of the sons only Feisul and Zeid will play square to us. Abdulla is an intriguer, and poor Sidi Ali, the eldest son, is a religious fanatic, and will be the tool of evil spirits. I do hope we play them fair.'[35]

During his stay in Jidda, Lawrence found time to make a surreptitious visit to Mecca. His strongest motive must have been curiosity, but he also wanted to order a new ornamental dagger. Previously, he had worn one given him by Abdullah in Wadi Ais, but during the recruiting before Akaba, Sherif Nasir had expropriated all the best daggers in his party, in order to use them as presents for Howeitat chiefs. Lawrence needed a replacement worthy of his special status, and knew that the craftsmen in Mecca produced very fine examples. In particular, he wanted to order one which was smaller and lighter than usual. He later wrote: 'My gold dagger . . . was made in Mecca, in the third little turning to the left off the main bazaar, by an old Nejdi goldsmith whose name I fancy was Gasein'.[36]

The journey to Mecca would have presented little difficulty at that time of year. A contemporary report states that there was a very safe and easy road from Jidda: the fifty-four-mile journey took about eight or nine hours by donkey. Long afterwards, Lawrence described the Holy City as 'a curious place, without trees or running water, a very hot town, in narrow valleys between limestone hills . . . it's not really so difficult to go there, if they know you, because the people are not fanatical. They keep Christians out because the other Moslems of the world (India and elsewhere) would be annoyed if we were allowed in: and if they were annoyed they might stop coming on pilgrimage, and the pilgrim traffic is all the revenue of the place. So if anyone asks me if I've been there I have to say "no" in public: but in private you can guess about it! It mustn't get into the papers, because it would do the old King's reputation harm.'[37]

On another occasion, he wrote: 'Yes, I've promised not to admit the Mecca jest. I did it because I wanted to choose my own gold dagger, and it was not serious for me. Hussein will never forgive it me.'[38] Lawrence's use of the word 'jest' may well be explained by an incident that had taken place soon after the capture of Wejh. In his notebook there is a jotting (dated 8th March 1917): 'One night we all swore not [to] go [to] Mecca till after we had seen Damascus. Great fun when I insisted on taking the oath too.'[39] Unlike the others who had been present on that occasion, Lawrence had now seen Damascus, and doubtless he enjoyed fulfilling the second part of his oath.

While he was still in the Hejaz, an alarming message was received from Egypt. In Clayton's words: 'It was reported by Agent "Y" during the week, that Auda Abu Tayi (who was Captain Lawrence's right-hand man during the recent operations in the Maan-Akaba area) had written to the Turks giving as his reason for rebelling, that presents had been given [by the Turks] to Nuri Shalaan and not to him, but that he was now willing to come in under certain conditions, and had written twice to the G.O.C. 8th Army Corps [in Maan] asking for a present.'[40]

This news was most disturbing. Auda had been entrusted with the defence of Guweira, an important post on the route from Akaba to Maan. The Turks had already recaptured Aba el Lissan, and were bombing the Arab forces closer to Akaba. If the Howeitat abandoned their positions before Feisal's regulars arrived, there would be little to prevent the Turks retaking the Wadi Itm. Such an outcome would be fatal to the whole northern campaign. Lawrence replied at once to Cairo that the treachery might possibly be 'a ruse on the part of Abu Tayi in order to gain time against the Turks.'[41] However, he travelled up to Akaba as quickly as possible and then went inland to confront Auda with knowledge of this apparent treachery. There were embarrassed explanations from both Auda and Mohammed el Dheilan, another Howeitat leader. Lawrence seems not to have been convinced of their innocence, but he laid stress on the bounty that Feisal would shortly distribute, and hoped that the shock of such rapid discovery would discourage them from further wavering. On August 6th he sent a calming message to Cairo, stating that the situation was 'absolutely satisfactory'.[42] He later admitted that 'This may have been hardly true, but the deception was mine, and I regularly reduced impolitic truth in my communications, as it was Egypt which kept us alive by stinting herself. To make her continue in sacrifice we must keep her confident and ourselves a legend'.[43]

After this hurried visit to Akaba, Lawrence spent a week in Egypt, where he and Wilson took part in further detailed discussions at the Arab Bureau. Although the northern operations were to be under Allenby's command, the Bureau would continue to act as a clearing-house for all dealings with the Revolt. For the time being, Clayton would remain in charge, although it had just been confirmed that he was to replace Sykes as British Chief Political Officer in Palestine.

Lawrence wrote home from Cairo: 'I am now going back to Akaba to look round at the country there . . . The average length of my last five visits to Cairo has been about five days! However it is more restful in Arabia, because one feels so nervous of what may happen if one goes away.

'I cannot ask for leave, as I know there is so much to do down there, and no one to do it. If I asked I would probably get it, but it would not be right at present. If ever things get safe there, it will be possible to rest. You know there are very few of us on the job . . .

'About writing:– please try to realise that one's thoughts for nearly two years have been fixed on one object. We have realised part of the scheme, and the situation is critical but hopeful. In the circumstances one has become a monomaniac, unable to do or think about anything else – and of the one thing I cannot write to you.'[44]

Despite this reticence in his wartime letters home, Lawrence had by this time decided that his experiences during the Revolt would make a magnificent subject for a book. The idea had been forming in his mind for some while, and ever since his permanent posting to Feisal in February, he had made descriptive jottings in his notebook. Many of these (such as the account of tribal feasting quoted on pages 408-9) had little or no relevance to military questions. It seems that he mentioned the book project to Wilson and others during their talks in Cairo. Lloyd, who was there briefly at this time, wrote afterwards that Lawrence would 'some day be able to write a unique book. Generally, the kind of men capable of these adventures lack the pen and wit to record them adequately. Luckily Lawrence is specially gifted with both.'[45]

There was also a more immediate writing project: in an attempt to pass on the secrets of his success in dealing with the Arabs, Lawrence drew up a set of guidelines called 'Twenty-seven Articles'. These were published in the *Arab Bulletin* later that month. They provide a remarkable insight into the methods he used to direct operations without being seen to do so, and they have since been used in the training of Western advisers for many other theatres of war. The full text is printed in Appendix IV.

Lawrence returned to Akaba on August 17th, just after his twenty-ninth birthday. Three days later Doynel de Saint-Quentin, of the French military liaison staff in Egypt, drew up a confidential summary of his career and achievements for the War Office in Paris. He wrote: 'This officer, whose name has often appeared in correspondence from Cairo, is probably the most outstanding figure of the British army or administration in the east.'[46]

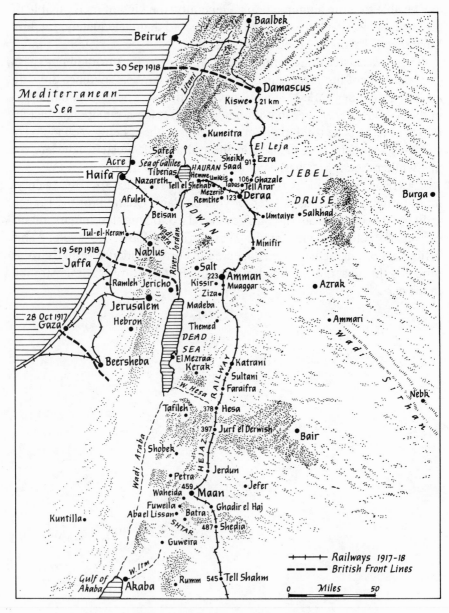

Map 7: *The Syrian Campaigns*

CHAPTER 21

The First Syrian Campaign
August – December 1917

BY mid-August the transformation of Akaba into a military base was well under way. The Navy had stationed HMS *Humber* there as guardship and headquarters, and the presence of a British warship did much to bolster Arab morale. Meanwhile, other vessels of the Red Sea Patrol ferried men, animals and stores up from Wejh.

On August 18th Jaafar Pasha arrived on HMS *Hardinge* with eight hundred Arab regulars. Two days later HMS *Dufferin* brought three hundred more. The French contingent at Wejh, now under the command of Captain Pisani, came too. On August 23rd, the *Hardinge* put in again, bringing Feisal with another five hundred men as well as a large quantity of stores. A quay for landing supplies was being built under naval supervision.

During the preceding weeks Nasir had been steadily recruiting, and when he was joined by Feisal hundreds of new volunteers came in every day. Lawrence wrote: 'The slide of Arabs towards the Sherif was obvious when Nasir was here, and has become immense, almost impossible, since Feisul arrived. He is unable even to see all the head sheikhs of the newcomers.'[1] One result of the increasing numbers at Akaba was that supply problems became acute.

Although the Turks had kept up some pressure against Arab outposts, there had not yet been any major offensive. It was known, however, that they were preparing for action, and in the meantime aircraft flying from Maan were doing a great deal of damage to Arab morale.

As there was not yet an RFC Flight at Akaba, it had been arranged that British aircraft from El Arish would strike back against Maan. For this purpose they needed a safe intermediate landing ground, and Lawrence's first task was to help prepare a temporary strip at Kuntilla, an old frontier fort in Sinai about fifty miles north-west of Akaba. In readiness for this, a supply of bombs and other stores had been brought to Akaba by sea. All these were now transported to Kuntilla, where a small garrison was installed in the old police post. On August 28th and 29th, acting on detailed instructions from Lawrence, the four RFC aircraft raided Maan, Fuweila and Aba el Lissan. In all, they dropped 116 bombs, inflicting severe damage on the railway and other targets. This unexpected attack again checked the Turks.

The Arab military situation was nonetheless worrying. Although Akaba itself could be protected from the sea, the important defensive line was far inland. The future of the Syrian campaign depended, therefore, on local bedouin who would fare badly if the Turkish forces at Maan launched a full-scale attack. The situation would have been better if Feisal's two thousand Arab regulars had been an effective force, but this was not yet the case. Their shortcomings were unsparingly described in a report by Captain MacIndoe of the Arab Bureau, who had recently arrived from Cairo: 'At the present moment the men are quite untrained and have little discipline, and no keenness to get more, and their one desire (which they have no hesitation in expressing) is to be left alone to eat and sleep. They, however, express a desire to fight the Turk, whom they are under the impression they can defeat with no previous training on their part.

'There is considerable friction between the Syrians and the Meccans, who chiefly compose the infantry regiments, which culminated a few days ago in a quarrel, which was only stopped by the Machine Gun Officer threatening to produce his machine guns and informing them he would open fire unless the affair stopped at once. There was no one hurt.

'Gaafar however, is proceeding with the training, and the men do a little Company Drill, but I think he quite realises that it would be useless putting them up against anything like an equal body of trained Turkish troops with any hope of success.'[2]

Lawrence, who had been asked by Feisal to remain in Akaba for the time being, was more optimistic. For the present the Arabs seemed to be favoured both by geography and by the psychology of warfare. He knew, for instance, that there was too little water between Aba el Lissan and Akaba to allow an attack on Wadi Itm in force. On August 27th he wrote to Clayton: 'The situation here has not changed in any way . . . Captain MacIndoe has shown me a report he has written on the local military situation. The facts are, I think, correctly stated, but he appears to overrate the man-power factor in this area. I have found hitherto that questions of Railway capacity, traffic conditions, camels, water and roads count for far more than the quantity or quality of troops on each side . . .

'Jaafar Pasha is on the whole fairly sensible I think, and shows more comprehension of the Arab point of view than any of the other Syrian

Officers. Captain MacIndoe criticises his force rather bitterly, but their
real object is not so much to engage Turkish forces on equal terms, as to
stiffen the Beduin resistance, by providing the comforting spectacle of a
trained reserve, and to impress the Turks with the fact that behind the
Beduin screen lies an unknown quantity, which must be disposed of
before they can conquer Akaba. The Turkish C.-in-C. cannot risk arriving
here with less than two thousand men, because Jaafar has two thousand
men: their quality, so long as it is not proved bad by premature action, has
of necessity to be estimated by the Turks as good. Of course it would be
nice and much simpler for us if the Arab Movement emerged from
the bluff-and-mountain-pass stage, and became a calculable military
problem: but it hasn't yet, and isn't likely to. Jaafar's force is serving its
moral purpose admirably, and if he can find reliable officers to handle the
men tactfully and improve their discipline, it may become of practical
value in the near future'.[3]

Lawrence had no intention of postponing action until Allenby's
offensive began. Moreover, he saw that offence might be the best form of
protecting Akaba from attack. He wrote: 'The Abu Tayi are owed two
months' wages. Till they receive this we can hardly ask them to undertake
a new job. However they will be the first charge on the funds the
Hardinge is bringing, and we will then undertake the Railway between
Maan and Mudowwara [113km farther south]. There are seven waterless
stations here, and I have hope that with the Stokes and Lewis guns we may
be able to do something fairly serious to the line. If we can make a big
break I will do my best to maintain it . . . As soon as the Railway attack is
begun a force of "regulars" will enter the Shobek–Kerak hills [north-west
of Maan] and try to occupy them.

'If these operations are part-successful, the Turkish force at Fuweileh
will probably be withdrawn, or reduced, and our position at Akaba
then becomes safe. We cannot attack Fuweileh, and its retention in
force by the Turks after the rains would be serious. At the same time I
have little fear of anything unfortunate happening, since by extended
threats on the Railway we can force the Turks to increase their forces
there, and I believe that the Hejaz line is already working to full capacity
to support the troops now between Deraat and Medain Salih. For this
reason I do not think they can at once defend it, and attack Akaba on
the necessary scale.'[4]

For the moment, Lawrence was busy on all kinds of tasks at the new
base. He wrote to his family: 'I have too much to do, little patience to do

it with, and yet things are going tolerably well. It is much more facile doing daily work as a cog of a machine, than it is running a campaign by yourself. However it's the maddest campaign ever run, which is saying quite a little lot, and if it ever works out to a conclusion will be imperishable fun to look back upon. For the moment it is heavy and slow, weary work, with no peace for the unfortunate begetter of it anywhere.'[5]

On September 1st, Clayton came down to Akaba and held lengthy discussions with Lawrence and Feisal about the strategic situation. While there, he produced a dramatic letter from Sykes, which raised all kinds of issues in Lawrence's mind. Sykes had been greatly upset to discover what had happened in London during his absence in the Middle East, and his letter began: 'On my arrival I found that the Foreign Office had been carefully destroying everything I had done in the past two years. Stimulating anti-*Entente* feeling, and pushing separate negotiations-with-Turkey ideas. Indeed I just arrived in the nick of time. Luckily . . . the plots to . . . negotiate a separate peace with Turkey in Switzerland were foiled . . . The situation has occupied my whole attention since I arrived. I had also to clean up my own position which had been heavily attacked in my absence by the Foreign Office pro-Turk gang . . . However such worms do not take much dealing with, a few right and lefts, a breakfast with the P.M. and a successful speech in the House laid them low, and I found myself myself again'.[6]

If Lawrence had not already heard rumours of the secret moves to make peace with Turkey, this letter provided sufficient warning. Even while Sykes had been writing, Aubrey Herbert had been holding discussions with a Turkish representative in Geneva.[7] In the event, nothing ever came of these talks, but contacts between Britain and Turkey were to continue throughout the remainder of the war, and at times it seemed that a peace treaty was within reach.[8]

Lawrence realised that the fate of the Arabs might be greatly influenced by such negotiations. He later wrote: 'I had always the lurking fear that Great Britain might . . . conclude its own separate peace . . . with the Conservative Turks. The British Government had gone very far in this direction, without informing her smallest ally. Our information of the precise steps, and of the proposals (which would have been fatal to so many of the Arabs in arms on our side), came, not officially, to me, but privately. It was only one of the twenty times in which friends helped me more than did our Government'.[9]

Sykes's letter to Clayton continued with an exhortation to uphold the Anglo-French alliance: 'The main thing is never to yield to Fashoda-ism French or British . . . Hogarth arrived and played hell by writing an anti-French anti-[Sykes-Picot] Agreement memorandum . . . there is only one possible policy, the *Entente* first and last, and the Arab nation the child of the *Entente*. Get your Englishmen to stand up to the Arabs on this and never let them accept flattery of the "you very good man him very bad man" kind. I am going to slam into Paris to make the French play up to the Arab cause as their only hope. Colonialism is madness and I believe Picot and I can prove it to them. Lawrence's move [i.e. the capture of Akaba] is splendid and I want him knighted. Tell him now that he is a great man he must behave as such and be broad in his views. Ten years' tutelage under the *Entente* and the Arabs will be a nation. Complete independence means Persia, poverty and chaos. Let him consider this, as he hopes for the people he is fighting for.'[10]

This anti-imperialist stance was a new element in Sykes's rhetoric, and it has to be seen in the context of events elsewhere in the world. On April 1st the United States had entered the war, infuriated by German attacks on merchant shipping. However, President Wilson had stated unequivocally that America would not tolerate a scramble for new colonies in the wake of victory. In a speech to the American Senate, he had warned: 'No peace can last, or ought to last, which does not recognize and accept the principle that governments derive all their just powers from the consent of the governed, and that no right anywhere exists to hand peoples about from sovereignty to sovereignty as if they were property.'[11]

A similar policy had been adopted by Russia, now under Kerensky's provisional government after the fall of the Tsarist regime in March. Kerensky demanded an assurance that Britain agreed with the policy of self-determination laid down in Wilson's speech. The British Government complied, fearing that Russia would be prompted to stop fighting; it also expressed its willingness 'to examine and, if need be, to revise' any existing agreements that were found to contravene Wilson's principles.[12]

Liberal-minded Englishmen readily accepted that if the Central Powers were defeated, the future of their colonies should be resolved according to the principle of self-determination. This new form of idealism had quickly entered the political debate about Britain's proper war aims, and Sykes was very sensitive about it. His secret agreement with Georges-Picot was a flagrant contradiction of Wilson's policy, and association with such an imperialist measure might pose a threat to his political career. A few days before writing to Clayton, he had drawn up a memorandum insisting that in future the Agreement 'should be called the Anglo-French-Arab Agreement . . . and not the Sykes-Picot Agreement.'[13] Moreover, he had sought to reinterpret it on more disinterested and benevolent lines: 'Our basis of action should . . . be founded on two axioms:– (i) The unalterable friendship of Great Britain and France. (ii) The duty of Great Britain and France towards oppressed peoples. If in spite of the pettiness of individual officers [Lawrence and Brémond were probably among those Sykes had in mind] . . . Great Britain and France stick to these two grand principles, then we may gain our temporal requirements without endangering our good name or running counter to the ethical sense of mankind as a whole.'[14]

Sykes's letter to Clayton also contained a passing reference to the Zionist question. It was well known that he was interested in this subject, and the British staff in Egypt also knew that some kind of discussions on the matter were taking place in London. Jewish ambitions in Palestine were common knowledge in Cairo, where Aaron Aaronson, a prominent figure in the movement, was hoping to set up a Zionist office. Lawrence had good reason to be interested in a question that so obviously affected the aspirations of the Palestinian Arabs.

On September 7th, he wrote to Sykes at length, asking both about Zionist aims and about the future of the Sykes-Picot Agreement. He sent this letter to Clayton, with the comment: 'Some of it is really thirst for information, and other is only a wish to stick pins into him . . . One must have the Jewish section cleared up: and I fancy we may (if we win) clear up the French section ourselves.'[15]

Lawrence wrote to Sykes: 'General Clayton showed me a letter from you which contained a message to myself – and this has prompted me to ask you a few queries about Near East affairs. I hope you will be able to give me an idea of how matters stand in reference to them, since part of the responsibility of action is inevitably thrown on to me, and unless I know more or less what is wanted there might be trouble.

'About the Jews in Palestine, Feisal has agreed not to operate or agitate west of the [Wadi] Araba–Dead Sea–Jordan line, or south of the Haifa–Beisan line . . .

'You know of course the root differences between the Palestine Jew and the colonist Jew: to Feisal the important point is that the former speak Arabic, and the latter German Yiddish. He is in touch with the Arab Jews (their H.Q. at Safed and Tiberias is in his sphere) and they are ready to help him, on conditions. They show a strong antipathy to the colonist Jews, and have even suggested repressive measures against them. Feisal has ignored this point hitherto, and will continue to do so. His attempts to get into touch with the colonial Jews have not been very fortunate. They say they have made their arrangements with the Great Powers, and wish no contact with the Arab Party. They will not help the Turks or the Arabs.

'Now Feisal wants to know (information had better come to me for him since I usually like to make up my mind before he does) what is the arrangement standing between the colonist Jews (called Zionists sometimes) and the Allies . . . What have you promised the Zionists, and what is their programme?

'I saw Aaronson in Cairo, and he said at once the Jews intended to acquire the land-rights of all Palestine from Gaza to Haifa, and have practical autonomy therein. Is this acquisition to be by fair purchase or by forced sale and expropriation? The present half-crop peasantry were the old freeholders and under Moslem landlords may be ground down but have fixity of tenure. Arabs are usually not employed by Jewish colonies. Do the Jews propose the complete expulsion of the Arab peasantry, or their reduction to a day-labourer class?

'You know how the Arabs cling even to bad land and will realise that while Arab feelings didn't matter under Turkish rule . . . the condition will be vastly different if there is a new, independent, and rather cock-a-hoop Arab state north and east and south of the Jewish state. I can see a situation arising in which the Jewish influence in European finance might not be sufficient to deter the Arab peasants from refusing to quit – or worse!

'Then about French help here in Akaba. They have offered some quick firing mountain guns, and Feisal will accept them. His inevitable comment was that they had asked for these guns for a year for the Hedjaz, without getting them, and that they were offered unasked, as soon as he got to Akaba. The Sherifs accept British help openly, since they believe it disinterested (gratis, if you like). They feel the spirit of bargaining, or the desire to confer an obligation, in the offers of French help. This is partly the fault of the clumsy agents France has used in the Hedjaz. The Arabs can put their revolt through without French help, and therefore are disinclined to pay a price only to be made known to them in the future. You say they will need French help afterwards in the development of Syria – but do you really imagine anyone in Syria (bar Christians) wants to develop Syria? Why this craze for change? A slow progress, utilising only the surplus resources of Syria itself, seems to me more desirable than foreign borrowing, and a forcing-bed of public enterprises; and I think this point of view will be uppermost in the minds of the Damascus Government.

'If the French put a tangible price on their help, the Sherif might pay for it. He is not going to sell "spheres of influence" etc. for gold or mountain guns. If the French want to annex a province, in return for "X" materials, let them say so. You can't buy gratitude by a secretly conditional gift.

'I see you saying "pre-Fashoda" again! But please remember that Fashoda occurred before my time, and so the gibe is a generation late. The Sykes-Picot Agreement was made before the Sherif revolted. It stipulates for the erection of a sort of Arab-Albania; and resigns to France a great deal of what British people in the Near East regarded as, at least, mutual areas. The agreement was based, apparently, on the idea that the Allies were going to destroy Turkey, and strip her of her foreign possessions in their favour. We thought you had been generous to the Arabs, and were told unofficially that the need of bolstering up French courage and determination in the war made it necessary to surrender to her part of our own birthright. This latter statement, if true, justifies our suspicion of French action in the Near East. They are to get something of ours out here in return for their help in France. If we show an anti-French bias, it is your fault, for not educating us in Egypt officially to the knowledge of how much the French do require to stiffen them to last out the war in the west. Then the Sherif's revolt took place, and what had been a generous attempt to revive an Arab state in Syria under the aegis of France and England, became the sphere which the Sherif might obtain if he succeeded. You observe that we gave him no reward for his efforts on our side. He might take – what we had given already.

'Therefore I don't think the Sykes-Picot [Agreement] can stand as things are. The Sherif will succeed, given time and a continuance of our help: he will take by his own efforts (don't assume virtue for the mules and cartridges we supply him: the hands and heads are his) the sphere we allotted to our foreign-advised "independent Syria", and will expect to keep it without imposed foreign advisers. As he takes this sphere of his, he will also take parts of the other spheres not properly allotted to an Arab state. His title to them will be a fairly strong one – that of conquest by the means of the local inhabitants – and what are the two Powers going to do about it? It seems to me that England and France can either take their areas first, or turn the Arabs out by force, or leave the Arabs there, or leave the Turks there (by ceasing to pay the Sherif's subsidy). It will be quite impossible for whoever is the military adviser of the Sherif to advise him to leave a B area [of French influence], or a blue area [of French rule] alone, if the Turkish army is using it as a military area against him: and military occupations have a queer habit of developing into political ones.

'This is probably enough for the time being. You know I am strongly pro-British, and also pro-Arab. France takes third place with me: but I quite recognise that we may have to sell our small friends in pay for our big friends, or sell our future security in the Near East to pay for our present victory in Flanders. If you will tell me once more what we have to give the Jews, and what we have to give the French, I'll do everything I can to make it easy for us. Feisal is as reasonable as a soon-to-be successful man can be, and now is the time to mould him to our wishes. The future seems to me all over thorns, since military action by the Arabs, independently, was not in our minds when the Sykes-Picot [Agreement] was made, and if it is to be a Mede and Persian decree, we are in rather a hole: please tell me what, in your opinion, are the actual measures by which we will find a way out.'[16]

Clayton decided not to send this letter on to Sykes. Instead, he wrote back to Lawrence: 'Mark has, as far as I can gather from Hogarth, rather dropped the Near East just now and the whole question is, for the moment, somewhat derelict. All the better, and I am somewhat apprehensive lest your letter to Mark may raise him to activity. From all I can hear the Sykes-Picot agreement is in considerable disfavour in most quarters viz: Curzon, Hardinge, D.M.I., D.I.D., etc. . . . I am inclined . . . to think that it is moribund. At the same time we are pledged in honour to France not to give it the *coup de grâce* and must for the present act loyally up to it, in so far as we can. In brief, I think we can at present leave it alone as far as possible with a very fair chance of its dying of inanition. As you know, I have been of this opinion from the beginning . . . The Sykes-Picot agreement was made nearly two years ago. The world has moved at so vastly increased a pace since then that it is now as old and out of date as the Battle of Waterloo or the death of Queen Anne. It is in fact dead and, if we wait quietly, this fact will soon be realized: it was never a very workable instrument and it is now almost a lifeless monument. At the same time we cannot expect the French to see this yet, and we must therefore play up to it as loyally as possible until force of circumstances brings it home to them.'[17]

On September 7th Lawrence set out from Akaba intending to raid the railway south of Maan. By far the most important target was Mudawara station, where there was the only significant water supply in 150km of the line between Maan and Dhat el Haj (itself 84km north of Tebuk). If the water installations at Mudawara could be destroyed, it would become extremely difficult for the Turks to work traffic over this section. To cross it, trains would have to carry so much water that they would be able to transport little else.

In Lawrence's eyes, an attack on Mudawara had several merits. First, it would divert Turkish resources that might otherwise be used in attempts to retake Akaba. Secondly, it would be a severe blow against the Turkish line of communication to Medina. Thirdly, a really successful raid would do much to re-establish Arab morale.

As so often in these bedouin operations, Lawrence found that his original plan could not be carried out. He had hoped to raise a force of three hundred Howeitat at Guweira, sufficient to capture the station at Mudawara. However, the scheme was frustrated by tribal friction, lack of commitment to Feisal, and the fact that some of the men he had hoped to recruit had not yet been paid by Auda for earlier services. Eventually, Lawrence was obliged to return to Akaba. After some negotiations, he managed to raise a smaller force, and when he reached Mudawara on September 17th he had only 116 men. He quickly realised that he would be unable to take the place. Instead, he moved to another point on the railway and the following day successfully mined a train, using for the first time an electric exploder rather than an automatic detonator. Two English machine-gun instructors working at Akaba had accompanied the expedition, and their accurate fire contributed greatly to the success of the operation.

Lawrence returned to Akaba on September 22nd, and a few days later he wrote a graphic account of the raid to an acquaintance on Allenby's staff: 'The last stunt was the hold-up of a train. It had two locomotives, and we gutted one with an electric mine. This rather jumbled up the trucks, which were full of Turks, shooting at us. We had a Lewis, and flung bullets through the sides. So they hopped out and took cover behind the embankment, and shot at us between the wheels, at fifty yards. Then we tried a Stokes gun, and two beautiful shots dropped right in the middle of them. They couldn't stand that (twelve died on the spot) and bolted away to the east across a hundred-yard belt of open sand into some scrub. Unfortunately for them the Lewis covered the open stretch. The whole job took ten minutes, and they lost seventy killed, thirty wounded, eighty prisoners, and about twenty-five got away. Of my hundred Howeitat and two British NCOs there was one (Arab) killed, and four (Arabs) wounded.

'The Turks nearly cut us off as we looted the train, and I lost some baggage, and nearly myself . . . I hope this sounds the fun it is . . . It's the most amateurish, Buffalo-Billy sort of performance, and the only people who do it well are the bedouin.'[18]

Behind this self-confident façade, however, there was diffidence and misgiving. At much the same time Lawrence wrote to his Oxford friend E. T. Leeds: 'I hope when the nightmare ends that I will wake up and become alive again. This killing and killing of Turks is horrible . . . you charge in at the finish and find them all over the place in bits, and still alive many of them, and know that you have done hundreds in the same way before and must do hundreds more if you can.'[19]

Although this operation achieved far less than Lawrence had hoped, there was praise from Egypt: the destruction of a Turkish locomotive was one of the most useful things a railway raid could achieve. Allenby sent congratulations, and Wingate wrote to London that this 'latest exploit in wrecking a train with two engines, south of Maan, containing a considerable number of Turkish troops . . . is only in keeping with the splendid work [Lawrence] has done hitherto in Arabia.'[20]

The success also provided much needed encouragement. Arab morale in Akaba was suffering badly in the face of the growing Turkish threat, because it seemed that the forces now concentrating at Maan might overwhelm Feisal at any moment. Joyce shared something of this despondency, writing that the Arabs 'declare the Turks must be defeated before they get to Akaba, but exactly who is going to defeat them is a problem.'[21]

During Lawrence's absence at the railway, discontent at Akaba had been greatly aggravated by a shortage of supplies. In part, the problem was that the Arab Bureau did not realise quite how many tribesmen were coming in to join Feisal's army. It seems, however, that the question of supplies was not being handled efficiently in Egypt. At one point Joyce was moved to write: 'I am tired of this hand to mouth existence and if nothing is going to be done here, you had better let us quit for we are only wasting our time and yours.'[22]

Feisal too was in low spirits. The continuing weakness of his position was putting Akaba at risk and holding up the Syrian offensive. To help remedy this, he asked Joyce to arrange for Sherif Zeid's forces to be brought to Akaba as quickly as possible. Joyce reported: 'Feisal is much worried on the subject. If the old Sherif could be induced to send [Zeid] definite orders it would probably hurry his movements. Feisal still considers that his father and brothers are taking no interest in the Syrian movement and it takes a lot of talk to prevent his getting very depressed on the subject. He is mad keen himself and the indications of an early rising are so promising that all these delays in bringing it about are particularly annoying. If things are not kept going happily the whole movement will probably fall through and the responsibility will not rest on Feisal.'[23]

Now that Lawrence had returned to Akaba, he helped Joyce to tackle the situation. Feisal was in a resentful mood, critical of Britain, of his brothers, and of Hussein. Three days later, Joyce reported that they had been having a very difficult time: 'He is not a very strong character and much swayed by his surroundings . . . Lawrence and I did a dreadful thing and only gave him £10,000 instead of £50,000. The other £40,000 remains on the *Humber* to be given him as occasion arises. We have now been through so many of these critical moments when we have been told success or failure depends on a few thousands that we know the absolute necessity of a certain amount on short call, and therefore dared to keep back the above amount. We hope you won't give us away to the police!!'[24] Joyce now understood how much the Arab campaign would depend on Lawrence personally, and he saw it as a 'great weakness' that there was 'no one except Lawrence with a thorough martial and theoretical knowledge of the situation. We can all perhaps help a bit, having gained some knowledge, but it is his intimate and extensive knowledge of the history and the tribes and the language that really counts.'[25]

On September 27th Lawrence set off for another raid on the railway. Following the success of the previous expedition, he was inundated with volunteers. In addition to the Arab tribesmen, he took Captain Pisani, the French gunner who had come to Akaba, and three educated Syrians who were to be taught to use explosives. He hoped that by training them he would free himself from the necessity of taking part in time-consuming attacks on the line. Experience during the last few weeks had shown that he would be more usefully employed carrying out his liaison duties at Feisal's headquarters.

Another problem with these raiding expeditions was that Lawrence repeatedly found himself cast in the role of tribal mediator. After this second operation he wrote: 'A feature of the Howeitat is that every fourth or fifth man is a sheikh. In consequence the head sheikh has no authority whatever, and as in the previous raid I had to be O.C. of the whole expedition. This is not a job which should be undertaken by foreigners, since we have not so intimate a knowledge of Arab families, as to divide common plunder equitably. On this occasion however the Beduin behaved exceedingly well, and everything was done exactly as I wished; but in the six days' trip, I had to adjudicate in twelve cases of assault with weapons, four camel-thefts, one marriage settlement, fourteen feuds, two evil eyes, and a bewitchment. These affairs take up all one's spare time.'[26] Nevertheless, the raid did severe damage to an engine, which Lawrence judged to be beyond repair.

When he returned to Akaba, on October 8th, Lawrence found a telegram requesting him to go to EEF headquarters in Sinai. An aeroplane was sent from Suez to collect him, and on October 12th he reached GHQ, at that time to the north of of El Arish. There he found Clayton and Hogarth, and was briefed on plans for a major autumn offensive. As expected, orders had come from London for the capture of Jaffa and Jerusalem, in the hope that this would induce Turkey to withdraw from the war.

The decision to advance left Lawrence in a depressing quandary. In July, when he had sketched out his ideas for Arab action, he had not foreseen the difficulty Feisal would have in establishing himself at Akaba. So long as the Wadi Itm route was insecure, it would be impossible for the Arabs to embark on large-scale action elsewhere in Syria. After these discussions, Hogarth wrote: 'Feisal does not get any bigger – even T.E.L. admits that . . . [Lawrence] is not well and talks rather hopelessly about the Arab future he once believed in.'[27]

Another difficulty was that Lawrence could not tell whether or not the EEF would advance very far. Only three weeks earlier, Clayton had warned him against precipitate Arab action: 'My visit to the front in Palestine confirms me in the idea that we cannot expect more from our offensive than a smashing blow to the Turkish army, an advance to the Wadi Hesi [just north of Gaza] and possibly subsequent mounted reconnaissances further afield to the north. This is the utmost, and transport difficulties preclude anything more. The result may give us much less'.[28] If the EEF achieved no more than this, an Arab rising in Syria would be dangerously isolated. Moreover, the Turks were much stronger in these northern districts than in the Hejaz, because their lines of communication were so much shorter. Clayton wrote: 'Feisal may take a large slice of Syria by means of a general revolt of the inhabitants, but can he keep it with the British army necessarily tied by the leg far to the south and in face of a strong Turkish concentration in the north? If he cannot keep it, what is the result?

'You and Feisal know far better than I the situation in Syria and its possibilities and have doubtless weighed the pros and cons fully, but I want to ensure that no action is taken without full appreciation of the situation and that nothing is done which will bring down upon Syria a storm which we cannot avert and for which we shall inevitably have to bear the blame.'[29] Despite Allenby's recent orders, Clayton had no reason to retract this warning, and he must have repeated it during the discussions with Lawrence at EEF headquarters.

If Allenby proved to be successful, it was important that the Arabs should be ready, on their side, to exploit any Turkish retreat that followed. By determined action in the north, they would be able to turn defeat into chaos. Lawrence later wrote: 'Such would be our moment, and we needed to be ready for it in the spot where our weight and tactics would be least expected and most damaging. For my eyes, the centre of attraction was Deraa, the junction of the Jerusalem–Haifa–Damascus–Medina railways, the navel of the Turkish Armies in Syria, the common point of all their fronts; and, by chance, an area in which lay great untouched reserves of Arab fighting men, educated and armed by Feisal from Akaba. We could there use Rualla, Serahin, Serdiyeh, Khoreisha; and, far stronger than tribes, the settled peoples of Hauran and Jebel Druse . . . We were certain, with any management, of twelve thousand men, enough to rush Deraa, to smash all the railway lines, even to take Damascus by surprise.'[30]

A decisive action against the railway junction at Deraa would help Allenby greatly and, as Lawrence knew, the tribes were only too willing to rise. On the other hand, if the EEF failed, a rebellion on this scale could not be adequately supported, and the consequences would be terrible. Lawrence was therefore faced with a dilemma which Clayton and Hogarth could well understand. In *Seven Pillars* he wrote: 'Not for the first time or last time service to two masters irked me. I was one of Allenby's officers, and in his confidence: in return, he expected me to do the best I could for him. I was Feisal's adviser, and Feisal relied upon the honesty and competence of my advice so far as often to take it without argument. Yet I could not explain to Allenby the whole Arab situation, nor disclose the full British plan to Feisal.'[31] In an early draft of this passage Lawrence continued: 'Of course, we were fighting for an allied victory, and if in the end the sake of the English – the leading partner – was to be forwarded only by sacrificing the Arabs on the field of battle, then it would have to be done unhesitatingly; but it was hard to know just when it was the end, and necessary; and, in this case, to cast the die and lose meant to have ruined Feisal's cause.'[32] If the Arabs took Deraa, and later had to give it up, there would be 'horrible massacres of all the splendid peasantry of the district. They would have formed the bulk of our forces in the operation and were not beduin, able to fall back into the desert when the raid ended or miscarried. They were prosperous townsfolk and villagers, who lay open, themselves, their families and their property, to the revenge of a peculiarly barbarous enemy. Accordingly they could only rise once, and their effort on that occasion must be decisive. To call them out now was to risk the best asset Feisal held for eventual success, on the speculation that Allenby's first attack would sweep the enemy before it'.[33]

Before leaving GHQ Lawrence decided, with Clayton's support, that such a rising could not at present be justified. Instead, he proposed to go himself with a bedouin raiding party and try to destroy one of the larger railway bridges in the Yarmuk gorge. If this could be carried out at the moment of Allenby's attack, the Turkish army in Palestine would be deprived of its line of communication and retreat towards Damascus at a most critical moment. Should the EEF then succeed, a more favourable moment might arise for calling a general revolt. This scheme was put to Allenby, who approved it, and asked that the bridge should be blown up on November 5th or one of the following three days. Lawrence therefore flew back to Akaba on October 15th to make his preparations.

Neither Hogarth nor Clayton was very sanguine about his chances of destroying the bridge. Hogarth wrote shortly afterwards: 'I doubt if he will manage to get north again. Recent successes have drawn rather too many troops down onto the Maan section of the railway.'[34] For Clayton, one of the greatest worries was Lawrence's personal safety. Raids on the desert railway involved little physical risk, except at the moment of action. What was now proposed, however, was a journey through an area of settled villages deep inside enemy territory. George Lloyd, who had gone to Akaba to see if he could be of any assistance, wrote to Clayton on October 20th: 'Lawrence is quite fit but much oppressed by the risk and the magnitude of the job before him. He opened his heart to me last night and told me that he felt there was so much for him still to do in the world, places to dig, peoples to help, that it seemed horrible to have it all cut off, as he feels it will be – for he feels that while he may do the job he sees little or no chance of getting away himself – I tried to cheer him up, but of course it is true . . . He is really a very remarkable fellow – not the least fearless like some who do brave things, but, as he told me last night, each time he starts out on these stunts he simply hates it for two or three days before, until movement, action and the glory of scenery and nature catch hold of him and make him well again.'[35] Clayton wrote back: 'I am very anxious about Lawrence. He has taken on a really colossal job and I can see that it is well-nigh weighing him down. He has a lion's heart, but even so the strain must be very great. Well, he is doing a great work and as soon as may be we must pull him out and not risk him further, but the time is not yet, as he is wanted just now. The first real issue in this theatre of the war is at hand and much will depend on the doings of the next month.'[36]

Lawrence spent ten days in Akaba before setting out on the Yarmuk expedition. Shortly before he was due to leave, the plans were radically changed when the Emir Abd el Kader arrived in Akaba offering the support of his followers. Abd el Kader was an Algerian who controlled a number of villages on the north side of the Yarmuk valley, peopled by Algerian exiles. With their support, a small raiding party could in effect control the central section of the Yarmuk line. The opportunity seemed too good to miss, and it was decided that Abd el Kader would join the expedition, despite his reputation as a Muslim fanatic. Afterwards, a warning came from Brémond that he was in the pay of the Turks. This added to Lawrence's anxiety, but there was nothing to substantiate the charge and in the end it was ignored: Brémond's feelings towards a declared enemy of France were naturally suspect.

The expedition left Akaba on October 24th with an experienced raider, Sherif Ali ibn el Hussein of the Harith tribe, as its Arab leader. Much of the force was to be recruited farther north, but Lawrence also took a party of Indian machine-gunners who had been serving for several months in the Hejaz. When the Yarmuk bridge was attacked, their steady fire could be used to hold back any Turkish reinforcements while the bedouin overpowered the guards. He also thought it wise to take an explosives specialist who would know how best to destroy the complex steel girder bridge, and he chose Lieutenant Wood, a sapper officer who worked as base engineer at Akaba. In this way, the operation would still have a good chance of success even if Lawrence were killed or wounded. Lloyd was also to accompany them for the first part of the journey.

The little group crossed the Hejaz Railway below Maan and made its way towards Jefer, where Lawrence hoped to recruit an escort from the Howeitat. During this ride he had ample time to talk about his ambitions for the Arabs, and impressed upon Lloyd the political obstacles which lay ahead. Lloyd wrote in his diary: 'He would like me best to go home to England for he felt that there was a risk that all his work would be ruined politically in Whitehall and he thought I could save this'.[37]

Lawrence went over the details of the Yarmuk plan again with Lloyd. By approaching from the north, the raiders would travel as far as possible through uninhabited country until they reached the Algerian villages where Abd el Kader would recruit helpers. According to Lloyd's report, Lawrence hoped to 'get them to put up a fight with the bridge guards while he sets the mines. His chances of escape are greater in a general confusion than in a solitary attempt where all fire would be directed on him. I hope his chances are really much better than would appear at first sight. I wanted him to take a horse from Azrak to get away on, but he says he cannot ride one.'[38]

Lloyd also made rough notes of Lawrence's further plans, to be implemented if the bridge raid were successful and the EEF broke through in Palestine. Lawrence would first return to Azrak, and from there send out influential messengers to call a rebellion in the whole area north to Damascus and west to the Mediterranean. He himself would meanwhile ride north to Palmyra and plan the capture of Aleppo, thereafter moving up by stages to Alexandretta.

Lawrence usually agreed with Lloyd on Arab questions and hoped that Lloyd could advance the Arab cause in Whitehall. The notes record his thoughts about what might happen if his plans succeeded: 'Situation resultant:– Sherif's flag flies along coast from Acre northwards; French protests? Our attitude? Feisal's attitude will be non-negotiatory – "What I have taken I keep" – Lawrence not working for Allies but for Sherif – Had no instructions except hamper communications.

'Neither Feisal or Sherif ever seen text of S-P Agreement and claim never had its contents put before them – Nothing in writing – Anyway not parties to it – Agreement at best one between France and England for partition of a country in armed occupation of forces of Sherif of Mecca.

'Alexandretta must be obtained for G.B. This can be done but can only be done by Sherif's good will – Who gave Alexandretta to the French? On what claims: no railways, no politics, not Syria – Do we partition Arab countries without consulting the Arabs?'[39]

When they reached Jefer, Lawrence found to his annoyance that it was impossible to raise an escort of tribesmen. In *Seven Pillars* he spoke in vague terms of Howeitat dissatisfaction. Lloyd's contemporary report, however, shows that Lawrence was unable to persuade them to join the Yarmuk raid because there was no prospect of loot.[40] The party moved from Jefer to Bair, where they were able to recruit some Beni Sakhr and then travelled on towards Azrak, the desert oasis from which the raiding party would set out.

Before arriving, the expedition encountered some Serahin tribesmen who directed them to their encampment near Azrak. The tribesmen were willing to join Feisal, but were very unenthusiastic about the proposed expedition. Moreover, their news about the local situation in the Yarmuk valley was disquieting. Lawrence's original objective had been the most westerly bridge, at Hemme, which he had reconnoitred in June. It tran-spired that this would now be impossible, as the surrounding district was filled with Turkish wood-cutters collecting fuel. Under the current plan, one of the central bridges was to be attacked using Abd el Kader's villagers; but the Serahin were doubtful of this scheme and extremely mistrustful of Abd el Kader. There remained a third possibilty: an attempt on the nearest bridge, at Tell el Shehab. This would be much more dangerous than Abd el Kader's scheme, because the approach would have to be made through settled country. If there were rain, it would be difficult to escape across the muddy terrain. In addition, there was a feud between the Serahin and local villagers.

With deepening reservations, Lawrence decided to keep to the existing plan, but it was then noticed that Abd el Kader had disappeared. Lawrence feared, correctly as it turned out, that he had gone over to the Turks. This put the whole expedition in jeopardy, since he knew all their plans. It would now be folly to approach the Algerian villages, and with acute misgivings it was agreed that the bridge at Tell el Shehab was the only remaining option.

The British staff at Akaba and in Cairo knew nothing of these develop-ments, but they were nevertheless extremely apprehensive. On November 4th (the day that Abd el Kader disappeared) Joyce wrote to Clayton: 'Lawrence by now must be very near his objective. I hope he is lucky. Fortunately he has got brains as well as dash and the two I trust will pull him through, but one cannot help feeling anxious.'[41] Hogarth too was worried: 'I only hope and trust TEL will get back safe. He is out and up against it at this moment. If he comes through it is a V.C. – if not – well, I don't care to think about it!'[42]

The distance from Azrak to Tell el Shehab was about eighty miles, of which the last section would be the most dangerous. This could not be attempted before dusk, leaving little time to carry out the attack and escape before dawn. Nevertheless, the expedition reached its objective safely on the night of November 7th, and the early stages of the operation went according to plan. Then, as the demolition party crept towards the bridge in the darkness, someone dropped a rifle. The noise alerted the Turkish guards, and in the firing that followed the Serahin tribesmen panicked. Fearing that the explosive would blow up if hit with a bullet, they threw it into the ravine. Without any means to destroy the bridge, there was no point in continuing the engagement, and Lawrence gave orders for everyone to leave as quickly as possible. He was bitterly disappointed, but grateful when the raiding party escaped without loss.

Lawrence was determined to find some way of compensating for this failure. He had told Lloyd that if the bridges proved impossible, he would blow up targets on the railway in the El Leja region between Deraa and Damascus. This would help Allenby, even though the damage could be repaired more quickly than in the Yarmuk valley. Now, however, he had little explosive, and his range of action was restricted because the expedition was running short of food. The best he could do was to blow up a train near Minifir on the line between Deraa and Amman. This would not affect traffic to Palestine, but it would be good for Arab morale.

The circumstances for this attack were not ideal: in order to save food he had been obliged to send the Indian machine-gunners back to Azrak, and this meant that the raiding party had no machine-gun cover. There were further problems when they reached the railway, and two trains went by unscathed before Lawrence managed to trigger the mine. The account in *Seven Pillars* shows how little glamour there really was in these raids: 'Round the bend, whistling its loudest, came the train, a splendid two-engined thing of twelve passenger coaches, travelling at top speed on the favouring grade. I touched off under the first driving wheel of the first locomotive, and the explosion was terrific. The ground spouted blackly into my face, and I was sent spinning, to sit up with the shirt torn to my shoulder and the blood dripping from long ragged scratches on my left arm. Between my knees lay the exploder, crushed under a twisted sheet of sooty iron. In front of me was the scalded and smoking upper half of a man. When I peered through the dust and steam of the explosion the whole boiler of the first engine seemed to be missing.

'I dully felt that it was time to get away to support; but when I moved, I learnt that there was a great pain in my right foot, because of which I could only limp along, with my head swinging from the shock. Movement began to clear away this confusion, as I hobbled towards the upper valley, whence the Arabs were now shooting fast into the crowded coaches. Dizzily I cheered myself by repeating aloud in English "Oh, I wish this hadn't happened".

'When the enemy began to return our fire, I found myself much between the two. Ali saw me fall, and thinking that I was hard hit, ran out, with Turki and about twenty men of his servants and the Beni Sakhr, to help me. The Turks found their range and got seven of them in a few seconds . . . We scrambled back into cover together, and there, secretly, I felt myself over, to find I had not once been really hurt; though besides the bruises and cuts of the boiler-plate and a broken toe, I had five different bullet-grazes on me (some of them uncomfortably deep) and my clothes ripped to pieces.

'From the watercourse we could look about. The explosion had destroyed the arched head of the culvert, and the frame of the first engine was lying beyond it, at the near foot of the embankment down which it had rolled. The second locomotive had toppled into the gap, and was lying across the ruined tender of the first. Its bed was twisted. I judged them both beyond repair. The second tender had disappeared over the further side; and the first three waggons had telescoped and were smashed in pieces.

'The rest of the train was badly derailed, with the listing coaches butted end to end at all angles, zigzagged along the track. One of them was a saloon, decorated with flags . . . The Turks, seeing us so quiet, began to advance up the slope. We let them come half-way, and then poured in volleys which killed some twenty and drove the others back. The ground about the train was strewn with dead, and the broken coaches had been crowded: but they were fighting under the eye of their Corps Commander, and undaunted began to work round the spurs to outflank us.

'We were now only about forty left, and obviously could do no good against them. So we ran in batches up the little stream-bed, turning at each sheltered angle to delay them by pot-shots. Little Turki much

distinguished himself by quick coolness, though his straight-stocked
Turkish cavalry carbine made him so expose his head that he got four
bullets through his head-cloth. Ali was angry with me for retiring slowly.
In reality my raw hurts crippled me, but to hide from him this real reason
I pretended to be easy, interested in and studying the Turks. Such
successive rests while I gained courage for a new run kept him and Turki
far behind the rest.

'At last we reached the hill-top. Each man there jumped on the
nearest camel, and made away at full speed eastward into the desert,
for an hour.'[43]

Lawrence was fortunate to have escaped with his life. Afterwards, the
party made its way back to Azrak, arriving there on November 12th.
Rather than return to Akaba, he decided to stay in the north until the
moment was right for another raid, and also in case some further action
might be appropriate, should the Turks collapse under Allenby's attack.
During November, however, the winter rains set in, and he was able to
guess that Allenby's advance had been halted by the bad weather.

For Lawrence, the Yarmuk failure was a bitter disappointment. In
July, he had offered Allenby a general rising to help the EEF advance.
In October, fearful that the British would fail, he had decided to hold
back, substituting the more limited bridge-blowing operation. In the
event, he had been able to achieve almost nothing. The Turkish line of
communication between Damascus and Palestine remained intact.

It was some time before messengers from Akaba brought news to Azrak
of Allenby's offensive. The EEF had been victorious on the Gaza–
Beersheba line but, as Clayton had prophesied, their advance had soon
been handicapped by difficulties in transporting water and supplies.
Despite severe casualties and losses of *matériel*, the Turks had retreated
in reasonable order and were soon fighting a strong rearguard action.
Allenby had not been halted definitively, but a further advance would be
a slow and more costly affair. In late November, a two-week pause was
necessary while reserves were brought up to the front; both sides were
preparing to fight for Jerusalem.

Even before the advance in Palestine ground to a halt, Clayton had
expressed his relief that the Arabs had not called a general rising. On
November 12th he wrote to Joyce: 'Tell Feisal that he must not be in too
great a hurry to rush off to Syria. All these things take time, and it is
no use striking until the proper moment arrives and success is really

probable. I know that he is impatient but I think that now he will realize that we were wise not to let him loose earlier, as, had he started his show before the victory in Sinai, he would have inevitably been crushed by the powerful reserves which were available at Aleppo . . . I dare say it has upset him to have to remain inactive, and of course, it is expensive, but it is very much better to do that than to have the whole show smashed up.'[44]

Clayton was less disappointed than Lawrence about the Yarmuk expedition. He took a wider view of the developing situation, and seems to have felt that Lawrence's personal safety was almost as important to the British as the fate of the Yarmuk bridges. Although Feisal had made no specific contribution to Allenby's attack, there was no doubting the general value of Arab operations, both now and for the future. The Sherifian forces were engaging troops that the Turks desperately needed to defend Jerusalem. British Intelligence received frequent reports about Turkish dispositions, and these showed the large numbers of troops that were being held down by the Arabs. Clayton wrote: 'the enemy forces operating at Medina and on the railway line of communications . . . or the greater part of them, would have been available to reinforce the enemy's Palestine armies, if it were not for the Arab Revolt.

'The [Turkish] Hejaz Expeditionary Force and the two Composite Forces with Headquarters at Tebuk and Maan have a ration strength of over twenty-three thousand. They are made up in the main of regiments containing, until lately, over 90% of Turks, and even now, rarely under 80%, and include the picked force of three thousand Anatolian troops sent down originally in spring 1916 . . . Although the Arabs have not yet succeeded in overcoming the resistance of Medina and the line of communication, the continuance of their Revolt has cost the enemy, through deaths, wounds, sickness and captures, quite a full Division, and at the present moment his strength is barely sufficient to hold on to what, for politico-religious reasons, he will not resign except in the last extremity. For example, on 7th November, the 2nd Composite Force was reported inadequate to hold its section of the line of communication owing to the large proportion of sick and useless men on its strength. At the same time the maintenance of these forces and of supplies to them makes a heavy call on railway plant and rolling stock and on the reserves of food and stores at Damascus, a great proportion of which would otherwise be available for the Palestine front.

'This being so, the [Arab] operations by which these enemy forces are being held in place (and their numbers, equipment and morale, are being so continuously reduced that reinforcements in men and material have constantly to be sent down from Syria) are of direct assistance to the Palestine campaign.'[45]

Now that Feisal's army had reached Azrak, Lawrence was determined that it should remain in their hands. In *Seven Pillars* he wrote: 'Partly it would be a preaching base, from which to spread our movement in the north: partly it would be a centre of intelligence: partly it would cut off Nuri Shalaan from the Turks . . . Azrak lay favourably for us, and the old fort would be a convenient headquarters if we made it habitable, no matter how severe the winter.'[46]

Messengers were soon travelling regularly down to Akaba, two hundred miles to the south-west. Lawrence used them to send reports to Joyce and Clayton. He also wrote to his family: 'I wonder if you can find this place:– it's out in the desert between Deraat and Amman – and if you do find it you will think it a most improbable place to live at.

'Living however is quite easy and comfortable here. We are in an old fort with stone roofs and floors, and stone doors of the sort they used in Bashan. It is a bit out of repair, but is improving in that respect every day . . . I am staying here a few days; resting my camels, and will then have another fling.'[47] His younger brother Arnold, now seventeen, was keen to serve in the desert campaign, and Lawrence approved of the idea: 'I told the people concerned in Cairo, and either Mr. Hogarth or myself can get it arranged quite easily if the time comes.'[48]

At Azrak much time was taken up in entertaining visitors and encouraging them to take part in the Revolt. Ali ibn el Hussein was far more suited to this than Lawrence, who decided to leave again after only two days. He was accompanied by Sheikh Tallal, from the village of Tafas south of Damascus. Tallal had been outlawed by the Turks, and his influence would be valuable to the rebel cause. Some time before, he had offered to take Deraa whenever Feisal wished. With Tallal as guide, Lawrence set out on a brief tour of the Hauran country, so that he could see the lie of the land for himself. After circling Deraa he decided to look at the defences and installations inside the town. On November 20th, therefore, he parted company with Tallal and took two villagers as companions. There seemed no great danger in wandering through the busy town dressed inconspicuously as a local Arab, and Lawrence was by this time well used to travelling among the peasantry behind Turkish lines.

His earliest account of what happened next is given in a letter to a fellow officer, written eighteen months later. It begins: 'I went into Deraa in disguise to spy out the defences, was caught, and identified by Hajim Bey, the governor, by virtue of Abd el Kadir's description of me. (I learned all about his treachery from Hajim's conversation, and from my guards.) Hajim was an ardent paederast and took a fancy to me. So he kept me under guard till night, and then tried to have me.'[49]

This is at variance with the later *Seven Pillars* version in one important respect: it states plainly that he was recognised, as indeed he must have been. Arab clothes were good enough as a disguise at a distance, but neither Lawrence himself nor any of his fellow-officers in the Revolt ever claimed that he could pass close scrutiny as an Arab.

Moreover, his identity was by this time well known to the Turks, who had long offered a reward for his capture. The hunt for him had recently been stepped up, and the price on his head increased to £20,000.[50] This was because the staff carriage in the train he had wrecked near Minifir nine days earlier had been occupied by the GOC of the Turkish VIIIth Army. Several senior officers had been killed.

It seems that Lawrence was first arrested in Deraa purely on suspicion of being a deserter from the Turkish Army. He countered by claiming to be a Circassian, exempt from military service, but this excuse was not accepted, and he was held in a guardroom. In the evening, when he was taken to the Bey, he found out that he was expected to submit to homosexual advances. He later wrote: 'Incidents like these made the thought of military service in the Turkish army a living death for whole-some Arab peasants, and the consequences pursued the miserable victims all their after-life, in revolting forms of sexual disease.'[51] He resisted the Bey's attentions, and eventually the soldiers were ordered to take him away 'and teach him everything'.[52]

He was severely beaten and, when he could resist no longer, he was sexually abused. The whole ordeal may not have lasted very long – an early draft of *Seven Pillars* suggests that the beating took no more than ten minutes – but it affected him very deeply. It stopped when Hajim Bey called, and the soldiers 'splashed water in my face, lifted me to my feet, and bore me, retching and sobbing for mercy, between them, to his bedside: but he now threw me off fastidiously, cursing them for their stupidity in thinking he needed a bedfellow streaming with blood and water, striped and fouled from face to heel . . . So the crestfallen corporal, as the youngest and best-looking of the guard, had to stay behind, while the others carried me down the narrow stairs and out into the street . . . They took me over an open space, deserted and dark, and behind the Government house to an empty lean-to mud and wooden room, in which were many dusty quilts. They put me down on these, and brought an Armenian dresser, who washed and bandaged me in sleepy haste. Then they all went away, the last of the soldiers whispering to me in a Druse accent that the door into the next room was not locked.'[53]

Despite the injuries he had received, the instinct of self-preservation drove him to explore this second room, which turned out to be a dispensary. A window on the far side offered a way out. His earliest account of the incident ended: 'I escaped before dawn, being not as hurt as [Hajim] thought. He was so ashamed of the muddle he had made that he hushed the whole thing up, and never reported my capture and escape. I got back to Azrak very annoyed with Abd el Kadir'.[54]

At the time, his strongest emotion must have been an overwhelming sense of relief that he had managed to get away. In the future, however, other aspects of the experience would cast a deepening shadow, and later events would show that this brutal homosexual rape had inflicted terrible psychological damage. Lawrence had been sexually inexperienced (in 1917 this was the norm among young men from the middle classes, not the exception). What had taken place left him with profound feelings of guilt and shame.

Immediately afterwards, there were few outward signs of this psychological injury: some of the consequences would take years to manifest themselves. As long as the Arab campaign lasted, his attention was focused almost entirely on his responsibilities, and he had little opportunity for introspection. It was only later, when the war was over, that the events at Deraa would come to dominate his most intimate thoughts.

As for his physical injuries, their after-effects were no worse than other hardships of the campaign, and in a few days he had recovered. During the previous twelve months he had endured repeated illness and had been wounded several times, but he had made it his practice to carry on as best he could.

He did not stay long at Azrak, but rode on down to Akaba, which he reached on December 3rd. When he got there, Joyce sent a wireless message to Cairo: 'With a view to discussion on further operations, Lawrence is anxious to see General Clayton and General Staff. Can you arrange for an aeroplane to take him to GHQ from here?'[55]

Lawrence was flown to the British advance headquarters, fully expecting to be criticised for the Yarmuk failure. However, the EEF was within sight of Jerusalem at last, and he was told 'all the news of [Allenby's] great stroke at Beersheba, the fall of Gaza, the pursuit and the battles in the Philistine Plain, and the stern wrestle with the entrenched Turks in the fastnesses of the Judean Hills. [Allenby] was so full of victories that my short statement that I had failed to carry a Yarmuk bridge was accepted as sufficient, and the rest of my failure could remain concealed.'[56]

While Lawrence was with Allenby, extraordinary news came in: the Turks had quite unexpectedly pulled out of Jerusalem during the night, and civilian officials had come to the British lines in search of someone who would accept their surrender.

Lawrence was still at headquarters on December 11th, when the ceremonial British entry took place 'in the official manner which the catholic imagination of Mark Sykes had devised. [Allenby] was good enough, although I had done nothing to forward his success, to allow Clayton to take me with him as his Staff Officer for the day. The personal Staff tricked me out in their spare clothes till I looked like an ordinary major in the British Army, and Dalmeny lent me red tabs, and Evans gave me a brass hat, so that for once I had the gauds of my appointment; and then I shared in what for me was the most memorable event of the war, the one which, for historical reasons, made a greater appeal than anything on earth.

'It was strange to stand before the tower with the Chief, listening to his proclamation, and to think how a few days ago I had stood before Hajim, listening to his words. Seldom did we pay so sharply and so soon for our fears. We would have been by now, not in Jerusalem, but in Haifa, or Damascus, or Aleppo, had I not shrunk in October from the danger of a general rising against the Turks. By my failure I had fettered the unknowing English, and dishonoured the unknowing Arabs in a way only to be repaired by our triumphal entry into a liberated Damascus. The ceremony of the Jaffa Gate gave me a new determination.'[57]

CHAPTER 22

The Dead Sea Campaign
December 1917 – February 1918

JERUSALEM had been ruled by Muslim powers since the Crusades, and Christians in Britain, France and America were elated by the news of its capture. When Allenby and his staff entered the Holy City on foot, the dignified and moving ceremony caught the imagination of the western world. Lawrence wrote to his parents: 'I was in fortune, getting to Jerusalem just in time for the official entry . . . It was impressive in its way – no show, but an accompaniment of machine-gun and anti-aircraft fire, with aeroplanes circling over us continually. Jerusalem has not been taken for so long: nor has it ever fallen so tamely before.'[1] He was encouraged by the ease and completeness of Allenby's victory: 'Jerusalem cheered all of us mightily. Casualties were so few, and the booty so immense . . . going up there we found the whole countryside strewn with the old store-heaps of the Turks. Twenty million rounds of small arms ammunition, and uncounted shells. Also there are thousands of deserters, and God knows what amount of stuff looted by the villagers before we came. It is the loss of the accumulated stores of two years to them: and it will take them six months to pile up such another lot, if they can concentrate all their efforts on the job. In actual prisoners, and in killed and wounded the show was not over great – but then there were not many Turks to begin with – and very few to end with.'[2]

This dramatic climax to the EEF advance into Palestine made the prospects for total victory in the East seem suddenly much more real. Writing to an Oxford friend, Lawrence began to speculate about his career after the war: 'one is getting terribly bound up in Eastern politics, and must keep free. I've never been labelled yet, and yet I fear that they are going to call me an Arabian now. As soon as the war ends I'm going to build a railway in South America, or dig up a South African gold-field, to emancipate myself. Carchemish will either be hostile (Turks will never let me in again) or friendly (Arab), and after being a sort of king-maker one will not be allowed to go digging quietly again. Nuisance. However the war isn't over yet, and perhaps one needn't worry one's head too soon about it.'[3]

The fall of Jerusalem opened a new phase in tension between the Allies over the future settlement in the Middle East. The French knew that their hopes in the region were threatened by the general growth of anti-imperialist sentiment and their own negligible contribution to the Palestine campaign. For this reason they were anxious to assert their political rights as rapidly as possible. It would be difficult to do so, as *de facto* military control of the conquered territory was exercised by Britain, and the French presence was little more than symbolic. However, Palestine was the first captured territory in which the French had any claim to political influence, and it was therefore an important test case. They were determined to secure a role in its administration at once, as this would create a precedent for implementation of the Sykes-Picot Agreement if Turkish authority collapsed in Syria.

British officials understood the French position, but had little sympathy. There was now a pronounced opposition to the Sykes-Picot terms in many quarters. Lloyd George had already decided that British control in Palestine would be preferable to an international administration there. As far as Syria was concerned, the British were increasingly sensitive about Arab views. If delay in implanting French political influence helped to undermine the Sykes-Picot scheme, might this not be wholly to the good? For Allenby's staff there was a further consideration: the introduction of French officials would inevitably lead to intrigue and suspicion. Such an atmosphere would be detrimental to the future of the campaign.

Before the start of the EEF advance, Clayton had looked for a way of freezing the question of political settlement for as long as possible. He had found a solution in the principle of non-political military administration. This could be maintained if necessary until the final peace terms were agreed. The arrangement would be disliked by France, but could not be objected to under international law or the existing Anglo-French agreements. Sykes-Picot outlined the final post-war settlement, but it said nothing about the administration of captured territory while hostilities were still in progress.[4] On this point the only relevant accord was the one reached in December 1916, when a British advance into Palestine was first planned. Under this agreement, a French political officer had been attached to the EEF in order to advise the British C.-in-C. about French interests; the officer subsequently appointed had been Georges-Picot. His role did not include administrative responsibilities, and he had returned to Europe after Murray's failure.

Georges-Picot had rejoined the EEF a few days before the fall of Jerusalem, and soon showed that he was determined to enlarge his role as far as possible. Even before he arrived, messages had come from the French Foreign Office making it plain that he expected to be given an active role in the civil administration of Jerusalem. Allenby and his staff, however, were equally determined to enforce the principle of a non-political military government. Georges-Picot was permitted to take part in the official entry, but only as a staff officer attached to the EEF. Neither Defrance, head of the French Mission in Cairo, nor Wingate, was allowed to attend.

By this time, Georges-Picot must have seen that any prospects for immediate political influence were evaporating before his eyes. At the picnic lunch which followed the official entry he made a desperate bid to assert himself. This was witnessed by Lawrence and described in *Seven Pillars*: 'Picot . . . said in his fluting voice: "And tomorrow, my dear general, I will take the necessary steps to set up civil government in this town."

'It was the bravest word on record; a silence followed, as when they opened the seventh seal in heaven. Salad, chicken mayonnaise and foie gras sandwiches hung in our wet mouths unmunched, while we turned to Allenby and gaped. Even he seemed for a moment at a loss . . . But his face grew red: he swallowed, his chin coming forward (in the way we loved), whilst he said, grimly, "In the military zone the only authority is that of the Commander-in-Chief – myself." '[5]

Before leaving GHQ, Lawrence discussed the strategic situation with Allenby. He was told that a further British advance would be impossible before mid-February 1918, because new supplies were needed, and casualties had to be made good. After that, the EEF would consolidate its position by moving against Jericho, so that its inland flank reached the northern end of the Dead Sea. No large-scale offensive would take place until later in the year.

In the meantime, however, the Arab forces could be usefully employed. The first objective Allenby laid down was to occupy the region at the southern end of the Dead Sea, closing that route to a possible Turkish attack on his army from the rear. This scheme had been mooted for some time and, as it happened, Lawrence had just heard from Joyce that operations were beginning. The idea of moving into this region appealed strongly to Feisal, who wished to establish support for the Revolt among the settled villages. The area would be valuable to the Arabs because it produced grain, and its loss would be a serious blow to the Turks, who depended on it for the timber used as fuel on the Hejaz Railway south of Maan. Lawrence explained that Arab forces were moving out of Akaba already, with the aim of taking first Shobek and then Tafileh, a village close to the southern end of the Dead Sea. An elaborate three-pronged operation for this purpose had been worked out by Joyce and Feisal some weeks previously. Sherif Nasir had left Akaba on December 9th with about a thousand tribesmen and 150 mounted regulars under Nuri as-Said. They would move northwards through the desert east of the railway and then attack the line between Deraa and Maan. This would prevent Turkish reinforcements from interfering while the two other forces moved on Shobek, one from the south and the other from the west via Wadi Araba. Afterwards, all three forces would combine for an attack on Tafileh.

Allenby's second request was that by the middle of February the Arabs should put a stop to Turkish lighter-traffic on the Dead Sea. This was being used to carry food from the Kerak region to Jericho.

Lawrence himself suggested a third objective: if possible, the Arabs would take control during March of the whole region between the Dead Sea and the railway. The EEF could then supply the Revolt directly from Palestine and, in preparation for the final offensive, Feisal's main force could be moved from Akaba to the northern end of the Dead Sea.

After these discussions at GHQ, Lawrence went to Cairo for a short rest, staying as Wingate's guest at the Residency. He found time during this period to experiment with explosives and different types of insulated cable. The detonating wire previously supplied was too stiff to be buried easily in the sand.

Hogarth now thought that Lawrence was 'looking much fitter and better than when I saw him last. He still looks absurdly boyish for twenty-eight!'[6] It seems, however, that Clayton was thinking of giving him a longer rest once the current operations had been completed. On December 14th Lawrence wrote to his parents: 'they are going to send me to England for a few days in the spring, if all works well then: so this is my last trip, possibly. Don't bank on it, as the situation out here is full of surprise turns, and my finger is one of those helping to mix the pie. An odd life, but it pleases me, on the whole.'[7]

In the same letter, he noted that the official ban on reporting the Revolt had been dropped. This was a welcome change, since publicity would strengthen Feisal's political case. Lawrence wrote: 'Pirie-Gordon is coming out, to write popular articles on the Arab war for the home papers – so you will soon know all about it. Secrecy was necessary while the fight was a life and death one in the Hejaz: but since the opening of Akaba the stress has been eased, and today we are as comfortable as any front. As public sympathy is desirable, we must try and enlist on our side a favourable press . . . it was quite impossible before. This show of ours began with all against it, and has had first to make itself acceptable to the elect. They converted, we can afford to appeal to a wider circle . . . [Arnie] should keep an eye on the illustrated paper soon. They are going to get an occasional photograph from us, to help keep the Sherif (and Feisul above all) before the public eye. The Arab Bureau have about five hundred excellent prints.'[8]

Popular interest in the capture of Jerusalem was very strong, and it presented an opportunity for favourable publicity about the eastern campaigns. Sykes, who had always believed firmly in the value of propaganda, took a personal interest in the way the victory was presented. EEF press material about the Holy Land tended to be dignified, but somewhat pedestrian. Sykes dismissed it as 'vile barren stuff,'[9] and cabled to Clayton: 'ring off the highbrow line. What is wanted is popular reading for the English church and chapel folk; for New York Irish; Orthodox Balkan peasants and Mujiks; French and Italian Catholics; and Jews throughout the world; Indian and Algerian Moslems.

'Articles should give striking actualities, and description of scenes; picturesque details. Rivet the British onto Holy Land, Bible and New Testament.

'Jam Catholics on the Holy Places, Sepulchre, Via Dolorosa, and Bethlehem; dim religious light, chant; Irish, English, Franks, Savoyards, and Sicilians once again in sacred Fane.

'Fix Orthodox on ditto, laying stress on peace in Holy Places now the Turk has gone.

'Concentrate Jews on full details of colonies and institutes and wailing places. *Vox humana* this part.

'Rally Moslems on absolute Moslem control of Mosque of Omar; quote Sherif's words.

'Perorate all races (not religions), acclaim justice, humility, and nobility of conquerors.'[10]

Lawrence's visit to Cairo also enabled him to catch up on Intelligence about recent political developments. Among the most serious questions to be faced were those which had been raised by the Bolshevik Revolution of early November. The new Russian regime was vehemently opposed to the war and had taken immediate steps to reach an armistice with the Central Powers. This meant that Turkey would soon be able to transfer troops from the Caucasus Front to Palestine and Mesopotamia.

The Revolution had another disconcerting consequence. Within days of seizing control, the Bolsheviks had published secret Allied treaties including the Sykes-Picot Agreement. During the following weeks, these texts had appeared in newspapers throughout the world. The Sykes-Picot terms were a gift to Turkish propaganda, and British officials had waited anxiously for Arab reaction.

This had not been slow in coming. On November 26th, Wilson reported that Hussein had 'hinted that H. M. Government possibly had some secret understanding with France and that Zeid and Feisal were being delayed by us from advancing north on this account . . . the King expressed his distrust of French policy and . . . stated that Syria was his . . . His honour was concerned . . . as he had promised the Syrians he would give them help and never desert them.'[11]

It was feared that Arab support might disappear completely unless the Allies took some step to counteract the damage done by the Sykes-Picot revelation. The situation was made still more fraught by the release, at much the same time, of the Balfour Declaration, which provided for a Jewish 'national home' in Palestine. Reviewing the situation, Clayton wrote to Sykes: 'The lack of any definite pronouncement against annexation, especially in Syria, is causing distrust and uneasiness . . . The general principles of the Anglo-French Agreement are known, but there is still no certain knowledge of *Entente* intentions for the future. As regards Syria, there is an impression that we may be only marking time until our military successes place us in a position to hand [it] over to France with as few pledges as possible. This suspicion is ever present in the mind of the Sherif of Mecca . . .

'The recent announcement of His Majesty's Government on the Jewish question has made a profound impression on both Christians and Moslems who view with little short of dismay the prospect of seeing Palestine and even eventually Syria in the hands of the Jews, whose superior intelligence and commercial abilities are feared . . .

'All the above facts tend to prepare the ground for German-inspired . . . propaganda and pave the way for an attractive proposal [to the Arabs] for independence under nominal Turkish suzerainty. There appears every prospect of such a proposal . . . being made before long . . . Until these suspicions are set at rest no amount of oratory or propaganda can produce any real Arab unity of purpose, nor can the position be secure'.[12] Clayton argued that it was essential for the Allies to forestall any Turkish offer of Arab self-government, and that France should therefore 'make a definite pronouncement disclaiming any idea of annexation in Syria (including the Blue area [i.e. Lebanon]) and emphasising their intention of assuring the liberty of *all* Syrians and helping them along the path towards independence . . . This is particularly urgent. We cannot hope for unity and enthusiasm amongst the various Arab factions until it is done.'[13]

While Lawrence was in Cairo, news arrived which confirmed that the Turks were trying to use Sykes-Picot as a means of detaching the Arabs from the Allied side. Hussein passed on to Wingate the text of a letter which Jemal Pasha had recently sent to Feisal, alluding to the Sykes-Picot terms and offering talks. Jemal had written: 'There is only one standpoint from which your revolt can be justified in the interest of the Arabs, and that is the possibility of establishing an independent Arab Government, which would secure the independence, dignity and splendour of Islam under its influence. But what sort of an independence can you conceive in an Arab Government to be established, after Palestine has become an international country, as the Allied Governments have openly and officially declared, with Syria completely under French domination and with Irak and the whole of Mesopotamia forming part and parcel of British possessions? . . . Perhaps you had not foreseen these results at the outset. But I am hoping that the spectacle of the British conquering Palestine will reveal to you this truth in all its nakedness. It is indeed very tragical to see these truths revealed so terribly. Only it is comforting to know that it is not yet too late to limit the disaster or remedy the errors committed. If you admit this truth there is nothing easier than to announce a general amnesty for the Arab revolt and reopen negotiations with a view to solving the problem in favour of Islam. I am convinced that in writing this letter I am discharging a religious duty.'[14]

No reply had been sent but, by passing the letter on to Cairo, Hussein was clearly warning the British that he now had the option of making peace with Turkey. Wingate decided that Lawrence should return to Akaba and discuss the matter with Feisal, in case 'any further confirmation of the new Turkish policy could be obtained by interchange of verbal messages between [Feisal] and Jemal.'[15] Lawrence himself may well have made this suggestion.

He reached Akaba on Christmas Day, and encouraged Feisal to send Jemal a reply. One reason for doing so was to exploit dissension in the Turkish staff. Jemal himself was a Muslim traditionalist who would do everything possible to retain the Arab provinces, but there were others who thought differently. Lawrence later wrote: 'We knew the rifts in Turkey, and that Jemal's Islamism was old-fashioned in the eyes of seven in each ten of his nation. By suitably guarded phrases we could throw the odium of the Revolt on the clerical party, and then perhaps the militarists might fall out with them.

'They were constitutionally inclined to quarrel. The Nationalists, our particular target, were . . . a great and growing faction. Their heads were the anti-German section of the General Staff, under Mustapha Kemal Pasha, a hero of Gallipoli. They were real Nationalists, logical believers in their principles. By writing carefully to Jemal we could enlist their dispassionate judgment on our side, showing them the Arab and Turk nationalists were agreed to rid Turkey of her incubus of alien provinces, the dead weight which crippled her "Turki" mission. Self-government to the Arabic speaking areas would set Anatolia free to cultivate the old cradle of its people's birth in Turkestan.'[16] If the nationalists began to favour Arab independence, Jemal would be obliged to follow suit. In this way Feisal might be able to obtain his goal whether Turkey was defeated by the Allies or not.

Lawrence saw the correspondence as an insurance, knowing as he did that Britain was secretly negotiating with Turkish conservatives. In the draft *Seven Pillars* (but not in the final text) he wrote: 'Feisal, with my full assistance, sent back tendentious answers to Jemal, argumentative enough to cause to continue the exchange: and it continued brilliantly.'[17] In due course, the nationalist officers began writing separately to Feisal, and Jemal was forced to concede more and more of the Arab demands. Very little about these 'long complicated negotiations' was disclosed either to Cairo or to Hussein. Lawrence wrote: 'We feared that the British might be shaken at Feisal's apparent mistrust of them in entertaining separate negotiations, after their own model. Yet, in fairness to the fighting Arabs, we could not close all avenues of accommodation with Turkey.'[18]

Lawrence's account of this correspondence fails to mention one important aspect of the situation. For a time, the Sykes-Picot revelations were very damaging indeed to Britain's relationship with the Arabs. It was inevitable that Arab leaders, threatened with European domination after the war, would open contacts with Muslim Turkey. If Lawrence had opposed such moves, he would not have prevented them, and the issue might have destroyed the trust between himself and Feisal. It must have seemed better that any exchanges took place with his full knowledge, and if possible under his influence.

Lawrence had returned to Akaba during a lull in Arab operations. The Shobek expeditions were on their way, but had not yet launched their attacks. Meanwhile another force was beginning to push forward against the Turks at Aba el Lissan.

During the preceding months, the Akaba base had been greatly developed. The armoured cars, no longer needed at Wejh, had been transferred there, and a motor-track had been constructed from Akaba through Wadi Itm up onto the Guweira plain. A permanent advance headquarters had been established there for Feisal's army.

At the end of December, Joyce decided to attempt an experimental raid on the railway with the cars. If they could manage the terrain between Guweira and Mudawara, a long stretch of the line would be at their mercy. A secondary objective was to divert Turkish attention from the operations at Aba el Lissan.

Joyce himself took charge of the expedition, which was not accompanied by an Arab escort of any kind. After the route had been reconnoitred by Rolls-Royce tenders, the armoured cars attacked the line at two points. The results were not very great, but the experiment of getting to the line had succeeded. Lawrence, who was keeping Joyce company, was delighted by this mechanised warfare. He wrote in *Seven Pillars*: 'for the first time I was at a fight as spectator. The novelty was most enjoyable. Armoured car work seemed fighting de luxe, for our troops, being steel-covered, could come to no hurt. Accordingly we made a field-day of it like the best regular generals, sitting in laconic conference on our hill top and watching the battle intently through binoculars.'[19] From this time on, the cars could dominate the line to Medina, and it would be possible to halt supplies to the Turkish garrison there at will. For the moment, however, Lawrence was happy to leave the line working intermittently.[20]

The raid had also succeeded in distracting the Turks from Aba el Lissan. By January 6th the pass was once again in Arab hands, and the Turks were soon forced back to within three miles of Maan itself.

On his return to Akaba, Lawrence began to form a personal bodyguard. The price on his head was steadily rising, and this greatly increased the risk to his safety when moving through areas where local allegiance was doubtful. Sooner or later someone would be tempted by the reward, and after the experience at Deraa he was determined never again to fall into Turkish hands alive. He wrote about the bodyguard in *Seven Pillars*: 'I began to increase my people to a troop, adding such lawless men as I found, fellows whose dash had got them into trouble elsewhere . . . I paid my men six pounds a month, the standard army wage for a man and camel, but mounted them on my own animals, so that the money was clear income: this made the service enviable, and put the eager spirits of the camp at my disposal. For my time-table's sake, since I was more busy than most, my rides were long, hard and sudden. The ordinary Arab, whose camel represented half his wealth, could not afford to founder it by travelling my speed: also such riding was painful for the man . . . Fellows were very proud of being in my bodyguard, which developed a pro-fessionalism almost flamboyant. They dressed like a bed of tulips, in every colour but white; for that was my constant wear, and they did not wish to seem to presume . . . In my service nearly sixty of them died.'[21]

Early in the new year Lawrence finished a political essay that he had been thinking about for some weeks. Like other British officials, he was worried by the activities of various groups of Syrian intellectuals living in exile. Some of these were opposed to the idea that Feisal might become leader of their country, and were putting out increasingly anti-Sherifian propaganda. In the wake of the Sykes-Picot disclosure, the protestors might well be susceptible to Turkish offers. Moreover, if the future of Syria were to be decided on the principle of self-determination, their complaints would at the very least confuse the issue, and might well obscure the extent of local support for Feisal.

In this essay, which he called 'Syrian Cross-Currents', Lawrence dismissed in turn the various anti-Sherifian elements. Some of these were Christians, 'whose "nationalism" is [no] more than a pretty name for a European control, loose enough to give their co-religionists excessive place in the administration.' Others were survivors of the pre-war Muslim intelligentsia, who 'spoke foreign languages as often as they could, wore European clothes, were often wealthy, used to entertain and be entertained by foreigners, and impressed themselves more deeply upon foreign visitors than their numbers or home influence warranted. Their political ideals were culled from books. They had no programme of revolt, but many ideas for the settlement after one. Such and such were the rights of Syria, such her boundaries, such her future law and constitution. They formed committees in Cairo, Paris, London, New York, Beyrout, Berlin and Berne to influence European Powers to go on spinning real dreams. Their habits made Syria uncongenial to them, and most of them lived in foreign countries.'[22]

After three years of Jemal's dictatorship, none of these vociferous intellectual nationalists was in touch with the situation in Syria. However, the warmth of Feisal's reception in the north had shown the real strength of Arab sentiment among the ordinary people there: 'Now that we can feel the full vigour, we realise how jejune the former political groups have become, and how little they can claim to represent the feeling of Syria to-day. The . . . factions go on blind-foldedly, balancing this party with that party, and offsetting this programme with that programme in memoranda and solemn interviews with European statesmen, while in the disputed country the Sherifians set their teeth and work . . .

'The phrase "Arab Movement" was invented in Cairo as a common denomination for all the vague discontents against Turkey which, before 1916, existed in the Arab provinces. In a non-constitutional country these naturally took on a revolutionary character, and it was convenient to pretend to find a common ground in all of them. They were most of them very local and very jealous, but they had to be considered, in the hope that one or other of them might bear fruit. The day the Sherif declared himself ended this phase of the question. We had found one Arab who believed in himself and his people, and fortunately it was the noblest family of them all. Since then there has been for us no question of any "Arab Movement." We have supported the Sherifian movement, and have tried to help him gather into his own society such Arab side and sub-currents as his progress encountered.

'Needless to say the Arab parties are not all ready to welcome an imposed head. The renegade Moslems, the Christians, and all other sects (there are few parties whose real platform is not sectarian) are dissatisfied.'[23] Lawrence argued that the real cause of their dislike for the Sherif was his orthodoxy in religious matters. However, compared to a leader such as ibn Saud, Hussein was a progressive: 'Even in the holy cities he dilutes the *Sheria* [Islamic Law]; in the provinces, he abandons it altogether for customary law. For a first offence in Wahabi Nejd the right hand is cut off, for the second the tongue is torn out, for the third the offender is banished to a desert without food or water. In Mecca the worst penalty is imprisonment.

'For his northern provinces, whose complex population and commerce make a simple code impossible, he has designated his more plastic son, Feisal, as administrator. His promised programme for Syria may not be sufficient to enlist . . . the support of Syrians in Europe and America; but the Syrians of Syria are enlisting by the thousands in the ranks of his armies. Arabs in Egypt and elsewhere have spoken and written against him. Feisal will not hear of a press propaganda of his ideas; but no free Arab has yet fired a shot against him or his forces, and every advance of his armies is done, not merely by consent, but by the actual brains and hands of the local people, in the strenuous field of rebellion. There is no "Hejaz force" in Syria. Feisal accepts any volunteer for his service, allowing him to preach what he pleases and pray as he pleases so long as he will fight against the Turks. He says always that neither England nor France nor Turkey will give over to the Arabs one square foot of unconquered ground, but that each new village occupied, each new tribe enrolled by Arab effort, is one more step forward towards the Arab state . . .

'The Syrians abroad are as anxious as the Syrians in Syria to obtain deliverance from the Turk, but desire more elaborate reforms when he is removed, and particularly desire a leading voice in the decision of what these reforms are to be. They have a pathetic belief in the idiot altruism of Britain and France. Themselves hardly capable of courage or unselfishness, they credit us with little else. For their sake (or rather for their words' sake) we are to pull down the new (and to us rather comfortable) Moslem Power we have so carefully set up, to launch armed expeditions into Syria, expel the Turks, and police the country at their direction, while they exhaust upon it the portfolio of constitutions that Abbé Sieyes [a leading constitutional theorist of the French Revolutionary era] must have bequeathed to them. In return we are to have their gratitude, afterwards. The only difference between the Sherif's conquest of Syria and theirs (and they call it such a little difference!) is that the Sherif achieves it by the hands of the Syrians themselves, and they wish it achieved by our blood . . . But from our point of view it may be argued that, in these times of crisis, our interests may lead us to support those who adventure their lives in arms on our side (even if they do not please all who call themselves our friends), rather than to rebuff the armed supporters in favour of wordy persons who claim to represent – behind our line – a higher form of culture.'[24]

This paper was not published in the *Arab Bulletin*, but was printed for even more restricted circulation as an 'Arab Bulletin Supplementary Paper'. In this form, it would not be seen by French officials.

On January 10th Lawrence set out for Aba el Lissan with his new body-guard: there he waited for news of the Shobek and Tafileh operations. When he heard that Nasir had successfully cut the line, he rode north to join the Arab forces. By the time he reached Tafileh the village had been in Arab hands for five days: the first objective of the Dead Sea campaign had been achieved. Sherif Zeid had now arrived to represent Feisal, bringing orders that the expedition should push on as soon as possible towards Kerak, about thirty miles farther north.

Lawrence soon realised that this might be difficult, as the local situation was far from satisfactory. Among the bedouin, tribal loyalty was everything, and the men could usually be relied upon to follow their chiefs. In settled villages like Tafileh, things were very different. Political loyalties were complex, and winning the populace over to Feisal's cause would be a long and delicate process. He reported to Clayton: 'Affairs are in rather a curious state here. The place surrendered (after two false reports and a little fighting at the last) on the 15th. The local people are divided into two very bitterly opposed factions, and are therefore terrified of each other and of us. There is shooting up and down the streets every night, and general tension . . . We have about five hundred men in the place, and are quite secure, of course. Flour and barley are, however, dear . . . and very difficult to find . . . There is a great lack of local transport . . . Zeid is rather distressed by the packet of troubles we are come in for (amongst other things a colony of besieged Moors and a swarm of destitute, but very well fed, Armenians) and is pulled here and there by all sorts of eager newcomers all intriguing against one another like cats.'[25]

Lawrence still hoped that Kerak and Madeba could be under Sherifian control by January 26th. However, this would depend on the attitude of local leaders farther north. If it were necessary to take the villages by force, more funds would be needed to raise a sufficient body of men, and this would involve further delay.

In the meantime he was preoccupied 'trying to find out who was for us, and where they were. The conflicts of ideas, local feuds, and party interests are so wild (this being the moment of anarchy the whole district has been longing for for years), that hardly anyone could straighten them out in a hurry.'[26]

On January 23rd the Turks quite unexpectedly sent out a large expedition to recapture Tafileh. The first contacts with Arab outposts took place during the following afternoon, and by nightfall the attackers were threatening the village itself. Next morning, however, the Arabs began a counter-attack which steadily grew in vigour. After a day of hard fighting, the Turks were driven back into Wadi Hesa, a precipitous ravine lying to the north of Tafileh. During the night the survivors of the attacking force were harried mercilessly by local Arabs, and many others died of wounds or exposure. Lawrence later estimated that up to a thousand Turks may have perished; some two hundred were captured, along with valuable field artillery. Arab losses were about twenty-five killed and forty wounded.

This was the first time that an Arab force to which Lawrence was acting as adviser had fought a battle on conventional lines. He had taken a key role in the day's events, overturning Jaafar Pasha's original idea of moving from the village to a defensive position farther south. After some indecision, Zeid had put his weight behind Lawrence's plan.

Although the outcome had been a crushing defeat for the Turks, Lawrence wrote in *Seven Pillars* of the bitterness he felt about the decision to fight an orthodox battle, when he could probably have avoided an engagement altogether. His chosen tactics had been 'villainous, for with arithmetic and geography for allies we might have spared the suffering factor of humanity . . . We could have won by refusing battle, foxed them by manoeuvring our centre as on twenty such occasions before and since . . . By my decision to fight, I had killed twenty or thirty of our six hundred men, and the wounded would be perhaps three times as many. It was one-sixth of our force gone on a verbal triumph, for the destruction of this thousand poor Turks would not affect the issue of the war . . . This evening there was no glory left, but the terror of the broken flesh, which had been our own men, carried past us to their homes.'[27]

Lawrence also saw that the battle would delay the northward advance, and the inevitable pause for recuperation would impose a heavy drain on the limited funds available. There had been a miscalculation at the outset about the money required, and both he and Zeid were now urgently appealing for more.[28] On the day after the battle Lawrence wrote to Clayton: 'The advance on Kerak has been delayed, partly because Zeid is fearful, partly for lack of money, partly because of the Turkish counter-attack, which developed yesterday into a warm affair . . . Victory upsets the Arab army, so I'm afraid we will stick here for a bit . . . If Zeid was not so timid, or if I had cash, we would be in Madeba tomorrow.'[29]

A few days earlier a small force under Abdullah el Fair had been instructed to destroy the Turkish lighters used to carry produce up the Dead Sea from Kerak to Jericho. Since then there had been no news, and as there was no immediate prospect of an advance, Lawrence decided to go himself and see what was happening. As a result of his prodding, the operation got under way. On January 28th, Abdullah el Fair led a force of seventy picked horsemen against the Turkish position at El Mezraa, on the Dead Sea coast west of Kerak, where a natural harbour was being used as the southern terminus for the supply traffic. The base huts were burned down and the boats (six dhows and a launch) scuttled in deep water: sixty Turkish prisoners were taken, along with ten tons of grain. The second of Allenby's requirements had been met two weeks ahead of time, with no Arab casualties.

Lawrence had calculated that some £30,000 would be necessary if the advance were to continue. When the winter weather turned to snow, making immediate action even less likely, he decided to return to Guweira and collect the money himself.

His arrival, on February 5th, coincided with a visit by Lieutenant-Colonel Alan Dawnay, who had recently been given responsibility for liaison between the EEF and the Revolt. The increasing scale and complexity of the campaign in Syria called for a good deal of staff work, and Dawnay's role would be to direct a small 'Arab Operations' team in Cairo. He would work closely with the Arab Bureau, which continued to handle Intelligence.

This appointment brought a strength to the Revolt which it had hitherto lacked. There would now be a relatively senior officer in Cairo working exclusively on the Arab campaign. Dawnay was able to translate the suggestions put forward by Lawrence and others into formal plans which could be acted upon swiftly at headquarters. In addition, he had the standing to see that requests for supplies, air reconnaissance, bombing raids, etc. were given prompt consideration. Lawrence later wrote: 'Dawnay was Allenby's greatest gift to us . . . He was a professional soldier and so had the class-touch to get the best out of the proper staff at G.H.Q. . . . He married war and rebellion in himself: in the way that . . . it had been my dream every regular officer would do it. Yet in three years' practice only Dawnay succeeded, and he on his first visit . . . He spent twenty days in Akaba and Guweira, and went back with despatches to

Allenby, showing all our needs (far more and other than we thought) in stores and funds and arms, and personnel and direction . . .

'Indeed, his taking charge of us was a revolution in our history. Hitherto the Arab movement had lived as a one-wild-man show . . . Henceforward Allenby counted it as . . . part of his tactical scheme, and the responsibility upon us of doing better than he wished, knowing that forfeit for our failure would be paid in his soldiers' lives, removed it from the sphere of joyous adventure, and often frightened us.'[30]

During this first visit by Dawnay to Arab headquarters there were wide-ranging talks. He reported to GHQ that he had been able to tour 'a considerable portion of the area of operations in company with Lt.-Col. Joyce and Djafer Pasha – respectively *de facto* and *de jure* commanders of the Northern Arab Army – also to discuss prospective plans in detail with Sherif Feisal and Major Lawrence'.[31]

On the basis of these discussions, Dawnay concluded that there was now scope for two quite different types of Arab operation. The first was loosely organised guerilla action, carried out mostly by local men. The Revolt had hitherto consisted almost entirely of such operations, and, in the near future, they would be used to complete the Dead Sea campaign. Secondly, there was now scope for more conventional action, to be carried out by Jaafar Pasha's Arab regulars. By the end of January the regular force at Akaba totalled more than three thousand men. It was equipped with artillery and machine guns, and could also call on the French artillery detachment, British armoured cars, and two British-crewed 10-pounder guns mounted on Talbot lorries. In addition, the RFC Flight of six aircraft at Akaba was by this time carrying out reconnaissance and bombing missions with great effect.

Hitherto, the regulars had served mainly to secure Feisal's base against attack from Maan. This danger had now passed, and Jaafar, Nuri, and other senior officers believed that the time had come to embark on more ambitious operations. Consequently, it was agreed at the Guweira talks that preparations should be made for an offensive against the Turkish forces centred on Maan. The objectives would be: 'The destruction of the enemy's 1st Composite Force and the capture of Maan, with a view to the permanent isolation of all Turkish forces south of the latter, the ultimate capitulation of whom should, in these circumstances, become merely a question of time.'[32]

The British officers had argued that a frontal attack on the Maan defences should nonetheless be avoided. Dawnay wrote: 'having in view the clearly defined limitations of the Arab Army and the material of which it is composed, it must be assumed that a direct attack upon the strong, prepared positions immediately covering Maan is impracticable, and, if attempted, would inevitably result in failure, if not actual disaster.'[33] Instead, the Arab regulars should try to cut the railway north of Maan compelling the Turks to leave their prepared defences in order to restore supplies. Fighting would then take place on ground more favourable to the Arabs. If, at the same time, the British armoured cars attacked the line south of Maan, the chances of reducing the garrison to surrender seemed excellent.

Before these operations could begin, however, the regulars would need another seven hundred camels as well as 150 transport mules. As soon as Lawrence could be spared from the Dead Sea operations, he was to visit the Azrak district and buy five hundred riding camels. The mules, with two hundred baggage camels, would be obtained from Egypt.

Another aspect of the Syrian operations which Dawnay sought to clarify was the structure of command among the various British officers involved. In a separate report, he noted that the existing arrangements had grown up piecemeal to meet immediate needs. As a result, some officers were carrying out duties which bore little relation to their original appointments, and there were also anomalies in rank.

In particular, the duties of Joyce and Lawrence clearly called for redefinition. During recent months, Lawrence had spent very little time at Feisal's headquarters, and Joyce had taken over much of his original role as military adviser. As Lawrence later wrote: 'It was Joyce who ran the main lines of the Revolt, while I was off on raids, or making plans for advances. I acted as his main source of Intelligence.'[34]

Similarly, when Joyce came to Akaba, his main duty had been to work as Base Commandant, responsible for supporting Feisal's army. He was also there to advise and control the Arab regulars training under Jaafar Pasha. Now that Feisal's headquarters had been moved inland to Guweira, and the regulars were about to undertake offensive operations, the actual work of Base Commandant at Akaba was being carried out by a subordinate, Major Scott.

Dawnay proposed that the British staff with Feisal should be established as a formal organisation, and that the officers involved should be given ranks and duties which corresponded more closely to the work they were actually doing. This would mean changes at all levels. He recommended that Joyce, who was in command of 'all British troops in the area, also *de facto* director of Arab operations in the field,'[35] should be reclassified as a Special Service officer, grade one, while Lawrence should be classified as a Special Service officer, second grade.

After the Guweira meeting, Lawrence returned to Tafileh with a small party of Arabs, each of whom carried two thousand of the thirty thousand sovereigns allocated to the Dead Sea operations. Rain and blinding snow turned the three-day journey northwards over muddy tracks into a test of endurance, and several of the camel-men dropped out. Some were delayed for several days.

By the time Lawrence reached Tafileh on February 11th, he was exhausted. To his disappointment, he found that no preparations had been made for an advance. It seemed that the tactical advantage of the Tafileh victory had been entirely wasted. He wrote to Clayton: 'Zeid hummed and hawed, and threw away his chance of making profit from it. He had the country from Madeba at his feet. These Arabs are the most ghastly material to build into a design.'[36]

After discussing the situation, Lawrence concluded that Zeid's force no longer had the capacity or the will to take the northern villages on their own. The Turks would first have to be weakened by bedouin attacks from east of the railway, which Lawrence decided to organise. He told Clayton: 'Zeid having lost his frontal chance, I am stirring up the Sukhur to cut across the line by Ziza, and raise Cain about Madeba, Wadi Sirr, Ghor el Riha. If I get them to taste I'll ride with them, but I am getting shy of adventures. I'm in an extraordinary position just now, *vis-à-vis* the Sherifs and the tribes, and sooner or later must go bust. I do my best to keep in the background, but cannot, and some day everybody will combine and down me. It is impossible for a foreigner to run another people of their own free will, indefinitely, and my innings has been a fairly long one.'[37]

He thought that the money he had brought up from Guweira would be sufficient to finance his own plan and also to meet Zeid's legitimate needs: 'This £30,000 will last the northern tribes this month, and have enough over to carry us into the middle of March.'[38]

Two days later the weather improved, and he set off on a reconnaissance of the south-eastern shore of the Dead Sea, to look at possible approaches to Kerak from this side. He was accompanied for part of the way by Lieutenant Kirkbride, who was visiting the area to gather information for EEF Intelligence. Kirkbride spoke Arabic, and was delighted when Lawrence suggested that he should transfer to the Arab forces.

Having successfully completed this journey, Lawrence decided to examine the lie of the land between Tafileh and the northern end of the Dead Sea. He took a sheikh from Kerak as his guide, and in two days they travelled to the edge of the Jordan valley and back. The results were entirely satisfactory. Lawrence later wrote that it had been 'a complete and profitable reconnaissance, very assuring for our future success. I felt that each step of our road to join the British to the north of the Dead Sea was possible for us: and most of them easy. The weather was so fine that we might reasonably begin at once: and we could hope to finish in a month.'[39]

He rode back to Tafileh on February 18th, but when he explained the favourable situation to Zeid, the latter was unimpressed. In the early draft of *Seven Pillars* there is an account of what followed which differs significantly from the published version: 'Zeid stopped me, and said, "But that will need a lot of money." I said not at all: that our funds in hand would cover it, and more. Zeid said that he had nothing: and when I gaped at him muttered rather shame-facedly that he had spent what I had brought. I thought he was joking, but he went on to say that so much had been due to Dhiab el Auran, sheikh of Tafileh, and so much to the men of Senefhe, Aima, Buseira and the other villages: and so much to the Jazi, and so much to the Zebn Beni Sakhr.

'All such expenditure would be entirely profitless for an advance, indeed, was conceivable only if we were on the defensive. The peoples named were the sedentary and nomad elements centring in Tafileh, men whose blood-feuds made them impossible for any invasion of Kerak, or for use northward of Wadi Hesa. The Sherifs, as they advanced, enrolled all the men of every district at a monthly wage: but it was understood on both sides that the wage was fictitious, paid only if some special reason made the area critical. Feysul had more than forty thousand on his Akaba books: and his whole subsidy from England would not pay seventeen thousand. The wages of the rest were nominally due and often asked for: but not a proper debt. However, Zeid said that he had paid them.

'I was aghast, for this meant the complete ruin of my plans and hopes: but remembered in time that [the last of] the money had only arrived twenty-four hours earlier, and that it was physically impossible to pay it out in so short a period. There were not enough clerks and secretaries available to count and enter it. But Zeid stuck to his word that it had all gone. We had an unpleasant scene, and afterwards I went off to Nasir, who was in bed with fever, and asked him for the truth. He was very despondent and said that everything was wrong – those about Zeid stupid and cowardly and dishonest, and Zeid too young and shy to counter them.

'All night I thought over what could be done, but found a blank wall staring me every way in the face: and when morning came could only send a last word to Zeid that, if he would not return me the money, I must go away: putting into words what had hitherto been better understood, that I was in no way under his orders or responsible to him; rather the contrary: that in all respects I expected to have my wishes considered, and not acted against without due and previous explanation: and that where the British provided, through me, the whole resources for a particular operation, it should follow, as exactly as possible, my instructions.

'He sent back a supposed statement of account of the spent money, and I had no choice but to leave at once.'[40]

For the second time, Lawrence would be unable to fulfil a promise he had volunteered to Allenby. The loss of such a huge sum meant that there was no longer any hope of taking the northern villages. Worse still, without a further advance, most of the territory already taken would soon be recaptured by the Turks.

He had always feared that the moment would come when one of the principal Arab leaders ignored his advice. This one act might destroy his authority completely. Only a week before, he had warned of the danger in his letter to Clayton. Now, he felt that his only course was to quit the Arab operations. Perhaps he would take the home leave he had already been promised, and return later to Intelligence duties at GHQ.

As he was preparing to set off, Joyce arrived unexpectedly with Marshall, the British doctor from Akaba: 'They had ridden here from Guweira to give us a pleasant surprise, and happened on this most inauspicious moment. I explained to them what Zeid had done, and that I was going across to Allenby to explain, and to put my further employment in his hands. There was no chance of me being sent back, since my explanation of the failure of our advance and of the loss of the money was the lame one that my faulty judgment had been still unable to distinguish between trusty and untrusty Arab agents: and I would be glad not to come back to the humiliation of being tricked in confidence, after such and so long service with the Arabs.'[41] Joyce tried to persuade Zeid to release the money, but had no success. He therefore agreed to close down Lawrence's affairs and disperse the bodyguard. On February 19th, Lawrence left for the British lines at Beersheba, accompanied by an escort of only four men.

When he reached Allenby's headquarters, he found Hogarth waiting for him. 'To him I said that I had made a mess of things: for me the play was over, and I had come to beg Allenby to find me some smaller part elsewhere. I had put all of myself into the Arab business, and had come to wreck in it just as the tide turned towards success. The fault lay in my sick judgment, bitterest because the occasion was Zeid, own brother to Feisal and a little man I really liked. I now had left no tricks worth a meal in the Arab market-place, and wanted . . . to pillow myself on duty and obedience, irresponsibly.

'Since landing in Arabia I had had options and requests, never an order: and I was surfeited, tired to death of free-will . . . For a year and a half I had been in motion, riding a thousand miles each month upon camels, with added nervous hours in crazy aeroplanes, or rushing across country in powerful cars. In my last five actions I had been hit, and my body so dreaded further pain that now I had to force myself under fire. Generally I had been hungry: and lately always cold: and that and the dirt had poisoned my hurts into a festering mass of sores.

'However, these worries would have taken their due petty place had it not been for the rankling fraudulence which had to be my mind's habit: that pretence to lead the national uprising of another race, the daily posturing in alien dress, preaching in alien speech: with behind it a sense that the "promises" on which the Arabs worked were worth what their armed strength would be when the moment of fulfilment came. The fraud – if fraud it was – was shared with Feisal in full knowledge: and we had comforted ourselves that perhaps peace would find the Arabs in a winning position (if such poor creatures, unhelped and untaught, could defend themselves with paper tools), and meanwhile we conducted their necessary, honourable war as purely and as cheaply as men could... but now by my sin this last gloss had been taken from me in Tafileh. To be charged against my conceit were the causeless and ineffectual deaths of those twenty Arabs and seven hundred Turks in Wadi Hesa. My will had gone, and I feared longer to be alone, lest the winds of circumstance or absolute power or lust blow my empty soul away.'[42]

Years later, Lawrence told Liddell Hart: 'I was a very sick man, again, you know: almost at breaking point.'[43]

CHAPTER 23

A False Start
February – May 1918

WHEN Lawrence saw Clayton, he realised at once that he would not be allowed to give up his work with the Arabs. There was no place for defeatism in the mood now prevailing at Allenby's headquarters.

Earlier that month, General Smuts had travelled out from England on the instructions of the War Cabinet. Now that the Russians had made peace, Britain was, in effect, the only Allied power fighting against Turkey. The Cabinet had therefore decided that victory in this theatre should be given first priority, even if this meant that no offensive could be undertaken on the Western Front. They hoped that a British advance to Damascus and Aleppo would force the Turks to sue for peace.

Smuts had reached EEF headquarters in mid-February, and spent several days in talks with Allenby and his staff. There was general agreement that the best hope of a rapid victory lay in Palestine, rather than Mesopotamia. Smuts therefore recommended that Mesopotamian operations should be placed on a defensive footing, releasing two infantry divisions and a cavalry brigade for Allenby's campaign. There were also plans to reinforce the EEF with Indian units brought from France.

Several attempts had been made to contact Lawrence so that he could take part in these discussions. However, none of the messages had reached him, and by the time he reached GHQ, Smuts had already left for Europe. He now learned that Allenby had been instructed to resume the offensive as soon as possible. Although Jericho had only just been taken, plans were already in train for an advance to Beirut, Damascus and beyond. Arab co-operation would be essential, and there could be no question of Lawrence resigning. He later wrote: 'I accepted the inevitable quietly'.[1]

In this new situation, there was no prospect of early leave either, and he wrote apologetically to his parents: 'This year promises to be more of a run about than last year even! As for coming back – no, not possible now. The situation has changed . . . and I'm to go back till June at least. One rather expected that, I'm afraid.'[2]

At a meeting on February 24th, Allenby told Lawrence of his new requirements. As the EEF moved northwards, there would be a lengthening eastern flank needing protection. Lawrence later explained: 'If he advanced up the coast, the Hejaz railway became a threat to his security, and a burdensome threat, for it lay behind such difficult country, and so far away that he could operate against it only with his full store of transport. Therefore, he called me to consider if the Arabs could play such a part there as to relieve him of care of it.'[3]

Feisal's army would not be able to concentrate on the north until it had closed down the present campaign. This meant disposing of the Turkish forces at Maan as rapidly as possible. Once this had been done, the whole of the Hejaz Railway southward to Medina would fall into Arab hands. Now that Allenby was aiming to secure a total victory within weeks, there was no longer any merit in Lawrence's earlier strategy of keeping the railway open.

Plans for the capture of Maan had been discussed only a few weeks previously, but nothing had yet been done to put them into effect because the problem of transport was still unresolved. To Lawrence's delight, Allenby now agreed to provide seven hundred camels from the Egyptian Camel Transport Company, together with their drivers, equipment and British officers. According to a contemporary memorandum: 'The C.-in-C. has discussed the matter with Major Lawrence, and has given his assent to these camels being placed at the disposal of the Hedjaz Operations on the understanding that they are not to be controlled by the Sherifian forces but by Colonel Joyce'.[4] With this transport, the Arab regulars could operate some eighty miles in advance of their supply base.

On February 26th, Lawrence attended a conference of Allenby's corps commanders. This approved both the plan for taking Maan and a small British operation to be carried out in conjunction with it. To divert Turkish attention from Maan, units of the EEF would make a thrust across the Jordan and attack the Hejaz line below Amman. The first objective would be the small town of Salt, which Allenby hoped to take and hold in order to help secure his inland flank. From there, a raiding force would attempt to blow up an important bridge and a long tunnel on the railway south of Amman. If either of these were destroyed, the Turks would find it difficult to send forces and supplies southward for some time.

Lawrence argued that it would be better not to involve local Arabs in this Amman raid; first, because of the risk of reprisals, and secondly because they might misconstrue the withdrawal of the Amman raiding party to Salt as a retreat. When the British operation was complete, however, he would raise a force locally and occupy the region between Madeba and the Jordan valley, immediately north-east of the Dead Sea. This would help Allenby to retain Salt, and prepare the way for Feisal's next move northward.

The first phase of Arab operations would come to an end with the capture of Maan. The regulars would then be moved to a new base in this area north-east of the Dead Sea, where they could draw supplies from Jericho. If the seven hundred camels lent by Allenby could be retained, this force would be in a position to raid a large section of the railway south of Deraa.

Lawrence's proposals for this latter part of the campaign (largely omitted from the published version of *Seven Pillars*) show that his view of Arab potential had been badly shaken by the experience of the past few months. In the euphoria following the capture of Akaba he had offered to isolate and perhaps even take Deraa. Now, his ideas about the Arab contribution were much more modest, and he hoped that British units would carry out some of the key operations east of the Jordan. He later wrote: 'the second phase of the operation . . . was to be Allenby's grand attack along the whole line from the Mediterranean to the Dead Sea. It was to lead to the capture of Damascus. The Arab role in this would be to cut the railway in the rear of the Turks in Palestine, probably near Deraa. Allenby suggested we ought to take Deraa, and be ready to fight the Turks in their retirement. This sounded like assault tactics, things of which I had no experience, and for which I thought the Arabs had no capacity. So I asked if he would consider lending me the Imperial Camel Brigade as shock troops.

'This splendid unit of picked Yeomen and Australians, mounted on Sudanese camels, had done good service in Sinai . . . but was out of the picture in Palestine proper, and not now in much favour with the great, since the camels were expensive to keep up, and (as they complained) slower than cavalry and little more durable. I . . . knew this heaviness was an accident, due to tactics and training, and that, in fact, any camel would outmarch every horse . . . G.H.Q. did not in the least understand the tactical abilities of camels, and, deceived by their apparent immobility had never given them a chance. They wished to save me from a bad bargain, and asked me, therefore, what I would do with the Brigade if I got it . . . ?

'I said I would march it from the Jordan into the desert, to Azrak, and fall upon Deraa unawares. With fifteen hundreds of such men we could not fail to carry it first try, and the rest of the programme would be easy. Their longest march would be only forty miles a day . . . Smith, the commander of the Camels was sent for to give his opinion. He was all for the effort, and swore that he would be fit on May the fifth, the appointed date. So this was agreed, and he went off with permission to reshape the Brigade for long distance desert riding.'[5]

When these matters had been settled, Lawrence travelled to Jerusalem, where he spent two days with Ronald Storrs, now Military Governor of the city. One irritation now faced by the incumbent of this historic post was a running conflict with Georges-Picot, the French 'High Commissioner for Palestine and Syria', who was still trying to increase French influence by every means at his disposal. Having been denied a role in the administration, Georges-Picot was placing great emphasis on his country's traditional right to protect Roman Catholic interests in the Holy Land. This led him into a series of tortuous intrigues with religious bodies, all of which were designed to underline the special status of France.

Needless to say, these activities were not encouraged by the British. The general disapproval is well conveyed by one official's complaint that 'French political claims in Palestine, disguised though these may be by French pretensions to be regarded as the exclusive protectors of all Latin Christians throughout the East . . . constitute a serious menace to our prestige and the satisfactory military administration of the occupied territories . . . they provoke the jealousy of the Italians, the hostility of Orthodox Christians, and arouse suspicions of bad faith in the minds of both Arab Moslems and Zionists . . . Ever since the anti-clerical regime in France . . . the Vatican has ceased to support French claims, which are essentially political. It is apparent that these French claims are not limited to the Holy Places, but to the whole of the "Holy Land".'[6]

Georges-Picot's intrigues were countered by the British with studied diplomacy, and this often led to situations which bordered on farce. Storrs doubtless gave Lawrence a very entertaining account of these manoeuvrings. According to one of his reports, he had recently been subjected to a 'somewhat prolonged visit' from Georges-Picot, who had 'embarked upon the question of the French "Protection" of the Eastern Latin Church, explaining that he had gathered . . . that persons had expressed surprise at the special honours paid to the French in this connection. He would like to point out that enormous stress was laid on this "Protection" by France . . . and the slightest infringement of it would cause the gravest results. I said . . . I could not see how the matter lay within my competence.

'He then returned to the charge by remarking that the posting of an Italian Guard outside the Holy Sepulchre and the Church of the Nativity at Bethlehem had produced a painful impression upon the Catholics in Jerusalem, an impression which would be intensified when the news became known in Paris. From time immemorial the right of protecting Catholics . . . had been by Treaty the prerogative of the French: the Italians were, he knew, intriguing in every direction, and although he fully admitted the special position of England for the moment, that could be no justification in allowing them to share this holy task. He would do his best to allay feelings both here and in Europe but was seriously afraid that when he reported the matter, as he immediately must, the question would be raised in London. What did I propose to do about it?

'I proposed that I was a Military and not a political Governor and had therefore no authority to concern myself with these distinctions . . .

'In conclusion, Monsieur Picot hinted that the Latin section of the Holy Sepulchre were about to celebrate a Te Deum in which it would be necessary for him to be received with the customary special honours, including the special throne or chair placed at his disposal. He himself was of course quite indifferent to and even averse from these externals, but was obliged to be strict in maintaining the prescriptive rights of his country.

'I said that I could not see that it was for me to intervene in the allotment of seats or pews by any religious community here.

'Not being a Roman Catholic, I have no intention . . . of attending this Te Deum, and if invited shall regret a previous engagement in some distant part of the Zone. It will probably be an affair of some considerable pomp and circumstance and I see no reason in any representative of the British Army, however low in rank, appearing before the public at a marked disadvantage.'[7]

The significance of Georges-Picot's move had only transpired later, when Storrs was visited by one of the Fathers of the Franciscan Convent. The friar had told him that while the Roman Catholic Orders were very willing to celebrate a Te Deum in recognition of the British victory, they were 'repelled by the French Consul General's insistence upon a special place of honour at a service commemorating a campaign in which not one drop of French blood had been shed . . . They were therefore in the dilemma of either appearing to fail in gratitude to the redeemers of the city or of being forced to render undue . . . honours to those who had nothing to do with its redemption'. Storrs had concluded: 'There is no doubt that the Franciscans would do a great deal to be quit of their "Protectors," and to be recognized for what they are, an international institution'.[8]

At some point during this brief visit to Jerusalem, Lawrence was introduced by Storrs to a young American who was gathering material for a series of illustrated lectures about the war. This was Lowell Thomas, an experienced journalist and skilled public speaker, who had arrived in Palestine a few weeks earlier with his photographer, Harry Chase. Thomas had been thrilled by rumours of the Arab Revolt and was delighted to meet one of the leading personalities engaged in it.

The Thomas mission was no ordinary exercise in wartime journalism. It had first been planned in the spring of 1917 with the express purpose of increasing popular support for the war effort in America, and it had the backing of influential figures in the US Administration. The authorities in Whitehall were also keen to help Thomas, in the hope that his work might promote a better appreciation of Britain's part in the struggle. American press coverage during the early stages of the war had sometimes given the impression that the Allied campaigns were being fought largely by Frenchmen and Canadians. In August 1917, the head of the British Bureau of Information in New York, one of whose tasks was to correct this misapprehension, had commended Thomas and Chase to the Department of Information in London: 'the two gentlemen, whose cards I enclose, are about to go to Europe for the purpose of getting material for so called "travelogues." These are very popular in this country and consist in a sort of penny reading illustrated with living and moving pictures . . . the Secretary of War [is] very anxious that these gentlemen should meet with success. Accordingly, anything that you could do for them would be well worth doing . . . I do think it is important to put our case through as many channels as possible . . . and as this project has the blessing of the Administration I think it would be wise to give them some really good interviews. Let them go to really interesting places and try to show up in a good light as compared with the French.'[9]

Thomas had first visited the Western Front, but found that the grim realities of trench warfare offered little material to suit his purpose. On December 10th, having learned of British successes in Palestine, he had written to John Buchan, then Director of the Department of Information in London: 'I am here in Europe at the head of a mission authorised by the United States Government, to gather data and photographic material for a series of illustrated patriotic lectures to be delivered throughout America to help arouse the country to complete support of the Allies . . . A bulletin received to-day states that your Army has captured Jerusalem. From the standpoint of the material we are gathering this event is of the greatest importance, and if it can be arranged, I want to go there at once, accompanied only by my photographer . . . These lectures are to be delivered by me, hence to make them effective pictures must, at least partially, be of things I see personally and which have not already been used for general publication. I have letters from the Secretaries of War, Navy and State requesting that all possible facilities be given my mission.'[10]

Clearly, Thomas was offering Britain an excellent opportunity to 'show up in a good light'. The Department of Information therefore applied to the EEF and the War Office, and on December 21st Thomas and Chase were given permission to visit Palestine. They sailed from Italy on about January 12th.

When Lawrence met Thomas in Jerusalem, the circumstances of the mission were explained to him. Lawrence was enthusiastic about publicity for the Revolt, and understood how important American opinion might be in the ultimate settlement. He talked about the progress of the campaign and the politics of Arab nationalism, and also agreed to pose for Harry Chase on the balcony of the Residency.

Thomas was intrigued by what he had learned and decided to pursue the matter further. Soon after Lawrence's departure he persuaded Allenby to authorise a visit to the Arab forces at Akaba. The decision to grant this request was probably influenced by pressure from London for more coverage of the Revolt. On March 2nd, for example, Sykes had cabled: 'Can you supply as soon as possible a good article on Feisal's operations for world consumption?'[11]

Lawrence next spent a few days in Cairo, where he helped the Arab Bureau with a new map of the region around Maan. He also discussed current plans with Alan Dawnay, whose Hejaz Operations staff was now operating very efficiently (Lawrence wrote in *Seven Pillars*: 'our affairs were now far from haphazard . . . We had supply officers, a shipping expert, an ordnance expert, an intelligence branch'.)[12]

On March 4th, he flew to Akaba to visit Feisal. He explained the new plans agreed with Allenby and discussed the problems he had experienced with Zeid. When he had left Tafileh a fortnight earlier, he had realised that the Turks would be able to recapture the village without difficulty. The latest news suggested a build-up of enemy strength in the region, but Lawrence no longer cared. According to an early draft of *Seven Pillars*, he told Feisal that Tafileh 'now meant nothing to us. In March the two interests were going to be in the extremes of his area, Amman and Maan: and Kerak and Tafileh would be included in their fate. They were not worth losing a man over; indeed, if the Turks moved there, and kept a main force there, they would weaken either the garrison of Maan or the garrison of Amman, and make our real work easier.'[13] Word soon came that Zeid had been forced to retreat, and Tafileh was in Turkish hands within a matter of days. After these discussions Lawrence returned to Cairo.

Some time before, it had been decided that an understudy would have to be found for Lawrence. His role with the tribes had become so important that he was unable to take leave, and there was no one who could replace him if he were killed or seriously wounded. He had suggested that Hubert Young might be a good choice. Young, who spoke Arabic fluently, was still serving in Mesopotamia, where the two had last met in April 1916. At that time he had resented Lawrence's manner and in particular, his disrespectful attitude towards regular soldiers. However, Lawrence now wrote that Young 'should be the right sort of man: the work is curious, and demands a sort of twisted tact, which many people do not seem to possess. We are very short-handed, and it will make things much easier if he fits in well.'[14]

Young arrived in Cairo early in March, and was surprised at the scale of Arab operations: 'I found that Lawrence was only one of the many British officers who were helping the Arabs . . . as soon as the Sherifian revolt took definite military shape, a special liaison staff was formed at General Allenby's G.H.Q. to deal with what were known as Hejaz operations . . . When I arrived at Cairo the "Hedgehog" staff consisted of Colonel Dawnay, G.S.O.1, Captain Pratt Barlow, G.S.O.3, Major Wordie D.A.Q.M.G., and Captain Bennett, staff captain. Dawnay was officially the chief staff officer, just as Joyce was officially the senior British officer with Feisal's army, but Lawrence really counted more than either of them with Allenby and Feisal, and used to flit backwards and forwards between G.H.Q. and Feisal's headquarters as the spirit moved him.'[15]

It was no doubt in recognition of this extraordinary role that Lawrence was promoted Lieutenant-Colonel on March 12th. Many years later he wrote that this was 'to put me on the level with Joyce, who was G.S.O.1. for liaison with the Arab Regular Army, as I was G.S.O.1 for liaison with Bedouins – a scheme worked out by Dawnay.'[16] However, the scheme Dawnay had recommended a month earlier had been different: he had proposed that Joyce should remain senior to Lawrence. It seems likely that the decision to promote Lawrence to equality owed something to Hogarth and Clayton. A telegram from Allenby to the War Office on March 9th stated that Joyce and Lawrence 'should be graded for pay as General Staff Officers, 1st Grade, one for conducting the independent operations of the Bedouin Arabs, the other those of the more regular Arab forces . . . the positions of the two Officers . . . involve great responsibilities, and the results of operations are entirely dependent on their skill and energy.'[17]

Lawrence also learned that he had been awarded a DSO, for his part in the battle of Siel el Hesa outside Tafileh. Later, he claimed to have proposed himself humorously for a naval DSO on the grounds that he had destroyed the Turkish Dead Sea fleet. He thought this much the more worthwhile of the two operations.[18]

On March 15th he returned to Akaba to finalise preparations for the new Arab offensive. It was agreed that the Maan operation should go ahead on the plan drawn up at Guweira three weeks previously. Jaafar Pasha's Arab regulars were to occupy the railway north of the town, while Joyce, with the British armoured cars, went south to Mudawara. Joyce hoped to do so much damage there that Turkish communications with Medina would be broken permanently. Lawrence, for his part, would be responsible for arranging the tribal follow-up to Allenby's thrust across the Jordan.

While waiting for the operations to begin, he travelled up to the Shobek region for a few days to look at the situation and to consult Zeid and Nasir. As the Turks had withdrawn their forces from the region of Tafileh a few days earlier, Zeid's cavalry had reoccupied the village.

During this tour, unpleasant news came from Ali ibn el Hussein, who had passed the winter at Azrak: two of the men there had died of cold. One was an Indian machine-gunner, the other Lawrence's young servant Ali. It was Ali's friend Othman who brought the news. The two had enrolled themselves in Lawrence's service during the journey to Akaba. In *Seven Pillars* (where they are called Daud and Farraj) Lawrence described their high spirits and incessant practical jokes, which must have appealed to his own sense of mischief. Now, however, Othman had changed: 'These two had been friends from childhood, in eternal gaiety: working together, sleeping together, sharing every scrape and profit with the openness and honesty of perfect love. So I was not astonished to see Farraj look dark and hard of face, leaden-eyed and old, when he came to tell me that his fellow was dead; and from that day till his service ended he made no more laughter for us. He took punctilious care, greater even than before, of my camel, of the coffee, of my clothes and saddles, and fell to praying his three regular prayings every day. The others offered themselves to comfort him, but instead he wandered restlessly, grey and silent, very much alone.'[19]

Lawrence returned to Akaba on March 21st. To his surprise, Lowell Thomas arrived shortly afterwards with Harry Chase, following up the story he had scented at Jerusalem. Chase began taking large numbers of photographs and asked Lawrence to sit for more portraits. Thomas doubtless explained that the impact of an illustrated lecture is greatly increased if the slides change frequently, and that he might therefore need several different photographs of some subjects. Lawrence agreed to the portrait sessions, but he saw to it that Chase also photographed the Arab forces and their leaders.

After the war, Thomas would imply that he and Chase had spent a considerable time with Lawrence, working as correspondents accredited to the Arab campaign. He would even claim to have been present during battles against the Turks.[20] The truth was rather different: he spent less than a fortnight with Feisal's army and saw Lawrence for only a few days. Before Thomas and Chase completed their work in Akaba, Lawrence had travelled inland. He later wrote that Thomas 'saw a scoop in our side-show, and came to Akaba (1918) for ten days. I saw him there, for the second time, but went up country to do some other work. He bored the others, so they packed him off by Ford car to Petra, and thence back to Egypt by sea.'[21]

As it happened, Thomas's visit took place during one of the dullest periods of the entire Revolt. The March War Diary of Hejaz Operations noted: 'Sherif Feisal's army did not succeed in attacking the Turks . . . A very sudden and deep fall of snow about March 24th in this area made further operations impossible . . . The main activity . . . has been in establishing supply dumps at Gueira and Abu Lissal, with a view to extended action against Maan.'[22] Two small expeditions earlier in the month had come to nothing because of snow and rain.

It would be eighteen months before Lawrence discovered the real reason that Thomas and Chase had come to Akaba. Thomas knew, with the instinct of a practised journalist, that there would be little popular interest in Arab military achievements and political claims to Syria. However, these would provide a romantic backdrop for the story that was really forming in his mind: that of a young English archaeologist who had become the 'Uncrowned King of Arabia'. Doubtless he was able, like all skilled journalists, to conceal the real drift of his enquiries by displaying profound interest in everything his interviewees talked about. Yet his true intentions are revealed in the glamorous portrait photographs of Lawrence taken by Chase.

It is doubtful that Thomas managed to get many personal details from Lawrence himself, but other British officers freely expressed their admiration for him, and unwittingly provided a great deal of material to fill out this 'human angle'. Thomas later wrote: 'During the time that Mr. Chase and I were in Arabia, I found it impossible to extract much information from Lawrence himself regarding his own achievements. He insisted on giving the entire credit to Emir Feisal and other Arab leaders, and to his fellow adventurers, Colonel Wilson . . . Joyce, Dawnay, Bassett, Vickery, Cornwallis, Hogarth, Stirling, etc., all of whom did magnificent work in Arabia. So to them I went for much of my material, and I am indebted to various members of this group of brilliant men whom General Clayton used in his Near Eastern Secret Corps. Eager to tell me of the achievements of their quiet scholarly companion, they refused to say much about themselves, although their own deeds rivalled those of the heroes of *The Arabian Nights*.'[23] Lawrence commented bitterly: 'His spare credulity they packed with stories about me. He was shown copies of my official reports, and made long extracts or summaries of them. Of course he was never in the Arab firing line, nor did he ever see an operation or ride with me.'[24]

On April 2nd Lawrence set out northwards from Aba el Lissan. He was accompanied by his bodyguard, a large convoy of baggage camels loaded with food and ammunition, and Mirzuk el Tikhemi, a prominent member of Feisal's entourage. They were unsure of the exact date that the EEF would raid Amman, and planned to stay in the desert east of the line until news came that the operation had been successful.

They would then cross the railway to Themed, a watering-place not far from Madeba.

Meanwhile, a large force of local tribesmen would take advantage of the distraction caused by Allenby's raid, and capture the railway stations between Amman and Katrani. The garrisons would be taken to Themed as prisoners. Lawrence later wrote: 'the taking of the four stations should be a picnic. We would then call to us . . . the main Faiz section of the Beni Sakhr and under cover of their cavalry would move to Madeba, and collect there temporary supplies to fit it as our headquarters . . . We ought to complete this work and link up with the British comfortably without firing a shot.'[25]

Although Lawrence did not know it, the EEF raid on Amman had gone badly wrong. Salt had been captured on March 24th, but bad weather hampered further progress. The Turks recognised the threat to the railway, and by the time the attack finally took place their positions had been reinforced. The raiders succeeded in blowing up the line on each side of Amman, but their prime targets, the viaduct and 140-metre tunnel just to the south, were too strongly defended. Worse still, the Turks then launched a strong counter-attack and forced the raiding party to retreat. The withdrawal was precipitate and there had been too little time to prepare adequate defences at Salt. By the morning of April 2nd, the day that Lawrence's expedition set out, the town had been abandoned.

He did not hear of this reverse until he was approaching Themed, and at first did not appreciate the scale of the British defeat. Knowing that the raiding force was supposed to fall back from Amman, he ignored the first rumours of a retreat and continued his part of the operation as planned. Before long, he was joined by the tribesmen who had attacked the line south of Amman. They brought with them some twelve hundred prisoners. Later, when he found out what had really happened at Amman, he realised that nothing useful could be done in the north. To minimise reprisals, the Turkish prisoners were released. Lawrence later wrote: 'We put them back in their stations with apologies for having troubled them.'[26] He returned to the desert east of the railway, and carried out a brief reconnaissance of Amman (then a small village) before going south with his bodyguard; he might yet be able to help with the attack on Maan.

On the way back towards Aba el Lissan, his party marched for some distance along the railway. Near Faraifra they came upon a small Turkish patrol and there was a brief skirmish. During this, Othman (Farraj of *Seven Pillars*) whose lifelong friend Ali had died only weeks before, rode forward in advance of the main party. As he neared the Turks, he fell from his camel. In *Seven Pillars*, Lawrence described what followed:

I was very anxious about Farraj. His camel stood unharmed by the bridge, alone . . . We reached it together, and found there one dead Turk and Farraj terribly wounded through the body, lying by the arch just as he had fallen from his camel. He looked unconscious; but, when we dismounted, greeted us, and then fell silent, sunken in that loneliness which came to hurt men who believed death near. We tore his clothes away and looked uselessly at the wound. The bullet had smashed right through him, and his spine seemed injured. The Arabs said at once that he had only a few hours to live.

We tried to move him, for he was helpless, though he showed no pain. We tried to stop the wide slow bleeding, which made poppy-splashes in the grass; but it seemed impossible, and after a while he told us to let him alone, as he was dying, and happy to die, since he had no care of life. Indeed, for long he had been so, and men very tired and sorry often fell in love with death . . .

While we fussed about him Abd el Latif shouted an alarm. He could see about fifty Turks working up the line towards us, and soon after a motor trolley was heard coming from the north. We were only sixteen men, and had an impossible position. I said we must retire at once, carrying Farraj with us. They tried to lift him, first in his cloak, afterwards in a blanket; but consciousness was coming back, and he screamed so pitifully that we had not the heart to hurt him more.

We could not leave him where he was, to the Turks, because we had seen them burn alive our hapless wounded. For this reason we were all agreed, before action, to finish off one another, if badly hurt: but I had never realized that it might fall to me to kill Farraj.

I knelt down beside him, holding my pistol near the ground by his head, so that he should not see my purpose; but he must have guessed it, for he opened his eyes and clutched me with his harsh, scaly hand . . . I waited a moment, and he said, "Daud will be angry with you," the old smile coming back so strangely to his grey shrinking face. I replied, "Salute him from me." He returned the formal answer, "God will give you peace," and at last wearily closed his eyes.[27]

When Lawrence arrived, he found that the fighting round Maan had already begun. Here too, there had been departures from the agreed plan.

British officers had consistently maintained that the Arabs should draw the Turks away from their prepared defences by cutting the railway farther north. Feisal and Jaafar Pasha had seen the wisdom of this idea, but Nuri as-Said and others in the Arab Army were determined to attack the town directly. A lengthy debate had taken place over these alternatives, and eventually a compromise had been agreed: the Arabs would send three mobile columns against Maan. Two of these would cut the railway, north and south of the town, while the third engaged the main defences. All three forces would then converge in a general attack.[28] The first stages of this modified plan were under way when Lawrence rode in from the north.

The two outer columns had achieved almost complete success. During the night of April 11th, the southern party had attacked and captured Ghadir El Haj station, ten miles from Maan, and on the following day a thousand rails and three culverts had been destroyed. At the same time the northern column had destroyed two hundred rails south of Aneiza station, before attacking the railway near Jerdun. This station too had been occupied and burned, and afterwards another three thousand rails had been destroyed. On April 13th the central column had attacked and captured Semna, a well-defended Turkish position just south of Maan. This was the latest news when Lawrence reached the Arab headquarters.[29]

The fighting around Maan continued indecisively for some days, while the RAF bombed the town and defences. Then, on April 17th, Nuri as-Said led a storming party into the main Turkish positions about the station. The defences here were formidable, and the Arabs found themselves caught in the fire of well-positioned machine guns behind concrete emplacements. There was insufficient artillery cover from their own side, and they were forced to retreat with heavy losses. This was exactly the kind of result the British advisers had feared. Afterwards, the Arabs could only entrench their positions outside the town, and the situation at Maan settled into a stalemate.

Despite this unsatisfactory outcome, Lawrence and the other British officers thought that the regulars had put up an impressive performance. He later wrote: 'we had never expected such excellent spirit and work from our infantry, who fought steadily and cheerfully under machine-gun fire, making clever use of their ground. The gunners worked well, and so little leading was required that we lost only three officers. The general conduct showed us that, given fair technical equipment, the Arabs were good enough for anything, with no need of British stiffening, however weighty the affair. This changed our course of mind for the future, and made us much more free to plan: so the failure was not wholly unredeemed.

'The criticism lay against the direction, which was at fault in undertaking so large a problem with such slender resources: and which had persisted in the face of the truth.'[30]

Another element in the plan was an attack by armoured cars on the railway farther south; this operation began on April 18th. Joyce was too ill to take part, and Dawnay stepped in as commander. The raid involved not only British and tribal forces, but also the newly formed Egyptian Camel Corps under F. G. Peake. Lawrence asked to go too, ostensibly as an interpreter because Dawnay spoke no Arabic. In reality, he was worried that there might be friction between the various racial elements. As he later wrote: 'I knew that one row would spoil the delicate balance of the Arab front: and that rows would come unless ceaseless vigilance were exercised. I was one of the very few people intimate enough with the Arabs to be ceaselessly with them without boring them into sulks. So I tried to god-father every mixed expedition. Dawnay didn't want me hanging about.'[31]

On this occasion his fears proved well founded. After the capture of Tell Shahm station on April 19th, the bedouin set about looting, as was their habit. According to Dawnay's report, while this was going on 'a somewhat dangerous situation arose between the Arabs and the Egyptians; serious consequences were, however, averted by skilful handling of the Bedouin by Colonel Lawrence.'[32]

Years later, Lawrence told his biographer Liddell Hart: 'This was really why I came down. The antipathy of the Egyptians and Bedouin was intense, and the Egyptian effort to save some of the loot from private plundering nearly started a fight. I had a very near call, but just managed to keep the Arabs in hand. Otherwise all the regulars would have been killed.'[33] Elsewhere, he wrote: 'We were all within a hair's breadth of getting scragged.'[34] The incident is described in *Seven Pillars*, but there is no hint there that it had been so serious.

During the following day the force moved southward along the line, and on the 21st it approached Mudawara. This appeared to be too strongly defended for an attack with the forces remaining at Dawnay's disposal, as most of the bedouin had gone back to their tents after the looting at Tell Shahm. However, demolition work on the railway itself continued for several days, and by April 25th a hundred kilometres of line between

Maan and Mudawara had been systematically destroyed. A few days later the *Arab Bulletin* noted: 'providing that the Arabs take advantage of the opportunity created, and by persistent harrying prevent the Turks from repairing the very extensive damage between Maan and Mudawwara . . . railway communication between Medina and the north should now permanently cease, a result which would entail the withdrawal of all Turks south of Maan into Medina and other isolated stations where they could be closely invested and eventually starved out'.[35]

Lawrence had not stayed for the second stage of these operations. When the irregular tribesmen went home, he had seen little risk of further trouble, and on April 22nd returned to Aba el Lissan. His concern now was that the Maan operations were vulnerable to counter-attack from the north. The limited damage done by the British at Amman had soon been repaired, and there was little to prevent the Turks bringing strong reinforcements down the line towards Maan, where Feisal's army was already facing superior numbers.

In order to delay such a move, Lawrence proposed that bedouin forces should mount frequent raids on the railway from Jurf el Derwish northwards. He himself was unable to organise this, as he was about to go to Palestine for meetings at GHQ. Instead, he asked Young to co-ordinate the various regular and tribal elements in the area. He later wrote: 'I wanted Young to try his prentice hand at it, so gave him the idea and my notions of what to use for the job.'[36] Not long afterwards, Dawnay reported: 'Sherif Zeid, accompanied by Captain Young, is operating with a mixed force of regulars and Beni Sakhr tribesmen together with the French artillery detachment and four guns, in the neighbourhood of Jurf el Derwish, the mission of this force being to destroy the railway north and south of Kutrani and to intercept the advent of enemy reinforcements to Maan from the north'.[37]

When Lawrence reached GHQ on May 2nd, he learned to his astonishment that General Bols, Allenby's Chief of Staff, had just launched a further attack on Salt. This had been prompted by Beni Sakhr envoys who had come to the EEF offering Arab help on a large scale. The British action had been taken on the spur of the moment, without reference either to Lawrence or to Dawnay's staff in Cairo.

Lawrence's reaction was one of alarm, because he knew that there was no likelihood of substantial help from the Beni Sakhr. A day later his worst fears were confirmed: the Arabs had done almost nothing. As a result the Turks had been able to seize the roads by which General Chauvel's expedition had advanced. It seemed trapped, and Lawrence was 'sent for and asked to be ready to fly over to Salt, land, and lead the cut-off cavalry via Madeba, Kerak, Tafileh, back to safety. It would have been possible, as there was lots of water and some food. The Turks would have been properly flummoxed! The Staff thought the Salt force were probably cut off from the Jordan by forces too strong to pierce.'[38] In the event, however, a withdrawal across the Jordan proved possible, and Chauvel's force was able to escape. By the time it got back, there had been 1,650 casualties. After this blunder, the General Staff resolved to leave future co-operation with the bedouin to Lawrence, who later wrote: 'They saw that moving irregulars was an art, like moving troops, and agreed to let me know if anything of the sort was ever required.'[39]

There was other disquieting news at British headquarters. Some weeks earlier the German Army had launched a major offensive on the Western Front. The War Office had begun to recall men and equipment to Europe, and by March 27th, Allenby had been told to fall back for the present on a scheme of active defence. During May, nine battalions would have to leave Palestine. Although they were to be replaced by native units from India, the change-over placed an awkward question mark over the timing of the coming offensive.

Any delay would be unwelcome to Feisal, whose confidence had been badly shaken by the earlier British retreat from Salt. The new fiasco would unsettle him further, and Lawrence decided to fly at once to Akaba and explain how it had happened. He later wrote: 'I feared a little its effects on Feisal. Our clean-cut movement had lost its way, since we arrived at Akaba, in a bog of contingencies, no longer alone face to face with a simple enemy, but tied to a leading partner, ever and again playing a self-effacing or self-sacrificing role for his advantage.

'Amman had hurt Feisal, and its grand repetition a month later might drive him to be foolish. Before him Jemal's traps of fair words were always open. It would be wise to get our version spread about Aba el Lissan before the Turkish songs of triumph sounded'.[40]

Lawrence soon learned that his anxiety on this point was justified. Two days earlier the Turks had sent out a messenger with a white flag to the Arab lines in front of Maan. He was carrying a letter to Feisal from Jemal Pasha, written immediately after the new British defeat at Salt. Jemal had written: 'At the present day, the Ottoman Government, the mightiest representative of Islam, has obtained supremacy over the

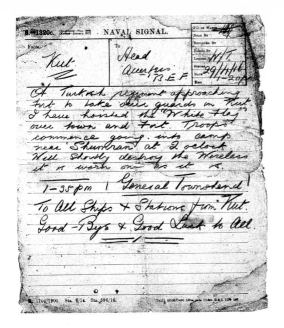

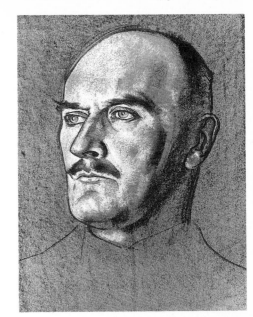

above: Tragic end to an impossible mission: the last radio messages from Kut, 29th April 1915
above right: Allenby by Eric Kennington, a portrait commissioned by Lawrence for *Seven Pillars of Wisdom* and later hung on the staircase at Clouds Hill
below: Gilbert Clayton, head of Cairo Intelligence during 1915 and 1916. One of the most important figures in Lawrence's career
right: S.F. Newcombe in the Hejaz as leader of the British Military Mission, 1917

The Hejaz railway ran through desert for hundreds of miles. Arab attacks forced the Turks to deploy thousands of troops to patrol it

Feisal's camp at dawn, photographed by Lawrence in January 1917. He wrote: 'Most sunrise pictures are taken at sunset, but this one is really a success'

above: Auda aby Tayi, the famous Howeitat
chief with whom Lawrence developed the
successful plan to attack Akaba

right: Emir Feisal, Hussein's third son.
Lawrence wrote: 'I felt at first glance that this
was the man I had come to Arabia to seek'

below: Hussein, Sherif and Amir of Mecca.
Very few photographs survive of this key figure
in the history of the Arab movement

The Arab force on its way to triumph at Akaba, 1917, one of the most important events of the Revolt

Lawrence with his Arab bodyguard, 1918. This personal bodyguard was recruited after Lawrence's capture at Deraa and subsequent escape

Lawrence at Damascus, October 1918: 'Our war was ended'. He left Damascus in the same Rolls-Royce tender after only four days

below left: Lawrence, D.G. Hogarth and Alan Dawnay in Cairo, 1918. Hogarth was then running a branch of the Arab Bureau in Palestine, and Dawnay was responsible to Allenby for liaison with the Arab forces. *below right*: T. E. Lawrence sketched by Augustus John during the Peace Conference in Paris. This drawing epitomised the popular image of 'Lawrence of Arabia'

Churchill, Gertrude Bell and Lawrence, from a larger group photograph taken during
an excursion on camel-back to the Pyramids, 20 March 1921

The Cairo Conference, March 1921. Front row centre, l–r: Sir Herbert Samuel, Winston Churchill, Sir
Percy Cox. Second row left: Sir Arnold Wilson, Gertrude Bell; centre: Jaafar Pasha, Lawrence

Feisal with his delegation and advisers at the Peace Conference. Second row l–r: Rustum Haidar (Feisal's secretary), Nuri Said, Capitaine Pisani (France), Lawrence, and Captain Hassan Kadri

Sherif Feisal by Augustus John, painted during the Peace Conference at Paris, 1919, and subsequently used by Lawrence as frontispiece to the subscribers' *Seven Pillars*

l–r: T.E. Lawrence, Sir Herbert Samuel and the Emir Abdullah in Transjordan after the Cairo Conference, 1921

greatest enemies of the Mohammedan religion. I am persuaded that I am honouring the Prophet's name by inviting His most excellent and noble grandson to participate in the protection and defence of Islam, for, by ensuring the supremacy of the Turkish Army, a safe and happy life will be obtained for all true believers.

'I have the honour to state that I shall be pleased to converse with Your Excellency in four days' time at Your Excellency's place of residence . . . I feel sure that we shall be able to fulfil the wishes of all Arabs.'[41]

After a difficult journey, Lawrence reached Feisal's headquarters at Waheida in the small hours of May 5th. His later account continues: 'I walked up in the dark to Feisal's tent . . . arriving about four in the morning, and crouched down outside it, feeling the shiver of the mountain dawn strongly upon me, waiting for the first light when he would be stirring. It was not my part to make too heavy my news by waking him specially. Actually I amused him by spinning a good story of it. He promised to admonish the Beni Sakhr . . . but could not understand why Allenby had not warned him, or asked him to help . . . Did the British mistrust him?

'He was comforted a little by my suggesting that at such short notice, and after the Amman accident, perhaps we might have been unable to help them very much: so that Bols' precipitancy had possibly saved us from confessing a failure. Then I walked back down the pass, and found my waiting car . . . turned round ready for me. A little after noon we were in Akaba, before sunset in Jaffa, and at Allenby's punctual table for dinner . . . This was important, for he was going to show me his new plans, and my suggestions for ourselves depended wholly on them.'[42]

If Lawrence was hoping for better news, he was disappointed. A second German offensive had begun in Europe on April 9th, and Allenby had now been asked to release another fourteen battalions without waiting for the Indian relief troops. Altogether, sixty thousand officers and men were being withdrawn from the EEF.

Allenby explained that the new Indian units he was expecting were not fully trained, and lacked any previous experience of warfare: 'When these drafts came he would reorganise or rebuild his army on the Indian model, and perhaps, after the summer, might be again in fighting trim; but for the moment this was too far to foresee: we must, like him, just hold on and wait.'[43] For Lawrence, ten weeks' planning lay in ruins: he would have to tell Feisal that the promise of an early victory had been false.

CHAPTER 24

Going it Alone
May – June 1918

LAWRENCE realised that the delay in Palestine would be a severe blow to
the Arabs. In the first place, he had been counting on Allenby's forward
movement to resolve the dangerous stalemate at Maan. Now, however,
the Turks would be free to concentrate their attention on Jaafar Pasha's
army. They were already building up their forces near Amman, and an
attack seemed imminent. If they were allowed to move south, the Arabs
might soon be driven back off the Maan plateau.

In the longer term, the delay could have even more serious consequences. Lawrence later wrote: 'We on the Arab front had been exciting
Eastern Syria, since 1916, for a revolt near Damascus, and our material
was now ready and afoot. To hold it still in that excited readiness during
another year risked our over-passing the crisis ineffectually.'[1] The risk of
declining morale among Feisal's present forces was no less worrying:
'This was now 1918, and stalemate across its harvest would have marked
the ebb of Feisal's movement. His fellows were living on their nerves
(rebellion is harder than war) and their nerves were wearing thin. Also the
big war was not looking too well.'[2]

These difficulties had to be seen in the context of a much wider
anxiety. Since the autumn of 1917, the Anglo-Arab alliance had been
under great strain. The cause was Arab knowledge of the Sykes-Picot
terms (greatly exploited by Turkish propaganda) and of the Balfour
Declaration. These agreements affected Syria, Lebanon, Mesopotamia
and Palestine. If they were implemented, only the Arabian Peninsula
would be autonomous. In other words, the richest and most fertile of
the Arab provinces had been reserved for the Allies, and political
independence was to be denied to the overwhelming majority of Turkey's
subject peoples. Arab leaders felt cheated of much that they had been
fighting for, and bitterly angry that they had not been consulted about
these agreements.

Their principal reason for continuing the alliance with Britain was a
belief that the Allies would win the war. During the spring of 1918,

however, even this seemed open to doubt. The EEF advance to Jerusalem and Jericho had been impressive, but there it had stopped, to be followed only by two disastrous raids across the Jordan which had done immeasurable damage to British prestige. Arab suspicions that the Allies might be weakening had been reinforced by news of the successful German offensive in Europe.[3]

It was inevitable that signs such as these would cause the Arab leaders to reconsider the likely outcome of the war they were fighting. Russia had made peace with Turkey, and the French commitment in the Middle East was nominal; America had not even declared war on the Ottoman Empire. Clearly, the only hope of an Allied victory in the East lay with Britain, yet with the massive troop withdrawals from Palestine, this hope was visibly dwindling. When the Arabs heard from Turkish sources that secret peace talks were taking place in Switzerland, they felt that this was conclusive proof of Britain's difficulties.

If Britain were forced to make peace with Turkey from a position of weakness, what would happen to Arab aspirations? Syria and much other Arab territory would end the war in Turkish hands, and the Arabs might be left to strike the best deal they could, having fought the war on the losing side. If this were the case, why should the Arabs wait so long? At present, a change in their allegiance would offer Turkey greatly improved military prospects: in exchange, they could surely obtain something better than the Sykes-Picot terms.

Lawrence was acutely aware of this danger and feared that a military standstill on both sides of the Jordan would precipitate an Arab *rapprochement* with the Turks. If nothing could be done in Palestine, Feisal must be persuaded to take the initiative himself.

This problem was on his mind when he paid another visit to GHQ on May 15th. While discussing the position with Allenby, he learned that the Imperial Camel Corps Brigade whose services he had asked for in February was soon to be reorganised as a conventional cavalry force. As he reflected on this news, it suddenly dawned on him that the change would release a large number of riding camels. If these could be given to the Arab regulars, Feisal would be able to strike at objectives much farther afield. Lawrence asked for the camels, saying that they would enable him to 'put a thousand men into Deraa'[4] whenever Allenby pleased.

This was, in essence, an adaptation of the earlier Camel Corps scheme using different riders: Lawrence believed that the Arab regulars had proved their worth at Maan. The logistics of the new scheme would be complicated, because the attacking force would have to make a long approach via Akaba and Azrak, rather than coming from Jericho in the west. On the other hand, the use of Arabs rather than Europeans would be far more acceptable to the local people, and the Arab force could afterwards be used for further operations east of the Jordan.

Lawrence set these ideas out in a written plan. The two thousand ICC camels would be used to send fifteen hundred soldiers and five hundred machine-gunners to the north. He wrote: 'The raiding force will concentrate behind Azrak and move via Jebel Druse on Deraa, which it is hoped to occupy temporarily'.[5] Before the attack on Deraa began, a small expedition would be sent to blow up the Hemme bridge at the western end of the Yarmuk valley. The bridge at Tel el Shehab, which had survived Lawrence's expedition in November 1917, could be destroyed with relative ease when the Turks had been driven out of Deraa. If the Yarmuk railway were cut, it would take the Turks a long time to send reinforcements up from Palestine. The only reserve they would be able to draw on quickly would be the force at Amman which was such a threat to Jaafar Pasha.

Lawrence had no doubt that the Turks would be able to retake Deraa, using these southern troops. However, before they did so, the camel-mounted Arabs would have disappeared eastwards into the hills, taking the local people with them. All being well, the raiders would soon be free to continue northwards: 'If we can persuade the peasantry of the Hauran to fall back, with their food, into Jebel Druse, there is no reason why they should not maintain themselves there against a Turkish force ten thousand strong, for a considerable time. If we were able so to retain Jebel Druse, and to gather there enough barley for our three thousand men and animals, the Sherifian regulars would be at once detached on a further raid in force to the northward. Suitable targets for the second raid are Damascus and Homs.'[6]

It seems that he had already mentioned this second stage of the scheme in conversation. He wrote in *Seven Pillars*: 'Exasperated one night at G.H.Q., I . . . blurted out that to me 1918 seemed the last chance, and we [the Arabs] could take Damascus, anyhow, whatever happened at Deraa or Ramleh'.[7] In his written plan, he clearly sought to allay any worries that this remark might have caused, saying that he was not prepared to guarantee that there would be operations north of Deraa. The only undertaking he could give was 'to raid the Hauran (preferably Deraa, though the corn stores are at Ezraa) with the Sherifian regulars . . . no more can be put definitely on paper . . . I hope [the further movement] will not be regarded as a plan, but only as a sketch of the line which an extension of the raiding programme, if successful, might take. It is most improbable.' Moreover, 'All Arab schemes have hitherto taken longer to execute than we have expected.'[8]

Despite this cautious statement, Lawrence must have thought that a larger breakthrough was feasible. He had always believed that the local forces available to Feisal in the Hauran would be a very powerful factor. With their support, it might well be possible for the raiding force to reach Damascus. His hope was that an Arab success in the east would put the Turks off-balance, opening the way for a parallel advance by the EEF in Palestine: 'I made up my mind to take the offensive . . . Allenby agreed, unofficially, while not promising to pass the Palestine boundary: but I felt that did I get on to near Aleppo he would come along, too.'[9]

This daring scheme seemed to involve great risks. If the raiders advanced to Damascus, but Allenby was still unable to move, they would be very exposed. Lawrence later wrote: 'I did not know if I could hold the city afterwards: but told [Allenby] it was better to have won and lost than never to have tried at all. The war was going against us, everywhere.'[10]

In reality, Lawrence knew that Feisal could avoid such an outcome. If Allenby left the Arabs to fend for themselves, they would save the situation by making a separate peace with Turkey.[11] He knew that the Arabs would see this too, and that they might therefore be attracted to his new plan. A successful raid on Damascus would in no way weaken their position *vis-à-vis* the Turks: on the contrary, Feisal's bargaining power might be greatly improved.

However, Lawrence did not intend to encourage such negotiations. While his scheme might appeal to some Arabs for the wrong reasons, what he really sought was a northward movement which Allenby would join. If that happened, the Anglo-Arab alliance would probably last until the final victory. If not, the Arabs would at least be fighting on Britain's side for as long as their efforts could be focused on the new offensive. That might turn out to be long enough for Allenby to prepare a new advance in Palestine.

When Lawrence returned to Akaba on May 21st, he appeared to be in a jubilant mood. He had decided to offset news of the EEF standstill by expounding on the immense possibilities opened up through Allenby's gift of the ICC camels. He reached Feisal's headquarters at Aba el Lissan the next day and met Joyce, who noticed that he 'could scarcely eat for eagerness, and yet his conversation was about a herd of wild ostriches which had crossed his path on the way over and . . . how his bedouin escort had fled after them . . . It was only afterwards, in Feisal's tent, that he announced the tidings of the gift of two thousand camels from GHQ, the essential link to the goal of his ambition: the great Arab drive north and the capture of Damascus. He was like a boy released from school that day'.[12]

There was, however, a major problem which would have to be solved before Lawrence's northern scheme could be put into effect. The men he had in mind for the ICC camels would have to be drawn from the Arab regulars at present serving outside Maan. But it would be most unwise to weaken Jaafar Pasha's forces there, which were already outnumbered by the Turkish defenders. To get over this difficulty Lawrence proposed to bring up most of the regular Arab units still serving with Ali and Abdullah in the Hejaz.

This seemed wholly justified, as the destruction of the railway between Maan and Mudawara in April had removed the need for attacks on the line farther south. In Lawrence's view, there was no longer any call for large-scale military action in the Hejaz, and little would be gained by sending further British supplies and subsidies to Hussein's southern armies. He wrote home a few weeks later: 'The two Sherifs down by Medina, Abdulla and Ali, allow their fancy very free play with their achievements, and keep on reporting that they have broken thousands of rails and bridges. The bridges are tiny culverts and the breaks in the rails only shorten them a few inches. Besides they break usually only 10% of their published figures . . . One thing . . . which I can tell you, is that from Maan southward for 100 kilometres there are no Turks, and the eight stations and all the rails and bridges have been smashed to atoms by us. This makes a break that I am sure they will not be able to repair so long as the war lasts, and thanks to it the very large body of troops from there to Medina are cut off from Turkey, as much as the little garrisons of Turks in South Arabia. Medina is a holy city, and the Arabs do not attack it: it has huge gardens and palm groves, and is quite self-supporting so far as food goes, so there is no definite reason why the troops there should ever surrender. We are not in any hurry about it, anyway, though the capture of the place might be a political gain to the Sherif.'[13]

Lawrence discussed his new ideas with Joyce and with Dawnay, who was again at Feisal's headquarters. Afterwards, Dawnay returned to

Palestine and put their conclusions to Allenby. He wrote to Joyce: 'I . . . went into the Deraa scheme, on the lines of our talk at Akaba, pointing out the various limitations and qualifications as they appeared to us, as the outcome of joint discussion and examination by the three of us. The Commander-in-Chief quite realises . . . that the proposition must be regarded in the light of a gamble, and, as a gamble, he is prepared to take it on; so we can now set to work, and do what we can, with easy consciences . . .

'I pointed out that should the Deraa operation . . . fall through, the provision of the additional camels would be none the less essential, in order to enable us to undertake the alternative of major offensive operations against the railway north of Maan . . .

'Next, I skimmed rather lightly over the general question of the lines upon which the operations might in the future be developed, by the closing down of the south, and the transfer of Abdulla with the whole of the regular army to the northern area . . . The discussion of all this was, of course, purely academic, the Chief realising that nothing could be done in this direction without the previous concurrence of the King . . . but the general policy, I think, appealed to him as sound, and he has told me to talk things over with the High Commissioner . . . with a view to moving on these lines later on, should the King prove amenable when Feisal has sounded him.'[14]

Lawrence hoped that with the reinforcements from the Hejaz, and the extra men now being recruited in Palestine and elsewhere, the number of Arab regulars in the north could be brought up to about ten thousand.[15] This army would then be divided into two, the larger part continuing the siege of Maan while a carefully picked force mounted on the ICC camels operated in the Deraa-Damascus sector, helped by Nuri Shalaan and the Druse peasantry.

As details of the opening offensive were worked out at Feisal's head-quarters, Lawrence became fairly confident that the initial movement would break the deadlock on the Palestine front: 'The long-distance mounted raid, by taking Deraa or Damascus, would compel the Turks to withdraw from Palestine one division, and perhaps a second, to restore their communications, and to blockade us securely in Jebel Druse or Azrak, whichever was our base.' These reductions might 'give Allenby the power to advance his whole line from Jordan to the sea – not, indeed, to Haifa and Damascus, as in the abandoned Smuts plan – but, at any rate, to Nablus.'[16] Even a small advance in Palestine would place the Turkish forces at Salt in an exposed position, and they would probably have to leave. This in turn would give the Arabs control of the hill country east of the Dead Sea, and allow them to link up with the British around Jericho for a final campaign.

Lawrence could only speculate about the outcome of the later stages of his offensive. In *Seven Pillars* he wrote that the ICC camels were 'an immense, a regal gift; the gift of unlimited mobility. The Arabs could now win their war when and how they liked.'[17] Privately, however, he must have known that the camel raiders might never reach Damascus. In this case, the gain would be slight and the cost very heavy. As he later wrote: 'Practically, I was proposing that we use up the Hauran Arabs to let us reach Jericho, half-way to our Damascus goal. It was an expensive plan therefore but the alternative was stagnation for English and Arabs in their present line throughout next winter.'[18]

It would be some time before these operations could begin. The ICC camels would not arrive from Palestine immediately, and when they did, they would need time to get accustomed to grazing (hitherto they had been given feed). Feisal and Lawrence would also have to arrange for the transfer of Arab regulars from the Hejaz.

In the meantime, it was necessary to protect the Arab position outside Maan from a Turkish counter-attack. For the moment, this was being done by repeatedly cutting the railway to the north. A force commanded by Zeid had been raiding the line around Jerdun for some weeks, and Sherif Nasir had now taken up a position about half-way between Maan and Amman. He was accompanied by Hornby, a British engineer officer who had now spent a year working with Arab raiding parties, as well as Peake's Egyptian Camel Corps and a corps of Egyptian labourers. On May 23rd the station at Hesa was captured, and an important water supply there destroyed. The following day Nasir's force moved north and took Faraifra station, attacked a train, and carried out further large-scale demolitions.

Co-ordination of these northern operations had originally been en-trusted to Young. However, it had soon become evident that he was unsuited to this delicate task. As Lawrence had seen in other instances, regular army training was of little help when working with Arab irregu-lars. In Young's case there was also a problem of temperament. He possessed too little patience to deal successfully with the bedouin: in his eagerness to get things done, he gave strings of exacting orders and expected them to be obeyed. This approach led to constant difficulties, and he had exhausted himself riding backwards and forwards trying to keep different groups working together in the most effective fashion. Eventually, he had fallen ill and was sent back to Egypt. Lawrence later wrote: 'He upset everybody by being too cast-iron, and wore himself out. Maximum of friction. So I was not sorry when he went sick, except that I then had to take over the push myself.'[19] For this reason, Lawrence left Feisal's headquarters on May 28th to join the northern operations. His object, according to a subsequent report by Joyce, was 'to assist Sherif Nasir and to endeavour to keep the tribes active'.[20]

Lawrence had already taken other steps to help safeguard the Arab position on the Maan plateau. During his last visit to GHQ he had asked for frequent bombing raids on Amman and Katrani, and had discussed this requirement in detail with General Salmond, senior RAF officer in the Middle East. The RAF responded very generously. In *Seven Pillars* Lawrence wrote: 'Routine attacks upon the Hejaz Railway were arranged, and the Royal Air Force kept at this dull and troublesome business from now till the fall of Turkey. They served a valuable strategic purpose, by causing heavy damage and uncertainty along the line, and so making any large concentration either of men or stores dangerous in the sector north of Maan. Much of the inactivity of the Turks in this our lean season was due to the disorganisation of their railway traffic by air bombing.'[21] Using an advance airfield near Guweira, the RAF flew missions as far north as Jurf, while aircraft from Palestine attacked the line south of Amman. The Air Force also flew very frequent reconnaissance missions which provided detailed information on enemy troop movements.

The cumulative effect of these operations on the ground and in the air was everything that Lawrence had hoped. He later told Liddell Hart: 'Nasir took the Turks completely by surprise – and Peake and Hornby, with the labour assistance of their stalwart Egyptians (not fighting men: line-breakers) made an awful mess of the Turkish stations and line. We turned over great lengths of it, bending rails and sleepers, and even blew in cuttings, besides wells, water towers, pumps, points – all the railway. Nasir stayed up there, in Wadi Hesa which was full of air-proof caves [safe from Turkish bombing], and as often as the Turks tried to mend a bit, he broke it again . . . the Turks had the proper wind-up. They thought we were coming on to Jericho . . .

'As for the effect of the bombing, the war showed me that a combination of armoured cars and aircraft could rule the desert'.[22]

After a short time with Nasir, Lawrence concluded that operations on the present scale would prevent any major Turkish counter-attack for at least two months. As there was little he could contribute to the raiding, he turned his attention to the forthcoming Arab offensive. One potential weak point now seemed to be the attitude of villagers in the area between the Dead Sea and the railway. Some of the headmen were still pro-Turk, and the local people were more inclined to listen to them after the two British failures at Salt. If the villages on this Moab plateau did not side with Feisal, it might be impossible to advance the Arab front line as far north as Jericho, which was the minimum objective. In order to assess the situation, Lawrence set out on May 31st to make a secret tour of the area.

While returning south a week later, he had a very unpleasant ex-perience. Near Jurf el Derwish, his party noticed a small column of Turks approaching from behind, and then, a moment later, more troops appeared in front: 'We were certainly caught. The Arabs jumped off their camels, and crouched in a covered place behind their guns, meaning to fight to the last like cornered animals, and kill at least some of the enemy before they themselves died. Such tactics displeased me, for when combats came to the physical, bare hand against hand, I used to turn myself in. The disgust of being touched revolted me more than the thought of death and defeat . . .

'Anyway, I had not the instinct to sell my life dearly, and to avoid the indignity of trying not to be killed and failing, rode straight for the enemy to end the business, in all the exhilaration of that last and terrific and most glad pain of death . . . When they saw me single, their horsemen galloped in advance, with their rifles out, but did not shoot when first I came up. Instead they reined back suddenly, stood still, and very slowly aimed at my body, calling to me a last warning in Arabic to testify. I said "There are no gods but God, and Jesus is his prophet." They gasped, stared, and then yelled "Urans" together, laughing'.[23] It turned out that they were not Turks, but Arabs wearing stolen Turkish uniforms. Lawrence arrived safely in Aba el Lissan on June 8th.

He was now satisfied that the wavering villagers on the Moab plateau could be brought out on Feisal's side. The dissenting voices would carry little weight if the population could be reassured that the coming Arab advance was to be permanent, and not merely a raid. In practical terms, this would mean sending in a column of Arab infantry to spearhead operations in the region. Lawrence concluded that two or three thousand

Arab regulars would be needed. This force would also serve to assure a reliable link with Allenby's front line at Jericho.

Accordingly, he modified the planned offensive, so that the regulars would be divided into three forces, rather than two. One would be required for Moab, another for Maan, and the third for Deraa and beyond. This new commitment made it even more necessary to obtain a large number of additional men from the Hejaz. However, Lawrence still felt that the scheme as a whole offered grounds for optimism. He later wrote: 'My plan for containing Maan, holding the Moab plateau, and simultaneously raising the Hauran was actually to capture Damascus, and so destroy the Turkish Palestine army between my hammer and Allenby's anvil.'[24]

While he had been away on this northern expedition, a further message from Jemal Pasha had reached the Arab headquarters. Without telling Lawrence, Feisal had begun to take these exchanges with the enemy very seriously. Lawrence later wrote: 'Djemal was willing to give independence to Arabia, and autonomy to Syria, and half the riches of Turkey to Feisal, if the Arab Army would rejoin the Turks against the British'.[25] On another occasion, Lawrence discussed these secret negotiations with Liddell Hart, who made notes of the conversation. These jottings are confused, probably because he only gave a condensed and somewhat vague summary. In part, however, they clearly refer to the situation in June: 'Feisal never told [Lawrence] about his negotiations in the summer of 1918 – Feisal was definitely "selling us". He thought the British were cracking . . . [Lawrence] heard through agents in camp. [He] stopped it when getting dangerous; pretended to take it as a piece of political tactics . . . Feisal could not carry on when the English knew.'[26]

After the war, Lawrence clearly thought it politic to conceal the seriousness of these Arab dealings with the Turks, and there are obvious discrepancies between his different statements on the subject. Contemporary records, however, suggest that he originally encouraged the correspondence, believing that he could control it. As contacts between the two sides were inevitable, it seemed best to know what was going on. During the spring of 1918, however, he discovered that Feisal was attempting to hide the negotiations from him. By devious means, he seems to have kept abreast of the situation.

Feisal replied to Jemal's latest approach on approximately June 10th. Lawrence managed to see this letter, and was alarmed by its contents. He passed details to Hogarth, who noted that a copy had been obtained 'from Feisal's secretariat without Feisal's knowledge'.[27] It set out specific conditions for a *rapprochement* between Arabs and Turks:

    a. that all Turkish troops south of Amman should be withdrawn there

    b. that all Arab officers and men serving in the Turkish Army in other provinces should be returned to Syria where they would join the Arab Army

    c. that if the Arab and Turkish armies fought side by side, the Arab Army should be under its own Commander

    d. that Syria's future relationship with Turkey should be modelled on the relationship between Prussia, Austria, and Hungary

    e. that all supplies and foodstuffs in Syria should be handed over to the Arab Army.[28]

There had been another important diplomatic contact while Lawrence was away in the north. This was a visit to Feisal's camp by Dr Chaim Weizmann, a leading British Zionist. Some weeks earlier, Weizmann had arrived in Palestine at the head of a Zionist Commission authorised by the Eastern Committee of the War Cabinet. The Commission's objects, according to a telegram to Wingate from the Foreign Office, were 'to carry out, subject to General Allenby's authority, any steps required to give effect to the Government declaration in favour of the establishment in Palestine of a National Home for the Jewish people . . . Among the important functions of the Commission will be the establishment of good relations with the Arabs and other non-Jewish communities in Palestine . . . It is most important that everything should be done to . . . allay Arab suspicions regarding the true aims of Zionism'.[29]

Clayton, who was closely involved in the administration of Palestine, hoped that the mission would help to reduce hostility between Jews and Arabs. He had written to Sykes on February 4th: 'I have urged Lawrence to impress on Faisal the necessity of an *entente* with the Jews. [Feisal] is inclined the other way, and there are people in Cairo who lose no chance of putting him against them. I have explained that it is his only chance of doing really big things and bringing the Arab movement to fruition.'[30] Subsequently, Lawrence had told Clayton: '[As] for the Jews, when I see Feisul next I'll talk to him, and the Arab attitude shall be sympathetic, for the duration of the war at least. Only please remember that he is under the old man, and cannot involve the Arab kingdom by himself.' He would advise Feisal to visit Jerusalem when the demands of the campaign permitted, and 'all the Jews there will report him friendly. That will probably do all you need, without public commitment, which is rather beyond my province.'[31]

In late May, a message had been sent to Akaba proposing a meeting between Feisal and Weizmann, who would be accompanied by a liaison officer: 'The interview would take place at Arab Headquarters, to which they would motor. Wire if this is convenient to Sherif Feisal and Lawrence. It is important the latter should be present at the interview.'[32] In the event, however, Lawrence had left to join Nasir before the date of Weizmann's journey to Akaba was telegraphed from Cairo. He was therefore absent when the meeting took place on June 4th.

His place was taken by Joyce, who afterwards reported that the discussions lasted about forty-five minutes: 'Sherif Feisal expressed his opinion of the necessity for co-operation between Jews and Arabs . . . As regards definite political arrangements, [he] was unwilling to express an opinion, pointing out that in questions of politics he was acting merely as his father's agent and was not in a position to discuss them . . . Dr. Weizmann pointed out that the Jews do not propose setting up a Jewish government, but would like to work under British protection with a view to colonizing and developing the country without in any way encroaching on anybody's legitimate interests . . . Feisal declared that as an Arab he could not discuss the future of Palestine, either as a Jewish colony or a country under British Protection. These questions were already the subject of much German and Turkish propaganda, and would undoubtedly be misinterpreted by the Bedouin if openly discussed. Later on when Arab affairs were more consolidated these questions could be brought up.

'Sherif Feisal personally accepted the possiblity of future Jewish claims to territory in Palestine . . . but he could not discuss them publicly'.[33]

It was only during a subsequent visit to Allenby's headquarters that Lawrence had an opportunity for significant discussions with Weizmann. Not long afterwards, when he was questioned on the topic by a member of Wingate's staff, he said: 'The real imminence of the Palestine problem is patent only to Feisal of the Sherifians. He believes that we intend to keep it ourselves, under the excuse of holding the balance between conflicting religions, and regards it as a cheap price to pay for the British help he has had and hopes still to have . . .

'Dr. Weizmann hopes for a completely Jewish Palestine in fifty years, and a Jewish Palestine, under a British façade, for the moment. He is fighting for his own lead among the British and American Jews: if he can offer these the spectacle of British help, and Arab willingness to allow Jewish enterprise free scope in all their provinces in Syria, he will then secure the financial backing which will make the new Judaea a reality . . . Weizmann is not yet in a position, as regards Jewry, to make good any promise he makes. In negotiating with him the Arabs would have to bear in mind that they are worth nothing to him till they have beaten the Turks, and that he is worth nothing to them unless he can make good amongst the Jews . . .

'Until the military adventure of the Arabs under Feisal has succeeded or failed, he does not require Jewish help, and it would be unwise on our part to permit it to be offered.'[34]

However, Lawrence thought that in the more distant future Feisal might have something to gain from co-operation with the Zionists. As soon as the Turks had been defeated, vociferous factions in Syria would turn against the Sherifians. Much of the upper-class intelligentsia would prefer autonomy, while the Maronite Christians and other pro-French elements would side with Paris in calling for the introduction of French advisers and capital. At this point Feisal might, with advantage, turn to the Zionists: 'If the British and American Jews, securely established under British colours in Palestine, chose this moment to offer to the Arab state in Syria help (1) against the Syrian autonomous elements, [and] (2) against the foreign railways, ports, roads, waterworks and power companies, Sherif Feisal would be compelled to accept the help, and with Anglo-Jewish advisers could dispense with the effendim and buy out the foreigners. This would give time for a development of an Arab spirit in Syria from below'.[35]

In June 1918, however, Lawrence was faced with more urgent questions than the future relationship between Arabs and Zionists. The plans for an offensive were complete, and he was shortly to go to Egypt to make arrangements with GHQ and to seek Wingate's support for requesting the transfer of regulars from the Hejaz.

In all his planning, Lawrence had placed great emphasis on accurate knowledge of local conditions and political loyalties. While working out details of the northern operations, he had studied the attitudes of tribes and leaders in the north, whose contribution would be essential. His findings were set out in a paper called 'Tribal Politics in Feisal's Area', which illustrates the extraordinary complexity of the situation. He wrote: 'The Howeitat remain absolutely loyal to Feisal, but are getting very weary of fighting, and have, besides, profited so materially in Sherifian service as to value their lives dearly. They still show splendid dash and courage when in action, but it is becoming ever more difficult to persuade them into the firing line. Auda is as good as ever, but more wayward, if it be possible. He has now proved to his own satisfaction that his descent from the Prophet entitles him to equality with ordinary sherifs . . . with Turkish prisoner-labour, he is building himself a great *kasr* [palace] of mud-brick at el-Jefer, and collecting two hundred telegraph poles along the railway to roof it with . . .

'The morale of the Beni Atiyeh is good; but their fighting efficiency is nullified by the sluggish incapacity of Sherif Mohammed Ali el-Bedawi . . . The Hejaya are considerably divided . . .

'It may now be said that, so far as Feisal can see, no element, indeed no individual, of the Beni Sakhr remains in active sympathy with the Turks . . . Hatmal is weak and unimportant; Nawaf, Nail, Trad, and Turki are enthusiastic. Indeed the last, on taking leave of Feisal at Aba Lissan, knelt down before all his tribesmen and kissed Feisal's feet, saying that as no Arab had so abased himself to the Sherif before, so no Arab would surpass himself in the extent of his services to the Sherifian cause in war or peace. Turki is a lad of seventeen, celebrated among the tribes for an almost insane courage in the field, and for his curious habit of shaving his face . . .

'Feisal is rather disturbed by this enthusiasm among the Beni Sakhr. They urge him day and night to put a headquarters at Themed, and to raise war against the railway between Amman and Kutrani. They would all – to the number of at least eleven thousand – join in, and ask only for two mountain-guns, and the presence of British aeroplanes . . . a Sherifian expedition in their country would put at Feisal's disposal the harvest of Kerak and Madeba . . . On the other hand, to maintain the Beni Sakhr in the field would cost Feisal an extra £30,000 a month . . .

'At Madeba . . . the Christians are much elated at the punishment which has fallen on the Arabs as a result of the British trans-Jordan raids, and have taken upon themselves to . . . denounce to the Turks casual Bedouins entering the town. A mischievous rumour which they spread, that the British had forcibly nailed up a hat [abhorred by Muslim Arabs] over every Moslem house in Jerusalem . . . has done much harm to British prestige . . .

'The Ruwalla have split into four. Nuri [Shalaan] insisted on neutrality till the Sherif should call them out, and is at Asrak . . . His letters to Feisal are loyal and sensible, and he has given a receipt for the Sherifian dumps at Asrak, while making his peace with the Turks by expelling thence Ali ibn Hussein. Nawaf Shalaan insisted on joining the Turks . . . Trad has moved to Rueishid and declared himself Sherifian, while Mijhem has come in to Aba Lissan with twelve hundred men . . . Nuri has been sent a further £5,000 by Feisal . . .

'As with the Beni Sakhr, so with the Ruwalla and the Druses, Feisal's chief care is, by diplomacy and delay and small payments, to restrain their eagerness to join him openly. A premature rising in the north, while he is enmeshed in the south, would break the frail fabric he is so carefully building up, by throwing upon his transport and his treasury a strain which neither of them could bear. Sherifian propaganda is complete to Damascus, and every possible supporter in that area is prepared for his coming. It remains to see whether there is fuel enough in their fire to keep them at rebellion pitch till he can use them . . .

'The Fadhl . . . have declared for Feisal, but are to take no action until called upon. This is the main agricultural tribe of the northern Hauran and eastern Jaulan . . . Nesib and Selim el-Atrash have . . . sworn allegiance to the Sherif. The Druse block is therefore complete, but will wait instructions.'[36]

Feisal was also gaining adherents within the Turkish administration of Syria. This was almost entirely staffed by Arabs: Turks occupied only the most senior posts. With these supporters, Feisal could hope that government would not break down entirely when the Turks withdrew. Joyce reported: 'Satisfactory letters have been received by Sherif Feisal from Deraa, showing that the personnel in most of the departments including the telegraph are Arabs, and are available to be utilised when required.'[37]

On June 10th Lawrence left Akaba. While passing through Cairo, he spoke to Wingate about bringing Arab regulars up from the Hejaz. Afterwards he travelled to GHQ, meaning to discuss final details of the northern offensive.

When he arrived, on June 19th, he found that the mood of Allenby's staff had changed completely. The Indian troops had arrived, and a programme of rapid training was yielding excellent results. As a result, plans had advanced much farther than had seemed possible a few weeks before, and it had just been decided that a new offensive could be launched in September. This meant that Lawrence's Arab initiative, with all its attendant risks, was no longer necessary.

CHAPTER 25

Third Time Lucky
June – September 1918

THE decision to launch a major attack in the autumn of 1918 had been taken only four days before Lawrence arrived at GHQ, and detailed plans had not yet been made. However, Allenby's requirement east of the Jordan had not changed since the spring. The main objective of the Arab forces would still be the railway junction at Deraa. If this could be isolated, Turkish lines of communication to their Seventh and Eighth Armies in Palestine would be cut.

In February, Lawrence had proposed that Deraa should be taken by the Imperial Camel Corps; but these units were now being disbanded and their camels transferred to Feisal. The operation would therefore have to be carried out by the new force of camel-mounted Arab regulars. In practical terms, the new scheme would incorporate many of the details that had been worked out for an independent Arab offensive.

From Lawrence's point of view, this change of plan brought both advantages and disadvantages. The chief benefit was that the Arabs' northern campaign would run far less risk of failure if there were also a major offensive in Palestine. The disadvantage, however, was that Feisal would again be the junior partner, taking orders from Allenby about timing and objectives.

In Cairo, Lawrence found the Arab Bureau mulling over a new Foreign Office declaration to the Arab nationalists. A few weeks earlier, not long after the second failure at Salt, a memorandum had been received from seven Syrians resident in Cairo. They claimed to represent the secret committees in Damascus and, hence, 'four-fifths and more of the total inhabitants of Syria'. The seven, who preferred after the first contact to remain anonymous, protested strongly about the division of Arab territory into British and French zones. They asked for clarification of recent pronouncements in favour of self-determination made in speeches by Lloyd George and President Wilson,[1] and they requested assurances that Britain intended to give the Arabs complete independence in Arabia,

Syria, and Mesopotamia. Despite professions of loyalty to Hussein, the writers gave clear hints that they were opposed to Sherifian rule in Syria, and asked whether the future regional governments would be decentralised, on the American model, or whether some leaders were to be given more influence than others.

Wingate had sent the memorandum to London, giving his view that it would be inadvisable either to dismiss it or to give a wholly disappointing answer. An unsatisfactory response might lead the signatories 'to modify their pro-Ally inclinations, and ultimately . . . to enter into communications with the enemy . . . I feel strongly that we should be ill-advised to ignore the aspirations towards independence and eventual political union . . . which are held, I believe, by a majority of the Moslem and a large proportion of the Christian Syrians: and I think it would be very advantageous to supplement, if possible, the very general – and, in native eyes, vague and consequently unsatisfactory – lines of our declared policy in regard to the future of the Arab peoples.'[2]

In London, the matter was passed to Sykes, who drew up a carefully worded reply. This began by dividing the Arab areas referred to in the memorandum into four categories. The first two were areas 'which were free and independent before the war', and areas 'emancipated from Turkish control by the action of the Arabs themselves during the present war'. In these cases, the British Government would 'recognise the complete and sovereign independence of the Arabs inhabiting those areas and support them in their struggle for freedom'.[3]

In the third category were areas 'occupied by the Allied forces during the present war.' Here, the undertakings were much more vague: it was Britain's 'wish and desire' that the future government should be based on 'the principle of the consent of the governed'. Finally, there were 'Areas still under Turkish control', where it was also Britain's 'wish and desire' that the Arabs should gain their 'freedom and independence'.At first sight, this document was a flagrant contradiction of the Sykes-Picot Agreement. On closer scrutiny, however, it can be seen to contain a subtle ambiguity.

The crucial issue was whether any further areas of Syria and Lebanon captured by the Arabs before war ended would be regarded as coming into the second category: 'areas emancipated from Turkish control by the action of the Arabs themselves during the present war'. If so, the British were now pledged to recognising 'complete and sovereign independence' in these regions, despite the earlier Sykes-Picot undertakings.

Sykes, however, meant the wording 'during the present war' to allow a second interpretation. While the obvious sense was 'during the whole of the present war', he had carefully phrased the document so that this vital clause could also be understood to mean 'during the present war up until now'.[4] According to this alternative interpretation, Syria was excluded from the area of guaranteed independence.

Sykes probably considered this ambiguity pardonable because he had persuaded himself that in the political atmosphere now prevailing, neither Britain nor France would attempt to impose colonial rule in their respective Sykes-Picot areas. At the time that he drafted this reply, he was hoping to obtain an assurance from Georges-Picot on that very point. Sykes's draft was approved by the Foreign Office, and telegraphed to Cairo on June 11th.

A few days later, Wingate received from Hussein's agent in Cairo an angry enquiry about the present status of the Sykes-Picot Agreement. As the Sherif had already known about the Agreement for some time, Wingate feared that this sudden reaction might be an attempt to pick a quarrel with Britain. He cabled to the Foreign Office saying that he had 'advised the agent to say that the Bolsheviks found . . . a [Russian] Foreign Office record of old conversations and a provisional understanding (not a formal treaty) between Britain, France and Russia early in the war to prevent difficulties between the Powers in prosecuting the war with Turkey. Jemal, either from ignorance or malice has . . . omitted its stipulations regarding the consent of the native populations and the safeguarding of their interests, and has ignored the fact that the subsequent outbreak and success of the Arab Revolt, and the withdrawal of Russia, has for a long time past created a wholly different situation.' He asked: 'Can I add that we regard the Agreement as dead for all practical purposes?'[5] The Foreign Office approved the line Wingate had taken, but had to refuse his final request, pointing out that until or unless the Sykes-Picot Agreement was modified, Britain was bound to uphold its terms.

A meeting with two of the Syrians was arranged for June 25th, and Hogarth read them the British Government's declaration as well as the reply Wingate had given to the Sherif's agent.[6] As a result, both statements gained wide circulation. Taken together, their content led many people, including Lawrence, to assume that the declaration should be taken at its face value and that the Sykes-Picot Agreement was a dead letter.

Although the role to be played by Feisal's army under Allenby's new scheme would be less onerous than an independent offensive, Lawrence still thought it would be advisable to obtain additional regulars from the Hejaz. The extra men would help to secure the position at Maan until the autumn, and would enable the Arabs to send a large force northwards when the offensive began. He decided to go ahead with his visit to the Hejaz and put the case to Hussein personally.

By this time, however, he was beginning to realise that it might be extremely difficult to persuade the Sherif to transfer these units. For one thing, the Hejaz was embroiled in a dispute with ibn Saud, the Wahhabi leader of the Nejd on Hussein's inland frontier. Like Hussein, ibn Saud had formally broken with the Turks, but this had involved him in little fighting. Turkish strength in Arabia lay along the Hejaz Railway, and that was in Hussein's territory. While the Sherifians had fought a long and hard campaign, ibn Saud had concentrated on increasing his influence in the Arabian Peninsula. Although he was nominally on friendly terms with the Sherif, there had been growing tension along their common frontier, and several incidents had taken place.

Hussein had made no secret of his aspirations to some kind of supremacy throughout the Arab world and, in his view, Britain bore a large share of the responsibility for the difficulties he was having with ibn Saud. The latter was receiving liberal support from the Government of India, which believed that 'divide and rule' was the safest policy, and was deliberately building up ibn Saud as a counterbalance to Hussein.

Not long after Wingate's statement about the Sykes-Picot Agreement, Wilson reported from Jidda: 'There is no reason to suspect weakening of the King's loyalty to his alliance with us: but he is nervous and tired and consequently very difficult to deal with.

'He is preoccupied with the Saud question and the tone of their recent letters is very acrid . . . the real ground of their disagreement is that the King regards Ibn Saud as his chief opponent to his personal ascendancy and to his scheme of unification in Arabia. His anxiety is increased by his uncertainty how far we shall be willing diplomatically to support his views . . .

'His present state of mind might lead him to a nervous breakdown or ill-considered action.'[7]

Another difficulty facing Lawrence was that Hussein's relationship with Feisal was not very close. In recent months it had deteriorated sharply, no doubt because of Feisal's increasing dependence on Syrian and Iraqi officers who were opposed to the Sherif's wider political ambitions. Since early May, Hussein had refused to allow Feisal to visit him, inventing one excuse after another.

Lawrence sailed for Jidda on June 21st, taking letters to the Sherif from Wingate and Allenby supporting the request to move troops to Syria. On arrival, however, he soon realised that his mission was hopeless. According to a contemporary report, following the most recent incident on the border with ibn Saud, 'a reinforcement of eighty-two men ... with two old Turkish guns and two machine-guns' had been dispatched to the border from Mecca on June 13th, 'and that was about all the King could send. His forces are, of course, all up in the north quite out of reach, and there is no doubt that Taif and Mecca lie dangerously open to attack from Central Arabia or from the south.'[8] The Sherif declined to meet Lawrence, on the pretext that it would not be correct to leave Mecca during Ramadan. They spoke by telephone, but Lawrence found that each time he tried to discuss the object of his mission, Hussein pretended that the line was faulty and broke off the conversation.

In a further attempt, Lawrence wrote a personal letter to Hussein, in Arabic, stressing both the achievements of Feisal's army and the difficulties of the present position: 'There are now four thousand Turkish soldiers at Maan entrenched in strong fortifications with cement machine-gun points and many guns. There is a good supply of water and sufficient food for three months ... Feisal's force of 3,500 will not be able to occupy Maan in direct assault. No commander could attack nowadays an entrenched force if he has not under him at least twice or three times the surrounded force ... The bedouin are no good for a continued siege and will not attack fortifications ... The British General Staff is of the opinion that rarely has an army accomplished what Jaafar's army has, under the command of Emir Feisal ... but we are a little afraid of the future ...

'The Turks are bound to lift the siege ... upon Maan within the next two months. The strength of the Turkish army at Amman is estimated at eight thousand and it is possible that the German General Staff would send a third of it from Katrani to Maan ... Sherif Nasir has now at Hesa seventy regulars and four hundred bedouins and has done admirably well ... but he cannot stand alone against three thousand Turkish regulars.

'After the railway to Maan is repaired, the Turks will be able to reinforce Maan with infantry and transport: then they will attack Aba el Lissan. The Arab fortifications there are in good condition and therefore your army will probably be able to defend itself. Otherwise the army should retreat to Guweira, a well-fortified position which the Turks will not be able to attack.'[9]

After repeating that it would be impossible to take Maan by direct assault, Lawrence concluded: 'In war it is more profitable for the Arabs to adopt the daring plan which the enemy does not anticipate.

'I have submitted to Sidi Feisal a plan which General Allenby might help us in implementing. If this plan succeeds, Maan and its garrison of four thousand Turks is now locked in with no hope of escape to north, south, east or west.'[10]

Hussein was unmoved by this appeal, and Lawrence decided that it would be useless to pursue the matter. The deciding factor had been Hussein's problems with ibn Saud. Lawrence left Jidda on July 1st and reached Cairo five days later. There, he submitted an account of the latest developments in the border conflict to the *Arab Bulletin*.[11]

From Cairo he went to Palestine, to discuss details of the forthcoming offensive with Allenby and Dawnay. The EEF had by this time a very considerable advantage in strength over the Turks, and Allenby knew it.[12] Nevertheless, the key to a cheap and speedy victory would be surprise. As it happened, the abortive raids on Amman and Salt that spring had persuaded the Turks that the EEF intended to attack in this sector. Allenby, who learned of this Turkish appreciation from Intelligence sources, decided to do everything possible to sustain it. Meanwhile, he would secretly build up his forces along the Mediterranean coast. The real plan was to attack there in overwhelming force on September 19th. He expected the Arabs to isolate Deraa three days beforehand. This would further convince the Turks that the weight of his attack was to be expected in the east.

By July 13th, Lawrence was back in Cairo, hoping to rest for a few days before returning to Akaba: 'We were going to have a busy autumn and . . . the two years' irregular work had used up some of my personal elasticity.'[13] He wrote to his parents: 'It is very nice to have finished one part of the show. We begin something fresh next month, and the change will be a pleasant one.

'Having said that much, that is all, I think, that I have got to say. You know I have nothing doing or to do which does not actually concern Feisal's campaign, and that, I make a rule to write nothing about. I cannot talk about books because I don't read any, or about people, because I meet only the Staff who deal with our operations, or places, because most of them are not to be made public property. So there you are'.[14]

During this lull in his activities, he replied to a letter from Vyvyan Richards, the friend with whom he had once planned to run a private press. Nine months before, in September 1917, he had mentioned to his parents that he might take up the printing scheme again after the war. He had then written: 'I can honestly say that I have never seen anyone doing anything so useful as the man who prints good books.'[15] Now, however, his plans were far less certain. He was convinced, as he explained wearily to Richards, that the kind of life he had thought of leading was forever closed to him. This is perhaps the earliest surviving document which reflects the mood that later took him into the ranks of the RAF. He wrote:

I have been so violently uprooted and plunged so deeply into a job too big for me, that everything feels unreal. I have dropped everything I ever did, and live only as a thief of opportunity, snatching chances of the moment when and where I see them. My people have probably told you that the job is to foment an Arab rebellion against Turkey, and for that I have to try and hide my Frankish exterior, and be as little out of the Arab picture as I can. So it's a kind of foreign stage, on which one plays day and night, in fancy dress, in a strange language, with the price of failure on one's head if the part is not well filled.

You guessed rightly that the Arab appealed to my imagination. It is the old, old civilisation, which has refined itself clear of household gods, and half the trappings which ours hastens to assume. The gospel of bareness in materials is a good one, and it involves apparently a sort of moral bareness too. They think for the moment, and endeavour to slip through life without turning corners or climbing hills. In part it is a mental and moral fatigue, a race trained out: and to avoid difficulties they have to jettison so much that we think honourable and brave: and yet without in any way sharing their point of view, I think I can understand it enough to look at myself and other foreigners from their direction, and without condemning it. I know I'm a stranger to them, and always will be: but I cannot believe them worse, any more than I could change to their ways . . .

Anyway these years of detachment have cured me of any desire ever to do anything for myself. When they untie my bonds I will not find in me any spur to action. However actually one never thinks of afterwards: the time from the beginning is like one of those dreams which seems to last for aeons, and then you wake up with a start, and find that it has left nothing in your mind. Only the different thing about this dream is that so many people do not wake up in this life again . . . Achievement, if it comes, will be a great disillusionment . . .

A house with no action entailed upon one, quiet, and liberty to think and abstain as one wills – yes, I think abstention, the leaving everything alone and watching the others still going past – is what I would choose today, if they ceased driving one. This may be only the reaction from four years' opportunism, and is not worth trying to resolve into terms of geography and employment . . .

Those words – peace, silence, rest and the others – take on a vividness in the midst of noise and worry and weariness like a lighted window in the dark. Yet what good is a lighted window? and perhaps it is only because one is overborne and tired . . . Probably I'm only a sensitised film, turned black or white by the objects projected on me: and if so what hope is there that next week or year, or tomorrow, can be prepared for today?

This is an idiot letter, and amounts to nothing except cry for a further change which is idiocy, for I change my abode every day, and my job every two days, and my language every three days, and still remain always unsatisfied. I hate being in front, and I hate being back and I don't like responsibility, and I don't obey orders. Altogether no good just now. A long quiet like a purge and then a contemplation and decision of future roads, that is what is to look forward to.[16]

Lawrence spent almost a fortnight in Cairo, and passed some of this time discussing details of the coming Arab campaign with Dawnay. The main concern was still the position around Maan, which would have to be held until the beginning of September without any reinforcements from the Hejaz. Jaafar Pasha's forces were not really adequate for this task, and his line of communication back to Akaba was slow and inefficient. Owing to poor supplies, shortages of ammunition, and an epidemic of fever, his men had achieved very little during the past few weeks.

On June 22nd his position had become even more insecure, when Nasir's force had been attacked by a mobile Turkish column and driven onto the defensive. By the beginning of July, the Arab blockade of the railway down to Maan had effectively been ended, and the Turks had begun repairs to the line. On July 15th Dawnay wrote to Joyce: 'Frankly I am nervous about the next four weeks – we cannot possibly make much use of the northern tribes much before the beginning of September, and until then Feisal will be sitting at Uheida with about 2,000 men, faced on the other side by roughly 3,000/4,000 Turkish troops in Maan plus anything up to 2,500 between Kutrani and Aneiza, all of whom (if they succeed in the repair of the railway) could be rapidly concentrated to make an offensive thrust . . .

'Should they do so, the result might well be disastrous. Meanwhile our greatest security lies in the fact that the Turks, at present, have no conception of Feisal's actual strength (or weakness), believing, in fact, that strong reinforcements are already commencing to arrive, and that his plans are rapidly maturing for a new offensive on a scale much larger than ever before . . .

'As long as we can encourage this impression by a sufficient show of offensive activity we are all right, but in present circumstances that . . . is not too easy and will not . . . become more so. And *if* we are found out, the old Turk might well take heart to have a whack which would not improbably send us spinning.'[17]

Both Dawnay and Lawrence knew that it was vital to prevent the Turks from mounting an attack on Jaafar's force before the autumn offensive began. Otherwise, the whole scheme might founder: Feisal could not be expected to move regulars towards Deraa as long as his line of communication from Akaba onto the Maan plateau was under threat. Thinking over this problem, Dawnay remembered that two companies of the Imperial Camel Corps had not yet been disbanded. He suggested to Lawrence that this mobile force of three hundred men might be used to put on a show of force east of the Jordan.

Lawrence took to the idea immediately, and Dawnay therefore asked for General Staff approval. This was obtained, with the stipulation that the men must, if possible, be returned to Palestine by August 25th, so that they would be available for Allenby's autumn offensive. For the same reason, they were not to be employed in any operation that might involve heavy casualties.

Dawnay and Lawrence worked out details of a long raid by the Camel Corps which would do as much as possible to worry the Turks in the short time available. They decided that the first objective should be the water installations at Mudawara station, and the second either the railway bridge or the tunnel near Kissir (the targets that the EEF had failed to blow up in the Amman raid). Little was known, however, about these northern targets, and if they proved impossible, the Camel Corps would try to do serious damage to the railway farther south.

The targets were important in themselves, but the real value of the expedition would be psychological. The Turks would probably not realise that these widely separated attacks had been carried out by the same force. As a result, they would be more uncertain than ever of Feisal's true strength. The natural reaction would be extra caution, and this would make them think very hard before launching an offensive southwards towards Maan.

To carry out the plan, the Camel Corps would march across Sinai to Akaba, then south to Mudawara, where there would be a night attack. Then the raiders would disappear eastwards into the desert. Some days later, they would descend on the second objective, two hundred miles to the north. After this, they would return to Palestine, arriving by August 30th. The total distance covered would be about nine hundred miles.

General Bartholomew, Allenby's Chief of Staff, reported favourably on the scheme: 'I take it that it is of great importance to stave off a Turkish attack on Feisal who Lawrence and Dawnay are quite convinced is in no condition to meet one. The Turks do not seem to have grasped the situation, and I think the question we have to ask ourselves is whether the appearance of the Camel Corps companies is likely to postpone the day when they will grasp it. Lawrence and Dawnay go farther and say the material damage that may be done is also very important.

'I think it would be a good thing to send the Camel Corps and that if they appear just at Mudawara and then in the area north of Maan we add considerably to our chance of fooling the Turk until after other events make it unnecessary to do so any longer.'[18]

Another matter discussed by Lawrence and Dawnay in Cairo was the plan to take Deraa. Several factors had changed since Lawrence had first developed his scheme for an attack by camel-mounted Arabs. Not least among these was the lack of reinforcements from the Hejaz: Jaafar Pasha could ill afford to deplete his force by sending the best of his Arab regulars to Deraa.

A second consideration was the very precise timing Allenby had asked for. Lawrence later wrote: 'Allenby . . . wanted us to lead off not more than four nor less than two days before he did. His words to me were that three men and a boy with pistols in front of Deraa on September the sixteenth . . . would be better than thousands a week before or a week after.'[19] Hitherto, few Arab operations of any scale had been carried out to such a precise timetable.

The final complication was that Nuri Shalaan had declared himself openly for the Revolt, having been bombed at Azrak by the Turks in mid-June. Nuri's support was vital, but the plan had been to call out his Rualla tribesmen when the Deraa raid took place, taking the Turks by surprise. Now that so few regulars could be spared from Maan, the Rualla would have to play a very large role in the northern operations. Nuri's premature action was therefore a cause for concern. If his tribesmen became involved in serious fighting, they would expect Feisal to support them by launching his northern offensive at once. Dawnay feared that this tribal activity might 'force our hand before the time is ripe'.[20]

Arab plans would have to be adjusted to these changed circumstances. Lawrence therefore proposed that only five hundred camel-mounted regulars should be withdrawn from Maan. They would march north to Azrak in a single journey, taking with them a supply column of fifteen hundred camels, the French artillery, machine guns, two armoured cars and two aeroplanes. The force would operate as a self-contained unit, carrying all the supplies it could not obtain locally. It would take a fortnight to reach Deraa, via Azrak, and another week to cut the railways with the help of the Rualla. As in the previous plan, the regulars would withdraw after the attack and re-form for further operations. This scheme was drawn up into a paper and submitted to the General Staff.

Some weeks earlier, Dawnay had seen the need for an additional British officer to organise the line of communications inland from Akaba. It was clear that Jaafar Pasha's operations would be greatly assisted if the supply caravans were run more efficiently, and any kind of northern offensive would place still greater strains on transport resources. In early June, Dawnay had suggested to Joyce that Hubert Young would be suited to this work: 'His clear military mind would be specially well adapted to this class of work: his knowledge of Arabic would not be wasted, as he would be dealing, largely, direct with the Arabs; moreover, his present nominal position as understudy to Lawrence has never up to now really panned out entirely satisfactorily, and I am not sure, taking the personal factor into account, that it is ever likely to; also, and lastly, one doesn't see any apparent alternative'.[21] Another British officer, Major Stirling, was about to join Joyce's staff, and Dawnay proposed the following division of responsibilities:

Yourself [Joyce], directly in charge of the whole show.
Lawrence, running his peculiar brand of Lawrentian stunt, and carrying on as usual.
Young, i/c communications and administrative understudy to yourself.
Stirling, in charge of the travelling circus [British units in the northern operation], and doing the bulk of the reconnaissance work and so forth.'[22]

Young had arrived in late June. As before, he proved to be an able but very demanding chief, who found it very frustrating to deal with the independent-minded Arabs in charge of supply caravans.[23] Joyce was worried by the constant rows, and Dawnay wrote to him in July: 'I was afraid that Young would prove difficult but I hope . . . that you will be able to overcome that – as, if only his *personality* can be kept in check, he should be extraordinarily useful . . . The great thing is to restrict opportunities of friction by the most *precise* definition of his duties and powers, by which it should be possible to prevent his getting up against other people to any great extent, as otherwise he inevitably will. It is a great pity, yet his temperament and his capacity are so ill matched – but I expect with your capacity of getting over difficulties you will manage it!'[24]

Joyce had also complained to Dawnay that he was not being sufficiently consulted about schemes submitted by Lawrence to GHQ, even though he would have to play a large part in their execution: 'I am quite prepared to accept any responsibility as regards all British and European personnel . . . being the senior officer here, that of course is my job. As regards the whole show, I think Colonel Lawrence must accept a share of the responsibility – he pipes the tune with GHQ and then disappears and leaves working out . . . details to other people, and these may or may not work when put into practice.'[25] Dawnay had replied that he had discussed the question with General Bartholomew, 'and I think that you may now feel absolutely assured that in future no scheme or plan will receive official sanction . . . until examined and recommended by yourself . . . That is to say, that although "wild cat" schemes may and will be discussed – academically – their acceptance will in future rest on your approval after thorough examination by us both.

'Moreover, that, I honestly believe, is what Lawrence himself would wish – as he is absolutely satisfied in his capacity of the inexhaustible fountain of ideas, and perfectly content to leave to others the more practical business of irrigating the fields.'[26]

Despite this assurance, Joyce was not consulted about the new plans for the Deraa operation and the Camel Corps raid until the main outlines had been finalised and submitted to GHQ. Details were taken to Akaba by Stirling, who arrived on July 19th. Dawnay had written a hurried covering letter giving reasons for the massive changes in the Deraa scheme: 'I am forwarding for your information . . . a copy of the paper I put up to GHQ as the basis of our discussion. The conclusions therein were generally accepted by the C-in-C . . . It is a pity we can't stick to the old plan, but we must make the best of things as they are. The show as we planned it rested on *surprise*, and surprise now that the Rualla have shown their hand prematurely is no longer possible – so the *character* of the operation must be adapted, and, instead of a regular army show supported by Bedouin co-operation we must now substitute a Bedouin show with regular army support – a difference in degree rather than in principle'.[27] As regards the Camel Corps, Dawnay explained that he had been obliged 'hurriedly to draw up a scheme with Lawrence which I put up to [the General Staff] in outline the same day . . . there was neither time nor opportunity to consult you before the plan was definitely approved.'[28] There was some basis for this excuse. Very secret information could not be transmitted by radio, in case it was decoded by the Turks. This was why Lawrence so frequently travelled across to GHQ.[29] Confidential messages had to be carried by a trusted messenger and were subject to delays, depending on the movement of ships and aircraft between Egypt and Akaba.

As soon as Joyce received the new Dawnay-Lawrence plans, he telegraphed Cairo asking that no final decision about the northern operations should be taken until an alternative, drawn up at Guweira, had also been considered. Thus, when Lawrence returned to Akaba on July 28th after a seven-week absence, he was shown an elaborate nine-page scheme, worked out largely by Young. It contained detailed schedules (down to the last camel-load) for transporting food, ammunition, and forage, which were to be stockpiled in dumps in advance of the movement of five hundred camel-mounted regulars northward to Azrak. The supply system envisaged was so complex that the 'flying column' could not even set out until September 29th, and would reach Azrak on October 7th or 8th.

Lawrence must have seen at a glance that the scheme was impossibly complicated. Its precise interdependent timetables would be reduced to chaos by the dislocation inevitable in Arab operations. He said plainly that he thought it unworkable. Moreover, even if by some miracle it did succeed, the regulars would arrive at Deraa three weeks too late to meet Allenby's requirement. He therefore insisted on the alternative he had worked out with Dawnay. Joyce was furious at this new *fait accompli*, and in the discussion that followed he sided with Young, who had spent many hours calculating the transport schedules. They argued, with some reason, that inadequate supply had always been the cardinal weakness of Arab operations. Lawrence refused to give way, and the atmosphere became very tense. There was also disagreement about the Camel Corps raid. The transport arrangements, as set out by Young, would be stretched to the limit by the forthcoming offensive, and it was argued that there was no spare capacity to put in the dumps required by the Camel Corps. Joyce said that the result would be a further delay to the main autumn campaign.

The argument seems not to have reached any immediate conclusion. Young later wrote: 'Relations between Lawrence and ourselves became for the moment a trifle strained, and the sight of the little man reading the *Morte d'Arthur* in a corner of the mess-tent with an impish smile on his face was not consoling.'[30] The documents suggest that it was three days before Joyce gave in. He cabled Dawnay on August 1st: 'It is evident after discussion with Lawrence, that operations must be accelerated . . . The scheme as outlined [by us] has as a result to be cancelled and a short raid with a reduced force substituted . . . Time does not permit of forward dumps being put in. Our supply [calculations] for personnel and animals are therefore quite unsound. In the past, unsupported raids . . . have had a bad effect on the Arab movement . . . Sherif Feisal is prepared to make the attempt but expects full support should premature action result in reprisals on the tribes concerned.'[31] He had also accepted the Camel Corps scheme.

Young resigned himself to doing things Lawrence's way, at any rate in this instance. He focused his attention on Jaafar Pasha's supply lines, and earned generous praise in *Seven Pillars*, where Lawrence wrote: 'Using his full power, he grappled with the chaos. He had no stores for his columns, no saddles, no clerks, no veterinaries, no drugs and few drivers, so that to run a harmonious and orderly train was impossible; but Young very nearly did it, in his curious ungrateful way. Thanks to him, the supply problem of the Arab regulars on the plateau was solved.'[32]

While preparations for the final offensive were being made in the Middle East, politicians in London made efforts to reconcile Britain's differing engagements in this region. At the end of June, Sykes met Georges-Picot in order to review 'the whole situation as it now stands in regard to the Anglo-French Agreement of 1916.'[33] During these discussions, Sykes explained his view that the Agreement should now be modified, not least because it contradicted American commitment to the principle of self-determination. Georges-Picot, however, insisted that the Agreement 'could not be abolished',[34] and Sykes was unable to obtain any kind of substantive modification. Instead, he tried to persuade Georges-Picot to join him in submitting two declarations he had drafted for consideration by the British and French Governments. One was an assurance to Hussein, very similar to the recent declaration to the seven Syrians of Cairo; the other, a statement expressing general support for the principle of self-determination, while insisting that in the immediate future an undefined 'period of tutelage must supervene'.[35]

In effect, these discussions were a bargaining process. Sykes was hoping to commit France to a less openly imperialistic stance, while Georges-Picot was hoping to secure real political power in Syria as rapidly as possible. Georges-Picot saw that Allenby's coming advance would take the EEF into areas designated for French direct rule or influence under the Sykes-Picot terms. After his frustrating experiences in Palestine, he feared that Britain would concede nothing in Syria either. Having complained bitterly to Sykes about the treatment he had received from Allenby in Jerusalem, he now sought practical commitments. He argued that in Syria, the British C-in-C should retain ultimate authority on military questions alone. French political officers should be appointed who would be 'wholly responsible for civil administration and who would have complete executive power on these questions.'[36] Sykes was persuaded to present this case in London.

On July 18th, the Eastern Committee of the Cabinet discussed Sykes's new ideas. These met with a mixed reception but it was agreed that, in view of Britain's obligation under the Sykes-Picot Agreement, Allenby should be consulted on the practical question of French administration in Syria. A few days later he was sent a telegram by the CIGS: 'The question has arisen as to what form of administration would be put into force in the event of your troops occupying any part of the Syrian areas which are regarded as of special interest to France. It is considered by the French that the Military administration in Palestine is virtually a temporary British Civil administration, and that an extension thereof to Syria would be liable to serious misconstruction both in France and in Syria. From a political point of view it would appear desirable that we should be able to give the French assurances that, subject to your supreme authority, French advice would be taken and French assistance accepted in regard to purely administrative affairs in areas of special interest to France . . . but of course it is realized that, in war, military considerations are paramount. I should be glad of your personal opinion and views on this question and hope you may be able to meet the French wishes.'[37] Allenby replied: 'While active military operations are taking place, the Civil Administration of any occupied territory must be included in the Military Administration, as is that of Palestine at present.

'In the event of part of the Syrian areas which are regarded as being of special interest to France being occupied by my Force, I shall be prepared to accept French advice and assistance in regard to purely administrative affairs, subject to my supreme authority, and so long as they do not conflict with military requirements.'[38] This arrangement offered France much less than Georges-Picot had asked for.

A few days later, having heard nothing more on this question, the French Embassy in London asked the Foreign Office for a response. The Eastern Committee therefore discussed the matter when it met on August 8th. It considered a suggestion developed by Sykes in collaboration with Lord Robert Cecil, the assistant secretary of State for Foreign Affairs, that Britain should reply to the French along the lines agreed with Allenby, but insert a significant proviso. As Georges-Picot had resisted all Britain's requests to modify the French position with regard to Arab nationalist aims in Syria, the proviso would aim to prevent the imposition of colonial rule. Administrative power would only be handed over to French officials if their Government would undertake to act in accordance with the spirit of a joint declaration, to be agreed between London and Paris, which would guarantee self-determination for these areas.[39] The declaration had been conceived, Cecil said, 'with a view to tying the French Government down'.[40] He explained: 'The point was to ensure beforehand that the French, if and when we entered Syria, should not make use of our military forces in order to carry out a policy which was at variance with our general engagements.'[41] The declaration would 'show our disinterestedness, and also . . . get rid of the objectionable "imperialistic" features of the Sykes-Picot Agreement.'[42]

After some discussion, the Committee agreed that once the wording of the proposed declaration had been studied by the Foreign Office, the matter should be considered again.

The Camel Corps raiding party reached Akaba on July 31st. Although Lawrence would not be involved in their attack on Mudawara, he guided them for the first stage of the journey, to Wadi Rumm. During this ride he became acquainted with their commanding officer, Robin Buxton who, like himself, had studied history at Oxford. Buxton wrote down his impressions of Lawrence: 'He is only a boy to look at, has a very quiet sedate manner, a fine head but insignificant body. He is known to every Arab in this country for his personal bravery and train wrecking exploits. I don't know whether it is his intrepidity, disinterestedness and mysteriousness which appeals to the Arab most, or his success in finding them rich trains to blow up and loot. After a train success he tells me the army is like Barnum's show and gradually disintegrates. At any rate it is wonderful what he has accomplished with the poor tools at his disposal.

'His influence is astounding not only on the misbeguided native, but also I think on his brother officers and seniors. Out here he lives entirely with the Arab, wears their clothes, eats only their food, and bears all the burdens that the lowliest of them does. He always travels in spotless white, and in fact reminds one of a Prince of Mecca more than anything. He will join us again later I hope as his presence is very stimulating to us all and one has that feeling that things can not go wrong while he is there.'[43]

On Lawrence's side, the thoughts provoked by this ride with the Camel Corps were later recorded in *Seven Pillars*: 'I stayed at Rum with the Camel Corps for the first day, feeling the unreality there of these healthy-looking tommies, like stiff-bodied schoolboys in their shirts and shorts . . . Three years of Egypt and Sinai had burned all the colour out of their faces, to a deep brown – in which their blue eyes flickered weakly like sky-gaps, against the dark possessed gaze of my men. For the rest they were a broad-faced, low-browed people, blunt-featured beside the decadent Arabs, whose fine-curved shapes had been sharpened by generations of breeding to a radiance ages older than these primitive, blotched, honest Englishmen . . .

'Late the next day I left them, and rode for Akaba, passing again through the high-walled Itm, but now alone with my silent, unquestioning fellows, who rode after me like shadows, harmonious and submerged in their natural sand and bush and hill; and a home-sickness came over me, reminding me vividly of my outcast life among these Arabs, exploiting their highest ideals and making their love of freedom one more tool to help us win England the victory over her enemies.

'It was evening, and the low sun was falling on the straight bar of Sinai ahead, its globe extravagantly brilliant in my eyes, because I was dead-tired of life, longing as seldom before for the peaceful moody sky in England. This sunset was fierce, stimulant, barbaric. Its intense glow revived the colours of the desert like a draught – as indeed it did each evening, yet seeming ever a new miracle of strength and heat – while my longings were for weakness and chill, and grey mistiness, that I might not be so crystalline clear, so sure of the wrong which I was doing.

'We English who lived years abroad among strangers . . . idealised our country so highly, that when we returned, sometimes the reality fell too short of our dreams to be tolerable. When away, we were worth more than other men by our conviction that she was greatest, straightest and best of all the countries of the world, and we would die before knowing that a page of her history had been blotted by defeat. Here, in Arabia, in the war's need, I was selling my honesty for her sustenance . . .'[44]

This sense of guilt about his role had never been far from his thoughts, and he could imagine the personal recriminations that would follow if, when the war was ended, the Arabs failed to obtain what he had promised them. These forebodings now came to him very strongly, because he was to see Nuri Shalaan in order to discuss the role to be played by Rualla tribesmen in the attack on Deraa. He could not forget the pledge he had given at their last meeting, a year before. Nuri now knew, because of the Sykes-Picot revelations, that Lawrence had not told the whole truth, and he might demand fulfilment of whatever penalty had been agreed between them. Lawrence later wrote: 'There was a particular and very horrible reason (not published) for my distress at this moment.'[45]

On August 7th, he was flown from Guweira to Jefer, where the talks were to take place. The anxiety he felt is clear from his description of the flight in *Seven Pillars*: 'The air was thin and bumpy, so that we hardly scraped over the crest of Shtar [the head of the pass near Aba el Lissan]. I sat wondering if we would crash, almost hoping it. I felt sure Nuri was about to claim fulfilment of our dishonourable half-bargain, whose execution seemed more impure than its thought. Death in the air would be a clean escape; yet I scarcely hoped it, not from fear, for I was too tired to be much afraid: nor from scruple, for our lives seemed to me absolutely our own, to keep or give away: but from habit, for lately I had risked myself only when it seemed profitable to our cause.

'I was busy compartmenting-up my own mind, finding instinct and reason as ever at strong war. Instinct said "Die", but reason said that was only to cut the mind's tether, and loose it into freedom: better to seek some mental death, some slow wasting of the brain to sink it below these puzzlements. An accident was meaner than deliberate fault. If I did not hesitate to risk my life, why fuss to dirty it? Yet life and honour seemed in different categories, not able to be sold one for another: and for honour, had I not lost that a year ago when I assured the Arabs that England kept her plighted word?'[46]

To his relief, when they reached Jefer, Nuri greeted him amicably, making 'no mention of my price'.[47] But the Rualla leader had not forgotten their previous discussion, and he brought out copies of the Sykes-Picot Agreement and the declaration to the seven Syrians of Cairo. Lawrence later wrote: 'Old Nuri Shalaan, wrinkling his wise nose, returned to me with his file of documents, asking in puzzlement which of them all he might believe. As before, I glibly repeated "The last in date", and the Emir's sense of the honour of his word made him see the humour. Ever after he did his best for our joint cause, only warning me, when he failed in a promise, that it had been superseded by a later intention!'[48]

Feisal was at this meeting also, and for two hours Lawrence shared with him the task of preaching revolt to the Rualla sheikhs. Afterwards, Lawrence was flown back to Guweira, and by nightfall he had travelled down to Akaba.

When he arrived there, he found that Dawnay had come down from Palestine. Someone at GHQ had remembered Lawrence's remark, back in May, that Feisal might use the Camel Corps mounts to take Damascus. France was now demanding the administration of Syria, and Allenby did not wish to become embroiled in a political wrangle; he had sent Dawnay to warn against any rush northwards.

The next day, therefore, Lawrence went up with Dawnay to Aba el Lissan, and Dawnay explained to Feisal how exposed the Arabs would be if the EEF advance were to founder: 'the British push was a chance, and if it failed the Arabs would be on the wrong side of Jordan to be given help. Particularly, Allenby begged Feisal not to rush upon Damascus, but to hold his hand till events were surely favourable . . . Feisal smiled wisely at Dawnay's homily, and replied that he would try this autumn for Damascus though the heavens fell, and, if the British were not able to carry their share of the attack, he would save his own people by making separate peace with Turkey.'[49] Dawnay was taken aback by this final comment, and Lawrence therefore told him something of Feisal's secret exchanges with the Turks. In the draft of *Seven Pillars*, he wrote: 'I made to Dawnay a clean breast of so much of the secret situation as he needed, to judge fairly of Feisal's strength to accord with Turkey after he had taken Damascus and before he had lost it again. He heard me out, and heard Feisal's appreciation of the internal state of the Turkish counsels, and gave us both reason in our hopes: but he thought he would not retail them too loudly in Palestine!'[50]

By this time, they knew that Buxton's Camel Corps had succeeded in taking Mudawara, the Turkish post that had survived so many previous expeditions. They had attacked before dawn that morning, and had captured the station with the loss of only seven men killed.[51] By evening, the wells and railway installations had been destroyed.

Afterwards, the British force had set off north-eastwards towards Jefer. Lawrence and Joyce drove out to meet it there on August 11th, and a conference was held to decide which of the northern targets to attack. In the end they chose the most difficult: the railway viaduct near Kissir, south of Amman. This meant making another 120-mile journey behind Turkish lines. Buxton wrote: 'It is not unlike an attempt on the part of the Huns to blow up Waterloo Bridge, as it is as many miles at the back of their lines and within five miles of their Army headquarters; but provided we can suprise them the matter should not be difficult.'[52] This raid would bring the units into contact with Arab tribesmen, and Lawrence was therefore to accompany it.

Having finalised these plans, Lawrence and Joyce parted company with the Camel Corps, in order to carry out an armoured car reconnaissance as far as Azrak. Three cars would go up there during the main offensive that autumn, and Joyce needed to calculate journey times and check the suitability of the terrain. They were also prospecting for a suitable advance landing ground for the aircraft that were to accompany the expedition.

They rejoined the British force at Bair on the evening of August 15th. Buxton, who had arrived a little earlier, had discovered that the dump of stores placed there in readiness had been looted by bedouin tribesmen. He wrote: 'You can imagine our dismay . . . Plans had to be quickly revised and the most abstruse calculation of rations gone into, everyone going on half commons immediately . . . I have had to send back one officer and fifty men and a hundred camels as I can't feed them . . . with the remainder we shall make a dash for it . . . I am hopeful we shall do the job . . . Lawrence makes one feel that the most impossible things are not really so impossible. [He] is a great source of wonderment to me and a great relief to the mind from purely military matters.'[53]

The next day was Lawrence's thirtieth birthday but, according to Buxton's notes, he was ill with a high temperature. He chose to pass most of his time alone, and he was therefore free to think about what he had made of his life. During the preceding months he had become prone to morbid introspection and, in his feverish state, this exercise in self-judgment gave him little satisfaction.[54]

The Camel Corps continued northwards, and on August 20th reached some ruined buildings near Muaggar, only eight miles south of Amman. It was from here that the raid was to be launched. During the final stage of the journey there had been an alarm when the column was sighted by two German aircraft: as a result Buxton knew that his attack could no longer take the Turks by surprise. To make matters worse, they now learned that a bedouin tribe which had yet to declare for the Revolt was camped in the area they would have to cross in order to reach the railway viaduct. They sent two Arabs forward to find out what the situation was, and in due course the men reported that there were also three strong Turkish patrols in the district.

Taken together, these factors greatly increased the risk of heavy fighting and casualties. Therefore, with great reluctance, the operation was abandoned. Buxton wrote: 'very sadly at sunset . . . I had to turn east and make for water sixty miles away. It was really heartbreaking, having come such a distance and having got our complete force there successfully, but Lawrence agreed with me that we could not risk a disaster, nor was the prize worth it.'[55]

Although the bridge itself had not been touched, Lawrence knew that the raiding party had already served the main purpose of its mission. The Turks would be alarmed by exaggerated rumours of its strength, and would soon turn their energies to preparing a defence of Amman rather than attacking Jaafar Pasha.

The Camel Corps returned south via Azrak, which Buxton saw for the first time. He wrote that the castle was 'a really wonderful old ruin . . . turreted and loopholed just like the latest Scottish baronial castle . . . in spite of its palm grove it stands black and forbidding, and it is wonderful to think that it has been an outpost of so many empires – and has seen the rise and fall of so many fates.

'Lawrence . . . talks of making the place his home after the war and after the Arabs have won their country. Feisal would give it him with his blessing I should think, and perhaps one winter we will cross the desert and we will stay with him for the winter duck shooting, which must be A1 . . . The Arabs won't go near it. They say it is haunted by the hunting dogs of the Shepherd Kings, who go prowling around it at night.'[56]

On August 26th Lawrence arrived back in Aba el Lissan, to find that preparations for the Deraa raid had been completed. Nuri as-Said had mounted the four hundred best regulars on camels, and was to lead the expedition himself. It was due to set out, together with its supply columns, in a few days' time.

At this critical juncture, however, Feisal's army was thrown into confusion because of an unexpected intervention by Hussein. The ageing Sherif had published in the *Qibla*, his newspaper at Mecca, a statement to the effect that Jaafar Pasha had never been appointed Commander-in-Chief of the regular Northern Army and held no such position.[57]

The truth was that Jaafar's appointment had been made by Feisal in 1917, but that Hussein had never approved of it. Lawrence saw the intervention as an attempt by Hussein to assert his authority over Feisal. He later wrote: 'This gross insult to all of us had been published by King Hussein . . . out of pique at his son's too-great success, and to spite the northern town Arabs, the Syrian and Mesopotamian officers, whom the King despised and feared. He knew they were fighting, not to give him dominion, but to set free their own countries to govern themselves'.[58]

As a result of the announcement Jaafar immediately resigned, and so did all his officers. Feisal might have been prepared to ignore the snub, but the Syrians and Iraqis in his army were opposed to Hussein's political ambitions, and seized the opportunity to humiliate the Sherif by forcing a retraction of the offensive statement. In view of their attitude, Feisal felt that he too must resign, which he did in a telegram to his father of August 29th. This development led in turn to problems with the irregular forces, who had previously been unaffected by the squabble. Buxton, passing through Aba el Lissan on his return journey to Palestine, wrote: 'I find a political crisis on here . . . Feisal and Gaafar and all his Arab officers have got the hump and handed in their portfolios. It really is a serious situation for the moment, and there is a danger of all the English work falling to the ground. But I think the situation is bound to clear, though everyone is acting rather childishly at present.'[59]

From the British point of view, the position was extremely worrying. Unless the columns moved off for Azrak without delay, the Deraa raid would fail to take place on the date Allenby had requested. Everything possible was being done to persuade Hussein to make a conciliatory gesture, but the northern operation could not be held up until he gave in. To get round the difficulty, the British officers at Aba el Lissan assumed direct command. Lawrence cabled to Cairo on August 30th: 'According to plan, the convoy and advanced guard of the September scheme are going forward on our orders, without Sherifian approval . . . I think that the situation can be held together another four days. If Feisal can be satisfied by then, operations may continue, if not I will do all possible to withdraw these advanced posts.'[60] In this manner a supply caravan and the first assault column set out, accompanied by Pisani's artillery, on September 3rd. They were one day late.

In the meantime there was a tedious correspondence with Hussein, who was in no hurry to withdraw his remarks. Lawrence was bitterly angry that so much planning had been put in jeopardy. This was the Arabs' one chance of victory in the north, and they would lose a great deal if they threw it away. He later wrote: 'King Hussein behaved truly to type, protesting fluently, with endless circumlocution . . . It was intolerable to be at the mercy of so crass a person. One would have wished such characters confined to Turkey, and indeed Hussein was a "palace Turk" in mind and manner, and in his habit of writing unintelligible nonsense and calling it official correspondence. To clear his mind we sent him some plain statements, which drew abusive returns.'[61]

On the day the first assault column left, Joyce cabled that Hussein's latest telegram 'did not restore the situation regarding Jaafar Pasha . . . the action of the King in disowning him . . . has shattered the authority of Faisal and has given him to understand that he has entirely lost the confidence of his father as regards northern operations. A telegram in Sherifian cipher yesterday from the King to Zeid described Faisal as a traitor and rebel and instructed Zeid and a council of three officers to carry on. Unless the King puts this matter right Faisal will not of course move north and Zeid is not competent to take charge. Nothing will restore the situation unless the King telegraphs to Faisal . . . urging him to continue his work in the north and stating that he has the full confidence of the King and that he will approve provisionally appointments made by Faisal until the matter can be adjusted by post.'[62]

Hussein's cipher messages passed through the hands of British radio operators and were decoded secretly before being passed to the Arab secretariat. Lawrence had been taking advantage of this to re-copy them, corrupting the most offensive passages so that they became unintelligible. Finally, on September 4th, he decided that no further delay could be tolerated. In *Seven Pillars* he wrote: 'there came a long message, the first half a lame apology and withdrawal of the mischievous proclamation, the second half a repetition of the offence in a new form. I suppressed the tail, and took the head marked "very urgent" to Feisal's tent'.[63]

This intervention quietly resolved a crisis which no one wanted to see prolonged. A few days later Joyce reported to Cairo: 'Lawrence and Nasir left for the north on September 6th . . . Recent satisfactory telegrams have greatly relieved the situation . . . unless anything unforeseen arises I confidently expect to leave on the 9th with Feisal.'[64]

CHAPTER 26

A Hollow Triumph
The Capture of Damascus: September – October 1918

LAWRENCE and Nasir travelled up to Azrak in an armoured car with Lord Winterton, an officer who had recently transferred to Arab operations from the now-defunct Camel Corps. Nasir, rather than Feisal, was to take charge of the Arab irregulars in this final campaign. As Lawrence later wrote: 'In accord with my year-old principle, Feisal would be kept in the background, in reserve, to be risked as a last card only if the situation was overtaxing our strengths, or if we were certainly victors. Until then, to fill his place, we needed an experienced and popular Sherif in command, since we would have contingents of Rualla, of Serahin, of Druses, and of Howeitat tribesmen . . . besides masses of peasant horse and foot from the villages of the Hauran'.[1]

During the next few days the Arab striking force assembled at Azrak in readiness for the assault. Lawrence's bodyguard came in on September 9th, two aeroplanes the next day, and then Joyce, Peake, Stirling, Young, and the rest of the armoured cars. On September 12th Feisal himself arrived with Nuri as-Said, Pisani, and the column of regulars: by this time Nuri Shalaan, Auda, and other tribal leaders were also there. According to Lawrence's report, there were 'four hundred and fifty camel corps of the Arab regular army, four Arab Vickers, twenty Arab Hotchkiss, a French battery of four mountain quick-firing .65 guns, two British aeroplanes, three British armoured cars with necessary tenders, a demolition company of Egyptian Camel Corps and a section of camel-ghurkas. Besides these, Sherif Nasir and myself had our private body-guards of Arab camel-men. This made our total force one thousand strong, and its prospects were so sure that we made no provision (and had no means) for getting it back [to Aba el Lissan] again'.[2]

Unless there was some wholly unexpected misadventure, the northern breakthrough Lawrence had worked towards for so long was about to take place. However, he found it impossible to share in the general mood of elation, for he had begun to lose the sense of purpose that had been driving him. In *Seven Pillars* he wrote: 'Everyone was stout and in health. Except myself. The crowd had destroyed my pleasure in Azrak, and I went off down the valley . . . and lay there all day in my old lair among the tamarisk, where the wind in the dusty green branches played with such sounds as it made in English trees. It told me I was tired to death of these Arabs; petty incarnate Semites who attained heights and depths beyond our reach, though not beyond our sight. They realised our absolute in their unrestrained capacity for good and evil; and for two years I had profitably shammed to be their companion!

'To-day it came to me with finality that my patience as regards the false position I had been led into was finished. A week, two weeks, three, and I would insist upon relief. My nerve had broken; and I would be lucky if the ruin of it could be hidden so long.'[3]

He was almost certain that the combined assault east and west of the Jordan would lead to a Turkish defeat. If that happened, there would be no reason for him to stay in the field. He had done more than his share of active service, and it was nearly a year since Clayton had first spoken of pulling him out.

The motivation that had sustained him until this final campaign had been largely personal. Ever since coming to Cairo Intelligence at the end of 1914 he had dreamed of bringing about self-government for the Arabs. The greatest obstacles to success had often been created by the Arabs themselves, rather than the Turks. Yet he had kept his eyes on the final objective, refusing to be distracted by the cultural differences which so infuriated his British colleagues.

This astonishing resolve owed much to Lawrence's clear vision of his goal and to a conviction whose strength seemed to lie in emotion rather than reason. His aim was noble and romantic: to bring freedom and dignity to the peasant villagers of Syria, a population which had for centuries been exploited by corrupt Turkish administrators.

It seems that in his mind he had distilled this idea into a simple, untarnished image: that of his friend and protégé at Carchemish, Dahoum – the boy who had once helped to save his life. When faced by the difficulties and horrors of the battlefield, most men drew moral strength from some such concept; a symbol of the values and loyalties they were fighting for that could be called to mind in an instant. Most found this image in religious belief or the memory of loved ones at home. But by this time Lawrence had few religious convictions, and he had lived away from his family since 1910. His strongest personal allegiances were not in Oxford, but in Carchemish, where he had lived so happily before the war.

At the end of *Seven Pillars* he wrote: 'The strongest motive throughout had been a personal one ... present to me, I think, every hour of these two years.'[4] This private motive also appears in the book's dedication: 'I loved you, so I drew these tides of men into my hands ... to earn you Freedom'.[5] The meaning of both passages is clarified in a letter written while he was drafting *Seven Pillars*: 'I liked a particular Arab very much, and I thought that freedom for the race would be an acceptable present.'[6]

By the time the final Arab offensive began, Lawrence knew that Dahoum was dead. This is clear from several post-war statements. He said, for example, that the personal motive referred to in the dedication had ceased to exist 'some weeks before'[7] the capture of Damascus. Other remarks suggest that this does not refer to the date of Dahoum's death but to the date he learned of it. He told Liddell Hart: 'The unhappy "event" happened long before we got to Damascus',[8] and two years after the Armistice he wrote: 'Dahoum died some years ago, during the war, of fever'.[9]

In reality, Dahoum may have died a long time before. In 1916 there had been a severe famine in northern Syria followed by a typhus epidemic. Leonard Woolley, who went to the Jerablus region at the end of 1918, found that nearly half of the old Carchemish labour force had perished, and it was reported to him that almost a third of the population had died during 1916.

Dahoum had remained at the site as one of the guards, and salary records for the first two years of the war show that he worked there on and off until October 1916. After this, no records survive; but post-war reports by Woolley state that, apart from Hamoudi, none of the men who had originally been appointed to watch the site had been there during the later part of the war.

Carchemish is some two hundred miles north of Damascus, and it is most improbable that Lawrence heard the news directly. On the other hand, British Intelligence received a constant flow of local information from Turkish prisoners and deserters. The Arab Intelligence office at Allenby's advance headquarters had been built up by Hogarth, who was interested in any news of Carchemish. If he had learned of Dahoum's death, he would have seen to it that Lawrence was told.[10]

The news that Dahoum was no longer alive removed the last prop from Lawrence's patience with the Syrian Arabs. Years later, when the journalist William Seabrook published his romantic *Adventures in Arabia*, Lawrence wrote: 'It just shows you how time and experience take the zest out of adventure. If I'd written the tale of my first travels in Syria, hunting crusader castles, I might have done this sort of thing. Indeed, I probably did it, cautiously, in letters home. Later I went to the very bottom of Arab life – and came back with the news that the seven pillars were fallen down.'[11] In the closing stanza of the *Seven Pillars* dedication he wrote bitterly:

> Men prayed me that I set our work, the inviolate house
> > as a memory of you.
> But for fit monument I shattered it, unfinished: and now
> The little things creep out to patch themselves hovels
> > in the marred shadow
> > > Of your gift.[12]

Lawrence knew that the presence of a large force at Azrak could not be kept secret from the Turks. He was confident, however, that they would see it as further proof that the Arabs were about to launch an attack on Amman, which was almost due west of Azrak and much closer than the real target, Deraa. This impression had been carefully fostered, as is clear from a report by Dawnay: 'Measures have been taken to spread among the local Arabs rumours of an impending attack by Emir Feisal on Amman from the east. The recent reconnaissance . . . by Lt. Col. Buxton's column has lent colour to these rumours'.[13]

This deception on the Arab side would reinforce the Turkish expectation, carefully nurtured by Allenby, that the EEF was planning a third attack on Salt. Lawrence wrote: 'we put in a strong bluff towards Amman. Money was sent to Mithgal [head of the Beni Sakhr] with very secret instructions to collect barley dumps for us and the British, in our combined surprise attack against Amman and Salt on the 18th. The Beni Sakhr were to mass at Ziza to help us. The rumour of this . . . confirmed by other factors supplied them from Palestine, kept the Turks' eyes fixed on the Jordan and east of it'.[14]

By the time the Arab forces were assembled, it was clear that they would not be able to attack Deraa in the way Lawrence had hoped. His plan had been to take the town by direct assault, under cover of an aerial bombardment; but messages from Palestine now warned that the RAF would be unable to provide very much air support. Moreover, the large force of Rualla irregulars which he had expected had not had time to gather, mainly because of the delays created by the *Qibla* affair.

At a conference held on September 11th, therefore, the original plan was dropped. Instead, the Arabs would 'carry out a flying attack on the northern, western, and southern railways at Deraa, with our regular troops, the Rualla horse . . . and such Hauran peasants as should be brave enough to declare for us.'[15]

The first step would be to make a break in the railway between Amman and Deraa. This would strengthen Turkish fears of a threat to Amman, and prevent the reinforcement of Deraa from the south. A raiding party consisting of Peake's Egyptians and the Gurkha Rifles left Azrak on September 13th to carry this out, assisted by the armoured cars.

At dawn the following morning, the main column set out northwards. When Lawrence joined them the following day, he learned that Peake's attack on the railway south of Deraa had miscarried. Guides had mistakenly led his raiders to a place where the line was guarded by a large force of Arabs in Turkish pay.[16]

As Peake's men would soon be needed north of Deraa for the attack on the Damascus line, there was no time to send them back for a second attempt. Lawrence therefore decided that the operation would have to be carried out by the armoured cars alone: they had enough speed to carry out both attacks on schedule. After a hurried reconnaissance, a bridge was selected as the new target. It seemed risky to carry out such an operation without any infantry support, but there was no alternative. Lawrence was to go in one car and lay demolition charges under the bridge while the other car drew the enemy's fire.

The attack took place on September 16th: 'we went down in all the cars we had to the railway and took a post of open-mouthed Turks too suddenly for them to realise that we were hostile. The post commanded a very pleasant four-arched bridge . . . with a very flattering white marble inscription to Abd el-Hamid [the former sultan of Turkey]. We wrecked all this with one hundred and fifty pounds of gun-cotton, and did what we could to the station.'[17]

While this was going on, the main column had continued its advance. Its object was to break the line between Deraa and Damascus. Lawrence rejoined it early the following morning in time to witness an assault on the Turkish post at Tell Arar, five miles north of Deraa. This was carried out successfully, with only one Arab killed. In *Seven Pillars* he wrote: 'So . . . ten miles of the Damascus line was freely ours . . . It was the only railway to Palestine and Hejaz and I could hardly believe our fortune; hardly believe that our word to Allenby was fulfilled so simply and so soon.'[18]

Large-scale demolitions continued throughout that day, despite bombing and machine-gun attacks from enemy aircraft based at Deraa.[19] It was hoped that the damage done would keep the line closed for some time.

Now that the railway north and south of Deraa had been cut, only the branch line into Palestine remained. Nuri's regulars were sent to attack this, and Lawrence joined them with his bodyguard. That afternoon they began an artillery bombardment of the station at Mezerib, west of Deraa, and this was later carried by assault. Lawrence reported: 'As our only demolition parties were on the Damascus line, still demolishing, we could not do anything very extensive, but cleared the station, burnt a lot of rolling stock and two lorries, broke the points and planted a fair assortment of "tulips" [mines] down the line.'[20] Lawrence and Young also cut the main telegraph lines into Palestine, an essential part of Turkish military communications. The damage would probably not be repaired before Allenby's surprise offensive began.

That night, Lawrence took a demolition party a few miles farther west, hoping to blow up the bridge at Tell el Shehab, where he had failed a year previously. As they approached, however, they learned that a trainload of German and Turkish reserves had just arrived from Palestine. For a second time, he was obliged to leave the bridge intact; but his disappointment was tempered by knowledge that these troops, sent up to reinforce Deraa against Arab raids, would weaken Turkish resistance west of the Jordan. On the next day, he moved eastwards again with Nuri's force. In the afternoon they reached the Hejaz line south of Deraa, and blew up a large bridge.

By the morning of September 19th, the expedition was safely back in the Arab camp at Umtaiye in Jebel Druse. A note in the war diary of the armoured-car unit reads: 'The Arab Army returned, having so successfully completed their operations that all means of communications between Deraa and the west of Jordan were completely destroyed, as also between Damascus and Amman.'[21] This was the day of Allenby's attack.

Although the Arab advance position at Umtaiye had seemed well chosen when the plans were made, it was proving to be very vulnerable to air attack. Against this, the Arabs were defenceless, since both of the British aircraft that had accompanied them had now been grounded (in one case after heroic action against enemy machines). Lawrence wrote in *Seven Pillars*: 'Our business was to hold on to Umtaiye. Strategically it was a wonderful place, which gave us command at will of Deraa's three railways. If we held it another week we would have strangled the Turkish armies by our own efforts, whatever fate Allenby was having in the west. Yet tactically Umtaiye was a dangerous place, only four miles from the railway, and an easy march from Deraa. A force made up of regulars without a guerilla screen could not safely hold it: and yet to that we would shortly be reduced, if our air helplessness continued . . . We were camped twelve miles from their aerodrome, in the open desert, about the only possible water-supply, with great herds of camels and many horses necessarily grazing round us. The Turks had found us out, and had made a beginning of bombing, enough to disquiet the irregulars . . . Unless they could be delivered from overhead risk, they would break up and go home, and our usefulness would be ended'.[22]

It had been arranged that an RAF machine would fly from Palestine to Azrak on September 21st, bringing news of the EEF advance. Lawrence travelled down to meet it, hoping to be able to fly across to Allenby's headquarters and arrange for extra air cover. When the aeroplane arrived, it brought news of a quite extraordinary victory. As planned, the EEF had attacked in overwhelming force in the early hours of September 19th. The onslaught had taken the Turks completely by surprise. It had occurred in the west and not, as they had been expecting, in the east. There had been little organised resistance and, by noon, all semblance of orderly retreat had ended. Allenby's cavalry had then broken through and swept northwards to close off the enemy's main lines of retreat. During September 20th the EEF had captured Beisan, Afuleh, and the enemy headquarters at Nazareth. The complete destruction of the Turkish 7th and 8th armies now seemed very probable. Their only remaining escape route was eastwards across the Jordan, and Allenby hoped that the Arabs would close it.

The aeroplane brought several messages. One, from Allenby to Feisal, read: 'I send your Highness my greetings and my most cordial con-gratulations upon the great achievement of your gallant troops about Deraa, the effect of which has, by throwing the enemy's communi-cations into confusion, had an important bearing upon the success of my own operations.

'Thanks to our combined efforts, the Turkish Army is defeated and is everywhere in full retreat . . . Prisoners already counted number eight thousand, and we have taken over a hundred guns, as well as a great mass of war material of every description, the extent of which it is not at present possible to estimate.

'Already the Turkish Army in Syria has suffered a defeat from which it can scarcely recover. It rests upon us now, by the redoubled energy of our attacks, to turn defeat into destruction.'[23]

There was also a letter from Dawnay to Joyce which enclosed Allenby's new instructions for the Arab forces. Dawnay wrote: 'On this side things have gone without the faintest hitch, and with amazing rapidity . . . The enemy was caught completely by surprise and simply boosted right off his feet before he began to realise what was happening.

'Now, with Afuleh and Beisan in our hands, and infantry pressing up to Nablus both from the east and the south, the whole Turkish army is in the net, and every bolt-hole closed except, possibly, that east of the Jordan by way of the Yarmuk valley.

'If the Arabs can close this, too – and close it in time – then, not a man, or gun, or wagon ought to escape – *some* victory!'[24]

He went on to spell out Allenby's requirements: '(1) he wants the railway *south* of Deraa smashed, *as completely as you are able* to smash it, in order to eliminate that flank once and for all; (2) he wants the tribes to close the gap across the Yarmuk valley between Lake Tiberias and Deraa, which may be used by parts of the 8th Army Corps from the Amman area and by remnants of other troops who succeed in making their way across from west of Jordan. (3) Above all he does NOT wish Feisal to dash off, on his own, to Damascus or elsewhere – we shall soon be able to put him there as part of our own operations, and if he darts off prematurely without General Allenby's knowledge and consent, to guarantee his action, there will be the very devil to pay later on, which might upset the whole apple cart. So use all your restraining influence, and get Lawrence to do the same, to prevent Feisal from any act of rashness in the north, which might force our hand and in the wrong direction. The situation is completely in our hands to mould now, so Feisal need have no fear of being carted, provided he will trust us and be patient. Only let him on no account move north without first consulting General Allenby – that would be the fatal error.'[25] The letter ended: 'All good luck to you, Joyce, again my *best* congratulations to you all. Give a good fruity message from me to Feisal, and my love to Lorenzo, and Frank Stirling.'[26]

Allenby's wish that the Arabs should not move northwards was underlined in the formal orders: 'The Commander-in-Chief wishes you to ensure that Emir Faisal . . . does not embark on any enterprise to the north, such as an advance on Damascus, without first obtaining the consent of the Commander-in-Chief. (In this connection you can, if necessary, quote King Hussein's definite statement that Emir Faisal and his Army are directly under the orders of the Commander-in-Chief.) . . . Close co-operation with the E.E.F. is essential and there must not be any independent or premature action by Emir Faisal.'[27]

As Lawrence had hoped, he was able to fly across to EEF headquarters. It was fortunate that he did so, because the military situation was changing from hour to hour and the information received at Azrak was already out of date. During the night of September 20th, a large part of the Turkish 7th Army, together with remnants of the 8th, had attempted to escape eastwards. This movement had been detected at dawn on the 21st when British pilots reported a long transport column moving down the Wadi Fara from Nablus towards the Jordan valley. Lawrence later wrote: 'The modern motor road, the only way of escape for the Turkish divisions, was scalloped between cliff and precipice in a murderous defile. For four hours our aeroplanes replaced one another in series above the doomed columns: nine tons of small bombs or grenades and fifty thousand rounds of S.A.A. were rained upon them. When the smoke had cleared it was seen that the organization of the enemy had melted away. They were a dispersed horde of trembling individuals, hiding for their lives in every fold of the vast hills. Nor did their commanders ever rally them again. When our cavalry entered the silent valley next day they could count ninety guns, fifty lorries, nearly a thousand carts abandoned with all their belongings. The R.A.F. lost four killed. The Turks lost a corps.'[28]

Those men who escaped from Wadi Fara amounted to little more than an exhausted rabble without transport or supplies. Although they had survived the bombardment, many would be picked off by Arab villagers. This meant that one of the main tasks Feisal had been requested to undertake was no longer necessary.

The victory in Palestine was so complete that Allenby decided to push forward immediately, before the Turks had a chance to establish a new line of defence. His next objectives would be Deraa and Damascus. To defend them, there were at present only the regular Turkish garrisons, plus any remnants that might reach these towns from the defeated armies in Palestine.

To the south, however, was the Turkish 4th army, based east of the Jordan at Maan, Amman and Salt, . This had not, so far, been involved in any of the fighting, except some skirmishes with Arab raiding parties around Deraa. As soon as its commanders realised what had happened in Palestine they would guess Allenby's next move and see the danger of being cut off. They would respond by pulling back northwards, hoping to make a stand at Deraa or Damascus. Allenby was very keen to forestall such a move, and this was why he had asked Feisal to destroy the railway south of Deraa.

He now told Lawrence that cavalry units of the EEF would shortly drive eastwards across the Jordan. The New Zealanders under Major-General Chaytor would occupy Salt and Amman, hoping to intercept the retreat of the 4th Army. An Indian force, under Major-General Barrow, would move on Deraa, while Australian troops under Lieutenant- General Chauvel would advance on Kuneitra, farther north. When these places had been taken, the forces under Chauvel and Barrow would close on Damascus, while Chaytor continued his holding operation at Amman.

For the present, the Arabs were to co-operate with these movements, and in particular with action against the Turkish 4th Army. Allenby again stressed that there was to be no independent Arab offensive. Lawrence was firmly told 'not to carry out my saucy threat to take Damascus, till we were all together.'[29] He was assured, however, that Feisal would be given the opportunity to set up an Arab government in Damascus.

Before leaving GHQ, he saw Salmond and asked for the air cover so badly needed by the Arabs. As a result, two fighting aircraft were sent out to the advance base near Deraa immediately; Lawrence flew back in one of them. In addition, it was arranged that a Handley-Page bomber would fly across bringing petrol and spares.

By this time, the Arab achievement at Deraa had been reported back to London. It was discussed at a meeting of the War Cabinet on September 20th: 'The Chief of the Imperial General Staff said that, from information received, it appeared that the Arabs had blown up a railway bridge seventy miles north of the position the British troops were now holding. If this were correct, the railway communication of the Turkish army would be cut, and General Allenby's operations would be greatly assisted. General Wilson explained the position on the map, and pointed out that, if the retreat of the Turkish army to Damascus was cut off it would be possible for General Allenby to capture the bulk of the enemy forces opposed to him, which consisted of from 13,000 to 15,000 Turks, and about 2,500 to 3,000 Germans.

'The attention of the War Cabinet was again called to the work which Colonel Lawrence was doing with the Arab forces, and General Wilson undertook to make enquiries with regard to suitable recognition being given to Colonel Lawrence for his valuable services.'[30]

While this was by no means the first time that Lawrence had been discussed by the Cabinet, he was still totally unknown to the general public. Four days later, however, his name was published in a French newspaper, the *Echo de Paris*, and its startling claims were immediately picked up by the London press. The *Evening Standard*, among others, translated the French report, heading it 'An historic Lawrence':

Side by side with General Allenby and the French Colonel de Piépape [commander of the French contingent in Palestine] we must mention Colonel Lawrence as having played a part of the greatest importance in the Palestine victory. The name of Colonel Lawrence, who placed at the disposal of the British leader his experience of the country and his talent for organisation, will become historic in Great Britain.

At the head of the cavalry force which he had formed with Bedouins and Druses, he cut the railway at Deraa, thus severing the enemy communications between Damascus and Haifa and the eastern side of the Jordan.[31]

As soon as these reports began to appear, the Censorship and Press Committee in London issued a warning to editors which read: 'The Press are earnestly requested not to publish any photograph of Lieutenant-Colonel T. E. Lawrence, C.B., D.S.O. This officer is not known by sight to the Turks, who have put a price upon his head, and any photograph or personal description of him may endanger his safety.'[32]

One result of Allenby's unexpected advance was that attention in London and Paris was suddenly refocused on the administrative arrangements to be made in Syria. On September 23rd, the French Ambassador in London called to see A. J. Balfour, the Foreign Secretary. Balfour noted afterwards that Cambon had spoken of 'the situation which seemed likely to be created in the immediate future by General Allenby's success in Palestine. The Turkish Armies in that country had apparently been now destroyed, and there seemed every probability that General Allenby would penetrate into Syria. Syria, as M. Cambon reminded me, was, by the Sykes-Picot Agreement, within the French sphere of influence, and it was extremely important from the French point of view that this fact should not be lost sight of in any arrangements that General Allenby, as Commander-in-Chief, might make for the administration of the country he was presumably about to occupy.'[33]

In response, Balfour had given Cambon a statement setting out the Cabinet's position: 'The British Government adhere to their declared policy with regard to Syria: namely that, if it should fall into the sphere of interest of any European Power, that Power should be France. They also think that this policy should be made perfectly clear both in France and elsewhere.

'The exact course which should be followed by the two Governments in case General Allenby takes his forces into Syria should be immediately discussed in Paris or London. But it is understood that in any event, wherever officers are required to carry out civilian duties, these officers should (unless the French Government express an opinion to the contrary) be French and not English; without prejudice of course to the supreme authority of the Commander-in-Chief while the country is in military occupation.'[34]

This statement was telegraphed to Allenby on September 25th, with a reminder of those clauses of the Sykes-Picot Agreement which applied to inland Syria. At the same time, he was sent the text of a Foreign Office message to Paris: 'If General Allenby advances to Damascus, it would be most desirable that in conformity with the Anglo-French Agreement of 1916 he should if possible work through an Arab Administration by means of French Liaison.'[35]

It is clear from the records that these steps were forced on the British Government by French demands that the Sykes-Picot Agreement should be applied at once. They did not reflect any enthusiasm in London for French ambitions, which were now seen to be an acute embarrassment *vis-à-vis* the Arabs.

On September 22nd Lawrence returned to Azrak where he met Feisal and explained the need to break the line south of Deraa, in order to hold up any northward movement by the Turkish 4th Army. During the following two days armoured cars, Arab regulars, and large forces of tribesmen attacked the railway many times, until it was impossible for trains to travel between Amman and Deraa.

As Allenby had foreseen, the Turks decided to abandon Maan and began to move northwards by train, but before they were able to reach

Amman, it too was evacuated. When the retreating forces reached the break in the railway, they were obliged to continue their journey by road. As a result, their movement soon became very slow and disorganised.

Now that the line south of Deraa had been damaged beyond repair, Lawrence made up his mind to press northwards. If the Arabs took up a position north of Deraa and prevented the railway there coming back into service, that garrison too would find itself in a difficult position. It would have to chose between a retreat by road, leaving most of its stores and equipment behind, or making a stand in the town itself, where it would soon be surrounded by Barrow's cavalry.

Lawrence planned, after cutting the railway, to move north-west of Deraa to Sheikh Saad , where the Arab force would be able to watch over the Turkish line of retreat. From this vantage point, they could attack any units of the Turkish 4th Army trying to go north, and also remnants of the Palestine Armies still moving up through the Yarmuk valley.

Once this scheme was under way, there would be no purpose in retaining the present base in Jebel Druse; the armoured cars, which could not operate in the Hauran. would be sent back to Azrak. Operations in the north would be carried out by Nuri as-Said's regulars and tribal forces under Nasir, Nuri Shalaan, and Tallal, the headman of Tafas with whom Lawrence had toured the Hauran a year previously.

On September 24th Lawrence wrote to GHQ: 'The Turks have given up the repair of the line, and are streaming up the Haj road to Deraa. In consequence we have closed down here. Sherif Feisal returns at once to Azrak . . . Sherif Nasir and Nuri Shalaan move to . . . Sheikh Saad to place the army there and get in touch with the British . . . The Turks are entrenching Deraa, but the country is such that they will easily be cut off there, if they delay, by your cavalry . . . If it is possible, after mid-day on the 25th and throughout the 26th we would like a continuous [air] patrol of Deraa, dropping bombs'.[36]

The next day he wrote again: 'The [Turkish] force coming up from Amman is presumably about four thousand strong. Of this we hope to knock out nearly half. I think the others will not stand at Deraa (where they will find about two thousand of the relicts of the Palestine Army) but will go off to Damascus at once. Please tell the C.G.S. that I am acting on this idea and raising the west side of the Hauran . . . In Deraa they have about five hundred men digging trenches. Of the fugitives they are arming and equipping such as are in lots with their officers. Those who are pure deserters, single men, are being sent north towards Damascus. I want to stop that, since our cavalry will no doubt encircle Deraa shortly. If they don't we can in a week's time . . .

'Will you get news to me as soon as you can of General Allenby's intentions as to following up the Turks? We can do it, and I think should do it to the Nth, but we would be glad to have a small force of British cavalry with us.'[37]

On the same day, Allenby issued new instructions to Feisal. He knew that the Arab forces had fulfilled much of their previous assignment and that Lawrence was moving north. The Foreign Office had now confirmed that there was to be an Arab administration in Damascus, and there no longer seemed any reason to stop Feisal going there. Allenby therefore sent an urgent message: 'There is no objection to Your Highness entering Damascus as soon as you consider that you can do so with safety.

'I am sending troops to Damascus and I hope that they will arrive there in four or five days from today.

'I trust that Your Highness' forces will be able to co-operate, but you should not relax your pressure in the Deraa district, as it is of vital importance to cut off the Turkish forces which are retreating North from Maan, Amman and Es Salt.'[38] This letter was taken to Feisal by air, but Lawrence seems not to have been aware of it for some days.

Allenby's administrative plans for Syria were set out in a résumé cabled to London shortly afterwards: 'It is not my intention to extend the jurisdiction of the occupied enemy territory administration . . . into the area of French influence.

'I shall appoint French Military officers wherever administration may be necessary in the French "Blue" area [i.e. Lebanon, see Sykes-Picot map, page 236]. They will be under my orders as C.-in-C. of the Allied Expeditionary Force . . .

'I am not extending the existing occupied enemy territory administration to places east of Jordan in the "B" area [of British influence], such as Es Salt and Amman, but until such time as an Arab administration be formed later I am merely appointing a British officer to safeguard the interests of the inhabitants.

'As regards the "A" area [reserved for French influence], notably the city of Damascus, I shall recognise the local Arab administration which I expect to find in existence and shall appoint a French liaison officer as required . . .

'I hope by the above procedure to safeguard French and Arab interests while ensuring that supreme control remains in my own hands as

C.-in-C.'[39] The way was now open, therefore, for Feisal to set up an Arab government in Damascus. It could assume responsibility for civil administration as soon as the Turks left.

Allenby took other steps to ensure that this was allowed to happen. At his final meeting of corps commanders, on September 26th, he made it clear that EEF forces were to stay out. Thus, the orders given to the forces who were to close in on the city included a specific instruction: 'While operating against the enemy about Damascus care will be taken to avoid entering the town if possible . . . Unless forced to do so for tactical reasons, no troops are to enter Damascus. Brigadiers will arrange a picquet on all roads from their areas in to the town to ensure this order being carried out . . .

'Damascus will be left under the . . . civil administration and no national flags will be flown.'[40]

As Lawrence had planned, the Arabs cut the railway north of Deraa again on September 26th, capturing the station at Ghazale and the grain stores at Ezraa. The line had only just come back into operation after the damage done in the original operations nine days earlier. It was now broken over a long stretch. Lawrence, who accompanied the expedition, later reported that the destruction penned six complete trains into Deraa.[41]

Soon after the Arab forces reached Sheikh Saad, news came that Deraa was being evacuated by road. A little later a British aeroplane dropped a message that two columns of Turks were approaching. Lawrence reported: 'One from Deraa was six thousand strong, and one from Mezerib, two thousand strong. We determined that the second was about our size, and marched the regulars out to meet it just north of Tafas, while sending our Hauran horse out to hang on to the skirts of the large column . . . We were too late (since on the way we had a profitable affair with an infantry battalion) to prevent the Mezerib column getting into Tafas. They strengthened themselves there, and as at Turaa, the last village they had entered, allowed themselves to rape all the women they could catch. We attacked them with all arms as they marched out later, and bent the head of their column back towards Tell Arar. When Sherif Bey, the Turkish Commander of the Lancer rearguard in the village, saw this he ordered that the inhabitants be killed. These included some twenty small children (killed with lances and rifles), and about forty women. I noticed particularly one pregnant woman, who had been forced down on a saw- bayonet. Unfortunately, Talal, the Sheikh of Tafas, who . . . had been a tower of strength to us from the beginning, and who was one of the coolest and boldest horsemen I have ever met, was in front with Auda abu Tayi and myself when we saw these sights. He gave a horrible cry, wrapped his headcloth about his face, put spurs to his horse, and rocking in the saddle, galloped at full speed into the midst of the retiring column, and fell, himself and his mare, riddled with machine-gun bullets, among their lance points.

'With Auda's help we were able to cut the enemy column in three. The third section, with German machine-gunners, resisted magnificently, and got off, not cheaply . . . The second and leading portions after a bitter struggle, we wiped out completely. We ordered 'no prisoners' and the men obeyed, except that the reserve company took two hundred and fifty men (including many German A.S.C.) alive. Later, however, they found one of our men with a fractured thigh who had been afterwards pinned to the ground by two mortal thrusts with German bayonets. Then we turned our Hotchkiss on the prisoners and made an end of them, they saying nothing. The common delusion that the Turk is a clean and merciful fighter led some of the British troops to criticize Arab methods a little later – but they had not entered Turaa or Tafas, or watched the Turks swing their wounded by the hands and feet into a burning railway truck, as had been the lot of the Arab army at Jerdun. As for the villagers, they and their ancestors had been for five hundred years ground down by the tyranny of these Turks.'[42]

That night, Arab horsemen were sent into Deraa 'with orders to scatter any Turkish formations met with on the road, and to occupy the place.'[43] Lawrence did not follow immediately, because he had to return to Sheikh Saad. Later, he accompanied Nuri as-Said's regulars for part of the way down to Deraa.

It seems that during the night Mustapha Kemal, commander of the defeated Turkish 7th Army, may have fallen in to Arab hands. He had left Palestine some days previously and was trying to reach Damascus. After narrowly avoiding capture by the Eleventh Cavalry Brigade on September 24th, he had crossed the Jordan south of Beisan and on the night of the 27th he was among those attempting to travel north-wards from Deraa.

It is recorded that, at some time before dawn on the 28th, Nuri as-Said captured Kemal's personal baggage. Nuri's biographer, Lord Birdwood, later wrote: 'It seemed they had missed the passage north of the great Mustapha Kemal by only a matter of hours.'[44]

It would be wrong to dismiss the possibility that Kemal was held briefly by the Arabs and interrogated by Lawrence before being released. Kemal had been corresponding with Feisal for several months, and the Arab nationalists saw his Pan-Turk party as a potential ally. As a prisoner, he would have been in no position to further their cause. Some years after the war, Lawrence told a Foreign Office official that 'by a curious accident he was able, in September 1918, to have several conversations with Mustapha Kemal Pasha'.[45] There were only two occasions during that month when Lawrence and Kemal were in the same locality: September 27th and 30th. If this meeting took place, it was almost certainly on the first of these dates.

Lawrence recalled that they had talked, among other things, about Turkish war aims and the aspirations of the Pan-Turk party. His statement gave the gist of these conversations in considerable detail. Kemal had told him that Turkey's real interests lay to the east. They had entered the war primarily to gain territory in Persia, Muslim Trans-Caucasia, and so on. He had confirmed that the Pan-Turks were not interested in the Arab provinces: 'Palestine, Syria and Mesopotamia . . . were not only valueless in the Pan-Turkish scheme of things (except in certain strategical aspects relating to the war) but would be positive dangers and encumbrances if they remained in Turkish possession. The Pan-Turks, he declared, would lose them without a regret; they would even be glad to be rid of them.'[46]

Although Kemal was a high-ranking enemy officer, the Arab leaders saw him as their best hope for future relations with Turkey, and with Lawrence's agreement he was released. The incident is not mentioned in *Seven Pillars*, but rumours about it circulated in London after the war.[47] Both Feisal and Lawrence were later to be staunch supporters of Kemal during his struggle for control in Turkey and for international recognition.

It was not until dawn on September 28th that Lawrence arrived at Deraa. He found the town in a state of chaos, with Arabs looting and killing. He later wrote that it had been 'one of the nights in which mankind went crazy, when death seemed impossible, however many died to the right or left, and when others' lives became toys to break and throw away'.[48] With Nasir, he now began to make the first administrative arrangements, appointing a military governor, forming a police force, and placing guards over the remaining stores.

After this, he went out westwards to make contact with General Barrow's forces, which were advancing on Deraa without knowing that the Turks had left. The task of halting a division engaged in preparations for an attack was not simple. Lawrence later told Liddell Hart: 'This was a difficult situation to carry off. I took one man with me, only . . . and behaved with histrionic nonchalance, being treated first as enemy, then as native, then as spy'.[49] Eventually, however, he found his way to Barrow's staff.

When Barrow went into Deraa there was a disagreement. Lawrence had always hoped to occupy the town before the EEF reached it and to establish an Arab administration there. Barrow, however, knew nothing about Arab politics and thought only in terms of restoring order to the situation. Many of the Arabs now in Deraa had been at Tafas and they were still wreaking vengeance on the Turks. Barrow was horrified to find them looting a hospital train that had been caught there by the cutting of the line. He later wrote: 'In the cab of the engine was the dead driver and a mortally wounded fireman. The Arab soldiers were going through the train, tearing off the clothing of the groaning and stricken Turks, regardless of gaping wounds and broken limbs, and cutting their victims' throats . . . it was a sight that no average civilised human being could bear unmoved.'[50]

Lawrence made it clear that he did not want Barrow to take control of Deraa. He later justified this by stressing the need to let the Arabs establish their own government: 'My head was working full speed in these minutes, since now or never was the moment to put the Arabs in control, to prevent those fatal first steps by which the unimaginative British, with the best will in the world, usually deprived the acquiescent native of responsibility, and created a situation which called for years of agitation and successive Reform Bills and riotings to mend.

'. . . my play was for high stakes, high beyond [Barrow's] sight, and I cared nothing what he thought of me so that I won. By being personally objectionable to the great men I transferred their anger from my cause to my manner, and gained from them all that I wanted, so long as it was not for myself'.[51] Despite Lawrence's protests, Barrow ordered his men to restore order at the station.

By this time, Lawrence's behaviour and judgment were almost certainly affected by exhaustion, as he had slept very little during the four preceding nights. He later wrote to Stirling, his companion during the final days of the advance: 'before the end I was very weary, and moved in a haze, hardly knowing what I did. Up to Deraa, perhaps, I fought: after that clearly the crisis was solved in our favour, and the last advance and entry into Damascus were almost formalities... things which had to be passed through, but which required no grip or preparation. Didn't you notice that I was three-parts vacant then?'[52]

On September 29th, Barrow's cavalry set off on the seventy-mile advance to Damascus. It had been agreed that Nuri's regulars would march up the railway to cover his right flank, while the irregulars continued to harry the Turkish columns attempting to retreat northwards. Lawrence stayed behind to see Feisal, who was due to arrive in Deraa later that day.

Early next morning he set off with Stirling in a Rolls-Royce tender to rejoin the Arab forces. According to a contemporary report, the roads they passed along were 'scattered with enemy who had died from exhaustion, and dead horses and broken down vehicles were strewn in every direction. It is estimated that two thousand of the enemy must have been accounted for between Deraa and Damascus'.[53] About ten miles south of the city, they caught up with the Arab irregulars, still on the tail of a surviving Turkish column. In his report on this final advance, Lawrence described the fate the Turkish 4th Army had suffered at the hands of the Arabs: 'In all, we had killed nearly five thousand of them, captured about eight thousand . . . and counted spoils of about one hundred and fifty machine guns and from twenty-five to thirty guns.'[54] One column of about a thousand men had nevertheless succeeded in escaping to the east. It was dealt with a few days later by forces from the EEF.

By the night of September 30th, the escape routes from Damascus were virtually closed, with Chauvel's Australians on the north and west, and Barrow to the south-west. The Arabs camped that night at Kiswe, a few miles south of the city. Those Turks inside who had not already fled were trapped.

There seemed no reason for the Arab forces to enter Damascus that night. The roads were dangerous, and the arrival of so many exhausted men would only add to the state of confusion. However, messengers were sent in to make contact with Feisal's secret supporters. Lawrence wished to make sure that a provisional administration was set up, so that the city should be under Arab control before representatives of the EEF went in. It seems also that he feared there might be physical opposition to Christian troops from fanatical elements angered by rumours of the Sykes-Picot terms. He later wrote: 'In their envelopment of Damascus the Australians might be forced, despite orders, to enter the town. If anyone resisted them it would spoil the future. One night was given us to make the Damascenes receive the British Army as their allies.'[55]

In any case, Lawrence knew that Feisal's army would be allowed to occupy the city. He later wrote: '[Allenby's] word to General Chauvel had been, "You will let the Arabs go first, if possible."

'The "if possible" had pleased me, for the great man knew that for weeks it had been physically possible for us to enter, and that we had waited only by his command, for his troops to march with us . . . the word meant that he never questioned our fulfilling what he ordered . . .

'He hoped we would go in first, partly because he was generous, and knew how much more than a mere trophy of victory Damascus would be for the Arabs: and partly for prudential reasons. Feisal's movement it was which made the enemy country friendly to the Allies as they advanced, which enabled convoys to go up and down without escort, towns to be administered without garrison: and Allenby valued and used the Arabs not for their fighting, but for their preaching . . . It was our burden to make each new yard of country ours in sentiment before we took it.'[56]

Nasir and Nuri Shalaan entered Damascus at about 7.30 a.m. on October 1st. Lawrence and Stirling had meant to accompany them, but had been detained on the way. As Stirling later recalled: 'We stopped the car by a small stream and got out to wash and shave. No sooner had we completed our ablutions than a patrol of Bengal Lancers appeared round the shoulder of the hill, galloped up, and made us prisoners.

'Lawrence was in full Arab kit. I had on the Arab head-dress . . . and a camel hair *abaya*, or cloak, which concealed the ordinary khaki uniform I was wearing underneath. Unfortunately I could not speak a word of Urdu, but I tried to indicate that I was a British officer by pulling back my cloak and displaying the red gorget patches on my collar. The only effect this had was to provoke a prod in the back with the point of a very sharp lance. We were driven as captives across country until we were lucky enough to meet a British officer of the regiment to whom we explained our identity.'[57]

It was 9 a.m. before Stirling and Lawrence drove into Damascus. Lawrence wrote that they found the streets 'nearly impassable with the crowds, who yelled themselves hoarse, danced, cut themselves with swords and daggers and fired volleys into the air. Nasir, Nuri Shaalan, Auda abu Tayi and myself were cheered by name, covered with flowers, kissed indefinitely and splashed with attar of roses from the house-tops.'[58]

When they reached the Town Hall, they learned that an Arab government had been proclaimed the previous afternoon, even before the last Turkish and German forces had left. Lawrence had expected that the new administration would be formed by Ali Riza Rikabi, whose nationalist sympathies had been so well disguised that he had been Mayor of Damascus under the Turks for most of the war.[59] However, Ali Riza had made his way to Barrow's headquarters on September 29th. His place had been taken provisionally by another respected nationalist, Shukri el Ayoubi. The Sherifian flag had been hoisted, and the new administration had declared its allegiance to Hussein, as King of all the Arabs.

Lawrence found that Nasir, Nuri, and Shukri were not the only Arab leaders at the Town Hall. There was also a rival group, led by the Algerians, Abd el Kader and his brother Mohammed Said. Lawrence had suffered personally from Abd el Kader's treachery, and he knew that the two Algerians had been actively working for the Turks right up to the end.[60] Before leaving Damascus, Jemal Pasha had appointed Mohammed Said governor. However, the brothers had thought it politic to change sides, and had put themselves at the head of the Arab administration. Lawrence reported: 'I found at the Town Hall Mohhammed Said and Abd el-Kadir . . . who had just assumed possession of the provisional civil government, since there was no one in Damascus who could fight their Moorish bodyguard. They are both insane, and as well pro-Turkish and religious fanatics of the most unpleasant sort. In consequence I sent for them, and . . . announced that as Feisal's representative, I declared Shukri el-Ayubi Arab Military Governor . . . and the provisional civil administration dissolved. They took it rather hard, and had to be sent home.'[61]

He gave further details of this incident in a letter to Stirling, written a few months later: 'Abd el Kadir and Mohammed Said were sitting in the Serail with their armed servants. Feisal had begged me to get rid of them, so I told them to go, and that Shukri el Ayubi would be military governor till Ali Riza returned. Abd el Kadir refused to go, and tried to stab me in the Council Chamber, Auda knocked him down, and Nuri Shalaan offered me the help of the Rualla to put him out. Mohhamed Said and Abd el Kadir then went away, breathing vengeance against me as a Christian.'[62]

Soon after this, General Chauvel drove into the city, knowing that Lawrence was already there. When they met, at the Town Hall, Lawrence introduced Shukri to him as the military governor, and said that the Arab forces would take responsibility for public order. He encouraged Chauvel to keep his Australian troops, if possible, outside the town.

Chauvel wrote to GHQ about these arrangements. As he understood them, his orders had been 'to instruct the Wali to carry on the civil administration of the city, providing such military guards and police only as were required for the protection of property'. His report stated: 'On arriving at the Serail at 9.30 a.m. I met Lieut. Col. Lawrence who introduced me to Shukri Pasha, whom he told me was the Military Governor. I understood that this official was the Wali, and I issued him instructions through Lt. Col. Lawrence to carry on the civil administration of the city, and informed him that I would find him any military guards and police that he required.

'Lt. Col. Lawrence offered to assist, to advise me of what guards were required, and to supervise the carrying out of these instructions. I asked Lt. Col. Lawrence to assist in these matters because I had no Political Officer at the moment at my disposal . . .

'Lt. Col. Lawrence returned . . . to my Headquarters about 5 p.m. and informed me that Shukri Pasha was not, as I thought, the original Wali, but had been appointed by him that morning . . . all Turkish officials had fled from Damascus about noon on the 30th. The Arabs of Damascus had declared for the King of the Hedjaz on the evening of the 30th.

'I said I could not recognise the King of the Hedjaz in the matter without further instructions, but I was agreeable to Lt. Col. Lawrence, with the Military Governor, carrying out the civil administration as a temporary measure pending instructions to the contrary being received from General Headquarters.'[63]

Lawrence too reported on the situation: 'Shukri Pasha el Ayoubi was appointed Arab Military Governor, as all former civil employees had left with Jemal Pasha on the previous day. Martial law was proclaimed, police organised, and the town picketed . . . I have no orders as to what political arrangements should be made in Damascus, and will carry on as before till I hear further from you . . . G.O.C. Desert Mounted Corps [Chauvel] has seen above, and agrees with my carrying on with the town administration until further instructions.'[64]

It is clear from the retrospective accounts given by both Chauvel and Lawrence that there was considerable tension between the two men. Chauvel knew no more than Barrow about the political status of the Arabs. He was shocked by the scenes of Arab indiscipline and looting in the city, and angered to find that Lawrence, a relatively junior officer, seemed to have taken control in Feisal's name. His own troops had been engaged in hard fighting during the previous days, and he was determined that they should be regarded as the captors of Damascus. Despite Allenby's orders, some of his units had found an excuse to pass through the outskirts of the city early that morning, and the Australians were loudly proclaiming the glory of having been 'first in'.[65] Chauvel was annoyed when Lawrence pointed out that the Arabs had taken possession of Damascus hours before any EEF troops had entered.[66]

Lawrence had already made up his mind to escape from his role with the Arabs as soon as possible. His thoughts on the evening of October 1st are recorded in *Seven Pillars*: 'I was sitting alone in my room, working and thinking . . . when it came to the Arab last prayer, and the Muedhdhins began to send their call through the warm moist night over the feasting and the illuminations of the city. From a little mosque quite near there was one who cried into my open window, a man with a ringing voice of special sweetness, and I found myself involuntarily distinguishing his words: "God alone is great: I testify there are no gods, but God: and Mohammed the Prophet of God. Come to prayer: come to security. God alone is great: there are no gods but God."

'At the close he dropped his voice two tones, almost to speaking level, and very softly added: "And He is very good to us this day, O people of Damascus." The clamour beneath him hushed suddenly, as everyone seemed to obey the call to prayer for this first night in their lives of perfect freedom: while my fancy showed me, in the overwhelming pause, my loneliness and lack of reason in their movement: since only for me of the tens of thousands in the city, was that phrase meaningless.

'I had been born free, and a stranger to those whom I had led for the two years, and tonight it seemed that I had given them all my gift, this false liberty drawn down to them by spells and wickedness, and nothing was left me but to go away. The dead army of my hopes, now turned to fact, confronted me, and my will, the worn instrument which had so long frayed our path, broke suddenly in my hand and fell useless. It told me that this eastern chapter in my life was ended. There was the morrow and the next day of unrelenting care, that Feisal might surely gain the fruits of battle: and that was all my work.'[67] That evening he wrote a brief report on the events of the past three days. He ended: 'If Arab military assistance is not required in further operations of the Desert Corps, I would like to return to Palestine as I feel that if I remain here longer, it will be very difficult for my successor.'[68]

During the next two days Lawrence struggled to ensure that the Arabs achieved some semblance of order. He wrote in *Seven Pillars*: 'Our aim was a façade rather than a fitted building. It was run up so furiously well that when I left Damascus . . . the Syrians had their *de facto*

Government'.[69] Above all, he wished to establish the principle that the Arabs should receive technical or other help only when they asked for it, rather than have European control imposed on them.

The task was not easy, partly because the Turks had left acute problems for their successors. By October 2nd, however, the electric lighting system was working again. The trams, disused since 1917, were soon put back into service. Clayton reported a few days later: 'In Damascus the former machinery continues under an Arab Military Governor, all officials being Arab. Sanitation, public lighting and tramways and police are being restored to peace standard, but the complete neglect of these in 1917 by the Turks, and the disappearance of all local draught animals in the last fortnight, make progress necessarily slow.'[70]

Another problem was public disorder. Much of this was caused by Druse peasantry from outside the city who saw the victory as an occasion for riot and plunder. However, there was also political conflict. On the night of October 1st, Abd el Kader and Mohammed Said attempted to raise a rebellion against the Sherifians and their Christian allies. This was put down by the Arab Army during the following morning,[71] and the situation was finally calmed at noon by a march-through of Chauvel's forces, with an Arab contingent at their head. Clayton, who visited Damascus on October 3rd, commented: 'Considering the size of the city and the great upheaval which its capture from Turkey has occasioned, the situation is wonderfully quiet.'[72]

By this time, Beirut had also been evacuated by the Turks. On September 30th, before Lawrence reached Damascus, Mohammed Said had sent a message to nationalists there, urging them to proclaim an Arab government. This move was warmly supported by other Damascene politicians including Ali Riza Rikabi, who had taken over the leadership from Shukri on October 2nd. Lawrence did not learn of this until the next day, and he regretted it, because he knew it would cause trouble with the French. He later wrote: 'I was grieved by their mistake, yet glad they felt grown-up enough to reject me.'[73]

When Allenby and members of his staff visited Damascus on October 3rd, he approved the arrangements Lawrence had set up and confirmed Ali Riza's appointment as governor. By this time he had received detailed instructions from London about the political status of the Arabs and the attitude he should take towards any administration they formed: 'In accordance with the engagements into which His Majesty's Government have entered with the King of Hejaz, and in pursuance of the general policy approved by them, the authority of the friendly and allied Arabs should be formally recognised in any part of the areas "A" and "B" as defined in the Anglo-French Agreement of 1916, where it may be found established, or can be established, as a result of the military operations now in progress.'[74] The 'belligerent status of the Arabs fighting for the liberation of their territories from Turkish rule' should now be recognised. Accordingly, 'in so far as military exigencies permit, the regions so liberated should properly be treated as Allied territory enjoying the status of an independent State (or confederation of States) of friendly Arabs . . . and not as enemy provinces in temporary military occupation . . .

'It would be desirable to mark the recognition and establishment of native Arab rule by some conspicuous or formal act such as the hoisting and saluting of the Arab flag . . .

'Our policy should be to encourage the setting up of either central, local or regional Arab administration, as the case may be, and work, at least ostensibly, through them entirely. For this purpose there need be no hesitation to accept a merely nominal authority when no other can for the moment be established.'[75]

Despite these concessions to the idea of self-determination, the instructions continued: 'if . . . the Arab authorities request the assistance or advice of European functionaries, we are bound under the Anglo-French Agreement to let these be French in Area "A". From this point of view it is important that the military administration should be restricted to such functions as can properly be described as military, so as to give rise to no inconvenient claim to the employment where unnecessary of French civilians. It is equally important to keep our procedure on the same lines in that of Area "B" which lies east of the Dead Sea and of the Jordan Valley depression, so as not to give the French the pretext for any larger demands in Area "A".'[76]

Allenby had come to Damascus to implement these instructions, and it had been arranged that Feisal would arrive in the city on the same day. They met for the first time at the Victoria Hotel. Also present were Chauvel, Nuri as-Said, Nasir, Joyce, Lawrence, Stirling, Young and Cornwallis.

Lawrence wrote little about this meeting in *Seven Pillars*, mentioning only that 'Allenby gave me a telegram from the Foreign Office, recognising to the Arabs the status of belligerents; and told me to translate it to the Emir: but none of us knew what it meant in English, let alone in Arabic: and Feisal, smiling through the tears which the welcome of his people had forced from him, put it aside to thank the Commander-in-Chief for the trust which had made him and his movement. They were a strange contrast: Feisal, large-eyed, colourless and worn, like a fine dagger; Allenby, gigantic and red and merry, fit representative of the Power which had thrown a girdle of humour and strong dealing round the world.'[77]

Much fuller notes of the meeting were made by Chauvel. Regrettably, these appear to survive only in a form written up some years later. There are discrepancies between this and the contemporary documents; Chauvel's account cannot, therefore, be regarded as completely reliable.[78] He wrote: 'Lawrence acted as Interpreter. The Commander-in-Chief explained to Feisal:

'(a) That France was to be the Protecting Power over Syria.

'(b) That he, Feisal, as representing his Father, King Hussein, was to have the Administration of Syria (less Palestine and the Lebanon Province) under French guidance and financial backing.

'(c) That the Arab sphere would include the hinterland of Syria only and that he, Feisal, would not have anything to do with the Lebanon, which would be considered to stretch from the Northern boundary of Palestine (about Tyre) to the head of the Gulf of Alexandretta.

'(d) That he was to have a French Liaison Officer at once, who would work for the present with Lawrence, who would be expected to give him every assistance.

'Feisal objected very strongly. He said that he knew nothing of France in the matter; that he was prepared to have British assistance; that he understood from the Adviser whom Allenby had sent him that the Arabs were to have the whole of Syria including the Lebanon but excluding Palestine; that a country without a port was no good to him; and that he declined to have a French Liaison Officer or to recognise French guidance in any way.

'The Chief turned to Lawrence and said: "But did you not tell him that the French were to have the Protectorate over Syria?" Lawrence said: "No Sir, I know nothing about it." The Chief then said: "But you knew definitely that he, Feisal, was to have nothing to do with the Lebanon?" Lawrence said: "No, Sir, I did not."

'After some further discussion, the Chief told Feisal that he, Sir Edmund Allenby, was Commander-in-Chief and that he, Feisal, was at the moment a Lieut.-General under his Command and that he would have to obey orders . . .

'After Feisal had gone, Lawrence told the Chief that he would not work with a French Liaison Officer and that he was due for leave and thought he had better take it now and go off to England.'[79] It is clear from other passages in this account that Lawrence wished to return to London so that he could argue the Arab case.

At first sight, the statements about Anglo-French arrangements attributed to Lawrence in this document seem curious. Chauvel implies that, when challenged, both Lawrence and Feisal denied any knowledge of the Sykes-Picot terms. But the Agreement had by this time been public knowledge for nearly a year, and it would have been absurd for either Feisal or Lawrence to pretend not to know about it (although Feisal could maintain that he had never been told officially). It seems likely that Chauvel misconstrued what he heard, and it has to be borne in mind that at that time he knew almost nothing about the political background to the discussion. The probable explanation of these exchanges is that Lawrence and Feisal now heard for the first time about the interim arrangements for Syria, which had only recently been agreed between London and Paris.[80] The details Allenby announced must have come as a shock. They seemed to amount to an imposition of the Sykes-Picot terms, yet Lawrence's superiors had repeatedly told him that the Agreement was as good as dead.

The remark Chauvel attributed to Feisal about the Lebanon must also be considered in its proper context. Feisal would not have been able to admit, particularly in front of other Arab leaders, that he was prepared to recognise any form of French claim to the Lebanon. Such a concession would have led to an immediate breach with his father, and would have alienated Arab nationalists throughout Syria. If, therefore, such a remark was made at this meeting, it must be regarded as evidence of a political stance, rather than a reflection of Feisal's private knowledge or opinion.[81]

At 7 p.m. on October 4th Lawrence was driven away from Damascus in the same Rolls-Royce tender that he and Stirling had used for their triumphal entry. He would never return. His wartime mission was now fulfilled: Turkey had been defeated and the Arabs were established in Syria, for the time being at least. Ahead lay a more difficult task: to persuade the Allies to let Feisal keep what had been won.

CHAPTER 27

The View from Europe
October – December 1918

As Lawrence drove away from Damascus, he knew that Feisal's position would be extremely difficult. There would be problems both with the French liaison staff and with Syrian politicians who had no wish to see their personal influencé diminished by a Sherifian head of state. The latter were now trying as hard as they could to assert their own authority.

The situation was inadvertently made worse by Allenby and Clayton, whose first instinct was to prevent Feisal getting involved in local politics. They therefore tried to restrict him to a purely military role, making Ali Riza Pasha governor of all the occupied territories in Sykes-Picot areas A and B. He was to report directly to Allenby. This proved to be a tactical error, as Ali Riza was a Syrian political leader with no reason to feel loyal towards Britain.

One of his first acts was to send Shukri el Ayoubi to Beirut, claiming to have done so in Feisal's name. This was a provocation to France and a challenge to Feisal, who could not disown a move that was popular throughout Syria. Lawrence later wrote: 'Upon the taking of Damascus, Feisal and myself lost control. The Syrians (Ali Riza and the Bekri brothers) took charge, and galloped (metaphorically) straight for the coast. My intention had been to occupy from the gap of Tripoli northward to Alexandretta, and I had told Feisal that in the welter which would follow victory he would stand a very decent chance of getting this area eventually allotted to the Syrian kingdom upon terms. I still think that it was a possibility, and that the precipitate occupation of Beyrout and Lebanon wholly threw away the local people's chances. Shukri was sent to Beyrout by Ali Riza. I was much too engaged in struggling with difficulties of Damascus to attempt to cope with Ali Riza . . .

'There was nothing either Sherifian or mine, therefore, in the occupation of Beyrout. I was opposed to it, on grounds of interest, and Feisal had ordered his people to have nothing to do with littoral Syria south of the Tripoli gap . . . no one of the Sherifs, or of the Arab army, or of us, went there. It was entirely a Damascus move: as was the fatuous proclamation of King Hussein in Damascus [on September 30th]. These things were as much anti-Feisal as anything. The Damascenes hoped to avoid the near activities of Feisal by appealing to the distant Hussein, who hated Feisal. I had no intention of proclaiming or creating any king in Damascus.'[1]

The Syrians had been encouraged to act because there were no soldiers, Turkish or Allied, along the coast. During the panic that followed Allenby's initial victory, the Turkish garrisons had fled; yet the British Army had not yet moved so far north (it did not occupy Beirut until October 8th). As a result, Lebanon was there for the taking. Having set up Arab administrations in the coastal towns before this, Ali Riza and his party would claim permanent possession under the terms of the declaration to the seven Syrians of Cairo. Allenby had cabled about this risk to London on October 6th: 'The fact that the Arab leaders are aware of the assurances contained in Foreign Office telegram 753 of June 16th 1918 [i.e. the declaration to the seven] . . . complicates the position at Beirut; in this wire His Majesty's Government recognised the Native Army and the sovereignty of independent Arabs inhabiting the areas emancipated from Turkish control by the action of the Arabs themselves during the present war.'[2]

Clayton thought that such a claim was doubtful: 'it may fairly be said that the evacuation of Beirut by Turkey was a direct consequence of the Commander-in-Chief's capture of Damascus and not due to Arab military action.'[3] The Arabs, however, might well have replied that Allenby's campaign through Syria had itself relied heavily on Arab action inland.

Lawrence reached Cairo on October 8th, and immediately submitted a long press release on the final Arab advance. His account of the capture of Damascus gave the impression that the victory had been very largely an Arab affair.[4]

During the following days, the activities of the Syrian nationalists acting in Feisal's name gave increasing cause for irritation. On October 11th, after discussing the position with Lawrence, Clayton wrote: 'I must go to Damascus and give Faisal a talking to, as he is getting rather out of hand. The Governor whom Faisal appointed at Beirut [i.e. Shukri el Ayoubi] . . . refuses to vacate [Beirut] and consequently a difficult situation has arisen between him and Colonel de Piépape, the French Military Governor appointed by the Chief [Allenby]. Also Faisal has tried to take over control in Damascus of railways and telegraphs, which must of course be under our control at present (this will be all to his advantage too, as we shall place them in good running order). I have told Faisal . . . that he will only prejudice his case before the Peace Conference if he tries to grab, and have warned him that the Lebanon (whose status has been for many years guaranteed by the Powers) is a very delicate question. He should devote all his energies to forming a sound and reliable administration in Damascus and the "A" and "B" areas, so that he may have something tangible to show at the Peace Conference.'[5]

The Turkish collapse had occurred so rapidly that no senior political officer had been available to represent French interests in Syria. Clayton saw that it would be difficult to introduce one at a later date, and that his own staff would have to uphold French aspirations in the meantime. He cabled to London: 'If the present unsatisfactory situation continues in which we have to hold the balance between French and Arabs, it must end in our being accused of bad faith by both. It is no use the French reiterating their claims unless they take the problem in hand seriously and produce the advice and material assistance which alone can conciliate the considerable body of Arab opinion which at the present moment is opposed to their Syrian policy.'[6]

As Clayton soon realised, Feisal's position of leadership without administrative authority was unworkable. If he lent his name to British demands over Beirut, Feisal would lose all credibility with the northern politicians. He refused to do so unless some kind of general undertaking was given about the future protection of Arab interests along the coast. To resolve this problem, Allenby gave Feisal his personal assurance on October 16th 'that whatever arrangements may be made now for districts in the coastal area, these are of a military nature and without prejudice to the final settlement which will be decided upon by the Allies at the Peace Conference.'[7] This calmed the situation, and control of the civil administration in Beirut was taken over by Piépape. Finally, on October 21st, Allenby reduced the status of Ali Riza Pasha, giving Feisal full authority, under the British military administration, for political matters in areas A and B. Mindful of the Sykes-Picot proviso, Feisal had meanwhile offered the services of his army in pursuit of the retreating Turkish forces, and the Arabs were represented at the fall of Homs, Hama, and Aleppo.

On October 15th, Lawrence left Egypt for England. Before going, he cleared up his remaining affairs in Cairo. Lady Allenby had asked him for a memento of the campaign, and he gave her one of his few trophies, a prayer rug.[8] He also wrote briefly to Major Scott, still Commandant at

Akaba: 'As we hoped we got to Damascus, and there I had to leave the Arabs – it is a pity to go, and it would have been unwise to stay. I feel like a man who has suddenly dropped a heavy load – one's back hurts when one tries to walk straight.

'I'm off, out of Egypt. This old war is closing, and my use is gone . . . My regards to the Staff – and my very best thanks to you and them. We were an odd little set, and we have, I expect, changed history in the Near East. I wonder how the Powers will let the Arabs get on.'[9]

Long afterwards, Lawrence wrote: 'all my thought was of going home, where I meant to get transferred to the French front. The eastern business was badly on my nerves.'[10] Later still, he said: 'What was in my mind, as I went towards London, was to begin again – as a junior officer – in France'.[11] It is possible that such a step occurred to him, perhaps as a final honourable solution if Syria was now, after all, to be given to France. However, there is no evidence of it in contemporary documents. On the contrary, he seems to have plunged himself immediately and with unswerving commitment into political discussions about the future of the Middle East.[12]

The process began even before he reached England. By chance, one of his fellow-passengers on the *Kaiser-i-Hind* during the voyage from Port Said to Taranto in Italy was Lord Winterton, who wrote to Lord Robert Cecil, assistant secretary of State for Foreign Affairs, on the second day out: 'Lawrence, as you probably know, has been chief political officer to Feisal and may be described as "the Soul of the Hedjaz" . . . But for him the Arab movement could never have succeeded as it has done.

'He is very anxious to see you and A. J. Balfour [the Foreign Secretary]. May I bring him to the F.O.? Could you let your secretary write to me at the House of Commons when I could see you. Lawrence is au fait with the whole Damascus-Beirut-Aleppo position as no-one else is and joins exceptional intellectual brilliance to a unique personal knowledge of the Arabs and Arab movement.'[13]

Lawrence travelled north from Taranto by rail. As the journey by troop train often took ten days, he had arranged before leaving Egypt for promotion to the 'special, temporary and acting' rank of full colonel.[14] This entitled him to take a sleeping berth on an express, which reached Le Havre in only three days: 'Sleeping berths were given only to full colonels and upward . . . I like comfort!'[15]

During a brief stop in Rome he encountered Georges-Picot, who was on his way to Syria as French High Commissioner. Their conversation left

Lawrence in no doubt about French intentions. Georges-Picot had been humiliated by the British in Palestine, but he now intended to claim control of Syria under the terms of the 1916 Agreement, which he had defended against all modification. Lawrence continued his journey home with fresh determination to lobby the Government on Feisal's behalf.

He arrived in England on about October 24th and went to Oxford to see his family. This was the first time he had been home in nearly four years. On the following Monday (October 28th) he set to work, making use of Winterton's introduction. His object was to see that the Sykes-Picot Agreement was overturned. After meeting him that afternoon, Cecil wrote: 'Colonel Lawrence . . . impressed upon me that Faisal and the Arabs (to whom he always referred as "we") had taken Beyrout, Latakia, and Antioch without any assistance by means of local risings. He also declared that Damascus had been militarily at the mercy of Faisal ever since November of last year, and that he could have taken it then and made peace with the Turks upon terms which would have been very favourable. He declared that he had seen letters which had passed between Djemal and Faisal, and which made this clear beyond a doubt. He denounced in unmeasured terms the folly (or, as he called it, the levity) of the Sykes-Picot Agreement, the boundaries of which were, he said, entirely absurd and unworkable.

'I showed him the proposed joint declaration by the French and British, which he thought quite satisfactory, but inconsistent with the Sykes-Picot Agreement: as undoubtedly it is.'[16] This joint declaration was the 'proviso' Cecil had first proposed three months previously (see p. 533), as a condition for allowing French political officers into Syria. It had been agreed in principle at an Anglo-French meeting held in London on September 30th.

Cecil's account of his talk with Lawrence continues: 'I spoke to him about Mesopotamia, and he urged that it should be put under an Arab Government of as little practical activity as possible. He suggested that one of King Hussein's sons should be Governor. Abdullah would do very well . . .

'He was violently anti-French, and he suggested that, if there were to be fresh conversations, it would be well to have both Arab and Zionist representatives present, as well as Americans and Italians.'[17]

Lawrence made other visits during this first week in England, hoping to win as many friends as possible for the Arab cause. Among the people he saw was General Sir George Macdonogh at the War Office.

Macdonogh was very well informed about Middle Eastern affairs, and he attached some weight to Lawrence's opinions. They evidently discussed the whole Arab problem in some detail.

Afterwards, Macdonogh circulated to the War Cabinet a memorandum titled 'Note on Policy in the Middle East', incorporating Lawrence's views. He began by pointing out that a review of British policy in the area was opportune, and then went on to present an almost unanswerable case for setting aside the Sykes-Picot Agreement: 'The chief obstacle to a satisfactory solution of the problems presented, at least so far as Syria is concerned, consists in the attitude of the French. They are intensely jealous of any interference by third parties in that area, while their claims are based on sentiment rather than on any solid foundation, such as that of military conquest. That difficulties would arise with the French in the event of British troops invading Syria has been foreseen since the early days of the war, and it was for the purpose of providing some *modus vivendi* both then and when peace was declared that the Sykes-Picot Agreement was concluded . . . It is doubtful if this Agreement could ever have been satisfactory. At any rate, owing to its inherent faults and to the vastly altered circumstances of the present time, it has become not merely unsatisfactory but a positive source of danger, likely to lead to constant friction with France, and not improbably, to an eventual rupture with that Power.

'The circumstances which have contributed most largely to the discrediting of the Sykes-Picot Agreement are the following:-

1. The Arab revolt, which has led to the expulsion of the Turks from Hejaz, and has been an important factor in the deliverance of Syria from the Ottoman yoke.
2. The conquest of Palestine and Syria by General Allenby with practically no military assistance from the French, but with important assistance from the Arabs.
3. As a result of (1) and (2), the establishment of Feisal and an Arab administration in Damascus and other parts of Syria.
4. The recognition of Zionism by the British Government.
5. The revolution and subsequent, and still existing, anarchy in Russia.
6. The further massacres of Armenians, which have greatly decreased the numbers of that people.
7. The British conquest of Mesopotamia.
8. The wave of democratic feeling which has passed over the world and which has expressed itself in the condemnation of secret

diplomacy, and of Imperial aggression, and in the acceptance of the principle, so loudly voiced by President Wilson, of popular determination.

9. The entry of the United States into the war.

'Every one of these circumstances has militated against the usefulness of the Sykes-Picot Agreement. The Arab revolt and the Anglo-Arab conquest of Syria have converted an academic exercise into a treaty fraught with the gravest practical consequences. Not least among the factors now apparent is the intensity of the mistrust of the French evinced by the Arabs and their resentment against the administration of Arab districts by Frenchmen . . .

'It seems unnecessary to elaborate this point any further, as for some months past the Eastern Committee has recognised the imperfections and dangers of the Agreement and has sought some means of cancelling it. It is suggested that the best means of achieving this result is through the intervention of President Wilson, whose principles are diametrically opposed to those of the Agreement. It will be by insisting on the principle of self-determination that the Agreement will best be avoided, and it is essential that in any Conference which may be assembled to consider the affairs of Syria, the Arabs should be represented equally with the Americans, British, French and Italians.'[18]

Macdonogh went on to suggest alternative frontiers between the various zones. He proposed to give Arab Syria control of the Mediterranean coastline from Tripoli to Arsus (it would then have the railway from Homs to Tripoli as a corridor to the sea). There should be a separate Arab state in northern Mesopotamia under Emir Zeid, while southern Mesopotamia would be made into a kingdom under Abdullah. As regards the question of European influence, Macdonogh wrote: 'Under the principle of self-determination it is almost certain that Great Britain would be given the controlling voice in the Arab area [i.e. in the sectors of inland Syria designated for both British and French influence under Sykes-Picot]; this area should be under the rule of Feisal.'[19] The French would receive two sections of the Mediterranean littoral: the Lebanon and an enclave around Alexandretta. Macdonogh's memorandum concluded with a strong warning against the dangers of giving inland Syria to France. Almost as an afterthought, it urged that all British policy towards Arab areas should be directed by a single authority in Egypt (thus curtailing the future influence of the Government of India in Mesopotamia and the Arabian Gulf).

On October 29th, Lawrence addressed the Eastern Committee of
the War Cabinet. To his irritation, Lord Curzon, chairman of the committee, began the proceedings with a eulogy of his achievements in
Arabia. Lawrence was in no mood for such praise, and his reply was
brusque. According to his own later account, he said: ' "Let's get to
business. You people don't understand yet the hole you have put us
all into." Curzon burst promptly into tears, great drops running down
his cheeks, to an accompaniment of slow sobs. It was horribly like a
mediaeval miracle, a *lachryma Christi*, happening to a Buddha.'[20]

The Committee then asked Lawrence about 'the views that were
entertained by the Arab chiefs concerning the settlement of the conquered
territories and Franco-Arab relations in particular'.[21] He began his reply
by describing Feisal's pro-British stance and successful co-operation
with Allenby; in the future, however, the Arab attitude would depend
on the extent to which Britain backed up French claims: 'The French
representatives had made it perfectly clear to Feisal that they intended to
build up a colonial empire in the east . . . Feisal and the Arab leaders relied
upon our declaration of [June] 1918 [to the seven Syrians] . . . regarding
the disposal of all territory actually captured by Arab arms. In this declaration we had promised unlimited Arab sovereignty for such areas'.[22]

Lawrence went on to make a series of suggestions which closely
followed those proposed in the Macdonogh memorandum: Abdullah
should be set up as ruler of Baghdad and lower Mesopotamia, with Zeid
in a similar position in upper Mesopotamia and Feisal in Syria. The
Committee minute records: 'In regard to Upper Mesopotamia, whence
most of the best officers and men in Feisal's [regular] army had been
drawn, [Lawrence] was convinced that a separate province or kingdom
would have to be established distinct from Lower Mesopotamia and from
Syria.'[23] The Arabs, Lawrence said, believed that France was 'getting into
Syria under General Allenby's wing, and although he did not like it, Feisal
would probably be content to leave Beirut and the Lebanon to French
tutelage provided that there was no question of French annexation. Tripoli
is the part which the Arabs will make a fight for, as . . . the Tripoli-Homs
railway is the only Syrian railway with real commercial possibilities . . .
The Arabs wanted a footing in the Bay of Alexandretta at Arsus, and
Colonel Lawrence thought that no one Power should have exclusive
control of this bay.'[24] As regards French advisers, 'Feisal took the view
that he was free to choose whatever advisers he liked. He was anxious to
obtain the assistance of British or American Zionist Jews for this purpose.

The Zionists would be acceptable to the Arabs on terms.'[25] Following this discussion, Curzon asked Lawrence to write a memorandum, setting out his suggestions in more detail.

Lawrence must have realised very soon that the Cabinet might find it difficult to give their full support to Feisal. Britain already had an embarrassing list of desiderata to lay before the Peace Conference. Among them were Mosul in northern Mesopotamia (allocated to France under the Sykes-Picot Agreement) and Palestine (placed by Sykes-Picot under an international administration). Both these cases would involve concessions by France, and it would therefore be awkward for Britain to oppose French ambitions in Syria as well. Although the Foreign Office might well sympathise with Feisal, the India Office would not. The Anglo-Indian lobby still intended to add Mesopotamia to the Empire, and were opposed to Arab nationalist leaders there or anywhere else. Lawrence saw that the best hope for Arab independence lay with the Americans at the Peace Conference. President Wilson would surely prefer the cause of Arab self-determination to that of European imperialism.

On the day after the Eastern Committee meeting, Lawrence went to Buckingham Palace for an audience with King George V. Allenby had recommended him for a knighthood, but Lawrence had already told the military secretary at the Palace that he would not accept any honours. There was nothing new about this decision, which had been taken during the journey to Akaba in 1917. In September that year he had written home: 'I'll never wear or use any of them. Please don't, either. My address is simply T.E.L., no titles please.'[26] When he arrived at the Palace, however, he discovered that the meeting was to be a private investiture. His discussions in Whitehall during the preceding days had done nothing to weaken his objections to taking decorations from the British Government. According to a contemporary note made by the King's private secretary, he told the King 'that he had pledged his word to Feisal, and that now the British Government were about to let down the Arabs over the Sykes-Picot Agreement. He was an Emir among the Arabs and intended to stick to them through thick and thin and, if necessary, fight against the French for the recovery of Syria.

'Colonel Lawrence said that he did not know that he had been gazetted or what the etiquette was in such matters, but he hoped that the King would forgive any want of courtesy on his part in not taking these decorations.'[27] The King seems to have taken no offence, and subsequent letters show that he bore Lawrence no ill-feeling. In later years, according to Lawrence, the incident was to become one of George V's favourite stories, developed into 'an account which tells how each time he pinned one on and turned round for the next, he found the last taken off.'[28] Lawrence admitted, however, that the Queen had been 'very huffy'.[29] He also recalled that he had told the King: 'Your Cabinet are an awful set of crooks'. The King, rather taken aback, had countered: 'Surely you wouldn't call Lord Robert Cecil a crook?'[30] It seems that Lawrence agreed to this single exception.

While Lawrence's feelings were sincere, his gesture was perhaps ill-considered. It was seized upon by political opponents who spread hostile gossip during the succeeding months, to the effect that he had refused the honours at a public investiture and that the King had been caused acute embarrassment.[31] This rumour did Lawrence much harm, although it drew attention in some quarters to the depth of his feelings about British conduct towards the Arabs.

He spent the weekend of November 1st-2nd working on his memorandum to the Eastern Committee, a most important opportunity to influence the Cabinet. The document was submitted on November 4th. It began with a summary of the historical events (written from memory and not entirely accurate) and presented the Sherifian case in strong terms. Lawrence stressed the risks taken by Hussein in rebelling against the Turks, the sacrifices made by the Arabs during the Revolt, and their contribution to Allenby's victory. He then examined the principal regions in which the Arabs aspired to independence. In his view the Arabian Peninsula would eventually be dominated by Hussein (he still underestimated ibn Saud, whose position was strengthening daily).

Lawrence then considered the north: 'In Syria the Arab movement becomes really important [to British interests] since its origin was to prevent the man-power and strategic advantages of that country falling into the hands of any continental power. For this purpose the Arabs require equal rights with any other power in the Gulf of Alexandretta, the coastline from there to Tripoli, the port of Tripoli and its railway to Homs, the Bukaa [Bekaa] from Homs to Lake Huleh, access by treaty to Haifa, and all the country east of this line and the Jordan. Further, Feisal requires to be sovereign in his own dominions, with complete liberty to choose any foreign advisers he wants of any nationality he pleases. These advisers will be part of the Arab Government and will draw their executive authority from it and not from their own Government. It may be possible to secure Arab recognition of the Turkish Dette in return for an equitable share of the Beyrout and Haifa customs receipts. Feisal will, however, not consider himself bound by any agreement to which he is not a party.

'His assets in Syria are not small. He controls most of the good corn land and the four industrial towns. He has 80% of the Moslems (including all the fighting men) on his side, all the Ansariya, all the Jews. He has inherited the old Turkish Civil Service, all of whose lower ranks, and many of whose upper ranks, are Arabs. He himself is clear-sighted and well-educated, and is capable of satisfying the needs of Syria in local self-government. If he fails, the responsibility will lie at the door of the European powers, in whose word he shows an undue simplicity of trust.

'In Palestine the Arabs hope that the British will keep what they have conquered. They will not approve Jewish Independence for Palestine but will support as far as they can Jewish infiltration, if it is behind a British as opposed to an international façade. If any attempt is made to set up the international control proposed in the Sykes-Picot Agreement, Feisal will press for self-determination in Palestine, and give the moral support of the Arab Government to the peasantry of Palestine, to resist expropriation.

'In Irak [southern Mesopotamia] the Arabs expect the British to keep control. The Sherif, relying on his Agreement with us, hopes for a nominal Arab administration there.

'In Jesireh [i.e. northern Mesopotamia] there are very vivid Arab Nationalists, but they are in an unsatisfactory geographical position, until a proportion of the nomadic and settled Kurds can be persuaded to join hands with the local government required there.

'I would suggest that [Irak and Jesireh] should be kept quite separate, at least administratively. The problems of Irak are those of great public works and of a highly developed agriculture. The problems of Jesireh are those of turbulent mountain villagers and semi-nomadic tribes . . .

'If representations of small nations are admitted to the Peace Conference the cry of self-determination is likely to be raised, and agreements made semi-secretly between the Powers previously may be regarded with some suspicion. For this reason I would suggest that no second edition of the Sykes-Picot Treaty be produced. The geographical absurdities of the present Agreement will laugh it out of court, and it would be perhaps as well if we spared ourselves a second effort on the same lines. If we do not, I hope that we will at least recognise our official inclusion of the Arabs among the belligerents, and make them a party to any decisions affecting Arab areas conquered by themselves.'[32]

On the day this memorandum was handed in, Lawrence continued his efforts to win friends for the Arab cause in Whitehall. For the past eighteen months Winston Churchill had been Minister for Munitions; but it was generally supposed that he would be offered an important Cabinet post after the general election in December. Lawrence called on Churchill, and in doing so made the acquaintance of Edward Marsh, his private secretary.

Marsh was already a figure of significance in the literary world, and Lawrence asked him if he knew Siegfried Sassoon, whose *Counter Attack*, a volume of anti-war poems, had recently been published. Marsh had known Sassoon since 1913, and arranged dinner with him and Lawrence at the Savoy on the following night. This was to be the first of Lawrence's post-war contacts with contemporary writers.

The Armistice was signed on 11th November 1918. That evening Lawrence met Charles ffoulkes (head of the new Imperial War Museum) with whom he had so often discussed mediaeval arms and armour before the war. Together they went in search of E. T. Leeds, now working in Military Intelligence. Leeds subsequently wrote: 'Years had gone by since we three had foregathered: it must have been Lawrence's idea to collect ffoulkes and come along to me. Amid the cheering of Armistice night we dined together quietly in the Union Club overlooking Trafalgar Square, a night of conversation never to be forgotten.'[33]

During the first days of November diplomatic events gathered pace, as the Allied governments and interested pressure groups all sought to increase their influence at the coming Peace Conference. On November 6th Georges-Picot had landed at Beirut and at once demanded Syria for France. He was soon urging his Government to ask Britain to hand the territory over: 'As long as the British Army is in occupation, there will be doubt in the mind of the people, and this will favour those who are hostile towards us. The only remedy is to send twenty thousand [French] soldiers to Syria and request Britain to pass to us the responsibility. At present, this would seem natural, whereas in a few weeks it will appear to be a hostile act towards the Arabs. If we delay, those who are not yet committed will take sides against us, and our position in Syria will be ruined as it was in Palestine.'[34] However, the French War Office did not immediately follow up this request for a large French garrison.

At the time, there was some prospect of talks about the Syrian question before the Peace Conference opened. On November 8th, Lawrence sent an urgent message on this subject to Hussein: 'I believe there will be conversations in Paris in fifteen days' time between the Allies about the question of the Arabs. General Allenby has telegraphed that you will want to have a representative there. If this is so, I hope you will send Feisal, since his splendid victories have given him a personal reputation in Europe which will make his success easier. If you agree please telegraph him to get ready to leave Syria at once for about one month, and to ask General Allenby for a ship to take him to France. You should meanwhile telegraph to the Governments of Great Britain, France, America and Italy telling them that your son is proceeding at once to Paris as your representative.'[35]

On the following day, the Anglo-French Declaration, mooted since August, was at last released. Though this brief statement was couched in legalistic prose, the Foreign Office hoped that it would calm Arab nationalist fears about Allied intentions. In its final form it read: 'The aim which France and Great Britain have in view in prosecuting in the East the war let loose by German ambition is the complete and final liberation of the peoples so long oppressed by the Turks and the establishment of national governments and administrations deriving their authority from the initiative and free choice of the native populations.

'In order to give effect to these intentions, France and Great Britain have agreed to encourage and assist the establishment of native governments and administrations in Syria and Mesopotamia, already liberated by the Allies, and in the territories which they are proceeding to liberate, and they have agreed to recognise such governments as soon as they are effectively established. So far from desiring to impose specific institutions upon the populations of these regions, their sole object is to ensure, by their support and effective assistance, that the governments and administrations adopted by these regions of their own free will shall be exercised in the normal way. The function which the two Allied Governments claim for themselves in the liberated territories is to ensure impartial and equal justice for all; to facilitate the economic development of the country by encouraging local initiative; to promote the diffusion of education; and to put an end to the divisions too long exploited by Turkish policy.'[36] Although, in British eyes, this Declaration would preclude direct imperial rule, the 'functions' claimed by the Allies were so vaguely defined that they could be used to justify almost any form of colonialism.

It was expected that fundamental decisions about the future of the Middle East would be taken during the coming weeks, and during the second half of November the Cabinet received a series of memoranda on the subject, each setting out the author's considered advice. These papers, written by leading British authorities, were taken very seriously by the Eastern Committee.

D. G. Hogarth's contribution, dated November 15th, was circulated by the Admiralty. As regards Syria, he wrote: 'Pending settlements with the French, whom no Syrian district, not even Lebanon and Beirut, will accept willingly (especially if Palestine and the Arab State are virtually British), the points to insist on provisionally seem to be these:

  a. That all inter-Ally agreements lose validity with the opening of the Peace Conference, if not before.
  b. That in all official inter-Ally conversations about any part of the Arab area henceforth, Arabs themselves must participate, as Allies.
  c. That meanwhile the Arab State must have a sea port, preferably Tripoli, in order to pay its way. Indirect taxation, through Customs, is its only reliable source of revenue . . .
  e. That Syria be treated as an entity apart from either Mesopotamia and Iraq or Hejaz.
  f. That Arab leaders receive, as soon as possible, explicit assurances on the above points. The recent Joint Declaration will not reassure any of them by any means. They will see that France can find an easy loophole to Protectorate or Annexation . . . and that wholesale tutelage is assumed in the wording of the last part.'[37]

In another section, Hogarth discussed Mesopotamia, adding his support to the idea of dividing north from south. The north, he wrote, 'must be distinct from Iraq – a separate native State with Mosul or Urfa for capital. How far it will extend north will depend on the Khurds. These last affect Arab manners, and may well throw in their lot with an Arab State in considerable numbers.'[38]

Three days later, a long telegram was received from Clayton. This began by setting out the attitudes of the local populations, area by area, and then discussed the implications of the Sykes-Picot Agreement: 'The arrangement for a division of the independent Arab area into an "A" and "B" sphere, the one controlled by France and the other by Great Britain, presents almost insuperable practical difficulties from an administrative point of view. If an Arab Government is to function with any degree of efficiency, it must have a system of administration applying equally to all areas under its control and operating from one central [point], which in this case must be Damascus.

'It is impracticable to divide the territories into two parts (one of which contains the capital) and to lay down that advice and assistance must come from France in the one half and from Great Britain in the other.

'For many years to come, advice and assistance to the newly formed Arab State must entail a considerable measure of actual administration. French and British methods of administration are widely different, and confusion and inefficiency must result. Worst of all, such an arrangement contains the seeds of future friction between France and Great Britain in a region where the policies of the two countries have been in opposition for many years.'[39]

In order to avoid such a clash, Clayton proposed that Britain should be the trustee of Palestine, and adviser to the independent Arab state based on Damascus (this should include the port of Tripoli and a coastal strip). France should be the trustee of an autonomous Lebanon including the Bekaa and Beirut, and also trustee and adviser to an autonomous Armenia (including the port of Alexandretta). Arrangements could easily be made to safeguard French economic interests in Syria, and any further concession to French imperial ambitions should be made elsewhere.

Clayton now had to deal with the practical consequences of the Balfour Declaration, and he added: 'a sound administration established at Damascus would permit . . . the development of the arable country to the east of the Jordan and the construction of communications to enable its produce to be exported with profit. The districts east of the Jordan are thinly populated and their development would allow . . . considerable emigration from Palestine thereby making room for Jewish expansion.

'It should be noted that it is essential to impress on the Zionists that the complete fulfilment of [their] aspirations cannot be looked for at once and that undue haste in pushing their programme will only react against their own interests.'[40]

There was thus unanimity among those who had dealt with the Arab question from Egypt during the preceding years. However, a long note from Monsieur Pichon, the French Foreign Minister, dispelled any illusion that his Government's policy had softened as a result of Feisal's contribution to the Allied victory. France now demanded that the Sykes-Picot terms, as agreed between Britain and France, should be fulfilled to the letter: 'on no point, whether at Damascus, Aleppo, or at Mosul, is [France] prepared to relinquish in any way the rights which she holds through the 1916 Agreement, whatever the provisional administrative arrangements called for by a passing military situation.'[41] Pichon's message ended in a familiar vein: 'The French Government agrees with the general principle that lasting peace must be based on satisfying the aspirations of the people. But it is well known that, in the East, local populations must be helped in order to prevent them from exercising tyranny on each other and thereby stoking a hotbed of perpetual strife which will threaten the general peace. It is by virtue of these principles, as well as . . . historical, geographical, and strategic arguments . . . that France and England have come to share between themselves the role of disinterested steward, a role that neither country, on account of its status as a major Moslem power, could assume with regard to the Arabs on its own.

'France, moreover, has a historic duty toward the peoples of Syria, whose indigenous elements and expatriates throughout the world have greeted our entry into Beirut with enthusiasm. The French Government cannot fail in this duty. It intends to maintain its stewardship of the Arab population settled in the areas assigned to France under the 1916 Agreement.'[42] The note was received with dismay by those in the Foreign Office and elsewhere who hoped that Feisal might obtain some measure of real independence in Syria. They now realised that there was little chance of winning such a concession as long as the Sykes-Picot framework was in place.

To complete its dossier on the Arab question, the Eastern Committee also took steps to seek the views of Colonel A. T. Wilson, the Acting Civil Commissioner in Mesopotamia. In the meantime, a paper was received from Sir Arthur Hirtzel of the India Office.

In effect, the Anglo-Indian lobby intended to turn Mesopotamia into a colony, and its statements show that any 'concessions' to the principle of self-determination were purely a matter of form. Hirtzel's views about the Sherifian Arabs were as unsympathetic as those emanating from Paris, and he chose to ignore the fact that Iraqi officers had played a prominent role in Feisal's army during the Revolt.

His attitude towards the Syrian question was unequivocal: 'The material interests involved in Mesopotamia are far too great to be jockeyed away merely for the sake of diplomatic convenience. We are not pledged to King Husain to prevent the French from establishing a protectorate: our pledges relate only to those areas in which we can act without detriment to French interests, and we ought to take our stand firmly on that ground, and not allow ourselves to be used by the Arabs to secure their interests in Syria at the expense of the French. That, however, is what we are doing at present; and in doing it we risk losing the fruits of the Mesopotamian campaign for the *beaux yeux* of King Husain and his scheming sons.'[43]

Hirtzel was no less strongly opposed to the suggestion that two of Hussein's sons should be given thrones in Mesopotamia: 'at the eleventh hour Lieutenant-Colonel Lawrence has come home with a proposal to put one of the sons of King Hussein in as King of Iraq, and another as King of Northern Mesopotamia with his capital at Mosul or Ras-el-Ain . . . Without in the least wishing to deprecate Colonel Lawrence's achievements and his undoubted genius, it must be said about him that he does not at all represent – and would not, I think, claim to represent – the local views of Northern Mesopotamia and Iraq; of the latter, indeed, he has practically no first-hand knowledge at all, and if His Majesty's Government wants to know what they are, they will naturally turn to the Civil Commissioner and his officers.'[44]

The paper continued: 'It is submitted . . . that Colonel Lawrence's scheme has nothing to commend it so far as Mesopotamia and Iraq are concerned, convenient as it may be as a means of providing for the embarrassing ambitions of King Husain's other two sons, when Ali has been installed at Mecca and Feisal at Damascus . . .

'I cannot see that we are bound by honour or interest to defend the Arabs against the French. That the French will allow themselves to be eliminated from Syria by any local option under the [Anglo-French] declaration – or that, if they do, they will allow us to take their place, as some imagine – is surely incredible. Syria is too deeply graven on the heart of France for that. If we support the Arabs in this matter, we incur the ill-will of France; and we have to live and work with France all over the world. We have no interests of our own in Syria at all commensurate with those in Mesopotamia; and if we had, and could eliminate the French in our own favour, could we possibly undertake the control of Syrian politics and administration in addition to our responsibilities in Mesopotamia and the Arabian peninsula?

'And if we cannot eliminate the French from Syria, neither can we weaken their hold there without, *pro tanto*, weakening our hold over Mesopotamia. But if Mesopotamia is to be developed, our control of the administration must be complete, for only so (to put it at its lowest) will the capital necessary for its development be forthcoming. Now, as I ventured to say when first writing on this subject nearly four years ago, "the Power which detaches these regions from the Ottoman Empire cannot stop at that. By its action it has made itself morally responsible to humanity and to civilisation for their reclamation and development; that is to say it must either undertake the work itself or make it possible for others to do so." It may be that a League of Nations will decide on the latter alternative. But in the meantime we dare not gamble away our responsibility for the sake of anyone's dreams in Syria'.[45]

On November 21st, Lawrence attended a further meeting of the Eastern Committee. The Peace Conference was imminent, and everyone present understood the need to reach a firm decision about policy without further delay.

Lawrence's chief ambition at this stage was to ensure that Feisal, now on his way to Europe, got a fair hearing in any international debate about the future of the Middle East. America would be in a position to dominate such discussions, and although President Wilson's militant idealism held little attraction for France and Britain, it might prove a lifeline to the Arabs.

He had evidently convinced key members of the Eastern Committee before this meeting that it would be in Britain's best interest for Feisal to attend the Peace Conference. Only Hussein, the argument ran, could reassure President Wilson that the Arabs wanted Britain to assume the stewardship of Mesopotamia and Palestine. Thus Lord Robert Cecil told the Committee: 'When it came to the Peace Conference we should undoubtedly have a very difficult case from the international point of view, particularly with regard to the presentation of it to the Americans; this especially so in regard to the Sykes-Picot Agreement . . . It would be very important if we could produce an Arab who would back up our claims, and it was essential that Feisal and the British Government should have the same story.'[46] Lawrence was delighted when the Committee agreed that Feisal's presence would be indispensable. Moreover, if the Americans accepted Hussein's endorsement of British control in Mesopotamia and Palestine, they would be obliged at the same time to take note of his opposition to French control in Syria.

This meeting took place on the very day that Feisal sailed from Beirut on board HMS *Gloucester*. Originally his destination had been Paris, but now it was arranged that Lawrence would go to France and meet him, bringing him to England as rapidly as possible.

In the event, the circumstances of Feisal's journey were less than fortunate. Due to misunderstandings between London, Cairo, and Jidda, his intended mission was not announced until the last minute, and meanwhile the French Government had learned of it through its own channels. By the time the Foreign Office informed the French officially that Feisal was coming, he was on the point of arriving at Marseilles.

The French Government was incensed by the news: Feisal's attitude towards their ambitions in Syria was well known, and it was obvious that his presence at the Peace Conference would influence American opinion against them. Their first response was to demand consultation between the Powers on the whole question of Hussein's right to representation. In itself this was not unreasonable, but the French went on to insist that even after such discussions, Feisal could only visit France 'as a private envoy of the King of the Hejaz in order to plead the cause of an Arab group which should only be constituted under the respective supervision of the English and French in zones where the two countries have defined their limits and their civilizing mission.'[47] Successive notes showed the determination of the French Foreign Office to reach a private arrangement with Britain about the Middle East on the subject of Syria before the Americans became involved. This was exactly what Lawrence now wished to avoid, as did many people at the Foreign Office. With Arab endorsement, the British case in Mesopotamia and Palestine was secure. There was nothing to be gained by making a new agreement with France, which would only risk giving offence to President Wilson.

The Foreign Office played for time, suggesting that France had misunderstood the reasons for Feisal's visit. Lawrence was dispatched to meet him, with instructions to call at the British Embassy in Paris and inform himself of the latest position before going south.

It was now obvious that the whole matter of Feisal's visit to Europe had been mishandled, and the Navy agreed that, if necessary, HMS *Gloucester* would bring him directly to England. However, the Foreign Office recognised that this might only serve to make matters worse, and Lawrence was told that such a move should be a last resort. If possible, he must smooth things over.

Despite further protests, France was obliged to recognise a *fait accompli*. It was hurriedly arranged that Feisal would be welcomed, not as his father's diplomatic representative, but merely as a distinguished military leader and the son of a friendly sovereign. Since the French Government anticipated that Feisal would in future have to deal with Paris rather than London, it was decided that he should be taken on a lengthy and impressive tour. The arrangement of an itinerary at such short notice was complicated, however, by a simultaneous visit by King George V.

Both were to see Paris and the battlefields, but Feisal's escort was instructed to see that their paths did not cross.

When Feisal arrived in France, on November 26th, he was met by Emmanuel Bertrand, a retired French Foreign Office official, who had received strict orders. What ensued was something of a farce. Two British attempts to put Feisal on a train for Paris and London were foiled with great diplomacy by Bertrand, who nevertheless had been prepared to achieve this, if necessary, by force. Lawrence, who arrived in Marseilles after HMS *Gloucester* had docked, was given to understand that he was not welcome. Nevertheless, he travelled with Feisal's party as far as Lyons, where Bertrand was joined by Colonel Brémond. At this point, Lawrence seems to have thought it best to retire gracefully, and he decided to go straight to Paris with some members of Feisal's staff.

On November 29th, he cabled to London about his meeting with Brémond at Lyons: 'He told me : . . . that his instructions are that Europe will be submerged by America at the Peace Congress and after, unless France and England present a solid front, and refuse to allow any third party a voice in the settlement of the Near East. For this purpose, France will insist on immediate force being given to the Sykes-Picot Agreement, and the United States will be given a free hand in Mexico to stop her mouth. He said that the recognition of Feisul's force as belligerents was temporary, and was ended by the conclusion of the Armistice. He takes exception to the coming of Feisul without permission of Sykes and Picot . . . He said that the erection by Great Britain of a local [i.e. Arab] government in the solid red area in Mesopotamia [which should have been under direct rule] would be regarded by [France] as an infringement of the [Sykes Picot] treaty.

'Bertrand, the French Government representative with Feisul, has not committed himself in any way, and did his best to stop Brémond opening himself on me. Feisul has played with them very successfully.'[48]

After Lawrence had left for Paris, the British Consul in Lyons received an unexpected visit from Nuri as-Said, who was travelling with Feisal. He explained that Feisal 'felt himself rather like a prisoner in the hands of his French hosts, and though it had been expressly enjoined upon him not to do anything to cause annoyance, he wished to know whether he should assert himself, with a view to cutting short his French tour.'[49] The British Consul-General advised him to allow the French to carry out their programme. Subsequent reports written by Bertrand and Lawrence show that each of them thought he had come out of the situation on top, but the real victor seems to have been Feisal, who behaved with great courtesy in very trying circumstances and left Bertrand feeling that he was successfully carrying out his mission.[50]

One of the principal French objectives was to impress upon Feisal that he was not recognised by France as a political negotiator. He was taken to see refrigeration plants, refineries, gun foundries, tank exercises, silk workshops, and so on, but there was no discussion of the Syrian question. Bertrand gave him to understand 'how complicated the situation was, and how thoughtlessly his [British] advisers had made him set out on this unforeseen journey, without prior discussion and agreement [with France].'[51] Feisal, with considerably more acumen than Bertrand gave him credit for, assured his French hosts that his only wish, after visiting the battlefields, was to pay his respects in Paris. He would then go to London with a similar purpose, before returning to Paris where he would await the decision of the Powers concerning his participation at the Peace Conference.

On December 1st, while Feisal and Lawrence were still in France, the French and Italian prime ministers arrived in London. They were honoured with a military procession which passed through cheering crowds. After arriving at the French Embassy, Lloyd George found himself alone for a time with Clemenceau, the French premier. According to a later note by the Cabinet secretary, Clemenceau had asked what they might talk about, and Lloyd George, seizing the opportunity, had replied: ' "Mesopotamia and Palestine" . . . "Tell me what you want" asked Clemenceau. "I want Mosul" said Lloyd George. "You shall have it" said Clemenceau. "Anything else?" "Yes, I want Jerusalem too" continued Lloyd George. "You shall have it" said Clemenceau "but Pichon will make difficulties about Mosul." '[52]

This episode was typical of Lloyd George, an artful politician who knew what he wanted and seized an opportunity when he saw one. Characteristically, he took this action without any kind of brief from the Foreign Office, and he made no formal report despite the importance of this verbal 'gentleman's agreement'. Worse still, he was vague about the concessions he had made in return. Clemenceau had asked that Britain should not oppose a unified French administration in the whole of Syria, including the inland area reserved for an independent Arab administration. As far as Lloyd George was concerned, no British interests were threatened by this request and he had readily agreed.

Doubtless he believed that he had secured a valuable bargain, for his heart had long been set on a British administration in Palestine. In reality, however, the agreement was worth far more to Clemenceau. France's greatest fear had been that America would overturn the Sykes-Picot Agreement. If this happened, and the future of the Middle East were decided on the principle of self-determination, the French would certainly lose Syria, and possibly Lebanon as well. Britain, on the other hand, with support from Hussein, would be very well placed to receive stewardship of Mosul and Palestine. Now, by handing Mosul and Palestine to Lloyd George, the French premier had simply given away what he would have lost anyway. In exchange, however, he had obtained a commitment which cut the ground from under the feet of those inside the Foreign Office who wanted to see the whole Sykes-Picot Agreement scrapped. This was exactly the kind of bilateral settlement Lawrence had been seeking to avoid. In two areas, it is true, British territorial desiderata had been met, but this had only been achieved by sacrificing the hopes of the Arabs.

Lawrence returned from Paris to London on the following day, knowing nothing of this extraordinary agreement. He was deeply anxious about the French position, as he understood it, i.e. that Sykes-Picot should be applied in its original form. Shortly after reaching the capital he called on Lord Robert Cecil, begging for a chance to speak to the Prime Minister. Cecil sent a note to Lloyd George which read: 'Colonel Lawrence (the Arabian) . . . tells me that Clemenceau has come over here with a Middle East policy fully worked out which if Lawrence is rightly informed would mean the wholesale destruction of all Arabian and Jewish interests and incidentally our own.'[53] Lloyd George knew better, and it is very doubtful that he agreed to see Lawrence.

Three days later, before the French concessions over Mosul and Palestine were known to any but Lloyd George's closest associates, Lawrence attended a meeting of the Eastern Committee. It was the third of a series of meetings whose object was to determine British policy at the Peace Conference.[54] On the agenda was Britain's future policy over Syria. The minutes show that most of those present had no idea that the matter had already been decided, over their heads, by Lloyd George.

Once again, there was scathing criticism of the 1916 Agreement. Lord Curzon, for example, said: 'When the Sykes-Picot Agreement was drawn up it was, no doubt, intended by its authors . . . as a sort of fancy sketch to suit a situation that had not then arisen, and which it was thought extremely unlikely would ever arise; and that, I suppose, must be the principal explanation of the gross ignorance with which the boundary lines in that Agreement were drawn. Let me give in passing only three illustrations of the extent to which that Agreement in relation to Syria at any rate, is not only obsolete, but absolutely impracticable. First . . . it brings the French sphere right up to Mosul and the Upper Tigris, and far into Kurdistan lying beyond; secondly, it splits up the Arabs in the Areas "A" and "B" by a most fantastic and incredible line of division; and, thirdly, if it were adhered to, I fear it could only be a source of incessant friction between the French and ourselves, and the Arabs as third parties, in the future.'[55]

If Lawrence drew any comfort from these views, it was dashed when A. J. Balfour intervened. He did not usually attend Eastern Committee meetings and it seems likely that he came on this occasion because he had been told privately of the arrangement reached by Clemenceau and Lloyd George. He took the position that Britain could not go back on Sykes-Picot, which was a signed commitment. The only hope for the Arabs was that President Wilson would insist at the outset that secret agreements of this kind should be scrapped. He was adamant that Britain must refrain from taking any initiative in the matter: 'I am quite certain that we ought to be most careful not to give . . . the French . . . the impression that we are trying to get out of our bargains with them made at an earlier and different stage of the war. If the Americans can get us out well and good. If the Americans . . . possessing very considerable powers of putting pressure on their various associated allies, choose to do it, we can only congratulate ourselves upon their success . . . If the Americans choose to step in and cut the knot, that is their affair, but we must not put the knife into their hand . . . I am not at all sure that whatever dexterity we use we shall be able to keep out of it altogether. I am sure we ought to try, and sincerely try.'[56]

By the end of this meeting it was clear that, as regards Syria, the Cabinet was not prepared to offer Feisal anything more than sympathy. On the other hand, it would be willing to help him obtain a hearing at the Peace Conference, on the tacit understanding that he would support British stewardship of Mesopotamia and Palestine. If he used this opportunity to appeal for American help over Sykes-Picot, that was his affair.

From this point onwards, therefore, Feisal would be on his own, and his aims during the Conference would be quite independent of those pursued by Britain. The Foreign Office nevertheless thought it important to attach someone to his entourage who could persuade him whenever possible to act in Britain's interests. On December 5th Sir Eyre Crowe, a senior Foreign Office official, minuted: 'I venture to recommend strongly . . . that we ought to have Colonel Lawrence available at the Peace Conference for purposes of advice in regard to [the] Arab question of which he knows more than anyone else.

'Colonel Lawrence himself is apparently anxious to be with Feisal, and we have everything to gain from such an arrangement. It is a question whether Col. Lawrence should be in Paris in the capacity of a member of Feisal's staff (he holds an appointment from him to this effect) or as an adviser of the British Delegation. I favour the latter arrangement, but perhaps this need not exclude the former.'[57] Lord Hardinge noted: 'Col. Lawrence should certainly be in Paris and available as adviser. Probably he would be able to give an opinion as to the position in which he could be most useful or whether he could combine both.'[58] Lawrence's name was added to the list of the British Delegation, Political Section, as 'one of the advisers on special subjects'.

While these deliberations had been taking place, Feisal had continued his tour of France. On December 7th, however, Lawrence travelled to Paris to accompany him to England, and they arrived in London three days later. At much the same time the French Embassy delivered a frosty note to the Foreign Office: 'M. Pichon hopes that during the prince's stay in England, the British authorities will refrain from discussing with him any questions concerning Syria from Damascus to Aleppo. If the Emir Feisal broaches these questions, it would be appropriate to tell him that they are the particular concern of the French Government, with whom alone he should discuss them.

'The Emir must come back to France after his stay in London. The French Government will take care of the arrangements for his journey back to Syria.'[59]

The only justification for this request lay in the concessions Lloyd George had made to Clemenceau. As yet, however, the Foreign Office knew little or nothing about these concessions, and was at a loss to understand why Britain (whose army was at that time occupying a large part of Syria) should not discuss this region with an Arab leader on Allenby's staff. The French note was acknowledged but otherwise ignored.

On December 12th, their second day in London, Feisal and Lawrence called on A. J. Balfour. According to a note Balfour wrote afterwards,

Feisal said that if the French attempted to take over Syria, the Arabs would 'attack them at once and without hesitation. [Feisal] well knew that the Arabs could not successfuly resist the military power of so great a country as France. But he and his followers would rather perish in the struggle than tamely submit without a blow.' In reply, Balfour 'begged him not to allow his mind to dwell upon these tragic possibilities', and tried to suggest that Feisal's anxiety about French intentions in Syria was unfounded.[60]

On the same day, there was a meeting between Feisal and Chaim Weizmann, during which Lawrence acted as interpreter. Both leaders were now in a position to help one another politically: the Zionists needed Arab acquiescence to their programme in Palestine, while Feisal knew that Jewish support during the Peace Conference might help to swing American opinion behind his cause. Lawrence had already impressed upon Feisal the potential value of Jewish capital and skills.

According to his own contemporary account, Weizmann assured Feisal that the Zionists in Palestine 'should . . . be able to carry out public works of a far-reaching character, and . . . the country could be so improved that it would have room for four or five million Jews, without encroaching on the ownership rights of Arab peasantry.'[61] Feisal replied that 'it was curious there should be friction between Jews and Arabs in Palestine. There was no friction in any other country where Jews lived together with Arabs . . . He did not think for a moment that there was any scarcity of land in Palestine. The population would always have enough, especially if the country were developed. Besides, there was plenty of land in his district.'[62]

Feisal was also received by King George V, who decorated him with the Chain of a Knight Grand Cross of the Royal Victorian Order. Here too, Lawrence acted as interpreter, this time wearing full Arab dress as a member of Feisal's staff. He later recalled that it was one of only three occasions that he did so in Europe after the war.[63]

Over the next few days, Lawrence and Feisal went on an official tour to Edinburgh and Glasgow, where they attended various civic functions. According to Lawrence, when Feisal was asked to give an address at one of these, he recited passages from the Koran while Lawrence, pretending to interpret, made an impromptu speech.[64]

By this time Lawrence had begun to promote Feisal's cause in the British press. On December 15th he sent an article on Arab affairs to *The Times*, and in a covering letter wrote: 'Feisul will probably be in London on Thursday and then I'll try and arrange you something useful.

'The points that strike me are that the Arabs came into the war without making a previous treaty with us, and have consistently refused to listen to the temptations of other powers. They have never had a press agent, or tried to make themselves out a case, but fought as hard as they could (I'll swear to that) and suffered hardships in their three campaigns and losses that would break up seasoned troops. They fought with ropes around their necks (Feisul had £20,000 alive and £10,000 dead on him. I the same: Nasir £10,000 alive, and Ali el Harith £8,000) and did it without, I believe, any other very strong motive than a desire to see the Arabs free. It was rather an ordeal for as very venerable a person as Hussein to rebel, for he was at once most violently abused by the Moslem press in India and Turkey, on religious grounds.'[65]

Lawrence also took this opportunity to set the record straight on another matter: 'Sir Henry McMahon did all the spadework of the entry of the Sherif into the war, and was sacked (largely for it) when things got bad in the early days of the rising. Now Wingate says he did it. It was really McMahon, advised by Storrs, Clayton, and perhaps myself.'[66] Lawrence doubtless saw McMahon's removal in December 1916 as a big enough injustice in itself, without the efforts Wingate was now making to claim all the glory for himself.

Lawrence still intended to write a full-length account of his own part in the Arab Revolt. Indeed, he had probably given a great deal of thought to the project, at odd moments during the sixteen months that had elapsed since he had first mentioned it. In a letter to C. M. Doughty written on Christmas Day, he said that he had 'been over much of your country, (more securely and comfortably, but in somewhat the same fashion) meeting many of the people and sons of the people who knew you out there. It has been a wonderful experience, and I have got quite a lot to tell.

'I'm afraid it is not likely to be written for publication, since some of it would give offence to people alive (including myself!) but I hope to get it put on paper soon.'[67]

The year 1918 did not end happily for Feisal, who was soon told officially that 'if the French Government insisted on its rights under the [Sykes-Picot] Agreement, Great Britain would not be in a position to refuse.'[68] He could only reply that the Arabs fully recognised 'the exigencies of the Anglo-French Alliance, and the obligation upon Great Britain to keep faith with her Ally. But this obligation should be discharged at the expense of Great Britain herself, not of the Arabs.'[69]

During the last days of December, Lawrence and Feisal worked on a memorandum setting out the Arab case. This document would be Feisal's principal submission to the Peace Conference, and its tone was no less important than its content. His only remaining hope of success lay with the Americans, and the memorandum was therefore addressed directly to the idealism that was thought to inspire President Wilson's policy. A heavily amended draft, in Lawrence's handwriting, survives, but the memorandum was to be signed by Feisal. In its final form, it read:

The country from a line Alexandretta–Persia southward to the Indian Ocean is inhabited by 'Arabs' – by which we mean people of closely related Semitic stocks, all speaking the one language, Arabic. The non-Arabic-speaking elements in this area do not, I believe, exceed one per cent of the whole.

The aim of the Arab nationalist movements (of which my father became the leader in war after combined appeals from the Syrian and Mesopotamian branches) is to unite the Arabs eventually into one nation. As an old member of the Syrian Committee I commanded the Syrian Revolt, and had under me Syrians, Mesopotamians, and Arabians.

We believe that our ideal of Arab unity in Asia is justified beyond need of argument. If argument is required, we would point to the general principles accepted by the Allies when the United States joined them, to our splendid past, to the tenacity with which our race has for six hundred years resisted Turkish attempts to absorb us, and, in a lesser degree, to what we tried our best to do in this war as one of the Allies.

My father has a privileged place among Arabs, as their successful leader, and as the head of their greatest family, and as Sherif of Mecca. He is convinced of the ultimate triumph of the ideal of unity, if no attempt is made now to force it, by imposing an artificial political unity on the whole, or to hinder it, by dividing the area as spoils of war among great Powers.

The unity of the Arabs in Asia has been made more easy of late years, since the development of railways, telegraphs, and air-roads. In old days the area was too huge, and in parts necessarily too thinly peopled, to communicate common ideas readily.

The various provinces of Arab Asia – Syria, Irak, Jezireh, Hejaz, Nejd, Yemen – are very different economically and socially, and it is impossible to constrain them into one frame of government.

We believe that Syria, an agricultural and industrial area thickly peopled with sedentary classes, is sufficiently advanced politically to manage her own internal affairs. We feel also that foreign technical advice and help will be a most valuable factor in our national growth. We are willing to pay for this help in cash; we cannot sacrifice for it any part of the freedom we have just won for ourselves by force of arms.

Jezireh and Irak are two huge provinces, made up of three civilised towns, divided by large wastes thinly peopled by semi-nomadic tribes. The world wishes to exploit Mesopotamia rapidly, and we therefore believe that the system of government there will have to be buttressed by the men and material resources of a great foreign Power. We ask, however, that the Government be Arab, in principle and spirit, the selective rather than the elective principle being necessarily followed in the neglected districts, until time makes the broader basis possible. The main duty of the Arab Government there would be to oversee the educational processes which are to advance the tribes to the moral level of the towns.

The Hejaz is mainly a tribal area, and the government will remain, as in the past, suited to patriarchal conditions. We appreciate these better than Europe, and propose therefore to retain our complete independence there.

The Yemen and Nejd are not likely to submit their cases to the Peace Conference. They look after themselves, and adjust their own relations with the Hejaz and elsewhere.

In Palestine the enormous majority of the people are Arabs. The Jews are very close to the Arabs in blood, and there is no conflict of character between the two races. In principles we are absolutely at one. Nevertheless, the Arabs cannot risk assuming the responsibility of holding level the scales in the clash of races and religions that have, in this one province, so often involved the world in difficulties. They would wish for the effective super-position of a great trustee, so long as a representative local administration commended itself by actively promoting the material prosperity of the country.

In discussing our provinces in detail I do not lay claim to superior competence. The Powers will, I hope, find better means to give fuller effect to the aims of our national movement. I came to Europe, on behalf of my father and the Arabs of Asia, to say that they are expecting the powers at the Conference not to attach undue importance to superficial differences of condition, and not to consider them only from the low ground of existing European material interests and supposed spheres. They expect the powers to think of them as one potential people, jealous of their language and liberty, and ask that no step be taken inconsistent with the prospect of an eventual union of these areas under one sovereign government.

In laying stress on the difference in the social condition of our provinces, I do not wish to give the impression that there exists any real conflict of ideals, material interests, creeds, or character rendering our union impossible. The greatest obstacle we have to overcome is local ignorance, for which the Turkish Government is largely responsible.

In our opinion, if our independence be conceded and our local competence established, the natural influences of race, language, and interest will soon draw us together into one people; but for this the Great Powers will have to ensure us open internal frontiers, common railways and telegraphs, and uniform systems of education. To achieve this they must lay aside the thought of individual profits, and of their old jealousies. In a word, we ask you not to force your whole civilisation upon us, but to help us to pick out what serves us from your experience. In return we can offer you little but gratitude.[70]

CHAPTER 28

The Peace Conference
January – September 1919

LAWRENCE arrived in Paris on about January 9th, and was given rooms in the Hotel Continental, some distance from the Majestic and Astoria which were the main hotels used by the British Delegation. He was to remain in Paris, fighting for the Arab cause, until late May. Long afterwards he would describe these months as 'the worst I have lived through: and they were worse for Feisal. However he learnt the whole art of politics, from them. Perhaps I did, too!'[1]

Since 1915, Lawrence had been living and working among people to whom the future of Syria was a central issue. In Paris, however, attention was focused on Germany and Austria. The disposal of the Ottoman Empire was of secondary importance, and the fate of Syria seemed peripheral; it featured rarely on the official agendas.

While there was little scope for formal discussion, there were many opportunities to argue Feisal's case for Arab independence in private meetings with statesmen and journalists. Most of Lawrence's work took place, therefore, behind the scenes. At first, there was a flurry of activity, arranging interviews and acting as Feisal's interpreter, but as the weeks went by the pace slowed. Lawrence used his free time to begin drafting an account of the Arab Revolt. Between January 10th and mid-May he wrote what are now Books 2-7 and Book 10 of *Seven Pillars of Wisdom*. Nothing of this original draft survives, but it seems that the text written in Paris amounted to some 160,000 words.[2] During these months he was so preoccupied with the book that he wrote very few private letters. None of them refer to *Seven Pillars*, and the only independent evidence of its existence is the fact that parts of the draft were read in Paris by another member of the British Delegation, Richard Meinertzhagen.[3]

For Lawrence, the first obstacle to be overcome at the Conference was French opposition to any arrangement that would give Feisal an opportunity to present the Arab case. Jean Gout, Assistant Director of the Asian section of the French Foreign Ministry, left Feisal in no doubt about the matter. A note of their conversations on January 16th reads:

Feisal. 'I cannot understand why I am omitted from the list of representatives to the Congress.'

Gout. 'It is easy to understand. You are being laughed at: the British have let you down. If you make yourself on our side, we can arrange things for you . . .

　'We recognise you only as a visitor and honoured guest, not as having any connection with the Peace Conference. The fault is yours; you came here without the permission of Picot, or informing him. You acted on local advice, which had nothing to do with you. For this reason we regard you as son of the King of Hejaz only.'

Feisal. 'Shall I inform my father?'

Gout. 'Yes.'

Feisal. 'I came here on my father's orders. He has been long one of the Allies. General Allenby in Damascus informed me that the French and British Governments recognised my troops as belligerents.'

Gout. 'That is a lie. We know nothing of an Arab army in Syria. We received a telegram from your father that you were his representative; but that telegram was long delayed, and we do not recognise it. You must understand that France is strong.'

Feisal. 'I know nothing of England or France. Allenby was the Allied Commander-in-Chief, and my superior officer, and he told me himself in Damascus I was a belligerent. I believed him.'

Gout. 'You had better understand that if you want to be friends with France you must get rid of everybody else.'

Feisal. 'I have not come here to make bargains, but to impress on the world that we have not escaped from Turkey to enter a new servitude, or to be divided up. I beg to inform you that I revolted to be free and sovereign, and we will die for that principle. I am not ready to hand any part of my country to England.'

Gout. 'In Mesopotamia and Syria are people working against France, and you are on the side of the British. So France will not abandon any of her interests, but is ready to discuss things with you privately.'[4]

Despite this unpromising attitude on the part of the French, the British Delegation argued successfully for two Hejaz delegates, much to Feisal's satisfaction.

　Another important decision made at this time, in deference to American opinion, was that the imperial possessions of Germany and Turkey should not be reallocated among the victors as colonies. Instead, they were to be held as 'Mandates' under the newly-formed League of Nations, and it would be the responsibility of the Mandatory Powers to help the ex-colonial peoples reach independence.

The following weeks saw little progress towards a resolution of the Syrian question, but a number of memoranda were submitted to the Conference by interested parties, and some of these papers were widely circulated and discussed. The attitudes of Britain, France, America and the Arabs can readily be summarised from these documents.

Whatever the private feelings of British Delegates, the Cabinet had decided to remain neutral in the Franco-Arab dispute. It was thought probable that France would gain Lebanon, but if America took a hand and the future of Syria was established on the principle of self-determination, the prospects for France seemed uncertain. Acting as a disinterested observer, Britain refused to take any action in Syria or to sanction any move by France that might prejudge the Peace Conference decision. In practice, this meant that the British Government refused to hand over military control of Syria to France, or even to allow an increase in the number of French troops stationed there. French participation in the administration of Syria was limited to the presence of the advisers appointed under the Anglo-French understanding reached just before the capture of Damascus. However, British taxpayers were bearing the cost of keeping Allenby in Syria, and Lloyd George made it clear early in the Conference that he hoped the future of these regions would be decided as rapidly as possible.

Despite the formal British position, there were widely differing views on the Syrian question within the British Delegation. The majority, concerned mainly with the future of Europe, felt that no vital British interests were at stake in Syria, and that the wrangle was harming Anglo-French relations.

Among those whose chief interest was Mesopotamia, there were two schools of thought. Hardline Anglo-Indian imperialists, represented by Sir Arthur Hirtzel, wished to turn Mesopotamia into a colony. They hoped that concessions to the principle of self-determination would be nothing more than cosmetic, and that the Arabs would be content with the vague assurances contained in the Anglo-French Declaration. France had similar ambitions in Syria, and, now that the Mosul question had been re-solved, there was little conflict between French and Anglo-Indian views. Hirtzel's advice was to accommodate France: 'I suggest that our policy now is to play the honest broker between French and Arabs. We should tell Feisal frankly that we cannot support him beyond a certain point; that he must come to terms with the French; and that we will help him to make the best [terms] possible. We should tell the French that they must make more generous recognition than they have yet done of the fact that the Arabs are now free . . .

'The French are in a weak position, and I believe they would be glad to make terms. At all events it seems to me worth trying for the sake of retaining the friendship of France.'[5]

Hirtzel, however, was not the only person in the British Delegation to speak about the relationship between Mesopotamia and Syria. Gertrude Bell visited Paris specifically to represent the Baghdad administration. Although she was interested primarily in Mesopotamia, her views about the future of the Middle East were much more in tune with Lawrence's, and she spent much of her time working with him.[6]

Another important figure was Clayton, whose opinions would doubtless have carried more weight if he had been free to leave his duties in the Middle East and attend the Paris Conference. As Allenby's chief political adviser, he had to deal personally with the situation that was developing in Syria and Palestine. He foresaw the consequences of an unsatisfactory settlement and, in a memorandum of March 11th, set out the British dilemma and its likely results. He wrote: 'We are committed to three distinct policies in Syria and Palestine:–

A. We are bound by the principles of the Anglo-French Agreement of 1916, wherein we renounced any claim to predominant influence in Syria.
B. Our agreements with King Hussein . . . have pledged us to support the establishment of an Arab state, or confederation of states, from which we cannot exclude the purely Arab portions of Syria and Palestine.
C. We have definitely given our support to the principle of a Jewish home in Palestine and, although the initial outlines of the Zionist programme have been greatly exceeded by the proposals now laid before the Peace Congress, we are still committed to a large measure of support to Zionism.

'The experience of the last few months has made it clear that these three policies are incompatible . . . and that no compromise is possible which will be satisfactory to all three parties:–

a. French domination in Syria is repudiated by the Arabs of Syria, except by the Maronite Christians and a small minority amongst other sections of the population.

b. The formation of a homogeneous Arab State is impracticable under the dual control of two Powers whose system and methods of administration are so widely different as those of France and England.

c. Zionism is increasingly unpopular both in Syria and Palestine where the somewhat exaggerated programme put forward recently by the Zionist leaders has seriously alarmed all sections of the non-Jewish majority. The difficulty of carrying out a Zionist policy in Palestine will be enhanced if Syria is handed over to France and Arab confidence in Great Britain undermined thereby.

'It is impossible to discharge all our liabilities, and we are forced, therefore, to break, or modify, at least one of our agreements.'[7]

Clayton foresaw serious consequences if Britain handed Syria to France, and then sought to impose Zionism in Palestine: 'The French will certainly meet with great obstruction, and possibly armed resistance from the Arabs who will doubtless be supported by the Arabs of the Hedjaz sphere. Great Britain, as the controlling Power in Palestine, will be pressed by France to enforce the neutrality of beduins in the Palestine hinterland and to close the lines of communication between Hedjaz and Damascus. Our influence with the Arabs will have been greatly impaired, firstly by the fact that we shall be held to have sold Syria to the French, and secondly by our support of the unpopular Zionist programme.'[8]

In this situation, Clayton argued, Britain would have to maintain a costly army of occupation in Palestine and, 'by definitely alienating Arab sentiment,'[9] would also incur very unfavourable consequences for British interests and influence in the Arabian Peninsula and even Mesopotamia.

This led to a conclusion which few British politicians at that time would have found palatable: if Britain did not take both Palestine and Syria, she should take neither of them: 'If France must have Syria it would be preferable that America, or some Power other than Great Britain or France, be given the Mandate for Palestine.' Clayton continued: 'The alternative is to offer to France such inducement as will lead her to renounce her claims in Syria, and to give to some other Power the mandate for both Syria and Palestine. It is only thus that a compromise might be arrived at, between Arab aspirations for a united and autonomous Syria and Zionist demands for a Jewish Commonwealth in Palestine . . . In these circumstances the Power entrusted with the Mandate can only be America or Great Britain.'[10]

As the weeks passed, it became increasingly clear that Clayton was right. Both the British and American Delegations could foresee the additional difficulties which would face the Zionist programme in Palestine if the Arabs were alienated in Syria. Yet there was one immovable factor which prevented a satisfactory solution: namely the attitude of France.

At the beginning of the Peace Conference the French position was that there would be no concessions in the Middle East beyond those already made by Clemenceau to Lloyd George. On the contrary, France was keen to gain recognition for the principle Lloyd George had accepted, that her colonial administrators would have a free hand to govern both coastal and inland Syria as one unit. For this reason, there were attractions in exchanging the Sykes-Picot arrangements for a Mandate over the whole of Syria. In this case, it might be possible to eliminate the distinction between the coast and the inland area reserved under Sykes-Picot for an independent Arab administration.

The French Foreign Office began to press for this modification, submitting a long memorandum on the subject to Britain for agreement. The new proposals seemed to allow for some measure of Arab self-government, but they contained no details, and no guarantee that anything acceptable to the Arabs would result. The French stated that by abolishing the difference between the coastal and inland areas, 'the zone of direct sovereignty disappears and is fused in [Sykes-Picot] zone A, whose regime is to be revised and subsequently defined.'[11] However, France expressed a readiness 'to accept at Damascus a regime approximate to that laid down for zone A in 1916, which would ensure for the Emir Feisal the situation in which the Allies desire to place him in the common interest of the Arab peoples and of modern civilisation.'[12]

To British eyes, this proposal appeared to be little more than a re-statement of French colonial demands. The friendly allusion to Feisal had obvious propaganda value, but it was offset by the antagonism towards him so frequently expressed by French politicians and newspapers. Moreover, French imperialist plans for Syria were clear from a secret document that had recently come into possession of the Department of Military Intelligence at the War Office.[13] The Foreign Office therefore chose to ignore the proposal, commenting: 'His Majesty's Government are ready to take their stand upon the self-determination of the Arabs and to leave to them in every case the free choice of the Power whose assistance they desire.'[14]

Britain's refusal to pre-empt Peace Conference decisions left French imperialists facing the possibility that their ambitions would be thwarted by American insistence on Syrian self-determination. To counter this threat, they encouraged pro-French Syrian groups all over the world to send in petitions to the Peace Conference demanding a French Mandate for Syria. This propaganda campaign achieved little except to generate ill-feeling, as it was obvious to anyone who examined the question that these pro-French groups were largely from the Christian minority in Syria, whereas the Muslim majority was overwhelmingly opposed to French rule.[15]

The intransigence of the French Government over Syria was greatly aggravated by domestic popular feeling. Pressure groups with special interests in the Lebanon launched a well-orchestrated campaign in the French press. As a result there were frequent articles attacking Britain, Feisal, and even Lawrence; the Syrian issue became a *cause célèbre*.

A particular source of resentment was the British refusal to withdraw Allenby's occupying force until the Peace Conference had reached its decision. Repeated requests to increase the number of French troops in Syria were refused, and Britain remained firmly in control. Without the full apparatus of a military government behind him, Georges-Picot could achieve very little. As anti-French feeling grew, he feared that the prospect of a French Mandate was diminishing. Yet he lacked any means to censor anti-French sentiment in the Syrian press or to counteract it with pro-French propaganda. He poured out his troubles in reports to Paris, accusing the British military administration of anti-French bias. These complaints were forwarded by Pichon to the Foreign Office in a series of increasingly blunt memoranda. On investigation, however, the allegations were almost always proved false, and the tenor of British denials became almost as offensive as Pichon's accusations.[16]

The background to Feisal's efforts at the Peace Conference was therefore one of deepening antagonism between Britain and France. At first, Arab prospects seemed reasonably good: with Lawrence's help, Feisal was able to put his case to leading members of the American Delegation and to the press.[17] It was not difficult for the Americans to feel sympathetic. The Arabs, who had made great sacrifices to fight off their Turkish oppressors, were now cast as victims of French imperial greed.

Feisal was almost always accompanied by Lawrence, who prepared the English drafts of his memoranda, correspondence, and telegrams, and acted as interpreter in private meetings and in public, for example on February 6th, when Feisal spoke before the Council of Ten. To the Americans, Feisal seemed elegant and gifted, while amazing stories circulated about Lawrence, 'that young successor of Mohammed . . . the twenty-eight year old conqueror of Damascus, with his boyish face and almost constant smile – the most winning figure, so everyone says, at the whole Peace Conference'.[18]

American accounts of Feisal and Lawrence at this time are infused with romanticism: 'Lawrence came in the uniform of a British Colonel, but wore his Arab headdress to keep his friend company . . . He has been described as the most interesting Briton alive, a student of medieval history at Magdalen College, where he used to sleep by day and work by night and take his recreation in the deer park at four in the morning – a Shelley-like person, and yet too virile to be a poet. He is a rather short, strongly built man . . . with sandy complexion, a typical English face bronzed by the desert, remarkable blue eyes and a smile around the mouth that responded swiftly to that on the face of his friend. The two men were obviously very fond of each other. I have seldom seen such mutual affection between grown men as in this instance. Lawrence would catch the drift of Feisal's humor and pass the joke along to us while Feisal was exploding with his idea; but all the same it was funny to see how Feisal spoke with the oratorical feeling of the south and Lawrence translated in the lowest and quietest of English voices, in very simple and direct phrases, with only here and there a touch of oriental poetry breaking through.'[19] Lawrence's strategy of befriending Americans was so successful that French observers became deeply concerned about it, and steps were taken to present the French view to President Wilson.[20]

Elsewhere, however, Feisal was confronted by many difficulties. The India Office was opposed to the tacit alliance once envisaged by the Eastern Committee, whereby Britain would help Feisal in exchange for Arab endorsement of British plans for Mesopotamia and Palestine. Feisal's views about the future of Mesopotamia were anathema to the Anglo-Indian administration at Baghdad (headed by A. T. Wilson) and also to Hirtzel.

As already noted, Hirtzel favoured a tactical alliance with France. He saw Lawrence as one of the chief obstacles to such an arrangement; in mid-February he wrote: 'The French press have latterly devoted a good deal of space to Syria and the Shereefial claims, and one paper attributes the discord between French and British policy to Colonel Lawrence, whose activities are much commented on. This is perhaps an over-statement. But undoubtedly the pro-Arab enthusiasm of Colonel Lawrence has afforded material to the Francophobe tendencies of the [British] General Staff and of some political authorities, and his ambiguous position as Feisal's political officer and technical adviser to H. M. Government is hardly likely to impress the French favourably . . . it is essential that Colonel Lawrence's position should be regularised. At present it is fair to none of the parties. Either he should return to military duty (but not in [an] Arab country); or, if Feisal strongly objects, he should resign his commission and sever his connection with the Foreign Office. H. M. Government do not require a special adviser. There are properly constituted authorities in Syria, Palestine, Egypt and Mesopotamia, whom it is their duty to consult when they require advice. At present there is a danger of the opinions of these authorities being overridden on the advice of an officer who necessarily becomes more out of touch with the local situation every day.'[21] This kind of India Office criticism was to be expressed more forcefully as time went by and, although it had little support among members of the British Delegation in Paris, it gradually created the impression in London that Feisal and Lawrence were entirely responsible for Britain's increasingly awkward predicament *vis-à-vis* the French.

Another problem for Feisal was the tactical alliance with Zionism. Although this had at first seemed to promise a great deal, it soon became more of a liability than an asset. The apparent moderation of Chaim Weizmann's views, and the measured undertakings of the Balfour Declaration, were overshadowed at the Peace Conference by much more extreme demands.[22] There was, moreover, a flagrant contradiction between the principle of self-determination, as applied to the existing Arab population of Palestine, and Zionist ambitions. Many Zionists spoke openly of their hopes to take over Palestine and govern it in the interests of a new Jewish community that had yet to arrive.

The Zionist lobby was powerful in America as in Britain, and the Great Powers continued to ignore this conflict of principle, discouraging those who drew attention to it. Stephen Bonsal, one of the aides in the American Delegation, was embarrassed when Lawrence brought to him a draft memorandum in which Feisal expressed mounting anxiety on the matter. In outline, according to Bonsal's memoirs, the memorandum ran: 'If the views of the radical Zionists, as presented to the [Peace Conference], should prevail, the result will be a ferment, chronic unrest, and sooner or later civil war in Palestine. But I hope I will not be misunderstood. I assert that we Arabs have none of the racial or religious animosity against the Jews which unfortunately prevail in many other regions of the world. I assert that with the Jews who have been seated for some generations in Palestine our relations are excellent. But the new arrivals exhibit very different qualities from those "old settlers" as we call them, with whom we have been able to live and even co-operate on friendly terms. For want of a better word I must say that new colonists almost without exception have come in an imperialistic spirit. They say that too long we have been in control of their homeland taken from them by brute force in the dark ages, but that now under the new world order we must clear out; and if we are wise we should do so peaceably without making any resistance to what is the *fiat* of the civilised world.'[23]

In addition to these difficulties, there were inherent problems in the case that Feisal had to present at the Conference. Hussein was still hoping to obtain some kind of personal authority over the whole area, not just the Arabian Peninsula. Speaking as his father's representative, Feisal was obliged to promote this concept of Pan-Arab union, although this was clearly unworkable in the foreseeable future. There is contemporary evidence that Feisal was out of sympathy with these Pan-Arab ambitions but, as Lawrence explained, he hoped to 'put off the breach between his father and himself as long as possible.'[24] This was a price Feisal had to pay for the opportunity to speak in Paris. If he had openly contradicted his father's views, he would rapidly have lost his status as representative of the Hejaz. Lawrence himself later wrote that Arab unity was 'a madman's notion – for this century or next, probably. English-speaking unity is a fair parallel. I am sure I never dreamed of uniting even Hejaz and Syria. My conception was of a number of small states.'[25]

Unfortunately, talk of Arab union offended not only France and the Anglo-Indian lobby, but also more moderate opinion in the Foreign Office, where such ambitions were seen as a potential threat to Britain's imperial communications. Whenever Lawrence was able to influence Arab speeches and memoranda, he saw to it that the Pan-Arab ideal was presented as an ideal for the distant future. It was invoked in the present circumstances purely as a long-term argument against dividing up the Arab world between incompatible colonial administrations. Nevertheless, opponents were quick to accuse him of supporting extreme Pan-Arab views at the expense of British interests. A critical profile of Lawrence in the French press is typical of the comment that appeared:

'An Englishman – and a cultivated Englishman, as he is an Oxford graduate – he belongs to the tradition of General Gordon: men who have contributed both greatness and misfortune to their country; mystics who are at the same time adventurers. Once they are possessed by their dream, nothing can stop them, not even the recognised interests of their own country.

'Colonel Lawrence's adventure was not to be as tragic as Gordon's but was no less remarkable. Having gone to the East as a historian, he fell in love with the country. He was at Feisal's side from the very first days of the Hejaz Revolt.

'There were also French officers whom France lent to the Sherif for the duration of the war. But what a contrast there was between the roles these Europeans played! The French (such as Captain Pisani, who was the Emir's most valuable helper during his famous raid from Maan to Damascus in September 1918) were all soldiers. They were there to give the Arab bands the appearance of an army and to teach them the art of defeating the enemy. They themselves fought, and with great effect. Without the little French guns commanded by Captain Pisani, would Feisal ever have reached Damascus?

'Colonel Lawrence's role, however, was above all political. He was the inventor, with Sir Mark Sykes (a Member of Parliament) of Pan-Arabism, and urged Feisal along the path of this great dream. And in the meantime he was well provided with British funds, which he handed out liberally with a disdain for gold worthy of the knights errant.

'But there was another difference between the two. An Arabist like Captain Pisani never forgot that he was French. He fought in the desert as he had previously fought in the Vosges: with method; with determination; his only aim being to win victory for his country. Colonel Lawrence, on the other hand, seemed to have become more Arab – or Pan-Arab – than English. He was serving his country, but he would hardly hesitate before doing it a disservice whenever his sacred mission demanded. In fact, he encouraged hopes and passions for independence among the Arabs which cannot fail to become a source of embarrassment for Britain, if only in Egypt.

'In this sense, one cannot help drawing another comparison with Gordon. At the time that this noble idealist was in Khartoum, Lord Cromer, one of the most thoughtful of the empire builders, was in Cairo.

Gordon's fantasies, recklessness, and perpetual dreaming caused Cromer the most thankless difficulties. They could scarcely get on with one another. Cromer was serving England, Gordon was serving a passion.

'Doubtless Colonel Lawrence will return to Arabia. Let us hope that he does not set it on fire.'[26]

It was ironic that Sykes too was castigated in the French press. At the end of January, after a disappointing mission to Syria during which he had attempted in vain to bring Arab leaders and Georges-Picot together in an atmosphere of friendly co-operation, he had come to Paris. He was ill and exhausted, and he soon found that there were few people at the Conference who were prepared to listen to him. As far as the British were concerned, he was totally discredited by the wartime policies associated with his name. On February 11th, he contracted influenza which led to pneumonia, and five days later he died. Lloyd George remarked not long afterwards: 'He was a worried, anxious man. That was the cause of his death. He had no reserves of energy. He was responsible for the agreement which is causing us all the trouble with the French . . . Sykes negotiated it for us with Picot, the Frenchman, who got the better of him. Sykes saw the difficulties in which he had placed us, and was very worried in consequence. I said something to him about the agreement, and at once saw how I had cut him. I am sorry. I wish I had said nothing. I blame myself. He did his best. I did not wish to emphasise his mistake or to make him more miserable. I did not know until I spoke to him that he had taken the matter so much to heart.'[27]

On March 20th the Powers took their first decision of any importance about Feisal's case. President Wilson suggested that an inter-Allied commission should visit Syria in order to establish the wishes of the people. This decision, which the Foreign Office had long been hoping for, promised to absolve the Cabinet from any further embarrassment over the question. Britain would go on maintaining a position of strict neutrality, yet the Commission was certain to find that France was unacceptable to the great majority of Syrians as a Mandatory Power. Feisal's wishes would then be granted.

The French employed every possible device to block this move. Clemenceau immediately suggested that the Commission should not confine its attention to Syria, but should also visit Mesopotamia and Palestine. When Zionists heard that it was to consult the Palestinian Arabs, they threw all their influence against it. Likewise, the India Office opposed a visit to Mesopotamia. Within days, a considerable body of opinion at the Conference had been mobilised against the Commission scheme. An unofficial meeting between interested parties from France and Britain was arranged by the editor of *The Times*, Wickham Steed. At this meeting (where the French outnumbered the British) no official minutes were taken, but an account given by Steed to the American Delegation shows that the real objective was to find a solution to the Syrian problem which would not involve sending a Commission to the Middle East. Lawrence had been invited to attend, and during six hours of discussions he was put under great pressure to help arrange a meeting between Feisal and Clemenceau. He agreed to do so, although he can have had few illusions about the likely outcome.[28]

It was three weeks before this meeting took place, and Lawrence meanwhile received very bad news. On April 7th, a telegram warned him that his father was seriously ill with pneumonia. He left for Oxford immediately, but arrived too late and shortly afterwards returned to Paris. A week later he went home again, and it was only then that the Hejaz Delegation learned what had happened. Feisal wrote in his diary: 'The greatest thing I have seen in him, which is worthy of mention as one of his principal characteristics, is his patience, discretion, zeal, and his putting the common good before his own personal interest. When he came to take leave I asked the reason for his departure. He said, "I regret to say that my father has died and I want to go and see my mother." I enquired when his father had died and he said, "A week ago – I received a telegram saying that he was ill, and left straightaway, but when I arrived I found that he had died two hours previously. I did not stay in England until the funeral because I realised that you were here alone and that there is much work to be done. I didn't want to be far from you, in case things happened in my absence. I didn't tell you this at the time in case it upset you, so I tell you now. I shall return on Friday." Consider such honesty, such faithfulness, such devotion to duty and such control of one's personal feelings! These are the highest qualities of man, which are found in but few individuals.'[29]

The Feisal-Clemenceau meeting eventually took place in mid-April, but it only served to show that the gap between the two sides was as wide as ever. Lawrence minuted: 'In a nutshell, nothing has passed. Clemenceau tried to make a bargain with Feisal to acknowledge the independence of Syria in return for Feisal's statement that France was the only qualified mandatory.

'Feisal refused. He said first that it wasn't true. France hardly understood the mandatory system. Secondly, if he said so he would only have to go away to Mecca, since he could not make his people [in Syria] agree with him. The French had now, by means of the Commission, to deal with the people, not with him.'[30]

A few days after this, Feisal left for Damascus to prepare for the Commission's arrival. As soon as he had gone, *Le Matin* announced that in his talk with Clemenceau he had agreed that France was 'the only European nation which can assure the independence of Syria'.[31] It was further claimed that he would from now on follow a common policy with France. Lawrence commented: 'There is hardly a word of truth in these statements. Feisal did leave in a French cruiser (after making his will) but will probably not return to France . . . He made no agreement with M. Clemenceau, and is persuaded that France is the only nation in Europe determined to refuse independence to Syria.

'I hope that the Sykes-Picot Agreement is given up – but not in the *Matin* sense of extending the French sphere over both Arab and British spheres of the integral Syria.

'It is rather amusing that the very tendentious French communiqué containing all these lies was solemnly published in England.'[32]

Now that Feisal had left Paris, there was little to distract Lawrence from writing his account of the Revolt. As he worked, he realised that he needed to visit the Arab Bureau in Cairo in order to check his narrative against the messages and notes in its files.

When he learned that the RAF was about to send fifty Handley-Page bombers from France to Egypt, he asked General Groves, the British Air Delegate at the Peace Conference, to allow him to travel with them. Groves agreed, and Lawrence left in mid-May with one of the first squadrons to set out. He told colleagues in the British Delegation that he was going to Cairo to get his belongings, 'and was coming back in a week.'[33]

On May 18th the British Embassy at Rome cabled to the Foreign Office: 'Two Handley-Page machines in one of which was Colonel Lawrence arrived last evening at Rome aerodrome after nightfall. [His aircraft] struck a tree and was wrecked. Colonel Lawrence escaped with a broken collar bone. Aviation Officer Prince was killed on the spot. Spratt [the 2nd pilot] died in hospital from skull fractures. Two mechanics escaped with shock. Lawrence will be in hospital for four or five days and remain here till convalescent. The second machine landed safely.'[34]

Two days later the British Air attaché sent a more detailed report on the accident, from which it emerged that Lawrence and the two other survivors had been very lucky to escape with their lives: 'On the 17th at 8.45 p.m. just as it was getting dusk, two machines . . . arrived at the aerodrome at Centocelle. [Aircraft] No. 5429 was the first to land. It is a very big aerodrome, but slopes down from west-south-west to east-north-east. The pilot, 2/Lt Prince, made a very good landing but ran on some way owing to the slope of the ground and to the lack of wind. Evidently thinking that he was running too far, he switched on again and attempted to get off again and make another circuit of the aerodrome. When about 20 feet up his right wing hit a tree and he crashed into a road on the edge of the aerodrome.

'2/Lt Prince was killed instantaneously. The second pilot 2/Lt Spratt was taken to hospital with a fractured skull and he died three hours after admittance . . . Colonel J. Lawrence [sic] was admitted to hospital with a fractured shoulder blade. He is getting on very well and will be about again in a short time. A/c Daw and A/c Tunley received very slight injuries from the concussion but will be quite fit again in a few days. The machine is a complete write-off, in fact there is practically nothing left of it.'[35] On the same day, official instructions were sent to pilots of other aircraft flying to Egypt that they should land in the uphill direction at Centocelle when no wind was blowing.

Lawrence's injuries were remarkably slight. On examination, he proved to have a cracked shoulder blade and some strained muscles. Four days after the accident the British Ambassador in Rome reported: 'He is at present in the military hospital but I hope to move him to the Embassy in a few days. The medical view is that the cure will take about three weeks. He is however anxious to proceed on his mission earlier if possible.'[36]

By May 29th, Lawrence was well enough to leave Rome with the next flight of Handley-Page bombers. Although his left arm was in plaster, he was able to write, and he passed his time drafting the introductory chapters of *Seven Pillars*. At Taranto there was a delay while the machines were overhauled. Afterwards, the squadron flew on by easy stages, spending a week in Athens. In early June it reached Crete, where Lawrence decided that he would visit the ruins of Knossos, completing the journey to Egypt with one of the later squadrons.

In mid-June, the Foreign Office learned that Lawrence was waiting at Suda Bay, in Crete, for an onward flight which had not yet arrived.

While he was still there, however, another aircraft called, carrying a diplomat from London to Egypt. This turned out to be another Arab specialist, H. St.J. B. Philby, who was on an urgent mission to mediate in the continuing frontier dispute between King Hussein and ibn Saud. Lawrence joined him for the flight to Cairo.

Hussein's quarrel with ibn Saud had been smouldering for months, with repeated border incursions by one side or the other. In late May, a Sherifian army under Abdullah had been attacked while sleeping in its tents, and was virtually destroyed. The British Government was embarrassed, since Hussein was a key figure in its Middle Eastern policy, while ibn Saud was a protégé of the India Office. It had therefore been decided that the parties should be persuaded to accept arbitration.

Lawrence himself would have become involved in the affair, had anyone been able to contact him earlier. On June 5th, the Foreign Secretary had cabled to Allenby (who had now effectively taken over as British High Commissioner in Egypt): 'In view of the paramount importance of checking the Wahabi threat to the Holy Places and the difficulty of providing King Hussein with adequate support, I consider that every effort should be made to assist him to organise his own forces to the best advantage. Colonel Lawrence from his unequalled experience in directing Arab operations would, in my opinion, be invaluable in the Hedjaz and I recommend that he should be [despatched] to Jeddah forthwith to assist in Hussein's operations if this has not already been done.'[37] Allenby had agreed with the suggestion, but was unable to do anything until Lawrence arrived. Later, it had been suggested in London that Lawrence should undertake the role of mediator, but as he had still not reached Cairo, Philby had been sent instead.[38]

By June 28th, both Lawrence and Philby were in Cairo, where they stayed at the Residency. As originally planned, Lawrence remained in Egypt for only a few days, most of which he spent searching the files of the Arab Bureau.

During his absence there were important developments affecting the Syrian question. France refused to participate in the Inter-Allied Commission unless the British forces in Syria were first replaced by French troops. This move placed Lloyd George in an embarrassing position, and he decided that if no French Commissioners went, the British should stay away also. Consequently, the only Allies represented were the Americans, whose Commissioners were Dr H. C. King and C. R. Crane.

Accompanied by a small staff, they had spent two weeks in Palestine before arriving in Damascus on June 25th for a visit which lasted ten days.

By that time, however, their conclusions were of purely academic interest. As most observers recognised, there was little likelihood that America would accept any of the Middle East Mandates. The Syrians were still clamouring for British stewardship, but Lloyd George was tied to the gentleman's agreement he had made with Clemenceau. He decided to clarify the position by stating that the Cabinet would under no circumstances accept a Mandate for Syria. The only possible outcome, therefore, was that Syria would go to France.

In Paris, the imperialist press, which was vehemently anti-British, prepared the ground for an adverse report by claiming that the King-Crane Commission was under the influence of English propaganda. Whatever the Commission's findings, it was clear that French politicians would reject them. By mid-July, when Lawrence returned to Paris, the final outcome was certain; the only question that remained was how, in practical terms, the hand-over to France would be achieved.

It is significant that Britain had finally given in to French demands while both Feisal and Lawrence were absent from Paris. Without an effective advocate to stir the British conscience, the Arab cause had been no match for a determined onslaught by the French, who were ably backed up by the India Office.

The Anglo-Indian lobby had been an increasingly valuable support for French ambitions. Lawrence had requested permission, during the spring, for some of Feisal's Iraqi officers to return to Mesopotamia. The administration in Baghdad had strenuously objected to this, claiming that they were being sent to spread nationalist propaganda. During the early summer, the India Office had seized upon this issue in order to attack Arab nationalism in general and Lawrence in particular. It had suggested that he was responsible for great and growing difficulties in Mesopotamia, and that his unexplained absence from Paris since mid-May was cover for some sinister activity. On June 19th Hirtzel had written a private note to Lord Curzon, ostensibly on the subject of Arab nationalism: 'The propaganda originates with Feisal and Lawrence, and I am convinced that there will be no peace in the Middle East until Lawrence's malign influence is withdrawn. He is advocating and actively supporting a policy which is contrary to the policy of H. M. Government both in Syria and in Mesopotamia viz. a British or American Mandate in the former, and Arab Emir in the latter; and he roams about Europe and

Asia at his own sweet will, playing off one party against the other. Is it not possible to control him? I tried hard to get something done in Paris four months ago, but no one would listen; and the situation is infinitely worse now.'[39] The letter was passed by Curzon to Cecil, and thence to Kidston, a Foreign Office official hitherto fairly well-disposed towards the Arabs. The following day Kidston minuted: 'Feisal is advocating independence and spreading propaganda in this sense to Mesopotamia, but his object, I understand, is to fling off the French and, once his independence is recognised, to turn to us and seek our help in organising the whole Arab Federation. This of course is the Lawrence scheme and I feel convinced that Lawrence is at the bottom of these excursions into Mesopotamia. He began his manoeuvres in Paris and his telegrams to Feisal on the subject of the return of the Baghdadi officers were sent to us officially by the Peace [Conference] Delegation for transmission. I am becoming more and more suspicious that Lawrence's interest in the archaeology of Crete may have been mere bluff and that he may have given us the slip and may be in Syria at this very moment. General Bols told me today that the Intelligence Division in Paris had ascertained that he had furnished himself with Arab naturalisation papers, whatever these may be.'[40]

As a result of these attacks, Lawrence found that there was no longer any great sympathy for Feisal among members of the British Delegation. Officials who had once supported Arab claims now preferred to criticise him rather than admit that Britain had abandoned a deserving ally. The whole Syrian question had been shelved, pending a final decision by the U.S. Congress as to whether America would accept Mandate responsibilities. Lawrence cabled to Feisal, who was still in Damascus: 'The settlement of Arab affairs is not being considered at present in Paris. Nothing will be done till about September. I recommend that you do not come here till then.'[41] Philip Kerr, the prime minister's private secretary, wrote next day that he had spoken to Lawrence, who 'said that Feisal was quite top dog in Syria; that the American Commission was reporting that the Syrian population desired, first independence; second, an American Mandate; third, a British Mandate; under no circumstances a French Mandate. The Commission . . . may be expected back shortly. I further gathered from him that the Palestine population is coming out strongly for union with Syria. Finally, he told me that he had received a letter from [Cabot] Lodge, who is the Republican leader in the Senate, stating that under no circumstances would America accept any Mandate in Turkey or its late territories and that he had a majority in the Senate with him on the point.'[42]

When Lawrence read some of the attacks on Feisal that had accumulated in the British Delegation files, he felt very bitter. On a paper about the Iraqi officers returning to Mesopotamia he noted: 'Some of these officers are resigning from the Arab army, and in that case they will presumably return to Mesopotamia as private citizens. As they are all the men in Mesopotamia who had the courage to fight for their country, I regret that they are apparently going to be driven into opposition to our administration there. It is curious that men useful (indeed necessary) to Allenby in Syria should be "spreaders of undesirable propaganda" in Mesopotamia.'[43]

There was nothing to do in Paris, and he returned to Oxford. On June 10th he had been been elected to a Research Fellowship of All Souls College. He had been approached about this months before, by Geoffrey Dawson of *The Times*, and had indicated his willingness to accept if a Fellowship was offered. The conditions had been drawn up by the Warden and D. G. Hogarth in as vague a fashion as possible: during his tenure he was to 'prosecute his researches into the antiquities and ethnology, and the history (ancient and modern) of the Near East'.[44] The Fellowship was worth £200 a year, a comfortable income for a single person. It would run for seven years, and carried the right to rooms in college.

By this time there was increasing controversy over Lawrence's official position. After Hirtzel's request that his activities should be curbed, the British Delegation had enquired from the War Office whether he was still a serving officer in the Army. There had been no immediate reply, but on July 15th a telegram from the Foreign Office reported that he claimed to have been demobilised, although no documents could be found to support this. On August 5th, a War Office official wrote: 'there appears to be some ambiguity as to the actual status of Colonel T. E. Lawrence . . . According to the information of the Army Council, he is still employed as a special service officer under General Allenby, and, as such, is presumably under their orders. A telegram had been despatched to the General Officer Commanding-in-Chief, Egypt, asking him whether he gave him any instructions regarding his return to Paris, but his reply states that no instructions have been issued by him to Colonel Lawrence.

'At the same time the Army Council understand that he is attached to the Foreign Office section of the British Delegation in Paris and would be glad to know if this is the case and, if so, under what authority this was done. I am to add that the Army Council have no wish to cause Mr. Balfour any inconvenience by asking for the recall of Colonel Lawrence in the event of his services being required by the Foreign Office in Paris, but, in the interest of the Service, they would be glad to have his status definitely defined.'[45]

This message was forwarded to the British Delegation in Paris, and on August 13th a reply by Robert Vansittart stated that Lawrence was attached to the Delegation as a technical adviser: 'For the present Mr. Balfour would be glad if Colonel Lawrence could still be regarded as technical adviser to this Delegation as his services here are likely to be required when the question of Syria comes to be discussed with the French and possibly with Feisal on the latter's return to Paris.'[46]

The vehemence of the response this drew from the Foreign Office shows how successful Hirtzel's propaganda had been: 'While fully appreciating the value of Lawrence as a technical adviser on Arab affairs, we regard the prospect of his return to Paris in any capacity with grave misgivings. We and the War Office feel strongly that he is to a large extent responsible for our troubles with the French over Syria and you know well enough what their present temper is.

'Hirtzel goes as far as to say that the India Office hope that Lawrence will never be employed in the Middle East again in any capacity.

'If Feisal comes to Paris later on in the autumn and Lawrence is allowed to bear-lead him, there is sure to be a recrudescence of all the past bitterness . . . [We] understand that Lawrence has already been in Paris since he came back from Egypt, but neither we nor the War Office ever know where he is.

'In any case we think that he should be definitely under orders either of the War Office or of the Peace Delegation. Hardinge says that Lawrence used to come and go quite irrespectively of any authority from himself or the Political Section of the Delegation.'[47]

Vansittart minuted on this: 'If we handle Lawrence and the French properly he may be of value. We have no other channel for influencing Feisal in the desired direction – unless we use General Allenby. In any case it would be a bad start if Feisal thought we were trying to keep him away from his adviser.

'I don't think we should panic about Lawrence. If he is to be definitely under anyone's "orders" it had better be ours not W.O.'s. He will not however prove amenable to "orders." It is not the best way to use him.'[48]

A reply to this effect was sent to the Foreign Office on September 3rd. For the moment, however, Feisal was in Syria and Lawrence in Oxford.

By the beginning of September there was still no prospect of an American decision about accepting Mandates, and President Wilson, now in failing health, was preoccupied by domestic political difficulties. Lloyd George was unwilling to finance Allenby's troops in Syria indefinitely, knowing that the territory would almost certainly go to France. He therefore announced that he would shortly travel to Paris to try and settle the Syrian question. At the suggestion of the British Delegation, Feisal was urgently requested to return to Europe, though he could not possibly arrive in time for the proposed discussions.

Lawrence was not recalled, and when he learned of the forthcoming meeting, he feared that France was at last to get the bilateral agreement with Britain she had been seeking since before the Conference. Under the guise of a Mandate, her imperial rule would be extended to cover the whole of Syria. Whatever the shortcomings of the Sykes-Picot Agreement, it had been better than this. On September 8th he wrote to the editor of *The Times*, arguing that the situation should be resolved through revision of the original Anglo-French Agreement, and that the Arabs themselves should take part in this process. His letter set out the commitments given in the McMahon-Hussein pledge, the Sykes-Picot Agreement, the Declaration to the seven Syrians of Cairo, and the Anglo-French Declaration. He claimed to see 'no inconsistencies or incompatibilities in these four documents . . . It may then be asked what all the fuss between the British, the French and the Arabs is about. It is mainly because the Agreement of 1916 . . . is unworkable and in particular no longer suits the British and French Governments. As, however, it is, in a sense, the "charter" of the Arabs, giving them Damascus, Homs, Hama, Aleppo, and Mosul for their own, with such advisers as they themselves judge they need, the necessary revision of this Agreement is a delicate matter, and can hardly be done satisfactorily by England and France, without giving weight and expression also to the opinion of the third interest – the Arabs – which it created.'[49] In an editorial commenting on this letter, *The Times* urged that British, French, and Arab representatives should negotiate an amicable solution.

The Foreign Office was not pleased by Lawrence's indiscretion, nor by a further article which appeared in the *Daily Telegraph* over the signature of Perceval Landon. Kidston minuted on September 12th:

'Lawrence claims that he has written all the recent articles in the [British] press . . . on the Syrian question, including no less than twelve contributions to *The Times*.'[50] Predictably, the *Times* letter also raised a chorus of protest in French newspapers.[51]

If Lawrence was hoping to delay any significant action over Syria until Feisal reached Europe, he failed. On September 13th, Lloyd George told Clemenceau that, in the absence of a Peace Conference decision about the Mandates, Britain would shortly have to withdraw her troops from Syria. An *aide-mémoire* on this subject was drawn up that day. It began: 'Steps will be taken immediately to prepare for the evacuation by the British army of Syria and Cilicia . . . Notice is given, both to the French Government and to the Emir Feisal, of our intentions to commence the evacuation of Syria and Cilicia on the 1st November 1919.

'In deciding to whom to hand over responsibility for garrisoning the various districts in the evacuated area, regard will be had to the engagements and declarations of the British and French Governments, not only as between themselves, but as between them and the Arabs.

'In pursuance of this policy, the garrison in Syria west of the Sykes-Picot line and the Garrisons in Cilicia will be replaced by a French force and the garrisons at Damascus, Homs, Hama, and Aleppo will be replaced by an Arab force.

'After the withdrawal of their forces, neither the British Government nor the British Commander-in-Chief shall have any responsibility within the zones from which the army has retired.

'The territories occupied by British troops will then be Palestine, defined in accordance with its ancient boundaries of Dan to Beersheba, and Mesopotamia, including Mosul, the occupation thus being in harmony with the arrangements concluded in December 1918 between M. Clemenceau and Mr. Lloyd George.'[52]

By coincidence, before learning the details of this policy, Lawrence had recommended a very similar solution .[53] He was therefore delighted at the first news of Lloyd George's decision. At the Foreign Office, Kidston minuted: 'Colonel Lawrence is jubilant at the Syrian arrangement just concluded in Paris, as reported in the press. He professes to regard it as a personal triumph for himself.'[54]

In his elation, Lawrence drafted a letter to Lloyd George which read: 'I must confess to you that in my heart I always believed that in the end you would let the Arabs down:– so that now I find it quite difficult to know how to thank you. It concerns me personally, because I assured them during the campaigns that our promises held their face value, and backed them with my word, for what it was worth. Now in your agreement over Syria you have kept all our promises to them, and given them more than perhaps they ever deserved, and my relief at getting out of the affair with clean hands is very great. If ever there is anything I can do for you in return please let me know.

'My first sign of grace is that I will obey the F.O. and the W.O. and not see Feisal again.'[55]

CHAPTER 29

In the Wings

September 1919 – December 1920

WHEN Lawrence learned more about the Lloyd George proposals, he realised that his jubilation about the transfer of military control in Syria was premature. Feisal arrived in London on September 19th and protested bitterly about the British withdrawal. It would leave his people cut off from the Mediterranean and at the mercy of the French authorities along the coast.

In the eyes of the Cabinet, however, Britain could no longer take responsibility for the affairs of Syria, and it was explained to Feisal that his only course was to reach the best settlement he could with France. Lawrence, who was anathema to the French, could play no role in such negotiations. He wrote privately to Curzon, setting out what he would do if asked to use his influence with Feisal. However, the offer was ignored, and after a month of fruitless negotiations in London, Feisal left for Paris.[1]

Lawrence was affected deeply by his sudden political isolation and the failure to win a better settlement for Feisal. In Paris, observers had been impressed by Lawrence's personality and intelligence.[2] By the autumn, however, the strain had taken its toll. He lived at Oxford, dividing his time between All Souls and his home in Polstead Road. His mother later related how he 'would sometimes sit the entire morning between breakfast and lunch in the same position, without moving, and with the same expression on his face.'[3] According to a contemporary, he spent many hours at All Souls reading and re-reading a book-length poem by Doughty, *Adam Cast Forth*. Its subject was the expulsion of Adam and Eve from the Garden of Eden.

Lawrence's depression must have been aggravated by the knowledge he had recently acquired about his father's true identity. Until his father's death, he had never discussed his illegitimacy with either parent. Now, however, he had heard his mother's version of the family history. It seems probable that since childhood he had doubted whether Mr Lawrence was his natural father (see pp. 29-30). If so, he must have learned with mixed feelings that the man he had known as Mr Lawrence had been Sir Thomas

Chapman, rightful heir to large estates in Ireland, and also his true parent. Chapman had abandoned his wife, children, social position, and fortune in order to spend the rest of his life with a woman he loved.

A letter written by Lawrence some years later doubtless reflects the things his mother now told him: 'My father was on the large scale: tolerant, experienced, grand, rash, humoursome, skilled to speak, and naturally lord-like. He had been thirty-five years in the larger life, and a spendthrift, a sportsman, and a hard rider and drinker . . . Father had, to keep with mother, to drop all his old life, and all his friends. She by dint of will raised herself to be his companion: social things meant much to him: but they never went calling, or on visits, together. They thought always that they were living in sin, and that we would some day find it out. Whereas I knew it before I was ten, and they never told me: till after my Father's death something I said showed Mother that I knew'.[4] When the references to his illegitimacy in Lawrence's letters are taken together, they leave no doubt that he was bitterly aware of the social standing that might, in other circumstances, have been his by right.

By a supreme irony, while Lawrence was trying to come to terms with the failure in Paris, London audiences were being treated to a romanticised version of his wartime career: 'At this moment,' they were told, 'somewhere in London, hiding from a host of feminine admirers, reporters, book publishers, autograph fiends and every species of hero-worshipper, is a young man whose name will go down in history beside those of Sir Francis Drake, Sir Walter Raleigh, Lord Clive, Charles Gordon, and all the other famous heroes of Great Britain's glorious past. His first line of defence against these would-be visitors is an Amazonian landlady who battles day and night to save her illustrious guest from his admirers . . . The young man is at present flying from one part of London to another, dressed in mufti, with a hat three sizes too large pulled down over his eyes, trying to escape from the fairer sex.

'His name is Thomas E. Lawrence.

'The Germans and Turks were so impressed with Lawrence's achievements in Arabia that they expressed their admiration and appreciation by offering rewards amounting to over one hundred thousand pounds on his head – dead or alive. But the wild sons of Ishmael regarded their quiet, fair-headed leader as a sort of supernatural being who had been sent from heaven to deliver them from their oppressors, and they wouldn't have betrayed him for all the gold in the fabled mines of King Solomon.

'During the winter of 1917-1918, shortly after Allenby captured the Holy City, I met Lawrence on one of the narrow streets near the Church of the Holy Sepulchre. He was dressed in the garb of an Oriental ruler, and at his belt he carried the curved gold sword worn only by the direct descendants of the prophet Mohammed. Previous to that day I had heard nothing but wild rumours about him, and as no one either in Egypt or Palestine seemed to have any definite knowledge regarding him, I suspected that he was merely a myth.

'From what I saw of him in the few days he remained in Jerusalem I became convinced that he was one of the outstanding figures of the War, and a little later Allenby consented to my joining Lawrence and the Arab Army.

'From personal observation and from the lips of a group of equally daring and adventurous British officers who were associated with him, I discovered that Lawrence had accomplished more toward unifying the peoples of Arabia than all of the sultans and emirs since the days of the Great Caliphs six hundred years ago.

'His success was largely due to his genius for handling men, and his peculiar training, which made it possible for him to transform himself into an Arab.'[5]

The speaker was Lowell Thomas, the American journalist who had visited Akaba in March 1918 looking for lecture topics that would encourage his countrymen to support the war. His project had never served its original purpose, because he had not returned to America until long after the Armistice. By then, there was little interest in the European battlefronts. He had given his illustrated talks in New York, but found that the only ones which were popular were the accounts of Allenby in Palestine and Lawrence in Arabia.

By chance, his lectures on Lawrence and Allenby had been heard by an English impresario, Percy Burton, who later recalled: 'I was literally thunderstruck. From the lips of an American I received my first real insight into the exploits of our great crusader.'[6] Burton was an astute businessman and realised that there would be a British public for these romantic tales of the campaigns in Palestine and Arabia. He had met the stiff terms demanded by Thomas, and the travelogue had opened at the Royal Opera House, Covent Garden, on August 14th.

Burton's expectations were rewarded. The *Daily Telegraph* wrote: 'Thomas Lawrence, the archaeologist, who went out to Arabia and, practically unaided, raised for the first time almost since history began a great homogeneous Arab army . . . we should have thought of merely as one of many who did their duty in these five stirring years. Even the fact that the Turks, under the instigation of their Teutonic masters, set a price of £50,000 on the head of this Englishman who was rousing Arabia from her long lethargy, would probably soon have been forgotten. Now, thanks to Mr. Lowell Thomas and his moving pictures, Thomas Lawrence is definitely marked as one of the elect. In the opinion of the young American lecturer, the name of Thomas Lawrence will go down to remotest posterity besides the names of half a dozen men who dominate history.'[7]

Lawrence, who had played no role whatsoever in bringing this publicity to London, was disconcerted. The lectures attracted full houses for month after month, and it would have been inhuman not to have been intrigued. Yet their style and content were distasteful. During his tour of Palestine, Lowell Thomas had been shown copies of the *Arab Bulletin*, and had noted details from some of Lawrence's raiding reports. In a series of articles published that autumn in the American magazine *Asia*, he claimed to have accompanied Lawrence on expeditions against the railway, giving vivid details. Lawrence called this 'red-hot lying',[8] and persuaded Thomas to omit the most outrageous inventions before the articles were published in England. In exchange, he told Thomas a little about his background, including a version of his father's family history that owed something to the truth he had recently discovered. When the articles appeared in the *Strand Magazine*, readers learned that: 'His father's name was Thomas also, and he was a large landowner in Ireland, and a famous sportsman a generation ago. At one time the family was wealthy'.[9] On the strength of these changes, Thomas would later claim that Lawrence had helped him with the articles.[10]

As Lawrence's fame grew, even the politicians who had failed him were keen to associate themselves with his legend. The *Strand Magazine* articles were prefaced by a comment from Lloyd George: 'Everything that Mr. Lowell Thomas says about Colonel Lawrence is true. In my opinion, Colonel Lawrence is one of the most remarkable and romantic figures of modern times.'[11]

Lawrence's true reaction to Thomas can be judged from a contemporary letter: 'I am painfully aware of what Mr. Lowell Thomas is doing. He came out to Egypt on behalf of the American Government, spent a fortnight in Arabia (I saw him twice in that time) and there he seems to have realised my "star" value on the film. Anyway, since, he has been lecturing in America and London, and has written a series of six articles about me, for American and English publications. They are as rank as possible, and are making life very difficult for me, as I have neither the money nor the wish to maintain my constant character as the mountebank he makes me.

'He has a lot of correct information, and fills it out with stories picked up from officers, and by imagination . . . [He] asked me to correct his proofs: but this I decided was impossible, since I could not possibly pass one tenth of it, and he was making his living out of it. He then asked me what view I would take about misstatements, and I said I would confirm or deny nothing in public. The stuff seems to me too obvious journalism to weigh very deep with anyone serious . . . I am sitting still while he calls me an Irishman, and a Prince of Mecca, and other beastlinesses, and it seems hardly possible to begin putting it straight.'[12] However, Lawrence also admitted to a certain influence with Thomas: 'I don't pay him... but I could kick his card-house down if I got annoyed, and so he has to be polite. As a matter of fact he is a very decent fellow – but an American journalist, scooping.'[13]

Lawrence's reputation had been so well established in Government circles by the end of the war that he could easily have obtained personal publicity before this, had he wished. However, he had rarely consented to be interviewed, except on Arab questions, and he had usually chosen to provide material for articles anonymously. A journalist interviewing him in December 1918, shortly after his return to England, had written: 'Colonel Lawrence, like most men who "do things," is a man of the most charming and unassuming manners, and his extreme modesty and dislike of talking about himself make the interviewer's task a somewhat difficult one. His first remarks, in fact, were directed to "throwing down" the stories concerning himself which had appeared in the press, on the ground that he was having too large a share of the limelight cast upon him. "The stories told about me are very often untrue," said the Colonel, "and they are not quite fair, as I was not the senior British officer out there. There were four or five colonels senior to myself, and the fact that they happened to stay out there and I came home has rather spoilt the perspective of my seniors, who have remained in the east.'[14] Paradoxically, a reputation for personal reticence was now fuelling his popularity.

More than a million people, including royalty and leading politicians, went to the Lowell Thomas travelogue in London. To make way for other bookings, it had to move from the Royal Opera House to the Albert Hall, then to the Philharmonic Hall, and finally to the Queen's Hall. At first, Thomas had called it 'With Allenby in Palestine, including the Capture of Jerusalem and the Liberation of Holy Arabia'. However, as the figure of Lawrence caught the popular imagination, the title became 'With Allenby in Palestine and Lawrence in Arabia'. The phenomenal success must be attributed in part to the skill of Thomas's delivery and the excellence of the slides and motion pictures. But there was also a romance about the war in Palestine and Arabia which provided audiences with a welcome relief from the horrors of the Western Front. The Palestine campaigns had been dubbed 'The Last Crusade', and it was in this almost religious context that Lawrence now found himself cast as a national hero. Thomas had expected that his visit to London would only last a week or two, but he was to lecture there for more than four months, and afterwards he toured the provinces and the British Empire. During the years that followed, more than four million people would hear him deliver his epic account of Lawrence's Arabian adventures.

One consequence of this sudden fame was that Lawrence began to receive large numbers of unsolicited letters. Some were from admirers, some from women who wanted to marry him, some from people who hoped that he would help them to find work, and some from the demented. He was invited by fashionable hostesses to attend their social functions, and by British and overseas universities to give lectures.

Understandably, he wanted none of this, and he replied to few of the letters. Almost every invitation was refused. He would much rather not have had the publicity in the first place, and he now studiously avoided the press. Percy Burton, the impresario who had brought Thomas to England, was offered a large sum by Lord Northcliffe if he would secure a personal interview with Lawrence for *The Times*. Lawrence declined, writing: 'I'm afraid I can't do this. I never care what people say of me or about me, but I try not to help them to do it, and I will not do it myself. It is unpleasant to see one's name in print – and, in spite of the very nice way Lowell Thomas does it, I much wish he had left me out of his Palestine show. I'm very sorry for appearing so sluggish.'[15]

The friendships Lawrence sought during this period were in the world of art and letters. Hoping to improve *Seven Pillars*, he was spending much of his time reading the work of contemporary writers and trying to analyse their technique. He hoped that by talking to writers about questions of style and composition he would improve his own work.

After a dinner at All Souls in November he met Robert Graves, who had become a member of St John's College. He showed great interest in Graves's poetry, and his comments were evidently of some value. Graves later wrote that he had been 'for years the only person to whom I could turn for practical criticism of my poems. He had a keen eye for surface faults, and though I did not always adopt his amendments, it was rarely that I did not agree that something was wrong at the point indicated.'[16] Through this friendship Lawrence was soon introduced to Robert Bridges, Edmund Blunden, Robert Nichols, and other poets. In the same way he sought out prose writers and painters.

Towards the end of the year, the draft of *Seven Pillars* was nearing completion: only the chapters covering the spring and summer of 1918 remained to be written. He had sent the manuscript piecemeal to Alan Dawnay, then at Sandhurst, asking for corrections. One day late in November he went down to Camberley to discuss Dawnay's criticisms with him. Afterwards, he was to take the draft back to Oxford. As he had nothing to carry it in Dawnay lent him an official attaché case. At Reading, Lawrence had to change trains, and while waiting he sat in the cafeteria. When he went out, to catch the Oxford train, he forgot the attaché case. On arrival at Oxford he phoned Reading station, but there was no sign of the missing case or its contents. It had been taken by a thief and was never recovered.[17]

The loss was serious: the bag contained all but three of the book's eleven sections as well as photographs, negatives, and wartime notes relevant to the later chapters. This would have been a terrible blow in any circumstances, but Lawrence was already depressed. When he phoned Dawnay that evening he seemed distraught.[18]

Within days, however, he had been persuaded by Hogarth (one of the three people who had read the lost text) that *Seven Pillars* must be rewritten. He began on December 2nd, redrafting from memory. The work was not done at All Souls, where there were many distractions, but in a room on the upper floor of 14 Barton Street, Westminster. This house, in a quiet street close to the Houses of Parliament, was the property of Westminster School but had been let as offices to Sir Herbert Baker, one of the leading architects of the day. Baker had met Lawrence in Oxford and, not needing the top floor of the Barton Street house, he had offered it to Lawrence as a London base.

During the first two months of 1920, Lawrence wrote out a new version of *Seven Pillars*. He later stated that he had recreated 95 per cent of the text in only thirty days, 'by doing many thousand words at a time, in long sittings. Thus Book VI was written entire between sunrise and sunrise. Naturally, the style was careless and so Text II (though it introduced a few new episodes) came to over 400,000 words.'[19]

A great help in this task was his set of the *Arab Bulletin*, which contained many of his best wartime reports. By incorporating almost everything he had written for the *Bulletin* somewhere in *Seven Pillars*, he was able to write large sections of the text very easily. The reports were detailed, and provided the basis for almost all the descriptions of raids and journeys contained in the book. He was also able to use the few notes of his own which had survived; some were original, others copied in 1919 from the Arab Bureau files in Cairo. Despite this, the new version owed much less to contemporary materials than the one that had been lost. To enrich it, he used lavish description: 'the sense of the country and atmosphere and climate and furniture of Arabia hung so tightly about me that I put too much of them into the story, in hopes that they would make it life-like.'[20]

Lawrence's life at Barton Street was deliberately frugal: he believed that his creative power was intensified by hunger and lack of sleep, and preferred to work at night, wearing a flying suit to keep warm. The attic room contained little furniture and no cooking facilities. He lived off sandwiches bought from refreshment stands in nearby stations, and washed at the local public baths. He later wrote: 'I thought that the mind I had, (and I've matched it competitively often against other fellows, and have an opinion of it), if joined to a revival of the war-passion, would sweep over the ordinary rocks of technique. So I got into my garret, and . . . excited myself with hunger and cold and sleeplessness more than did de Quincey with his opium.'[21]

During the spring he set about correcting the text, as best he could; here again, the *Bulletin* was a valuable source. He tried very hard to make the book historically accurate. Years later he would write: 'All the documents of the Arab Revolt are in the archives of the Foreign Office, and will . . . be available to students, who will be able to cross-check my yarns. I expect them to find small errors, and to agree generally with the main current of my narrative.'[22] Nevertheless, he remained deliberately silent about certain aspects of the story. He carefully refrained, for example, from giving specific details of the methods and equipment he had used. Some years afterwards he explained this in a note for inclusion in a biography (referring to himself in the third person): 'A casual reading of his books might lead one to suppose that he fought his battles with bluff and crimson banners for main armament . . . his reasons for darkening counsel as to the means he used are connected with the political relations between the Syrian Government and the French in 1919 when he wrote his book. Both sides were preparing for armed struggle in Syria, and Lawrence apparently determined not to contribute anything to their conflict . . .

'He had to select the materials to be used from his two active years severely, to compress the history of them into a single volume (his self-imposed limit for the work): and whenever possible it is the details of fighting which have been sacrificed. He apparently fought some fifty armoured-car actions, enough to evolve a whole system and scheme of battle for them . . . We can only gather, by casual allusion, that he did not leave the tactics of the desert as he found them.

'He founded his strategy on an exhaustive study of the geography of his area; of the Turkish Army; of the nature of the Beduins, and the distribution of their tribe-masses. So he founded his desert tactics on the raiding-parties of the Arabs. He shows us this self-education, repeated again and again, till after the occupation of Akaba. Only by graduating in the Beduin school could he gain the competence and the prestige to modify its practice.

'Exactly what he did is nowhere explained. His English companions knew the difference between an Arab raid when he was present, and when he was not present: but they were not . . . students of war, and he himself, except in the battle of Siel el Hesa before Tafileh, slurs over the spectacle of himself in command . . . his reliance was on automatics, not on rifles. Bayonets he rejected . . . Machine guns, except when armoured, were too heavy for the *tempi* of his battles. Automatics (Lewis, or preferably Hotchkiss, since the Hotchkiss endured mud and sand) were his choice, and the files of Egyptforce were full of his demands for them . . . He himself carried an "air-Lewis" in a bucket on his camel saddle. He said once that he would supersede the rifle, if he could get control of an arms factory to make his Hotchkiss guns.

'His use of heavy machine guns (Vickers), in the armoured cars developed from the first tentative efforts after Akaba, till he could undertake combined operations of camels, armoured cars, and aeroplanes. Likewise he was able to refine upon the regulation uses of high explosive. He was able to fire electrical mines along the telegraph wires, and to introduce petards into the fire-boxes of railway locomotives by "salting" their wood-fuel piles with infernal contraptions. But he always saw his own ingenuities as things alien and incongruous in the Arab setting: and so we are left with only shadowy clues as to their importance and effectiveness in the more native scheme of things.'[23]

This was not the only way in which *Seven Pillars* reflected his concern about French ambitions in Syria. The book had now assumed a strongly political role: it was to serve as a record of the Arab war effort, justifying Feisal's claims to self-government. Lawrence did not entirely conceal the Arabs' failings during the war, but his treatment was sympathetic, and there was much that he glossed over. The documents show that *Seven Pillars* often tells less than the whole truth, concealing politically damaging matters such as the weakness of character displayed on occasion by Feisal. Lawrence also played down the enormous contribution made to the Revolt by non-Arab personnel. He did not assess the achievements of the Indian machine-gunners, the armoured cars, and above all the RAF, whose bombing and reconnaissance had been a decisive factor during the northern campaign.

This emphasis on the Arab achievement cannot be excused by the claim that Lawrence was writing only about his experience of the war. In his liaison role he had been directly and continuously involved with the non-Arab contribution. His decision to present such a one-sided account doubtless reflects the bitterness of his experience at the Peace Conference and his own commitment to the Arab cause. Yet the same political message might have been put across, with less risk of criticism, by stressing that there had been a large degree of interdependence. While Feisal's success owed much to British help, Allenby also owed much to Feisal. The needs of the Western Front had starved him of troops, and without the contribution made by Arab forces east of the Jordan the advance through Palestine would have been difficult, if not impossible.[24]

In late April, when he had roughed out most of the new *Seven Pillars* draft, Lawrence returned to Oxford for a month. Before long, he had become involved in Middle Eastern politics again.

The Paris Conference had produced no agreement over Mandates, and the matter was being settled at an Allied meeting then taking place in San Remo. As expected, Britain was to get Palestine and Mesopotamia, while France took the whole of Syria. After negotiating some kind of *modus vivendi* with Clemenceau at the end of 1919, Feisal had returned to Damascus in January to find himself attacked by extreme nationalists for selling out to the French. During his long absence in Europe the local support had begun to fade, and the internal situation showed signs of deteriorating.

If the Syrian politicians had been less short-sighted, they would have realised that their only hope of preserving any form of autonomy was to reach an accommodation with France. As it was, however, Feisal gave in to the extremists. After wavering for a few weeks, he disowned the understanding he had reached with Clemenceau, thereby earning lasting mistrust from the French.

On March 8th, the 'General Syrian Congress' had proclaimed Feisal King of an 'independent and integral Syria', which was supposed to include not only Lebanon, but also northern Mesopotamia and Palestine. The claim to these latter regions caused as much irritation in Britain as it did in France, and was roundly dismissed at San Remo. Both the Foreign Office and the India Office now viewed Damascus as a hotbed of rabid nationalism which threatened to unsettle the whole region.

Worse still, Feisal's control over inland Syria had weakened. Attacks on French personnel and property occurred with increasing frequency. The French administration made it clear that they would not tolerate such conduct, and the end of Feisal's regime seemed therefore merely a question of time.

As far as France and the Government of India were concerned, the allocation of Mandates at San Remo was simply a sharing-out of imperial gains. This action denied the claims of Arab nationalism and made nonsense of all that had been said in Britain and the United States about self-determination. Lawrence later wrote: 'The Sykes-Picot treaty was the Arab sheet-anchor. The French saw that, and worked frantically for the alternative of the mandate. By a disgraceful bargain the British supported them, to gain Mesopotamia. Under the Sykes-Picot treaty the French only got the coast: and the Arabs (native administration) were to have Aleppo, Hama, Homs, Damascus, and Trans-Jordan. By the mandate swindle England and France got the lot. The Sykes-Picot treaty was absurd, in its boundaries, but it did recognise the claims of Syrians to self-government, and it was ten thousand times better than the eventual settlement.'[25]

To Lawrence, at least, Arab fury about the San Remo Mandates was predictable. He had already warned, seven months previously, of his disquiet about the effect of Anglo-Indian methods in Mesopotamia, writing: 'if we do not mend our ways, [I] will expect revolt there about March next.'[26]

There were others who thought that the Anglo-Indian administration in Mesopotamia should go. Among them was Sir Hugh Trenchard, head of the RAF. Air power had proved a successful and relatively cheap method of maintaining order in Somaliland, and Trenchard was keen to extend the operations of his fledgling Service by taking over similar duties in Mesopotamia. On April 21st he discussed his ideas with Lawrence, who afterwards wrote to Lord Winterton (then a Conservative member of the House of Commons): 'I think he is right in all points, and after quite a lot of talk I feel inclined to back his scheme. It means Salmond as High Commissioner in Bagdad (a happy deliverance from the Indian Civil Service tradition) with probably the Colonial Secretary nominally responsible, and with an Arab army under an Arab–British administration to defend the country.

'Trenchard sounded to me clean and honest . . . and means to play fair by the local people. He thinks as little of the worth of bombing as we did!

'I told him Joyce would make the Arab army for him: it would be pleasant to see Nuri and Jaafar and the rest doing their job over again.'[27]

A month later Lawrence was one of the most prominent figures among an informal group of politicians and experts who urged Lloyd George to take control of Britain's Middle Eastern interests out of the hands of the Foreign Office and the India Office. Instead, it proposed that policy and administrative responsibilities for the whole area should come under a new authority.

Lawrence helped to canvass for signatures to this appeal. Writing to Philby, he said: 'It happens to be – politically – the right moment for pressure towards a new Middle East Department, since some re-shuffling of spheres is certain to happen quite soon: and the enclosed [draft letter to Lloyd George] is a step taken under advice, to add pressure from outside, to what is going on inside. They have asked me to get your name on the list: other "experts" invited are Hogarth, [Lionel] Curtis, [Arnold] Toynbee, and myself. I have no doubt you will agree, so I won't bother to argue. It is a step necessary before a new policy can be put in force, and when we get it through, then we'll have to open up a battery of advice on the new men.

'There are five peers in it (*pour encourager...*) and two or three of each House of Commons group [Lloyd George's government was a coalition] . . . all chosen for "weight" reasons in the present balance of power.'[28]

Now that he wanted to influence the Government, Lawrence suddenly found his popular reputation useful. Newspapers were only too willing to publish anything he wrote about the Middle East. On May 28th he began a press campaign with a piece in the *Daily Express*.

He had doubtless chosen the *Daily Express* because its editor, R. D. Blumenfeld, was associated with a group of Conservative Members of Parliament who felt critical of Britain's record in the Middle East.[29] His essay (concluded in a second part a few days later) exposed the absurd and costly results of Britain's muddled policy, taking as an example the conflict between Hussein and ibn Saud.

Despite the seriousness of the topic, the article was prefaced by an unsigned eulogy in the style of Lowell Thomas, which read: 'There is no greater authority on the subject than this temporary Colonel in the British army, Fellow of All Souls, formerly a scholar of Jesus, and afterwards Senior Demy of Magdalen, archaeologist, "uncrowned king of Arabia", Prince of Mecca, organiser of the Arab revolt against Turkey, and leader of irregulars under the Emir Feisal . . . His daring and his deeds, his extraordinary genius for handling wild natives, his complete assimilation of the East . . . his modesty and unconventionality, have become almost legendary.

'A slight and boyish figure "he is thirty, and might be mistaken for seventeen", a shy and nervous manner, a face not to be forgotten, with mind and character oozing through the eyes, boyish smile, boyish enthusiasm, and a venerable, unquestionable force of implacable authority – such is Lawrence, the man who will count for even more than he has yet accomplished in the contact of Western civilisation with Arabian tradition. He is entitled to be heard.'[30]

The *Express* editorial also discussed the suggestion that a single Middle East Department should be created: 'Those who have signed the letter to the Prime Minister affirm their opinion that the present arrangement, which places Mesopotamia, Central and Southern Arabia and Aden under the control and direction of the India Office, Egypt, Palestine, the Sudan, and the territory of the King of the Hejaz under the Foreign Office, and Cyprus and Somaliland under the Colonial Office, has resulted in a serious conflict of policy, which has all the seeds of permanence. None of the three existing departments, it is pointed out, has the qualification, in special organisation and personnel, to cope successfully with the new situation. India Office methods and direction are not suited to the conditions obtaining in Mesopotamia, and can only lead to political embarrassment among all the Arabic people. Similarly, the Foreign Office, bound by its own particular methods and diplomacy, is not a department designed to administer in complete harmony the territories at present under its sphere. The letter to the Prime Minister boldly advocates a new Ministry, staffed with a new Civil Service: self contained, and inspired, moreover, with the new spirit which is so greatly needed.

'It is argued that, far from increasing expenditure, the creation of this new Department would lead to economies. The aim of such a new Ministry would be to discharge British responsibilities in the Middle East with minimum garrisons and the minimum personnel, and to seek to bring about the maximum development of native administration and dependence.'[31]

Lawrence followed this up with another article, in the *Sunday Times* of May 30th which described him more modestly as 'the authority on Middle East affairs, whose brilliant exploits with our Arabian Allies during the war excited universal admiration'.[32] Rebellion had broken out four days earlier in northern Mesopotamia, and he pointed out sarcastically that this would provide a training opportunity for tens of thousands of troops. Some sections of the Army, he wrote, 'are pleased with the situation, and will hold up the offer of another British Government Department [i.e. the RAF] to maintain the administration for one fourth the price.'[33] These and other remarks were deeply embarrassing to the Foreign Office, the India Office, and to the War Office.

Although the changes Lawrence hoped for did not immediately occur, his press articles attracted many supporters. Their number grew during the summer when the rebellion in Mesopotamia began to impose a heavy strain on British resources. Early in July he wrote to Blumenfeld: 'In those short pushes the *Daily Express* achieved some things which I wanted very much, and I am still therefore deeply in your debt.'[34] He told a friend shortly afterwards that there would probably be a separate Middle East Department, but 'not till after the Imperial Conference next spring'.[35]

During the interval between the Peace Conference and this new involvement in Eastern politics, Lawrence had made plans for his own future. In fulfilment of a promise made years before, he had bought during the summer of 1919 the land which his friend Vyvyan Richards was renting at Pole Hill in Essex, on the edge of Epping Forest. It was here that, as young Oxford graduates, the two had planned to set up a private press. With the income from All Souls and the £5,000 given to him by his father in 1916, the dream of printing fine editions seemed at last to be within

Lawrence's grasp. His rooms at All Souls were soon furnished with books from the great private presses: a series of Kelmscotts, including the famous Chaucer, a Doves Press Bible, the latest titles from the Ashendene, and works from many other well-known craftsmen. He began to talk of producing an edition of poems by Meleager and other Gaderene poets, translated from the original Syrian.

Richards was still teaching at a school in Chingford, and by this time they were thinking of putting up a building at Pole Hill to house the press and provide simple living accommodation . First, however, it would be necessary to acquire more land adjoining the fields Lawrence had already bought, and to secure proper rights of access. They did not expect to begin work before 1921 at the earliest.

Lawrence offered to raise enough money to finance the building, and his letters show that as early as February 1920 he was intending to do this by publishing a popular abridgement of *Seven Pillars* in the United States. By the end of June the scheme had taken definite shape, and he offered the book to the American publisher F. N. Doubleday, whom he had met in London shortly after the war: 'I propose to . . . produce an edition 150,000 words long. This I'll have typed, and then you shall have a copy. Only it's just a boy-scout sort of book, not very good or deep (the strong bits all left out), produced in the hope of making enough money to build my house in Epping Forest. [A. S.] Watt [a London literary agent] must read it first and put a price on it. I called on him yesterday, and introduced myself. He sees no difficulty in preventing a British Isles edition, and talks hopefully about serials and films. However it will wait until about September or October, when I'll have (perhaps) done my part . . . I haven't any illusions about the rotten book it is, and will feel delighted if you find it below your standard. However perhaps its faults may help it sell, and I'm a well-advertised person, so that the necessary money may be raised by it. If it fails I'll have to go and work, which will be disgusting'.[36]

By midsummer he felt that the redrafted text of *Seven Pillars* written in the spring had been corrected sufficiently to serve as a basis for the abridgement, and he decided to spend August and September at All Souls, working on the shorter text. He invited Richards to visit him there whenever possible: 'Your critical faculty would be invaluable: because though it's only a cheap book written to buy Pole Hill and build its house, yet it's got to have my name on it – therefore I don't want it to be despicable.'[37]

Before beginning this abridgement, he wrote to Doubleday asking for advice: 'The original-and-to-be-kept-secret version was finished on July 12. On August 1 I start the American or boy-scout version. It should be ended by September 30 . . . I want to publish only one volume, and propose to leave out half, mending the gaps skilfully, and making it fit for family reading. The boy-scouts will be my best public, for my reputation is of a melodramatic and very bold swashbuckler. May I ask you a few questions, as publisher-to-be (*Inshallah*) without prejudice to you, to me or to Watt . . .

1. Is 150,000 words too many? I want eleven or twelve point type, no leading: about a 400-word page, if possible. No head lines . . .

2. I propose seven books of seven chapters each. The paragraphs are rather long, and there is no dialogue or broken lines.

3. Maps. I would like one double-page and two half-page maps. I would have to supervise the drawing of them, and it could be done either in London or in Cairo. They will have to be finely done, for my maps were supposed to be the best Staff maps of the war, and I helped in the Gallipoli, Sinai, and Syria series. Is there any reason why they should not be end-papers to the book? I do not want any folders.

4. Illustrations. Do *you* (any publisher...) want illustrations? I have many photographs, but half-tones do not harmonise with type. If you want illustrations I'll have them drawn decently in black and white by a proper artist. Would ten be enough in that case? Augustus John, who is famous, will lend me a drawing of Feisal [made during the Peace Conference]: do you want one of me? (John also in that case: he did a very pretty pencil head of me in Arab dress). I don't want too many drawings, for they will cost a fair amount to have drawn.

5. Season: by when should it be given you (any publisher) allowing that I want to keep my first proofs (galley, I hope) for six weeks, since Allenby must read them?

'Apologies for this awful string of questions.'[38]

During August, Lawrence completed several chapters of the abridge-ment. Then, during the first week in September, the work abruptly stopped. There is very little evidence relating to this decision, which was nevertheless a turning-point in his career. The most likely explanation, however, is the simplest one: his sole purpose in writing the book was to raise money to finance the press at Pole Hill and if, as seems probable, he began to doubt that it would earn the sum he needed, he had no reason to go on with it.

Lawrence's financial position at this time was much less secure than most people believed. In principle, his annual revenue amounted to £200 from All Souls and roughly another £150 interest from the £5,000 investments given to him by his father in 1916. At that time £350 was a very adequate income for a single person, and as recently as March 20th Lawrence had confidently described himself as 'a person who doesn't care sufficiently about money to try hard to make any. My father was kind to me, and spent none of the capital he received from his father... and unless I marry non-self-supporting wives or have children, all will be well with me.'[39]

In addition to these sources of income, he should have had a sizeable capital sum resulting from the accumulation of unspent army pay during the five years between October 1914 and August 1919. This surplus might well have amounted to £2,000 and, if he had invested it, his total income would have been over £400. However, he had not done so. Immediately after the war, he had begun to purchase land at Pole Hill. He had probably invested more than £2,000 in the fields bought there in September 1919 and May 1920. During the same period, he had built up a valuable collection of private press books, costing hundreds of pounds, even at the prices then prevailing. He had also acquired one of Augustus John's two oil portraits of Feisal. What he paid is not recorded (there is even a story that he exchanged the painting for a diamond). At that time, however, the market value of the portrait was about £600.[40]

It seems therefore that by the summer of 1920 all Lawrence's savings from his wartime pay had been spent. This would not have been a very serious matter, but at about this time he also gave away a large part of the capital received from his father. In doing so he was acting in the spirit of a request made by his brother Will who had been killed during the war.

In 1915, Will had appointed him executor, saying that he wanted all his money given to Janet Laurie (see pp. 226-7). This had been a confidential arrangement between the two brothers: there was no mention of Janet in the written will, which named T. E. Lawrence as sole beneficiary. After his brother's death, Lawrence had doubtless carried out this private request, but the sum involved was negligible because Will had died shortly before his father had divided £15,000 between the brothers.

During the spring of 1920, Lawrence must have learned that Janet Laurie, now married, was in need of money. It seems that he then gave her the £3,000 that Will had expected to receive from his father. This extraordinary act of generosity must reflect his affection for Will, who had been the closest of his brothers, and also for Janet, perhaps the only girl to whom he had ever felt a deep attachment.

His mother, who had always disapproved of the relationship between Will and Janet, would have been bitterly angry if she had known. Will had consulted Janet before deciding to return from India to fight on the Western Front, and Mrs Lawrence had always held her responsible for his death. Some years later, Lawrence wrote guardedly to Hogarth: 'My father's £5,000 (I don't want my mother or other brothers to know about it: they think I still have it). One of those killed left a tangle behind, and it took £3,000 to straighten it'.[41]

The gift of so much capital reduced Lawrence's income, and there is ample evidence of this sudden poverty in letters written during the summer and autumn of 1920. In his new financial circumstances he would have needed a much larger sum than before if he were to set up a private press at Pole Hill with Richards. He had never expected the press itself to be profitable, and in addition to the capital cost of the building and equipment, he would require a sufficient investment income to cover all his personal expenses. To meet these outgoings he now needed a capital sum of at least £5,000.

A. S. Watt, Lawrence's literary agent, would not have been willing to hazard a guess about likely earnings from the abridgement until he had seen a sample. By the end of August, Lawrence had seven chapters ready, and he must have sent them to Watt for evaluation before meeting Doubleday, who was due to arrive in Britain in the middle of September.

Lawrence wanted to confine publication to America and, because of this, Watt's estimate was almost certainly very disheartening. 'Lawrence of Arabia' was famous in Britain, but still relatively unknown in the United States. Yet to earn the money required, the 'boy scout' book would have to be a best-seller there. This was something no literary agent would have been prepared to guarantee, and Watt must have told Lawrence that the income he was hoping for could only be assured if the book were published in the British market.

Lawrence was totally opposed to this. He had earlier written: 'Unless I am starving (involuntarily) there will be no London publisher. My whole object is to make money in U.S.A. and so avoid the notoriety of being on sale in England.'[42] He saw that there was little point in continuing the abridgement. Moreover, the task he had set himself was proving more difficult than he had expected: after more than a month, barely a quarter of the proposed 150,000-word text had been completed. He abandoned the project and, in its place, began at the beginning of September to write a new polished draft of the complete *Seven Pillars* text.

While working on the 'boy scout' book, Lawrence had continued his press campaign against the Middle East settlement. In late July, he had written at length to *The Times* about the rebellion in Mesopotamia, then at its height. He pointed out that the Anglo-Indian administration had done nothing to cultivate Arab sympathy: 'The Government we have set up is English in fashion, and is conducted in the English language. So it has 450 British executive officers running it, and not a single responsible Mesopotamian. In Turkish days seventy per cent of the executive civil service was local. Our eighty thousand troops there are occupied in police duties, not in guarding the frontiers. They are holding down the people. In Turkish days the two army corps in Mesopotamia were sixty per cent Arab in officers, ninety-five per cent in other ranks. This deprivation of the privilege of sharing the defence and administration of their country is galling to the educated Mesopotamians. It is true we have increased prosperity – but who cares for that when liberty is in the other scale? They waited and welcomed the news of our mandate, because they thought it meant Dominion self-government for themselves. They are now losing hope in our good intentions.

'A remedy? I can see a cure only in immediate change of policy. The whole logic of the present thing looks wrong . . . I would make Arabic the Government language. This would impose a reduction of the British staff, and a return to employment of the qualified Arabs. I would raise two divisions of local volunteer troops, all Arabs, from the senior divisional general to the junior private. (Trained officers and trained N.C.O.'s exist in thousands.) I would entrust these new units with the maintenance of order, and I would cause to leave the country every single British soldier, every single Indian soldier. These changes would take twelve months, and we should then hold of Mesopotamia exactly as much (or as little) as we hold of South Africa or Canada. I believe the Arabs in these conditions would be as loyal as anyone in the Empire, and they would not cost us a cent.'[43]

He returned to this theme with added ferocity in the *Observer* of August 8th. The French Army had driven Feisal out of Damascus a few days previously, and Lawrence accused the Anglo-Indian administration in Mesopotamia of sharing responsibility for this: '[The French] have only followed in very humble fashion, in their sphere of Syria, the example we set them in Mesopotamia. England controls nine parts out of ten of the Arab world, and inevitably calls the tune to which the French must dance: if we follow an Arab policy, they must be Arab. If we fight the Arabs, they must fight the Arabs. It would show a lack of humour if we reproved them for a battle near Damascus, and the blotting out of the Syrian essay in self-government, while we were fighting battles near Baghdad, and trying to render the Mesopotamians incapable of self-government, by smashing every head that raised itself among them.'[44] Another article, in the *Sunday Times* of August 22nd, spoke bitterly of the Anglo-Indian officials in Baghdad: 'The sins of commission are those of the British civil authorities in Mesopotamia . . . who were given a free hand by London. They are controlled from no Department of State, but from the empty space which divides the Foreign Office from the India Office. They availed themselves of the necessary discretion of war-time to carry over their dangerous independence into times of peace. They contest every suggestion of real self-government sent them from home.'[45]

When Feisal was expelled from Damascus, it was suggested in many quarters that he should head a new Arab administration in Mesopotamia. The question was put to Lawrence in an interview published in the *Daily News* on August 25th. His reply was non-committal: 'perhaps, but the proposal must come from the people of Mesopotamia. We don't even know whether he would be willing to accept the position, and I am certain that he would not make himself a candidate. It is a fantastic mistake to suppose that he is a personally ambitious man.' Nevertheless, he agreed that Feisal was well qualified: 'Remember that Feisul, though an inspired leader at a time of crisis, is a mild and kindly man. He is not a true Bedouin of the desert; he has only lived in the desert during the three or four years of the war, when he worked with Allenby. He is much better educated than any Arab. He is inspired by one ambition – and that is to produce somewhere an independent Arab Government.'[46]

During the two previous years Lawrence been a regular visitor to London art galleries, and had sat for Augustus John, William Orpen, Derwent Wood, and William Rothenstein. He had thought of using portraits rather than photographs to illustrate the *Seven Pillars* abridgement, and he now hoped to commission portraits for an edition of the complete text.

For this purpose he made contact with Eric Kennington, whose work as one of the official war artists was very highly regarded. He asked whether it might be possible to draw portraits based on photographs of the Arab personalities in *Seven Pillars*. Kennington, whose previous knowledge of Lawrence had been derived from the Lowell Thomas lectures, was fascinated by the project, but he rejected the idea of working from photographs. Instead, he suggested that he should visit the Middle East and draw the Arabs from life. Lawrence explained how much this would cost, but Kennington said that he would shortly have earned enough from his other work to pay his own way.

At the beginning of October, Lawrence wrote an introduction to a new edition of Doughty's *Travels in Arabia Deserta*. This marked the successful conclusion of a long campaign to have the book reprinted. During the war, the Arab Bureau had possessed a copy of the original very small edition. Doughty's account had proved to be an invaluable source of information, and ever since returning to England Lawrence had been urging it on publishers: 'The whole book is a necessity to any student of Arabia, but it is more than that. It's one of the greatest prose works in the English language, and the best travel book in the world. Unfortunately it's solidly written (not dull at all, but in a queer style which demands care at first), and because of its rarity is far too little known . . . It has of course an immense reputation amongst the elect.'[47]

At first he had thought of having a new edition produced by the Government Press in Cairo, but this had proved impossible. However, he had been more fortunate when he approached the Medici Society, which had published a number of fine limited editions. There he had met Jonathan Cape, who was working for the firm but was keen to set up an imprint of his own. It had eventually been agreed that Cape and the Medici Society would co-publish a new edition, provided that Lawrence wrote an introduction. It was to be issued in January 1921 at nine guineas. If the first printing (of only five hundred copies) sold out rapidly, the cost of typesetting would be paid off and further impressions could be issued at a much lower price.

In November 1920 the Colonial Secretary, Lord Milner, let it be known privately that he would like to retire. An obvious choice for successor was Winston Churchill, who as Minister of War during the previous two years had been responsible for military garrisons throughout the Empire. Churchill had strong views on the Middle East, and had not hesitated to advocate a change in the administration of Mesopotamia. Although the rebellion had been quelled by mid-October, a large army was still considered necessary to maintain the peace.

On December 4th, Edward Marsh wrote inviting Lawrence to see Churchill: the subject of their conversation is not recorded. A month later, however, Churchill accepted the Colonial Office with a brief to set up a new Middle East Department, and on January 8th he invited Lawrence to join him there as an adviser on Arab Affairs.

CHAPTER 30

Adviser to Churchill

January – December 1921

LAWRENCE'S response to the idea of joining the Colonial Office was less enthusiastic than Churchill had hoped. After his failure at the Peace Conference he had resolved not to seek any further personal role in Arabian diplomacy or administration, and his present thoughts were mainly of writing and printing. Only a week before, he had written: 'I've long given up politics.'[1] However, he agreed to help unofficially. Churchill was convinced that an economical solution could be found in Mesopotamia if Feisal, who had now come to London, was made ruler there. He wished to know Feisal's reaction to this scheme before making a formal approach, and Lawrence agreed to discuss it privately. On January 17th he reported: 'Concerning Feisal this is how it stands:

'He has agreed to make no reference to the French-occupied area of Syria in his talks with H. M. Government.

'He has agreed to abandon all claims of his father to Palestine. This leaves four questions:

    a. Mesopotamia: for which he claims a watching brief in respect of the McMahon papers.

    b. Trans-Jordan [the area of inland Syria to be under British influence according to the Sykes-Picot terms]: where he hopes to have a recognised Arab state with British advice.

    c. Nejd: where he wants the Hussein–Ibn Saud question regulated.

    d. Yemen: on which he has a suggestion to make.

'The advantage of his taking this new ground of discussion is that all questions of pledges and promises, fulfilled or broken, are set aside. You begin a new discussion on the actual positions today and the best way of doing something constructive with them. It's so much more useful than splitting hairs. Feisal can help very much towards a rapid settlement of these countries, if he wants to: and if we can only get them working like a team they will be a surprising big thing in two or three years.

'I think all he asks in a.b.c.d. can be made useful to ourselves. They tend towards cheapness and speed of settlement.'[2] In the event, the content of this note was to foreshadow with remarkable accuracy the objectives Churchill would seek to achieve in the Middle East during the next twelve months.

Lawrence seems to have held further private discussions during the remainder of January and during this period he saw Marsh, Churchill's secretary, at least twice. On January 28th he wrote to Doughty: 'I have had a great deal to do lately, and am still very busy.'[3]

During the first week in February, Churchill made up his mind to call all the principal British officials working in the Middle East to a conference in Egypt. The object of this meeting would be to determine future arrangements for all the British mandated territories in the Middle East. Lawrence did not at first intend to go. Instead, he was planning to accompany Eric Kennington on a private journey through Trans-Jordan and the Hejaz, collecting Arab portraits to illustrate *Seven Pillars*. He applied for a passport authorising him to go to Petra, Azrak, Maan and possibly Medina. On February 12th the Foreign Office cabled to Sir Herbert Samuel, British High Commissioner in Jerusalem, and to Allenby in Cairo, asking for their views about this request; Lawrence was 'prepared to guarantee that he will refrain from unauthorised political activity, but even so we are doubtful of the wisdom of allowing him to visit Trans Jordania in the present circumstances, since his mere presence there will be regarded by the French as a political move on our part.'[4]

Although Churchill had been given responsibility for a large part of the Middle East in early January, he did not take over at the Colonial Office until February 14th. By this time, he had persuaded Lawrence to join the new Middle East Department. He knew very little about the Arab world and, if he was to succeed in his difficult assignment, he would need expert assistants. Lawrence would be valuable both for his knowledge of the region and for his friendship with Feisal.

Lawrence did not agree very willingly, and tried to make it a condition that Britain's wartime promises to the Arabs would be honoured. The condition was refused, and he later wrote that he had only accepted because 'Winston . . . offered me direct access to himself on every point, and a free hand, subject to his discretion. This was better than any condition, because I wanted the best settlement of the Middle East possible, apart from all the promises and treaties.'[5]

On February 13th Churchill drew up a list of the appointments he intended to make in the new Department. The Permanent Under-Secretary was to be J. E. Shuckburgh, previously a senior official at the

India Office. Lawrence was to be adviser on Arabian affairs, and Hubert Young head of the political and administrative branch. Lawrence's appointment would be for one year only, at a rank and salary equal to Young's. It was Lawrence who had suggested Young for the Department. Young's difficulties handling the Arabs during the Syrian campaign had in no way diminished Lawrence's admiration for his intellect. Moreover, since 1919 Young had been working in the Foreign Office, steadfastly advocating the policies that both he and Lawrence believed in.[6]

The proposal to appoint Lawrence did not meet with universal approval. One senior Colonial Office official wrote: 'Are you sure that Col. Lawrence would come? I had gathered the impression (but perhaps wrongly) that he did not wish to hold a Government appointment in connection with the Arabian problem. He is not the kind of man to fit easily into any official machine . . . I gather that Col. Lawrence has got used to dealing with Ministers – and Ministers only – and I see trouble ahead if he is allowed too free a hand.'[7] Churchill, however, saw things differently. After moving into his new offices, he wrote to his wife with satisfaction that he had 'got Lawrence to put on a bridle and collar'.[8]

On February 16th Lawrence saw Feisal again. Afterwards he reported to Churchill: '[I] explained to him that I had just accepted an appointment in the Middle Eastern Department of the Colonial Office. This would necessarily alter our relations, and particularly would prevent his asking me certain questions: but the appointment had not changed my opinions and I hoped he would take it as an indication that H. M. Government were not wholly adverse to our past policy.

'He replied that he would like to lose all his friends in the same way.

'I then spoke of what might happen in the near future, mentioning a possible conference in Egypt between the Secretary of State and his British lieutenants, in which the politics, constitution, and finances of the Arabic areas in Western Asia would come up for discussion in whole or part. These were all of direct interest to his race, and especially to his family, and I thought present signs justified his being reasonably hopeful of a settlement satisfactory to all parties. I mentioned specially the Mesopotamian, and Trans-Jordan questions'.[9]

Churchill knew that France was acutely hostile towards the idea of making Feisal ruler in Mesopotamia. Furthermore, Anglo-French tension over the Middle East had been aggravated during the winter by Abdullah. In November 1920 he had moved to Maan, at that time within the boundaries of the Hejaz, with the avowed intention of raising an army to drive the French out of Syria. Alarming rumours about his activities were picked up by both French and British Intelligence.

Churchill hoped that Feisal would use his influence to calm the situation. After Feisal's talk with Lawrence, a telegram was sent to Hussein in his name. It read: 'I hear rumours of anti-French movements and actions in the Belka district (Trans-Jordan). I request you to take immediate steps to prevent all hostile movements of any kind against anyone. Trouble in Trans-Jordan will ruin our negotiations in London which otherwise will go well. I take complete responsibility for this statement, which please forward at once to Abdullah.'[10]

Lawrence began work in the Colonial Office on February 18th. On that day a seven-point outline agenda for the Cairo Conference was drafted, and he spent most of the following week adding detail to this framework. In this he worked closely with Young, who shared a room with him at the Colonial Office.[11] They saw to it that the agenda was framed in such a way that the conference would arrive at the desired conclusions. Some years afterwards, Lawrence told his biographer Liddell Hart that everything had been staged before the meetings began. He had settled not only the questions to be considered, but the decisions to be reached: 'Talk of leaving things to the man on the spot – we left nothing'.[12]

Lawrence's appointment meant that he would be unable to accompany Kennington to the Middle East. He wrote to Graves on February 19th: 'I'd just got as keen as mustard on going out . . . when Winston Churchill in his third effort to get me to join his new Middle Eastern Department used arguments which I could not resist.

'So I'm a Government servant from yesterday: and Palestine goes fut (or phut?)....

'Kennington is going all the same: (that man is a great man) and as an official I'll be able to help him even more than ever: but what a beastly mess.'[13] He sent Graves some chapters from the abandoned 1920 abridgement of *Seven Pillars* which he had been adapting as magazine articles for sale: 'I had meant to publish the enclosed muck in USA, to raise £1,000: and now I have written to say that I have made other arrangements. Will you read them now they are born to blush unseen?'[14] In due course, Graves replied that he liked the chapters very much and Lawrence, knowing that he and his family were leading a very precarious existence, allowed him to sell four of the articles to an American magazine.[15]

On February 26th the Cairo Conference Agenda was discussed and approved by an inter-departmental meeting held at the Colonial Office. Shortly afterwards Lawrence suggested that it would be a good idea to arrange a meeting between Churchill and Abdullah, to take place in Jerusalem after the conference had ended.

Four days later Lawrence set out for Egypt. Before leaving, he wrote to Wilfred Scawen Blunt, a noted anti-imperialist campaigner: 'I'll get my way or resign – or even do both things . . . Winston is a new and very keen mind on the Middle East business, and I hope will take it the right way. It's a very great chance given me.'[16]

He had done everything possible to ensure that the settlement he hoped for was adopted. As long as Churchill continued to back him, he could not fail. If he had worries on this count, they were groundless. Churchill's performance was everything that he could have hoped for, and item after item on the Cairo Conference agenda was settled by unanimous agreement. The meetings began on March 12th, and after only one day Churchill was able to telegraph to Lloyd George asking the Cabinet to approve Feisal's candidature for the throne of Mesopotamia (henceforward known as Iraq): 'The formula would be: "In response to enquiries from adherents of Emir Feisal the British Government have stated that they will place no obstacles in the way of his candidature as ruler of Iraq, and that if he is chosen [by the people of Mesopotamia] he will have their support" . . . On receipt of your assent to this formula I shall tell Lawrence he can communicate the formula to Feisal. On this, Feisal will at once proceed to Mecca, passing through Egypt on the way. We do not want any announcement, even in guarded terms, of the formula if it can be possibly avoided until Feisal is at Mecca and Sir P. Cox [British High Commissioner in Iraq] at Baghdad about the middle of April.'[17]

Feisal and his Iraqi supporters were thus to be rewarded at last for their wartime role. Lawrence later explained how, by 1919, he had already concluded 'that the centre of Arab Independence will eventually be Bagdad not Damascus, since the future of Mesopotamia is great and the possible development of Syria is small. Syria now has 5,000,000 inhabitants, Irak only 3,000,000. Syria will only have 7,000,000 when Irak has 40,000,000. But I envisaged Damascus as the capital of an Arab state for perhaps twenty years. When the French took it after two years, we had to transfer the focus of Arab nationalism at once to Bagdad'.[18]

As far as the implementation of the agreed policy in Iraq was concerned, only two problems remained. One was a matter for Sir Percy Cox, who had to ensure that his own staff as well as the people of Iraq would accept Feisal as ruler. The second was equally delicate: when Feisal had been asked in London about the possibility of accepting a throne in Baghdad, he had insisted that Abdullah must first relinquish any personal claim there. The Conference was agreed that Feisal would be a much better ruler in Iraq than Abdullah, and the question was, therefore, what other role Abdullah might be asked to play, and where?

The immediate solution was, in effect, imposed on the Conference by Abdullah himself. In early March, while the Cairo discussions were in progress, news came that he had crossed the frontier into Trans-Jordan, and was now in Amman. It was decided that he should be offered some kind of political role as governor there or, if he refused, that an alternative Arab governor should be appointed with his approval.

This policy was opposed by Herbert Samuel, as the Zionists had been hoping to open up the eastern region, then inhabited entirely by Arabs, to Jewish colonisation. Churchill, however, refused to countenance such an idea. It had been agreed in London at the outset that Trans-Jordan should be governed by some kind of Arab administration, in accordance with the McMahon-Hussein undertakings and the Sykes-Picot Agreement.

On March 18th, Churchill cabled to Lloyd George that the Conference had decided that an arrangement would have to be reached with Abdullah about the future of Trans-Jordan: 'As we cannot contemplate hostilities with Abdullah in any circumstances, there is no alternative to this policy.'[19] If the Cabinet approved, Churchill would now try to negotiate a suitable arrangement with Abdullah.

When the Cairo discussions were nearly over, Lawrence wrote home saying: 'it has been one of the longest fortnights I ever lived . . . we live in a marble and bronze hotel, very expensive and luxurious: horrible place: makes me Bolshevik. Everybody Middle East is here, except Joyce and Hogarth. We have done a lot of work, which is almost finished. Day after tomorrow we go to Jerusalem for a week: after that don't know: perhaps home: perhaps I return to Egypt for a further fortnight . . .

'We're a very happy family: agreed upon everything important: and the trifles are laughed at.'[20]

He sent a message to London for Feisal (it was delivered on March 24th): 'Things have gone exactly as hoped. Please start at once for Mecca by the quickest possible route . . . I will meet you on the way and explain details. Say only that you are going [to see] your father and on no account put anything in the press.'[21]

At Churchill's request, Lawrence travelled from Egypt to Trans-Jordan, where he met Abdullah and explained the main lines of Britain's future policy in the region. Both men then went to Jerusalem, where a series of meetings with Churchill took place. The result was that Abdullah agreed to act as ruler in Trans-Jordan and to do his best to halt all anti-French activity. In exchange for this he would receive British financial and military aid. The arrangement was to run for a period of six months while Feisal sought popular approval in Iraq.

One of the principal decisions of the Cairo Conference had been to adopt Trenchard's scheme of using air power to enforce law and order in Iraq. This overseas role would be very important to the status of the RAF during the coming years, and Trenchard would not forget that Lawrence had been one of his most influential supporters. It was hoped that an equally economical solution could be applied in Trans-Jordan, which had sunk into a state of near-anarchy after the end of Feisal's administration in Damascus. Effective policing would be necessary in order to halt the continuing raids into French Syria, and a local force of Arab regulars was already being trained by Peake. Meanwhile Abdullah's authority was to be established with armoured cars and RAF support from Palestine.

Lawrence cabled to the Colonial Office on April 1st: 'As the High Commissioner [Samuel] has asked me to begin things with Abdullah while he is arranging the appointment of a Chief Political Officer for Trans-Jordania, I move to Amman tomorrow for about a week.'[22]

He spent eight days at Abdullah's camp in Amman, which he later described in a letter to his mother as 'rather like the life in war time, with hundreds of Bedouin coming and going, and a general atmosphere of newness in the air. However the difference was that now everybody is trying to be peaceful.'[23] On April 9th he drove back to Jerusalem and reported on the situation to Samuel: 'The position in Trans-Jordania seems to me fairly satisfactory. With the tribal elements of the eastern part, Abdullah's position is very strong. The people seem contented and comfortable and numbers of them are paying him visits and submitting to his judgment their tribal and family disputes. Ali ibn Hussein and Shakir help him in this side of the work . . . For the present the attitude of the Beni Sakhr is good I consider and there is no possibility, so long as Abdullah believes we are sincere, of any large movement against the French or against our Zionist policy and little possibility even of small incidents. In public Abdullah has taken a strong line about this and his injunctions have been well received.'[24] On the next day, he went across to Amman with a flight of RAF aircraft to demonstrate British support for the new régime. Afterwards he wrote: 'Abdulla had been longing for aeroplanes, and gave us a great reception and a large lunch. Then we went back to Ramleh, and I went up to Jerusalem to dinner.'[25]

On April 11th Lawrence flew down to Egypt to wait for Feisal, whose ship from England was shortly to arrive at Port Said. Four days later he reported: 'I had a long interview with Feisal today, quite secretly. I read him first Mr. Churchill's statement of policy to Abdulla . . . then explained the timetable as drawn up by Sir P. Cox . . .

'Feisal expressed his appreciation of the general policy outlined, and promised to do all he could to make his part of it work. He will guarantee neither to attack nor intrigue against the French . . . He will agree to establish friendly relations with Bin Saud on condition of Hedjaz immunity from Wahabi attack. He thinks that if he is given a free hand for the first few weeks after Ramadan in Bagdad and neighbourhood, there should be little doubt of the success of his candidature, but he thinks that his position as an outside candidate *vis-à-vis* the British admin- istration there may be very delicate, and to keep him in proper touch with Sir P. Cox and his wishes he asks for a British adviser on his personal staff. This must not be an official of the Mesopotamian Government for many reasons, but it must be a person of weight in whose judgement he can trust, and he asks for the loan of Colonel Cornwallis from the Egyptian Government to accompany him to Mesopotamia. He makes this a condition of his going . . .

'He regards the people of Irak as not fitted yet for responsible Government, and if he is left at the mercy of the local people in all things there will be a disaster. He will require British help sometimes against his own people, and he hopes his opinion on a permanent garrison will be taken eventually. He hopes that you and Sir P. Cox will accept these points, and will notify him of the date in May when he should reach Suez to embark for Basrah . . . When his election is a fact he will ask Sir P. Cox to arrange a friendly accord between himself and Bin Saud, and will do his best to bring in his father as a third party. Abdulla warns me this will be difficult, since Hussein flies into hysterics and resigns whenever any suggestion of an accommodation is pressed upon him.'[26]

After this meeting Lawrence went north to Jerusalem again, and then across to Amman, where he spent three days with Samuel and the newly appointed Chief Political Officer for Trans-Jordan. On April 21st, at

Churchill's request, he flew back to Egypt for a further unpublicised meeting with Feisal, which took place at Suez the next day.

This seemed to complete his work in the Middle East, and he cabled to Churchill: 'I leave tomorrow by air for Jerusalem, and I think that I might, unless you have other wishes, return thence to England.'[27] Churchill approved this suggestion and by May 11th Lawrence was back in London. Everything he had hoped for when he joined the Colonial Office had now been achieved. In Mesopotamia, the administration was taking the steps necessary to ensure that Feisal would be chosen by the people as their ruler, while in Trans-Jordan 'we kept our promises to the Arab Revolt and assisted the home-rulers to form a buffer principality'.[28] The India Office victory of 1919 had been overturned.

He later wrote: 'I take most of the credit of Mr. Churchill's pacification of the Middle East upon myself. I had the knowledge and the plan. He had the imagination and the courage to adopt it and the knowledge of the political procedure to put it into operation'.[29] The settlement was 'the big achievement of my life: of which the war was a preparation.'[30] At the time, however, he was less certain. He wrote to Graves: 'Our schemes for the betterment of the Middle East race are doing nicely: thanks. I wish I hadn't gone out there: the Arabs are like a page I have turned over: and sequels are rotten things'.[31]

Although Lawrence had agreed to remain with Churchill for a year he had no further personal ambitions regarding the Middle East. Many people expected him to take some role as adviser to one of the new Arab administrations. Thus on April 30th Maulud el Mukhlus, one of Feisal's bravest wartime commanders, had been to see the British consul in Damascus and had told him 'in the name of all the Mesopotamian Deputies, that they earnestly desired Col. Lawrence's appointment to some high or the highest post in Iraq; as they had heard rumours of Sir P. Cox's possible retirement from our Government service.'[32] However, Lawrence had made up his mind before the war had ended that he wished to play no such part.

Daily routine in Whitehall held no appeal for him either, and he was relieved to learn that he would shortly be sent abroad again, even though the main purpose of his new mission was very unattractive. His services were to be lent to the Foreign Office so that he could negotiate a treaty between Britain and Sherif Hussein.

Diplomacy was not the only career open to Lawrence at this time. During the summer of 1921 he turned down at least two offers from the academic world. On June 1st he had lunch with his old Oxford tutor, L. C. Jane, who tried to persuade him to accept some kind of position at the University of Aberystwyth. Jane reported that during their talk he had discovered that Lawrence had just refused the rectorship of McGill University in Montreal.[33]

In any case, whether he liked it or not, Lawrence would have to work a further nine months at the Colonial Office. On June 12th he wrote to Kennington, apologising once again for having been of such little use in Trans-Jordan. The results of Kennington's journey were nevertheless magnificent. Lawrence later wrote: 'He was to have had me as his guide, but circumstances prevented this, and plunged him alone into a great Arab camp . . . I had meant to help him in his selection of subjects to draw: as events turned out he was thrown on his own judgment. It is interesting to see that instinctively he drew the men of the desert. Where he was there were ten settled men to every nomad: yet his drawings show nearly ten desert men to every peasant. This has strengthened in me the unflattering suspicion that the nomad is the richer creature.'[34] Lawrence now told Kennington of his own forthcoming journey to Jidda, where he would have to spend July: 'the most stinking month in the year: and then Aden for August. Enough said. I'm fixed and finished and very sorry.'[35]

He knew from his experience of diplomatic negotiations during the Peace Conference that he might have a great deal of spare time during his coming mission. He therefore decided to take the rough draft of *Seven Pillars* with him, so that he could continue working on the new version. He had decided to print the book when this polished draft was complete. Although little is known about the kind of edition he had in mind, it must have been some kind of private printing. He now sent four of the Kennington Arab portraits to the printers Whittingham & Griggs Ltd., with instructions to prepare them for reproduction by colour lithography in a quarto format.

Shortly before setting out for the Middle East again, he was alarmed to learn that Hutchinsons, the London publishers, had announced to booksellers that they would be publishing a book about him by Lowell Thomas in the spring of 1922. Lawrence had hoped that there would be no more of the unwelcome publicity caused by Thomas. He could guess well enough the kind of book Thomas would write, and feared that its contents might handicap his work as a diplomat. He sent a note to the Foreign Office explaining the situation: 'I understand that the book will be founded on a series of articles by Mr. Thomas, published in the

American magazine *Asia* a year or two ago. They were published in America, and by an American, so that I took no notice of them. They were however about 70% inaccurate, and about 10% both inaccurate and offensive to those Arabs and Englishmen who took part in the Arab Campaigns. They were partly impure imagination, partly perverted quotation of articles (by myself or others) printed in the *Arab Bulletin*.

'Mr. Thomas saw the *Arab Bulletin* by the unfortunate error in judgement, (. . . entirely without F.O. authority), of an officer at G.H.Q. in Cairo. He made extracts from it: and has adapted them to his present purpose, regardless of the truth (which was often sufficiently offensive) or of the feelings of the persons named in them.

'As the *Arab Bulletin* was Foreign Office property, and a secret document, I feel that the Foreign Office might intervene with Messrs. Hutchinson, and suggest to them that they submit the proofs of the book for examination before they publish it, in order to prevent later complications under the Official Secrets Act. We could not possibly correct the book: but we could remove many offensive expressions. I think that Messrs. Hutchinson would probably respond very sensitively to any suggestion of this sort from the Foreign Office.

'If this is not done the book is quite likely to give offence to King Hussein, and to Feisal, and to some of their more influential followers. It would certainly weaken my position among them, if the book was published in its probable form without official contradiction by me, and I am unwilling to do this if it can be helped, since it would only tend to advertise an already bad book. The Foreign Office are now (by Mr. Churchill's liberality) proposing to use my position as an asset in trying to bring King Hussein to reason. Mr. Churchill has made use of it in Trans-Jordan and with Feisal, and may, unfortunately, require it on yet other occasions. So that I think I may call it a semi-official matter, and ask the F.O. to help me preserve it.'[36]

Three days later, on the eve of his departure, he sent another note to the Foreign Office, reminding them of his request: 'It really matters to me quite a lot. If you do write, Hutchinson will certainly send you the proofs for censoring. In that case may I suggest they be passed to Hogarth, who knows about books, edited the *Arab Bulletin*, and understands what is offensively true or false, and what is just or silly? He'd do the necessary excising and correcting willingly and save you much trouble.'[37]

After discussing the situation with Lawrence, the Foreign Office decided that the legal position was not very strong. However, the desired effect might be achieved by sending Hutchinson an intimidating letter signed by a senior official, and this was duly done. It read: 'I am directed by the Marquess Curzon of Kedleston to inform you that he has learnt of the impending publication by your firm of a book by Mr. Lowell Thomas dealing with the campaign in Arabia during the late war. His Lordship understands that this book will be based on certain articles by Mr. Thomas which appeared in an American magazine a short time ago. These articles contained a number of statements which were inaccurate on points of fact, and were also of such a nature that their publication in this country in book form would be likely to cause considerable embarrassment to H. M. Government in their relations with the rulers of the Arabian Peninsula and in the Near East generally.

'Quite apart from the possibility of the publication of the statements in question constituting an offence under the Official Secrets Act, his Lordship is confident that you would not wish that any book issued by your firm should be of a nature to embarrass H. M. Government in the conduct of the foreign relations of this country, and I am therefore to express the hope that you will be willing to submit the proofs of the book in question to this Department with a view to the elimination of any passages whose publication might be considered undesirable from this point of view. You will understand, of course, that in that event, the fact of any particular passage having been left untouched would not imply any guarantee by this department of the accuracy of the statements of fact contained therein but merely that its publication would not be considered objectionable.'[38] Some weeks passed before Hutchinsons replied to this letter, and when they did so, it was to state that Thomas's manuscript appeared to have been lost in the post. It was to be four years before the book was finally published in England, a postponement which Lawrence attributed entirely to his intervention through the Foreign Office.[39]

Another question raised by Lawrence before he left for the Middle East was the future of H. St J. B. Philby, who had been posted some months previously to Mesopotamia. On July 6th Cox telegraphed from Baghdad that he had been obliged to dismiss Philby, who objected so strongly to Feisal's enthronement in Iraq that he had been unable to work wholeheartedly for British policy. Lawrence, who had come to know Philby quite well during 1919 and 1920, had foreseen that such a problem might arise. He now wrote: 'Philby is a very powerful and able person, and I'm sorry he has crashed himself in this way. We have often thought of him for Trans-Jordan, which he would do splendidly if he would play

fair. His trouble is an uncertain temper'.[40] The suggestion was cabled to
Baghdad, and Cox agreed to it. Later that year Philby would be sent to
Amman as Chief British Representative.

When the Middle East Department was formed, Churchill had hoped
that the Hejaz would be included in the area it dealt with. However,
the Foreign Office had pointed out that this might be taken by some
as evidence that Hussein's kingdom was not fully independent. The
Colonial Office was nevertheless obliged to take Hussein's attitude into
account and to secure, if possible, his agreement to the Cairo Conference
settlements in Mesopotamia, Trans-Jordan, and Palestine. A draft treaty
covering these points had been drawn up by the Foreign Office. In
exchange for Hussein's co-operation, it offered financial subsidies and
guarantees against military incursions by ibn Saud.

As early as mid-April, Churchill had raised the possibility of sending
Lawrence to negotiate with Hussein, and the Foreign Office had agreed
that he would be the best person to send. On July 8th, therefore, he set out
for Jidda bearing what Curzon described as a 'special full power under
the Royal Sign Manual and Signet, authorising and empowering you to
negotiate and conclude, with such Minister or Ministers as may be vested
with similar power and authority on the part of His Majesty the King of
the Hejaz, a treaty between the United Kingdom and the Kingdom of the
Hejaz, for the settlement of matters now under discussion between the
two countries.'[41] In the event that Hussein found clauses of the draft
treaty unacceptable, Lawrence was to refer the matter back to Curzon. In
addition, he was to persuade Hussein to sign the Treaty of Versailles and
a declaration recognising the French position in Syria. While in the
region, he might also be sent to Aden, which had recently become a
Colonial Office responsibility, to negotiate a settlement between Britain
and the Imam of the Yemen.[42]

The final stage of his mission would be a return to Trans-Jordan. The
six-month period during which Abdullah had agreed to act as ruler would
end in September, and there was uncertainty as to what would happen
afterwards. One difficulty was the continuing influence of exiled Syrians
in Abdullah's entourage. Churchill cabled Samuel about this aspect of
Lawrence's forthcoming journey: 'While at Jeddah, Colonel Lawrence
should endeavour to effect a reconciliation between Abdullah and
Hussein [who did not approve of Abdullah's agreement to halt action
against the French in Syria]. He should then proceed to Trans-Jordania

and in consultation with you devise a means for getting Abdullah temporarily out of the country and engineering in his absence the removal of the Syrians. The plan which recommends itself to me is:– Abdullah should be invited to England towards the end of his six months . . . Shakir should then be approached to displace the Syrian officials. Whether Abdullah should return to Trans-Jordania or not will depend partly on his own views and partly on Lawrence's success in effecting a reconciliation between him and his father.'[43] If Abdullah did not return to Trans-Jordan, he might go to Mecca, where he could help Hussein negotiate settlements with the Imam of Yemen and the Idrisi.

Lawrence arrived at Jidda on July 29th (having spent nearly a fortnight in Egypt on the way).[44] At his first meeting with Hussein he learned that the King would have to leave for Mecca in five days' time for the pilgrimage, and would remain there until the end of that month. Lawrence cabled London asking whether he should take advantage of this interval to visit Aden. This suggestion was approved.

On August 2nd he sent Curzon a résumé of his talks up to this point: 'Have had several meetings with the King, who has not referred to the draft Treaty since he saw it. He urged his claims to the Kingship of Mesopotamia, but collapsed and gave up the idea when I discussed the practical effect of the move. He has announced his abandonment of a position founded on the McMahon letters, but raises absurd new ideas daily. The old man is conceited to a degree, greedy, and stupid, but very friendly, and protests devotion to our interests. His entourage are anti-British, except for Fuad el Khatib and [Emir] Zeid, who are helping us continually, and all sorts of interests are begging him not to conclude any treaty. However he shows such reluctance to quarrel with me that I suspect his own mind to be divided: but until he introduces the subject of the Treaty again I cannot say whether there is any hope of it. If he could be kept here for a month he would become biddable: but he will go off the rails as soon as he is back in Mecca.'[45] Two days later, Lawrence cabled again: 'Have had more conversations with the King. He was only playing with me so I changed tactics and forced him to make exact statements. After some questions he made clear that he refused absolutely all notion of making a treaty but expected acknowledgement of his kingship in Mesopotamia and Palestine, priority over all rulers in Arabia who were to be confined to their pre-war boundaries, and cession to himself of Asir and Hodeida. His ambitions are as large as his conceit, and he showed unpleasant jealousy of his sons.

'I gave him my candid opinion of his character and capacity. There was a scene, remarkable to me in that not only the Foreign Secretary [Fuad] but the King also burst into tears. I walked out with parting remarks which brought Zeid to me last night with a rough draft of a treaty based on ours for my consideration.

'The King is weaker than I thought, and could, I think, be bullied into nearly complete surrender. Reason is entirely wasted on him since he believes himself all-wise and all-competent, and is flattered by his entourage in every idiotic thing he does. The difficulties of using force are the short time, and the fear that if I hurt him too much he will sulk in Mecca. I shall not be able to finish anything before the pilgrimage, but his draft, if he submits it formally to me today, will give me grounds for returning here at the end of the month.'[46]

The talks progressed in a similar manner for a day or two, as Lawrence reported: 'On my next visit King Hussein went back on his previous suggestions and disclaimed any idea of considering a treaty. I got up and walked out. This flustered them, the King saying he thought no one could treat royalty so. His titles have turned his head and made him complacently absurd.

'Marshall [British Representative in Jidda] saw him next day after many messengers had come to us, and explained how regrettably the breaking off of negotiations would affect the prosperity of the Hejaz. The King thereupon yielded and sent last night an alternative draft and comments on a treaty which he is today anxious to make with us. It contains too much rubbish to wire to you, but in a final interview I hope to throw out some of this and will then refer it, but as the old man forgets yesterday tomorrow the issue is still uncertain. The need is not so much to secure his signature as to break down his convictions that we are dependent on him for our prestige in the East, and will pay any price and swallow any vexation to keep his friendship. If he is beaten over this business he will come easier next time.'[47]

Later on the same day, Lawrence cabled again to say that Hussein had accepted fifteen of the nineteen articles in the draft treaty, 'with unimportant modifications which will be sent you if you wish me to continue.' Two further articles had been rejected because 'they offer benefits not coveted by him.' There remained substantive disagreement over two clauses in the Treaty (Articles 14 and 15) which covered the status of British subjects in the Hejaz and the crucial question of recognising the British Mandates in Mesopotamia and Palestine. Hussein

had offered to 'recognise British "Guardianship" or "advice and assistance" or any word except "Mandate".' Lawrence added: 'I gave him a
loan of eighty thousand rupees in advance of subsidy at the end of today's
interview, on my own responsibility. He was in urgent need of it, and so
proportionately grateful: and will be in as great need the next time we
meet and as prepared to be grateful. Now he has gone to Mecca, leaving
Zeid to continue the argument. [HMS] *Clematis* which is probably
detailed to take me to Aden is due here about August 12th, so you have
time to consider Articles 14 and 15 and instruct me. I might get a little
more out of him but prefer to keep some dregs of my influence for
discussion of the Versailles treaty ratification.'[48] Nothing further was
achieved before Lawrence left for Aden.

It had been agreed at the Cairo Conference that if a more satisfactory
relationship could be established with the Imam of the Yemen, it would
probably be possible to reduce the British garrison at Aden. During the
war, the Yemen had been under Ottoman suzerainty, and while the Imam
had not fought alongside the Turks, he had refused to take action against
them. Thus, using Yemen as a base, Turkish forces had made deep
incursions into the Aden Protectorate and had come into direct conflict
with British troops at the isthmus of Aden itself. At the end of the war, ·
the Protectorate was the only part of the British Empire where enemy
troops had yet to surrender. When they did so, in December 1918, the
Imam had replaced the departing troops with his own men. There had
been two further years of unrest before indications that a settlement might
be possible led to Lawrence's mission. He had already encountered one
of the Imam's representatives while at Jidda, and on arrival in Aden he
discussed the situation with the British Resident. It was agreed that the
opening move should be to send the Imam a Ford car as a personal gift,
and that an educated Muslim should be sent to his remote capital to inform
him about conditions in the outside world 'and enable him to realise the
advantages of making terms.'[49]

As far as the Imam was concerned, there was little more that Lawrence
could do for the present. However, he had to remain in Aden for about a
week, waiting for a ship to take him back to Jidda. While there, he met
various notables and tried to form an idea of the state of the colony. Some
months later, at Churchill's request, he wrote a brief summary of his
impressions: 'The first thing I saw was the point of view, or rather the
angle, from which its people regarded it – as a calling place for the Indian
mail steamers. This may have been its main role in the past, but today

Perim, which is six hours nearer the direct line, is beginning to intercept many steamers, and this tendency must I think increase till the bulk of the through shipping leaves Aden alone. The harbour rights of Perim are, I believe, let on contract to a company for a term of years. On the expiry of this they will be a very profitable business for us.

'This growth of Perim will put Aden in what I fancy is its proper place as the only free port in Arabia, and the trade-capital of Yemen and all the southern Red Sea and Gulf. It is an admirable harbour, splendid both for coastal steamers and dhows, and its banks and merchants can offer great encouragement to export and import trade and to exchange.

'In the Turkish days their empire faced ours here, with hostility. They forced Yemen trade to Hodeida and Mokha [the old port for Yemen coffee, 125 miles south of Hodeida]. The Idrisi has now closed Hodeida to the Imam. Mokha is only a dhow port, and very distant from Sanaa. The result is that under the new conditions Aden has as many political as it has always had geographical advantages over the Red Sea ports. The history of south-west Arabia, which is full of the recurrent hostility of plain and hill (Idrisi and Imam) gives no reason to expect the present conditions to endure.

'There is a stump of railway going north from Aden through Lahej [about twenty-five miles distant] and beyond. It serves as a useful tramway between Lahej and Aden, but is too short to affect camel traffic from the interior, as its cheaper carriage is not yet advantage enough to justify a break in bulk. The geographical difficulties of extending the line are small. Before the war a French Company was formed to under-take a Hodeida–Sanaa railway. An Aden–Sanaa scheme should show a better prospectus.

'However all this suggestion of finding Aden's commercial future in Yemen is not practical politics, while the town regards itself as a Gibraltar, secure only in as far as it is cut off in interest from its mainland. I gathered that the Morley régime begat the present spirit, by forbidding British officers to go into the interior [the reference is to Viscount Morley, Secretary of State for India 1905–10]. My view is that if there were more pleasure trips there might be need of fewer garrisons.

'As for these garrisons, they told me the Lahej Sultan, though loyal, was served by such unwarlike subjects that he was powerless in his own defence. He has a few hundred soldiers, whose look I liked, and I have a notion that if armed and encouraged by us, they might serve our purpose. Unwarlike people often make the best-drilled troops, as distinguished from the irregulars, who certainly require self-confidence. A pre-eminent Sultan of Lahej might simplify the problem of the Protectorate.

'As for the defence of Aden town: the Turks might have assaulted it, probably without success: but I do not see any Arab ruler attempting such a thing. That peninsula is child's play to defend, with cars, aeroplanes and machine guns.

'The administration of Aden sounds odd. It is run in compartments, some under the G.O.C., some under Bombay. It is quite beyond the general's power to drive the whole government down the road of one policy, nor can any large revenue be disposed of except by a conference in Aden and Bombay. General Scott told me of some astonishing anomalies: and thought that the presence of a skilled maker of adminis-trations there for a little while to recast the local government scheme would be a necessary preliminary to any reform.

'These are very slender notes: but the place was so attractive, and I thought promising, that I spent nearly all my time instructing myself, and had no time to check my notions.'[50]

While in Aden Lawrence also found time to work on *Seven Pillars*, and to write the preface to an exhibition catalogue for Eric Kennington, who was about to show his Arab portraits in London.

Lawrence was depressed by the prospect of further attempts to negotiate with Hussein, and wrote to Kennington: 'This is the beastliest trip I ever had.'[51] He was back in Jidda by August 30th, and a week later sent Curzon news of his latest talks: 'On my return the King went back on his decision and demanded

1. Return of all states in Arabia except his to their pre-war boundaries.
2. Cession to him of all areas so vacated.
3. Right to appoint all Cadis and Muftis in Arabia, Mesopotamia, Palestine.
4. Recognition of his supremacy over all Arab rulers everywhere.

'My reply made him send for a dagger and swear to abdicate and kill himself. I said we would continue negotiations with his successor. [Sherif] Ali then took a strong line, and formed a committee of himself, Zeid, Haddad, and Fuad, to discuss with me. Things are now going in a most friendly and rational way. The King is not formally superseded but has certainly lost much of his power. The sons report to him and the Queen, who is of our party and lectures him at night. I look upon the assumption of responsibility by Ali as a most happy event and am taking the opportunity to get his ideas on paper concerning all outstanding Arab questions without committing either side in any way.'[52]

By the following day, he and Ali had agreed a final text for the treaty, and he cabled the amendments to London for approval. As an additional bonus, Ali had agreed to ratify the Treaty of Versailles. More difficulties, however, ensued.

On September 16th Lord Curzon cabled to say that the Colonial Office were anxious for Lawrence to go north for discussions with Samuel about the future of Trans-Jordan. Lawrence was asked to conclude the negotiations with Hussein as rapidly as possible or, alternatively, to allow them to be continued by Major Marshall.

Six days later Lawrence reported: 'King Hussein had approved each clause in the treaty and announced publicly his forthcoming signature of it. When Ali presented him with the text for ratification he shouted and struck at him and then set us eight contradictory sets of prior conditions and stipulations, all unacceptable. Ali says that the old man is mad, and is preparing with Zeid to obtain his formal abdication.

'Ali and Zeid have behaved splendidly, and they may change things in the next week. I have left Marshall the text of the treaty, and if King Hussein climbs down he will receive the signature; but meanwhile, or till I reach England and report, I suggest that no changes or no new line of policy be taken by you.

'I have asked King Hussein to return the 80,000 rupees paid him in advance of subsidy on his promise to sign.'[53] In a further message, he gave his opinion that Hussein's signature could probably be purchased, 'but I have told his sons that I will not take any action until King Hussein sends me the signed Treaty. He talks of abdication and telegraphed Feisal to keep Wakf money [revenue designated for religious purposes] until his successor had been appointed. The feeling in Jeddah is strongly against the King.'[54] By the time this was received by Curzon, Lawrence was on his way north, profoundly disappointed by the failure, after so much effort, to secure a treaty. The bitterness towards Hussein expressed in the draft of *Seven Pillars* he was working on almost certainly reflects this episode.

Abdullah's six months as Emir of Trans-Jordan expired on September 30th, before Lawrence reached Jerusalem. Samuel cabled London that day urging that a decision about the future should be taken as rapidly as possible, both for political and administrative reasons (for example, Abdullah's monthly allowance was about to cease). From the outset,

Abdullah had expressed little enthusiasm for his role in Amman, and the consensus of opinion was that he would have to be replaced. Lawrence, now evidently in a state of depression, wrote to Kennington from Cairo on October 1st: 'Tomorrow I go to Trans-Jordan, to end that farce. It makes me feel like a baby-killer. The last two months I've been in the Red Sea, and things are not ended there . . . I'm bored stiff: and very tired, and a little ill, and sorry to see how mean some people I wanted to respect have grown. The war was good by drawing over our depths that hot surface wish to do or win something. So the cargo of the ship was unseen, and not thought of.'[55] In the same letter, he told Kennington that he had cabled to Whittingham and Griggs, halting reproduction of the four plates for *Seven Pillars*, because: 'A lump of money I was expecting has not (probably will not) come. My house in Epping has been burnt down. In the leisure hours of this trip I have read half the manuscript: and condemned it. Not good enough to publish, because it isn't as good as I can make it (unless I deceive myself).

'The stoppage is only to prevent too big a bill this year. Next year I will have more money, and will be able to carry on. Meanwhile I'll be barely solvent . . . The job will go through none the less.'[56]

Lawrence arrived in Jerusalem on October 2nd and after ten days there went on to Amman. To his surprise, he found that the situation in Trans-Jordan was better than he had been led to expect. Taxes were being paid, and local policing was satisfactory. Abdullah, who doubtless saw little in prospect elsewhere, had changed his mind about going, and Lawrence reported that he might remain until March or even longer. Samuel cabled to London: 'Lawrence has discovered that Abdullah does not want to leave Transjordania now though he would like very much to visit London later.'[57]

Lawrence took over as British representative in Trans-Jordan, working to consolidate Abdullah's position there. After another month he discussed the situation with Samuel again. The latter reported to London: 'The Emir Abdullah, although an attractive personality and of honourable character, is not a competent administrator. There is a general consensus of opinion that the machinery of government would work better without him. There are, however, different views as to the degree to which his personal influence contributes to maintaining order in the country. Abdullah states definitely that he does not wish to stay in Trans-Jordania, but apparently he feels it his duty not to leave unless some other personal link with the Sherifian movement takes his place. King Hussein, it appears, has sent him instructions in that sense.'[58] Lawrence had also, by this time, arranged to take up the Hejaz Treaty negotiations with Abdullah. During the last week in November further modifications to the text were agreed, and on the 28th he cabled Churchill: 'Abdulla being only plenipotentiary, his signature without royal ratification is as valueless as my own. Abdulla accepts the treaty as modified by my telegrams . . . He swears that Hussein will ratify . . . but I, like Marshall, have my doubts. It may, however, seem to you worth letting [him] try. If I receive your concurrence . . . we can sign it in the next few days before I start home. Philby has arrived and I am handing over.'[59] The treaty was signed by Lawrence and Abdullah on December 8th. Four days later Lawrence left for Egypt, and by Christmas Eve he was back in London.

By the end of 1921, Feisal was King in Iraq, where he reigned until his death in 1933; Abdullah had been established as ruler in Trans-Jordan, where he too would become a monarch in 1946. Hussein refused to ratify the Anglo-Hashemite Treaty and in 1924, deprived of British support against the growing power of ibn Saud, he was forced to abdicate; he died in exile seven years later. Mecca was taken by ibn Saud's forces in 1924, and the Hejaz was eventually absorbed into the new Kingdom of Saudi Arabia. French rule in Syria encountered increasing difficulties, and one administration after another collapsed in the face of local opposition. Eventually, in 1936, France set up an Arab administration on the lines that Lawrence and Churchill had initiated in Mesopotamia.

For Lawrence, the Arabian chapter was closed. In the last days of 1921 he returned to the Colonial Office, knowing that the year he had promised Churchill had only two more months to run.

CHAPTER 31

The Decision
January – August 1922

AT the beginning of January 1922, Lawrence wrote to Sir Hugh Trenchard: 'You know I am trying to leave Winston on March the first. Then I want about two months to myself, and then I'd like to join the R.A.F. – with the ranks, of course.

'I can't do this without your help. I'm thirty-three and not skilled in the senses you want. Probably I couldn't pass your medical. It's odd being too old for the job I want when hitherto I've always been too young for the job I did. However my health is good: I'm always in physical and mental training, and I don't personally believe that I'd be below the average of your recruits in either respect. If you think so that will end it.

'You'll wonder what I'm at. The matter is that since I was sixteen I've been writing: never satisfying myself technically but steadily getting better. My last book on Arabia is nearly good. I see the sort of subject I need in the beginning of your Force... and the best place to see a thing from is the ground. It wouldn't "write" from the officer level.

'I haven't told anyone, till I know your opinion: and probably not then, for the newspapers used to run after me and I like being private. People wouldn't understand.

'It's an odd request this, hardly proper perhaps, but it may be one of the exceptions you make sometimes. It is asking you to use your influence to get me past the Recruiting Officer! Apologies for making it: if you say no I'll be more amused than hurt.'[1]

Other letters written at about this time show that he was not planning to remain in the RAF for very long. He had strong personal ambitions which he would not be able to fulfil from the ranks: it is clear, for instance, that he intended after an interval to return to *Seven Pillars* and to his scheme for a private press. Not long after this approach to Trenchard, he wrote to Eric Kennington: 'The real trouble is about my book, which is not good: not good enough to come out. It has grown too long and shapeless, and I haven't the strength to see it all in one piece, or the energy to tackle it properly. After I've got out of the Colonial Office and have been fallow for a time my interest in it will probably come back and then I'll have another go at it'.[2]

Likewise, he wrote to St John Hornby, proprietor of the Ashendene Press: 'When my press starts we will exchange products (enormously to my profit, for I'll be working just soon enough to get a gratis *Faery Queene* in return for my printed prospectus)'.[3] The Ashendene edition of Spenser's *Faery Queene* was to be published two years later. Still another indication of his plans was the fact that he went to much trouble and expense, during the remaining months of 1922, to commission further illustrations for *Seven Pillars*. When he asked Clayton to sit for a portrait, he wrote: 'I think there is no chance of its being published for years . . . I'd have it stored away.'[4] In the same vein, he instructed Whittingham & Griggs to keep the four colour plates they had begun to work on.

The motives that lay behind his decision to enlist were complex. He himself recognised that there was no easy explanation, and wrote some months later to a friend: 'Honestly I couldn't tell you exactly why I joined up: though the night before I did . . . I sat up and wrote out all the reasons I could see or feel in myself for it, but they came to little more than that it was a necessary step, forced on me by an inclination towards ground-level, by a little wish to make myself a little more human . . . by an itch to make myself ordinary in a mob of likes: also, I'm broke, so far as money goes . . . All these are reasons, but unless they are cumulative they are miserably inadequate. I wanted to join up, that's all . . . It's going to be a brain-sleep, and I'll come out of it less odd than I went in'.[5]

As his decision stemmed from both conscious and subconscious motives, there is little to be gained by attempting to set these out in a logical fashion. Nevertheless, it is possible to identify many of the factors which influenced him at this time.

One was his disinclination to follow a conventional career – an attitude he had doubtless inherited from his father. His years in the East had reinforced this outlook, leaving him with a contempt for possessions and wealth: 'The gospel of bareness in materials is a good one', he had written in 1918.[6]

Thus he had no ambition to remain in the Colonial Office: in any case, his mentality was that of a crusading politician rather than a Civil Servant. Now that the special circumstances of the war had passed, he was free to please himself, and he did not like having to advocate or implement ideas he disagreed with. He later wrote: 'the life of politics wearied me out, by worrying me over-much. I've not got a coarse-fibred enough nature for them: and have too many scruples and an uneasy conscience. It's not good to see two sides of questions, when you have (officially) to follow one.'[7]

Academic life might have seemed a natural alternative, but he had never felt attracted to the idea of a university post, and had rejected this option before the war. He had tried living at All Souls during 1919 and 1920, but felt ill at ease there and had spent most of his time at Barton Street. He now decided to give up his rooms in the college.

As an archaeologist, his enthusiasm had been for field-work rather than academic study. Shortly after the Armistice he had spoken of rejoining Woolley for further excavations at Carchemish. By the end of the Peace Conference, however, France had taken control in Syria, and it was obvious that he would not be allowed to go back.[8]

Finally, it is worth noting that Lawrence sometimes spoke of himself as a person only rarely moved by ambition. Years later, he wrote: 'When I want a thing, I'm prepared to lose everything to get it. Hence I succeed, *when I want to*. But that is, fortunately for my peace and comfort, seldom.'[9]

In 1922 he had only one wish: despite the problems he was facing with *Seven Pillars*, he still hoped to make a reputation for himself as a writer. There was nothing new about this ambition. Ever since leaving Oxford in 1910 he had toyed with literary projects of some kind. His latest scheme, for a book about the RAF, was certainly real; and at that time the idea of writing a study of the Air Force as seen from the ranks was a novel one. While it is unlikely that Lawrence would have enlisted for this reason alone, he undoubtedly took the project very seriously and it seems to have played a significant part in the conscious reasoning behind his decision.[10]

Another motive was probably fear of solitude. He did not have a close relationship with any surviving member of his family, nor did he have dependents of his own or hope of marrying. After the homosexual rape at Deraa in November 1917, the consummation of a marriage would have been utterly abhorrent to him. The incident had left him with an aversion for physical contact, which was noticed by many of his friends. Nevertheless, since the end of the desert campaigns he had often felt intensely lonely. The popular reputation created for him by Lowell Thomas had driven him increasingly into isolation, and he had spent months on his own in Barton Street working on *Seven Pillars*. On other occasions he had been hurt when cold-shouldered by political adversaries. Like many other ex-servicemen, he began to long for the spirit of comradeship that he had known during the war: a spirit that is rarely found in civilian life.

According to Lawrence, the idea of enlisting had first occurred to him when working with British units during the later stages of the desert campaign: 'These friendly outings with the armoured car and Air Force fellows were what persuaded me that my best future, if I survived the war, was to enlist.'[11] He also wrote: 'My ambition to serve in [the Air Force] ranks dates – concretely – from 1919: and nebulously from . . . 1917, before there was an Air Force.'[12] There is some evidence to confirm that enlistment had been in his mind during 1919,[13] but at that time he was still considering other possibilities such as the printing scheme. The final decision to join the RAF seems to date from the beginning of 1922.

As he himself admitted, these rational motives for his enlistment were barely sufficient, and he was undoubtedly influenced by other factors which were to some degree subconscious. Among these were psychological problems that had existed for some time. Although he usually made light of his illegitimacy, he would occasionally speak of it with great bitterness to close friends.[14] Likewise, he was acutely aware of his short stature. In the draft of *Seven Pillars*, he wrote: 'I was . . . ashamed of my awkwardness: and of my physical envelope: and of my solitary unlikeness which made me no friend or companion, but an acquaintance: complete, angular, uncomfortable'.[15] He probably knew that people referred to him slightingly as 'little Lawrence', and he seems to have regarded both his illegitimacy and his short stature as real handicaps which would in some way prevent him from taking a more prominent place among the ruling élite.

His sensitivity over these questions was heightened by the state of depression from which he was suffering when he returned to England in December 1921. For some time he had been in poor health, and this had aggravated his sense of disillusion with Hussein and the other Arab leaders. He had drifted into a negative mood which left him disappointed with the outcome of his diplomatic negotiations and irritated by the shortcomings he now saw in his *Seven Pillars* draft. A friend observed: 'In the winter of 1921-1922 Lawrence was in a very nervous condition, [and] did not eat or sleep enough'.[16] In addition to his work for Churchill, he had been draining his energies for months in a struggle to improve *Seven Pillars*. The book revived the worst of his wartime experiences, and the stress of recreating them under such unfavourable conditions had disturbed the balance of his mind. Subconscious forces, which he might otherwise have been able to cope with, began to play an increasingly important role in his motivation.

Like many soldiers who have lived through horrific battlefield experiences he was suffering from the after-effects of war, and for several years he had dreadful nightmares.[17] Although relatively common, this malaise was inadequately understood by the medical profession at that time, and went largely untreated. Lawrence recognised it, both in himself and in his friends. Some time after his enlistment he wrote to Graves: 'What's the cause that you, and Siegfried Sassoon, and I . . . can't get away from the war? Here are you riddled with thought like any old table-leg with worms: S.S. yawing about like a ship aback: me in the ranks, finding squalor and maltreatment the only permitted existence: what's the matter with us all? It's like the malarial bugs in the blood, coming out months and years after in recurrent attacks.'[18]

In his depressed condition, one incident in particular had come to dominate his thoughts. He had been able to put the Deraa episode out of his mind during much of the Syrian campaign, but since returning to civilian life he had found himself brooding over it. The experience had left him with profound feelings of uncleanliness, confusion and guilt. His account of it was among the first *Seven Pillars* chapters he had drafted, and he later said that he had rewritten the description nine times. In the version he finished in 1922, he wrote that he had been left feeling 'maimed, imperfect, only half myself. It could not have been the defilement, for no one ever held the body in less honour than I did myself. Probably it had been the breaking of the spirit by that frenzied nerve-shattering pain which had degraded me to beast level when it made me grovel to it, and which had journeyed with me since, a fascination and terror and morbid desire, lascivious and vicious, perhaps, but like the striving of a moth towards its flame.'[19] Such thoughts gave rise to a new and very damaging sense of personal worthlessness.

In Lawrence's mind, the destruction of his sense of integrity at this most intimate level seemed to reflect the moral degradation he had accepted during his wartime role with the Arabs. Churchill's settlement could not absolve him from responsibility for the lies he had told, nor from their terrible consequences. He would never be able to forget the sacrifices made by those who had believed in him. His memories of events such as the death of his young servant Othman, so painfully described in *Seven Pillars*, must have been an insistent reminder of what he had done.

It was this tormenting knowledge that made public adulation so intolerable. The association between praise and guilt had been forged at Damascus, where the populace had welcomed him as a liberator, believing that he had helped to bring them lasting freedom. There was deliberate irony behind his description of this triumph in the *Seven Pillars* draft: 'Every man, woman and child in this city of a quarter-million souls was out in the streets and as the miracle of victory was at last confirmed, they waited only the spark of our appearance to unchain their spirits. Damascus went mad with joy. The men tossed up their tarbushes to cheer, the women tore off their veils. Householders threw their flowers, their hangings, their carpets, into the road before us. Their wives leaned through the lattices and splashed cups and vases, even bath-dippers of scent at us.

'The poor dervishes came together, and made themselves our running footmen in front and behind, howling and cutting themselves with frenzy; and over all the local cries and the shrilling of the women, there came the measured roar of men's voices, chanting, "Feisal, Nasir, Shukri, Urens" . . . We English had been too long free to keep even a memory of its first delirious taste: so that this named gratitude and thanks from a hundred thousand voices broke us with the humiliation of over-great honour . . . From this cup I drank as deeply as any man should do, when we took Damascus: and was sated with it.'[20]

He was now desperate to escape from his popular reputation, and believed that he could do so by enlisting under an assumed name. The idea seemed intriguing in itself. In *Seven Pillars* he wrote: 'There was a special attraction in a new beginning, an everlasting endeavour to free my personality from its accretions, and to project it unencumbered on a fresh medium . . . The hidden self was reflected clearest in the still water of another man's yet incurious mind. Considered judgments, which had in them of the past and the future, were worthless compared with the first sight, the instinctive opening or closing of a man as he looked at the stranger. Whence came our pleasure in disguise or anonymity'.[21]

The wish to submerge his real identity was one aspect of the 'inclination towards ground-level' and 'itch to make myself ordinary in a mob of likes' he spoke of at the time of his enlistment. This feeling too is discussed in the draft of *Seven Pillars*, where he wrote: 'I liked the things beneath me and took my pleasures, and my adventures, downward. There seemed a level of certainty in degradation, a final safety. Man could rise to any height, but there was an animal point beneath which he could not fall. It was a solid satisfaction on which to rest. The force of things, and an artificial dignity, denied it me more and more, but there endured the after-taste of a real liberty from one youthful submerged fortnight in Port Said, coaling steamers by day with other outcasts of three continents and curling up by night to sleep on the breakwater by [the statue of] de Lesseps, with the sea surging past my head.'[22]

Lawrence chose to spend large parts of his adult life among people who shared none of the advantages of his background. He recognised this fact and sought to understand it; yet his explanations of this 'downward urge' seem inadequate, especially in relation to his enlistment. If he had thought about it deeply, he would surely have realised that his education and experience would always guarantee him a special position among the men in the ranks. In practice, therefore, his 'inclination towards ground level' would take him into situations where his intellectual superiority would be effortless and unrivalled. It is clear from his post-enlistment letters that he made no attempt to evade this special status: on the contrary, he seems to have cultivated it. This pattern of behaviour suggests that Lawrence suffered from a deep sense of insecurity.

In the draft *Seven Pillars* he also described a longing for roles that were truly subservient and self-abasing: 'Always in working I had tried to serve . . . It was part of my failure never to have found a chief to use me. All of them were weak, and through incapacity or fear or liking, allowed me too free a hand. I was always hoping for a master [for] whom I could have fought till I dropped at his feet to worship . . . I used myself as I would have let no man use another: but needed over me one yet harder and more ruthless, who would have worn me to the last fibre of my strength. To him I could have given such service as few masters have had, and I would have given it zealously, for voluntary slavery was a deep pride of a morbid spirit'.[23]

This curious statement seems to invite two quite different comments. First, it is clear from 'Twenty-seven Articles' and other writings that Lawrence had been far from subservient when acting as confidential adviser to influential men. Throughout his military and diplomatic career he had tried to manipulate his superiors in order to attain his personal objectives. With both Feisal and Churchill, he had seen himself as a 'power behind the throne'. Allenby had known nothing of Lawrence's personal motives in the Arab Revolt, yet, through Lawrence, he had helped to advance the cause of Arab freedom. In this respect, therefore, the passage quoted above must be regarded as misleading.

By 1922, however, a confused desire for some form of self-abasement seems to have become a powerful element in Lawrence's emotional condition. In a letter to a friend written shortly after his enlistment, he said: 'partly I came in here to eat dirt, till its taste is normal to me'.[24] There were to be many further references to this motive during the next few years, and these later allusions suggest that it formed part of an essentially masochistic disorder unleashed by his experience at Deraa.

Such was Lawrence's state of mind in January 1922. He appears to have believed that a spell in the ranks would help cure his malaise, and told Robert Graves that enlistment was little different from going into a monastery. It would also provide subject matter for a new book.

Trenchard replied to his letter about enlistment on January 11th: 'With regard to your personal point, I understand it fully, and you too, I think. I am prepared to do all you ask me, if you will tell me for how long you want to join, but I am afraid I could not do it without mentioning it to Winston and my own Secretary of State, and then, whether it could be kept secret I do not know . . . What country do you want to serve in, and how? I would make things as easy as anything.

'Let me know if I may mention this to my two Secretaries of State and come and see me.'[25]

Lawrence did not immediately press the matter: he was still employed by the Colonial Office, and before taking any new direction he wished to complete the revision of *Seven Pillars* he had been working on for so long. Having lost the previous draft, he decided to make copies of the new version. He learned that for little more than the cost of having it typed, the *Oxford Times* printers could typeset the whole text in double-column and run off a small number of copies on a proofing press. He was attracted by this unusual idea, and arranged for eight sets of proof pages to be printed.

He began sending text to the *Oxford Times* before the end of January. Chapters were submitted in a random order without their proper numbers so that the printers would be unable to assemble the book. For this purpose he had to write out a fair copy of the complete text, leaving the pages and chapters unnumbered. He kept back until last all the sections where the subject matter was potentially sensational.

It soon transpired that Churchill was unwilling to let him leave the Colonial Office. In mid-February Lawrence wrote to his mother: 'I told him I was open to hold on for a little till his first difficulties were over . . . but not in a formal appointment. Probably I'll get leave on the first of

March, and not go back again . . . There was a question of me for [British High Commissioner in] Egypt, if Allenby came away: but that of course I wouldn't accept. I don't think ever again to govern anything.

'If I get away finally from the Colonial Office about May my plans are to do nothing for a little, and then perhaps to consider the Air Force. Of course I'm too old to join it, but I think that the life and the odd mind (or lack of mind) there, might give me a subject to write about. This long-drawn-out battle over my narrative of the campaigns of Feisal has put an ink fever into me. I find myself always going about trying to fit words to the sights and sounds in the world outside me.

'However all this remains uncertain, and will remain uncertain for me till I do it'.[26]

Churchill finally agreed that he should stop work on March 1st and take three months' leave. During this time off, Lawrence intended to 'put a final end to the millstone, as it now is, of this Arabian book. So will sit at Barton Street till it is finished. It will take till sometime in May.'[27] In the event, however, it proved difficult to extricate himself from the Colonial Office, and twelve days into his 'leave' he told a friend that he was still going in to work regularly. By April the position had improved, but he had still not obtained his full release. He wrote: 'I've had my tenth resignation to Winston rejected, and am sitting in my attic, writing at the never-to-be-presentable-published-or-finished book.'[28]

It took him another two months to complete the new manuscript, the length of which he reckoned to be almost 330,000 words. As he later admitted, the effort almost drove him out of his mind. At Easter he told Newcombe: 'I spend whole days sitting at a table writing out my *Seven Pillars* straight enough for a printer to read, and after I get too blind to see, stagger out into the street, and get slowly pushed by taxis and buses up Whitehall into the National Gallery, where the Italian Rooms are good: or down Millbank to the Tate Gallery where the two modern rooms are good: and so to work again.'[29]

At the beginning of June the *Oxford Times* returned the penultimate block of text, and he began to prepare sets of the chapters for binding. He had not risked sending the title or other preliminary pages to be printed, and, to complete the copies, he now had these typed out.

Among the preliminaries was the dedication, which was addressed 'To S.A.' The earliest surviving outline of its content is a note jotted down in 1919: 'A(?) I wrought for him freedom to lighten his sad eyes: but he had died waiting for me. So I threw my gift away and now not anywhere will I find rest and peace.'[30] There can be little doubt that the initial 'A' represented Dahoum, whose real name was Ahmed.

By 1922 Lawrence had given a great deal of thought to this dedication. In conscious imitation of Shakespeare, whose sonnets were dedicated to an unidentified 'Mr. W.H.', he became evasive about the identity of 'S.A.' It is difficult to reconcile the various statements he made on the subject, but it seems that 'S.A.' had by this time become a wider concept which embodied both his affection for Dahoum and his feeling for Syria and its peoples. The text of the dedication now read:

> I loved you, so I drew these tides of men into my hands,
>   and wrote my will across the sky in stars
> To gain you freedom, the seven-pillared worthy house,
>   that your eyes might be shining for me
> When I came.
>
> Death was my servant on the road, till we were near
>   and saw you waiting:
> When you smiled, and in sorrowful envy he outran me,
>   and took you apart
> Into his quietness.
>
> So our love's earning was your cast-off body,
>   to be held one moment
> Before Earth's soft hands would explore all your face,
>   and the blind worms transmute
> Your failing substance.
>
> Men prayed me to set my work, the inviolate house,
>   in memory of you:
> But for fit monument I shattered it unfinished, and now
>   The little things creep out and patch themselves hovels
>   in the marred shadow
> Of your gift.[31]

Earlier in the year he had sent this poem to Robert Graves, asking whether it was prose or verse: Graves had answered that it was part one and part the other. Lawrence was dissatisfied with this reply, and sent the dedication to Laurence Binyon, whose poem 'For the Fallen' contained one of the most famous of all the stanzas inspired by the Great War. A draft of his letter to Binyon, whom he did not know personally, reads: 'Dear Sir, I have in me no poetry (unnecessary disclaimer): yet a poignant sequence of events drew from me, almost against my will, the stuff enclosed. Its content I am not ashamed of, since it expressed well enough my meaning and experience: but the form? It is quite short, and I will be most grateful if you are good enough to cast the eye of your experience rapidly over it, and tell me whether in *form* it is utterly contemptible – a jangle which a self-respecting man would stifle in silence? I suspect so, but would prefer your opinion to my own.'[32] Binyon's reply was reassuring, and Lawrence decided to include the poem in his bound copies of *Seven Pillars*. By the end of June, the only task that remained was to correct the last batch of printed chapters and insert them in their proper sequence. However, he did not expect them from the printers until late July, and in the meantime he went to spend a few days with friends in Cornwall.

Churchill finally allowed him to leave the payroll of the Colonial Office on July 1st, while retaining him for a time as an honorary adviser. Afterwards Lawrence wrote: 'I liked Winston so much, and have such respect for him that I was determined to leave only with his good-will:– and he took a long time to persuade!'[33] On July 4th he sent in his formal resignation, to which Churchill replied a few days later. Both letters were published in the *Morning Post*.[34]

As soon as he had secured his independence, Lawrence contacted Trenchard, who invited him to a private meeting to discuss the steps necessary if he really wished to join the ranks. Soon afterwards Lawrence wrote to Kennington that he had been offered 'a job which I have wanted to do since 1919. I don't know if it will come off yet or not: but I think it will: and in that case it will hold me in London for at least a year. No money in it, but keep, and very interesting work.'[35]

By July 21st both Churchill and the Secretary of State for Air had agreed to the enlistment. Three weeks later Lawrence arranged with Trenchard that he would present himself at the recruiting office on August 22nd. This date was later put back, at his own request, until the end of the month.

In his last weeks of freedom, Lawrence commissioned further portraits for *Seven Pillars*. The subjects were to be his British colleagues in the Revolt. He told Clayton: 'Kennington went east for me, and did about twenty Arabs: and I want about a dozen Englishmen to balance them.

'English people all look alike, in dress anyway: so to make an extra variety I'm out to have the dozen drawn by different artists. They include Newcombe, Alan Dawnay, Hogarth, Boyle (R.N.) . . . Bartholomew, and that sort of man.'[36] These five sitters were to be portrayed by William Roberts, William Rothenstein, Augustus John, Eric Kennington and Colin Gill. Clayton's portrait was to be by William Nicholson, and Lawrence commissioned others from John Singer Sargent, Henry Lamb, Frank Dobson and Gilbert Spencer.

He also needed landscape illustrations, and in early August wrote to Paul Nash: 'If you are full of work and money don't bother to read further – but if you are not, I'm going to suggest much of the first and a little of the second, to be gained in a quite dishonourable way:– drawing from photographs. If this professional prostitution drives you mad, please convey to Mrs. N. my regrets for inconveniencing her. If it doesn't, then please read the next paragraph.

'I wrote a book about Arabia. To publish it would involve me in as many libels as there are characters . . . Also it isn't good enough to publish – but it's good enough for me to make better, till it can be published in the course of years . . .

'One way of hiding its faults is to cover it liberally with illustrations . . . I wanted some scenes of real action. I had no artist with me: but there were photographs. I took one to Colin Gill who made a most spirited drawing of the represented scene. Roberts is trying to do another. They agreed that it was blasting, humiliating, dishonourable, damnable, to draw from photographs: but said that if I gave them complete freedom (no rules or truth or exactness to bother about) it might be done. It was.

'There remain landscapes. Valleys, Hills, Ports, Deserts: all Arabian. Thorn trees, palms, tamarisks. Ruins. There are about a hundred photographs, some good, some bad: but I have one rule: that no photograph shall be reproduced in my book. So I want a landscape artist to translate them into life.'[37] Nash wrote back at once, accepting the commission.

In the process of gathering illustrations for *Seven Pillars*, Lawrence was gradually becoming one of the most significant private patrons of contemporary artists in Britain. Moreover, this generosity was not exclusively related to his book: he did his best to place their work in national collections. For example, he purchased a bust of Osbert Sitwell by Frank Dobson for the Tate, and presented a portrait of Doughty by Augustus John, which he had himself commissioned, to the National Portrait Gallery.

In late August the binders delivered the first three copies of *Seven Pillars*. Lawrence sent one of them privately to Edward Garnett, a very experienced editor and judge of contemporary writing. Garnett was working as a consultant to Jonathan Cape's new publishing house and, even before finishing the book, he raised the question of publication. Lawrence replied: 'I should have warned you before I sent it . . . that if your opinion was favourable it would be wasted on me. Perhaps as you haven't yet finished it, this is still not too rude to say . . . So please don't consider the point of publication. That never came into my mind when writing it: indeed I don't know for whom I wrote it, unless it was for myself. When it came to the point of printing it, several passages had to come out, for fear of the compositor, and I cannot imagine showing it except to a few minds (like yours) already prejudged to kindness.

'If that Deraa incident whose treatment you call severe and serene (the second sounds like a quaint failure to get my impressions across, but I know what you feel) had happened to yourself you would not have recorded it. I have a face of brass perhaps, but I put it into print very reluctantly . . . For weeks I wanted to burn it in the manuscript: because I could not tell the story face to face with anyone, and I think I'll feel sorry, when I next meet you, that you know it. The sort of man I have always mixed with, doesn't so give himself away.

'I shall hope for help from your pencilled notes, and am very grateful for your goodness in reading it, and for what praise you have given it: only please don't do more, because it only underlines what I know to be my failure. Hitherto I've always managed, usually without trying my hardest, to do anything I wanted in life: and it has bumped me down, rather, to have gone wrong in this thing, after three or four years' top-effort . . .

'When you have had enough of it I'd like to come down and ask you some technical questions.'[38]

On the following day, he wrote to Garnett again, reporting that he had received 'an offer (running up to about £7,000) for serial rights and royalties (England and America) on not more than 120,000 words of that war-monument of mine – the thing you are reading or trying to read. It would be rather fun cutting it down to forty chapters, out of one hundred and forty. However I've said "nothing doing". I'd rather sink with all hands than build a raft out of the wreck.'[39]

On August 26th, after further praise from Garnett, Lawrence wrote very frankly about his literary ambitions: 'Confession is in the air. Do you remember my telling you once that I collected a shelf of "titanic" books

'Aircraftman Ross' by William Roberts, autumn 1922. Probably the only portrait of Lawrence during the period at RAF Uxbridge described in *The Mint*

Charlotte Shaw, wife of the playwright, who developed a very deep affection for Lawrence. She sent him countless presents and poured out her soul to him in letters. Every one of his replies is noted in her diaries

T.E. Lawrence by Augustus John, 1923. When Lawrence saw this picture on exhibition in London he said that it made him look like a 'budding sergeant'

Thomas Hardy by Augustus John, painted at Lawrence's suggestion in 1923. Hardy was delighted to learn that the portrait had been given to the Fitzwilliam Museum

Turkish concentration of troops, earmarked for Maan when supply Nasir conditions would let them move. This supply reserve was being put forward in by rail from Damascus, as well as the bombing attacks of the Royal Air Force from Palestine permitted.

To make head against them, Nasir, our best guerilla general, had been appointed, in advance of Zeid, to do something great against the railway. He had camped in Wadi Hesa, with Hornby, full of explosives, and Peake's trained section of Egyptian Army Camel Corps to help in demolition. Time, till Allenby recovered, was what we had to fight for, and Nasir would very much help our desire if he secured us a month's breathing space by playing the intangible ghost at the Turkish Army. If he failed we must expect the relief of Maan and an onslaught of the reinvigorated enemy upon Aba el Lissan.

New Chapter

For six weeks we marked time Zaid & Jaffar, with their regulars, continued a profitable Battering upon the Maan sector Sherif Nasir, accompanied by Peake & Hornby moved forty miles northward and occupied eight miles of railway in one happy thrust. By intensive demolition the very foundations of the line thereabout were destroyed and the Turkish contemplated offensive against Feisal in Aba-el-Lissan was brought to nought. Dawnay and myself took advantage of the lull to go up again to Allenby.

A proof page from the subscribers' *Seven Pillars* marked up by Lawrence for *Revolt in the Desert*. This is from the original pencil draft, not the fair copy sent to Jonathan Cape

Lord Trenchard, who did his best to help Lawrence serve in the RAF despite opposition from successive Air Ministers

above: Lawrence very rarely signed photographs but two signed prints of this one survive. *above right*: Lawrence at Miranshah in December 1928. He had broken his wrist at Cranwell and wrote on the back of this photograph, 'nursing my right wrist which hurt for so long that nursing it became a habit'

Lawrence at Karachi, reading *Ulysses*. He was pleased to find that his fellow airmen appreciated good books, and lent freely

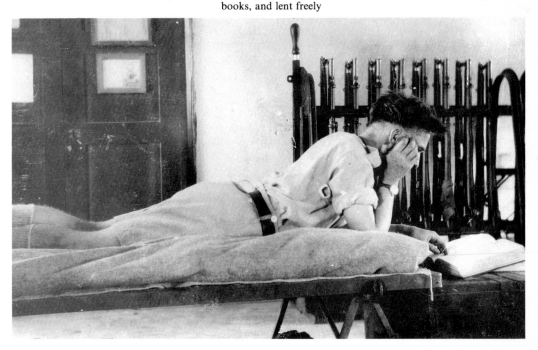

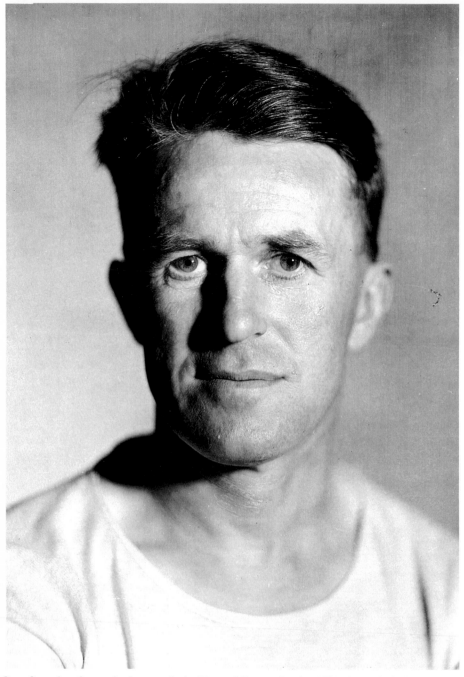

One of a series of portrait photographs by Howard Coster, October 1931. Coster had always wanted to photograph Lawrence, and recognised him one day in London. He chased after Lawrence and persuaded him to sit (those distinguished by greatness of spirit, "sublimity" as Longinus would call it): and that they were *The Karamazovs*, *Zarathustra*, and *Moby Dick*. Well, my ambition was to make an English fourth. You will observe that modesty comes out more in the performance than in the aim! . . . I had hopes all the while that it was going to be a big thing, and wrote myself nearly blind in the effort. Then it was finished (pro tem) and I sent it to the printer, and when it came back in a fresh shape I saw that it was no good . . .

'Please don't read this as a *cri de coeur*. I'm perfectly cheerful. If I'd aimed low I could have hit my target as squarely as Max Beerbohm or Belloc hits it: but their works are only a horrid example, and I'm much happier to have gone high and flopped than not to have tried, or to have tried half-measures. It's only that my weathercock of a judgement, which would like, in secret, to believe the *Seven Pillars* good, blows round that way whenever it finds a fair wind from someone else. I go on exercising the poor bird wantonly, by thinking to send the copy to more people for comment. You happen to be the first person to have read it: but there is Kennington half-way through and chuckling over it, and another man, whose work I admire, has got it on loan by his own request. So I'll go on veering about the point of publication, as with you, so often as any of them praise it: but at the end I'll say, No, once more – and it's the right decision.'[40] One of these further critics Lawrence hoped would read the book was Bernard Shaw, whom he had met by chance not long before. When he wrote asking whether he could send it, Shaw agreed, but asked for a delay until September.

The date for Lawrence's enlistment was now approaching, and he received detailed instructions from Air Vice-Marshal Sir Oliver Swann, the RAF officer responsible for personnel. He was to go to the Air Force recruiting office in Covent Garden at about 10.30 a.m. on August 30th: 'You will say that you wish to see Mr. Dexter from whom you have had a letter. Flight Lieut. Dexter will interview you and will fill up the necessary forms – you should tell him the particulars we have arranged upon (not the whole truth, nor your real name). He will advise you as to the age to give and what trade to enter in – (Dexter knows you are being specially entered and will help, but does not know all the facts, which do not concern him).

'You will then be medically examined at Henrietta Street. Do not mention any disability. If you are failed, Fl.L. Dexter will arrange matters.

'You will have to produce two references as to character and previous employment during the last two years. They will not be investigated but it is necessary for you to have them in order that someone may not say that your papers are not correct.

'You will be sent to Uxbridge with a draft of recruits. At Uxbridge you will be attested and medically inspected. You will have to declare that what you have stated on the attestation form is correct and you will have to swear allegiance to the Crown. You will have a slight educational exam if you are entering as an aircraft hand.

'I think there will be no difficulty after leaving Henrietta Street. No one will know about you . . . but if any difficulty arises, as a last resort, ask that Mr. Dexter of Recruiting Depot be communicated with by telephone.'[41]

Lawrence had already been in poor health when he approached Trenchard about the enlistment in January. By the end of August, after the further stress of completing *Seven Pillars*, he was not far from a nervous breakdown. He later wrote: 'I nearly went off my head in London this spring, heaving at that beastly book of mine.'[42] In this precarious state of mind, he had lived for several months without adequate food or sleep. As a result he was in no condition to pass the RAF medical examination, still less to face the rigours of the recruits' training course.

Part III

Writer and Serviceman

1922-35

Writing has been my inmost self all my life, and I can never put my full strength into anything else. Yet the same force, I know, put into action upon material things would move them, make me famous and effective.

T. E. Lawrence to E. H. R. Altounyan 9th January 1933

CHAPTER 32

Aircraftman Ross
September 1922 – January 1923

ON 4th September 1922 the *Daily Mail* reported that: 'Colonel T. E. Lawrence, the British officer who organised and led an Arabian army against the Turks during the war, has . . . left London for a destination abroad. It is thought that, in view of the unsettled position in Palestine between the Arabs and the Zionists, his departure has a special significance. Six months ago he returned from a mission to Aden and Trans-Jordania.'[1] This misleading statement was probably suggested to the press by Lawrence. In reality, he had presented himself on August 30th at the RAF recruiting office in Henrietta Street, Covent Garden.

There he answered questions about his previous career. With the blessing of higher authority he gave his age as twenty-eight and his trade as an 'architect's clerk'. He had doubtless picked up enough knowledge of architecture from his discussions with Herbert Baker in Barton Street to support this latter claim if necessary. According to his stated age, he should have fought in the Great War, but he said he had done no previous military service. He told the recruiting officer that he had been a civilian in Smyrna at the beginning of the war, and had been interned there by the Turks as an enemy alien (if discovered, such perjuries would normally have incurred two years' imprisonment with hard labour). He named Vyvyan Richards, a 'cousin', as his next-of-kin.

Lawrence had hoped to pass into the RAF without calling on the special arrangements that had been set up in advance, but he failed the medical examination. Afterwards he wrote to Swann: 'the mess I made of Henrietta Street demands an apology. I thought I was fitter: but when it came to the point, walked up and down the street in a blue funk, and finally went in with my nerves dithering, and my heart dancing. My teeth never were any good, so the doctors threw me straight downstairs again. There Dexter caught me, and lent me what was no doubt his right hand to steer me past the medical, and through other rocks of square roots and essays and decimals. However I was obviously incapable of getting through on my own, so he got another chit from you, and that did the trick satisfactorily. If I'd known I was such a wreck I'd have gone off and recovered before joining up: now the cure and the experiment must proceed together.'[2] As 352087 A/c Ross, he was posted to the RAF training depot at Uxbridge for three months' basic training.

He immediately started work on his projected book about the Air Force. The first section was to be a description of the training course, and he began to write notes: 'Every night in Uxbridge I used to sit in bed, with my knees drawn up under the blankets, and write on a pad the things of the day. I tried to put it all down, thinking that memory and time would sort them out, and enable me to select significant from insignificant.'[3]

The experience he recorded during these weeks came as a shock. He had pictured himself leading the kind of life he had seen in wartime service units; but the reality of the recruits' training was nothing like these expectations. Basic training in the RAF was much the same as in the other two services. Its purpose was to instil the fundamentals of military conduct, and it used techniques which had been proved in the training of mass conscript armies during the Great War. In the first few weeks at Uxbridge, recruits were subjected to rigorously disciplined physical training and spent much of their time on 'fatigues'. Many of their tasks were distasteful, and some had little point except to keep the men occupied. Recruits were made to understand that their time belonged to the RAF. Whether they were usefully employed or not, their duty was unhesitating and unprotesting obedience.

Lawrence now found himself among men whose motives and ambitions were quite different from his own. Few of them would have had any prospects in civilian life, and they saw the training as a stepping-stone to a secure career in the RAF. They had committed themselves willingly for a minimum of seven years, whereas Lawrence could obtain immediate discharge on request.

Lawrence's friends must have realised how unsuited he was to the Uxbridge regime, both physically and by temperament. Training that was designed to toughen men who were younger and fitter drove him almost to breaking point, and he bitterly resented the many deliberate humiliations. He could never forget that his presence at Uxbridge was voluntary, and this coloured his views on every aspect of the depot. When the training was severe, the others had to make the best of it; Lawrence, however, often felt the temptation to escape. He had to meet harsh discipline with stronger self-discipline, and it was typical of him that he refused to give up: 'My determined endeavour is to scrape through with it, into the well-paid peace of my trade as a photographer to some squadron.'[4]

The self-imposed task of recording this experience gave him many opportunities to put his mounting resentment into words. His account of Uxbridge, always self-conscious, had a rebellious tone which reached a climax when he described the abuse of authority: 'Tonight's crash of the stick on the hut door at roll-call was terrific: and the door slammed back nearly off its hinges. Into the light strode Raper, V.C., a corporal who assumed great licence in the camp because of his war decoration. He marched down my side of the hut, checking the beds. Little Nobby, taken by surprise, had one boot on and another off. Corporal Raper stopped. "What's the matter with YOU?" "I was knocking out a nail which hurts my foot." "Put your boot on at once. Your name?" He passed on to the end door and there whirled round, snorting "Clarke". Nobby properly cried "Corporal", and limped down the alley at a run (we must always run when called) to bring up stiffly at attention before him. A pause, and then curtly, "Get back to your bed."

'Still the Corporal waited and so must we, lined up by our beds. Again, sharply, "Clarke". The performance was repeated, over and over, while the four files of us looked on, bound fast by shame and discipline. We were men, and a man over there was degrading himself and his species, in degrading another. Raper was lusting for trouble and hoped to provoke one of us into some act or word on which to base a charge. Nobby limped submissively up and down perhaps eight times, before the other door admitted Corporal Abner. Raper wheeled and vanished.'[5]

The distractions of this Uxbridge training had not made Lawrence forget about *Seven Pillars*, and during the autumn of 1922 he found time to commission further portraits for his collection. He briefed each artist carefully before the sittings, as when he arranged for William Rothenstein to draw Alan Dawnay in September: 'He's a very perfect person, and when you have met him all will run easily . . . He's Eton and Magdalen, Oxford, and the Guards: and is everything that is absolutely right: and the best of it is that he looks like it, and will look like it in your drawing'.[6] Kennington was commissioned to paint Captain Boyle: 'A good face (hot as mustard, red-haired, socialist, thinker, disciplinarian: thinks the world made for Naval Officers: very decent: full of laughter of a slightly sharp sort: restless, impatient); a real bad sitter: but a first-rate face. Sinew and fire and tight skin.'[7]

Roberts was sent to draw McMahon: 'He is very tired, very shrewd, very kindly, and has been badly treated by the Government. A dapper carefully-decorative little man, who lives in Wilton Place.'[8] Also, 'He's got a jolly red nose – like blotting paper:– don't tell him I said so!'[9] Lawrence also wanted Roberts to sketch 'old General Wingate – Sir Francis Wingate, ex-Governor of Sudan, High Commissioner of Egypt etc. Do you think you could draw a courtly old man, broken and disappointed now because his career ended badly, a man who was never much more than a butter-merchant and great-man's friend, even in his best days, but whose administration was so successful that it gave him confidence, and for a while he believed himself great . . . please be very gentle with him, if you do him. He's not so much a butterfly as a ghost of one, a thing by no means to be broken on a wheel.'[10]

These portraits did not always please their subjects, and Lawrence often sent apologies in advance. For instance he warned Buxton (now his bank manager) that Roberts 'has done a wonderful study of Newcombe, fierce almost to the point of terror. I think he might do something rather subtle of you, because you don't look like an officer . . . You may not like the result, but it will be Art (with a capital A).'[11] In October, when Buxton's portrait was finished, Lawrence wrote consolingly: 'It must have been an effort: and the result is astonishing: you have become severe, abstracted, slightly sorry: with the laughter gone from your face. It is before Mudowwara, rather than after it! A wonderful drawing . . . It's exceedingly good of you to have endured it all: and the result is worth it, however much you find it hateful. I'm employing this week in writing such apologetic letters to Newcombe and McMahon and Boyle also. It's a dreadful business drawing friends' heads.'[12] Roberts's next victim was to be Lord Winterton: 'Try and make him look hot-tempered! He is',[13] Lawrence wrote, 'he'll be an impatient and unconscionable sitter.'[14]

Lawrence waited with excitement as the first group of readers passed judgment on the 'Oxford' *Seven Pillars*. To his surprise, one reaction was a series of comic sketches: 'Kennington was moved to incongruous mirth, reading my book, and a dozen Bateman-quality drawings came of it. To my mind they are as rare, surprising and refreshing as plums in cake . . . and lighten up the whole. It's good that someone is decent enough to find laughter in a stodgy mess of mock-heroic egotism . . . It's Kennington pricking the vast bladder of my conceit.'[15]

Edward Garnett had been the first 'literary' reader to see the book, and, as he worked through it, his letters continued to be full of praise.

Lawrence was delighted by this approval, knowing Garnett's reputation for recognising and encouraging literary talent (he had 'discovered' Joseph Conrad and many other distinguished writers). Lawrence was especially pleased that Garnett had sensed 'the veracity of the story.' He wrote: 'It was written in dead earnest, and with as much feeling as a "don possessed" can muster: and I think it's all spiritually true. Kennington tells me however that some of the incidents will strain people's credulity to snapping point. He finds them improbable.'[16]

Some years previously Garnett had abridged Doughty's *Travels in Arabia Deserta* to about half its length for a popular edition. Taking his cue from the letter Lawrence had written on August 23rd, mentioning a possible abridgement of *Seven Pillars*, Garnett wrote offering to shorten the text for this purpose.[17] While Lawrence was still dissatisfied with the book as a whole, a well edited abridgement would provide him with a private income. He cautiously agreed: 'It's very good of you to be willing to try and cut it down. I think that I may have to publish something after all: for I'm getting too old for this life of rough and tumble, and the crudeness of my company worries me a bit. I find myself longing for an empty room, or a solitary bed, or even a moment alone in the open air. However there is grand stuff here, and if I could write it... what mania is it that drives a man who has half-killed his brain for four years over one book, so soon as it is finished, to contemplate another? . . . However I was thanking you for offering to edit the old thing. Isn't there a certain cowardice in publishing for money (the only motive: a means of escape from the crowd) less than the whole facts I found it needful to put on record? I can understand editing it for artistic reasons: but not for others: and I rather think that should be our standard . . . It's very good of you, amongst all your work, to think of attempting it for me: and you will think me very ungrateful if after all I say "No"... I hope I won't, but things are variable, and myself most of all: and I must have the deciding word over my own writing while I'm alive.'[18]

On September 9th Garnett replied with more praise: 'Supposing you heard a new composer and recognised at once in the fibres of the work that he was doing something nobody had done before, a new approach, a new combination of things in him. I feel somehow that your analysis of life may carry us *further*: there's a quality in your brain that suggests a new apprehension of things, or rather a very *special* apprehension of things that will be lost to us if you don't communicate it to us. And you can only do that through writing; by The *S.P.* and by things to come.

'Well, *that's* your work, this *special apprehension* of things. I didn't criticise your going into the R.A.F.C. for I felt you are a law to yourself and you might extract from *that* just what you were needing. And I can quite *see* "your study of man in the ranks of the R.A.F." . . . But manual work will tire you out too much to write. I think you will want more and more "an empty room" and "a solitary bed" to express yourself.'[19] As an escape route from Uxbridge, he offered Lawrence the job of editing a new literary magazine to be called *Belles-Lettres*. Lawrence found it ironic to receive such a suggestion while serving in the ranks, and turned the offer down: 'I don't really know why I don't want to do it'.[20] He sent Garnett one of the unbound copies of the 'Oxford' *Seven Pillars*, and Garnett set about reducing the text by more than half, to about 150,000 words. Once this had been completed, Lawrence intended to go over it again, aiming at a final length of about 130,000 words for the abridgement.

It was a fortnight before he heard from another of the *Seven Pillars* readers. This was Vyvyan Richards, who wrote a long philosophical letter which ended with a perceptive remark that Lawrence was often to repeat in other contexts: 'it seems to me that an attempted work of art may be so much more splendid for its very broken imperfection revealing the man so intimately.'[21] Lawrence replied: 'Positively I know that it's a good book: in the sense that it's better than most which have been written lately: but this only makes me yet sorrier that it isn't as good as my book should have been.

'If you dig malevolently behind these last sentences you will realise that I have a tolerable opinion of myself. The criticisms miss their aim in me, partly because I have made them all (and many others) in a far stronger sense, to myself: and the reason why the book isn't different is because my will-power to persevere with it failed. I don't know if it will return. A book dropped behind a man is so soon left behind . . . I agree that the *Seven Pillars* is too big for me: too big for most writers, I think. It's rather in the titan class: books written at tiptoe, with a strain that dislocates the writer, and exhausts the reader out of sympathy. Such can't help being failures, because the graceful things are always those within our force: but, as you conclude, their cracks and imperfections serve an artistic end in themselves: a perfect picture of a real man would be unreadable.'[22]

Garnett worked hard at the abridgement and completed a first draft in only five weeks. Lawrence visited him in London on October 15th to collect the marked-up sheets. A fortnight later he wrote: 'With all the drawings (over fifty now) I feel less and less inclined to publish the whole work, and almost decided not to publish anything. My mind wobbles between the need for money and the desire to be withdrawn, and it's a pitiable exhibition on my part. I wish the beastly book had never been written. Garnett's reduction is in my hands, and is a good one: but it's a bowdlerising of the story and the motives of it, and would give the public a false impression. I don't like the notion of doing that. It's a favourably-false impression, you see.'[23] During the next few weeks he could not make up his mind whether or not to publish the abridgement, but he continued revising it nevertheless.

On November 7th, after only ten weeks on the recruits' course, Lawrence was posted away from Uxbridge to the RAF School of Photography at Farnborough. Before leaving Uxbridge he had begun to see the basic training in a new light. It had achieved something he had not anticipated: 'We have come, unknowing, to a corporate life. Today we think, decide, act on parade without a word said. Men are becoming troops when like one body they are sluggish (to a bad instructor), mulish (when angered), willing (to an open-hearted man). We have attained a flight-entity which is outside our individualities. The self-reliance each has singly lost is not lost to us all. As a flight we're stiff-necked and spirited as though the excellencies of Sailor and Snaggle [the nicknames of two aircraftmen] had been buttered thinly over all the fifty heads. The person has died that to the company might be born a soul.'[24] By the time he was posted to Farnborough he was 'getting keen on the R.A.F. Was writing freely about Uxbridge when they snatched me away from it.'[25]

By mid-November, Lawrence had recognised that the notes he had made at Uxbridge would form a harsh opening to his study of the RAF. The book had been one of his main justifications for going into the ranks, but he now felt uncertain about its future. For the time being he lost interest in the project and gave up writing notes. Instead he was becoming reconciled to the idea of publishing the *Seven Pillars* abridgement, 'and I shall very much despise myself if I do. Only to face thirty-five years of poverty hurts even more than to smash my self-respect. Honestly I hate this dirty living: and yet by the decency of the other fellows, the full dirtiness of it has not met me fairly.'[26] At the same time, the thought of asking to leave injured his pride: 'Isn't it a sign of feebleness in me, to cry out so against barrack-life? It means that I'm afraid (physically afraid) of other men: their animal spirits seem to me the most terrible companions to haunt a man: and I hate their noise. Noise seems to me horrible. And yet

I'm a man, not different from them; certainly not better. What is it that makes me so damnably sensitive and so ready to cry out, and yet so ready to incur more pain? I wouldn't leave the R.A.F. tomorrow, for any job I was offered.'[27]

During these weeks he had only given a part of himself to the Air Force. For example, while A/c Ross was at the beck and call of any RAF Corporal, T. E. Lawrence, the hero of the Arab Revolt, was able to obtain a civil list pension for C. M. Doughty through his contacts in Whitehall. He told Doughty: 'There were muddles in the giving of it. Normally a memorial is presented to the Prime Minister signed, by influential people, recommending the "victim" to his attention. It seemed to me that in your case the procedure was unnecessary, since your work put you *hors concours*. So I suggested to Lloyd George that the pension be awarded just like that:– and he agreed to it . . . Of the present Ministry, three or four are fellows of All Souls, and most of the others are friends of mine. The Duke of Devonshire, and Lord Salisbury, and Amery, and Wood and three or four others would be glad to serve you in any way you wished. Please don't delay to let me know if, or when, anything comes to your mind. You are a public character, and can make any claim you like on the public. That's one of the privileges of greatness!'[28]

In the general election of November 15th Winston Churchill lost his seat at Dundee. This was, in the words of the *Daily Telegraph*, 'perhaps the most sensational defeat of the whole election'.[29] Three days later Lawrence wrote Churchill a letter of commiseration, and sent another to Sir Edward Marsh: 'I'm more sorry about Winston than I can say. I hope the press comment is not too malevolent. It's sure to hurt him though.'[30] On the same day Lawrence drafted a preface to Garnett's abridgement of *Seven Pillars* in which he paid generous tribute to the part Churchill had played in 1921: 'He set honesty before expediency in order to fulfil our promises in the letter and in the spirit. He executed the whole McMahon undertaking (called a treaty by some who have not seen it) for Palestine, for Trans-Jordania, and for Arabia. In Mesopotamia he went far beyond its provisions, giving to the Arabs more, and reserving for us much less, than Sir Henry McMahon had thought fit. In the affairs of French Syria he was not able to interfere . . . I do not wish to publish secret documents, nor to make long explanations: but must put on record my conviction that England is out of the Arab affair with clean hands. Some Arab advocates (the most vociferous joined our ranks after the Armistice) have rejected my judgment on this point. Like a tedious Pensioner I showed them my wounds (over sixty I have, each scar evidence of a pain incurred in Arab service) as proof I had worked sincerely on their side. They found me out-of-date: and I was happy to withdraw from a political milieu which had never been congenial.'[31]

The thought of publishing an abridgement of *Seven Pillars* made Lawrence increasingly careless of his future in the RAF. In November he wrote with great self-assurance to Swann, complaining about his training. He had arrived at Farnborough one day too late for the beginning of a photography course; instead of allowing him to join it, the Commanding Officer had ordered him to wait until the next course two months later. Lawrence wrote a second letter of protest on November 19th: 'I'd have no difficulty in joining even a class earlier than the November one, for except in enlarging and mosaic work, (learned in two of the later months) I'm already as good as the men passing out. My father, one of the pioneer photographers, taught me before I was four years old, and I've done the photographic work of several British Museum expeditions, and exhibited a good deal at the Camera Club, regularly.

'I asked, accordingly, if you could put me straight into the School, for my technical training. Except for that, Farnborough doesn't offer me much scope. The camp isn't quite the sort of R.A.F. I want to write about! At the same time the technical work is A.1. and I'd like to watch the growth of a class'.[32] He told Swann plainly that unless he could join the class already in progress he would like to be posted somewhere else. Swann (mindful that Lawrence's presence in the ranks had Trenchard's blessing) dutifully requested the Farnborough CO to see that A/c Ross proceeded at once with photographic training.

This initiative on Lawrence's part was one of the actions which helped to give away his identity. The CO at Farnborough, Wing-Commander W. J. Y. Guilfoyle, was surprised that Swann should be so interested in the affairs of A/c Ross. When he looked at Ross more closely, he thought that he saw an uncanny resemblance to the famous Colonel Lawrence. Not long afterwards this suspicion was confirmed when Ross was identified as Lawrence by a visiting officer who had served in Cairo during the war. Guilfoyle and his adjutant Charles Findlay agreed to keep their discovery to themselves, hoping that Lawrence's course of training at the School of Photography would pass off without incident.

By this time, however, Lawrence seemed to be inviting exposure. He told relative strangers that he was now serving in the ranks. Some people, including Edward Garnett, knew his pseudonym and address. Incredibly,

Lawrence had written a tantalising letter about his secret enlistment to his acquaintance R. D. Blumenfeld, editor of the *Daily Express*: 'This letter has got to be indiscreet – shockingly so . . . please keep it as a personal one, from me to you . . . I found I was quite on the rocks: and so I enlisted, as a quick and easy way of keeping alive, and alive I am, in the ranks, and not always miserable. It's a varied life, often very bad, but with spots of light, very exciting and full of freshness. You know I always was odd, and my tastes my own. Also the only way I could escape politics entirely was to cut myself sharply off from my former way of living: and making a living with one's fingers is joyful work, and as clean as possible, after politics – to which not even the *Express* shall drag me back! . . . Do keep this news to yourself. No one in camp knows who I am, and I don't want them to'.[33] Revelations of this kind made it almost certain that gossip about his enlistment would reach the wrong ears.

On November 20th Lawrence sent the draft *Seven Pillars* abridgement with his corrections back to Garnett: 'The total is about 160,000 words. I've taken out more than I expected, when I began it . . . But for the public I'm sure the abridgement will be better than the full text. Your cuts have the effect of speeding up the action in a remarkable fashion . . . You will laugh at the vanity of an author, who read the whole surviving text from end to end last night, and got up from reading with a sense that the barrack room was gone dead quiet. It was half an hour before outside things came home to me once more. I wonder what I would think of the work, if I read it again in 1940? It is certainly uncommon, and there's power sensible under its peculiarly frigid surface.'[34]

In order to be able to visit London from Farnborough, Lawrence had bought a motorcycle and sidecar, 'an old crock of a Triumph'.[35] He would often give other airmen rides into town and back. This mobility was to become increasingly important to him. On November 23rd Garnett wrote to him: 'I think now the abridgement is done it should be put in the agent's hands without delay'.[36] It was to be called *War in the Desert*. Lawrence's long-standing commitment to offer the book to Doubleday presented Garnett with a problem. He asked Lawrence: 'Shall I tell Cape about the abridgement and that it is ear-marked for another publisher? The fact that I am his "reader" etc., makes it necessary for me to be clear and definite with him. You can of course say that you *may* have something later for him – if you should ever do "Uxbridge". Or we can say nothing at all, as like all publishers he lives on great expectations of the most nebulous order.'[37]

Garnett was not the only person concerned for Lawrence's well-being. Blumenfeld, temporarily convalescing from an illness, had now written offering him work. On the day Lawrence received Garnett's letter about publishing the abridgement, he replied to Blumenfeld with something close to recklessness.

Dear Blumenfeld

Your offer is a generous and very kind one: and you will think me quixotic to refuse it: but I ran away here partly to escape the responsibility of head-work: and the *Daily Express* would expect me to take it up again. Had I had fewer wits I would have been a merrier person. My best thanks all the same.

No, please don't publish my eclipse. It will be common news one day, but the later the better for my peace in the ranks: and I'd be sorry to have to render reasons for it. As you say, it reads like cheap melodrama, and my life so far has been that, nearly, since the odd circumstances of my birth. Some day I'll tell you stories about myself – if you will hear them.

Meanwhile I'm excogitating a new book – in no way personal – on the spirit of the Air Force; a most remarkable body: and am hoping to take advantage of my obscurity to produce an abridgement of my old war-book on Arabia. This latter book I printed, privately (5 copies) a while ago: and if the abridgement is approved by a publisher I'll find myself rich – according to my standard. Whether I'll continue in the R.A.F. then, or return to London life – I don't know.

I hope the nursing home, (now half over, I suppose, for my post comes spasmodically, with long delays) will go prosperously for you. It's beastly, the being in any way ill. By the way don't you think it's good for me at my great age, after a ragged life, after seven bad air-crashes, after nine war-wounds, and many peace-ones, to be able to enlist and hold my own with a lusty crowd? I'm contented with myself.

Yours ever

T E Lawrence[38]

People often move towards a decision subconsciously long before they are prepared to admit to themselves that they have made up their minds: while still claiming to be undecided, they begin to behave in a way which not only displays their new intention, but closes the door on the course they have subconsciously rejected. From all the evidence available it seems that Lawrence had reached such a position. Overtly he was still willing to remain for a while in the RAF. For example, on November 28th he wrote to William Roberts (who wanted him to sit for a portrait): 'It seems as if I might be sent abroad to a squadron in India or Mesopotamia in the spring.'[39] But this intention is belied by the many references to publishing Garnett's abridgement, and to living in future on its proceeds. Letters such as that to Blumenfeld suggest that he had become indifferent to the risk of exposure.

At much the same time, Lawrence's behaviour in the ranks began to invite a confrontation with the authorities. It was inevitable that a man with his qualities would acquire some kind of special status in the barrack room, and the senior officers, aware of his identity, watched uneasily as this began to happen. Charles Findlay, the adjutant, later wrote: 'he could not escape the fact of being Lawrence; the end of the war was too recent for this to be unimportant. It was a form of vanity, I think, that made him draw mentally apart from his fellows, wrap himself in an aura of mystery, and rejoice in the excitement his presence created in the barrack room.' But, Findlay added, 'His assumption of mental leadership among the rank and file mattered little while his identity was unrevealed'.[40]

There is little doubt that Lawrence began to abuse this position. He thought the calibre of the officers at Farnborough too low for them to have moral authority over the very able men under their command. Later, he would write to Trenchard: 'I had an uncomfortable feeling that we were better than the officers: and this feeling was strengthened, if not founded on the fact that the officers were treated by the men, off parade, as rather humorous things to have to show respect to. The officers played up to this impression by avoiding all contact with us.'[41]

Findlay recalled an occasion when 'I had to reprimand him for the part he played in a silly and pointless incident. The Orderly Officer, a young lad, was carrying out the usual inspection of dress and arms before mounting the guard, in the course of which he told an airman that he was not satisfied with his turn-out. The airman (it was Ross) replied to the officer in a foreign language, which elicited the inevitable titter from the other members of the guard. This was certainly not in keeping with his expressed desire to remain unnoticed.'[42]

Lawrence could risk the consequences of such insolence because he had now decided to publish the abridgement. He told Bernard Shaw on

November 30th not to trouble himself unduly about reading the complete *Seven Pillars*: 'I don't want to bore you (nice of me!) and if you say it's rot I'll agree with you and cackle with pleasure at finding my judgement doubled. Please laugh and chuck it.'[43] Two days later he wrote to Garnett again, about the abridgement: 'Mention the book to Cape, by all means: but tell him that it will be a costly production, and that I am making Curtis Brown my agent in disposing of it. Of course I'd be very glad if he got it: but it seems to me a speculation unjustifiably large for his resources. The thing may be a complete frost, and will cost £3,000 to produce: and I reckon that would about bust him.'[44]

In due course Lawrence heard from Shaw: 'Patience, patience . . . The truth is, I havnt read it yet. I have sampled it . . . My wife seized it first, and ploughed through from alpha to omega. It took months and months and months; but it carried her through. But the time it took warned me that I must dispose of certain other reading jobs, in respect of which I was tied to time, before tackling it . . . However, I know enough about it now to feel rather puzzled as to what is to be done with it . . . Obviously there are things in it that you cannot publish. Yet many of them are things that WONT die . . . One step is clear enough. The Trustees of the British Museum have lots of sealed writings to be opened in a hundred years . . . You say you have four or five copies of your magnissimum opus. At least a couple should be sealed and deposited in Bloomsbury and in New York . . . Think this over: I am sure to suggest it when I am through with the reading, which is now under weigh. Destruction of the work is out of the question: if I thought you capable of that I should take the book to London, burn down my house here, and tell you that the book had perished in the flames . . . But an abridgment will have to be made for general circulation. There is a need for the main history of the campaign for working purposes.'[45]

Shaw's advice about an abridgement must have seemed a valuable endorsement of the Garnett project, and if Lawrence still entertained any doubts about publication, he set them aside. He replied: 'The book is being abridged. Edward Garnett, a critic, has cut it to 150,000 words, and I'm going to see if a publisher will pay for these miserable orts. If so I'll become a civilian again. You have no idea how repulsive a barrack is as permanent home. It reconciles me to the meanness of the abridgement.'[46] Earlier in this letter he had told Shaw about his enlistment, making only a half-hearted plea for secrecy: 'I'm now an airman in the Air Force: one of those funny little objects in blue clothes who look forlorn when they walk

about the Strand. It keeps me alive (just) and keeps me out of mischief . . .
At present I'm stationed by Aldershot. As the Press would talk rot about
my eccentricity, please don't talk very much of it. It's not a secret, and not
common knowledge.'[47] On the same day he wrote to Garnett that the RAF
'still interests me, and as long as it does I'll stick to it: though my
hankering after flesh-pots is, I fear, too strong to be resisted when there
shall be an alternative livelihood, of a workless character, within reach. So
I won't ask for a loan, thanks: and my puritan self hopes that the *War in
the Desert* will be a failure, to compel me to dwell longer in barracks.'[48]
This letter also contained a hint about Lawrence's plans if he returned to
civilian life: 'The private press has been a life-dream of mine – and has
been twice . . . on the point of coming true. It will come, and will, I hope,
be as good as my expectations.'[49] A week later he wrote to Jonathan
Cape about the proposed abridgement contract: 'I don't want advance
royalties:– at least only about 200 to 300 pounds for immediate necessities'. He added: 'My address is 14 Barton Street, as before: though I can't
at present afford to live there. I'm most completely broke!'[50]

Eventually, Fleet Street papers began to investigate the rumours
of Lawrence's enlistment. It did not take them long to trace him to
Farnborough. On December 16th Guilfoyle reported to Swann that reporters from the *Daily Mail* and *Daily Express* had visited the camp:
'They interviewed two of the junior officers and learning from them that
Colonel Lawrence was not in the Mess and as far as they were concerned
not on the Station, they then asked to see the Adjutant and requested
permission to visit the airmen. This was not granted but they apparently
waited outside the gates and were seen talking to airmen.

'Do you think that all the conjecture and talk is in the best interest of
discipline? As Station Commander I do hope that some definite procedure
will be taken either way.'[51] It was a matter of time before the story became
front-page news, and Guilfoyle could only wait for the storm to break.

On receiving news of the proposed *Seven Pillars* abridgement,
Bernard Shaw had begun to take initiatives of his own. On December 17th
he wrote to Lawrence: 'I knew of course all along that publication was
inevitable in the simple operation of the laws of nature; but until you told
me about the Garnett abridgement and so forth I held my tongue. A day or
two after, I happened to have to discuss a question as to the price of some
new editions of my books with Constables; so I blew in there on that
business, and, being in conference with William Meredith and Otto
Kyllmann, the two senior partners, I led the conversation eastward to

Yemen and Colonel Lawrence. It turned out then that Meredith had met you and knew about the Sybilline copies. I naturally said "Why in thunder didn't you secure it? It's the greatest book in the world". He said he should have very much liked to, but felt that he could not push for it without indelicacy, and could only hope that it would come his way.

'I then expatiated on the qualities of the work, and said that it really ought to be published in the good old eighteenth century style in twelve volumes or so to begin with, the abridgement coming afterwards. This is not at all so impossible as it would have been ten years ago; for people are buying very expensive books now on an unprecedented scale . . . Anyhow, they became intensely interested; and yesterday I received a letter from Kyllmann. He had been rather afraid of cutting in across any arrangement that you might have made, and had accordingly seen Garnett and ascertained that he was acting in his private capacity and not as reader to an already selected publisher.' Shaw concluded that his initiative 'abolishes all approaches and preliminaries in case you would care to deal with Constables: you have nothing to do but come straight to business with them. If not, there is no harm done. But I don't think you can do better unless you would prefer a brace of thoroughgoing modern ruffians who would begin with exploiting the serial rights in the American and English papers with headlines and pictures and all the rest of it.'[52] Since Shaw knew that Garnett was working for Jonathan Cape, the last sentence can only be an unflattering reference to Cape and his partner G. Wren Howard. The letter continued with a long and bantering attack on Lawrence's presence in the Air Force: 'Nelson, slightly cracked after his whack on the head in the battle of the Nile, coming home and insisting on being placed at the tiller of a canal barge, and on being treated as nobody in particular, would have embarrassed the Navy far less'.[53]

Shaw was handing out this typically forthright advice and personal criticism to a man he hardly knew. He had met Lawrence only once, and there had been no more than a brief correspondence between them, mainly to do with Shaw's delayed reading of *Seven Pillars* (even now, he had only just begun to tackle it). Someone more sensitive might have hesitated before writing to a relative stranger in these terms, and might well have guessed that this kind of comment was likely to strengthen rather than weaken Lawrence's resolve to remain in the ranks. However, reticence in such matters was not Shaw's custom.

The letter did not reach Lawrence until Christmas Day, and his publishing arrangements were meanwhile advancing. On December 21st he had written to Cape: 'I left answering you till I had seen Savage [the manager of Curtis Brown's literary agency] because he is in charge of all the business arrangements of my book, till the moment the contracts want signing, and I can't interfere with his discretion to any extent.

'However yesterday I saw him, and what he said makes me hope that you will get the thing . . . Your course is to get hold of Savage; if you meet with difficulties there ask him to consult me, and I'll do what I can (it isn't more than an expression of opinion) on your side . . . I'd enjoy discussing format with Howard, and will hope to have the fun of it in the spring! . . . As for an advance cheque – yes, when the contract is signed I'd be very glad of one: but not till then. I can hold on for a while yet: but the prospect of having some money soon will make me spendthrift.'[54] On the same day Lawrence wrote to Buxton: 'I've decided to sell an abridgement (rather less than one third) of my Arabian narrative, and this will bring in some thousands (perhaps £6,000) next year. After that I'm quite likely to chuck the R.A.F. but meanwhile I hang on to it with no more expenses than artists and a motor-bike'.[55] He was now full of self-confidence. On Christmas Day he wrote to Herbert Baker that he was 'at Farnborough, suffering many things just lately, and provoking my persecutors by laughing at them. It isn't quite so provoking as being meek – but I can't do the meek touch.'[56]

Two days after this, however, the story of his presence in the ranks finally broke. A front-page headline in Blumenfeld's paper, the *Daily Express,* read ' "UNCROWNED KING" AS PRIVATE SOLDIER : LAWRENCE OF ARABIA : FAMOUS WAR HERO BECOMES A PRIVATE : SEEKING PEACE : OPPORTUNITY TO WRITE A BOOK.'[57] Despite the sensational opening, the article gave no precise information about his whereabouts, stating wrongly that he was serving in the Army: 'Colonel Lawrence, archae-ologist, Fellow of All Souls, and king-maker, has lived a more romantic existence than any man of the time. Now he is a private soldier, un-known and unrecognised, performing humdrum barrack routine, in a dull garrison town.'[58]

A follow-up article the next day was far more damaging. It revealed that Lawrence was serving in the RAF at Farnborough as A/c Ross: 'He rises at 6.30 each morning, washes and shaves in cold water, and does physical "jerks" till breakfast time. After breakfast he parades with rifle and bayonet and does a hard day's work.' Nevertheless the article was largely based on speculation. It claimed that: 'Sometimes in the evening he would tell astonishing stories of the East, of wild tribes and exciting fights, of tight corners and marvellous marches over desert sands.'[59] It is conceivable that R. D. Blumenfeld provided the tip-off for this exposure, although he was still in a nursing home. Later, in a rather confused account he claimed that while he was away 'someone in the office learned the story which could not of course be a secret long, and "the beans were spilled." '[60]

On December 27th, the day of the first *Daily Express* story, Lawrence replied to Bernard Shaw's letter about *Seven Pillars*. He was keen to hear critical opinions on the book, but his rejection of Shaw's publishing advice was unequivocal: 'About business. Curtis Brown – or rather Savage, his manager – served with me in the war, and is doing my money-worries on the usual 10% terms. I hate business, and would be child's play for any publisher. I believe Cape, a new publisher of the respectable sort (he runs that divine book of extracts from yourself) is first in the running for my thing: but I've told Savage that I want £300 a year, to live on, and have left it at that, with only two conditions: a. that I have the last word as to type, paper and format. b. that it be a royalty not an out and out sale. It's good of you to have worked up Meredith to the point of offering, and I'll tell Savage about it: but Garnett reads for Cape, and liked parts of the book: so that Cape has a special wish for it. I fancy film and serial rights are worth more than royalties: and my only motive in publishing a scrap of the book is money'.[61]

On December 28th, before receiving this letter, Shaw learned from an article in the *Daily News* that negotiations with Cape for *Seven Pillars* were already well advanced. He seems to have been extremely put out: it appeared that Cape had pre-empted the book, frustrating his own *démarche* on behalf of Constable. He wrote again to Lawrence, enclosing the article from the *Daily News*: 'The cat being now let out of the bag, presumably by Jonathan Cape with your approval, I cannot wait to finish the book before giving you my opinion and giving it strong. IT MUST BE PUBLISHED IN ITS ENTIRETY UNABRIDGED. Later on an abridgment can be considered . . . But anyhow you must not for a moment entertain the notion of publishing an abridgment first, as no publisher would touch the whole work afterwards; and I repeat THE WHOLE WORK MUST BE PUBLISHED. If Cape is not prepared to undertake that, he is not your man, whatever your engagements to him may be. If he has advanced you any money give it back to him, (borrowing it from me if necessary), unless he has undertaken to proceed in the grand manner with a library edition in several volumes. But you can borrow all you want from your banker on the security of the book without being obliged to anybody'.[62]

Shaw offered no excuse for this volte-face, but went on to criticise Cape's edition of *Arabia Deserta*: 'when I was on the point of the outrageous extravagance of ordering it I was told that it was very carelessly proofread. You must be very careful about the Seven Pillars on this point, because corrections are now very expensive; and you may easily get let in for them unless you know your way about as an author.

'The truth is, I am anxious lest you should have committed yourself already. I had ten years on the managing committee of the Society of Authors, and learnt that there is no bottom to the folly and business incompetence of authors or to the unscrupulousness of publishers, who, being in a gambling business, where one live book has to pay for ten duds, cannot afford to lose a single opportunity.

'You must not mind my shoving into your affairs like this. How else can I be of any service? Still, it's rather maddening; and I feel quite as apologetic about it as I ought . . . PS Did you get my last quite recent letter?'[63]

It is difficult not to read, behind Shaw's repeated criticisms of Cape, a determination to secure *Seven Pillars* for his own publisher. His central argument, that the issuing of an abridgement would prevent any kind of fuller publication, could not have been better calculated to influence Lawrence. But just four weeks earlier he had told Lawrence that an abridgement should be published and copies of the whole text placed under embargo in selected libraries. Even now he had not read the book, so there was no new factor to influence his opinion except the approach he had made to Constable. Despite its superficial appeal, his argument about the correct publication sequence was in this instance very weak. Events were to prove him totally wrong: abridgements of *Seven Pillars* would eventually be published in most European languages, yet when the whole text finally became available publishers fell over themselves to secure the rights.[64]

Whatever the motivation behind this letter, the effect on Lawrence of such a harangue from Bernard Shaw must have been devastating. Shaw was one of the most influential literary figures of the age. Garnett, hitherto Lawrence's trusted adviser, earned his living by working for a publisher, whereas Shaw was the outspoken champion of authors' rights. Lawrence had always felt some misgivings about the abridgement. Now he began to fear that he was being manoeuvred by Cape and Garnett into a commercial trap; worse still, that he had to choose between giving permanence to the abridgement or to the full text of *Seven Pillars*. During the last weekend in the year he discussed the position with Raymond Savage, and then on January 1st he wrote to Cape withdrawing from the project; he gave no reason.

If Lawrence had received Shaw's letter a few days later, the contract for the abridgement would already have been signed. He would then have had the money he needed to leave the Air Force and pursue his other plans. Withdrawal from the project left him without an income and meant that he would have to remain in the ranks or seek some other kind of paid work. Without realising it, and for motives which were at best trivial, Shaw had checked Lawrence at the very moment of decision. By doing so he changed the course of Lawrence's life.

Shaw, however, had little thought for the harm he might be doing. On December 31st his wife Charlotte had written to Lawrence, for the first time, in what was clearly an attempt to support her husband's point of view: 'How is it *conceivable, imaginable* that a man who could write the *Seven Pillars* can have any doubts about it? If you don't know it is "a great book" what is the use of anyone telling you so... I devoured the book from cover to cover as soon as I got hold of it. I could not stop. I drove G.B.S. almost mad by insisting upon reading him special bits when he was deep in something else. I am an old woman, old enough at any rate to be your mother; I have met all sorts of men and women of the kind that are called distinguished; I have read their books and discussed them with them. But I have never read anything like this: I don't believe anything really like it has been written before... it is one of the most amazingly individual documents that has ever been written...

'You have been the means of bringing into the world a poignant human document, and now – have faith in the Power that worked through you. About these *** Publishers... I am told I must be "very careful": that anything I say is sure to be libellous. I only want to say one thing. I am greatly honoured by your phrase "divine book of " *selections*, please, not "extracts", since it was I who selected them, but the fact that Cape has that book is an accident. He did *not* publish it, but took it over from a little friend of mine (A. C. Fifield) who, to my great regret, gave up business. I had practically no say in the matter. The reprint of Doughty's *Arabia Deserta* was not uncriticized, was it? . . .

'Your book must be published as a whole. Don't you see that? . . . Publish the book practically as it is, in good print, in a lot of volumes. I am sure Constables will do it for you that way. Both G.B.S. and I have lots of experience about books and we would both *like* to put it at your service.'[65]

Not content to let the matter rest, Shaw wrote again on January 4th, replying to an earlier letter. He displayed little concern for the sensitivities of the man he was writing to: 'Like all heroes, and, I must add, all idiots, you greatly exaggerate your power of moulding the universe to your personal convictions. You have just had a crushing demonstration of the utter impossibility of hiding or disguising the monster you have created. It is useless to protest that Lawrence is not your real name. That will not save you. You may be registered as Higg the son of Snell or Brian de Bois Guilbert or anything else; and if you had only stuck to it or else kept quiet, you might be Higg or Brian still. But you masqueraded as Lawrence and didn't keep quiet; and now Lawrence you will be to the end of your days, and thereafter to the end of what we call modern history. Lawrence may be as great a nuisance to you sometimes as G.B.S. is to me, or as Frankenstein found the man he had manufactured; but you created him, and must now put up with him as best you can.

'As to the book, bear two things in mind about me. First, I am an old and hardened professional; and you are still apparently a palpitating amateur in literature, wondering whether your first MS is good enough to be published, and whether you have a style or not. Second, I am entitled to a reasonable construction; and when I say, as I do, that the work must be published unabridged, I do not mean that it shall be published with the passages which would force certain people either to take an action against you or throw up their jobs. The publisher would take jolly good care of that if you were careless about it. But these passages are few, and can be omitted or paraphrased without injury or misrepresentation . . . You must get used to the limelight. I am naturally a pitiably nervous, timid man, born with a whole plume of white feathers; but nowadays this only gives a zest to the fun of swanking at every opportunity . . . And the people have their rights too, in this matter. They want you to appear always in glory, crying "This is I, Lawrence, Prince of Mecca!" To live under a cloud is to defame God.

'Moral: do your duty by the book; and arrange for its publication at once. It will not bounce out in five minutes, you know. You have the whole publishing world at your feet, as keen as Constables, who have perhaps more capital than Cape. Subject to that limitation you can choose where you will.'[66]

Cape, unaware of Shaw's activities, protested strongly to Lawrence over the sudden and unexplained refusal to publish the abridgement. But Lawrence was now under mounting pressure, and thought it safer to do nothing. Trenchard visited Farnborough on January 3rd and warned him that his position in the Air Force was becoming untenable. Four days later Lawrence wrote to Cape that he could not publish anything while he remained in the RAF: 'That rules out this year, at any rate.'[67] His mind was now in a state of confusion. He had often said that the purpose of the abridgement was to escape from the Air Force, but now something had changed. For the first time, he had discovered what it was like to be the object of sensational press exposure. Hitherto, journalists had eaten out of his hand, and this had led him to the dangerous illusion that he could influence them as he pleased. None of the publicity he had received after the war had prepared him for the shock of his present situation. The RAF now suddenly appeared to be a haven, and he clung to it desperately. He apologised deeply to Cape: 'I'm very sorry to behave in this way, and to do harm to your firm and its prospects. The initial fault was mine, in agreeing to publish the abridgement: and it's another fault to cancel it so late:– but I feel that the fault of letting the thing go to press would be far greater than any of the others, and is one to be avoided at all costs.'[68]

On the same day he wrote to his agent, Savage: 'I came up yesterday and saw Cape and Garvin [who was to have serialised the abridgement in the *Observer*] and made up my mind (is it final? The beastly thing has wobbled so that I despair of its remaining fixed for life) not to publish anything whatever: neither abridgement nor serial, nor full story: at least this year: and probably not so long as I remain in the R.A.F.'[69]

It was now that the Shaws learned how badly their plans had miscarried. Lawrence wrote that he had 'refused to sign any contract for any part of the *Seven Pillars*, to Cape or anyone else. I'd like to publish the whole, but that's as improbable as that I'd walk naked down Piccadilly: not that I'd like that either, but the whole is the only honest thing.'[70] Had Shaw taken the time to read the book himself, he would have understood that it could not be widely published without a great many cuts. As Lawrence remarked on January 7th: 'I'm too fed up with the *Daily Express* to endure the thought of giving away the remainder of myself to them.'[71] The omissions needed if the book were to be issued for general circulation in his lifetime would devalue it, in his eyes, to the same status as the abridgement. Moreover, he had decided before enlisting that the 'Oxford' text was not good enough to issue without further revision.

If he had published the abridgement, he would probably, as Garnett hoped, have improved the longer text at his leisure. There would have been no shortage of buyers for a subscription edition illustrated with the portraits he was still collecting. In January 1923, however, these hopes lay in ruins, and Lawrence's only safe future seemed to be in the ranks of the Air Force. This new dependence suddenly made the RAF much more attractive to him. When his identity was revealed the officers felt awkward and embarrassed, but most of the men stood by him and shielded him from the press with friendly solidarity. By the time the news broke they had worked alongside Lawrence for seven weeks; they greatly admired the splendid Brough Superior motorcycle he had now bought, and they were also well disposed towards him because he lent them money when they were short.

He accepted their admiration and uncomplicated friendship, telling himself that they knew his true qualities too well to be influenced by his 'Lawrence of Arabia' reputation. 'This last adventure in the R.A.F.', he wrote, 'is a chapter in itself. It would be hard to remain inhuman while jostling all days and nights in a crowd of clean and simple men. There is something here which in my life before I'd never met – had hardly dreamed of.'[72]

Though he did not realise it, some aspects of his position began to resemble the life he had enjoyed so much at Carchemish. He told Robert Graves: 'I think I'm going to stay on in the R.A.F. which has the one great merit of showing me humanity very clear and clean. I've never lived commonly before, and I think to run away from the stress of it would be a failing.'[73] Most of Lawrence's fellow aircraftmen at Farnborough were in their early twenties, and he found them 'like Oxford undergraduates in their second term... buds just opening after the restraint of school and home. Their first questioning, their first doubt of an established convention or law or practice, opens a flood-gate in their minds: for if one thing is doubtful all things are doubtful: the world to them has been a concrete, founded, polished thing: and the first crack is portentous. So the Farnborough fellows used to come to me there, after "Lights out," and sit on the box by my bed, and ask questions about every rule of conduct and experience, and about mind and soul and body'.[74]

Lawrence was certain that he would never have a family of his own, yet he retained a normal capacity for affection. He saw how much he could help these younger men whose backgrounds had denied them the education he himself had enjoyed. Like many other people working in a community younger than themselves, he soon had favourites. Two in particular at Farnborough were A. E. Chambers and R. A. M. Guy. 'Jock' Chambers had an intelligent and enquiring mind which nowadays would undoubtedly have won him a place at university. Lawrence recognised his ability and encouraged him to educate himself through reading (Lawrence gave him a subscription to the London Library). Guy was less intellectual, though he too liked reading. Lawrence enjoyed his company, and once wrote of him: 'the little man embodies the best of the Air Force ranks as I picture them.'[75]

It has been suggested, by writers who have seen only a small part of the surviving correspondence between Lawrence and Guy, that the basis of this friendship was homosexual. This claim raises two issues: first about the nature of Lawrence's relationship with Guy, and secondly the more general question of Lawrence's sexual inclination during these years in the ranks. As regards Guy, the suggestion of homosexual attraction rests on three pieces of 'evidence': Guy's good looks, the nicknames by which Lawrence addressed him, and a passage from one of Lawrence's letters.

The first question, of Guy's appearance, was discussed in the biography by John Mack: *A Prince of our Disorder*. He quoted Jock Chambers as saying that Guy was 'beautiful, like a Greek God'.[76] A few weeks before Mack's interview, Chambers made a very similar statement to me: that Lawrence had once joked to him of Guy's looks, saying 'they were almost angelic, but the effect was shattered by his vile Birmingham accent'.[77] Taken on its own, this observation is hardly evidence for homosexual passion.

Guy, who was short and fair-haired, was called 'Rabbit' or 'Poppet' in the ranks, where nicknames based on physical appearance are very common. The choice was often cruel: on occasions Lawrence himself had to tolerate being addressed as 'Shortarse'. Mack and other biographers such as Desmond Stewart imply that 'Rabbit' and 'Poppet' were used exclusively by Lawrence, apparently without realising that these were Guy's ordinary service nicknames.

The final piece of 'evidence' is a letter to Guy in which, according to Stewart, Lawrence 'wrote ecstatically about their closeness'.[78] It is misleading, however, to cite this letter without explaining the context. The letter was written about a year after Lawrence had left Farnborough. He had met Guy briefly some weeks previously, and in parting must have said something which Guy took to imply that they would not meet again. It is quite possible that this was in fact what Lawrence had meant to say, because his subsequent correspondence with Guy shows that he made little effort to continue their friendship once they had ceased to serve at the same station.[79]

Guy valued his friendship with such a famous personality, but this was not his sole motive for wishing to keep in touch with Lawrence. He was planning to marry a girl in Birmingham, and Lawrence had already given a modest sum of money to help the young couple. After Lawrence's rather definite farewell, Guy had evidently written a letter of protest. When Lawrence replied (as it happened this was at Christmas), he clearly meant to reassure Guy while confirming the distance between them. Hence the frequently quoted remark: 'When I said "This is the last" I meant that again for an overwhelming time we were going to be apart. Letters don't work, nor do casual meetings, for the shadow of the near end lies over them, so that the gaiety is forced and the talk foolish. You and me, we're very un-matched, and it took some process as slow and kindly and persistent as the barrack-room communism to weld us comfortably together. People aren't friends till they have said all they can say, and are able to sit together, at work or rest, hour-long without speaking.

'We never got quite to that, but were nearer it daily... and since S.A. died I haven't experienced any risk of that happening'.[80] Thus, when taken in context, the meaning of Lawrence's remark is exactly the opposite of Stewart's interpretation.

None of the evidence cited as proof of a homosexual affair between Lawrence and Guy stands up to examination.[81] While Guy seems to have been very ready to ask for money, he was only one of the many people Lawrence helped financially.[82] A letter written not long after leaving Farnborough shows Lawrence's assumption that Guy and Chambers (who both later married) were heterosexual. A female admirer had sent Lawrence a gift, addressed to Farnborough; Guy had forwarded it, and Lawrence, who did not want the gift, sent it back to Guy, writing: 'The enclosed is the letter which you and the postman so kindly sent me. It will please you and Jock [Chambers]. She says she is sending something else. Please keep it. Probably a knitted tie, or a pin cushion: or a photograph. I've blotted out her name to prevent accidents. Some of you youths are so impulsive.'[83] Lawrence's later letters contain amicable references to Guy's wife and children.

There has been a good deal of speculation about the more general question of Lawrence's sexual orientation during these service years.

Close friendships between people of the same sex are common in all walks of life and inevitable in all-male communities such as the armed services. It is patently absurd to suggest that all such friendships must be homosexual, yet this is the essence of many allegations about Lawrence. There is a popular belief that the service environment is attractive to homosexuals but, as a matter of fact, the lack of privacy would make it far more difficult to conduct a homosexual affair in the ranks than in civilian life. Lawrence dealt with this misconception in *The Mint*: 'Report accuses us of sodomy, too: and anyone listening in to a hut of airmen would think it a den of infamy. Yet we are too intimate, and too bodily soiled, to attract one another. In camps all things, even if not public, are publicly known: and in the four large camps of my sojourning there have been five fellows actively beastly. Doubtless their natures tempted others: but they fight its expression as the normal airman fights his desire for women, out of care for physical fitness.'[84]

Throughout his life Lawrence was deeply influenced by the ethical standards he had learned in childhood, and he set a great value on integrity in his dealings with other people, especially those who would naturally have looked up to him. He would probably have been shocked and bitterly ashamed if he had suspected that there was any sexual motive behind his friendships in the ranks. In later years, when he came to believe that carnality played an important role in all human motivation, he seems to have avoided close friendships with anyone.

In 1927 Lawrence would describe himself in a letter to a friend as 'really celibate'; he went on to say: 'Celibacy is unnatural, in the real sense, and it overturns a man's balance: for it throws him either on himself (which is unwholesome, like sucking your own tail, in snakes) or on friendship to satisfy the urge of affection within... and such friendship may easily turn into sex-perversion. If I have missed all these things, as I hope and you seem to suggest – well then, I'm barrenly lucky. It has not been easy: and it leads, in old age, to misery'.[85]

All the evidence suggests that during these post-war years Lawrence felt a deep revulsion towards the physical aspects of sex; yet despite the strength of this personal view, he refrained from criticising other people's conduct provided that he was unaffected by it. In part, this may have been a reaction against the prescriptive moral stance adopted by his mother and elder brother. Tolerance, however, does not imply personal approval or involvement. On this issue, as on the question of imperialism, Lawrence's attitude was ahead of his time.

During January 1923 the publicity about his presence in the RAF continued. His future in the ranks seemed extremely uncertain, and he again toyed with the idea of making money from *Seven Pillars*. Taking Shaw's advice into account, he 'began to think of publishing, not an abridgment, but the whole story . . . So I sketched to Cape the possibility of a limited, privately-printed, subscription edition of two thousand copies, illustrated with all the drawings made for me by some twenty of the younger artists. Cape was staggered for the first moment, but then rose to it – suggesting half-profits, and a serial-issue of a quarter of it in *The Observer*, and American copyrights, and all the necessary decorations'.[86] In mid-January he wrote to Graves that the book 'may be printed privately, in a limited subscription edition, next year. A sort of 15 guinea book, almost unprocurable. I hovered for a while this year with the notion of a censored version: but that seems dishonest, until the whole story is available.'[87]

Cape responded quickly, sending a new contract to sign; but before Lawrence had done so, the RAF decided that A/c Ross placed junior officers at Farnborough in an impossible situation. Sir Samuel Hoare, Secretary of State for Air, later wrote: 'I was horrified at the [Press] disclosure, and so were the Air Force officers who were drilling the new recruit . . . How, they not unnaturally asked, were they to deal on the barrack square with a private who was a Colonel and a D.S.O., and one of the most famous of war heroes? The position, which had been extremely delicate even when it was shrouded in secrecy, became untenable when it was exposed. The only possible course was to discharge Airman Ross.'[88] Lawrence was sent briefly on leave, and by the end of January he was a civilian once more.

These events changed the nature of Lawrence's life in one important way. From now on he would be regarded by the world's press as an enigmatic figure, whose motives and influence were open to endless speculation; his actions would be watched and reported, and casual acquaintances would find a ready market for 'revealing' articles about their friendship with him. The journalists who hounded him liked to claim that he enjoyed 'backing into the limelight',[89] but his behaviour does not bear out this claim. Before 1922 he had sought press attention on behalf of the Arab cause, but this campaign had now served its purpose and the resulting publicity seemed to have died. Following the discovery of his enlistment, however, popular interest refocused inescapably on his own life. He clung to a naïve conviction that the Fleet Street editors he had befriended in the past would help him, and from time to time he would plead with them to be left alone; but the effect was never lasting. This unwelcome publicity soon imposed very real restrictions on his personal freedom, yet his attempts to escape from it almost invariably made matters worse.

CHAPTER 33

Tank Corps Private
January – December 1923

ALTHOUGH Lawrence had half-expected the RAF decision, it still came as a shock. He began to see it as a personal defeat, quite different from leaving the service of his own volition. Later he claimed bitterly that the story had been sold to the press by one of the Farnborough officers, but there is no evidence to support this allegation.[1]

Considering the willingness he had previously shown to leave the Air Force, and the opportunity to secure an income for life from *Seven Pillars*, his reaction to dismissal must have owed a great deal to wounded pride. The press publicity had ceased within days of the first scoop headlines, and there was no follow-up story. Yet he seems to have become utterly obtuse, refusing to consider his real options or to sign Cape's new contract. He insisted to anyone who would listen that his only possible course was a return to the ranks of the RAF.

Depressed by the collapse of all his plans, he saw no need to rethink his position; instead he fell back on his original decision to enlist. His letters began once again to talk of a downward urge; he was 'determined not any more to be respectable.'[2] He appealed for reinstatement in the RAF, first to Trenchard and then to Hoare, with whom he dined on January 27th. Hoare was adamant, and hoped that Lawrence would find a job more suited to his talents. Leo Amery, who was also present, recalled that there was 'a tremendous talk' after dinner about the future role of the RAF in Mesopotamia: 'Lawrence insisted that there was no difficulty once we had peace with the Turks in withdrawing all the troops and keeping only such Air Force as was required for Imperial purposes.'[3] Amery, at that time First Lord of the Admiralty, said half-jokingly that it might be possible to find him a quiet job in the Naval Air Wing.

The following day Lawrence, who had gone into hiding at a small hotel in Frensham, Surrey, sent another appeal to Trenchard: 'I've been looking round, these last few days, and find an odd blank:– there is nothing I can think of, that I want to do, and in consequence, nothing that I will do! And the further I get from the R.A.F. the more I regret its loss.'[4]

He asked to be given another chance in some remote station, where his identity would be known from the start by the CO: 'The last thing I wish to seem is importunate: but I'm so sure that I played up at Farnborough, and did good, rather than harm to the fellows in camp there with me, that I venture to put in a last word for myself.'[5]

Trenchard replied two days later: 'I would like to agree with all you have written but the trivial circumstances have been too much for me, and for you. It is the smallness in it that has brought about the decision to finish it, and I know you will accept it however much you hate it.'[6] Trenchard had already offered Lawrence a commission in the Air Force, and now he suggested work as an Armoured Car officer. But Lawrence was determined to return to the ranks. He went to see Amery, hoping to find something in the Navy. Amery noted in his diary: 'He wants to be quite clear of the Middle Eastern business for the present, more particularly when his book appears, as he hates the idea of having to discuss things with everybody, being invited out to dinner, etc. What he would like to do is to look after the Naval Stores at Bermuda or something harmless of that sort for a few years. A very strange creature.'[7]

At the end of January Lawrence wrote telling Garnett that he had abandoned the idea of publication: 'Of course everything in connection with Cape and the *Seven Pillars* is over. I now feel that I was an ass ever to have dreamed of publishing anything.'[8] Yet the book had become his main interest in life, especially since prospects of writing about the RAF now seemed hopeless. When he went to lunch with the Shaws on February 1st (this was only the second time he had met them) he tried hard to discover what they really thought about *Seven Pillars*. But Shaw 'would only say cryptic words, all of commendation. These are nice, like chocolate éclairs or cream puffs, but not a meal. Mrs. Shaw praised even more than he did. I hung on until nearly four o'clock, but not even boredom would show through his courtesy, so that my curiosity came away unfed. My private opinion is that she's read it, and he hasn't: and can't: but is much afraid to shock her by letting on.'[9]

Although Lawrence had very little money, he now wrote to several artists and sitters about work on new portraits: 'I'm hoping for about fifty heads in all.'[10] On February 6th he asked Colonel C. E. Wilson if he was willing to be painted by Kennington, and the next day told William Roberts that Wingate, who had proved very elusive until now 'will write to you shortly and suggest a time.'[11] He explained his financial difficulties to Paul Nash: 'About cash. I'd told you my hope in February to have more money for drawings – and I haven't. I'll just be able to pay those I have commissioned in anticipation, and that's all. I'm very sorry . . . I'm still hoping for money soon: and will let you know at once if, or rather when, I get it: but a necessary condition of a surplus is that I should have no personal expenses: and I'm rather particular about what I do.'[12] Nine days later, however, he asked Kathleen Scott if she would paint Hubert Young, and told Roberts: 'I *do* want to get the whole lot finished this year.'[13] He also wrote happily to C. E. Wilson: 'I've just scored an excellent head of Clayton, by Nicholson, and a good Alan Dawnay, by Rothenstein. Hogarth, Wingate, and Winterton are being drawn at the moment. There are only six or seven more to do . . . the portrait drawings will . . . make the eventual book magnificent!'[14] Hearing that Jafaar Pasha was in London, Lawrence contacted Eric Kennington and arranged still another portrait.

On 17th February 1923 Sir Philip Chetwode wrote from the War Office to say that it would be possible for Lawrence to enlist in the Tank Corps as a private soldier. The Tank Corps did not seem a bad substitute for the RAF. It was a technical branch, and Lawrence had understood the value of armoured cars during the desert campaigns. More important, however, he also knew that men had sometimes been allowed to transfer from the Tank Corps to the Air Force. Chetwode wrote that Colonel Sir Hugh Elles, who commanded the Tank Corps Training Centre at Bovington in Dorset, would be in London the following week and had suggested that he and Lawrence should meet. Chetwode concluded: 'If you come to a satisfactory arrangement, would you call here at the War Office to see General Vesey the Director of Organisation, as there are certain matters which he would have to arrange with you before the affair is carried through.'[15]

One of these matters was the question of a new pseudonym. The previous one, John Hume Ross, had been chosen for him by the Air Ministry, but when Lawrence went to make the administrative arrangements for enlistment 'the recruiting Staff Officer in the War Office said I must take a fresh name. I said, "What's yours?" He said "No you don't". So I seized the *Army List*, and snapped it open at the Index, and said "It'll be the first one-syllabled name in this" '.[16] He was to become 7875698 Private T. E. Shaw.

Before returning to the ranks, Lawrence took the surviving manuscript of *Seven Pillars* to Oxford and presented it to the Bodleian Library. He had known the librarian, Dr Cowley, since before the war. Afterwards he wrote: 'In giving my MS to the Bodleian I acted perhaps unhumorously, taking myself a little too seriously as a classic. Cowley was equal to the occasion, and never smiled at all throughout the transaction. Whether he has a treasure or not the next century can tell. It rids me of a bulky weighty volume.'[17]

On 12th March 1923 Lawrence arrived at Bovington Camp, where all Tank Corps recruits had to go through their eighteen weeks' basic training. A few days later he wrote to Jock Chambers: 'The camp is beautifully put – a wide heath, of flint and sand, with pines and oak-trees, and much rhododendron coming slowly into bloom. When the heather flowers in a few weeks there will be enough to please me'. But he was not enthusiastic about army life: 'One of my sorrows is the recruits' course . . . and a consequent imprisonment in the camp for a month, being damnably shouted at.'[18]

Lawrence now had time to take stock of his position and to reflect upon the sequence of events that had brought him to Bovington. His letters became more gloomy as he began to adjust to the realities of the situation in which he now found himself. In this regard, it was unfortunate that his first enlistment had been in the RAF. At that time the Air Force had only existed as an independent service for four years, and there were those who thought it should be reintegrated with the Army. As a result Lawrence had been subjected to a good deal of anti-Army propaganda at Uxbridge: 'Day and night the distinction between airmen and soldiers is dinned into us by all comers . . . We identify the Army with its manner of life and already sincerely despise and detest it . . . Soldiers are part of a machine and their virtue is in subordinating themselves within their great company.'[19] Before he reached Bovington he was already expecting to dislike what he found.

After a week he wrote to Lionel Curtis, whom he had first met in 1918: 'My mind moves me this morning to write you a whole series of letters, to be more splendid than the *Lettres de Mon Moulin* . . . What should the preliminaries be? A telling why I joined? As you know I don't know! Explaining it to Dawnay I said "Mind-suicide": but that's only because I'm an incorrigible phraser. Do you, in reading my complete works, notice that tendency to do up small packets of words foppishly?

'At the same time there's the reason why I have twice enlisted, in those same complete works: on my last night in Barton Street I read chapters

113 to 118 [the series of very introspective chapters in *Seven Pillars*, XCIX-CIII in current editions] and saw implicit in them my late course. The months of politics with Winston were abnormal, and the R.A.F. and Army are natural. The Army (which I despise with all my mind) is more natural than the R.A.F.: for at Farnborough I grew suddenly on fire with the glory which the air should be, and set to work full steam to make the others vibrate to it like myself. I was winning too, when they chucked me out: indeed I rather suspect I was chucked out for that. It hurt the upper storey that the ground-floor was grown too keen.'[20]

The letter (which was followed over several months by four others in the same vein) reveals only too clearly the confusion in Lawrence's mind: 'perhaps there's a solution to be found in multiple personality. It's my reason which condemns the book and the revolt, and the new nationalities: because the only rational conclusion to human argument is pessimism such as Hardy's, a pessimism which is very much like the wintry heath, of bog and withered plants and stripped trees, about us . . . Lorde what a fog of words! What I would say is that reason proves there is no hope, and we therefore hope on, so to speak, on one leg of our minds'.[21] He was now re-reading Thomas Hardy's novels, and the mood of this letter probably owed something to their influence. Hardy lived only a few miles from Bovington, and Lawrence was eager to meet him. On March 20th (the day after writing to Curtis) Lawrence wrote to Robert Graves asking him for an introduction.

A week later, in another letter to Curtis, Lawrence reflected upon the differences he saw between the enlisted men at Bovington and those he had known in the RAF: 'There we were excited about our coming service. We talked and wondered of the future, almost exclusively. There was a constant recourse to imagination, and a constant rewarding of ourselves therefore. The fellows were decent, but so wrought up by hope that they were carried out of themselves . . . There was a sparkle round the squad.

'Here every man has joined because he was down and out: and no one talks of the Army or of promotion, or of trades and accomplishments. We are all here unavoidably, in a last resort, and we assume this world's failure in one-another, so that pretence would be not merely laughed at, but as near an impossibility as anything human. We are social bed-rock, those unfit for life-by-competition: and each of us values the rest as cheap as he knows himself to be.'[22]

He went on to sketch out the conclusions he had now drawn about the shallowness of civilisation: 'Can there be profit, or truth, in all these modes and sciences and arts of ours? The leisured world for hundreds, or perhaps thousands of years has been jealously working and recording the advance of each generation for the starting-point of the next – and here these masses are as animal, as carnal as were their ancestors before Plato and Christ and Shelley and Dostoevsky taught and thought. In this crowd it's made startlingly clear how short is the range of knowledge, and what poor conductors of it ordinary humans are.'[23]

Lawrence then applied this argument to himself with profound bitterness, seeing intellectual activity as a deceptive superstructure which served to conceal a 'black core ... of animality.' He reached a conclusion that had never previously appeared in his writing: 'It isn't the filth of it which hurts me, because you can't call filthy the pursuit of a bitch by a dog, or the mating of birds in springtime ... but I lie in bed night after night with this cat-calling carnality seething up and down the hut, fed by streams of fresh matter from twenty lecherous mouths ... and my mind aches with the rawness of it ... We are all guilty alike, you know. You wouldn't exist, I wouldn't exist, without this carnality. Everything with flesh in its mixture is the achievement of a moment when the lusty thought of Hut 12 has passed to action and conceived ... A filthy business all of it, and yet Hut 12 shows me the truth behind Freud. Sex is an integer in all of us, and the nearer nature we are, the more constantly, the more completely a product of that integer. These fellows are the reality, and you and I, the selves who used to meet in London and talk of fleshless things, are only the outward wrappings of a core like these fellows.'[24]

The romantic Victorian concepts that he had so willingly adopted in his youth were one by one falling away. His evangelical Christianity had faded before the war; at Uxbridge he had written: 'Hungry time has taken from me year by year more of the Creed's clauses, till now only the first four words remain. Them I say defiantly, hoping that reason may be stung into new activity when it hears there's yet a part of me which escapes its rule'.[25] The vision of the 'noble savage', which had been a guiding principle during his Carchemish years, had crumbled during the Arab Revolt: 'I was tired to death of these Arabs; petty incarnate Semites who attained heights and depths beyond our reach, though not beyond our sight'.[26] He had abandoned one of the fundamental tenets of his Victorian upbringing: belief in the progress of mankind,[27] and now he had concluded that romantic love, a concept he had been brought up to revere, was nothing more than animal lust. Like many others of his generation he had accepted these values uncritically, without questioning their validity or logical consistency. He lacked both the intellectual bent and the interest in moral philosophy that might have helped him to build up an alternative set of values; yet he was by nature deeply introspective, and the disintegration of his beliefs had taken him to the brink of nihilism.

As soon as the new recruits were allowed out of camp, Lawrence brought his motorcycle to Bovington, finding a release from his grim thoughts by riding through the Dorset countryside. Alec Dixon, a corporal at the camp, later wrote: 'One Wednesday afternoon Shaw appeared in the lines with a powerful Brough motor-cycle of the latest design, the cost of which represented, to a private soldier, about two years' pay . . . Now where, the N.C.Os. asked one another, did that bloke Shaw get hold of that bike?

'Three days later the Brough again appeared in the lines, but this time with a side-car, a rakish affair of polished aluminium. The N.C.Os. goggled, and did some more mental arithmetic. The recruits, dazzled and impressed by these toys, were much too excited to count their cost. They stood in an admiring circle round the Brough and watched enviously while its owner wriggled himself into a flying suit of sleek black leather. There was a shy murmuring among the spectators; someone whispered "joyrides". Shaw, now gloved and helmeted, turned to them with a grin. "Joyrides?" he said thoughtfully. "Of course! Who's going to be the first?"

'So, one by one, the recruits were taken out in the sidecar... Seventy miles an hour was nothing to Shaw... and *couldn't* that little bloke ride a motor-bike! . . . Within a week he was known throughout the camp as "Broughie" Shaw, a nickname that clung to him for the remainder of his stay at Bovington.'[28]

It was now possible for Lawrence to make visits outside camp, and on March 25th he wrote to Thomas Hardy's wife: 'A letter from Robert Graves (to whom I had written) tells me that I'm to get into communication with you. It feels rather barefaced, because I haven't any qualifications to justify my seeing Mr. Hardy: only I'd very much like to. *The Dynasts* and the other poems are so wholly good to my taste.

'It adds to my hesitation that I'm a private in the Tank Corps, at Wool, and would have to come across in uniform. You may have feelings against soldiers. Also I'm therefore not master of my own time. They let us off on Wednesdays, Saturdays, and Sundays at noon: and I have a motor cycle so that getting over to Dorchester is only a matter of minutes. I must be in camp again at 9.30 P.M: but between that and noon on any one of those three days for the next three months I should be free, if you are good enough to offer me a time.'[29] Mrs Hardy replied favourably, and on March 29th Lawrence went to tea at Max Gate. It was the first of many visits.

There were other matters to distract Lawrence from camp life. The five *Oxford Times* copies of *Seven Pillars* were still circulating, and successive readers told him that it was a remarkable work. Reassured of his skill as a writer, he wrote at the end of March to Jonathan Cape: 'If you, as a publisher, ever have anything in French which needs translating (for a fee!) please give me a chance at it. I've plenty of leisure in the Army, and my French is good, and turning it into English is a pleasure to me: also the cash would be welcome, however little it was'.[30]

Garnett must have heard of this request, for he wrote trying patiently to bring Lawrence back to serious writing. Lawrence replied on April 12th: 'Revise the book? Do you know, I've now reached the happy point of being really sorry that ever I wrote it! Apologies: I must be exasperating to work with: but what can I do about it? Any idea of working over it again must wait. Projects of epochal writings flit – or flash, through my head. If I can take one on the wing I'll look at it carefully... but this atmosphere is hostile to everything.'[31]

On a smaller scale, he was now taking immense care over the literary quality of his letters, which were sometimes redrafted more than once.[32] Many of them contain polished descriptions which are little short of essays. One piece of writing that survives from this period was probably written in the Tank Corps classroom at Bovington. It describes part of the flight Lawrence had made to Egypt in the spring of 1919.

A Sea Trip, Essay, Pte. T.E.Shaw, 18.IV.23.

We were in Crete, at Suda Bay, when there came a wireless message that a Handley-Page, with an urgent diplomat on board, would arrive in the afternoon, halting with us on its way to Egypt. We stood by all day, to fill it up, but it arrived too late to reach Africa before sunset: so that perforce it stayed the night on our aerodrome.

The new pilots told us that their starboard engine was uncertain, and that therefore they would be glad of convoy across the wide sea. One of our flying-boats was ready, and its commander agreed to go with the Handley as far as Sollum in Africa, and to let me accompany him.

We started at dawn, rising from the harbour after a run of about six hundred yards:– but the Handley was not ready. We circled round, waiting for her. She got up, made a short flight, descended, and signalled 'a breakdown' to us. We returned to the harbour, where after half an hour the diplomat-passenger arrived by car to suggest that the flying-boat take him straight through to Alexandria. Our commander worked out the distances and found it possible.

Accordingly an hour later we were off again, flying over Canea, round the western tip of Crete, in towards Messara, and then took a due southern course, out across the open Mediterranean, towards Sollum two hundred miles away. The engines (twin R.R. eights) were beating perfectly, with that slow harmonic "munch munch" of aero engines exactly tuned: and as the minutes passed we forgot their roar, forgot the rush of wind past our heads, and had attention only for the views about us.

After a while even the views faded from our minds. We had risen high, to some eight thousand feet, and the sea beneath us was specklessly blue, and the sky above us was specklessly blue, and the two elements mirrored each other so precisely that even the horizons were indistinguishable. Lacking a sky-line, our pilot had to fly only by instruments, and we in the machine were like souls suspended motionless in unchanging ether, conscious of no movement, of no space, hardly of time – for comparing notes with one another afterwards we could not rightly say if the four hours of our crossing had seemed to us a moment or an age. For that space our minds had ceased to exist.

The landfall was ideal. Our azure world was suddenly cut, in front of us, by a burning yellow bar, the sandy coast of Africa, steeped in sunlight. Our plane swooped down in exciting circles, splashed into the sea outside the little bay of Sollum, and ran, a black knife in a plume of spray, alongside the breakwater. A launch was ready waiting with petrol, we refilled, and flew calmly along-shore to Alexandria.[33]

The quality of this essay alone would have raised questions about Lawrence's past. Alec Dixon recorded that: 'My idle speculation about Private Shaw quickened to curiosity when I found that he exerted – or appeared to exert – a remarkable influence over his fellow recruits. It was significant that the recruits eschewed swearing and smutty backchat whenever Shaw paid them a visit . . . Scarcely a day passed but I heard some new and fantastic tale of this new recruit, and it was significant that most of the gossip came not from the young soldiers but from the N.C.Os. Sergeants and corporals were heard to say, peevishly, that they couldn't "place" the fellow, which meant that they wanted to label Private Shaw because he was gravely disturbing their peace of mind. An unclassified recruit is, as any soldier will tell you, a constant menace to authority, a fly in the ointment of good order and military discipline . . . it was clear to me that his quiet manner and non-commital grin had captured the imagination of the men with whom he lived.'[34] From his experience at Farnborough, Lawrence knew that revelation of his identity would do him no harm in the ranks, and after a few weeks at Bovington he let the secret out.

While he was keen to hear literary opinions of *Seven Pillars*, he also sent the draft to friends who had first-hand knowledge of the campaign. Knowing that parts of the book had been written from memory, he asked them to correct any mistakes they found. For example, he wrote to Buxton: 'I wonder what you will think of the work. Anything critical (moral, intellectual, military, or merely on a point of fact) which you please to write in the ample margins will be very useful to me. Please correct with special severity the account of the Camel Corps march in Book IX. By accident of fate and my pen, the Imperial Camel Corps may have to rely mainly on this book for their future fame: so let's have it right.'[35] Occasional slips were to be expected, and seemed to Lawrence inevitable. Also, he had been 'wrapped up in my burden in Arabia, and saw things only through its distorting prism: and so did third parties wrong. It wasn't meant: just the inevitable distraction of a commander whose spirit was at civil war within himself'.[36]

A letter written on May 11th to A. P. Wavell set out Lawrence's own assessment of *Seven Pillars* at this time, and is particularly interesting since his opinion would change radically not long afterwards: 'though (as of a son) I can see and say no good of my book, yet I'm glad when others praise it. I hate it and like it by turns, and know that it's a good bit of writing, and often wish it wasn't. If I'd aimed less high I'd have hit my mark squarer, and made a better little thing of it. As it stands it's a great failure (lacking architecture, the balance of parts, coherence, stream-lining): and oddly enough among my favourite books are the other great failures – *Moby Dick, Also sprach Zarathustra, Pantagruel,* – books where the authors went up like a shoot of rockets, and burst. I don't mean to put mine into that degree of the class: but it is to me as *Zarathustra* was to Nietzsche, something bigger than I could do.

'Apart from literature, how does it strike you as history? It's hard to see another man's campaign – but you saw as much of mine as I saw of yours... does my record of mine stand up, so to speak, upon its military feet? I've never posed as a soldier, and feel that the campaign side of the book may be technically weak. That's why I was glad you asked to read it, because I hope you'll have an opinion (critical not laudatory) on your professional side. Bartholomew made no comment. That's the worst of writing too long a book... it gets beyond criticism, by being too abounding in weak and strong points . . . As for holding it private – well I've suffered more than I can bear of public discussion and praise, and the insufficiency and obliquity of it are like a nightmare of memory. To publish the whole book might cause a new clamour, for I don't hide from myself that it might be a successful book, as sales went. To censor it would mean practical re-writing, and I'm weary of the work put into it already: also it feels a little dishonest to hide parts of the truth. Further I remind myself that the feelings of some English, some French and some Arabs might be hurt by some of the things I tell of. Against these instincts you have to set the vanity of an amateur who's tried to write, and would like to be in print as an author: and my need of money to live quietly upon. It's a nice calculation, with the balance just against, and so I bury all my talents!'[37]

Lawrence found that the Tank Corps made few demands on his time: 'it will do to pass a while in,' he told Buxton, 'and next year I'll have a fair chance of getting to India.'[38] He was moving towards a new stance: that service life, while uninteresting, was also undemanding, providing him with food and lodging yet leaving him free to give his mind to other things. On May 12th he spelt out the philosophy which was to sustain him for some years: 'I'm fit, and the sort of job I do doesn't worry me, since the only adventures and interests I have are in my head, and the army leaves you all your thinking-time to yourself . . . I quite agree that you can't get satisfaction for life out of working for a living . . . but can't you work for something else? In my case I try to write, and read half my spare time, and get interest in looking at the others doing things, and wondering why they do them... it's what they call the reflective mind . . . I've . . . found that the way out lay in the freedom of my mind. Give the world the use of your body and keep the rest for yourself.'[39]

Despite this intellectual self-justification Lawrence suffered from fits of deep depression. Two days later he wrote to Lionel Curtis: 'I consume the day (and myself) brooding, and making phrases and reading and thinking again, galloping mentally down twenty divergent roads at once, as apart and alone as in Barton Street in my attic. I sleep less than ever, for the quietness of night imposes thinking on me: I eat breakfast only, and refuse every possible distraction and employment and exercise. When my mood gets too hot and I find myself wandering beyond control I pull out my motor-bike and hurl it top-speed through these unfit roads for hour after hour. My nerves are jaded and gone near dead, so that nothing less than hours of voluntary danger will prick them into life: and the 'life' they reach then is a melancholy joy at risking something worth exactly 2/9 a day.'[40]

At the end of May, Jonathan Cape took up Lawrence's request for translation work, sending an awesome proposal: an English rendering of J. C. Mardrus's four-thousand-page *Mille et une Nuits* (*The Arabian Nights*). Lawrence had owned and discarded the translation Sir Richard Burton had made from the original Arabic. He replied on June 4th: 'I've been thinking over Mardrus – it's a big idea: and a good one, I believe. Much the best version of the "nights" in any language (not excepting the original which is in coffee-house talk!) and it's ambitious to make a still-better English version: and yet I think it's possible. Better, I mean, as prose. The correctness of Mardrus can't be bettered. The rivalry in English isn't high. Payne crabbed: Burton unreadable: Lane pompous: if yours gets the name of the best version it will sell now, or at long last: but it's a long book, and means a good deal of money down. I can't think the French publishers will ask much for the English rights.

'As for time – I'd like to do it very well... into as good English as we moderns can write... for the essence of the "nights" lies in their goodness as stories, and the better to read the better they will feel:– and I don't know how long Mardrus is. Less than Burton, I know, but it's years since I read him, and then it was in a picture filled folio, and I never noted its length.

'I've lots of time, and could do up to two thousand very decent words a day, average: and would like doing – well some of it, for there are dull patches! However it's a great chance and if you can satisfy your end I'll do my best my end. Anonymous of course? You will pass yours as "Mardrus" for he has the reputation.

'I'll be eager to hear how the idea grows with you.'[41]

In the meantime Cape asked Lawrence to translate *Le Gigantesque*, a novel by Adrien le Corbeau describing the life cycle of a giant sequoia tree. Lawrence agreed, but also pressed for the Mardrus, a fitting sequel for Cape to Doughty's *Arabia Deserta*: 'I'm glad you still think of carrying it out: it's a fine thing . . . Wouldn't the Medici [Society] do a de luxe [edition] for you? Or could you get the Chiswick [Press] people to give you some proportion on hand-made [paper]? There exists no luxury edition of the proper *Nights* today.

'How about bawdy parts? Toned down, omitted, or left to stand?'[42]

Lawrence soon found, however, that literary translation was more demanding than he had anticipated. As he worked on *Le Gigantesque* he realised that a translator very clearly sees shortcomings in the original. After a month he wrote to Cape: 'I started gaily: did about twenty pages into direct swinging English then turned back and read it, and it was horrible. The bones of the poor thing showed through.

'So I cancelled that, and did it again more floridly. The book is written very commonplacely, by a man of good imagination and a bad mind and unobservant. Consequently it's banal in style and ordinary in thought, and very interesting in topic.

'I've dressed up about a third of it in grand-sounding prose to hide its hollowness. And am not pleased with it. What hurry are you in? I'll finish translating it in about ten days – and would like then to set it aside for a week and then paraphrase the whole thing again from end to end . . . Sorry for making a mess of it: but it's infuriating to find second-class meta-physics, and slip-shod writing, on so extraordinarily good a theme. I'd like to wring Le Corbeau's neck.'[43]

He sent Cape the first half of the manuscript on August 11th: 'I still feel it very deficient, both as English and as a work of fiction. However I also feel that it's better than the French. If the man had had a grain of humour.'[44] To follow this work, which Lawrence titled *The Forest Giant*, Cape proposed a book called *Sturly*, by Pierre Custot. The *Arabian Nights* project fell through because Cape discovered that a translation had already been made by E. Powys Mathers and was on the point of publication. Lawrence was very disappointed: 'I'm sorry about Mardrus. I'd have done you something very good there.'[45] This was another turning-point: if he had committed himself to *The Arabian Nights* in 1923, the work would have filled his off-duty time for several years, and would have kept him from the final revision of *Seven Pillars*.

Lawrence was constantly reminded of *Seven Pillars*, for instance when the Hardys read and praised it. On August 15th Lawrence wrote to Mrs Hardy: 'It is meant to be the true history of a political movement whose essence was a fraud – in the sense that its leaders did not believe the arguments with which they moved its rank and file: and also the true history of a campaign, to show how unlovely the back of a commander's mind must be.

'So what you said cuts right across my belief, and has puzzled me. Will you tell me what you would do – publish or leave private – if yourself or Mr. Hardy had written such a book? Apologies for bothering you: but the value of the book would give me an income which would keep me out of the army: and I'm wondering since Sunday whether perhaps I may be able to enjoy it.'[46]

At about this time Gertrude Bell strongly urged Lawrence to issue the book in some form, and he began to contemplate the idea again. Shortly afterwards he wrote to Kennington: 'My book isn't coming out: but I've asked some friends to see if there isn't an interested millionaire who would put up £2,000 and let me produce a privately printed edition with all the portraits complete. There is a chance of this in the fairly near future.'[47] D. G. Hogarth, Alan Dawnay, and Lionel Curtis, who all lived in Oxford, discussed the position and decided that the best plan would be a subscription edition of three hundred copies priced at ten guineas. Lawrence, however, was not very enthusiastic about raising the money through subscriptions; he wrote to Gertrude Bell that he was 'turning over in my mind the alternative – to publish Garnett's abridgement . . . and do the subscription edition with its profits.'[48]

He asked Cape to send him the draft of *War in the Desert*: 'I'd like to read it again and see if I can screw myself up to let it appear. So if you (or Garnett) have it will you post it down? I promise nothing, of course, but you will probably want at least the refusal if I decide to loose something.'[49] Then, on August 23rd, he wrote to Hogarth: 'What am I to do? Publish the Garnett abridgement after all, with such restrictions as seem fit to me, and use its profits to publish a limited illustrated complete edition... publish nothing... or print privately?

'Hardy read the thing lately, and made me very proud with what he said of it. Shaw (have you seen him?) praised it. Alan Dawnay compares it, not unfavourably, with the lost edition. I still feel that it's a pessimistic unworthy book, full of the neurosis of the war, and I hate the idea of selling it. If I won't make profit of my war-reputation, still less should I make profit of my war-story. Yet Lowell Thomas lurks still in the background, and if his book is the fulsome thing I expect, he will force the truth out of me. It might be better to get my blow in first.

'You have read the original and the abridgement... will you tell me what, in my place, you would do?'[50]

During the summer Lawrence's new friendship with the Hardys had deepened. He now visited Max Gate, their home near Dorchester, at least once a fortnight. Robert Graves wrote to ask for Lawrence's impressions of the 83-year-old writer. In reply Lawrence sent an essay which shows, amongst other things, that his writing style had now moved towards a much greater simplicity.

. . . you said 'Tell me about Max Gate' – and I can't!

The truth seems to be that Max Gate is very difficult to seize upon. I go there as often as I decently can, and hope to go on going there so long as it is within reach: (sundry prices I've paid in Company Office for these undefended absences) but description isn't possible. Hardy is so pale, so quiet, so refined into an essence: and camp is such a hurly-burly. When I come back I feel as if I'd woken up from a sleep: not an exciting sleep, but a restful one. There is an unbelievable dignity and ripeness about Hardy: he is waiting so tranquilly for death, without a desire or ambition left in his spirit, as far as I can feel it: and yet he entertains so many illusions, and hopes for the world, things which I, in my disillusioned middle-age, feel to be illusory. They used to call this man a pessimist. While really he is full of fancy expectations.

Then he is so far-away. Napoleon is a real man to him, and the country of Dorsetshire echoes that name everywhere in Hardy's ears. He lives in his period, and thinks of it as the great war: whereas to me that nightmare through the fringe of which I passed has dwarfed all memories of other wars, so that they seem trivial, half-amusing incidents.

Also he is so assured. I said something a little reflecting on Homer: and he took me up at once, saying that it was not to be despised: that it was very kin to *Marmion*... saying this not with a grimace, as I would say it, a feeling smart and original and modern, but with the most tolerant kindness in the world. Conceive a man to whom Homer and Scott are companions: who feels easy in such presences.

And the standards of the man! He feels interest in everyone, and veneration for no-one. I've not found in him any bowing-down, moral or material or spiritual . . .

Yet any little man finds this detachment of Hardy's a vast compliment and comfort. He takes me as soberly as he would take

John Milton (how sober that name is), considers me as carefully, is as interested in me: for to him every person starts scratch in the life-race, and Hardy has no preferences: and I think no dislikes, except for the people who betray his confidence and publish him to the world.

Perhaps that's partly the secret of that strange house hidden behind its thicket of trees. It's because there are no strangers there. Anyone who does pierce through is accepted by Hardy and Mrs. Hardy as one whom they have known always and from whom nothing need be hid.

For the ticket which gained me access to T.H. I'm grateful to you – probably will be grateful always. Max Gate is a place apart: and I feel it all the more poignantly for the contrast of life in this squalid camp. It is strange to pass from the noise and thoughtlessness of sergeants' company into a peace so secure that in it not even Mrs. Hardy's tea-cups rattle on the tray: and from a barrack of hollow senseless bustle to the cheerful calm of T.H. thinking aloud about life to two or three of us. If I were in his place I would never wish to die: or even to wish other men dead. The peace which passeth all understanding:– but it can be felt, and is nearly unbearable. How envious such an old age is.

However, here is enough of trying to write about something which is so precious that I grudge writing about it. T.H. is an experience that a man must keep to himself.[51]

By this time Lawrence had made friends with one or two men in the Tank Corps who shared his interest in literature, and he occasionally took them with him to Max Gate, where they found a welcome which disregarded social class. Lawrence himself had the unusual distinction of being liked by Hardy's ferocious dog. That autumn he persuaded Augustus John to paint a portrait of Hardy, and there were several sittings in the study at Max Gate. Afterwards Lawrence wrote: 'John has painted (at my request) a very beautiful portrait of him. The old man is delighted, and Mrs. Hardy also. It is seldom that an artist is so fortunate in his sitter's eyes.'[52] When the portrait was finished Sydney Cockerell found a benefactor who purchased it for £3,000 on behalf of the Fitzwilliam Museum in Cambridge. Afterwards Mrs Hardy wrote that her husband 'was genuinely delighted' that the picture had gone to Cambridge; 'he said he would *far* rather have had that happen than receive the Nobel prize – and he meant it.'[53]

On September 13th Lawrence completed *The Forest Giant* and sent it to Cape: 'At last this foul work: complete. Please have typed and send down that I may get it off my suffering chest before I burst. Damn Adrien le Corbeau and his rhetoric. The book is a magnificent idea, ruined by jejune bombast. My version is better than his: but dishonest here and there: but my stomach turned. Couldn't help it.'[54]

Lawrence sent the translation fee to Guy, whose family in Birmingham was in some financial difficulty: 'hoping that you won't take offence. I made it in less than a month, so that it is no great gift which I offer you.'[55] His generosity to those in financial need became proverbial among his service friends. Their difficulties were inescapable, whereas he could make money easily if he chose. Although he refused offers of well-paid jobs and projects, the knowledge that these opportunities existed gave him a sense of security. This fact, together with the option to leave the ranks at will, meant that he enjoyed a freedom of choice open to no other serviceman. For this reason he would never truly experience a sense of being imprisoned in the ranks.

It was almost impossible for Lawrence to concentrate on translation work in the camp. For a few weeks while working on *The Forest Giant*, he had shared an attic room rented by Alec Dixon in a private house in Moreton, a few miles away. Dixon was due to be posted away from Bovington, and Lawrence looked for somewhere else to work. He soon heard of a cottage at Clouds Hill, a mile north of Bovington Camp. It belonged to the Moreton estate and had been built in 1808 as a farm labourer's cottage. Since the early years of the war it had been unoccupied and it was in a very dilapidated condition. A Tank Corps sergeant, Arthur Knowles, had leased the cottage with some neighbouring land where he had built a bungalow for his family. It was a condition of the lease that the original cottage should be restored, and work had already begun when Lawrence first heard that the old cottage would become available. During the summer a new agreement was made under which Lawrence paid for the completion of the repairs and then rented the cottage for ten shillings a month. It would provide him with 'a warm solitary place to hide in sometimes on winter evenings. This district is unusually desolate (of good company) and I covet the idea of being sometimes by myself near a fire.'[56]

When Lawrence had finished *The Forest Giant* he looked more closely at Cape's next translation project, *Sturly*. The novel described life under the sea. In a draft for the dust-jacket blurb, Lawrence wrote that its author, Pierre Custot, had 'used his beloved fish as a vehicle to convey to us his comments on the world, and nature, and human kind; but with so much skill that the fish always keep the fore-front of the view, and tinge the whole story with a vivid strangeness.'[57] On September 25th Lawrence told Cape: 'It's plainly a true tale of how fish live, very well told: but English people like hearing of fish that were caught, hardly of fish *qua* fish, minus humanity. I can translate it, if you wish, and make it respectable. It's something different, you know, from the ordinary book, and rather honourable. Very difficult too, because the author was not solid upon his own simplicity, and has chased off after rare words and images to buttress out his nervousness. To put them into English will be hard, but interesting.'[58]

A year had gone by since Lawrence's first enlistment, during which he had twice passed through a basic training course. At Bovington he found himself employed on menial duties: 'We do unskilled house-work, mostly, with short spells of navvying.'[59] For the moment there was no sense of personal direction in his letters, although the pursuit of achievement in some form had always been important to him. His principal ambition, endlessly repeated, was to become just like the other men; yet he must have known that this would be impossible.

During the autumn he ran short of money and had to lay up his motorcycle. This kept him from pleasures such as visiting the Hardys, and from the exhilaration of putting the Brough through its paces; he had begun to see the thrill of speed as a necessary release from the irritations of the camp. Worse still, he was giving much of his spare time to translation, and as a result he had little time for reading, one of the few pleasures that distracted his thoughts. It was also months since he had been to a concert or listened to a gramophone record. In a fit of depression he wrote to Lionel Curtis: 'My thoughts are centering more and more upon the peace of death, with longing for it. Is it, do you think, that at last I am getting old? Do old people secretly dwell much upon their inevitable end?'[60]

His one remaining pleasure was writing. He told Garnett of the 'frenzied aching delight in a pattern of words which happen to run true. Do you know that lately I have been finding my deepest satisfaction in the collocation of words so ordinary and plain that they cannot mean anything to a book-jaded mind: and out of some of such I can draw deep stuff. Is it perhaps that certain sequences of vowels and consonants imply more than others: that writing of this sort has music in it? I don't want to affirm it, and yet I would not deny it: for if writing can have sense (and it has: this letter has) and sound why shouldn't it have something of pattern too? My sequences seem to be independent of ear... to impose themselves through the eye alone. I achieved a good many of them in *Le Gigantesque*: but fortuitously for the most part.'[61]

At the beginning of October Robin Buxton suggested an alternative scheme for *Seven Pillars*. A hundred and twenty copies could be printed and illustrated with all of Lawrence's pictures, for sale to subscribers for about £25 each. Lawrence asked Lionel Curtis to see Buxton and discuss the idea: 'My preference is for the fewest copies which will tot up to £3,000 (supposing £3,000 is to be the cost of production).'[62] Buxton's hundred and twenty copies appealed much more than the three hundred copies proposed by Hogarth, Dawnay and Curtis. But the £25 subscription seemed very high, and Lawrence suggested that some copies should be set aside to give away to 'the dozen or so worthy men on the adventure with me. They aren't twenty-five pound or even ten pound men.'[63] He now wrote to Whittingham & Griggs, the colour-plate printers, to ask for a new estimate for the illustrations.

While these plans were being considered, Lawrence would have time to tackle *Sturly*, and he wrote to Cape accepting the task on October 11th, with the warning that 'It will take a while to do well, for the wretched man catalogues innumerable French fishes... and my French never extended into scientific ichthyology!'[64]

By the end of October the roof of the cottage at Clouds Hill was completed. The building was extremely simple: the ground floor and first floor were each divided by the central chimney which had a single flight of stairs beside it. At each level there was a large room with a fireplace on one side of the chimney, and a smaller room on the staircase side. To begin with Lawrence used only the upstairs rooms, storing lumber and firewood below. He sold the gold Arabian dagger he had carried during the Revolt to Lionel Curtis and used the money to pay for improvements at Clouds Hill. There were even plans for a bathroom, but this scheme was postponed. A more immediate task was the replacement of old floorboards. On November 5th he wrote to Jock Chambers: 'At present one chair and a table there. Am hoping for a book case this week, and a bed next week but cash isn't too plentiful and needs are many.'[65]

By this time Lawrence had more or less accepted the Hogarth-Dawnay-Curtis scheme for a three-hundred-copy edition of *Seven Pillars* priced at ten guineas: 'A subscribed edition of course, without publishers or booksellers or reviews.'[66] By selling direct to subscribers, the bookseller's profit margin of 33 per cent could be avoided. The £3,000 subscription money would cover the cost of printing the text and illustrations. Lawrence had already paid nearly as much to the artists who had painted portraits for the book and, though he knew that in most cases the resale value of the pictures would be far lower than the cost, he had no plan to recover this money from subscribers. The text was to be shortened and revised: 'the fourth [version of the text], if it comes out, will be widely different – and better, if my skill has not wholly gone.'[67] There would be time for revision because Whittingham & Griggs would need a year to reproduce the pictures by the high-quality colour collotype process. On October 27th Lawrence wrote to Sydney Cockerell: 'Whether it will come off or not will depend on how many people Curtis finds willing to subscribe for it. I'd be glad to get the burden of the worthy production of the work off my chest: that's all. There will be no profit and no noise about it. Incidentally, no public-library copies, (B.M. Bodley, Cambs, etc.), and no subscription to which I take exception will be permitted.'[68]

Meanwhile, however, Robin Buxton was still canvassing friends about the possibility of finding one hundred and twenty subscribers at thirty guineas. Lawrence encouraged him: 'I'd rather the few copies: I had rather one copy at £3,000 than 10 at £300, or 30 at £100 or 300 at £10... it is only what people will subscribe. I hate the whole idea of spreading copies of the beastly book'.[69]

The scheme to publish *Seven Pillars* in an expensive subscription edition had led Lawrence to take a radical decision. He could not stomach the idea that subscribers might think that the high price reflected personal greed on his part. No one must say that he was making money out of his own legend, and he therefore decided not to take a royalty from the book. Lawrence presented this extraordinary decision, which had unquestionably been made for reasons of pride, as a matter of principle. He now repeatedly told people that he could not accept money from the book or any other part of his share in the Arabian adventure. Thus in November he wrote to Hellé Flecker (after seeing a stage version of her husband's *Hassan* in London one weekend): 'My joining up was quite direct and plain. I hate the semi-politics to which my Eastern efforts in the war had seemed to doom me: and to break away from them, to make myself quite independent of them and their glamour, I changed my name, and had consequently to begin rather low down. I'm not worth much money apart from Arabia: and to that I'll not return. I won't even make money by publishing my beastly book upon the war-period, because that's all of a piece with it.'[70] Hitherto *Seven Pillars* had been an investment which Lawrence could have turned at any moment into a personal fortune, simply by signing a publication contract. The subscription scheme would allow him to print *Seven Pillars* lavishly, but it would also deny him the book's earning-power. In future, if he wished to escape from the ranks, he would have to obtain money some other way.

During November Hogarth, Curtis, and Buxton weighed the chances for their subscription schemes, while Cape was hoping to find a single millionaire who would underwrite the edition. Lawrence fitted up a writing room at Clouds Hill where, he told Hogarth, 'I can revise my text, in about a twelve-month, allowing say two hours average per day. More than this is too much. I've got into an "employed job" here, which will keep me in camp a year or two. I can let you (or whoever edits) have the revised text a book at a time, gradually. The pictures will take about a year to do, I expect. So that the whole project may be complete within eighteen months.'[71] At this stage Lawrence thought that the text could be printed by a commercial firm, and he suggested the Oxford University Press. He had revived the ideas about format and typography discussed in 1920 with Vyvyan Richards at All Souls: 'I want Caslon eleven point or its nearest monotype equivalent . . . The book's size is determined by the ready plates (10 x 8 I think it is, a large quarto . . .) If I can get it to 250,000 words it will go in one vol. of 450 words a page.'[72]

In late November Lawrence heard from Buxton that a hundred thirty-guinea subscribers could certainly be found. However, subscribers could not be asked to pay the whole thirty guineas in advance, and Buxton's support was therefore crucial. Liverpool & Martin's Bank, where he was a branch manager, would help finance the book's production.

Another boost to Lawrence's morale came a day or two later, in the form of a letter from Siegfried Sassoon, who was reading the 'Oxford' text. His praise concluded: 'It is a GREAT BOOK, blast you. Are you satisfied?, you tank-vestigating eremite.

'And thank all gods, heathen deities, fetiches, Theocracies, inter-cessors, and Emmanuels for a man who writes a good book and doesn't sell it for his soul to a pimp of a publisher!'[73]

It was arranged that Lawrence, Curtis, Hogarth and Dawnay would meet in Oxford on December 9th and take a final decision about which subscription scheme to adopt. Having looked at *Seven Pillars*, Oxford University Press had declined to print the text, on the grounds that it contained many libels. Eric Kennington, however, told Lawrence that he had met a newly qualified printer, Manning Pike, who might be willing to tackle the job privately. Lawrence replied that a decision about the edition was about to be taken: 'Till after that it's no good bothering a printer: but a private man (such as you indicate) would be a great luxury: much better than a firm.'[74]

Shortly before the meeting Lawrence wrote to Hogarth: 'I expect Dawnay will have told you that I'm coming down to Oxford on Saturday night . . . to stay till early Monday morning: and in that Sunday I hope to put my point of view as to the *Seven Pillars* before you and Curtis.

'It is, briefly, that I'm aiming at a public that will pay but not read... and from what one hears the plutocrats should be of that sort. If as many as 300 copies were sent out, the book would have to be severely cut down, and that means another edition some-day, and consequently no rest now. The fewer the copies the less the cuts.'[75] It is clear from this letter that the task he had set himself was to win his three Oxford backers round to Buxton's thirty-guinea scheme.

CHAPTER 34

Tribulations of a Publisher
December 1923 – December 1924

ON 13th December 1923 Lawrence sent Eric Kennington a summary of the decisions reached in Oxford: 'At a meeting last Sunday Hogarth, Dawnay, Curtis, and I decided to produce 100 copies of the *Seven Pillars*, at thirty guineas a copy, if so many subscribers can be found.

'I am to be solely responsible . . . will pay all bills, and sign all papers and copies. Hogarth will help edit my proofs: you, edit my pictures (I hope).

'Production to start as soon as £200 has been subscribed: ("starting" means sending four Arab pastels to Whittingham & Griggs).

'Intending subscribers are to write to me (under any name) to Clouds Hill . . . for details and conditions. I'll reply personally to each . . .

'I estimate the job might take a year at the shortest, two at the longest'.[1]

After giving details of the format, typography, and paper to be used, Lawrence continued: 'Book will run between 300,000 and 330,000 words: preferably the lesser number.

'Matter will be sent in in sheets of the book you have [the *Oxford Times* text], hand-corrected (scissors and paste). So it will be a very legible MS to set up from.

'Will you ask your printer how this proposition appeals to him... what sample experimental type-panels and margins he would set up: how long he would be before he could start the job: how many words per week he would be prepared to set up: how many sheets he would be prepared to hold in type, what he would charge per thousand words? . . .

'I would interfere with the sample pages a good deal, with the accepted format very little. Author's corrections almost nil. Matter sent in regularly'.[2] It had been agreed that in addition to the subscribed edition, about twenty copies of the text containing incomplete sets of the illustrations would be given to British soldiers who had fought in the Arab campaign.

Lawrence told Robin Buxton that he himself, 'a man of straw,' was 'to be solely responsible for the printing, production, and distribution of the book. This because it must inevitably be libellous. Civil Libel Actions break down because I have no money: criminal, because prison wouldn't seem to me worse than the Tank Corps . . . I propose, in my letter of conditions to each subscriber, to explain that my proposed edition of 100 copies is based on the estimate of £3,000 for the cost of production, with a 10% margin for eventualities: but that if the book costs less I'll distribute fewer than 100 copies: and if more as many more as are required to meet the bill: the price always remaining thirty guineas, and the total proceeds always equalling the total cost.'[3]

He also wrote to Bernard Shaw, telling him that the text would be 'corrected only in blemishes of prose: uncensored and unimproved' (Lawrence thought that the length would not be reduced by more than ten per cent). He added: 'The business will be done as crazily as you feared'.[4] Shaw was taken aback by the high subscription price, and argued that the book would have to be made very special to justify such a figure, though this might be achieved through the quality of its illustrations. However, 'it is quite certain that there will be cheap editions of the book before very long . . . Restricting the book to a hundred copies is nonsense, and you know it as well as I do.'[5]

In the same letter Shaw mentioned his attempts to persuade the Prime Minister to award Lawrence a state pension. Shaw had put the idea to Stanley Baldwin seven months earlier, and had even arranged meetings with Hogarth and Baldwin to discuss Lawrence's predicament. Hogarth had written to Shaw: 'The fact is that money weighs much less with [Lawrence] than mode of life. I cannot now conceive of any Government post, such as the P.M. could offer, which Lawrence would accept, or if he accepted, retain. He begins at once to talk of "moral prostitution" and quits! . . . Lawrence is not normal in many ways and it is extraordinarily difficult to do anything for him! In some measure, the life of letters is best suited to him. He will not work in any sort of harness unless this is padlocked onto him. He enlisted in order to have the padlocks rivetted onto him.'[6] The scheme for a pension had proved difficult because Lawrence was not technically eligible for any kind of state award, and a special Act of Parliament would therefore have been required.[7] Shaw's hopes were further dashed when Baldwin's party lost its parliamentary majority in the general election at the beginning of December.

On December 20th Lawrence wrote to Shaw: 'It seems I'm to regret the fall of Mr. Baldwin: and to thank you very much for the attempt at a pension. It was exceedingly good of you. Hogarth gave me no idea of it. Why did you think I wouldn't take it? It's earned money which sticks in the throat:– that a man should come down to working for such stuff... The Government have been very decent to me. They would give me political employ (only I won't look upon the Middle East again) or a commission (only I won't again give an order): and at my asking have twice let me enlist, against their judgement.'[8]

The decision to publish *Seven Pillars* gave Lawrence a substantial project to work on. Hogarth, Curtis and Dawnay doubtless hoped that the work would prove therapeutic, or that by the time it was finished he would be ready to take up some new literary project. The subscription scheme placed Lawrence in a position of great personal responsibility. At thirty guineas, *Seven Pillars* would be a very expensive book. The modern equivalent of this price can be estimated by relating it to the average cost of a novel, then 7/6d. On this basis, the *Seven Pillars* subscription in 1989 would be approximately £650, and the gross projected turnover of the edition equivalent to about £65,000. This was a business venture of some scale for a private soldier, and it would involve a good deal of administrative work in addition to the tasks of revising the text and supervising the book's production.

Hogarth, Curtis and Buxton now set about finding subscribers, demonstrating their confidence that Lawrence would see the project through. If he failed, their only security was the Garnett abridgement, which could be published to meet his financial obligations although it would hardly recompense the disappointed subscribers. For this reason Lawrence had agreed to appoint Hogarth his literary executor at the Oxford meeting. Clearly Hogarth believed in December 1923 that Lawrence was in a state of mind which would enable him to handle the responsibility of *Seven Pillars*. A few weeks later Hogarth wrote to Geoffrey Dawson, who had put Lawrence up for the All Souls fellowship, 'the most that Dawnay and I can get T.E.L. to do about his Arabia book is to let 100 copies be issued privately . . . We guarantee nothing: but T.E. is getting on with the reproductions and revising his text; and we trust he'll go through with it this time.'[9]

While friends looked for subscribers, Lawrence put the production work in hand. He wrote to Kennington telling him where to find the forty-four portraits and other illustrations needed for reproduction. He also arranged with Manning Pike, the printer introduced by Kennington, to buy printing machinery and equipment. From the detailed estimates it seemed that £2,800 would be sufficient to pay for the printing of text and plates and for the press machinery. A further £200 would cover the cost of binding. Once the portrait plates had been printed, he planned to sell some of the most valuable originals, notably John's oil of Feisal. Since the pictures were his own property he expected the balance in his personal bank account to be handsomely in credit within a year.

Lawrence found these arrangements for producing *Seven Pillars* very satisfactory: 'It will be rather a fine volume, and unless I'm wrong, a celebrated one some day.'[10] Cheered by the prospect, he bought a new Brough Superior, his second. The old one had been borrowed without permission by one of the Bovington soldiers and wrecked: 'I've tried now for a valiant six weeks to do without a motor bike... and I find that it was indeed the safety valve I'd thought it.'[11] The new Brough would cost £150, and Lawrence raised part of the cost by selling a copy of the Fourth Folio Shakespeare from his library. It made £80 at auction.

By mid-January, a month after the decision to publish, a dozen subscribers had been accepted. Among them was Lord Grey, who wrote from Fallodon: 'Your campaign was such a remarkable and unique part of the war that I should value very much having the account of it in the library here, so I will take all risks up to thirty guineas'.[12] In addition to the Shaws, who subscribed at once, enquiries came in from Sydney Cockerell, Harley Granville-Barker, Hugh Walpole, Edward Garnett and J. M. Barrie.

Had Lawrence been living in other circumstances, his commitment to the new work might have had the effect Hogarth had hoped for. But the grim realities of life in the Tank Corps were inescapable. He wrote to Hogarth in January: 'The Xmas spectacle of camp took out of me the zest I had won at Oxford'[13], and told Wavell that the festivities had been 'like sleeping – or lying rather – in a public lavatory with choked drain... and it was even worse than the usual lavatory... for there seemed to be a heavy sea on, and all the *habitués* were in need of stewards with little basins. The old army, in my recollection, did at least carry its drink.'[14] Clouds Hill had become an essential refuge: 'When things are unspeakable I fly out in the evening and debauch myself with canned music till my mind is sick'.[15]

On January 2nd, while the Shaws were visiting Bournemouth, they had come across to see Lawrence at the cottage. A few days later he received a parcel of books from Charlotte Shaw, the first of many such gifts. He began to accumulate a small library at the cottage, although the valuable private press books he had collected after the war remained in storage with Vyvyan Richards at Pole Hill.

Pike would soon need revised text to begin work on *Seven Pillars*, but Lawrence was still busy with other writing. The translation of *Sturly* should have been finished at the end of December 1923, but it was held up while he made arrangements for *Seven Pillars*. In addition he was asked by Edward Garnett to write an introduction to *The Twilight of the Gods*, a collection of short stories by Garnett's father, Richard, now to be issued in a new illustrated edition.[16] There was a possibility of still further commitment when Cape suggested following *Sturly* with a translation of Flaubert's *Salammbô*. Lawrence felt unable to refuse it: 'one of my favourite books: there is a copy on the table by me, as I write: and it's the description of Hanno's leprous body, after twelve days on the cross which has finally conquered me.'[17]

By the end of January he had hardly started to revise *Seven Pillars*. Realising that he had over-committed himself, he abruptly dropped the time-consuming translation work, writing to Cape: 'Tonight I've read through my *Sturly*, since I'd got to the penultimate chapter... and I've burned it page by page. There is something about this book which I can't get.

'This will throw you out... but there are translators more careful than myself, and it is a short book. I've spent days over a single chapter, and yet not got the essence of any . . . Is it any good, after this failure, my thinking of doing *Salammbô* ? I fear not.'[18]

When Lawrence at last tackled *Seven Pillars* he was shocked by the quality of his own writing which he now saw from a different standpoint. He later wrote: 'I'll never forget the despair with which I read my *Seven Pillars* . . . after forgetting it for two years. It was so incredibly unlike what I'd thought my talents (of which I'd had too good an opinion) would bring forth, that I then and there swore I'd never try again. If there'd been any redeemable feature... but the whole thing was unwholesome.'[19] He had written *Seven Pillars* immediately after the Great War. Its style had been influenced by intense reading, but the notions of good writing he had formed owed far more to the nineteenth century than to the twentieth. By 1924 Lawrence's views about style had changed radically, and the epic manner he had once striven for seemed overwrought and false. Translation work had taught him to see instantly through literary pretension. Moreover, his mind had become attuned to a far simpler form of English through daily contact with men in the ranks. He saw that *Seven Pillars* was written in a style very unlike that of the contemporary literature he now admired.

This change in Lawrence's opinion is clear from a letter written to Harley Granville-Barker in February, commenting on his new play *The Secret Life*: 'I rather like the pemmican of letters, or rather I used to like it, when my head was at ease . . . And yet, and yet... your leisure is so abundant that perhaps you have been cruel to the larger audience. I don't see you somehow as only a highbrow for highbrows: but haven't you been forgetful of the duties of the many. I get up in the morning, and clean boots and make beds and carry coal and light fires... and then all day long I work till five o'clock... and when in the evening the choice lies between an easy thing, like *Methuselah*, and a hard thing like yours: why without my will my hand strays to the left, and I read Shaw. It's not out of sheer laziness: predigested food is wholesome to a stomach which is weary.'[20]

Lawrence had kept the letters Garnett and others had written to him about *Seven Pillars* and, rereading them, he must have realised that they avoided the question of its style. Their comments had been on generalities, praising such qualities of the book as his observation and self-revelation. Now that Lawrence saw the text so differently, he found little to comfort him in such opinions.

In mid-February, however, he received a very different type of letter about *Seven Pillars*. It was sent by E. M. Forster and contained detailed comment: 'you probably prefer criticisms, tips. I will try and send some, on the faint chance of their helping you'.[21] Forster wrote at great length, illustrating his criticisms with passages from the text. He took, for example, a paragraph commenting on the Sykes-Picot Agreement, in which Lawrence had written: 'The control of the Arab movement was left lying, like a golden apple, between the contestants, but the charm was cogged. One of the two powers was given all the deserts – the sources of originality; all the holy places – the sources of fervour; all the great rivers – the sources of power; in the Arabic-speaking world. With these assets it might safely invest for the future whose outlines revealed themselves so inevitably a client growth: though the time of fruit had not nearly come.'[22]

Forster wrote: 'It starts with a metaphor of the sort I don't much like – a rhetorical allusion to poetry for a historical purpose, which will only be justified, will only pay its way, if it oils the sentence's wheels. This it fails to do. I am pulled up by "contestants" a little, and a good deal more by a "cogged charm". Is the apple cogged, or is a die being thrown for the privilege of picking it up? The second sentence raises no such questions. It runs through on pure poetry and from far far away – from ch. III to be precise. I like it, but, by throwing me off my guard, it is going to increase my trouble over sentence three. Here Clio is herself again. She opens as a company-promoter, coquets for a word or two with some charm or vision, and then re-enters the vegetable kingdom. Of what is this here new growth a client suitor or sucker? Can't decide. Of England, of the Arabs, or of the original apple (*control* of Arabs)? And – though it's a small point – client as adj. is unusual, my mind has had to do that extra work. I think the paragraph means that the Franco-British understanding practically left the control of an Arab movement to England and that England was well advised to exercise such control. But I've had to read it over several times. It strikes me as an example of the pseudo-reflection, of the process of incrustation going on mechanically, without the writer's full conscious-ness, and therefore adding nothing to his effect . . . I suggest you go through some other backwater paragraphs (which are necessarily numer-ous in such a work) and see if you can't make them go more simply. Don't let the reflective apparatus function unless it has something to reflect about.'[23] Forster summarised the drift of these comments by saying: 'The criticism I'd offer is that your reflective style is not properly under control. Almost at once, when you describe your thoughts, you become obscure, and the slightly strained sense which you then (not habitually) lend words, does not bring your sentence the richness you intended, imparts not colour but gumminess.'[24]

Lawrence was extremely grateful for such detailed criticism. He replied: 'This book is my only one, and I have a longing (which I seldom admit) to hear what men say of it.

'In your case it is wonderful. Writers and painters aren't like other men. The meeting them intoxicates me with a strangeness which shows me how very far from being one of them I am. Of your work I only know *Howards End* and *Siren* and *Pharos*: but that's enough to put you among the elect... and yet you bother to write to me whole pages about my effort. No one else has done that for me, and I'm abnormally grateful'.[25] Forster had suggested that Lawrence's descriptions of people could be improved by putting in more dialogue. Lawrence replied that *Seven Pillars* set out to be 'a complete narrative of what actually happened in the Arab Revolt . . . it was compiled out of memory (squeezing the poor organ with both hands, to force from it even the little lively detail that there is). If I invent one thing I'll spoil its *raison d'être*: and if there are invented con-versations, or conversations reconstructed after five years, where will it be? . . . the revise I'm going to give the *Seven Pillars* in the next ten months can be one of detail only: for the adventure is dead in me'.[26]

Lawrence had now not only recognised the problem of style, but found someone who could help him. He later said: 'detailed criticism is the only stuff worth having – plain praise being the most useless and boring stuff in the world – but the only people who can give you detailed criticism fit to help you are other craftsmen working themselves upon your job.'[27] He later wrote in the same vein to James Hanley: 'I found Forster a very subtle and helpful critic, over my *Seven Pillars*. Hardly anybody else (of the dozens of critics . . .) said anything that wasn't just useless pap.'[28]

Lawrence told Forster that he would like to meet him and discuss revisions of the text. Forster, who had just finished *A Passage to India*, offered to come in March: 'I can't cheer you up over the book. No one could. You have got depressed and muddled over it, and are quite incapable of seeing how good it is. The only thing is to get rid of it and I should feel very happy indeed if I could help you towards doing that.'[29]

Forster first visited Clouds Hill on 23rd March 1924; he described the cottage in a letter as: 'A charming place in a hollow of the "Egdon Heath" described by Hardy at the opening of *The Return of the Native*. It is all among rhododendrons which have gone wild. We worked for a couple of hours at his book, then had lunch on our knees – cold chicken and ham, stewed pears and cream, very nice and queer; a fine log fire. I like Lawrence though he is of course odd and alarming'.[30] There is no doubt that Lawrence found these discussions on *Seven Pillars* helpful, and in due course he was to invite Forster to come and look over later sections of the revision.

Several of Lawrence's letters written in February and March 1924 refer to an illness which was sufficiently serious to put him on the camp sick list, and from which he did not fully recover for some weeks. At the time he was preoccupied, not merely with *Seven Pillars*, but with an overload of clerical duties. He suffered a deepening malaise from this time on. Despite flashes of good humour directed towards particular correspondents, the overall mood of his letters was to grow blacker and blacker. One factor was despair that he was still attracting attention as 'Lawrence of Arabia'. He had again been discovered by a *Daily Express* reporter, who, on February 27th, published details of his life at Bovington: 'Now he is Private Shaw. He performs the ordinary duties of a trained soldier of the Tank Corps. It is believed that he is writing a book. He has a bungalow which he rents to the north of the camp. He mixes freely with the other men. He possesses a motor-bicycle, and makes frequent journeys. Also he has visitors periodically. The men in the battalion know who he is and what he has been.

'When I accosted him by the name of Shaw today he made an evasive answer, saying that there was no one by the name of Shaw there whom he knew, and he walked away hurriedly. A few minutes later he left the camp on his motor-cycle.'[31]

Another influence on Lawrence's mood was the constant sense of degradation he felt in the Tank Corps. On March 1st, a year after his dismissal from the RAF, he appealed to Trenchard to be allowed back: 'Forgive me this letter. I'm ashamed of it already, since I know that you sacked me for good, and it's perverse of me not to take it so. Yet the hope of getting back into the R.A.F. is the main reason for my staying in the Army. I feel eligible, there, for transfer or re-enlistment. You once took over some Tank Corps fellows'.[32] Lawrence argued that his dismissal from Farnborough was due more to the CO's weakness than to any fault in his own conduct, adding: 'I don't mind the present discomfort (as long as I can hope to reach the R.A.F. at the end): but the filth is a pity, for no fellow can live so long in it and keep quite clean.'[33]

His depression was aggravated by the task of revising *Seven Pillars*, whose subject matter was painful to him, and whose style was such a constant disappointment. Moreover, during the first months of 1924 it seemed as though the plans for a thirty-guinea subscription edition had been over-optimistic. By mid-March, three months after the start of the project, only twenty-six subscribers had been found, whereas the detailed estimates that he had now obtained were higher than expected. The reproduction of the pictures would cost £2,405; the cost of printing and binding would be £970, and there was now to be the additional expense of printing a small edition in America to protect copyright there. Allowing £200 for this last item, the total came to £3,575, and 120 subscribers would be needed. Before starting work Pike would need £300, and he could not continue without at least £40 monthly thereafter. When this was added to the bills due in from Whittingham & Griggs, it was clear that the bank would have to advance a large sum if Pike were to proceed. Lawrence wrote to J. G. Wilson, manager of Bumpus's bookshop in London, 'and asked if he, on his own account and not as Bumpus, would like to place twenty copies at the thirty guineas price. I explained that it was not book-selling, and I was offering him no commission or reward.'[34]

As he grappled with these worries, Lawrence's thoughts turned inwards. On March 26th, having recovered from what appeared to be a mixture of malaria and influenza, 'all but the weariness after',[35] he sent a letter to Charlotte Shaw which clearly displays his deepening depression, and the morbid direction his introspection was taking: 'it rankles in my mind to be called proud names for qualities which I'd hate to possess... or for acts of which I'm heartily ashamed'.[36] Referring to Hogarth, he wrote: 'All my opportunities, all those I've wasted, came directly or indirectly, out of his trust in me'. The core of the letter, however, is a passage which shows that his outlook on life was still profoundly influenced by the homosexual rape he had suffered at Deraa six years earlier: 'I'm always afraid of being hurt: and to me, while I live, the force of that night will lie in the agony which broke me, and made me surrender. It's the individual view. You can't share it.

'About that night. I shouldn't tell you, because decent men don't talk about such things. I wanted to put it plain in the book, and wrestled for days with my self-respect... which wouldn't, hasn't, let me. For fear of being hurt, or rather to earn five minutes respite from a pain which drove me mad, I gave away the only possession we are born into the world with – our bodily integrity. It's an unforgiveable matter, an irrecoverable position: and it's that which has made me forswear decent living, and the exercise of my not-contemptible wits and talents.

'You may call this morbid: but think of the offence, and the intensity of my brooding over it for these years. It will hang about me while I live, and afterwards if our personality survives. Consider wandering among the decent ghosts hereafter, crying "Unclean, Unclean!" . . . There's not a clean human being into whose shape I would not willingly creep. They may not have been Colonel Lawrence... but I know the reverse of that medal, and hate its false face so utterly that I struggle like a trapped rabbit to be it no longer . . . it's my part to shun pleasures... through lack of desert. There's expiation to be made: and the weak spirit is only too ready to lunch with you, or to enjoy a book, or to hide a quiet while in a cloud-defended cottage: any alleviation of the necessary penalty of living on'.[37] This tone of bitter self-denial must reflect a moment of particularly deep depression, but such thoughts lay behind his everyday mood. He was spending almost all his free time at Clouds Hill, where he was safe from the drunken violence that often broke out among Tank Corps men off-duty. By contrast the cottage was calm. He would go there to work or to read and listen to gramophone records. Since the early post-war years in London, classical music had become increasingly important to him. From this time onwards he would escape mentally from life in the ranks through good music and books, and there are many references to records and composers in his letters.[38]

The friends he had made in the Tank Corps were exceptions to the general type. Alec Dixon was interested in writing (and eventually published two books). Privates Palmer and Russell were both 'outsiders' in the camp; they too liked reading and listening to classical music and were frequent visitors to Clouds Hill. Earlier that year Lawrence had told Mrs Hardy: 'Some of the fellows are making it their habit to drop in: but mostly they are quiet men . . . You see the cottage is unlike camp, and it gives them a sense of healthy change to visit me, and I like them to like coming.'[39] He sometimes referred to these young soldiers as 'the children', or 'the family', and he lent them books freely. Through Lawrence some of them met writers such as Thomas Hardy, Bernard Shaw, and E. M. Forster. On April 30th Lawrence sent Charlotte Shaw a description of tea at the cottage: 'It's streaming with rain against the western window, and the trees are tossing:– not as if they were playing, but wearily, as though this fourth day of the wintry weather was too much against their longing to turn green: and inside it is calm as ever. We went out in the drift and looked under the rhododendron for dry stakes: and have got enough to make a red fire, in whose heat the damp fir-logs burn away freely: and Palmer is sitting in front of it with his hands folded waiting for the *Rosenkavalier* waltz to end. After it he wants a little bit of Mozart as played by the Lener [string quartet]. Palmer gets drunk on music:– likes the sort which makes him most drunk. Russell is reading the *Dream*: and shocking Palmer out of his peace by elbow digs now and then, when he comes on an extra-juicy paragraph.

'Meanwhile I'm out over by the very wet window (but on its dry side) writing to you. There'll be tea when I've finished the letter . . . and more and more animal contentment after that: till we wind up, when the dark comes, with a movement out of a Bach thing for two violins. We always finish with that, if the time is dark enough.'[40]

At their meeting in March, Forster had told Lawrence about some short stories he had written, which were at that time unpublishable because their theme was homosexual. Lawrence agreed to read them, and Forster sent him a typescript of 'The Life to Come'.[41] On April 30th Lawrence wrote about the story, trying to offer the kind of helpful criticism Forster had given on *Seven Pillars*. To Forster's consternation Lawrence's first reaction was of schoolboy humour: 'Comment? Oh, it's very difficult.

How much, you will see by my confessing that in my first avid reading of it I ended it, and laughed and laughed. It seemed to me, in the first instance, one of the funniest things I'd ever come across.'[42] The letter continued with detailed criticisms, evading the central problem of its sexual content until near the end, where he wrote: 'Contrary to your opinion I incline to consider it quite fit to publish. Perhaps other people's improprieties come a little less sharply upon one? It doesn't feel to me nearly so bad as my true story.

'Incidentally we're different, aren't we? I make an awful fuss about what happened to me: and you invent a voluntary parallel, about which the two victims make no bones at all. Funny the way people work.'[43]

Forster replied on May 3rd: 'Yes, we're different all right, and your admission that you laughed at 'The Life to Come' makes me laugh and laugh . . . I don't understand much of your letter.'[44] After discussing Lawrence's criticisms, Forster added: 'I am glad you wrote, as I had assumed you were disgusted, and was sorry, though I knew that in such a contretemps neither the disgusted nor the disgusting party would be the least to blame. I think the story as good as any I've written, so does Siegfried [Sassoon]. Lowes Dickinson [of King's College, Cambridge] doesn't like it. Scarcely anyone else has seen it.'[45]

In late April Trenchard responded to Lawrence's appeal for readmission into the RAF with an unexpected offer. The Secretary of State for Air, now Lord Thomson, a socialist, was as unwilling as Hoare had been to allow Lawrence to rejoin the Air Force. Instead, at the beginning of May, Trenchard offered Lawrence the job of finishing an official history, *The War in the Air*, whose author had died after completing the first volume.[46] Hogarth had worked on the project briefly, but had abandoned it owing to ill-health. After refusing Trenchard's offer, Lawrence wrote to Hogarth: 'I took thought for a night, and then declined. The job is a hazardous one (Trenchard wants a "literary" history, the Committee of Imperial Defence a "technical"), attractive, very, to me by reason of its subject. The terms (three years) compare unfavourably with the six which the Army offers: and the responsibility is one which I'd regret as soon as I had shouldered it. Also it's no use, having gone through the grind of climbing down to crowd-level, at once to give it up for three years' decent living. It would leave me older, less strung up to make another effort at poor living.'[47] Now that he thought there would be no return to the RAF, he speculated grimly about the future: 'If I can complete my seven years in the Army I should be able to slip quietly into a job of some sort at the end. There is a garage near here which might take me on . . . Here at Bovington I seem to sit still: so still that often I fancy the slow passing of time about me can be heard. Isn't it rare for a person, who has been as unsparing as myself, to be purged quite suddenly of all desire? Even the longing or regret for the R.A.F. sleeps now, except when I come suddenly at a turn in the road, on its uniform. *That* was another bar to the job: because I'd have had to visit aerodromes, and each time the homesickness would have made itself felt afresh.'[48]

There is ample evidence in other letters of his increasingly depressed state of mind, which was aggravated by continuing poor health. He told Graves: 'I've cured myself of every wish to do anything or see anyone; unless the thing is ordered, it slides, so far as I am concerned. Nirvana perhaps: but there isn't a desire for nescience... it's just a letting slide off all myself except the physical.'[49]

By the middle of May, five months after the decision to reprint *Seven Pillars*, there were only thirty-four subscribers, barely a quarter of the number needed. Buxton began to fear that the target would never be reached. Lawrence had chosen the type size, and Pike was starting work, but there now seemed a risk that the project might end in a large financial loss. Moreover, the original scheme to complete the project within about a year was clearly unrealistic. Lawrence had failed to take into account the time needed for administrative work. He could not give more than his off-duty hours to the project, and by then he was already tired after a full day's work for the Tank Corps. In five months he had managed to revise only two of the book's eleven sections, and the printing of the text had not begun.

His progress was also slowed by depression, almost certainly in this case an illness brought on by the combination of poor health, worry, and over-work. He did not understand what was happening to him, and could in any case have done little to alleviate the problem. His state of mind could have been cured only by some radical change in the factors that were causing it, but he was committed to the *Seven Pillars* project and to remaining in the ranks. He began to suffer from a feeling of listlessness, and his thoughts drifted increasingly into paths of self-destructive introspection.

One of the matters which he reflected on was his illegitimacy. By a strange coincidence the Moreton estate from which he rented Clouds Hill belonged to the Fetherstonhaugh Framptons, relatives of his father's family in Ireland. They were well aware that 'Lawrence of Arabia' was Sir Thomas Chapman's natural son. In January 1924 Mrs Hardy had visited the cottage when Lawrence was not there, and in a well-intentioned gesture left a picture of Killua Castle, the Chapman family seat in County Westmeath.[50] Lawrence wrote to her: 'Am I to think of it as a gift (once I meant to earn money and buy the place: now I'm wiser and want only to buy Clouds Hill . . .): it's one I'd value very much, but I hardly like to assume it, when it may be only a loan.

'If it's a gift, then please whose gift – for I'd owe a letter of thanks. Will you be good enough to enlighten my darkness?'[51] By May, Lawrence had found out much more. He wrote to his mother: 'the Fetherstonehaugh people want to give me this little cottage (. . . quaint how these people are settled all about here. The daughter of the rector (?) of South Hill parish it was who knew all about us. She had kept in touch with affairs, and is living in camp, being the mother-in-law of one of our officers) and I've told them that my movements are too uncertain to make me wish for more property than I already own'.[52]

Many of his letters at this time reflect this renewed awareness of his illegitimacy. He wrote to Harley Granville-Barker: 'My genuine, birth-day, initials are T.E.C. The C. became L. when I was quite young and as L. I went to Oxford and through the war. After the war it became a legend: and to dodge its load of legendary inaccuracy I changed it to R. In due course R. became too hot to hold. So now I'm Shaw: but to me there seems no virtue in one name more than another. Any one can be used by anyone'.[53] On August 3rd, writing to Jock Chambers, he signed himself 'T.E.S. (ex J.H.R. ex T.E.L. ex E.C.)'[54] For some months he had been signing letters simply 'T.E.', and occasionally 'T.E.?' and from now on he told people quite readily that Lawrence had been an assumed name.[55]

On May 18th, while recovering from another attack of fever, he summarised his predicament in a letter to Edward Garnett: 'I'm sick just at present – in mind and body – and hate myself and all the circumstances of life. If only there was some way out of the *Verboten* notice-boards which stand in thickets about all my roads.'[56] On the same day he wrote to Granville-Barker: 'as for my being in the Army, the reasons for that go back a long way, as far as an unpresentable chapter (87) of my white elephant.'[57] Chapter 87 of the 'Oxford' text contains the account of his experience at Deraa in November 1917.

By the beginning of June, he was making some headway with the revision of *Seven Pillars*. Progress was 'very slow: but not so slow as the printer . . . I expect proofs of about the first 10,000 words tomorrow . . . Whittingham & Griggs haven't done the first eight illustrations yet.

'I'm trying to shorten the lumbering thing by 10%. Simplest way is to cut out eighteen lines from the 180 which make up each double-columned page of the old edition: but the simplest way doesn't always work. Sometimes I cut out fifty lines, and elsewhere only one or two. The experience of the book is gone foreign and remote from me, so that I can't do more than darn and trim it... no new matter. I haven't yet re-written a word: but will try when I get into the stodgy stuff. If I can't improve I'll erase. There will always remain too much for the stoutest-stomached reader.

'It's the most awful tosh of a book. Am I really so hysterical and fiddling a nincompoop? (Clearly I don't believe I am: that's what they call a rhetorical question: but the book is a show-up of a mean man on the rack of action.)'[58]

On June 20th Forster again came to Clouds Hill for a weekend to discuss the revision. Lawrence asked the Hardys over to join them for Sunday tea. A week later he told Buxton that two of the eleven Books of *Seven Pillars* had been passed for typesetting. Charlotte Shaw offered to help with the proof-reading and he gladly accepted, but it was to be three months before he sent her anything. In the meantime he worked with Pike to produce a first section of page proof, printed to his chosen typeface and page design. Most writers limit revision to literary matters, but Lawrence's enthusiasm for fine printing made him equally concerned with the appearance of the printed pages. In many cases this involved altering what he had written. He told Charlotte Shaw on July 10th: 'The text is being a little worked over, and all possible redundancies taken out – often too we have to alter things, to dress the ends of the paragraphs neatly. Also I don't wish any words divided at the ends of lines. These things all lead to rearrangement. So I have the text sent me in galley, for first check, and paged later. So far only six pages are finished.'[59]

The number of subscribers gradually crept upwards, and by the end of July there were about fifty. Lawrence became more confident that there would be enough before the book was finished. At the beginning of August he decided that it might be a good idea to send out a page proof of the introductory chapters to each subscriber as a sample. He ordered a hundred extra copies of one of the first colour plates for this purpose, but it was to be much longer than he anticipated before even this first section of the book was ready. In mid-August he promised Charlotte Shaw some proofs to read 'in a few days (which is perhaps three weeks, to be prosaic)'.[60] He expected that the work would become easier and quicker: 'It's the beginning, the settling things, which is so difficult.'[61]

By this time the project had incurred additional costs, some of which were due to Lawrence's perfectionism. The text was initially set up in galleys by a commercial typesetting house, the Westminster Press. Pike corrected it, removed the more obvious typographical blemishes, and sent a proof to Lawrence, who then suggested further changes. After eight months not a single section of the book had been run off. It was clear that more subscribers would be needed to cover the mounting costs, and Lawrence decided to print two hundred copies of the text and plates. At the end of August he apologised to Charlotte Shaw again: 'The proofs are not coming so soon. Pike, the printer, is taking a holiday in Cornwall, and meanwhile the work halts for our joint reflections.'[62] A fortnight later he wrote to Garnett: 'did you hear of my difficulty in cutting it down only 12%? I'm like a parent who has been converted to four-toed children, but can't make up his mind which of the five is best off.'[63]

By the middle of September J. G. Wilson had added a block of subscriptions and the total suddenly jumped to eighty. A week later the introductory Book of eight chapters was in page proof at last, and on September 27th Lawrence sent copies out to several people who were qualified to criticise the standard of printing. One of these was St John Hornby, a partner in W. H. Smith who was also proprietor of the Ashendene Press, one of the finest private presses in England. Lawrence wrote: 'I want to ask you to look over the enclosed proofs, technically!

'It's a good deal to ask: but I'm keen that the printing, (type-setting and press-work) should be respectable: and this is the first section to be put in shape . . .

'Pike, a new man who is setting it for me (using a monotype base, and rearranging by hand) is very keen, but this is his first book, and mine, and we are both doubtful whether it is well done . . .

'We vary the type-panel length, by a line or two, as the paragraphs demand: and cut about the text, so that no word shall be divided at a line-ending, and so that all paragraphs shall finish in the second half of the line . . . Do you think that all chapters should end at the foot of a right-hand page? . . .

'You realise that my book isn't even aiming at being sumptuous or splendid: I will be more than content if it just reaches the line which people who like fine printing find bearable. It won't be good enough to give pleasure... but I want it to avoid giving pain: to be in the insensible middle region.'[64]

Lawrence also sent a copy of the proof to Sydney Cockerell, who had worked with William Morris at the Kelmscott Press: 'The aim of it is to strike mid-way between printing so good (like the Ashendene) that it dazzles the eye to the imperfections of the matter: and printing so bad that it deforms the matter. In fact we aim at "vehicular" printing, if such there can be.'[65]

Another copy went to Charlotte Shaw: 'I hope that Cockerell and Hornby will criticise the printing... and that you will reassure me upon the text. It's an awful job to put words into type, anyhow: and I think that Pike has done excellently... only there it is: we are both beginners, and he trusts me as writer, and I trust him as printer, and each of us knows that the other is leaning on a broken reed . . . Please alter, mark, erase, add, abuse anything which hits you: either technical, or literary, or moral, or intellectual. I haven't any illusions about the thing, and the very hottest condemnations won't hurt even a secret feeling.

'Once we get this first lump passed there will be no delay or difficulty in setting up the rest.'[66]

To Lawrence's delight she gave the proof chapters to her husband, and reported soon afterwards that he had taken to them 'like a duck to water, and is working at them as if they were his own'.[67] It seems quite likely that this was the first time Shaw had given serious attention to any part of the book. He returned the proof after ten days with a forthright letter:

> My dear Luruns
>
> Confound you and your book: you are no more to be trusted with a pen than a child with a torpedo.
>
> I have gone through the proof; and as it would be quite impossible to discuss it point by point in a letter, I have just corrected it exactly as I should correct a proof of my own, and made notes where the corrections were on non-technical points. Charlotte has also made some corrections . . .
>
> I invented my own system of punctuation, and then compared it with the punctuation of the Bible, and found that the authors of the revised version had been driven to the same usage, though their practice is not quite consistent all through. The Bible bars the dash, which is the great refuge of those who are too lazy to punctuate . . . I never use it when I can possibly substitute a colon; and I save up the

colon jealously for certain effects that no other stop produces. As you have no rules, and sometimes throw colons about with an unhinged mind, here are some rough rules for you.

When a sentence contains more than one statement, with different nominatives, or even with the same nominative repeated for the sake of emphasising some discontinuity between the statements, the statements should be separated by a semicolon *when the relation between them is expressed by a conjunction*. When there is no conjunction, or other modifying word, and the two statements are placed baldly in dramatic apposition, use a colon. Thus, Luruns said nothing; but he thought the more. Luruns could not speak: he was drunk. Luruns, like Napoleon, was out of place and a failure as a subaltern; yet when he could exasperate his officers by being a fault-less private he could behave himself as such. Luruns, like Napoleon, could see a hostile city not only as a military objective but as a stage for a *coup de théâtre*: he was a born actor.

To put it another way, when the second statement is a reaffirm-ation or illustration of the first, use a colon. When it is a modification of it, or a contradiction, or a condition, or a mere correlation, the outward and visible sign being a conjunction, use a semicolon.

Colons are needed for abrupt pull-ups: thus, Luruns was con-genitally literary: that is, a liar. Luruns was a man of many aliases: namely, Private Shaw, Colonel Lawrence, Prince of Damascus &c &c &c.

You will see that your colons before buts and the like are contra-indicated in my scheme, and leave you without anything in reserve for the dramatic occasions mentioned above. You practically do not use semicolons at all. This is a symptom of mental defectiveness, probably induced by camp life.

But by far the most urgent of my corrections – so important that you had better swallow them literally with what wry faces you cannot control – are those which concern your libels. I spent fifteen years of my life writing criticisms of sensitive living people, and thereby acquired a very cultivated sense of what I might say and what I might not say. All criticisms are technically libels; but there is the blow below the belt, the impertinence, the indulgence of dislike, the expression of personal contempt, and of course the imputation of dishonesty or unchastity which are and should not be privileged, as well as the genuine criticism, the amusing goodhumoured banter, and (curiously) the obvious "vulgar abuse" which *are* privileged. I have weeded out your reckless sallies as carefully as I can.

Then there is the more general criticism about that first chapter. That it should come out and leave the book to begin with chapter two, which is the real thing and very fine at that, I have no doubt whatever. You will see my note on the subject . . .

ever

G. Bernard Shaw[68]

The idea of dropping the first chapter caused Lawrence some misgivings. The chapter contained an important, if over-modest, statement about his position in Arabia, and paid tribute to the other British officers who had served there: 'This isolated picture throwing the main light upon myself is unfair to my British colleagues. Especially I am most sorry that I have not told what the non-commissioned of us did. They were inarticulate, but wonderful, especially when it is taken into account that they had not the motive, the imaginative vision of the end, which sustained the officers. Unfortunately my concern was limited to this end, and the book is just a designed procession of Arab freedom from Mecca to Damascus. It is intended to rationalise the campaign, that everyone may see how natural the success was and how inevitable, how little dependent on direction or brain, how much less on the outside assistance of the few British. It was an Arab war waged and led by Arabs for an Arab aim in Arabia.

'My proper share was a minor one, but because of a fluent pen, a free speech, and a certain adroitness of brain, I took upon myself, as I describe it, a mock primacy. In reality I never had any office among the Arabs: was never in charge of the British mission with them.'[69] The chapter went on to name the other British officers involved. Lawrence now wrote to Charlotte Shaw: 'I'm sorry to lose the list of names . . . It was my only homage to the fellows who helped the show. Perhaps it can be stuck in somewhere, someday. I began the book with that flat chapter, since those usual trumpet-like sentences are too loud for my manner. I like things which creep in silently. The book really begins in Chapter 10, which has not yet been sent you, as it isn't ready.'[70] He was less willing to accept Bernard Shaw's ideas about punctuation: 'The hatred of semi-colons was born in me: and I've never consciously used one at all. Pike must have put in the three you saw. There shall be an acknowledgement of the others to you in a preface somewhere . . . May I go on sending the proofs? Please be gentle with the semi-colons, for they hurt my sense of fitness.

'G.B.S.' punctuations strike me as literary, not conversational. Stops aren't necessary really, at all . . . Please give G.B.S. my most astonished thanks: and accept the same directly for yourself.'[71]

Further progress with the printing was held up while Lawrence thought over comments sent him by Hornby, Cockerell, Hogarth, and Shaw. On balance the technical judgments were favourable. He wrote to Hornby: 'I'm very glad you like Pike's part of the work. It is his first piece of printing, and he is spending all his time and energy on it, and so we can afford to balance paragraphs and re-set pages as often as seems necessary. He's not like a skilled workman who knows that his stuff has reached the technical standard and resents alteration'.[72] However, the effect of the criticisms was that Pike had to reset a good deal of the forty-page sample.

The page proof had also gone to Robin Buxton, who had shown growing concern about the finances of the project and its very slow progress. In a letter of October 7th Lawrence admitted to Buxton that the revenue from a hundred and ten subscriptions would no longer cover the cost of the edition. He was expecting Pike's expenses to be fifty per cent higher than the original estimate, and there were other additional costs. He wrote: 'It's very good of you to have borne the load so long, and if you will have patience a little longer . . . I'll make arrangements . . . I've been peacefully drawing without ever thinking of a reckoning, and probably it'll be a month now before I get clear.'[73]

To ease his problems with the bank, Lawrence offered the land he owned at Chingford as security. He had acquired the land in several different pieces, and he now had some difficulty locating the various title-deeds. In addition, he once again raised the possibility of issuing an abridgement: 'The idea in my mind was that I could assign to the Bank, in case of my death or disappearance, the right to publish an abridgement (as approved by D. G. Hogarth . . . acting as editor) of as much of the *Seven Pillars* as seemed necessary or fit: and to apply the profits of such transaction to meeting any charges they had against either of my accounts... any surplus going, of course, to my brother, who is to inherit my debts and assets, if there are any assets ever.

'Is this a possible document? It won't be necessary if I go on all right... but I might go off, just as easily. A burst front tyre, or weariness, or the other fate I'm always fearing. You know, Robin, I'm hardly sane at times.'[74]

By the end of the year it was certain that publication of the book would leave a considerable debt. On December 5th Lawrence told a friend: 'The bills grow ominously: it is clear that my estimates were too low.'[75] The same day he wrote to Lionel Curtis: 'I think I've about done with the Tank Corps, since I now fit it smoothly... and the next step must be considered with circumspection. That's the worst of having once been fool enough to have been 'somebody'. At times I fear that my news value may not end till the day after I'm dead.'[76]

These financial difficulties and the effects of a year's overwork compounded the depressive illness from which Lawrence was suffering. It seems that by the end of 1924 his mind was no longer balanced. Early in the New Year he wrote to Lionel Curtis that he would probably remain in the Tank Corps 'till the labour of this reprint is past: say November 1925. After that, if I feel as at present, I'll look for some safer employment... but it will be difficult to find . . . In the next stage there may be obeying of orders... no objection to that... but there must be no scope for voluntary effort supplementary to, or apart from, orders. That's where I fail here: the leisure lets me carry on another life when I'm off duty.

'It's selfish of me to worry you to help me think of some compulsory life which shall be 24-hour in the 24... but as I say the finding is difficult, and your *savoir-faire* may show me some roads to it'.[77]

In this fragile state of mind, the complex forces driving Lawrence downwards led him to even more extreme self-degradation. It was to be many years before this came to light: in May 1968 John Bruce, who had served with Lawrence in the Tank Corps, approached the *Sunday Times* with sensational testimony. He claimed to have been a key figure in Lawrence's life between 1922 and 1935. After some negotiations the newspaper acquired an eighty-five-page typed account of the alleged events in which Bruce had been involved.

Parts of the document were clearly invention, for instance it was stated that Bruce had accompanied Lawrence on spying expeditions in India disguised in native dress. Other parts, which contained extraordinary claims, could not possibly be verified. To protect itself the *Sunday Times* requested Bruce to make a legal declaration that he was telling the truth. In consequence any attempt to point out the inventions in Bruce's testimony would amount to an accusation of perjury.[78]

Extracts from the Bruce document, omitting obvious errors, were published in the *Sunday Times* on 23rd June 1968. It was alleged that Bruce had met Lawrence in 1922, that he had been engaged to act as a kind of bodyguard and that, while serving in the Tank Corps, he had administered the first of a series of beatings.

There is independent evidence for one aspect of the Bruce narrative. Lawrence did arrange to have himself beaten, on a small number of occasions and over a period of several years (Bruce claimed to have administered nine beatings between 1923 and 1935). This evidence has been discussed by John E. Mack, a professor of psychiatry, in his book *A Prince of our Disorder*. Put simply, Mack's conclusion was that the beatings were a form of penance through which Lawrence attempted to come to terms with the homosexual rape at Deraa in 1917. Mack does not, however, suggest that this was Lawrence's only motivation; he points to other psychological factors that may have been involved (some factors of this kind are evident in letters from the Bovington period quoted here).

The matter is clearly very complex. Since Lawrence himself left no explanation, and there is no opportunity for detailed psychiatric questioning, further speculation as to the causes of this behaviour can lead to no conclusive result. Doctors have told me that someone who goes through a deeply traumatic experience will react in a way which is determined by factors in that person's unique psychological make-up. Such a reaction may involve 'abnormal' private behaviour which appears to verge on insanity. Yet, however strange it may seem to others, this course is probably the surest path by which that individual can attain psychological equilibrium.

There is no case for attempting to deal in this historical biography with a psychological question already discussed by Mack with much greater professional authority. The argument for not doing so is particularly strong because psychiatrists stress that private behaviour of this nature is usually totally independent of a person's everyday life. In Lawrence's case, no one knew of it except for a handful of people directly involved, and there appears to be no way in which it affected his career. It was a symptom rather than a cause of his state of mind. As Mack has written: 'There is a temptation in this age of science and psychology to try to explain everything about human beings, or to show how each of the parts of a person's personality relates to the others. There is a false scientism in this, for we are not integrated in our personalities to nearly the same extent as we are in our bodies. Some qualities in all of us – in Lawrence certainly – must stand by themselves without explanation.'[79]

CHAPTER 35

Escape from the Tank Corps
January – August 1925

LAWRENCE was spending a great deal of time on *Seven Pillars*, but the printing had made little progress. By the beginning of 1925, a year after the project had started, only the first three of the eleven Books were in type, and not a single page had passed its final proof. Nevertheless, he told Charlotte Shaw of his hopes to have the text printed by September and the book distributed soon after. Events were to show that this new estimate was as wildly optimistic as the first. In February, when Pike finally printed the forty-page Introduction, the fourth section of text was still not typeset. To make matters worse, Pike was using a small press operated by a treadle. It was not large enough to print more than two pages at once, and as a result *Seven Pillars* would require a very large amount of press time (in a book of this format, four or eight pages would normally have been printed together). Some of the sheets carried black and white illustrations which could not, for technical reasons, be printed at the same time as the text, and these had to go through a second laborious printing.

Lawrence's mental state was now deteriorating rapidly, and he had begun to think that, once *Seven Pillars* was finished, re-entry into the RAF would be the only future worth living for. He was totally obsessed with this idea, and it is difficult to comprehend the importance he attached to it. On February 6th he wrote to Trenchard: 'February is "supplication month"... so for the third time of asking – Have I no chance of re-enlistment in the R.A.F., or transfer? It remains my only hope and ambition, dreamed of every week, nearly every day. If I bother you only yearly it's because I hate pestering you on a private affair.

'Last year I said all I could in my favour, and have no eloquence left. My history hasn't changed. Clean conduct sheet since then, which (in a depot) shows that I have been lucky as well as discreet. I've kept my job as storeman in the recruits' clothing store, except for intervals of clerking (for the Q.M.), a Rolls-Royce Armoured Car Course, and a month in company store. Official character (from the Q.M. who is good to me) "Exceptionally intelligent, very reliable, and works well." A descending scale, you will note: but I so loathe the Army that I might not work at all. Even in better days I was not laborious. "Intelligent" was because I got 93% on my Rolls course: the highest marks ever given. "Reliable" because when a company stores went wrong they borrowed me to enquire, check, make new ledgers, and wangle deficiencies.

'I've lived carefully, and am in clean trim, mind and body. No worse value, as an Aircraft Hand, than I was . . . The war-worry and Middle East are finished: and I'd be peaceful and moderately happy, if I weren't always seeing the R.A.F. just out of reach.

'Your objections to me lay on the point of discipline. Yet I pass . . . all right and the R.T.C. being weakly can less afford exceptions than the R.A.F. [I] don't say that I fit in, exactly:– any more than I did at Uxbridge or in Arabia or at All Souls or in any Officers' Mess. But I'm not the only misfit one meets (and is usually sorry for). There is nothing portentous about my small self. If I had the greatness you alone see in me would I write you begging letters year after year? It's true I wasn't brought up as a mechanic: but I've learned the way (nearly three years, you know) and can pass muster, and avoid their dislike. Being "bottom dog" isn't a whim or a phase with me. It's for my duration, I think.

'Please don't turn me down just because you did so last year and the year before. Time has changed us both, and the R.A.F. since then. I could easily get other people to help me appeal to you: only it doesn't seem fair, and I don't really believe that you will go on refusing me for ever. People who want a thing as long and as badly as I want the R.A.F. must get it some time. I only fear that my turn won't come till I'm too old to enjoy it. That's why I keep on writing.'[1]

Two weeks later Lawrence wrote to Buxton thanking him for his help with the *Seven Pillars* overdraft. But although the bank was prepared to continue the existing level of borrowing, it was opposed to any increase. Lawrence knew that he would have to raise further money in some other way since he was powerless to speed up the work of printing or revision: 'I am cutting out much, changing some, and smoothing out many of the stylistic roughnesses . . . the most I can manage is a page a day, and any extra duty (such as we have sometimes) or a visitor, or an urgent letter from outside, breaks the current of my corrections, and makes their progress slower. It is really hard work, since it's grudged work.'[2] In the short term he could only plead with Buxton for funds to help him through while he took other steps to resolve the problem: 'If you can give me a hundred extra, please do, since it will take two months for my second remedy to work. This is a sale of some books I possess. Sotheby will do it I hope . . . and the yield from them should be in the neighbourhood of £300. This should see me through to the end of this year . . . The first copies should be ready in November: and I hope the whole by Xmas.

'I'm prepared for a loss of about a thousand pounds on the edition. This added to the overdraft of £1,300, with interest, will leave me about £2,500 to find in January next... I have two irons in the fire for the clearing up. Chingford is up for sale, and might bring the whole figure. If it has not done so by Christmas I'll take the offer of an abridgement of about half *Seven Pillars* to Cape, who was willing to go £7,000 last time, and would probably go £3,000 this time, for a limited agreement, which would suit my scruples better than outright disposal.'[3]

The difficult situation was made worse by the temperament of his printer. Manning Pike, an American from Minnesota, had an unhappy marriage and was given to fits of extreme depression during which he would do no work at all. Despite the many delays, Lawrence knew that the only hope of progress was to flatter and encourage him. On February 23rd, for example, he wrote: 'This is merely a scribble, because your letters sound despairing – and I hope that isn't true. There is nothing to despair about, though the job is very big and long and difficult. It is being superbly done, you know: better than I had dreamed of before you began work. Forster thought those eight pages were the most beautiful he had seen, as printed type-faces, and for legibility . . . now I'm going to get ahead with Book V. Do you realise that we are half-way? Or at least that I'm half-way with corrections, and you have been held up by the Shaws' slowness in returning their page proof of Bk.ii, and galley of Bk.iii.

'We aren't doing at all badly, as to quantity: and beautifully, as to quality. While the second is true, blow the first!'[4]

Much of the praise was sincere. Lawrence told Kennington: 'I'm rather non-plussed: if I go on writing him cheerfully, the letters will lose force, out of monotony. Yet he is doing glorious work. The crispness and brilliance of the finished proofs of Book i. are wonderful. As good press-work as has ever been done. The man is a treasure, and shall take as long as he likes . . . Cheer him up, please, if you see him.'[5] Forster came down to Clouds Hill for a third visit on February 18th. From then on proofs went for criticism to him as well as to Charlotte Shaw.

In March, Lawrence decided to approach Jonathan Cape and sound out the idea of an abridgement. Despite previous disappointments Cape was interested, and on March 23rd Lawrence met him in London and offered

125,000 words, less than half of *Seven Pillars*, to be published under a different title in spring of 1927, about a year after the subscribers' edition of the complete text was due to be issued. Cape suggested a contract under which he would pay £1,500 on signature and a further £1,500 six months later. Lawrence undertook to complete the abridgement by March 1926, which meant that he would tackle it after work on the subscribers' *Seven Pillars* had been finished. When the abridgement contract was agreed, he cancelled the sale of his private press books: 'I'd rather keep them than anything I've ever had.'[6]

Later that month the appeal to Trenchard seemed to bear fruit. The previous year it had been Lord Thomson rather than the Air Ministry who had rejected the idea of Lawrence returning to the Air Force. After only a few months in office, however, the minority Labour Government had fallen, and in October 1924 the electorate returned the Conservatives with a large majority. Since Lawrence was already in the ranks, it could surely not matter which branch he served in. Samuel Hoare was once again appointed Secretary of State for Air, and Trenchard promised to raise the question of a transfer when the new Minister returned to England in May after a lengthy visit to the Middle East.

This news was a great boost to Lawrence's morale. He told Buxton on March 26th: 'Brough has brought out a new and most wonderful 'bike, which will do 112 m.p.h. so long as the tyres will stand it. I'm going to blow £200 of Cape's on that.'[7] Hearing something of his financial difficulties, Bernard Shaw had sent a telegram offering to guarantee the *Seven Pillars* overdraft. But he had misunderstood the problem; his proposal would only have helped if the money from subscribers would eventually have repaid the whole debt. This was not the case, and Lawrence could not possibly accept the offer. Instead, he told Charlotte Shaw about the possibility of returning to the Air Force: 'Such a thing would push me up into the seventh level of happiness. May is to be the month of decision. Perhaps a good thing may at last happen!'[8] He asked Edward Marsh to canvass Churchill, now Chancellor of the Exchequer, on his behalf. The support of such a senior minister might help to sway Hoare, whose unsympathetic attitude was already known.

Lawrence was beginning to think farther ahead. He did not like the idea of publishing an abridgement of *Seven Pillars* in England, where it would bring him continued publicity. He had therefore built a clause into the contract with Cape which would enable him to halt publication once the bank overdraft had been repaid. In exchange, Cape was to receive a larger share of the American royalties than was usual. Lawrence also had reservations about the standard clause in the contract giving Cape first refusal of any subsequent book. He had been asked confidentially by Thomas Hardy's wife whether he would like to edit for publication a diary Hardy had written during his youth. Lawrence wrote to Cape, explaining his difficulty about the 'next book' clause, saying that the diary showed, 'very wonderfully, the growth of [Hardy's] mind and the slow accumulation of its knowledge', but the book 'would be Macmillan's [Hardy's publishers] in any case.

'I haven't said either yes or no: and will not, for a long time yet. "No", probably, since I haven't much desire to undertake so difficult a scissors and paste job... but its anonymity appeals to me: and if I felt at a loose end, say two years hence, then I might try my hand as an editor.'[9]

Lawrence had shown the draft contract for the abridgement to Bernard Shaw, who still disapproved of Cape. Shaw amended it radically and told Lawrence that the edition would bring publicity and a new press scandal. Worse still, without saying anything to Lawrence, Shaw wrote once again to Stanley Baldwin pressing the case for a pension: 'Lawrence has landed himself in a corner from which he cannot extricate himself without a blazing publicity'. Shaw went on to explain that Lawrence had run up debts in producing the subscribers' *Seven Pillars* 'which he proposes to meet by an abridged edition to be published by Jonathan Cape after being exploited, like Lady Oxford's memoirs, by the American press at large and by the Rothermere-Beaverbrook Sunday papers here.

'If this comes off – and I do not see any means of preventing it – Private Shaw and his ungrateful country will be all over the shop. There will be paragraphs, snapshots, reproductions of the Augustus John portraits and drawings, interviewers besetting the camp in Dorset, and deuce knows what not . . . Meanwhile the man remains as impossible as ever. He will not make money out of his book. He has just sent me a draft of his agreement with Cape designed to prevent this – an absurd document of no practical value if brought into court.' Shaw suggested that 'this is the moment to blackmail the Treasury into putting on their minutes a pension to him for extraordinary and diplomatic services in Arabia during the late war.'[10] Baldwin almost certainly discussed this letter with Churchill, Lawrence's former chief at the Colonial Office. The effect of such threats of publicity on the impending decision about Lawrence's transfer to the RAF may well be imagined.

While waiting for Hoare's decision, Lawrence wrote to Hornby about Pike, who was still making heavy weather of the printing: 'Lately he has been looking at your books, paper and vellum, and he can't make out how your press-work on vellum is done. As I told you, mine is his first book, his apprenticeship to what he hopes will be commercial printing. It is my luck to have found a mature beginner who is willing to take every possible trouble with the composition and printing: but of late he has been over loaded – we are half-way in the job, and want to finish it, and he must have an assistant.

'This is where I hope you will come in. May Pike meet you, or your workmen, to get hints, and if they know of anyone, to get the name of someone who would double him where he is weak? It will be about a five or six months job, of an interesting character to anyone who likes good work.'[11]

On May 16th Lawrence heard that Hoare had again refused to allow him back into the RAF. He was shattered by the news: 'I have the feeling in my bones that this time the decision is final. Am I a pessimist? Not too quickly, anyway, for it has been nearly three years since my rejections began. Odd, to have tried so many ways of living, to have found only one of them thinkable as a permanency, to have endeavoured for seven years consistently to follow it, and to have achieved it for exactly six months in those seven years. Exactly what effect the disappearance of my last ambition will have upon my course I can't say yet, since for the rest of this year all my attention must be upon finishing the revise of the *Seven Pillars*. About Xmas I will have to make up this very veering and fickle mind, afresh.'[12]

He wrote to Buxton on the same day: 'The R.A.F. has finally made up its mind, that I am not, and will never be, considered fit to serve in it again. This, of course, affects my stay in the army, by removing the motive of it. So I may buy myself out in the autumn, to have full-time for the last three months, to finish the *Seven Pillars* business. After it is over I will be able to square up its account and to pay off any deficit there may be in my private account . . . I'm most grateful to you and your Bank for making this last two years possible: and your reliance on my not pegging out (deliberately that is) without settling all up, shan't be disappointed.'[13]

News of the rejection by the RAF dashed the hopes that had been sustaining Lawrence during the preceding weeks. His black depression returned: he saw no point in living on once *Seven Pillars* had been finished. However, he was prepared to try any steps that might reverse the decision. Knowing that John Buchan was friendly with the Prime Minister, he had written to Lionel Curtis a few days earlier: 'John Buchan: do you ever see him? Could I? Without seeming to wish to? Naturally, in other words.'[14] It had been impossible to arrange a meeting before Hoare had made up his mind, but on Sunday May 17th, the day after he had learned about the refusal, Lawrence met Buchan in London. He evidently begged for help, and he followed this up two days later with a letter: 'I don't know by what right I made that appeal to you on Sunday. It happened on the spur of the moment. You see, for seven years it's been my ambition to get into the Air Force . . . and I can't get the longing for it out of my mind for an hour. Consequently I talk of it to most of the people I meet.

'They often ask "Why the R.A.F.?" and I don't know. Only I have tried it, and I liked it as much after trying it as I did before. The difference between Army and Air is that between earth and air: no less. I only came into the army in the hope of earning my restoration to the R.A.F. and now the third year is running on, and I'm as far away as ever. It must be the ranks, for I'm afraid of being loose or independent. The rails, and rules and necessary subordination are so many comforts. Impossible is a long word in human dealings: but it feels to me impossible that I should ever assume responsibility or authority again. No doubt any great crisis would change my mind: but certainly the necessity of living won't. I'd rather be dead than hire out my wits to anyone, importantly.

'The Air Ministry have offered me jobs: a commission, and the writing of their history. These are refinements of cruelty: for my longing to be in the R.A.F. is a homesickness which attacks me at the most casual sight of their name in the papers, or their uniform in the street: and to spend years with them as officer or historian, knowing that I was debarring myself from ever being one of them, would be intolerable. Here in the Tank Corps I can at least cherish the hope that I may some day justify my return. Please understand (anyone here will confirm it) that the Battalion authorities are perfectly content with me. Nothing in my character or conduct makes me in any way unsuitable to the ranks: and I'm fitter and tougher than most people.

'There, it's a shame to bother you with all this rant: but the business is vital to me: and if you can help to straighten it out the profit to me will far outweigh, in my eyes, any inconvenience to which you put yourself!

'I think this last sentence is the best one to end on.'[15]

Buchan wrote to Baldwin. His letter, coming so soon after the one from Bernard Shaw, brought an invitation from Baldwin to 'Come and see me about that exceedingly difficult friend of yours.'[16] However, Buchan's appeal carried too little weight to change Hoare's mind.

The printing of *Seven Pillars* began to run more smoothly when Hornby found an experienced pressman, Herbert Hodgson, to help Pike with the work. Hodgson's first act was to have an electric motor fitted to the press, and he proved to be as good a craftsman with presswork as Pike was with typesetting. As a result the text and delicate line illustrations of *Seven Pillars* were printed with great skill.[17]

Now that there was to be money from the abridgement, Lawrence decided to commission more illustrations for *Seven Pillars*. As the typeset text was divided into pages, he could see where there were blank spaces at the ends of chapters. He set about getting tailpiece drawings to fill these spaces, asking Kennington, Paul Nash, and Wyndham Lewis. To the last he wrote: 'My thing is written in many short chapters. So far as I can these are squared to end far down their page: but every now and then one comes with a long blank white space ending it . . . I don't like such voids, and I'm filling them with any line drawings I can get hold of. Kennington did me some actual "illustrations", rather in the manner of Bateman, to what seemed to him funny episodes of the book. I have about seven of these, and they are being inserted near their contexts. Other people have done me vegetable sorts of drawings, just formal designs, which can be cut on wood or put on zinc, as tailpieces.'[18] Wyndham Lewis accepted £50 in advance for the work, but despite several reminders never produced any illustrations for *Seven Pillars*.

Lawrence was still busy revising the 1922 text for typesetting, but in addition he now had to correct three or four stages of proof. The work was taking him five hours a day, over and above his Tank Corps duties. By mid-June he was little more than half-way through the revision, having just completed the section in which he described the distressing events at Deraa. He wrote to Edward Garnett: 'You asked me long ago how I was correcting the old text... since when I've had nothing convenient to send you. Here at last is a section (Book VI) ready for Pike, to whom please forward it when you have looked at it (if you want to trouble yourself still with the rake's progress of this deplorable work).

'This, being the best written section, is less cut about than any yet: and has lost fewer lines: only a bare 15%: though a good many lines usually come out in the next stage (galley) and in the first page-proof which succeeds the galley. So not all that I have now left will survive to the end. My judgement gets furry, by dint of staring at the familiar pages.

'What muck, irredeemable, irremediable, the whole thing is! How on earth can you have once thought it passable? My gloomy view of it deepens each time I have to wade through it. If you want to see how good situations, good characters, good material can be wickedly bungled, refer to any page, passim. There isn't a scribbler in Fleet Street who wouldn't have got more fire and colour into every paragraph.

'Trenchard withdrew his objection to my rejoining the Air Force. I got seventh-heaven for two weeks: but then Sam Hoare came back from Mesopotamia and refused to entertain the idea. That, and the closer acquaintance with the *Seven Pillars* (which I now know better than anyone ever will) have together convinced me that I'm no bloody good on earth. So I'm going to quit: but in my usual comic fashion I'm going to finish the reprint and square up with Cape before I hop it! There is nothing like deliberation, order and regularity in these things.

'I shall bequeath you my notes on life in the recruits' camp of the R.A.F. They will disappoint you.'[19]

It seems certain that Lawrence wrote this letter with the intention of making his friends take some action about his predicament. Suicide threats, especially when they are issued such a long time in advance, are generally a *cri de cœur*. Whether or not Lawrence would, in the event, have taken his life cannot be known, but the great majority of people who threaten to commit suicide never do so. Moreover, Lawrence must have known that such a threat would be a potent weapon against Hoare.

Garnett was naturally alarmed by this letter and immediately wrote to Bernard Shaw appealing for help. Shaw forwarded Garnett's letter to Baldwin, pointing out that if Lawrence carried out his threat there would be an appalling scandal.

As it happened, public interest in Lawrence was running high at that moment. In May, Hutchinson had published a popular biography by Lowell Thomas called *With Lawrence in Arabia*, based on his earlier slide lectures. The book was of little comfort to Lawrence. When Forster had the idea of reviewing it, Lawrence sent him some notes, saying of Lowell Thomas: 'I resent him: but am disarmed by his good intentions. He is as vulgar as they make them: believes he is doing me a great turn by bringing my virtue into the public air'. A great deal of the book, according to Lawrence, was 'either invention or gossip. Some of the invention is deliberate, though much that he put into his American magazine articles (red-hot lying it was) has been left out of the American edition of his book. I've not seen the English edition. I thought the American version so disjointed and broken-backed as to be nearly unintelligible, as a history of me in Arabia or of the Arab Campaign above my head! However perhaps I am biased.

'His details are commonly wrong. My family isn't Irish from Galway (we were an Elizabethan plantation from Leicestershire in Meath without a drop of Irish blood in us, even)... and they hadn't any ancestors called Lawrence (which is a very recent assumption, no better based than Shaw or Ross or any other of my names). His school and college yarns are rubbish: ditto his story that I was medically unfit, or a child when war began. I was employed in the Geographical Section of the General Staff in the War Office till December 1914.

'I was never disguised as an Arab (though I once got off as a Circassian: and nearly got on as a veiled woman!)

'My height is five foot five and a half inches! Weight ten stone. Complexion scarlet. I have not been pursued by Italian Countesses.

'If I had the book handy I would amend other points: these are only contradictions of things which Posh [Palmer, Lawrence's Tank Corps friend] flings in my teeth . . . do please, above all, say that the Arab Revolt was a pretty scabious business, in which none of the principals can take any pride or satisfaction: and that my disgust with it expresses itself in my refusal to profit in any way by the spurious reputation I (most unjustly) won in it.'[20]

He was now determined to complete *Seven Pillars* as quickly as possible. With Hodgson's assistance, Pike could finish printing the text in October. Lawrence wrote to Whittingham & Griggs to enquire about progress on the colour plates. About twenty were ready, and he asked when he could expect the remainder.

Then, unexpectedly, he heard from Buxton that Air Vice-Marshal Sir Geoffrey Salmond (whom Lawrence had known since the war) had intimated that the RAF was reconsidering the question of a transfer. Lawrence, still contemplating suicide, wrote to Buxton by return: 'Will you ask him about it? I gathered that I was finally turned down, and have been making all my plans on that basis. Till I hear from you I'll hold up the American book-contract, since I can (if I'm continuing to hope) arrange another £4,000 from that source. Otherwise I've got enough, in the further £2,350 coming, to frank me over the book-bills, and over the time in which I mop the mess finally up.'[21] A week later he knew that a transfer was possible, and wrote to Charlotte Shaw: 'I live in suspense. Trenchard, the Air Chief has told me to come and see him on Wednesday, to receive a sugar-plum. I can't think what it is. He knows that I want a bad job from him, not a good one. However I will know on Wednesday. Meanwhile I work nearly five hours a day on the various stages of various sections of the proofs . . . I cut 55% out of the last corrected section of the Oxford text (Book viii)! . . . Two more books only to end the first revise.'[22]

There were difficulties over this final section of *Seven Pillars*. In the 1922 draft Lawrence had put a dramatic pause after Book VII: 'a dull area, describing a dull period, before the final effort against Damascus.'[23] However, several readers had said that this 'flat' interlude (Books VIII and IX) was much too long, and Lawrence decided to cut it savagely. He did not like Book X either, and wrote: 'It was my ambition to rewrite the last book, the advance on Damascus, hoping to key it up a bit, and make it more warm with excitement than the others (excitement perhaps isn't the right word: I'm a very cold-blooded person: but I wanted the text of it to vibrate with feeling of some sort, to mark it off from the frigid procession of all the other chapters. That unending deadness of correct style and sober judgement is enough to freeze a wombat).'[24]

At his meeting in London on July 1st he was told that he could rejoin the RAF. In giving the news to Charlotte Shaw he made no reference to the letter he had sent to Garnett threatening suicide: 'John Buchan seems to have worked the oracle: anyway Trenchard and Hoare have agreed to let me back into the ranks, any terms I please: and the matter will be put in hand straight away and completed – some time before October. I think Mr. Baldwin said something to Hoare.

'This has made the world feel very funny. The first effect was like a sunset: something very quiet and slow: as if all the fuss and trouble of the day was over. Now I feel inclined to lie down and rest, as if there was never going to be any more voyaging. I suppose it is something like a ship getting into harbour at last. The impulse to get that book finished by Christmas is over. I may be living on for years now, and so why hurry it? Also there isn't any longer any need for the book. I was consciously tidying up loose ends, and rounding the oddments off... and now it seems there aren't any loose ends or oddments.

'Don't get worried over this: a few days will see me square again, and I'll realise that it will be as well to finish all the consequences of the Arabian business before pushing off into the R.A.F. You see, if I can clean up the Arab mess, and get it away, behind my mind, then I can be like the other fellows in the crowd. Perhaps my mind can go to sleep: anyway I should be more ordinary than I have been of late. The relief it will be, to have the fretting ended.'[25]

Lawrence also wrote to Buchan about the transfer, offering his 'very deepest thanks. I've been hoping for this for so many years, and had my hopes turned down so regularly, that my patience was completely exhausted: and I'd begun wondering if it had ever been worth waiting and hoping for . . . Formalities will take some weeks: but I should change skins in September at latest.'[26] However, twelve days later he wrote to Garnett: 'You know, I expect, that they have at last revised their decision, and I am to be transferred shortly. My sense is of something ineffable; like ship *Argo* when Jason at last drew her up upon the beach; surely nothing but time and physical decay will uproot me now.'[27]

During his last weeks at Bovington Lawrence worked hard at revising the remaining text of *Seven Pillars* and correcting proofs. There would be little time for working on the book if, as he expected, he had to repeat two months' basic training when he rejoined the RAF. By July 27th the first seventy-nine pages (fourteen chapters) had been printed, and the text up to the end of Book VIII (another eighty-three chapters) was in various stages of proof. He had completed the revisions to Book IX, and told Garnett that he had cut the principal introspective chapter (chapter CIII in current editions) by a quarter: 'It . . . being concentrated, can be skipped. Whereas had I embodied its matter in incident, as you suggest, the poor worms would have had to read it all . . . Judgements upon this chapter vary. Gertrude Bell, a woman of enormous heart and whirling head, of the book said, "Approved: all but the libellous, untruthful description of yourself." Very nice of Gertrude. Alan Dawnay, a very cultivated garden, said, "Whenever anybody is puzzled about you, I lend them your chapter upon yourself. It is crystal-clear, so that afterwards they always understand." Very nice of Alan D.'[28]

CHAPTER 36

Ambition Fulfilled

August 1925 – December 1926

LAWRENCE rejoined the RAF at Uxbridge on 18th August 1925, just after his thirty-seventh birthday. He had abandoned the idea of rewriting Book X, the final section of *Seven Pillars*, knowing that he could not complete it before his transfer, and fearing that it would be a while before he had any free time. Instead he had merely revised the text, and before leaving Bovington had sent the two final Books for typesetting: 'but adjustments and corrections will last on till October perhaps. Depends a good deal on the R.A.F. Pike is now quicker than I am, with the help of his assistant.'[1] On August 21st, after only a few days at Uxbridge, orders came for Lawrence's immediate posting to the RAF Cadet College at Cranwell in Lincolnshire. He was delighted with the news. When he arrived there three days later, he celebrated by ordering a Brough motorcycle of the latest type. It would be his fourth Brough Superior.

At Cranwell he joined B flight, which consisted of fifteen men, a sergeant, and a corporal. Their duties were to look after six of the aircraft used for training cadets, and consequently their workload was much lighter during the college vacation than in term time. Ten of the flight were technicians, and five were unspecialised aircraftmen. Lawrence acted as runner and clerk.

Although he was happy to return to the Air Force he missed the beauty of the countryside around Bovington and the friends he had made there. He wrote to Palmer: 'Odd that a man should be so ungrateful, for the R.T.C. was very good to me, and I've jilted her without a regret.'[2] One link with Bovington remained. His younger brother Arnold had recently married, and the couple had moved into Clouds Hill during July. Lawrence had great affection for the cottage, and his brother, now an archaeologist working mainly overseas, wanted a base for his possessions in England. They soon decided to buy Clouds Hill, and Arnold began negotiations with the Moreton estate.

Now that Lawrence was back in the RAF and the subscribers' *Seven Pillars* was nearing completion, he had time to take stock. There was no longer an easy escape route from service life: he had so frequently rejected the idea of accepting any benefit from the Arab Revolt that he could not take any profit from Cape's abridgement, however successful. Moreover, he would now be morally compelled to stay in the RAF, having fought so hard to return to its ranks. In effect, he had been trapped by his own actions and would have to make the best of his five remaining years of enlistment. He professed to be happy with this prospect, yet within five weeks of reaching Cranwell he sent Charlotte Shaw one of his most despairing letters: 'Do you know what it is when you see, suddenly, that your life is all a ruin? Tonight it is cold, and the hut is dark and empty, with all the fellows out somewhere. Every day I haunt their company, because the noise stops me thinking. Thinking drives me mad, because of the invisible ties about me which limit my moving, my wishing, my imagining. All these bonds I have tied myself, deliberately, wishing to tie myself down beyond the hope or power of movement. And this deliberation, this intention, rests. It is stronger than anything else in me, than everything else put together. So long as there is breath in my body my strength will be exerted to keep my soul in prison, since nowhere else can it exist in safety. The terror of being run away with, in the liberty of power, lies at the back of these many renunciations of my later life. I am afraid, of myself. Is this madness?

'The trouble tonight is the reaction against yesterday, when I went mad:– rode down to London, spent a night in a solitary bed, in a furnished bedroom, with an old woman to look after the house about me: and called in the morning on Feisal, whom I found lively, happy to see me, friendly, curious [Feisal was on a brief visit to England]. He was due for lunch at Winterton's (Winterton, with me during the war, is now Under Secretary of State for India). We drove there together, and had lunch in Winterton's lovely house, a place of which I'm splendidly fond, because it has been his for hundreds of years, and is so old, so carelessly cared for. Winterton of course had to talk of old times, taking me for a companion of his again, as though we were again advancing on Damascus. And I had to talk back, keeping my end up, as though the R.A.F. clothes were a skin that I could slough off at any while with a laugh.

'But all the while I knew I couldn't. I've changed, and the Lawrence who used to go about and be friendly and familiar with that sort of people is dead. He's worse than dead. He is a stranger I once knew. From henceforward my way will lie with these fellows here, degrading myself (for in their eyes and your eyes and Winterton's eyes I see that it is a degradation) in the hope that some day I will really feel degraded, be degraded, to their level. I long for people to look down upon me and despise me, and I'm too shy to take the filthy steps which would publicly shame me, and put me into their contempt. I want to dirty myself outwardly, so that my person may properly reflect the dirtiness which it conceals... and I shrink from dirtying the outside, while I've eaten, avidly eaten, every filthy morsel which chance threw in my way.

'I'm too shy to go looking for dirt. I'd be afraid of seeming a novice in it, when I found it. That's why I can't go off stewing into the Lincoln or Navenby brothels with the fellows. They think it's because I'm superior, proud, or peculiar, or "posh", as they say: and its because I wouldn't know what to do, how to carry myself, where to stop. Fear again: fear everywhere.

'Garnett said once that I was two people, in my book: one wanting to go on, the other wanting to go back. That is not right. Normally the very strong one, saying "No", the Puritan, is in firm charge, and the other poor little vicious fellow, can't get a word in, for fear of him. My reason tells me all the while, dins into me day and night, a sense of how I've crashed my life and self and gone hopelessly wrong: and hopelessly it is, for I'm never coming back, and I want to'.[3]

Despite this deep unhappiness about his present course, the majority of Lawrence's letters show that he soon found contentment at Cranwell. He made no secret of his identity, and the men's curiosity quickly wore off. The Cadet College was an attractive station in other ways. Lawrence made friends among members of the teaching staff and helped one of them, Rupert de la Bère, to edit the college journal.

The *Seven Pillars* printing went on steadily. Lawrence had less free time for proof-reading than at Bovington, and allowed himself more distractions. On November 3rd he wrote to Edward Garnett: 'I'm in the R.A.F. Absurdly happy. Such content feels *brittle*, in the light of my past histories. Perhaps it will last.

'The *Seven Pillars* are at Book VIII. The joy of living is hindering its road. People only work when profoundly miserable. Profoundly but not hopelessly. In March perhaps it will be ready for issue. The poor subscribers . . . Have read again: *War and Peace, The House of the Dead, The Brothers Karamazov*'.[4]

Lawrence was now working on the last pages of *Seven Pillars*. As he told an acquaintance: 'I cut it off at the end like a knife: since that was how I cut myself off the Arabian adventure.'[5] He had placed a brief epilogue after the end of the narrative, and on November 17th he sent a revised draft of this to Charlotte Shaw: 'Something is urgently required at the end, to leave people who get so far in the book with a harsh taste in their mouths. You will say that this isn't necessary: that the bitterness is sensible all through: but remember that no one will ever again read the book as carefully as you have done: and that your knowledge of it, and understanding of it, will remain deeper and sharper than anyone else's . . .

'Isn't it wonderful? the job is nearly over. Your part finishes with what you have in your hand. Mine is to 1st revise IX (nearly through) and X, and to page-proof VI, VII, VIII, IX and X. After that index and map: and binding: and then peace.'[6]

As the typesetting progressed there were more opportunities to use tailpieces, many of which were drawn by William Roberts. Lawrence sent him a batch of proofs: 'I don't suggest your reading all this, but the pages [indicated] would do with tail-pieces and if your imagination prompts you to anything fitting – why fire away!

'Designs needn't be *illustrations*. Abstract designs will do. Ditto remote things, like vegetables or trees, hills, sunsets, clouds: dead fishes, apples on a plate.

'*Not* Pierrots à la Beardsley. *Not* Ballet dancers à la Laura Knight. *Not* Café scenes à la Sickert.'[7]

Lawrence spent Christmas alone, since the rest of B flight were on leave. He passed the time correcting proofs and reading T. S. Eliot's *Poems 1909-1925*: 'It's odd, you know, to be reading these poems, so full of the future, so far ahead of our time; and then to turn back to my book, whose prose stinks of coffins and ancestors and armorial hatchments. Yet people have the nerve to tell me it's a good book! It would have been, if written a hundred years ago: but to bring it out after *Ulysses* is an insult to modern letters – an insult I never meant of course, but ignorance is no defence in the army!'[8]

By the close of the year it seemed that the new text of *Seven Pillars* would be completed, at long last, within a month. But there was still work to be done on the illustrations. Lawrence suggested that the cost of extra tailpieces should be covered by accepting more subscribers. In any case, he didn't 'want to make the number exactly a hundred, for one of my dislikes is the bibliophile, and that sort of man makes a fetish of numbers. To defeat him I am not numbering my copies, nor disclosing to anyone quite how many have been printed, nor making any two just alike'.[9]

Under the terms of his contract with Jonathan Cape, Lawrence had to deliver the new abridgement by the end of March 1926. He began work on it in January, deleting passages in pencil on a proof of the subscribers' *Seven Pillars*. The task was easy, for he had twice before (in 1920 and with Garnett in 1922) shortened the text in this way. Much of the new version was broadly equivalent to Garnett's 1922 contraction of the Oxford text.

Lawrence was subsequently to make statements implying that he had given little thought to this Cape abridgement. These deliberately concealed the truth. Having charged subscribers thirty guineas for the complete text, he would have been tactless to suggest that the shortened version shared its merits. Also, it was to be expected that he would be less enthusiastic about the abridgement than about the full text of *Seven Pillars*. Yet Cape's popular edition was extremely important to him. He cared greatly about writing, and his nature forced him to make as good a job of the new version as possible. This was the first significant work under his own name to be published for general circulation, and he would not have risked hostile reviews by slipshod editing.

Indeed, the Cape project was a special challenge. Lawrence felt that in *Seven Pillars* he had failed to create a work of the 'titanic' class: his aim in the abridgement was more modest and therefore more attainable. There was magnificent material in *Seven Pillars* for an uncomplicated adventure story, and Lawrence was determined to succeed in this easier genre. Success would be extremely important, not merely for reasons of self-esteem, but because he was relying on the shortened version to clear his debts. A letter written to Cape at the end of January shows that he had already given a good deal of time to it: 'I'm not pleased with the abridgement . . . as now in my hands; I've done the first 500 pages, and it reads queer. The details are too large for the body.

'How would you view my dictating a more colloquial contracted narrative to some shorthand scribe? I'd take the subscriber version, page by page, and miss out or boil down rapidly in my mind each sentence as it came to the eye. The result would be unceremonious, swift-moving, rough perhaps.'[10] Jonathan Cape probably thought that the scheme was not serious, for he rejected it. But three years earlier Lawrence had made a similar suggestion to Aubrey Herbert with very good results. Herbert, by then nearly blind, had written a travel book based on earlier diaries. On reading the draft Lawrence had written: 'it's not a book yet. In your place I'd retire to a solitary place and have the stuff read to me by a slave, again and again. Then I'd dismiss the slave and dream over those times until all the adventures came together. Then I'd dictate a slow story of my progress: avoiding so far as possible, what is here put: then I'd use this as the bag of plums and sift them slowly into a new cake, and stir them together with a third version, which would be a book of books.'[11] Herbert had followed this advice and the result, *Ben Kendim*, became a minor classic of Middle Eastern travel.

As work on *Seven Pillars* drew to a close, Lawrence began to consider further literary projects. The scheme to edit Hardy's early autobiography was especially attractive. He told Mrs Hardy: 'I had been reading it deliberately, tasting it all over: and I swear that it's a very good thing. There is a strange *individual* taste about the story of those early days. It's very beautiful. Rarely so . . . I was seeing, every page I read, little things which might be done to polish the jewel more excellently. I do hope you will send it me back. I'll tackle it most humbly and honestly.'[12]

Cape too thought that Lawrence should start some new project. C. M. Doughty had died in January (Lawrence had taken a day's leave in order to attend the funeral in Golders Green). Shortly afterwards Cape suggested a biography to Lawrence, who replied: 'I've thought of that "life" idea, up and down: and I'm sorry that I can't touch it. I would not have delayed so in considering the life of anyone else: but for C.M.D. I have a very real regard.'[13]

On March 8th he finished correcting the last proofs of the *Seven Pillars* text, but the illustrations were still well behind. Whittingham & Griggs told him they could not complete their part of the work before July, and he replied that this was too late: 'Will you let me know which are the laggard plates? and I'll cancel them, if possible . . . I want all the illustrations completed by the first week in June.'[14]

It was as well that he had finished the text corrections, for ten days later he broke his right arm. He was turning the starting-handle of a car when the engine backfired, breaking off the tip of his radius and dislocating his wrist. Fortunately, by this time he had also completed the Cape abridgement as far as the final Book of *Seven Pillars*. He was never to recover full movement of his right hand, and for the next month could only write with difficulty, often asking one of the other aircraftmen to act as secretary.

When he finished making the Cape abridgement in late March he decided to keep the pencil working draft. With help from two friends, another proof of *Seven Pillars* was marked up with all the cuts and linking passages for the abridgement. This operation, which consisted mainly of blacking out the deleted passages with Indian ink, provided the basis for a deliberately misleading statement Lawrence later gave to Cape's house journal *Now and Then*: 'The abridgement . . . was made by him in seven hours at Cranwell in Lincolnshire on March 26 and March 27 1926, with the assistance of two airman friends, A/A Knowles and A/c Miller'.[15] The text they produced was submitted to Cape on March 30th.

When Lawrence first agreed to the Cape abridgement, he had planned that it would appear several months after *Seven Pillars* had been issued; but work on the illustrations was still holding up the subscribers' edition. In April 1926 Whittingham & Griggs postponed their completion date until August, and Lawrence heard that the Ordnance Survey was too busy to tackle his maps, so he had to look for an alternative printer. In the meantime he had commissioned more tailpieces, including a group from Blair Hughes-Stanton. At the beginning of May progress with the remaining work was briefly held up by the General Strike, but Lawrence felt that the end was in sight. He expected to issue *Seven Pillars* in September. Friends in the rare book trade told him that its value would go up to £50 within a month.

In late May he learned that he was to be posted to India that autumn. This seemed to be for the best, because it meant that he would be out of reach of the publicity surrounding Cape's issue of the abridgement. But the posting did not please him personally; he wrote to a Tank Corps friend then serving at Quetta: 'I will be low in India. Living on my pay, and trying to be an airman. The *Seven Pillars* will have been built by then, and my hybrid existence ended. In some way it will be a relief. So long as I am in England I cannot avoid sometimes bridging the classes. The writers and artists are intoxicating to meet and talk to. For a while with them I imagine myself to be an artist: they feel somehow (presumptuous it sounds) to be of my own sort. With these fellows in the service I'm very happy; but the play-times are rather a strain. I don't play – not at anything: so that the more hours work they give us the better life goes'.[16]

Within two months of receiving the abridgement draft, Cape produced a set of galley proofs for correction; as a result Lawrence had this additional preoccupation in June. Work on *Seven Pillars* was not going so smoothly. The continuing industrial unrest was affecting power supplies, and Whittingham & Griggs were held up still further. He resigned himself to the possibility that they might not finish the plates until September. On June 21st he wrote to Mrs Hardy: 'Everything else is printed and ready, and I'll send the copies out before I go abroad, whether all the possible pictures are finished or not.'[17]

In mid-August he went to Edinburgh to see Bartholomews, the map publishers, who had agreed to adapt and print the War Office maps he wanted to use for *Seven Pillars*. By then the colour printers were working on their last three plates. He wrote to Charlotte Shaw: 'One has twenty-three colours upon it. Lord save us! Kelman, a Constable partner, was admiring some of the prints at Chiswick and said to the printer "Now why shouldn't you give *us* some work of that quality?" "We will," said Newbery [of Whittingham & Griggs], "if you'll pay ten shillings a print"! Exit K.'[18] Most of the plates were to be placed at the end of *Seven Pillars*, and Lawrence, who had the idea of making each copy different, thought of changing their order. Later, however, he abandoned the idea since it would have made a nonsense of the list of illustrations.

On August 24th he sent Charlotte Shaw a description of his journey back from Edinburgh which conveys both the pleasure he took in motor-cycling, and his happiness that work on *Seven Pillars* was so nearly over:

> This morning dawned on me in Durham . . . after a mile or two I said to Boanerges ['sons of thunder', the name he had given his motorcycle] "We are going to hurry"... and thereupon laid back my ears like a rabbit, and galloped down the road. Galloped to some purpose too: Cranwell (160 miles) in 2 hrs 58 minutes. It seemed to me that sixty-five miles an hour was a fitting pace. So we kept down to that where the road was not fit for more: but often we were ninety for two or three miles on end, with old B. trumpeting ha ha like a war-horse.
>
> The rest of the north of England did not seem to love us. The Great North Road: (what a dream, what a drunkenness of delight of a name!) is, as you know, very wide and smooth, and straight. So that you can biff along it safely, without any tactics in meeting or overtaking traffic. Traffic this morning was mainly Morris Oxfords, doing their thirty up or down. Boa and myself were pioneers of the new order, which will do seventy or more between point and point. Like all pioneers we incurred odium. The Morris Oxfords were calculating on other traffic doing their own staid forty feet a second. Boa was doing 120. While they were thinking about swinging off the crown of the road to let him pass, he had leaped past them, a rattle and roar and glitter of polished nickel, with a blue button on top. They

waved their arms wildly, or their sticks, in protest. Boa was round the next corner, or over the next-hill-but-two while they were spluttering. Never has Boa gone better. I kept on patting him, and opening his throttle, knowing all the while that in a month or two he will be someone else's, and myself in a land without roads or speed. If I were rich he should have a warm dry garage, and no work in his old age. An almost human machine, he is, a real prolongation of my own faculties: and so handsome and efficient. Never have I had anything like him.[19]

At that time Lawrence thought that copies of *Seven Pillars* would be ready for dispatch to the binders on September 15th. However, there were yet further delays and the text was still not ready on September 25th when he learned that he had inadvertently libelled Ronald Storrs. The offending passage had to be rewritten, and then, since the type had been distributed, four pages had to be reset, proofed and reprinted. To add to his problems, Kennington found fault with some of the plates. As a result, the binding date had to be postponed until the end of October. There was good news, however, when Raymond Savage obtained offers worth £2,000 from the *Daily Telegraph* and *Asia Magazine* for serial rights in the Cape abridgement. This would help greatly with the *Seven Pillars* overdraft, and Lawrence accepted.

On November 4th Lawrence began the month's leave to which he was entitled before going to India. He had planned a last visit to many friends before this five-year absence overseas. But work on *Seven Pillars* took priority, and he meant to spend the first few days helping Pike get the sheets off to the bookbinders: 'Then I'll be free for ten days to say goodbye to everyone: then a week distributing the bound volumes'.[20] He wrote to Pike on October 18th: 'Keep at it. We are really last-lapping. Get the Table of Contents done: make a title-page which pleases you, and don't send it me: and then print and print and print.'[21]

Despite the care he had given to producing *Seven Pillars*, Lawrence, like William Morris, did not regard fine binding as part of the publisher's responsibility. He divided the work among several London binderies, asking them to do each copy differently so that owners could, if they wished, rebind them in another style without affecting their value. As a result some subscribers got much better bindings than others: one surviving estimate shows a variation in the cost of work on different copies ranging from eighteen to forty-two shillings.

Savage had arranged that the American copyright edition of *Seven Pillars* should be set up and printed by George H. Doran, who was publishing the Cape abridgement in New York. The contract was for twenty-two copies, two of which would be needed for copyright deposit. The remainder were to be so expensive that none would sell; in this way *Seven Pillars* would remain in print on Doran's list, and copyright would be secure.

A few copies of the English *Seven Pillars* were completed by the binders during November. Lawrence sent the very first of these to the Royal Library at Windsor. Some months previously he had learned that the library had taken out a subscription and had told J. G. Wilson, through whom the order had been placed: 'The Windsor copy will be duly sent: but I'm an old-fashioned person, to whom it seems improper that Kings should buy and sell among their subjects. You told me that the advance cheque was Fortescue [the Librarian at Windsor Castle]: and I mean to return it gently to him with the book when it is ready. Fortescue is decent, and will not tell his owner: for I should prefer Him to think He is paying for it, since that is His notion of propriety.'[22]

Another free copy, with a special inscription, went to Trenchard, who wrote: 'the part I like almost best is the expression "from a contented admirer and, whenever possible, obedient servant". This is a delightful touch from the most disobedient mortal I have ever met.'[23]

The month's leave passed very quickly. Lawrence had to spend most of it helping Pike collate the remaining copies of *Seven Pillars*, making up the individual sets of pages and plates. He managed a brief visit to Clouds Hill and spent an hour with the Hardys; Kennington had asked him to pose for a bronze portrait bust, and somehow Lawrence made time for five sittings. In London he saw the Shaws and a few other friends. As a leaving present Charlotte gave him a notebook she had filled with philosophical meditations. He wrote to thank her: 'Your little book will be very valued, for your sake, and I hope for its own. I tremble rather, upon this second head, for my tastes are not very catholic and not speculative. However I'll write and tell you just how it takes me, after I've studied it.'[24]

He sold his motorcycle, which had been damaged in a skid during this leave. Not long before he had sent a testimonial to George Brough, its manufacturer, writing that he had 'completed 100,000 miles, since 1922, on five successive Brough Superiors, and I'm going abroad very soon, so that I think I must make an end, and thank you for the road-pleasure I have got out of them. In 1922 I found George I (your old Mark I) the best thing

I'd ridden, but George II (the 1922 SS 100) is incomparably better. In 1925 and 1926 (George IV & V) I have not had an involuntary stop, and so have not been able to test your spares service, on which I drew so heavily in 1922 and 1923. Your present machines are as fast and reliable as express trains, and the greatest fun in the world to drive:– and I say this after twenty years' experience of cycles and cars.

'They are very expensive to buy, but light in upkeep (50-65 m.p.g. of petrol, 4,000 m.p.g oil, 5,000-6,000 miles per outer cover, in my case) and in the four years I have made only one insurance claim (for less than £5) which is a testimony to the safety of your controls and designs. The S.S. 100 holds the road extraordinarily. It's my great game on a really pot-holed road to open up to 70 m.p.h. or so and feel the machine gallop: and though only a touring machine it will do 90 m.p.h. at full throttle.

'I'm not a speed merchant, but ride fairly far in the day (occasionally 700 miles, often 500) and at a fair average, for the machine's speed in the open lets one crawl through the towns, and still average 40-42 miles in the hour. The riding position and the slow powerful turn-over of the engine at speeds of 50 odd give one a very restful feeling.

'There, it is no good telling you all you knew before I did: they are the jolliest things on wheels.'[25]

During the last days in London, Lawrence made over the copyright of the Cape abridgement, to be called *Revolt in the Desert*, to a charitable trust, appointing Robin Buxton, D. G. Hogarth and Edward Eliot (a London solicitor recommended by Buxton) as Trustees. He later told Hogarth that he had 'made the Trust final, to save myself the temptation of reviewing it, if *Revolt* turned out a best seller.'[26]

This renunciation would eventually deprive Lawrence of a consider-able fortune, but it was implicit in the decision he had taken in 1923 not to take any personal royalty from the subscribers' edition of *Seven Pillars*. He could not now revoke his many statements that he viewed the book as a consequence of his wartime role, and that he would take no money from it. Moreover, it would be unthinkable to profit from an abridgement which some subscribers feared would devalue their costly investment. He suggested that if publication produced surplus revenue, as seemed likely, the major beneficiary should be the RAF Benevolent Fund set up by Trenchard in 1919. In due course the *Revolt* Trustees would establish an Anonymous Education Fund, administered by the RAF Benevolent Fund, 'for the benefit of children of Royal Air Force officers, past and present, preference being given to the children of officers who lost their lives or were invalided as a result of service.'[27]

In another letter to Hogarth, Lawrence set out his ideas for the Trust's management: 'The Trust Deed left the disposal of the money to the charitable discretion of the Trustees: my idea was that the R.A.F. should get it all: except when any case turned up, for which in the ordinary way money would not be available from any source: some really interesting thing, for which we could gladly use a thousand or so: a new instance such as C. M. Doughty's sudden shortage of money. I don't want the Trustees to work at the fund: the line of least resistance is the R.A.F. Memorial, and that will take anything up to a £100,000 gladly: but if a bright idea occurs to me I won't hesitate to send it in to Eliot, and I think he won't refuse to consider it, at least. There is no power on earth which can call in question your disposal of the cash: so let's have some fun with it: so far as fun can be had without bothering Eliot, Robin and yourself. Simple fun. Let's hope there will be thousands of pounds. The more, surely, the merrier. Chucking away things is the best of sport. Here in the ranks I see many hard cases, which could be palliated by a cheque: however I promise not to bother you. I rather envy you the job. It will, as you say, go on for years: till I die and the *Seven Pillars* is reprinted'.[28]

On December 1st he wrote to his mother: 'This is my last free night in England, and I'm writing to you, very late, in the top of Barton Street, where Baker has let me stay during this month. It should have been leave, preparatory to going overseas: but for me it has been a very hard month of work on that big book of mine. It is not finished: but every copy is at the binders, so that my share is over. All that remains is to send off the copies, and that my printer, Pike, will do for me . . . Getting it over has been a big relief. I have spent £13,000 on it, altogether, and the responsibility of that has been heavy'.[29] A week later Lawrence sailed for India on board the troopship *Derbyshire*.

CHAPTER 37

A Fresh Start
India: January – June 1927

THE journey by troopship was worse than anything Lawrence had expected. Afterwards he wrote to a friend at Cranwell: 'This worm dares to advise any airmen of B Flight who may be posted overseas to make up their minds to suffer every human misery during the trooping voyage. If they expect hell they may be merry to find themselves treated little worse than cattle, packed little tighter than sardines, fed little worse than charity. The best training for a trooper is to haunt a Tube Station during the rush hour. This worm, being old and hardened and wicked did not spew out its guts into the sea. The fishes were sufficiently fed by other airmen, however. Better food would have been wasted on the airmen; and wasted on the fishes.'[1] He also wrote pointedly to Edward Marsh, Churchill's secretary at the Treasury, that the voyage out 'was something vigorous in the way of experience. Your improper department has ruled that at sea three airmen can be packed into the airspace of two sailors. Kindly meant, no doubt, to keep us warm and comfortable. But in the Red Sea and the Gulf we grew sick of each other's smell.'[2]

The *Derbyshire* called at Port Said. Lawrence had arranged to meet Stewart Newcombe and was taken ashore for a brief respite. Afterwards, the ship left Egypt with fewer men on board and conditions were less disagreeable. The next port of call was Basra, where they spent three days. Lawrence stayed on board; he had taken *War and Peace* and Samuel Pepys's *Diary* with him to occupy his time during the month-long voyage. To his disgust the ship was full again for the last leg of the journey, from Basra to India.

On January 7th he reached his destination. This was the RAF depot at Drigh Road, Karachi, seven miles outside the town. The first letters written there show mixed reactions: the accommodation was 'comfortable, almost magnificently-built, and cool . . . It seems a quiet place, though the stone floors and high ceilings are noisy and distant, hospital-like, after the homeliness of Cranwell.'[3] A fortnight later, however, he was finding the depot 'dreary, to a degree, and its background makes me shiver. It is a desert, very like Arabia: and all sorts of haunting likenesses (pack-donkeys, the colour and cut of men's clothes, an oleander bush in flower in the valley, camel-saddles, tamarisk) try to remind me of what I've been for eight years desperately fighting out of my mind. Even I began to doubt if the coming out here was wise. However there wasn't much chance, and it must be made to do. It will do, as a matter of fact, easily.'[4]

Lawrence was posted to the Engine Repair Section, where all the RAF aircraft engines in India were sent for overhaul, but he was not employed on mechanical work: 'This wrist still makes me afraid of tools. Instead I'm a half-baked clerk. I follow the course of each engine which comes in . . . and note on a large form all that is done to it, by each man, by name, with what new parts are fitted in replacement, what results it gives on test, and how many hours its rebuilding and adjustment occupy. A technical record which is referred to whenever anything happens in the future flying of its machine, or whenever the time comes to overhaul it again. You know that aero-engines have to "come down" occasionally, perhaps after 200 hours running, for complete overhaul.'[5] As a result of this work, Lawrence was to extend greatly the knowledge of engines he had acquired in the Tank Corps, and he would learn to write clearly about mechanics. He wrote : 'This is not a hard job, though it is more difficult and tricky than most. We get up at 6: breakfast at 6.30: go to work at 7.30: knock off at 1: eat a plateful of soup: sleep or read till 4: a mug of tea, slice of bread: sleep play walk or read till 7: dinner: sleep walk or read till reveille next morning. The food is satisfactory, allowing me to eat cereals or grass, instead of meat, which is a taste, not a principle, of mine, especially in hot places.'[6] There was no work on Thursdays and Sundays, but unfortunately the Commanding Officer was 'mad on parades, so that we do double the drill (and half the work) of an ordinary station.'[7]

Indian servants made their beds and cleaned their boots and brasses. Lawrence had no taste for this racial servitude and wrote to Fareedeh el Akle, who had taught him Arabic at Jebail before the war: 'This country, India, is not good. Its people seem to feel themselves mean. They walk about in a subdued, repressed way. Also it is squalid, with much of the dirty industrialism of Europe, with all its native things decaying, or being forcibly adjusted to Western conditions. I shall be happy only when they send me home again'.[8] Not long afterwards he told Lionel Curtis that he had not been out of the camp since arrival: 'The India business is too big for me to tackle: and I don't see myself following my inclination to stand, hat in hand, before every educated Indian, and murmur that it isn't my fault; that I'm not an intelligent, nor a deliberate, cog of the governmental machine. So it's better to stay in, and not meet anyone.'[9] The airfield at Karachi was two or three miles square, and this gave Lawrence enough space for exercise. He maintained this self-imposed confinement to barracks throughout his time there.

Unlike most of the airmen he found the Indian climate cool. The daytime temperature stayed fairly constant at about 90°F. At night it dropped by about ten degrees in summer, but sometimes fell by thirty degrees in winter. There was little direct sun: 'the nearness of the sea gives us so much mist and there are such continual dust-storms in the Gulf, that the light comes to us always filtered, indirectly. I go about perversely wishing for a really hot day, one which would show the grumbling crowd how fortunate is the climate they have fallen into.'[10]

He had been trying for some time to persuade his mother and elder brother Bob to give up missionary work in China, to which they had devoted their lives since the early 1920s. Renewed contact with a subject race seems to have added bitterness to his views. He was glad to see the 'anti- foreign' bias of Chinese politics and wrote to his mother: 'Salvation comes from within a nation, and China cannot be on the right road till, like Russia, she closes her eyes and ears to teaching, and follows her own instincts to their logical and absurd limits. So long as she permits outsiders to teach or preach in her boundaries, so surely is she an inferior nation. You must see that. People can take from one another, but cannot give to one another.

'It seems to me that the inevitable victory of the Canton party may be delayed yet a long while, and that the disorder is nearly bound to spread slowly up the river till it reaches you. The journey is unwholesomely long, even in peaceful conditions. In war conditions it might be very hard, even if not dangerous to you – and I have noticed that there are no foreign casualties in all this unrest, which means probably that there is little danger – and therefore I'd urge strongly that it's Bob's business to get you out before you are both compelled to go . . . Of course you will do as you like: remembering always that you are guests of China, and that guests should leave their hosts before the hosts are replete, so that their leaving shall be yet regretted.'[11]

Lawrence needed a pastime to fill the off-duty hours at Karachi. Soon after arriving he had sent to Cranwell for some of his books, and while waiting for them he read through *Ecclesiastes*. At the end of January he

told Charlotte Shaw: 'After fourteen days consideration of this unwelcome leisure I've sent for some Greek books. My Greek has nearly
perished, and I will sharpen it for six months. That may partly fill
the void. After Greek? German perhaps, or shall I try and translate
another French novel'?[12]

Ironically (since he had signed away a potential fortune in making
over the copyright of *Revolt* to a charitable Trust) Lawrence now found
himself short of cash. The men were kept on low pay until their documents arrived from England, and postage alone was costing him a great
deal. He also wanted to build up a new collection of gramophone records.
On February 1st he wrote to Cape asking about translation work. If Cape
offered nothing Lawrence thought of tackling Heinemann, which was
owned at that time by F. N. Doubleday.

The first mails to arrive from England brought letters from recipients
of *Seven Pillars*. Among them was one from Allenby, who wrote: 'I
congratulate you on a great work; fit record of your splendid achievements in the war.

'I am grateful for the kind way in which you refer to my part in our
collaboration, and am happy to think that to our unity of thought and
intention can be attributed, in great measure, the success obtained.'[13]

Lawrence was relieved by Allenby's letter. He told Charlotte Shaw: 'it
has been a fear of mine that his sense of proportion (a very sober and
stern quality in him) somehow associated my person with the ridiculous
reputation raised about it by the vulgar. You see, my campaign and
fighting-efforts were entirely negligible, in his eyes. All he required of us
was a turn-over of native opinion from the Turk to the British: and I took
advantage of that need of his, to make him the step-father of the Arab
national movement – a movement which he did not understand and
for whose success his instinct had little sympathy. He is a very large,
downright and splendid person, and the being publicly yoked with a
counter- jumping opportunist like me must often gall him deeply. You and
G.B.S. live so much with poets and politicians and artists that human
oddness attracts you, almost as much as it repels. Whereas with the senior
officers of the British army conduct is a very grave matter.'[14]

Eric Kennington sent photographs of the new bust, which Lawrence
liked immensely: 'It represents not me, but my top-moments, those few
seconds in which I succeed in thinking myself right out of things . . . a
most convincing portrait of a person very sure of himself who had
convinced the artist that he really was sure of himself . . . Yet I can't

remember much about the sittings except that I went off into a day-dream whenever we were left alone: and that I was usually dog-tired before I ever came. It was such a pity that I had to leave your sittings to the bitter end of my last month'.[15]

The *Revolt* Trustees had arranged to exhibit the originals of the *Seven Pillars* illustrations at the Leicester Galleries, where Kennington had shown his Arab portraits in 1921. They hoped that sale of the pictures would raise money to help pay off the overdraft. Without consulting Lawrence, Bernard Shaw had written a preface to the catalogue, and this contained several factual errors, including a statement that the subscribers' *Seven Pillars* was a limited edition of one hundred copies. There were in reality 170 'complete' copies, and Lawrence had given away a further thirty-two 'incomplete' copies, lacking some of the colour plates. Shaw's inaccurate claim helped to boost the second-hand value of the subscribers' edition, which climbed within weeks to more than ten times the original price.[16]

Shaw also used the Leicester Galleries preface to repeat his view that the Government should provide Lawrence with an income: 'Any country with a Valhalla or a spark of gratitude would have rewarded him with a munificent pension and built him another Blenheim. The British Government left him to pension himself like any ex-Minister by writing a book about it all'.[17] Lawrence told Kennington: 'It's a pity people don't generally realise that I can make the most lovely bubble and squeak of a life for myself, without their contributing any ingredient at all.'[18] He also remonstrated to Charlotte Shaw: 'I devoutly hope that G.B.S. does not get his pension scheme through. I manage my own life beautifully, it seems to me. Surely you and G.B.S. don't want me to take bachelor quarters in some Blenheim or other . . . As a general rule, you must agree, money matters do not enter hugely into my thinking.'[19]

In another context, however, money matters were very much in his thoughts. Everything he owned was mortgaged to the bank, legally or morally, against the *Seven Pillars* overdraft. His financial position in future years would depend entirely on the success of *Revolt in the Desert* which was to be published in March. If *Revolt* failed, Lawrence would 'be hopelessly in debt, and forced to leave the R.A.F. (which is my condition of contentment) to earn money and become solvent.'[20] Unless he did so, the bank would sell his land at Pole Hill. He could not afford to let that happen, since he hoped that this capital would one day provide a modest income for his retirement.

Nevertheless he put on a brave face and, despite the chequered financial history of the subscribers' *Seven Pillars*, told Charlotte Shaw a few days before *Revolt* was published: 'As it happens there should not be any worry about money. My overdraft was £7,000 when I sailed, and now it is less than £4,000. The Bank has the deeds of my Chingford land, which has been valued at nearly £4,000. So the position is covered, even if Cape and Doran don't roll up another penny of royalty. And the odds are that they will eventually double their advance of £3,000. Occasionally I regret my moderation in not putting a little more money into decorating the *Seven Pillars*. However it doesn't matter. It's finished.

'Surely the whole business of the *Seven Pillars* entitles me to gloat. I've written it, with generous assistance, on the whole not so badly as my circumstances (a retired Colonel, educated at Oxford) would reasonably have made G.B.S. fear. I've had it beautifully printed, and strikingly illustrated. It has been financed from the slenderest resources, and distributed (to subscribers considerately judged able to afford an extravagance) without accident or public rumour. Only one review, isn't it? and that in *The Times*, which I had not the right to refuse Geoffrey Dawson. Now, if nobody buys an American copy, or pirates it anywhere, or films it... let's hope the story ends happily, as it has begun. Pike and the colour printers, and the artists, and the bookbinders have all been properly paid, and I cannot miss the money I have never had. The alternatives, a Government appointment, or the receipts of a publishable book would have benefited me only, and only for my lifetime. *A bas* the next thirty years! What do they matter to anybody else?'[21]

His friends were concerned about what he would do to occupy himself, now that *Seven Pillars* was finished. Lawrence himself must have been pondering this question and he was at no loss for a reply when Buxton wrote inviting him 'to divulge your feelings about your life'.[22] 'Well: I feel that the writing complication is past: and with it the last vestige of responsibility for what I did in Arabia. Under Winston I put in order the actual situation in the Middle East, to my full content. In the *Seven Pillars* I've put on record my "why" and "how". So now that is all over, and I'm again a private person, and an insignificant one.

'It remains for me to do something with the rest of my life. Having tried the big things and collapsed under them, I must manage something small. The R.A.F. in England suits me perfectly. If I could be always fit and at home and not grow old I'd stay in it for ever. India is exile, endured for a specific purpose, to let the book-fuss pass over. After India I may be still fit enough for a little more service in the R.A.F. at home. When my health drives me out of it (or Trenchard drives me out!) I'll try and get some quiet job, near London, which is the place I like. A night-watchman, door-porter, or else something like a chauffeur: though I will soon be too old for anything exposed. Perfection would be to do nothing: to have something like a pound a day from investments, and live on it, as I very well could. I've learnt a lot about living in the last five years: and have a curious confidence that I need not worry at all. Desires and ambitions and hopes and envy... do you know I haven't any more of those things now in me, for as deep down as I can reach? I am happy when I'm sitting still, in complete emptiness of mind. This may sound to you very selfish... but the other fellows find me human, and manage to live with me all right. I like so much the being left alone that I tend to leave other people alone, too.'[23]

Trade editions of *Revolt in the Desert* were published in England on 10th March 1927, and in America on March 29th (there were also large-format limited editions in both countries). The book was advertised in dramatic terms, especially in America, where the tone of Doran's publicity owed much to Lowell Thomas:

LAWRENCE OF ARABIA – By Himself !

REVOLT IN THE DESERT
By T. E. Lawrence

The most spectacular and mysterious figure of modern times, he relates one of the strangest stories ever written. "With his own hands and in his own way," says George Bernard Shaw, "he exploded Turkish dominion in Arabia." He did more: he united under himself tribes and nations which had not joined together since the last Crusade; he led them in revolt to victory – the white genius of the desert legions.

Matchless in its fierce action, the story of *REVOLT IN THE DESERT* is yet matched by the brilliant prose of its telling. Whether its tale is harsh, staccato, desperate in battle, or melancholy with the sombreness of the desert, its writing is classic. Few volumes have ever combined such fascinating qualities.

Into the book has gone the spirit of this extraordinary man. Adventurer, poet, mystic, military genius – you must know him.[24]

In England a serialisation of *Revolt* had begun in the *Daily Telegraph* two months before the book was published,[25] and advance orders exhausted three printings. At thirty shillings the book cost nearly four times as much as a novel. Cape's partner Wren Howard had spared no reasonable expense to produce a volume that would meet Lawrence's demanding standards. After publication reviewers heaped praise on *Revolt*, and within days Cape had put together an advertisement which ran:

The following are extracts from some of the first reviews
"A great story, greatly written. Below a standard higher than most men's best he never falls; and the book leaves from first to last an impression of absolute truth." *Times Literary Supplement*

"The description of that last crescendo of confusion and fury and fighting, of desperate adventure and hair breadth escapes, and of the culminating triumph at Damascus, is a masterpiece. It is a marvellous record, clear, incisive, utterly unsentimental, burking nothing." *The Times*

"*Revolt in the Desert* is the great story of a truly great adventure . . . It has lasting value as a war record. It certainly stirs one's emotions . . . Its literary technique is of a high order. It will be avidly read, for page follows page giving one of the most stirring stories of our times." *Daily Telegraph*

"If myths and stories go from mouth to mouth about him, it is because Lawrence is a man of extraordinary and unclassifiable genius as surely as was George Borrow or Sir Richard Burton . . . There has, probably, been no English soldier so astonishing in his character and circumstances since Byron was at Missolonghi. And like Byron he has the genius of literature as well as the genius of adventure." *Daily News*

"I venture to think it has gained in power and vividness by compression. It is a work of literature cleared for action, monumental and momentous as Doughty's masterpiece. It has at times the epic touch of *Arabia Deserta*." *Morning Post*

"An extraordinary man, and an extraordinary book; but a book which should rank, in the future, both with the best of war books and with *Arabia Deserta* itself." *Westminster Gazette* [26]

When *Revolt* was published Charlotte Shaw took out a subscription to 'T. E. Lawrence' newspaper cuttings from an agency, and she regularly sent him a selection of these clippings while he was in India. On April 7th he wrote to her: 'The knock-out of the week was your sheaf of reviews of *Revolt in the Desert* . . . It feels altogether incredible: because I know that I'm not any of the things they call me.'[27]

His first reaction was one of self-questioning: 'I think the book reviews . . . have worried me. You say you have seen some common note in them. I've only been jarred by the improbabilities they spray out. "Genius" comes once in each, ten times in some. Who are they to judge genius? I haven't the slightest awareness of any in myself. Talent, yes, a diversity of talent: but not the other quality which dispenses with talent, and walks by its own light . . . It's odd that I should pay attention to these cuttings, when I would not, probably, pay any attention to the reviewers' opinions if I met them in the flesh. I take it as a sign that perhaps my mind is not sound on the belief that my writing is no good at all'.[28] Indeed, the praise, which was almost universal, soon strengthened his self-confidence about writing. He became fascinated by the reviews, and commented in great detail on the various criticisms. Yet he found them unhelpful in the very area which mattered to him most: their assessment of his ability as a writer. He sent Charlotte Shaw an abstract of their conflicting opinions about his style:

"Obscure to the point of affectation"
> *Tatler*

"Positively breezy"
> G.B.S.

"So imitative of Doughty as to be near parody"
> L. Woolf

"Has none of Doughty's archaisms"
> J. Buchan

"Affectedly abrupt and strenuous"
> E. Shanks

"As easy, confident, and unselfconscious as a duck's swimming"
> G. Bullett

"Gnarled texture, twisted with queer adjectives"
> *Nation*

"Simple, direct, free from ornament"
> Nevinson

"Like music"
> C. F. G. Masterson

'Now, I ask you, what is a plain, modest, would-be author to make of advices like those?'[29]

Leonard Woolf had compared Lawrence's style to Doughty's in a way that was not entirely flattering, saying that it was 'so imitative . . . as to be near parody. It imitates Doughty even to the sweeping itself absolutely bare of conjunctions, so that every sentence begins again with a full breath and ends with a really full stop. It often acquires the same gnarled texture with the same habit of an order twisted with queer adjectives and adverbs. On one page you read:-

"We slept where we were, in the mud; rose up plated with it at dawn; and smiled crackily at one another";

and on the next:-

"Step by step I was yielding myself to the slow ache which conspired with my abating fever and the numb monotony of riding to close up the gate of my senses. I seemed at last approaching the insensibility which had always been beyond my reach: but a delectable land for one so slug-tissued that nothing this side of fainting would let the spirit free."

'But the moment of irritation at this sham Doughty soon passed. After all, why should not a man imitate Doughty? The more you read *Arabia Deserta*, the more you feel that it is Arabia itself that has made the style, that nothing could give so immediately the feel of its sands and its nomads than those gnarled and twisted sentences, so swept and bare of even a conjunction . . . At any rate it did not take fifty pages before I had lost my irritation with Colonel Lawrence's style.'[30]

The comparison with Doughty was raised by so many reviewers that Lawrence defended himself to his friends: 'Leonard Woolf put it strongest: but showed an ignorance of Doughty, whose "style" isn't Elizabethan in any sense. It is Scandinavian, pure and simple, in its syntax (the inversions, the queer verbs, the broken directness) and very eclectic in vocabulary. He used words from any language, Saxon, Latin, Arabic, Greek, where his sense demanded them: and had an exquisite sense of the right word. Many of his adjectives are final, so far as fitness goes, if my judgement is worth anything: and some of these adjectives I've used, because no better ones will ever be found to fill their place.

'In that sense I've copied Doughty: but I don't like his style, his syntactical style, any more than I like his recondite vocabulary, or his point of view. You will find no Norse constructions in my book, no Arabic or archaic English words, and none of C.M.D.'s uncharitable narrowness of mind . . . People who call Doughty's book a perfect and polished whole have not read it. He had less sense of design even than myself: his book is invertebrate, shapeless, horrific: a brick-yard rather than a building. So is mine: and my sentences are abrupt, and do not flow, one from the other: but those are my misfortunes. I did my best to write accurately and well, and couldn't manage it. Conjunctions are very difficult words to fit in.

'I expected people would link C.M.D. and myself: that was inevitable in the circumstances. It's not fair to me, or to him. He was a real and tremendous poet. I'm a much smaller-built creature. His faults are big: due often to too much power of mind. My faults are due to a smallness of character.

'Doughty was a very curious person, who took his politics and feelings about politics direct from the *Morning Post*. He had no personal friends, and no bonds or nerves uniting him to his own generation, or his fellow-men. His hardness of eye closed him up, apart from life. That led to the inhuman arrogance of his work – himself being the meekest and gentlest of men. It takes a saint to judge the whole world wrong: a god to cast it into hell.'[31]

Although few copies of *Revolt in the Desert* reached Karachi, Lawrence soon heard that it was a best-seller in Britain and America. He had predicted that the combined royalties from Cape and Doran would pay off his debt within two or three years; in the event the overdraft was covered within a few weeks, and *Revolt* would earn a huge surplus before the end of 1927.

Reactions to *Seven Pillars* were no less pleasing. Churchill wrote in May, comparing it with the third volume of his own war memoirs, *The World Crisis* (which had been published a week before *Revolt* and was another of the season's best-sellers): 'when I put down the *Seven Pillars*, I felt mortified at the contrast between my dictated journalism and your grand and permanent contribution to English literature. I cannot tell you how thrilled I was to read it. Having gone on a three days' visit to Paris, I never left my apartment except for meals, and lay all day and most of the night cuddling your bulky tome. The impression it produced was overpowering . . . No wonder you brood in haughty anti-climax! I think your book will live with *Gulliver's Travels* and *Robinson Crusoe*. The copy which you gave me, with its inscription, is in every sense one of my most valuable possessions. I detected one misprint, but to torture you I will not tell you where.

'I am always hoping some day to get a letter from you saying that your long holiday is finished, and that your appetite for action has returned. Please do not wait till the Bolshevik Revolution entitles me to summon you to the centre of strife by an order "from the Imperial Stirrup"!

'All your many friends always ask about you, and I wish I had more news to tell them.'[32]

As Lawrence had forecast, the reviews of *Revolt* brought a new wave of public curiosity about his life. The extreme flavour of the legend at that time can be judged from an American advertisement for Lowell Thomas's *With Lawrence in Arabia*: 'An amazing story of intrigue and danger and audacious adventure. A complete history of the Silent Englishman who overthrew the power of the Turks and ruled the desert . . . This book will keep you up o'nights. You will want to return to it after the last stirring chapter is done. If you wore uniform in the Great War, or if you have a touch of wanderlust and adventurous passion in your blood, you will want this story of Lawrence on your shelf of most treasured books. What a book for a man to own – and to let his sons read! Now – when the whole world is talking about Lawrence – is the time to secure Lowell Thomas's amazing story.'[33]

This extraordinary publicity brought many letters from strangers, although Lawrence had asked Cape not to forward mail from unknown admirers; he rarely replied to them. On the other hand his isolation at Karachi led him to write more than ever before to his friends. One correspondence in particular found a new basis during the first few months of 1927. For two years he had been exchanging letters regularly with Charlotte Shaw about the proofs of *Seven Pillars*. Now that he was in India, Charlotte sent him parcels of books. Lawrence read and commented on them: 'Such a comfort: one can write about books. That will solve the problem of our continued correspondence: which otherwise would have been difficult'.[34]

The Shaws had no children, and Lawrence was young enough to be Charlotte's son. He liked her and admired G.B.S., and Charlotte gradually became one of his most intimate correspondents. It has been suggested that it was Lawrence who took the initiative in this friendship, but the reverse is true. It was of her making: she wrote far more frequently than he did, and showered him with gifts of books, gramophone records and luxury foods. She attached great importance to their relationship, using symbols in her private diary to note the dates she sent him letters and parcels, and those on which she received his replies.

On his side there was always an element of reserve. For example, in April 1927 he wrote to E. M. Forster: 'Her valuation of my work amazes me: and makes me fear that she hangs it as a cloak about the peg of my personality, and wants to over-estimate the cloak, for the sake of being able to over-like the peg. Woe's me. This peg distrusts all human affection.'[35] In return for her generosity he had given her a copy of *Seven Pillars* and the best known of several portrait drawings Augustus John had sketched in Paris during the Peace Conference. In June 1927 he wrote to acknowledge her 'weekly toil, of choosing, packing, posting, writing. Not anybody can feel, every week, in the mood to send or give. Sometimes it must be labour. You have never missed a mail. That gives me a guilty feeling.'[36] He wrote to her regularly, but often had difficulty finding something interesting to say: 'Perhaps if I keep a pencilled sheet handy I may be able to jot down enough in the course of a week, for it to be worth posting you. It isn't right that I should just report a bald existence to you. What's the good of two people communicating, if they haven't anything to say to one another? Feeling, you say? Yes, in England, where we were near enough to feel: but Drigh Road is outside the world . . . You send me so much, in the way of books and cuttings and letters: and I must try and be adequate, to my ability, in return . . . I can only write about your books and letters, back to you.'[37] Although she knew that Lawrence destroyed almost all her letters to him, she carefully preserved his replies.

Lawrence accepted Charlotte Shaw's presents but made sure that he was never in her debt. Over the years he gave her several manuscripts, in addition to a copy of the 'Oxford' *Seven Pillars* which he left with her on indefinite loan. Ultimately, the financial value of these gifts would far exceed the cost of her presents to him.[38] He would have found the notion of receiving charity from her repugnant. Indeed, he was using his own resources to help needy friends in England. Now that *Seven Pillars* was finished, Manning Pike, who lacked business acumen, was drifting into financial difficulties. Lawrence persuaded Cape to offer Pike some printing work, and when it became clear that *Revolt* would pay off the *Seven Pillars* overdraft, asked Buxton to set aside money from the Leicester Galleries picture sale to help. Another beneficiary of the picture money was Private Palmer, who wanted to leave the Tank Corps and find a civilian job so that he could live at home with his wife. Palmer had kept in touch with E. M. Forster, whose writing he admired, and both Forster and Lawrence arranged to help in various ways. For example, the sale of a special proof copy of *Seven Pillars* raised £400. During 1927 Lawrence gave very large sums of money to both Palmer and Pike.

Lawrence was also concerned about members of his family. That spring his mother and elder brother travelled home from China, and he wrote to Arnold Lawrence on May 5th: 'I wonder in what mind they will reach England, and where they will settle to live. It struck me, thinking it over, that some such place as Dumfries or Edinburgh might please them. London does not care for the things they care about, and the solidity of parts of Scotland might appeal to Bob. Mother, herself, was always Scotch in inclination. You might suggest it to them, as a chance idea of mine. I am sure that neither London, nor any of the usually-considered-habitable parts of England, will suit.'[39] Ten days later he wrote to Jonathan Cape, for whom Arnold was now doing occasional work: 'If you'd cast an occasional kindly eye on the activity of my little brother you'd gratify me much. I feel a responsibility, which I can't in any way support.'[40]

In April Lawrence wrote to Edward Eliot, the solicitor who had been appointed Trustee of *Revolt in the Desert*, asking about the formalities required to change his surname legally to Shaw. When Eliot replied that the process was simple and could be carried through without publicity, Lawrence decided to go ahead with it. The letter he wrote to Eliot on June 16th, in which he described his parents' situation, reveals something about his sense of ancestry: 'I'm in some doubt as to my previous name, for I've never seen my birth certificate . . . My father and mother . . . called themselves Lawrence, at least from 1892 onwards. I do not know whether they did so when I was born or not . . . Of course if Father registered me as Chapman, that will do, and there's no need to have the intermediate stage of Shaw, between Lawrence and it: for eventually, I suppose, Chapman it will have to be. There is a lot of land in that name knocking about: and I don't want to chuck it away, as Walter Raleigh, for whom I have a certain regard, gave it to my father's first Irish ancestor. I have a feeling that it should be kept in the line.'[41]

There is other evidence of a revival in Lawrence's private ambition to buy Chapman family land, referred to but apparently abandoned during the Tank Corps period. On 15th March 1927 he wrote to a friend: 'Lady Chapman has kept South Hill, my father's own house, near Killua. But

I'm told she and the daughters generally live in Earl's Court or some such place! I have the fancy, if money ever comes my way, to buy some square yards of Ireland for myself, and dig myself in there: after the old lady dies. The daughters will not bear me malice, probably. Having experienced a mother, they will not lament the absence of a father!'[42]

In part, Lawrence's decision to change names in 1927 was taken to end the awkwardness of using a name in the RAF that was not legally his own. However, there is no evidence that the pseudonym caused him any real difficulties, and it is clear from his letter to Eliot that he would have been prepared to continue the position if it turned out that he had been registered at birth as Chapman. Perhaps at one level the change symbolised a determination to reject his public image as 'Lawrence of Arabia'. At another, he saw the name Lawrence as a vestige of his parents' situation and a reminder of his illegitimacy.

CHAPTER 38

Life at Karachi
June – December 1927

LAWRENCE felt increasingly, during the early summer of 1927, that the completion of *Seven Pillars* had marked the close of a period of his life. When he realised that his overdraft would be paid off before the end of the year, he set about persuading the three Trustees to halt English publication of *Revolt* as soon as possible, hoping that this would quell public interest in him and bring forward the date at which he could return to England. He feared that it might not be easy to persuade the Trustees, since continuing sales of *Revolt* would raise a large sum for the RAF charity. On May 12th, he wrote to Buxton about stopping publication, adding: 'I'm aware that Trustees are less limber (and possibly less eccentric) than owner-writers: so perhaps the idea of turning off the stream of gold won't please them.'[1] A week later he again urged cancellation in letters to Eliot and Hogarth. The three Trustees met on May 31st and agreed that they would support Lawrence if he wrote to Cape invoking the clause in the *Revolt* contract that would end its sale in England.

He was delighted when he heard about this decision: 'Great news. My trustees, angels and archangels they are, agree to try and withdraw *Revolt in the Desert* . . . I never thought the trustees (three persons of infinite and utter sobriety, scandalously conscientious) would have the guts to do it. Hooray!'[2]

As he had feared, however, Eliot was unhappy with the decision; he sent Lawrence a long and eminently reasonable letter urging continued publication. Lawrence had foreseen this reaction, as he confided to Charlotte Shaw: 'I've only seen Eliot twice. I liked him. He is the only Trustee, really: but I added Hogarth and Buxton so that I could carry any point against him and common sense, if I wished it deeply.'[3] On June 23rd Lawrence wrote to Buxton, enclosing a formal letter to Cape which would in due course bring English publication to an end, although editions of *Revolt* would continue overseas.

Sales in America astonished no one more than the publisher, George H. Doran, who concluded that Lawrence 'had a capacity for a superbly arrogant modesty that brought him into a limelight that would have gratified the soul of P. T. Barnum as one of the great publicity triumphs of all time.'[4] When Lawrence had set the price of the American copyright *Seven Pillars* at $20,000 a copy, he cannot have guessed how Doran would use it: 'Never was better publishing publicity conceived', Doran later wrote: 'Not a copy was sold, but they were all exhibited in leading book-stores throughout the country, and the public flocked to purchase the slightly abridged . . . book for $3. Frankly, so far as his book is concerned I never could understand the stampede for it. Interesting and somewhat spectacular, yes, but great or permanent, decidedly no.'[5]

It was not just in English-speaking countries that *Revolt* sold well. Translation rights were sold for many languages, and during Lawrence's lifetime the abridgement was reprinted several times in French, German and Italian. As early as June 1927 *Revolt* had sold 30,000 copies in England and 120,000 in America. Lawrence must have reflected wryly from time to time that if he had published Garnett's abridgement five years earlier he would now be living in very different circumstances.[6]

Whatever his reservations about *Revolt*, Doran like Cape was keen to exploit Lawrence's commercial value. The two publishers decided to commission a popular biography and began to approach possible authors. When Hogarth wrote to Lawrence about this in mid-May, Lawrence was alarmed: 'Dimly behind my mind lay the certainty that some Lytton Strachey of the future would attempt a life of me: but I did not expect more than Lowell Thomas' futile effort in my life-time. And there are so many things in my life that I do not want told. When I heard that Doran was touting literary London for someone to write on me I had a spasm of fear that it would be Mrs. Ffoulkes or something horrible.'[7] His thoughts turned to Robert Graves, who had once again appealed to him, a few months previously, for a substantial sum of money.[8] Lawrence replied to Hogarth: 'If Doran wants my plain life, send him to Robert Graves, who'd be glad to earn a fee. I don't suppose that you or Buchan would be bothered with it. A bit too soon, anyway, to write it. Lowell Thomas and *Revolt* between them should satisfy the sheep and the goats.'[9]

Lawrence, now approaching his thirty-ninth birthday, was entitled to feel that a 'life' was premature; in fact, his career had nearly taken an entirely new direction the previous week when the station adjutant had sent for him and asked whether he would be prepared to serve as airman-clerk to the British attaché in Kabul. This was a two-year posting and would have put Lawrence back into civilian clothes. Lawrence told

Charlotte Shaw in confidence about the offer: 'Probably the British military attaché in Kabul is only a glorified kind of spy.'[10] He had been taken aback by the adjutant's suggestion and 'explained that I wasn't a clerk, and couldn't undertake to make myself one at short notice.'[11] Yet the posting had evidently interested him, and he also mentioned it when writing to Edward Marsh about Churchill's views on Russia: 'He alarms me a little bit, for I feel that he wants to go for Russia, and the ex-bear hasn't yet come into the open. It's hard to attack, for its neighbours, except Germany, aren't very good allies for us. We can only get at her, here, through Turkey, or Persia, or Afghanistan, or China, and I fancy the Red Army is probably good enough to turn any one of those into a bit of herself, as the Germans did Rumania. Persia certainly: Turkey will be very strong, soon, and should be our ally, if common interests make for anything. China I know nothing of, but she is too huge for anyone to swallow. The most dangerous point is Afghanistan. Do you know I nearly went there, last week? . . . the Depot would have put my name forward, if I'd been a bit nippier on a typewriter. I'll have to mug up typing: for from '14 to '18 I served a decent apprenticeship in semi secret / secret work, and Russia interests me greatly. The clash is bound to come, I think.'[12]

Lawrence's reaction to this offer suggests that he no longer felt the need to 'lie fallow' in the ranks; and with *Seven Pillars* behind him was ready for some greater challenge. A turning-point had been passed, and he was seeking more rewarding personal activities. In this case, however, he told Charlotte Shaw: 'It seems to me that I'd better stick as tight to Karachi as I can: or to Drigh Road rather . . . It would have been interesting to have seen the whole of the Khyber Pass: and I might have liked Afghanistan. However, it won't be. Safety first, as they say in 'busses. Better the camp you know... and Drigh Road is as hidden a place as any in the world.'[13] Nevertheless a few weeks later he began to teach himself to type.

Lawrence was preoccupied with several matters during June and July 1927, but his dominant concern was the new biography. The idea of offering the job to Robert Graves had also occurred to friends in England, and on June 3rd Graves sent Lawrence a telegram: 'Cape and Doran want schoolstory of Revolt shall I decently to prevent others no formal imprimatur from you but veto for manuscript Kennington will illustrate'.[14] Lawrence cabled back the one word 'yes' by return, and wrote: 'There may be money in it: which is my reason for wishing you to get it. From all other points of view I'm sorry. Doran should have had more sense . . . I would like to see your text, if time admits, before it goes to press: preferably in typescript. There are certain things which must not be said. Not that I care, but other people have such odd views. And politically about Arabia, there may be a touch or two which I'd suggest your adding. Your book quite likely won't be just a school edition: and if so I may try and persuade you to act as a vehicle in correcting some mistakes the public have made about the direction of my hopes.'[15] To save time he suggested that batches of typescript should be sent out to India by air mail. He would go through them as quickly as possible and return them to Graves by air.

Graves followed his cable with a letter which explained more about the terms: 'I am to get £500 advanced royalties and what is also good, Cape and Doran will publish other work of mine and Laura [Riding]'s which is waiting for a publisher and spoiling our appetite for further writing. The Muses are grateful.'[16] The book envisaged in the contract was a short account for children. According to Graves, Cape and Doran had 'deduced from the interest in Lawrence created by *Revolt in the Desert* among adults that a *Lawrence's Adventures* for boys could profitably be published as a Christmas book.'[17] Both publishers feared that another writer might jump on the Lawrence bandwagon, and they asked Graves to deliver his text in only six weeks.

As soon as he received Lawrence's cabled agreement, Graves set to work. On June 5th he wrote to Siegfried Sassoon: 'I am getting information from Hogarth, Buxton, Lloyd, Arnie Lawrence, etc., and have even written to Allenby. Also to Mrs. Hardy, E. M. Forster; and Kennington is going to illustrate.

'I have to work against time to get it out before anyone else can, and to make it authoritative to discourage imitations. Please get your wits together and put down on paper what you remember of T.E.'s reminiscences or accounts you've had from others of his doings . . . I want you to help me with the writing; with blue pencil and red.'[18] Graves also appealed for help to Bernard Shaw; but Shaw refused bluntly, having confused Robert Graves with his brother Charles, a noted journalist. Shaw later confessed to Lawrence: 'I wrote very unceremoniously to Robert Graves under the impression that he was Charles, whom I treat *sans façons*.'[19]

Nearly three weeks passed before Lawrence received Graves's letter explaining the urgency of the project. To save time Lawrence sent Graves about five thousand words of autobiographical notes covering his life before and after the war, and suggesting people Graves should contact for information. He mentioned both Lionel Curtis and Charlotte Shaw as useful sources for letters. One of Lawrence's chief worries about an independent and possibly sensational biographer must have been the question of his family background, since the truth could quite easily have been uncovered. Graves was not only a friend, but also very substantially in Lawrence's debt. The autobiographical notes were therefore quite open about the problem: 'My father didn't like his wife: so he left her for my mother. No divorce. Wife took all property, by agreement, and title, when succession eventually fell due. You'll find him in Debrett's *Baronetage*, under Chapman, of Killua and South Hill. Father took name of Lawrence (not even my mother's name) when he left Ireland. As widow and mother are both yet alive this story is not for publication. You'll have to dodge the birth somehow.'[20]

Lawrence also included for Graves's use a long description of his 'object with the Arabs', ending with an account of the Colonial Office negotiations: 'The work I did, constructively, in 1921 and 1922, was the best I've ever done. It redresses, to my mind, the risks I took with others' lives and happiness in 1917 and 1918 . . . So, as I say, I got all I wanted, and have quitted the game. Whether the Arab national spirit is permanent and dour enough to make itself into a modern state in Irak I don't know. I think it may. Its success will involve the people of Syria in a similar experiment. Arabia will always stand out of the movements of the settled parts: and Palestine too, if the Zionists make good. Their problem is the problem of the third generation. Zionist success would enormously reinforce the material development of Arab Syria and Irak . . . do make clear how from 1916 onwards, and especially in Paris, I worked against the idea of an Arab Confederation (politically, before it had been effected commercially, economically, and geographically) whether under Hussein in Mecca, or Feisal in Damascus, or X in Bagdad. How I worked to give the desert Arabs a chance to be on their own and the settled Arabs a chance to set up their provincial governments, whether in Syria, or in Irak. And how in my opinion . . . Winston's settlement has fulfilled our war promises, and my hopes.'[21]

The information Lawrence gave to Graves was both helpful and almost entirely accurate. Graves cannot have hoped for so much assistance. At this stage Lawrence seems to have believed that Graves could be relied upon to exercise discretion and good taste: 'He is a decent fellow, does not know too much about me: will think out some psychologically plausible explanation of my spiritual divagations: and will therefore help to lay at rest the uneasy ghost which seems to have stayed in England when I went abroad'.[22] With a little subtle direction, Graves might produce an acceptable, even useful book. As Lawrence wrote candidly in August: 'Graves is smaller than I am, and so will do mainly what I have asked him.'[23]

There were nevertheless areas of reticence in Lawrence's autobiographical notes. He did not mention that he had once planned to earn money from *Seven Pillars*, and even claimed that he had put his Colonial Office salary 'to official purposes'. (In reality he had paid £1,920 of his Colonial Office salary to Kennington for the Arab portraits. However, the statement was essentially true, from Lawrence's point of view, since he had derived no personal benefit when the portraits were ultimately sold.[24]) He also repeated the misleading half-truth that 'The abridgement, *Revolt in the Desert*, was made entirely at Cranwell, in two evenings' work, by myself, with the help of two airmen, Miller and Knowles.'[25] In accounting for his knowledge of Arabic, Lawrence did not mention that he had taken formal lessons from Fareedeh el Akle. He probably suspected that Graves would seize the opportunity to imply a romantic relationship.[26] However, these reticences were exceptional, and to some degree necessary in the circumstances; besides, the matters concerned were of relatively little importance.

Graves worked long hours at the project, which almost immediately became much larger than he had expected. Lowell Thomas's publishers suddenly announced a children's version of his book *With Lawrence in Arabia*, to be called *The Boys' Life of Colonel Lawrence*, and published in September. Since there was unlikely to be a market for two children's books on Lawrence that autumn, Cape and Doran agreed that Graves's book should be transformed into a longer popular study. Graves felt that this plan would meet with approval from Lawrence, who had indeed written: 'Your book quite likely won't be just a school edition'.[27]

From Jonathan Cape's point of view there was another compelling motive for this change. *Revolt in the Desert* was by far the most successful book he had yet published, and its impending withdrawal would be a severe blow. He readily agreed with Graves that the biography should be expanded to three times the length originally proposed: just over three-quarters of the text would be a hasty paraphrase from *Seven Pillars*.[28] In this way, by the time *Revolt* had sold out, Cape would have a profitable substitute; Graves too would benefit from the new scheme.

Lawrence heard nothing more of the project for some weeks, but he had other things to think about. For the past year the *Spectator* had been trying to persuade him to contribute book reviews, and on May 5th he had at last agreed (though he had refused to write about anything on the Middle East, on political subjects, or archaeology): 'If you want poems reviewed, anonymously, or literature, (biography, criticism, novels of the 20th century sort of Forster's, Joyce's, D. H. Lawrence's, etc.) at an interval of three months from the fountain-head:– but of course you don't'.[29]

On June 1st Francis Yeats-Brown, literary editor of the *Spectator*, had sent Lawrence a parcel of books to review, including some volumes from Secker's new pocket edition of D. H. Lawrence's novels. The books took five weeks to arrive in India, but Lawrence wrote at last on July 8th: 'I enclose you a note on D.H.L. Your books came to me on Wednesday . . . I read the three D.H.L's on Thursday, and have written this today. Too quickly, no doubt, but I did not want to keep you longer without a sample: besides I've been reading him since before the war, so that my mind was made up before this week.'[30] For these *Spectator* contributions Lawrence had settled on the pseudonym Colin Dale, a name derived from Colindale, the last London Underground station he had entered before leaving England. He now wrote that he had signed the first review 'C.D.': 'because it's the first, if you do print it, after all. I'd suggest the first five or six things worth signing be restrained to their initials. If the miracle continues after that (surely either your forebearance or my endeavour will break down) we might climb so far as Colin D., keeping the full truth about the D. till it was certain that the fellow could write and had a character.'[31] In spare moments he worked on other books Yeats-Brown sent, and during the next few months he contributed five reviews to the *Spectator*.[32] The D. H. Lawrence piece was published on August 6th and earned him four guineas. It was a polished study of the novelist's growth, containing an interesting comparison of work by D. H. Lawrence and E. M. Forster. There was an unexpected consequence: Martin Secker wrote to the anonymous 'C.D.' care of the *Spectator*, 'to say that he had read my review, and would be glad to know if "C.D." would undertake a short critical book on D. H. Lawrence! Either Secker is badly off for someone to write about D.H.L... or? What is the "or"...? I give it up.'[33]

Reassured by the success of *Revolt*, Lawrence now had other writing projects in mind. On June 16th he wrote to F. N. Doubleday asking for translation work: 'I'd like to make pocket money, to supplement my

R.A.F. pay of a pound a week, out of writing . . . the trouble is I live so far from London that there's great delay in anything I do. However if Heinemann ever contemplate a leisurely translation of a French book, by an anonymous translator, I'd be grateful for the chance of doing it.'[34]

Before he received Doubleday's reply, however, Lawrence had taken up a literary project of his own. The notes he had made in 1922 on the RAF recruits' training depot at Uxbridge had been untouched for a long time, but soon after arriving in India he had asked a friend to post them out to him. On June 10th he wrote to Edward Garnett that they were 'waiting the time when I gather strength to write them out for you. They are not, however, a book. Only my idea of what notes I might have wanted to write a book about the R.A.F.'[35]

Garnett replied on July 18th in encouraging terms, praising the final text of *Seven Pillars*, and reassuring Lawrence: 'you have another book in you, at least as good as the *S.P.* and one that should be much easier to write, one that should also be a masterpiece. It should be a book from the personal side, dictated by the unofficial you – a book of episodes, like beads on a string. Say, episodes from your life as an archaeologist, of your pre-war life in Syria, your fruitless journey to Syria during the war – etc. You should write it without thinking of yourself or of the public – only critically anxious to set down what you thought and felt in each particular episode . . . You are a born writer, fearfully handicapped by fixed ideas and all sorts of complexes, which the great achievement of *The Seven Pillars* should have dissipated . . . I suggest that you write the "Episodes" for your own pleasure as a writer, after you have let me see the "Notes on Uxbridge" – which is overdue from you to me, if I may make this mild remark.'[36]

During June and July, while Graves worked on the biography in England, Lawrence began the difficult task of transforming his original pencil jottings into prose. On August 1st he described to Garnett the evolution of the notes up to this point: 'I wrote them pell-mell, as the spirit took me, on one piece of paper or another. Then I cut them into their sections, and shuffled them, as Joyce is supposed to have shuffled *Ulysses* . . . You would have thought them the raw material of a paper-chase. So I began at Clouds Hill to stick each class in some sort of order on to sheets of paper, meaning to have them stitched for you. But that did not work, for the sections were too intertwined.'[37] Lawrence planned to give Garnett the final version written out neatly in a handsome manuscript book, but first he had to edit the sixty pages of pasted-up notes: 'I add nothing, but take away repetitions, where vain. I "did" three church parades for example: and I believe they can be boiled to two: or even to one, which would be the quintessence and exemplar of all my church parades.'[38] By the beginning of August Lawrence had transformed about a third of the notes into a new pencil draft.

He did not immediately tell Charlotte Shaw about this work on the Uxbridge notes, but he acknowledged his urge to write again in a letter of July 14th: 'That ambition to have written only one thing, one little thing, with life in it, comes back to me despairingly here and now. Yet when I was fresh and strong I attempted it, with all my might and sincerity, and failed. And now that I'm a dry tree, what is there to do?'[39]

Lawrence was now to learn something of Charlotte Shaw's true feelings towards him. As he had suggested, Robert Graves had written to her asking for help with the biography: 'I have just had a 5,000 word letter from T. E. Shaw giving me details about himself for inclusion in the book I am writing about him. I gather that your husband is still against my undertaking: I am sorry. Anyhow, he has suggested my applying to you for the two diaries that are in your hands and for any letters of his that you may have kept which are at all illuminating. He is anxious that I should make a decent show of it. Will you be good enough to help me in this? And please keep your husband from writing me pre-breakfast postcards which arrive to spoil my supper: for I'm largely Irish too, and write back.'[40]

Charlotte Shaw was enraged by this letter, which reached her while she was on holiday in Italy. She replied deceitfully: 'I had letters from him when my husband and I were reading the proofs of his book: but, as far as my recollection goes, they were scraps relating to the proofs and not at all biographical material.'[41] She went on to say that the letters were inaccessibly locked up in England, together with the diaries he had asked for. She sent Graves's letter to Lawrence, noting that it was so badly phrased that it was not clear who had suggested approaching her. When Graves wrote again, telling her of the urgency of the project, she replied coldly: 'I am amazed at your celerity. I am sure a book of this importance would have taken my husband quite a long time to write.'[42] By chance, however, she had just received from Lawrence a copy of a long letter he had written to Vyvyan Richards during the war. This was on the back of an equally long letter to her. As a gesture she re-copied the Richards letter for Graves, and sent it to him with the untruthful remark that she could not send on Lawrence's copy 'as T.E. has written on the back of it business notes which I must keep . . . I also have had a few letters sent to me. I will read them carefully through, and if there is anything I think likely to be useful to you in these, I will send it.'[43]

Charlotte must have told Lawrence in no uncertain terms how deeply she resented the request to see her private correspondence with him. Lawrence destroyed this letter, but the strength of her protests is clear from his tactful replies: 'More anger last week. An exquisite tact and smooth sense of social values were never my two salients: but it seems to me that in both I could give R. Graves a stroke a hole, and yet carry off the prize. His letter . . . is the poorest effort at gaining a favour that ever any sane man put up. He is a good poet, and a decent fellow, nevertheless . . . Any letters I send you are yours, to destroy, to keep, to make public, according to your sense of fitness . . . I've not written any letters of this sort to anyone else, since I was born. No trust ever existed between my mother and myself. Each of us jealously guarded his, or her, own individuality, whenever we came together. I always felt that she was laying siege to me, and would conquer, if I left a chink unguarded. So when Graves asked me about letters I told him that only you (for the recent period) and Lionel Curtis (for the Tank Corps period) held anything illuminating. Curtis' letters are essays in misery, for I felt like Lucifer just after his forced landing, at that stage of my career. Yours are – well I don't know – you know more of them than I do, for they are thrown off quickly, and never dwell in my mind. But I never have to be conscious of an audience in writing to you . . . Graves has misunderstood, probably, what may have been an ambiguity in my letter to him. People who are as sure of themselves as I am upon the ownership of letters, give great scope for misunderstanding when they write to strangers without context. Yet I don't read his letter as an attempt to get yours: it was sent in a fit of temper, to annoy you: and to crow at having got from me a long letter of details, about rocky patches of my life, to show him what to avoid. This book of Graves' may be useful to me, in underlining errors of Lowell Thomas, and in unsaying some of the things which the Press have said.'[44] This misunderstanding with Charlotte Shaw had told Lawrence something he had hardly suspected about the strength of her feelings towards him. He would have good cause to remember it when another biography was written a few years later.

Lawrence received the first third of Graves's typescript on July 26th and returned it four days later with his comments. He told friends that he was disappointed by the amount of paraphrase from *Seven Pillars*, and remarked to Graves that he had seen 'a few questions of fact, where

Woolley or Lowell Thomas or someone had led you astray. I put a few bright bits in the margin, in case you want to hunt the popular taste . . . I wish you were not hurried. With time you could have written a decent *history* of the Arab Revolt, which would have put my personal contribution in the background.'[45]

In his notes Lawrence made it clear that he did not want Graves to use material from *Seven Pillars* that was omitted from *Revolt*. Predictably, Graves had included a version of the Deraa incident in the draft. Lawrence deleted it, with the note: 'As you'll readily imagine I'm dead against any of this coming out with your authority. If you say so much someone else will say a little more:– and then what will have been the use of my careful refusal to publish the *Seven Pillars*?'[46] Graves had not been able to resist the temptation to include other material from *Seven Pillars* which would be unfamiliar to readers of *Revolt*, and he had borrowed Kennington's longer 'Oxford' text to work from. To Lawrence's dismay, the second batch of typescript contained even more of this unwelcome matter. He wrote to Graves on August 3rd: 'I . . . will, I fear, have troubled you with my suggestion that you "go easy" on *Seven Pillars* material. But it seems to me only logical. I chose not to give this to the public: my reasons may have been bad, but in any case they were my reasons . . . [*Revolt*] contained all that I wanted the public to know . . . Regard *Revolt* as your maximum, rather than as something to be supplemented by the *Seven Pillars*. Please don't set the example of nibbling at its copyright!'[47] The following day Lawrence wrote about the typescript to Charlotte Shaw: 'I hate reading it. I correct little, excise little: add less. He avoids G.B.S.' prophecy that he would only be retelling my story in his words, by telling it in my words. I have begged him to confine himself to *Revolt* and leave the *Seven Pillars* in peace. I fear this may be too high an ordeal for him.'[48]

After he had seen the final batch of typescript Lawrence wrote a brief letter to Graves which barely conceals his disappointment with the work: 'Of course you have "done me very well" – but I don't really care a hoot about that. The thing that was really important was for you to do yourself really well, and I don't feel that it's up to the level of your other prose. In the rushed circumstances it could not be: and you will doubtless pull it together in the revise'.[49] A letter to Charlotte Shaw the following day is more frank: 'Every page of R.G.'s own had inaccuracies. I corrected it till I was sick: and let as much more slip. Eighty per cent of the book was what I'd call a bare parody or précis of *Revolt*: I do not think it was quite right to make so free with another's work.'[50]

Lawrence's last long letter to Graves about the biography, written some time later, again expressed his disappointment at the opportunity that had been missed: 'I had hoped to find someone who would retell the story of the Arab Revolt from the available eye-witnesses, leaving the "I" of *Revolt in the Desert* out of it: whereas you only turned first to third person.

'There are plenty of people about to tell you the whole story: Winterton put four articles in *Blackwood's*, years ago. Young put something (which I never saw, except in extract) in the *Cornhill*. Besides there are so many people who rode with me, each of whom could say something: Joyce, most of all: Stirling, who has a bright eye and a sense of colour, and liveliness: Wood, who rode with me to the Yarmuk bridge: Alan Dawnay: Peake, who lives at Amman, and has kept his memories of the war alive by continuing to campaign in its later area: Goslett, who lived at Akaba: his friend Makins, an active R.A.F. pilot: etc. there are dozens of them: besides people like Jaafar, Nuri Said, Zeid, and of course Feisal himself. If Doran and Cape had financed you to go round and see some of these, and collate their stories with the reports of the *Arab Bulletin*... then you'd have produced that most valuable thing, a cross check on my accuracy or inaccuracy. A history of the Arab Revolt would have been definitive. Whereas a "life" of me cannot be. I've not finished: and the last five years are a closed book, unless I write it.

'Yet of course what the publishers want is a cheaper edition of *Revolt*, to tap the wider public without 30/- or 3 dollars to spare: and yet with enough of shape and new material about it to be worth reading on the part of those who liked *Revolt*. This, I fancy, you have provided, and I hope that it will sell hugely...

'Don't stress too much the part I have had in the production . . . I can't accept responsibility for any of your judgements. I've tried to correct your text, where I thought it significantly wrong. Where it was merely one of those idle stories which every man collects about him as he journeys through life, as a ship collects barnacles – well, then I haven't often bothered.'[51]

Despite his reservations, Lawrence's attitude towards the biography was philosophical. It would extend the British publicity he had hoped to quell by withdrawing *Revolt in the Desert*; but some such book was unavoidable, and he could console himself with the thought that it 'might have been done 5,000 times worse by someone merely sensation-hunting'.[52] As it was, even Graves's commercial instincts had proved unexpectedly crude. After this, their relationship never recovered its former intimacy. When *Lawrence and the Arabs* was eventually published in December 1927 at 7/6d, less than a quarter of the price of *Revolt*, Lawrence told Graves that it was 'the only book about myself in which I will lend help';[53] but a few years later he would give wholehearted assistance to a more serious study by the military historian Liddell Hart.

Lawrence appears nevertheless to have drawn some benefit from the Graves project. The task of reviewing his life, particularly the Arab period, seems to have helped him come to terms with the moral issues that had troubled him for so long. At no time after this did he express the bitterness and remorse about his wartime role that occurs so frequently in the early post-war letters.

Working in the office of the Engine Repair Section, Lawrence had quickly proved himself 'a little gift from Providence to the paper-laden officer in charge.'[54] The station adjutant noted a distinct literary polish in memoranda coming from the engineering section, and Lawrence was brought in, at first on a part-time basis, to help with paperwork in the Orderly Room. In late August he wrote to Doubleday: 'Don't send me any translation jobs, yet a while, please. They have moved me from the engine shop, here, into the office, as a sort of pen-and-ink clerk: but there is a typewriter on the next table, and I aim to fill up the next few months of my leisure in learning how to knock it about. Typing might, in circumstances, be a useful accomplishment . . . It is very good of you to consider me for the chance of turning something French into English for Heinemann, some day. I shall write as soon as I'm free (after Christmas I expect) and suggest it again. It is not at all a bad job, such as your letter seems to imply. I've done two, of late, and found the getting a naturally French expression, like a French novel, into a naturally English expression, like an English novel, was difficult, interesting, and curious, and I do it in my spare time, after our day's work is over, in small doses. I dare say it would be a rotten way of earning bread and butter: but the R.A.F. gives me that, and the earnings of my spare time are so much gain. Jam, excellent stuff, spoils itself if it is as thick as the bread.'[55]

There was another reason why Lawrence could not undertake any new projects before Christmas. He intended to spend the autumn editing his Uxbridge notes. On September 22nd he wrote to Edward Garnett saying that he was making slow progress: 'I am trying not to rewrite: but I have to rearrange extensively, and to cut out repetitions and expand the sentences which are in an esoteric shorthand. It seems to me that it may in all be fifty thousand words long: but it is soon to say that. There is not much more than a quarter of it in shape: and even that I dare hardly call in shape: for as I dig further into the loose sheets I continually find my self of 1922 returning to earlier subjects, re-doing them better, or correcting what had seemed to him hasty. I think the job may be worth its trouble. It seems to me to convey some of the reality of the Depot at Uxbridge.'[56] Three weeks later the work had hardly progressed. When about twenty thousand words were done Lawrence was given extra clerical work, bringing his RAF commitment up to nine and a half hours a day. However, as practice for his typing he produced a new intermediate draft, based on a pencil rearrangement he had made from the original notes. Once the text was in this form he found it fairly easy to polish it for the manuscript fair copy he had promised Garnett: 'a posh manuscript, in my most copper-plated hand.'[57]

By the end of October, he had decided that the Uxbridge material could not stand on its own; it painted too bleak a picture of life in the ranks of the RAF. To counter this he now planned a final section describing his experiences as a qualified aircraftman at Cranwell. He wrote to Charlotte Shaw telling her about the work: 'I promised Edward Garnett my notes on Uxbridge – the history of the three months breaking-in to the R.A.F. which we all have been through . . . I feel I daren't send them him without just a few pages about the real R.A.F. – the Cranwell season – which after Uxbridge was like the sun breaking through.'[58] He had made a few pages of notes while at Cranwell, some of which he had sent her: 'little yellow slips, dealing with colour-hoisting parade, and a guard, and Wing Commander Jago's sermon about Queen Alexandra . . . There are only a few hundred words, in all, I think.'[59] He asked her to copy these for him so that they could be included. Another chapter was to be based on an article he had written at Cranwell about racing an aeroplane on his Brough motorcycle. Months before, he had sent the article, anonymously, to a motorcycling magazine, and to his chagrin it had been rejected.[60] This had helped to convince him that his writing was bad, and that publishers would only accept it because of his 'Lawrence of Arabia' reputation.

On November 15th he wrote telling Garnett that he had written sixty pages of the Uxbridge manuscript, which would perhaps run to 110 pages in all: 'They shall be finished for you in the next burst of energy I get. I really want to do them for you. It is the last thing I'll ever write: and most justly your property, since you were my first critic.'[61]

By this time he had settled down fairly comfortably at Karachi. He found it a 'good place in which to mark time, for the food is good, and there is no attempt to control our deportment in camp . . . I have found a sheltered occupation, which delivers me from working parade, first thing in the morning, and from most of the ceremonials. This is an extraordinary place for ceremonies. An average of one posh visitor a month seems to come here, or to Karachi, and no performance is complete without the presence of the R.A.F. And India is a country of rifles, so that a parade is a military occasion . . . From all these diversions of temper my little job as key-orderly preserves me.'[62] He had even improvised a water-heating system using a fifteen-gallon drum and a blow lamp, so that he could take hot baths every day.

Friends such as Charlotte Shaw, Jonathan Cape and J. G. Wilson were sending books out to India regularly, and Lawrence lent them freely to the other men. That autumn he wrote to Charlotte Shaw: 'Very special things I can keep, under lock and key, in my box. The rank and file have to stand out on a wall-shelf, beyond my bed. We have all things in common, you know, in our life. So it is as if there was an invisible notice on the wall "Please take one". All the book-hungry men (hungry for more than the fiction library can give them) slide quietly in and out of my end of the room, borrowing or returning. We are rough, and dirty handed, so that some of the volumes are nearly read to death. You can tell the pet ones, by their shabbiness. I suppose I have had 150 in all, here: of which nearly two-thirds are from you. Of them perhaps fifty are now on loan: I have just counted the survivors – eighty-eight – including many of my pet things. Spenser, and Malory and Morris do not go out much. Though a Glasgow marine-boiler expert, who has read only the *Scientific Engineer* since he came to our room, and scowls drunkenly at the rest of us, took up the *Well at the World's End* once, and read it for nearly six weeks, millimetre by millimetre. It made him beam at me with happiness. Reminded him, he said, of Glasgow. Upon no other reader, probably, has it had that effect.'[63] Lawrence enjoyed recommending books to the airmen: 'They would read, avidly, anything in their reach. Only there are no guides for them, to books: and so many books . . . Everybody reads rubbish when he is tired, and isolated in camp: it would be an insult to give a good book only the dregs of our attention. So magazines and shockers are read: but my little library of queer books is almost as much used as the thousand-volume fiction library which the H.Q. maintains. It's because I tell 'em about books, and make them see them, as they reflect us.'[64]

In October the publication of Gertrude Bell's *Letters*[65] and reports of a visit by Feisal to London gave Lawrence cause to look back on the past. Charlotte Shaw met Feisal and sent Lawrence her impressions. He replied: 'I'm awfully glad you liked him. For so long he was only my duckling: and I crow secretly with delight when he gets another inch forward on his road. When you think of the harassed and distant figure of Wadi Safra in 1916 – and then to the Hotel Regina Palace in 1927: why it is very wonderful.

'After your letter came I lay awake all the Sunday night, arguing my position (in Arabic: how much of it I have forgotten!) with an imaginary Feisal. I made a distinct impression on him, and completely convinced myself. I don't think he wants me, really. Not even the nicest man on earth can feel wholly unembarrassed before a fellow to whom he owes too much. Feisal owed me Damascus first of all, and Bagdad second: and between those stages most of his education in kingcraft and affairs. When with him I am an omnipotent adviser: and while that is very well in the field, it is derogatory to a monarch: especially a monarch who is not entirely constitutional. Feisal often has to lead his people: which is seldom the conduct of G.R. [King George V].

'Also peoples are like people. They teach themselves to walk and to balance, mainly by dint of trying and falling down. Irak did a good deal of falling between 1916 and 1921: and since 1921, under Feisal's guidance, has done much good trying and no falling. But I don't think it yet walks very well. Nor can any hand save it from making its mess: there is a point where coddling becomes wicked. All my experience of the Arabs was in the god-father role: and I think they have outgrown that. If they are to make good as a modern state (how large an "if") then it must be by virtue of their own desire and excellence.

'So that I remain unrepentant. I was right to work for Arab self-government through 1919 and 1920: and my methods then, though not beyond criticism, were I think reasonably justifiable. The settlement which Winston put through in 1921 and 1922 (mainly because my advocacy supplied him with all the technical advice and arguments necessary) was, I think, the best possible settlement which Great Britain, alone, could achieve at the time. Had we waited for the French to come to their right mind and co-operate in a complete settlement, we would be waiting yet. And after June 1922 my job was done. I had repaired, so far as it lay in English power to repair it, the damage done to the Arab Movement by the signing of the Armistice in November 1918.

'The people who want me to go on keeping my hand on the plough are either unfair to the existing ploughmen, or unfair to the plough. The class of work I was doing is finished. Had I continued to be connected with Arab affairs I should have had to change my style and subject and status. I thought it easier – no, I thought it imperative – to change roles altogether. Hence the clean break with my past which the R.A.F. represents.

'It's because I've chosen the R.A.F. that people make a fuss of my abdication from Arab affairs. If I'd accepted a Governorship – of Cyprus, or Jamaica, or Borneo – they would have taken for granted my leaving the Arab sphere . . .

'I'm happy, indeed, that you liked him. He is one of the best people I know. Your remark about his tenacity interested me. He is both tenacious and weak: perhaps these qualities always go together. It is easy to swing him off his point: and when released he tends to swing back to it. Therefore the French called him treacherous. He was (and perhaps is still) quite weak: but, I agree, tenacious. Very gentle, you know, and very kind, and very considerate, and outrageously generous to friends, and mild to his enemies, and cleanly and honest and intelligent: and full of wild freakish humour: though I suppose that is a little overlaid with kingliness, now. He has been king for six years, which is a deep experience. I wish you could have known him, as I did, when he was Feisal, just. One of the most attractive human beings I have ever met . . .

'You know, without my telling you, how much I liked him. I talk of him always in the past tense, for it will be a long time before we meet again. Indeed I hope sometimes we never will, for it would mean that he was in trouble. I've promised myself to help him, if ever that happens. As for Irak... well, some day they will be fit for self-government, and then they will not want a king: but whether 7 or 70 or 700 years hence, God knows. Meanwhile Feisal is serving his race as no Arab has served it for many hundred years. He is my very great pride: and it's been my privilege to have helped him to his supremacy, out there, and to have made him a person, for the English-reading races'.[66]

There were many people who thought Lawrence's talents were wasted in the ranks, especially after the completion of *Seven Pillars* and the success of *Revolt in the Desert*. For the first time since 1923, he was in a position to earn a large amount of money if he chose, and during 1927 he received several proposals for well-paid work. In November, for example, he was offered $100,000 for a seven-week lecture tour in the United States, and a month later an American offered him £5,000 (enough capital for him to retire on) for one of the five surviving 'Oxford' copies of *Seven Pillars*. But his only stated ambition, after completing his years in the ranks, was to take a night-watchman's job in London. From time to time he reminded his friends of this: 'Don't forget I rely on someone to recommend me as bachelor-night-caretaker of a block of city offices or buildings in 1935: it is March 1935 which sees my sorrowful departure from the R.A.F.'[67]

The most persistent offers of help came from an American, Ralph Isham, who had served on the British staff during the war and had encountered Lawrence at the Colonial Office. Isham, now a banker in New York, had written at the end of June pointing out that *Revolt* was selling very well in America: 'there are a dozen ways that you can make ten or twenty thousand quid within the next year, by writing what you *want* to write.'[68] A week later he had written again: 'Your book has an enormous sale here. I have made enquiries from the booksellers and I find it has gone as well as any best-selling novel. This is remarkable, for books of a serious nature do not generally have a large sale. It must have done proportionately as well in London. It is iniquitous that you are not making a lot of money on it, but be that as it may, the fact is that your book and you are being widely talked about at this time from one end of the country to the other. The result of this situation is that American publishers would pay enormous sums for anything from your pen, and you must know that literary work is paid for at very much higher prices here than in England.'[69] Isham was an astute businessman, and seems to have wished to represent Lawrence in some way. He suggested magazine articles for the American market on any subject Lawrence chose, although topics linked with the Middle East would be the most profitable: 'The *Saturday Evening Post* I know would pay from $2,000 to $5,000 apiece for such articles from you, and you will remember that $5,000 is £1,000 . . . If you would undertake to write another book I am sure I could find publishers here who would pay you immediately at least £2,000 advance royalties'.[70]

Lawrence did not receive these letters until August, and he then wrote: 'It is exceedingly good of you to want to help me so much, and I'd not hesitate to take advantage of it if my sense of fitness would allow me to profit by you. But experience has taught me that I will inevitably turn down every job I'm given the chance of getting – the truth being, I fancy, that the service has become a second nature to me, and that I'll feel lost if (or when) it chucks me out.'[71]

Scholarly periodicals took some time to comment on *Revolt in the Desert*. During the summer of 1927, however, a scathing review by Sir Arnold Wilson appeared in the *Journal of the Central Asian Society*.[72] Many of the journal's readers would have known the reason for Wilson's blatant hostility; in Lawrence's own words: 'When Winston put into my power the re-shaping of the Middle East I told him that A. T. Wilson must go: and as there had been a more or less declared war between Egypt and Irak during the war, the final victory of the Arab Bureau policy was bitter for him. Wilson is a thrusting, confident, official administrator, who was very ambitious for a career in power: and he does not find the Persian management of the Anglo-Persian Oil Company a good exchange for his lost High Commissionership of Irak. And I fancy that my own retirement, when I had got all I wanted out of the British Government, was a new offence in his eyes. He is a decent fellow, all the same: and if he had been wicked enough to keep his temper, could have written a damaging review. His article should certainly not be answered. A controversy would only revive the dead interest in *Revolt* and make it more difficult to kill finally.'[73] Robert Graves, no doubt keen to protect his forthcoming biography, wrote a letter to the *Sunday Times* in Lawrence's defence. Lawrence asked Graves to desist, and also wrote to Eric Kennington: 'If you see Graves again, do urge on him, as an independent authority, the undesirability of anyone's championing me or my doings in the Press. As if it mattered a damn what sort of a creature I was or what I did or didn't do. It is history now, and the judgement is out of the hands of A.T.W. and myself. I suppose you know the friction at Cairo was because he had just got the sack from the political service. This was inevitable, when my policy conquered. I was sorry for him, or would have been, had he taken it better.'[74] Lawrence cared much more about the success of his policy than his personal reputation. He told Charlotte Shaw: 'If the Wilsons of the world like to shoot at me, why they are welcome to waste their ammunition. I would I might gather all the spite of politics into my arms, as the Swiss champion gathered the spears of the Austrian phalanx, and snap the heads of it off.'[75]

At Karachi, Lawrence was now, in effect, carrying out the duties of two men. Long hours in the office left him with little time or energy for revising the Uxbridge notes, which he had hoped to finish by Christmas. Then, on November 9th, he received a telegram from Buxton that D. G. Hogarth had died two days earlier. He was deeply saddened by the news: 'Somehow I never thought that special thing would happen.'[76] He wrote: 'the background of my life before I enlisted has gone. Hogarth sponsored my first tramps in Syria – then put me on the staff for Carchemish, which was a golden place – then moved me to Sinai, which led to the War Office: which sent me to Cairo on the Staff: and there we worked together on the Arab business, until the War ended: and since then whenever I was in a dangerous position I used to make up my mind after coming away from his advice. He was very wise for others, and very understanding, and comfortable, for he knew all the world's vices and tricks and shifts and evasions and pretexts, and was kindly towards them all. If I might so put it, he had no knowledge of evil: because everything to him was fit to be looked at, or to touch. Yet he had his own position and principles, and was unmoveable on them. Till I joined up he did everything for me. It was the first thing I did entirely on my own. So lately I have seen little of him: but I always felt that if ever I went back to living I'd be able to link up with him again.'[77]

While he was still depressed by this news, Lawrence received another letter from Isham containing an extraordinarily flattering offer. Isham had recently acquired a long-lost archive of manuscripts by James Boswell, the biographer of Dr. Johnson. These had been discovered at Malahide Castle in Ireland, and Isham was now offering Lawrence the task of editing them for publication. Lawrence felt honoured rather than seriously tempted. As a medievalist at Oxford he could hardly have acquired a deep knowledge of eighteenth-century England, and he felt no great enthusiasm for scholarly editorial work. Yet his thanks were sincere when he wrote to Isham on November 22nd turning the offer down: 'I cannot imagine how you get through life, if it's your principle to lend a hand to every breakdown you see on the road. Meanwhile, please believe that there's one very grateful one, here.'[78]

During November and December 1927, in the aftermath of Hogarth's death, Lawrence made little progress with the Uxbridge notes. He seems, however, to have decided on a title for them during this period, since they are referred to as *The Mint* in a letter to Edward Garnett written on November 30th.[79] The title was meant to convey the way in which raw recruits were transformed at Uxbridge into airmen. Lawrence later told Trenchard that he had called the notes *The Mint*, 'because we were all being stamped after your image and superscription.'[80]

Lawrence's friendship with Trenchard was known to his superiors and often resented. There were few difficulties with junior officers who had daily contact with him, but senior commanders feared that his letters to the chief of the RAF might contain criticisms of their administration. On December 22nd Lawrence wrote to Trenchard: 'Do not allow my confession of pleasure at your letters to make them more frequent. Each one makes me feel guilty, and they are dangerous. "I fancy he writes to Headquarters" said a very important person, of me, to a Depot person slightly less important. "Will you try to find out?" Person II, being bull-honest, came and asked me. I showed him the letter you had sent me, and the one Salmond sent me about the same time... both obviously private affairs. Person II was pleased. V.I.P. was not yet feeling safe, so I was sent for, cursed, and condemned to go up country as a Bolshevik.'[81] The 'V.I.P.' was the Commanding Officer at Karachi, who had previously ignored Lawrence: 'I think he must have been reading Robert Graves, and felt that I was a worm. Fortunately Salmond happened along next day, and told him I was all right. So my sheet remains clean. I have a terror about that sheet: if I get a mark on it someone will hoof me out into the street again: and I am too old to go wandering any more.'[82]

Lawrence explained more about this incident in a letter to a friend: 'After a year of rather evident non-notice the C.O. sent for me, and stepped heavily on my face. However, he's mad, or used to be (we arranged his return, under supervision, from Mudros in 1916. Wonderful how they get back, isn't it?) and Salmond, knowing that, stepped in and saved me.'[83] In March the officer concerned was sent home, 'not recommended for further employment'.[84]

During the autumn of 1927 Lawrence spent much of his free time reading. Among the books he commented on was *The Wild Body*, a collection of short stories by Wyndham Lewis. Lawrence had always found Lewis's work impressive, though he thought the man himself 'slovenly and lazy'.[85] The combination of the camp's Christmas festivities and *The Wild Body* provoked a cynical letter to Charlotte Shaw. He thought Lewis's stories: 'untidy, obscene, and nasty. The psychology is very acute, and the studies are exact and rare. But I do not interest myself in such types. He is himself, you know, large and flaccid, and is white-faced and unwholesome to the touch. Apparently such gawky things engross his interest. To me, his gallery is a shocking one. I live in a society of men who take habitual care of their bodies, and temper them by games and exercise and diet to a certain dry splendour of activity. There are exceptions of course: a matter of fifteen or twenty creatures with pendulous bellies and loose cheeks haunt the wet bar midday and evening, and reel about the camp roads in ungainly forgetfulness of their bodies. But the 90% are always thinking of themselves, and are a satisfaction to watch. I like to see a man well in control of his limbs: and that is easy and natural for the young. Athletic ambitions have, indirectly, their use!

'Not at Christmas. These three days have been miserable: not as regards myself, but for my eyesight. All the fellows one normally likes and enjoys have been making fools of themselves – fools if not beasts – and I get very sick seeing them. In England the Tank Corps was like this... almost worse than this... one Christmas. At Cranwell there was nothing horrible. Last year I was on the boat at this time, and there were not so many drunks: nor were they conspicuous on the troopship, which was itself a home of bestiality at normal times. But Drigh Road has been a degraded place this week-end.'[86]

The men had been paid two weeks' wages on December 23rd, and by January 4th everyone in Lawrence's room, except Lawrence himself, had run out of cash. He wrote: 'I don't drink, and (expecting the shortness) hoarded my money, which I have been lending in small items to everyone for the last few days, to buy them cigarettes and suppers.'[87] This willingness to help out with cash had always given him a special status in the ranks. In a few cases men took advantage of his generosity, but most of the loans were discreetly repaid.

His popularity rose still further when two large hampers arrived just after Christmas from Fortnum & Mason. As was the custom, they were shared: 'I was out when they came. They clustered about them like vultures about a corpse. The cake was exactly divided into fourteen: and as two fellows were away (hospital etc.) I was given three shares. Likewise of all the other things. I returned to find my bed hidden under *marrons glacés* and chocolates, and almond icing. All the hut was merry: and voted it the best cake they had ever eaten'.[88] The gift had been sent anonymously, but Lawrence had no doubt that it came from Charlotte Shaw, to whom he wrote: 'They advised me to write to all the friends I know, and thank them for the kindness. I don't think I have to search very far. You would have been very rewarded if you could have listened in to us for that day and night.'[89]

CHAPTER 39

New Projects and Old
January – May 1928

UNKNOWN to Lawrence, another proposal had been taking shape in America. Its origins lay in the set of *Seven Pillars* proofs which he had sent to Doran in New York eighteen months previously to serve as a text for typesetting the US copyright edition. When the American printing had been completed, Doran passed the English proofs to a friend, who in turn gave them to Bruce Rogers.

Rogers was one of the world's outstanding typographers. He was almost as well known in England as in America, since he had been for a time printing adviser to the Cambridge University Press. In 1927 he was working independently, and had been commissioned by Random House to design and print a fine edition of any important book he chose. After some thought he had decided on Homer's *Odyssey*. He began reading the various English renderings, but concluded 'that all the available translations were lacking in speed, primarily, however admirable they might be in other respects.'[1]

At first, as he later explained to Lawrence, he had thought of using Samuel Butler's well-known rendering into colloquial English, first published in 1900; but then he had seen another by George Herbert Palmer, 'which at once seemed to me superior to Butler's while not quite so "literary" as Leaf and Myers . . . But still his translation didn't march, and was pretty dull in spots . . . Then it suddenly came to me that if the swing and go of your English in the *Seven Pillars* which held me to it when I was not specially interested in some of your expeditions, could be applied to the *Odyssey*, we would get a version that would out-distance any existing translations.'[2]

Rogers had never met Lawrence, but by a happy coincidence he was consulted by Ralph Isham about printing the projected edition of Boswell's papers. When Rogers mentioned his *Odyssey* scheme during a dinner with Isham, he learned that the latter was in touch with Lawrence. As a result, Isham had written to Lawrence on December 6th explaining the project, for which a fee of £800 was proposed: 'They want to get away from the old translation; they want this to be a free translation – rather a new interpretation of the *Odyssey*.

'You will be glad to know that it is not your name they want but your translation. They are willing either to give the name you now use, as translator, or to give no name at all, whichever you wish. I do not know how you are at Greek but I thought this scheme might just fit into your present scheme of things and the honorarium of £800 is not to be grown on every tree in India.

'There is no particular hurry about the translation itself but I should like to know soon if you are willing to undertake it.'[3]

The offer reached Lawrence in India nearly a month later. It was extremely attractive to him: he knew the *Odyssey* well, and had the Greek text with him. His work on *The Mint* was nearly complete, and for some time he had been thinking of taking on a new translation project. The *Odyssey* was not just an ephemeral novel like *The Forest Giant* and *Sturly*: it was one of the world's great works of literature, and the task would be worthy of all the effort he could give. The *Odyssey* appealed to him as Cape's abortive *Arabian Nights* proposal had done in 1923. He replied to Isham modestly on January 2nd that the offer had 'knocked me out, temporarily . . . The money suggested is wonderful, but that only shows how well they expect it to be done: and I have no trust whatever in my writing. Agreed the reviewers spoke highly of it, when *Revolt* came out: but they speak as well of seventy per cent of the books they notice, so one discounts that: and in my case they were also astonished that a practical man could write at all. "So clever of him, my dear, to be able to sit up"... as they'd say of a toy dog.

'When your letter came, I took the *Odyssey* down from the shelf, (it goes with me, always, to every camp, for I love it) and tried to see myself translating it, freely, into English. Honestly, it would be most difficult to do. I have the rhythm of the Greek so in my mind, that it would not come readily into straight English. Nor am I a scholar; I read it only for pleasure, and have to keep a dictionary within reach. I thought of the other translators, and agreed that there was not a first-rate one. Butcher and Lang... too antique. Samuel Butler... too little dignified, tho' better. Morris... too literary. That only shows the job it is. Why should my doing be any better than these efforts of the bigger men?'[4]

Lawrence was delighted at the chance to work with Bruce Rogers: his 'dressing of the book will make it glorious, so that even an inferior version would pass muster . . . I have for years admired him from ground level;

and have even been able at intervals to buy books of his production: of course I've never met him:– but you know, and he knows that he's the ideal of all those who have tried to produce books. Or perhaps I should say, of all who have gone far enough in the direction of producing books, to know what a job it is.'[5] Lawrence concluded: 'let me make stiff terms, in the hope of being refused an honour which I feel too great for me to carry off successfully. I cannot refuse so profitable an offer bluntly.

'1. I should need two years in which to complete the translation, after I began work on it.

'2. I do not feel capable of doing it as well as Homer would have liked; and shall feel unhappy if it turns out botched.

'3. I could not sign it with any one of my hitherto names. It must go out blank, or with a virgin name on it.

'4. I would do the first book, within six months of having concluded the agreement with the publishers; and if they were not satisfied with it, I would agree to let the contract go, upon their paying me the fraction of £800 which the first book bears to the whole . . .

'My strongest advice to you is to get someone better, to do you a more certain performance: I am nothing like good enough for so great a work of art as the *Odyssey*. Nor, incidentally, to be printed by Bruce Rogers.'[6]

Lawrence knew that it would be several weeks before Isham's reply to this letter could reach India, and he decided to use this time to finish *The Mint*. Charlotte Shaw, who had known about the Uxbridge notes since November, had written asking if she could see them. Her letter arrived at much the same time as the hampers she had ordered from Fortnum & Mason, and Lawrence immediately sent her the first part of his typed working draft, warning her, however, of the raw barrack-room descriptions and uncensored language: 'Please regard yourself (in reading it) as being in an equivocal position, eavesdropping in a men's barrack. Those of us who live publicly together have to depend on each other's common decency to respect our inevitable confidence. We are all in the mire, together. The rest relied on me, to keep their custom, and I break it. What is given away is not myself, as in the *Seven Pillars*, but my fellows. I take you into their confidence, showing only just so much of myself as seems to illuminate their dark places. I fear you will not like them. Yet I have censored out their secretest things, their best or worst intimacies. So many of them came to confide in my greater age and experience . . . They talked like this to me, because I was one of them. Before you they would have been different: and they would be angry to think that a woman had shared their life. They cannot have the privilege of knowing you: nor could all of them have the largeness to understand you, if they did. It has been bred into them that a woman is different: holy almost, despite the soilings they receive when men handle them.'[7] He told her that he might finish the notes in a month or two, 'if I begin on it again: for really the changes I make are formal. But in such a work I must wait for the mood.'[8]

The remaining sections of *The Mint* were tackled in earnest during January. His incentive to finish them grew more urgent when still another project was imposed upon him. When Hogarth died, he had been working on a life of Doughty, to be published by Oxford University Press. The manuscript was at an advanced stage and Sydney Cockerell had written on the family's behalf asking whether Lawrence would be prepared to complete the work and see it through the press. Lawrence felt that he could hardly refuse. He had already realised 'that circumstances might point me out as the one person to oversee and smoothen D.G.H.'s draft chapters'.[9] He agreed in principle to take on the job, provided that his work could be strictly anonymous. However, it was not immediately clear what remained to be done, and during the spring of 1928 Lawrence waited for more definite information. On February 2nd, for example, he told Charlotte Shaw that matters were still unsettled: 'Cockerell (whom I distrust: he feels always as if he were trying to "get at" some-thing) wants me to write a preface, about Doughty and Hogarth as two formative influences upon my life. This seems to me a vulgar, almost immoral, suggestion.'[10]

It turned out that the Press was in a hurry to have the book finished, and that Hogarth's son was able to undertake the remaining work. Lawrence declined to write a signed introduction, and the book was finally printed without any contribution by him.

He felt even more apprehensive about a second possibility: that he might be asked to write Hogarth's biography. Charlotte Shaw evidently raised this with him, because Lawrence replied: 'As for writing a book on Hogarth... why heaven forbid. D.G.H. expressed himself in his speech, and in his face, and personal warmth. His letters are all right, of course, but too correct to be worthy of him. His career did not fit his character. A life of him will therefore belittle him: it cannot fail to: for he left nothing of his size behind him except the inexpressible image in our eyes. I hope they will not do a life of him. To be forgotten is not a penalty. He would not have thanked me for trying to beat up my memories of him into an image: because it would not be a good image. I can pay him back the debt

I owe him in many better ways than that. He lived more than he wrote: that was his way.'[11] Before the question of the Doughty book had finally been resolved, the suggestion of writing such a biography was put to Lawrence, as he had feared, by Hogarth's widow: 'Some day will you do David's life for us? There is *no* one else. I ask this very seriously.'[12]

On January 15th Lawrence learned that Thomas Hardy also had died, and he was reminded once again of their last meeting in November 1926, just before he had sailed for India. Hardy had stood in the porch at Max Gate to see Lawrence leave, but the Brough had not started straight away, and fearing the cold Hardy had gone indoors. Lawrence had written afterwards: 'The afternoon was raw and miserable, like the day, and when T.H. turned back into the house to get a shawl (as I guessed) instantly I ran the bicycle out into the road and away, so that no possible reproach might lie against me for having helped him into the danger of a chill.'[13] Hardy, then eighty-six, had been greatly affected by the parting, knowing that they were unlikely to see each other again. Mrs Hardy later wrote: 'Returning a few moments after, Hardy was grieved that he had not seen the actual departure, and said that he had particularly wished to see Lawrence go.'[14]

Lawrence was struck by the difference between his feelings about Hardy's death and Hogarth's: 'I am sorry for T.H.'s going, too, though less so, for T.H. had perfected himself in his work, and went into the grave very poor in spirit. Whereas Hogarth put so much of his force into the acts of living.'[15] Charlotte Shaw attended the funeral service in Westminster Abbey on January 16th, and afterwards sent Lawrence a vivid description of the occasion:

And now I have come from the burial of Thomas Hardy's ashes in the Abbey. I went thirty-five minutes early and found nearly all the places filled up, but got a seat almost in the middle of the South transept. By the cuttings you will see that G.B.S. was a pall-bearer. He walked to pair with Mr. Galsworthy, but, as the catafalque was high and great they were completely separated from one another. It seemed absurd to have an immense bier and a great and splendid pall, white, embroidered with royal crowns and many other emblems, to enclose one small casket, but it made its effect. The service was very beautifully sung, and I have never heard anything better read than the lesson "Let us now praise famous men." . . . When the procession came down the South transept they all passed quite near me. I was curiously impressed by Baldwin. I had never seen him before: he is far stronger than I thought. He was the only one who looked entirely unimpressed – I almost fancied he looked amused – I was terribly afraid G.B.S. would "act": but no, he did it perfectly. Kipling I thought looked sinister.

The clergy came first – and shocked me. All except one looked full of worldly pomp and disdain; self-conscious jacks-in-office – but that one – young, appeared wrapped from the world. Then came the catafalque, and after some men friends: finally Mrs. Hardy with Mr. Cockerell. The first time they passed she looked erect and calm, but was so completely swathed in crape that her face was invisible: as she passed back she was hanging on Mr. Cockerell's arm, and seemed completely broken. The service at the grave (I could not see it) must have been terribly trying for her. All the rest of the time, they tell me, she was hidden in some recess; but there, of course, she had to stand out prominently. Mr. Cockerell was splendid: a rock of strength and most dignified. He gives the impression (sometimes) of restrained emotion; but I don't think he feels anything very deeply really.

Before me was Jack Squire with his pretty young wife. He looked old and battered – getting grey on the top of his head . . . Behind me was Mr. Tomlinson. I am very fond of Mr. Tomlinson. I felt him there all the time, and, at a very moving moment I just turned slightly to catch his eye and I saw him transfixed, with tears rolling slowly down his face . . .

Then a wonderful thing came. On that glorious organ an almost divine organist played the Dead March from *Saul*. I say advisedly that was among the most splendid things of my life. He began very low and soft and gradually opened out, making one's whole being thrill to each great phrase, up to a most marvellous burst of great chords – confident, assertive, triumphant.[16]

Whatever reservations Lawrence had about Charlotte Shaw's attitude towards him, he must have been interested by letters such as this. She mixed with leading figures in the intellectual and literary world, and the correspondence kept him in touch with a society he had abandoned.

By the end of January he was about two-thirds of the way through the *The Mint*. As with *Seven Pillars*, he was now finding it difficult to recapture the spirit of his original draft: 'These are painful chapters. I wonder how I came to write them. They are so much too emotional for my present mind.'[17] A fortnight later the typescript of the middle section had been finished, and the final chapters were taking shape. He aimed to have the book completed by the end of March. His letters show that he was now thinking increasingly of the *Odyssey*. For example, on February 25th he wrote: 'Translating Homer is playing with words, which, as you know, have always fascinated me: playing with them like a child with bricks . . . Meanwhile the old *Mint* staggers on. I think it has a certain historical interest, as the document of a recruit of 1922. The R.A.F. makes documents for every one of its airmen: I have made a document for it: only it might not say thank you! Still, even that's only fair, for we don't thank it for ours: they're mostly records of the poor little faults it calls "crimes". I hope, though, that something of my feeling for the R.A.F. will carry across the mass of contrary examples in which I seem to dissemble my love!'[18]

By March 1st he had finished the fair copy of *The Mint* up to the end of the Uxbridge section, two-thirds of the way through. He sent the typescript draft to Charlotte Shaw, thanking her for her comments on the earlier chapters: 'I try to hope that the essence of the book is clean . . . What you and G.B.S. think about the tightness and spareness of it pleases me more than pages of praise. Think of the tightness and spareness of our uniform: and for its bare severity, look at a barrack room. That is the scene, this the manner, those the figures. Service life is not freedom. It can be a contented slavery, though.

'You write almost as though it were a book. It is the re-arrangement of notes: with no more than detailed changes: I have moved a long way, given up much pugnacity, since that time, and couldn't write the book it was the notes for. I expend days and days of time, and hours of patience, and some skill, piecing the scattered sentences together. A literary jig-saw. And I tell myself that order is coming out of the chaos'.[19]

The notes were completed on the evening of March 14th, and he wrote to Charlotte Shaw two days later: 'I have looked back through the book: I sat up very late last night, trying to judge it: and found it good prose. It is monotonous. So is life in the R.A.F. Monotony in life is good: in books apparently bad . . . Anyway I have successfully made this unprintable. The people are all real, though the names are not: or only a few of the names, White, Cunningham, Tim, Stiffy. Those are the four realities, the last two nick-names. I have mixed up the others. I don't know why. Nobody will read so much of my handwriting.

'I wonder what Garnett will do with the book. It is an embarrassing gift, surely? When he asked me for it, in 1922, I was nobody: and he didn't think it was as big a thing as this. He will get a shock.'[20]

Instead of sending Charlotte the last section in typescript, he posted Garnett's manuscript fair copy to her so that she could read it in its final version. He sent her the typescript only when he knew that the Garnett manuscript had arrived safely (in that way there was no risk of losing part of the text, as had happened with *Seven Pillars* in 1919). However, he did not want Garnett to realise that she had seen the manuscript first: 'Do not let Garnett know where it comes from: don't use a bit of wrapping paper with Mr. Shaw's name on it; and post it from London, not Ayot. I am asking E.G. not to lend it anyone except his son David: and he is more likely to do as I wish, if he does not know that you have seen it. This book must be kept secret: though its existence had already been proclaimed in the press years before I wrote it!'[21]

Lawrence was very concerned that *The Mint* should not be widely gossiped about. In 1928 its contents would have caused a public scandal and greatly damaged the RAF: 'Any word used in barrack rooms has been judged good enough to go in; wherefore Scotland Yard would like to lock up the author. The general public might be puzzled, and think I didn't like the R.A.F. whereas I find it the only life worth living for its own sake.'[22] He wrote to Trenchard, explaining that he had put the Uxbridge notes into a readable form, and offering him the opportunity to read them. He had little doubt that Trenchard would find the book disturbing: 'Uxbridge was bad, and I'd have written and told you so, only that it seemed implicit, in your letting me join, that I should take my stuff quietly.'[23]

Lawrence did not tell Charlotte Shaw that Trenchard might see *The Mint*. If each recipient of the draft thought that they were uniquely privileged, they would be less likely to let others into the secret. Doubtless Charlotte Shaw enjoyed the intrigue about Garnett's copy, but she would have been surprised by the letter Lawrence sent him explaining away the English postmark of his parcel, and claiming that this was the only copy of *The Mint*: 'I have today posted (as yesterday I finished) the R.A.F. notes. They will come to you, round about through the parcel mail, in some ten days: I sent them by an official by-pass, for safety; as there is no copy and the making this long manuscript has hurt my eyes exceedingly. I never want to write a thing again.

'The notes eventually worked out at seventy thousand words: the Uxbridge part was fifty thousand: and I added twenty thousand on

Cranwell, (built up out of contemporary letters and scraps of writing which I'd hoarded against such a need) to redress the uniform darkness of the Depot picture. Cranwell was a happy place . . . This afternoon I am going out into the desert with some paraffin and the original draft, to make sure that no variant survives, to trouble me as those two editions of *The Seven Pillars* do. So before you get it your copy will be unique.'[24]

Lawrence told Garnett to offer the book to Cape for publication 'without one word excised or moderated. Can you, as his reader, arrange this? I'd rather no one read it but you (and David Garnett . . .): and I want him to refuse it, so as to free me from the clause in his contract of the *Revolt in the Desert*, tying me to offer him another book. I hate being bound by even an imaginary obligation.'[25]

This secrecy was quite proper, given the damage that might be done if the contents of *The Mint* became public; but nevertheless it seems curious that he should so casually have deceived two of his friends. The truth appears to be that he had become an extremely isolated person, and after Hogarth's death there was no one he trusted completely. Since childhood he had chosen to lead a solitary life, and this tendency had been greatly reinforced (as in many other cases) by fame. While he knew many people, he held himself at a distance from all of them. He enjoyed his contacts with intellectuals, yet rejected their view of his life. He always suspected that their admiration for him owed much to his reputation as 'Lawrence of Arabia'; few of them could hide their conviction that he was wasting his talents in the ranks. The RAF provided a simpler companionship which grew naturally through shared activity. He excelled in his service work and thereby won respect from both officers and men. Their admiration was based on personal knowledge rather than exaggerated legend. On the other hand none of these companions shared his intellect and education. They were cut off from many of his wider interests, and to this extent he could form no fully satisfying friendships in the ranks.

Lawrence was reticent about different areas of his life when writing to different people. In any period, there was no single correspondent to whom he revealed everything that he told to others: in each one of these pen-friendships there were important reservations.

This may seem an unexpected conclusion, because many of his letters have an air of great intimacy, giving the reader (and doubtless the original recipient) the impression of a close friendship. But even with relative strangers Lawrence was prepared to discuss in letters subjects which most people would regard as intimate or confidential. He showed his lack of concern for this kind of privacy when he wrote *Seven Pillars*, and allowed it to go into circulation (albeit limited) during his lifetime. Nevertheless he had an inner core of privacy. For example, he never mentioned his pre-war affection for Janet Laurie, nor that he had later given her the greater part of his inheritance.

His contact with intellectuals was especially important to him while he was in India. During these months he sent letters every week to Charlotte Shaw, and about once a month to Edward Garnett and E. M. Forster. When Forster wrote that he was dedicating a volume of short stories 'To T.E. in the absence of anything else',[26] Lawrence remarked: 'That is rather beautiful of him, I think. How very fortunate I have been in the people I know. They are like a lot of rivers, relieving my dryness. The pity is that I can't tell them how much they make me glad and happy. There is nothing in oneself unknown, or producing a fresh joy. But when I travel in others' minds there are infinite and joyous adventures. I seem to have been able to collect, like beads on a string, just the rarest things alive.'[27] He was now also exchanging letters from time to time with Edward Garnett's son David, and with F. L. Lucas, an English don at Cambridge. In January 1928 he read a page proof of Henry Williamson's *Tarka the Otter* sent by Edward Garnett, and wrote a long criticism in reply.[28] As a result he also began to correspond with Williamson.

Lawrence was still receiving letters from appreciative readers of *Seven Pillars*. Wavell, who had first read the book in the 'Oxford' text, wrote: 'I can't tell you how much pleasure your magnificent gift of the *Seven Pillars* affords me. It is a constant joy to be able to read your beautiful prose. I am your most grateful admirer.'[29] Sir Herbert Samuel was even more generous: 'Prophecies about contemporary literature are almost always wrong, but I will risk the prophecy (since I shall not suffer any penalty) that a hundred years hence, and perhaps five hundred years hence, of the books of travel and adventure and descriptions of foreign peoples that have been written in our period, your book and Doughty's are the only two that are likely to be read.

'I do not see why you should be diffident about it either as a writer or as a man. The public appreciation of all that you did is much better founded than your own depreciation. Nor can I understand why you should think that you were a party to any deception of the Arabs. As to Palestine, there may have been a difference of opinion, though I do not suppose that the desert sheikhs and tribes ever had Palestine very much in mind. For the events in Syria you were in no degree responsible. And if you compare the present position in the Hejaz, Iraq and Trans-Jordan with what it was before the War, those who fostered or participated in the Revolt have no ground for remorse – or indeed for anything but pride.'[30]

When *The Mint* reached England in April, Lawrence began to receive letters about that as well. Trenchard had agreed to read the book, although he had considerable misgivings about its content: 'I feel rather that what you have probably written is what is quite comprehensible to you and to me as we both understand the position, but it would be seized upon immediately by the Press *if they got hold of it*, and they would say what a hopeless Air Force it was – how badly it was run – what hopeless officers we had, etc., when I know that is not what you mean at all, *though I have not seen what* you have written. I am certain you will believe that this is the sort of thing the Press will do *if what* you have written is ever published.

'And the Air Force is still young. It cannot go on continually being abused by everybody, and I have enough of it as it is regarding accidents and one thing and another.

'I do not feel a bit annoyed with you. I feel I always thought you would do it, though I hoped you would not. Anyhow, I am going to see Garnett when I can, and I hope he will not publish it or let it be published'.[31]

Charlotte Shaw had commented on the text sections as she had received them. On April 12th her husband wrote about *The Mint* at great length. He made little attempt to hide his distaste for the book: 'As it cannot be published as a work of literary art (except possibly by Werner Laurie in a three guinea subscription edition as pure bawdry) the only thing to be considered is how and where to place it on record and to secure it from destruction . . . This being done, everything will be done that you could possibly have contemplated when you did the job; and you may dismiss it from your mind and go on to something else . . . Still, though you are wobbling between your conceptions of the thing as a verbatim report for the archives and a work of art, I think you had better discard the latter unless you are prepared to rewrite a good deal of it with humour enough to make it bearable and decency enough to make it presentable'.[32] Shaw suggested various ways of preserving the text for the historical record, but his letter showed clearly that *The Mint* had run up against a streak of prudishness in his character.[33]

Garnett had no such reservations. He received the manuscript (sent on by Charlotte Shaw) on April 18th, and soon afterwards cabled Lawrence that it was 'a classic'. He followed this with an enthusiastic letter: 'Well, you've gone and done it this time! And knocked all your feeble pretences of not being a writer, etc. etc. into final smithereens . . . It is a most *perfect* piece of writing. I call it a *classic*, for there's not a word too much. It's elastic, sinewy, terse: and spirit and matter are the inside-out of its technique, perfectly harmonious throughout – inseparable, as in all first-rate stuff. It's very original in its effect, for having given us the essential in its living body, it smites one much harder than if you had made "a book" of it, or told us more. That terse, sinewy, yet elastic form, all lean and athletic, is just what is right: the descriptions of the men . . . are wonderfully drawn, mere thumbnail sketches, with the lines bitten in with a marked precision. Then, the atmosphere that grows more hard and bitter and north-easterly as the men get branded, or "minted" in the struggle. There's nothing like it in the least in English: there may be in French? . . . The *book has a perfect spiritual balance*. For a *book* it is. One has no feeling of "notes" at all. The "lubricant" you have added, does right away with any scrappiness. It all flows, one out of another perfectly . . . The feeling of the hut and fatigue life, sweeping out of existence all former states of consciousness rivets one horribly – and the sensations of the breathless struggle with time, to get things done *in time*, is nightmarish. The Cadet College comes as a relief to the blackness, and it's also admirably written: but you grow a little sententious in your Airman propaganda. Yes, that's overdone a trifle. I don't mind that because luckily it dries up: and you wind up with three fine last chapters, fine in their ease and naturalness. Well, you've done it, now! . . . I haven't exhausted the subject in any sense – but now I'll remain your exultant and "told you so" critic . . . Yes by God, its extreme naturalness and concise simplicity and frankness make it a masterpiece.'[34] Fearful that Trenchard might destroy the *Mint* manuscript after reading it, Garnett immediately arranged to have typescript copies made.

This letter crossed with one from Lawrence, sent in response to Garnett's telegram, in which he set out his own views about *The Mint*: 'Do not let your enthusiasm for new notes in writing run away over *The Mint*. It is a new note, I fancy: I've never read any other book of exactly the same character. It is fragmentary, and has the dry baldness of notes: none the worse for that, for the *Seven Pillars* was prolix: and this *Mint* is not long-winded: or not often long-winded . . . It is well-written, I fancy, as prose. The labour of the *Seven Pillars* taught me a good deal about writing: and I have worked very hard at other people's books and methods. So by now I must have acquired the rudiments at least of technique. I'd put *The Mint* a little higher than that: and say that its style well fitted its subject: our dull clothed selves; our humdrum, slightly oppressed lives; our tight uniforms: the constriction, the limits, the artificial conduct, of our bodies and minds and spirits, in the great machine which the R.A.F. is becoming. I had to hold myself down, on each page, with both hands.

'A painted or sentimental style, such as I used in the *Seven Pillars*, would have been out of place in *The Mint*, except in the landscape passages, where I have used it. But I doubt whether any un-versed reader would be able to connect the two books by any tricks of authorship.

'The form of the book took a lot of settling. I worked pretty hard at the arrangement of the sections, and their order. Mainly, of course, it follows the course of our training, which was a course: but where I wanted monotony or emphasis, I ran two or three experiences together, and where I wanted variety I jogged 'em up and down. I got all the material out into a skeleton order, and placed it, so near as I could: then I fixed in my own mind the main curves of idea which seemed to arise out of the notes: and re-wrote them with this intention in the back of my mind. So I fancy there are probably hundreds of tiny touches (perhaps only an adjective or comma) of a tendentious nature, which help to guide your intelligence to the ends I had in view. Only here again I was hampered, as in the *Seven Pillars*, by having true experiences to write about. I took liberties with names, and reduced the named characters of the squad from fifty odd to about fifteen: else there'd have been too many fellows in the book, and they'd have confused the picture. Otherwise it is exactly true.

'Force – oh yes, I expect parts of it are forcible. That's the worst of feeling things as strongly as I do. Only I hope that some of my contentment and satisfaction in the R.A.F. appears, as well as the abuses I saw. So often we tend to take the sweets for granted . . . Don't let the snare of ownership stifle your judgement. It is not a classic: but the précis of an (unwritten, and never to be written) book: and as it is not to be published, itself, you and I will never be able to check our judgements by public opinion. So:– regard it as a notebook of mine, given to you because you liked my *Seven Pillars*, and because I had no further room nor reason for it. I won't tell you it's rubbish: for I wouldn't have given you what I believed to be rubbish, but it's pretty second-rate, like me and my works: it's the end of my attempts to write, anyhow . . . I'd so like something of my creating to be very good: and I bask for the moment in the illusion of your praise.'[35]

On 19th April 1928, or shortly before, Lawrence abruptly decided to apply for transfer to another camp. He wrote to Sir Geoffrey Salmond, the AOC in India, asking to be sent up-country, perhaps to Peshawar on the North-West Frontier. A week later he explained the request in a private letter to Trenchard: 'Nothing has gone wrong yet: but since you are far away, and not entitled to do anything I'll tell you why. A conversation between an officer and a civilian in a club after dinner was improperly repeated to me. The officer has never spoken to me. Our section officers – there have been six in all in E.R.S. in the sixteen months – have been very decent to me. I think I deserve it, for I work hard, and intelligently.

'However this one is reported to have sworn he "had me taped" and was "laying to jump on me" when he got the chance. It was after dinner. They had all dined. I have no means, or wish, to check the story.

'But I'm pretty tired of fighting, and of risks: and my past makes my service character brittle. People easily believe ill of a man who has been an unconventional officer . . . and now prefers not to be an officer. So I'm going to run away to a squadron. They are small, and officers mix with airmen, and aren't so likely to misjudge a fellow. I told Salmond I had private reasons.

'Don't think me a funk. At worst it's only over-caution.'[36]

In reality, Lawrence had good reason to be alarmed by what he had heard, even though he was uncertain whether to take it seriously. The person involved, whose identity he did not reveal either to Salmond or to Trenchard, was the new station Commanding Officer.[37] Only four months earlier Lawrence had been instrumental in the previous CO's departure after a similar incident. This time it was his turn to leave.

He had settled in very well and was happy at Karachi, despite the long working hours. Once again, however, present contentment had been threatened by the reputation of his previous life. As the move approached he was saddened by the personal consequences of the transfer: 'I lose a lot of books, and music (only gramophone music, but the potted stuff is very well, for people away abroad), and the little conveniences I've arranged myself in the last fifteen months; and begin again: I'm stared at, a good deal, my first month in a new camp.'[38] The impending move provoked a depressed and introspective letter to Charlotte Shaw, although this kind of self-deprecation was becoming increasingly rare in his correspondence: 'All this finishing and finishing for ten years: without the faintest desire or stirring to begin anything anywhere again. I have no more notes for books in my bag: and no urge to join the Boy Scouts or the House of

Commons. The R.A.F. seems natural somehow, as a way of living: and no other life seems natural: or is it that no energy to attempt any new life remains? *Nunc dimittis*... if I had a Lord, and he were a decent fellow, he would tell his servant to go to sleep, in reward for having worked "over-time", and very hard, for forty years: or I think he would. It is what his servant (if profitable) would ask as reward.

'Of course G.B.S. at forty was just beginning to get into his stride, with plays: but between the power and courage of G.B.S., and my weariness, how great a gap! And when I think of lives for which I am very grateful: for poor Dowson, who wrote ten lovely poems, and died; for Rossetti, who wrote a few more, and died; for Coleridge, who wrote for two years, and then ran dry; why surely duration and bulk aren't the first considerations? It seems to me that the Arab Revolt, of activities of the body: and the *Seven Pillars* and *Mint*, of activities of the mind, may be all that my tissues can do. Certainly for the moment, it is all. I just labour, grudgingly, through the daily duty the R.A.F. compels from me: and lie restlessly on my bed (restlessly for the flies and prickings of external difficulty) during the other, very long, hours of this interminable day.'[39]

Despite his protests to the contrary, it seems that Lawrence was now weary of his purposeless existence in the ranks. He was ready for some new and challenging activity, and the seven years which lay ahead were to be among the busiest of his life. He had at last put the Arabian period and its bitter consequences behind him.

CHAPTER 40

The Edge of the World

May 1928 – January 1929

ACCORDING to Lawrence's RAF record, he was moved from Karachi to Peshawar on 26th May 1928. He stayed there only two days, and was then sent to Miranshah, an outpost in Waziristan near the Afghan border, seventy miles to the south-west. The RAF detachment he joined was the smallest in India: 'We are only twenty-six, all told, with five officers, and we sit with seven hundred India Scouts (half-regulars) in a brick and earth fort behind barbed wire complete with searchlights and machine guns. Round us, a few miles off, in a ring are low bare porcelain-coloured hills, with chipped edges and a broken-bottle skyline. Afghanistan is ten miles off. The quietness of the place is uncanny – ominous, I was nearly saying: for the Scouts and ourselves live in different compartments of the fort, and never meet: and so there's no noise of men: and no birds or beasts – except a jackal concert for five minutes about 10 p.m. each night, when the searchlights start. The India sentries flicker the beams across the plain, hoping to make them flash in the animals' eyes. So sometimes we see them.

'We are not allowed beyond the barbed wire, by day, or outside the fort walls, by night. So the only temptations of Miranshah are boredom and idleness. I hope to escape the first, and enjoy the second: for, between ourselves, I did a lot of work at Karachi, and am dead tired.

'Here they employ me mainly in the office. I am the only airman who can work a typewriter, so I do Daily Routine Orders and correspondence: and act postman, and pay clerk, and bottle-washer in ordinary. Normally flights do two months here, and get relieved: but I will try and get left on. It's the station of a dream: as though one had fallen right over the world, and had lost one's memory of its troubles. And the quietness is so intense that I rub my ears, wondering if I am going deaf.'[1]

The reduction in Lawrence's RAF workload was very welcome. When he left Karachi, two men working the standard five and a half hour day were needed to replace him. He was now a proficient typist, and his reputation for handling routine correspondence and administration meant that he was posted to the office as soon as he reached Miranshah. He took pride in clerical work, and had written jokingly to Trenchard six months before: 'The gods have my style taped. When the section people put up one of my drafts of letters they say "This is more Shaw"... and are so pleased at their prescience that they always take my wording. Sometimes your Air Ministry Weekly Orders make me wonder if I have found my widest sphere of usefulness. Wouldn't you like the future anthologies of English prose to include passages from Technical Orders? Think of the score it would be over the War Office! (Incidentally it takes a pretty good clerk to get an exclamation mark out of this machine.)'[2]

Lawrence used his extra time to begin working on a specimen section of the *Odyssey* for Bruce Rogers. The sample was to be Book I (there are twenty-four Books in all) which he hoped to finish by the end of July. It would take him five drafts to reach a satisfactory working text, and he planned a final revision when the Book was completed. The calm at Miranshah was a perfect setting for this kind of work, and Charlotte Shaw helped by sending him a selection of *Odyssey* translations. A week after arriving at Miranshah he wrote to her: 'If there is a spare hour it goes on the *Odyssey*, of which I have already rendered the first fifty lines into English which seems to me tolerable . . . The first pages are the hardest, for I have to find my style. Butler has missed, I find, all the picturesque side: the bric-à-brac: and most of the poetry has evaporated with Homer's queer, archaic, dignity. He or she [Butler had speculated that the author was a woman] was not telling a contemporary story, any more than I am.'[3] The work had not detracted from his admiration for the *Odyssey*: 'I like doing it. Translating is an ingenious game, very exciting for a man who has no originalities of his own to express.'[4]

Progress with the sample was quicker than he had expected, and he sent the completed Book I off to Ralph Isham on June 30th. He assured Isham that he would not be offended if the specimen were rejected, even though it had been hard work: 'Only the unusual size of the translation fee would reconcile me to doing twenty-four Books like this: and I shall, on the whole, be glad if they call it not good enough. Homer is a very great and exacting leader.'[5] The slow postal services between India and the United States meant that it would be at least two months before Lawrence had news of the publishers' decision.

In the interim he did a great deal of reading. Before leaving Karachi he had given many of his books away, packing the remainder into parcels to be sent on. These now began to arrive, and were supplemented by others

from friends in England. There was a library of about sixty books at
Miranshah when he arrived, but within four months the total had risen to
two hundred. He was put in charge of the Fort's library, which gave him
another retreat where he could read and work.

His chief regret about Miranshah was that there was no gramophone.
Of all the records he had collected at Karachi, he had brought only Elgar's
Second Symphony with him, expecting to receive the others later. After a
fortnight he wrote sorrowfully to Charlotte Shaw about the lack of a
gramophone, and predictably she offered to send him one. Lawrence was
a little conscience-stricken when he received her letter: 'If you sent me the
good Columbia portable it would run to £20, by the time it got here: and
I do not think that a justifiable expense. Remember that I have chosen to
be quite poor: and can only be happily poor if I have a poor man's
ambitions and standards of desire. Books do not seem so dear . . . and I
read them, and let them go: but £20 is hardly decent, is it? It is four
months' pay, for me: and appreciable, even to you.'[6] The 'protest' was in
vain, for the machine was already on its way. It arrived on Lawrence's
birthday: 'Thursday, August 16th was a red letter day. For one thing it was
the only fortieth birthday I shall ever have: for another, when I went
across in the afternoon to fetch the mail, I found the tiny post-office filled
with parcels addressed to me. Of course it was your gramophone, arrived
on the anniversary . . . The gramophone is a sumptuous-looking effort in
scarlet and gold. "OOO" called all the airmen when it came suddenly out
of its packing. Russian leather, the covering smells like. It is delicious but
far too good-looking. As for good-sounding, it could not be that. The
records I have to play on it ask for more than the world has yet invented
in the way of gramophones, to play them. Yet its tone is a clear and clean
one, as good or better than the Karachi one which was the best of my
hitherto possessing: and its volume is tremendous. You will scoff at
volume, perhaps, a little; but I like it, not out of vulgar wish to make
a noise, but because we live in such enormous rooms, and for their
demands noise is essential.

'To sum up, it is a lovely thing, everything the heart of any man in
camp could wish. Its portability ensures my never being sent away from
it, in future. It is working overtime, even now while I am down at the
Office. When one man falls away from its handle, exhausted, another
takes his place, like the sailors on a leaking ship, at the pumps. The airmen of Miranshah are envious of me, and very grateful to you for it.
They are even grateful to me for letting them play it so soon. It would

have been etiquette in camp to have reserved it for myself during the first three or four days.

'It went through the Elgar Symphony today. Nearly a month since I had heard it. Perhaps because it is English, that piece of music is coming to seem more meaningful to me than any other. As I listen to it I feel always on the exciting brink of understanding something very rare and great. Of course it slips away. Music cannot be understood in words or by the mind, in that fashion. But it makes me lean into it with extremity of trying to catch what it is going to say. And I hear it end with a singleness and solitariness of feeling which is very wonderful . . . I was wondering how my time would find some meal to fill it up, for the *Odyssey* has not been heard of since it went to the U.S.A. Now I know that the music is going to leave me with never enough time on hand.'[7]

Lawrence had now found a new contentment. He was enjoying life at Miranshah and the prospect of interesting literary work. For the present, no other life seemed as attractive, and he decided to extend his stay in the RAF for as long as possible. His seven-year period of enlistment was calculated from the date he had joined the Tank Corps, 12th March 1923, rather than his transfer to the RAF in 1925. He could therefore expect to be discharged on 12th March 1930. It was possible, however, to extend his service by a further five years, and he wrote to Trenchard on August 5th: 'In the winter you get my application to be allowed to carry my five reserve years across into active, which gives me till 1935 to be happy'.[8]

In the first week of September he at last heard about the specimen Book of the *Odyssey*. Isham wrote: 'I am very enthusiastic over your translation as are also the publishers and I am afraid that there is little chance of your getting out of this job of work through any hope that you may have entertained that the answer would be "no".'[9] Although arrangements for publication had yet to be settled, Isham asked Lawrence to go ahead with the work, offering his personal guarantee that the terms of the contract would be satisfactory. His scheme was that Rogers would print a limited de luxe edition, to be followed by general trade publication for which Lawrence would receive additional royalties over and above the initial £800 fee.

Isham enclosed a £35 cheque for the sample, and also an American newspaper article which claimed that Lawrence was engaged in covert diplomacy: 'Disguised in Arab garb, but known to every chieftain in the desert plains and hills between the Suez Canal and the Afghanistan frontier, the former Colonel Lawrence is continuing his peregrinations in the Middle East.'[10] Such reports were common and often originated in the French press, which habitually presented Lawrence as a secret agent working to undermine French imperial ambitions (for example, it had been claimed a few years previously that Lawrence was trouble-making in Morocco during the Riff rebellion there).

Lawrence also heard from Bruce Rogers about the *Odyssey* sample: 'It is just the vein I hoped for and I am most enthusiastic over it.'[11] Rogers's plans for the project had now changed. Instead of doing the book for Random House, he had decided to publish a limited edition in England. It would be printed there by Emery Walker, who had worked with William Morris and had been a founding partner of the famous Doves Press. Walker, now working with Wilfred Merton, was running a commercial printing firm which specialised in high-quality process engraving. Rogers told Lawrence about the company, describing Walker as 'my oldest friend in England . . . As they are not professional publishers [J. G.] Wilson thought (as I do) that the best chance of preserving anonymity lay with them. They *have* acted as publishers for several books (chiefly on art) and are of course well-known as engravers and printers, all over the world. Both Walker and Merton are as enthusiastic as I about the prospect of doing the book here. The greatest difficulties seem to lie in the protraction of time necessary to make the translation – and, in view of your present location and occupation, of the chance of the translation's being interrupted half-way through . . .

'There is no one I had rather work with than Walker and Merton and they will leave the book-making *entirely* in my hands. Walker is now over seventy-five (though almost as vigorous as ever) and it would be a great pleasure to him to have his name on one more important book, before he stops printing for good – and in my eyes this will be the *most* important, except perhaps the Doves Bible – no, I won't except even that . . .

'As Walker's plant is small we would set your copy as fast as received and send you proofs for correction and revise . . . The illustrations, or rather, decorations, (whatever they are to be) could go on simultaneously . . . I shall have much better assistance here, in every line, than I would have in New York . . . Wilson wanted me to warn you that it would be almost a superhuman task to prevent *all* leakage of your authorship – for a very long period. *He* is quite safe, I am confident, and Walker and Merton are entirely to be relied upon. But we can only guarantee that no announcement or hint of your connection with the book will be given before or after its publication – by anyone concerned with the making or marketing it – i.e. Walker, Merton and myself. None of the workmen need know what they are engaged upon.

'And here arises another point. You are very much mistaken, I think, in assuming that no one will be interested in the text as translation, instead of, or in addition to, the book-making. Wilson says it would not be pirated by any reputable publisher here, but would most likely be in America. So it seems to me necessary to copyright it there and print at least a few copies there to secure copyright. I feel sure that your version is going to be of far more general interest than you think, and my idea is to submit it to the Cambridge University Press for publication in – say – eight shilling form and at the same time to some University Press in the U.S. for publication there – either Harvard, of which I am official Printing Adviser, or Yale, where they gave me an Honorary M.A. in June. In either case I would not divulge authorship to anyone connected with the press – the copyright would be in my name, and I would stipulate 10% royalties for you and 5% for myself . . . I am not surprised at what you say of the difficulties of the job – it is probably the most difficult thing in the world to translate – you literally have to build the book over with Homer as raw material – but your opening book – or at least what I have by me – doesn't *show* the labour, and that to me is the main thing. It reads as though it were a new tale – fresh and unstudied.'[12]

Rogers sent a draft contract for the work, and Lawrence wrote on October 10th: 'Your terms suit me – if Isham agrees – and I'll do my best to earn the money you offer for a version of the *Odyssey*, which shall be as good a version as I can do'.[13] He stressed the need for anonymity: 'The twenty-fifth English version of the *Odyssey* is hardly a literary event; so I hope to get away with it, without publicity, of which I have had a surfeit. We must think out some humdrum name to put to it, if anyone asks a question about the person who did it.

'Also, I am not a scholar. If I read Greek, it is for pleasure. I fear my version will inevitably try harder to convey my pleasure, than to be an exact mould of the Greek. Yet accuracy is a good thing, in its way. Will you try to find a hidebound scholar, and ask him to snout through the sample chapter for literal errors? I'd like to avoid howlers.'[14]

Lawrence expected the translation to be complete in 1930: 'Your sample took me just over a hundred hours and it is not yet properly finished. Agreed that later books will go easier. The finding a style is hard, and it is not yet fully found. But remember that it is done after I have done the usual day's work of an airman in the workshop or office, and that on days when the R.A.F. give me overtime to do, I shall not be able to touch the Greek. It is a common tale that no fellow in the Services works:– but I think it is not true. We go to bed very tired, as a rule.'[15]

The Indian press had already referred to the fact that Lawrence was serving on the North-West Frontier. On September 26th, however, under a four-decker headline, the London *Evening News* published a fantastic account of his activities:

LAWRENCE OF ARABIA'S SECRET MISSION.
COUNTERING RED ACTIVITIES IN THE PUNJAB.
POSE AS A SAINT.
WARDING OFF THE EVIL EYE AND CURING ILLNESS.

Evening News Telegram.   BOMBAY, Wednesday
Lawrence of Arabia – one time of Oxford University, then the "Uncrowned King of the Arabian Desert" and a Colonel in the British Army, next a plain mechanic in the R.A.F., in which he enlisted in 1922 for a term of seven years as Aircraftman Shaw – has undertaken a new job now.

Like most of the jobs that Lawrence has undertaken in his picturesque life, it is an out-of-the-ordinary one.

He is, according to messages from Lahore, moving about the Punjab in disguise studying the activities of Bolshevist agents, whose secret headquarters are said to be in Amritsar. It has long been known that the Bolshevists have an eye – a very wide-open eye – on India.

Lawrence's present home is in a queer house in a remote street in Amritsar. It is luxuriously furnished, and women in quest of wonder-working charms are among his frequent visitors. They bring their babies to him to ward off the Evil Eye; they ask his advice in the curing of illness.

Lawrence poses as a great Pir (Mohammedan saint or spiritual guide) who has visited many Moslem lands and the tombs of all the great saints. The native gossips say that he is such a religious man that he is always recounting his own deeds.

It is so unlike Lawrence to "recount his own deeds" that of a certainty he must have some hidden purpose in doing so.[16]

The article was so patently absurd that it could cause little harm; indeed it provoked letters to newspapers from people knowledgeable about India pointing out that 'spying in Amritsar is valueless. There is nothing to spy on.'[17] Nevertheless, it was repeated in America and elsewhere. Rival popular newspapers were keen to pick up the story, and four days later the fiction was given a new twist by the *Sunday Express* under the headline 'LAWRENCE OF ARABIA'S SECRET AFGHAN MISSION'. It was claimed that: 'The everlasting mystery of the movements of Colonel T. E. Lawrence . . . was deepened last night by a statement circulating in well-informed quarters in London that he is engaged on a secret mission in Afghanistan attempting to facilitate the negotiation of a treaty between Great Britain and that country.

'Earlier in the week it was reported that Colonel Lawrence was in Amritsar, posing as a Mohammedan saint, and investigating Communist activities in the district.

'The opinion is expressed in authoritative circles that such an investigation could serve no useful purpose, and that the story might have been circulated to veil his real mission.

'It is, in fact, confidently asserted that this Colonel Lawrence, the romantic figure who gathered the wandering tribes of the Arabian desert and led them against the Turks, is in Afghanistan studying Afghan life for the British Government . . . Colonel Lawrence, it is explained, is making an intimate study of the views of the hillmen, the merchants, and the peasants. He is living with them, concealed beneath a mocha stain and the turban and robes he knows so well.'[18] The article ran on in the same vein, exploring the possible implications of Lawrence's supposed new role. It too was repeated in American newspapers, but no further evidence was produced, and the story seemed to die.

Since these allegations involved British government policy, they were noted in the India Office, and in the ensuing weeks the *Sunday Express* claims were the subject of a futile series of exchanges between the India Office, the Foreign Office, and the British Minister in Kabul, Sir Francis Humphrys. Two days after the story appeared, an India Office minute commented: 'The article is absurd, but it is just as well that Sir Francis Humphrys should know about it and be consulted as to a denial.'[19] On October 6th, Sir Francis cabled back recommending that a 'denial of the report be published if practicable by *The Times*, which Afghans regard as an authentic newspaper.'[20]

The Foreign Office duly contacted Charles Graves at *The Times*, but he wanted to write: 'The F.O. requests us to state . . . that Colonel Lawrence has not been in Afghanistan.'[21] The Foreign Office felt unable to authorise this without more information, and although Graves promised to try to have a general denial inserted, none appeared. The editor had decided that there was no case, without a formal Foreign Office request, for denying a nonsensical rumour published a week earlier in another newspaper.

Neither Sir Francis Humphrys nor the India Office were pleased by this apparent inaction. The unwillingness of the Foreign Office to take stronger measures was explained in a minute by E. M. B. Ingram: 'The whole of this rumour has lost its "news value" and we have already made such large drafts on our credit with *The Times* this week over the Anglo-French compromise and Abyssinia, that I am most reluctant to press them to meet our convenience in this matter.

'It is surely more important that the *démenti* should appear in the Indian papers. (In this connection I may add that only the other day Sir R. Lindsay [permanent under-secretary at the FO] said that F.O. *démentis* were to be reduced to their minimum and issued only in cases of emergency.) However if the Northern Department will draft a statement to be circulated to the press as a whole, we will circulate it but we can't force papers to publish it, least of all *The Times* who never published the original rumour and have a certain pride in keeping their columns free from such material.'[22] In the end, no action at all was taken. Lancelot Oliphant noted in a Foreign Office memorandum of October 10th (marked 'NOT to be copied to the I.O.'): 'If we start denying every rumour that gets about, the possible disadvantages are obvious.'[23] In due course the India Office wrote formally telling Sir Francis Humphrys that: 'on consideration here it was felt that the story had become rather old, and that, as it appeared to have attracted no particular notice, it was perhaps hardly worthwhile to draw attention to it again by issuing a denial'.[24] Within a few weeks, however, all concerned would have reason to wish that more positive action had been taken.

Lawrence was unaware of these absurdities, and his life at Miranshah that autumn was very calm. A new flight came to the station every two months, but he managed to stay on as one of five permanent staff. The only worry was a threat by the Government of India to close down the fort in the spring of 1929 as an economy measure. He worked in the Wireless Office 'a fifteen foot square white washed cube, with cement floor. In the centre is the fan: underneath it the officer's table: against the far wall my table, covered with white American cloth, and carrying the typewriter, which I've taught to produce pages of Homer, as well as Daily Routine

Orders!'[25] Every spare hour went on the translation. On October 30th he wrote: 'Book II is harder than Book I. I have done three hundred lines this month: only three lines per hour! And those aren't finished . . . The tale is very dignified: told for chiefs, and masters of households, to pass dark evenings. Butler is too parlour-like. Morris wanted to avoid the idea of translation. His version is neither free enough nor bound enough. He does not help me: for I want to keep the mediaeval city-state feeling out of it. The thing is Greek island, I feel sure.'[26]

Although he had insisted that the translation should be anonymous, he began to mention it frequently in letters to friends. As a result, his work on the *Odyssey* must soon have been well known in English literary circles. For example, he wrote to Forster: 'Did I tell you I'm making the twenty-fifth (rotten) translation of the *Odyssey* into English? They offered me £800 to do it all (anonymously!), and I fell for the cash, and do not yet regret it, though it is an impossible job to do well, and a heart-breaking job to botch. However botched it certainly is.'[27] He wrote in similar terms to Edward Garnett, adding, 'I find the *Odyssey* very hard to do . . . it's not like the *Iliad*: it's only mock-heroic: *Sigurd the Volsung*, not the *Volsunga Saga*: very literary, very skilled: only the modern bones keep on showing through their Wardour-Street fleshings. And the harder I try to keep it to one date, the more it swings up and down the centuries. *Marmion* is a genuine *Iliad*, a heroic poem: *Sigurd* is self-conscious: and the *Odyssey* enormously so: but the work of a great poet.'[28] (The mention of Wardour Street alludes to the trade in imitation antique furniture for which this street was once famous; it had first been used by William Morris, referring to a translation of the *Odyssey*.)

Lawrence aimed to complete the first three Books by the end of the year, and as a result he neglected his correspondence: 'I'm a man buried 125,000 words deep in the ground, who's got to scrape his way to daylight and the sunny face of the earth. Through this thick covering you won't hear any sharp or distinct noises till I'm almost through: and when I'm through (April 1930) it will be in so tired a state that I'll just moon about, happy to have open eyes and a shut head.

'However, there may be £800: and after all, if I don't get it, and if my *Odyssey* is no good, I shall be no worse for having lived so tightly with a great book all these months. It is a great book: and I am a very small creature, whose trotting up and down is not important except to itself.'[29] To keep to his schedule meant working fourteen hours a day, divided equally between the *Odyssey* and RAF duties.

The translation was especially demanding because Lawrence believed that the spirit of the original would be lost if it was put into plain English: 'I would have a version of Homer mannered, certainly'.[30] He found it a considerable challenge to write consistently in a style which would be acceptable yet slightly archaic.

In England, Lawrence's *Mint* was being seen by an increasing number of people, though always under the promise of strict secrecy. During 1928 he himself suggested it to Forster, H. S. Ede, Eric Kennington, Robert Graves, Sir Herbert Baker, Alan Dawnay and John Buchan. Edward Garnett showed it to H. M. Tomlinson, Herbert Read, and a young literary protégé, H. A. Manhood. Most of these readers wrote to Lawrence about the book, and several (not knowing about his work on the *Odyssey*) urged him to take up new writing projects. Jonathan Cape offered a translation of Rousseau's *Confessions*; David Garnett suggested that he should try to write a fairy-tale, and Forster suggested a book about women. Lawrence made a collection of the *Mint* 'reviews', as he called them. One of those he found most interesting was a letter sent by Manhood to Garnett, who forwarded it to Lawrence. Manhood's criticisms, drafted with the care of a writer whose reputation was not yet firmly established, were remarkably perceptive:

> Rather against will and nature I've re-read *The Mint* (well named!) There is a compelling, almost an obscene rawness of spirit in it. I have been startled into self-examination. Substantially it is rich, naked, honest stuff, invigorating for all its starkness and inartistry. The prose, well-born of a singularly acute, observant and analytical mind, is careful, conversational, occasionally memorable, occasionally deplorable, overdone: ('whose precipitous tenement walls pushed the night-cap dome of London's smoke-mist almost sky-far away'). The shaping of sheer fact, the will to 'let well alone' has all my admiration. At first glance I was led, shortsightedly, to write the author down as unromantically imaginative, to write: 'were this not so he would have broken himself on another, more common wheel, shaped his vision in a more universally palatable form, become an entertainer in the Temple instead of lavatory attendant'. This is nonsense. He is exquisitely romantic in a large, chivalrous and religious sense: he alone, I imagine, has found pure poetry in a severely practical service. His vision is single and complete, is the cause of his pre-occupation. I cherish 'My nature persists in

seeing all things in the mirror of itself and not with a direct eye'. Here is the hallmark . . .

An unflattering head and shoulders of the author appears from the book. Obviously he is never unaware of self, is never surprised, is self-conscious almost to the degree of morbidity. A little very human vanity is there. He postures with consistent, disarming honesty: ('Though sometimes I've laughed aloud while I cried hardest into my note-paper'). He is well aware of his rarity; his solitariness amuses when it doesn't pain. He declares himself knowing what he is to receive. His course was very natural in one 'wearied of abstractions', of intellectual bull-shit. The R.A.F. certainly offers an effective surface cure for loneliness, disillusion, which is all that was wanted... a respite from sophistry, a return to normality, to body-contact. The 'growing pains' afforded the required contrast, though truly, 'there's a defiance of common-sense in every faith'. No other life could hold so much so exactly. The cure, characteristically, was in the brush of a known, orderly life, in the writing out of fevers. I question 'no more loneliness', wonder if he can claim, or would wish to, a complete relationship, in the Christ sense, with anyone of his own race. He writes, I imagine, more frankly than he would ever talk, even in hysteria or in an improbable state of drunkenness. A natural man in his fundamental simplicity, seeming-abnormal only when judged possessively. He has come to live largely on little. He has got what he wanted, but for how long?[31]

Lawrence was interested by this criticism, and wrote to Garnett: 'Manhood's opinion of *The Mint* is flattering, isn't it? I'm sorry he speaks of its "inartistry". I tried ever so hard to cobble it together decently for you. The sentence he calls deplorable, about the tenement-court in London, was meant as a jest, to upset the gravity of Corporal Williamson's fatuous story about the prostitute and her dead baby. "Too discursive" he says too. I had suspected that, and had tried to cut out loose words.

'That cursed running on is a main vice of my writing. "Wonder if he can claim, or *would wish to*, a complete relationship, in the Christ sense, with anyone of his own race". The second guess got it. I have, he says, got what I wanted (*Yes*) but for how long? Why, for seven years, anyhow: six of them are past, and I have just asked Trenchard to sign me on for five more.'[32]

Trenchard agreed to Lawrence's request on November 30th, although, he wrote: 'Various people at home have been to see me, rather to implore me not to allow you to re-engage, but to bring you back to England. I have said that when you like to write to me or my successor and say you are tired of the Royal Air Force, I will agree to your going, but I will not take it from any of your friends that you really want to leave.'[33] The friends in question were Lionel Curtis and Sir Herbert Baker, who wanted Lawrence back from India, and had succeeded in persuading the Bank of England to offer him a job as a night-watchman. When Lawrence received the letter from Trenchard he commented: 'As for the friends and enemies who try to steer a course for me:– neglect them. They seem to disbelieve in my capacity to lay out a good course for myself; and refuse to understand that I prefer my course (however peculiar) to all their offers. Being in the R.A.F. for instance, though some people didn't want me there, has paid *me* excellently. Today I'm healthy, and sane, and happy at odd times. If you hadn't let me back in 1925, I shouldn't be alive now.'[34]

However, Lawrence's peace of mind at Miranshah was about to be shattered by a train of events that had begun in Afghanistan in mid-November. Local unrest in the east of the country had rapidly grown into a major rebellion by the Shinwari tribe. This soon threatened the position of the reforming national leader, King Amanullah.

Although Miranshah was close to the Afghan border, the frontier was a range of mountains, and life on the Indian side remained completely peaceful. But elements in the Indian press, knowing how close Lawrence was to Afghanistan, began to whip up speculation that he was working to promote the Shinwari cause. On December 5th, the London *Daily News* carried a report from Bombay which was a typical combination of truth and sensational fantasy: 'Colonel Lawrence has been located in Tochi [the region of Waziristan around Miranshah]. The Peshawar correspondent of the *Times of India* says that under the assumed name of Shaw, Colonel Lawrence is leading an obscure life as an Army clerk at Miranshaw, in a Tochi agency, on the North-West Frontier of India.

'In an interview Colonel Lawrence is reported to have said that he was tired of public life and wanted to lead a quite obscure existence among the barren hills of Tochi, in Waziristan.

'He is busy learning the Pushtu language, and it is inferred that he intends to move into Afghanistan.'[35]

The question of Lawrence's activities was taken up by *Pravda*, which commented: 'The appearance of Colonel Lawrence in any Mussulman country always marks a new British Imperialist intrigue and provocation.'[36] A few days later, an India Office official minuted: 'It would not be a bad thing if this Aircraftman could be found employment in the R.A.F. elsewhere than on the N.W. Frontier.'[37] The minute was passed to Field Marshal Sir Claude Jacob, secretary of the Military Department of the India Office. Jacob had served in India for much of his career, and his opinion of Lawrence was typical of the views of the Anglo-Indian hierarchy. Jacob added sourly to the India Office minute: 'I quite agree – I look on Lawrence as a fraud – and I am wondering when his bubble will burst.'[38]

On December 13th, Sir Francis Humphrys telegraphed from Kabul that the *Sunday Express* article of September 30th, which had never been denied, had now been reprinted with a pointed commentary by the Afghan press: 'This article has aroused great interest and speculation among my colleagues. I should like to be informed by telegram of Lawrence's whereabouts and be authorised to give an absolute denial to the statement that he is in the neighbourhood of the Afghan frontier or that he has visited Afghanistan.'[39]

By now the Shinwari rebellion had become a news story in the international press, and it was clear that a firm response would be needed if allegations about Lawrence's involvement were not to be a diplomatic embarrassment. A semi-official *démenti* in strong terms was published in India, where all the rumours were originating, and on December 14th Humphrys was authorised to deny categorically that Lawrence had ever been in Afghanistan. By now, however, circulation of the story was beyond control. On December 16th, the *Empire News*, a thoroughly sensationalist newspaper based in Manchester, published the confirmation of Lawrence's presence in Afghanistan which the world's press had been waiting for. It appeared in a long report allegedly based on information provided by Dr Francis Havelock, 'the well-known medical missionary who has just returned from the wild Afghan hills'. The article stated that Havelock had encountered in Afghanistan both Lawrence ('the most mysterious man in the Empire . . . the ultimate pro-Consul of Britain in the East') and Trebitsch Lincoln ('ex-spy, ex-British M.P., ex-forger, the tool of the Soviet Government in China').[40] The article was a complete fiction, but its substance was repeated on December 27th by a press agency, the Free Press Mail Service, and distributed throughout the world. It was claimed that Lawrence and Lincoln were fighting on opposing sides in Afghanistan: 'The battle is now joined between the Apostle of

Hatred and the Apostle of Peace. Lincoln has gold and rifles. Hillmen love both. Lawrence has unknown resources and a silver tongue'.[41]

For a while, Lawrence remained unaware of the growing storm. By late December he had completed Books I–III of the *Odyssey*. After reading them through, on Christmas Day, he wrote to Emery Walker: 'I have spent five hundred hours over these fourteen thousand words, and have reached a sort of finality – arriving at that negation of improvement, when after a cycle of alternatives one returns to the original word.

'The *Odyssey* is very difficult. It is clever, in the real sense, which held no derogatory meaning. A very skilful literary performance, not simple, not primitive: very, very artful and artificial. It's full of tags out of the *Iliad*, but is not epic at all. It's a narrative, and all its persons have character. That in itself would save it from epic, for the persons of an epic should be on the stupid scale and the grandeur of it come from a relentless march of events.

'Nor is there much poetry about the story, so far as it has gone. The author writes in metre, as that was the consecrated form of the early novel, or *chanson de geste*. He was a poet – oh yes, a great poet, I fancy: but this was a story he was telling.

'He was also an antiquarian and filled in his background with lots of quaint furniture, to give it the antique feel. Quite Wardour Street, as I said before, with the modern bones showing through the fancy fleshings.

'His naivety is sham too: he laughs in his sleeve at his puppets. Line after line is ironical, as if he wasn't sure if it should be 'Sir Topas' [Chaucer's mock-heroic knight] or not. Perhaps the first part of *Don Quixote* is a nearer parallel...

'I think my version is richer, on the whole, than the original: as Samuel Butler's version is balder. Butler was the realist, telling a tale. Thereby I think he did the *Odyssey* too much honour. The author was picking flowers, on the way, also.

'He or she? Honestly I don't care. No great sexualist, either way: no great lover of mankind. Could have been written by a snipped great ape. A marvellous crafty tale, mixed just to the right point with all the ingredients which would mix in. The translators aren't catholic, like their master. Each of us leans towards his private fancy.'[42] He started work on Book IV on Boxing Day, hoping to be able to maintain his pace and finish Book VI by the end of March.

Long before this, however, his tranquil existence at Miranshah came to an abrupt end. On 3rd January 1929, Sir Francis Humphrys cabled to

Delhi and London pointing out that the increasing speculation about Lawrence's activities now appearing in the Indian press was being repeated in Afghanistan, where suspicions about covert British support for the Shinwari rebellion were 'naturally encouraged by Russian and Turkish Ambassadors and, I am told, even by my French colleague . . . Contradiction of this nonsense will no longer produce the desired effect, and I should be relieved of much embarrassment if Lawrence could be transferred to a place distant from the frontier until the civil war in Afghanistan subsides.'[43]

As a result, the Government of India in New Delhi took up the issue with Salmond, while the India Office in London contacted Trenchard. Salmond cabled Trenchard on January 4th and again the following day, reporting the mounting pressure to have Lawrence removed and asking for instructions. Trenchard replied on January 5th: 'I agree that whatever we do the propaganda re Lawrence will go on whether we move him or not; people would not believe us. However in view of the definite request I concur in Lawrence being transferred from India, but I want to help Lawrence as much as I can and I would ask you to find out from him whether he would like to go to Singapore for a year, to Aden, or to a small detachment of two or three men in Somaliland, or whether he would rather come home.

'I am ready to do anything I can to help Lawrence... Please wire me where Lawrence wants to go.'[44]

On the same day he wrote to Sir Arthur Hirtzel at the India Office: 'I . . . have sent instructions to India that Lawrence is to be transferred from India to some other Air Force station. I will let you know in a few days to what station they will be instructed to send him.

'Both ourselves and Lawrence are anxious that there should be as little publicity as possible . . . I feel that a communication to the Press will set everybody ringing up to know where he is going.'[45] Hirtzel, who shared Sir Claude Jacob's opinion of Lawrence, noted wrily on Trenchard's letter: 'This is an astonishing business.'

On January 8th, Lawrence was flown from Miranshah to Lahore. *The Times* reported his move, adding: 'He flatly denied that he had had the faintest connexion with events in Afghanistan'. An official communiqué issued in Delhi had 'stated that in view of the currency obtained by the unfounded and preposterous rumours connecting the name of Aircraftman Shaw with events in Afghanistan, the Government had decided to transfer him from Miranshah.'[46]

Lawrence's disgust at this latest press fantasy was tempered by pleasure: it had given him the chance to cut short a five-year posting overseas. He opted to return home, and was put on board a passenger liner, the SS *Rajputana*, which sailed for England on January 12th. By this time allegations and denials of his role in Afghanistan were appearing almost daily in the world's press.

CHAPTER 41

Plymouth
January – September 1929

THERE were few passengers on the SS *Rajputana*. Lawrence had a second-class cabin to himself, and rarely left it. He spent most of the voyage to England working on the *Odyssey*, and was able to translate three more Books.

At Port Said there was a distraction: an official in the local police force, acting in the belief that Lawrence was a dangerous spy, sent officers on board to search the ship and arrest him. Lawrence took pleasure in evading them, and afterwards wrote happily to a service friend: 'They were fair flummoxed, it seems, that night: and reported that I was probably not on the *Rajputana* after all.'[1]

In England, the allegations about Lawrence had now been seized upon both by journalists and radical socialists. The *Army & Navy Gazette* of January 24th reported: 'The latest manifestation on the part of organisations somewhat grandiloquently describing themselves as "The International Class War Prisoners' Aid Society and the League against Imperialism" at a meeting held on Tower Hill was the burning in effigy of Aircraftman Shaw, with the egregious Mr. Saklatvala [Communist MP for Battersea North] in the role of the chief stoker.'[2]

The Air Ministry, knowing that the press would try to interview Lawrence as soon as he reached England, decided to take him off the *Rajputana* when she put in at Plymouth on February 2nd, before reaching her final destination at Gravesend. At Plymouth, a naval duty officer boarded visiting liners as a matter of course, and it was arranged that Lawrence should be taken ashore in his launch. The pressmen, however, were ready for such a manoeuvre, and Lawrence was photographed and filmed as he climbed down a rope ladder into the waiting naval pinnace.

He was met by Wing Commander Sydney Smith, whom he had first met in very different circumstances during the Cairo Conference of 1921. At that time, Smith had been commander of an RAF station in Egypt, and had helped to entertain the visiting delegates. Later, during 1926, they had both been stationed at Cranwell.

Smith handed Lawrence a note from Trenchard which warned: 'I don't want to see a lot of placards to the effect that the Air Ministry have spirited you away in fast motor-boats and cars'.[3] However, their attempts to keep Lawrence's whereabouts secret failed at almost every step. In order to avoid Plymouth railway station, they drove to Newton Abbot, but as soon as they boarded the London train they were recognised, and by the time it reached Paddington a crowd of journalists was waiting. Trenchard had asked Lawrence to: 'Endeavour as much as possible to avoid being interviewed.'[4] They therefore pushed through the pressmen with hardly a word. After this, there was a farcical chase in taxis, which lasted nearly an hour. The driver of their cab went so slowly that the pursuers had no difficulty in following (Smith later concluded that he had been bribed). Lawrence could not help being amused, but he was also deeply worried that this new deluge of publicity would cost him his place in the RAF.

In the end, the journalists were disappointed. A paragraph in the *Manchester Guardian* next morning read: 'Aircraftman Shaw was hunted through the London streets last night with real Arabian fervour, although the hunters were only newspapermen and photographers. They tracked him to a flat in Cromwell Road, but the only interview with him that has appeared contains no more than these words, "No, my name is Mr. Smith." He said little more, indeed, than his effigy said when it was burnt the other day at Tower Hill'.[5] In due course, Lawrence had been spirited away to his old haunt above Herbert Baker's offices in Barton Street, and the following morning (a Sunday) he went to stay with the Trenchards at their house in Barnet.

By this time, the confusion about Lawrence's activities had spread to the House of Commons. On January 28th, Ernest Thurtle, Labour MP for Shoreditch, had asked a question about Lawrence's enlistment under a false name. This had been dealt with by the Air Minister, Sir Samuel Hoare, whose irritation can be imagined. He had consistently opposed Lawrence's reinstatement in the Air Force, until overruled in 1925. Now he found himself at the centre of yet another Lawrence controversy. More Parliamentary questions followed, and there seemed little prospect that the issue would die down. Lawrence, who could foresee the likely consequences, decided to tackle Thurtle personally. On February 4th, he went to the Houses of Parliament and tried to find Thurtle, but without success. Finally, late in the evening, he managed to make contact by telephone. After a long conversation, Lawrence arranged to visit the House of Commons to talk with Thurtle and some of his Labour Party colleagues.

The following day, Lawrence wrote to Trenchard excusing himself for taking a step which involved a risk of still further publicity: 'I want to tell you . . . that I have explained to Mr. Thurtle, privately, the marriage tangles of my father (*you* probably know of them: *he* didn't, and is asking questions which might have dragged the whole story into the light) and I hope he will respect my confidence, and stop asking questions in the House. Probably an airman shouldn't discuss his family tree with an M.P. but I can hardly ask the Secretary of State to intervene and save me from curiosity.'[6] Thurtle and Saklatvala had already given notice of more questions, which were dealt with on February 6th, but after this, parliament lost interest in the affair.

Lawrence also tried to arrange a meeting with his acquaintance R. D. Blumenfeld, editor of the *Daily Express*, hoping to discourage further press attention. Before he could do so, however, the Air Ministry intervened. Trenchard feared that Lawrence was courting press attention and reprimanded him. After a difficult meeting at the Air Ministry, Lawrence wrote to Thurtle: 'I have been told by the Powers that my visit to the House was not approved: told very distinctly, I'm afraid.'[7]

He did not, however, give up his newly made political acquaintances. He lent Thurtle both *Seven Pillars* and *The Mint*, writing: 'I'm delighted to have had the chance, by lending you those two books, to give myself away to you completely. If Mr. Maxton [Labour MP for Glasgow, Bridgeton, and a renowned popular orator] will read some of them, he'll never be nervous about me, either, again.'[8]

Lawrence was now told that he would be posted to Sydney Smith's station, RAF Cattewater, at Plymouth. First, however, he was due for a month's leave, and he planned to spend the time living at Barton Street and visiting old friends. The problem of reaching them was resolved when he unexpectedly found himself in possession of a motorcycle: he received a letter informing him that a new Brough SS-100 was waiting for collection, paid for by an anonymous group of friends.

The motorcycle was very welcome as it would enable him to travel, yet he deeply resented the idea of accepting it. He calculated that it must have cost about £220, at that time a very large sum. Although he could easily have earned a substantial income, he had chosen to live in poverty. A gift of this size seemed to be charity and he felt that he had no right to it. He wrote: 'So large a present (valued at three years of my pay) pauperises me a bit, in my own sight, for accepting it.'[9] He guessed rightly that Charlotte Shaw was behind the scheme. For more than five years she had been showering him with expensive presents, and he saw that the Brough would put him under a still deeper obligation. He made up his mind to refuse the motorcycle, thus making it clear that there was a limit to the indebtedness he could tolerate.

On his second free day in London he visited Charlotte Shaw and spoke to her about the gift. Afterwards she wrote: 'he volunteered to me that he had had a letter to say there was a bicycle for him: and asked my advice as to his taking it!'[10] She had urged him to accept it, and wrote contentedly to Lionel Curtis: 'The Lord be praised, and Glory be, *he will take it*! He has just said so. But he bargains to repay later on . . . It is going to be a splendid thing for him, and will be his salvation if they throw him out of the Air Force.

'I suppose you haven't seen him yet? He looks, I think, worn and tired, but is in splendid form mentally, and very gay and hopeful.'[11]

In reality, Lawrence had overestimated the value of a new SS-100. Its list price was just under £185, and Robin Buxton had negotiated a £40 discount. The final cost, therefore, was only £144 4s. 6d. of which Charlotte Shaw had intended to contribute £100. The balance was to be paid in equal shares by Buxton, Lionel Curtis, Francis Rodd, and C. J. Holland-Martin, one of Buxton's banking colleagues.

The 'friends' had named Buxton as their spokesman, and on February 6th Lawrence went to see him to discuss the motorcycle. He was adamant about the terms on which he would accept it. Buxton reported: 'He would not move the bike, anxious as he was to do so, until he was assured he might pay for it himself and his face cleared up wonderfully when I said I would let them [the friends] know his views.'[12]

Buxton was able to tell Lawrence that the money in his bank account was sufficient to pay for the machine. However, Lawrence was also planning to complete the purchase of Clouds Hill. If he used his reserve now, for the Brough, he would probably need to borrow money for the cottage. Buxton offered to provide an overdraft for this purpose, and the question of accepting the motor-cycle as a gift was dropped. Charlotte Shaw was pleased, nevertheless, that because of her scheme Lawrence now owned a Brough, and that he had been given a handsome discount.[13]

Despite this new-found mobility, Lawrence chose to spend most of his leave in London. He was worried that the unwelcome publicity would continue, since he knew that the RAF could not be expected to tolerate such problems. Hoare's patience was already stretched to the limit, and Trenchard had warned that there was a real risk of dismissal from the service. Lawrence was expecting a further crisis in the summer, because he had heard rumours of a film being made about his part in the Arab Revolt. He wrote to Newcombe: 'I am in London, rather distractedly and jerkily, with one suit of plain clothes, and two suits of uniform, and a motor-bike: I see hardly anyone, and don't know what to say to them, when I do see them.

'On March 10 R.A.F. life begins again – at Cattewater, which is Plymouth. It will be a blessed relief. Now, it's like being lost.'[14]

After his two-year absence from Britain, he was keen to see his closest friends. He made several visits to the Shaws, and on February 7th met Bruce Rogers for the first time. Rogers later wrote to a friend: 'For two hours we both talked as hard as we could . . . Lawrence isn't at all a disappointment – quite the reverse. He is small and quiet and self-contained and extremely modest. His letters were so interesting that I own I was almost regretful when I heard he was coming back to London – but he's a great success personally.

'You already know about the *Odyssey* so I can write of it to you (*sub rosa*). Lawrence has four books done and they are in my hands – a whacking translation, I think – the best ever. He has two more books pretty well roughed out, but he goes over it and re-writes six or eight times . . . He's coming in again on Thursday and hopes to be in civilian clothes so that he can lunch with me'.[15]

On the day he met Rogers, Lawrence also visited Clive Bigham, who had been on the British staff in Cairo during the war. Bigham was now writing a series of historical studies, and the conversation was mainly about Crusader castles. Afterwards he wrote in his diary that Lawrence was 'alert enough, but melancholy and seems to live in another plane'.[16] A week later, Lawrence had lunch with Sir Philip Sassoon, whom he had also met at Miranshah in 1928. The other guests included Sir Hugh and Lady Trenchard, Winston Churchill, Sir Louis Mallet and Charlotte Shaw.

In mid-February he took his new motorcycle to the Brough works in Nottingham for modifications. The weather since his return had been extremely cold, and he wrote to Alan Dawnay: 'I am frozen in to London. The bike is at Nottingham, and the roads all ice and snow. So she cannot travel them. The first day of melting I will go up there, by train, and ride her down. But will it ever melt?

'If God is good, I'll try and call in at Aldershot on my way down to Plymouth:– about March 8. If only it were tomorrow! I do not think I shall ever go on leave, for pleasure: only to dodge publicity is the misery justified. Something's gone wrong with the works, and I find myself breaking every engagement, and avoiding everyone.'[17]

When his leave came to an end, Lawrence wrote thanking Herbert Baker for the use of the flat in Barton Street, which had again served as a sanctuary from the press: 'Your people have been very good. Nobody has found me at Barton Street, despite efforts by callers and telephones. Harvey [a member of Baker's staff] has been like a rock, and so the house has always felt safe.'[18]

He called in to see Clouds Hill again on his way down to Plymouth, finding it 'as lovely as ever'.[19] That day, he paid the balance of the purchase price, £350, and from then on he regarded it as his property. It would be several months before the legal conveyance was finally completed, on October 12th.

RAF Cattewater was to be one of the most enjoyable of Lawrence's postings. The station itself was small and isolated. He wrote to H. S. Ede: 'Cattewater proves to be about 100 airmen, pressed tightly on a rock half-awash in the Sound; a peninsula really, like a fossil lizard swimming from Mount Batten golf-links across the harbour towards Plymouth town. The sea is thirty yards from our hut one way, and seventy yards the other. The Camp officers are peaceful, it seems, and the airmen reasonably happy. That is good hearing for me, as I am to share their good fortune.'[20]

The original military base at Cattewater had been closed down shortly after the Great War, and Sydney Smith had now been sent there to reopen it as a seaplane station. It would be manned by 104 Squadron, but as yet no aircraft had arrived. Lawrence was attached to the headquarters section, and during the first weeks his duties were mainly clerical. His experience as clerk to the Engine Repair Section at Karachi proved valuable in setting up the new station workshops. When not in the office, he was to serve as crewman in one of the motorboats used as tenders to ferry personnel round the seaplane anchorage.

After three weeks, he sent his impressions of the station to Corporal Easton, the wireless operator whose room he had shared at Miranshah: 'There is an H.Q. flight (Office and Motor-boat and transport personnel and W/T [wireless]) and a Squadron . . . They are going to add a second Squadron, later. This one has no flying-boats yet, but hopes for them, this month . . . I'm typing Daily Routine Orders for a living. "What a change" you'll say: that's about all I do, too: but I'm to go to the Marine Section, and do something on a motor-boat, this month . . . My poor old Greek book is a bit held up. This hut is rather a beer garden, with wireless and gramophones and what-not: and I find it almost impossible to work: no, hardly that: I did pretty well this week: finished another book, one twenty-fourth of the whole: so perhaps, if the new job proves easy, I may get it done by this time next year.'[21]

There was much less free time at Cattewater than in India. Weekend leave was from 1 p.m. on Saturday until midnight on Sunday, and after one or two visits to London, Lawrence decided that there was little attraction in going there for such a short time (the journey took him at least five hours each way). This was a great disappointment: at Bovington and Cranwell he had been within easy reach of friends in the capital, whereas at Plymouth he was not.

One compensation was friendship with his CO. As Sydney Smith already knew and liked Lawrence, he was able, in private, to set aside the formal relationship between a Wing Commander and an A/c 1. Smith's work was very demanding, and he saw in Lawrence a highly capable and trustworthy assistant. He therefore delegated to Lawrence work that was well beyond the level of responsibility normally accorded to an aircraftman. Moreover, Lawrence frequently visited the Smiths' house, and soon became a close family friend. This unusual state of affairs attracted much less attention in the small headquarters section than it would have done in a squadron, and the friendship made a great deal of difference to Lawrence's life at Cattewater.

Apart from his station duties, Smith had been nominated by the RAF as its representative on the Royal Aero Club committee set up to organise the international Schneider Trophy seaplane race. The competition was scheduled to take place over the Solent early in September. Smith took Lawrence as his personal assistant for this work, and during April both men became engaged in what proved to be a major administrative task. It involved a heavy correspondence, as well as frequent meetings in London and Calshot (an RAF base at the mouth of Southampton Water). Lawrence drafted countless letters and minutes and looked after an increasing number of files.[22]

In his role as clerk to the marine and workshop section, Lawrence was soon given an attic office of his own. Although there was little free time, he managed to rough out Books VII and VIII of the *Odyssey* during March and April. He planned to get them to Emery Walker by the end of that month.

On April 13th, however, his growing contentment was shattered by a hostile piece in the popular weekly magazine *John Bull*:

> Aircraftman T. E. Shaw – your old friend "Lawrence of Arabia" – has signed on for a further five years with the R.A.F.
>
> At present he is stationed at the seaplane depôt, Cattewater, Plymouth, where he is not much troubled with duties, but divides his time between "special leaves of absence" in London, tinkering with a "super sports" motor-bicycle and literary work.
>
> The last takes the form of translating Homer's *Odyssey* into English. This version will be published anonymously in America in the autumn book season this year.
>
> Rumours that Lawrence will soon be posted back to India are rife. Don't believe them.
>
> He proved too much of a nuisance on his last visit by providing material for Russian propaganda.[23]

This was the first time that Lawrence had been subjected to such belittling treatment at the hands of the British press, and he was hurt by it. After a second article in the same vein he wrote to a service friend: 'as for choking off the Press – he will be my friend for life who finds how to do that. I do nothing – and they talk. I do something – and they talk. Now I am trying to accustom myself to the truth that probably I'll be talked over for the rest of my life: and after my life, too . . .

'That snobbery "He does not associate with the other airmen, except a few of the more intellectual" – God, it's poisonous. If I could get that reporter by the neck he would want a new one in five minutes.'[24]

The renewed publicity left him in no mood to apply himself to the *Odyssey*. On two occasions since December 1922, journalists had put his service position in jeopardy, and his reaction to the press had become progressively more defensive. Three days after the *John Bull* article appeared, he found an excuse to write to Trenchard, stressing the contribution he was making to the RAF at Cattewater.

On May 1st he wrote about the situation to Bruce Rogers: 'Today I had meant to send you Books VII and VIII: instead of which I must tell you of my worries. It's been published (in *John Bull*, of all the world's press!) that I'm doing an *Odyssey*: and since that day I haven't done a stroke. Up till then I'd been trying to get on with it. Seven is complete, all but the last look-over. Eight is having its third revise. Nine is started: but that was all March work: and since, as I say, there has been nothing . . .

'I had not expected this trouble, before publication: *After*, yes: but somehow that didn't matter. You'll realise, I hope, that I can't carry on as it is.

'Will you see Walker and Merton, and present them the difficulties as they stand? I want to be as reasonable and helpful as possible, and only hope that their more sober experiences may find a road out of what seems, to me, rather a deep hole.'[25]

This letter, which contained a broad hint that Lawrence might abandon the translation, was hardly fair. During the preceding months he had described the project openly to friends in the English literary world, many of whom had links with the press. The fact that the author of *Seven Pillars* was now working on the *Odyssey* must by this time have been common literary gossip, and wider publicity was therefore inevitable. Lawrence had been warned by Bruce Rogers at the outset that anonymity could only be preserved if everyone concerned took great care, and he must surely have realised that he himself had probably been responsible for letting the news out. However, by this time other factors were involved in his reaction. One of the most important was the knowledge that further press comment might lead to his dismissal from the RAF.

Bruce Rogers drafted a careful reply, discussing the problems he himself had experienced with the press, and continued: 'Aren't you a little too heedful of the rumour and gossip that must necessarily attend the doings of anyone who has attracted the attention of the public at large – or of even a small section of it? In my opinion (which you have only indirectly asked), you lay too much stress on the supposed importance of this present project, in the public eye. I don't suppose that one person in a thousand who reads newspapers of the *John Bull* type has ever even heard of the *Odyssey* – and in every thousand that one person is probably not in the least interested in what you may or may not do, and dismisses it at once from his mind. In a year and a half, at any rate, if a new *Odyssey* appears, no one will remember or care whether you did it or not. No copies will be sent to reviewers and in my opinion the appearance of the volume will not cause a ripple in the book world.'[26]

Rogers was bemused by the importance Lawrence attached to anonymity, not least because the draft translation had been praised by everyone who had seen it. He also emphasised that people other than himself were involved in the scheme: 'I have given your letter to Walker and Merton to read and they were both tremendously upset by it.'[27]

Substantial sums had already been spent on typesetting and special paper. He concluded: 'I think we shall have to go on, somehow. If you cannot produce any more at present, let it rest for a time. We have already enough copy to go on with for some time, and my own part of the work is far behind its schedule . . . These rumours will not persist (they don't *know* anything definitely) and they will be forgotten before the book appears.'[28]

If Lawrence was shamed by this letter, he did not show it. He told Charlotte Shaw that Rogers had written 'a typically wise and sensible letter (all wrong of course!) holding me to my contract, which of course I must keep, if they insist upon it.'[29] It was a week before he replied to Rogers, and the terms of this letter suggest that another reason for his attempt to drop the translation may have been his increasing RAF workload. He wrote: 'I understand, and shall complete the translation as well as I can do it, and (if possible) by April next year. Only they put extra jobs on me here, one after the other, and so I have little spare time. I have not done anything since I wrote you that letter trying to get off the job.'[30]

On March 23rd, Lawrence had briefly visited London to hear Bernard Shaw read *The Apple Cart* at the home of Lord and Lady Astor in St James's Square; the American Ambassador and Philip Kerr were also present. Nancy Astor, who was Conservative MP for Plymouth, Sutton, told Lawrence that she would be in Plymouth throughout May to defend her seat at the forthcoming general election. In late April he discovered that she had already arrived, as he reported to Charlotte Shaw: 'I was in Plymouth, paying a reluctant call, when a pea-hen voice screamed "Aircraftman" from a car: and it was her. Next day she rang up the Wing Commander, and was allowed all over the station. We sparred verbally at each other. She got on my motorcycle: I drove with her and Michael [Astor] to her housing estate, to her house (supper), to a children's club she runs in Plymouth. It has since been in the papers. Serves me right for walking about with a talkie sky-sign.

'She was very nice: at her swiftest and kindest: one of the most naturally impulsive and impulsively natural people. Like G.B.S., more a cocktail than a wholesome diet.'[31] A few days later he referred to her again: 'I like her: and admire her, even more: but, for living beside, commend me to some vegetable.'[32] After this, Lawrence and Nancy Astor began to write to one another regularly and, from time to time, they met. Her vitality and lack of affectation appealed to his sense of humour, and his letters to her have a mischievous touch which had been absent from his correspondence since the pre-war letters to E. T. Leeds. He seems, moreover, to have felt a more general mood of contentment. Just as he had once described Carchemish as 'a wonderful place and time: as golden as Haroun al Raschid's in Tennyson',[33] he would later refer to Sydney Smith's years at Plymouth as 'the golden reign'.[34]

One of Smith's friends was Major A. A. Nathan, with whom he shared the ownership of a Moth aircraft fitted with seaplane floats. Lawrence, who helped to maintain it, enjoyed flying and during that summer he often accompanied Nathan. They began planning to make a European tour in the Moth during his autumn leave.

Lawrence was fascinated by the possibilities opened up through the great expansion of military and commercial flight which was then taking place. On July 12th he sent Trenchard a letter passionately advocating that one of the latest British airships (the R.100 or R.101) should be diverted on its trial flight to Karachi so as to cross the unexplored Empty Quarter of Arabia. He wrote: 'This is immensely important . . . I have been saving it up for you for years . . . by going just a few miles out of their course to the southward they can pass over the *Ruba el Khali*, the so-called "Empty Quarter" of Arabia. This is a huge area of many hundred thousand square miles. No European has ever crossed it, nor any Arab any of us has actually questioned. All the geographers refer to it annually as the great unsolved question of geography.

'Now, I want the trial trip of the airships to settle the *Ruba el Khali* . . . On the first trip they will be inhabited mainly by their crew, and it will be easy to deflect them. To go over the Empty Quarter will also be an enormous advertisement for them: it will mark an era in exploration. It will finish our knowledge of the earth. Nothing but an airship can do it, and I want it to be one of ours which gets the plum.

'If you consult the map you will see that it is a very slight diversion from their course between Karachi and Ismailia. I would like it to be an unheralded diversion. Not a newspaper stunt exhausted before it begins. Take the geographical world by surprise.

'The Navigator of the airship will be getting his W/T bearings and time signals all the way, and will plot his course exactly. I do not think there will be anything much to see – sand, sand, and hills, perhaps – but the comfort of having finished, in twelve hours, what man has been projecting for fifty years....

'Do think it out, properly, and say yes. I do not ask to be let go, myself. I'd love it, of course: but the important thing is to get it done, without talk'.[35]

A few days later, Lawrence was in London to attend Schneider Trophy committee meetings. He dined with the Shaws and spoke enthusiastically about the airship scheme. Afterwards, Shaw wrote recommending it to Lord Thomson, Air Minister in the new Labour Cabinet, and suggested that Lawrence should take part. Thomson replied that such a diversion would probably not be possible on the first trial flight, but would nevertheless be seriously considered: 'I am especially keen on this aspect of aviation and regard surveys of this sort as one of the principal uses of airships.

'As regards including Lawrence, or Private Shaw, as you yourself described him, I will consider the matter. His passion for obscurity makes him an awkward man to place and would not improve his relations with less subtle members of the crew. However, as a friend of yours he will be remembered.'[36]

As the time for the Schneider Trophy approached, Lawrence became busier and busier, and in the early summer his letters often spoke of tiredness. At the end of July, he wrote to Bruce Rogers explaining that the *Odyssey* translation had been held up by his 'long immersion in Schneider Cup Race details'. All the preparations were complete, on paper, but, 'Next month we start doing the things, and will be frantically busy till mid-September: and then I want to get some leave, and break the back of the *Odyssey*. . .

'It is wonderful to see how much work the R.A.F. give me here. Of course I like doing their work, and would be quite happy doing it, if I hadn't agreed to do the *Odyssey* for you, at the same time. In India there were heaps of leisure hours. Here too few: but after September it will be easier. I have told my officer that I must have my winter evenings free.'[37] Lawrence was concerned that the typesetters would soon overtake him: 'You will be clamouring at the hut door for copy: and I'll be inside polishing boots, or otherwise being unhelpful. I'll do my best, as soon as this flurry of R.A.F. work passes.'[38]

From the beginning of August he was occupied working on the RAF boats that were to go to Calshot. He expected to be sent there himself, any day, but did not finally leave Plymouth until August 24th, a fortnight before the race.

He did not travel directly to Calshot, but rode first to London and then to the Malvern Festival to see a performance of *The Apple Cart*. Afterwards he went south, spending a day with Augustus John, who took the opportunity to paint a head and shoulders portrait in oils.[39] John later presented him with the picture, writing: 'My only condition is that you will sit again, for your face as you say is a good wearer and should be periodically recorded.'[40]

By this time, the Schneider Trophy had become the world's premier air race and received international attention. New machines had been built for the 1929 event, and it was confidently expected that the speed record would be broken, as it had been in every preceding Schneider contest. The race was always flown over water, because aircraft specially built for competition could not fly at low speeds, and therefore needed a long unobstructed surface for take-off and landing. Moreover, as the engines were subjected to great stress, mechanical failures were quite common, and it would have been unsafe to hold such events over land. The competing aircraft were all fitted with seaplane floats.

The rules required a race over at least 150 nautical miles. That year, the competitors took off in succession to fly seven laps round a fifty-kilometre diamond-shaped course in the Solent, starting, and finishing, off Ryde on the Isle of Wight. Although four nations had originally entered, the French and American teams had been withdrawn, and only Britain and Italy competed. The trophy was won, for the second time in succession, by a British machine.

In the organisation of this famous event, the reputation of the Royal Aero Club was at stake. Smith and Lawrence played central roles during the final preparations at Calshot and on the yacht *Karen* that was used as race headquarters. Lawrence later wrote that 'the actual days and nights at Calshot were unmixed work. I hardly slept, and do not remember eating much'.[41] To everyone's relief, however, the event passed off without a hitch.

The *Karen* had been lent by Major Colin Cooper. One of its tenders, used on ferry duty during the contest, was a Biscayne Baby speedboat built in America by the Purdy Boat Company This should have been capable of 45 knots, but the 100hp engine needed attention. Lawrence, who had greatly enjoyed driving the boat, offered to give it an overhaul, and was surprised when Major Cooper decided to make a present of it, jointly to Lawrence and Sydney Smith. They renamed it the *Biscuit*.

Lawrence's presence at the contest had involved some risk of publicity, but the accredited press had been told not to photograph him, and neither pictures nor stories were published in British newspapers.[42] Unfortunately, this was not enough to satisfy Lord Thomson. While visiting Calshot he spotted Lawrence acting in a supervisory role and talking to visiting VIPs, including the Italian Marshal Balbo. Thomson, who had been a high-ranking army officer before and during the war, was even more vehemently opposed to Lawrence's presence in the ranks than Samuel Hoare had been. He spoke briefly with Lawrence, whom he had not previously met, and the encounter seems to have left him with a strong desire to rid the Air Force of this unconventional serviceman. Lawrence returned to Plymouth from Calshot with uneasy premonitions, and a week later these were confirmed. On September 16th Trenchard wrote: 'Since writing a letter to you today about your [proposed] trip with Major Nathan round France, Italy and Germany, and after having seen the Secretary of State I am writing to say you cannot go on this trip.

'You must come and see me as soon as you get your leave as I want to speak to you.'[43]

Lawrence's leave began four days later and he immediately went to London. As he had feared, his future in the RAF was again in doubt, and he called on influential friends asking them to take up his case. One of these was Sir Robert Vansittart, now private secretary to the Prime Minister. Vansittart did not like Lawrence very much, but he knew that they were second cousins (on Lawrence's father's side), and he offered to put in a good word. Another acquaintance with useful contacts was Captain B. H. Liddell Hart, the military historian and strategist, whose correspondence with Lawrence had begun in 1927 over a contribution to the *Encyclopaedia Britannica*. As military correspondent of the *Daily Telegraph*, Liddell Hart was well placed to put in a discreet word with high-ranking officials in Whitehall.

On September 30th, Lawrence was told by Trenchard that he would be reprieved, but there were conditions: in future his employment in the RAF was not to go beyond the duties of an aircraftman; he was not to leave the United Kingdom, and he was not to visit or speak to any of the 'great', notably opposition politicians such as Winston Churchill and Lady Astor. Lawrence was pleased to learn that the ban did not extend to Bernard Shaw; but apparently Shaw, when he heard of this, felt rather slighted.

For the second time that year, Lawrence had narrowly avoided dismissal from the ranks.

CHAPTER 42

Odyssey and the Biscuit
October 1929 – February 1931

LAWRENCE was entitled to a long leave and he decided to stay in London for nearly seven weeks. His intention was to spend all this time working on the *Odyssey* in Barton Street. However, there were many friends whom he had not seen for three years, and he soon began to call on them.

During a visit to Liddell Hart on October 25th, he learned that Jonathan Cape had suggested that there was room for another biography about him. The proposal was for a study that would 'supplement and round off the picture presented first by Lawrence himself in *Revolt in the Desert*, and next by Robert Graves. What has so far been left undone is an estimate not only of Lawrence and his work, but of the relation of this work to the immense affairs of which it was an important part, and in which Lawrence was one of the leading figures'.[1]

Liddell Hart was interested in the idea, and asked Lawrence what he thought about it, emphasising his own interest in the military history of the Revolt. As Lawrence did not condemn the project outright, Liddell Hart wrote to him the following day asking whether he would be prepared to help with such a biography. This time, Lawrence's reply was un-enthusiastic, and in particular he drew attention to the likelihood that a new book would increase his difficulties with the RAF. While offering to do what he could to prevent errors, he wrote: 'your difficulty will be that your sole source is my *Seven Pillars*. That was not intended as a military manual. It leaves out vital parts (vital as tactics: not as narrative) and slurs lots of things. The *S.P.* is a private publication: copyright. You can't quote it'.[2] He suggested that Liddell Hart could contact Alan Dawnay, who might have documents, but he himself had not 'the time, or the inclination, or the heart, to dig very much into my own memories of those times for anyone's sake.' He ended: 'I don't care a bit, either way.'[3] Liddell Hart must have been discouraged by this response, because he shelved the project for three years.

By this time, Lawrence was beginning to look ahead to 1935, when his term of enlistment in the RAF would end. He had recently decided to sell his land at Pole Hill, near Chingford, as Vyvyan Richards had moved to a new job in Wales. Lawrence hoped that if the capital which Pole Hill represented was invested, it might produce enough income to live on.

The land would have been worth about £7,000 if sold to a builder, but he had always hoped that it would one day become part of Epping Forest, which it adjoined. In the spring he had offered it to the Forest for the £4,000 he had spent on it, and the purchase had now been agreed in principle. He visited it for the last time on October 26th, and wrote afterwards: 'It was marvellously beautiful. Our oak "cloister" [built by Richards] has settled into the hill-side, and grown moss, and dignity. My poor trees have added three feet to their stature since a year ago, all except the cypresses, which were to have been an avenue, for my walking when I felt sad; but the drought has browned three of them to death. However they are not wanted: I will not be there when they (and myself) become old: and for the sadness, it was very presently with me this afternoon, in the knowledge that I had lost these fields. I wonder why we get so fond of fields? Commonplace fields, you might call these, only that no common place could afford so proud a view. Today it was perfection, for the mist and the cold air held all the smoke of all the chimneys, so that every ridge was sharpened at the top by the waves of grey vapour rising from the next valley. All the sky-lines were remote, and lovely, and it would have been enough for the rest of my day's thinking just to have sat there till dark and watched everything blur into one blackness, starred with lamps. Only of course I couldn't stop, for the place won't be mine next month'.[4]

On the way back to Plymouth he called at Clouds Hill. With money in prospect, both from the Chingford sale and from the *Odyssey*, he had begun to think of improvements to the cottage, and he now asked a local firm to draw up plans for a two-room extension: 'A new wing will not harm either the smallness or the quietude of Clouds Hill, or its simplicity.'[5]

In a letter written after his return, Lawrence expressed the sense of contentment and security he now felt about his life in Plymouth: 'it is good to be here again, though there is a wind from the north-east which rattles our roofs, and the impact of the rain is like small shot. They have put a new stove in our office, so that life will be warm all day: it *is* warm, now, but smelly as the paint burns off: and in bed it is warm all night, and the bath water is always hot. Accordingly I see no difference in comfort between myself and the best of people: and there are books and music . . . and the camp is happy.'[6] The station had even lost its unattractive name:

a letter from Sydney Smith to the Air Ministry, suggested and drafted by Lawrence, had persuaded them to change it from RAF Cattewater to RAF Mount Batten.

That winter he settled down in earnest to complete the *Odyssey*. By the beginning of December he had managed to complete the two Books (VII and VIII) he had started that spring. He wrote: 'I want to do six, and then send the batch to Bruce Rogers: February or March, perhaps, if I am left alone. I am so bored with the resourceful Odysseus: yet these two books . . . have been better done than any of the earlier ones. With nine we get over the chit-chat and begin the adventures of Odysseus, as he tells them. I am trying to increase the rapidity of the style, here and there, to feel like a narration. *Odyssey*-Homer is worse than [George] Borrow, as described by Sidney Webb. He (or she) does describe every cup of wine, every man, every wave, of the world. Intolerably slow, and yet so delicate, so subtle, so sophisticated, so civilised. Hoots.'[7]

When he sent Books VII and VIII to Rogers, on December 12th, he felt that he had got back into the habit of translating. By the middle of the month he had finished Book IX, and started Book X: 'not a favourite book'.[8] He worked at it every night in his attic office until 10 pm when the keys had to be handed in.

As with *The Forest Giant* six years earlier, he found that the effort to make a good translation gave him unexpected insights into the original text. Satisfaction with his work was therefore tempered by what he felt were shortcomings in the Greek: 'what a set of worms the ancient Greeks paint themselves to be. In my version I underline all strong words, and fade away the weakness, so that my translation will be not so much a copy as an intensification, dramatically. I try to make the poor yarn take up its bric-à-brac and walk. Vainly, I think: but that is meeter than Butler who threw all the muck out of the window before he began to English it.

'I have got into a rhythm in the work. The fair copy represents the fourth writing, and is the fourteenth revision; by and large I do five lines an hour, if you take the length of a book, and the total hours I have spent before the fair copy is ended . . . During the last three or four working weeks I have got in forty hours each week on *Odyssey*, and done my forty-eight R.A.F. hours too: and I feel as though I had not had a moment off: yet that leaves eighty hours unallotted. Say fifty-six for sleep:– I've wasted twenty-four somehow, frittered on feeding and dressing and washing myself. Absurd how much time goes to waste, even when we are trying to work hard.'[9]

He was so busy with the *Odyssey* that he hardly noticed the effect of Lord Thomson's restrictions. In any case, after two years in India he was happy just to be back in England. That spring, he had written: 'There is something about southern England which makes me, in every valley, on every ridge, say "Oh, I want to have a room here, and sit in it looking and looking!" If my name was Rockefeller, I'd have 3,428 cottages, and spend my time flitting from one to the other (a different name in each) round every ten years' spell of my unendurably long and slow life.'[10] This affection for England was expressed again at the end of 1929, when he wrote to Robert Graves, who was now living in Majorca: 'The Mediterranean sounds good . . . but there's a streak of vulgarity in me which passionately enjoys English gutters and mud and wet winds and fire-sides. Pure Dickens, all of that, yet it makes me want to live in England for ever. My Clouds Hill cottage should be cheap to live in; not as cheap as where you are, but cheap. Soon I hope to have an assured £3 a week, the invested proceeds of my Epping Forest land . . . That might be enough for independence at Clouds Hill; and I'd prefer that to independence out of England, anywhere.'[11]

During the next few months he continued to give most of his spare time to the *Odyssey*. The project was viewed without enthusiasm by his literary friends, who thought that he should write something new of his own. Embarrassed, he frequently told them that the translation was only a pot-boiler, undertaken to raise cash. Letters to Charlotte Shaw and Bruce Rogers, however, show the immense care he took over it. Many previous translators had tried to capture the spirit of the *Odyssey* in English but, as he worked on through the text, he felt increasingly that they had failed. For the time being his ambition was to create a new and better rendering.

Just after Christmas, he wrote to Charlotte Shaw that he had spent several days 'wrestling with about four lines of Anticleia's speech in Book XI: behind some wall or curtain in my mind I know there is the perfect English for these words: and I cannot get in to feel and drag it out. If I didn't know of these, there are fifty other words that would do as well: I have a sheet of them on my table all written down one under the other: but the real ones will not come. Sometimes it is like that, and I can't account for it: I am no more tired than usual, no stupider than usual, not ill or distracted or lazy: it is just like a knot in the grain of wood: a nuisance to the carpenter.'[12] He now began to send her draft sections of the *Odyssey*, and she made critical notes on them. In late January he thanked her for reading Book XI: 'I have been over it three or four times since it came back, and have managed about 100 minor alterations. That is for the good. I changed, so far as I could, all the places you had marked. It is very difficult.

'What you say about it is about what I feel: a sense of effort, of hard work: of course there must be this. I never wrote (for printing) an easy line in my life. All my stuff is tenth-thoughts or twentieth-thoughts, before it gets out. Nice phrases in letters to you? Perhaps: only the differences between nice phrases in a letter (where one nice phrase will carry the thing) and an *Odyssey* where one phrase not nice will spoil it all, is too great to carry a comparison . . . "Don't", you say, "work too hard at it, all at once". Why it has to be finished this year! I am at Book XII, only half-way . . . Last night I spent five hours doing five lines – not doing them, for they were already on paper, but re-grouping and re-tensing and re-mooding them, to make them stand up: it's deadly hard. There cannot be any of my own exciting little adjectives or words: for I am translating Homer, most word-for-wordly, and Homer has been too long the possession of the educated world for any surprise to remain in him. We know all Homer: digested him generations back . . .

'Other news? Why none at all. Homer covers all that. I do not think there will be any other news till next Christmas, when I may be a free man again. Book IX, the Cyclops book, is V.G. Even I say that. V.G. compared to Butler, or Laing or Palmer.'[13]

It is impossible to reconcile such letters with his disparaging comments to other friends. Forster had written in December: 'I trust that the *Odyssey*, to which I feel unreasonably frivolous, nears completion. I see no reason you shouldn't do a novel.'[14] Lawrence replied: 'the experience of the *Odyssey* is going, I think, to be the last straw upon the back of my writing hopes. They will just crush flat to the ground and wither. I'm sorry, for I have grown to envy the writing blokes. They have the only immortality worth owning.'[15] Henry Williamson wrote, praising the style of *Seven Pillars* and offering to read proofs of the *Odyssey*. Lawrence said there were no page proofs, but enclosed a few sample sheets, writing that they were 'not sent for criticism: but to show you that no one can help in them. Translations aren't books, for in them there is no inevitable word: the whole is approximation, a feeling towards what the author would have said: and as Homer wasn't like me the version goes wrong whenever I let myself into it. Consequently the thing is a pot-boiler only, a second-best'.[16]

During the spring of 1930, some of the pressure eased. Lawrence wrote to Charlotte Shaw in late February that he was still revising Book XIII, 'in a leisurely way, as though Homer were short, or life long. Bruce Rogers has told me not to hurry.'[17]

He had found little time for reading during these months, although he usually liked to follow the work of contemporary novelists. At the end of January 1930, however, he had to spend three days on RAF business in London, and while there he bought a copy of *Her Privates We*, a novel about life in the trenches on the Western Front published under the pseudonym 'Private 19022'. He was fascinated by the book: '*Her Privates We* knocked me all of a heap with delight. It's the true and honourable thing, so far as the "other ranks" are concerned. I never thought to see it. That's what my little *Mint* should have been and wasn't.'[18] When his RAF work was completed, he went to see J. G. Wilson at Bumpus: 'I said to him "Who wrote *Her Privates We* . . . for I know his touch?" He said "I think it begins with M"... and rang up Peter Davies [who had published it]. That let a flood of light in: So to P.D. I said "You haven't heard of me, my name is Shaw: but perhaps you've read a thing called *Revolt in the Desert* . . . Did the author of *Scenes and Portraits* [Frederic Manning] write *Her Privates We?* He was flabbergasted, having promised not to give it away. In the sequel Peter Davies, Wilson and your servant lunched at [J. M.] Barrie's and talked much shop. (Barrie in excellent wit: likened George Moore to a decayed gold-fish!)

'*Scenes and Portraits* . . . has been one of my friends since undergraduate days, so of course *Her Privates We* is bound to make me happy . . . It is a war book, of course, but with a difference. There is so much laughter and happiness in it: and it is beautiful. The troops in it are real, at last.'[19]

Lawrence wrote enthusiastically to Manning, and as a result they soon became friends. He liked Peter Davies too, and allowed publication of a leaflet quoting his praise of *Her Privates We*;[20] he also lent both of them a typescript of *The Mint*. Other readers at this time were Maurice Baring, F. L. Lucas, and Francis Yeats-Brown.

Although he often said that he had put his 'Arabian' life behind him, there were many indications during these years that Lawrence had not lost interest. In early March he was invited by a wartime colleague to meet Jaafar Pasha, who was returning home after two years representing Iraq in Britain. He replied: 'I'd have liked to . . . All my memories of the war, whenever he is in the picture, are pleasant ones. You know, he made even Tafileh in winter-time a joke. When the papers told of his coming to Weymouth, lately, I looked up the times and distances, wondering if my motor-bike would get me there and back in the half-day. I might have tried it, if it had been summer time . . . Will you give him my best regards? I imagine, somehow, that he is going back to Bagdad soon: in that case I'd like him to remember me to Nuri [as-Said] and the others: and especially to tell the King that I watch the history of Irak with great pride. It is a lasting pleasure to me that so much construction should have come out of all the destruction and effort of the war. It was in places like Jerdun and Deraa that the new Irak was founded'.[21]

If Lawrence enjoyed the irony of sending word from the barrack room to a King, he did not show it. Indeed, the tone of his letters during the following months was of increasing depression. He had chosen life in the ranks because it offered security, but it could not protect him from financial troubles. Having used up his bank balance, a year earlier, to pay for the Brough motorcycle, he had been obliged to borrow in order to pay for Clouds Hill. He had expected that this expense, together with others that had followed, would be covered by the sale of Pole Hill; but the Epping Forest authorities had postponed the purchase, and although five months had passed, no end to the delay seemed in sight. Lawrence's overdraft was now £600, and increasing steadily through accumulated interest charges. His morale seems to have suffered badly, as it had done in 1925 when he ran into difficulties over the production cost of *Seven Pillars*. The anxiety showed in many ways, but most obviously in a reluctance to leave camp. Whenever he did so, he spent money he now needed to save. Knowledge that he was famous and could easily earn all the money he needed should have been a comfort, but instead it was an irritation. He wrote bitterly to Jonathan Cape: 'Gods, I have written twenty letters this week. At £20 each [their value to collectors at that time], that's £400 I've given away: not to speak of the labour in vain'.[22]

His public reputation remained an embarrassment, as when, for example, he received a letter from the University of St Andrews offering him an honorary doctorate. At first he thought the proposal was a student hoax, and he returned it with a none-too-formal rejection. Soon afterwards, however, a second letter arrived, this time from J. M. Barrie, Lord Rector of St Andrews, who wrote: 'I hear from the Principal . . . that when Mr. Baldwin goes there to be installed as Chancellor on May 10th, which will be a great occasion, he has intimated a great desire that you should be there also to receive the LLD. degree. The degree does not matter to you, but Mr. Baldwin is keen about it and all the professors, and I believe you would have the undergraduates riotous with joy. I do wish you would let them see you.'[23]

Lawrence realised that his first response had been a gaffe, and appealed to John Buchan to pass on his apologies. However, he had no intention of accepting the degree. Apart from the difficulty of getting leave for the ceremony and the cost of going, there would inevitably be unwelcome publicity. The Labour Air Minister would surely dismiss him if he appeared on such a public platform at Baldwin's side: 'The Labourites think I'm an imperial spy, and the Die-hards thought I was a bolshie, and Lord Thomson says I'm a self-advertising mountebank. So it would be better for me if the matter could quietly drop. The mere being taken into consideration for an honorary degree is the honour of it. They've conferred that on me: won't they drop the actual degree, as it would do me harm?'[24]

Despite his troubles with Lord Thomson, Lawrence had remained on friendly terms with Ernest Thurtle. Now that Labour was in power, Thurtle was campaigning against the wartime death penalty for cowardice. Lawrence wholeheartedly supported this cause. Throughout his years in the RAF he had done his best to improve the conditions of service, for example by urging Trenchard to modify the uniform worn by the other ranks. He encouraged Thurtle's present efforts, even sending a statement that could be quoted in Parliament ('I would love to be taken advantage of, in this cause!')[25] The statement read: 'I have run too far and too fast under fire (though never fast enough to suit me at the time) to dare throw a stone at the fearfullest creature. You see, I might hit myself in the eye.'[26] He was delighted when the reform eventually passed into law, and suggested further changes, including the end of compulsory church parade.

By late March, he was again giving most of his time to the RAF. During the previous four months the Brough had only clocked up eighty-six miles. He wrote: 'Even Homer has flopped. The Wing Commander has given me more work lately, and the America speed-boat [the *Biscuit*] . . . is now approaching readiness, and the last touches are given to her by my little party as and when we have spare time . . . *Odyssey* is left undone because I do not feel up to doing it, just now . . . I don't think I have read anything, either, of late, except the official files, which rain down upon the offices. Our new wireless has been improved beyond all notion by the fellows, and gives me occasional moments of real joy'.[27]

In part, this tendency to remain inside the base at Mount Batten must have reflected the two years' voluntary confinement to camp in India. This long period of isolation from the outside world had reinforced his dependence on the closed RAF community: 'Now I can't get to feel safe, wandering about.'[28] In the spring of 1930 he lacked both the money and the inclination to break this habit. There was, however, another reason for spending so much time at Plymouth during the spring and summer of 1930. By the beginning of April, work on the *Biscuit* was completed, and possession of this speedboat gave him a new kind of freedom. He began to spend hours exploring the creeks off Plymouth Sound, sometimes going even farther afield. At Easter he wrote that the *Biscuit* was 'really a sea-car, a two-seater. I get a great deal of new satisfaction out of her.'[29] Often, he went alone, but sometimes he took Mrs Sydney Smith or one of her friends. As with the Brough, he liked occasionally to open out the throttle and experience the thrill of speed, but usually he was content just to know that the power was there.

Progress on the *Odyssey* had halted at Book XIV. Bruce Rogers was now sending him batches of proofs to correct, and this distracted him still more from the translation. Lawrence had originally asked for two years to complete it, but it was already obvious that he would be late. He wrote to Lionel Curtis: 'This cloud of translation hangs over me yet, and will hang till some day next year. It has thrown me out of gear, so that I feel wrong whenever I leave camp'.[30] During the early summer, his work for Sydney Smith occasionally took him to London, and this gave him opportunities to see some of his friends there. But as long as his financial troubles continued, he could not afford to pay for journeys of his own.

Despite these worries, there was one important respect in which Lawrence was now more at ease than in the earlier post-war years. The immorality of his wartime role no longer troubled him deeply, He wrote to Manning: 'We do these things in sheer vapidity of mind, not deliberately, not consciously even. To make out that we were reasoned cool minds, ruling our courses and contemporaries, is a vanity. Things happen, and we do our best to keep in the saddle . . . Now-a-days my mind does not concern itself greatly with abstractions. Hence the red face and round belly and comfortable port. I think I am happier than most people.'[31]

In May, he looked over the draft of a book called *Red Dust*, sent to him by Edward Garnett. It was a memoir by an Australian trooper who had served in the Palestine campaign. Lawrence sent it back, noting that he had 'tried in the first two or three chapters to clean up some of the writing, which is not rare or good.'[32] Donald Black, the author, had described some of the more horrific aspects of desert warfare. Lawrence commented: 'The one outstanding element in him seemed to be his sensibility. He is more moved by death and pain than were most soldiers. That comes out powerfully in the last few pages, when he sorrows for his dead horse [which, like other cavalry animals, had been shot when the campaign was over] . . . This latrine-stuff comes from Germany [a reference to E. M. Remarque's *All Quiet on the Western Front*], and feels forced in English, *pace* Joyce. Yet it comes off, always . . .

'I will not write a foreword or a back-word, or a middle piece, or any old piece, for anyone for anything, I hope. I always say "I hope", because I daren't say "never": that word would ring down the curtain on too many hopes. I propose to go on fancying that I could, in some circumstances, and under certain impulses, write: and so long as I don't disabuse myself by trying to write, that makes a nice warm fiction to cherish under one's breath. After the *Seven Pillars* I gave up writing for four years: and it will take me longer than that to forget the disillusionment of re-reading *The Mint*.'[33]

During one of his visits to London on RAF business, Lawrence called on Peter Davies and asked how much it would cost to print twelve copies of *The Mint*. Davies replied in due course with an estimate of £120. By June 24th, Lawrence had decided to go ahead with this very small edition as soon as he could find the money. In odd moments he began working through one of the typescripts, lightly correcting the text. He planned to work on it more seriously, as well as on the *Odyssey* translation, as soon as the summer was over.

Meanwhile, he was giving a large part of his free time to the *Biscuit*: 'it runs well when my work on it has been momentarily successful. The sea cuts so white under the stern, and is so blue and green each side: and there is a little galloping of the boat when the swell from the sea comes in: and the spray is salted and cooling, and the sparkle of the sun leaps off the water into my eyes'.[34] Maintenance, however, was difficult, since parts for the American machinery could not readily be obtained in Britain. On July 2nd, he wrote to his American friends the Doubledays (whom he had seen a few days earlier in London) asking permission to give their names

T.E. Lawrence on one of his Brough Superior motorcycles, talking to the manufacturer, George Brough, in October 1930

T.E. Lawrence during his last RAF years, at Scott Paine's Yard in Southampton.

An RAF 200 Class seaplane tender. The success of this innovative planing-hull design soon led to the introduction of similar but larger launches. All these high speed RAF boats were used for Air-Sea rescue work during the Second World War.

The RAF 200 Class design modified and armour-plated to serve as a target for bombing practice. When the press publicised Lawrence's association with these boats in October 1932 he was returned to more mundane duties

ground floor plan.

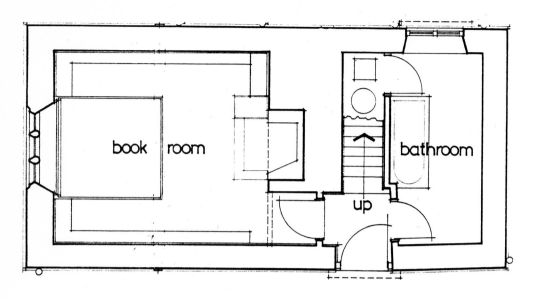

first floor plan.

Clouds Hill: (*top*) ground floor plan; (*below*) first floor plan

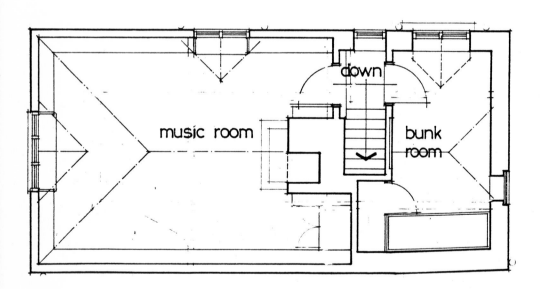

Clouds Hill, 1935. Lawrence had written, 'it will be a very habitable and restful place. I am fond of it, and hope to live there after I leave the RAF'

The music room at Clouds Hill, photographed shortly after Lawrence's death. During the preceding years he had modified the cottage to suit his requirements exactly

T.E. Lawrence, photographed by Flight Lieutenant R.G. Sims at Hornsea near Bridlington during the winter of 1934–5. Sims, a keen photographer, took what was to be the last series of portrait photographs

T.E. Lawrence sketched by Augustus John at Friern, near Fordingbridge, in January 1935. Lawrence had 100 collotype plates made from this drawing as the frontispiece for an edition of *The Mint*, but he was destined never to print it.

T.E. Lawrence photographed as he left the RAF at Bridlington in February 1935. When he reached
Dorset he found Clouds Hill besieged by the press

as a reference when ordering from the manufacturers: 'My boat's maker is the Purdy Boat Co. Inc. of Port Washington, Long Island: and its *class* name is the Biscayne Baby. There were six of them made, with Scripps 120 h.p. Junior Cup model engines in them. They are the six best things the States have made, I think. I had a gorgeous run in mine late last night (we put a head-lamp on her for night work a while ago) in very rough water which she rode like a cork. She drenched me through and through, but it was glorious. I'm going to write to the maker soon for some spare parts, and will venture to quote him your names. Then he will send me the things on credit'.[35] The difficulty of getting spares, and also the very lightweight construction of the hull, meant that repairs were often necessary, and Lawrence spent much time dealing with them. Nevertheless, he enjoyed the speedboat enormously, and even raced it in a local regatta.

By the beginning of August, Book XIV of the *Odyssey* was at last finished, and XV was waiting only to be copied out legibly. Lawrence wrote apologetically to Bruce Rogers: 'I am so sorry: but having begun trying to do it very well I feel that it would be dishonest now to spare pains upon it. Alas & alack! I am not going to be really proud of my *Odyssey*.'[36] He was now equally despondent about *The Mint*, and gave up trying to make improvements. In his critical mood, he found it 'scrappy and arty and incompetent'.[37] The idea of printing a few copies was abandoned.

On the evening of August 12th, after a brief visit to Northamptonshire on RAF business, he saw Charlotte Shaw in London. The following day he had lunch with Philip Sassoon and George Lloyd, who took him to meet Noël Coward and watch a rehearsal of *Private Lives*. Lawrence later wrote to Charlotte Shaw that he had found Coward 'not deep but remarkable. A hasty kind of genius . . . His prose is quick, balanced, alive: like Congreve's probably, in its day. He dignifies slang when he admits it. I liked him: and suspected that you probably do not. Both of us are right.'[38] He lent Coward *The Mint*.

At this juncture, the German press announced that Lawrence was in Kurdistan. According to *The Times*, 'the average German newspaper reader is convinced that the Afghan revolt was fomented by Great Britain working through T. E. Lawrence, and he will receive the same impression about the Kurdish revolt from the irresponsible statements being published . . . The German editorial writers, from whom nothing is concealed, have discovered Colonel T. E. Lawrence in Kurdistan. He is credited with extraordinary powers.'[39] On this occasion, the nonsensical story drew a protest from King George V, and a Foreign Office minute spoke wearily of 'the fatal influence of the Lawrence legend on the Continental mind'.[40]

Soon after returning to Plymouth, Lawrence left again, this time by air, for a weekend at Lympne as a guest of Philip Sassoon; three days later he went to the Malvern Festival, to see one of Shaw's plays performed. Despite this sudden flurry of activity, he was still depressed. In late August he wrote to Edward Garnett: 'No news with me. A thin poor year and I feel low about it'.[41] Likewise, he told H. S. Ede: 'This has been a bad summer, meteorologically and morally, and I shall be glad when the cold weather closes down on us and the fires are lit. For the first time in my life I have not liked the out-of-doors. I wonder what is happening?'[42] The same theme appears in a letter to Henry Williamson: 'I wish I knew what was the matter with me. Some unformed impulse keeps me in camp. I am always putting in passes, and saying "I will go out this weekend": and when the time comes I cannot get into breeches and puttees, so the bike rusts in the garage and I moon about the water's edge in camp, dreaming or dipping inconsequentially into books. It has come to this, that I feel afraid and hesitant outside. The camp itself is like a defence to me, and I can't leave it. I think I have only been outside three times this summer. As for the speed-boat, that is joyous, when it goes: but except to take other people about I never start it. I am like a clock whose spring has run down.'[43]

He had arranged to see Robert Graves during the first weekend in September, but the meeting was not successful. Graves, who was accompanied by Laura Riding, had not met Lawrence for some years. He later wrote: 'The most striking change in him . . . was that his speaking intonation had changed: from Oxford University to garage-English . . . the accent was that pleasant compound of (perhaps) North London and Birmingham and Sheffield that one associates with men who drive lorries or have to do with mechanical bits and pieces.'[44]

Lawrence disliked Laura Riding intensely, and feared that Graves's infatuation with her might destroy him as a poet.[45] He felt that both of them had allowed their lives to be dominated by carnality: 'I cannot have patience with people who tickle up their sex until it seems to fill all their lives and bodies. I'd as soon tickle up my appetite for beer'.[46]

The sale of Pole Hill went through at last on September 9th, shortly before the beginning of Lawrence's leave. He asked Buxton to clear the overdraft and invest the balance so that it would bring 'about £70 or

£80 per annum, perhaps, and grow fatter with the years, . . . leaving me about £200 in current account. Time enough to think about money when I'm discharged'.[47] After this he left Plymouth to spend a few days at Collieston on the Scottish coast, but just before setting out, he heard that F. N. Doubleday was seriously ill. On September 18th, he sent Doubleday a long descriptive letter from Scotland:

> Come northward many miles above Aberdeen, and then strike towards the sea across the links, which are sand-tussocked desolations of charred heather and wiry reeds, harbouring grouse to whirr up alarmingly sideways from under-foot, and rabbits so lazy that they will hardly scuttle their snow-white little tail-flags from the path. Add a choir of larks and a thin high wind piping over the dunes or thrumming down the harsh stems of heather.
>
> They are three miles wide, these links, and ever so desolate till they end abruptly in a rough field whose far side is set on edge with a broken line of cottages. Behind their roofs seems to be pure sky, but when you near them it becomes sea – for the cottages have [been] built round all the crest of the grassy sea-cliff and down it too, cunningly wedging their places into its face wherever there was a flat of land as wide as two rooms. Almost to the beach the cottages fall. Beach, did I say? It is a creek of sand, cemented along one side in a grey quay wall from which and from the opposing rocks up run the grass-grown cliffs in heart-comforting bastions to the houses fringed against the sky. The creek's a fishing port. You could find room to play a game of tennis in it, perhaps, if the tide went dry. So there are no bigger boats than dinghies and no room for any: nor heart for any with the jaws of greycold reefs champing white seas outside, all day and night.
>
> Imagine whole systems of slate-like slabby rocks, flung flatwise and acres square, thrusting out into the maddened North Sea which heaves and foams over them in deafening surges. The North-Easter, full of rain and so misted that our smarting eyes can peer only two or three hunched yards into it, is lifting the waves bodily into the air and smashing them upon the rocks. There is such sound and movement out there in the haze that our eyes keep staring into its blindness to see the white walls rolling in. The concealed sun makes all white things half-luminous, so that the gulls become silvered whenever they dip suddenly to turn a knife-edged cartwheel in the spray: and

the thunder of the seas enforces a deafened silence on all other things, so that we feel as much as see the energy let loose. Each big wave makes the air quiver and sends a shading reverberation across the shore about our bodies.

That is the fighting of the sea against the land: and the sea's casualties have filled the port, around the elbow that the jetty makes. There the water is stifled and heaves sickly under a mat of sea-suds one foot thick. You know the creamed and bubbly foam that blows up a beach when the wind rises and the sea, together? Well, that flocculent stuff is all impounded in our bay, filling it so full that black water and jetty and steps and rocks and beach are all invisible, buried under it like a corpse in a blanket.

'Curse the fellow and his seascape' you are saying. 'Am I paid to read his manuscript?' Peace, Mrs. Doubleday will take it away and burn it, so soon as you roar in anger.

What are we doing here? Nothing, practically. There are three of us – Jimmy who used to work in Canada but came home in 1914 and was a gunner for four years in France: now he jobs horses in Aberdeen: Jock [Bruce], the roughest diamond of our Tank Corps hut in 1923;– and me. We have Mrs. Ross' cottage lent to us and reluctantly in turn sweep its floor and fetch the water and coal. For meals thrice a day we spread our coats to the wind and fly to the cliff-top, where the Mrs. Baker-and-butcher feeds us in her parlour. Then, heavy inside, we slide down hill to the cottage again in the cove: for ours is the nearest hovel to the high-tide mark. That is good in fair weather and exciting today. Great flocks of surf beat tattoos on the roof till the tide turned.

But what do we do? Why nothing, as I said. Jimmy has his horses to groom and feed and exercise. Sometimes we do the last for him. Jock fishes: boys bring him mussels and he waves a pole from the quay at the wild wild waves. Once up came a codling from the yeasty deep, the poor orphan taking pity on him. He brought it us in silent manly pride, and we made him clean it. Scrape scrape his knife went, like a man cleaning a flower-pot. We helped him eat it, too. Most of our food is fish . . .

The cottage has three rooms. Jock took the middle one with big bed and fire-place. Ours open from it and are cold. So we make his our sitting room, and have pushed the bed into the corner, farthest from the fire where I sit and think all day, while turning

over the swimming suits to dry. Also I eat pounds of peppermints
. . . or read . . .

Our tea-time now. The winds have stopped, but the waves
increase. They are so big that only two roll in to the minute now. I
wish you could hear the constancy and fresh repetition of their
thunder, and the sharpness and loneliness of the gulls questing
through the spume. The poor gulls are hungry from the storm and
beset our roof for the food-scraps we throw away. They have the
saddest, most cold, disembodied voices in the world.'[48]

It is hard to reconcile the pastoral tone of Lawrence's letter to Doubleday
with other evidence, which shows that this visit to Collieston formed
part of a self-prescribed therapy for the *malaise* he had been suffering
from that year. John Bruce, whom he had paid to administer beatings in
the Tank Corps some years before, had been hired to organise a gruelling
daily routine of swimming and riding. At the end of the stay, according to
Bruce, Lawrence received a severe birching.

This episode seems to have been another manifestation of the abnormal behaviour referred to in Chapter 34. During the coming years, he
arranged to have himself instructed in a number of outdoor pursuits under
very peculiar conditions. For example, he would write under a false name
to a swimming or riding instructor, requesting private lessons for an adult
'nephew', and asking for full reports on the nephew's progress and
conduct; the nephew was Lawrence himself. These activities were not
physically punitive, but he was always to be observed and reported on.
The reports sent back to the fictional uncle were seen only by Lawrence.

These fantasy-world arrangements might suggest that Lawrence was
mentally unbalanced, were it not for the undoubted sanity of his everyday
life and work. It therefore seems likely that they were subtle forms of the
masochistic disorder caused ultimately by the violent homosexual rape he
had suffered at Deraa in 1917. They may have been a substitute for
birchings, to which he submitted himself very rarely, or perhaps for the
rigorous barrack-room discipline which was no longer a dominant feature
of his service life.

After a week in Scotland, Lawrence travelled south. He left his
motorcycle at Nottingham for an overhaul and continued on to London
by train. During the week he spent in the capital he visited friends and
saw the second night of *Private Lives*. Afterwards, he went back to

Nottingham and then to Mount Batten, where he arrived on the evening of October 2nd.

Three days later, rumours began to spread in the camp that the new British R.101 airship had crashed. Many famous passengers had been on board. When the news was confirmed, Lawrence wrote: 'Last night was an awful night. I tried to do *Odyssey*, and then to read: but the wind and the rain (I was duty crew, and so partly responsible for the craft at moorings in the Cattewater) prevented any hope of quietness. We never dreamt the airship would leave. I knew so many people in her. I wonder who are saved.'[49] Among those killed in the disaster was Lord Thomson.[50]

Now that the Chingford property had been sold, Lawrence began thinking of improvements to Clouds Hill, where he planned to live when he left the RAF in five years' time. He wrote to Buxton: 'I am in love with Clouds Hill . . . and have a head-full of plans for it. So that will be my future H.Q. . . .

'Investments: don't let the interest come over £70 a year, otherwise I shall be due for income tax and that is to join the wealthy classes. I want a mild capital accumulation, instead, for among my Clouds Hill plans is a new room, to house my books, and that might call for £400-£500, in 1932. Half this I can make on Homer. The rest should come from investment'.[51]

Later that month he visited the cottage to see about a new shed in which to house the Brough. At the time, his mother and elder brother Bob were living there, and he did not altogether approve of their changes. He wrote: 'The little people at Clouds Hill seem queerly contented . . . I tried to tell them that it was sad and isolated in the winter, when the rains closed down, for I think they would be better off at Max Gate: but they would not be convinced. My mother is an enraged house-wife. She has cleaned all the cottage remorselessly and takes a pride in polishing it. So there we are! I still hope she may realise that it is too summery a place.'[52]

At the beginning of November he suddenly received an urgent appeal from Bruce Rogers about the *Odyssey*: the delays were beginning to cause serious difficulties. He replied that he would try to finish by March, 'subject to the R.A.F. leaving me alone to work all my spare time. It will, of course, be done as well as I can do it.'[53] Little time had been spent on the translation during the previous two months, but he now returned to it in earnest, working on it about forty-five hours a week, over and above his forty-eight hours' RAF duty. By November 6th, he had finished Book

XVII; three weeks later he told Charlotte Shaw that he was 'at work at the very dull XIX. What an impossible family is this of Arcesius! Husband a cold-blooded bore, son a pig, wife a sly cat. I regret having come to know them so well. Book XIX shows them at the impossible worst. However, I feel that the end is getting more attainable: XX, XXI, XXII, XXIII, and then the release. Alas, I was twelve months in India doing five books, and I want to end this in March coming.'[54]

He was unwilling to skimp the work and told Bruce Rogers: 'Eventually, and by passage of time, one reaches a certain finality: one gets as far as one can: and it is at that stage the fair-copy should be made and passed to you: to hurry the revisions means only too many corrections in typescript or proof, and that is a bad mark on a writer. He should find out what he wants to say before he says it.'[55]

Although he tried to give as much time as possible to the translation, there were many small distractions. One that he found particularly distressing at this moment was a show trial in Soviet Russia, where his name had been used in incriminating 'confessions'. He asked Ernest Thurtle whether it might not be possible to rebut the allegation: 'I am rather troubled over this Russian business, where some unfortunates are being tried for, amongst other things, treasonably associating with me as British Government Agent in London in 1927!

'I know they do not much believe any English official word: but I was demonstrably in India all the time from December 1926 to February 1929. Would it be any good getting some private person they trust to tell them so? Or could anything be done? They may hang these poor creatures for all I know, else: and I would like to do something for them, if there is anything. Now Lord Thomson is gone the Air Ministry will not be so tender on my subject.'[56]

Thurtle arranged to have a formal question asked in Parliament. In reply to this the Under-Secretary of State for Air gave a record of Lawrence's postings. There were cries of 'Hear, hear' and general laughter when Lady Astor then asked: 'Is it not true that Aircraftman Shaw is leading a quiet, respectable, and useful life?' One humorist shouted back: 'That's more than you are.'[57]

Lawrence had told friends that he would take no more holiday until the *Odyssey* was completed in the spring, and that he was looking forward afterwards to 'a lazy summer with full pocket and no liabilities!'[58] However, this did not prevent him from spending the weekend of December 20th with the Astors at Cliveden.

As the end of 1930 approached, he began to feel that the previous months had not been a bad time, after all: 'I have nearly finished the Greek and it has been a quiet year, of no publicity at all. This has been the first year for ten years to leave me quite at peace. I think that is very good. One or two more, and my existence will be taken for granted.

'So that is to my credit: and so is the *Odyssey*: and so is the speed-boat. And I have read several books which delighted me. In music I have been less fortunate . . . A Delius cello sonata, an Elgar symphony, a Brahms double concerto: one cannot go on hoping for wonders indefinitely . . .

'I am sensibly older, with more aches and pains, and a lesser inclination to extend myself. That perhaps is the worst sign. Only a strong man can live heedlessly, as I wish to do. A single man who is poor has difficulty when he is old. Only I am not old yet: just older.

'I have not met, this year, people I much wish to meet again. Noël Coward perhaps. But I have seen Manning after some years [they had first met just after the war], and Siegfried Sassoon.'[59]

On December 29th, he sent off Books XVIII-XX of the *Odyssey*, completed during the slack period over Christmas. He still hoped to finish the translation in March: 'I wish I felt its standard rise as it goes forward: but all I can hope is that it does not perceptibly worsen, through my being tired.'[60]

In January, however, work on the translation suffered a setback. He had to spend several days at the beginning of the month on RAF duties in London. Then, soon after his return to Plymouth, his mother came to stay nearby for a ten-day visit. The projected delivery date moved forward into April.

While in London, he had visited H. S. Ede at the Tate Gallery. Ede was about to publish *Savage Messiah*, a study of the sculptor Henri Gaudier-Brzeska. Lawrence hoped to persuade literary editors to review the book. He told Ede on January 26th: 'Eddie Marsh is going to try and wangle *The Times*. He said Charles Marriott would have to do it. I do not think that the best possible: but *The Times* is a beast I cannot myself approach . . . Yeats-Brown, of the *Spectator*, is excited over it. He wants a reviewer's name. Do you know anyone who would do it particularly well . . . The *Spectator* will give it a page, and the nature of the book demands that the serious people should commit themselves in its favour. I would like James Douglas to review it! Don't suggest him to Yeats-Brown. I do not know whom to suggest: except E. M. Forster . . . who has promised to do his best over it for some paper. Forster is a good man. Very. And a good critic.'[61]

This was by no means the first time Lawrence had helped friends with their books. Among other works he had taken an interest in were *Scarlet and Khaki* by T. B. Marson and *Singapore Patrol* by Alec Dixon. In these two instances he had not only helped to find a publisher, but also edited (and in parts rewritten) their texts.

Lawrence helped Dixon in other ways as well. When he learned in February that Dixon had financial troubles, he immediately arranged for Buxton to cable £40 out to Singapore for him. However, his philanthropy was becoming more selective. The previous year, when R. A. M. Guy had written asking for £350, Lawrence sent only a very small sum. He seems to have felt that Guy's requests for help had become too regular and too extravagant. From now on he would frequently plead poverty when responding to begging letters, although he still managed to find cash to help really worthy cases.

On February 4th, Lawrence happened to be standing on some rocks by the shore at Mount Batten when he saw an RAF Iris III flying boat crash into the sea while coming in to land about six hundred yards offshore. He ran to the rescue launch, which was one of the first boats to arrive on the spot. The aircraft had sunk in about twenty-six feet of water. Six of the crew managed to escape, but the remainder were trapped inside the hull. A scribbled note found among Lawrence's papers after his death probably refers to this crash: 'sea molten-visioned aluminium. Poor Paddy drunk with foolish laughter, like captive balloon whose gas wobbles it drunkenly as the strands that tether it to the earth are parting, one by one. Rest drawn, bleak, grey-faced, tardily quarrelling amongst themselves. No joy but Paddy laughingly. We got onto him, he promised betterment. Six of us crushed together in the crushed canister of the hull were bubbling out their lives. Great belches of air spewed up now and then, as another compartment of wing or hull gave way.'[62]

This horrific crash caused much bitterness at Mount Batten. The pilot at the time had been a senior officer, Wing Commander Tucker, who was under instruction. He had refused to hand over the controls to his instructor, Flight-Lieutenant Ely, for the landing. Lawrence commented that the crash was 'due to bad piloting, on the part of a man who (as we all knew) should never have flown with passengers. He would not be convinced of that. Fortunately he died with the rest.'[63] It was hoped that by bringing out the truth at the subsequent enquiry, regulations about senior officers under instruction would be changed. Lawrence wrote to a friend: 'I propose to say just what I saw, and what it meant, in the endeavour to bring the responsibility home upon an Air Marshal Webb-Bowen at the Air Ministry, who refused to listen to reports, made him on three separate occasions, regarding this officer's unfitness to fly. I shall try to do it without getting myself into trouble, if I can. If not – well, I think such a case had better not happen again, and I have facts enough to prevent it happening again, if I publish them.'[64]

In addition to the Air Ministry Inquiry, there was a public inquest in which Lawrence was called as a witness. Under questioning, several people voiced doubts about Tucker's competence, and the whole matter was reported in the press. When Lawrence was asked whether he, personally, would have objected to flying with Tucker, he replied: ' "Had I been ordered to do so I should have flown with him."

"But you would not have flown with him as a matter of choice?"

"No Sir, not as a matter of choice." '[65]

The crash and its aftermath had taken still more of Lawrence's time, and on February 25th he wrote to Bruce Rogers: 'I have yet a confession of delay to make. First a delay in London then a visit of some people to Plymouth: then another business trip to London: then a crash of a Flying Boat, followed by its Court of Inquiry and an Inquest: and tomorrow a detachment to near Southampton for ten days to test a new fast motor boat for the R.A.F.

'The upshot of all this is no more *Odyssey*. I am still working on Book XXI and it will be the end of April before I finish, if all goes well after this ten days'.[66]

CHAPTER 43

A Taste of Freedom
February 1931 – March 1933

THE 'new fast motor boat' Lawrence was sent to test had been designed and built by the British Power Boat Company at its yard in Hythe, on the western shore of Southampton Water. At that time, high-speed boats from this small company led the field in Britain. It had been founded in 1927 by Hubert Scott-Paine, one of the pioneers of the British seaplane industry.[1] He had always been fascinated by the sea, and at Hythe he applied his knowledge of aircraft to hull design and construction, developing successful racing boats such as *Miss Britain III*. His other great strength was salesmanship, and during the winter of 1929-30 he had suggested to the RAF that his firm's new 35ft hard-chine hull design would make an excellent fast seaplane tender, much faster and cheaper to build than the traditional displacement hull types then in use.[2] At first the reply was noncommittal: the 35ft boats used American engines, and this was not acceptable to the Air Ministry. The only suitable British alternative (the 100hp Brooke) was very heavy in relation to its power. Nevertheless, Scott-Paine offered to install Brooke engines in a proto-type boat for the RAF. After further discussions, the RAF ordered an experimental 37ft 6in boat powered by two 100hp Brooke engines. At the preliminary trials, held in Stokes Bay on 19th February 1931, the boat achieved almost seventeen knots. As a result, it had been decided to undertake service trials with a seaplane squadron.

Scott-Paine was anxious to conceal these trials for as long as possible from rival yards in the Solent, and it was therefore agreed that the new boat, known as RAF 200, should be sent to Plymouth for evaluation. This choice was no accident. Ever since Lawrence and Sydney Smith had acquired the *Biscuit*, they had deplored the slowness of the boats used for work with seaplanes. The value of faster craft in rescue work had been underlined by the recent Iris flying boat crash. Lawrence had drafted letters to the Air Ministry on this subject for Sydney Smith, and he had already met Flight-Lieutenant W. E. G. Beauforte-Greenwood, Head of the RAF Marine Equipment Branch, during one of the latter's visits to

Plymouth. One of the three RAF officers who had taken part in the preliminary trials of RAF 200 was Flight-Lieutenant Jinman, an engineering officer from 209 Squadron at Mount Batten.

When putting together a trials crew for the prototype, it was natural for Beauforte-Greenwood to ask for Lawrence, whose experience in high-speed boats was probably unique in the lower ranks of the RAF. Lawrence's personal enthusiasm for faster RAF craft would be an asset during the trials. Other important qualifications were his flair as a mechanic and his ability to write clearly about technical matters.

Before the boat could be brought to Plymouth, the four-man RAF crew had to receive instruction in handling and maintenance at the British Power Boat Company yard. There, for the first time, Lawrence met Scott-Paine, who was three years his junior, but an equivalent, in the world of fast motorboats, to George Brough in the world of motorcycles. Lawrence was impressed by the yard and the innovations in design and production that Scott-Paine had introduced. He spent just over a week there, returning to Plymouth on March 7th. RAF 200 would be delivered to Mount Batten ten days later.

In the meantime, garbled versions of the Iris flying boat inquest were circulating in the world's newspapers. *The Times* reported on March 12th that the Turkish press, 'not content with accusing Colonel Lawrence of having instigated the Menemen disorders . . . now affirms that Lawrence was killed in the accident to the Blackburn Iris III flying-boat at Plymouth on February 4.' *The Times* noted, however, that one Turkish paper, 'on the strength perhaps of the fact that Aircraftman Shaw was able to give evidence about the accident a fortnight after it had happened, goes to the length of warning its readers that although it is believed that Colonel Lawrence is dead it is not inconceivable that he may again be heard of.'[3]

Once the new boat arrived at Plymouth, an exhaustive programme of tests began which left Lawrence little time for any other activity. After a week he wrote: 'I stay here testing the new RAF motor boat . . . We run her for hours daily and try all sorts of things, with a view to an exhaustive report on her performance. She is very good. Today we have been towing loads and boats and testing her pull. Tomorrow likewise. Then, I hope, some coasting trips, perhaps as far as Salcombe. Bright, east-windy weather, roughish cold sea, sunny: but pale sunlight, with no burn in it . . . Picture me just as a sailor, now-a-days, working so hard all the bright hours that in the evening I just bath and bed. No Homer: and no letters'.[4]

By April 2nd, RAF 200 had completed fifty hours' running, and Lawrence was asked to draft a report. He concluded: 'The boat has been found to behave extremely well in all weathers including broken 19ft. seas. In one run up-channel from Falmouth to Plymouth against a strong south-east wind and in breaking water she only shipped solid sea once; an average of 12 m.p.h. was achieved on this run . . .

'She does not roll and is an exceptionally clean sea boat. In winds of up to 20 m.p.h. the deck can be kept dry by careful steering. The very deep V [hull-]section below the wheelhouse prevents the boat from hammering into every wave like the ordinary hard chine speed boat. She is lively and dances, but seldom knocks and is therefore comfortable across a chop. She runs excellently before a sea and is not difficult even then to keep steady.

'She has been tried in all the duties normally performed by Marine Craft at this station and can be fairly pronounced a cleaner sea boat than anything yet, to be safer than all but the 56ft Pinnace, to be the finest towing boat and the most exactly manoeuvred. She takes 50% more passengers than the 35ft motor-boats and her sturdy construction qualifies her to withstand hard work.'[5]

While the RAF was pleased with the prototype, it had been recognised at the outset that the heavy Brooke engines were not ideal. Scott-Paine had therefore worked with the Meadows Company, of Wolverhampton, to develop a marinised version of their 100hp tank engine. This was christened the 'Power' engine, and had a much improved power-to-weight ratio. It had been designed for easy installation and maintenance, and when perfected was considered to be the most up-to-date marine engine in the world. It was also much cheaper than the Brooke alternative.

Once the Plymouth trials had been completed, RAF 200 was returned to Hythe so that two of the 'Power' engines could be fitted. While the necessary structural alterations were carried out, Lawrence was sent to the yard with the trials mechanic, Corporal Bradbury, to put the engines through fifty-hour tests. For this purpose the new units had been mounted temporarily in an open 28ft hull. Lawrence wrote: 'We buzz . . . up and down Southampton Water, the Spit and the Solent, each of us (two on the job) taking the wheel in turn, while the other checks gauges.'[6] The work was 'very noisy, very wet and very cold. The weather is wintry, with drizzles and blizzards and attempts at sleet . . . high north and north-east winds, and the sea is at its roughest . . . Bad weather is the ideal condition for testing motor-boats, and we have got it. Our endeavour is to do fifty hours running in the week – and that is difficult, taking tides, breakdowns, adjustments etc. into account.'[7]

During these weeks there had been no progress with the *Odyssey*, still at Book XXI: 'Homer finds life difficult. I have the books here, and my eyes smart too much, by night fall, with spray to welcome the crabbed Greek characters or my pencil drafts.'[8] However, Rogers had meanwhile written asking Lawrence to put down any thoughts about the translation that might be incorporated in a prospectus. On April 16th Lawrence replied, sending a draft essay which he described as 'my notes on translating the *Odyssey*, copied from the back of the book over the flyleaves of which I scribbled my comments as I worked at it. I wonder if you will find they mean anything? Use anything you like'.[9] The notes began thus:

> This version of the *Odyssey*, while not a crib, is essentially a translation. Whenever choice offered between a poor and a rich word I have preferred riches, to heighten my colour. I have transposed; the order of metrical Greek being unlike plain English. Not that my English is plain enough. 'Wardour-Street' Greek like the *Odyssey*'s defies honest rendering. Also I have assumed liberty with moods and tenses; allowed myself to interchange adjective and adverb; and dodged over poverty of preposition, limitations of verb and pronominal vagueness by rearrangement. Still, syntax apart, this is a translation.
>
> It has been made from the Oxford text, uncritically. I have not pored over contested readings, variants or spurious lines. However scholars may question the text in detail, writers (and even would-be writers) cannot but see in the *Odyssey* a single, authentic, unedited work of art, integrally preserved. Thrice I noted loose ends, openings the author had forgotten: one sentence I would have shifted, in time: five or six lines ring false: one speech seems to come before its context. These are specks on a tale which is neat, close-knit, artful and various, as nearly word-perfect as midnight oil and pumice can effect.
>
> 'Crafty, exquisite, homogeneous.' Whatever great art may be, these are not its attributes. In this work every big situation is burked and the writing is soft. The shattered *Iliad* yet makes a masterpiece; while the *Odyssey* is merely easy and interesting, the oldest book

worth reading for its story and the first novel in Europe. Gay, fine and vivid it is: never huge or terrible. Book XI, the Underworld, verges towards *terribilità* – yet runs instead to the seed of pathos, that feeblest mode of writing. The author misses his every chance of greatness, as must all his translators.

For this limitation of the book's scope is apparently conscious. Epic belongs to early man, and this Homer lived too long after the heroic age to feel assured and large. He shows exact knowledge of what he could and could not do. Only through such superb self-criticism can talent rank beside inspiration.

In four years of living with this novel I have tried to deduce the author from his self-betrayal in the work. I found a book-worm, no longer young, living from home, a mainlander, city-bred and domestic. Married but not exclusively, a dog-lover, often hungry and thirsty, dark-haired. Fond of poetry, a great if uncritical reader of the *Iliad*, with limited sensual range but an exact eyesight which gave him all his pictures. A lover of old bric-à-brac, though as muddled an antiquary as Walter Scott in sympathy with which side of him I have conceded 'tenter-hooks' but not railway-trains.

It is fun to compare his infuriating male condescension towards inglorious woman, with his tender charity of head and heart for serving-men. Though a stickler for the prides of poets who never misses the chance to cocker up their standing, yet he must be (like much later writers) the associate of menials, and make himself their friend and defender by understanding. Was it a fellow-feeling, or did he forestall time in his view of slavery?

He loved the rural scene as only a citizen can. No farmer, he had learned the points of a good olive tree. He is all adrift when it comes to fighting, and has not seen deaths in battle. He had sailed upon and watched the sea with a palpitant concern, seafaring being not his trade. As a minor sportsman he had ran wild boars at bay and heard tall yarns of lions ...[10]

When Rogers read this note, he wrote to a friend that 'with some touching up, [it] is I think too fine a piece of both writing and criticism to print only in a circular. I hadn't contemplated a Preface at all – but don't you think this is worthy of being made a permanent addition to the volume? At any rate it expresses my own feeling about Homer, accurately'.[11] In due course, therefore, the blurb was polished and titled 'Translator's Note'. It was printed, by Lawrence's request, at the end of the text, rather than the beginning.

At much the same period as this critical essay on Homer, Lawrence also wrote a piece of pure science fiction, at the request of Robert Graves and Laura Riding. The two were collaborating on a novel, and asked him to contribute the description of a futuristic autogiro. Lawrence was delighted by the challenge and worked out details of the machine with Bradbury. The result illustrates his skill in producing well written technical descriptions:

> For the benefit of air-minded readers a short account may here be given of this admirable little machine . . . All structural members were drop-forgings of cellular colloidal infra-steel, rubber-faced. The monocoque hull was proofed against sound and temperatures by panels of translucent three-ply crodex, between whose films were managed the ducts and condenser areas of the evaporative-cooling system for the eleven Jenny-Ruras picric-electric motors in the under-body.
>
> Their power units were universally coupled by oil transmission and magnetic clutches alternatively to the lifting vanes (for hover or direct ascent) or to the propulsive rotor for horizontal travel. The vanes were geared into centrifugal governors which automatically varied their lifting angle according to load and air resistance.
>
> In the rotor, the blade-pitch was adjustable at will, for speed and air density. The blades were set (with a clearance at maximum protrusion of .05m.) in the internal drum of a rotor-turbine of (tractor) Townend type, revolving about the nose of the fuselage which was paired for lead-in and baffled for internal turbulence. The slipstream was deflected by scoops at the exit upwards against the bearing surfaces of the vanes, to increase lift in rare atmospheres or from salt water. A syphon-regulated ballast tank was fitted, to trim by the tail when taxying in rough water. The aircraft's landing springs were castored for ease of garaging and retractable for marine use. Landing speeds as low as 4 k.p.h. (downward) and 2 k.p.h. (forward) were attained. The maximum speed at 22,000 m. was .... k.p.h.
>
> All controls were of course directional operated, at will, and gyroscopically stabilised. Baehlen beam-antennae (of four-cycle frequency) were energised by the rotor-brushes. These were set to indicate by sound-signal to the pilot the presence of any body of more

than atmospheric density within 300 metres. At 200 metres they began to induce deflection in the controls, and absolutely refused nearer approach than eighteen metres until the motors were throttled back to landing speed. Antaeus indicators recorded height and earth-direction continuously and nitro-generators supplemented the power-units at great elevations.[12]

Lawrence had not expected to stay at Hythe very long, but he went on from one task to another, and it was not until June 6th that RAF 200 was ready for further trials at Mount Batten. By then the new engines had been fitted and many minor improvements had been made and tested. Lawrence was one of the five-man RAF crew that took the boat along the south coast to Plymouth.

After these trials on Southampton Water, Beauforte-Greenwood wrote to Sydney Smith thanking him for the part Lawrence had played: 'May I express to you my great appreciation for all the assistance you have been good enough to afford my branch by allowing Shaw to run the trials of the new speed-boat for the R.A.F. at Hythe. I can assure you that the help which has been given, together with the reports, have been most useful and resulted in bringing us up to date and at least 4-5 years ahead of the Admiralty. Such an advance would have been impossible without the aid which you have so readily given us, and I thank you very much indeed . . .

'As you know Shaw carried out fifty-hour running trials of this new machinery in an experimental hull belonging to the firm, and as a result of the satisfactory running and favourable report of this machinery we have ordered eight launches which will be ready for delivery by the end of July, in time for the Schneider Trophy'.[13]

This letter leaves no doubt that Lawrence rather than Corporal Bradbury was considered to be responsible for the trials, even though he was merely an aircraftman in rank. Afterwards he wrote to Beauforte-Greenwood: 'We did all we could, I think, as things went; and Mr. Scott-Paine let us into most of his business, so there seemed nothing bad to hide up. That eased our job a lot. We both feel that hull and engines are sound and strong; and that their performance is away above that of the older boats: accordingly I would . . . like to see what [Scott-Paine] could do in designing a slightly larger and more powerful craft – perhaps a 60-footer. The [existing RAF] pinnaces, for all their safety and strength, are so dear.'[14]

Beauforte-Greenwood sent Scott-Paine a copy of Lawrence's report on the voyage from Hythe to Plymouth, and wrote thanking everyone at the yard for their work: 'To say No. 200 is a success does not sufficiently express one's views. She is more than a success, both from the hull point of view and the machinery. If all the remaining boats are as great a success I think it can be said that we shall have achieved something.'[15]

For Lawrence, however, there was still a fortnight's testing in Plymouth before RAF 200 could leave for the Marine Craft Training Section at Calshot, where Air Force coxswains were to be instructed in handling the new boat. There were other distractions, too, notably a mountain of letters which had accumulated while he had been away. He began to write replies to the most urgent, and had to apologise once again to Bruce Rogers about the long-delayed Book XXI. It would now be impossible to complete the translation before July. Even this prospect was dashed when he learned that he was shortly to return to Hythe for trials of the eight follow-on 200 Class boats under construction.

By June 17th, when RAF 200 left for Calshot, Lawrence was occupied with further experiments. The object this time was to develop a floating target that could be towed behind a fast launch and used for bombing practice. The most successful trials were with a naval fog buoy, designed to throw up a visible splash when towed behind a warship in foggy conditions (thus acting as a distance marker for a vessel following behind). Trials with this buoy had not been completed when RAF 200 left, and he reported to Beauforte-Greenwood on June 18th: 'I am sorry about the inconclusive trial . . . It seemed to me extraordinarily promising. The splash was like all the Trafalgar fountains rolled together, and it towed beautifully . . . The Calshot party wanted to get away, so would not leave 200 here to go on testing . . . The only day we had for testing it opened in driving mist, which turned to heavy rain and wind. The Sound was quite impossible, being full of sheltering ships. So we waited for high tide at 6 p.m. and went up past Saltash, where the lake was only choppy, and visibility about half a mile. There could not have been worse conditions, for man and boat, and the test was therefore unfair on everything. If we can go on playing with it, and get the wire right, I shall try some fast towing behind my own boat, and see if the board does "take off" at speed . . . In any case, whether you leave the target here or not, I hope you will continue to try it. It seemed to me like the best bombing target yet.'[16]

A month later Lawrence wrote again, having tested the buoy behind the *Biscuit*: 'It is very good for its proposed job, I think, the only difficulty being spotting . . . The rough days (everybody said the wire would break in bad water) were great fun . . . Once I got it up to 35 m.p.h: but 20-25 is really its fastest decent speed. For a fast target you would have to re-design, with flared bows and a flattened after-moulding, I think, to plane; with scoop-tubes like air intakes thrust through the floor amidships. You could make it weigh only half of this target's weight . . . The Flying Boat very much enjoyed bombing at it. The towing is dead easy: you can turn anyway you please, as slow or as fast as you like. I have doubled back . . . within fifty yards of the target, with it proceeding blissfully in the former direction while I dashed by!'[17]

At the end of July he began twenty-eight days' leave. He was determined to finish the *Odyssey* and had arranged to seclude himself once again in Barton Street. By working day and night on the translation, he managed to finish by August 15th, dedicating the final page to 'Sir Emery Walker, Knight, Wilfred Merton, Treasurer, Bruce Rogers, Printer, Miss Saunders, scribe'. Underneath, he wrote: 'This last page of my version of the *Odyssey* upon which I have spent almost as long as Odysseus and travelled further... Which has furnished me with luxuries for five years and so wholly occupied my hours off duty that I have had no leisure to enjoy them... is affectionately, kindly, gratefully and gladly and with enormous relief and glee *presented*.'[18] After this, he went to spend a few days on holiday with the Sydney Smiths, who were soon to be posted away from Mount Batten to RAF Manston in Kent.

Lawrence had expected to be sent to Hythe as soon as his leave ended, but a fire at the British Power Boat Company's works on August Bank Holiday had destroyed all but one of the 200 Class boats then nearing completion. Scott-Paine promised to replace them as quickly as possible, but it would be some weeks before there was any more testing to do. During the autumn, therefore, Lawrence was to carry out normal duties at Mount Batten.

In late August 1931 the Labour Government was forced to relinquish power because of a severe economic crisis. A National Government was formed which immediately abandoned the gold standard. Another of its first acts was to cut salaries in the Civil Service and armed forces. RAF pay went down by ten per cent, which was an inconvenience to Lawrence, but a terrible blow to many in the ranks. He was able to save money by making less use of his motorcycle and the *Biscuit*, but he had little to spare for friends who turned to him for help. For several weeks he remained quietly in camp, with little to do in his free time except read and correct occasional proofs of the *Odyssey*.

The new Commanding Officer arrived in early October, and shortly afterwards Lawrence wrote: 'I think it is going to be all right. The routine has stiffened, with the going of Group Captain Smith, and I, at least, feel less secure: but the present C.O. (Wing Commander Burling) shapes well. He will do, I fancy. I'm going to keep more to myself this time, as with the last C.O. I had too much to do.'[19]

By this time Lawrence was reading and helping to improve the draft of *Arabia Felix* by Bertram Thomas, who had recently made history by crossing the Empty Quarter of Arabia. This was the unexplored region which Lawrence had once suggested a British airship should fly over, and when he first heard of the crossing, he had suggested that Thomas should receive a knighthood. Now, having helped prepare *Arabia Felix* for publication, he allowed himself to be persuaded to contribute a foreword.

With the pause in boat construction, it seemed as though he would spend several months at Mount Batten and wrote: 'I hope to be able to read a lot this winter, and hear some gramophone music, and ride the bike, and drive the boat: it is rather fine to be owner of all one's 24 hours daily again . . . It is going to be so good, being on my own . . . I hope there will be good books published.'[20] However, the 200 Class boat (No. 201) that had been completed just before the British Power Boat Company fire arrived at Mount Batten during October for more trials with bombing targets. Lawrence wrote to Beauforte-Greenwood: 'The old fashioned sailors still look sideways at her. Nothing but performance will convince them of her superiority for aircraft work. That makes me all the more eager to keep her running. Up to date we have trained two coxswains to handle her, both successes. They swear by her. The others will do the same, when they have had their turn. I am staying on board with each, for his first six or seven hours, giving hints.'[21] A week later he wrote again, evidently pleased with the new Commanding Officer: 'He encourages experiment . . . and is keen on our doing all we can.'[22]

Soon afterwards, Lawrence was involved in another development. Meadows had produced a new marinised engine suitable for the 16 ft. fast dinghies recently introduced by the RAF Marine Branch. By November 21st he was back in Hythe, testing one of the first dinghies fitted with this engine. He found the work exhausting, and wrote to Charlotte Shaw: 'We drive all the daylight hours, and by night are dirty, tired, with salt-smarting eyes. Not fit for letters, of the real sort. A novel or even a magazine, perhaps. Nothing worthy, anyhow. Testing a marine engine, in a new and open hull, is hard work, and difficult. On a rough day it is utterly comfortless: and what I call comfortless, probably is! The others do not drive on bad days, so I get all of it, then.

'This engine seems a very good one. It is too good for its hull, I fear. We will have to strengthen the boat for it. Another week or ten days here, I fancy. Do you know, in testing these new R.A.F. boats I have driven the distance to New York and back! . . .

'As soon as I regain Plymouth I shall let you know, and ask for . . . books. Meanwhile I repeat lines of poetry to myself, while I drive: and try to pass the evening somehow, till bed just after 9. Active, concerned, acute, enduring, judicious. That is what a marine tester should be, I think, to his ability.'[23]

His hopes of returning to work at Mount Batten were premature. In December trials began on a new type of engine control system (known as the Hyland control) for the 200 Class. A great deal of development work was needed before this could be put into service and, apart from a short break at Christmas, Lawrence had to remain at Hythe. By the New Year he foresaw that testing of one kind or another would go on until April or May. He was staying in lodgings next to the yard, and worked 'at all odd hours . . . A queer, mixed, uncertain life, living always with a half-packed kit-bag. Yet I like the testing and modifying and inventing. It gives scope for ingenuities.'[24]

News of his involvement in marine activities had reached the press, and on January 8th a brief news story appeared in the *News Chronicle*. It stated that Lawrence, who 'has proved himself to be an excellent motor-cyclist . . . is now developing into a skilful speed-boat pilot.

'Officially known as Aircraftman T. Edward Shaw, attached to Mount Batten Air Station, he is now engaged as part of his normal Royal Air Force duties, in trying out boats on Southampton Water.

'The development of fast boats is of great importance to the flying-boat and seaplane squadrons. Lawrence is to be seen frequently speeding down the Solent when employed on these motor-boat tests.'[25] The day after this appeared, a journalist from the Associated Press came to the yard trying to obtain photographs and a story about Lawrence and RAF boats. Lawrence reported to Beauforte-Greenwood: 'I refused, for what concerned me, and told them to get Mr. Robertson's visa [i.e. Air Ministry permission] before proceeding with the boats. They did not come back. If they want their yarn badly they can hire a Southampton launch, and snap us off the yard. Perhaps you might ask Robertson to warn the Associated Press against this, if it is still, as I hope, desired not to make a song about the boats. I would like my personal part . . . to be minimised, anyway.'[26]

He also reported that, despite several modifications, the Hyland control was still not perfect: 'Each edition registers an advance, definite but small. I see probably one or two more changes yet . . . Mr. Scott-Paine is unwilling to have anyone from Calshot see all the trouble we are having. So he, Leonard [one of Scott-Paine's employees] and me are the crew, normally: and I have not yet called upon W/Cmdr. Watkins [of Calshot] for a coxswain. I will do so as soon as the boat is ready for running tests. These yard exercises, which is what we have done so far, make one unnecessary, really.'[27]

Many of the letters Lawrence wrote during these months were concerned with technical matters, and it is clear that he was working in a field which gave him great satisfaction. In the past, service life had merely been a refuge: his main interests had been elsewhere, in reading, writing, and a voluminous correspondence. Now, however, he was personally committed to his work, not only because it was worthwhile, but because he enjoyed helping to solve mechanical problems. He was proud of the boats, and if they were damaged by carelessness he complained bitterly. In late January he reported that '202 has now done fifteen hours with the Hyland gears. Today was too foggy to risk going out, so we passed the day trying to invent some means of protecting the reverse from too sudden engagement. We had not realised the need for this till yesterday, when for the first time I got the crew from Calshot and took her down on exhibition. W/Cmdr. Watkins "bumped" the reverse eight times, stalling the engine one time in two. His Flight Sergeant bumped once, his first try, and after that did sixty-eight changes beautifully, and said that there was no difficulty whatever in it. My Corporal coxswain drove for thirty-three minutes, without a single bad mark, though he had had only the normal ten-day course on 200 previously. Welsh, the civilian instructor, did four bumps, but seemed confident, and said he liked the gears: as did W/Cmdr. Watkins, who admitted outright that he had not mastered their operation perfectly. I was able to agree with him. It is clear to me that the instructional boat, at least, must have some spring preventors to save the reverses from becoming scrap iron in a month. After training there will be no need for it'.[28]

The new boat referred to in this letter, RAF 202, was the first 200 Class hull to be built since the boatyard fire. Many small improvements had been incorporated and the service personnel were delighted. Now that the Class was in production again, Lawrence had begun work on an instruction book. At first he thought this a simple project, but it kept growing in scale: 'I have tried to meet the needs of boat builders, fitters, electricians and drivers, in all points of repair and maintenance and every half-hour I remember something else!'[29] By mid-February the notes had reached about fifteen thousand words, but it was to be another month before the final text was sent to the Air Ministry. Meanwhile he had typed it out on stencils and circulated it to the stations that needed copies.

In early February, George Brough wrote offering a very attractive trade-in price for his present motorcycle in exchange for a new SS-100. Lawrence replied: 'Thank you very much. I have £80 already, and can get the balance shortly, I think. It is a very good offer, for my present bike is very rusted and chattery. It hasn't been down, and is quite good-running yet: but looks its age, fully. The only perfect thing is the tank, which can be transferred to George VII [the present machine was nicknamed George VI], if you are short'.[30] He collected the new machine three weeks later, and afterwards wrote gratefully to Brough: 'I think this is going to be a very excellent bike. The crowds that gape at her, just now, will stop looking after she gets dirty: and that may be soon, if only the R.A.F. give me spare time enough to use the poor thing.'[31]

There was, in reality, little hope that he would have free time for motorcycling. Sixteen boats (200 Class and dinghies) had to be tested, and the earliest possible completion date seemed to be the end of March. After that there would be another nine dinghies, one of which would be specially equipped with tanks for refuelling work. This last would have to be exhaustively tested in all weathers. Later there were to be two special boats, based on the 200 Class hull but armour-plated for work as bombing targets (an alternative to the towed targets Lawrence had been experimenting with). He was looking forward to working on these, as they promised to be 'curious and rather exciting'.[32]

He hoped to spend some time at Plymouth once this demanding programme had been completed: 'Not the *Biscuit*, particularly. I shall be half-dead of motor-boating, and longing for books and armchairs and fleshpots. A queer mixed life mine is . . . After Easter . . . I should at least get a weekend. But until the sixteen boats are passed, not a day or hardly an hour. The irony was that I lately spent five days in London, and did nothing – saw nobody. All the time I was in E.6 [at the Air Ministry] typing these blessed *Notes on the...* [200 Class seaplane tender] and answering questions about them and other boats. I become learned about boats, and meanwhile, there are no books, no music, no easements.'[33]

After Easter, however, there was further work in store. At the end of March, Lawrence set out in RAF 210 on a long voyage to Donibristle on the east coast of Scotland. According to his log, the 740-mile journey from Calshot was completed in just over thirty-five hours' running time, despite appalling conditions, at an average speed of 18.3 knots. He was kept in Scotland for two weeks, giving instruction, and did not return to Hythe until mid-April. Soon afterwards *The Times* published an account of the voyage which, like an earlier piece on the development of the 200 Class, was based very largely on notes Lawrence had provided.[34]

In mid-April work began on the two target boats. They would have to be armour-plated, to withstand the impact of eight-and-a-half pound practice bombs dropped from ten thousand feet, which would have a striking velocity of 890 ft/second. After research at Woolwich Arsenal, Beauforte-Greenwood decided that an armour plate produced in Sheffield by Hadfields Ltd. would provide the best ratio of protection to weight.

The boats were to be based on the 200 Class, but the height of the hull above the water line was to be cut down as far as possible in order to reduce the exposed area and hence the weight of armour. According to Beauforte-Greenwood, the final design 'was the result of confidential discussions and collaboration of ideas of Mr. Scott-Paine, myself, T. E. Shaw, Captain Nicholson (of Hadfields) and very probably many other Heads of Departments and employees.'[35] Occasional references to the project in Lawrence's letters show that these discussions had been going on for some months. To support the armour, the hulls were strengthened internally with box girders, and a third engine was fitted so that speed would not be drastically reduced by the extra weight. The whole project was experimental, and as the boats went into construction Lawrence wrote: 'the problems of them are strange to everybody, and we can only guess hard for the moment.'[36] When completed, they were to be taken to Bridlington, in Yorkshire, for trials.

On June 3rd, he set off along the coast from Hythe with the new refuelling dinghy (referred to as No. 1376), hoping to reach Dover. He was accompanied by an RAF pinnace. The voyage proved to be quite an adventure; he later reported that once they had left the Solent, they went 'deep across the bay for Beachy Head. There was a brisk off-shore breeze, and twenty miles out, as we were, quite a sea running. The Pinnace and 1376 had the same top speed, brought down by the sea to about ten knots.

Pinnace was taking it over freely, in the bows. I was bone dry, but had to steer most carefully, to keep 1376 from bumping. With her 350lbs of tanks she is too heavy to throw about. I am getting good with dinghies – only bumped her badly [into a wave] three times all the morning.

'On the Pinnace was 201 Squadron's dinghyman [whose name was Bond], who was supposed to take turn-about with me. Because of the bad weather I kept the boat to myself for the first six hours. The Pinnace hailed me several times, offering relief. Finally I got near enough to explain that it was too rough out there for Bond, and that I would not transfer till we were in the lee of the land . . . about 2.30 we were off Newhaven or Seaford. The sea moderated immediately, and I came aboard the Pinnace and gave Bond the dinghy, asking him to take care not to bump her. He has done no open sea work at all. I watched him, and he drove very well; but after half an hour we were coming round Beachy Head and a little cross-swell worked up. He began to bump in this. After a few minutes I waved him to follow in the Pinnace's wake, where the rollers of her wash gave a constant gradient, upon which I had driven for hours across the swell without a splash or bump. He came in to the wash but fell behind. We stopped for him, and he came near and shouted that the engine was running all right, but the speed no good. I jumped into the dinghy, and he into the Pinnace; then I found 1376 six inches deep in water in the bilges. This was more than the bilge-pump could cope with; so I unshipped the Zwicky [pump] . . . and pumped about 100 gallons out. It came in faster than that. I looked for a leak, but couldn't find one. Not much of the bottom is visible, between the tanks, and she was now very wet, too. Water was cascading up off the shaft-coupling.

'Mr. Jones [the officer in charge of the pinnace] said "Newhaven" and I put back for it as hard as I could, about 5 m.p.h. Before half an hour had passed the water was up to the thwart, and running away over the two corners of the transom. It swilled in as fast, over either bow, as she wallowed in the following swell. There was no buoyancy in the hull, of course, but she was navigating nicely, if sluggishly, on her tanks. The engine went on for nearly ninety minutes, the oil pressure slowly rising as the sump filled. It was an odd experience. Dampish, too.

'The engine finally sputtered out (wet plugs) in the mouth of New-haven Harbour, and the Pinnace towed me up river to the Southern Railway Wharf, where we lifted her on an electric crane, to find the starboard garboard strake split over nearly five feet, under the engine. The lips of the split had mounted on one another, making a huge opening . . .

'I am sorry. Had I driven on it would not have happened: but I felt selfish at hogging all the fun. I am kicking myself now.'[37]

The first armoured boat began trials in June. Lawrence found it 'a great success – and it bristles with new ideas. That may keep me longer on boats. Had it failed, or done no more than was asked for, they would have sent me back to Plymouth. But it did 36 m.p.h. and is completely stable.'[38] On July 11th the two boats, one with Lawrence on board, set off for Bridlington. They arrived three days later, and immediately started further trials. At first, he had expected to be back at Hythe within a fortnight, but he had to remain at Bridlington for nearly six weeks. Five of the boats normally stationed there were in poor mechanical repair, having suffered 'from misfortune and ignorance, in equal doses'.[39] He worked long hours to put things right. Near the end of his stay, he wrote to Charlotte Shaw: 'I shall be so glad to get away and taste change and hear talk and think about immaterials for a spell. Bridlington life is all nuts and split pins and oil pressures.'[40]

During the holiday months in summer there is rarely much interesting news, and the press has often made up for this by printing exaggerated or far-fetched stories. The summer of 1932 was no exception. In mid-August the Chinese Legation in London was disturbed by reports emanating from Germany that Lawrence had gone to Tibet on a mission for the British Government or the Government of India. Commenting on this, the secretary of the Political Department at the India Office wrote: 'During the last few years his wraith has appeared in Kurdistan, Southern Persia, Afghanistan, and, I think, Soviet Turkistan, and in fact, almost everywhere where there was trouble which could be attributed to the Machiavellian designs of the imperialistic British Government. If the legend has struck deep roots in proportion to the extent of its branches, it seems likely to enjoy quite a respectable spell of immortality!'[41]

This nonsense was harmless compared to an outburst in the *Sunday Chronicle*. This paper, which liked to print 'human news-features of a colourful, picturesque and unusual type about living people'[42] ran a large headline on August 28th which read: 'COLONEL LAWRENCE : MAN BEHIND BRITAIN'S PLANES, CARS, AND SPEEDBOATS : HIGH-SPEED PROBLEMS FOR "AIRCRAFTMAN SHAW" : THE EXPERT IN THE COLLEGE.'

Beneath this was an article which could hardly have been better calculated to offend the Air Ministry: 'Colonel Lawrence, once the Uncrowned King of Arabia, is now the uncrowned King of speed . . .

Aircraftman Shaw . . . is living in a little red-brick cottage in the village of Hythe, near Southampton. The real secret reason why Colonel Lawrence is here is that he is the Government speed expert, the man to whose steely brain the most abstruse problems of speed, either in the air or on the water, are referred . . . "Aircraftman Shaw is a great authority on internal-combustion engines" a noted expert told me to-day. The truth is that his brain is the ultimate Government testing shop for all problems affecting high-speed aero and marine engines. It is whispered that more than half Britain's success in the races for the Schneider trophy was due to his research work . . . his true identity is unknown even to his landlady. She knows him merely as a shy reserved young man . . . He is just "Our Mr. Shaw in the sitting room." She regards him simply as a somewhat mysterious young man who suddenly disappears without warning, remains away for months, as suddenly reappears perhaps at mid-night, and neither drinks nor smokes – with two notable exceptions . . . He smokes twice a year – on Midsummer Eve and on Christmas Eve. Always at midnight.

'He possesses only one intimate friend, a humble fitter in a nearby works; the two spend hours together discussing abstruse mechanical problems. His one hobby is his motor-cycle, the most powerful one in Hampshire. It is a monster capable of 110 m.p.h. . . .

'Sometimes Aircraftman Shaw takes classes of young officers in technical instruction. Their embarrassment is comic. They do not always know his identity, but they realise that the man of technically far inferior rank is obviously an authority and clearly a person of great importance.'[43]

Anyone who read this carefully would realise that the interview material was entirely unexceptional. All the sensational claims were made by the 'special correspondent' who had written the story. The sensible reaction would have been to ignore it, but it was inevitable that some officers thought differently. Protests were made at the Air Ministry, and eventually it was decided that Lawrence should be returned to normal duties at Plymouth as from September 8th.

He was not immediately aware of this, because on August 31st he had left for a few days' holiday. His first stop was Malvern and on September 1st, he went to see a new play by Bernard Shaw, *Too True to be Good*. It was not popular with the critics or the public, but was particularly interesting to Lawrence because he himself was parodied in the second act as 'Private Meek', a soldier who always knew much more about what was going on than his Commanding Officer. During the preceding months he had read the play in draft, and had amused himself suggesting the kind of things that Meek might have said to his superiors.

On September 22nd he had lunch with the Shaws and the artist Laura Knight. Afterwards, the Shaws took him to Worcester, for tea with Sir Edward Elgar. That evening he went on to London. It was only when he reached Hythe that he heard of the change in his RAF fortunes. He wrote bitterly to a correspondent: 'You will note that I am returning to my Plymouth address in a day or two. Please forget the Hythe one.'[44] However, the move had compensations. After working on boats for several months, he was happy with the thought of spending time reading and catching up with his correspondence. After a few days in Plymouth, he wrote: 'I am settling into place at Mount Batten, slowly. My old place had gone, of course, and it will take time to find a new one, and make it fit me comfortably: but there is a feeling of relaxation, like a hulk settling again into the sand after a spring tide . . . Now I am going to read all the books which have been sacrificed for speed boats since 1931: where to begin? There are so many.'[45]

Among the mail he found at Plymouth was an invitation from a new organisation to be called the Irish Academy of Letters. At its first meeting, on September 14th, Lawrence's name had been put forward as a possible Associate, and W. B. Yeats had written inviting him to accept. Hitherto, Lawrence had shown little feeling for his origins, but he had always regarded England as his home, and at one time had taken pains to point out that his father's family had never inter-married with the Irish. In recent years, however, his sense of loyalty to Ireland had grown because Charlotte Shaw had frequently written to him about Irish topics and sent him the work of Irish writers. He now replied to Yeats accepting the nomination: 'I am Irish, and it has been a chance to admit it publicly – but it touches me very deeply that you should think anything I have done or been to justify this honour . . . Thanks again. It's not my fault, wholly, if I am not more Irish: family, political, even money obstacles will hold me in England always. I wish it were not so.'[46]

Public recognition of Lawrence's writing increased at the beginning of November, when the Bruce Rogers *Odyssey* was published. In England there was hardly any reaction, but an American trade edition, in which he had allowed his name to be given as translator, was issued by Oxford University Press. It was instantly successful.

Although the Emery Walker edition attracted little notice in the British press, it was a magnificent example of book production. The text was set in Centaur, which Rogers had developed from a typeface used in the fifteenth century. It was printed in special ink on pale grey paper, and the beginning of each Book was marked by a drawing based on a Greek vase painting, reproduced in black on a roundel of gold leaf. The black morocco binding was elegant and simple. After receiving an advance copy, Lawrence wrote to Wilfred Merton, Walker's partner: 'I had a little kick, in first opening it. Well, well. That is for the second time in my life. *Revolt in the Desert* was the first, in 1927 . . . This is a good-looker, this book. The binding is very chaste. I tried to read a page of it, but failed. Awful muck, the text, alas.'[47]

As examples of book production, the Bruce Rogers *Odyssey* and Lawrence's *Seven Pillars* were very different. While the solid, 'craft' appearance of *Seven Pillars* reflected Lawrence's passion for William Morris, the *Odyssey* was essentially classical. It is not surprising, therefore, that Rogers's work was not entirely to Lawrence's taste. To one correspondent he wrote that it was 'ever so dove-mild and boudoiry',[48] and to another: 'As for his roundels, the mass of gold and black fills the empty chapter-heading well enough. I am not fond of vase-painting, I must admit; and so the style of them disappoints me: but he enjoyed fitting them together. If you half-shut your eyes and look at them, you will like their balance and tone.'[49]

After a while in Plymouth, Lawrence began to regret that he was no longer testing motorboats: 'there is all the difference between looking after one, and embodying one's idea in new types. I've been at the building job for eighteen months, and we have got out a new dinghy (speed 21 m.p.h. instead of the five of our old type) and a new standby boat (37 footer, speed 30 m.p.h. instead of 12 m.p.h., the old type). I had in mind a new refuelling boat: and then a new pinnace 50 foot to do 50 m.p.h. and be an all-weather boat, instead of our present 12-knot Diesel-naval things.'[50] However, all this was now a pipedream. The Air Ministry had told the Marine Equipment Branch that they could only continue employing Lawrence if they could guarantee that there would be no more newspaper publicity. This was, he said, 'an absurd condition, like stipulating that it should rain no more. So I told them to have nothing to do with it. It was a bad way to leave.'[51]

Far from enjoying his rest, Lawrence caught bad flu which dragged on for several weeks. Depressed by this illness, he began to think of leaving the Air Force. He hinted at this possibility in a letter written only five weeks after his return to Plymouth: 'My R.A.F. time runs out on March 12 1935: so that is quite a bit yet. I have been not at all well lately and am wondering if I can stick it out.'[52] He had spent several months living away from camp, for the first time since his enlistment, and he had enjoyed the freedom and responsibility of the speedboat work. By comparison, he found life at Mount Batten unpleasantly restricted. He began to talk about his plans to retire to Clouds Hill. The cottage was soon to be unoccupied because his mother and elder brother had decided to take up missionary work in China again.

During the winter, he instructed builders to repair the Clouds Hill roof and damp-proof the walls of the large downstairs room, hitherto used as a kitchen. His plans to add on a room for books had been abandoned because of the recession. Instead, he decided to have shelving installed downstairs. On November 24th he wrote: 'By the end of January it should be again habitable. Slowly the certainty that I shall inhabit it permanently sinks in. Once it seemed incredible that I should have a real habitation.'[53]

If he chose to leave the Air Force, he already had a guaranteed income from investments. It would be meagre, but probably sufficient. In addition, however, there was now money from the *Odyssey*. The American trade edition was selling well, and Lawrence was entitled to a third share of the royalties. He began to think of bringing a water supply to the cottage and installing a water heater and bath.

While this work was going on, the cottage was uninhabitable, and he would have to remain at Mount Batten. To occupy himself, and earn a little money, he agreed to edit for Cape a book by an unknown author, Ian Tyre, about experiences in Palestine and Syria during the war. At first he was cautious, and wrote to Edward Garnett: 'Are you committed to publishing it? It's authentic, and all that; but very penny-plain: and if much edited, it might lose its flavour . . . An editor, as I see the job, would have to gorge a good deal: for one couldn't footnote so transparent a tale. It would have to be corrected inside itself, by re-writing bits in the style of the plain man: and how would the author take that? His politics, for instance, aren't good enough or bad enough to leave as they stand. The French and British are both ignorantly traduced. He didn't understand, poor creature. His tale is well told and full of himself. I liked bits of it very well: but it wants quite a lot of cutting about and altering, and the author would have to agree.

'I don't know, as I said, if it is worth your while. I could do it, subject to the author's consent: but it's a queer job, or it will be!'[54]

Soon afterwards, Cape forwarded a letter from Tyre, giving the publishers a free hand, and Lawrence began work. After ten days, however, he wrote to Cape: 'The job is harder than I thought, for my writing won't mix with his, so that forgery is impossible. I'm trying to do a page or two as trial, and will send them to you for sample as soon as they are done. After that you must make up your mind. I have a suspicion that they were better before I started to mangle them. My work must be completely anonymous, if you take it'.[55]

As the end of 1932 approached, he became increasingly uneasy about his future at Mount Batten. When it was learned that Wing Commander Burling would leave on January 3rd, Lawrence wrote: 'He has been a very quiet and uninterfering C.O. and we are all very sorry he is going . . . Mount Batten is not very cheerful at the moment. It is to be up-graded on April 1st and so there's yet another change in prospect. All very unsettling.'[56]

He was now wavering between the alternatives of transfer to another station or leaving the RAF altogether. On January 11th he wrote to Charlotte Shaw, who was travelling abroad: 'Life for me has been unrelieved Mount Batten since you went. And that word unrelieved will give you the notion that the R.A.F. is no longer my perfect home. Partly because the station is changing, with three new commanding officers in three weeks, and two more coming soon: partly because our hut is full of noisy newcomers, and is sometimes like bedlam and sometimes like a beer-garden. I have to wander out of it often, for peace of ear: and it is cold and wet outside. Also I have been not well at all this winter, and that is probably at the root of other discomforts.

'Anyway I have been seriously wondering if I ought not to go out. Only what will "out" mean? My cottage... but that's a gamble. If it proved not good to live in, where then would I be?

'I suppose these changes come to everybody, and it is wrong of me to spread them over you. Only the next change is my last, I think: it marks retirement age: and I wanted it to be compatible.'[57]

On the following day he sent an appeal for help to Sir Philip Sassoon, the under secretary of State for Air: 'We have trebled the speed of the stand-by flying boats, with increased reliability and seaworthiness, at reduced cost. So I have earned my two years' pay and pleased myself. There were two or three other types of boats to revise, and I was hoping... but the Sunday press stepped in with an article and your very sensitive Ministry sent me back to station duty.

'Mount Batten is full of ghosts and sad. You once told me I might think of coming to 601 at Hendon to see the Air Force of the future. Is the offer still open? An A.C.H. [aircraft hand] is not hard to fit in, usually...'[58]

Although he found little interest in his RAF work, Lawrence was not idle. He spent his time reading, editing the Tyre book, and tackling an enormous backlog of letters. He wrote frequently to Bruce Rogers about the *Odyssey*, and to Charlotte Shaw on literary topics; but there were many other correspondents. During the winter of 1932-3, these included Nancy Astor, Herbert Baker, Maurice Baring, John Brophy, Robin Buxton, Jonathan Cape, F. N. Doubleday, H. S. Ede, Edward Elgar, Feisal, L. Frere-Reeves (of Heinemann), David and Edward Garnett, Robert Graves, James Hanley and C. J. Greenwood (Hanley's publisher), Mrs Thomas Hardy, Wyndham Lewis, L. B. Namier, Stewart Newcombe, William Rothenstein, A. P. Wavell, Henry Williamson, and Lord Winterton. Lawrence knew that these friendships, which contributed so much to his contentment, had nothing to do with his life in the RAF: they would continue whether he remained in the Service or not.

Just before Christmas he told Bruce Rogers: 'The large sale for our *Odyssey* will, as you say, mean a big royalty payment next March. I had, in my more hopeful moments, dreamt of its being adopted as a school text-book in the States. Our Oxford Press here makes a better income out of obscure text-books than most publishers do out of novels. They sell and sell for twenty years, making a clear £100 or so a year. However in our case we'll net a purse-full our first year and then forget it . . .

'I can't enlist again – too old, which is a sad word to write. So it is cottage inevitably for me. I have nearly my £2 a week from investments, and therefore it can happen any moment. I do not rely in any way upon Odysseys or other suches to supply my bread and butter. Only if I run short of jam, in the future, I would try and do another something to help me forward . . . I don't think I'm reckless, exactly, about money. If I could afford the attitude I'd stand aside and ignore it. As I cannot, I have been very parsimonious and careful for some years until I have collected the minimum that should meet my needs for the future... and there I want to stop.'[59]

By mid-February he knew that the American *Odyssey* had sold eleven thousand copies, and that there had been a fifth printing in January. This-success was beyond his wildest expectations, and publishers were urging him to authorise a trade edition in England. He consistently refused to do so: the money earned in America was more than sufficient for his needs, and even enabled him to find £200 to help a friend who was facing bankruptcy.

He wrote to Buxton on February 16th that he was 'repairing and altering my cottage, against the day of retiring, which may be very soon. This station is not pleasant, now.'[60] Twelve days later, however, he was still thinking he might go to another unit: 'I still wonder about moving, but will not settle that for a month yet, and might retire into civil life instead.'[61] In the event, he made up his mind after only a week, and on March 6th submitted a formal request for discharge: 'I, No.338171 A/C Shaw, E., respectfully request that I may be granted an interview with the Commanding Officer, to ask him to forward my application to be released from further service in the Royal Air Force as from the sixth of April, 1933.'[62] The request was approved.

CHAPTER 44

Last RAF Duties
March 1933 – February 1935

NO sooner had Lawrence committed himself, than he began to regret it. He wrote to Charlotte Shaw: 'This morning I decided I had better end my self-argument, so I have put in a request to be discharged from the R.A.F. . . . and am homesick already, with the change and loneliness to come.

'I'm not telling people yet: they would want to know why, and all I can say is that the shortening of my R.A.F. time (for 1935 March was my ultimate date) with so much not done, and not tasted, left me aching inside every time I remembered it: and better end it now, shortly, than linger two years like that . . . Tell G.B.S., please, that Meek is now out of his conceit.

'My move will be to Clouds Hill, where I shall try to stay till my heart and head settle down again. I have not been into ways and means, so cannot say how I shall live: but the *Odyssey* has postponed that question till next year.'[1]

Within a few days, news of the decision found its way into the newspapers. Geoffrey Salmond, who was to be the next Chief of Air Staff, was very ill (he died soon afterwards), but he immediately wrote to Lawrence: 'I am alarmed to see in the Press that you are now proposing to leave the R.A.F. . . . I do not know what is going on at the Air Ministry but you have now become an Institution in the R.A.F. [and] it seems difficult to imagine you as anything else.'[2] Lawrence went to see him, but did not change his mind, although he offered to stay on if further special work could be found for him.

At the end of March he was called in by his Commanding Officer who asked him whether he had any grievance. The Secretary of State wanted to know the reason for his decision to leave. Afterwards, Lawrence wrote to Sir Philip Sassoon directly: 'I could no longer be content to do station duty at Mount Batten. My present job is looking after the boats and their engines here, and that is purely routine and not a day's work . . . I am a reasonably skilled mechanic, after all these years, but without ambitions to excel in it.

'My feeling was that I should do something more if I was to justify my staying on in the R.A.F. At Karachi, for instance, they let me revise the procedure of engine-overhaul in the Depot. At Batten, Sydney Smith gave me the Schneider Cup ground-organisation. Then the D[irectorate] of E[quipment] gave me the R.A.F. fleet to put on new lines, and I did eighteen months on that and got half-way in it . . . The only thing that troubles me is that there is much I could yet do. In these eleven years I have learned every square inch of the R.A.F. and it seems a pity to leave so much knowledge unused . . . I saw Geoffrey Salmond lately, and told him almost what I have said above. "I will not go on at Batten, doing routine work. I would like to do more boats," or to see the auxiliary airmen (the R.A.F. of the future, I think!) or best of all, to do a long flying-boat voyage and write a log of it.'[3]

By this time the Air Ministry had formally approved his premature discharge (which would not normally have been granted to a serving airman). He was to be allowed to buy himself out for the nominal sum of £17-10-0.

Lawrence was half-expecting the offer of more interesting work, and on April 3rd he wrote: 'Here is Monday come, and my discharge due on Thursday, and not an indication from Air Ministry if I am to or not. Extraordinary people.

'I am carrying on as if to go, and have got rid of all my kit, except what I stand in. This last Saturday I ran a car-load of books, records, clothes and tools to my cottage, which is still in the throes of the builders, but looking peaceful despite it. I think it will do, as a harbour.

'Gramophone already there, and the acoustics of the room wonderful. Strings are really "woody" and ripe, in the cottage. All my records are there assembled, yards of them. But only a few books, as yet. The rest in London await the shelving's completion.'[4]

On April 15th the *Daily Mail* reported that he had left the RAF. Four days later, however, he was called to the Air Ministry and offered a posting to the RAF Marine Aircraft Experimental Establishment, at Felixstowe, where he would continue to work on the boat-building programme under Beauforte-Greenwood and Jinman. This he accepted, and the necessary orders were issued two days later. To reduce the risk of publicity, it was also decided that in future Lawrence would wear plain clothes whenever he was working away from an RAF station.

He arrived at Felixstowe on April 28th, and told friends that it seemed to be pleasant. However, he was destined to spend very little time there during the twenty-two months' service that remained. His new duties were laid out in a memorandum dated May 2nd. They were:

a. Generally to watch the Air Ministry's interests at contractors' yards during the construction of marine craft, various types of bombing target, moorings, engines, and equipment.

b. Assist in preparation of trial reports and notes on running and maintenance of various types of craft.

c. Assist in production of craft and equipment generally and in particular the high speed vessel for crashwork, life saving and also salvage of boat planes.'[5]

At the outset, Lawrence hoped that the job would prove less gruelling than his previous spell in boats. He wrote: 'I have warned them that I am not very energetic, now'.[6] Soon, however, he was giving many more hours to the job than duty required and when, some months later, the RAF began to consider his ultimate replacement, it was thought that two men would be needed to carry on with his work.[7]

After two weeks at Felixstowe he was sent to Manchester, and thereafter he travelled frequently, visiting different boatyards, engine builders and other suppliers. He spent much of his time watching over construction work at Hythe, or at East Cowes on the Isle of Wight. There were also frequent meetings at the Air Ministry in London.

One result of his new posting was that his letters became short and obviously hurried. Another was that, for the first time since 1919, he gave up any thought of literary work. He had finished editing Ian Tyre's book in March,[8] and refused to start anything else, saying repeatedly that all such projects would have to wait until after he had left the Air Force: 'With these boats always cutting into my weekends and evenings, and preoccupying my thoughts, I have made up my mind not to undertake any sort of outside job till my R.A.F. days end in the beginning of 1935. It seems almost certain that I shall be boat-building till my service ends, and I shall do nothing but boat-build. Plenty of leisure, afterwards. Let us work while we can.'[9]

He took very few days off, but if he was within reach of Dorset he would visit Clouds Hill at the weekend: 'And there I potter about, like any other retired Colonel, doing little jobs about the place. It is not quite equal to my past reputation, but fits well enough with my present.'[10] The cottage was the only outside interest to which he gave any time during 1933. Its downstairs room was now damp proofed and shelved, and during the summer he arranged to have his books brought there. They had been left in the care, first, of Vyvyan Richards, and later of Richards' brother. When they finally reached Clouds Hill, Lawrence was distressed to find that many were missing. He wrote to Charlotte Shaw: 'I had posted off to my deposit all the books – over twelve years – which I had liked and wanted to re-read. There were dozens of yours, dozens of everybody's. But someone has been dishonest or careless with them: the private press luxury books are there, but the exciting works are gone. It is not theft but stupidity, I fear: for instance Vol. 2 of the set of *Arabia Deserta* inscribed to me by Doughty is missing; not the inscribed volume, but the plain one. The *Intelligent Woman*['s *Guide to Socialism*] and the *Too true* [*to be Good*] remain: but the [*St.*] *Joan*, [inscribed] from public Shaw to private Shaw is gone: also many other inscribed books. I hope they will not think I have been selling them. Of the first seven D. H. Lawrence prose books only two survive. Of the James Stephens, all the prose is gone. Mostly the poems are saved, and the prose lost. I am going round the old book shops, wherever I visit, and making up the casualties. It is heart-breaking work. My own fault, I suppose, but to lock up books that people may want to read is a selfish sort of sin: only I wish whoever has removed them had had more conscience. I had so enjoyed – in imagination – this little library. It was to have been all the worth-whiles of thirty years of reading. There are good things, still, of course – but the incompleteness shames me.'[11]

The most important improvement Lawrence was now planning at Clouds Hill was a water supply, which would enable him to install a bath. The only water source within reach was a stream on the far side of the road, about a hundred feet from the cottage and thirty-five feet below it. To bring this supply uphill without power (there was no electricity at Clouds Hill) Lawrence bought a small water-ram which would be driven by the stream itself. This would be sufficient to deliver thirty-five gallons of water every twenty-four hours. At the end of August the work was completed, and Lawrence wrote: 'Yesterday was a DAY. At 1.45 p.m. water, driven by the smallest ram ever installed anywhere, began to flow into my cottage at Clouds Hill. The pipes are a hundred yards long: the ram was turned on at 10 a.m. without public ceremony: it worked steadily for hour after hour: and at 1.45, as I have said, the water arrived at its destination. The single, oldest and only inhabitant of Clouds Hill took off his R.A.F. cap with a simple gesture (to avoid knocking it against the roof-beam) and collected the first pint in a pint mug. It arrived in four minutes, and the S.O. and O. inhabitant then drank it. The taste was of red lead and galvanised iron: but the quality was wet, indubitably: and they say that in four weeks the taste will be unalloyed water. I hope so: for otherwise my drinking water will come from the spring by bucket!

'If a pint in four minutes seems to you little, reflect that it works all day and all night at that rate. It is copious; excessive. Indeed I have laid down a spill-pipe, which will feed the kitchen of my neighbour, Mrs. Knowles, with my surplus. Both of us are henceforward endowed with running water. We feel so rich and happy.

'Now for the bath. It has arrived, but must wait for fixing till its boiler, cistern and burner are in order. Some date in October, I hope, there will be the sound of a hot bath at Clouds Hill . . . Imagine that a mere translation of the *Odyssey* does me all this good!'[12]

In addition to these improvements, the staircase was to be sheathed in oak three-ply and the bathroom fitted out. Lawrence also began to think of turning the smaller of the two upstairs rooms into a study.

Unfortunately, these plans soon ran into difficulties. The dollar exchange rate fell, and the sterling value of his *Odyssey* receipts became much lower than he had reckoned on. By the autumn he was obliged to borrow in order to continue the building work. In September he wrote: 'all my money has gone on the changes to the cottage. To finish the water and heating business I will probably have to anticipate my next payment of American royalties on the *Odyssey*. Until it is finished I cannot say exactly what will be the total cost – more than I had expected, but then I have done more than I meant. Improvements suggest themselves, and it was now or never to put them in. So I have plunged, rather. All bills are paid, to date, but little remains . . . I get to the cottage only for a few hours a fortnight: hardly ever for a night. The place needs living in, badly. I would like to find a tenant for the winter, but cannot well offer it, without kitchen or bedroom: and will the water-works be finished? They are so slow, these firms.'[13] Towards the end of the year, when the main work had been completed, Lawrence decided to get rid of the builders. There was more he wanted to do, but Pat Knowles, the eldest of Mrs Knowles's sons, was now living with her, and he offered to do the work much more cheaply.

In April 1933 Liddell Hart at last began writing the military biography of Lawrence that Cape had proposed three years earlier. During the spring

and summer he asked Lawrence to answer detailed questionnaires, sometimes in writing, sometimes verbally, and afterwards he sent sections of
the book in typescript, on which Lawrence wrote further comments and
corrections.[14] Liddell Hart was more thorough and discerning than Graves
had been, and he was not under the same pressure over deadlines. He was
able to consult British officers who had served in the Middle East during
the war and he obtained access to some of the military documents.
Lawrence quickly realised that this was to be a serious work of history and
decided to give Liddell Hart all the help he could.

One difficulty proved to be Charlotte Shaw, to whom Lawrence had
sent his surviving war notebooks and his set of the *Arab Bulletin*. As she
had reacted so badly to the Graves biography, Lawrence did not expect
her to help Liddell Hart. However, he needed some of the material she
was holding, particularly the *Bulletin*. On June 16th he wrote cautiously:
'Oh, by the way, Liddell Hart, the military biographer, is doing for
Cape a book on my military significance, in the fields of strategy and
tactics. I am sorry. There is so little in it – in my military significance, I
mean.'[15] Nine days later, while reading the first section of Liddell Hart's
draft, Lawrence wrote to her again, saying: 'He has made a detached
examination of the Arab Revolt – as warfare – and we all come well out
of it! Only I think it a pity to traverse those worn subjects again.'[16]
On June 29th he plucked up the courage to ask for the *Bulletin*. He
began by attempting to engage her sympathy: 'Liddell Hart is tall, thin,
and flame-hot on his pet subject, which is the deficiency of thinking
in the British Army. He lives for the avoidance of battle and murder,
and for winning campaigns by wise dispositions. A tenuous sincerity
about him. Good, I think, within reason. He carries his revulsion against
Clausewitz too far.

'I think he is really interested in generals of individuality, and his
books on Sherman and Scipio were excellent: really excellent. And one
chapter of his study of war-from-the-British-angle was almost the only bit
of abstract military philosophy in English. Yet he is not a philosopher: all
his knowledge applies itself.

'If you see him will you press on his attention those three volumes of
the *Arab Bulletin* that were at Ayot? Nobody should study our revolt in
print before mastering those: but I think there are no other sets in private
hands.'[17]

Liddell Hart was in Denmark when this was written. By the time he
had returned, Charlotte Shaw, who probably hoped to avoid giving the

impression that she held other important materials, had sent the *Bulletin* volumes back to Lawrence. She agreed to meet Liddell Hart for lunch, but told him that Lawrence 'had taken away the copies of the *Arab Bulletin*'.[18] Lawrence probably realised that this was all the help that could be expected from her. He wrote thanking her for the *Bulletin*, but made no mention of the war diaries and notebooks.

Having read Liddell Hart's military chapters, Lawrence was sufficiently impressed to send detailed suggestions for a conclusion: 'You talk of a summing up to come. Will you (if you agree with my feeling) in it strike a blow for hard work and thinking? I was not an instinctive soldier, automatic with intuitions and happy ideas. When I took a decision, or adopted an alternative it was after studying every relevant – and many an irrelevant – factor. Geography, tribal structure, religion, social customs, language, appetites, standards – all were at my finger-ends. The enemy I knew almost like my own side. I risked myself among them a hundred times, to *learn*.

'The same with tactics. If I used a weapon well, it was because I could handle it. Rifles were easy. I put myself under instruction for Lewis, Vickers, and Hotchkiss (Vickers in my O.T.C. days, and rifles and pistols) . . . To use aircraft I learned to fly. To use armoured cars I learned to drive and fight them. I became a gunner at need, and could doctor and judge a camel.

'The same with strategy. I have written only a few pages on the art of war – but in these I levy contribution from my predecessors of five languages. You are one of the few living Englishmen who can see the allusions and quotations, the conscious analogies, in all I say and do, militarily.

'Do make it clear that generalship, at least in my case, came of understanding, of hard study, and brain-work and concentration. Had it come easy to me I should not have done it so well.

'If your book could persuade some of our new soldiers to read and mark and learn things outside drill manuals and tactical diagrams, it would do a good work. I feel a fundamental, crippling, incuriousness about our officers. Too much body and too little head. The perfect general would know everything in heaven and earth.

'So please, if you see me that way and agree with me, do use me as a text to preach for more study of books and history, a greater seriousness in military art. With two thousand years of examples behind us we have no excuse, when fighting, for not fighting well.'[19]

All went well with the Liddell Hart project until August, when Cape, having read the draft, suddenly asked 'for less military consideration and more life'.[20] Lawrence protested, both to Liddell Hart and to Cape, but to little avail. Later he wrote angrily to Charlotte Shaw: 'I like Liddell Hart, yet I fear him. He is too serious. His book on me is very interesting, where it is military, and *awful* (to my hidden self-regard) where it deals with me as a human being. I wish it had not been done.'[21]

Despite his praise for the military analysis, he wrote elsewhere that Liddell Hart's biography 'is heavy, and contains no criticism. He is a very good and keen military writer – but unfortunately my tactics and principles happen to support the theory of war which he urges, in and out of season. So he uses me as the stalking horse to air the merits of his ideas and this makes even the well-founded parts of his book feel improbable.'[22]

In fairness to Liddell Hart, it must be said that the lack of criticism had not been entirely his doing. Where his draft had been less than favourable, Lawrence had quite naturally defended himself, usually by supplying additional information. This left Liddell Hart in an awkward predicament. After working over one batch of Lawrence's annotations, he had written: 'I'm a bit sorry that you provide facts that knock out some of my few criticisms of your action, for to tell the truth I was becoming almost anxious to find something critical to say as an offset and for the reader's satisfaction. The more I've studied your campaign, the more my admiration has grown, until I have begun to feel that I must temper it lest my tribute be discounted.'[23]

Little else interrupted Lawrence's RAF work in 1933. His daily routine is described in a letter to Forster written from his lodgings in Southampton: 'rise 0730 hrs: breakfast: and leave for Hythe or Cowes at 0830. Work all day in one of those shipyards, generally at Hythe. Return to Southampton about 6 p.m. (1800 hrs) eat again. Sleep after reading about 11 p.m. (2300 hrs).

'Saturday is different. Cease work at noon: and if Sunday is clear, ride to Clouds Hill and camp in the reconstructing cottage, amidst the riot of builders' men and their mess of material: returning to Southampton p.m. on Sunday.

'Periodically and abruptly I am called by telephone to London to the Air Ministry; or sent to one or another of five or six R.A.F. stations, for a day or two days: once for four days. All duties in connection with boat-building.'[24]

This itinerant work gave him opportunities to see some of his friends and, conversely, an excuse to avoid many of the people who wanted to meet him. Feisal visited London in June, and Admiral Snagge, who had served in the Red Sea Patrol, wrote telling Lawrence how he had stood on Horse Guards Parade 'and watched Feisal pass in State . . . on his return from the Guildhall with his sovereign's escort of Life Guards and the whole paraphernalia, and my thoughts rather naturally wandered back into the past'.[25] Snagge was invited with Lawrence and Newcombe to a lunch given by Feisal at the Hyde Park Hotel. Lawrence wrote to him beforehand: 'Your company will (or would) strengthen me for the ordeal: for I have no civil clothes even imaginable for Hyde Park, or its hotels: and airmen (unless in company of unimpeachable correctness) find it hard to gain access to kings.'[26]

Although Feisal was only fifty, he suffered from heart disease. After leaving London he went to Switzerland to receive medical treatment. He died there on September 11th. Not long afterwards Lawrence wrote: 'I think of his death almost with relief – as one would see enter the harbour a good-looking but not sea-worthy ship, with the barometer falling. He is out of it, intact'.[27]

Towards the end of the year, Lawrence had further irritating experiences with the press. The November issue of the *British Legion Journal* contained an article called 'Service Life', which he himself was alleged to have contributed. In reality, the text had been taken from three of the Cranwell chapters in *The Mint*. These had been sent in to the journal by someone who had been allowed to read the typescript without Lawrence's knowledge. The RAF authorities were very angry, and feared that some of the less acceptable Uxbridge chapters might also find their way into print. Lawrence wrote: 'I've got into awful trouble: with the Air Ministry, for publishing opinions about service matters without permission – with Lord Trenchard, for publishing part of *The Mint* against my most solemn promise to keep it private till 1950 at least – Jonathan Cape, for piece-meal disclosure of matter upon which they hold an option. In fact my name is mud, everywhere, and I may be civvy next week because of it . . . They all want me to let the police follow it up – and that would mean courts and reports.'[28] Eventually, the matter was smoothed over without any further action, and the *British Legion Journal* published an apology in a later issue.

Soon after dealing with this problem, Lawrence was confronted with an absurd story about his work on target launches. It was first published in America, but a British newspaper repeated it under the heading: 'Human Target for Bombs: Men risk Death in Speed-Boats'. The article read: 'Using two heavily-armoured, unsinkable speed-boats, Aircraftman Shaw – "Lawrence of Arabia" – and two other R.A.F. men, have risked their lives as human targets for bombing 'planes, it was revealed yesterday.

'Daily for nearly a year the men have been cruising in the North Sea, offering themselves as targets. Although dozens of bombs have been dropped on the boats from heights varying from 1,000 to 15,000ft., they have been hardly damaged and the crews absolutely unhurt. The reason is that the boats have been specially designed to withstand air attack, being composed mainly of rubber and protected by steel armour plating . . . Aircraftman Shaw was in one of these boats during all its early trials, and had the nerve-racking experience – an experience unique in the annals of any Air Force – of being directly bombed during practice exercises.'[29]

This was exactly the kind of publicity Lawrence had been asked to avoid. Moreover, it was embarrassing to the RAF, which had banned all coverage of the target launches during the international disarmament negotiations that were then taking place in Geneva. Privately, Lawrence thought the embargo absurd, and he told a friend that the RAF had brought this nonsense upon itself. When Liddell Hart asked him to provide accurate information about the boats as a basis for a corrective article in the United States, he agreed readily, pointing out that, 'Picture postcards of these boats are on sale in the shops at Bridlington, and everybody there knows of them . . . Robertson, the Air Ministry press lord, has had orders to prevent any publication . . . He can stop the *Daily Telegraph* [of which Liddell Hart was military correspondent] but not U.S.A., of course! We have tried, for long enough, to get the ban removed. It is just silly.'[30] In the event, the RAF lifted its embargo and Liddell Hart's corrective was published by the *Daily Telegraph*.

It was now some months since Lawrence had contemplated any kind of literary project. In early December, however, he wrote to Charlotte Shaw: 'something happened to me last night, when I lay awake till five. You know I have been moody or broody for years, wondering what I was at in the R.A.F., but unable to let go – well, last night I suddenly understood that it was to write a book called "Confession of Faith" . . . embodying *The Mint* and much that has happened to me before and since as regards the air. Not the conquest of the air, but our entry into the reserved element "as lords that are expected, yet with a silent joy in our arrival". It would include a word on Miranshah and Karachi, and the meaning of speed, on land and water and air. I see the plan of it. It will take long to do. Clouds Hill, I think. In this next and last R.A.F. year I can collect feelings for it. The thread of the book will only come because it spins through my head: there cannot be any objective continuity – but I think I can make it whole enough to do. *The Mint*, you know, was meant as notes for something (smaller) of the sort. I wonder if it will come off. The purpose of my generation, that's really it. Anyway I shall tell no one else . . . Three years hence we'll know.'[31]

Lawrence made no further reference to this project, and it might be tempting to dismiss it; but he was due to leave the Air Force in fourteen months, and had begun to think seriously about what he would do next. He had recently told another friend: 'When I have left the R.A.F. and entered upon the emptiness of my cottage, desperation may well make me write something, and seek an anonymous printing of it.'[32]

One piece of writing he did undertake at this time was a dust-jacket blurb for Liddell Hart's biography. When Wren Howard, Cape's partner, sent a draft for his comments, he replied: 'Rotten effort, I call it. No zipp, and some misleading words'.[33] He sent a version of his own, which was used when the book was first published; he was also concerned about the proposed title 'Lawrence', protesting that this created confusion with D. H. Lawrence. To make matters difficult, he demanded pedantically that the name Lawrence, if used, should be placed between inverted commas. When Cape settled on *'T. E. Lawrence' in Arabia and After* he was still dissatisfied, and wrote: 'Your title is rotten. Why not get away from Lawrence and his Arabia? Lowell Thomas and Robert Graves both had a skim of that; only thin milk is left. Call it "The third Vomit". Call it "Third time lucky". Call it "Colonel Lawrence – and after". Call it "Long after Colonel Lawrence". Call it "Too long after"... call it – oh, call it anything you don't like; being careful to keep my "L" name in inverted commas. Call it "Cape's Good Hope". Forget it.'[34]

On December 17th he wrote telling his mother that Clouds Hill was at last finished. The only work remaining was a cement-lined reservoir which he had asked Pat Knowles to build. It would collect water from the stream on the far side of the road and contain enough to help the fire brigade fight any heath fires threatening the cottage.

He spent Christmas week at Clouds Hill, which was warmed by its two log fires. Much of his time was passed upstairs, reading, writing letters, and listening to the gramophone. Sometimes in the evening Pat Knowles and another local friend would join him. On December 23rd Jock Chambers, one of Lawrence's friends from his first RAF enlistment, arrived unexpectedly. They spent the holiday clearing up after the builders, taking long walks, chopping wood for the fire. On the evening of Christmas Day he shared a tinned chicken with Chambers and Pat Knowles.

He found this relaxed company agreeable, having received a surfeit of over-affectionate messages from some of his other acquaintances. Not long afterwards he wrote to Lady Astor: 'Probably it would be wholesome for me to lose my heart – if that monstrous piece of machinery is capable of losing itself: for till now it has never cared for anyone, though much for places and things. Indeed I doubt these words of "hearts". People seem to my judgement to lose their heads rather than their hearts. Over the Christmas season two men and four women have sent me fervent messages of love, love carnal, not love rarified, you know: and I am uncomfortable towards six more of the people I meet, therefore.'[35]

He left Clouds Hill on Boxing Day, and after a brief visit to London returned to his Southampton lodgings. On the last day of the year he reflected on the changes that had taken place in his life during 1933, and wrote to H. S. Ede: 'Do you ever feel that there is a wall of glass between you and the street? You see the people scurrying and waving their arms – but no noise, no eddy of air and no touch? Well, that's been me since I left off living in barracks.'[36]

During 1934 Lawrence was to have little energy to spare for anything except his RAF duties. He told a friend: 'These boats occupy too much of my time. Yet I feel, as I do them, that they will be the last tangible things I do.'[37] In January the British Power Boat Company began building five more target launches, and he did not expect them to be finished before late March. Meanwhile, despite mounting expense, work continued at Clouds Hill. The water reservoir was completed in February and Pat Knowles began building a glass roof over it. Lawrence wrote: 'Pat goes on, charging me almost nothing, yet more than I have got. The bank has made me a heavy loan, on which we will finish it all, in about a month more. Then I shall not be able to afford to live there, alas! My last visit to London I went the round of the publishers I know, sounding them for a job in twelve months' time, when the R.A.F. leaves me. Sad, for I had hoped to live on my hump, and taste leisure at last. I try, however, for a job that will let me stay most of the time in Dorset.'[38] He had now decided to extend the roof over the water tank at one end to provide a kind of conservatory where he could work. Pat Knowles was to install there a pair of ornately carved doors Lawrence had brought back from Jidda in 1921, facing inwards so that they formed the end wall. On the outside they were to be protected by a second pair of doors. When the building was finished, it would be possible to open them, 'and then they will throw the study and the tank into connection with the air and the bushes'.[39]

By early April, this further work was almost finished, and he felt that the cottage would be ready for him to move into when he left the RAF in ten months' time. He wrote to his mother: 'The book-room lacks only its fender-cum-log-box. Then it is complete. The bath-room lacks only its bath-mat; and the boiler its final lagging of asbestos plaster. The upstairs room is complete, but for its beam-candle-sconce. The food-room alone remains to arrange, I plan to sheath its walls with aluminium foil; to fit an old ship's-bunk across the dark end, complete with drawers: to arrange its food-shelf, its table, perhaps a chair. Then Clouds Hill cottage is finished – no, I forgot a cast-iron fire-back for the book-room, and an air-vent to make the fire draw. But these are all small jobs, and could be finished in two months, if I had the time for them. As it is, I can attend to the place only by fits and starts, and so it drags on interminably.

'Our last doing was to sheath the bath-room walls in sheet cork, laid on in slabs of twelve inches by seven, and a sixteenth of an inch thick.

'We have also hung the door-leathers to the book-room and the upstairs room, on hinged door-rods of wrought iron. They are in natural cow-hide, and very successful.

'Pat works steadily at roofing the water-pool, which has now been full for six weeks, and does not leak at all. That is 7,000 gallons of water.

'The pool is not finished: it has still to be rendered over inside in fine cement; but we will not do that till the roof is finished, as rain or cold or the dust of a high wind would damage the final cementing. So Pat is now roofing it, slowly and single-handed. He has nearly finished the wooden framing and the sash-bars. Next week the floors of my little study at its north end and of the entrance-porch at the south end will be laid. Then the Jeddah gates go in'.[40]

In late March, after the new target launches had been completed, Lawrence had gone to Northwich, in Cheshire, for the acceptance trials of a small cargo vessel which the RAF had purchased for use in Singapore.

By the time the *Aquarius* sailed for Plymouth, with Lawrence on board, the press had learned of his presence. Journalists were reassured that 'there was no mystery about the visit. The Air Ministry had been looking for a small ship to carry stores for the Air Force, and the *Aquarius* was exactly suitable.'[41]

Press interest in Lawrence had been reawakened by the appearance of Liddell Hart's biography in early March. Shortly after his return from Northwich to Southampton, Lawrence complained that 'a gent, describing himself as the French Consul, rang the bell this morning and then produced a *News Chronicle* card. If it develops I shall have to move.'[42] A week later his name was in the papers again, this time because he had helped at a demonstration of high-speed boats given by the British Power Boat Company.

Far more alarming, however, was a news story in the *Daily Express*, based on a careful reading of Liddell Hart's book. It read:

NEW MYSTERY OF 'LAWRENCE OF ARABIA' WHAT IS HIS REAL NAME?'

A new mystery has arisen concerning Lawrence of Arabia – the famous Colonel T. E. Lawrence, who after the war changed his name by deed-poll to Shaw, and became Aircraftman Shaw.

The question now is this: was his real name ever Lawrence, or was it something else? It is one of Lawrence of Arabia's friends – Captain B. H. Liddell Hart – who creates the new mystery. He has written a book about Lawrence . . . and he begins by putting the name in quotation marks – thus 'T. E. Lawrence' – as the title. Then, on the first page, he says this:– 'The friends of his manhood called him "T.E.," for convenience, and to show that they recognised how *his adopted surnames – Lawrence*, Ross, Shaw, whatever they were – did not belong.'

Captain Liddell Hart says that Lawrence of Arabia's family were related to Sir Walter Raleigh, but he does not say what their name was . . . *Who's Who* does not say whose son Lawrence of Arabia was. The *Encyclopedia Britannica* says he came of an old Leicestershire family – presumably they were in Leicestershire before the time of Queen Elizabeth, when they settled in Ireland.

Lawrence of Arabia's father left Ireland, and 'T.E.' was born near Portmadoc.[43]

This piece of deduction led readers unpleasantly close to a secret that Lawrence did not want publicised. If someone thought of spending a few hours with Debrett, where the Chapman entry mentioned both the Leicestershire and Raleigh connections, they would probably deduce that Lawrence was related to this family. The probing and exposure that might result would be quite intolerable. Although weeks passed without a follow-up, he knew that the cutting would be on the files of every major newspaper, and that the quest for his true identity could be taken up again at any time. When he had insisted that Liddell Hart put Lawrence in inverted commas, he had expected people to assume that this was because he had changed his name to Shaw. He would surely not have made such a stipulation if he had thought that it would set journalists prying into his ancestry.

He now grew more fearful than ever of publicity and was perturbed to hear in late April from one of the trustees of *Revolt in the Desert* that another scheme was afoot to film the book. He found the idea of a film hateful and his letters show that he was beginning to drift into a state of depression. In early May he wrote: 'I'm tired. I want to get away and be at peace, so badly. That is what defeat means.'[44] A fortnight later he again complained that he was tired: 'So would you be if you had been thinking for months how to better so vague and intractable a thing as a boat. The mere driving them at 30 m.p.h. into the wind and spray is work. No matter. On March 12 next my service ends... and Clouds Hill is a hushed green place, noisy with birds only, and fertile only with weeds. There are twelve hundred books there (. . . all read once at least, and worth reading again) and four hundred gramophone records. "No books before 1850 and no music since" I say at rash moments: but it isn't true.'[45] The prospect of living in the cottage was increasingly in his thoughts. He told Charlotte Shaw: 'I feel rooted now, whenever I pass its door. Such a lovely little place, and so plain. It is ingenious, comfortable, bare and restful: and cheap to maintain.'[46]

By the mid-thirties extreme right-wing politics were gathering strength all over Europe. In England, there was Oswald Mosley's British Union of Fascists. As with all such movements, some adherents spent their time trying to attract famous people who might be persuaded to endorse the political programme. In May, Lawrence refused an invitation to a Fascist dinner, commenting frivolously: 'I want your movement to hurry up, and put an end to the license of the daily Press. It will be glorious to dance on the combined cess-pit that holds the dead *Daily Express*, *Daily Chronicle* and *Daily Herald*.

'My dictatorship programme would also uproot all telegraph poles and bury the wires, assume ownership of all the sea-beaches – and scrag the police.' He signed the letter: 'Yours not very seriously, T. E. Shaw'.[47] At the time, he was trying to get some telegraph wires that ran along the road outside his cottage put underground.

As his reply was not totally negative, the Fascists tried again. This time he wrote more firmly: 'Politics in England mean either violent change (I care not enough for anything to lead me into that) or wasting twenty years of one's time and all one's strength on parading to the House of Commons. The meanest Government servant has more power than any unofficial M.P. [i.e. a Member of Parliament not holding Ministerial office]. So I can't afford politics, either.

'I'm sorry you think the youth now growing up lacking in character and guts. I have now served for twelve and a half years in the R.A.F. and nearly lost what withered heart I possess, (at forty-five), to my fellows, here. They are so definite and happy, I think. They seem to get much more out of life than my contemporaries did, twenty-five years ago. I should have called them a cleaner and better generation. I don't see how anybody in daily touch with working fellows could have dismal thoughts of England . . .

'No, please don't make me any part of your Club. I'm prepared only to serve. . . and I'm very tired: even of serving.'[48]

Some weeks later an American commentator put the suggestion to Liddell Hart that Lawrence might become 'the symbol of a fascist type of movement in Great Britain.' He asked: 'If this possibility exists I should appreciate being informed as to his actual and potential influence on political developments. If such an interpretation is beside the mark, I should appreciate a candid appraisal of his status in British and Imperial affairs.'[49]

Liddell Hart had recently discussed the Fascist movement with Lawrence, and his reply lays to rest the speculation which has so often been raised on this point. He wrote: 'With regard to your enquiry, I have had numerous suggestions and approaches from the spokesmen of the younger generation of this country, concerning the possibility of Lawrence taking the lead in a new movement which would break away from ordinary party lines, and those approaches have come from the Fascist side, as well as from young Liberals, Conservatives and Socialists.

'But, from my knowledge of him, I doubt whether he would lend himself to such a proposal, at any rate in the propagandist stages of any such movement. Should events ever come to a real crisis, then it is possible that he might agree to take an active role – if only for a few weeks.

'That at present he is, in the eyes of a great number, a symbol of their ideals, is an undoubted fact but it cannot be said that he has any actual influence, still less any part, in British and Imperial affairs.'[50]

The last word should rest with Mosley himself, who wrote in his autobiography: '. . . Neither did I meet nor have any communication with T. E. Lawrence, despite many later rumours to the contrary . . . I knew nothing of him apart from reading the *Seven Pillars of Wisdom*'[51]

In November Lawrence received another proposal for his future. It too was wholly inappropriate to his talents and ambitions. Montagu Norman, Governor of the Bank of England, had conceived the idea that he would make an excellent Secretary for the Bank. Norman had never met Lawrence, but asked a mutual acquaintance, Francis Rodd, to act as intermediary. Lawrence refused the offer graciously but firmly.[52]

That month he had moved to Bridlington for what was to be his last RAF work, supervising the winter overhaul of ten fast launches. There was a great deal of work to be done and barely enough time to do it. He saw little prospect of getting away until the spring, and wrote: 'As for my ever being free to call on anybody, while I'm still R.A.F., it doesn't look probable. This twelve years' compulsory grind and absence from the world has made a basic difference in me, I think. Now I take it as natural, and even after I'm free, I fancy I shall still keep apart, and let alone the people I used to know. I mean the important people. When I meet one now by chance I feel so hopelessly out of it. My sort seems to be the plain sort, for with them I can chat away and reach common ground.'[53]

As the end of Lawrence's Air Force service drew near, he quite frequently referred in letters to his uncertainty and anxiety about the future. He did not write obsessively about it, but repeated similar thoughts to many different correspondents. From these remarks it is possible to discern the main lines of his thinking about the years ahead.

His final two years' work on boats had been extremely tiring, and he knew, above all, that he needed a rest. Fatigue is a constant refrain in his letters during 1934. He also believed that it would be foolish to take any major decision before he needed to: 'I have determined to keep my mind wholly blank about futures, till the time comes.'[54] His friends were

showering him with suggestions of literary work, Government appointments, and so on, but he refused to make any commitment. If he waited
long enough, someone was certain to make a proposal that appealed
to him very strongly. For the present, that had not happened, and he
told a friend: 'I wish there was any one thing in the world that I wanted
to do. Perhaps vacancy will breed a wish'.[55] Likewise, he wrote at the
end of the year: 'here I am still strong and trenchant-minded, but with
nothing in my hand.'[56]

Until he knew what he wanted to do, he would live at Clouds Hill. He
believed that the 'last thing desirable is activity for the sake of activity. I
hope I have enough mind for it to be quietly happy by itself. So I shall not
do anything until it becomes necessary: or at least that is my hope.'[57]

This first stage of his retirement was to be a deliberate experiment. He
wrote to Cape: 'don't conceive of me as needing immediate work . . . I am
promising myself a huge rest and sample-time, to see if (a) I am happy
doing nothing, and (b) if I have money enough for it. Granted (a) and (b)
you'll hear no more of me. My heart tells me that I am finished.'[58] Yet he
had also written: 'The finding myself outside what has been my frame and
support for thirteen years will be a test of my stability: and we shall see
what happens. I am very much afraid for myself, and rather miserable.'[59]

The reason for this fear is apparent from other letters: despite his
elaborate preparations at Clouds Hill, he was not sure whether he would
be able to bear living on his own. The risk, as he told Charlotte Shaw, was
that he would 'go back to the self of 1920 and 1921, a crazy pelican
feeding not its young but its spirit-creations upon its bodily strength. I had
hoped, all these years, that I was not going to be alone again.'[60]

Another problem would be lack of money. He had hoped that by 1935
his accumulated capital would produce an income of £3 a week. However,
he had spent lavishly on Clouds Hill and in helping needy friends. Then
the interest rate had fallen and, as a result, he would have to live on only
twenty-five shillings a week, just over a third of what he had planned.
This would be a very real handicap. He wrote to Frederic Manning:
'Candidly, the prospect of unalloyed leisure terrifies me, for I shall not
have enough money to kill time with travel and motor cars and calls and
meals.'[61] The sacrifices would be greater than that: he would be unable to
afford much use of his Brough, and he therefore bought a pedal cycle.
For the same reason, he would have to cut down the number of letters
he wrote. He began to tell friends that he would in future spend only
three pence a week on postage. If it proved impossible to live within

twenty-five shillings weekly, his experiment with freedom would come to an ignominious end: he would be forced to take up paid work, probably editing, reviewing, or translating.

Meanwhile his own larger projects hovered at the back of his mind: he could write a major work about the RAF, or try a biography of Roger Casement, the Irish patriot hanged as a traitor by the British in 1916. He had mentioned this last project several times to Charlotte Shaw during recent years.

The one thing that was certain was that he would miss the Air Force, which had provided him with a home and companionship and interesting work for twelve years. As the date for leaving approached, he would write: 'I'm still all amazed at what to do next. I want a rest, and time to think about things, and I'd like a holiday, and to wander about England for a bit... and I don't think I'll have enough cash even for bread and butter, after the first year. However, we'll see.'[62] He told another friend that, after February, 'I've got to look after myself: not immediately, for I have enough for at least six months, but as soon as is convenient. I have not an idea in my head: various jobs have been offered, but none of them attractive. Possibly I shall fall back on my cottage and see how much – or rather how little – I really need.'[63]

During the weeks he spent at Bridlington, Lawrence lived at a small hotel that was let to the Air Force for billets during the winter months. He became friends with Flight-Lieutenant Sims, a retired officer working as Adjutant at the RAF training station of which Bridlington was an outpost. They had in common an interest in photography and a love of classical music, and Lawrence was soon spending most of his weekends with the Sims family at their cottage in the village of Hornsea.

On December 21st he had to go to London for a meeting at the Air Ministry, and afterwards he went briefly to Clouds Hill. Jock Chambers was expected, but the weather was bad and he did not come. Lawrence shared his Christmas chicken with Pat Knowles. They talked about his plans for the cottage and also for installing a small printing press, which was to be in operation by the beginning of 1936. It was to be housed in a first-floor building constructed over the water tank. Lawrence intended to print a small edition of *The Mint*, followed by a book of poetry: probably the edition of Meleager he had thought of after the war.

By the end of the year he was back in Bridlington, but in late January he went south again to see Alexander Korda, who was responsible for the new plan to film *Revolt in the Desert*. Lawrence was determined to stop it, if at all possible, and found to his delight that Korda made no difficulty: 'He was quite unexpectedly sensitive . . . seemed to understand at once when I put to him the inconveniences his proposed film of *Revolt* would set in my path . . . and ended the discussion by agreeing that it should not be attempted without my consent. He will not announce its abandonment, because while he has it on his list other producers will avoid thought of it. But it will not be done. You can imagine how this gladdens me.'[64]

Afterwards he went to Fordingbridge, where he sat for Augustus John, who 'painted with great ease and surety . . . a little head-and-shoulders of me in oil. R.A.F. uniform, with cap on head. I think it much the best thing of me he has ever done. It sparkles with life, is gay-coloured and probably not unlike my real face, when thinking. So lively and clean. He himself agreed that it had come off and was comforted, as lately he has found it hard to finish anything. In his pleasure he went on to do two charcoal drawings of me, three-quarter lengths, standing – and then gave me the better of them. I have put it with [Wilfred] Merton, who took over the business from Emery Walker, and have asked him to copy it, for safety. A fine swagger drawing: small head, thin body and big knees!'[65] He asked Merton to produce a hundred prints of the portrait. They were to be the frontispiece to his private edition of *The Mint*, the first book printed at Clouds Hill.

In late January, he received a letter from Robert Graves, who had been asked by *The Times* to draft a two-thousand-word obituary of Lawrence which would be held on their files in case of need. Graves suggested that Lawrence might like to write it himself, promising that no one would know. During these last weeks of his RAF service Lawrence had been thinking deeply about his life, and the request provided an opportunity to put his conclusions on paper. He wrote back: 'Yes, Hogarth did the morgue-men a first sketch of me in 1920, and they are right to overhaul their stocks . . . I won't touch it myself, but if you do, don't give too much importance to what I did in Arabia during the war. I feel that the Middle Eastern settlement put through by Winston Churchill and Young and me in 1921 (which stands in every particular... if only the other Peace Treaties did!) should weigh more than fighting. And I feel too that this settlement should weigh less than my life since 1922, for the conquest of the last element, the air, seems to me the only major task of our generation; and I have convinced myself that progress to-day is made not by the single genius, but by the common effort. To me it is the multitude of rough transport drivers filling all the roads of England every night, who make this the mechanical age. And it is the airmen, the mechanics, who are overcoming the air, not the Mollisons and Orlebars [two renowned pilots]. The genius raids, but the common people occupy and possess. Wherefore I stayed in the ranks and served to the best of my ability, much influencing my fellow airmen towards a pride in themselves and their inarticulate duty. I tried to make them see – with some success.

'That for eight years, and now for the last four I have been so curiously fortunate as to share in a little revolution we have made in boat design. People have thought we were at finality there, for since 1850 ships have merely got bigger. When I went into R.A.F. boats in 1929, every type was an Admiralty design. All were round-bottomed, derived from the first hollow tree, with only a fin, called a keel, to delay their rolling about and over. They progressed by pushing their own bulk of water aside. Now (1935) not one type of R.A.F. boat in production is naval... We have found, chosen, selected or derived our own sorts: they have (power for power) three times the speed of their predecessors, less weight, less cost, more room, more safety, more seaworthiness. As their speed increases, they rise out of the water and run over its face. They cannot roll, nor pitch, having no pendulum nor period, but a subtly modelled planing bottom and sharp edges.

'Now I do not claim to have made these boats. They have grown out of the joint experience, skill and imaginations of many men. But I can (secretly) feel that they owe to me their opportunity and their acceptance. The pundits met them with a fierce hostility: all the R.A.F. soldiers, and all the Navy, said that they would break, sink, wear out, be unmanageable. To-day we are advising the War Office in refitting the coast defences entirely with boats of our model, and the Admiralty has specified them for the modernised battleships: while the Germans, Chinese, Spanish and Portuguese Governments have adopted them! In inventing them we have had to make new engines, new auxiliaries, use new timbers, new metals, new materials. It has been five years of intense and co-ordinated progress. Nothing now hinders the application of our design to big ships – except the conservatism of man, of course. Patience. It cannot be stopped now.

'All this boasting is not to glorify myself, but to explain; and here enters my last subject for this letter, your strictures upon the changes I have made in myself since the time we felt so much together at Oxford.

You're quite right about the change. I was then trying to write; to be perhaps an artist (for the *Seven Pillars* had pretensions towards design, and was written with great pains as prose) or to be at least cerebral. My head was aiming to create intangible things. That's not well put: all creation is tangible. What I was trying to do, I suppose, was to carry a superstructure of ideas upon or above anything I made.

'Well, I failed that. By measuring myself against such people as yourself and Augustus John, I could feel that I was not made out of the same stuff. Artists excite and attract me; seduce me. Almost I could be an artist, but there is a core that puts on the brake. If I knew what it was I could tell you, or become one of you. Only I can't.

'So I changed direction, right, and went into the R.A.F. after straightening out that eastern tangle with Winston, a duty that fell to me, I having been partly the cause of the tangle. How well the Middle East has done: it, more than any part of the world, has gained from that war.

'However, as I said, I went into the R.A.F. to serve a mechanical purpose, not as leader but as a cog of the machine. The key-word, I think, is machine. I have been mechanical since, and a good mechanic, for my self-training to become an artist has greatly widened my field of view. I leave it to others to say whether I chose well or not: one of the benefits of being part of the machine is that one learns that one doesn't matter!

'One thing more. You remember my writing to you when I first went into the R.A.F. that it was the nearest modern equivalent of going into a monastery in the Middle Ages. That was right in more than one sense. Being a mechanic cuts one off from all real communication with women. There are no women in the machines, in any machine. No woman, I believe, can understand a mechanic's happiness in serving his bits and pieces.'[66]

The content of this letter reflects Lawrence's particular relationship with Graves in two important respects. The final paragraph quoted refers to his differences with Laura Riding, which had been discussed at length by Graves in the letter to which this was a reply. Also, there is little here about Lawrence's books or his continuing ambition to write. He had long been reluctant to discuss his work with Graves, and in any case it was for Graves, rather than himself, to pass judgment on his literary achievement. His true feelings may be gathered from a statement made to Edward Garnett some years previously: 'And in the distant future, if the distant future deigns to consider my insignificance, I shall be appraised rather as a man of letters than as a man of action.'[67]

A few of the Englishmen who had taken part in the Arab Revolt liked to keep in contact with Lawrence, and when they wrote to him he generally made a point of replying. One of these was T. W. Beaumont, who had served as a gunner in the Hejaz Armoured Car Company.

It seems that Beaumont wrote to Lawrence for the first time in 1931, as Lawrence's reply to this letter indicates that there had been no contact between them since the war. Beaumont wrote again, and Lawrence sent him three further replies, in December 1933, June 1934, and on 31st January 1935. None of these letters was of any consequence, but in the last, Lawrence mentioned his impending retirement.

A few days after sending it, he was warned by the Air Ministry that someone from the press had been making enquiries about his movements. Then, on February 17th, the *Sunday Express* published an article which read:

LAWRENCE OF ARABIA
LEAVING THE AIR FORCE ON MARCH 1
'REALLY SORRY'

Lawrence of Arabia, now Aircraftman T. E. Shaw, is to leave the Royal Air Force on March 1, when his discharge becomes effective.

In a letter to a Yorkshireman who served under him in Arabia, he wrote: 'My time runs out a month hence, and I shall be very sorry. The work passes my time. The last twelve years would have been long without it. Yes, I shall be really sorry.'

The letter, dated January 31 last, from Bridlington, was received by Mr. T. W. Beaumont, now a foreman in a Dewsbury textile mill. Mr. Beaumont was a machine-gunner in the 'Suicide Club', a detachment of twenty-six men, sent to Arabia in 1917 for secret service work under Lawrence.

FEELING OF PEACE

Lawrence plans to retire to his cottage in Dorset. This is how he describes it in his last letter to Mr. Beaumont. 'It is a cottage in the middle of a great heath of bracken and heather. Two rooms, no bed, no kitchen, and no drains, but a spring in the garden and a feeling of utter peace. I may go there for a while after my discharge.' . . .

T. E. Shaw has written four times to Mr. Beaumont since 1931. All the letters reveal uncertainty as to the future. 'I shall be rather lost in charge of myself after all these years,' he writes.

A collector has offered Mr. Beaumont £20 for one of these letters, but although he is a poor man he refuses to entertain the offer.[68]

This article alerted every newspaper to Lawrence's imminent retirement, with consequences that Lawrence cannot have begun to imagine as he worked out his last days at Bridlington. Just before the end of his service he wrote: 'I've been frantically busy, working all the time to finish these RAF boats – and successfully too. They are in the water two days ahead of schedule. It is comforting to plan a campaign of overhaul, and work it all out according to rule. And a minor benefit has been that in the rush I have not had time to listen to my last minutes in the Air Force ticking out.'[69] He wrote to Pat Knowles that he would 'push off by bike in a day or two for Clouds Hill, travelling by very slow stages, but arriving there in very scruff order some time in early March.

'I shall be glad to get away, now.'[70]

CHAPTER 45

Clouds Hill

March – May 1935

LAWRENCE cycled away from Bridlington on 25th February 1935, five days earlier than the date announced by the *Sunday Express*. He was able to go early because he had not used up his annual entitlement to leave. The night before he left, he had written a mild rebuke to Beaumont, whose lack of discretion had so unfortunately stirred up newspaper interest in his doings: 'Your contribution sent the pressmen scurrying about Bridlington, I believe: but vainly. They are proper tripe hounds, keep clear of them, for your own sake.

'If it's true that you got a good offer for my letters by all means take it! They are your property but the copyright (that is the right to publish) remains mine always. Sell them cheerfully but for the Lord's sake don't let the pressmen read or repeat them, it's pretty beastly to have them snooping around the place.'[1]

Had Lawrence's departure from the RAF been unnoticed for a few weeks, it would have become 'old news,' hardly worth reporting. As it was, the advance warning turned his retirement into a news event. Journalists from every popular paper were now on his track, determined to secure at least as much coverage as their rivals.

As he cycled southwards, Lawrence had little idea of the reception that was in store for him when he reached Clouds Hill. But for the moment the press was unable to locate him, and had to make do with snippets culled in Bridlington. Under the headline 'Lawrence of Arabia cycles into the "Unknown" ', the *Evening Standard* reported: 'Somewhere between Bridlington and the Dorset coast is a cyclist, hatless and with a rucksack on his back, seeking peace and quietness in little villages where he is unknown. The cyclist is Colonel Lawrence of Arabia, who, until a few days ago, was also Aircraftman Shaw . . .

'His first act when he received the official R.A.F. papers of his discharge was to ask his fellow men in the marine section to help him to spend his gratuity before he left the town. He bought two rows of stalls in the local picture theatre, and afterwards there was a celebration in the hotel where Aircraftman Shaw and the other men were billeted . . . During his career he had appeared, in some strange way, in many R.A.F. stations where secret and important experiments were being carried out . . . Bridlington, with its power boats and targets, is still a "hush hush" station of the Air Ministry . . . he did not reveal to any person where he went when he was given various leaves of absence . . .

'A friend came up to him when he was about to cycle away, and Shaw said:

"I don't know where I am going, except that eventually I shall be reaching my country home in Dorset, but it may be a month before I arrive there.

"I am going to cycle each day and sleep each night in some village which appeals to me because of its peace and quietness.

"If I find a village which really pleases me I may stop there several days. I am sorry to be leaving the R.A.F., but I am also happy in the thought that I shall now have real freedom.

"I have made no plans for the future, and I am leaving it to take care of itself." '[2]

Lawrence meant to visit Frederic Manning in Lincolnshire and then go on to Cambridge and London. On February 28th, however, he learned that Manning had died. The news seemed to bear in some peculiar way on his own predicament. He wrote to Peter Davies: 'Some friends of mine, in dying, have robbed me; Hogarth and Aubrey Herbert are two empty places which no one and nothing can ever fill. Whereas Doughty and Hardy and Manning had earned their release. Yet his going takes away a person of great kindness, exquisite and pathetic. It means one rare thing the less in our setting. You will be very sad.

'My losing the R.A.F. numbs me, so that I haven't much feeling to spare for the while. In fact I find myself wishing all the time that my own curtain would fall. It seems as if I had finished now.'[3]

When he reached Clouds Hill he found, to his horror, that journalists and photographers were waiting for him. He left again immediately, and cycled to London. Sir Herbert Baker had moved out of Barton Street, and Lawrence no longer had free lodgings available there. Instead, he rented a room in Richmond as 'Mr. T. E. Smith.' In the belief that the journalists would eventually grow tired of watching Clouds Hill, he decided to pass some time touring southern England on his bicycle. He told a friend: 'Probably I shall wander for most of this year about England'.[4]

This unexpected press attention was an additional strain at a moment in his life which he would in any case have found very difficult. His dislike of publicity had grown steadily since 1922, when it had cost him his place in the RAF. Unscrupulous journalists had caused him great difficulties in 1929 and again in 1933. Now, they had shattered the privacy of his only home.

He had foreseen that the transition to solitary retirement at Clouds Hill would call for calm and mental fortitude. However, his fragile mental equilibrium had been dealt a heavy blow, and his fear of the press became almost irrational. The sense of being hunted added to his unhappiness about leaving the Air Force. He was afflicted with a growing sense of hopelessness, and during the next few weeks his letters became increasingly depressed. Nevertheless, he was still able to see his predicament from a rational viewpoint. Thus he wrote to T. B. Marson on March 6th: 'At the moment I'm hiding in London, with pressmen besieging my cottage in Dorset... and I feel lost and aimless and *cold* somehow. Ah well, that will pass.'[5]

On March 14th he paid five shillings for a year's membership of the Youth Hostels Association, and set off for Dorset to explore the situation at Clouds Hill. When he arrived the following day he found no pressmen, and sent a telegram to Ralph Isham, then visiting England, inviting him to come down. On March 17th, however, a Sunday, the journalists and photographers appeared again. They shouted at him to come out and speak to them, banging incessantly on the door. Eventually, in a state of utter rage, he made his escape through the rear of the garden, after hitting one of his persecutors in the eye. He cycled as far as Romsey that night and on the next day reached London.

It was obvious that whenever he returned to Clouds Hill the press would soon come after him. The only solution would be to use what was left of his influence, and appeal directly to those who were really responsible for this nuisance. He therefore spent March 19th visiting the Press Association and London photographic agencies, begging them to call off their men. Afterwards he wrote optimistically to Pat Knowles: 'There are good hopes, I fancy, of persuading all of them to leave me alone . . . I shall know for certain in about three days' time; and if successful, I shall try to get back to Clouds Hill early next week.'[6] On the same day he wrote to Churchill: 'My R.A.F. discharge happened about three weeks ago, and I've since had to run three times from my cottage in Dorset (where I want to live) through pressure of newspaper men. Each time I've taken refuge in London, but life here is expensive, and I cannot go on moving about indefinitely.

'My plan is to try and persuade the press people, the big noises, to leave me alone. If they agree to that the free-lances find no market for their activities.

'What I am hoping from you is a means of approach to Esmond Harmsworth, who is the new Chairman of the Newspaper Proprietors Association. He used to know me in Paris, sixteen years ago, but will have forgotten. If you could tell him I exist, and very much want to see him, I could put my case before him in ten minutes and get a Yes or No . . .

'I'm sorry to appeal in this way; but they have got me properly on the run. I blacked the eye of one photographer last Sunday and had to escape over the back of the hedge!'[7]

A week later, he was more confident about the situation. With the help of an official at the Newspaper Society, he had been to see the heads of several press agencies and had reached working agreements with them. He had also seen Harmsworth, who had asked him for a letter to put before the Newspaper Proprietors Association. A surviving draft of this letter reads: 'I am presuming on a brief acquaintance of many years ago to approach you now (as Chairman of the N.P.A.) on a personal matter.

'You may have heard that about a month ago I was discharged from the R.A.F. upon completion of my engagement for twelve years with the colours.

'I take it this discharge marks the end of the active part of my life. I returned to this cottage, which has been mine for many years, with the intention of settling quietly in retirement.

'Unfortunately, the quietude has been a complete failure. Reporters and press photographers have visited the place in some numbers, anxious to photograph it and me, or to ascertain my future intentions. This is a very simple district and their enquiries after me have given my country neighbours only too much to talk about. Their eagerness to find me drove me out: and after I had gone it led them to break the tiles of my roof, split the door and trample all over my patch of land in search of me. I have had to ask the local police to patrol the place, in my absence.

'I am writing to you to ask if your Association can help to relieve me of some of this attention? I quite realise that many of the visitors are freelance: but even these find their market in the biggest newspapers. It would be a great comfort to me if editors could generally deny me further space.

'As I said at the beginning of this letter, my retirement is, I hope, for good. I am not under any further obligation to the Government. I am not looking for any employment. I am not writing, or intending to write, any other books: nor am I likely to go abroad again. I have saved just enough money to keep me by myself in modest idleness, and I am very much looking forward to doing nothing. I think I can promise you never again to earn a paragraph, and if you can do anything to help keep me out of sight I shall be most grateful.'[8]

By the beginning of April Lawrence was back at Clouds Hill. There was no sign of any pressmen and he began trying to settle down. He told a friend that he was 'hoping to stay here quite a while, finishing off my cottage after my own liking. There is pleasure (and engrossment) in arranging and fixing one's surroundings. I find I spend nearly the whole day, beginning job after job and laying them aside, part-done. The sense of infinite time, all my own, is so new.'[9]

One thing that cheered him was a letter about *The Mint* from John Buchan, who had written: 'It is the kind of document which has never been produced before about any service. One thing is clear to me, that you are a great natural writer.

'I have been thinking a great deal about what you told me – that you feel an impulse to write a book of some kind. The easiest form would be a set of pictures and reflections. Your pictures will always be brilliant, and your reflections are the most thought-provoking things I have come across for many a day. But that kind of thing is not a recognised literary form, and one naturally thinks of fiction. Fiction demands a certain kind of shape in the way of a story, for which you may not be very much inclined; but if you condescend to adopt the story form you would write a very great novel. You can write brilliant narrative when you try, as parts of the *Seven Pillars* showed.

'The other literary form I have thought of is biography. If there is any historic figure who really interests you, you would be the perfect biographer, for you can see a long way into the human heart, and you have an amazing power of imaginative construction.'[10]

Lawrence's reply shows that the idea of writing was still very much in his thoughts: 'I take it from what you say that if ever a subject does arise to excite my writing faculty, I shall be doing no harm in letting rip. At the moment there is no such excitement. All my twelve years in the Air Force I'd hoped to be let go on a long Flying Boat cruise, to keep its log à la Hakluyt. A novel – no, I think not: my writing practice has all been to put down more and more exactly what I have seen or felt: invention would come very hard. A biography – yes, I had wanted to write Casement, Sir Roger; but the obstacle is that the Government refuse all access to those confiscated diaries from which purported extracts were circulated to influential people when he was condemned; and without them there cannot be a life of him written.'[11]

Although he had settled for the moment at Clouds Hill, he had not given up the idea of travelling round England that summer. He told George Brough that he had only ridden his motorcycle twice since the beginning of the year: 'The pushbike is a reality, though. I came down here from Yorkshire on it and have toured much of the south of England on it in the last three weeks. It is dull hard work when the wind is against: but in lanes, and sheltered places and in calms or before winds, wholly delightful. So quiet: one hears all the country noises. Cheap – very! not tiring, up to sixty or seventy miles a day, which is all that I achieve, with sightseeing: and very clean on a wet road.

'The loss of my R.A.F. job halves my income, so that my motor cycling would have been much reduced for the future, even without this 30 m.p.h. limit idea. I had half-thoughts of a touring sidecar, for long jaunts, with the push-bike for leisured local trips, but we shall see.'[12]

The cost of running the Brough was a very real problem. On the same day he wrote to another friend that his present life at Clouds Hill was an experiment: 'have I saved enough to live on in decency, or must I make more? The sooner I can find the answer to that, the better for me . . . As for the Brough, that is easy. I have licensed it, and yesterday I rode into Poole to buy some necessary fittings for the house. It goes like stink, and is altogether a marvellous machine. But I should hesistate to call it necessary . . . If it is, I shall have to save somewhere else, live below estimate, or make more; to be able to afford it. My earning power is potentially considerable: but I hate using it.

'You will observe that the whole essay is deliberate, an endeavour to enjoy idleness. That is (by modern standards) not a very moral aim. I do not care. I feel that I have worked throughout a reasonably long working life, given all I can to every cause which harnessed me, and earned a rest. My "expectation" is less than twenty years, and the last few years of that twenty will be diminishingly pleasant, as infirmities increase. If I am to taste the delights of natural England, as has been my life's wish, I must do it before I grow really old. And I must do it on my own: not at others' expense.

'I have no dependents, no sense of public spirit, or of duty to my neighbour. I like to live alone for 80% of my days, and to be let alone by 80% of my fellow-men, and all my fellow-women below sixty years of age. The golden rule seems to direct me to live peacefully in my cottage.'[13]

After a few days at Clouds Hill he was beginning to settle into a régime. He started inviting friends down to stay, telling them: 'I think I am going to be happy and comfortable here'.[14] Jock Chambers promised to stay for a fortnight, arriving in late April; in May his place would be taken by E. M. Forster, and after that Lawrence was expecting a friend from Cranwell. In the meantime he worked at improvements to the cottage. He wrote to a service friend: 'I sleep in a sleeping bag, anywhere on the floors: and go to Bovington for a daily meal. That is called the simple life. I think I shall like it, but for the moment the place is in an awful mess, and I have so many odd jobs to do that I can finish nothing. So the general confusion grows. By midsummer I hope to be tidier and cleaner and more comfortable.'[15]

His latest project was to install a porthole in the smaller of the upstairs rooms, and he wrote to find out if T. B. Marson, who lived at Inverkeithing in Scotland, could obtain one from a shipbreaker: 'It is for a slip of a roomlet upstairs in my cottage – too small for any manufactured bed: so I built into it a bunk, of ship-cabin type, with drawers beneath for my clothes. A rough job I made of it, but it works. Only it is too dark. A window is not desirable, just there: but a ship's port-hole would be perfectly in keeping . . . It should be the gunmetal frame (circular) and hinged glass: size – largish, if possible . . . I would like it cut out complete with a square of plating . . . My notion is to cement the four edges into the brick wall and so have the job complete . . .

'I hope this eccentric proposal will not lead you into great trouble: abandon it, if it offers to become arduous. Only the notion of a real port-hole by my imitation bunk in my simili-cabin strikes me as happy in the last degree. Should they be cutting up some ship or other in the harbour, it might be easily obtained.

'Finishing off, or rather fitting up the cottage is the only pursuit that interests me, at the moment. I am grateful for its quiet and the loneliness: but lost, all the same.'[16] Marson duly obtained a porthole, from HMS *Tiger*. It arrived at Clouds Hill on April 17th. Meanwhile, Lawrence had acquired some aluminium foil to line the bunk-room walls.

Even though he was doing most of the work himself, there were further costs. He explained to Buxton that he had 'embarked on this new building, and on a fire pump and other things. By the end of May all these capital expenses will be over. I shall then again sum up the situation and decide how I stand. My true living expenses the last three weeks have been 22/- weekly, which is encouraging . . . I shall not ask you to send me a regular allowance down here till after this capital expenditure is over . . .

'My little cottage is charming, I think, for what it is. What ails me is this odd sense of being laid aside before being worn out. However I mustn't bore you with that, and Time is on my side.'[17]

By April 20th, after three weeks without interference from the press, Lawrence was beginning to recover his balance. Letters continued to arrive from literary friends, all of whom were willing to suggest interesting projects. For the time being, however, the only thing Lawrence felt certain about was that he wanted to remain at Clouds Hill. He wrote to Bruce Rogers on May 6th that he was 'sitting in my cottage rather puzzled to find out what has happened to me, is happening and will happen. At present the feeling is mere bewilderment. I imagine leaves must feel like this after they have fallen from their tree and until they die. Let's hope that will not be my continuing state.

'Money is very short, and this is the only spot, apparently, where I can afford to live: but it is too soon to judge of that. In a few months' time I will know for sure if my savings are enough, or not. Meanwhile I am practising a not un-amusing penury – or parsimony, rather. Also I work enough at wood cutting and gathering, pipe-laying and building, to tire me out thoroughly by each early afternoon... and then follows a heavenly laze, in the sun, if available, or by my fires if not.'[18]

The following day he wrote contentedly to E. M. Forster: 'Your arrival will be marked by the setting of a white stone into the new wall. Wool Station: taxi to here: any day after the 14th. Superb.

'Clouds Hill has now two inhabitants: Pat Knowles and me. He lives west end [i.e. the cottage on the far side of the road], and I east end. We feed in his place and very simply. We will try to make you[r stay], if not comfortable, at least endurable for a few days. Splendid.'[19] Like many of the other letters he had sent since retiring to Clouds Hill, this was written on the back of a printed card which read: 'To tell you that in future I shall write very few letters. T.E.S.'

It was on this day that he learned there were real prospects of further work for the Government. Ramsay MacDonald was shortly to retire as head of the National Government, and Stanley Baldwin would take over. Lawrence received a letter from Nancy Astor, who wrote: 'I believe when the Government re-organizes you will be asked to help re-organize the Defence forces. I will tell you what I have done already about it.

'If you will come to Cliveden Saturday, the last Saturday in May [actually June 1st], you will never regret it. Please, please come. Lionel [Curtis], Pat [Mrs. Curtis], Philip [Lord Lothian], and, for the most important, Stanley Baldwin. Please think about this.'[20] He replied by return: 'No: wild mares would not at present take me away from Clouds Hill. It is an earthly paradise and I am staying here till I feel qualified for it. Also there is something broken in the works, as I told you: my will, I think. In this mood I would not take on any job at all. So do not commit yourself to advocating me, lest I prove a non-starter.

'Am well, well-fed, full of company, laborious and innocent-customed.'[21] A few days later he wrote to another friend that he was 'sitting in my cottage and getting used to an empty life.'[22] However, he expected this spell to come to an end, and when it did, he would begin to get about again.

On May 11th, a Saturday, Lawrence received a letter from Henry Williamson, announcing that he would be driving from Devon to London in three days' time, and proposing to call at Clouds Hill unless the weather was wet. Williamson wrote that he wanted to leave the typescript of an unpublished work by the late V. M. Yeates, whose *Winged Victory*, a book about air fighting in the war, had been greatly admired by Lawrence.

The only way Lawrence could be sure of getting a reply to Devon before Williamson set out was to send a telegram. In mid-morning of Monday May 13th, he rode his Brough to the post office at Bovington Camp and sent a wire which read simply: 'Lunch Tuesday wet fine cottage one mile north Bovington Camp'.[23] At the same time he sent off a parcel of books to Jock Chambers, who had returned to London.

On the way back to the cottage, while riding at about 40 m.p.h., he suddenly came upon two boy cyclists in a dip in the road. He swerved to avoid them, but one was knocked down and fell without serious injury. Lawrence himself was thrown from his machine. When help arrived, he was taken unconscious to the camp hospital at Bovington.

Lawrence had suffered very severe brain damage in the accident. He remained in a coma for six days while his strength gradually failed and finally, on 19th May 1935, he died. Had he lived, he would have been almost completely paralysed, and would have known nothing whatsoever of his past.

His funeral took place at St Nicholas' Church in Moreton, on May 21st. Six friends from different periods of his life acted as pall bearers. They were Ronald Storrs, Eric Kennington, Corporal Bradbury, Private Russell, Pat Knowles, and Stewart Newcombe. Among those present were Winston Churchill, Nancy Astor, Alan Dawnay, Lord Lloyd, Lord Winterton, Sir John Salmond, Philip Graves, Lionel Curtis, Mrs Thomas Hardy, A. P. Wavell, Jonathan Cape, Bruce Rogers, B. H. Liddell Hart, Augustus John, and Siegfried Sassoon.

That day a message from George V to A. W. Lawrence was published in The Times. It read: 'The King has heard with sincere regret of the death of your brother, and deeply sympathizes with you and your family in this sad loss.

'Your brother's name will live in history, and the King gratefully recognises his distinguished services to his country and feels that it is tragic that the end should have come in this manner to a life still so full of promise.'

Envoi

As for harnessing to my go-cart the eternal force – well, no:
I pushed my go-cart into the eternal stream, and so it went
faster than the ones that are pushed cross-stream or
up-stream. I did not believe finally in the Arab movement:
but thought it necessary, in its time and place.
It has justified itself hugely, since the war, too . . .
I am still puzzled as to how far the individual counts:
a lot, I fancy, if he pushes the right way.

T. E. Lawrence to Frederic Manning
May 15th 1930

His best epitaph is perhaps from Pliny's letter to Tacitus (xvi. 6):

Equidem beatos puto quibus deorum munere datum est aut facere scribenda aut scribere legenda; beatissimos vero quibus utrumque.

Happy are those who can do things worth recording, or write things worth reading: most happy those to whom it is given to do both.

Sir Arnold Wilson

I am not a very tractable person or much of a hero-worshipper, but I would have followed Lawrence over the edge of the world. I loved him for himself, and also because there seemed to be reborn in him all the lost friends of my youth. If genius be, in Emerson's phrase, a 'stellar and undiminishable something', whose origin is a mystery and whose essence cannot be defined, then he was the only man of genius I have ever known.

John Buchan

I think he would always have grinned at the idea of anyone 'mothering' him. But, in the end, he was very dreadfully lonely. The strangest contact of my life.

Charlotte Shaw

APPENDIX I

Note on T. E. Lawrence's Ancestry

Lawrence's Father

Thomas Robert Tighe Chapman, Lawrence's father, was born on 6th November 1846. He was the second son of William Chapman (1811-89) and Martha Louisa Vansittart.

Lawrence's early knowledge of the Chapman family history seems to have been derived from *Debrett*. According to the 1918 edition: 'This family was originally settled at Hinckley, in Leicestershire; but John Chapman, and his brother William, through the influence of Sir Walter Raleigh, their cousin-german, received large grants of land in Ireland, and settled in that country. Benjamin, the son of William Chapman, was an officer of cavalry in Cromwell's army, and for his services received the castle and estates of Killua, sometime the seat of the family. The 3rd baronet sat as M.P. for Westmeath . . . 1830-41. Sir Benjamin James, 4th baronet, sat as M.P. for Westmeath . . . 1841-7 and was Lord-Lieutenant of that county. The 5th baronet, Sir Montagu Richard, was High Sheriff of County Westmeath.' (*Debrett's Illustrated Baronetage*, London, 1918, p. 135). The Chapman family motto is curious, both in itself and as a comment on Lawrence's life after the First World War. Translated from the Latin, it reads: 'Virtue thrives under oppression'.[1]

Lawrence's father was brought up to the life of a gentleman landowner, at a large manor house called South Hill, near the village of Delvin, County Westmeath. The family also maintained a town house in Dublin. The size of the Chapman fortune should not be judged by the relatively modest South Hill estate (173 acres). When the family land was sold in 1949 it totalled over 1,230 acres, in nine different locations. A better indication of the family's wealth is given by the valuation at probate of the estate of Francis Robert Chapman, Lawrence's uncle, who died in 1915. This amounted to £120,296, equivalent in today's terms to a sum of more than £3 million. All sources show that the Chapman family belonged to the upper tier of the Anglo-Irish landowning class. Through successive generations it had intermarried with families of comparable stature in England and Ireland. Thus Lawrence was a blood relative, on his father's side, of many Englishmen from distinguished backgrounds. For example Robert Vansittart, later Baron Vansittart, was his second cousin.[2]

Thomas Chapman was educated at Eton (as were his two brothers). It was expected that he would run the family estates and from 1866-8 he studied at the Royal Agricultural College at Cirencester. His elder brother, William, joined the army and served in the 15th Hussars, but in May 1870 he died. Thomas then assumed the position of eldest son, and his younger brother Francis was trained to run the estates. In 1873 Thomas married Edith Sarah Hamilton, from another landowning family in County Westmeath. There were four daughters: Eva Jane Louisa (b. 1874); Rose Isabel (b. 1878); Florence Lina (b.1880) and Mabel Cecele (b. 1881).

Lawrence's Mother

At some time in the late 1870s, a young Scotswoman known as Sarah Lawrence entered the Chapman household, having been engaged to work as governess to the daughters. Her industry, capability and cheerfulness were much appreciated.

This was by stark contrast to the conduct of Edith Chapman, who developed an increasingly militant obsession with religion which made life extremely difficult for those closest to her. Most accounts agree that by the mid-1880s Edith Chapman had become a bitter and vindictive woman who subjected her family and servants to very frequent prayer meetings and disapproved of all but the most genteel pleasures. Thomas Chapman, for his part, had by that time become a heavy drinker. In due course he fell in love with Sarah Lawrence, who was fifteen years his junior.

While the history of the Chapman family is well documented, much less is known about Sarah Lawrence. She was herself illegitimate, born on 31st August 1861 in Sunderland, County Durham and registered at birth as Sarah Junner. Her mother's name was Elizabeth, and census records for Sunderland made in April of that year show that Elizabeth Junner was at that time working as a servant in the household of one Thomas Lawrence, who was by profession a Lloyd's surveyor.

There can be little doubt that Sarah Junner was the child of Thomas Lawrence's eldest son, John. Her birth certificate gives the name Junner both as the maiden name of the mother and as the surname of the father. As the name is unusual, this in itself is curious. However, Elizabeth Junner had been listed in the census only four months before the birth as an unmarried servant living in the Lawrence household. The profession of the child's father is given on the birth certificate as shipwright journeyman, and this corresponds to the profession given in the census for John Lawrence: that of ship's carpenter. The girl was given the name Sarah, which was the name of John Lawrence's mother (and also of one of his sisters). It must also be significant that when Sarah Junner grew older, she used the name Lawrence rather than the name Junner. It may be that the Lawrence family concerned itself with her education after her mother, who became an alcoholic, had died.

The 1861 census reveals a little more about Sarah Lawrence's parents. John Lawrence was born at Chepstow in 1843; his father Thomas at Swansea in 1808; his mother Sarah at Chepstow in 1811. Sarah appears, therefore, to have been half-Welsh. Elizabeth Junner, Sarah's mother, was born in Scotland in 1833. A family called Junner is mentioned in the 1861 census, living in Sunderland at 14 Hamilton Street. As the name is so uncommon it seems possible that these were her parents. If so, her father was John Junner, a retired master mariner born at Franfield, Sussex, in about 1807, and her mother Jane Junner, born at Monkwearmouth in about 1813.

The break-up of the Chapman household

In 1885 Sarah Lawrence became pregnant. She therefore left the Chapman household to live in rooms Thomas Chapman rented for her in Dublin. In December that year a son was born. He was christened Montagu Robert; both names are found in the Chapman pedigree.

For a time, Thomas Chapman continued to live at home while also seeing Sarah and his child. Eventually, however, Mrs Chapman discovered what had taken place. When faced with the choice of leaving his wife and daughters or giving up Sarah and his son, Thomas decided to go with Sarah. Soon afterwards he took her to live in Tremadoc in Wales, where their second son, christened Thomas Edward, was born in August 1888.[3]

Thomas Chapman's subsequent financial position

On March 30th of that year, Chapman had signed an Indenture under the terms of which he assigned his life interest in the family estates to his younger brother Francis (their father, William Chapman, did not die until 1889). In exchange, Thomas Chapman was to receive an annuity of £200 for the rest of his life. It seems that he also possessed or afterwards inherited other capital. According to his own statement, this amounted by the beginning of 1916 to rather more than £20,000. It would have produced, at prevailing interest rates, an income of about £1,000 per annum. This substantial figure contradicts Lawrence's later claim that his parents lived in straitened circumstances (see chapter 1 note 28): it seems that Mr Lawrence's revenues during the boys' childhood amounted in reality to much more than the £400 per annum that Lawrence spoke of to his biographer Liddell Hart.

In 1914 Mr Lawrence became the seventh and last Chapman baronet. When he had separated from his wife, twenty years previously, it would have been difficult to foresee that the title might pass to him. At that time it was held by an uncle, Benjamin Chapman, who had two sons. They were each in turn to inherit it (becoming respectively 5th and 6th baronets) but neither had children.

Lawrence's father probably expected that the five sons Sarah bore him would eventually inherit a reasonable share of the Chapman fortune. He must therefore have been disappointed when his younger brother Francis, who died in 1915 without having married, bequeathed to him only £25,000 of the £120,296 Chapman estate. (Other specific bequests under the will included £10,000 to the Adelaide Hospital in Dublin, and £25,000 divided between the four Chapman daughters, Lawrence's half-sisters, who were also the residuary legatees.) When

Mr Lawrence received this £25,000 inheritance, he shared part of it among his sons (see pp. 226 and 252). In a draft of the letter he sent to Lawrence he wrote: 'I am glad to say that circumstances allow me to hand over to Bob, you and Arnie exact equal portion of the same Securities as described on another page . . . I should mention that my capital will be increased by less than a third, so that I can never make any of you wealthy but I am very thankful I can do what I am doing and by your having this money now it enables you when this war is over to decide more freely on your future proceedings.'[4] Mr Lawrence stated that the securities given to each of his sons would provide them with incomes of about £270 per annum.

Caroline Margaret Chapman

The last part of this history concerns Mr Lawrence's younger sister, Caroline Margaret Chapman (Lawrence's aunt). She had married her cousin, Montagu Chapman, who became 5th Chapman baronet. He died in 1907 without children, and four years later she drew up a will setting out the terms under which the Killua estate was to be broken up. In this will she arranged to bequeath £20,000 to her brother Thomas (Lawrence's father), making further generous legacies to his daughters in Ireland.

This separate provision for the Chapman girls leaves little doubt that she intended Mr Lawrence's £20,000 to pass, ultimately, to his sons. It is not unreasonable to suppose that he knew of these legacies and that he would have discussed them with Sarah Lawrence. If this is the case, it might account for some otherwise unexplained remarks in Lawrence's letters (see below).

Caroline Margaret Chapman was seriously ill for several years: a codicil to her will dated June 1916 was signed with a cross and witnessed by two nurses. She died in 1920, some months after the death of Lawrence's father. As he had predeceased her, the £20,000 bequest was passed, not to his sons, but to the residuary legatees under her will: his four Chapman daughters.

It seems possible that, following his father's death, Lawrence had learned from his mother of this bequest, and that this explains his remark in a letter to Eric Kennington of 1.10.1921: 'A lump of money I was expecting has not (probably will not) come.' (see p. 662). The loss of the bequest may also explain the bitterness of the allusion to the Chapmans inserted by Lawrence in Liddell Hart's biography: 'The father's family seemed unconscious of his sons, even when after his death recognition of their achievement might have done honour to the name.'[5]

If Lawrence did know of his aunt's bequest to his father (and I can discover no other 'lump of money' that he could have been expecting at that time) then it is less surprising that he should previously have given £3,000 of his earlier inheritance to Janet Hallsmith (née Laurie, see pp. 637-8).

Report by F. Willoughby Smith

American Vice and Deputy Consul-General at Beirut,
to W. Stanley Hollis, American Consul-General.

9th December 1912.[1]

Sir,

Since I had the honor to submit my report of Dec. 7th, 1912, on the political situation in North-Eastern Syria, I believed it prudent to have another conversation on the subject with Mr. Woolley and Mr. Lawrence of the British Museum, and have been able to obtain from these gentlemen the following report:–

The Melli-Kurds have not forgiven the death of their leader [Ibrahim Pasha], who was poisoned by the Young Turks.[2] Recently one of his sons died suddenly at Diarbekr [100 miles north of Urfa], and this also is attributed to poison and will further irritate the Kurds. Ibn Ibrahim Pasha is said to be more capable, more powerful and more ambitious than was his father, and he is certainly looked up to by the Kurds as their common leader. He has rebuilt his father's capital Wiransehr, which the Turks had destroyed.

Mr. Lawrence, some time ago (about 12 months),[3] was shown, by the Sheikh of Harran, the vaults of the old crusader castle there stocked with eight or ten thousand Martini rifles and ammunition. All the confederacy was of course equipped by [Sultan] Abdul Hamid as an irregular army of Hamidieh, and they are supplied with rifles and ammunition, which, though not of the modern type, are as good as the Turks would be likely to use against them.

The Sheikh of Harran told Mr. Lawrence that the weapons would be used when Ibn Ibrahim Pasha went to Aleppo to avenge his father. From what Mr. Woolley and Mr. Lawrence were told by a certain Busrawi Agha . . . this vengeance is to be fairly soon, and is to be part of a bigger move. He and the leaders like him talk freely of getting rid for good and all of the Turkish Government. They believe that the opportune moment has come, or is coming, and that the power of the central government at Stamboul is broken for good.

They talk of a conspiracy into which have entered the Khedive of Egypt, the Sherif of Mecca, the Sheikh es Senussi, and Ibn Rashid, whose object is to expel the Turks and to set up an Arab Sultan, apparently at Baghdad as capital. The Kurds say they are not strong enough to set up a Sultan of their own. It is heard that since the terms of peace with Italy were made known, there have been secret meetings of the leading Arabs in Aleppo, Damascus and elsewhere, condemning Turkey's betrayal of the Arabs and proposing to turn out the Turks and take over the Government. How far this is true is not known, but it agrees with the statement made by the Kurds as to Arab co-operation.

Around Aleppo among the Kurds and Bedouins the news of Turkish defeats and the rumoured fall of Stamboul are received with undisguised satisfaction. As long as the Sultan was also the Khalifa the religious bond that held the Kurds and Arabs to the Empire was strong; but with Abdul Hamid's deposition this bond was snapped; the only Khalifa recognised is the Sherif of Mecca, and the new Government's attempt at a Pan-Islam rally has wholly failed.

The Bulgarian victories have not even raised ill-feeling against foreigners. If a smash comes, it is undoubtedly the Kurds who will take the initiative. They frankly state their intention of rising and spoke of hostilities as imminent; in fact they are already on the move. But their plans seem to be cleverly enough concealed. During the [Balkan] war the Kurds have not raised a finger to help the Turks; the few so-called volunteers who joined did so with orders from their chiefs to desert as soon as they had had guns served out to them.

Now they have in a body volunteered for service at the front, and have actually risen in arms to make good their words. In private they continue to talk treason and say that they have not the slightest intention of going against the Bulgarians or of helping the Government. They all (those interviewed) agree that their object is Aleppo, and they freely talk of looting that town and of sacking the German railway (*Bagdadbahn*, Aleppo–Jerablus) and of killing the engineers; individuals have told Mr. Woolley precisely what loot they hoped to get out of a particular German settlement, and they are rather annoyed because they believe that Shatun Bey's son has gone to Aleppo (where Mr. Woolley saw him last week) to make out the best houses for plunder. But if asked directly why they are going to Aleppo they say 'to eat'. The facts are that Ibn Ibrahim Pasha with four thousand men having been reported as on his way to Bitlis [80 miles west of Van] to repel Russian agressions, suddenly turned up at Biridjik, where he was a week ago, with his men well in hand. Derai with 945 men was in Biridjik twelve days ago, moved to Nizib, where his men did some small and decent looting and when they met the Government Doctor sent by the Aleppo authorities to accompany them, Derai finding that he was an Armenian and a Christian, shot him in the street, where his body was still lying when Mr. Lawrence was there two days later. Incidentally, Mr. Lawrence found that the Kurdish hill villagers north of Nizib were in a state of great excitement, running round with guns and looking for another Christian to kill. It was only the fact that Mr. Lawrence was in disguise that saved him from serious trouble. In Nizib and Biridjik the Christians are all in hiding.

From Nizib Derai went to Aintab, where he does not seem to have done any harm; he left there the other day and nothing has been heard of his movements. Mustapha Pasha, with a force estimated at from seven thousand to nine thousand men, is marching slowly westwards from the Tigris . . . Busrawi Agha and Shatun Bey have not yet moved, but are waiting orders from Ibn Ibrahim; it is noteworthy that the blood feud that has lasted for years between these clans was suddenly patched up about a fortnight ago, and these two now profess to be friends, whereas when Mr. Woolley was there during Bairam the followers of the one did not venture near the dwellings of the others. Busrawi can put some two thousand men into the field, Shahin twelve hundred; all these numbers refer to mounted men armed with Martinis; a vastly greater number could be called out, and if foot soldiers are taken also then Busrawi ought to lead out about twenty thousand men (if they can all be armed), and the others in proportion. All these men are wild fighters in their own way and deadly in street fighting; they wouldn't be any good against good European troops. At present the Kurds in the field are just wandering about. They are more or less in hand, each force is accompanied by a Turkish officer, and they claim to be loyal volunteers. As such they have to be fed at government expense, or at any rate are licensed by the Government to feed at the expense of others.

This doubtless is one of their objects, the awful winter of two years ago frightened them, as well as impoverished them greatly; and so long as they live well at Government cost they are not likely to make trouble, but will be glad to tide so cheaply over the winter.

Moreover, not all their forces can get under arms, and perhaps the conspiracy is not just ripe, also they are still waiting on news, from Europe, and if that should favour the Turks the whole trouble may yet pass over and the Kurds retire harmlessly to their homes. Mr. Woolley and Mr. Lawrence don't think they will, but believe it is possible. The reasons above given may keep them in check for a while, unless an accident happens; at least until they see what the winter is going to be like. It seems that their idea is to wander about (possibly they may go to Zeitoun [120 miles north-west of Aleppo]), until their forces are out, and quietly concentrate on Aleppo. Probably till the last moment they could pose as volunteers and when they are all there – or when their men could no longer resist the temptation – could sack the place.

Apart from the idea of avenging Ibrahim Pasha, the leaders have chosen Aleppo as their first place of attack with a view to securing field guns, for they are fully aware of the need of artillery if they are to fight the Turkish Regulars. As to their chances, most of the artillery at Aleppo is served by Kurds who would go over at a word from their tribal chief; there are a few Christian soldiers there, practically no Turks; the mass are either Kurds, who would at once rejoin their tribal chief, or Arabs who would, in so far as they are drawn from the coast towns, run away, and in so far as they come from the interior, join the Kurds. The Arabs of the villages Anezzeh and Beni-Suyrd, near the excavations, openly state that they would join in the rising as soon as the signal was given, and they would materially strengthen the revolutionary party. Mr. Woolley has very little doubt that they could sack Aleppo and drive the Turkish officials out of North Syria; but greatly doubts whether they have the cohesion and the powers of organisation to build up anything on the destruction which they would cause. On the other hand a certain foresight was shown by Busrawi's remark to these gentlemen that it was too late to do away with the railroad, but it might be made to serve Arab rather than German interests by acting as a link to tie more closely the Kurds and Arabs of the North with those of Bagdad and the Yemen.

The whole country is Anglophile and the leaders certainly very much so, nor do they intend violence against foreigners as such, only the engineers on the German railway are marked out for murder. This is due to their personal unpopularity. The moral effect of the construction of the line has been bad; it has for the first time introduced to the country Arab a low class of European, Greek and Italian foremen, and some of the higher German officials have earned the hatred of the people by their arrogant and even brutal treatment of them. But it is almost certain that if they are killed the leaders would not have their men sufficiently in hand to prevent a more general massacre, in which not only native Christians but all foreigners would be involved.

Mr. Woolley's and Mr. Lawrence's conclusions appear to me correct. I have long observed the dissatisfaction of the bedouins and of many city Arabs (Moslems), with Turkish rule. The lack of a suitable leader and their mistrust of each other, has in the past, and may now as well, prevent their concerted action. The Sherif of Mecca, whom I met last year, appears to lack the qualities of a leader, his brother, however, is a stronger man, and has a very considerable influence [Willoughby Smith has probably confused Sherif Hussein with one of his sons, Feisal or Abdullah, whom he could have met in Turkey]. Some of the young men of the family have been encouraged to study English, and have adopted European customs and dress.

With the return of Izzet Pasha, the Arabs will have an adviser well accustomed to unite and conciliate opposing factions.

The outcome may not be as serious as prognosticated in Mr. Woolley's report, but the facts given undoubtedly reveal the present political sentiment of the country.

Intelligence. I.E.F. "D"

T. E. Lawrence's report on Mesopotamia, May 1916 [1]

In Mesopotamia there is a strict divorce between the political and military sides of Intelligence. The Political Department is a separate organisation under the Chief Political Officer, Sir Percy Cox. The Military Intelligence is under Colonel Beach. To preserve a fiction of control Sir P. Cox has been made a Colonel on the staff of the G.O.C. He works well with Colonel Beach personally, and each keeps the other somewhat 'au fait' with what he is doing. Their staffs are, however, quite separate, and hardly know each other.

THE MILITARY INTELLIGENCE
Colonel Beach is very excellent but he has never been in Turkey, or read about it, and he knows no Arabic. This would not necessarily matter, but unfortunately his staff do not supply the necessary knowledge. They are good men, but all beginners or amateurs at Intelligence work. None of them knows a word of Turkish, only one can speak Arabic. This one is an office man, who sits in Basra and runs the Secret Service work. He has a separate house and office of his own, and seldom sees Colonel Beach, who therefore gets no advice from him.

(1a.) It is rather difficult for us to realise that the Intelligence Staff at such places as Basra, Amara, Ali Gharbi, Sheikh Saad, Nasiriya, Ahwaz, and with the Corps in the fighting line, cannot speak any of the local languages. They do all their examination of agents, prisoners and refugees, through interpreters. They have never learnt or read anything of the manners of Turk or Arab, or of their customs. They know nothing of the country beyond them: they cannot test an agent by cross-questioning: the supply of good interpreters is very limited, so that many of the finer points that make the difference between obvious truth and falsehood are missed. Also you get gross errors of place or number, besides confusion of technical military terms.

They get their knowledge of Turkish communications from the various military reports (none of them has served on a railway, or knows much about supply or transport work): they learn the Turkish Army from the *Turkish Army Handbook*, and they follow events in Turkey from the Cairo *Bulletin*, which is a sort of Bible to them. They receive practically nothing from London except the 'Marsh' telegrams from Tiflis. They are mostly anxious to pick up all they can, and they make very good use of all they get.

I think we might make our *Bulletin* a little simpler for their sakes. It strikes me – in Mesopotamia – as a little too specialist. There should be more summaries of what we know of Turkish finance, trade statistics, crops, and notes on the produce of particular *vilayets*, and the habits and peculiarities of districts and races.

Also we must send them a linguist or two, who knows the inside of Turkey. Heny would be the best man if he is available. We should henceforward take anything they send us, such as train time-tables, march-rates, agents' information, and identifications of units opposed to them (other than by contact) with reserve, since many of their sources are so uncritical.

(1b.) The Secret Service work done by Intelligence Officers outside Basra is not well done. The man at Amara is trying very hard to work up a system. His agents, through his interpreter, spend their time telling wild fictions, or denouncing their private or tribal enemies as Turcophiles.

Capt. More

In Basra the S.S. work is being run by Captain J. C. More, the solitary member of the Intelligence Staff who speaks Arabic. He also knows Persian. He has lived and travelled in Syria, understands the Arabs, and gets on well with them.

The scheme of getting agents into Syria, which we put up to them some months ago, is in his hands. He has a big system afoot, with men going to Jauf, Damascus, Aleppo, Diarbekir, Mosul, Deir and Baghdad. He also gets in a good deal of local information and was, I thought, very sound indeed. He is doing all this single-handed, and if anything happened to him there is nobody to take his place.

We discussed S.S. work, and worked out a number of common schemes, which I will not write down. They have unlimited funds, and *carte blanche*: also they are willing to do anything or everything.

(1c.) There are two separate mapping sections.

Survey of India

One is under Colonel Pirrie, of the Survey of India. It consists of four or five officer surveyors, a dozen Indian surveyors, many chainmen, a vandyke section, and a printing section with two or three machines. It is quite independent of Colonel Beach, but in touch with him and does any special jobs he wants. This survey work seems very good. They have triangulated from Fas to Ali Gharbi, on a half-inch scale, going three miles each side of the river. Also from Kurna to Nasiriya. They are doing Basra–Nasiriya, and Basra–Kuwait. They also did a patch round Kut. They would have done other areas but the Army makes difficulty about escorts. I do not think the work could be bettered, except in the matter of collecting place names. These are awful. On the field sheet nearly every name is wrong, and broader errors such as villages called 'Place', 'I don't know', 'Tents', 'Mound' are pretty common. When a selection of names has to be made, they generally put in the ephemeral ones, and miss out the permanent. I am afraid this fault is unavoidable with the native surveyors. Fortunately they have now recognised that a careful checking of the names is necessary before reproduction, and Miss Bell is getting the correct Arabic form of each one, so far as she can.

Vandyke Section of Survey of India. The vandyke section sent out by the Survey of India said there was oil on the surface of the Tigris and struck work. I don't think they knew their job. There has been a good deal of difficulty with Indian skilled labour. They now use autograph transfer for everything. The draughtsman (Indian) is very bad. He loses most of the character of the field sheets in copying them, and his pen work and writing are wretched. The results are, therefore, unnecessarily poor. It struck me that the transfer paper was stretching a good deal. The air of Basra is rather moist.

Printing Section The printing machines are old. I think there was something wrong with the bed of one: with another you get the pressure by screwing down, for each pull, a boxwood block with a knife edge, on to the cover plate. Four men then grind it through. They can do seventy pulls a day on this machine (a decent machine will do two thousand). They use zinc plates, which they grain locally by hand. They seemed very badly done. They have also run out of paper and are using cheap sheets, supplied by the *Basra Times*.

It seems a pity that such good survey work should be spoiled by bad machinery and labour in reproduction. They excuse it by saying that their copies are only provisional, and that India will produce the final. Only India seems to take six months to do the work, so that enough corrections have come in to justify a new edition before the first one comes out.

R.E. Litho and Printing Section.
The Military Intelligence (Colonel Beach) have also a Map Section. Most of this is attached to the Corps Headquarters, and works up at the firing line. What is left at Basra confines itself to issuing corrections to degree sheets. It does these rather nicely. The Section with the Corps produces all the large-scale operations maps and all the artillery maps and trench maps. There is no surveyor belonging to it.

By some unfortunate mistake the trig. survey from Basra was stopped at Ali Gharbi, and began again at Kut. All the fighting between Sheikh Saad and Kut has therefore been over unsurveyed country. The only maps available were the quarter-inch degree sheets. These show almost nothing but the main stream of the Tigris. Captain Hamilton's survey seems to be the main authority. He did his work half-surreptitiously, drifting down the river, and checking his distances by a stop-watch and the estimated speed of the river. In the circumstances his results were wonderfully good – but you get a constant error of two or three hundred yards, and local errors up to 1,500 yards or a mile.

When artillery maps were first called for, the Corps produced them by enlarging the degree sheet twelve times, to 3 inch. The originals are slight enough, and of course the enlargement was mostly white paper. The Corps then began to fill these maps in from aeroplane photographs. Planes were sent up to observe, or drop bombs, or food, and they used to take trench photographs incidentally. These were, therefore, necessarily scratch productions, taken from all angles, usually without overlap, at any time of day, and on half a dozen scales. The prints were sent up to the Corps (some miles from the aerodrome) and were handed over to the G.S.O.3. to be drawn up in his spare time. He had no instruments except pencil, dividers, and an army protractor. He had never drawn anything before. He used to guess where the photographs fitted, guess what scale they were on, and adjust them to the old degree sheet (with its error of 1,200 yards or so). He worked very hard at them but he was no topographer, and used carefully to leave out every natural feature. The results are trench diagrams only.

It is then drawn by hand on stone (they have only three stones, so that one map has to be rubbed out before another can be done) and printed in a press like a mangle which does up to three hundred a day. Editions of three thousand are sometimes produced. The maps are a great advance on the degree sheets, and are improving steadily; but they are still too inaccurate to be of much use; are confused and difficult to read, and are printed on very soft paper which tears at once in a wind.

Colonel Beach asked me to give him a note on what could be done to improve things. I suggested:-

1. That the trig. survey be extended as soon as possible to the firing line, and beyond, as in Gallipoli. It will not be hard to fix some points in the Turkish lines, for the country, though flat, has a lot of minor detail in it: and until these control points are in, it will be impossible to fit your photographs perfectly.
2. That whenever serious photography is required, an aeroplane be sent up to do nothing else. Massy backed me up very warmly in this and other suggestions.
3. That some form of correcting apparatus, like our 'Bahel' be installed. I promised to consult Dowson about it, and let Colonel Beach know the latest developments.
4. That a special officer be told off to compile the air photographs. The present one has to do his ordinary work as well, and in consequence it is all scamped. I would like Dowson to lend them Hayes for a couple of months. He has had more air-photograph compilation than anyone alive, does it magnificently, and besides would teach them what draughtsmanship means.
5. That a decent tent be provided as a drawing office. Careful work is impossible in the present dusty conditions.

6. That the compilation and drawing be done at the aerodrome, to ensure the co-operation of observers and compiler. You can cross-question the observers on details and they will get keen on the map they see being drawn, and will take pains to get the right photographs.

7. That zinc plates be used instead of stones. They will crack a stone soon – besides it will save continual redrawing of the same area, if the originals of former maps are kept ready.

8. That a vandyke section be set up, if possible. It would save hours (or days) in time, and the results are neater and more accurate. It will have to be run by soldier labour. If Dowson could spare Cowan he would do it, or Buttanoni could be lent perhaps as a teacher.

9. That a new printing machine be bought. The higher proportion of British troops means more maps, and the force in Mesopotamia should be independent of India at a pinch, so far as map production goes.

   With an up-to-date machine doing two thousand or three thousand copies a day you could print in colours. A blue on the artillery maps, to bring out rivers, lakes, floods and marsh, would make them twice as attractive, and much clearer to use.

10. That all maps to be used for any length of time in the field be printed on linen-backed paper. I have promised thirty reams of our own to start them.

11. Until accurate maps are obtainable I suggested the use of balloon theodolites with smoke balls. They were very pleased with some trials they made of these.

   The areas that require correct artillery maps are I think:-

   (1) The present front-line (by air-photo checked on advanced trig. points)
   (2) Nasiriya (Survey)
   (3) Sheikh-Saad to Um el Hanna (Survey).

This is not a very large programme, as survey in Mesopotamia is quick and easy. The aeroplanes have no trouble in identifying the ground, as there is a great deal of shape in it.

   I would have liked to have got them a camera for enlargement or reduction, but I am afraid it would be too ambitious. I suggested taking a 60-foot barge for the mapping section, and getting the new machine, the dark rooms, and the drawing office into it. But barges are very scarce, and they say too hot in summer for working in.

(1d.) Colonel Beach said the Censor Department was working excellently.

THE POLITICAL DEPARTMENT

The Political Department under Sir Percy Cox wears khaki uniform and white tabs. Some of its people are officers, and some civilians. Most of them know Arabic or Persian, and one (Bullard, Levant Consular Service) knows Turkish well, and most of Turkey and its politics. Another of them is Leachman, the Arabian; also Noel, and Young and Eadie. As far as expert knowledge goes the Political Department is as well served as the Military Intelligence is badly served.

'Political Department' is rather a false name. It is really a civil service and is mostly taken up in administration. Under it are the Customs, Excise, Land Revenue, Taxation, Crown Lands, the Judiciary, the Police, River-Conservancy. Headquarters is at Basra, but there are assistants at all large centres in our occupation. They are, of course, entirely distinct from the Military Intelligence Officers at the same places.

Capt. Wilson
Of the politicals only Sir Percy Cox (and his assistant, Captain Wilson) do politics proper. They deal with Ibn Saoud, Ibn Rashid, Kuwait, Mohammerah and the rest.

Sir P.Z. Cox
Sir Percy Cox is High Commissioner except in name. He is absolute dictator in the Gulf, and will remain so as long as he is there. He is delightful to work with. His fear of us was mostly because he thought we aimed at getting the Sherif a temporal ascendancy over the Arab-speaking world. When I gave him a sketch of our ideas on a united Arabia he was pleased – and relieved. However, he will not take orders or suggestions about his policy from anyone but London, and he knows London so well that I feel sure this is only a diplomatic way of taking no orders at all. He would like a round-table conference with you, and would send Dobbs to it: I think more for Dobbs' sake than his own, for it looks as though Dobbs would succeed him out here when he goes.

[H. R. C. Dobbs]
Dobbs is one of the most interesting people I met in Mesopotamia. I think he is probably an Indian civilian. They made him Chief of the Revenue Department, as which he had to settle land disputes, and oversee the sub-letting of the Crown lands. The Turks left him vast confusion in the province. They got away most of the official registers: what they left were ill-kept, and their system had been to enter on paper enormous rents for the various estates, and in practice to hold in check the tribal leaders by the accumulation of unpayable arrears. Also they had an odd habit of entering the name of a dead man as formal tenant.

The statelands are let on leases (average term of four or five years) in great blocks to rich Pashas and chiefs of tribes. These sub-let their holdings to contractors, who sublet to farmers – under whom are the peasants or fellahin. Some fellahin are tenants at will, others adscript for a term. The latter are the better off, for they cannot be dismissed without compensation. The crops are usually rice, barley and wheat, sometimes two crops a year, sometimes one only.

The year of change of lease is usually a fallow, and the river silt deposited in flood is the only food the land gets. Dobbs and Bullard (I don't know the precise virtue of each) went into this question, gave title-deeds, assessed rents, solved disputes of succession, rights of way, water, estimated the values of crops disposed of or spoiled, granted compensation for the events of war, and at the end of their year they not only showed a profit in administration, but left a contented province behind them. They both understand and like the natives, took the right manner with landlords and landowners, and scored a tremendous success for the British, in what was one of the most important (as it was certainly the most difficult) things we had to do. They are both reading men (Dobbs perhaps forty-five, Bullard perhaps thirty) with strong tastes in history and literature. Bullard is merely keen to get something done, but Dobbs has definite views in politics and differs from Cairo on several issues, for reasons thought out and made precise in his own mind. I think he will come into agreement when he has learned more (he suffers, like all the rest, because there is no one out there who knows what is going on, or what the rest of the Arab world is like), and in any case it is well worth while trying to make him a convert, for he will act vigorously on his opinions, and on him will, I think, depend very largely the line of our future policy in Mesopotamia. He is due for leave in August for some months and Sir Percy is quite willing to let him off in mid-June, if we can have him in Cairo for a bit, and discuss the Near East with him and a man from Aden.

ARAB BUREAU

When notes on this first came out Sir Percy Cox said he would have nothing to do with it, and so Colonel Beach had to undertake it. He appointed a Major Blaker, of the Military Intelligence, who was at a loose end, to act as local correspondent of the Bureau.

Major Blaker is very intelligent and quite ready to be interested in local politics, but has never been in the East before. I went to Sir Percy, explained that the Bureau was a Foreign Office affair, and insisted that its correspondent must be intimate with the work of the political side. I told him we would want notes on public opinion in Basra or the villages, especially when it was dissatisfied: also on all religious movements, tribal affairs, with estimates of the personal character and importance of leading sheikhs or politicians; details of our negotiations with Ibn Rashid, Ibn Saoud, and the others; geographical distributions of tribes, trade statistics, figures of local taxation, summaries of land settlements, and notes on any trials or legal cases of political interest.

As every item of the above is dealt with by the Political Department, and is never heard of by Colonel Beach or his office, Sir Percy Cox eventually agreed to alter his decision. Major Blaker will continue to exist, as a sort of pillar-box, and because I think it is a happy way of drawing the attention of the Military Intelligence to a side of the work which it has missed, but the actual collection and selection of information for us will be done for the present by Miss Gertrude

Bell. She will work up the connections we require with the various Political Officers and will see that extracts from the Political files are sent us regularly. Meanwhile she will search for a good successor to herself from among the politicals (Bullard or George Lloyd seemed to me possibles), and will later write and tell us who it might be. She is already doing the tribal and geographical work the Bureau needs, herself, as there is no officer in Basra qualified to do it. I have a feeling that no one person will be able to supply us with all we want, unless his fellow politicals get interested and send him in special stuff, and I think Miss Bell, by her sex and energy and lack of self-consciousness, is peculiarly likely to persuade Political Officers to send her what she asks for. At present what I would describe as the social side, the particular province of the Eastern Bureau, is being entirely neglected officially in Basra:– though men like Leachman, Young, Eadie, and Dobbs are doing magnificent work in keeping in friendly touch with the people, and winning their respect for our administration.

The Eastern Bureau is going to be so useful to them on its publicity side, that I think it may make all its activities welcome in the end. At first, though, we should go very easy with the Mesopotamians: they feel that we will use them and what they have conquered as a bribe to make our policy acceptable elsewhere, and make their area a dumping ground for theories and theorists of a nationalism inconvenient in Egypt.

LOCAL FEELING

Basra
Basra itself has no politics. It does not appeal as a residence to the leisured class, and is itself not one town, but the sum of a number of overgrown villages. In consequence it has none of the corporate feeling of Baghdad, Aleppo or Damascus; and the date crop, rice and foreign trade are its interests. You can get individual opinions in Basra, but no common point of view.

Marsh Arabs
I think the hostility of the tribal Arabs towards us has been greatly overdrawn. Of course there are the Maadan, the Arabs of the marshes, who are impure savages, without any code of manners or morals to restrain them. Their hand is against every stranger – but even among them there is no antipathy to the British as such. They hate us perhaps more than they do the Turk, in so far as they see our rule will be more efficient, and therefore worse for them. They cut up our wounded and the Turkish wounded, raid our convoys and the Turkish convoys, steal our rifles and the Turkish rifles – but to know how to estimate the Maadan, ask a tribesman his opinion of them. We cannot condemn them in stronger terms than do the real Arabs living round them, and if we make their hostility typical (as the second-rate local 'eye-witness' does) we only show up our own lack of understanding.

Hai Tribes.

The great block of Arab irreconcilables are the tribes along the Shatt el Hai. These are independents, rich, well organised, with tribal customs, but of Shia stock. They have fought the Turks incessantly and driven back three formal expeditions made against them. Recently they claimed a fourth victory (over us this time) when General Brooking retired from Butuniyah. They are a confederation who mean to be free and undisturbed, who would be friendly to us only if they thought our rule so weak as to allow of general anarchy. If we remain outside their borders they will let us alone (I do not believe they will even attack Nasiriya); if we invade them they will fight us – if the Turks invade them in force I believe they will drive them back – on the other hand, I think they would allow a small Turkish contingent to come down and raid our communications, as it is only conquest they are afraid of. I rather sympathise with them, though of course their pretensions to remain an independent little state of freebooting freelancers in the middle of Mesopotamia is absurd. To put them down by force will probably cost us more than we could profit. By damming the north end of the Hai we will subdue them inevitably; and by carrying out the irrigation scheme we put an end to their present existence.

Of the other Arabs, in tribes or villages or towns, the rule is that those in front of us are hostile and those behind friendly. Hostility to us does not in this case mean friendship with, but only subjection to, the Turk. In truth all these people (like the 35th and 38th Divisions) do not want to fight, and are indifferent to the change of masters. If we had played our cards better at first, I do not think there would have been even the fighting there has been – but we have entered their country (for it is their country, and not the Turks') like sphinxes, never saying why we came or what we meant to do. A public declaration, properly explained, of our intentions and policy would even now give them a clear issue, and rank them with us or against us.

At present the rule for the doubting is to stand in with the Turks. They know the best and worst of them and we are an incomprehensible quantity. Also the Turks punish a backslider much more savagely than we can do: for one thing they are not our rebels, and again it is not our manner.

In considering Mesopotamia and the tribes, I think one should bear in mind how transient all these things are. We will presumably not remain there unless we are in a position to carry out a full irrigation scheme. When we regulate the rivers we also drain the lakes and swamps, and prevent marshes and floods. With these latter go the present livelihood of the marsh tribes. We will be able to starve a rebellion by shutting down a sluice, or drown it by opening them too wide. When the country is parcelled out by orderly roadways and canals, and watered by an irrigation inspector, in accordance with the bye-laws and local water regulations, the style and mode of living of the farmers there will have changed as much as their system of land tenure. The increase of land values will make the burden of great estates like the present ones too heavy for any man to bear, and the sheikh and the tribal organisation will have no more chance than it would have in Egypt today. In place of his present occupations of blood feud and foray, the landowner of the future will drive his motor car and gamble in margins in the pit at Basra. The Government will be very prosperous at that time – for about half of Mesopotamia is Crown land, and the annual value of it will be staggering.

Complaints

I saw something of many kinds of Arabs, and heard their grievances. None of them had anything very serious though of course few of them love their government (even some English people don't). We have been very fair to them in compensating them for the loss of crops. Owing to shortage of river transport they have been unable to sell the surplus of their harvests, and in some districts the necessity of making or breaking the dykes that control the river has prevented a rice crop. One tenant of Crown lands whose normal rents are £40,000 a year has been excused some £17,000, and others in fit proportion. This is some loss to us, but the province has still shown a profit, and the concessions have been very much appreciated.

We have been conservative in settling disputes. We have decided that no decision of a Turkish Appeal Court may be revised. This measure is perhaps justified in expediency, by the feeling of security and continuity it gives the rich man who has bought favourable but iniquitous verdicts in the past. We have introduced the Indian code of law into Basra, and by translating it at once into Arabic have given the people for the first time courts in their own language. They are grateful.

There is a current of British opinion which favours the introduction of a tribal law (as in Sinai) for the country districts, when the time comes for us to administer them.

The Police are unsatisfactory, from our standard, perhaps because the native officer is inefficient. Still, they are better than they were, so the local people do not feel aggrieved. It is a compliment to us that they judge us by a higher standard than they did the Turks, in most things.

I think we made a mistake in driving Ajaimi into the other camp. Before the war he was generally disliked, and could hardly visit his estates. We are going about now to make him a popular hero – and all for the lack of a bit of politeness and a small burnt-offering to the absurd family pride of the Saaduns. Politeness is still associated with greatness, by the Arabs. Basra itself has one grievance, which, silly though it sounds, is actually doing us some harm. The local Pashas and Beys have no great one on whom they can go and call. The town notables long for a leisured and dignified vali, who would rise from the divan to meet them, and would give them cigarettes or coffee, and do them little unimportant favours.

It would certainly be to the advantage of our government if they did receive the formal entertainment they crave for. The attitude of the Pashas means a good

deal on their estates, and in the current of general public opinion in the towns –
and at present the Pashas feel themselves slighted. It is no use in the East being
friends only with the common inarticulate people.

Our present Headquarters in Basra is all Indian, without even an A.D.C. who
can speak three words of Arabic, or a servant who could hand a cup of coffee or
a cigarette to a great man in the proper form. This was all well when we were an
invading Indian army – but in our second year we should have sobered down into
occupation and ownership.

Religious Questions

For us now these resolve themselves almost entirely into questions of Waqf. The
population is composed of some Sunni landowners, and a few tribes of Sunni
Beduin, but the rest are all Shias. Perhaps 70 or 80 per cent of the total population
is Shia. Dogmatic rivalry is fairly strong.

The only official Waqf is Sunni, and it is showing a considerable annual
surplus. Sir Percy Cox, and Dobbs, proposed to hand this over at once to the
Sherif of Mecca, for relief of pilgrims, etc., but were refused permission by India
and home. In peace times the Waqf surplus belonged to the Sultan, and was
absorbed by the Waqf Ministry in Constantinople. If the money is kept in hand
till the end of the war it will certainly (under pressure of the Indian Moslems) be
disposed of in the traditional way. This would be a wanton strengthening of the
hands of Turkey, and as well an acknowledgement by us of the Khalifate of the
Sultan, which conflicts with the attitude of non-interference with that vexed
question, strictly maintained by us lately. To assign the Waqf surplus to the
promotion and relief of pilgrimage is a neutral way out of an unpleasant
difficulty and I hope may yet be approved.

Besides the Sunni Waqf there is in Basra some landed property belonging to
the Sherifate of Mecca, and administered directly by his representatives in Basra.
The question of the Shia Waqf is coming to the fore. The Turks refused to allow
it, and the Shias therefore constituted private trusts to the same end. They have
now asked to be allowed a public Waqf. No answer was returned, but private
instructions were given to the Land Department to accept such trusts.

I think we should go a little further than this, in pursuit of a fiction of religious
equality. The difficulty before us will be if a surplus occurs, to whom to pay it.
A solution proposed locally is that we should elevate the President of the College
of Mullahs at Kerbela to be a kind of Shia Sherifate. This would presuppose a
British overlordship of Kerbela and Najf. In view of the coming importance of
Persia and the tremendous pull over the Shia world such a position would give
us, it may be worth consideration. The Turks were of course too orthodox to gain
a political profit from their possession of the Shia shrines, but as a Christian
Power there is nothing to hinder our getting out of it all the prestige we can – and
keeping on good terms with Mecca meanwhile, so that the two sects will play for
our favour.

Twenty-Seven Articles
by T. E. Lawrence, August 1917 [1]

The following notes have been expressed in commandment form for greater clarity and to save words. They are, however, only my personal conclusions, arrived at gradually while I worked in the Hejaz and now put on paper as stalking horses for beginners in the Arab armies. They are meant to apply only to Bedu: townspeople or Syrians require totally different treatment. They are of course not suitable to any other person's need, or applicable unchanged in any particular situation. Handling Hejaz Arabs is an art, not a science, with exceptions and no obvious rules. At the same time we have a great chance there: the Sherif trusts us, and has given us the position (towards his Government) which the Germans wanted to win in Turkey. If we are tactful we can at once retain his good will, and carry out our job – but to succeed we have got to put into it all the interest and energy and skill we possess.

1. Go easy just for the first few weeks. A bad start is difficult to atone for, and the Arabs form their judgements on externals that we ignore. When you have reached the inner circle in a tribe you can do as you please with yourself and them.

2. Learn all you can about your Ashraf and Bedu. Get to know their families clans and tribes, friends and enemies, wells, hills and roads. Do all this by listening and by indirect enquiry. Do not ask questions. Get to speak their dialect of Arabic, not yours. Until you can understand their allusions avoid getting deep into conversation, or you will drop bricks. Be a little stiff at first.

3. In matters of business deal only with the commander of the army, column or party in which you serve. Never give orders to anyone at all, and reserve your directions or advice for the C.O., however great the temptation (for efficiency's sake) of dealing direct with his underlings. Your place is advisory, and your advice is due to the commander alone. Let him see that this is your conception of your duty, and that his is to be the sole executive of your joint plans.

4. Win and keep the confidence of your leader. Strengthen his prestige at your expense before others when you can. Never refuse or quash schemes he may put forward: but ensure that they are put forward in the first instance privately to you.

Always approve them, and after praise modify them insensibly, causing the suggestions to come from him, until they are in accord with your own opinion. When you attain this point, hold him to it, keep a tight grip of his ideas, and push him forward as firmly as possible, but secretly so that no one but himself (and he not too clearly) is aware of your pressure.

5. Remain in touch with your leader as constantly and unobtrusively as you can. Live with him, that at mealtimes and at audiences you may be naturally with him in his tent. Formal visits to give advice are not so good as the constant dropping of ideas in casual talk. When stranger sheikhs come in for the first time to swear allegiance and offer service, clear out of the tent. If their first impression is of foreigners in the confidence of the Sherif, it will do the Arab cause much harm.

6. Be shy of too close relations with the subordinates of the expedition. Continued intercourse with them will make it impossible for you to avoid going behind or beyond the instructions that the Arab C.O. has given them on your advice: and in so disclosing the weakness of his position you altogether destroy your own.

7. Treat the sub chiefs of your force quite easily and lightly. In this way you hold yourself above their level. Treat the leader, if a Sherif, with respect. He will return your manner, and you and he will then be alike, and above the rest. Precedence is a serious matter among the Arabs, and you must attain it.

8. Your ideal position is when you are present and not noticed. Do not be too intimate, too prominent, or too earnest. Avoid being identified too long or too often with any tribal sheikh, even if C.O. of the expedition. To do your work you must be above jealousies, and you lose prestige if you are associated with a tribe or clan, and its inevitable feuds. Sherifs are above all blood-feuds and local rivalries, and form the only principle of unity among the Arabs. Let your name therefore be coupled always with a Sherif's, and share his attitude towards the tribes. When the moment comes for action put yourself publicly under his orders. The Bedu will then follow suit.

9. Magnify and develop the growing conception of the Sherifs as the natural aristocracy of the Arabs. Inter-tribal jealousies make it impossible for any sheikh to attain a commanding position, and the only hope of union in nomad Arabia is that the Ashraf be universally acknowledged as the ruling class. Sherifs are half-townsmen, half-nomad, in manner and life, and have the instinct of command. Mere merit and money would be insufficient to obtain such recognition: but the Arab reverence for pedigree and the prophet gives hope for the ultimate success of the Ashraf.

10. Call your Sherif 'Sidi' in public and in private. Call other people by their ordinary names, without title. In intimate conversation call a Sheikh 'Abu Annad', 'Akhu Alia' or some similar by-name.

11. The foreigner and Christian is not a popular person in Arabia. However friendly and informal the treatment of yourself may be, remember always that your foundations are very sandy ones. Wave a Sherif in front of you like a banner, and hide your own mind and person. If you succeed you will have hundreds of miles of country and thousands of men under your orders, and for this it is worth bartering the outward show.

12. Cling tight to your sense of humour. You will need it every day. A dry irony is the most useful type, and repartee of a personal and not too broad character will double your influence with the chiefs. Reproof if wrapped up in some smiling form will carry further and last longer than the most violent speech. The power of mimicry or parody is valuable but use it sparingly for wit is more dignified than humour. Do not cause a laugh at a Sherif except amongst Sherifs.

13. Never lay hands on an Arab: you degrade yourself. You may think the resultant obvious increase of outward respect a gain to you: but what you have really done is to build a wall between you and their inner selves. It is difficult to keep quiet when everything is being done wrong, but the less you lose your temper the greater your advantage. Also then you will not go mad yourself.

14. While very difficult to drive, the Bedu are easy to lead, if you have the patience to bear with them. The less apparent your interferences the more your influence. They are willing to follow your advice and do what you wish, but they do not mean you or anyone else to be aware of that. It is only after the end of all annoyances that you find at bottom their real fund of good will.

15. Do not try to do too much with your own hands. Better the Arabs do it tolerably than that you do it perfectly. It is their war, and you are to help them, not to win it for them. Actually also, under the very odd conditions of Arabia, your practical work will not be as good as perhaps you think it is.

16. If you can, without being too lavish forestall presents to yourself. A well placed gift is often most effective in winning over a suspicious sheikh. Never receive a present without giving a liberal return, but you may delay this return (while letting its ultimate certainty be known) if you require a particular service from the giver. Do not let them ask you for things, since their greed will then make them look upon you only as a cow to milk.

17. Wear an Arab headcloth when with a tribe. Bedu have a malignant prejudice against the hat, and believe that our persistence in wearing it (due probably to British obstinacy of dictation) is founded on some immoral or irreligious principle. A thick headcloth forms a good protection against the sun, and if you wear a hat your best Arab friends will be ashamed of you in public.

18. Disguise is not advisable. Except in special areas let it be clearly known that you are a British officer and a Christian. At the same time if you can wear Arab kit when with the tribes you will acquire their trust and intimacy to a degree impossible in uniform. It is however dangerous and difficult. They make no special allowances for you when you dress like them. Breaches of etiquette not charged against a foreigner are not condoned to you in Arab clothes. You will be like an actor in a foreign theatre, playing a part day and night for months, without rest, and for an anxious stake. Complete success, which is when the Arabs forget your strangeness and speak naturally before you, counting you one of themselves, is perhaps only attainable in character: while half success (all that most of us will strive for – the other costs too much) is easier to win in British things, and you yourself will last longer, physically and mentally, in the comfort that they mean. Also then the Turks will not hang you when you're caught.

19. If you wear Arab things, wear the best. Clothes are significant among the tribes, and you must wear the appropriate, and appear at ease in them. Dress like a Sherif – if they agree to it.

20. If you wear Arab things at all, go the whole way. Leave your English friends and customs on the coast, and fall back on Arab habits entirely. It is possible, starting thus level with them, for the European to beat the Arabs at their own game, for we have stronger motives for our action, and put more heart into it than they. If you can surpass them, you have taken an immense stride toward complete success, but the strain of living and thinking in a foreign and half-understood language, the savage food, strange clothes, and still stranger ways, with the complete loss of privacy and quiet, and the impossibility of ever relaxing your watchful imitation of the others for months on end, provide such an added stress to the ordinary difficulties of dealing with the Bedu, the climate, and the Turks, that this road should not be chosen without serious thought.

21. Religious discussions will be fairly frequent. Say what you like about your own side, and avoid criticism of theirs, unless you know that the point is external, when you may score heavily by proving it so. With the Bedu Islam is so all-pervading an element that there is a little religiosity, little fervour, and no regard for externals. Do not think, from their conduct, that they are careless. Their conviction of the truth of their faith, and its share in every act and thought and principle of their daily life is so intimate and intense as to be unconscious,

unless roused by opposition. Their religion is as much a part of nature to them as is sleep, or food.

22. Do not try to trade on what you know of fighting. The Hejaz confounds ordinary tactics. Learn the Bedu principles of war as thoroughly and as quickly as you can, for till you know them your advice will be no good to the Sherif. Unnumbered generations of tribal raids have taught them more about some parts of the business than we will ever know. In familiar conditions they fight well, but strange events cause panic. Keep your unit small. Their raiding parties are usually from one hundred to two hundred men, and if you take a crowd they only get confused. Also their sheikhs, while admirable company commanders, are too set to learn to handle the equivalents of battalions or regiments. Don't attempt unusual things, unless they appeal to the sporting instinct Bedu have so strongly, or unless success is obvious. If the objective is a good one (booty) they will attack like fiends: they are splendid scouts, their mobility gives you the advantage that will win this local war, they make proper use of their knowledge of the country (don't take tribesmen to places they do not know), and the gazelle-hunters, who form a proportion of the better men, are great shots at visible targets. A sheikh from one tribe cannot give orders to men from another: a sherif is necessary to command a mixed tribal force. If there is plunder in prospect, and the odds are at all equal, you will win. Do not waste Bedu attacking trenches (they will not stand casualties) or in trying to defend a position, for they cannot sit still without slacking. The more unorthodox and Arab your proceedings the more likely you are to have the Turks cold, for they lack initiative and expect you to. Don't play for safety.

23. The open reason that Bedu give you for action or inaction may be true, but always there will be better reasons left for you to divine. You must find these inner reasons (they will be denied, but are none the less in operation) before shaping your arguments for one course or other. Allusion is more effective than logical exposition: they dislike concise expression. Their minds work just as ours do, but on different premises. There is nothing unreasonable, incomprehensible, or inscrutable, in the Arab. Experience of them, and knowledge of their prejudices will enable you to foresee their attitude and possible cause of action in nearly every case.

24. Do not mix Bedu and Syrians, or trained men and tribesmen. You will get work out of neither, for they hate each other. I have never seen a successful combined operation, but many failures. In particular, ex-officers of the Turkish army, however Arab in feelings and blood and language, are hopeless with Bedu. They are narrow-minded in tactics, unable to adjust themselves to irregular warfare, clumsy in Arab etiquette, swollen-headed to the extent of being incapable of politeness to a tribesman for more than a few minutes, impatient,

and, usually, helpless on the road and in action. Your orders (if you were unwise enough to give any) would be more readily obeyed by Beduins than those of any Mohammedan Syrian officer. Arab townsmen and Arab tribesmen regard each other mutually as poor relations – and poor relations are much more objectionable than poor strangers.

25. In spite of ordinary Arab example avoid too free talk about women. It is as difficult a subject as religion, and their standards are so unlike our own, that a remark harmless in English may appear as unrestrained to them, as some of their statements would look to us, if translated literally.

26. Be as careful of your servants as of yourself. If you want a sophisticated one you will probably have to take an Egyptian, or a Sudani, and unless you are very lucky he will undo on trek much of the good you so laboriously effect. Arabs will cook rice and make coffee for you, and leave you if required to do unmanly work like cleaning boots or washing. They are only really possible if you are in Arab kit. A slave brought up in the Hejaz is the best servant, but there are rules against British subjects owning them, so they have to be lent to you. In any case take with you an Ageyli or two when you go up country. They are the most efficient couriers in Arabia, and understand camels.

27. The beginning and ending of the secret of handling Arabs is unremitting study of them. Keep always on your guard; never say an inconsidered thing, or do an unnecessary thing: watch yourself and your companions all the time: hear all that passes, search out what is going on beneath the surface, read their characters, discover their tastes and their weaknesses, and keep everything you find out to yourself. Bury yourself in Arab circles, have no interests and no ideas except the work in hand, so that your brain shall be saturated with one thing only, and you realise your part deeply enough to avoid the little slips that would undo the work of weeks. Your success will be just proportional to the amount of mental effort you devote to it.

T. E. Lawrence's Published Writings

Note

For further bibliographical information see: P. M. O'Brien, *T. E. Lawrence, a Bibliography* (Winchester, St. Paul's Bibliographies; Boston, G. K. Hall, 1988). This bibliography of works by and about Lawrence contains extensive listings. See also J. M. Wilson, *T. E. Lawrence, a Guide to Printed and Manuscript Materials* (Fordingbridge, Hampshire, Castle Hill Press, 1990), for an annotated listing of primary manuscript and printed sources.

Major Works and Translations, listed in order of completion
Editions listed contain the most complete texts

The Influence of the Crusades on European Military Architecture – to the End of the XIIth Century

Lawrence's BA thesis (1910) published as *Crusader Castles* (first published 1936). Oxford, Clarendon Press, 1988 (contains additional material by Lawrence and an introduction and notes by D. Pringle).

The Wilderness of Zin

By C. L. Woolley and T. E. Lawrence (first published 1915). London, Jonathan Cape, 1936.

Seven Pillars of Wisdom

'Oxford text' (1920-2). Eight copies of this draft were printed for Lawrence in 1922 by the *Oxford Times*. The text contains important historical material omitted from the final version and an edition is now being prepared for publication.

Revised text (privately printed 1926, first published for general circulation 1935). London, Jonathan Cape, 1973 (contains passages omitted from earlier editions while retaining the dates in the page headlines omitted from later Cape printings).

The Forest Giant

Translation of *Le Gigantesque* by Adrien le Corbeau (first published 1924). London, Jonathan Cape; Garden City, N.Y., Doubleday, Doran, 1935 (contains material not in the original edition).

Revolt in the Desert
Abridgement of *Seven Pillars of Wisdom* (1926). London, Jonathan Cape; New York, George H. Doran, 1927.

The Mint
Manuscript given to Edward Garnett (1927-8). Garden City, N.Y., Doubleday, Doran & Co., 1936 (fifty copies privately printed to secure American copyright).
Revised text (1929-35, first published 1955). London, Jonathan Cape, 1973 (paperback, with a preface by J. M. Wilson, Harmondsworth, Middlesex, Penguin Books, 1978).

The Odyssey of Homer
Translation (1928-31, first published in an edition of 530 copies in 1932) New York, O.U.P., 1932, London, O.U.P., 1935.

Essays, introductions, articles, contributions to books by other writers, and other minor works (excluding serials and reprints of articles from one journal in another). Listed under date of writing

1904

'Playground Football'
School magazine contribution, signed 'Goalpost', presumed to be by T. E. Lawrence, *O.H.S. Magazine* Vol I, No. 5, March 1904.

'Playground Cricket'
School Magazine contribution, signed 'L.ii.' (1904), *O.H.S. Magazine* Vol II, No. 2, July 1904.

1906

'The Bastion'
School magazine contribution, signed 'Two Calcotripticians' [i.e. T. E. Lawrence and C. F. C. Beeson], *O.H.S. Magazine* Vol. III, No. 5, February 1906.

1907

How to Win a Scholarship
Contribution to a school magazine article compiled by C. F. C. Beeson, *O.H.S. Magazine* Vol. IV, No. 3, March 1907.

1910

Two Arabic Folk Tales
Privately printed, Corvinus Press, 1937 (30 copies).

1911

Mores Romanorum
   Printed pp. 93-4 above.

The Diary 1911
   Privately printed, Corvinus Press, 1937 (reprinted in *Oriental Assembly*,
   1939, see collected writings).

'Vandalism in Upper Syria and Palestine' [Letter to the editor]
   The Times (London) 9.8.1911 (reprinted pp. 92-3 above).

1912

'The Kaer of Ibu Wardani' [sic]
   Jesus College Magazine Vol. I, No. 2, January 1913. The title should read
   'The Kasr of Ibn Wardani'.

1914

Carchemish, Report on the Excavations at Jerablus . . .
   Contains contributions by T. E. Lawrence (written between 1911 and 1922):
   London, The British Museum, 3 vols, 1914-52.

Military Report on the Sinai Peninsula
   Compiled by T. E. Lawrence (originally published for restricted circulation
   by the War Office General Staff, Geographical Section, in 1914). Fordingbridge, Castle Hill Press, 1990, introduction by J. M. Wilson.

1916

Arab Bulletin (1916-19)
   Lawrence edited the first numbers, and contributed regularly thereafter (a
   very small edition of this secret Intelligence publication was published by the
   Arab Bureau). Facsimile edition: Gerrards Cross (Buckinghamshire),
   Archive Editions, 1986 [500 copies]. (Most of Lawrence's contributions
   have been reprinted elsewhere, see collected writings: *Secret Despatches
   from Arabia*, 1939, and collected letters: *Wartime Diaries and Letters*, 1990).

1917

Military Handbook on Palestine
   Unsigned contributions by T. E. Lawrence, two or three printings, G.S.(I),
   E.E.F. and Arab Bureau, 1917.

1918

H. Pirie-Gordon (ed): *A Brief Record of the Advance of the Egyptian
Expeditionary Force*

Contains unsigned contributions on the Arab Revolt by Lawrence. Cairo, *Palestine News*, 1918.

'Release of Damascus'
Palestine News (Cairo) 10.10.1918 (reprinted in *Wartime Diaries and Letters*, 1990, see collected writings).

'The Arab March on Damascus'
The Times 17.10.1918 (reprinted in *Wartime Diaries and Letters*, 1990, see collected writings).

'The Arab Campaign: Land and Sea Operations: British Navy's Help'
The Times (London) 26.11.1918 (reprinted in *Evolution of a Revolt*, 1968, see collected writings).

'The Arab Epic: Feisal's Battles in the Desert: On the Threshold of Syria'
The Times (London) 27.11.1918 (reprinted in *Evolution of a Revolt*, 1968, see collected writings).

'The Arab Epic: Doom of Turk Power in Syria: Wrecking the Hedjaz Railway'
The Times (London) 28.11.1918 (reprinted in *Evolution of a Revolt*, 1968, see collected writings).

1919

'Demolitions under Fire'
The Royal Engineers' Journal (Chatham) Vol. XXIX, No. 1, January 1919 (reprinted in *The Essential T. E. Lawrence*, 1951, see collected writings).

'Diary of the Peace Conference'
See collected letters: *The Letters of T. E. Lawrence*, 1938.

'Sidelights on the Arab War'
The Times (London) 4.9.1919.

'The Syrian Question' [Letter to the editor]
The Times (London) 11.9.1919.

1920

'Secrets of the War on Mecca'; 'The War of the Departments'
Daily Express (London) 28-9.5.1920 (reprinted in *Evolution of a Revolt*, 1968, see collected writings).

'The Middle East: How We are Losing Prestige'
Sunday Times (London) 30.5.1920.

'With Feisal at Court and Afield', 'Arabian Nights and Days' (etc)
Extracts from the uncompleted first abridgement of *Seven Pillars of Wisdom*, (1920) *The World's Work,* Vol. XLII, Nos 3-6, July - October 1921 (reprinted in *Evolution of a Revolt*, 1968, see collected writings).

'A Set Piece, January 1918'
Extract from the unpublished first abridgement of *Seven Pillars of Wisdom* (1920) *Army Quarterly* Vol. II, No. 1, April 1921.

'Sherif Feisal, King of the Irak'
Biographical note written in the summer of 1920, *The Landmark* (London) Vol. III, No. 10, October 1921.

'France, Britain, and the Arabs'
Observer (London) 8.8.1920.

'Ferment for Freedom'
Daily Herald (London) 9.8.1920.

'Emir Feisal'
The Times, London, 7 and 11.8.1920 (reprinted in *Evolution of a Revolt*, 1968, see collected writings).

'Mesopotamia: the Truth about the Campaign'
Sunday Times (London) 22.8.1920 (reprinted in *The Letters of T. E. Lawrence*, 1938, see collected letters).

'The Egyptian Problem'
Review of a book of the same title by Sir Valentine Chirol, *Observer* (London) 19.9.1920.

'The Changing East'
The Round Table Vol. X, No. 40, September 1920 (reprinted in *Oriental Assembly*, 1939, see collected writings).

'The Evolution of a Revolt'
Army Quarterly (London), Vol. I, No. 1, October 1920 (reprinted in *Evolution of a Revolt*, 1968, see collected writings).

Travels in Arabia Deserta by C. M. Doughty
Introduction by T. E. Lawrence, London, Jonathan Cape and the Medici Society, 1921.

1921

'If you keep unstained the honour of your house . . . '
Translation of a poem in Arabic by Emir Feisal written in Sir Edward Marsh's commonplace book and dated 26.1.1921, L. Russell (ed), *The Saturday Book* 11, London, Hutchinson, 1951.

Catalogue of an Exhibition of Arab Portraits
　　Preface by T. E. Lawrence (written in Aden, August 1921). London, The
　　Leicester Galleries, 1921 (the preface was also used in an abridged form for
　　a second exhibition held in 1927. It was reprinted in its original form in
　　Oliver Brown: *Exhibition*, London, Evelyn, Adams & Mackay, 1968; and in
　　its abridged form in *Oriental Assembly*, 1939, see collected writings).

1922

'Arabian Politics: Resignation of Colonel T. E. Lawrence as Adviser'
　　Letter from T. E. Lawrence to Sir J. E. Shukburgh 4.7.1922, published in the
　　Morning Post (London) 20.7.1922 (reprinted in *The Letters of T. E.
　　Lawrence*, 1938, see collected letters).

1923

'A Sea-Trip'
　　Printed pp. 715-6 above.

Dust-jacket blurb for *Sturly* by Pierre Custot
　　(Written for Jonathan Cape in October 1923). London, Jonathan Cape, 1924.

1924

The Twilight of the Gods and other Tales by Richard Garnett
　　Introduction by T. E. Lawrence. London, John Lane, the Bodley Head; New
　　York, Dodd, Mead, 1924.

1925

'My estimate of the time required . . . '
　　(Privately printed letter to the subscribers of *Seven Pillars of Wisdom*, dated
　　1.6.1925.)

Essay on Flecker
　　(Written about 1925, first published privately in 1937, reprinted in *Men in
　　Print*, 1940, see collected writings).

1926

'Ramping'
　　Article signed 'J.C.', submitted anonymously to motorcycling journals but
　　rejected, published in *Journal of the Royal Air Force College* (Cranwell),
　　Vol. XI, No. 1, Spring 1931.

1927

'History of *Seven Pillars*'
　　(Bibliographical note dated 1.1.1927) *Texas Quarterly* Vol. V, No. 3, 1962.

Some Notes on the Writing of the Seven Pillars of Wisdom
> (Privately printed 1927, reprinted in editions of *Seven Pillars of Wisdom* after 1935).

Lawrence and the Arabs by R. R. Graves
> Extensive contributions and corrections by T. E. Lawrence (see collected letters: *T. E. Lawrence to his Biographer Robert Graves*, 1938). London, Jonathan Cape, 1927; Garden City, N.Y., Doubleday, Doran, 1928 (US title *Lawrence and the Arabian Adventure*).

'Seven Pillars of Wisdom' [note on the text]
> *Now and Then* (London) No. 25, autumn 1927.

'D. H. Lawrence's Novels'
> Book review signed 'C.D.', *The Spectator* (London) 6.8.1927 (reprinted in *The Essential T. E. Lawrence*, 1951, see collected writings).

'Mixed Biscuits'
> Book review signed 'C.D.', *The Spectator* (London) 19.8.1927.

'A Critic of Critics Criticised
> Review of the works of Walter Savage Landor signed 'C.D.', *The Spectator* (London) 27.8.1927 (reprinted in *Men in Print*, 1940, see collected writings).

'Hakluyt – First Naval Propagandist'
> Book review signed 'C.D.', *The Spectator* (London) 10.9.1927.

1928

'The Wells Short Stories'
> Book review signed 'C.D.', *The Spectator* (London) 25.2.1928

The Imperial Camel Corps with Colonel Lawrence . . . and, Lawrence and the Arab Revolt, by D. G. Pearman
> Lecture slide notes, with a prefatory letter by T. E. Lawrence received by Pearman on 5.3.1928. London, Newton & Co, 1928 (Lawrence's letter reprinted in *The Letters of T. E. Lawrence*, 1938, see collected letters).

1931

Arabia Felix, by Bertram Thomas
> Foreword by T. E. Lawrence. London, Jonathan Cape; New York, Charles Scribners' Sons, 1932.

1932

The 200 Class Royal Air Force Seaplane Tender, Provisional Issue of Notes
> (Restricted circulation 1932, first published in *A History of Royal Air Force Marine Craft 1918-1986* by G. D. Pilborough, Appendix 1b: 'The 200 Class Seaplane Tender' London, Canimpex, 1986.)

No Decency Left by Barbara Rich [pseud. of R. R. Graves and L. Riding]
(Novel, containing an unsigned description of an imaginary autogyro by T. E. Lawrence written in April 1931) London, Jonathan Cape, 1932 (Lawrence's contribution reprinted in *T. E. Lawrence to his Biographer Robert Graves*, 1938, see collected letters).

1933

'T. E. Lawrence' in Arabia and After by B. H. Liddell Hart
Extensive contributions and corrections by T. E. Lawrence (see *T. E. Lawrence to his Biographer Liddell Hart*, 1928) London, Jonathan Cape, 1934; New York, Dodd, Mead, 1934 (US title *Colonel Lawrence, the Man behind the Legend*).

1934-5

'Leaves in the Wind'
Notes probably destined for a book about the RAF, published in *The Letters of T. E. Lawrence*, 1938, see collected letters.

River Niger by S. Jesty
Prefatory letter by T. E. Lawrence [to C. J. Greenwood, Jesty's publisher, dated 20.5.1934] London, Boriswood, 1935.

'Myself'
(Notes for his own obituary sent to R. R. Graves on 4.2.1935). *Evening Standard* (London) 20.5.1935 (original text reprinted in *The Letters of T. E. Lawrence*, 1938, see collected letters).

Collected Writings, listed in order of first publication.

A. W. Lawrence (ed.), *Secret Despatches from Arabia*
London, Golden Cockerel Press, 1939, 1,000 copies. (Lawrence's dispatches are reprinted with much additional material in *Wartime Diaries and Letters*, 1990, see below).

A. W. Lawrence (ed.), *Oriental Assembly*
London, Williams & Norgate, 1939; New York, E. P. Dutton, 1940.

A. W. Lawrence (ed.), *Men in Print, Essays in Literary Criticism*
London, Golden Cockerel Press, 1940 (500 copies).

D. Garnett (ed.) *The Essential T. E. Lawrence*
London, Jonathan Cape; New York, E. P. Dutton, 1951.

S. Weintraub (ed.) *Evolution of a Revolt: Early Post-War Writings*
University Park and London, Pennsylvania State University Press, 1968.

Works edited by Lawrence

J. M. Wilson (ed.), *Minorities*
(Commonplace-book of poetry collected by Lawrence, 1919-27). London, Jonathan Cape, 1971; Garden City, N.Y., Doubleday, Doran, 1972.

Ian McKinnon [pseud. of I. Tyre] *Garroot, Adventures of a Clydeside Apprentice.*
(Edited for Jonathan Cape by T. E. Lawrence.) London, Jonathan Cape, 1933.

Collected letters, listed in order of first publication.

Letters from T. E. Shaw to Bruce Rogers
Privately printed, 1933, 200 copies. Letters reprinted in J. M. Wilson: *T. E. Lawrence, Bruce Rogers, and Homer's Odyssey*, 1990, see below).

More Letters from T. E. Lawrence to Bruce Rogers
Privately printed, 1936 (300 copies, letters reprinted in J. M. Wilson: *T. E. Lawrence, Bruce Rogers, and Homer's Odyssey*, 1990, see below).

Letters from T. E. Shaw to Viscount Carlow
Privately printed, 1936, 17 copies.

D. Garnett (ed.), *The Letters of T. E. Lawrence*
(First published 1938) London, Spring Books, 1964 (incorporating corrections, with a foreword by B. H. Liddell Hart).

R. R. Graves and B. H. Liddell Hart (eds.), *T. E. Lawrence to his Biographer Robert Graves*, *T. E. Lawrence to his Biographer Liddell Hart*
Issued in a limited edition as companion volumes in 1938; first published for general circulation as *T. E. Lawrence to his Biographers Robert Graves and Liddell Hart* (two volumes in one): London, Cassell; Garden City, N.Y., Doubleday, Doran, 1962.

Eight Letters from T.E.L. [to Harley Granville-Barker]
Privately printed, 1939, fifty copies.

C. Sydney Smith, *The Golden Reign*
(Contains fifty letters from Lawrence to Sydney Smith) London, Cassell, 1940.

Henry Williamson, *Genius of Friendship, 'T. E. Lawrence'*
Letters from T. E. Lawrence to Henry Williamson, with a commentary by Williamson. London, Faber & Faber, 1941 (letters from T. E. Lawrence reprinted in *Letters between T. E. Lawrence and Henry Williamson*, 1991, below).

H. S. Ede (ed.), *Shaw–Ede*, T. E. Lawrence's Letters to H. S. Ede 1927-1935
London, Golden Cockerel Press, 1942, 500 copies.

M. R. Lawrence (ed.), *The Home Letters of T. E. Lawrence and his Brothers*
    Oxford, Basil Blackwell; NY, Macmillan, 1954

T.E.L. Five Hitherto Unpublished Letters [to R. V. Buxton]
    Privately printed, 1975, fifty copies.

H. Montgomery Hyde, *Solitary in the Ranks, Lawrence of Arabia as Airman and Private Soldier*
    (An account of Lawrence's service life built around his correspondence with
    Lord Trenchard.) London, Constable, 1977; New York, Atheneum, 1978.

J. M. Wilson (ed), *Letters from T. E. Lawrence to E. T. Leeds*
    Andoversford, Whittington Press, 1988, 750 copies.

M. Brown (ed), *The Letters of T. E. Lawrence*
    London, Dent, 1988; NY, Norton, 1989.

J. M. Wilson, *T. E. Lawrence, Bruce Rogers, and Homer's Odyssey*
    (Contains the surviving correspondence between T. E. Lawrence and Bruce
    Rogers.) Wakefield, Fleece Press, 1990 (limited edition).

J. M. Wilson and J. Law (eds.), *T. E. Lawrence: Wartime Diaries and Letters*
    N. Helari, 1990.

Editions of Lawrence's correspondence with Henry Williamson and with
Bernard and Charlotte Shaw are in preparation.

References and Notes

Manuscript materials: File and, in most cases, page number or document identification are given. In the case of the embargoed T. E. Lawrence papers at the Bodleian Library, file numbers are not listed as they will change when the papers become generally available.

In many instances originals or transcripts of documents are available in more than one location. The source listed here is the source I have used. For example, there are few references to the many original T. E. Lawrence letters held at the University of Texas because transcripts of these letters made for David Garnett's *Letters of T. E. Lawrence* (1938) were available to me among the T. E. Lawrence papers at the Bodleian Library.

Dates of letters and other documents are given in the standard British sequence: day-month-year, e.g. 9.11.1916 for 9th November 1916.

When quoting letters by T. E. Lawrence published in one of the standard collections, I have indicated this by using one of the abbreviations listed below. When quoting passages partially or wholly omitted from the letter as published in such a collection, this fact is indicated.

When quoting telegrams which were not signed by name, I have nevertheless given the name, followed by the sender's identification (usually an abridged military title or telegraphic address) as stated on the document: e.g. 'Sir A. J. Murray (Chief Egypforce)'.

Printed books: American as well as English editions are listed where the page references apply in both.

Abbreviations used in the Notes

AB	*Arab Bulletin* (Cairo), secret Intelligence journal issued by the Arab Bureau, 1916-19. Facsimile reprint (Gerrards Cross, Archive Editions, 1984).
ADM	Archives of the British Admiralty in the Public Record Office, London.
AE	Archives of the French Foreign Office, Paris.

AFGG   [France] Ministère de la Guerre, Etat-Major de l'Armée –
              Service Historique: *Les Armées Françaises dans la Grande
              Guerre*, Tome IX – premier volume, Volume d'Annexes (Paris,
              Imprimerie Nationale, 1935).

AIR   Archives of the Royal Flying Corps and Royal Air Force in the
              Public Record Office, London.

Arbur   Telegraphic address of the Arab Bureau, Cairo.

Ashmolean A   Ashmolean Museum Archives, Oxford.

BL   British Library, London.

B:LH   *T. E. Lawrence to his Biographer Liddell Hart* (London, Faber
              & Faber, 1938; Garden City NY, Doubleday, Doran, 1939).

BM/A   Papers of F. G. Kenyon in the British Museum Archives relating
              to the excavations at Carchemish.

BM/WAA   Archaeological papers relating to the Carchemish excavations in
              the British Museum, Department of Western Asiatic Antiquities.

Bodleian   Bodleian Library, Oxford.

Bodleian R   Categories of embargoed material in the Bodleian Library,
              including the T. E. Lawrence papers embargoed until the year
              2000.

B:RG   *T. E. Lawrence to his Biographer Robert Graves* (London, Faber
              & Faber, 1938; Garden City NY, Doubleday, Doran, 1939).

CAB   Archives of the British Cabinet in the Public Record Office,
              London.

CO   Archives of the British Colonial Office in the Public Record
              Office, London.

DBFP 1/4   *Documents on British Foreign Policy 1919-1939*, First Series,
              Vol. IV, 1919, ed. E. L. Woodward and R. Butler (London,
              HMSO, 1952).

DG   D. Garnett (ed.), *Letters of T. E. Lawrence* (London, Jonathan
              Cape 1938; Garden City NY, Doubleday, Doran, 1939).

Dirmilint   Telegraphic address of the Director of Military Intelligence,
              War Office, London.

Durham   Durham University Library.

EoR   S. and R. Weintraub (eds.), *Evolution of a Revolt* [collected
              minor writings of T. E. Lawrence] (University Park and London,
              Pennsylvania State University Press, 1967).

ETEL	D. Garnett (ed.), *The Essential T. E. Lawrence* (London, Jonathan Cape; New York, E. P. Dutton, 1951).
FO	Archives of the British Foreign Office in the Public Record Office, London.
Friends	A. W. Lawrence (ed.), *T. E. Lawrence by his Friends* (London, Jonathan Cape; Garden City NY, Doubleday, Doran, 1937).
Hedgehog	Telegraphic address of A. C. Dawnay's Arab Operations staff in Cairo. Some telegraph operators abbreviated this to 'Hedghog'.
HL	M. R. Lawrence (ed.), *The Home Letters of T. E. Lawrence and his Brothers* (Oxford, Blackwell; New York, Macmillan, 1954).
HGM	E. Brémond, *Le Hedjaz dans la Guerre Mondiale* (Paris, Payot, 1931).
Houghton	Houghton Library, Harvard University.
HRHRC	Harry Ransom Humanities Research Center, University of Texas, Austin.
Intrusive	Telegraphic address of the Military Intelligence Department, Cairo.
IWM	Imperial War Museum, London.
KCL	The Liddell Hart Centre for Military Archives, King's College, London.
LAA	K. Morsey, *T. E. Lawrence und der arabische Aufstand 1916-18* (Osnabrück, Biblio Verlag, 1976. A revised English edition is in preparation)
LH:*TEL*	B. H. Liddell Hart, *'T. E. Lawrence' in Arabia and After* (London, Jonathan Cape, 1934).
L-L	J. M. Wilson (ed.), *Letters from T. E. Lawrence to E. T. Leeds* (Andoversford, Whittington Press, 1988).
L/P&S	Political and secret papers of the British India Office in the India Office Library, London.
LTEL	A. W. Lawrence (ed.), *Letters to T. E. Lawrence* (London, Jonathan Cape, 1962).
MB	M. Brown (ed.) *Letters of T. E. Lawrence* (London, J. M. Dent, 1988).
The Mint	T. E. Lawrence, *The Mint* [revised unexpurgated text] (London, Jonathan Cape, 1973).

MOEP	*Military Operations in Egypt and Palestine* ('Official History of the Great War' series) Vol. I by Sir G. MacMunn and C. Falls; Vol. II (Parts 1 and 2) by C. Falls and A. F. Becke; with two cases of maps (London, HMSO, 1930-9).
OA	A. W. Lawrence (ed.), *Oriental Assembly* [collected minor writings of T. E. Lawrence] (London, Williams & Norgate, 1939; New York, E. P. Dutton, 1940).
PEF	Archives of the Palestine Exploration Fund, London.
PRO	Public Record Office, London. Also a file class at the PRO designating collections of private papers held there.
SIR	H. M. Hyde, *Solitary in the Ranks* (London, Constable, 1977; New York, Atheneum, 1978).
SP	T. E. Lawrence, *Seven Pillars of Wisdom* (London, Jonathan Cape; Garden City NY, Doubleday, Doran, 1935).
SP(O)	*Seven Pillars of Wisdom*, 1922 draft, known as the 'Oxford' text.
WSC	Documents volumes published as companions to *Winston S Churchill* by R. S. Churchill then M. Gilbert (London, Heinemann, 1966-) For example *WSC* Docs 4/2 denotes *Winston S. Churchill* Volume IV, Companion Part 2, Documents July 1919–March 1921 (London, Heinemann, 1977).
WO	Archives of the British War Office in the Public Record Office, London.

Prologue

1. K. Morsey, *T. E. Lawrence und der arabische Aufstand 1916/18* (Osnabrück, Biblio Verlag, 1976). Originally written as a doctoral thesis. A revised English-language edition is in preparation. The book compares Lawrence's own account of the Arab Revolt in *Seven Pillars* with the evidence of contemporary documents, and also discusses criticisms made by biographers such as R. Aldington and S. Mousa.

2. T. E. Lawrence to V. W. Richards n.d. (1922). Bodleian R (transcript).

3. W. S. Churchill, address given at the City of Oxford High School for Boys on the occasion of the unveiling of a memorial to T. E. Lawrence, 3.10.1936 *HL* p. xiii.

4. At one time it was suggested, by J. Meyers and others, that I was commissioned to write this biography as a corrective to J. E. Mack's *A Prince of our Disorder* (Boston, Little, Brown, 1976. For Meyers's views see *Virginia Quarterly Review*, Vol. 52, No. 4, Autumn 1976).

   In reality, the project of a major historical biography was put to me some years before Mack's book was written, and I agreed to take on the commission before I had seen his text in any form. I had, however, already discussed Lawrence with him on many occasions during his research and I knew that his book would be a subjective interpretation of Lawrence, written from the unusual and interesting viewpoint of a professional psychiatrist.

   The biography I have written is a historical study based on far more extensive examination of contemporary records (especially British Government papers) than Mack was able to undertake. Consequently there have been many revisions (some of them substantial) in the factual narrative of Lawrence's life. In particular, I have dealt in greater depth with the history of the political, military, and literary activities which are at the core of Lawrence's reputation. These revisions and additions have considerably altered the biographical record given by Mack, and have sometimes placed his argument in question; but in no sense did I set out to overturn his specialist analysis and judgments.

5. T. E. Lawrence to R. R. Graves 28.6.1927 *B:RG* p. 58.

6. M. J-M. Larès, *T. E. Lawrence, la France, et les Français* (Université de Lille III, Service de Réproduction des Thèses, 1978; abridged edition: Paris, Imprimerie Nationale [Publications de la Sorbonne, 7] 1980). K. Morsey, *op. cit.* note 1 above. For an annotated list of American studies of Lawrence's writing see J. M. Wilson, *T. E. Lawrence: A Guide to Printed and Manuscript Materials* (Fordingbridge, Castle Hill Press, 1990).

7. In the past, some of the most outrageous allegations about Lawrence have been made by writers in France and Italy, but all in all there has been far more sensational comment about him in Britain than overseas.

8. H. Williamson, *Genius of Friendship* (London, Faber & Faber, 1941).

9. The letter to Alister Kershaw used as an introduction to Aldington's biography of Lawrence has left many readers with the impression that Aldington was a Lawrence admirer when he began research for the book, and that his views changed as he 'discovered the truth'. The letter is skilfully written to suggest this, but it does not actually contain any such statement. In reality, Aldington's published and unpublished correspondence clearly shows that dislike of Lawrence permeated his research from the outset. For his true attitude see *A Passionate Prodigality, Letters to Alan Bird from Richard Aldington* (New York, New York Public Library and Readex Books, 1975); *Literary Lifelines: the Richard Aldington–Lawrence Durrell*

Correspondence (London, Faber & Faber, 1981), and Aldington's unpublished letters to his wife Netta, BL Add. MS 54211.

10. Historians working on more recent events have met with difficulties where contemporary documents have contradicted accounts by the surviving participants. In some cases these conflicting versions have raised the possibility of action for libel. For a discussion of this delicate problem see C. Cruikshank, 'People or Papers' in *The Author* (London) Vol. XCVIII, No. 4, Winter 1987, pp. 105-6.

11. J. Bruce, 'I knew Lawrence' in the *Scottish Field*, (Glasgow) August 1938, pp. 20-1.

12. P. Adam, *Les Echecs de T. E. Lawrence* (privately printed, *c.* 1962, p. 9) author's translation.

13. J. M. Wilson, *T. E. Lawrence: A Guide to Printed and Manuscript Materials* (Fordingbridge, Castle Hill Press, 1990).

14. T. E. Lawrence to C. F. Shaw 29.3.1927 *MB* p. 321. BL Add. MS 45903. This comment is slightly at odds with the impression often given by Lawrence when discussing the use of documents. For example, after reading John Buchan's life of Montrose, he wrote: 'I am glad you allow common-sense to interpret the documents. A fetish of the last-school-but-one was to believe every document. As one who has had the making of original historical records I know how weak and partial and fallible they are. Fortunately you have been a man of affairs, and so are not to be taken in, like a scholar pure.' (26.12.1928 *DG* pp. 627-8) Elsewhere, his remarks were even stronger: 'One of the ominous signs of the time is that the public can no longer read history. The historian is retired into a shell to study the whole truth; which means that he learns to attach insensate importance to documents. The documents are liars. No man ever yet tried to write down the entire truth of any action in which he has been engaged. All narrative is *parti pris*. And to prefer an ancient written statement to the guiding of your instinct through the maze of related facts, is to encounter either banality or unreadableness. We know too much, and use too little knowledge.' (T. E. Lawrence to L. G. Curtis 22.12.1927 *DG* p. 559). However, I view with caution the extreme statements on the same theme reported by Ralph Isham (*Friends*, bottom of p. 298). Only the first of the passages cited by Isham comes from any letter I have seen. The remainder appear to be paraphrase, or memories of conversations with Lawrence. I am particularly doubtful about the weight that should be attached to the statement: 'What does [the truth] matter? History is but a series of accepted lies.' As Lawrence admitted in *Seven Pillars*, he enjoyed provoking people with outrageous assertions so that he could observe their reaction. This remark, made to an American banker who was investing huge sums in research on the Boswell papers, seems a typical instance (assuming that it was reported correctly).

In considering Lawrence's views, one must first of all recognise that his enthusiasm had been for medieval history. The documents relating to that period are notoriously undependable, and have often been contradicted by archaeological evidence. As a field archaeologist he would have been well aware of such conflicts. Secondly, he was by nature an interpretative historian. This does not mean that he was indifferent to the factual record other people had worked to establish. That record is, after all, the raw material for all worthwhile historical interpretation. Lawrence was urging intelligent use, not total disregard, of the documents. He himself used contemporary documents very extensively when writing *Seven Pillars*. Few historians of the twentieth century would accept his suggestion that researchers do not recognise partiality in written records. The archival sources for this period are very great, and it is usually possible to read so widely that the bias and inaccuracy of individual documents become obvious. Lawrence himself had no experience of, or taste for, this kind of research. It is therefore wrong to treat his comments as though they were the carefully considered views of a qualified research historian.

15. P. Adam, *Les Echecs de T. E. Lawrence* (Privately printed, *c.* 1962); A. Malraux, [unpublished biography of T. E. Lawrence], extract published as 'N'était-ce donc que cela?' in *T. E. Lawrence Studies* (n.pl.) Vol. I, No. 1, 1976, pp. 21-32; V. Ocampo, *338171 TE (Lawrence of Arabia)* (Buenos Aires, Sur, 1942; English translation: London, V. Gollancz, 1963). All three of these intellectual works on Lawrence (including Ocampo's) were originally written in French.

16. For the circumstances under which Lawrence's various portraits were painted see C. Grosvenor, *An Iconography: the Portraits of T. E. Lawrence* (Pasadena, The Otterden Press, 1988). There were only three major series of photographic portraits during Lawrence's adult life. All were taken at the photographers' request.

17. D. Stewart, *T. E. Lawrence* (London, Hamish Hamilton, 1977). See for instance Stewart's claims about Lawrence's relationship with Ali ibn el Hussein, which include the suggestion that Ali was responsible (under different circumstances) for the flogging described by Lawrence in *Seven Pillars* ch. LXXX. Not a shred of evidence is offered for these extraordinary allegations.

18. W. S. Churchill, *Life of Lord Randolph Churchill* London, Macmillan, 1906, pp. x-xi.

19. T. E. Lawrence to C. F. Shaw 27.11.1928. BL Add. MS 45904.

Chapter 1. Childhood
December 1891 – October 1907

1. *Baedeker's Northern France* (London, 1894) pp. 216-17.
2. T. E. Lawrence to R. White 10.6.1931 *DG* p. 721. According to M. J-M. Larès (*T. E. Lawrence, la France et les Français*, Paris, Imprimerie Nationale, 1980, p. 8 n. 9), contemporaries recalled only two large yachts at Dinard, neither of which belonged to Mr Lawrence. At that time, however, a 'yacht' was a sizeable vessel, and it is possible that Mr Lawrence had a smaller sailing boat of some kind.
3. Langley Lodge is about seven miles north-west of the village of Langley. The lease to Mr Lawrence survives, showing that on 1st May 1894 the Lawrence family took up a furnished tenancy of the house, 'with the kitchen garden and two Paddocks, coach house and Stabling' for two guineas a week. The lease, dated 27th April 1894, is signed T. Laurence [sic], showing that at that date Mr Lawrence was not fully accustomed to using this pseudonym. He also purchased game licences from the New Forest authorities for £20 per annum, at that date a large sum of money. (Information courtesy of Maggs Bros., rare book dealers, see Maggs Bros., *Catalogue 1091*, London, 1988, p. 49 #238.)
4. T. E. Lawrence, introduction to *Travels in Arabia Deserta* by C. M. Doughty (London, Jonathan Cape and the Medici Society, 1921) p. xxviii.
5. *Ibid.*
6. A. T. Pollard, first headmaster of the Oxford High School, quoted in *Reminiscences*

1881-1981 – *City of Oxford High School* – *Oxford High School* (in *Phoenix*, Oxford, No. 15, 1981, p. 22).

7. An analysis of parental occupations made in 1906 states that 108 pupils had fathers in categories given as 'independent means', professional, merchants, bankers, and retailers. Forty-six pupils had fathers who were clerks; just three fathers were artisans. See Board of Education: *Report of First Inspection, 15th-16th March 1906* in the Oxford City Library local history collection.

8. *Op. cit.* note 7 above.

9. H. R. Hall, 'T. E. Lawrence' in *Oxford High School Magazine* (Oxford) 1935, pp. 40-1.

10. T. E. Lawrence to C. F. Shaw 24.8.1926. BL Add. MS 45903.

11. T. E. Lawrence, amendments to the typescript of R. R. Graves, *Lawrence and the Arabs*, 1927 *B:RG* p. 61. Houghton fMS Eng 1252 (367).

12. *Oxford High School Magazine* (Oxford) Vol. II, No. 1, May 1904, p. 5.

13. *Ibid.* Vol. I, No. 5, March 1904, pp. 100-1.

14. *Ibid.* Vol. II, No. 2, July 1904, pp. 29-30.

15. E. F. Hall in *Friends* p. 46.

16. A. W. Lawrence to J. E. Mack 1.11.1968, quoted in Mack's *A Prince of our Disorder* (Boston, Little, Brown, 1976) p. 474 n. 70.

17. A. W. Lawrence to J. M. Wilson 12.5.1985.

18. Oxford Local Examinations Board, *Division Lists for the Year 1904: Junior Candidates* and *Tables Supplementary to the Division Lists* [etc.] (Oxford, James Parker & Son, 1904). Also 1904 Junior candidates' mark sheets, Oxford University Archives.

19. C. F. C. Beeson in *Friends* p. 52.

20. T. W. Chaundy in *Friends* p. 41.

21. C. F. C. Beeson in *Friends* p. 52.

22. 'Report of the Keeper of the Ashmolean Museum to the Visitors', in *Oxford University Gazette* (Oxford) Vol. xxxvii, No. 1203, 30.4.1907, pp. 552-6.

23. See J. E. Mack, *op. cit.* note 16 above, pp. 26-7: 'Arnold Lawrence told me that Lawrence wrote either to his friend Lionel Curtis or his mentor David Hogarth that when he was four and a half he began to discover what the situation was from trying to understand a discussion his father was having with a solicitor about managing the estate in Ireland' (source: Mack interview with A. W. Lawrence 15.7.1968). However, neither Mack nor I have found such a letter to Curtis or Hogarth.

24. T. E. Lawrence to C. F. Shaw 14.4.1927: 'They thought always that they were living in sin, and that we would some day find out. Whereas I knew it before I was ten, and they never told me'. BL Add. MS 45903. See also Mack, *op. cit.* note 16 above, p. 27: 'Arnold Lawrence is convinced his brother understood the fact of their illegitimacy by the time he was nine or ten years old' (source: Mack interviews with A. W. Lawrence 13.3.1965 and 15.7.1968).

25. C. F. Bell, notes on LH:*TEL*. BL Add. MS 63549.

26. A. W. Lawrence to J. M. Wilson 12.5.1985.

27. T. E. Lawrence to his family 19.5.1911 *HL* p. 160. Bodleian MS Res C13.

28. In 1933, when Lawrence had long known the truth about his parents' relationship, he wrote the following sketch of them for inclusion in Liddell Hart's biography: 'The father's self-appointed exile reduced his means to a craftsman's income, which the landowning pride of caste forbade him to increase by labour. As five sons came,

one after the other, the family's very necessaries of life were straitened. They existed only by the father's denying himself every amenity, and by the mother's serving her household like a drudge.

'Observers noted a difference in social attitude between the courtly but abrupt and large father, and the laborious mother. The father shot, fished, rode, sailed with the certainty of birthright experience. He never touched a book or wrote a cheque. The mother kept to herself, and kept her children jealously from meeting or knowing their neighbours. She was a Calvinist and ascetic, though a wonderful housewife, a woman of character and keen intelligence, with iron decision, and charming, when she wished' (*B:LH* p. 78).

In later life many people develop unreal views about their family circumstances as well as their parents' personalities and relationship with each other. These views, heavily coloured by the child's own relationship with its parents, can be very inaccurate indeed. This retrospective comment by Lawrence is clearly inconsistent with information contained in the Lawrence brothers' early letters home. Mr Lawrence's income was as great as that of middle-class professional families [see Appendix I] The parents took regular holidays both in Britain and abroad. A. W. Lawrence recalls that when still very young, 'I had to be lifted up to see "an extraordinary animal" in a glass case on a hotel mantelpiece, and said "it's only a duck-bill platypus"; that was not the first of a vast number of holidays, mostly in expensive hotels. There was never the least shortage of excellent food. My father denied himself no amenities (except drink, and that because he had become teetotal . . .). I accompanied one or both parents all over the south of England, Wales and (repeatedly) the Channel Islands.' He has also pointed out that the first paragraph in the statement to Liddell Hart is contradicted by the second, especially by its second sentence (A. W. Lawrence to J. M. Wilson 8.6.1987).

Even the statement 'he never touched a book or wrote a cheque' should not be taken literally. While Lawrence's father did not read a great deal for pleasure, Lawrence warmly commended Ruskin's architectural study *Stones of Venice* to him, in letters of 1906 (for details of Mr Lawrence's education see Appendix I). Lawrence's portrait of his mother is still more misleading. A. W. Lawrence has written: 'I emphatically deny that my mother served "like a drudge"; she kept two maids, a charwoman, a gardener; spent the mornings shopping (mainly for food) and seldom did any housework. She did not attempt to keep her children from the neighbours, and met them herself freely. She was neither a Calvinist nor ascetic.' (*Ibid.*)

29. T. E. Lawrence to C. F. Shaw 14.4.1927. BL Add. MS 45903.
30. B. H. Liddell Hart's notes on a conversation with Lawrence, weekend of 12.5.1929 omitted from *B:LH* p. 24. See also Lawrence's written reply to Liddell Hart's 'Queries I', partially omitted from *B:LH* p. 51. Bodleian R (transcript).
31. T. E. Lawrence to D. Knowles 7.12.1927 *DG* p. 553.
32. T. E. Lawrence, *The Mint*, Part 2, ch. 11, p. 132.
33. T. E. Lawrence, written reply to B. H. Liddell Hart's 'Queries I' *B:LH* p. 51.
34. A painting by H. S. Tuke found among Lawrence's possessions at his death would appear to show the young Lawrence in RGA uniform sitting on a beach. It has been suggested that the painting, which is now at Clouds Hill, provides evidence for Lawrence's pre-war enlistment. However, Tuke kept a detailed register of his works, and both the Tuke paintings Lawrence is known to have possessed were

entered in 1922 (see *The Registers of Henry Scott Tuke*, annotated by B. D. Price, Falmouth, Royal Cornwall Polytechnic Society, 2nd. ed. 1983). Lawrence's pictures have been identified as entries R987: 'Picture of Gray', and R988: 'Small bathing picture'. Both these paintings were purchased by R. F. C. Scott, but a marginal note by Tuke reads: 'When R. F. C. Scott died "Gray" bought these two at the sale of his effects for a fiver!' It is not known how the paintings came into Lawrence's possession, unless he is the person referred to by the pseudonym 'Gray'.

Lawrence probably knew of Tuke's work through C. F. Bell, a life-long friend of Tuke's who owned several of his paintings. It seems possible that Lawrence met Tuke in Cornwall after the war, during the period when he was making contact with artists who might illustrate *Seven Pillars*. He certainly visited Cornwall in June 1922 (see *B:RG* p. 20).

There is a cryptic reference in a letter from Lawrence to another artist, Elsie Falcon (who had asked Lawrence to sit for her) which may refer to this Tuke painting: 'if you are like the artist who said "Do sit: I really can't afford a proper model"... then by all means. He worked what was left of his study of me into a beach picture after, giving me a new head, several sizes smaller. Apparently I am shaped rather like a tadpole.' (undated, but 1928. Bodleian MS Eng. Lett. c. 213).

35. T. E. Lawrence to C. F. Shaw 26.12.1925. BL Add. MS 45903.
36. T. E. Lawrence, written reply to B. H. Liddell Hart's 'Queries I' *B:LH* p. 51 (where four words are omitted). Bodleian R (transcript).
37. T. E. Lawrence to Mrs Rieder 8.3.1914. Bodleian R (transcript).
38. T. E. Lawrence to his family 14.8.1906 omitted from *HL* p. 20 and from *MB* pp. 8-9. Bodleian MS Res C13.
39. T. E. Lawrence to his family 28.8.1906 *HL* p. 43. Bodleian MS Res C13.
40. T. E. Lawrence to his father 20.8.1906 *HL* p. 23. Bodleian MS Res C13.
41. T. E. Lawrence to his mother 17.8.1906 *HL* p. 21. Bodleian MS Res C13.
42. T. E. Lawrence to his mother 24.8.1906 *HL* p. 27. Bodleian MS Res C13.
43. T. E. Lawrence to his father 6.8.1906 *HL* p. 8. Bodleian MS Res C13.
44. *Ibid. HL* pp. 9-10.
45. T. E. Lawrence to his mother 24.8.1906 omitted from *HL* p. 32. Bodleian MS Res C13.
46. T. E. Lawrence to C. F. Shaw 14.4.1927. BL Add. MS 45903. Lawrence has confused the Episcopal Church of Scotland, which is in communion with the Church of England (though historically distinct from it), with the much larger Church of Scotland, a Presbyterian body.
47. T. E. Lawrence to his father 20.8.1906 omitted from *HL* p. 24. Bodleian MS Res C13.
48. T. E. Lawrence to his mother 24.8.1906 omitted from *HL* p. 30. Bodleian MS Res C13.
49. T. E. Lawrence to his father 6.8.1906 *HL* p. 9. Bodleian MS Res C13.
50. T. E. Lawrence to his mother 26.8.1906 omitted from *HL* p. 35. Bodleian MS Res C13.
51. T. E. Lawrence to C. F. Shaw 10.7.1928. BL Add. MS 45904.
52. T. E. Lawrence to his mother 14.8.1906 omitted from *HL* p. 20 and from *MB* pp. 8-9. Bodleian MS Res C13.
53. T. E. Lawrence to W. G. Lawrence 16.8.1906 *HL* pp. 22-3. Bodleian MS Res C13.

54. T. E. Lawrence to his father 20.8.1906 omitted from *HL* p. 24. Bodleian MS Res C13.
55. See for example C. L. Woolley in *Friends* p. 88.
56. T. E. Lawrence, 'Twenty-Seven Articles', in the *Arab Bulletin* (Cairo) No. 60, 20.8.1917, p. 348.
57. T. E. Lawrence to his mother 24.8.1906 omitted from *HL* p. 27. Bodleian MS Res C13. The opinions expressed on Baden-Powell and Churchill, though amusing in retrospect, were quite widely held at that time. Baden-Powell had enjoyed popular adulation as the hero of Mafeking, but high military circles had little regard for his talents and thought his reputation as a soldier unjustified. He did not launch the Boy Scout movement until 1908. Churchill had entered Parliament as a Unionist in 1900 but had crossed the floor to join the Liberal party in 1904; most Conservatives thought this unpardonable. He had been returned as a Liberal MP in the general election of January 1906.
58. T. E. Lawrence to his father 20.8.1906 omitted from *HL* p. 24. Bodleian MS Res C13.
59. T. E. Lawrence to his mother 24.8.1906 *HL* p. 30. Bodleian MS Res C13.
60. T. E. Lawrence to his mother 26.8.1906 *HL* p. 35. Bodleian MS Res C13.
61. T. E. Lawrence to his father 31.8.1906 *HL* p. 45. Bodleian MS Res C13.
62. T. E. Lawrence to his mother 14.8.1906 *HL* p. 19. Bodleian MS Res C13.
63. T. E. Lawrence to his mother 28.8.1906 *HL* p. 42. Bodleian MS Res C13.
64. T. E. Lawrence to his mother 26.8.1906 *HL* pp. 34-5. Bodleian MS Res C13.
65. C. F. C. Beeson in *Friends* p. 54.
66. *Ibid.*
67. T. E. Lawrence to his mother 9.8.1906 *HL* pp. 11-12. Bodleian MS Res C13.
68. T. E. Lawrence to his family April 1907 *HL* p. 50. Bodleian MS Res C13.
69. T. E. Lawrence to his mother 24.8.1906 *HL* p. 29. Bodleian MS Res C13.
70. T. E. Lawrence to his mother 14.8.1906 omitted from *HL* p. 20 and from *MB* pp. 8-9. Bodleian MS Res C13.
71. T. E. Lawrence to his father 31.8.1906 *HL* p. 45. Bodleian MS Res C13.
72. Oxford Local Examinations Board: *Division Lists for the Year 1906: Senior Candidates* and *Tables Supplementary to the Division Lists* [etc.] (Oxford, James Parker & Son, 1906). Also 1906 Senior candidates' mark sheets, Oxford University Archives.
73. T. E. Lawrence to his mother 24.8.1906 *HL* p. 31. Bodleian MS Res C13.
74. T. E. Lawrence to his mother 6.4.1907 partially omitted from *HL* p. 52. Bodleian MS Res C13.
75. T. E. Lawrence to D. G. Hogarth 14.1.1926 *DG* p. 491.
76. T. E. Lawrence, written reply to B. H. Liddell Hart's 'Queries I' *B:LH* p. 51.
77. T. E. Lawrence to D. Knowles 14.7.1927. Bodleian R (transcript).

Chapter 2. Oxford University

October 1907 – June 1909

1. Source: *Oxford University Undergraduate Register, 1908*. Oxford University Archives.

2. In Lawrence's lifetime and the years immediately following his death relatively few people had been to university. Consequently it appeared to the general public that

Lawrence's reported eccentricities at Oxford were exceptional. Some of his contemporaries, notably Vyvyan Richards, fuelled this legend by telling stories about him which were clearly exaggerated.

3. For accounts of this expedition see H. F. Mathers in *Jesus College Magazine* (Oxford) Vol. IV, No. 49, June 1935, p. 344; E. F. Hall in *Friends* pp. 47-8; T. W. Chaundy in *Friends* p. 42.

4. A. T. P. Williams, 'Lawrence in Oxford' *The Oxford Magazine* (Oxford) Vol. 53, Feb.-June 1935, p. 696.

5. A. G. Prys-Jones, 'Lawrence of Arabia: Some Personal Impressions' (typescript). Jesus College, Oxford.

6. T. E. Lawrence, *The Mint*, Part 2, ch. 2, p. 109.

7. T. E. Lawrence, *SP* ch. LXI p. 348.

8. E. F. Hall in *Friends* pp. 46-7.

9. T. E. Lawrence, written reply to B. H. Liddell Hart's 'Queries I' *B:LH* p. 50.

10. *Ibid.* pp. 50-1, cf. *SP* ch. XXXIII p. 188.

11. L. C. Jane to R. R. Graves 26.7.1927. Bodleian R.

12. *Oxford University Examination Statutes* 1908, p. 97.

13. T. E. Lawrence to his mother 23.7.1908 *HL* p. 61. Bodleian MS Res C13.

14. *Ibid. HL* pp. 61-2.

15. T. E. Lawrence to his mother 2.8.1908 *HL* pp. 63-4; *MB* p. 14. Bodleian MS Res C13.

16. *Ibid. HL* p. 64.

17. *Ibid.*

18. *Ibid.* omitted from *MB* p. 14.

19. *Ibid. MB* p. 15.

20. *Ibid. HL* pp. 65-6.

21. T. E. Lawrence to his mother 6.8.1908 *HL* p. 67. Bodleian MS Res C13.

22. *Ibid.*

23. *Ibid.*

24. *Ibid.* pp. 67-8.

25. T. E. Lawrence to his family 9.8.1908 *HL* p. 69. Bodleian MS Res C13.

26. *Ibid. HL* pp. 70-2.

27. T. E. Lawrence to his mother 16.8.1908 *HL* p. 73. Bodleian MS Res C13.

28. T. E. Lawrence to C. F. C. Beeson 16.8.1908 *DG* p. 60.

29. T. E. Lawrence to his mother 16.8.1908 *HL* p. 73. Bodleian MS Res C13.

30. T. E. Lawrence to C. F. C. Beeson 16.8.1908 *DG* p. 61.

31. T. E. Lawrence to his mother 23.8.1908 *HL* p. 76. Bodleian MS Res C 13.

32. *Ibid.*

33. T. E. Lawrence to his mother 28.8.1908 *HL* p. 80; *MB* pp. 16-17. Bodleian MS Res C13.

34. *Ibid.*

35. *Ibid. HL* pp. 80-1.

36. C. F. Bell, notes on LH:*TEL*. BL Add. MS 63549. This conversation probably took place very shortly after Lawrence's return to Oxford: he consulted C. M. Doughty's *Travels in Arabia Deserta* in the Bodleian on October 20th and 23rd 1908 (Bodleian readers' records).

37. R. R. Graves, *Lawrence and the Arabs* (London, Jonathan Cape, 1927) p. 18. It has frequently been claimed that Lawrence's first meeting with D. G. Hogarth was

earlier than January 1909. There are two sources for this error. The first is B. H. Liddell Hart's biography *'T. E. Lawrence' in Arabia and After* (LH:*TEL*) in which it is stated (p. 19): 'Contrary to what has been said, T.E. had known Hogarth some time before he conceived this visit to Syria'. Liddell Hart was incorrect, however, and appears to have based this statement on a misreading of his own jottings of a conversation with Lawrence (*B:LH* p. 72): 'Knew Hogarth long before he went to Syria'. It is clear from the context of this note that Lawrence meant 'long before I went to Carchemish'. The other source of confusion is Lawrence's letter to Dick Knowles of 7.12.1927 (*DG* p. 553): 'I owed [Hogarth] everything I had, since I was seventeen'. In this case Lawrence was simply wrong about his age when he met Hogarth. Apart from the reference in Graves, the date of the first meeting between Lawrence and Hogarth is confirmed independently by both E. T. Leeds (*L-L* p. 4) and C. F. Bell (BM Add. MS 63549). Hogarth spent very little time in Oxford in the years immediately before taking up his appointment as Keeper of the Ashmolean in January 1909.

38. C. M. Doughty to T. E. Lawrence 3.2.1909 *LTEL* p. 37.
39. T. E. Lawrence to C. M. Doughty 8.2.1909. Gonville and Caius College, Cambridge.
40. T. E. Lawrence to C. F. C. Beeson 16.8.1908 *DG* p. 61.
41. G. G. A. Murray, preface to *The New Loggan Guide to Oxford Colleges* (Oxford, Basil Blackwell, 1932) p. 5.
42. T. E. Lawrence, written reply to B. H. Liddell Hart's 'Queries I' *B:LH* p. 52.
43. W. Morris: *A Note by William Morris on his Aims in Founding the Kelmscott Press* . . . (London, Kelmscott Press, 1898) p. 1.
44. L. H. Green in *Friends* p. 68.
45. V. W. Richards, *Portrait of T. E. Lawrence* (London, Jonathan Cape, 1936) p. 43.
46. Bodleian readers' records.

Chapter 3. First Steps in the East

June 1909 – December 1910

1. T. E. Lawrence to his mother 'about' 6.7.1909 *HL* p. 86. Bodleian MS Res C13.
2. T. E. Lawrence to his mother 2.8.1909 *HL* p. 94. Bodleian MS Res C13.
3. *Ibid. HL* p. 97.
4. *Ibid.*
5. *Ibid. HL* pp. 98-9.
6. *Ibid. HL* p. 89.
7. *Ibid. HL* pp. 91-2.
8. T. E. Lawrence to his family 13.8.1909 *HL* p. 102; *MB* p. 18. Bodleian MS Res C13.
9. *Ibid.* omitted from *MB* p. 18.
10. T. E. Lawrence to his father 15.8.1909 *HL* p. 103. Bodleian MS Res C13.
11. T. E. Lawrence to his mother 29.8.1909 *HL* p. 105; *MB* p. 19. Bodleian MS Res C13.
12. T. E. Lawrence to his mother 7.9.1909 *HL* p. 107. Bodleian MS Res C13.
13. *Ibid.*
14. T. E. Lawrence to his mother 29.8.1909 *HL* p. 105; *MB* p. 20. Bodleian MS Res C13.
15. T. E. Lawrence to his mother 7.9.1909 *HL* p. 106. Bodleian MS Res C13.

16. *Ibid.*
17. T. E. Lawrence to E. T. Leeds 19.9.1909 *L-L* pp. 5-7. In ignorance of this letter, first published in 1988, some of Lawrence's biographers have suggested that during the final stage of his Syrian tour he was carrying out secret Intelligence work. See, for example, D. Stewart, *T. E. Lawrence* (London, Hamish Hamilton, 1977) p. 46: 'This third phase was fogged from beginning to end with the mystery that still hangs around the clandestine activities controlled by Hogarth.'

    For a note on Hogarth's alleged 'clandestine activities', see chapter 5 note 30 and chapter 10 note 96.
18. T. E. Lawrence to his family 22.9.1909 *HL* pp. 107-8; *MB* p. 20. Bodleian MS Res C13.
19. T. E. Lawrence to Sir John Rhys 24.9.1909 *DG* p. 81.
20. T. E. Lawrence to his father 15.8.1909 *HL* p. 103. Bodleian MS Res C13.
21. T. E. Lawrence to his family 22.9.1909 *HL* p. 108. Bodleian MS Res C13.
22. This account of Lawrence's expenses is included in a letter to his mother of 9.10.1909 omitted from *HL* p. 109 but published in *MB* pp. 21-2. It does not refer to any *baksheesh* paid out after he was attacked and robbed while collecting Hittite seal stones (see p. 61). It seems likely that he replaced this money by working for a few days in Port Said on the return journey. Many years later Lawrence told Liddell Hart that he had worked there briefly as a coal checker in about 1909 (see *B:LH* pp. 84, 166). Lawrence also sold his Mauser for £5 in Beirut when leaving Syria, making a small profit. The account gives additional information about the third stage in his Syrian journey and further refutes the suggestions made by biographers such as Desmond Stewart (see note 17 above).
23. T. E. Lawrence to his mother 9.10.1909 omitted from *HL* p. 109; *MB* p. 22. Bodleian MS Res C13.
24. *Ibid.*
25. After Lawrence's death his college friend Vyvyan Richards wrote that the head had been found 'in a rubbish heap in Italy', and that Lawrence thought it 'so precious that it travelled in his bunk while he himself slept on deck. It was . . . twin almost to that in the British Museum; indeed he was asked to exchange them as his seemed the more perfect. But it was found after to be a reproduction'. (*Portrait of T. E. Lawrence*, London, Jonathan Cape, 1936, pp. 23-4). This kind of yarn casts doubt on much that Richards wrote about Lawrence. I have been told by A. W. Lawrence that his brother's Hypnos appeared to have been cast from a free-hand copy of the British Museum example, and was not identical. Its present location is not recorded.
26. T. E. Lawrence to C. F. Shaw 12.5.1927. BL Add. MS 45903.
27. T. E. Lawrence to his family 16.3.1916 *HL* p. 315.
28. L. C. Jane to R. R. Graves 26.7.1927. Lawrence papers, Bodleian R.
29. T. E. Lawrence to his mother late August 1910 *HL* pp. 110-11. Bodleian MS Res C13.
30. Relatively few of the drawings that illustrate Lawrence's BA thesis were his own work. He was very short of time when preparing the final draft of the thesis and Beeson helped with the illustrations. Beeson and Lawrence searched through a number of sources for drawings to copy. The majority came from M. Viollet-le-Duc, *Dictionnaire Raisonné de l'Architecture Française du XIe au XVIe Siècle* (10 vols, Paris, B. Bance, 1858-68). Others, however, came from sources such as *A Little Tour in France* by Henry James (London, Heinemann, 1900, illus. by Joseph

Pennell). Beeson pointed out to me that his version of the illustration on p.183 of this latter work is reproduced as Lawrence's sketch in *HL* p. 65. The two drawings reproduced in *A Touch of Genius, the Life of T. E. Lawrence* by M. Brown and J. Cave (London, Dent, 1988, pp. 24-5) as examples of Lawrence's work were copied by Beeson from Viollet-le-Duc.

31. There was no undergraduate course in archaeology at Oxford. Many students undertaking postgraduate archaeological studies at the university had graduated in history or classics.

32. T. E. Lawrence to V. W. Richards 10.12.1913 *DG* pp. 160-1.

33. T. E. Lawrence to C. M. Doughty 30.11.1909 *DG* p. 82. Gonville and Caius College, Cambridge.

34. T. E. Lawrence to his family 24.1.1911 *HL* pp. 129-30; partly quoted in *MB* pp. 28-9. Bodleian MS Res C13.

35. V. W. Richards, *Portrait of T. E. Lawrence* (London, Jonathan Cape, 1936) p. 20.

36. Quoted in P. G. Knightley and C. Simpson, *The Secret Lives of Lawrence of Arabia* (London, Nelson, 1969) p. 29.

37. V. W. Richards in *Friends* p. 383.

38. T. E. Lawrence to his family 31.1.1911 *HL* pp. 131-2. Bodleian MS Res C13.

39. Cf. R. R. Graves, *Lawrence and the Arabs* (London, Jonathan Cape, 1927) p. 13: '[Mrs Lawrence] told me once: "We could never be bothered with girls in our house".' This statement should be regarded with some caution: Graves had been irritated by Mrs Lawrence, who had not co-operated with his research for a popular biography of her son.

40. Quoted in J. E. Mack, *A Prince of our Disorder* (Boston, Little, Brown, 1976) p. 65. The information given here about Lawrence's friendship with Janet Laurie is based on Mack's interview with her on 25.3.1965. I did not myself meet her, but a number of people who knew her well have suggested to me that her story of a proposal may be exaggerated. There is, however, no doubt that Lawrence was strongly attracted to her and spent time in her company while at Oxford, since this was observed independently by his friend E. F. Hall.

41. T. E. Lawrence to W. G. Lawrence 11.5.1911 *HL* p. 207 (printed out of sequence with a wrongly inferred date of 11.5.1912). Bodleian MS Res C13.

42. L. C. Jane to R. R. Graves 26.7.1927. Bodleian R.

43. C. T. Atkinson to the President of Magdalen College, Oxford 18.6.1935. Liddell Hart papers 9/13/33, KCL.

44. W. H. Hutton to R. R. Graves 21.11.1927. Bodleian R.

45. E. Barker in *Friends* p. 62.

46. Lawrence attended the Oxford University OTC summer camp (23 officers and 441 men) which was held on Farnborough Common, June 20th-July 2nd 1910. Regular reports of its activities (which included a mock battle against Cambridge University OTC) were published in *The Times*.

In *DG* p. 84, David Garnett states that Lawrence paid *three* visits to France during the summer of 1910. However, his only evidence for the first of these is an undated postcard of Beauvais Cathedral. According to Garnett, the postmark on this reads 19.6.1910. There is no other evidence whatsoever for a visit to France at this time, and I believe that the postmark date must in reality be 19.8.1910, when Lawrence was certainly at Beauvais (see F. H. Lawrence to M. R. Lawrence 19.8.1910 *HL* p. 598).

47. F. H. Lawrence to M. R. Lawrence 19.8.1910 *HL* p. 601.
48. F. H. Lawrence to F. Messham 25.8.1910 *HL* pp. 604-5.
49. T. E. Lawrence to his mother, late August 1910 omitted from *HL* p. 109. Bodleian MS Res C13.
50. F. H. Lawrence to F. Messham 25.8.1910 *HL* p. 606.
51. T. E. Lawrence to V. W. Richards 29.8.1911 *DG* p. 87.
52. Jesus College, Oxford, Minute Book, 15.10.1910.
53. Jesus College, Oxford, Minute Book, 19.10.1910.
54. A meeting of the Modern History Faculty on 28.10.1910 received a report from the sub-committee on B. Litt. approvals in which Lawrence's thesis title was accepted as a subject for a B. Litt. thesis. Oxford University Archives.
55. C. F. Bell, notes on LH:*TEL*. BL Add. MS 63549.
56. T. E. Lawrence to E. T. Leeds 2.11.1910 *L-L* p. 12. Leeds papers. The scope of the thesis is misstated in this letter, presumably due to a slip of the pen. The thesis title he had registered included pottery of the 16th century.
57. *Ibid.*
58. J. E. Mack (*op. cit.* note 40 above) p. 67, suggests that Janet Laurie's rejection of Lawrence's proposal of marriage had something to do with his change of plans in the autumn of 1910: 'I am of the impression that this disappointment played a significant part in Lawrence's turning to Syria and to Carchemish, where a congenial life among men, the archaeologist's world of the dig, the camp and the campfire, without the need to relate seriously to women, provided what Lawrence claims were the pleasantest years of his life.' However, Lawrence had expressed his hope of returning to Syria ever since first going there in 1909. Also, the two events linked by Mack were separated by some months: her rejection (if it occurred: see note 40 above) seems to have taken place between October 1909 and June 1910, whereas Lawrence's request to go to Carchemish dates from late October 1910. At that point Lawrence could not, of course, have known that the excavations at Carchemish would last for a long time, since only a single season was planned.
59. H. Maundrell: *Journey from Aleppo to Jerusalem*, supplement to the third edition titled: 'An Account of the Author's Journey to the River Euphrates, the City Beer, and to Mesopotamia', p. 3 (Oxford, printed at the Theater, 1699).
60. Quoted in D. G. Hogarth, *Carchemish* Vol. I (London, The British Museum, 1914) p. 6.
61. P. Henderson to E. A. Bond 4.9.1880. BM/A.
62. D. G. Hogarth, 'The Excavations at Carchemish: First Report' in *The Times* (London) 1.7.1911, p. 5.
63. E. Wallis Budge, British Museum internal memorandum 1.2.1908. BM/A.
64. D. G. Hogarth, *op. cit.* note 60 above, p. 12.
65. D. G. Hogarth: 'The Excavations at Carchemish: First Report' in *The Times* (London) 1.7.1911, p. 5.
66. E. T. Leeds, 'Recollections of T. E. Lawrence' (p. 82 of manuscript), see *L-L* p. 11. Leeds papers.
67. D. G. Hogarth, *Accidents of an Antiquary's Life* (London, Macmillan, 1910) p. 1.
68. C. F. Bell, notes on LH:*TEL*. BL Add. MS 63549. Both Bell and Hogarth were Fellows of Magdalen College at the time.
69. T. E. Lawrence to his family 24.1.1911 *HL* p. 130; *MB* p. 29. Bodleian MS Res C13.
70. T. E. Lawrence to his family 14.1.1911 *HL* p. 126. Bodleian MS Res C13.

71. T. E. Lawrence to Herbert Baker 20.1.1928 *DG* p. 568.
72. See T. E. Lawrence to R. V. Buxton 22.9.1923 *DG* p. 431; *MB* p. 245. Jesus College, Oxford.
73. The first reference to this title is in a letter from T. E. Lawrence to his family 24.1.1911 *HL* p. 130; *MB* p. 29. Bodleian MS Res C13.
74. T. E. Lawrence to his family 14.1.1911 *HL* p. 126. Bodleian MS Res C13.

Chapter 4. Beginnings at Carchemish

December 1910 – June 1911

1. T. E. Lawrence to his family December 1910 *HL* pp. 115-16; *MB* pp. 26-7. Bodleian MS Res C13.
2. F. G. Kenyon to the Lords Commissioners of the Treasury, late December 1910. BM/A holds Kenyon's manuscript drafts of this and other letters. His secretary normally added the exact date to the draft when typing out a letter, but in this instance did not.
3. D. G. Hogarth to F. G. Kenyon 21-23.2.1911. BM/A.
4. T. E. Lawrence to his family 26.2.1911 *HL* pp. 135-7. Bodleian MS Res C13.
5. D. G. Hogarth to F. G. Kenyon 2.3.1911. BM/A.
6. D. G. Hogarth, report to the British Museum 20.5.1911, pp. 3-4. BM/A.
7. *Ibid.* p. 3.
8. D. G. Hogarth to F. G. Kenyon 16.3.1911. BM/A.
9. *Ibid.*
10. D. G. Hogarth to F. G. Kenyon 2.3.1911. BM/A.
11. D. G. Hogarth to F. G. Kenyon 10.5.1912. BM/A.
12. T. E. Lawrence to his family 1.3.1911 *HL* p. 138. Bodleian MS Res C13.
13. T. E. Lawrence to his family 20.3.1911 *HL* pp. 141-2. Bodleian MS Res C13.
14. R. D. Barnett in *Carchemish* Vol. III (London, The British Museum, 1952) p. 258.
15. T. E. Lawrence to E. T. Leeds 27.3.1911 *L-L* pp. 17-18; *MB* p. 31-2. Leeds papers.
16. T. E. Lawrence to his family 31.3.1911 *HL* p. 143; *MB* p. 33. Bodleian MS Res C13.
17. D. G. Hogarth to F. G. Kenyon 1.4.1911. BM/A.
18. *Ibid.*
19. T. E. Lawrence to his family 11.4.1911 *HL* p. 148; *MB* p. 35. Bodleian MS Res C13.
20. T. E. Lawrence to his family 16.4.11 *HL* p. 149. Bodleian MS Res C13.
21. T. E. Lawrence to his family 11.3.1911 omitted from *HL* p. 140; *MB* p. 30. Bodleian MS Res C13.
22. T. E. Lawrence to his family 11.4.1911 omitted from *HL* p. 147; *MB* p. 34. Bodleian MS Res C13.
23. D. G. Hogarth to W. M. F. Petrie 10.7.1911. Ashmolean A.
24. D. G. Hogarth to F. G. Kenyon 24.4.1911. BM/A.
25. T. E. Lawrence to his family 29.4.1911 *HL* pp. 150-1; *MB* pp. 35-6. Bodleian MS Res C13.
26. T. E. Lawrence to his family 11.5.1911 *HL* pp. 206-7 (where the date is wrongly inferred as 11.5.1912). Bodleian MS Res C13.
27. D. G. Hogarth, *The Life of C. M. Doughty* (London, OUP, 1928) p. 176 n. 1.
28. D. G. Hogarth, report to the British Museum 20.5.1911, pp. 39-40. BM/A.
29. *Ibid.* p. 20.
30. T. E. Lawrence to his family 23.5.1911 *HL* pp. 161-2; *MB* pp. 36-7. Bodleian MS

Res C13. Lawrence's closing remarks were meant seriously. Gertrude Bell was already influential. She was twenty years older than Lawrence and eight years older than Thompson.

31. G. M. L. Bell to her family 18.5.1911 *The Letters of Gertrude Bell*, ed. Lady Bell (London, Ernest Benn, 1927) Vol. I, pp. 305-6.
32. T. E. Lawrence to E. T. Leeds 2.6.1911 *L-L* p. 22. Leeds papers.
33. T. E. Lawrence to D. G. Hogarth 8.6.1911 *MB* p. 38.
34. R. C. Thompson to F. G. Kenyon 14.6.1911. BM/A.
35. R. C. Thompson to F. G. Kenyon 24.6.1911. BM/A. Kenyon's telegram, as received in Carchemish, actually read: 'Thomanson care of Britsch Consul Alep. When palace with norwth acropovliot and houses and tombs well tested shop work. Kenyon'.
36. T. E. Lawrence to his family 24.6.1911 *HL* p. 172; omitted from *MB* p. 39. Bodleian MS Res C13.

Chapter 5. An Undecided Future

June 1911 – June 1912

1. Minutes of the Standing Committee of the British Museum Trustees, 8.7.1911. BM/A.
2. R. C. Thompson to F. G. Kenyon 24.6.1911. BM/A.
3. R. C. Thompson: 'The Excavations at Carchemish: Second Report' in *The Times* (London) 9.10.1911.
4. Published as 'Diary of a Journey across the Euphrates' in *OA* pp. 5-62, where it is illustrated by Lawrence's photographs taken on this journey.
5. See D. G. Hogarth, 'The Excavations at Carchemish: First Report' in *The Times* (London) 1.7.1911, p. 5.
6. *The Times* (London) 9.8.1911.
7. T. E. Lawrence, 'Mores Romanorum'. Bodleian MS Res C13. Haj Wahid was an Arab, not a Kurd; Lawrence may have made this change to disguise the location of the incident, since he evidently intended to publish the story pseudonymously. The term 'Moghreby' means Moroccan, but may have the sense Lawrence attributes to it in northern Syria. For another account of this incident, see T. E. Lawrence to his mother 23.5.1911 *HL* p. 163.
8. T. E. Lawrence, diary entry for 29.7.1911 *OA* p. 46.
9. T. E. Lawrence, diary entry for 31.7.1911 *OA* p. 48.
10. T. E. Lawrence to his family 24.6.1911 *HL* pp. 173-4; *MB* pp. 39-40. Bodleian MS Res C13.
11. T. E. Lawrence to his family 6.1.1912 *HL* p. 184. Bodleian MS Res C13. *The Centaur*, by A. Blackwood, concerned the progress of a city clerk to a mythical world untouched by the evils of human 'civilisation'.
12. T. E. Lawrence to Mrs Rieder 4.7.1911 *DG* p. 115; *MB* p. 42.
13. T. E. Lawrence to Mrs Rieder 11.8.1911 *DG* p. 119; *MB* p. 42.
14. T. E. Lawrence to D. G. Hogarth 24.6.1911 *DG* p. 114.
15. T. E. Lawrence to Mrs Rieder 11.8.1911 omitted from *DG* p. 119 and from *MB* p. 42. Lawrence papers, Bodleian R (transcript).
16. T. E. Lawrence to D. G. Hogarth 6.8.1911 *DG* pp. 118-19.
17. T. E. Lawrence to N. Rieder postmarked 12.8.1911 *DG* p. 120.

18. T. E. Lawrence to F. el Akle 14.8.1911. Bodleian R (photocopy of original).
19. See T. E. Lawrence, *Crusader Castles*, with an Introduction and Notes by Denys Pringle (Oxford, Clarendon Press, 1988): 'After the examination . . . one of the judges of the thesis urged the University Press to publish it in book form, saying however that not one of the illustrations could be spared; the cost was considered prohibitive' (from the Foreword by A. W. Lawrence, p. vi).
20. This account is based on correspondence in BM/A.
21. T. E. Lawrence to V. W. Richards 26.8.1911 *DG* pp. 120-1.
22. T. E. Lawrence to Mrs Rieder 26.9.1911 *DG* p. 123.
23. D. G. Hogarth to F. G. Kenyon 4.10.1911. BM/A.
24. Sir L. du P. Mallet to F. G. Kenyon 21.11.1911. BM/A.
25. T. E. Lawrence to C. M. Doughty 11.12.1911. Gonville and Caius College, Cambridge.
26. T. E. Lawrence to his family 11.1.1912 *HL* p. 185. Bodleian MS Res C13. In 1933 Lawrence told his biographer Liddell Hart that he had met Lord Kitchener in 1913, when Kitchener was British Agent in Egypt (also in 1914, presumably during the first months of the war when both were at the War Office in London). I have found no other evidence relating to the first of these meetings. It could have occurred during this 1912 visit to Egypt, or during a second brief visit made the following year. The dates given by Lawrence, so long after the event, are not necessarily reliable. The full text of his remarks about Kitchener, partially quoted in *B:LH* p. 55 is: 'He was boss-eyed and wooden, and normally as dull as ditch water: but every now and then he would appear to have second-sight, and be quite dogmatic about something utterly problematical – and was then as often right as wrong. A very limited imagination, selfish, greedy: ignorant and sure of himself: not honest according to ordinary men's codes. He inspired very little personal devotion.' Bodleian R (transcript).
27. T. E. Lawrence to his family 18.1.1912 *HL* p. 186. Bodleian MS Res C13.
28. T. E. Lawrence to D. G. Hogarth 12.2.1912. Bodleian R (transcript).
29. T. E. Lawrence to his family 31.1.1912 *HL* pp. 190-1. This passage is one of several in Lawrence's letters which have lent themselves to misinterpretation through very abridged quotation. See, for example, J. E. Mack, *A Prince of our Disorder* (Boston, Little, Brown, 1976) p. 79.
30. D. G. Hogarth to F. G. Kenyon 1.2.1912. BM/A. A number of recent biographers, seeking to show that the Carchemish excavations were in reality cover for a British Intelligence operation, have made much of the secrecy surrounding this funding. However this was Morrison's habitual practice, also adopted in many cases where there is no possibility of a connection with Intelligence.
31. T. E. Lawrence to E. T. Leeds 7.2.1912. *L-L* pp. 33-5. Leeds papers.
32. T. E. Lawrence to J. E. Flecker 18.2.1912 *MB* p. 44. Houghton bMS Eng 1252 (7).
33. C. L. Woolley, report, enclosed with his letter to F. G. Kenyon of 31.3.1912. BM/A.
34. T. E. Lawrence to D. G. Hogarth 20.2.1912 *DG* p. 137.
35. T. E. Lawrence to E. T. Leeds 18.3.1912 *L-L* p. 39. Leeds papers. For Woolley's flamboyant account of these events see his *Dead Towns and Living Men* (London, OUP, 1920) pp. 151-76. For Lawrence's account see letters to his family of 25.2.1912 *HL* p. 195; 17.3.1912 *HL* p. 196; 20.3.1912 *HL* pp. 197-8, and 6.4.1912 *HL* p. 199. Bodleian MS Res C13. See also letters from T. E. Lawrence to E. T. Leeds of 18.3.1912 and early April 1912 *L-L* pp. 39-43.

36. T. E. Lawrence to his family 29.4.1912 *HL* p. 203. Bodleian MS Res C13.
37. D. G. Hogarth to F. G. Kenyon 10.5.1912. BM/A.
38. D. G. Hogarth to F. G. Kenyon 10.4.1912. BM/A.
39. D. G. Hogarth to F. G. Kenyon 10.5.1912. BM/A.
40. *Ibid.*
41. D. G. Hogarth to F. G. Kenyon 19.5.1912. BM/A.
42. *Ibid.*
43. T. E. Lawrence to his family 2.6.1912 *HL* p. 211. Bodleian MS Res C13.
44. T. E. Lawrence to Mrs Rieder 20.5.1912 *DG* p. 139.
45. T. E. Lawrence to his family June 1912 *HL* p. 212. Bodleian MS Res C13.
46. *Ibid. HL* p. 213.

Chapter 6. Learning from the Arabs

June 1912 – June 1913

1. T. E. Lawrence to his family 23.6.1912 *HL* pp. 215-17. Bodleian MS Res C13.
2. T. E. Lawrence to his family 24.6.1912 *HL* pp. 218-19. Bodleian MS Res C13.
3. See T. E. Lawrence to J. Buchan 20.6.1927: 'All my walking tours in Syria were done in European clothes: and four months was the longest. I only wore Arab kit on one or two short treks after forbidden antiquities.' (Queen's University, Kingston, Ontario.) He told Liddell Hart that disguise 'was easy in north Syria, where the racial admixture has produced many fair natives and many with only a broken knowledge of Arabic. I could never pass as an Arab – but easily as some other native speaking Arabic.' (*B:LH* p. 85).

   It seems that on one of these journeys in Arab dress, his disguise was too successful, and he was arrested on suspicion of trying to evade Turkish military service. Little is known about this incident, but it appears that Lawrence was beaten up and had to be taken to hospital (see *SP* ch. LXXX p. 446: 'myself . . . a timid recruit at Khalfati', and *SP*(O) ch. 87: 'myself in hospital at Khalfati'). Khalfati is between Aintab and Urfa, and this led D. Garnett to believe that Lawrence was referring to the occasion in 1909 when he was attacked during his first visit to Syria (see *DG* p. 80). Lawrence himself placed the incident in about 1912 (see *B:LH* p. 141).
4. T. E. Lawrence to his family 24.6.1912 *HL* p. 219. Bodleian MS Res C13.
5. T. E. Lawrence to his family 21.7.1912 *HL* pp. 223-4; omitted from *MB* p. 46. Bodleian MS Res C13.
6. T. E. Lawrence to his family 3.8.1912 *HL* p. 227. Bodleian MS Res C13.
7. H. Flecker (ed.), *Some Letters from Abroad of James Elroy Flecker* (London, William Heinemann, 1930) p. 59.
8. T. E. Lawrence to W. G. Lawrence 12.9.1912 *HL* p. 230. Bodleian MS Res C13.
9. *Ibid. HL* p. 229.
10. For an amusing but probably embellished account of this episode see C. L. Woolley, *Dead Towns and Living Men* (London, OUP, 1920) pp. 100-5.
11. T. E. Lawrence to M. R. Lawrence 12.9.1912 *HL* p. 231. Bodleian MS Res C13.
12. T. E. Lawrence to his family 13.9.1912 *HL* pp. 232-3. Bodleian MS Res C13.
13. T. E. Lawrence to M. R. Lawrence 12.9.1912 *HL* p. 230. Bodleian MS Res C13.
14. T. E. Lawrence to his family 18.9.1912 *HL* p. 233. Bodleian MS Res C13.
15. T. E. Lawrence to his family 2.10.1912 *HL* p. 235. Bodleian MS Res C13.

16. T. E. Lawrence to his family 8.10.1912 *HL* p. 236. Bodleian MS Res C13.
17. *Ibid.*
18. T. E. Lawrence to D. G. Hogarth 29.5.1913. BM/WAA.
19. T. E. Lawrence to his family 15.10.1912 *HL* p. 237. Bodleian MS Res C13.
20. *Ibid.*
21. D. G. Hogarth to C. L. Woolley 22.10.1912. BM/WAA.
22. T. E. Lawrence to his family 22.10.1912 *HL* p. 239; omitted from *MB* p.47. Bodleian MS Res C13.
23. T. E. Lawrence to his family 22.2.1913 *HL* p. 248. Bodleian MS Res C13.
24. T. E. Lawrence to V. W. Richards 15.7.1918 *DG* p. 244; *MB* p. 150.
25. 'The Kaer of ibu Wardani' [*sic*], by C.J.G. [pseud. of T. E. Lawrence] in *Jesus College Magazine* (Oxford) Vol. I, No. 2, January 1913, pp. 37-9. The title should have been printed: 'The Kasr of Ibn Wardani'.
26. T. E. Lawrence to his family 22.10.1912 *HL* pp. 239-40. Bodleian MS Res C13.
27. C. L. Woolley (*op. cit.* note 10 above) p. 188.
28. C. L. Woolley to F. G. Kenyon 1.11.1912. BM/A.
29. C. L. Woolley to F. G. Kenyon 9.11.1912. BM/A.
30. *Ibid.*
31. T. E. Lawrence to his family 10.11.1912 *HL* pp. 242-3. Bodleian MS Res C13.
32. T. E. Lawrence to his family 14.11.1912 *HL* p. 243. Bodleian MS Res C13.
33. C. L. Woolley, report to the Trustees of the British Museum for November 1912. BM/A. Sinjirli, excavated by German archaeologists in 1882-92, is an important Hittite site at the foot of the Amanus mountains in Turkey.
34. T. E. Lawrence to Mrs Rieder 7.1.1913. Bodleian R (transcript).
35. D. G. Hogarth to F. G. Kenyon 3.12.1912. BM/A.
36. T. E. Lawrence, note for inclusion in Liddell Hart's biography *B:LH* p. 87.
37. D. G. Hogarth to F. G. Kenyon 20.12.1912. BM/A.
38. F. G. Kenyon to D. G. Hogarth 27.12.1912. BM/WAA.
39. *Ibid.*
40. D. G. Hogarth to F. G. Kenyon 29.12.1912. BM/A.
41. F. G. Kenyon to D. G. Hogarth 10.1.1913. BM/A.
42. T. E. Lawrence to C. L. Woolley 25.1.1913. BM/A.
43. T. E. Lawrence to his family 2.2.1913 partially omitted from *HL* p. 245. Bodleian MS Res C13.
44. T. E. Lawrence to D. G. Hogarth 2.2.1913. Leeds papers.
45. T. E. Lawrence to his family 22.2.1913 *HL* p. 248; omitted from *MB* p. 47. Bodleian MS Res C13.
46. Lawrence wrote to his family on 22nd February 1913: 'At Aleppo I stayed five days more than I need[ed] entertaining two naval officers, who became partners in my iniquity of gun-running at Beyrout. The consular need of rifles involved myself, the Consul General at Beyrout, Flecker, the Admiral at Malta, our Ambassador at Stamboul, two captains, and two lieutenants, besides innumerable *cavasses*, in one common law-breaking. However Fontana got his stuff, and as he was too ill to entertain the porters, I had to trot them over Aleppo. And we did trot over it all, all day and all night, and out to Jerablus *en prince*, and back laded with Babylonian gems, and Greek coins, and Roman bronzes, and Persian carpets and Arab pottery... all going to a warship, a modern engine of efficiency and destruction... what will their captain say to their stuffed bags?' (Bodleian MS Res C13, omitted from *HL* p.

248; *MB* pp. 47-8). His parents must have been shocked by this dramatic account, because in a subsequent letter Lawrence wrote: 'About gun-running – it was ten rifles for the defence of the Aleppo consulate; sent up by the *Medea*. We are using both ships this week for the export of the first part of our Phoenician collection.' (28.3.1913. Bodleian MS Res C13, omitted from *HL* p. 252).

The circumstances of this gun-running expedition are explained in a letter from R. A. Fontana to Sir G. A. Lowther, British Ambassador in Constantinople, of 15.6.1913: 'I had exchanged correspondence between November and February with His Majesty's Consul General at Beyrout with regard to the supply of rifles for this Consulate, but owing to apprehended difficulties with regard to landing the arms, the matter remained in abeyance. During February Mr. Lawrence, one of the excavators at Jerablus in the employ of the British Museum, passed through Aleppo on his way to Beyrout. Mr. Lawrence, who knows the country well, offered of his own accord to bring the rifles to Aleppo, provided they were landed at a sea-side house in the vicinity of Beyrout belonging to friends of his. And I gave him a letter in this sense to Mr. Consul General Cumberbatch. The Senior Naval Officer, after consulting with His Majesty's Consul General, who read him the letter, decided to land and forward the rifles in charge of two Naval Lieutenants accompanied by a Consular *Cavass* . . .

'In view of the extremely critical situation prevailing in this region subsequent to the outbreak of war with the Balkan States, owing to the imminent menace of a Kurdish rising accompanied by a wide Arab tribal movement . . . I thought it necessary that this Consulate should be provided with arms for its protection and for that of British Subjects who would take refuge therein in the event of an outbreak. Six Army rifles and twelve revolvers were supplied to the United States Consul, and rifles were also supplied to the Russian Consul at Aleppo by his Government previous to the war between Turkey and the Balkan States. This Consulate . . . is particularly exposed in situation and in construction to attack by a mob. And the presence of warships at Beyrout and Alexandretta, although a sure safeguard for those ports, cannot be considered as affording a guarantee for the safety of foreign subjects at Aleppo in exceptionally critical times.' (FO 371/1812, fos. 101-2).

47. T. E. Lawrence to E. T. Leeds 25.5.1913 *L-L* p. 70. Leeds papers.
48. T. E. Lawrence to D. G. Hogarth end of February 1913 *MB* pp. 48-9. BM/A.
49. C. L. Woolley to F. G. Kenyon 4.3.1913. BM/A.
50. T. E. Lawrence to his family 23.3.1913 *HL* p. 251. Bodleian MS Res C13.
51. C. L. Woolley, report to the Trustees of the British Museum for March 1913. BM/A.
52. T. E. Lawrence to Mrs Rieder 5.4.1913 *DG* p. 152.
53. T. E. Lawrence to F. Messham 18.4.1913 *DG* p. 153.
54. T. E. Lawrence to his family 26.4.1913 *HL* p. 254. Bodleian MS Res C13.
55. C. L. Woolley, report to the Trustees of the British Museum for April 1913. BM/A.
56. T. E. Lawrence to D. G. Hogarth 14.5.1913. BM/A.
57. C. L. Woolley, report to the Trustees of the British Museum for April 1913. BM/A.
58. C. L. Woolley in *Friends* p. 87.
59. C. L. Woolley, report to the Trustees of the British Museum for April 1913. BM/A.
60. *Ibid.*
61. T. E. Lawrence to E. T. Leeds 13.5.1913 *L-L* pp. 68-9. Leeds papers.
62. T. E. Lawrence to E. T. Leeds 15.5.1913 *L-L* p. 71. Leeds papers.
63. T. E. Lawrence to E. T. Leeds 1.6.1913 *L-L* p. 73. Leeds papers.

64. C. L. Woolley to D. G. Hogarth 6.6.1913. BM/WAA.
65. T. E. Lawrence to his family 11.6.1913 *HL* p. 256 (where 'kept' is mistranscribed 'left'). Bodleian MS Res C13.
66. T. E. Lawrence to his family 15.6.1913 *HL* p. 257. Bodleian MS Res C13.
67. *Ibid. HL* p. 258.
68. T. E. Lawrence to his family 20.3.1911 *HL* p. 142. Bodleian MS Res C13.
69. T. E. Lawrence to his family 13.3.1913 *HL* p. 249. Bodleian MS Res C13.
70. T. E. Lawrence to his family 26.4.1913 *HL* p. 254. Bodleian MS Res C13.
71. T. E. Lawrence to his family 15.6.1913 *HL* p. 258. Bodleian MS Res C13. On this occasion his revulsion from food may have had a particular explanation. The following day he wrote to Leeds, 'A camel died next to our house last week, and the wind is setting in strongly from its remains'. (16.6.1913 *L-L* p. 74. Leeds papers).

Chapter 7. Achievement at Carchemish

June – December 1913

1. T. E. Lawrence to C. F. Bell 12.8.1913 *MB* pp. 50-1. BL Add. MS 63550. Of these portraits only the first survives. Lawrence also spent a day during this brief visit to England reading about Oriental carpets. Records preserved in the Bodleian Library show that he consulted five works on the subject on August 6th. His letters from Carchemish display an increasing interest in carpets, which could be bought fairly cheaply in Arab towns and villages. During these years he seems to have acquired a number for his family and friends.
2. T. E. Lawrence to his family 29.8.1913 *HL* p. 262. Bodleian MS Res C13.
3. T. E. Lawrence to his family 9.9.1913 *HL* p. 262. Bodleian MS Res C13.
4. T. E. Lawrence to E. T. Leeds 9.9.1913 *L-L* p. 81. Leeds papers.
5. T. E. Lawrence to his family 9.9.13 *HL* pp. 262-3. Bodleian MS Res C13.
6. W. G. Lawrence to a friend 14.10.1913 *DG* p. 158.
7. W. G. Lawrence to his family 16.9.1913 *HL* p. 442.
8. W. G. Lawrence to his family 27.9.1913 *HL* p. 447.
9. See H. W. Young, *The Independent Arab* (London, John Murray, 1933) p. 18.
10. T. E. Lawrence to C. F. Bell 1.10.1913. BL Add. MS 63550.
11. T. E. Lawrence to W. G. Lawrence 21.10.1913 *HL* pp. 270-1. Bodleian MS Res C13.
12. C. L. Woolley to D. G. Hogarth 12.10.1913. BM/WAA.
13. C. L. Woolley in *Friends* p. 89. Another reference to the carving occurs in Eric Kennington's contribution to *Friends*: 'I . . . asked if he had ever done some creation with his hands, and how he knew he had no creative power. He said, "I carved eight life-sized figures in soft stone in Syria, using knives, and forks, and a hatchet. My servant was my model. They had no merit." ' (p. 276). The conversation referred to had probably taken place fifteen years before Kennington wrote this account, so the exaggerated number of figures is not surprising.
    For evidence that Lawrence was seriously interested in sculpture, see the letters to his family of 16.6.1915 (*HL* p. 305) and 16.3.1916 (*HL* p. 315).
14. *Ibid.*
15. In a printed notice addressed to people who knew Lawrence, requesting contributions to *Friends*, A. W. Lawrence described the book as 'a collection of . . . portraits of one man's mind'. Since the articles were to be mainly about Lawrence's

personality, rather than factual accounts, it could be argued that Woolley was not asked to describe what Lawrence actually did at Carchemish. However, he was surely wrong to leave the reader with such a false impression.

16. T. E. Lawrence to F. el Akle 3.1.1921 omitted from *MB* p. 183. Bodleian R (photocopy of original).

17. E. T. Leeds, 'Recollections of T. E. Lawrence' pp. 92-3 of the manuscript (edited text in *L-L* p. 49). Leeds papers.

18. T. E. Lawrence to D. Garnett 14.2.1930 partially omitted from *DG* p. 681. Bodleian R (transcript).

19. T. E. Lawrence to R. R. Graves 28.6.1927 partially omitted from *B:RG* p. 51. Houghton fMS Eng 1252 (347). After D. G. Hogarth's death in 1927, some archaeologists thought that Woolley should be appointed Keeper of the Ashmolean. Lawrence wrote to one of them pointedly: 'Your idea that Woolley may get the Ashmolean surprised me: Evans was a great archaeologist, Hogarth a great man: and that has set a standard for the Museum.' (T. E. Lawrence to E. Mackay, 2.12.1927. Bodleian R, transcript).

20. T. E. Lawrence to his family 3.10.1913 *HL* p. 267. Bodleian MS Res C13.

21. C. L. Woolley, report to the Trustees of the British Museum for October 1913. BM/A.

22. *Ibid.*

23. C. L. Woolley to D. G. Hogarth 3.11.1913. BM/WAA.

24. C. L. Woolley to F. G. Kenyon 6.11.1913. BM/A.

25. C. L. Woolley, report to the Trustees of the British Museum for November 1913. BM/A.

26. C. L. Woolley to F. G. Kenyon 6.12.1913. BM/A.

27. T. E. Lawrence to V. W. Richards 10.12.1913 *DG* pp. 160-1.

28. T. E. Lawrence to R. V. Buxton 22.9.1923 *DG* p. 431; *MB* p. 245. Jesus College, Oxford.

29. T. E. Lawrence, 'History of *Seven Pillars*' reproduced in *Texas Quarterly* (Austin, Texas) Vol. V, No. 3, Autumn 1962, pp. 48-9.

30. T. E. Lawrence to R. V. Buxton 22.9.1923 *DG* p. 431. Jesus College, Oxford.

31. C. L. Woolley to F. G. Kenyon, telegram *c.* 10.12.1913, quoted in F. G. Kenyon to Sir Charles Watson, 11.12.1913. PEF.

32. C. L. Woolley to F. G. Kenyon 17.12.1913. BM/A.

33. T. E. Lawrence to his family 17.12.1913 *HL* p. 277. Bodleian MS Res C13.

34. T. E. Lawrence to F. Messham 20.12.1913 *DG* p. 162.

35. T. E. Lawrence to his family 26.12.1913 *HL* p. 278 (where 'Arabia' is misprinted 'Arabic'). Bodleian MS Res C13.

36. T. E. Lawrence to C. F. Bell 26.12.1913; *MB* p. 55. BL Add. MS 63550.

Chapter 8. The Wilderness of Zin

January – August 1914

1. Sir Charles Watson to C. L. Woolley 16.12.1913. PEF.

2. C. L. Woolley to Sir Charles Watson 1.1.1914. PEF. In his book *The Illicit Adventure* (London, Jonathan Cape, 1982), H. V. F. Winstone makes the astonishing claim that Lawrence and Gertrude Bell met secretly for Intelligence reasons on 5th January 1914 and again later that month. As evidence for the first

'undoubted' meeting, Winstone states (p. 418) that Lawrence and Bell were both at Ziza on January 5th. In reality, while Bell was at Ziza on that date, Lawrence was visiting Gezer, an archaeological site many miles distant. The only evidence for the second alleged meeting is a photograph by Bell reproduced by Winstone (facing p. 273). He claims that Lawrence appears in this photograph disguised as an Arab woman; I find this identification preposterous. *The Illicit Adventure* is a highly speculative and contentious book in which the discussion of Lawrence's role is rendered valueless, in my opinion, by a great many factual errors.

3. S. F. Newcombe in *Friends* p. 105.
4. T. E. Lawrence to his family 4.1.1914 *HL* p. 280; *MB* p. 56. Bodleian MS Res C13.
5. Director of Military Operations to the Under-Secretary of State for Foreign Affairs 19.9.1913. FO 371/1812 fos. 279-80. The background to the Sinai Survey is described in greater detail in my introduction to Lawrence's *Military Report on the Sinai Peninsula* (Fordingbridge, Castle Hill Press, 1990), where the official documents referred to here are printed *in extenso*.
6. Sir L. du P. Mallet to Foreign Office London, telegram 527(R), 29.10.1913. FO 371/1812 fo. 285.
7. Sir C. R. Watson to W. C. Hedley 5.11.1913. PEF.
8. F. G. Kenyon to Sir C. R. Watson 21.11.1913. PEF.
9. L. W. King to Sir C. R. Watson 26.11.1913. PEF.
10. T. E. Lawrence to his family 24.1.1914 *HL* p. 283. Bodleian MS Res C13.
11. T. E. Lawrence to E. T. Leeds 24.1.1914 *L-L* p. 89; *MB* p. 56. Leeds papers.
12. T. E. Lawrence to his family 29.1.1914 *HL* p. 284. Bodleian MS Res C13.
13. S. F. Newcombe to Sir C. R. Watson 3.1.1914. PEF.
14. D. G. Hogarth to F. G. Kenyon 17.2.1914. BM/A.
15. C. L. Woolley to Sir C. R. Watson 17.2.1914. PEF.
16. H. C. Trumbull: *Kadesh Barnea: Its Importance and Probable Site, Including Studies of the Route of the Exodus and the Southern Boundary of the Holy Land* (New York, Charles Scribner's Sons, 1884) pp. 272ff.
17. C. L. Woolley to Sir C. R. Watson 17.2.1914. PEF.
18. C. L. Woolley and T. E. Lawrence, *The Wilderness of Zin* (Palestine Exploration Fund *Annual* No 3, 1914-1915, London, Palestine Exploration Fund, 1914) pp. xv-xvi.
19. *Ibid.* pp. 11-12.
20. T. E. Lawrence to his family 25.2.1914 *HL* p. 287. Bodleian MS Res C13.
21. T. E. Lawrence to E. T. Leeds 28.2.1914 *DG* p. 166; *L-L* p. 95; *MB* p. 59. Leeds papers.
22. *Ibid. DG* p. 167.
23. T. E. Lawrence to his family 28.2.1913 partially omitted from *HL* p. 287.
24. D. G. Hogarth to F. G. Kenyon 8.2.1914. BM/A.
25. C. L. Woolley to F. G. Kenyon 14.3.1914. BM/A.
26. R. A. Fontana to the British Ambassador in Constantinople 26.3.1914, enclosed in Sir L. du P. Mallet to Foreign Office London, dispatch N. 240, 8.4.1914. FO 371/2132 no. 16157.
27. *The Times* (London) 25.3.1914. See also *The Times* 26.3.1914: 'Kurdish Labour on Baghdad Railway'.
28. D. G. Hogarth to F. G. Kenyon 30.3.1914. BM/A. See T. E. Lawrence to J. E. Flecker *DG* pp. 171-7, for a long description of this incident written in June 1914.

29. C. L. Woolley to F. G. Kenyon 5.4.1914. BM/A.
30. D. G. Hogarth to E. T. Leeds 10.4.1914. Leeds papers.
31. T. E. Lawrence to his family 23.4.1914 *HL* p. 295. Bodleian MS Res C13.
32. T. E. Lawrence to Mrs Rieder 24.4.1914 *DG* p. 170.
33. T. E. Lawrence to his family 4.5.1914 *HL* p. 296. Bodleian MS Res C13.
34. *Ibid.*
35. T. E. Lawrence to his family 17.5.1914 *HL* p. 299. Bodleian MS Res C13.
36. C. L. Woolley to D. G. Hogarth 25.5.1914. BM/WAA.
37. C. L. Woolley to F. G. Kenyon 31.5.1914. BM/A.
38. C. L. Woolley, preface to *Carchemish* Vol. III (London, British Museum, 1952) p. [5].
39. C. L. Woolley, *As I Seem to Remember* (London, Allen & Unwin, 1962) p. 93. See also the article by S. F. Newcombe and J. P. S. Greig, 'The Baghdad Railway' in *The Geographical Journal* (London) Vol. XLIV, No. 6, December 1914, pp. 577-80.
40. D. G. Hogarth, address to the Royal Geographical Society, 14.4.1927, quoted in *The Letters of Gertrude Bell* ed. Lady Bell (London, Ernest Benn, 1927) Vol. I, p. 353.
41. D. G. Hogarth to C. L. Woolley 6.7.1914. BM/WAA.
42. J. E. Flecker to T. E. Lawrence 27.7.1914 *LTEL* p. 57.
43. T. E. Lawrence to D. Knowles 7.12.1927 *DG* p. 553. (In this letter Lawrence gives the date of his first journey alone to France incorrectly as 1905.)

Chapter 9. London and Cairo

August – December 1914

1. T. E. Lawrence to R. V. Buxton 22.9.1923 *DG* p. 431; *MB* p. 245 (where 'indiscretion' is mistranscribed 'indiscretionary'). Jesus College, Oxford. In this and other letters Lawrence stated that he burned the manuscript when he joined up (i.e. October 1914). Elsewhere, however, he said that it was destroyed in August 1914.
2. T. E. Lawrence to Mrs Rieder 18.9.1914 *DG* p. 185. During the autumn of 1914 the War Office was inundated with applications for Intelligence work, see C. E. Callwell: *Experiences of a Dug-out* (London, Constable, 1920) pp. 25-6.
3. Minutes of the Standing Committee of the Trustees of the British Museum, 10.10.1914. BM/A
4. T. E. Lawrence to Mrs Fontana 19.10.1914 *DG* p. 187.
5. Lawrence's commission appears in the Army List for December 1914, dated 23.10.1914. It is, however, clear from contemporary letters that he worked for some time at the War Office as a civilian. The commission was probably backdated to October for administrative reasons, so that he would be entitled to army pay; see *B:LH* pp.192-4, and the Army List for December 1914 cited in 'Some Notes on the Military Career of T. E. Lawrence' by G. W. Nichols, in *T. E. Lawrence Studies Newsletter* (Fordingbridge) No. 2, 1981-2, p. 14.
6. T. E. Lawrence to A. E. Cowley 29.10.1914 *MB* p. 66. Bodleian Ms Autog. d.24 fo. 92.
7. C. L. Woolley and T. E. Lawrence, *The Wilderness of Zin* (Palestine Exploration Fund Annual No. 3, 1914-1915, London, Palestine Exploration Fund, 1914).
8. T. E. Lawrence to F. G. Kenyon 2.11.1914. BM/A.

9. The arrangements made by Fontana very soon went wrong. Money could not be sent directly to Turkey, and Akras suggested that the Museum should transfer funds via the British office of one of his suppliers (presumably a company with neutral nationality). Unhappily, at this point the ex-dragoman was forced to go into hiding as a suspected British spy. This must have affected his business, because the supplier refused to pay him the Museum's money, pointing out that he owed them a considerably larger sum. Although the headmen at Carchemish remained loyally at their posts, no pay arrived and they were soon in dire straits. Eventually the Museum was able to make alternative arrangements through the American Embassy in Constantinople.

10. T. E. Lawrence to E. T. Leeds 16.11.1914 *L-L* pp. 104-5; *MB* pp. 66-7. Leeds papers.

11. *Ibid.*

12. T. E. Lawrence to J. D. Crace 21.11.1914. PEF.

13. T. E. Lawrence to Mrs Fontana, envelope postmarked 4.12.1914 *DG* p. 189.

14. *Ibid.*

15. C. E. Callwell to Sir J. G. Maxwell 19.11.1914. Quoted from extracts printed in an unidentified rare-book dealer's catalogue.

16. R. E. M. Russell, 'Précis of conversation with Abd el Aziz el Masri, on 16th August 1914' 17.8.1914. FO 371/2140 no. 46261.

17. G. F. Clayton, report, 30.10.1914. FO 371/2140 fos. 180-1.

18. *Ibid.* fo. 183.

19. Sir P. Z. Cox, 'Proclamation issued on behalf of the General Officer Commanding the British Forces in occupation of Basra, to the notables and public of the town' 22.11.1914. English translation given in Sir A. T. Wilson, *Loyalties: Mesopotamia 1914-1917* (London, OUP, 1930) Appendix I, p. 311.

20. M. Cheetham to Sir E. Grey, telegram 264, 13.11.1914. FO 371/2140 fo. 158.

21. Sir E. Grey to M. Cheetham, telegram 347, 14.11.1914. FO 371/2140 fo. 159.

22. M. Cheetham to Foreign Office London, telegram 274, 16.11.1914. FO 371/2140 fo. 165.

23. Unsigned undated memorandum on Sayid Taleb. FO 141/736/2475.

24. Sir P. Z. Cox to Secretary to the Government of India, Foreign and Political Department, telegram 82-B, 3.12.1914. FO 371/2479 fos. 308-9.

25. *Ibid.* fo. 309.

26. P. P. Graves, 'Note on conversation with Aziz Ali Bey el Masri' 6.12.1914. FO 371/2140 fo. 235.

27. *Ibid.*

28. *Ibid.* fo. 236.

29. Foreign Office London to M. Cheetham, telegram 432, 18.12.1914. FO 371/2140 fo. 200.

30. Lord Kitchener to R. H. A. Storrs, for Sherif Abdullah, repeated in Foreign Office London to M. Cheetham, telegram 219, 24.9.1914. FO 371/2768 fo. 76.

31. Sherif Abdullah to Lord Kitchener, repeated in M. Cheetham to Foreign Office London, telegram 233, 31.10.1914. FO 371/2139.

32. Lord Kitchener to M. Cheetham, repeated in Foreign Office London to M. Cheetham, telegram 303, 31.10.1914. FO 371/2139.

33. *Ibid.* The message was rephrased and embellished by the British staff in Cairo before transmission to Abdullah, and it has been suggested that in the process the

intention of Kitchener's cable was distorted (see E. Kedourie, *In the Anglo-Arab Labyrinth*, Cambridge University Press, 1976, pp. 17-20). Specifically, Kedourie denies that Kitchener intended to encourage any Arab aspirations beyond the Hejaz: i.e. in writing 'the Arab nation', Kitchener meant only the Hejaz Arabs. This interpretation is contradicted by the evidence: for example, a few days later Kitchener wrote to Grey suggesting that the whole of Syria should be included in the new Arab Caliphate (Kitchener to Grey 11.11.1914, FO 800/102). It is clear from the surviving documents that Kitchener's views were fully understood by the Cairo officials. These were experienced civil servants who had been in daily contact with him as members of his own staff until a few months previously. They had discussed the Arab question with him in person, and there can be no basis for suggesting either that they were ignorant of his views or that they would wilfully have misrepresented them. Kedourie presents no evidence to support this allegation, nor does he explain why Kitchener did not protest when the full Cairo text of the message to Abdullah was subsequently received in London.

Chapter 10. Intelligence Duties
December 1914 – August 1915

1. T. E. Lawrence to D. G. Hogarth 20.12.1914 *DG* p. 190.
2. Force in Egypt, GHQ General Staff, War Diary entry for 22.12.1914. WO 95/4360.
3. T. E. Lawrence to E. T. Leeds 24.12.1914 *L-L* p. 106; *MB* pp. 68-9. Leeds papers. The identity of the fifth officer in the original Intelligence group is uncertain. In this letter he is named as Hay, whose responsibility was 'the Tripoli side of Egypt'. I have found no further references to Hay, but a letter from Lawrence to his family of 12th February 1915 (*HL* p. 301) mentions 'Hough ex-Consul at Jaffa'. This may not be the same person as 'Hay', since several people had joined the Intelligence Department in the intervening weeks.
4. T. E. Lawrence to W. G. Lawrence 21.1.1915 *HL* p. 301. Bodleian MS Res C13.
5. Diary entry by S. P. Cockerell, a close friend of Lloyd's, for 27.12.1914. Lloyd papers GLLD 9/1, Churchill College, Cambridge.
6. T. E. Lawrence, *SP* ch. VI p. 57.
7. S. F. Newcombe, note, 1927. Bodleian R (I have substituted 'Lawrence' where Newcombe wrote 'T. E.', because Lawrence was neither referred to nor addressed in this way prior to 1923).
8. Sir J. G. Maxwell to Lord Kitchener 4.12.1914 quoted in *MOEP*, Vol. I, p. 20 n. 2.
9. T. E. Lawrence to D. G. Hogarth 20.12.1914 *DG* p. 190.
10. M. Cheetham to Foreign Office London, telegram 251, 9.11.1914. FO 371/2141 fo. 65.
11. Sir J. G. Maxwell to Lord Kitchener, telegram 332E, 27.11.1914. FO 371/2139 no. 77224.
12. Lord Kitchener to Sir J. G. Maxwell, 28.11.1914. FO 371/2139 no. 77224.
13. Quoted in M. Fitzherbert, *The Man who was Greenmantle* (London, John Murray, 1983) p. 149. This is probably from a letter by Herbert to Sir Mark Sykes. No date is given.
14. G. F. Clayton, 'Note', 3.1.1915. FO 371/2480 fos. 137-42.
15. Cairo Intelligence Department, unsigned memorandum, 5.1.1915. Wingate papers W/134/9/12-15, Durham. The memorandum places great emphasis on the scope for

native assistance (Armenian and Arab) and suggests prophetically that this could be led by British officers. However, the proposed plan clearly displays its origin in 'Intelligence' rather than 'Operations'. It provides valuable geographical, political and ethnic details, but contains few suggestions about the actual execution of the military operation.

16. T. E. Lawrence, note on a proof of *The Decisive Wars of History* by B. H. Liddell Hart, March 1929 *B:LH* p. 17.

17. Cairo Intelligence Department, unsigned memorandum, 5.1.1915. Wingate papers W/134/9/12-15, Durham.

18. T. E. Lawrence, note on a proof of *The Decisive Wars of History* by B. H. Liddell Hart, March 1929 *B:LH* p. 17.

19. Sir M. Cheetham (Residency) to Foreign Office London, telegram, *c.* 5.1.1915. Clayton papers 693/9/1, Durham.

20. 'Expedition to Alexandretta' prepared by MO2, 11.1.1915. WO 106/1570. The figure of 21,000 troops included sufficient men to hold Alexandretta and to form a mobile column for operations against the Baghdad Railway. This paper does not mention the possibility of an Arab rising, but like the Cairo Intelligence Department memorandum it expresses the hope that the local Armenian population would revolt against the Turks.

Another memorandum entitled 'Note on Mr. Cheetham's proposal for Operations in Syria', prepared by the General Staff, January 1915 (WO 106/1570) gives the size of the required force as 12,000.

21. 'Alexandretta', unsigned memorandum 19.1.1915. WO 157/689.

22. T. E. Lawrence to D. G. Hogarth 15.1.1915 *DG* p. 191.

23. T. E. Lawrence to D. G. Hogarth 2.2.1915 *DG* p. 192. For 'the Man who was Friday' see G. K. Chesterton, *The Man who was Thursday* (Bristol, Arrowsmith, 1908).

24. Diary entry by S. P. Cockerell (see note 5 above) for 27.12.1914. Lloyd papers GLLD 9/1, Churchill College, Cambridge.

25. Quoted in M. Fitzherbert, *The Man who was Greenmantle* (London, John Murray, 1983) p. 144.

26. T. E. Lawrence to his family 12.2.1915 *HL* p. 302; *MB* p. 70. Bodleian MS Res C13.

27. Several editions of the *Turkish Army Handbook* had been printed by the War Office in London before the war. The most recent of these formed the basis for the first Cairo printing.

28. T. E. Lawrence to C. F. Bell 18.4.1915 *MB* p. 71. BL Add. MS 63549.

29. T. E. Lawrence, *SP* ch. CIII p. 566.

30. A. N. H. M. Herbert, diary entry quoted in M. Fitzherbert, *The Man who was Greenmantle* (London, John Murray, 1983) p. 144, where no date is given.

31. E. M. Dowson in *Friends* p. 138.

32. *Ibid.* p. 136.

33. R. H. A. Storrs, *Orientations* (London, Ivor Nicholson & Watson, 1937) p. 229. See also Storrs's disparaging comments on the way Philip Graves dressed, *ibid.* p. 56.

34. S. F. Newcombe, note, 1927. Bodleian R (transcript).

35. Sir A. H. McMahon to Sir E. Grey, dispatch 117, 9.10.1915. FO 371/2480 fos. 196-7.

36. *Ibid.* fos. 197-8. See also chapter 11 note 14.

37. G. F. Clayton to Sir F. R. Wingate (Governor-General, Khartoum) telegram 70, 28.1.1916. FO 882/12 fo. 6. The date 1898 refers to the Fashoda incident, when

Britain obliged a French military expedition to withdraw from the Sudan under humiliating circumstances.

There is no basis for the claim by P. Knightley and C. Simpson that Georges-- Picot was 'very pro-British' (*The Secret Lives of Lawrence of Arabia*, London, Nelson, 1969, p. 67).

38. Sir A. H. McMahon to Sir E. Grey, dispatch 117, 9.10.1915. FO 371/2480 fo. 198. See also chapter 11 note 14.

39. *Ibid.* fos. 198-9.

40. Sir A. H. McMahon to Sir E. Grey, telegram 23, 15.2.1915. FO 371/2480 fo. 152.

41. *Ibid.*

42. T. E. Lawrence to his family 20.2.1915 *HL* p. 303. Bodleian MS Res C13.

43. Foreign Office London to Sir A. H. McMahon, telegram 91, 17.2.1915. FO 371/2480 fo. 145. The demise of the Alexandretta scheme at this time was due to a combination of political and logistical factors. In late January, as preparations for the Dardanelles action went forward, Britain and France had agreed on areas of naval command in the Mediterranean. As a result, the Alexandretta region passed into the control of a French vice-admiral commanding in the Levant. Churchill, then First Lord of the Admiralty, had written on January 26th: 'Any military operation on the Levantine coast should be a subject of discussion first between the two governments, and the French wish to participate in any occupation of Alexandretta. Lord Kitchener informs me that he cannot now fix any date for the Alexandretta expedition, so it appears unnecessary to make precise conditions about it.' (to Sir E. Grey and Lord Kitchener, 26.1.1915, *WSC* Docs. 31 p. 458.) Grey had noted against this: 'I think it important to let the French have what they want in this Memo even about Alexandretta. It will be fatal to cordial co-operation in the Mediterranean and perhaps everywhere if we arouse their suspicions as to anything in the region of Syria.' (*Ibid.*) Kitchener's uncertainty about timing was caused by a shortage of transport, since the available shipping was heavily committed at that moment to the Dardanelles operation. Unaware of this problem, Churchill and others had earlier argued that the Dardanelles and Alexandretta schemes should go ahead almost simultaneously, so that if the Dardanelles action failed it would appear to have been a feint to divert Turkish attention from the landings at Alexandretta.

The turning-point in British plans is clear from a diary kept by Wyndham Deedes, at that time a member of the War Office Intelligence staff. On February 10th he noted: 'If they can get the ships the Alexandretta scheme is now particularly in favour, and likely to come off before long.' (Deedes papers, St Antony's College, Oxford.) A week later, however, it had been recognised that the two operations would over-stretch British resources. Deedes wrote: 'The Alexandretta scheme seems likely to die a temporary death owing to lack of transport.' (*Ibid.* entry for February 17th.)

The Alexandretta scheme had been studied in Paris, as in London. For details see *AFGG*, '*Projet de Débarquement d'un Corps Expéditionnaire en Orient*' 20.1.1915 (pp. 15-19), and '*Hypothèse d'un Débarquement à Alexandrette*' 8.2.1915 (pp. 28-37).

44. Foreign Office London to Sir A. H. McMahon, telegram, 8.3.1915. FO 800/48 fo. 321.

45. T. E. Lawrence to E. T. Leeds 9.3.1915 *L-L* p. 107. Leeds papers.

46. Lord Kitchener, 'Alexandretta and Mesopotamia' 16.3.1915. CAB 27/1, quoted as

Appendix X to the report of the de Bunsen Committee, p. 103. Kitchener wanted British possession of Mesopotamia in order to prevent Russia expanding to the Arabian Gulf. If Mesopotamia were to be annexed, it would be very desirable to possess a railway from the Mediterranean, so that military reinforcements could be sent overland very quickly. Such a railway already existed: the Baghdadbahn, whose western end was at Alexandretta. For this reason, Kitchener argued that Alexandretta should be annexed by Britain.

47. *Ibid.*
48. 'Meeting of the War Council' 19.3.1915, secretary's notes. CAB 22/1 fos. 5-6.
49. *Ibid.* fo. 7.
50. *Ibid.*
51. Sir E. Grey to Sir F. L. Bertie, telegram 250, 23.3.1915. FO 371/2486 fo. 2.
52. T. E. Lawrence to D. G. Hogarth 18.3.1915 *DG* pp. 193-4.
53. *Ibid.*
54. *Ibid.*
55. G. F. Clayton to Sir F. R. Wingate, undated, but March 1915. Wingate papers W/134/5/10, Durham.
56. T. E. Lawrence to D. G. Hogarth 22.3.1915 *DG* pp. 195-6. Lawrence's suggestion was not as fanciful as it might seem. The Idrisi was known to be extremely ambitious, and before the war he had attempted to form anti-Turkish alliances with other chieftains in the Arabian Peninsula. His negotiations had come to nothing, however, and in 1915 he was an isolated figure viewed with some suspicion by his neighbours.
57. T. E. Lawrence to E. T. Leeds 18.4.1915 *L-L* p. 109. Leeds papers.
58. T. E. Lawrence to D. G. Hogarth 20.4.1915 *DG* pp. 195-6.
59. T. E. Lawrence, 'Syria: the Raw Material . . . written early in 1915' *AB* No. 44, 12.3.1917, p. 110.
60. *Ibid.*
61. *Ibid.* pp. 110-12.
62. *Ibid.* p. 112.
63. *Ibid.* pp. 112-13.
64. *Ibid.* p. 113.
65. *Ibid.*
66. *Ibid.* p. 114.
67. *Ibid.*
68. T. E. Lawrence to D. G. Hogarth 26.4.1915 *DG* p. 198.
69. *Ibid.*
70. Sir E. Grey to Sir A. H. McMahon, telegram 173, 14.4.1915. FO 371/2486 fo. 7.
71. *Ibid.*
72. *Ibid.*
73. Sir A. H. McMahon to Sir E. Grey, telegram 188, 14.5.1915. FO 371/2486 fo. 9.
74. T. E. Lawrence to D. G. Hogarth 20.4.1915 *DG* p. 196.
75. T. E. Lawrence to C. F. Bell 18.4.1915 *MB* pp. 71-2. BL Add. MS 63549. The daily Intelligence Bulletins were typed on stencils and (though written by various members of the Intelligence staff) issued in Newcombe's name. After the war, when the *Daily Telegraph* inadvertently attributed an article by Newcombe to Lawrence, Newcombe remarked, 'after all, very many of your articles appeared with my signature below them in 1915, so that's quits!' (letter to T. E. Lawrence 25.11.1920,

transcript in Bodleian R). In practice, when Newcombe was out of the office the bulletins were signed on his behalf by the most senior officer present. On many occasions this was Lawrence.

76. T. E. Lawrence to E. T. Leeds 18.4.1915 *L-L* p. 109. Leeds papers.

77. For the wartime development of aerial photography in Egypt as a source for map-making, and Lawrence's contribution, see Dov Gavish, 'An Account of an unrealized aerial cadastral Survey in Palestine under the British Mandate' in *The Geographical Journal* (London) Vol. 153, No. 1, March 1987, pp. 93-8. (Note, however, that one article referred to, 'Map making by Air Photography', in the *Daily Telegraph* 30.10.1920, was published in error over Lawrence's name; it was in reality by Newcombe, see note 75 above.) See also 'Co-operation of Survey of Egypt in fuller application of air photography to map making' (FO 371/5139/E3680 fos. 93-5); H. Henshaw Thomas, 'Geographical reconnaissance by aeroplane photography, with special reference to the work done on the Palestine Front' in *The Geographical Journal* (London) (Ref) 1920, pp. 349-76. For a more general study of the principles involved at that time in making maps from aerial photographs, see C. A. Hart, *Air Photography applied to Surveying* (London, Longmans, Green, 1940).

78. T. E. Lawrence, note on the typescript of '*T. E. Lawrence' in Arabia and After*, by B. H. Liddell Hart, 1933 *B:LH* p. 91.

79. T. E. Lawrence to D. G. Hogarth 15.1.1915 *DG* p. 191.

80. See T. E. Lawrence to his family 4.1.1916: 'I can get no news of Dahoum: indeed I am afraid to send and ask. Most of the men (and boys) from that district have been sent to Constantinople, where they still are. Few have been in firing lines as yet.' (*HL* p. 311). Surviving documents show that Dahoum worked intermittently as a site guard at Carchemish until at least October 1916.

81. Cairo Intelligence Bulletin 23.5.1915. WO 157/691. This statement considerably weakens the position of those writers who have suggested (without offering any evidence) that the Carchemish excavations were begun and kept in being in order to observe the building of the Euphrates railway bridge.

82. T. E. Lawrence to D. G. Hogarth 20.4.1915 *DG* p. 197.

83. *Ibid.*

84. R. H. A. Storrs, *op. cit.* note 33 above, p. 219.

85. T. E. Lawrence to his family 4.6.1915 *HL* p. 304; *MB* p. 72. Bodleian MS Res C13.

86. T. E. Lawrence to his mother, undated, *HL* p. 304; *MB* p. 73. Bodleian MS Res C13.

87. See for example T. E. Lawrence to D. G. Hogarth 2.2.1915: 'Confidential work doesn't tend to letter writing' *DG* p. 192; T. E. Lawrence to his family 1.7.1916 *HL* p. 327 (quoted on page 291); T. E. Lawrence to his family 16.9.1916: 'Another letter – and as usual an absolute blank. I have come to the conclusion that as I do nothing but work, and the work I cannot tell you about, that there is precious little hope of my ever having anything to say.' *HL* p. 328.

88. T. E. Lawrence to his family 23.6.1916 *HL* pp. 305-6. Bodleian MS Res C13. In another letter to his family, of 3.7.1915 (*HL* p. 306), Lawrence stated that the total number of maps printed had reached 140,000.

89. Cairo Intelligence Bulletin 1.7.1915. WO 157/693.

90. Cairo Intelligence Bulletin 23.8.1915. WO 157/694. Lawrence also wrote an entertaining account in this article of a German, Dr Lotyved of Damascus, whose father had held the Danish Consulate in Beirut: 'The son went to Germany, where

he took a medical degree. He then began his practice in Beyrout, holding an administrative post in the German Hospital there. His manipulation of the funds was however unsatisfactory, and in consequence he left the country.

'His father repaired the damage, and Lotyved returned to Syria, and began a private practice in Beyrout. His clientele was entirely native, and his speciality venereal diseases. His operations were of a character considered illegal in England . . . When the Bagdad Railway came, he applied for and obtained the post of chief Medical Officer to the Aleppo section'.

In November 1914 Lotyved was given the German Consulate of Haifa. Lawrence wrote: 'He went to Damascus on his way to Haifa, and in the courtyard of the great mosque there, he made an impassioned speech in favour of a jehad, and the killing of all except Teutonic Christians. The Damascenes were not favourably impressed with the exception . . . In Haifa he collected a band of roughs to diffuse German ideas, and made a register of desirable *Entente* women in the town, for distribution to his followers. He was responsible for the great bitterness of feeling in Haifa against the English and French. His crowning achievement was the opening up, and defiling (in the traditional manner) of the graves of Napoleon's soldiers on the top of Mount Carmel. The French in pique bombarded his house, and destroyed it with its collection of antiquities, which he valued. They were only Palmyrene sculptures.

'He has now been made German Consul in Damascus, to succeed von Padel, who was respectable.

'In person Lotyved is very fat, blotchy, and short-winded. He takes bribes, and has blackmailed his patients on occasion. He is much more Levantine than German in character and appearance.'

91. Sir A. H. McMahon to Foreign Office London, telegram 306, 30.6.1915. FO 371/2486 fo. 44.
92. Lord Hardinge (Viceroy) to Foreign Office London, telegram, 23.6.1915. FO 371/2486 fo. 33.
93. Sir T. B. M. Sykes to C. E. Callwell, dispatch 11, 12.7.1915. FO 371/2476 no. 106764.
94. Sir T. B. M. Sykes to C. E. Callwell, dispatch 14, 14.7.1915. FO 371/2490.
95. See E. Kedourie, *In the Anglo-Arab Labyrinth* (Cambridge University Press, 1976) p. 61 n. 1, citing a note by Lieutenant de Saint-Quentin (of the French staff in Cairo), no. 63, 28.7.1915 '*Visées anglaises sur la Syrie*'. AE, Guerre 1914-1918, Vol 869.
96. D. G. Hogarth's difficulties in finding war service appropriate to his specialist knowledge must surely be proof that he had no pre-war connections with British Intelligence. For the first few months of the war he remained in Oxford. His visit to Cairo in August 1915 led to nothing. When he reached Athens he met Compton Mackenzie, who had arrived there in mid-August to work in Intelligence under Major Samson. Mackenzie later wrote that when Hogarth came 'in search of an Intelligence job . . . I remember suggesting that he should make for Bucharest at once and start up a Bureau there for military information' (*First Athenian Memories*, London, Cassell, 1931, pp. 254-5).

Shortly afterwards, Hogarth returned to England where he joined the new Geographical Section of the Naval Intelligence Division, set up to produce a series of geographical handbooks. Sir Reginald Hall, head of Naval Intelligence, was at that time recruiting a number of experts from the academic world for this Division.

The historian H. A. L. Fisher, whose brother was a senior naval officer, later claimed to have been responsible for Hogarth's recruitment. Some writers (e.g. H. V. F. Winstone in *The Illicit Adventure*, London, Jonathan Cape, 1982, p. 79) have alleged that Hogarth was already working for Naval Intelligence in 1910. There is no evidence whatsoever to support this claim, which appears to be inferred from Hogarth's wartime role. In reality the section of Naval Intelligence that Hogarth joined in 1915 was not created until that year. During the war he specialised in geographical, historical and political questions related to his specialist area, the Middle East. Among the reference works he compiled was the secret Naval Intelligence *Handbook to Arabia*, a comprehensive two-volume study issued in 1916-17 which ran to more than 1,200 pages. After March 1916 he was responsible, for some months, for co-ordinating work on these publications at the Geographical Section of Naval Intelligence in London and the Arab Bureau in Cairo. He was never formally appointed Director of the Arab Bureau in Cairo, although he acted as its head during the first few weeks of its existence in the spring of 1916 and worked there extensively at various times during that year. In 1917, however, he took charge of a parallel organisation attached to Allenby's advance headquarters in Palestine. For Lawrence's assessment of Hogarth's influence in Cairo, see *SP* ch. VI p. 58.

97. Major Samson ('R') to S. F. Newcombe 3.8.1915. WO 158/922.
98. T. E. Lawrence to his family 19.8.1915 *HL* p. 307. Bodleian MS Res C13.
99. T. E. Lawrence, note on the typescript of *Lawrence and the Arabs* by R. R. Graves, 1927. *B:RG* p. 82. Houghton fMS Eng 1252 (367).
100. Sayed Ahmed, a leader known as the Senussi, was head of a Muslim sect which had great influence in the desert west of Egypt. In the spring of 1915 he was invited by the Turks to call a jihad against Britain, France and Russia. For an account of his hostile activities, see *MOEP*, Vol. I.

Chapter 11. The McMahon Pledge

August – October 1915

1. B. H. Liddell Hart, note of a comment by Lawrence made during an interview in 1933 *B:LH* p. 59.
2. R. H. A. Storrs, 'Note on communication of the Sherif of Mecca' 19.8.1915. FO 371/2486 fo. 150.
3. *Ibid.*
4. Sir A. H. McMahon to Foreign Office London, telegram 450, 22.8.1915. FO 371/2486 fo. 101.
5. A. Hirtzel, for Sir J. A. Chamberlain, to the Under-Secretary of State, Foreign Office, letter P.3061, 24.8.1915. FO 371/2486 fo. 104.
6. *Ibid.*
7. *Ibid.* Minute on the above by G. R. Clerk, Foreign Office, 25.8.1915. FO 371/2486 fo. 103.
8. *Ibid.*
9. Sir A. H. McMahon to Foreign Office, dispatch 94, 26.8.1915. FO 371/2486 fo. 129.
10. In his book *In the Anglo-Arab Labyrinth* (Cambridge University Press, 1976, pp. 69-71) E. Kedourie argues that the wording of this Cairo reply departed from

Foreign Office instructions. The passage he singles out for criticism reads: 'we confirm to you the terms of Lord Kitchener's message . . . in which was stated clearly our approval of the Arab Khalifate when it should be proclaimed. We declare once more that His Majesty's Government would welcome the resumption of the Khalifate by an Arab of true race.' (Sir A. H. McMahon to Sherif Hussein 30.8.1915, *Correspondence between Sir Henry McMahon . . . and The Sherif Hussein of Mecca*, London, HMSO, 1939, Cmd. 5957, p. 4).

Kedourie points out that McMahon's statement about the Caliphate is less cautious than that suggested by London officials. While McMahon's text did not use the exact wording suggested by the Foreign Office, he had not (as Kedourie claims) been 'instructed' to do so. The suggested text was prefaced by the remark: 'If you think it advisable, you may add a private message to the following effect'. (Sir E. Grey, Foreign Office London, to Sir A. H. McMahon, telegram 598, 25.8.1915. FO 371/2486 fo. 109). Although the matter may seem trivial, it is by repeated touches such as this that Kedourie builds up an impression that Cairo officials were pursuing a policy at variance with that agreed in London.

Kedourie fails to produce any evidence of the kind of protest which would have followed if McMahon's letter had contradicted Foreign Office or Cabinet views. Instead he quotes criticism by a civil servant, Sir Arthur Hirtzel, Secretary of the Political Department at the India Office.

Throughout his study, Kedourie presents India Office criticisms of Cairo policy as though they were disinterested statements. In reality the views of the India Office (and of the Government of India itself) on the Arab question were known to be extremely partial. To ignore this, as Kedourie does, is to suggest ignorance of the mechanics of inter-departmental relationships in Whitehall. It is wrong to imply that India Office criticisms reflected either the policy or, necessarily, the best interests of the British Government.

See also chapter 9 note 33 above.

11. R. H. A. Storrs, *Orientations* (London, Ivor Nicholson & Watson, 1937) p. 178.

12. T. E. Lawrence to his family 31.8.1915 *HL* p. 307. Bodleian MS Res C13. Parker had been working at the Foreign Office in London that spring, and Lawrence assumed incorrectly that he had been in some way responsible for shelving the Alexandretta scheme (see T. E. Lawrence to D. G. Hogarth 18.3.1915 *DG* p. 194). Parker was not in charge of the Intelligence Department for very long; he was back in London in October.

13. French Embassy London to Foreign Office London 31.8.1915. FO 371/2480 fos. 187-9 (author's translation).

14. Sir A. H. McMahon to Foreign Office London, dispatch 117, 9.10.1915. FO 371/2480 fos. 200-1. This reply was probably drafted for McMahon by the Intelligence Department, and the tone in places suggests that Lawrence himself may have had a hand in it. See for example the passages quoted on pp. 176-7 above.

15. Foreign Office minute 10.9.1915 concerning a letter from the War Office of 8.9.1915. FO 371/2490 no. 128226. This letter had forwarded to the Foreign Office Sir I. Hamilton's report on Faroki, of 25.8.1915.

16. E. Kedourie's claim that Clayton and the Cairo Intelligence Department were unable to subject Faroki's story to any kind of independent verification (*op. cit.* note 10 above, p. 76) is clearly much exaggerated.

Kedourie also questions the wisdom of placing any confidence in the claims of a young lieutenant. Faroki was then in his mid-twenties, an age at which men were considered fit to shoulder considerable responsibility during the First World War. The power and influence of young officers in the Ottoman Army had been demonstrated some years previously by the Young Turk movement, which had succeeded in bringing down the Sultan. Some British officials sensed a parallel, and indeed referred to Faroki's party as the 'Young Arabs'. In a different context, Faroki's integrity was later to be proved doubtful, but there is no reason why this should have been apparent to British officials in Cairo during the autumn of 1915 (see note 20).

17. Al Ahd, being strongest in Mesopotamia, saw British protection as a necessary alternative to Turkish colonial rule. Al Fatat, being primarily a Syrian organisation, had no particular reason to be pro-British, and every reason to be passionately anti-French.

18. See also G. Antonius, *The Arab Awakening* (Beirut, Khayats, n.d.) pp. 157-8. Antonius gives the text of the document known as the 'Damascus Protocol' in which the secret co-ordinating committee's demands were set out.

19. 'Statement of Captain X [Faroki]' 12.9.1915. FO 141/732.

20. *Ibid.* Faroki added other qualifications to this statement about his potential role in negotiations. The first omission from the text quoted on p. 200 reads: '. . . keeping in mind the complications of social problems of the Arabs amongst themselves and the political complications between us and one of the Powers of Europe (France), for the above reasons and for the confidence in myself and my party and all Arabs, and the good wishes of the English towards the Arabs, and my conviction that England does not wish to alienate the Arabs from her'.

Cairo officials had little reason to suspect Faroki's integrity, and within a few months he became Hussein's agent there. Subsequently, however, there was to be considerable dissatisfaction with his performance. It was found that he was misrepresenting British statements in his reports to Hussein, perhaps in a wish to appear more successful as an intermediary than he actually was. In retrospect, therefore, it seems possible that during these first Cairo interviews he exaggerated the influence and capability of the secret nationalist societies in Syria. The truth of the matter cannot be known, because the secret societies were never put to test. *At the time*, there was nothing to suggest that the essentials of his testimony were inaccurate.

21. Report from G. F. Clayton (Director of Intelligence, Cairo) forwarded by the DMO London to the Under-Secretary of State for Foreign Affairs 27.9.1915. FO 371/2490, no. 139665.

22. T. E. Lawrence to G. A. Lloyd 19.9.1915 *MB* pp. 77-8. Lloyd papers GLLD9/1, Churchill College, Cambridge.

23. T. E. Lawrence to A. B. Watt 29.8.1915 *DG* pp. 199-200.

24. Cairo Intelligence had considered the possibility of taking some kind of action against the Turkish coast during the previous two months. On August 1st, Lieutenant Doynel de Saint-Quentin, the French military representative in Cairo, had reported to the French War Office that Maxwell doubted the success of operations in Gallipoli and had asked his staff to study ways to cut off the Turks in Anatolia (*AFGG* p. 45). The project is discussed in more detail in a further telegram of September 22nd: 'The Intelligence Department is considering, above all, a raid against the Baghdad Railway to isolate Syria from Anatolia; they hope to destroy

either the Toprak Kaleh junction with the Alexandretta branch line, or the Baghche tunnel and the nearby power station.' (*AFGG* p. 47, author's translation).

A draft telegram to London in the Clayton papers, also dated September 22nd, reads: 'As far as I can ascertain from information obtained by our Military Intelligence Branch here the garrison of Alexandretta and the immediate neighbourhood, including the Adana plain, cannot much exceed 5,000 men.

'The garrison of Cilicia and North Syria consists of little more than two Divisions of second class troops with but few guns. In central and southern Syria are some 8,000 to 10,000 men distributed chiefly on the Sinai frontier and in the Lebanon . . . Operations on our part at Alexandretta might perhaps afford an opportunity of employing mounted troops.' (Clayton papers 693/9/4, Durham).

Maxwell noted: 'I concur. We have however nothing definite that inactivity at the Dardanelles during the winter is contemplated.' (Clayton papers 693/9/5, Durham).

On September 23rd Saint-Quentin cabled to the French War Office that Maxwell 'has spoken to me of an expedition to Cilicia as a necessary operation in the likely case that the Allied army cannot make progress in the Dardanelles. In his opinion 15,000 men would be sufficient to occupy the Taurus region and isolate Syria. These remarks appear to be the expression of a personal opinion which he has held for a long time.' (*AFGG* p. 49, author's translation).

25. T. E. Lawrence to G. A. Lloyd 19.9.1915 *MB* p. 78 (where 'unarmed battalions' is transcribed as 'unmarried battalions', and '10,000 rifles' as '1,000 rifles'). Lloyd papers GLLD9/1, Churchill College, Cambridge.

The question of forming an Armenian corps at this time is discussed extensively in the French documents. See D. de Saint-Quentin to Ministre Guerre, Paris 18.9.1915 *AFGG* p. 45, and the reply 22.9.1915 *AFGG* p. 46; Saint-Quentin to Guerre Paris 22.9.1915; Contre-Amiral Darrius to Ministre de la Marine Paris, 22.9.1915 *AFGG* pp. 48-9; Ministre de la Guerre to Saint-Quentin 10.11.1915 *AFGG* p. 57. Eventually, in March 1916, a definite British plan was made, to use a volunteer force of 100 Armenians in a raid to destroy the Raju viaduct on the railway 100 km. north of Aleppo. The proposal was abandoned, however, at the request of the Armenian Patriarch, who feared that the expedition would lead to Turkish reprisals against the surviving civil population in Armenia (see Saint-Quentin to Ministre de la Guerre Paris 8.4.1916 *AFGG* pp. 95-6).

26. *Ibid. MB* p. 77.

27. T. E. Lawrence to his family 29.9.1915 *HL* pp. 308-9. Bodleian MS Res C13. Tribal notes drafted by Lawrence at this time are published in *The Diaries of Parker Pasha* ed. H. V. F. Winstone (London, Quartet, 1983) pp. 94-8. The Parker papers also contain a list of Pan-Arabs drawn up by Lawrence, probably based in part on information provided by Faroki, who is included in the list (*op. cit.* pp. 99-100). Winstone's editorial comment states incorrectly that Faroki deserted in late October, and did not reach Cairo until the end of that month. This leads Winstone to the false conclusion that Lawrence's October notes may reveal inside knowledge of the Damascus Committee prior to Faroki's arrival. On this basis Winstone goes on to suggest that Lawrence may have infiltrated the Arab secret societies as part of his hypothetical Intelligence activity before the war. Without better evidence than this, such allegations have to be dismissed.

28. See Cairo Intelligence Bulletin 19.8.1915. WO 157/694.

29. Arab unease about Britain's prospects was well-founded. Had the United States not entered the First World War in April 1917, the Allies might have been obliged to sue for peace with Germany and Turkey from a position of relative weakness.

30. Sherif Hussein, translation of unsigned undated letter to the Grand Cadi of the Sudan, enclosed with G. S. Symes to G. F. Clayton 7.10.1915. FO 141/461/1198 fo. 60. A subsequent letter from Hussein to the Grand Cadi spelled out even more clearly the consequences for Britain of failing to meet Arab aspirations. This second letter reached Cairo on 5.11.1915 (copy enclosed in G. F. Clayton to the Residency 5.11.1915. FO 141/461/1198 fos. 94-6).

These contemporary documents refute claims by Arab historians that the possibility of an Arab realignment on Turkey's side was a 'bogey', either imagined or invented by Cairo officials in their enthusiasm to put pressure on the British Government (see for example A. L. Tibawi, *Anglo-Arab Relations and the Question of Palestine, 1914-1921,* London, Luzac, 1978 p. 78).

31. Sir F. R. Wingate to G. F. Clayton, telegram 721, 5.10.1915. FO 141/461/1198 fo. 51.

32. Quoted in G. F. Clayton to Sir F. R. Wingate 9.10.1915. Wingate papers W135/4/10, Durham.

33. *Ibid.*

34. *Ibid.*

35. G. S. Symes to G. F. Clayton, telegram 37, 10.10.1915. FO 141/461/1198 fo. 55.

36. G. F. Clayton, 'Memorandum', 11.10.1915. FO 371/2486 fos. 224-8.

37. *Ibid.* fos. 224-5. A. L. Tibawi claims that Clayton grossly distorted Faroki's position by attributing ideas to him not found in his original statement (see Tibawi, *op. cit.* note 30 above, pp. 76-81). This assumes that the original interview and statement dated 12.9.1915 is the only reliable record of Faroki's views and that he neither added to nor modified his opinion during his time in Cairo. It is very clear from the documents, however, that there were further conversations between Faroki and Cairo Intelligence, and that these formed the basis for Clayton's report. When Tibawi's account is viewed alongside the documents, his historical bias is as evident as that of some pro-Zionist historians: readers should treat the claims of either side with a great deal of caution.

38. R. H. A. Storrs to O. A. G. Fitzgerald 12.10.1915. Kitchener papers PRO 30/57/47 QQ/46.

39. Sir J. G. Maxwell to Lord Kitchener (S of S, War Office), telegram 2012E, 12.10.1915. Wingate papers W135/4/18, Durham.

40. A. N. H. M. Herbert, report, 30.10.1915. FO 371/2486 fo. 287. The outline of this report had been drafted in Cairo at Clayton's request. See M. Fitzherbert: *The Man who was Greenmantle* (London, John Murray, 1983) p. 169.

41. Lord Kitchener to Sir J. G. Maxwell, telegram 8784, 13.10.1915. FO 371/2486 fo. 190.

42. Lord Kitchener (S of S for War) to Sir J. G. Maxwell, telegram 8813, 14.10.1915. WO 33/747 p. 697.

43. War Office to G. F. Clayton (DMI Cairo), telegram 8858, 15.10.1915. WO 33/747 p. 699.

44. For Lawrence's article on the Syrian, Palestine and Baghdad railways see Cairo Intelligence Bulletin 19.8.1915. WO 157/694. Liddell Hart included in the typescript draft of his biography *'T. E. Lawrence' in Arabia and After* a passage

which read: 'Already, in October [1915], when the evacuation of Gallipoli was in the air, [Kitchener] had urgently demanded from Maxwell a report on the Turkish communications in Asia Minor and Syria.' Lawrence noted beside this: 'Don't I know it. Gave me a lot of unnecessary work.' (*B:LH* p. 88).

45. G. F. Clayton (DMI Egypt) to War Office London, telegram 908, 16.10.1915. WO 33/747 p. 701.

46. Sir J. G. Maxwell (GOC Egypt) to Lord Kitchener (S of S for War) telegram 2026E, 15.10.1915. WO 33/747 p. 698.

47. Sir J. G. Maxwell to Lord Kitchener, telegram 2030E, 16.10.1915. FO 371/2486 fo. 197. The telegrams sent by Maxwell at this time bear out to some extent a later statement by McMahon, who said that his positive response to Hussein's demands had been made at the behest of the military leadership: 'At that moment a large portion of the [Turkish] force at Gallipoli and nearly the whole of the force in Mesopotamia were Arabs, and the Germans were then spending a large amount of money in detaching the rest of the Arabs, so the situation was that the Arabs were between the two. Could we give them some guarantee of assistance in the future to justify their splitting with the Turks? I was told to do that at once . . . we were forced to do it at the military request, to assist Gallipoli and Mesopotamia and also as a relief for Egypt.' (Minutes of a conference held at Ismailia on 12.9.1916. FO 882/4 fo. 342). Note, however, that these remarks were addressed to Maxwell's successor as C-in-C in Egypt, General Sir Archibald Murray, on an occasion when Murray had spoken very critically of McMahon's handling of the Arab Revolt. McMahon therefore had particular reason to stress the Army's responsibility for the diplomatic moves which culminated in the Revolt.

48. Sherif Hussein to Sir A. H. McMahon 9.9.1915, English translation from *Correspondence between Sir Henry McMahon . . . and the Sherif Hussein of Mecca* (London, HMSO, 1939, Cmd. 5957) pp. 5-6. Although dated September 9th, this message was not received in Port Sudan until about October 10th. There is therefore no basis for A. L. Tibawi's allegation that McMahon deliberately left the note unattended 'on his desk' for a month before doing anything about it (see Tibawi, *op. cit.* note 30, pp. 73, 79, 82).

49. *Ibid.* p. 6.

50. Sir A. H. McMahon to Foreign Office London, telegram, 18.10.1915. FO 371/2486 fo. 206.

51. *Ibid.*

52. T. E. Lawrence to his family 19.10.1915 *HL* p. 310. Bodleian MS Res C13.

53. D. G. Hogarth, 'Mecca's Revolt against the Turk' from *Century Magazine* (New York) Vol. 78, July 1920, p. 409.

54. D. G. Hogarth, 'T. E. Lawrence', in *Encyclopædia Britannica*, 13th ed., supplementary Vol. 2 (London and New York, 1922) p. 674.

55. Sir E. Grey to Sir A. H. McMahon, telegram 796, 20.10.1915. FO 371/2486 fo. 208.

56. Report of the de Bunsen Committee, June 1915. CAB 27/1, p. 28.

57. Sir A. H. McMahon to Sherif Hussein 24.10.1915, see *Correspondence between Sir Henry McMahon . . . and The Sherif Hussein of Mecca* (London, HMSO, 1939, Cmd. 5957) p. 8.

The exact region McMahon intended to delineate by this phrase has been hotly disputed. His intentions become quite clear, however, if his letter is read alongside the original presentation of the four towns idea in Lawrence's paper 'Syria: the Raw

Material', written early in 1915 (*AB* No. 44, 12.3.1917, pp. 107-14). Because of the essentially 'Arab' character of Damascus, Homs, Hama and Aleppo, the Cairo officials intended to include them and their immediate economic districts at the western border of a proposed independent Arab region.

Despite certain problems of translation between English and Arabic, the debate as to what exactly was meant in McMahon's letter by the term 'districts' seems to me to be misconceived. When the reference to these towns in McMahon's letter is seen in the light of Lawrence's analysis, it becomes clear that no allusion to pre-war Turkish *vilayets* or other administrative areas was ever intended.

Academic writers who have not understood the original context of the four towns idea have misconstrued Cairo's intentions. Thus Kedourie has placed a quite different interpretation on McMahon's phrase, incorrectly attributing the naming of the four towns to Storrs (Kedourie, *op. cit.* note 10 above, pp. 86-7). As the list of the four towns is so well known to Middle East historians, it is surprising that he should have overlooked Lawrence's discussion in 'Syria: the Raw Material', which predates any reference to the towns that he cites. The memorandum has long been available to scholars in Lawrence's *Secret Despatches* (London, Golden Cockerel Press, 1939, pp. 70-9) which is included by Kedourie among his references. Tibawi also gives *Secret Despatches* as a source, but he too overlooks Lawrence's discussion of the inland Syrian towns, attributing the phrase to Clayton (Tibawi, *op. cit.* note 30, p. 85).

58. An Anglo-Arab committee set up to consider the McMahon-Hussein correspondence in 1939 heard evidence to the contrary (see *Report of a Committee set up to consider certain Correspondence between Sir Henry McMahon . . . and the Sherif of Mecca* (London, HMSO, 1939, Cmd. 5974). British representatives on the Committee argued that the wording of McMahon's letter had effectively excluded all territory west of the Damascus-Aleppo line, which should have been interpreted as extending from the Cilician border in the north to the Gulf of Akaba in the south. On this basis they claimed that Palestine had been excluded from the Arab area both by the Damascus-Aleppo clause and by the reservation in favour of French interests.

59. Sir A. H. McMahon to Foreign Office London, dispatch 131, 26.10.1915. FO 371/2486 fos. 274-5.

60. Sir T. B. M. Sykes to C. E. Callwell, dispatch 11, 12.7.1915. FO 371/2476 no. 106764.

61. It may seem curious that McMahon's communications to London about the reply to Hussein nowhere refer specifically to Palestine. There are two relevant considerations. First, as a matter of fact, his views on Palestine had recently been placed on record. Secondly, he knew that there would probably be major delays if it were thought that the reply to Hussein involved any kind of commitment about the future of Palestine. In such a case the matter would have been referred to the Cabinet, and it was unlikely that any decision could have been reached without consulting France. Such steps would have precipitated exactly the kind of diplomatic confrontation that McMahon wished to avoid.

The Cairo staff therefore took care to ensure that reservations in McMahon's reply gave no legal basis for an Arab claim to Palestine. At the same time it is possible that they deliberately refrained from drawing attention in London to this aspect of the affair. No one in the Foreign Office raised it with the Cabinet, presumably because McMahon's reservation about French interests covered the question adequately. It is thus wholly unreasonable to deduce from McMahon's silence on the issue in his communications to London that he meant to include Palestine in the independent Arab area.

62. Sir A. H. McMahon to Foreign Office London, dispatch 131, 26.10.1915. FO 371/2486 fos. 275-6.
63. G. F. Clayton to Sir F. R. Wingate 27.10.1915. Wingate Papers 135/4/77, Durham.

Chapter 12. Tackling the French

October 1915 – March 1916

1. A. N. H. M. Herbert, report, 30.10.1915. FO 371/2486 fo. 290. For Clayton's influence on this report see chapter 11 note 40.
2. Sir J. A. Chamberlain (S of S for India) to Lord Hardinge (Viceroy, Foreign Dept), telegram, 22.10.1915. FO 371/2486 fo. 254.
3. Lord Hardinge (Viceroy) to Sir J. A. Chamberlain (S of S for India), telegram, 4.11.1915. FO 371/2486 fo. 297.
4. Sir J. E. Nixon (GOC Force D) to Foreign, Simla, telegram Ig160X, 9.11.1915. Houghton Library bMS Eng 1252 (372).
5. Sir A. Hirtzel, minute on a telegram of 5.11.1915 from Sir A. H. McMahon to Foreign Office London. L/P&S/10/524 fo. 206. The phrase quoted refers specifically to the FO reply to McMahon of 6.11.1915.
6. Sir J. A. Chamberlain, quoted in Foreign Office to Sir A. H. McMahon (High Commissioner, Egypt), telegram 874, 11.11.1915. FO 141/732.

    Two India Office representatives would be appointed to the inter-departmental Nicolson Committee. It was probably for this reason that the Committee decided at its first meeting on November 13th to tell the French that 'all promises to the Arabs depended on the Arabs at once giving serious proof of their break from Turkey' (FO 371/2486 fo. 350).
7. Sir F. R. Wingate, note on a paraphrase of Sir A. J. Chamberlain's views (see note 6 above) contained in G. F. Clayton to Sir F. R. Wingate, telegram 992, 13.11.1915 (misdated 13.10.1915). Wingate papers W135/5/103, Durham.
8. Foreign Office London to Sir A. H. McMahon, telegram [860], 6.11.1915. FO 371/2486, fo. 304.
9. Sir A. H. McMahon to Foreign Office London, telegram 677, 7.11.1915. FO 141/732/62.
10. *Ibid.*
11. Sir J. G. Maxwell to Lord Kitchener, telegram 2125E, 4.11.1915. WO 33/747 p. 770.
12. *Ibid.* In this printed version of the telegram 'Maan' has been transcribed 'Wean'.
13. T. E. Lawrence to N. Bentwich 4.11.1915. Bentwich papers, Central Zionist Archives, Jerusalem.
14. Sir J. G. Maxwell to Lord Kitchener, telegram 2141E, 6.11.15. WO 33/747 p. 779.
15. See LH:*TEL* pp. 54-5. See also *B:LH* p. 88: Lawrence noted on Liddell Hart's typescript: 'This reply was due to action of myself upon Guy Dawnay!' (a senior officer on Maxwell's staff).
16. Lord Kitchener to H. H. Asquith (Prime Minister), telegram 29, 13.11.1915. WO 33/747 p. 810. These exchanges reflect the long-standing dispute between Easterners and Westerners.

17. *Ibid.*
18. *Ibid.*
19. Note given by Col. de La Panouse, military attaché at the French Embassy in London, to Sir W. R. Robertson (CIGS), quoted (in English translation) in H. J. Creedy to O. A. G. Fitzgerald, telegram 9885, 13.11.1915. WO 33/747 p. 811.

    In this connection see *'Note sur un projet d'opérations dans la région d'Alexandrette'* prepared by the French War Office on 22.10.1915 (*AFGG* pp. 49-53). While admitting that the operation presented little difficulty, this memorandum argued that it would have little effect on the Western Front and on the Serbian campaign. A second paper: *'Rapport sur un projet d'opérations à Alexandrette'* (*AFGG* pp. 54-7) notes that France could not at present undertake such an operation alone; that Britain had much more reason than France to be interested in cutting Turkish communications at Alexandretta, and that French interests were relatively unaffected by any Turkish threat to the Canal. Paragraph 6 stated that: 'For political reasons which it is unnecessary to spell out, any scheme involving action at Alexandretta by England alone is out of the question.' (author's translation).

    This episode shows that when confronted with questions of conflicting imperial ambition, the wartime Alliance was as tenuous on the French side as the British. Commenting on the note delivered in London by de La Panouse, Liddell Hart would later write: 'This must surely be one of the most astounding documents ever presented to an Ally when engaged in a life and death struggle. For it imposed what was really a veto on the best opportunity of cutting the common enemy's life-line and of protecting our own . . . The British General Staff may also be considered as accessories to the crime. It was no less – when we count the large force engaged and losses incurred in the frontal advance into Palestine that had alternatively to be undertaken.' (LH:*TEL* p. 56).
20. The formal communication from the French Government is quoted in H. H. Asquith (Prime Minister) to Lord Kitchener, telegram 9918, 14.11.1915. WO 33/747 p. 815.
21. For a discussion of these events see *MOEP*, Vol. I, pp. 76-85. See also 'A Statement of Military Considerations as to the advisability of undertaking an expedition . . . for the purpose of severing and keeping severed, the Turkish communications from Asia Minor . . . to Baghdad and ... to Syria and Egypt [etc.]'. WO 106/1570.
22. G. F. Clayton to Sir F. R. Wingate 12.11.1915. Wingate papers W135/5/91, Durham.
23. *Ibid.* W135/5/91-2.
24. T. E. Lawrence to W. G. Lawrence 17.7.1915, omitted from *DG* p. 199 and from *MB* p. 76. Bodleian R.
25. T. E. Lawrence to E. T. Leeds 16.11.1915 *L-L* p.110; *MB* pp. 78-9. Leeds papers.
26. Faroki did not become Hussein's official representative in Cairo until the following year, and at this date had still not had any contact with him. Faroki introduced himself to Hussein in a letter of 7.12.1915, quoted in A. L. Tibawi, *Anglo-Arab Relations and the Question of Palestine, 1914-1921* (London, Luzac, 1978) pp. 498-9. Sykes's biographer, R. Adelson, claims incorrectly that at the time of these talks Faroki had already visited Hussein for discussions on a future Anglo-Arab understanding. Had this been true, Sykes would have been more justified in attaching such weight to his conversation with Faroki (see R. Adelson, *Mark Sykes: Portrait of an Amateur*, London, Jonathan Cape, 1975, p. 194).

27. Sir T. B. M. Sykes to DMO London, telegram 707, 20.11.1915. FO 882/13 fo. 437. Sent in McMahon's cipher and listed in London as a message forwarded by Sir A. H. McMahon via the Foreign Office (see FO 371/2486 fos. 379-80).

28. *Ibid.* fo. 438.

29. Liddell Hart's note of a conversation with Lawrence records that, in Lawrence's recollection, Sykes himself had requested to make this tour. I have not found documents which specifically confirm this, but it seems characteristic of Sykes (see *B:LH* p. 60).

30. In this connection see 'Evidence of Lieut. Col. Sir Mark Sykes . . . at a meeting held at 10 Downing Street, on Thursday, July 16th 1916'. At one point Sykes said: 'I suggested the matter [a scheme for reorganisation in Egypt] to Lord Kitchener – at least, I did not; I could never make myself understood; I could never understand what he thought, and he could never understand what I thought. I say this because whenever I wanted to say anything I always passed it through Fitzgerald [Kitchener's secretary].' (CAB 42/16). Sykes seems to have been unconscious of the fact that this statement might be taken as a criticism of his own powers of reasoning and self-expression.

31. T. E. Lawrence, *SP* ch. VI p. 58.

32. 'Results of Second Meeting of Committee to discuss Arab Question and Syria' (the Nicolson Committee) 23.11.1915. FO 882/2 fo. 156. Georges-Picot continued by saying 'that the whole of the Damascus *Vilayet* must be included, as defined by the Turks; that the line must thence go to Deir el Zor and from there eastwards to the south of Kirkuk, turning east of that place and running north to include the whole of the Mosul district; thence west to include Diar Bekr, and on to include the whole of Cilicia.' *Ibid* fos. 156-7.

33. *Ibid.* fo. 157.

34. *Ibid.*

35. *Ibid.* fo. 158.

36. G. M. L. Bell arrived in Cairo on 26.11.1915 and not on 30.11.1915 as has often been stated. The latter date cannot be correct as she wrote a letter from Cairo to Lord Cromer on 29.11.15 (see note 38 below).

    The confusion seems to have arisen from *The Letters of Gertrude Bell* ed. Lady Bell (London, Ernest Benn, 1927) Vol. 1, p. 359, where a letter dated 30.11.1915 begins: 'I telegraphed to you this morning after my arrival'. Here 'this' is probably a mistranscription of 'the' (her handwriting can be very difficult to read). Other remarks in the same letter make it clear that she arrived on a Friday, which could only be 26.11.1915.

37. G. M. L. Bell to her family, *The Letters of Gertrude Bell* ed. Lady Bell (London, Ernest Benn, 1927) Vol. 1, p.360.

38. See G. M. L. Bell to Lord Cromer 29.11.1915. WO 79/64.

39. G. M. L. Bell to her family, *op. cit.* note 37 above, p.360.

40. Sir A. H. McMahon to Foreign Office London, telegram 736, 30.11.1915. FO 371/2486 fo. 447.

41. *Ibid.* fo. 448.

42. A. C. Parker to G. F. Clayton, enclosing minutes of the second Nicolson Committee meeting, 25.11.1915. Wingate papers W135/6/34, Durham. On 29.11.1915 Parker and Calwell signed a joint 'Note on the Arab Movement' (FO 371/2486 fos. 434-6). It read in part: 'it should be pointed out to the French that their refusal to act as we

wish may endanger all British possessions in the East, and may thus necessitate the removal of a very large part of the British army from France'.

43. G. F. Clayton to Sir F. R. Wingate, 6.12.1915. Wingate papers W135/7/33, Durham.

44. Sir A. H. McMahon to Foreign Office London, telegram 761, 10.12.1915. FO 371/2486 fo. 480.

45. Foreign Office London to Sir A. H. McMahon, telegram 961, 10.12.1915. FO 141/732.

46. Sir A. H. McMahon to Sherif Hussein 14.12.1915, English translation in *Correspondence between Sir Henry McMahon . . . and the Sherif Hussein of Mecca'* (London, HMSO, 1939, Cmd. 5957) p. 12. This goes somewhat farther than the reply suggested to McMahon by the Foreign Office, which stated that future arrangements in Mesopotamia would depend on 'the extent and success of Arab co-operation' (Foreign Office London to Sir A. H. McMahon, telegram 961, 10.12.1915. FO 141/732). The notion of such a proviso had by this time been generally accepted in London.

47. G. W. Clerk, minute dated 11.12.1915 on telegram 761 from Sir A. H.McMahon to Foreign Office London of 10.12.1915. FO 371/2468 fos. 478-9.

48. *Ibid.* fo. 479.

49. Sir T. B. M. Sykes, introductory 'Note' to a memorandum headed 'Arab Question' 5.1.1916 (later generally known as the Sykes-Picot Memorandum). FO 371/2767.

50. Sir T. B. M. Sykes to G. F. Clayton 28.12.1915. FO 882/2 fo. 10.

51. Sir T. B. M. Sykes and F. Georges-Picot, memorandum headed 'Arab Question' (i.e. the Sykes-Picot Memorandum) 5.1.1916. FO 371/2767.

52. Message from Sir T. B. M. Sykes to DMO London, telegram 707, 20.11.1915. FO882/13 fo. 437 (see note 27 above).

53. G. M. W. Macdonogh to Sir A. Nicolson 6.1.1916. FO 371/2767. See also an untitled memorandum of the same date headed 'Communicated by D.I.D.' FO 371/2767 no. 2989, in which similar arguments are advanced.

54. W. R. Hall, 'Memorandum on the Proposed Agreement with the French' enclosed in W. R. Hall to Sir A. Nicolson 12.1.1916. FO 371/2767.

55. *Ibid.*

56. Sir A. Nicolson to Lord Hardinge 16.2.1916. FO 800/381 fos. 134-5.

57. Minutes of a meeting of the Nicolson Committee 21.1.1916. FO 371/2767 no. 14106.

58. Draft of the Sykes-Picot terms enclosed with Sir A. Nicolson to Sir E. Grey 2.2.1916. FO 371/2767.

59. T. E. Lawrence to his family 24.1.1916 *HL* p. 312. Bodleian MS Res C13.

60. T. E. Lawrence to E. T. Leeds 18.1.1916 *L-L* p. 111. Leeds papers.

61. T. E. Lawrence, verbal statement noted by B. H. Liddell Hart *B:LH* pp.61-2.

62. In 1927 Lawrence commented to Robert Graves that 'the Erzeroum capture had been "arranged" (*Greenmantle* has more than a flavour of truth)' *B:RG* p. 82. John Buchan's novel *Greenmantle*, published in the autumn of 1916, gives a fictional account of the fall of Erzurum in which a military plan showing a weak point in the Turkish defences is smuggled out of the city and across to the Russian lines. Buchan had at that time such good connections inside the Foreign Office and War Office that he could well have heard rumours that something unusual had taken place. By coincidence, in February 1916 he was looking after a Russian delegation to Britain.

63. See T. E Lawrence, *SP* ch. VI pp. 59-60. For other references see *B:RG* and *B:LH*.

64. B. H. Liddell Hart, notes made of a conversation with T. E. Lawrence. Lawrence suggested that Liddell Hart should write: '[the] half-hearted defence of Erzerum [was] possibly to be explained by Secret Service reasons.' *B:LH* p. 141.

65. T. E. Lawrence to his family, 24.1.1916 *HL* p. 312. Bodleian MS Res C13. British Intelligence in Athens had reported on 30.11.1915 that the German staff at Constantinople had agreed with Enver (one of the Turkish ruling triumvirate) that a campaign against Egypt should be launched straight away. On 1.12.1915 further reports reaching the War Office indicated that the offensive had been prepared and that troops were already being assembled in order to take part. See the Intelligence information about the movement of troops in Asia Minor reported to Paris by the French military attaché in London on 2.12.1915, *AFGG* p. 69. These plans were evidently stalled by the Russian Caucasus campaign.

66. Note by T. E. Lawrence on the manuscript of B. H. Liddell Hart, *'T. E. Lawrence' in Arabia and After B:LH* p. 92. See also *B:LH* p.89, where Lawrence is quoted as saying that the exaggeration by Murray's staff of the Turkish threat 'was misrepresentation by our chief of Intelligence in Egypt [i.e. Holdich], against the protests of Philip Graves, Jennings Bramley, and myself – the three active Intelligence staff officers.' See also *DG* p. 203 on Lawrence's relationship with Holdich, whom he described as having 'a lunacy streak'.

67. Sherif Hussein to Sir A. H. McMahon 1.1.1916, English translation, *op. cit.* note 46 above, p. 13.

68. *Ibid.* p. 14.

69. W. H. Deedes, diary entry for 26-28.1.1916, quoted in J. Nevakivi, *Britain, France and the Arab Middle East 1914-1920* (London, Athlone Press, 1969) p. 29. Shortly after his arrival in Egypt with the Intelligence staff from Gallipoli, Deedes had written: 'Cairo . . . are wondering whether they will have to give way before us or vice-versa and altogether it's a pretty good muddle. I personally got a very nice *acceuil* from the Intelligence here. Clayton . . . a most charming and very clever man whom I knew before, is now running Intelligence here with Philip Graves . . . and others I know, also Gertrude Bell! who knows more about Arabs than most people. All a very happy and able party wondering whether they are to be turned out. They would willingly have me in too. How it will all plan out I don't know, I personally should much like to do some time here in this very interesting country.' (W. H. Deedes to his mother 8.1.1916. Deedes papers).

70. Sir A. H. McMahon to Foreign Office London, telegram 70, 26.1.1916. FO 141/734.

71. Sir T. B. M. Sykes to Sir A. Nicolson 24.1.1916. FO 371/2767 no. 15352.

72. Sir A. H. McMahon to Foreign Office London, dispatch 16, 24.1.1916. FO 371/2767 no. 20954.

73. Sir A. Nicolson to Sir E. Grey 2.2.1916. FO 371/2767 no. 23579.

74. Minute (headed 'Arab Question') of a meeting held on 4.2.1916. FO 371/2767. Although this passage is rarely quoted as part of the Sykes-Picot text, it was again incorporated as a preamble to the Agreement in a formal exchange of notes between Britain and France. See Sir E. Grey to P. Cambon 16.5.1916 *DBFP* 1/4 p. 245.

75. Minute by Sir A. Nicolson (undated but 5.2.1916) on Sir A. H. McMahon to Foreign Office London, dispatch 70, 24.1.1916. FO 371/2767 no. 20954.

76. Minute added to the above by Sir E. Grey.

77. Sir A. Nicolson to Sir A. H. McMahon 16.2.1916. FO 800/381 fo. 198. By agreeing

to postpone negotiations over French ambitions in Syria, Hussein himself had left the way open for this convenient Foreign Office gambit.

78. G. F. Clayton to W. R. Hall 13.1.1916. FO 882/2 fos. 24-5.
79. T. E. Lawrence, 'The Politics of Mecca', sent to the Cairo Residency on 1.2.1916 and to the Foreign Office on 7.2.1916. FO 141/461 fo. 146. This is one of several wartime and political documents by Lawrence which biographers have mis-construed. By quoting such material entirely out of context, they have suggested that he was wholly cynical in his attitude towards the Arabs. This illustrates the danger of research which focuses too narrowly on Lawrence without seeking a fuller understanding of contemporary events. See for example M. Yardley, *Backing into the Limelight* (London, Harrap, 1985) pp. 70-2. Note that Yardley does not, as he claims, print Lawrence's report in full: the extract he uses is from pp. 4-5 of the original document, and amounts to about a quarter of the text.
80. Minute signed [?]'HCN' dated 16.2.1916 on T.E.Lawrence's 'The Politics of Mecca'. FO 371/2771 fo. 150.
81. L. Oliphant, minute added to the above dated 19.2.1916.
82. Abdul Aziz ibn Saud, quoted in Cairo Intelligence Bulletin 10.2.1916. WO 157/751.
83. T. E. Lawrence, 'Cairo Note' on the above.
84. T. E. Lawrence to his family 21.2.1916 *HL* p. 314. Bodleian MS Res C13.
85. W. H. Deedes, diary entry 21-29.2.1916, quoted in J. Presland, *Deedes Bey* (London, Macmillan, 1942) p. 244.
86. Sir A. Nicolson to Sir A. H. McMahon 8.3.1916. FO 800/381 fo. 205.
87. Foreign Office London to Sir A. H. McMahon, telegram 173, 9.3.1916. FO 141/461/1198.
88. Sir A. H. McMahon to Sherif Hussein 10.3.1916, English translation, *op. cit.* note 46 above, p. 17.
89. T. E. Lawrence to his family 16.3.1916 *HL* p. 315. Bodleian MS Res C13.
90. *Ibid.*

Chapter 13. Witness to Tragedy

March – April 1916

1. This was soon noticed by the IEF commanders. In early March the CGS India commented to Robertson: 'I regard the enemy's fighting value as small if we can get him in the open but behind trenches he is distinctly formidable and he has now a much larger proportion of Anatolian Turks than formerly.' (Chief India to Sir W. R. Robertson, repeated in Chief India to Sir P. H. N. Lake [General Force 'D'] telegram 43304, 13.3.1916. WO 158/669 fo. 46.) The following day Lake commented: 'The C.I.G.S. [Robertson] probably under-estimates the comparative fighting value of the army now opposing us. It is immeasurably superior to that of the Arab troops encountered during the earlier operations in this country.

'Of the six Divisions now in the Kut area, the bulk of five Divisions is composed of European and Anatolian Turks of the best quality, at least the equal in fighting power of those who successfully held the Dardanelles against us. Their operations are directed largely by German officers and they are well supplied with machine guns and small arms ammunition.' (Sir P. H. N. Lake [General, Force D] to CGS Delhi and Sir W. R. Robertson [Chief London], telegram 1008/527/0, 14.3.1916. WO 158/669 fo. 54.)

Lawrence later wrote: 'By brute force [the IEF] marched . . . into Basra. The enemy troops in Irak were nearly all Arabs in the unenviable predicament of having to fight on behalf of their secular oppressors against a people long envisaged as liberators, but who obstinately refused to play the part. As may be imagined, they fought very badly. Our forces won battle after battle till we came to think an Indian army better than a Turkish army. There followed our rash advance to Ctesiphon, where we met native Turkish troops whose full heart was in the game, and were abruptly checked. We fell back, dazed; and the long misery of Kut began.' (*SP* ch. VI p. 59).

2. Quoted (in French) in C. V. F. Townshend to GHQ and Corps, telegram 69/258/G, 11.3.1916. WO 158/669 fo. 4 (author's translation).

3. C. V. F. Townshend to GHQ and Corps, telegrams 69/257-260/G, 11.3.1916. WO 158/669 fos. 2-6.

4. Sir P. H. N. Lake (GHQ) to C. V. F. Townshend (6th Division and Corps), telegram 1008/519/0, 13.3.1916. WO 158/669 fo. 36. Townshend replied the following day, adding on 15.3.1916: 'Please inform the C. in C. that I never intended negotiation with the Turks unless the Army Commander had any doubt regarding the possibility of my relief and then only with the approval of him and the Government.

'My idea was to come away from Kut without any lost prestige and save the Government humiliation in case Kut has to fall. Very possibly the Turks would not give such terms in which case I would take no others but would stand until overpowered or there is no food left when I should try to cut my way out with any who volunteered to come with me.' (C. V. F. Townshend [6th Division] to GHQ. WO 158/669 fo. 66).

5. C-in-C India to Sir W. R. Robertson (CIGS London), telegram 43397, 14.3.1916. CAB 22/13/2.

6. Sir W. R. Robertson (CIGS London) to C-in-C India, telegram 14396, 14.3.1916. CAB 22/13/2. Repeated to Lake in CGS Delhi to General Force 'D', telegram 43685, 16.3.1916. WO 158/669 fo. 107. For further expressions of optimism by London and Delhi see: Chief India to Sir P. H. N. Lake (General, Force 'D'), telegram 43304, 13.3.1916. WO 158/669 fos. 45-6.

7. *Report of the Commission appointed by Act of Parliament to enquire into the Operations of War in Mesopotamia* (London, HMSO, 1916, Cmd. 8610) p. 113.

8. W. H. Deedes, diary entry for 18.3.1916. Quoted in J. Presland, *Deedes Bey* (London, Macmillan, 1942) p. 251. Kitchener may well have nominated Deedes for this task because in February 1915 Deedes himself had suggested that he might be able to weaken the Turkish Army through bribery. Turkish prisoners had begun to arrive in Cairo in large numbers, and he asked to go there in order to try and bribe 'certain surrendered Turkish officers to return to Syria or other parts and cause dissension in the Turkish army and effect the desertion of others' (W. H. Deedes, diary entry for 6.2.1915. Deedes papers). The suggestion came to nothing. This, however, was a very different proposal to that adopted by Kitchener in March 1916.

9. *Ibid.* The idea of seeking Arab nationalist help to ease the situation in Kut seems to have occurred to several people at much the same time. See for instance Sir A. H. McMahon to Foreign Office London, telegram 152, 1.3.1916, and Sir T. B. M. Sykes to DMI London (sent via Sir G. Buchanan), telegram 355(K), 13.3.1916. L/P&S/10/525 fos. 119-20.

10. *Ibid.*

11. See *SP* ch. VI pp. 59-60: 'our Government . . . for reasons not unconnected with the fall of Erzerum, sent me to Mesopotamia to see what could be done by indirect means to relieve the beleaguered garrison.' See also Lawrence's written answer to a question by B. H. Liddell Hart, *B:LH* pp. 61-2: 'I had put the Grand Duke Nicholas in touch with certain disaffected Arab officers in Erzerum. Did it through the War Office . . . So the War Office thought I could do the same thing over Mespot., and accordingly wired out to Clayton.'

12. G. M. L. Bell to T. E. Lawrence 18.3.1916. FO 882/13 fo. 261.

13. *Ibid.*

14. T. E. Lawrence: *SP* ch VI p. 60. Kerbela and Nejef, on the western edge of the Euphrates marshes, are approximately 50 and 90 miles south of Baghdad. Both are centres of pilgrimage for Shia Moslems. For a description (probably by Lawrence) of the Arab unrest there at this period see *AB* No. 1, 6.6.1916, pp. 5-7.

15. T. E. Lawrence to his family 20.3.1916 *HL* p. 315. Bodleian MS Res C13.

16. Sir A. H. McMahon to Sir P. Z. Cox 20.3.1916. Houghton Library, bMS Eng 1252 (372).

17. A. N. H. M. Herbert to G. A. Lloyd 22.3.1916. Lloyd papers GLLD 9/2, Churchill College, Cambridge.

18. Sir A. H. McMahon to Foreign Office London, telegram 204, 21.3.1916. FO 371/2767 no. 54229.

19. Foreign Office London to Sir A. H. McMahon, telegram 215, 22.3.1916. L/P&S/10/525 fo. 106.

20. India Office to Viceroy, Foreign Department, repeated to Sir P. H. N. Lake (GOC Basra), telegram [1196], 24.3.1916. FO 371/2768 no. 57783.

21. W. H. Deedes to T. E. Lawrence 26.3.1916. Unsigned copy in FO 882/15 fos. 68-9. These instructions arrived in Basra after Lawrence had left, probably in the care of Aubrey Herbert, who travelled from Egypt with Admiral Wemyss. On reaching Mesopotamia, Wemyss and Herbert went up-river to advance headquarters, first on HMS *Imogene*, and then on board a smaller naval vessel, the *Snakefly*. As it happened, they overtook the river steamer in which Lawrence was travelling, and reached Lake's headquarters first. By the time Lawrence received Deedes's letter, its instructions were out of date.

22. *Ibid.* fo. 69.

23. *Ibid.* fo. 70. Lawrence was also told in this letter that General George MacMunn, who was passing through Cairo on his way to a staff posting in Mesopotamia, had been fully briefed on the scheme and would help if necessary. Lawrence seems, however, to have had no contact with him.

24. Sir P. H. N. Lake to Secretary of State for India, telegram 1040B, 30.3.1916. FO 371/2768 fos. 36-7. Something of Lake's attitude towards the natives of Mesopotamia may be gathered from his use of the word 'pabula', i.e. animal feed.

25. W. H. Deedes, quoted in J. Presland, *op. cit.* note 8 above, p. 256. No date given, but probably 31.3.1916.

26. Sir A. H. McMahon to Foreign Office London, telegram 232, 1.4.1916. FO 371/2768 fos. 46-7.

27. T. E. Lawrence, *SP* ch. VI p. 60.

28. Sir W. R. Robertson (Chief, London) to Sir P. H. N. Lake (GOC Force D) repeated to Intrusive Cairo, telegram 14895, 29.3.1916. Cairo text FO 882/13 fo. 279. The incomplete text received by Lake is in Houghton, bMS Eng 1252 (372).

29. Sir P. H. N. Lake (General, Basrah) to the War Office (Troopers, London), telegram IG 2375, 30.3.1916. Houghton Library bMS Eng 1252 (372).

30. W. H. Beach to C. V. F. Townshend (6th Division), telegram IG 2376, 30.3.1916. Houghton bMS Eng 1252 (372).

31. C. V. F. Townshend to Sir P. H. N. Lake (HQ), telegram 69/361/G, 31.3.1916. Houghton bMS Eng 252 (372).

32. Campbell Thompson seems not to have distinguished himself at Basra. In a letter written a few weeks later, Gertrude Bell wrote of him to Hogarth: 'if you will let me say so, he isn't any damned use – I think I have never come across anyone just like him before, so amiable and so entirely futile.' (G. M. L. Bell to D. G. Hogarth, undated but April 1916. FO882/13 fo. 285).

33. G. M. L. Bell to F. Bell 9.4.1916 in *The Letters of Gertrude Bell* ed. Lady Bell, Vol. I (London, Ernest Benn, 1927) p. 372.

34. T. E. Lawrence to G. F. Clayton (Intrusive, Cairo), telegram MS 1, 8.4.1916. FO 882/15 fo. 73. See also P. P. Graves, *The Life of Sir Percy Cox* (London, Hutchinson, 1941) pp. 202-3. Following a misunderstanding created by one of Cox's subordinates, Lawrence later sent an apologetic cable to Cox, in which he said: 'The general impression I had was that your practice agreed perfectly with our theory and that if Clayton and yourself met there would be no conflicting opinion at all' (*op. cit.* p. 203, telegram, no date given, but sent in reply to a telegram from Cox of 1.6.1916).

35. Sir P. Z. Cox to W. H. Beach 7.4.1916. Published in P. P. Graves *op. cit.* note 34 above, pp. 200-1.

36. *Ibid.* An account of Lawrence's dealings with Arab nationalists in Basra can be found in the memoirs of Sulayman Fayzi. See S. Mousa, 'T. E. Lawrence and his Arab Contemporaries' in *Arabian Studies*, VII (London) 1985, pp. 7-8. Fayzi recalled that he was asked to see Lawrence on April 7th 1916. Lawrence offered him money and weapons if he would start an Arab revolt in Mesopotamia. The memoir gives a detailed account of their conversation and confirms that Fayzi and his associates declined.

37. T. E. Lawrence to G. F. Clayton (Intrusive, Cairo), telegram MS3, 9.4.1916. FO 141/461/1198 fo. 247. A contemporary note by Deedes reads: 'Several interesting telegrams from Lawrence, general trend of which shows that purely *locally* there is no Pan-Arab or pro-war following. This applies, I fancy, to Basra, though the Pan-Arab and pro-British [following] is to be found further to the north at Baghdad.' Presland (*op. cit.* note 8 above, pp. 251-2) remarks that Lawrence's telegrams seem to have been inconsistent with his assessment of the prospects for an Arab revolt in *Seven Pillars* (quoted on p. 258 above). In reality they are wholly consistent.

38. T. E. Lawrence to his family 18.5.1916 *HL* p. 323; omitted from *MB* p. 82. Bodleian MS Res C13.

39. Sir P. H. N. Lake (General, Basrah) to Sir W. R. Robertson (Chief, London), telegram IG2508, 16.4.1916. Houghton bMS Eng 1252 (372).
For Sulayman Fayzi see note 36 above.

40. Sir P. H. N. Lake (GOC Force D) to Sir W. R. Robertson (CIGS London), telegram 129/408/O, 23.4.1916. WO 33/768 p. 1111.

41. *Ibid.* quoting C. V. F. Townshend to Sir P. H. N. Lake. It may have been the wording of this message which led the Official Historian and others to believe that the bribery scheme was originally proposed by Townshend. In reality, Townshend's

original suggestion of a negotiated and honourable release had nothing to do with bribery, an idea that had now been put to him by Lake.

42. *Ibid.*

43. *Ibid.* See also Sir W. R. Robertson (CIGS London) to Sir P. H. N. Lake (GOC Force D), which crossed with the above, suggesting that if the current relief efforts failed 'it is for consideration whether we should not think about negotiating terms'. WO 33/768 pp. 1111-12.

44. Lord Kitchener (S of S for War) to Sir P. H. N. Lake (GOC Force D), telegram 15736, 25.4.1916, 12.10 pm. CAB 22/18.

45. C. F. V. Townshend to Sir P. H. N. Lake (Army Commander), telegram 69/465/G, 27.4.1916, 10.15 am. Houghton bMS Eng 1252 (372).

46. C. F. V. Townshend to Sir P. H. N. Lake (HQ), telegram 69/466/G, 27.4.1916, 1.20 pm. Houghton bMS Eng 1252 (732).

47. *Ibid.* Lake had already cabled to the War Office asking permission to arrange an exchange of prisoners. See Sir P. H. N. Lake (GOC Force D) to Sir W. R. Robertson (CIGS London), telegram 1008/691/O, 26.4.1916. CAB 22/18.

48. C. F. V. Townshend to Sir P. H. N. Lake (HQ), telegram 69/468/C, 27.4.1916, 9.15 pm. Houghton bMS Eng 1252 (372).

49. A. N. H. M. Herbert, diary entry 28.4.1916. Herbert papers.

50. C. F. V. Townshend to Khalil Pasha 28.4.1916, translated from the original French in Sir P. H. N. Lake (GOC Force D) to Sir W. R. Robertson (CIGS London), telegram IG2671, 29.4.1916. WO 33/768 p. 1143.

51. Enver Pasha to Khalil Pasha, English translation in Sir P. H. N. Lake (GOC Force D) to Sir W. R. Robertson (CIGS London), telegram IG8471, 29.4.1916. WO 33/768 p. 1143.

52. C. F. V. Townshend to Sir P. H. N. Lake (HQ), telegram 69/474/G, 28.4.1916, deciphered 7.50 pm. Houghton Library bMS Eng 1252 (372).

53. C. F. V. Townshend to Sir P. H. N. Lake (HQ), telegram, 29.4.1916. IWM.

54. A. N. H. M. Herbert, diary entry 30.4.1916. Herbert papers. In *Leachman, 'OC Desert'* (London, Quartet, 1982) H. V. F. Winstone claims that Beach, Herbert and Lawrence were led through the enemy lines to Khalil's camp by Lt-Col Gerard Leachman on April 25th. This date is wrong; furthermore the claim that Leachman was present contradicts the accounts by Herbert and Beach, and was not made by Leachman's earlier biographer N. N. E. Bray. The statement, for which Winstone offers no source, appears therefore to be incorrect.

55. W. H. Beach to his wife 4.5.1916. Private collection.

56. A. N. H. M. Herbert, diary entry 30.4.1916. Herbert papers.

57. *Ibid.* In Robert Graves's draft of *Lawrence and the Arabs* (1927), he wrote that Lawrence had refused to take part in any exchange of courtesies, and had ended the conference with Khalil by remarking that 'a million dead Armenians' stood between Britain and the Turks. Lawrence deleted the passage about courtesies, and noted beside the Armenian comment: 'It was Aubrey Herbert who said this'.

When publishing this note (*B:RG* p. 83) Graves stated that his authority for attributing the Armenian remark to Lawrence had been Herbert, and added: 'I am inclined to believe Herbert. Lawrence may have wished not to seem responsible for the failure of the conference by having given way to private feelings.'

There is no contemporary record that Lawrence made any such remark, and whether or not it was made, it was certainly not responsible for the 'failure' of the meeting. Graves should have checked his facts before making such a serious charge. Nothing of the kind is reported by Herbert in his autobiography *Mons, Anzac and Kut* or in his contemporary diaries. Herbert had died three and a half years before Graves started research for the Lawrence biography, so he is most unlikely to have been Graves's source (I have found no record to suggest that the two ever met). If, while researching his book, Graves had really heard that Lawrence had behaved in such a way, it can only have been third-party gossip. His repetition or invention of this sensational allegation shows that he did not possess the integrity needed for worthwhile historical work.

58. T. E. Lawrence to his family 18.5.1916 *HL* p. 324; *MB* p. 82. Bodleian MS Res C13.

59. W. H. Beach to his wife 4.5.1916. Private collection.

60. A. N. H. M. Herbert, diary entry on 30.4.1916, published in *The Man who was Greenmantle*, by M. Fitzherbert (London, John Murray, 1983) p. 181.

61. W. H. Beach to his wife 4.5.1916. Private collection.

62. *Ibid*.

63. Sir P. H. N. Lake (GOC Force D) to Government of India, telegram IG2857, 22.5.1916, quoted in Viceroy, Foreign Department, to Foreign Office London, telegram, 28.5.1916. FO 371/2771. For Lawrence's observations on the question of co-operation between the Arab Bureau in Cairo and the authorities in Mesopotamia see his subsequent report to Clayton, Appendix III, pp. 949-59 above.

64. T. E. Lawrence to his family 18.5.1916 *HL* p. 324; *MB* pp. 82-3. In both these published texts 'Cork' is mistranscribed as 'Abingdon'. Bodleian MS Res C13.

65. T. E. Lawrence, note on the typescript of B. H. Liddell Hart, *'T. E. Lawrence' in Arabia and After*, June 1933 *B:LH* p. 92.

66. G. F. Clayton to Sir F. R. Wingate 10-13.6.1916. Wingate papers W/137/2/38, Durham.

67. W. F. Stirling, 'Tales of Lawrence of Arabia' in *Cornhill* (London) Vol. LXXIV, No. 442, April 1933, pp. 494-5. In June 1933 Lawrence noted on the typescript of Liddell Hart's biography *'T. E. Lawrence' in Arabia and After*: 'I was not distressed at their editing it, for Webb Gillman . . . had discussed every page of my original with me, before starting to write down his own submissions.' *B:LH* p. 92. This claim is borne out by Gillman's evidence after his return to London. See 'Memorandum on the Intelligence Service in Mesopotamia' (undated, but mid-June 1916. WO 106/1510 fos. 19-21). Much of this (e.g. comment on map-printing) seems to have been closely based on Lawrence's report.

68. W. H. Beach to his wife 4.5.1916. Private collection. It has often been claimed that Lawrence behaved insufferably in Mesopotamia and was universally unpopular there. This may be inferred partly from his own remarks in *Seven Pillars* (ch. VI p. 60), but the only relevant evidence seems to be in the recollections of Hubert Young, a career officer in the Indian Army. Young had visited Carchemish in 1913 and had enjoyed Lawrence's company. When they met again in Mesopotamia in 1916 both men were in uniform. Young then found Lawrence's unmilitary manner hard to accept. Moreover, Lawrence, though only a Captain, had earned a position of some importance. Young wrote: 'He seemed to me thoroughly spoilt, and posing in a way that was quite unlike what I remembered of him at Carchemish. It was then that I first noticed his anti-regular soldier complex, and, perhaps not unnaturally, resented it hotly.' (*Friends* p. 123).

69. T. E. Lawrence, suppressed introductory chapter of *Seven Pillars*, published in *OA*

pp. 143-4 (this chapter was included in English editions of *Seven Pillars* published after 1940).

Chapter 14. The Revolt Begins

May – September 1916

1. T. E. Lawrence to his family 18.5.1916 *HL* p. 326; MB p. 83. Bodleian MS Res C13.
2. Sir T. B. M. Sykes to G. F. Clayton, enclosed in Foreign Office London to Sir A. H. McMahon telegram 287, 14.4.1916. FO 371/2768 fo. 105.
3. *Ibid.*
4. *Ibid.* fo. 106.
5. In March, when Sykes had suggested sending al Masri or Faroki to London, 'where I could enter into formal discussion with them and when the ground was prepared bring them into contact with Picot', he had warned: 'Keep the actual terms of the provisional [Sykes-Picot] agreement from the knowledge of Arab leaders.' (Message from Sir T. B. M. Sykes to unidentified recipient, forwarded in Sir G. Buchanan to Foreign Office London, telegram 377 (K), 16.3.1916. FO 371/2767 no. 51288.)

    Sykes's purpose in trying to bring these Arabs to London was evidently to get a particular concession from the French, not to reach an agreement acceptable to Hussein. It is, however, difficult to see how he could have achieved even this much without running the risk of a confrontation between the Arabs and Georges-Picot.
6. Message from G. F. Clayton to Sir T. B. M. Sykes, in Sir A. H. McMahon to Foreign Office London, telegram 278, 20.4.1916. FO 371/2768 fo. 123.
7. *Ibid.* fo. 122. For Clayton's reaction to the proposal to send Syrians to London, and to the first intimations of the Sykes-Picot Agreement, see his annotations on the Cairo copy of Sir E. Grey to Sir A. H. McMahon, telegram 287, 14.4.1916. FO882/16 fos. 18-20.
8. Sir A. H. McMahon to Foreign Office London, telegram 284, 22.4.1916. FO 371/2768 fo. 132.
9. *Ibid.* fo. 133.
10. Sir A. H. McMahon to Foreign Office London, dispatch 83, 19.4.1916. FO 371/2768 fo. 160.
11. For information about Deedes's Turkish schemes see J. Presland, *Deedes Bey* (London, Macmillan, 1942) pp. 258-63. See also Sir A. H. McMahon to Foreign Office London, telegram 284, 22.4.1916. FO 371/2768 fos. 132-3, and telegram 286, 23.4.1916. FO 371/2768 fos. 142-3.
12. L. Oliphant, minute dated 23.4.1916 on Sir A. H. McMahon to Foreign Office London, telegram 284, 22.4.1916. FO 371/2768 fo. 129.
13. In essence, Sykes told the War Committee that while McMahon had been adequate as a temporary replacement for Lord Kitchener, he was too weak to impose the leadership now required in Egypt (see War Committee, 'Evidence of Lieut.-Col Sir Mark Sykes . . . at a Meeting held . . . on Thursday, July 6, 1916.' CAB 42/16). Sykes also proposed the transfer of Cox's administration in Mesopotamia to the Foreign Office. After the meeting, Clayton, who had been present, dissociated himself from Sykes's views. See Minutes of the War Committee Meeting held on 11.7.1916. CAB 42/16, where Sir J. A. Chamberlain is reported as saying that 'he had had a conversation with General Clayton after that meeting from which he

gathered that the latter did not take Sir M. Sykes' views entirely. General Clayton volunteered this information. He was not in favour of the change which Sir M. Sykes advocated.'

14. Sir A. Nicolson, minute dated 24.4.1916 on Sir A. H. McMahon to Foreign Office, telegram 284, 22.4.1916. FO 371/2768 fo. 130.

15. W. H. Deedes, diary entry, probably 24-28.4.1916, quoted in J. Presland, *op. cit.* note 11 above, pp. 261-2.

16. D. G. Hogarth, 'Anglo-Franco-Russian Agreement', memorandum for W. R. Hall, 3.5.1916. FO 882/14 fo. 35.

17. *Ibid.* fo. 36.

18. Intrusive Cairo to Dirmilint London, telegram ER 524, 3.5.1916. FO 882/2 fo. 207.

19. Sir F. R. Wingate (Governor-General Sudan) to G. F. Clayton, telegram 402, 16.4.1916. FO 882/4 fo. 90.

20. *Ibid.*

21. G. F. Clayton to Sir F. R. Wingate (Governor-General Sudan), telegram 299, 22.4.1916. The final paragraph is omitted from the copy in FO 882/4 (fos. 92-3) but is quoted in an Arab Bureau history of the Revolt prepared for McMahon in the autumn of 1916: *Summary of Historical Documents from the Outbreak of War between Great Britain and Turkey 1914 to the Outbreak of the Revolt of the Sherif of Mecca in June 1916*, FO 882/5 (see 'Part II – January to June 1916' p. 185; the pagination differs in other copies of this report preserved at the PRO).

22. Sherif Hussein to Sir A. H. McMahon 18.4.1916. English translation in FO 141/461/1198 fo. 303.

23. Sir A. H. McMahon to Sherif Hussein 8.5.1916. Quoted in *Arabia in Asia* No. XVIIIA, week ending 5.6.1916, p.1. WO 158/625. A more forceful message in this vein was sent on 22.5.1916, see FO 141/461/1198 fos. 323-4.

24. Sir F. R. Wingate (Governor-General Sudan) to G. F. Clayton, telegram 402, 16.4.1916. FO 882/4 fo. 90.

25. G. F. Clayton to Sir F. R. Wingate 22.5.1916. Wingate papers W/136/6/103, Durham.

26. G. F. Clayton to Sir F. R. Wingate 29.5.1916. Wingate papers W/136/6/152, Durham.

27. *Arabia in Asia*, No. XVIIIA, week ending 5.6.1916, p.2. WO 158/625.

28. T. E. Lawrence to his family 1.7.1916. *HL* p. 327; *MB* p. 84. Bodleian Ms Res C13.

29. D. G. Hogarth, report, 10.6.1916. FO 882/4 fos. 117-18.

30. Sherif Hussein to R. H. A. Storrs, undated but *c.* 5.6.1916. Translation in FO 882/4 fo.139.

31. Sir A. H. McMahon to Sherif Hussein 23.6.1916, draft letter to be telegraphed to Port Sudan for translation and transmission. FO 882/19 fos. 104-5.

32. Sir A. J. Murray (Chief Egypforce) to Sir W. R. Robertson (Chief London), telegram AM652, 15.6.1916. WO 158/625.

33. Sir W. R. Robertson to Sir A. J. Murray, telegram 17939, 16.6.1916. Quoted in Sir A. J. Murray (Chief Egypforce) to Sir F. R. Wingate (Sirdar), dispatch 1550, 25.6.1916. WO 158/625.

34. T. E. Lawrence, *SP(O)* ch. 22.

35. Sir A. J. Murray to Sir A. H. McMahon 19.6.1916. FO 141/738/3818.

36. The British Government and French representatives in London were anxious to hear about the Arab Revolt from Clayton himself. He left for England on June 20th, and

attended a meeting of the War Committee on July 6th. Another important issue discussed with the Government was the deportation to England of certain Egyptians suspected of hostile activities, for which Clayton was personally responsible in his role as head of Egyptian civil Intelligence. He was back in Cairo by July 22nd.

37. EEF Intelligence Diary 24.6.1916. WO 157/705.
38. D. G. Hogarth, 'Arab Bureau report for June 1916', 30.6.1916, p. 2. FO 141/738/3894.
39. T. E. Lawrence to his family 1.7.1916 *HL* p. 327; *MB* p. 84. Bodleian Ms Res C13.
40. A. L. Lynden-Bell to Cairo Branch, GHQ Intelligence, undated, but late June or early July 1916. WO 158/602.
41. A. C. Parker to Sir F. R. Wingate 6.7.1916. Wingate papers W138/3/69, Durham.
42. C. E. Wilson, report, 7.7.1916. Wingate papers W/138/5/14, Durham.
43. *Ibid.*
44. War Office memorandum, 'The Sherif of Mecca and the Arab Movement', 1.7.1916. FO 371/2773 no. 131897.
45. War Committee Minute WC-53 of 6.7.1916, quoted in a Committee of Imperial Defence memorandum to Sir M. P. A. Hankey, 24.1.1917. CAB 21/10.
46. Sir A. J. Murray to Sir W. R. Robertson 14.7.1916. CAB 44/15. It seems that Hussein expected to succeed rapidly in the Hejaz: after this he would himself need the Railway as the Revolt extended northwards into Syria.
47. T. E. Lawrence, *SP*(O) ch. 41. Years later Lawrence wrote to Liddell Hart: 'One of my first jobs for Holdich had been to make out a tactical scheme for the occupation of Akaba by amphibian expedition – and I had confessed that such a landing party could nohow cover itself. The proposed operation was indefensible. I said this in Jan. 1915, in my paper on an Akaba landing.' (*B:LH* p. 97). The January 1915 date for this paper is almost certainly wrong: at that period the only landing schemes considered seriously by Cairo Intelligence were on the Mediterranean coast of Syria. It is possible that Lawrence may have written some notes on Akaba, but his major paper – the one commissioned by Holdich – was unquestionably written in August 1916. Its conclusions may be judged from a report to the French War Office by D. de Saint-Quentin, dated 25.8.1916: 'General Murray's Chief of Staff told me, "We would be obliged to disembark into a narrow steep-sided valley, and could lose 2,000 men. Even if we got a foothold without meeting any resistance, the Turks would attack us in force three weeks later. A division would be needed to hold the heights which command the town, and in the meantime we would be blocked, immobile. As for a temporary occupation to encourage the tribes to raid the railway, the outcome is too uncertain to justify such a large cost and risk. For the moment we have neither surplus troops nor ships." ' *AFGG* p. 137 (author's translation).
    The extreme difficulties of the Wadi Itm road had not been evident from the maps available to Murray's staff. Lawrence's judgment, based in part on new aerial surveys, is borne out by an earlier reconnaissance attempt made by French seaplane pilots in December 1914, see *AFGG* pp. 7-8. The report, a French naval document, seems to have been unknown to the British and French army officers who advocated a landing at Akaba later in the war. It noted that (according to information from various sources) the gorge narrowed in places to seventy metres, and that the track had to cross a 1,400-metre pass. It concluded that 'this route presents very great difficulties for an army' (author's translation).
48. C. E. Wilson, 'Report on meeting with Sherif Feisal Bey at Yanbo, August 27th and

28th 1916', 1.9.1916. FO 882/4 fo. 309.

49. *Ibid.* fo. 312.

50. 'Translation of a Proclamation issued in the Hejaz by Sherif Haidar on August 9, 1916' *AB* No. 20, 14.9.1916, pp. 237-8.

51. C. E. Wilson, *op. cit.* note 48 above, fo. 311.

52. *Op. cit.* note 50 above, p. 238.

53. A. C. Parker to GHQ Intelligence 10.9.1916. FO 882/4 fo. 325.

54. 'Conference held at the Commander-in-Chief's Residence, Ismailia, at 12 noon, Tuesday 12th September, 1916, to discuss the Hedjaz question' verbatim minutes. FO 882/4 fo. 345.

55. *Ibid.* fo. 347.

56. *Ibid.* fo. 336.

57. *Ibid.* fo. 338.

58. Sir A. H. McMahon, memorandum, 12.9.1916, telegraphed by Sir A. Murray (Chief Egypforce) to Sir W. R. Robertson (Chief London), with additional comments, at 11.50 p.m. that evening, telegram AM1026, WO 158/602.

59. *Ibid.*

60. Sir W. R. Robertson to Sir A. J. Murray, telegram, 17.9.1916. Quoted in *op. cit.* note 21 above, fo. 266.

61. Lawrence gives a somewhat inaccurate account of this affair in *Seven Pillars* (ch. XIII, p. 94). He had not been in the Hejaz at the time, and when writing *Seven Pillars* probably relied on incomplete contemporary reports printed in the *Arab Bulletin* (at this time the Bureau was receiving little reliable information from the Hejaz). The version given here is based largely on A. C. Parker's diaries (see *The Diaries of Parker Pasha* ed. H. V. F. Winstone, London, Quartet, 1983, pp. 120, 129).

There had long been reservations about Hussein ibn Mubeirik, see for example G. F. Clayton to Sir F. R. Wingate, telegram 299, 22.4.1916: 'The High Commissioner deprecates sending arms to Sultan Hussein of Rabegh. He is an old arms dealer and "O's" [Sheikh Oreifan's] close connections with him may account for his pressing the matter. The High Commissioner would prefer that anything he gets comes from the Sherif.'(Quoted in *Summary of Historical Documents from the Outbreak of War between Britain and Turkey 1914 to the Outbreak of the Revolt of the Sherif of Mecca, June 1916*, Part II, undated but late 1916. FO 882/4 fo. 185. This part of the telegram is omitted from the version in FO 882/4 fos. 92-3.) Oreifan took part in Zeid's attempts to bring Sheikh Hussein to heel.

62. T. E. Lawrence to his family 22.7.1916 *HL* p. 328; *MB* p. 85. Bodleian MS Res C13.

63. *Ibid.*

64. Memorandum by the Survey of Egypt for the Sherif of Mecca, 1.10.1916, printed in *A Short Note on the Design and Issue of Postage Stamps Prepared by the Survey of Egypt for His Highness Hussein, Emir and Sherif of Mecca and King of the Hejaz* (El-Qahira, 1918) pp. 19-21.

65. T. E. Lawrence to his family 24.9.1916 *HL* p 329. Bodleian MS Res C13.

66. T. E. Lawrence, *SP(O)* ch. 9.

67. *Ibid.* Lawrence's studied eccentricity at Murray's HQ is noted in a French report on Lawrence, dating from August 1917, quoted in M. J-M. Larès, *T. E. Lawrence, La France et les Français* (Paris, Imprimerie Nationale, 1980) p. 97.

68. G. F. Clayton to Sir F. R. Wingate 9.10.1916. Wingate papers W/141/3/35, Durham.

In *Seven Pillars* (ch. VII) Lawrence concealed the fact that his journey to the Hejaz was really an Intelligence mission for Clayton. The account he gives there repeats the 'cover story' which he offered to his superiors at GHQ. There are two possible motives for the concealment. One was literary convenience: the *Seven Pillars* version saved a lot of explanation about his earlier Intelligence role, and may have seemed attractive, in dramatic terms, since it suggested that his involvement stemmed from a casual visit (at the time GHQ staff probably thought this was the case). There was probably, however, another motive: *Seven Pillars* was first drafted in 1919. At that period, when the future of the Middle East had yet to be settled, Lawrence may well have felt that it would be improper to reveal this kind of detail about wartime Intelligence work.

R. H. A. Storrs, in his autobiography *Orientations* (London, Ivor Nicholson & Watson, 1937, p. 199) endorsed Lawrence's *Seven Pillars* version, although contemporary documents show that this is much less than the truth. Storrs even claimed to have invited Lawrence to Jidda. In the light of Clayton's statements this seems improbable. In later life, Storrs was delighted to find himself cast in *Seven Pillars* as the man who introduced Lawrence to Arabia, and he probably had no wish to renounce such a flattering role.

69. T. E. Lawrence, *SP*(O) ch. 9.

Chapter 15. Intelligence Mission to the Hejaz
October – November 1916.

1. Arab Bureau, 'Summary of the Military Achievement of the Sherif of Mecca, June to October 1916', October 1916. FO 882/5 fos. 80-1.
2. Sir A. H. McMahon to Lord Hardinge 13.10.1916. Lloyd George papers E/3/12/1, House of Lords.
3. *Ibid.*
4. Although there had been criticism of McMahon in London for some time, the particular issues which seem to have precipitated his removal were the organisation of military supplies to the Hejaz and the question of his relationship with Wingate. During the early stages of the Revolt, arrangements to meet its needs had not been handled very efficiently from Egypt, and this fact had been reported to London. Thus Lawrence wrote in *SP*(O) (ch. 9): 'Sir Ronald Graham [a Foreign Office official who was adviser to the Ministry of the Interior of the Egyptian Government] whose six years' inconclusiveness in Egypt wrecked the Ministry of the Interior and prepared the disorders of 1919, made up his mind for the first time, and when sent down to Suez to report on the situation to Lord Hardinge [now Permanent Under-Secretary of State at the Foreign Office] was only able to beg him to remove McMahon. It was less diplomatic of him to boast of this exploit across Cairo in the evening of the very day he had solemnly assured Sir Henry McMahon of the profoundly favourable impression his exposé had made upon the [ex-]Viceroy.'

On October 3rd McMahon received a telegram from London which read: 'The question of military control and supervision of all arrangements for assisting Sherif has been made the consideration of War Committee, who have decided that they should be entrusted to the Sirdar who should be instructed to take the steps necessary to keep himself in close communication and co-operate with Admiral Commanding Naval Forces in Red Sea. War Office will inform Commander in

Chief [Egypt] to the above effect and he will be instructed to assist Sirdar in provision of stores and supplies so far as his own requirements permit. (Foreign Office London to Sir A. H. McMahon, telegram 787. FO 141/738/3818).

McMahon replied the following day: 'I much regret the decision arrived at for the strong reason that the proposed arrangement has already been given a full trial and found quite impracticable. In agreement with C.-in-C., the Sirdar at my request undertook last June control and supervision of Military arrangements for assistance of the Sherif. The arrangement after some weeks had to be abandoned much to relief of Sirdar and myself as it led to endless correspondence and confusion without any compensating advantage.

'Circumstances necessitate provision of assistance in matter of stores supplies equipment arms munitions and other material from here. The base is necessarily Suez and sea transport must be arranged here.

'The centre of Military Intelligence, the Arab Bureau, and, in the case of stores etc which have to be purchased, the financial control, are all here.

'The Naval C. in C. is in close touch with C.-in-C. Egypt and myself and cannot under any circumstances be so with Sirdar at Khartoum . . .

'Political and military aspects of question are so intermixed that there must be every facility for rapid personal interchange of views between those responsible . . .'(Sir A. H. McMahon to Foreign Office London, telegram 844, 4.10.1916).

McMahon's arguments served only to convince his critics that the Sirdar should be moved to Cairo. On 12.10.1916 Grey cabled to Wingate: 'Lord Kitchener's death has made the consideration of an appointment necessary which can be substantive and continue after the war. In my opinion there is no one so well fitted as yourself, by your special knowledge, experience, and personal qualities, to fill the post' (Sir R. Wingate, *Wingate of the Sudan*, London, John Murray, 1955, p. 201).

Lawrence later wrote: 'Wingate, whose rather facile mind had believed itself the home of political insight in the Arab East, foresaw credit and great profit for the country in the new development [the Arab Revolt]; but as criticism slowly beat up against McMahon he dissociated himself from him, and at the same time came hints of how much better use might be made by an experienced hand of so subtle and involved a skein.' *SP*(O) ch. 9.

5. Viscount Grey to D. Lloyd George 2.11.1916. Lloyd George papers E/2/13/12, House of Lords (Lloyd George was at that time Minister for Munitions). McMahon's dismissal was handled with little tact: he received a personal 'decypher yourself' telegram from the Foreign Office informing him that Wingate would take over. The news came as a complete surprise, not only to McMahon but to most of the British staff in Cairo. Many (e.g. Admiral Wemyss) were saddened by it, and especially by the way it had been done. G. A. Lloyd wrote from Cairo on 4.11.1916 that the McMahons were 'taking it quite splendidly, but they are puzzled and pained about it, for it does not appear from the information that they have received that the change is being made on account of any dissatisfaction with his work, but on the grounds that the appointment was only a temporary one and that the time has now come to appoint someone permanently. Of course Lord Kitchener had kept a reversionary interest in the post. That was almost common knowledge, but he [McMahon] had not considered that the appointment, subject to this one proviso, was in any way anything but permanent . . . one cannot but be sorry for him, especially as there is no present prospect of any alternative post. One rather wonders

how far India will feel disposed to do much for him in view of the fact that he was identified with an Arab policy which they considered disagreeable.' (to S. P. Cockerell, Lloyd papers GLLD 9/13). Both in this letter and in an appeal to Austen Chamberlain written on the same day, Lloyd stressed the value and difficulty of McMahon's work in Cairo, and the unjustness of dismissal without offer of some other employment.

One rumour current in Egypt was that the Foreign Office had disliked McMahon because he was not one of their own career staff. Sykes, who had vociferously urged McMahon's dismissal, was happy to foster this myth. After meeting Sykes some months later, Wemyss wrote home: 'It appears that poor McMahon was ruthlessly chucked out from here simply because he had been an Indian official and the Foreign Office were jealous. They had been furious at his being given the appointment at all and had intended it for one of their out-of-job people! Mark Sykes's remarks on the Foreign Office are indeed withering.' (Lady Wester Wemyss, *The Life and Letters of Lord Wester Wemyss*, London, Eyre and Spottiswoode, 1935, p. 340.)

6. T. E. Lawrence, 'The Sherifs', 27.10.1916. FO 882/5 fos. 40-1.
7. R. H. A. Storrs, diary entry for 16.10.1916. Transcript headed 'Extract from Diary' and dated 25.10.1916 in FO 171/462/1198 fos. 294-5. On October 3rd the British Government had confirmed its decision not to send any troops. It recommended holding a brigade of Sudanese troops in readiness at Port Sudan in case of urgent need, but there was little likelihood that they could be transferred to the Hejaz in time if a crisis developed. For the text of Wingate's message to Wilson about the decision, see Sir F. R. Wingate (Sirdar Khartoum) to Arbur, telegram 439, 15.10.1916. WO 158/602. As no troops were to be sent it became impractical to send the flight of aeroplanes authorised on September 25th. Wingate cabled to Murray: 'You should instruct Parker on the arrival of the officer commanding the flight to notify him that pending further orders he should not land the flight'. Sir F. R. Wingate (Sirdar Khartoum) to Sir A. J. Murray (Chief Egypforce), telegram 442, 15.10.1916. WO 158/602.
8. T. E. Lawrence to G. F. Clayton 18.10.1916. Clayton papers 693/11/1-2, Durham (photocopy of original). The War Committee decision not to send troops to Rabegh was reconfirmed on October 17th. See Sir W. R. Robertson, 'Despatch of an Expeditionary Force to Rabegh' 13.11.1916, Appendix II (WO 106/1511) for an account of the circumstances.
9. T. E. Lawrence, *SP* ch. VIII p. 70.
10. *Ibid.* p. 71.
11. T. E. Lawrence to G. F. Clayton 17.10.1916, included in Arbur to Sir F. R. Wingate (Sirdar Khartoum) telegram AB30, 18.10.1916, WO 158/602. In the section of *Seven Pillars* describing the voyage from Suez to Jidda (ch. VIII p. 65) Lawrence mentions a conversation between Storrs and al Masri. As the latter had arrived in Jidda some time previously this conversation must have taken place during the later journey from Jidda to Rabegh, which all three made together. The conversation (about music) has no historical significance, and this trivial error is only worth noting because *Seven Pillars* contains few such lapses.
12. T. E. Lawrence, memorandum 17.11.1916. Clayton papers 694/4/42-46 (misdated 18.11.1916). It is possible that Lawrence had not had any serious discussion with Brémond before this visit to the Hejaz, although it seems likely that they had already

encountered one another in Cairo. In *Seven Pillars*, however, he mentioned no meeting with Brémond before mid-December 1916 (see ch. XXVIII). There he gave a summary of conclusions about French policy which he had, in reality, reached rather earlier.

There is ample evidence of Lawrence's meetings with Brémond in October: Storrs noted having dinner with Brémond and Lawrence on October 16th (see R. H. A. Storrs, 'Extract from Diary' FO/171/462/1198 fo. 296; Brémond alludes to Storrs's discussions in a telegram of 20.10.16, see *AFGG* pp. 192-3). A further meeting took place at Jidda on Lawrence's return journey. On 3.11.1916 Brémond sent a long report of Lawrence's news to Paris (see E. Brémond Djeddah to Ministre de la Guerre Paris, no. 40, *AFGG* pp. 202-4). Wemyss's diary shows that he dined with Lawrence and Brémond that evening (Wemyss papers WMYS 12/4, Churchill College, Cambridge).

The British were uncertain at this time whether any route between Medina and Mecca other than the Sultani Road via Rabegh would be practicable for a Turkish advance. It was later established that the alternatives were too mountainous to be suitable for a large force, and that the Rabegh route alone had sufficient water all year round to provide for an army.

13. E. Brémond to A. Defrance (head of the French diplomatic mission in Cairo) 16.10.1916. Service Historique de l'Armée, Box 17 N. 498, file 2. Quoted in M. J-M Larès: *T. E. Lawrence, La France et Les Français* (Paris, Imprimerie Nationale, 1980) p. 156 (author's translation). On 23.11.1916 Brémond repeated this caution in a telegram to Paris, see *AFGG* p. 219. He believed that this policy would be in Britain's best interests too, because a Sherifian victory in the Arabian Peninsula would be followed by a nationalist campaign in Mesopotamia. See also *HGM* p. 96, where Brémond lists his suggestions at a meeting with Wingate on 14.12.1916: '*Il est désirable de ne pas prendre Médine, qui permettrait au panarabisme de se développer de manière nuisible pour les Alliés.*'

14. T. E. Lawrence, 'Military Notes', 3.11.1916. FO882/5 fo. 61.

15. T. E. Lawrence to G. F. Clayton 18.10.1916. Clayton papers 693/11/1-2, Durham (photocopy of original).

16. *Ibid.*

17. R. H. A. Storrs, diary entry for 19.10.1916. Transcript headed 'Extract from Diary' and dated 25.10.1916 in FO 141/462/1198 fo. 307.

18. T. E. Lawrence, 'The Sherifs', 27.10.1916. FO 882/5 fo. 40.

19. A. C. Parker to G. F. Clayton 24.10.1916, *The Diaries of Parker Pasha* ed. H. V. F. Winstone (London, Quartet, 1983) p. 158.

Ali insisted that Lawrence should travel inland disguised in an Arab cloak and headcloth. Commenting on this after Lawrence's return, Brémond wrote: 'Captain Lawrence travelled dressed as an English officer . . . on his head he wore an *agal*, the bedouin head-dress. He claims that he passed everywhere, thanks to his knowledge of the Syrian dialect, as a Syrian officer in the Sherif's service. Although he has a very good knowledge of Syrian Arabic, Lawrence has a marked English accent which would seem to make such confusion difficult.' (E. Brémond, Djeddah, to Ministre de la Guerre Paris, no. 40, 3.11.1916. *AFGG* p. 203). Lawrence himself later wrote: 'I never heard an Englishman speak Arabic well enough to be taken for a native of any part of the Arabic-speaking world, for five minutes' (*B:RG* p. 57). There were, however, races on the northern fringes of Syria whose first language was not Arabic, and Lawrence might have been taken for someone of this kind.

Parker arrived in the Hejaz on 6th September 1916 and spent three months there. His original mission, carried out with the help of an engineer officer and a pilot, was to study the possibility of setting up an airfield at Rabegh. He continued to act as a liaison officer, mainly at Rabegh, where he gathered information about Arab requirements and the progress of the campaign. He handed over to Major P. C. Joyce on December 5th. Winstone (*op. cit.* above, pp. 158-9) states wrongly that Wingate had 'little time' for Parker and wanted to replace him with Newcombe. Parker was withdrawn from the Hejaz at Murray's request, in anticipation of an advance across Sinai. In a letter to Wilson of 30.11.1916, Wingate referred to the 'struggle I had to try and keep Parker at Rabegh,' adding, 'but I fully appreciate Murray's point and of course Parker's knowledge and local experience in Sinai will be invaluable when the push comes.' (Wingate papers W/143/6/100, Durham).

In his edition of Parker's diaries, Winstone gives the impression that Parker was Lawrence's superior in the Hejaz. In reality Parker's stay there overlapped very little with Lawrence's, and during this brief period Parker, although of senior rank, was neither his commanding officer nor responsible for his activities. Parker had, however, been one of Lawrence's seniors for short periods in the Cairo Military Intelligence organisation.

20. T. E. Lawrence, *SP* ch. XI, p. 84.
21. T. E. Lawrence, report 29.10.1916, *AB* No. 31, 18.11.1916, p. 458. This contemporary account of Lawrence's first meeting with Feisal gives a different impression to the version in *SP* (ch. XII pp. 90-1) where Feisal's entrance is made to seem more heroic. It is clear that the first appearances of Feisal, Auda and Allenby in *Seven Pillars* were dramatised to give an impression fitting to their central role in the story.

A small Egyptian artillery unit under Hassan Zeki Bey had been sent by Wingate to strengthen Feisal's tribesmen. Lawrence was soon pressing to have the Egyptians removed, leaving their guns behind. One of his contemporary notes reads: 'Egyptians say forbidden to kill Moslems, so they could not fight the Turks. Egyptian officers all pro-Turks, as they are not aware of Turkish tyranny: also all turning to politics. Their battery took 362 camels to carry their goods: same battery afterwards went off with 31 camels, when manned by Arabs. They all wanted Turkey to take Egypt.'(BM Add. MS 45914, fo. 6) See also T. E. Lawrence to A. C. Parker 24.10.1916, Parker *op. cit.* note 19 above, p. 163.
22. T. E. Lawrence, 'The Sherifs', 27.10.1916. FO 882/5 fo. 41.
23. T. E. Lawrence, *SP*(O) ch. 14.
24. There is no evidence about the date at which Lawrence first heard of the Sykes-Picot Agreement and the proviso about Damascus, Homs, Hama, and Aleppo. However, in the absence of proof to the contrary it seems reasonable to assume that he learned of the Agreement at some point between his return from Mesopotamia in May 1916 and his first mission to the Hejaz in October. He had been privy to discussions about the McMahon-Hussein correspondence and, as a key member of Clayton's staff, he would surely have been told of this new development. Others in the Department, for example Deedes, certainly knew about it by then (see p. 283).

Seven Pillars (ch. XLVIII p. 275) contains a curiously-worded statement which gives the impression, at first reading, that Lawrence had known nothing of these political moves until some later stage in the war. He wrote: 'I had had no previous or inner knowledge of the McMahon pledges and the Sykes-Picot treaty, which were both framed by war-time branches of the Foreign Office.'

As regards the McMahon-Hussein negotiations, this statement is plainly incorrect. Contemporary evidence shows that Lawrence was aware of the correspondence while it was taking place.

This statement in *Seven Pillars* is also misleading as regards the Sykes-Picot Agreement. While it is true that Lawrence had no knowledge of the negotiations that had taken place in London, he certainly knew about the Agreement long before this, and in all probability before the the Revolt began.

His claim may owe something to the impression he formed when the terms of the Anglo-French Agreement were finally made known to Cairo. He assumed wrongly that the Agreement predated the McMahon-Hussein correspondence and later made several statements to this effect (see for example *DG* p. 266. This is also implied in *Seven Pillars* ch. XLVIII p. 275).

The context of the remark in *Seven Pillars* has led many readers to suppose that he knew nothing about the Sykes-Picot negotiations until Nuri Shalaan confronted him with conflicting documents in June 1917. However, such an inference is contradicted elsewhere in *Seven Pillars*, for example in the much later chapter (ch. CI p. 555) where Lawrence stated that he had revealed the essentials of the Anglo-French arrangement to Feisal early in the campaign and in ch. XXXVI pp. 212-13, where he contrasted his own knowledge of the political situation with Abdullah's confidence in British promises. The discussion referred to took place in early April 1917. In any case, he cannot have learned of the Sykes-Picot terms from Nuri Shalaan in June 1917, because Nuri himself did not know of them until they were revealed by the Bolsheviks at the end of that year (in this connection see *B:LH* p. 126).

Lawrence's disclaimer in chapter XLVIII of *Seven Pillars* must therefore be ignored. As will be clear from later chapters, it formed part of a stance which he adopted after the war, when he found it politic to imply that the Arabs had not known of the Sykes-Picot terms during the war.

25. T. E. Lawrence, *SP*(O) ch. 41.
26. T. E. Lawrence, report 29.10.1916. FO 882/5 fo. 72.
27. T. E. Lawrence to A. C. Parker 24.10.1916, Parker *op. cit.* note 19 above, pp. 161-2. Parker papers.
28. T. E. Lawrence, report, 29.10.1916. FO 882/5 fo. 73.
29. T. E. Lawrence, 'Hejaz Administration', 3.11.1916. FO 882/5 fo. 54.
30. T. E. Lawrence, 'Military Notes', 3.11.1916. FO 882/5 fos. 56-8
31. T. E. Lawrence, 'Feisul's Operations', 30.10.1916. FO 882/5 fos. 45-6.
32. *Ibid.* fos. 49-51.
33. A. C. Parker, diary entry for 31.10.1916, Parker *op. cit.* note 19 above, pp. 167-8.
34. Sir F. R. Wingate (Sirdar Khartoum) to Arbur for transmission to the Foreign Office, telegram 627, 2.11.1916. WO 158/602.
35. *Ibid.*
36. This translation of the note from the French Embassy to the Foreign Office of 1.11.1916 appears in *Arabian Report* (London), No. XVI, 2.11.1916, p. 2. CAB 17/177.

The *Arabian Report* was a weekly digest of Middle East news and opinion prepared by Sir Mark Sykes, who in June had joined the secretariat of the

Committee of Imperial Defence as expert on Arab affairs.

37. Foreign Office London to Sir F. R. Wingate 2.11.1916, quoted in Sir A. J. Murray (Chief Egypforce) to Sir F. R. Wingate (Sirdar Khartoum), telegram AM1214, 3.11.1916. WO 158/603.

38. Sir W. R. Robertson (Chief London) to Sir A. J. Murray, telegram 24574, 2.11.1916, quoted in Sir A. J. Murray (Chief Egypforce) to Sir F. R. Wingate (Sirdar Khartoum), telegram AM1214, 3.11.1916. WO 158/603.

39. Quoted in Sir W. R. Robertson, 'Despatch of an Expeditionary Force to the Hejaz' Appendix II, p.7, 13.11.1916. WO 106/1511.

40. A. C. Parker to C. E. Wilson, quoted in Arbur to Sir F. R. Wingate (Sirdar Khartoum), telegram AB140, 2.11.1916. WO 158/603.

41. T. E. Lawrence, suppressed introductory chapter of *Seven Pillars*, first published in *OA*, pp. 139-46.

42. Most members of the Arab Bureau had a high personal regard for McMahon. However, they recognised that Wingate was strongly committed to the Arab cause, and that the previous arrangements for supporting the Hejaz revolt had been cumbersome. Wemyss wrote on 13.11.1916: 'I am bound to say that I think affairs in the Hedjaz will be better managed under the new régime than formerly. This will not be owing altogether to Wingate's replacement of McMahon, but to the fact that at last the Government seem to have realized that more co-ordination is necessary, and I am in hopes that Wingate will have a freer hand.' (letter to an unidentified recipient, quoted in Lady Wester Wemyss, *The Life and Letters of Lord Wester Wemyss* London, Eyre and Spottiswoode, 1935, p. 338).

43. Sir F. R. Wingate to Sir A. J. Murray, telegram 'private and personal', 23.11.1916. WO 158/627.

44. For details of this force see *HGM* p. 64.

45. N. N. E. Bray, report, 18.10.1916. Wingate papers W/141/6/117-120, Durham. Bray had visited the Hejaz with an Indian Army mission (see N. N. E. Bray, *Shifting Sands*, London, Unicorn Press, 1934, p. 67).

H. V. F. Winstone, editor of *The Diaries of Parker Pasha* (*op. cit.* note 19 above) is incorrect in stating (p. 131) that Bray was at that time a Staff Officer (I) to Colonel Wilson. Bray did not go to Jidda for this purpose until his return from London in late December.

46. Sir F. R. Wingate (Sirdar Khartoum) to Arbur, telegram 9, 7.11.1916. WO 158/603. In early October Clayton had suggested sending Newcombe to Jidda as an assistant to Colonel Wilson, whose workload was very heavy.

47. A. C. Parker, report to Arab Bureau 8.11.1916. Wingate papers W/143/7/7-8, Durham.

48. N. N. E. Bray, report 18.10.1916. Wingate papers W141/6/117-120, Durham. Bray's observations are supported by those of other British officers. A month later P. C. Joyce wrote: 'We went round the so-called defences of Rabegh yesterday, mere scratchings they are, and quite useless as they stand, against an army with any sort of artillery. I pointed out a few obvious improvements to Nuri Bey . . . he entirely concurred with my suggestions but I heard from Parker afterwards that the Sherif [Ali] did not approve of any criticisms at all being made and so of course one is rather checked.' (to G. S. Symes, Akaba archive I/2, H8, KCL). Joyce's reports and telegrams during his time as senior British officer at Rabegh often show an acute sense of frustration in his dealings with Ali and the other Arab leaders.

49. Sir W. R. Robertson (Chief London) to Sir F. R. Wingate (Sirdar Khartoum), telegram 24923, 11.11.1916. Wingate papers W/143/2/142-143, Durham. The suggestion of sending Lawrence and Lloyd had been made at the War Office by C. French (see C. French to G. A. Lloyd 10.12.1916, Lloyd papers GLLD 1/16, Churchill College, Cambridge).
50. Arab Bureau Report 31.10.1916. FO 371/2781. Lawrence was destined never to take up this full-time position in the Arab Bureau. There is no suggestion here that he had been visiting the Hejaz while on leave, and the details of his itinerary included in the report show that Clayton had been kept closely informed of his progress.
51. Sir F. R. Wingate to G. F. Clayton, telegram 781, 12.11.1916. Wingate papers W/143/2/144, Durham.
52. Sir F. R. Wingate to C. E. Wilson 12.11.1916. Wingate papers W/143/1, Durham.
53. Arbur to Sir F. R. Wingate (Sirdar Khartoum), telegram AB205, 13.11.1916. Wingate papers W/143/2/190-192, Durham.
54. T. E. Lawrence, *SP* ch. VIII p. 66. Wilson's views are clear from a note he attached to a letter from Hussein of 19.8.1916 asking him to wear Arab dress while in the Hejaz: 'I informed the Sherif I could not dress like an Arab . . . I told him there was nothing about not wearing helmets in the Koran. I took this line about dress because I consider that to have complied with the request *in toto* would not be in keeping with the prestige or custom of British officers, and the sooner the Arabs knew this the better' (FO 686/33). This attitude amazed both Lawrence and Storrs, who commented: 'Wilson . . . is conscientious, hard working, and generally admirable, if a little lacking in imagination. I cannot for instance conceive why he should object to the temporary adoption of Arab costume over his uniform when going well inland to meet Feisal.' (R. H. A. Storrs to G. A. Lloyd 5.9.1916. Lloyd papers GLLD 9/8, Churchill College, Cambridge). In time, Wilson's views moderated, at any rate as regards others. In March 1917 Lawrence was to note: 'Colonel Wilson at Wejh told the Armoured Car squad that they should always wear their *keffiyehs* and *agals* when ashore. This is different to September 1916!' (notebook, BL Add. MS 45914, fos. 31-2).
55. T. E. Lawrence to G. F. Clayton 18.10.1916. Clayton papers 693/11/1-2, Durham (photocopy of original).
56. Sir F. R. Wingate (Sirdar Khartoum) to G. F. Clayton 14.11.1916. Wingate Papers W/143/2/193-4, Durham.
57. French Embassy London to Foreign Office 8.11.16, author's free translation. Quoted in French in Sir W. R. Robertson, 'Despatch of an Expeditionary Force to Rabegh' Appendix III, 13.11.1916. WO 106/1511.
58. Sir W. R. Robertson, 'Despatch of an Expeditionary Force to Rabegh, 13.11.1916, p. 1. WO 106/1511.
59. See Sir W. R. Robertson (Chief London) to Sir A. J. Murray (Chief Egypforce), telegram 24903, 11.11.1916: 'Rabegh once more under consideration. Please say how your prospective operations would be affected if your force was reduced by (a) one infantry brigade, (b) two infantry brigades, two artillery brigades and two camel corps companies' (WO 158/627). Murray replied the following day, referring to his forthcoming operations against El Arish and proposed raids into Syria: 'I thus hope to attract to myself Turkish forces which would otherwise be engaged against the Sherif . . . By acting on the defensive-offensive I hope to gain full value from my

Egyptian Field Force which a purely defensive role would not achieve. The sending of any detachment to Rabegh weakens my offensive and has the natural drawbacks inherent in dispersions of force, and if the larger force you mention were sent to Rabegh I doubt the possibility of undertaking any serious offensive from El Arish' (Chief Egypforce to Chief London, telegram AM1251, 12.11.1916. WO 158/627).

Although Murray strongly opposed landing troops at Rabegh, which he saw as the start of a new 'side-show', he was by no means indifferent to the outcome of the Arab Revolt. Hussein's rebellion was already drawing Turkish troops away from Sinai and Palestine. Some weeks previously he had suggested a different scheme for assisting the Arabs. The Hejaz Railway was beyond the range of aircraft flying from Egypt, but if the RFC could send aircraft to Jauf, a remote oasis on the edge of the Nefud desert nearly two hundred miles to the east of the Railway, it might be possible to attack the line with impunity. Though nominally in Turkish-held territory, Jauf was far from any Turkish forces, and it would be some time before the Turks could act against a temporary base there. The plan was greeted with enthusiasm by the RFC and steps were taken to see whether Feisal could arrange for petrol and other supplies to be transported and stockpiled at Jauf.

After an exchange of messages with Nuri Shalaan, the Rualla chief at Jauf, consignments of petrol were sent to the Hejaz for forwarding inland. The scheme was dropped, however, when Feisal's army moved up the Red Sea coast to Wejh in early 1917; after this, aircraft operating from Wejh could attack inland targets, and there was no longer any need for a base at Jauf.

60. T. E. Lawrence, note on the typescript of LH:*TEL*, June 1933 *B:LH* p. 93.
61. T. E. Lawrence, memorandum, 17.11.1916. Quoted from a typescript in the Clayton papers misdated 18.11.1916 (Clayton papers 694/4/42-6, Durham). The date on this copy is clearly wrong, since a version was transmitted by Murray to London on 17.11.1916 (GOC-in-C Egypt to DMI, telegram IA 2629. WO 106/1511 fos. 34-5).

Lawrence's confidence in the hill tribes was not shared by Parker, who had written on November 8th: 'Captain Lawrence, who has seen the country, I think exaggerates the difficulties [in the way of a Turkish advance]. In India it has been proved that provided a force can move sufficiently rapidly, it can carry out its objective in face of opposition of the hill tribes, probably a more efficient enemy than the Arabs.' (A. C. Parker to Arab Bureau, Wingate papers W/143/7/7-8, Durham).

Lawrence was to be proved wrong shortly afterwards when the hill tribes scattered to their villages in panic. He later wrote: 'While we were training the [Arab] regulars . . . the Turks suddenly put my appreciation to the test by beginning their advance on Mecca. They broke through my "impregnable" hills in twenty-four hours, and came forward from them towards Rabegh slowly. So they proved to us . . . that irregular troops are as unable to defend a point or line as they are to attack it. This lesson was received by us quite without gratitude, for the Turkish success put us in a critical position.' (T. E. Lawrence, 'Evolution of a Revolt', *The Army Quarterly*, London, Vol. I, No. 1, October 1920, p. 56).

It should be said, however, that the hill tribes subsequently harassed the Turkish lines of communication in a very effective manner; this seems to have been one of the reasons for the ultimate Turkish withdrawal to Medina.

62. *Ibid.* fo. 36. The section of this report dealing with Brémond's ambitions is quoted on p. 309.

63. G. F. Clayton, note (almost certainly 17.11.1916). Clayton papers 694/4/42, Durham (this copy dated 18.11.1916).

64. Lawrence's memorandum is quoted *in extenso* in Sir A. J. Murray (GOC-in-C Egypt) to DMI, telegram IA2629, 17.11.1916. WO 106/1511 fos. 34-6. The text was circulated to the Cabinet, see CAB 17/177. See also Sir A. J. Murray (Chief Egypforce) to Sir W. R. Robertson (Chief London), telegram AM1272, 17.11.1916. WO 158/627.

Immediately afterwards Murray cabled Wingate: 'I have just seen Lawrence on his return from visiting Feisal, and his opinion, in which I understand you and Feisal concur, is so strongly against the despatch of white troops to Arabia that I venture to suggest for your consideration that [Robertson] should at once be informed.' (telegram AM1274. WO 158/627). As Murray's telegraph operator had sent Lawrence's views to London fifteen minutes previously, this 'consultation' with Wingate was clearly a diplomatic precaution. Two days later Murray cabled to Wingate that Lawrence's memorandum had been sent to the DMI 'as a matter of ordinary daily routine'. In the margin of this telegram Wingate wrote 'OH !!!' (Sir A. J. Murray [Chief Egypforce] to Sir F. R. Wingate [Sirdar Khartoum], telegram AM1282, 19.11.1916. Wingate papers W/143/3/115, Durham.)

65. Sir R. E. Wemyss to Sir F. R. Wingate 19.11.1916. Wemyss papers, Churchill College, Cambridge.

66. T. E. Lawrence, *SP* ch. XVI p. 111.

67. Sir F. R. Wingate to Sir W. R. Robertson 12.11.1916. Quoted in Sir F. R. Wingate (Sirdar Khartoum) to Sir A. J. Murray (Chief Egypforce), telegram [number illeg.], 18.11.1916. WO 158/627.

68. Sir A. H. McMahon to Lord Hardinge 21.11.1916. Transcript in Lloyd George papers E/3/12/2, House of Lords. See also Sir A. J. Murray to Sir W. R. Robertson 28.11.1916. CAB 44/15: 'I am certain that the French are not in the least desirous of affording us cordial support in the Hedjaz but have sent their troops to secure political advantages . . . Colonel Wilson elicited from Colonel Brémond a statement that in the latter's opinion the longer the Arabs took to capture Medina the better, and for that reason he was reluctant to give any assistance in personnel for work inland. Wilson further reported that Colonel Brémond had said that he had no intention of hurrying the despatch of the contingent from Suez. Again, later, mention was made by Colonel Parker of a salient remark by Colonel Cadi [of the French mission] to the effect that the French had no intention of endeavouring to train any of the Arab troops . . . The French fear that if the Sherif is successful in turning the Turks out of the Hedjaz they will find that the Arabs propose to operate in Syria. This would not suit them . . . I have seen Brémond today. He is going back to Jeddah to watch matters for his Government but his troops do not leave Suez. He is a very pleasant clever man.' For Brémond's account of the negotiations about sending French troops to Rabegh see *HGM* pp. 64-7; pp. 69-74; pp. 81 *et seq.* See also *AFGG* for a selection of the messages between Jidda, Cairo, and Paris during this period. In communications to the French War Office, Brémond's arguments for landing Allied troops at Rabegh were couched in purely military terms, but there is ample proof elsewhere of his political motivation.

While there was unanimity within the French hierarchy about France's goals in Syria, there were at this time differing views as to the best policy towards Hussein; Brémond belonged to the more extreme school. When Lawrence's account of

Brémond's objectives was circulated in London, Sykes commented: 'Captain Lawrence's statement in regard to the French attitude to the Arabs, and his reference to their larger schemes of policy, must be the result of some misunderstanding, either by Captain Lawrence of the French, or by the French officers of their own Government's intentions, as it seems in no way to fit in with anything said or thought here or in Paris' (*Arabian Report* No. XVIII. CAB 17/177). Sykes always preferred to believe that the French moderates would prevail.

69. T. E. Lawrence, *SP* ch. XVII p. 114.
70. G. F. Clayton to Sir R. F. Wingate (Sirdar Khartoum), telegram AB230, 19.11.1916. Wingate papers W/143/3/93-94, Durham.
71. Sir F. R. Wingate (Sirdar Khartoum) to G. F. Clayton, telegram 885, 19.11.1916. Wingate papers W/143/3/106, Durham.
72. Abdul Aziz al Masri had arrived in the Hejaz during September, and on October 20th was formally appointed Commander in Chief of the Sherifian forces. He was given the task of training a force of Arab regulars which could defend Rabegh in lieu of the proposed European brigade. They were to be recruited from townsmen, villagers and slaves, rather than bedouin tribesmen. There would, however, be a nucleus made up of Arab defectors or prisoners who had served in the Turkish Army.

Despite al Masri's high appointment, his relationship with the Sherif was very difficult from the start, as Hussein was not prepared to give him any measure of control. Al Masri also found it impossible to secure any co-operation from Ali at Rabegh. By late October 1916, Ali's obstruction had brought him to the point of resignation. There were difficulties in attracting volunteers, and it soon became clear that there was little hope of raising the proposed force of 5,000 men. On October 30th, McMahon cabled to London that Parker had reported: 'that the situation did not improve, and that the Rabegh force was entirely unready either to defend that place or to advance. Aziz Masri had been trying to get Ali to approve his various schemes; the latter generally approved in principle and then hindered passively' (*Arabian Report* No. XVI, 2.11.1916. CAB 17/177).

As a result of these difficulties, al Masri decided that the only practical course would be to move his activities from Rabegh to Yenbo, relying on Feisal rather than Ali for co-operation. In effect, he had abandoned the original scheme, and hoped to get an independent command of his own. Thus, on November 2nd, Parker wrote in his diary: 'Aziz appeared more hopeless of organising anything in face of constant obstacles. The original plan of the 5,000 regulars has become to him a Castle in Spain and his intention as now expressed is to form as soon as possible a reliable and mobile camel corps of 800 men, and with them to lead raids on Turkish communications and on the railway. He feels himself entangled in a mesh of responsibility without control, and command without authority, and wishes to cut himself loose in however small a way', Parker *op. cit.* note 19 above, p. 170.

This makeshift proposal was given a much grander status many years later by Nuri as-Said, who had been al Masri's second-in-command at Rabegh. In lectures on Arab military tactics during the Revolt, Nuri presented the 1916 mobile force idea as though it had been a significant new strategy. Sadly, however, the documents show that al Masri was simply grasping at straws, and he never put the scheme into effect.

Abdul Aziz raised the mobile column scheme at a meeting with Ali and Feisal on November 16th. After this meeting Feisal began to form a force of Arab regulars at Yenbo. However, Wingate successfully opposed attempts by al Masri to move there, believing that Rabegh had greater strategic importance and a better harbour.

S. Mousa, quoting from Nuri's lectures, claimed in his book *T. E. Lawrence, an Arab View* (London, OUP 1966, p. 22) that it was al Masri who had devised the mobile tactics Lawrence was to apply in Syria during 1917. This *post hoc ergo propter hoc* argument is untenable. The idea of using mobile raiding parties in the north would have been obvious to any military commander, given the facts of Syrian geography, the distribution of settled population there, and the traditions of bedouin warfare. Lawrence would have been just as aware of these factors as al Masri. The remarkable aspect of Lawrence's role during the Syrian campaigns was not the principle behind his actions, but his ability to ensure that at least some of the plans involving Arab irregulars were actually carried out.

73. G. F. Clayton to Sir F. R. Wingate 20.11.1916. Wingate papers W/143/6/2-3, Durham. Note, however, that Clayton wrote five weeks later: 'it makes me sick to see 12,000 Turks still (after six months) sitting at Medina waiting to be taken.' (G. F. Clayton to G. A. Lloyd 28.12.1916. Lloyd papers GLLD 9/8, Churchill College, Cambridge).

74. Sir A. J. Murray to Sir W. R. Robertson 14.11.1916. CAB 44/15. This remark seems to have been justified, at least in Wilson's case. During the meeting to discuss the Rabegh question held at Ismailia on 12.9.1916, Wilson had shown little perception of the military realities facing Murray (see pp. 298-9, above, and the minutes of this meeting, 'Conference held at the Commander-in-Chief's Residence, Ismailia . . . 12th September, 1916, to discuss the Hedjaz question'. FO 882/4).

75. Sir F. R. Wingate to C. E. Wilson 23.11.1916. Wingate papers W/143/6/54-56, Durham. Wingate suspected that Clayton's views had been influenced by al Masri, who had recently visited Cairo. Whether or not this was the case, the opinions expressed in Clayton's letter seem a logical conclusion from the observations in Lawrence's recent reports.

76. Lawrence later told Liddell Hart incorrectly that Clayton had taken responsibility 'for having asked my views' (*B:LH* p. 93). Wingate took over as High Commissioner in Cairo on 27th December 1916.

77. Earl of Cork and Orrery, *My Naval Life* (London, Hutchinson, 1942) p. 99. Boyle later concluded that Lawrence's manner was due to shyness. This first meeting is alluded to in *Seven Pillars*: 'I failed to make a good . . . impression. I was travel-stained and had no baggage with me. Worst of all I wore a native head-cloth, put on as a compliment to the Arabs. Boyle disapproved' (ch. XVI p. 109). Lawrence also wrote that Boyle was: 'a very professional officer, alert, businesslike and official; sometimes a little intolerant of easy-going things and people. Red-haired men are seldom patient'(ch. XXIII p. 143). Major Joyce, whom Lawrence met for the first time when passing through Port Sudan with Admiral Wemyss, was equally unimpressed. Many years later he said: 'the memory of this meeting merely recalls the intense desire on my part to tell him to get his hair cut and that his uniform and dirty buttons sadly needed the attention of his batman. I should most certainly have done so had he not been surrounded by such distinguished people.' P. C. Joyce, BBC radio talk (transcript) 30.4.1939. Akaba Archive II/18, KCL.

78. C. E. Wilson to G. F. Clayton 22.11.1916. Clayton papers 470/4, Durham.

Chapter 16. Temporary Posting with Feisal
December 1916 – January 1917

1. T. E. Lawrence to C. E. Wilson 6.12.1916. Houghton bMS Eng 1252 (228). At the beginning of December, George Lloyd visited both Rabegh and Yenbo, from whence he wrote to Clayton: 'I have also softened down the rather prickly relations between Wilson and Lawrence which never amounted to much, but were a pity and they are now all right.' (G. A. Lloyd to G. F. Clayton 2.12.1916. Lloyd papers 9/8, Churchill College, Cambridge). Lloyd discussed the Rabegh question with Lawrence, and in his letter to Clayton he expressed views about landing troops which are identical to those Lawrence had held for some time.

2. T. E. Lawrence, 'The Arab Advance on Wejh' *AB* No. 41, 6.2.1917, pp. 60-2.

3. T. E. Lawrence, *SP* ch. XX p. 126. Feisal also gave Lawrence a British rifle which had been captured by the Turks at Gallipoli. It had been presented to him, with a handsome engraved inscription, before the Arab Revolt. On the butt of the rifle Lawrence carved the date he received it from Feisal: 4.12.16. The rifle is now in the Imperial War Museum, London.

4. T. E. Lawrence, 'Twenty-Seven Articles' *AB* No. 60, 20.8.1917, pp. 347-53 (reprinted here as Appendix IV, pp. 960-5). The passage quoted is from Article 19. Lawrence also knew that Captain W. H. I. Shakespear, killed during a tribal battle in January 1915 while serving as an adviser to ibn Saud, was believed to have been picked out as a target because of his British uniform.

5. When Zeid began his retreat on Yenbo, on about 3.12.1916, he sent a message to Garland asking for aeroplanes and ships to defend the town. Garland forwarded this request to Colonel Wilson without making any recommendation, but decided to keep HMS *Dufferin* and a French cruiser at Yenbo for the time being. Lawrence did not reach Yenbo until the night of 4th-5th, when he told Boyle of Feisal's difficulties. As a result of this further message, Boyle brought in extra naval strength. See H. Garland to C. E. Wilson 3.12.1916, repeated in C. E. Wilson to Arbur, telegram [number illegible], 6.12.1916. WO 158/604. Also T. E. Lawrence, *SP* ch. XX p. 127.

6. T. E. Lawrence to Director Arab Bureau 5.12.1916 *MB* p. 92. FO 882/6 fo. 6.

7. *Ibid.* fos 6-7 largely in *MB* pp. 92-3.

8. *Ibid.* fo. 7 omitted from *MB*.

9. *Ibid.* fos. 7-8 *MB* pp. 93-4.

10. A. C. Parker, report to the Arab Bureau 6.12.1916. FO 141/825/1198. For an account of the difficulties facing al Masri see chapter 15 note 71.

11. C. E. Wilson to Arab Bureau (Arbur), telegram W221, 7.12.1916. WO 158/604. Wilson had telegraphed to Lawrence on December 5th, but Lawrence was unable to reply immediately by radio because atmospheric conditions at Yenbo had caused a backlog in naval signals.

12. Sherif Feisal to Sir A. J. Murray, forwarded in T. E. Lawrence to C. E. Wilson, telegram L28, repeated in C. E. Wilson to Arbur, telegram W825, 7.12.1916. WO 188/604.

13. T. E. Lawrence, undated postscript to diary notes ending 5.12.1916. FO 882/6 fo. 15. Boyle's autobiography records that Lawrence went on board HMS *Suva* to help arrange the naval contribution to the Yenbo defence. See Earl of Cork and Orrery, *My Naval Life* (London, Hutchinson, 1942) p. 100 (where the chronology is

slightly incorrect; for example, Lawrence returned to Yenbo before Feisal's army, not, as stated by Boyle, with it).

14. See C. E. Wilson to Sir F. R. Wingate (Sirdar Khartoum), telegram W836, 7.12.1916, repeating a message presumed to be from W. H. D. Boyle. Quoted in Arbur to Sir F. R. Wingate (Sirdar Khartoum), telegram AB379, 9.12.1916. WO 158/604.

15. W. H. D. Boyle to R. E. Wemyss (Admiral C-in C) 9.12.1916, paraphrased in Arbur to Sir F. R. Wingate (Sirdar Khartoum), telegram AB385, 10.12.1916. WO 158/604.

16. Sir W. R. Robertson (Chief London) to Sir A. J. Murray (Chief Egypforce), telegram 26175, 9.12.1916. WO 158/627.

17. T. E. Lawrence to C. E. Wilson, telegram L41, repeated in C. E. Wilson to Arbur, telegram W873, 12.12.1916. WO 158/604.

18. T. E. Lawrence to Director, Arab Bureau, undated but evidently written on 11.12.1916 *MB* p. 95. FO 882/6 fo. 123.

19. R. H. A. Storrs, diary entry for 11.12.1916. Signed transcript titled, 'Extract from Diary: Visit to Grand Sherif'. FO 882/6 fo. 36.

20. *Ibid.*

21. C. E. Wilson to Arbur, telegram W873, 12.12.1916. WO 158/604. Hussein's claim caused some consternation in Egypt, and on 29.12.1916 Lynden-Bell wrote: 'The question as to who promised to cut the Hejaz line is being gone into pretty thoroughly by us in order to clear up the responsibility. All we know is that the Commander-in-Chief never held out any hopes of it, but yet, nevertheless, was prepared to try. Each time he was about to put his plans to the test they were stopped by the intervention of the Arab Bureau, acting on behalf of the Sherif himself [see for example pp. 293-4]. There is, therefore, nothing on our side. The Residency side swear equally that despite the Sherif's assurance that he could produce a letter from them in which it was stated, as a condition of his rebelling, the line should be cut, no such letter has ever been written.' (A. L. Lynden-Bell to G. A. Lloyd. Lloyd papers GLLD 9/2, Churchill College, Cambridge).

As the war progressed, British officials in Jidda were to become accustomed to Hussein's fantasies about the content of British written undertakings. In this instance, however, his delusions may well have been caused by Faroki, who had served for a while as his agent in Cairo (this arrangement came to an end when the Cairo staff discovered that Faroki was sending Hussein fictitious accounts of his diplomatic contacts). For events which point to Faroki as the originator of the misunderstanding about a British promise to intervene, see pp. 228-9 and pp. 284-5.

22. R. H. A. Storrs, diary entry for 13.12.1916. Signed transcript titled 'Extract from Diary: Visit to Grand Sherif'. FO 882/6 fo. 40.

23. T. E. Lawrence, *SP* ch. XX p. 130. Dakhilallah el Gadir, a senior member of the Juheina tribe, was at that time acting as a guide to the Turkish expedition. He subsequently joined the Arab cause, and Lawrence met him during a visit to Sherif Abdullah's camp, see p. 386 above and *SP* ch. XXXV.

24. T. E. Lawrence to Director, Arab Bureau, undated but evidently written on 11.12.1916 *MB* pp. 94-5. FO 882/6 fos. 122-3. Lawrence had already made these complaints about his role at Yenbo in a letter to C. E. Wilson of 6.12.1916 (Houghton bMS Eng 1252 (228)). He was not alone in feeling that his position was undefined. Both Garland and Joyce made similar protests during this period. See P. C. Joyce to H. Garland 10.12.1916. Akaba Archive I/8, H23, KCL.

25. A week earlier Lawrence had written to the Arab Bureau: 'One of the things not fixed when I came down here was my chief, and my manner of reporting. It is probably through Colonel Wilson, but as there is a post going to Egypt tonight I am sending this direct in advantage of the omission.' (T. E. Lawrence to Director, Arab Bureau 5.12.1916 omitted from *MB* p. 92. FO 882/6 fo. 6).

26. R. H. A. Storrs, diary entry for 13.12.1916. Signed transcript titled 'Extract from Diary: Visit to Grand Sherif'. FO 882/6 fo. 41. S. Mousa remarks that Storrs 'in writing about this journey, makes no reference to Lawrence' (*T. E. Lawrence: An Arab View*, London, OUP, 1966, p. 46 n. 43) and goes on to suggest that Storrs omitted to mention Lawrence because he thought him unimportant. Long before the official documents became available, it was clear from *HL* p. 332 that Lawrence was not in Yenbo during Storrs's visit: Mousa's comment is therefore without foundation.

27. Sir F. R. Wingate (Sirdar Khartoum) to Foreign Office London, telegram 83, 14.12.16. WO 158/604.

28. *Ibid*. J. Charmley states incorrectly that Lloyd managed to dissuade Wingate from the landing scheme (see *Lord Lloyd*, London, Weidenfeld and Nicolson, 1987, p. 60). Lloyd sent an account of these discussions to General Lynden-Bell, in which he specifically stated that Wingate had accepted Brémond's arguments in preference to his own (he also reported his favourable impression of Hussein, whom Brémond had described to him as a '*vieux ramolli*' and a '*salaud*'). G. A. Lloyd to A. L. Lynden-Bell 22.12.1916. Lloyd papers GLLD 9/8, Churchill College, Cambridge.

29. T. E. Lawrence, *SP*(O) ch. 18.

30. Sir F. R. Wingate to C. E. Wilson, telegram W289, 14.12.1916. FO 882/6.

31. *Ibid*.

32. C. E. Wilson to Sir F. R. Wingate, telegram W915, 15.12.1916. FO 882/6 fo. 44.

33. *Ibid*.

34. Sir F. R. Wingate (Sirdar Khartoum) to Foreign Office London, telegram 86, 16.12.1916. WO 158/604.

35. Foreign Office London to Sir F. R. Wingate (Sirdar Khartoum), undated, but probably 16.12.1916, repeated in Sir W. R. Robertson (Chief London) to Sir A. J. Murray (Chief Egypforce), telegram 26663, 16.12.16. WO 158/627.

36. T. E. Lawrence to C. E. Wilson 19.12.1916 *MB* p. 97. Transcript in FO 882/6 fos. 48-9. Wilson sent a copy of this letter to the Arab Bureau with the remark 'Please call attention of the proper authorities to remarks *re* field guns, which . . . Garland confirms.' (C. E. Wilson, note on 'Extracts from letter from Captain T. E. Lawrence'. WO 158/605.)

37. T. E. Lawrence, *SP* ch. XVII pp. 114-15 (on p. 115 Lawrence implies incorrectly that Garland died during the war: he died in 1921). See also chapter 17 note 40.

38. T. E. Lawrence to C. E. Wilson 19.12.1916 *MB* p. 96. Transcript in FO 882/6 fo. 48. Wilson added the note: 'I trust Sgt Garland will be sent back to Yenbo as soon as possible; his work has been of the greatest value.' (C. E. Wilson, note on 'Extracts from letter from Captain T. E. Lawrence'. WO 158/605) Garland had been promoted from Sergeant to Major at the beginning of his service in the Hejaz. See also page 375 above and chapter 17 note 40.

39. An evacuation was considered at a conference in Rabegh on Christmas Eve: see T. E. Lawrence *SP* ch. XXI p. 134. In his reports to the Admiralty, Wemyss stated

that the Navy could defend an area near the shore but not the wells, some way inland, which were the most important feature of Rabegh. See also E. Brémond to the French War Office (Guerre, Paris), telegram, 25.12.1916 *AFGG* p. 235.

40. T. E. Lawrence, *SP*(O) ch. 24.
41. T. E. Lawrence, 'The Arab advance on Wejh' *AB* No. 41, 6.2.1917, pp. 60-2.
42. T. E. Lawrence, *SP*(O) ch. 23.
43. In *Seven Pillars* Lawrence appears to give credit to Feisal for the idea of sending Abdullah to Wadi Ais: 'A first idea was that [Abdullah] might come to Kheibar . . . but Feisal improved my plan vastly, by remembering Wadi Ais . . .' (ch. XXII p. 138). In the *Arab Bulletin*, however, Lawrence wrote: 'It was pointed out to Feisal how effective Abdullah might be made if he was moved to Wadi Ais . . . Feisal saw the point'. ('The Arab Advance on Wejh' *AB* No 41, 6.2.1917, p. 62).

Liddell Hart must have been puzzled by this discrepancy, because he asked Lawrence who had been responsible. Lawrence's reply, jotted down by Liddell Hart, was: 'It arose thus: in discussing the project [Lawrence] said that on second thoughts he doubted if Abdullah could maintain himself at [Khaibar]. Feisal said, "You mean Wadi Ais". Until then T.E. had never heard of Wadi Ais but on learning about [it] he at once saw possibilities and the fact that it would make a move possible. So jumped at it.' (*B:LH* p. 63).

Liddell Hart's brief note-taking did not always transmit the full sense of what had been said (see chapter 2 note 37). It is clear from contemporary documents that Lawrence already knew of Wadi Ais; see his telegram L15, repeated in C. E. Wilson to Sir F. R. Wingate, telegram W759, 2.12.1916. Wingate papers W144/1/46, Durham, also sent to Arbur. WO 158/606. Both these telegrams were badly corrupted in transmission, but in conjunction they give the whole text of Lawrence's message, which concerned the proposal to move Nuri as-Said to Wadi Ais. It may have been this which prompted a request for geographical information from Kinahan Cornwallis, at that time revising the Arab Bureau's *Hejaz Handbook*. On 27.12.1916 Lawrence wrote to him: 'When I have someone to take over from me here I'll go off. Wadi Ais is the unknown area of north Hejaz, and I want to drop in and see it – anything behind Rudkwa will be worthwhile.' (*MB* p. 98. FO 882/6).

References to Wadi Ais in Wilson's report of his meeting with Feisal and Lawrence on 27th December show that the scheme to move Abdullah was conceived before Wilson's visit and not, as would appear from *SP*, afterwards. Lawrence did not begin to keep a regular diary until January 1917, and this must have proved a handicap when working out the chronology for the early sections of *Seven Pillars*.

Many years later Abdullah claimed in vague terms that the move to Wadi Ais had been his idea, but contemporary documents and the timing of the move suggest very strongly that this was not so (see *The Memoirs of King Abdullah of Transjordan* ed. P. P. Graves, London, Jonathan Cape, 1950, p. 156). Abdullah cannot have been pleased by Lawrence's remarks about him in *Seven Pillars*, and in statements made on various occasions after the war he sought to diminish Lawrence's role in the Revolt. The documents also show that there was jealousy between Abdullah and Feisal during the war. These factors should be taken into account when reading Abdullah's memoirs.

44. T. E. Lawrence, 'The advance on Wejh' *AB* No. 41, 6.2.1917, p. 62.
45. *Ibid.* p. 61.

46. T. E. Lawrence to K. Cornwallis 27.12.1916 *MB* p. 98. FO 882/6.
47. T. E. Lawrence to R. Fitzmaurice (Commander of HMS *Espiègle*) 2.1.17. Houghton fMS Eng 1252 (352).

   Contemporary documents show a one-day discrepancy in the chronology of Lawrence's movements at this point. During 1917 and 1918 Lawrence kept pocket diaries in which he wrote the name of the place he spent each night. This diary (most of which is reproduced as Appendix II to *SP*) suggests that Lawrence took part in a raid on the night of January 2nd. However, Lawrence's report to C. E. Wilson of 8.1.1917 (FO 882/6), gives a detailed account of his movements during early January, and here the dates differ slightly. I have used the dates given in this second source, because the most likely explanation for the discrepancy is that Lawrence did not acquire his pocket diary at the beginning of January 1917, but after his return to Cairo later that month. Having no copy of his report to Wilson of 8.1.1917, he made a small error when reconstructing his movements for the new pocket diary.

48. T. E. Lawrence to C. E. Wilson, report, 8.1.1917. FO 882/6 fos. 127-8.
49. Lawrence's statement to this effect in *SP* (ch. XXIII p. 143) is confirmed in *AB* No. 39, 19.1.1917, p. 28: 'On January 10, we received a telegram from Yambo that communication had been established between Sidi Abdullah and Sidi Feisal'.
50. C. E. Wilson to Arbur, telegram W126, 6.1.1917. WO 158/627.
51. Sir R. E. Wemyss to Secretary of the Admiralty, dispatch 26/1139, 10.1.17. ADM 137/548 fos. 106-7.
52. C. E. Wilson to Arbur, telegram W194, 11.1.17. WO 158/627. Wingate's ultimatum, agreed by the Foreign Office on December 16th, seemed to produce a clear-cut answer on December 27th, when a message came from Hussein appearing to refuse Allied Christian troops. Wilson passed this news on to Wingate, who informed Murray that the British brigade held in readiness at Suez could be released.

   Wilson then went to Cairo on leave and was replaced for a time at Jidda by an engineer officer, Major H. Pearson. It seems that Pearson immediately struck up a cordial relationship with Brémond, who later wrote that Pearson was 'used to International Relations, because he was the soul of every mission on frontier demarcation; modest and full of merit, he was a perfect neighbour.' (*HGM* p. 103 n. 1). After further exchanges with Hussein a cipher telegram came from Mecca on January 3rd, couched in vague terms. This seemed to reverse the earlier message and accept the scheme for a landing by Allied troops, but at the same time it put all responsibility for the decision and its consequences onto Wingate. It was signed not by Hussein but by one of his officials, Fuad el Khatib.

   Pearson, according to a contemporary comment by Lloyd, was 'an excellent fellow whose knowledge of things Arab however is slender . . . he has not Wilson's gift of dealing with men which matters here.' (G. A. Lloyd to W. H. Deedes 29.12.1916. Lloyd papers GLLD 9/13, Churchill College, Cambridge). With Brémond's encouragement, Pearson interpreted this latest message as positive approval by Hussein for an Allied landing (see H. Pearson to Arbur for Sir F. R. Wingate, telegram W099, 4.1.1917. WO 158/627). Wingate took the same view and applied to Murray on January 5th for the embarcation of the British brigade, under the command of Brigadier General Mudge. Murray replied: 'I need hardly say what a blow your letter and the Sherif's telegram is for me. It is not for me to criticise your actions or views in this matter, but I do consider that the Sherif has been more or less obliged to accept this assistance.' (Sir A. J. Murray to Sir F. R. Wingate

5.1.1917. WO 158/627.) Now that the English force was set to go, Brémond agreed that the French North African units held at Suez should accompany them. Embarcation was fixed for January 9th.

On January 6th, however, Colonel Wilson arrived back in Jidda. According to Brémond, Wilson had called in at Yenbo on the way, and returned to Jidda 'determined not to disembark Europeans at Rabegh . . . To cut a long story short, he had gone back to the viewpoint held by Lawrence, whom he had seen at Yenbo' (*HGM* p. 109).

On reaching Jidda, Wilson examined Fuad's cipher message and judged its wording insufficient to justify landing Allied troops. He tried to get a more satisfactory document, but none was forthcoming, and the Sherif chose not to make himself available by telephone.

Learning of this, the War Cabinet decided on January 8th that the brigade should not be sent unless Hussein requested it both in writing and by public declaration, accepting full responsibility for any adverse consequences. After repeated enquiries by Wilson and Pearson a reply finally came on January 11th. Hussein stated that he did not at present need Allied troops, and accepted that they might not be available in future. The Rabegh question was closed.

For French documents relating to this episode see *AFGG*.

53. T. E. Lawrence to his family 16.1.1917 *HL* p. 333; *MB* p. 102. Bodleian MS Res C13.
54. D. G. Hogarth to E. T. Leeds 23.1.1917. Leeds papers.
55. Earl of Cork and Orrery, *My Naval Life* (London, Hutchinson, 1942) p. 102. A passage in *SP*(O) ch. 25 refers to this incident, but was omitted from the final text. It read: 'During lunch . . . there was an unfortunate lapse, when Vickery pulled out a great flask of whisky and mixed himself a hearty drink. We were not alone as guests, and it was tactless; but long residence in the Sudan, which had no educated class or Press or public opinion, took the fine edge off some Englishmen.'
56. T. E. Lawrence to S. F. Newcombe 17.1.1917 *MB* pp. 102-3. National Museum, Ankara.
57. T. E. Lawrence, notebook entry dated 18.1.1917. BL Add. MS 45915 fo. 2.
58. In his report 'Um Lejj to Wejh' (*AB* No. 41, 6.2.1917, p. 66) Lawrence gave a number of elaborate excuses for this delay, but concealed the real reason. Long after the war, however, when the truth could no longer damage the Arab cause, he admitted to Liddell Hart that it had been: 'Because the Arabs jollified over the news of Abdullah's victory.' (*B:LH* p. 63). Wemyss stated merely that the 'occupation of Wejh was originally to have taken place on the 21st, but for some Arabian reason was postponed until the 23rd.' (Sir R. E. Wemyss to Sir F. R. Wingate 25.1.1917. FO 141/825/1198.)
59. Sir R. E. Wemyss to the Admiralty 30.1.1917. ADM 137/548 fos. 114-15.
60. T. E. Lawrence, notebook entry dated 23.1.1917. BL Add. MS 45914 fo. 7. The entry is written in abbreviated form and, as with telegrams, several obvious words omitted for brevity have been silently restored in this transcription.
61. C. E. Vickery, 'Memorandum on the general situation in Arabia (Hedjaz) and the Policy and Organisation of the British Mission to Grand Sherif' 2.2.1917. FO 882/6 fo. 152.
62. *AB* No. 40, 29.1.1917, p. 41.
63. Sir F. R. Wingate to Sir W. R. Robertson 21.2.1917. FO 882/6 fos. 189-90.

64. Sir R. E. Wemyss to Sir F. R. Wingate 25.1.1917. FO 141/825/1198. On March 12th the *Arab Bulletin* (No. 44, p. 115) reported that al Masri, 'whose admitted political aspirations suited neither the views of the King of the Hejaz nor of ourselves, has been removed from his command and has retired to his village in the Delta.'

65. C. V. Vickery *op. cit.* note 61 above, fos. 152-4.

66. *Ibid.* fo. 156. Arab historians have cited numerous plans as evidence that Hussein's armies were acting in concert during the early stages of the Revolt. Contemporary documents, however, show that while there were many schemes for combined action, usually in the medium or long term, these were rarely (if ever) carried through. The fundamental reason was doubtless that bedouin tribesmen could not be relied upon to behave as a disciplined army.

   Arab plans bore little relation to anything that actually occurred until the emphasis was switched from conventional engagements to *ad hoc* guerilla action, in which British advisers and technical personnel often played a crucial role.

67. R. H. A. Storrs, *Orientations* (London, Ivor Nicholson & Watson, 1937) p. 221.

68. J. C. Watson, RFC, to GOC Middle East Brigade RFC 11.1.1917. WO 158/605. Watson had been serving as an observer with the RFC flight at Rabegh.

69. *Ibid.*

70. T. E. Lawrence to C. E. Wilson 19.12.1916 *MB* p. 97. FO 882/6 fo. 49.

71. T. E. Lawrence, *SP*(O) ch. 30.

72. T. E. Lawrence, *SP* epilogue p. 661.

73. C. E. Wilson [transmitted 'Weldon'] to Arbur, telegram W300, 25.1.1917. FO 141/736/2475.

Chapter 17. Looking Northwards

January – March 1917

1. T. E. Lawrence to his family 31.1.1917 *HL* p. 334; *MB* p. 103. Bodleian Ms Res C13.

2. Lawrence was by no means the only person to have complained about this. There is ample testimony in the records that Brémond's activities had caused deep irritation at all levels in the British hierarchy. The person who had to deal with him most was Colonel Wilson, also based at Jidda. On 5.3.1917 he wrote to Clayton: 'Damn Brémond and his nasty ways. He creates more beastly situations for me than one would have thought possible.' (Clayton papers 470/6/18, Durham)

   In May 1917 the British authorities in Cairo decided that Brémond's activities were intolerable, and a formal request was made to the French Government that its Military Mission should be withdrawn from the Hejaz. After protracted negotiations it was agreed that Brémond himself would go. He went to France 'on leave' in the autumn of 1917 and did not return.

   It should be stressed that Brémond's activities did not reflect the ambitions of the entire French leadership (see for example the personal rebuke from the French War Office published by Brémond himself in *HGM* p. 97). In the same way, opposition to his policies by the British in Cairo and the Hejaz did not represent, as has been claimed, an uncritically Francophobic attitude on their part. The Cairo staff opposed both French and Anglo-Indian imperialism. However, they were intelligent men who knew that the imperialist lobby was only a particular element in French politics and popular opinion, as was also the case in Britain.

3. The origins of this proposal are evident from *AFGG*. It was suggested in Paris by A. Briand (then French Foreign Minister and Président du Conseil) in a letter to the French Minister for War of 5.1.1917 (*AFGG* pp. 244-5). See also French Foreign Office comments on the proposal 9.1.1917 (*AFGG* p. 249) and the instruction to French representatives in London and Cairo reported on 13.1.1917 (*AFGG* pp. 256-7).

4. A report from Colonel de La Panouse on the British War Office rejection is contained in his dispatch of 14.1.1917 (*AFGG* p. 259). However, this did not reach the French War Office in time to halt the instructions sent to Saint-Quentin in Cairo on 17.1.1917 (*AFGG* pp. 260-1). By the time these instructions reached Brémond, Paris had ceased to promote the scheme (see *AFGG* p. 262).

Brémond's advocacy of the Akaba scheme was reported to the Arab Bureau by H. Pearson (Jidda), telegram W250, 20.1.1917. WO 158/67 fo. 108A. For Murray's reaction see Sir A. J. Murray to Sir F. R. Wingate 22.1.1917. WO 158/627. For Wingate's message to Brémond rejecting the scheme see Arbur to H. Pearson, telegram AB681, 24.1.1917. FO141/736/2475. The message was not very forcefully expressed, and may have led Brémond to hope that he could reverse the decision. It read: 'You can confidentially inform Brémond that we have already given the fullest consideration here to the proposal to land troops at Akaba, but in view of our present military commitments in Sinai and elsewhere it must be discarded. We fully recognised the advantages of this scheme but the troops and transport necessary to undertake a successful expedition against the railway are not available. Plans to promote and extend the scope of raids to the railway by aircraft are therefore being considered.' An Allied landing at Akaba was one of the options that had been discussed by Brémond, Wingate, and Lloyd at their meeting on 14th December 1916. Brémond probably guessed, therefore, that Wingate would be favourably disposed towards some such scheme. On the day his message was sent to Brémond, Wingate wrote to Murray advocating the establishment of an airfield at Akaba with a view to bombing the railway (see Sir F. R. Wingate to Sir A. J. Murray 24.1.1917. WO 158/627).

The composition of Brémond's contingent at Suez on 12.1.1917 is given in *AFGG* p. 253. These documents also show that since the contingent was idle, the French War Office was already thinking of redeploying some or all of it in other theatres (see *AFGG* p. 270).

5. An account of Brémond's visit to Wejh 30.1.1917 is printed in *HGM* p. 133, but the date is given wrongly as 31.1.1917. The correct date is apparent from a report by S. F. Newcombe to C. E. Wilson 4.2.1917: 'Colonel Brémond called at Wedj for one hour on January 30th, saw Feisal, and I acted considerably as interpreter. He said he was going to Egypt to inspect his men at Suez for two days and to Cairo for one day to get one British brigade to Akaba plus aeroplanes, when he would send his two battalions from Jibuti to Akaba, provided British troops were there. Feisal afterwards told me that he would like British troops to help him, but did not want any help from the French or to have anything to do with them.' (Lloyd papers, GLLD 9/9, Churchill College, Cambridge).

Brémond was by this time alarmed at what he saw as anti-French collusion between Britain and the Arabs. He resented the fact that French help had not been called on for the movement to Wejh (see *HGM* p. 120). The interview with Feisal on 30.1.1917 confirmed his fear that a further northward movement might be undertaken by the Arabs without French participation. Note that he had only just been told of the terms of the Sykes-Picot Agreement (see *HGM* p. 130). It was an essential feature of all French policy that in any operations to liberate Syria the French flag should be present.

Brémond seems to have assumed that Feisal's operation to take Akaba would be very similar to the operation at Wejh. Lawrence later wrote: 'He did not know the impossible coast between Wejh and Akaba, and feared that I would go forward again in such a march' (*SP*(O) ch. 30).

6. T. E. Lawrence, *SP* ch. XXVIII p. 168. According to Lawrence's pocket diary, this meeting took place on February 3rd: 'Met Colonel Brémond in morning. St-Quentin to lunch. Decided go Suez in afternoon and strarted by 6.15 train.' (BL Add. MS 45983). Contemporary documents show that Brémond's record in *HGM* of his movements at this period is incomplete and not always accurate.

The account of this meeting in *SP* suggests very strongly that Brémond gave Lawrence a partial account of his talk with Feisal and Newcombe at Wejh. It would have damaged Brémond's own case to admit that Feisal had opposed the French scheme. Lawrence's account of the conversation, given in *Seven Pillars*, shows that he had no idea of the line Feisal had taken.

The fear Lawrence described there (that the Arabs would support Brémond) was not unreasonable, and his thinking was probably as follows:

Hussein had frequently requested such a landing in the past, and a few months earlier Feisal himself had favoured the scheme. Feisal was now keen to spread the rebellion into Syria. He knew that the Hejaz Revolt was secure, and Akaba, 270 miles farther up the Red Sea coast, had long been considered the next objective. It was therefore entirely possible that he would view the prospect of an Allied force at Akaba (under British control) as a step that would accelerate his own campaign. He might not find this in the least alarming, as he expected in any case to be in direct contact with British forces once the Arab campaign reached Akaba. Thus he had written to Hussein on 15.1.1917: 'all that therefore remains for us to do is capture Akaba and effect a junction with the British army there.' (cited by S. Mousa, *T. E. Lawrence: An Arab View*, London, OUP, 1966, p. 51).

On the other hand Brémond probably told Lawrence that Newcombe had approved of using Akaba as a base, implying (as he did in *HGM* p. 133) that this was support for the Anglo-French scheme. Lawrence would have been extremely perturbed by such news.

It is also possible that Brémond deliberately set out to make Lawrence uneasy about events at Wejh, in order to get him out of Cairo while the Anglo-French scheme was under discussion. The French Mission was well aware of the part Lawrence had played in securing Murray's rejection of the Rabegh landing scheme. They must therefore have suspected that he would be an influential opponent to the Akaba scheme. In *Seven Pillars*, Lawrence states that Brémond 'ended his talk ominously by saying that, anyhow, he was going down to put the scheme to Feisal in Wejh.' ch. XXVIII p. 168.

7. T. E. Lawrence, *SP* ch. XXXVI p. 214. The statement appears in a passage praising Colonel Wilson's honesty in dealings with the Arabs.

8. Some Arab historians have vehemently denied that Feisal knew about the Sykes-Picot terms at this time. The contemporary evidence strongly supports Lawrence's

statement that he explained the matter to Feisal at Wejh. See note 9 below.
9. T. E. Lawrence, *SP*(O) ch. 115 (cf. *SP* ch. CI p. 555).

The exact time and place of this discussion cannot be determined from any single contemporary or later document I have found. *Seven Pillars* is of only limited help, since Lawrence's references there to this sensitive political matter were deliberately obscure. However, there are a number of pointers which place the discussion in the early part of February 1917.

One can deduce *a priori* that Lawrence must have had an important conversation with Feisal on future Arab strategy in Syria at about the time that he took up his permanent post as Feisal's British liaison officer. This question had not been of immediate interest prior to the capture of Wejh in January 1917: until then the Arab forces had been too far south for action in Syria to have been a realistic part of their current planning. Feisal had sent diplomatic messages to northern leaders before this, but the documents show that the only northern scheme given any *practical* consideration between October 1916 and February 1917 was the abortive plan to station British aircraft at Jauf (see note 23 below, and chapter 15 note 59).

In any serious discussion about French interests and Arab plans in the north, Lawrence would have been obliged to reveal the main lines of the Sykes-Picot terms. Had he not done so, much of his advice about proper Arab objectives would have seemed groundless. Even if he had seen a way to skate over this problem in the early days, deception would have become wholly untenable once the Revolt progressed northward, and Lawrence knew far too much to risk embarking on such a foolish course. This is not the place to discuss the complicated ethics of confidentiality (an issue inextricably linked to Lawrence's sense of the immorality of his position, discussed in chapter 19). No one should underestimate, however, the difficulties he would have faced if Feisal had learned the truth from some other source. It is worth noting a significant parallel: for very similar reasons he took Feisal into his confidence, against Clayton's instructions, a few weeks later. On that occasion, also, the matter was of extreme delicacy (see pp. 378-9).

There are a number of specific allusions to this important discussion between Lawrence and Feisal which, when taken together, narrow down the likely date to a period of only a few days. Taking these in turn:

a. In *SP* (ch. LVII p. 324) Lawrence described a conversation with his British superiors in July 1917 about the future Arab role in Syria. On this occasion he told the British staff that Feisal's army would be prepared to act in concert with the EEF's advance in Palestine, protecting the British right flank from east of the Jordan. To ensure proper co-ordination, he recommended putting the northern Arab Army under Allenby's command. He confidently affirmed that Feisal would be willing to serve in this role, because 'I had talked it over with him in Wejh months ago'. As this conversation with his British superiors took place soon after the fall of Akaba, Lawrence must have been referring to a discussion with Feisal that had taken place at Wejh. However, Lawrence had not been there since May 9th.

b. Also in *SP*, Lawrence stated obliquely that he had salved his conscience about Britain's duplicity towards the Arabs by explaining the position to Feisal: 'In Hejaz the Sherifs were everything, and I had allayed my conscience by telling Feisal how hollow his basis was.' (*SP* ch. XLVIII p. 276). For this remark to have any meaning, the discussion must have taken place before Lawrence's role in the Arab Revolt took him northwards *out* of the Hejaz, i.e. before early May 1917.

Taken together, these two passages in *SP* show that the conversation referred to must have taken place at Wejh prior to May 9th.

c. If this discussion was at Wejh, it cannot have taken place before January 25th when the town fell. It is, moreover, very improbable *a priori* that Lawrence would have held such talks before he returned to take up his permanent liaison appointment, on February 6th.

d. There is other evidence which helps to establish the *latest* date at which this conversation could have taken place. In the spring of 1917 British officers at Wejh observed a marked change in Feisal's plans and outlook. He became almost obsessed with the need to mount an Arab campaign in Syria as quickly as possible. This was particularly remarkable in view of his earlier anxiety about the risk of moving north from Yenbo to Wejh, and his caution in all military matters. The cause must have been some very important new factor, and the only explanation which is both sufficient and probable is that he now knew about the Sykes-Picot proviso. In this connection, one memorandum in particular, dated April 5th, is revealing. Based on information from Newcombe, it refers specifically to Feisal's schemes for taking urgent action in the regions of Damascus, Homs, Hama, and Aleppo, the four Syrian towns named in the Sykes-Picot proviso (the text is quoted on p. 392) At that time Lawrence had been absent from Wejh for nearly a month. The *latest* date on which he could have discussed Sykes-Picot with Feisal was before his departure on March 10th.

e. This narrows the possible time of the discussions to a date between February 6th and March 10th. However, Lawrence had been in Wejh for only two brief periods between these dates: February 6th-19th and March 3rd-10th. There is good reason to believe that the discussion must have taken place during the first of these visits: Lawrence had returned to Wejh on February 6th with the *specific* intention of warning Feisal about French scheming and in particular that Brémond's devious activities were intended to keep the Arabs out of Syria. To deal with these subjects adequately, Lawrence would have been obliged to discuss the Sykes-Picot proviso. This conversation almost certainly took place at the very beginning of his visit, since he expected Brémond to arrive any day.

f. The case for placing this discussion during the February 6th-19th visit is strengthened still further by a report written during Lawrence's subsequent stay in Cairo. This proves that a discussion of future Arab strategy in the north had already taken place, as Lawrence told Clayton of Feisal's agreement that 'Arabs should not operate west of the River Jordan and the Dead Sea – Wadi Araba line' (the report is quoted extensively on pp. 373-4). Elsewhere, Lawrence implied that it was on *his* advice that Feisal had adopted this 'east of Jordan' strategy (see p. 442) This policy correlates exactly with the Sykes-Picot terms and with the need for Feisal to concentrate on taking Damascus, Homs, Hama and Aleppo.

g. It is worth noting two further statements. In *SP* (ch. CXXII p. 658) Lawrence again refers to discussions at Wejh: 'As long ago as Wejh I had warned [the Arabs], when they took Damascus to leave Lebanon for a sop to the French and take Tripoli instead; since as a port it outweighed Beyrout, and England would have played the honest broker for it on their behalf in the Peace Settlement.' A similar statement occurs in a letter from Lawrence to W. Yale written on 22.10.1929 (*DG* p. 670): 'About the Lebanon and Beyrout. I had secured a promise, from Feisal and his staff, that they would leave it alone, for the European allies to occupy. This promise was made me in Wejh . . . My intention had been to occupy from the gap of Tripoli northward to Alexandretta, and I had told Feisal that in the welter which would follow victory he would stand a very decent chance of getting this area eventually allotted to the Syrian kingdom upon terms.' It seems that in these retrospective comments (more especially the second), Lawrence is referring to discussions held in or near Wejh on two different occasions. The first must have been a private talk with Feisal which, according to the evidence above, took place in February 1917. The second was probably a more official conversation with Feisal's staff which took place in July 1917 shortly before the Arab Army moved to Akaba (see p. 429). This second meeting was at an advance base inland.

I have found no contemporary evidence proving conclusively that the possibility of gaining the littoral north of Tripoli was discussed in February 1917, but this seems extremely probable. The only questions on which Lawrence could have held out any hope of an improvement in the Sykes-Picot terms were, first, the nationality of European advisers in Syria and, second, the acquisition of a Syrian port. As implied in the *SP*(O) (see p. 363) it would have been tactful diplomacy to hold out such prospects when revealing the Anglo-French agreement to Feisal.

10. These plans are described in Newcombe's report to C. E. Wilson of 4.2.1917. Lloyd papers GLLD 9/9, Churchill College, Cambridge. The operations against Dhaba and Muweilah were carried out one day later than planned, on 8.2.1917. For details of the operation see R. W. Wemyss to the Admiralty 22.2.1917. ADM 137/548; see also *AB* No. 42, 15.2.1917, pp. 81-2, and Lawrence's notes dated 16.2.1917. FO882/6 fo. 172. The idea of taking Dhaba and Muweilah as steps to the capture of Akaba was not new. It had been discussed in principle even before the taking of Wejh.

11. S. F. Newcombe, report to C. E. Wilson, 4.2.1917. Lloyd papers GLLD 9/9, Churchill College, Cambridge. Newcombe's enthusiasm for this scheme must reflect ignorance of the difficulties of advancing up the Wadi Itm towards the railway. He had visited Akaba before the war, but had never seen the Wadi Itm. During the summer of 1916, when Lawrence had written his study of the Wadi Itm problem for Murray, Newcombe had not been in Cairo. Brémond was therefore wrong to attach great significance to the views Newcombe expressed about Akaba on 30.1.1917 (see *HGM* p. 133).

12. No other supply route to the desert regions of inland Syria had the advantages of Akaba. Wejh was 270 miles farther south, and owing to geographical factors, supplies destined for the north would have had to travel by a long and very circuitous overland route. This difficulty ruled out Wejh, or any port south of Akaba, as a long-term supply base for inland Syria. Supply across Sinai or from the Mediterranean coast would remain impossible as long as the Turks controlled Palestine and the Lebanon. The only other access to inland Syria was from the east, but the difficulties of transporting large amounts of *matériel* for 500 miles across the Syrian desert from Mesopotamia would be immense (for a study of possible routes see 'Euphrates Route to Syria' by D. G. Hogarth, *AB* No. 47, 11.4.1917, pp. 158-61).

13. The capture of Akaba proved so important to the Arab Revolt that anti-Lawrence polemicists (e.g. Aldington) and some Arab historians (e.g. Mousa) have done their best to deny him the credit for the successful plan to capture Wadi Itm. However, there can be very little doubt that Lawrence was responsible for the essentials of this

scheme, although he had to rely on local Arab knowledge and Arab tribal forces for the detailed planning and execution (and he made no claim to the contrary).

Questions remain as to the exact date when the idea first occurred to him, and when he first mentioned it to Feisal. There is no direct contemporary evidence, probably for the reasons discussed in note 14 below. *Seven Pillars* (ch. XXVIII p. 168) suggests that Lawrence had already conceived the idea by early February when he discussed the Anglo-French landing scheme with Brémond. It is again alluded to (ch. XXX pp. 174-5) in his account of Feisal's messages in February to Nuri Shalaan and Auda abu Tayi. Now that the whole account in *Seven Pillars* can be compared with contemporary documents, it is clear that Lawrence was a reliable witness, and there is little reason to doubt his specific statements about Akaba. Moreover, the idea of taking the Wadi Itm road from its inland end is essentially a very simple one, which should have been obvious to someone with Lawrence's training and lifelong interest in military strategy. It may well have occurred to him a considerable time before, for example when he studied the Wadi Itm problem for Murray during the early autumn of 1916. He already knew by the end of that year that Feisal was in touch with the northern chiefs whose co-operation would be needed.

Though indirect, the evidence about the date on which he first discussed the scheme with Feisal is very strong. Newcombe's report of February 4th (*op. cit.* note 9 above) describes the ill-judged plans for an Arab landing at Akaba which Feisal was making at that time. This bears out the statement in *SP* (ch. XXVIII p. 168) that Lawrence had not previously discussed the Akaba problem with him. Had he done so, he would have discouraged such a scheme.

When Lawrence returned to Wejh on February 6th, he *had* to discuss the question of Akaba. This had been one of his principal reasons for hurrying down from Cairo. He was delighted to find that Feisal had rejected Brémond's Anglo-French proposal, but he had nevertheless to advise against the Arab landing scheme as well: he knew that it could not succeed. There is evidence that he did this, because the plans for an Arab landing (as described a few days earlier by Newcombe) were halted. Lawrence's contemporary notes, cited elsewhere in this chapter, show that no attempt was made to capture the Red Sea coast farther north than Dhaba and Muweilah, and that the coastal Howeitat were instructed not to occupy Akaba.

It was obvious to Lawrence that Akaba would be the key to further progress northwards (see note 12 above), and he would surely not have turned down Feisal's scheme for an Akaba landing unless he was ready with a better idea of his own. It is reasonable, therefore, to infer that he must have discussed the idea with Feisal in early February 1917, and that this accounts for the changes in Arab plans recorded in contemporary documents.

In passing, it is worth noting that Newcombe's report of February 4th on Arab plans for a landing at Akaba refutes the suggestion by Suleiman Mousa that by mid-January 1917 Feisal had envisaged the inland scheme (see Mousa's *T. E. Lawrence: an Arab view* London, OUP, 1966, pp. 50-1). The letter from Feisal to Hussein of 15.1.1917 cited by Mousa clearly refers to the plan for a landing at Akaba, and not to the inland scheme.

It has also been suggested that the capture of Wadi Itm and Akaba was an opportunist action, not planned before the expedition set out. Evidence to the contrary is given in chapter 19.

14. The free passage of information between the Arab and Turkish armies is referred to on several occasions in *Seven Pillars*, for example ch. LXIX p. 385. Lawrence took pains not to counsel Feisal when other Arab leaders were present: to have done so would have diminished Feisal's stature in their eyes. In this connection see Lawrence's *Twenty-Seven Articles* (printed here as Appendix IV), especially paragraphs 3, 4, 6, 11.

15. Lawrence's reticence about Akaba in reports to Cairo cannot possibly have been unintentional. He seems to have offered no comment on several documents in which the Akaba question was discussed: examples are Newcombe's report of 4.2.1917, Vickery's report of 1.3.1917 (see pp. 376-7), and Clayton's reply to this of 8.3.1917 (see pp. 393-4).

16. W. H. D. Boyle (SNO Red Sea Patrol) to Sir R. E. Wemyss (Naval C-in-C Red Sea Patrol), telegram, 11.2.1917. FO 141/736/2475 fo. 427.

17. See T. E. Lawrence, notebook entry dated 13.2.1917. FO 882/6 fo. 169 and entry dated 18.2.1917 quoted on p. 371.

18. T. E. Lawrence to his family 12.2.1917 *HL* p. 335; *MB* pp. 104-5.

19. *Ibid.*

20. T. E. Lawrence, notebook entry dated 14.2.1917. FO 882/6 fo. 171.

21. T. E. Lawrence to his family 12.2.1917 *HL* p. 335; *MB* p. 104.

22. T. E. Lawrence, notebook entry dated 16.2.1917. FO 882/6 fos. 172-3.

23. In view of the large claims made by S. Mousa (*op. cit.* note 13 above, p. 51) for Feisal's far-sighted contacts with northern leaders prior to February 1917, it is worth examining these contacts in the light of the British documents.

   Feisal had sent a messenger to the Rualla chief Nuri Shalaan as early as the spring of 1916. However, serious contact does not seem to have begun until mid-November, when ibn Sheddad (described by Lawrence as 'Feisul's self-appointed messenger to the north') left for Nuri Shalaan's principal settlement at Jauf (see T. E. Lawrence to C. E. Wilson 5.1.1917 *MB* p. 100. FO 882/6 fo. 12.

   In early December Lawrence met Feisal's preferred messenger, Faiz el Ghusain, and discussed with him the Jauf scheme (see chapter 15 note 59). Faiz was at that date waiting for a messenger to come from Nuri Shalaan as a result of the previous visit by ibn Sheddad, after which he would himself go to Jauf to act as Feisal's agent. Meanwhile, Faiz visited Cairo to see the Arab Bureau and to provide it with geographical information.

   On 28.12.1916, while Faiz was in Egypt, a message from Feisal to Hussein was reported to Cairo. It read: 'Messenger from north just come. Nuri Shalan, Nawaf, Auda abu Tai, Sinaitan, ibn Awaja, Ferhan ibn Ayda, with all the Anazeh, Beni Sakr, are your obedient servants.' (H. Pearson to Arbur, telegram W201. FO 141/736/2475). Hussein replied: 'You should give a warm welcome to these tribes and pay each Chief from 500 to 1,000 pounds. You should also express to them my warmest greetings' (reported in H. Pearson to Sir F. R. Wingate, telegram W203, 29.12.1916, repeating Lawrence to Pearson, telegram L65. FO 141/736/2475).

   During his stay Faiz seems to have been persuaded by the Arab Bureau to attempt to set up a system of regular communications with Arab chiefs in southern Syria, and this idea was now developed as a result of the news from Jauf. A telegram from Cairo on January 4th informed Lawrence of the scheme: Faiz would inform the chiefs, 'in writing, if feasible, of the latest news of the situation in the Hejaz and of the British advance and will enquire of them of their preparedness to rise, what material assistance they need, and how this can best be sent.' (Arbur to T. E. Lawrence, telegram AB529, 4.1.1917. FO 141/736/2475) The same message asked Lawrence to obtain from Feisal letters to northern leaders including Fawaz ibn Faiz, Nuri and Nawaf Shalaan, Mohammed ibn Milhem, and Nesib el Atrash: 'It should be stated in these letters that Faiz el Ghusein is working for the Sherif through us and that in arranging help for us he has a free hand.'

The following day, Lawrence sent Wilson 'a hurried note on northern politics', describing the results of Feisal's recent contacts with Nuri Shalaan. According to this, ibn Sheddad had met Nuri and several other sheikhs in Jauf: 'They held a committee meeting and came to the decision that they would break off all relations with the Turkish Government at once. They will not, however, commit themselves to an active policy, until Feisul has established himself at El Ula, and has opened up direct communication with them . . . El Ula is the first possible point with which they can have direct contact with supplies from the Sherif.'

'The tone of the messages sent by Nuri and Nawaf to Feisul is excellent. They are quite ready to do their work, as soon as it gives a fair chance of success . . .

'Faisul will not send ibn Sheddad north again except from El Ula, when he has reached there himself. Matters stand over till then. I will get from Feisul when I see him next letters for Faiz in the sense of Arbur telegram 539 [*sic*, for 529, see above]. Please try and arrange a successor to Faiz when possible, as he will go forward from El Ula. I hope you will avoid our share in things as far as possible in his letters.' (T. E. Lawrence to C. E. Wilson 5.1.1917. FO 882/6 fo. 12 partially quoted in *MB* p. 100.)

There seem to have been no further contacts between Feisal and the northern chiefs until after the capture of Wejh on January 25th. Thus, Feisal's messages prior to that date were purely exploratory, and cannot have had anything to do with such a delicate and secret project as the capture of Wadi Itm from inland. At this stage none of the northern tribes were prepared to take any action until Feisal's army had captured El Ula.

24. T. E. Lawrence, notebook entry dated 17.2.1917. FO 882/6 fos. 177-9. For another account of these events, giving additional details, see *SP* ch. XXX pp. 178-80.
25. T. E. Lawrence, notebook entry dated 17.2.1917. FO 882/6 fo. 179.
26. T. E. Lawrence, *SP*(O) ch. XXXII.
27. T. E. Lawrence, notebook entry dated 17.2.1917. FO 882/6 fo. 179.
28. *Ibid.* 18.2.1917 fo. 181.
29. *Ibid.* 14.2.1917 fo. 171.
30. T. E. Lawrence, report, 11.2.1917. FO 882/6.
31. T. E. Lawrence, notebook entry dated 18.2.1917. FO 882/6 fos. 179-80. This sketchy account is filled out in *SP* ch. XXVIII pp. 168-9.
32. *Ibid.* fo. 180.
33. T. E. Lawrence to his family 25.2.1917 *HL* pp. 336-7; *MB* pp. 105-6. Bodleian Ms Res C13. Lawrence's variations in rank are confusing. In general, due to the structure of the military hierarchy, Intelligence officers held a relatively junior rank which belied their true influence. In this connection see FO 882/15 fo. 423: 'Temporary naval or military rank held by officials of the [Arab] Bureau is in no way indicative of their political status or duties.'

The *London Gazette* records that Lawrence was promoted Captain on 20.3.1916, and that he held this rank until he was promoted Major on 5.8.1917.

However he had also at various times held 'local and temporary' rank in Cairo.

34. T. E. Lawrence to G. F. Clayton 28.2.1917. FO 882/6.

35. 'Weekly newsletter from Arbur to DMI [London]' 3.3.1917. FO 882/6 fos.208-9.

36. H. Pearson to Sir F. R. Wingate 4.3.1917. FO 882/6 fo. 196.

37. Note enclosed in a letter from G. F. Clayton to Sir F. R. Wingate of 7.9.1916. Wingate papers W140/2/106, Durham. This note may well have been written by Lawrence, who was the department's principal expert on the railway.

38. H. Garland, 'Report on the Raiding Party sent to the Hejaz Railway line under Bimbashi Garland, February 1917' 6.3.1917. FO 882/6 fo. 40.

39. *Ibid.*

40. T. E. Lawrence, verbal reply to a question from B. H. Liddell Hart *B:LH* p. 63 (where the words 'not very good' are omitted). Extracts from Garland's report of 6.3.1917 printed in *AB* No. 61, 1.9.1917, p. 359, began with the words 'The difficulties I experienced during this trip afford so good an example of those under which one has to work in this country that they are probably worth recording.' In his copy of the Bulletin, Lawrence put an asterisk beside this, and wrote across the foot of the page: 'This confession justifies the withdrawal of Major Garland from Hejaz. TEL'. In *SP*, however, Lawrence's remarks about Garland are very generous, concealing the problem of his unsuitability for work with the bedouin forces as well as the question of his withdrawal. Doubtless Lawrence felt that Garland should not be pilloried for a difficulty which other British regulars (including Newcombe, Joyce and Hornby) also experienced.

41. C. E. Vickery, report, 1.3.1917. FO 886/6 fos. 47-8. Although Vickery did not give a very detailed account of Feisal's scheme, it seems beyond question that this was a reversion to the landing plan that Lawrence had rejected in his discussions with Feisal a month earlier. Feisal had probably allowed himself to be swayed back to this plan because reports showed that neither Akaba nor the Wadi Itm were, at that moment, strongly held by the Turks.

42. Feisal and his brothers had been educated in Constantinople, where they would doubtless have acquired some rudimentary knowledge of military affairs. According to *SP*, 'when they came back to the Hejaz as young effendis in European clothes with Turkish manners, the father ordered them into Arab dress; and . . . gave them Meccan companions and sent them out into the wilds, with the Camel Corps, to patrol the pilgrim roads . . . He would not let them back to Mecca, but kept them out for months in all seasons guarding the roads by day and by night, handling every variety of man, and learning fresh methods of riding and fighting.' (ch. XIV pp. 98-9).

In *SP*, and to some extent in contemporary reports, Lawrence did his best to give the impression that Feisal was successful both as a military and political leader. The documents offer little evidence to support this representation. Feisal was undoubtedly skilled in recruiting tribal leaders to the Arab cause and in reconciling their disputes, and this ability was essential to the success of the Revolt. However, he showed little talent for other aspects of military leadership, and after the end of 1916 he relied heavily on his British advisers.

43. B. H. Liddell Hart, notes on a conversation with Lawrence 31.10.1933 *B:LH* pp. 188-9. On another occasion Lawrence remarked that Feisal 'takes too easily the colour of his company' (T. E. Lawrence to F. Manning 1.9.1931. Public Library of New South Wales, Australia). A contemporary remark in exactly the same vein was

made by Joyce in September 1917: 'I had a very difficult time with Feisal for a few days. He is not a very strong character and much swayed by his surroundings.' (P. C. Joyce to G. F. Clayton 25.9.1917. Akaba Archive H77-8, KCL). See also Lawrence's letter to C. F. Shaw of 18.10.1927, quoted on p. 807.

This weakness must be taken into account when estimating the influence of British advisers such as Lawrence (and later Joyce) in decisions nominally taken by Feisal during the Arab Revolt.

44. T. E. Lawrence, *SP*(O) ch. 30. See also *B:LH* p. 36.

Vickery had neither qualifications nor enthusiasm for leading demolition parties to the railway. On February 2nd he had written a memorandum which argued against such work: 'It is assumed that the duties of the [British] Military Mission were to advise and report, and it was not intended that they should take an active part in leading and assuming military control of small raiding parties.' (FO 882/6 fo. 150). Instead, he advocated setting up a conventional military hierarchy in the Hejaz which would control all British activities there. In passing, this paper displays a personal distaste both for the Arab rebels and for (unnamed) political liaison officers. Vickery argued that with centralised command: 'The officers attached to armies would advise the Sherif with whom they had to deal in accordance with the general line of conduct as formulated by the O.C. British Staff. This would do away with the present absurdity of officers with divergent views and opinions each advising his Sherif to adopt a different plan or line of operation.' (*ibid.* fo. 151) The allusion was clearly to Lawrence. Another remark was even more specific: 'It appears, at present, that any officer may requisition articles of equipment if he considers them necessary. Hence one sees a motor bicycle lying on the beach' (*ibid.*) A Triumph motorcycle, which Lawrence had asked for, had been sent to Yenbo from Egypt on December 30th 1916. This was probably the first motorcycle he used regularly.

S. Mousa and others have suggested that Vickery was removed from the Hejaz through Lawrence's influence, but this seems most improbable. Newcombe, head of the Military Mission, must have realised that both Vickery and Cox were unsuited to the new requirements. Wingate's retrospective dispatch to the Secretary of State for War of June 25th notes their departure in these terms: 'Early in March 1917 I was able, in view of the improved situation and having regard to the necessity for experienced Artillery Officers in other theatres, to dispense with the services of Majors Vickery and Cox' (FO 141/668/4332). In April 1917 the Sherifian forces were joined by another British engineer officer, Lieutenant H. S. Hornby.

45. T. E. Lawrence to R. Fitzmaurice 5.3.1917. Houghton fMS Eng 1252 (352).

46. In writing his account of this incident, Liddell Hart expressed some uncertainty as to whether British Intelligence had interpreted the message correctly (LH:*TEL* p. 158). According to Liddell Hart, it could not be deciphered completely. He did not state his source for this information, and it seems likely that his enquiries had met with deliberate official evasiveness. Contemporary documents referring to 'an absolutely reliable source' suggest that news of the Turkish order came from a British agent occupying a high place in the Turkish command (probably the one usually referred to as 'Agent Y'). The intended withdrawal is confirmed in German Foreign Office documents quoted by K. Morsey *LAA* pp. 153 *et seq.*

First news of the Turkish orders had evidently reached Cairo by March 6th, when a telegram from Wingate asked Pearson in Jidda to 'instruct Newcombe and

Lawrence confidentially to urge on Feisul and Abdulla the vital necessity at this critical juncture of maintaining the utmost possible pressure with all the forces at their disposal all along the railway.

'The telegraph line should be continually kept cut from Medina as far north as possible; this is most important.

'The necessity of efficient Intelligence is also very urgent. Fullest and earliest information of enemy troop movements either by rail or march route should be obtained both by agents and contact.' (Arbur, for High Commissioner, to Pearson, Jidda, telegram AB887, 6.3.1917. FO 141/736/2475 fo. 649).

Two days later Murray cabled Robertson: 'The failure of the Turkish campaign in Arabia and the approaching withdrawal of the Hedjaz Expeditionary Force to Palestine is of course now obvious. It is naturally of vital importance in view of the source from which our information has been obtained, that no premature announcement of any kind should be made on the subject either in the Press, in Parliament, or elsewhere. I have therefore asked the High Commissioner to make no communication to the Foreign Office on the subject for the present.' (Sir A. J. Murray (Chief Egypforce) to Sir W. R. Robertson (Chief London), telegram AM1868, 8.3.1917. WO 158/605 fo. 59a.) See also *AB* No. 45, 23.3.1917, p. 125.

In passing, it seems appropriate to comment on the article by E. Kedourie, 'The Surrender of Medina, January 1919' (*Middle Eastern Studies* Vol. 13, No. 1, January 1977, pp. 124-43). One of the principal implications of this article is that the Arab forces were so weak and disorganised that they were unable to capture Medina at any time during the war. Here, as in many other instances, Kedourie's conclusions are based on a very partial reading of the evidence. In particular, his article makes no reference whatsoever to the fact that the Turks would have abandoned Medina to Hussein in March 1917, had they been able to do so. This fact contradicts the impression Kedourie is seeking to give, and its omission seems regrettable.

47. See *SP* ch. XXXI p. 177.
48. T. E. Lawrence to C. E. Wilson, undated, but 8.3.1917. Houghton bMS Eng 1252 (230).
49. T. E. Lawrence, notebook entry dated 10.3.1917. BM Add. MS 45914.
50. *Ibid.*

Chapter 18. Wadi Ais

March – April 1917

1. *SP* ch. XXXI p. 181.
2. T. E. Lawrence, notebook entry dated 13.3.1917. BL Add. Ms 45915 fo. 22. In seeking traces of this execution in contemporary documents, K. Morsey (*LAA* p. 158) points out that there are discrepancies between *SP*, Lawrence's route notes, and a later report, as to the exact number and tribal origin of the men who accompanied him to Wadi Ais. However, the discrepancies between contemporary and later documents do not seem to prove anything except a slight error of memory, which is in itself unsurprising as Lawrence was very ill at this time. The only truly contemporary source is his notebook of the journey, which contains two possible indications that the execution took place. First, the entry quoted here, and secondly

the deliberate and total obliteration of one name in a list of men in the party written later on March 13th. (*op. cit.* fo. 25).

3. *SP*(O) ch. 33.

4. *SP* ch. XXXVIII p. 225.

5. *Ibid.* ch. XXXIII p. 193.

6. T. E. Lawrence, notebook entry dated 22.3.1917. BL Add. MS 45914 fo. 34. Under this date his notebook contains copies of two messages addressed simply to 'Wejh' (he evidently did not know which British officer had taken over there). The two are typed out as one document in FO 686/6 fo.9 and printed from that source in *MB* pp. 106-7.

7. B. H. Liddell Hart, notes after a conversation with T. E. Lawrence 31.10.1933 *B:LH* p. 188.

8. J. C. Watson to GOC Middle East Brigade RFC 11.1.1917. WO 158/605.

9. T. E. Lawrence, notebook entry dated 22.3.1917. BL Add. MS 45914 fo. 33.

10. T. E. Lawrence to C. E. Wilson 16.4.1917. FO 882/6. Abdullah later implied that he had crossed the Hejaz Railway to Wadi Ais with a force of 20,000 men (*The Memoirs of King Abdullah of Transjordan* ed. P. P. Graves, London, Jonathan Cape, 1950, p. 163). This figure is hard to reconcile with the estimated 3,000 men noted in Lawrence's report. Figures for Arabs actively taking part in the Revolt at any one time tend to be confused with the total tribal force available. Lawrence wrote in 1919: 'The numbers of the irregulars are difficult to estimate. They came up to fight when called, and went home after the action. The whole male populace of the districts in which he happened to be operating were at the disposal of Feisal, and we used to summon few or many according to the object we had in view . . . I have never seen more than 11,000 of them together, and more often we had only a few hundreds. The total who bore arms for the Sherif at one time and another must have been very large, and probably ran into hundreds of thousands: but nothing like this was ever under arms at one time' (memorandum to S. Bonsal, of the U.S. Delegation to the Peace Conference, January 1919. This long document, one of Lawrence's earliest accounts of the Arab Revolt, is printed in full in J. M. Wilson, *T. E. Lawrence*, London, National Portrait Gallery, 1988, pp. 50-4. Houghton MS Eng 1146.1).

    Abdullah's *Memoirs* also suggest (p. 173) that at this time he favoured a joint attack on Medina, after which the united Arab armies would march north into Syria and Iraq. This notion takes no account of the constantly changing composition of the Arab forces. The tribesmen available in the Hejaz could not have been used in Syria or Iraq. Furthermore, this northern ambition, recorded many years after the event, is incompatible with Lawrence's contemporary statement that Abdullah was looking south. The Algerian captain Raho was also present when Abdullah told Lawrence of his Yemen scheme. Brémond gives the following account, evidently based on Raho's report: 'In a conversation on March 20th . . . [Abdullah] said that after the capture of Medina he would turn towards the Yemen, in order to liberate it from Turkish rule, leaving Syria and Anatolia to others.'(*HGM* p. 119, author's translation). Brémond goes on to comment, perhaps with some reason, that there were so many variations in Abdullah's statements that 'it was impossible to be certain of the Emir's plans; and doubtless this was his intention'.

11. *Ibid.* Lawrence later wrote that Abdullah: 'regarded the autonomy of the Northern Arabs as assured by the promises of Great Britain to his father, and was inclined to

rest quietly on this security. I longed to tell him that the half-witted old man had obtained from us no concrete or unqualified undertaking of any sort, and that their ship might founder on the rock of his political stupidity; but that would have been to give away my English masters, and the mental tug of war between honesty and loyalty, after swaying a while, settled again expediently into a deadlock.' (*SP*(O) ch. 38). Lawrence knew, of course, that there was a great deal of difference between frank discussion with Feisal, who was remote from Mecca, and similar discussion with Abdullah, who was Hussein's principal confidant in political matters.

12. *Ibid.*
13. *Ibid.*
14. T. E. Lawrence to 'Wejh' 22.3.1917. BL Add. MS 45915 fo. 33.
15. T. E. Lawrence to C. E. Wilson 16.4.1917. FO 882/6.
16. *Ibid.* fo. 257. On March 10th Raho had written telling Brémond that Abdullah wanted Claude Prost in Wadi Ais. Prost's departure for Abdullah's camp is confirmed by a telegram from Brémond to the French War Office of 18.3.1917 (*AFGG* p. 289). Brémond's letter to Abdullah was alluded to by Feisal during an interview with Joyce in early April. Feisal said that he had recently heard from his brother, who was annoyed with the French about a letter that had been sent abusing British policy in the Hejaz and criticising the conquest of Baghdad (see notes by P. C. Joyce of a conversation with Feisal 11.4.1917. Akaba Archive I/123, B36, KCL). See also Lawrence's account of the Prost incident in *SP* ch. XXVI pp. 213-14.
17. T. E. Lawrence, report, April 1917. FO 882/6 fo. 339.
18. *Ibid.* fo. 340.
19. T. E. Lawrence, 'Raids on the Railway *AB* No. 50, 13.5.1917, pp. 216-17.
20. T. E. Lawrence to C. E. Wilson 16.4.1917. FO 882/6.
21. Feisal to T. E. Lawrence 30.3.1917. The original of this letter, which is in indifferent French, is in the Codrington Library, All Souls College, Oxford. It reads: '*Cher Capitaine Lawrence! J'ai beaucoup regretté lorsque j'ai appris que vous étiez indisposé. J'espère que vous vous êtes déjà rétabli et que vous voulez nous rejoindre dans peu de temps et le plus tôt possible. Votre existence avec moi est très indispensable, vue de la rapidité de demandes et de marche des affaires. Ce n'était du tout votre promesse de résider là si longtemps. Donc j'espère votre départ vers nous dès que vous receviez cette lettre. En attendant je vous salue sincèrement. Votre sincère* Feisal' [signed in Arabic].

An English rendering of a similar but even more urgent letter sent at much the same date exists in FO 882/6 fo. 18a: 'I am waiting for your coming because I want to see you very much because I have many things to tell you. The destruction of the Railway is easy. Major Garland has arrived and we can send him for this purpose.

'You are much needed here more than the destruction of the line because I am in a very great complication which I had never expected.'

In *HGM* (p. 72 n.3) Brémond claims that Feisal spoke fluent English. This statement is not based on Brémond's personal contacts with Feisal, but on a remark by the German general Liman von Sanders. In his memoirs *Fünf Jahre Türkei* (Berlin, Scherl, 1920, p. 260) Sanders wrote: 'I knew Sherif Feisal well from the summer of 1914 in Constantinople. He was a typical Arabian *grand seigneur*. He had received a European type of education and spoke good English' (author's translation; the English rendering published in 1927 by the US Naval Institute is unreliable).

This cannot be correct. Feisal may have known a few words of English, but his note to Lawrence shows that he cannot have had sufficient fluency to send even a simple message. His French was clearly rather better. French was at that time the principal diplomatic language, and the only European tongue widely used by the Turkish élite.

Feisal always needed interpreters when English was spoken, and he was also unsure about his French. Brémond records that in May 1917 Feisal 'began to learn French' with Lamotte, a French officer (*HGM* p. 158). This can only mean that Feisal wanted to improve his command of the language. Brémond's inaccurate statements on this subject may have been intended to emphasise Feisal's pro-British orientation.

22. T. E. Lawrence to C. E. Wilson 16.4.1917. FO 882/6.
23. P. C. Joyce to C. E. Wilson 26.11.1916. Akaba Archive I/3 H13, KCL.
24. P. C. Joyce to C. E. Wilson 23.3.1916. Akaba Archive I/78 H55, KCL.
25. Sherif Feisal to C. E. Wilson, repeated in C. E. Wilson to Arbur Cairo, telegram W717, 30.3.1917. FO 882/6 fo. 130A.
26. P. C. Joyce to C. E. Wilson 1.4.1917. FO 886/6.
27. *Ibid.*
28. C. E. Wilson to G. F. Clayton 5.3.1917. Clayton papers 470/6/18, Durham.
29. For information on French projects to send a force to Syria see 'Projet d'Intervention en Syrie' 26.1.1917 *AFGG* pp.265-6; also 'Rapport du chef de bataillon Sarrou sur la situation en Syrie' 15.3.1917 *AFGG* pp. 283-7. On 9.1.1917 Sykes, then in Paris, warned the War Office that he had 'learned there is now a desire here to use ten to fifteen thousand men from Salonica for the occupation of Tripoli in Syria. You will recollect the proposal was mooted some weeks ago and the question was asked whether such a force could be victualled from Egypt. Your then reply ran that no answer could be given unless a concrete scheme was put forward. I believe that a proposal will now be made. The military-political factor is that the French believe such a landing could precipitate a rising of Ansarie and Lebanon population. The former seems possible, the latter unimportant. A purely political factor is that such a move has the advantage of engrossing French attention in legitimate spheres and tends to disentangle both our policy and interests paving way for sounder basis of military and military-political co-operation than heretofore.' (Sir T. B. M. Sykes to DMO, War Office London, telegram 1A, 9.4.1917. Sykes papers, St. Antony's College, Oxford). Note that Sykes displayed absolutely no concern in this message about the possible effect on Arab opinion and military effort of a French invasion of Syria.
30. At an Anglo-French conference held in London on 28.12.1916 the British Government had agreed that 'when the British forces now operating in the Sinai Peninsula enter Palestine a French Moslem detachment should be associated in the operations, and a French Political Officer should be attached to the British Commander-in-Chief. The British Government undertook to warn the French Government as to when the eventuality referred to was likely to occur.' (quoted in 'Notes of a conference . . . to consider the instructions to . . . Sir Mark Sykes' 3.4.1917. Sykes papers, St Antony's College, Oxford. For French plans to send a force to Palestine, see *AFGG* pp. 236, 243-4, p. 246, 263, 267, etc.

News of this French contingent was unwelcome in Cairo. Lynden-Bell wrote to Lloyd on 17.3.1917: 'we have now got a demand from the French to allow a base to be formed at Port Said for three battalions of French troops and some artillery, who are to be used, we understand, for Line of Communication work in Palestine. At the present moment we have heard nothing officially about it, but no doubt that will come, as I have had a preliminary intimation from St. Quentin on the subject. Of course, it is impossible to decline to have these French troops, but you can imagine what a terrible nuisance they will be to us.' (Lloyd papers GLLD 9/3, Churchill College, Cambridge).

31. E. Brémond to Guerre, Paris, telegram, 3.4.1917, *AFGG* p. 297 (author's free translation). In repeating his request for mountain guns, Feisal was touching on a sensitive issue. Since the early days of the campaign, Brémond had promised that although Britain had failed to provide modern mountain guns, he would have some sent from France. However, the French War Office had not released any, and the original offer was now having an effect exactly opposite to Brémond's intention: the Arab leaders had concluded that the guns were being deliberately withheld for political motives.

This suspicion was caused by the fact that Brémond was thought to be holding back suitable guns in the French encampment at Suez. Lawrence wrote in *SP*: 'Brémond had some excellent Schneider sixty-fives at Suez, with Algerian gunners, but he regarded them principally as his lever to move allied troops into Arabia. When we asked him to send them down to us, with or without men, he would reply, first that the Arabs would not treat the crews properly, and then that they would not treat the guns properly. His price was a British brigade for Rabegh; and we would not pay it.

'He feared to make the Arab army formidable . . . In the end, happily, Brémond over-reached himself, after keeping his batteries idle for a year at Suez. Major Cousse, his successor, ordered them down to us, and by their help we entered Damascus. During that idle year they had been, to each Arab officer who entered Suez, a silent incontrovertible proof of French malice towards the Arab movement.'(*SP* ch. XXVIII p. 166)

Maurice Larès has pointed out that Lawrence's accusation is only partially correct. Larès reproduces a number of telegrams about artillery between Brémond and Paris which show that there were in reality no 65s at Suez until January 1918 (see his *T. E. Lawrence, la France, et les Français*, Paris, Imprimerie Nationale, 1980, pp. 90-5). Until then, Brémond's artillery at Suez consisted of relatively unsophisticated weapons: one 80mm field battery and one 80mm mountain battery (see *AFGG* p. 164). During the Rabegh crisis, as Lawrence correctly claimed in *SP*, this artillery had remained at Suez. By 9th March 1917 Brémond had moved one of these batteries to the Hejaz (see *AFGG* p. 278).

Lawrence (who rarely encountered Brémond face-to-face) was unaware that the Frenchman's attitude about Arab success at Medina had changed during the spring of 1917. This change was the result of instructions from Paris (see *HGM* p. 97) and also of news about the Sykes-Picot treaty, whose terms Brémond had been unaware of until January 1917 (see *HGM* pp. 130-1). After this, Brémond made strenuous efforts to obtain modern guns for the Hejaz, although in Feisal's case he clearly had ulterior motives for doing so (he did not view the prospect of Arab operations farther north with any enthusiasm). In the end he was granted two 65s for Feisal, but (as Lawrence observed) they did not arrive until Cousse had taken over. Lawrence's inaccurate statements in *SP* reflect his own misunderstanding at the time: he knew that during the Rabegh crisis guns had been held back in the French camp at Suez, and that 65s were sent to Feisal after Brémond had been replaced. His error was in assuming that these were the same guns.

32. 'Note on Information received from Col. Newcombe dated 5th April'. WO 158/606. Brémond had arrived in Wejh from Cairo, and would therefore have been aware of French projects for sending a force into Palestine and possibly for landing troops in Syria.
33. *Ibid.*
34. *Ibid.*
35. *Ibid.*
36. *Ibid.*
37. *Ibid.*
38. G. F. Clayton, memorandum to the Arab Bureau 8.3.1917; copied to Sir F. R. Wingate, C. E. Wilson and T. E. Lawrence. Lawrence did not see this memorandum before his return to Wejh in mid-April.
39. See p. 397.

Chapter 19. 'A Useful Diversion'

April – July 1917

1. T. E Lawrence to C. E. Wilson 16.4.1917 *MB* p. 110. FO 882/6 fo. 256.
2. P. C. Joyce to Director, Arab Bureau 15.4.1917. FO 686/6 Part 2 fo. 157-8.
3. See passage from document cited in note 2 above quoted on p. 404.
4. T. E. Lawrence to C. E. Wilson 16.4.1917 *MB* p. 110. FO 882/6 fo. 256.
5. N. N. E. Bray puts this case forcefully in his book *Shifting Sands* (London, Unicorn Press, 1934, pp. 136-42). Although written much later, this account probably summarises the arguments used by Bray and other British officers at the time. Bray confirms that Lawrence's attitude towards the El Ula scheme and the capture of Medina had 'mysteriously' changed since his visit to Abdullah's camp.

For examples of British optimism about an early surrender of Medina see: R. E. Wemyss, report, 20.4.1917. ADM 137/548 fo. 167; Sir F. R. Wingate to Sir W. R. Robertson 1.5.1917. FO 141/811/4526 no. 4526/3; C. E. Wilson to G. F. Clayton 20-24.5.1917. Lloyd Papers, Churchill College Cambridge.

In April 1917 Lawrence too thought that Medina could probably be captured without great difficulty. Reports coming into Abdullah's camp had led him to believe that much of the Turkish garrison had now been withdrawn. He wrote to Wilson: 'As regards the situation at Medina, I think the great bulk of the troops and practically all stores have been evacuated northward in small parties by rail. The programme for a route march of the main body to El Ula has (wisely I think for the Turks) been abandoned, and the fall of Medina is now merely a question of when the Arabs like to put an end to the affair. They have little food – but so small a garrison that the question has less importance. No food is going in from the north, so that sooner or later starvation will ensue. Till it does the Arabs will probably not enter the town since the Emirs are all anxious to avoid warlike action against the place itself, for religious reasons.'(T. E Lawrence to C. E. Wilson 16.4.1917 omitted from *MB* p. 110. FO 882/6). For Lawrence, the supposed weakness of Medina was an argument for leaving it alone, not for stepping up the offensive.

By late April it had become clear that no significant Turkish withdrawal had taken place. On the 28th Clayton reported to the DMI: 'it is evident that the original [Turkish] plan of withdrawing considerable quantities of troops from the Hejaz to reinforce in Palestine has not been put into execution yet. Whether this is due to Arab activity or a change of plan is not known . . . The [Turkish] Hejaz Expeditionary Force is evidently still in Medina.' (G. F. Clayton to Sir G. M. W. Macdonogh, DMI War Office. FO 882/6 fo. 380.)

Hopes that combined Arab operations could bring about an early surrender in Medina were very soon dashed. In the event, the garrison there held out until the beginning of January 1919, several weeks after Turkey had surrendered.

6. T. E. Lawrence, *SP* ch. 38 p. 225.
7. T. E. Lawrence, 'The Howeitat and their Chiefs' *AB* No. 59, 24.7.1917, pp. 309-10. This report is based largely on diary jottings made in May and June.
8. G. F. Clayton to Sir F. R. Wingate 29.5.1917. FO 882/6 fo. 388. See also note 17 below for references to Akaba in reports by Wilson and by Newcombe during May. Clayton's comment was provoked by the latter.
9. T. E. Lawrence, *SP* ch. XXXVII p. 226. Lawrence stated that before leaving on the Akaba expedition he 'wrote a letter full of apologies to Clayton, telling him that my intentions were of the best'. If Lawrence did write such a letter it has not been found, and in view of Clayton's complete surprise when Akaba was taken, it seems extremely unlikely that he received it.
10. T. E. Lawrence, *SP(O)* ch. 41. These arguments would have meant little to the Arabs, and suggest very strongly that the decision to go to Akaba was indeed Lawrence's (and not, as some Arab historians have suggested, Feisal's or Auda's).
11. *Ibid.* The comment in note 10 above applies here also.
12. The evidence suggests that all the essentials of the Akaba plan were worked out before April 20th. This was the latest date on which Wilson and Auda could have left Wejh to attend the conference at Fagair. On the basis of conversations with Auda during this trip, Wilson submitted a report in which the main outlines of the Akaba scheme are described (see p. 401). Likewise, the account in *Seven Pillars* (ch. XXXVIII pp. 225-6) suggests that the plan was more or less agreed by the time Captain Boyle brought naval intelligence from Akaba, ie. 20.4.1917 (see p. 400).
13. T. E. Lawrence, *SP* ch. XXXVIII p. 225-6.
14. R. E. Wemyss, report, 20.4.1917. ADM 137/548 fo. 167. See also T. E. Lawrence to C. E. Wilson undated but *c.* 21.4.1917. FO 686/6 Pt. II fos. 88-9. Lawrence's possession of this crucial information in late April is further evidence against the view that Akaba was not the original goal of the expedition.
15. Lawrence later told Liddell Hart that he had 'arranged with Boyle to put in there when possible. The ship had actually been there and departed about an hour before I reached Aqaba' (*B:LH* p. 64). Naval patrols went up and down the Gulf of Akaba quite regularly, and Lawrence probably made a loose arrangement with Boyle that ships passing Akaba should keep an eye open for friendly Arabs.

In the draft *Seven Pillars* he wrote that shortly before the Arabs entered Akaba 'there had been an armed tug, H.M.S. *Slieve Foy*, off the town, but she had not seen our signals, and, after firing a few shots at the hills, had steamed away again. That meant no other patrol-visit for a fortnight' (*SP(O)* ch. 59).
16. Note by T. E. Lawrence on the typescript of LH:*TEL*, *B:LH* p. 97.
17. See C. E. Wilson, 'Note on the proposed Military Plan of Operations of the Arab Armies' 1.5.1917. FO 882/6 fo. 351. Although Wilson ascribed curiously little

significance to the idea that Akaba might be captured, his report confirms beyond doubt that this was the objective of the expedition from the start.

See also 'Note by S. F. Newcombe, D.S.O.' 24.5.1917, Wingate papers W145/7/37-40, Durham. This account of Feisal's plans mentions all the main elements of the Akaba scheme, without reaching the conclusion that Akaba was the real objective of Lawrence's expedition. Newcombe stated that Lawrence and Auda were intending to make a base east of Maan, and (in another part of the note) that the Howeitat had been asked to clear out the posts at the head of Wadi Itm. He also noted Feisal's statement that Akaba was indispensable, and that it was hoped to ship men there at the end of July. Yet Newcombe clearly took Feisal to mean that the Arabs were planning to capture Akaba from the sea. Presumably Feisal had been somewhat vague about the true plan during these discussions.

18. Lawrence did not mention the expedition to find the aeroplane in Wadi Hamdh in *Seven Pillars*. It is, however, referred to in his contemporary notebooks and diaries (now in BL).

19. For the origins and purpose of the Political Mission see 'Notes of a Conference held at 10 Downing Street . . . on April 3 1917'. CAB 24/9. See also letters from Sir T. B. M. Sykes to Sir F. R. Wingate 22.2.1917 and 6.3.1917 (Sykes papers, St Antony's College Oxford); G. A. Lloyd to A. L. Lynden-Bell 28.2.1917, and Lynden-Bell's reply of 17.3.1917 (Lloyd papers GLLD 9/3, Churchill College Cambridge).

20. Sir T. B. M. Sykes to Sir G. M. W. Macdonogh (DMI, War Office), telegram 18, 30.4.1917. FO 882/16. See also note 25 below.

21. Sykes travelled on to Jidda, and returned a few days later. Colonel G. Leachman, who had accompanied him from Cairo, spent this interval at Wejh. This was the only meeting between Leachman and Lawrence, two men who had each won a reputation for their work in the Middle East. It seems from later remarks that Lawrence did not get on with Leachman. He wrote: 'Leachman was a thin jumpy nervous long fellow, with a plucked face and neck. He was full of courage, and hard as French nails. He had an abiding contempt for everything native (an attitude picked up in India). Now this contempt may be a conviction, an opinion, a point of view. It is inevitable perhaps, and therefore neither to be praised nor blamed. Leachman allowed it to be a rule of conduct. This made him inconsiderate, harsh, overbearing towards his servants and subjects: and there was, I stake my oath, no justification for the airs he took. Leachman was an ordinary mind, but a character of no ordinary hardness. I do not say a great character, for I think it made its impression more by its tough skin and unyielding texture than by any great spread or degree. I should call him a man too little sensitive to be aware of other points of view than his own: too little fine to see degrees of greatness, degrees of rightness in others.

'He was blunt and outspoken to a degree. Such is a good point in a preacher, a bad point in a diplomat. It makes a bullying judge, too. I think he was first and foremost a bully: but not a fleshy bully. He had no meat or bulk on him: a sinewy, wasted man, very yellow and dissatisfied in face. He was jealous of other people's being praised.

'For his few days with us in Hejaz we were not prepared. "Leachman", it was a great name and repute in Mesopotamia (a land of fourth-raters) and we thought to find a colleague in him. After less than a week we had to return him on board ship, not for anything he said, though he spoke sourly always, but because he used to chase his servant so unmercifully that our camp took scandal at it. The servant was a worm, a long worm, who never turned or showed a spark of spirit. Any decent servant would have shot him.

'Leachman lasted a long time after that: but one day [12th August 1920] he spat in a sheikh's face at a time when the veil of terror under which we had worked in Mespot had worn thin. The chief upped and shot him in the back, as he was running out of the tent [the incident occurred at a khan]. Both insult and reprisal were almost unprecedented in the history of the desert. Then Leachman wasn't quite what you call a decent fellow, and the sheikh ([Sheikh Dhari] whom I met a year later) was febrile. As Leachman died tragically we must hide his fault. Don't make him a hero . . . He was too shrill, too hot-tempered, too little generous.' (T. E. Lawrence to A. Dixon 29.12.1929 *DG* pp. 490-1).

It had not been intended that Leachman should remain in the Hejaz: he had written just before setting out: 'I am off . . . in a man-of-war down the Red Sea for ten days, and return here' (G. Leachman to his family 29.4.1917 quoted in N. N. E. Bray *A Paladin of Arabia* London, Unicorn Press, 1936, p. 295). He was in poor health at this time, and this may have contributed to his dislike of the Hejaz. Soon after returning to Cairo, he wrote: 'commend me to the Arabian coast of the Red Sea for absolute hopelessness. Not a blade of grass or bush, but miles of volcanic desert and stones. Most vile form of Arab, worse than the worst Mesopotamian specimen.' (10.5.1917 *op. cit.* p. 296).

In mid-May Leachman accompanied Sykes to Jidda, travelling afterwards to Aden and thence back to Mesopotamia. During the call at Jidda Wilson arranged for him to meet Hussein, but at the last minute Leachman gave a very weak excuse and cut the meeting. Wilson was angered by this and reported the whole matter to Cairo, commenting: 'What Leachman did in Cairo I don't know but as far as the Hedjaz is concerned his visit in my opinion has done harm rather than good if it has done anything at all, whereas it was really an excellent opportunity for advantageous discussion.' (C. E. Wilson to Sir F. R. Wingate 21.5.1917. Wingate papers W145/7/46, Durham).

22. *AB* No. 50, 13.5.1917 p. 207. In Lawrence's own copy of the *Bulletin* he wrote against this: 'S-P treaty explained in general terms'.

23. Sir T. B. M. Sykes to Sir F. R. Wingate 6.5.1917. FO 141/654 fo. 243.

24. *Ibid.*

25. C. E. Wilson to G. F. Clayton 21.3.1917. FO 882/12 fo. 198. The immediate subject of this protest was Britain's failure to inform Hussein about the true purpose of the Sykes-Picot Mission. At the time, Wilson himself was under a misapprehension: he seems to have assumed that the Mission was coming out to finalise an Anglo-French agreement about Syria. In reality, the matter had already been settled, and the role of the Mission was not to engage in fresh negotiations but to begin the implementation of Sykes-Picot. Wilson was, however, correct in thinking that Hussein was being kept in the dark. He ended his letter to Clayton: 'I earnestly trust that it will be decided to take him into our confidence as fully as possible regarding the settlement of the Arab territories, and that he will be as generously treated . . . as may be found possible'.

In the same letter, Wilson expressed alarm at Sykes's idea that a Sherifian delegate should be attached to the Mission and involved in a charade of 'consultation'. He had seen a telegram in which Sykes advised Wingate: 'The Hejaz delegate should be, if you concur, a venerable but amenable person who will not want to ride or take much exercise.' (Sir T. B. M. Sykes to Sir F. R. Wingate 22.2.1917. Sykes papers, St Antony's College Oxford.) Wilson protested: 'If we press for a man who is practically a nonentity we will only make trouble for ourselves and cannot I think be surprised if the Sherif becomes suspicious.

'For Heaven's sake let us be straight with the old man; I am convinced it will pay in the end.' (C. E. Wilson to G. F. Clayton 21.3.1917. FO 882/12). In the event, Hussein declined to send a representative.

26. P. C. Joyce to Director, Arab Bureau 15.4.1917. FO 686/2 Part II fos. 157-8.
27. Quoted in *HGM* p. 142.
28. *Ibid.*
29. 'Note by Lt. Col Newcombe D.S.O.' 20.5.1917. Wingate papers W145/7/66, Durham. See also pp. 431-2 and ch. 20 note 33 below.
30. T. E. Lawrence, pocket dairy entry for 13.5.1917. BL Add. MS 45983.
31. T. E. Lawrence, *SP* ch. XLII, pp. 246-7.
32. T. E. Lawrence, *SP* ch. XLIV, p. 254.
33. T. E. Lawrence, notebook jottings, undated but 23-4.5.1917. BL Add. MS 45915 fo. 52 (the first part of this quotation is written upside down on the page). An entry in the same notebook dated 24.5.1917 reads: 'entered el Biseita, an absolutely bare barren plain . . . wasted hour and a half looking for Gasim'(fo. 53).

Ali and Othman had volunteered for Lawrence's service during the first week of the Akaba expedition, see *SP* ch. XL pp. 236-7 (where the two are called Daud and Farraj).
34. T. E. Lawrence, notebook entry 28.5.1917. BL Add. MS 45915 fos. 54-5.
35. T. E. Lawrence, notebook entry 30.5.1917. BL Add. MS 45915 fo. 55.
36. T. E. Lawrence, notebook jotting, undated but *c.* 31.5.1917. BL Add MS 45915 fo. 55v. (compare *SP* ch. XLVII p. 271). This note was written in pencil and later almost obliterated by a draft report which Lawrence wrote on the same page. A version appears in *A Touch of Genius* by M. Brown and J. Cave (London, J. M. Dent, 1988) p. 103. In this case, however, the text has been mistranscribed and therefore misinterpreted.
37. T. E. Lawrence, notebook entry, 2.6.1917. BL Add. MS 45915 fo. 56.
38. T. E. Lawrence, *SP* introductory chapter, first published in *OA* p. 145.
39. T. E. Lawrence, notebook jotting, undated but *c.* 31.5.1917. BL Add. MS 45915 fo. 55v. Compare the descriptions of Wadi Sirhan in *SP* ch. XLVII p. 271 and *AB* No. 66, 21.10.1917 p. 421. According to Lawrence, the wadi was infested with poisonous snakes and contained a number of important salt-works: the wells were also salty.
40. T. E. Lawrence, pocket diary entry, 5.6.1917. BL Add. MS 45983. Lawrence may well have realised that this was the first anniversary of the beginning of the Revolt. If he did, this can only have added to his bitterness.
41. T. E. Lawrence, notebook jotting, undated but *c.* 5.6.1917. BL Add. MS 45915 fo. 55v. Lawrence later tried to obliterate this entry, but it can still be read.

In *T. E. Lawrence, An Arab View* (London, OUP, 1966) pp. 72-9, S. Mousa claims that Lawrence invented the whole story of this northern ride. He offers no contemporary evidence for this allegation, supporting it principally by statements made by Nesib el Bekri some fifty years after the event.

When I began to do historical research at the London School of Economics, one of the first things I was taught was to mistrust published reminiscences and information gained in interviews. All memory is fallible, but, in addition, politicians are noted for giving highly distorted versions of past events. This problem is general, and applies as much to British politicians as to those of any other nationality.

There can be no justification for accepting Nesib el Bekri's retrospective statements rather than those contained in contemporary documents. Nesib had two understandable motives for contradicting Lawrence. The Revolt is now regarded by many Arabs as a great event in their history and, quite naturally, Arab politicians and historians have sought to diminish the British contribution to its success. Secondly, Lawrence had criticised Nesib scathingly in *Seven Pillars*. The book was available to Arabic readers long before Nesib and Mousa spoke.

Mousa's other arguments on this point are adequately refuted by A. W. Lawrence in his 'Comment', published as an appendix to Mousa's book (pp. 281-3).

Lawrence's notebook and pocket diary confirm beyond all reasonable doubt that the journey took place. Remarks already quoted show that by June 5th he had decided to ride north from Wadi Sirhan (see above p. 410). Although the diary entries for 5th to 19th June were intentionally cryptic and have in places been erased, they support the account given in Lawrence's report to Clayton (10.7.1917 *DG* pp. 225-30. FO 882/16 fos. 246-9). The entries for 7th, 9th and 11th June, for instance, confirm that he visited Burga, the Metawila tribe, and Ras Baalbek.

Other documents now available further weaken Mousa's case. Firstly, there is confirmation from a Turkish source of Arab unrest in northern Syria at the precise date Lawrence was there. The report specifically mentions action against the railway at Ras Baalbek (see p. 412). Secondly, on 28th July 1917, only weeks after this journey, Lawrence visited Sherif Hussein in Jidda. The prime object of their discussion was to make arrangements for a northern revolt. On July 22nd, when writing to set up their meeting, Wilson told Hussein: 'Captain Lawrence of whom your Highness has heard has arrived here today, he was with Sherif Nasir, and has himself been north of Damascus and seen various Sheikhs . . . The situation north of Maan is very promising for your Highness's cause and after the present operations it is necessary to make a scheme for the future' (FO 686/35). Hussein had been personally in touch with some of the men Lawrence had talked to on the northern journey, and it is inconceivable that Lawrence could have bluffed his way through a discussion with him on these matters.

42. T. E. Lawrence, *SP* ch. CIII p. 562.
43. T. E. Lawrence to V. W. Richards, undated but *c.* autumn 1922. Bodleian R (transcript).
44. T. E. Lawrence, *SP(O)* ch. 51.
45. *Ibid.*
46. For Lawrence's quarrel with Nesib see *SP* ch. XLVIII pp. 273-5. In this account, Lawrence implies that he began his northern ride *after* Nesib's departure for Jebel Druse. However, this seems to be a mistake: according to Lawrence's contemporary report Nesib did not set off until 18.6.1917 (T. E. Lawrence to G. F. Clayton 10.7.1917 *DG* p. 226 FO 882/16 fo. 247). It is possible, of course, that Nesib made more than one journey.

When Nesib left for the north on 18th June, Lawrence gave him written instructions about the steps he should take. In his report to Clayton, Lawrence commented: 'Nessib El Bekri is volatile and short-sighted, as are most town Syrians, and will not carry them out exactly – but no other agent was available.' (*DG* p. 226. fo. 247).

In *Seven Pillars* Lawrence chose not to stress the personal crisis which led him to undertake the northern journey and, as a result, the main emphasis falls on his wish to foil Nesib's plans. At the time, this was probably only a secondary motive.

47. T. E. Lawrence to G. F. Clayton 10.7.1917 *DG* p. 225. FO 882/16.

48. Miscellaneous Military Report No. 148, 7.7.1917. L/P&S/11/24, file P. 2885. See also the EEF GHQ Intelligence Summary of 16.7.1917, WO 157/717.

49. T. E. Lawrence, *SP* ch. XCIX p. 546.

50. T. E. Lawrence, *SP* ch. XXX p. 174.

51. T. E. Lawrence, *SP*(O) ch. 51.

52. T. E. Lawrence, verbal answer to a question by B. H. Lidell Hart, 24.2.1933. Bodleian R (transcript). The matter is alluded to, somewhat cryptically, in *SP* ch. XCIX pp. 545-6. See pp. 535-6 above.

This distressing incident was probably one reason for Lawrence's refusal to be explicit about the details of this northern journey in comments made after the war. When Robert Graves pressed him on the matter, Lawrence replied: 'During [the journey] some things happened, and I do not want the whole story to be made traceable. So on this point I have since darkened counsel . . . my reticence upon this northward raid is deliberate, and based on private reasons . . . I have found mystification, and perhaps statements deliberately misleading or contradictory, the best way to hide the truth of what really occurred, if anything did occur.' (T. E. Lawrence to R. R. Graves 22.7.1927 *B:RG* p. 88, 90.).

Lawrence was also concerned after the war to avoid causing any risk of danger or embarrassment to the people he had conferred with at that time. The meetings had taken place in conditions of strict confidence.

53. T. E. Lawrence, *SP* introductory chapter, first published in *OA* pp. 145-6.

54. In his report to Clayton, Lawrence stated that he visited Um Keis on June 23rd. This seems to be confirmed by an entry in his pocket diary which reads: 'Slept in a hollow valley in the hills just SE of the railway post of Hemme' (23.6.1917, BL Add. MS 45983). Hemme is very close to the bridge at Um Keis.

The visit to Um Keis is not alluded to in Lawrence's notebook entries for late June, which deal only with his operations against the Hejaz railway between Amman and Deraa. This silence, however, is probably due to Lawrence's fear that his notes might fall into the wrong hands. The visit is not mentioned in the *Seven Pillars* account of this expedition either (chs. L-LI), but many small expeditions were omitted. The railway raiding described in the notebook took place within easy reach of Um Keis, and there are several gaps in the narrative long enough for such a visit to have taken place. Lawrence later mentioned a journey to the Yarmuk valley in June 1917 when talking to Liddell Hart (*B:LH* p. 205. See also *B:RG* p. 89).

It is difficult to make an exact comparison of the different versions of these journeys because Lawrence lost track of the correct date during late June: a number of the dates recorded in his notebook are wrong (e.g. 'Saturday June 21st' – Saturday was the 23rd.)

55. T. E. Lawrence, *SP*(O) ch. 108. In his report Lawrence described Fawaz as 'fair spoken, but I am convinced pro-Turk at heart and treacherous.'(T. E. Lawrence to

G. F. Clayton 10.7.1917, FO 882/16 fo. 247 fo. 8). Lawrence is correct in stating that Fawaz died not long after this visit (although it was a matter of weeks not days), and his suspicions of foul play were widely shared at the time. See *AB* No. 64, 27.9.1917, p. 393, and No. 65, 8.10.1917, p. 399. These reports suggest, however, that Fawaz was murdered at the instigation of the Turks, not by members of his own family.

In his report to Clayton, Lawrence implied that he visited Ziza between June 20th and June 23rd, on the outward stage of the expedition against the railway near Amman. This is almost certainly incorrect, as it is difficult to reconcile such a visit with his notebook entries for these days. On the other hand his pocket diary contains the following entry under the date June 28th: 'At Bair till noon when Z. till midnight.' (BL Add. MS 45983). This suggests that he made a quite separate journey to Ziza and back immediately after his return from the railway raid on June 28th.

A remark in *Seven Pillars* ch. LII confirms this view. Lawrence here describes his return to Bair from the railway, and adds: 'My hopefulness misled me into another mad ride which miscarried' (p. 295; nothing further is said about the ride.) The error in the report to Clayton is quite understandable: Lawrence simply confused two journeys made from the same place, in the same direction, only days apart.

See also the comment about chronology in note 54 above.

56. 'Fighting Instructions', General Staff 4th Cavalry Division, 5.8.1918. WO 95/4510. For Lawrence's fullest contemporary account of this battle see *AB* No. 59, 12.8.1917, pp. 336-8. He later told Liddell Hart: 'My alternative plan – for I hardly expected to crush the battalion at Aba el Lissan – was to hold them on the defensive, and force them to fight their communications open again to Ma'an. This would take all their reserve and transport.' While the Turks at Aba el Lissan were being contained in this way, part of the Arab force would have taken the opportunity to slip down to Akaba. (*B:LH* p. 98).

57. T. E. Lawrence, *SP*(O) ch. 57.

58. G. F. Clayton to Sir G. M. W. Macdonogh (Director of Military Intelligence) 5.7.1917. FO. 882/7 fo. 2.

Chapter 20. The Consequences of Akaba
July – August 1917

1. S. F. Newcombe, report, undated but *c*. 10.5.1917. FO 686/6 Part 2 fo. 72. This file contains a series of extremely pessimistic reports from Newcombe and other British officers in the field. See, for example, Newcombe's report of 3.4.1917, fo. 163, and his Intelligence notes 25.4.1917 fos. 107-12; See also H. S. Hornby to S. F. Newcombe, undated but *c*. 17.5.1917; H. Garland to Wejh, 22.5.1917, fos. 54-6; W. A. Davenport to Jidda, 8.8.1917, fos. 26-8; H. Garland, two reports to C. E. Wilson both dated 14.8.1917, fos. 13-17 and 17-20; H. Garland to C. E. Wilson 16.8.1917, fos. 20-23; H. Garland to S. F. Newcombe, undated, fos. 118-21.

2. *Ibid* fo. 73.

3. S. F. Newcombe, report, undated but *c*. 4.5.1917. FO 686/6 Part 2 fos. 82-4.

4. S. F. Newcombe, report, 4.5.1917. FO 686/6 Part 2 fos. 80-1.

These reports cast an interesting light on the account of Newcombe's raiding exploits in *SP* ch. XLI pp. 239-40, where Lawrence wrote: 'Newcombe had constant difficulties owing to excess of zeal, and his habit of doing four times more than any other Englishman would do: ten times what the Arabs thought needful or wise . . . "Newcombe is like fire" they used to complain; "he burns friend and enemy"; and they admired his amazing energy with nervous shrinking lest they should be his next friendly victims.

'Arabs told me Newcombe and Hornby would not sleep except head on rails, and that Hornby would worry the metals with his teeth when gun-cotton failed . . . They were wonderful, but their too great excellence discouraged our feeble teams, making them ashamed to exhibit their inferior talent: so Newcombe and Hornby remained as individualists, barren of the seven-fold fruits of imitation.' In this manner, Lawrence presented Newcombe's failure with the Arabs in the most favourable light possible.

5. In the late spring of 1917 British officers with Feisal had noticed that he was more preoccupied than ever with the idea of a revolt in Syria. They did not, however, see the true connection between this renewed interest and the small expedition which left Wejh on May 9th. On May 1st Wilson reported to Cairo: 'When Medina and El Ula are captured the Emir Feisal proposes to start for the north himself, taking with him all the Syrians and probably the trained Meccans which are now with the armies of his brothers . . . His present proposal is not to follow up the railway beyond Maan but to keep well to the east of it and strike the railway at or near Hama. He states that there is a very large bridge over a river gorge which, if destroyed, would stop all railway communications for several weeks if not months . . . he expresses himself as confident that once he appears on the railway near Hama, a general revolt in Syria will break out. He proposes to act southward from Hama to Damascus, and otherwise act as the situation admits.

'The above may be considered a too ambitious plan; ambitious it is, but in my opinion one by no means impossible of carrying out.

'Feisal has received letters or representatives from most of the chief northern tribes and the Druses, all expressing their willingness to join his cause at the proper time . . . A messenger from the local Arabs at Hama arrived recently and he has returned with instructions to prepare the Arabs for the day of revolt . . .

'If the plan of operations outlined above materialises it should prove of considerable assistance to the British army in Palestine.' (C.E. Wilson, 'Note on the proposed Military Plan of Operations of the Arab Armies' 1.5.1917. FO 882/6 fos. 351-2.)

The issues raised by this note were discussed at a meeting in Cairo on May 12th. Those present included Wingate, Clayton, Wilson, Sykes and George Lloyd. Wilson now argued that Feisal's plans for action in Syria should go forward without delay, irrespective of the outcome in the Hejaz. Although this represented a major shift in policy, the idea was agreed, subject to Murray's approval. The meeting decided to look into the possibility of supplying an Arab offensive in the north from Mesopotamia, via Jebel Druse. ('Note of a Meeting at the Residency, Cairo, on 12th May 1917'. Wingate papers W145/6/62-3, Durham.)

It seems that the main reason for this change of heart was the failure of the EEF to break through at Gaza. An Arab offensive in Syria would have a direct effect on the Turkish position in Palestine, and for this reason would be well worth backing. According to Lloyd's record of this meeting, those present agreed that 'in operating against the Damascus-Deraa section of the railway results would be obtained that would not only assist in the reduction of Medina, but seriously hamper Turkish communications on the Palestine line – [the] Damascus–Deraa section being of course the single line on which both the Palestine and Hejaz lines depend.' (G. A. Lloyd to CGS, 12.5.1917. Lloyd papers GLLD 9/9. Churchill College, Cambridge.)

When Wilson brought this news back to the Hejaz, Feisal told him that a northward move would not be possible for some weeks at least, and that he would meanwhile be happy to go ahead with his part in the El Ula scheme. Preparations for action in Syria could go forward simultaneously (C. E. Wilson to G. F. Clayton 20-24.5.1917. Wingate papers W145/7/33-4, Durham.) Although Feisal gave various reasons for the delay, he did not mention the most important: that he was waiting to learn the outcome of the move against Akaba, upon which his hopes in the north depended.

Feisal told Newcombe that once the El Ula operation had been carried out he would begin to move forces overland to Jebel Druse by stages (a very similar plan had been discussed briefly at the beginning of April, see pp. 392-3). However, when the Arabs were established in the north, the main problem would be to find a workable supply route. Newcombe suggested that the solution was either to capture Akaba from the sea or to secure the road which ran from El Arish to the country south-east of the Dead Sea. ('Note by Colonel Newcombe, D.S.O.' 24.5.1917. FO 882/6 fos. 363-6.)

These plans met with a cool reception in Egypt. One staff officer commented: 'It is somewhat difficult to examine in any detail Sherif Faisal's plan for a preliminary advance . . . which is characterised throughout by a remarkable freedom from conventional restrictions in regard to time, space, arrangements for supply, or the disposition and possible action of the enemy.' (A. G. C. Dawnay to CGS, General Headquarters EEF, 29.5.1917. WO 158/606). The idea of supplying the Arabs across Sinai was rejected as hopelessly impracticable, and Clayton argued that an Arab occupation of Akaba was undesirable on political grounds (his remarks are quoted on p. 397).

Although the possibility of Arab action in Syria was discussed on several occasions during the following weeks, it was now taken for granted that nothing could be done until the El Ula operation had run its course. It was also assumed that some means would have to be found of bringing supplies from Mesopotamia to Tudmor in Jebel Druse. (See C. E. Wilson to G. F. Clayton 17.6.1917. FO 882/16 fos. 237-9; C. E. Wilson to G. F. Symes 21.6.1917. FO 882/16 fos. 243-5; G. F. Clayton, Brig Genl., General Staff, to Sir G. M. W. Macdonogh, DMI War Office. FO 882/6 fos. 426-7.) Feisal evidently played along with the Tudmor scheme while he was waiting for news of Akaba: he may also have felt that, in the last resort, some such arrangement could serve as a fallback. The idea of supplying Syrian operations from Mesopotamia was dropped as soon as Lawrence arrived with news that Akaba was in Arab hands.

6. T. E. Lawrence, *SP* ch. LVII p. 323. Lawrence commented on this statement to Liddell Hart: 'I did not ask for command: but that *my* policy and tactics should be adopted by those of us who were working in the Arab area. In other words, I wanted the northern plan to be adopted as the official one.' (*B:LH* p. 99).

7. T. E. Lawrence, report to G. F. Clayton 10.7.1917 *DG* p. 228-9. FO 882/16 fos. 248-9. Earlier in this report Lawrence stated that one of the main objects of his

Syrian reconnaissance was to 'meet the Bishr and compose their feud with the Howeitat with a view to working between Homs and Aleppo. The plan failed' (*DG* p. 225).

With his report and sketch-map Lawrence also enclosed an 'Abstract of Instructions given to Nesib Bey el Bekri at Kaf on 18th June, 1917' (*DG* pp. 230-31). Taken together, these show that Lawrence was now proposing Arab action in parts of the Lebanon.

8. D. Lloyd George: *War Memoirs* (London, Odhams Press, n.d.) Vol. 2, p. 1090.

9. G. F. Clayton, memorandum, 15.7.1917. WO 158/634.

10. *Ibid.*

11. *Ibid.*

12. Sir E. H. H. Allenby (Chief Egypforce) to Sir W. R. Robertson (Chief London), telegram EA61, 16.7.1917. WO 158/634.

13. *Ibid.*

14. C. E. Wilson to G. F. Clayton 22.11.1916. Clayton papers 470/4, Durham.

15. C. E. Wilson to Arbur for Sir F. R. Wingate, telegram W12.10, 13.7.1917. FO 882/7 fo. 28.

16. Sir F. R. Wingate (HC) to Sir W. R. Robertson (CIGS War Office) 11.7.1917. FO 882/7 fo. 21.

17. Sir F. R. Wingate to T. E. Lawrence 14.7.1917. FO 882/7 fo. 29.

18. Sir F. R. Wingate to Sir W. R. Robertson (C.I.G.S) 14.7.1917. L/P&S/11/124, file P. 2884/1917. Wingate also expressed his wish that Lawrence be awarded the V.C. in letters to C. E. Wilson (15.7.1917, Wingate papers W146/1/15, Durham) and to Sir Mark Sykes (16.7.1917, Wingate papers W146/1/17, Durham). A letter from the Director of Military Intelligence to Sir A. Hirtzel at the India Office (undated) bears the comment: 'The D.M.I. sends you his account of Lawrence's wonderful journey. Was ever V.C. better earned?' (L/P&S/11/126, file P. 3733/1917). A minute on this letter reads: 'His splendid performance shows *inter alia* what Arabs can do when led by the right man.'

A few months later, the French Government conferred on Lawrence the *Croix de Guerre avec palme et citation à l'ordre de l'Armée*: 'for gallant service with a Beduin contingent and the capture of Akaba.' (Sir F. R. Wingate to War Office, Troopers London, telegram 43W, 27.11.1917. Wingate papers, Durham).

After the war Lawrence told Robert Graves: 'I was gazetted a C.B. for taking Akaba, and promoted to field rank (Maj.) from Capt. so as to be eligible for the C.B. Wingate recommended me for the V.C. instead, but it was quite properly (and much to my relief) refused. My report to Clayton admitted no individual effort of the V.C. character. It is not given for good staff work, or brainy leadership, but for courage of the fighting sort – and I am not a fighter.' (*B:RG* p. 93).

19. Sir F. R. Wingate to C. E. Wilson 15.7.1917. Wingate papers W146/1/15, Durham.

20. Sir F. R. Wingate (High Commisioner Egypt) to Sir W. R. Robertson (Chief London), telegram 959 AB, 13.7.1917. FO 141/668/4332.

21. Lawrence despised the medals gained in his dishonest role with the Arabs. He asked his family not to put titles or letters before or after his name. See, for example, his letters home of: 5.9.1917 (*HL* p. 340; *MB* pp. 121-2); 24.9.1917 (*HL* p. 341; *MB* p. 123), and 14.12.1917 (*HL* p. 345; *MB* p.133).

22. T. E. Lawrence, *SP*(O) ch. 65.

23. Sir E. H. H. Allenby (Chief Egypforce) to Sir W. R. Robertson (Chief London),

telegram EA70, 19.7.1917. WO 158/634.

24. Sir W. R. Robertson to Sir C. C. Monro 1.8.1917. Monro papers, MSS Eur. D783/2 (b), India Office Library.

25. G. F. Clayton to Sir T. B. M. Sykes 22.7.1917. FO 882/16 fo. 144-5. Clayton's statement that no European personnel apart from Lawrence were required 'in the north' is curious, since moves were already afoot to transfer most of the British staff at Wejh to Akaba. Presumably he meant 'in the Syrian interior'. This letter also exaggerates the independence Feisal would enjoy under the new arrangement with Allenby. Clayton's remarks seem to be designed to allay any suspicions that the British were using the Arab campaign to undermine French hopes in Syria.

26. See *SP* ch. LVII p. 324-5. This meeting may have been the occasion when Lawrence told Feisal and his staff that they should avoid any operations in Lebanon (see ch. 17 note 9*g*).

27. C. E. Wilson: 'Note on Memorandum dated Cairo 15th July, 1917, by Brigadier General Clayton' 28.7.1917. Wingate papers W146/2/28, Durham.

28. C. E. Wilson to G. F. Clayton 29.7.1917. Wingate papers W146/2/26, Durham. Lawrence later commented: 'Newcombe was a bigger man than Joyce, and better – but not for my base commandant. He was too enterprising, too keen, too active. What I needed was a man glad to stay behind me' (comment by T. E. Lawrence on the typescript of LH:*TEL*, partially ommitted from *B:LH* p. 104. Bodleian R, transcript).

29. G. F. Clayton to General Staff 'Operations' 9.8.1917. WO 158/629.

30. C. E. Wilson to Sherif Hussein 22.7.1917. FO 686/35.

31. Sherif Hussein to C. E. Wilson ('The Honourable British Agent') 28.7.1917. WO 158/629. Note that it is not stated that Feisal would be under Allenby's orders.

32. T. E. Lawrence: 'The Sherif's Religious Views' 29.7.1917. FO 686/8.

33. The first meeting between Sykes, Georges-Picot, and Hussein took place in Jidda on 19th May: Feisal and Fuad el Khatib, Hussein's Foreign Secretary, were also present. According to Sykes's brief report, Georges-Picot introduced the notion that France's position on the Syrian coast should be equivalent to Britain's in Baghdad. Questions about the status and authority of European advisers were also raised. As there was no agreement on either point, the interview 'closed most inconclusively, Monsieur Picot being unfavourably impressed by the King' (Sir T. B. M. Sykes to Sir F. R. Wingate [High Commisioner Egypt], telegram 38, 23.5.1917. Sykes papers.)

This outcome seems to have dented even Sykes's confidence. Wilson reported that during a private conversation afterwards, Sykes 'stated that Picot was apparently of the same mind as Brémond, was anti-Sherif and appeared not to wish the Arab movement to succeed. Sykes gave me the impression that things were not going at all well owing to Picot's attitude, and that if [this] was not materially altered it appeared hopeless to try and bring France and the Sherif together'. (C. E. Wilson to G. F. Clayton 21-25.5.1918. Wingate papers W145/7/45, Durham.)

A second meeting took place on May 20th. The same people were present, with the addition of Wilson. The previous day's deadlock was broken when Fuad, on behalf of Hussein, read out a statement which delighted both Sykes and Picot. The text of this statement was not handed over and no verbatim minutes of the meeting were taken. The exact wording is therefore not recorded. According to Wilson, the gist was that: 'the relations between the Arab Government and France should be the same in Syria as those between the King and British in Baghdad.' He went on to comment: 'I am not clear, and probably Picot and the Sherif are not clear, whether Syria i.e. including Damascus etc. is meant; or merely the Syrian coast claimed by France: one may have meant Syria, the other only the Syrian coast.' (Wilson report cited above, W145/7/47). According to Georges-Picot, the suggested parallel was between Baghdad and 'Moslem Syria', while according to Sykes it was between Baghdad and something called 'the Moslem Syrian littoral' – an incomprehensible phrase (Sir T. B. M. Sykes to Sir F. R. Wingate, telegram 38, 23.5.1917. Sykes papers).

Wilson came away from the meeting feeling very uneasy about the ambiguous 'understanding' that had been reached. He reported to Cairo: 'Although Sykes and Picot were very pleased with this happy result and the Sherif had made the proposition himself, I did not feel at all happy in my own mind and it struck me as possible that the Sherif . . . was verbally agreeing to a thing which he would never agree to if he knew our interpretation of what the Iraq situation is to be . . . My own opinion is that the terms on which we hold Baghdad etc. should have been clearly stated at the meeting . . .

'As you know, I have all along been a strong advocate of being as open as possible with the Sherif. My considered opinion is that we have not been as open and frank as we should have been at this last meeting'. (C. E. Wilson to G. F. Clayton 21-25.5.1918. Wingate papers W145/7/48-50, Durham.)

Later that evening, Wilson learned that the formula read out by Fuad had *not* originated with the Sherif. It had been pressed on Hussein by Sykes after the failure of the first interview. Wilson commented: 'By urging the Sherif to agree to the formula re France and Syria, Sykes has undoubtedly taken a very heavy responsibility on his shoulders, and if I had known . . . that the Sherif had only agreed to the formula on Sykes's urgent persuasion, I should certainly have tried hard to get some principal facts re our position in Iraq stated at the meeting.

'From George Lloyd [who had accompanied Sykes to Jidda] I gather that Baghdad will almost certainly be practically British; if this is so then I consider that we have not played a straightforward game . . . for it means that the Sherif [agreed] verbally to Syria being practically French, which I feel sure he never meant to do . . .

'Is the Sherif living in a fool's paradise? If so he will have a very rude awakening, and once his trust in Great Britain has gone we will not get it back again . . . If we are not going to see the Sherif through and we let him down badly after all his trust in us, the very "enviable" post of Pilgrimage Officer at Jeddah will be vacant because I certainly could not remain . . . this letter can be shown to anyone you like' (report cited above, W145/7/50-54).

Although Wilson's distaste for these proceedings is understandable, he was probably wrong to assume that the Sherif was an innocent dupe. Hussein's 'ignorance' of British ambitions in Iraq may have been tactical. He had always believed that the MacMahon letter of October 1917 gave him a firm claim to Baghdad, and on this basis he could now argue that the verbal agreement with Georges-Picot assured his position throughout Syria and Lebanon.

Sykes's curious behaviour also stands in some need of explanation. The equivocal Baghdad/Syria formula seems to have had two main advantages in his eyes. In the short term, it would serve to prevent an open rupture between Hussein and Georges-Picot – a danger which had seemed imminent after the first meeting.

Secondly, Sykes now found certain aspects of the 1916 Agreement embarassing and he hoped to be able to recast it on less overtly imperialistic lines (some reasons for this change in his attitude are given on pp. 441-2). He seems to have believed that the new formula might contribute to this process. During the spring, he had written several papers arguing that Britain would have to make some concessions to Arab nationalism in Baghdad and that the idea of annexation ought to be renounced (see, for example, a memorandum read to the War Cabinet on 12.3.1917, CAB 23/2). These suggestions had been rejected by the War Cabinet, but Sykes's confidence that such a policy would in the end prevail may help to explain his manoeuvrings in Jidda. If, as he hoped, Britain took a more liberal approach in Mesopotamia, then the Baghdad/Syria formula would lose most of its sting as far as the Arabs were concerned. Indeed, it might well operate in their favour, by preventing the French from adopting an openly imperial policy in Syria. Surviving documents suggest that some such idea was forming in Sykes's mind.

What Hussein was told about the Sykes-Picot Agreement during the Jidda meetings is unclear. Sykes's brief report says nothing on this crucial point. Although some key elements of the Agreement were alluded to during the first meeting, their real significance may not have been explained. Sykes's methods when dealing with Arab representatives in Cairo (see p. 403) lead one to suspect that he concealed unpleasant truths whenever he thought he could get away with it.

According to a contemporary statement by Fuad el Khatib: 'The results of the Mission are solely that the King has agreed to [Sykes's] propositions thinking that Baghdad is entirely his . . . Beyond the above, no fresh information has been given the King as to the country's future except a hasty perusal and explanation (with little opportunity given him to think it over or criticise) of the Sykes-Picot agreement. Any criticsms or exclamations were stopped by Sir Mark Sykes asking me to induce the King to agree to the . . . propositions [i.e. the Syria/Baghdad parallel].' ('Note by Sheikh Fuad el Khatib taken down by Lt Col Newcombe', undated but 20-23.5.1917. Wingate papers W145/7/61, Durham).

After the second meeting, Fuad and Feisal discussed these matters with Stewart Newcombe, who reported: 'Nothing was written, and the Sherif has no copy of the Sykes-Picot agreement: the full text of which he was apparently told yesterday and asked to give a final decision upon at a moment's notice: while French and English Governments have had months to consider their point of view . . .

'As regards the agreement . . . several large questions have never been touched upon or mentioned to the Sherif: not that he necessarily would have the knowledge to criticise or discuss them, but an interview of a few hours debarring all investigation of the subject entails throwing great responsibility on our Government, to see the Sherif or Arab cause through to the end'. ('Note by Lt. Colonel Newcombe D.S.O.' 20.5.1917. Wingate papers W145/7/66, Durham.)

34. T. E. Lawrence, 30.7.1917. FO 686/8. On Lawrence's return to Cairo, Wingate sent a copy of this report to the Foreign Secretary with the comment: 'A verbatim report of the conversations . . . between King Hussein, Monsieur Picot and Sir Mark Sykes does not exist, and Lieutenant-Colonel Wilson has expressed some uncertainty as to how correctly the King has interpreted the present intentions of ourselves and France . . . It will probably be advisable to postpone further discussion with the King of these political issues . . . but we must eventually take steps to correct any erroneous impression he may have, or profess to have' (Sir F. R. Wingate to A. J.

Balfour 16.8.1917. FO 371/3054 fos. 370-1). With characteristic optimism, Sykes minuted: 'When all is said and done it seems to me that there is no real cause for either apprehension or action. I presume if all goes well we in Irak intend to set up some kind of Arab Government under our auspices . . . Similarly the French are quite ready (though they naturally won't say so) to do the same on the Syrian littoral. As to the Lebanon, I do not believe that the distance between the King of Hejaz and the French is so great as it might appear . . . I am certain the French do not desire to annex the Lebanon, which means Maronite deputies in the French chamber' (minute on the above dated 15.9.1917, fo. 368).

35. T. E. Lawrence to his family 12.8.1917 *HL* p. 338; *MB* p. 113. Bodleian MS Res C13.

36. T. E. Lawrence to S. C. Cockerell 27.5.1927 *DG* p. 519. S. Mousa argues that this journey did not take place, claiming Lawrence could not have visited Mecca without Hussein's consent, and that his movements gave him no opportunity to do so. In reality, it would have been perfectly possible for Lawrence to travel surreptitiously from Jidda to Mecca and back (see *T. E. Lawrence, An Arab View* London, OUP, 1966, pp. 272-3).

The timing of Lawrence's visit becomes clear from a letter he wrote to Lionel Curtis about the various daggers he had owned: '*Dagger I*, of silver gilt, was given me by Sherif Abdulla in Wadi Ais . . . I wore it thereafter, and up to Wadi Sirhan with Nasir and Auda on our way from Wejh to Akaba. In Wadi Sirhan, Nasir wanted to give gifts to the Howeitat chiefs, and collected all the honourable daggers of our party, therefore.

'Accordingly, I arrived at Cairo (from Akaba) daggerless and half-naked: and took advantage of my visit to Jidda, to argue with King Hussein . . . to arrange the manufacture in Mecca of *Dagger II*, (gold) . . . Dagger II was not finished when I left Jidda abruptly for Akaba . . . to see Nasir and Auda. Nasir there presented me with *Dagger III* (silver-gilt) . . . Dagger III I wore for some weeks, round Akaba, till Dagger II arrived from Mecca. It (III) was a heavy thing, and I discarded it with pleasure for the gold one (II), which had been made small by my order: and the gold one . . . I wore for the rest of the war, except when it was being repaired or re-belted.' (T. E. Lawrence to L. G. Curtis 22.2.1929. Bodleian R, transcript).

37. T. E. Lawrence to H. R. Hadley 25.9.1920 *DG* p. 320.

38. T. E. Lawrence to A. P. Wavell 21.5.1917 *DG* p. 423.

39. T. E. Lawrence, war notebook entry dated 8.2.1917 (BL Add. MS 45914 fo. 25b). According to *Seven Pillars*: 'The King, an enthusiast for the revolt, believed that his servants should work as manfully. So he would not allow visits to Mecca, and the poor men found continual military service heavy banishment from their wives. We had jested a hundred times that, if he took Akaba, Nasir would deserve a holiday; but he had not really believed in its coming' (ch. LVII p. 236). When Lawrence met Hussein in July, one of his objects was to negotiate a month's leave for Nasir. This must have reminded him of the oath sworn at Wejh, and the fact that, according to its terms, only he himself was 'entitled' to visit Mecca.

40. G. F. Clayton (Brig. Gen., Cairo) to Sir G. M. W. Macdonogh (DMI) 28.7.1917. FO 882/7 fo. 44. See also: Clayton to DMI 4.8.1918. FO 882/7 fo. 58; *AB* No. 58, 5.8.1917 pp. 321-2; *AB* No. 61, 1.9.1917, p. 359. These contemporary documents refute Mousa's suggestion (*op. cit.* note 36 above, p. 85) that Auda's treachery was a product of Lawrence's imagination. For Lawrence's account see *SP* ch. LVII

pp. 325-6.

41. *Ibid.*, citing Lawrence's opinion.

42. C. E. Wilson to Arbur, telegram W.006, 6.8.1917. WO 158/634.

43. T. E. Lawrence, *SP*(O) ch. 61.

44. T. E. Lawrence to his family 12.8.1917 *HL* p.338; *MB* p. 113. Bodleian MS Res C13.

45. G. A. Lloyd to Sir F. R. Wingate 17.8.1917. Lloyd papers GLLD 9/13. Churchill College, Cambridge. A few weeks later, Lawrence wrote to Colonel Wilson: 'The Hejaz show is a quaint one, the like of which has hardly been on earth before, and no one not of it can appreciate how difficult it is to run . . . and if ever I can get my book on it out, I'll try to make other people see it.'(2.9.1917 *DG* p.236; *MB* p. 121.)

46. D. de St-Quentin to Guerre, report 70, Paris 20.8.1917 Quoted in M. Larès, *T. E. Lawrence, la France et les Français*, Paris, Imprimerie Nationale, 1980, p. 158 (author's translation).

Chapter 21. The First Syrian Campaign

August – December 1917

1. T. E. Lawrence to G. F. Clayton 27.8.1917 *MB* p. 118. FO 882/7 fo. 89. Lawrence continued: 'all have to be fed while here, and for the return journey, and the imposition (unavoidable) is very serious.

2. D. Macindoe, 'Report on present Situation at Akaba' 27.8.1917. FO 882/7 fos. 103-4.

3. T. E. Lawrence to G. F. Clayton 27.8.1917. FO 882/7 fos. 88-92. The report contains a remark which appears to be a reflection on Macindoe: 'I don't think that any apprecation of the Arab situation will be of much use to you unless its author can see for himself the difference between a national rising and a campaign.'(*Ibid.* fo. 92.)

4. *Ibid.* fo. 88.

5. T. E. Lawrence to his family 27.8.1917 *HL* pp. 338-9. Bodleian MS Res C13.

6. Sir T. B. M. Sykes to G. F. Clayton 22.7.1917. Sykes papers, St Antony's College, Oxford.

7. See M. Fitzherbert, *The Man Who was Greenmantle* (Oxford, OUP, 1985) pp. 192-4. On his return from Switzerland, Herbert had interviews with both the Foreign Secretary and the Prime Minister.

8. See FO 371/3388 for documents relating to secret contacts between British and Turkish representatives in Switzerland during 1918.

9. T. E. Lawrence, *SP* ch. CI p. 556. Lawrence's private source of information may well have been Arab: it was in the Turks' interests to let the Arab leadership know something of these discussions. Feisal seems to have known about the existence of Anglo-Turkish negotiations during the spring of 1918.

10. Sir T. B. M. Sykes to G. F. Clayton 22.7.1917. Sykes papers, St Antony's College, Oxford. 'Fashoda-ism' is a reference to the Fashoda incident of 1898, when Britain forced a French military expedition to withdraw from the Sudan in humiliating circumstances. Sykes often used this term to denounce what he saw as unreasoning suspicion and hostility between the *Entente* powers.

11. President W. Wilson, speech to the United States Senate 22.1.1917, published in J. B. Scott (ed.), *President Wilson's Foreign Policy: Messages, Addresses, Papers*

(New York, OUP, 1918) p. 250.

12. 'British reply to Russian Note regarding the Allied War-Aims', undated, but given in response to a Russian enquiry of 3.5.1917. FO 371/3062.

13. Sir T. B. M. Sykes, 'Memorandum . . . on Mr. Nicolson's Note regarding our Commitments' 18.7.1917. FO 371/3044 fo. 294. Sykes later protested at a dispatch from the Foreign Secretary describing him as the 'joint author' of the 1916 Agreement: 'I . . . desire to point out that I cannot properly be described as joint author of the Anglo-French Agreement of 1916 (here called the "Sykes-Picot" Agreement). I was responsible only for giving advice as far as concerned the Arabic-speaking areas, under direct instructions from Lord Kitchener. The military and strategic side was entrusted to General Callwell; the commercial and economic questions to Sir H. Llewellyn Smith . . . The general policy was supervised by Lord Carnock [Sir Arthur Nicolson]' (Sir T. B. M. Sykes to Sir E. A. B. W. Crowe 28.9.1918. FO371/3383 fo. 479.)

14. *Ibid.* See also Sykes's 'Memorandum on the Asia-Minor Agreement' 14.8.1918. FO371/3059. Here, he observed: 'When the agreement was originally drawn up . . . certain concessions were made to the idea of nationality and autonomy, but an avenue was left open to annexation. The idea of annexation really must be dismissed, it is contrary to the spirit of the time, and if at any moment the Russian extremists got hold of a copy they could make much capital'.

15. T. E. Lawrence to G. F. Clayton 7.9.1917. Clayton papers 693/11, Durham (photocopy of original).

16. T. E. Lawrence to Sir T. B. M. Sykes 9.9.1917, enclosed with the above. Clayton papers 693/11, Durham (photocopy of original). I have omitted from the second paragraph quoted here Lawrence's statement that he 'fixed these areas on military grounds only'. It would not have been politic for Lawrence to tell Sykes the truth about his confidential discussions with Feisal.

17. G. F. Clayton to T. E. Lawrence 20.9.1917. Clayton papers 693/11/9-12, Durham.

18. T. E. Lawrence to W. F. Stirling 25.9.1918 *MB* pp. 125-6. Bodleian R (transcript).

19. T. E. Lawrence to E. T. Leeds 24.9.1917. *L-L* p. 113; *DG* p. 239; *MB* p. 124. Leeds papers. In the same letter, Lawrence wrote: 'I'm not going to last out this game much longer: nerves going and temper wearing thin, and one wants an unlimited account of both'.

20. Sir F. R. Wingate to Lord Hardinge 26.9.1917. Wingate papers W146/5/54, Durham. For Allenby's congratulations see Assistant Military Secretary to Arbur, telegram MS 381, WO 158/634.

21. P. C. Joyce to G. F. Clayton 24.9.1917. Akaba Archive H70-1, KCL.

22. P. C. Joyce to G. F. Clayton 14.9.1917. Akaba Archive H69, KCL. Joyce seems to have had second thoughts and decided not to send this message.

23. P. C. Joyce to G. F. Clayton 17.9.1917. Akaba Archive H72-3, KCL. See also Joyce to Clayton 25.9.1917, Akaba Archive H74, KCL.

24. P. C. Joyce to G. F. Clayton 25.9.1917. Akaba Archive H77-8, KCL. Feisal's morale remained low throughout the early autumn of 1917. His tendency to become fretful during periods of military inactivity was by this time a recognised problem. Thus when George Lloyd visited Akaba at the end of October he reported to Clayton: 'Feisal is very jumpy and difficult but so long as Lawrence is here all goes well' (G. A. Lloyd to G. F. Clayton 20.10.1917. Lloyd papers GLLD 9/13, Churchill College, Cambridge.) At much the same time, Clayton wrote to Joyce: 'I have had

one or two gloomy letters from Feisal but I realize his peculiar mentality and I do not attach any great importance to them, and you may be sure that I shall not take any action . . . unless they are backed up by you or Lawrence.' (G. F. Clayton to P. C. Joyce 24.10.1917. FO 882/7 fo. 175.) Lawrence does not allude to these difficulties with Feisal in *Seven Pillars*.

25. *Ibid.*
26. T. E. Lawrence to G. F. Clayton 10.10.1917. FO 882/7. In the draft *Seven Pillars*, Lawrence commented: 'These decisions had to be arrived at by me unaided, without experience, with my very imperfect knowledge of the Arabic language. The fraudulence of the whole business stung me deeply. Here were more fruits – very bitter fruits – of that decision on the way to Akaba, that I must become, not an instigator, but a principal, of the Arab Revolt. It . . . involved me . . . in an assumption of false authority over the lives and habits of my dupes.' (*SP*(O) ch. 74.)
27. D. G. Hogarth to W. G. A. Ormsby-Gore 26.10.1917. FO 371/3054 fo. 388.
28. G. F. Clayton to T. E. Lawrence 20.9.1917. Clayton papers 693/11/10, Durham.
29. *Ibid* 693/11/11. See also G. F. Clayton to General Staff Operations 9.9.1917. FO 882/7 fo. 99; G. F. Clayton to P. C. Joyce 24.10.1917. FO 882/7 fo.176.
30. T. E. Lawrence, *SP* ch. LXIX p. 385.
31. *Ibid.*
32. T. E. Lawrence, *SP*(O) ch. 76.
33. *Ibid.*
34. D. G. Hogarth to W. G. A. Ormsby-Gore 26.10.1917. FO 371/3054 fo. 388.
35. G. A. Lloyd to G. F. Clayton 20.10.1917. Lloyd papers GLLD 9/13, Churchill College, Cambridge.
36. G. F. Clayton to G. A. Lloyd 25.10.1917. Lloyd papers GLLD 9/10, Churchill College, Cambridge.
37. G. A. Lloyd: 'Diary of Journey with T.E.L. to El Jaffer, 28.10.1917'. Typescript in Clayton papers 694/5/31, Durham.
38. G. A. Lloyd to G. F. Clayton 5.11.1918. Lloyd papers GLLD 9/10, Churchill College, Cambridge.
39. G. A. Lloyd, notes, undated but *c*. 25.10.1917. Lloyd papers GLLD 9/10, Churchill College, Cambridge.

According to these notes, Lawrence's own role in the later stages of the campaign would be as follows: 'ride north Tadmor . . . stay and plan taking Aleppo – if successful send party out to Jerablus, march to Kalma, raise Antioch and have a go at Marmourique – if succesful go on to Chak al Dere (bridge between Adana and Toprah Kali) then come to Alexandretta.' These contemporary notes support Lawrence's statement, in the epilogue to *Seven Pillars*, that his ultimate goal lay far beyond Damascus. The objective at Jeralbus was the railway bridge into Mesopotamia, a vital link in Turkish supplies to that theatre.

Lloyd's notes also make it clear that Lawrence was at this time prepared to act in a part, at least, of Lebanon. This readiness to defy Sykes-Picot probably owed something to recent assurances from Clayton that the Agreement was virtually dead.

Lloyd did not mention these politically sensitive plans in his subsequent report to Clayton. On the contrary, he stated that Lawrence and he discussed 'the necessity of tying down the Arab movement to its military purpose, its original aims and objective, and to risk no breach of faith with the Arabs by raising hopes beyond it'. (G. A. Lloyd: 'Diary of Journey with T.E.L. to El Jaffer, 28.10.1917'. Typescript in

Clayton papers 694/5/31, Durham.)

In a later account of this journey, Lawrence said that he told Lloyd of a plan for spreading the Revolt eastwards to Mesopotamia from a base in Jebel Druse. This might be tried if the overall military situation deteriorated and a rapid victory in Palestine and Syria began to look impossible (*SP*(O) ch. 78).

40. See G. A. Lloyd to G. F. Clayton 5.11.1918. Lloyd wrote: 'Anyone who can hold up a train and enable the Arabs to sack it commands temporarily their allegiance. Joyce does not quite agree here, but if not all the truth it is the mainspring of influence at this game. It is . . . by no means the only but a great part of the secret of Lawrence's success, and he will admit this privately with a smile. Newcombe, it is true, had not Lawrence's gifts but he knows more than the average man about Arabs. His game was merely cutting the line. Would the Arabs help him? Not they . . . Lawrence conceived the necessity of giving them instant reward and loot and stopped trains . . . The moment he did this the Arabs showed reckless courage. To them he is Lawrence, the arch-looter, the super-raider, the real leader of the right and only kind of *ghazzu* [raid] – and he never forgets that this is a large part of his claim to sovereignty over them. At El Jaffer he was greeted effusively until they learnt he was not on *ghazzu* . . . when all interest died down'. Lloyd papers GLLD 9/10, Churchill College, Cambridge.

This is clearly not an adequate explanation of Lawrence's ability to get results from the Arabs where others failed. The capture of Akaba offered no more prospect of loot than did Newcombe's operations against the line, but was incomparably more successful. Nor is it true that Lawrence was the first British officer to attack trains, or that the main motive for doing this was to provide an incentive for the bedouin.

41. P. C. Joyce to G. F. Clayton 4.11.1917. FO 882/7 fo. 199.

42. D. G. Hogarth to his wife 11.11.1917. Hogarth papers, St Antony's College, Oxford.

43. T. E. Lawrence, *SP* ch. LXXVIII pp. 431-3.

44. G. F. Clayton to P. C. Joyce 12.11.1917. FO 882/7 fo. 204.

45. G. F. Clayton to War Office London 12.11.1917. WO 158/637.

46. T. E. Lawrence, *SP* ch. LXXIX p. 435.

47. T. E. Lawrence to his family 14.11.1917 *HL* pp. 342-3; *MB* p. 130.

48. *Ibid*. p. 343.

49. T. E. Lawrence to W. F. Stirling (Deputy Chief Political Officer) 28.6.1919 *MB* p. 166. Bodleian R (transcript).

At first sight, it seems curious that, when writing about this incident in *Seven Pillars*, Lawrence should have concealed the fact that he had been recognised. There are, however, several likely reasons. First, he wanted his treatment by the Turks to form the dramatic content of the Deraa chapter. If he had stated at the outset that he was recognised, the entire nature of the chapter would have changed, because readers would have been concerned to know how he would escape. Secondly, the fact that he *had* managed to escape made the question of recognition irrelevant to the story he was telling in *Seven Pillars*. Thirdly, by the time he came to write the book, the homosexual rape he had experienced at Deraa had begun to influence him deeply. By comparison, the matter of his recognition must have seemed trivial.

When these events took place, however, Lawrence must have been acutely anxious to escape. Had he failed to do so, he would have been subjected to very unpleasant interrogation and would probably have been shot. It is therefore significant that in this 1919 account to Stirling, written only eighteen months after the event, the question of recognition is given so much prominence.

In recent years it has become fashionable to ask whether the events at Deraa described in *Seven Pillars* really happened. As there is no independent evidence, there can be no direct proof. However, there are strong indications that such an event took place in Lawrence's life at this time. Taking these in turn:-

a. Lawrence's post-war attitude towards all matters linked to sex appears typical of a male rape victim. For example, he developed a horror of physical contact; he could not accept that sexual activity is enjoyable to both partners (he saw it as an intolerable abuse of the woman by the man) and he became obsessed with cleanliness, going to great lengths to bath daily at successive RAF stations (he also installed a gleaming bathroom at Clouds Hill, but no kitchen or lavatory). Lastly, the incident left scars on his body which were later seen and commented upon by men in the Tank Corps and RAF.

b. As regards the timing of this incident: first, it is worth noting that as soon as he returned to Akaba he recruited a personal bodyguard. Secondly, those who doubt that the event took place at this time are accusing Lawrence of an elaborate and pointless lie. Such accusations were commonplace after the publication of R. Aldington's *Lawrence of Arabia: a Biographical Enquiry* (London, Collins, 1955). However, I have found that Lawrence was not as Aldington claimed, a habitual liar, and that *Seven Pillars* is remarkably accurate on questions of fact. Those who wished in the 1950s to show that Lawrence was pathologically dishonest hoped that the contemporary documents would eventually demonstrate that they were right. In the event, the documents have done exactly the opposite.

50. This figure was given by Lawrence himself after the war, see page 594.
51. T. E. Lawrence, *SP*(O) ch. 87.
52. *Ibid*. 'Him' has here been substituted for 'me' in Lawrence's text.
53. *Ibid*.
54. T. E. Lawrence to W. F. Stirling (Deputy Chief Political Officer) 28.6.1918 *MB* p. 166. Bodleian R (transcript).
55. P. C. Joyce to Arbur, telegram 209, 3.12.1917. WO 158/634. The operations alluded to here are those described on pp. 465-6. In *SP* ch. LXXXI p. 453, Lawrence states incorrectly that he was ordered to fly to Palestine.
56. T. E. Lawrence, *SP*(O) ch. 87.
57. T. E. Lawrence, *SP*(O) ch. 88. In the final text of *Seven Pillars*, the last paragraph quoted here was omitted. As a result the ending of the chapter became more dramatic: 'Dalmeny lent me red tabs, Evans his brass hat; so that I had the gauds of my appointment in the ceremony of the Jaffa gate, which for me was the supreme moment of the war.' *SP* ch. LXXXI, p. 453.

Chapter 22. The Dead Sea Campaign
December 1917 – February 1918

1. T. E. Lawrence to his family 14.12.1917 *HL* p. 343; *MB* p. 131. Bodleian MS Res C13.
2. T. E. Lawrence to E. T. Leeds 15.12.1917. *L-L* p. 114-5; *MB* p. 134. Leeds Papers.
3. *Ibid. L-L* pp. 115-6; *MB* p. 135.

4. Two months earlier, when the advance into Palestine was about to begin, Clayton had arranged for Colonel Parker to be appointed Military Administrator of Sinai. He had written to Wingate: 'my point in this is that, unless [the EEF] have a ready made and cut-and-dried system *before* they advance, they will find themselves faced with many political difficulties with our Allies. I foresee proposals for an international gendarmerie and even perhaps an international provisional government for Palestine etc. etc. These can best be countered by the C. in C. saying that he *has* a military administrator of occupied enemy territory, working in accordance with the "Laws and Usages of War", and that, having regard to the safety of his lines of communication and the security of his army, that is the only system which he can permit while military operations are in progress . . . When the military situation is fully developed, it may be time for politics – but not now' (G. F. Clayton to Sir F. R. Wingate 12.10.1917. Wingate papers W146/6/68, Durham).

A few days later, Clayton had written to Sykes: 'As the situation develops, it becomes more and more evident that the French will never make good their aspirations in Syria unless they take some more active military part in this theatre. It cannot be disguised that they are unpopular with both Arabs and Syrians as a whole – their colonial and financial methods are disliked, and they have never been able to live down the seizure of Picot's papers by the Turks [these incriminated Arab nationalists, and had been left behind in the French consulate at Beirut at the beginning of the war] and the consequent execution and ruin of various notables. Every effort on our part to put [the French] in the forefront of the Syrian picture is met by the retort "what have they done, except propaganda in Cairo, to warrant consideration as the saviours of Syria or to establish any claim on either Syrian or Arab. The fight against the Turk is being maintained by Great Britain and by the Arabs with the help of Great Britain".

'As the situation develops and time goes on, this attitude becomes more and more general and difficult to combat.

'I do not speak in any anti-French spirit. As you know, I am doing my utmost to help them and to act up to the spirit of our Agreement, but it is impossible to get round solid facts.

'I think Picot realized this when he left and that was the reason of his anxiety to procure real French military co-operation here – he himself said to me "It is a *fait accompli* only which will solve this question."

'A victory in Palestine combined with further success of the Arabs under Faisal (guided by Lawrence) will still further weaken the French political position – it is unavoidable that it should do so, and it is the knowledge of this which makes them anxious regarding the scope of Faisal's operations and desirous of having a Frenchman to co-operate with Lawrence. At the present time with important military developments pending, this latter proposal cannot be accepted. Lawrence's chances of success (and his life) cannot be jeopardized, which would be the case were he hampered by the presence of any European officers other than such exceptionally qualified men as might be really useful (and these do not exist). At the present moment the military problem of beating the Turk must be paramount in our consideration' (G. F. Clayton to Sir T. B. M. Sykes 18.10.1917. FO 882/16 fos. 152-3).

Hogarth too was pondering over the situation that might emerge if the Palestine offensive succeeded. He wrote to an acquaintance in the Foreign Office: 'Till it has taken place . . . it is hard to believe in either ourselves or the French being the ultimate arbiters of Syria's fate. And if it should be very successful, with a collapse also east of Jordan and a rising of Arabs generally, it will be still harder to believe seriously in French arbitrament. A British Force can hardly advance up Syria with a French flag at its head, the French doing absolutely nothing, beyond the contribution of a grey-headed battalion, an Armenian Legion, some obsolete ships and Picot. What can and will the Syrians think? I don't say – since, as soon as any autonomy has come into being in Syria, it will at once be found that it can neither protect itself against the Turkish remnant in the North, nor organise its own Government – that we may not have to give the French a mandate, if we don't want to see the thing through ourselves. But beyond question, it is we, and not the French, who will be asked for by the Syrians, and the latter will take over, if at all, under very unfavorable conditions' (D. G. Hogarth to W. A. G. Ormsby-Gore 26.10.1917. FO 371/3054 fo. 387).

The true nature of the administration the British set up in Palestine is clear from a letter written to Allenby some months afterwards by a Foreign Office official. This cites a passage in an earlier letter (of 23rd March 1918): 'For reasons of international politics it is not desirable to set up a separate civil administration under British control and . . . the administration will therefore be military in form and under the direction of the General Officer Commanding-in-Chief, subject to the instructions of His Majesty's Government conveyed to him through the War Office.' The Foreign Office letter comments: 'The military character of the administration being therefore confined rather to its external form, as distinct from its essential features and the functions which it will perform, it will be clear that matters connected with the actual working of the administration must be referred by the War Office to the Foreign Office' (B. B. Cubitt to Sir E. H. H. Allenby [GOC-in-C EEF] 11.5.1918. FO 371/3389 fo. 154).

5. T. E. Lawrence, *SP* ch. LXXII p. 455.
6. D. G. Hogarth to his son, William, 16.12.1917. Hogarth Papers, St Antony's College, Oxford. Hogarth was mistaken about Lawrence's age.
7. T. E. Lawrence to his family 14.12.1917 *HL* p. 344; *MB* p. 132. Bodleian MS Res C13.
8. *Ibid. HL* pp. 344-5. See also T. E. Lawrence to his family 8.1.1918 *HL* pp. 346-7; *MB* p. 137. C. H. C. Pirie-Gordon was a traveller, scholar, and journalist. Lawrence had first met him in 1909, when preparing to visit Crusader castles in Syria (see p. 55).
9. Sir T. B. M. Sykes, minute on a draft sent by G. F. Clayton for press publication, contained in Sir F. R. Wingate to Foreign Office London, telegrams 100-105, FO 371/3383 fo. 18. See also Sykes's minute on Sir F. R. Wingate to Foreign Office, telegram 95, repeating the first part of this message to the press (FO 371/3383 fo. 10).
10. Sir T. B. M. Sykes to Sir F. R. Wingate, for G. F. Clayton, telegram 75, 16.1.1918. FO 371/3383 fo. 14. Sykes was probably the author of the following telegram, sent to Cairo a few weeks later: 'It appears from your article on Religious Jerusalem that "the grotto of Notre Dame de Lourdes" was turned into a latrine by the German Commander at Bethlehem. This sort of information is very valuable as propaganda and if authenticated, should have been reported officially.
   'Please report any similar cases in future.' (Foreign Office London to G. F.

Clayton, telegram 68, 11.4.1918. FO 371/3383 fo. 201.)

11. C. E. Wilson to Arbur for Sir F. R. Wingate, telegram W1966, 26.11.1917. FO 141/654/356.

12. G. F. Clayton to Sir T. B. M. Sykes, transmitted in Sir F. R. Wingate to Foreign Office London, telegram 1281, 28.11.1917. Sykes Papers, St. Antony's College Oxford.

13. *Ibid.*

14. Jemal Pasha to Sherif Feisal, undated but November 1917, translation in Sir F. R. Wingate to Foreign Office London 25.12.1917. FO 371/3395 fos. 402-3. Wingate also enclosed a letter from Jemal to Jaafar Pasha, dated 13.11.1917 (fo. 401). For D. G. Hogarth's comments on these letters see *AB* No. 74, 24.12.1917, pp. 509-11.

15. Sir F. R. Wingate to Foreign Office London, telegram 1394, 24.12.1918. FO 371/3062, no. 243033.

16. T. E. Lawrence, *SP*(O) ch. 115. Lawrence later told Liddell Hart: 'Negotiations between Feisal and Kemal in 1918 were separate from those with Jemal – began with correspondence between subordinates and then extended to principals' (*B:LH* p. 189).

17. *Ibid.*

18. *Ibid.* In *SP* (ch. CI p. 554) Lawrence states that both Wingate and Hussein tried to prevent Feisal from sending any reply to the Turkish overtures. Contemporary documents show that this is the case. By the time Lawrence arrived at Arab headquarters in late December 1917, Feisal had already drafted a possible reply and sent it to Hussein for approval. This was passed on to Wingate, who commented: 'I consider it would be dangerous to give the impression that we might contemplate an arrangement with the Turks in regions where Arab interests are involved . . . I have advised the King that no official acknowledgement . . . should be sent to Jemal Pasha.' (Sir F. R. Wingate to A. J. Balfour, dispatch 316, 25.12.1917. FO 371/3395 fo. 400.) A few days later the *Arab Bulletin* reported: 'King Hussein has instructed Feisal by telegraph that he should reject without hesitation all proposals from Jemal' (*AB* No. 75, 3.1.1918, p. 521).

According to Lawrence, it was this 'disappointing issue of our first confidence' which led Feisal and himself to be much more circumspect about later exchanges with Turkish leaders (*SP* ch. CI p. 556). The documents show that Lawrence told his superiors something about the continuing correspondence with Jemal; on the other hand, the contacts between Feisal and Kemal seem to have been entirely unknown to the British. They are not alluded to in any contemporary document I have seen.

19. T. E. Lawrence, *SP* ch. LXXXII p. 459, where Lawrence stated that the Arab success at Aba el Lissan preceded (and permitted) the armoured car action south of Maan. In reality, it was the other way around. For a contemporary report which makes this clear see P. C. Joyce to A. G. C. Dawnay 6.1.1918, Akaba Archive II 6, KCL.

20. In the draft *Seven Pillars* Lawrence wrote: 'The certainty that in a day from Guweira we could be on the line, operating along it, meant that the traffic lay at our mercy, to be held up at a day's notice for so long as we could keep the cars in petrol and water and food and ammunition. All the Turks in Arabia could not fight an armoured car in open country. If they tried, it would be a massacre: but I hoped not to have to prove it, except in the event of their withdrawing the Medina garrison, and that, though much talked-of, and frequently ordered, was now almost beyond

their power to do, as our mining operations had reduced their rolling stock below the capacity to put in dumps for so great an operation.

'To cut the line here prematurely was . . . to put the railhead at Maan, and great strength there just now would inconvenience us. We preferred to keep the bulk of our Turks at Medina, five hundred miles from anywhere' (*SP*(O) ch. 89).

At the end of January, Davenport reported from the Hejaz: 'About three weeks ago, I believe . . . the Turks began an attempt to evacuate Medina; my opinion is that this was frustrated by Sherif Feisal's operations in the north.' (W. A. Davenport to the Director, Arab Bureau, 29.1.1918. FO 141/668/4322.)

21. T. E. Lawrence, *SP* ch. LXXXIII, pp. 462, 465, 467.

22. T. E. Lawrence: 'Syrian Cross-Currents' printed as *Arab Bulletin Supplementary Paper* No. 1, 1.2.1918, p. 1. FO 882/14 fo. 206. The writing of this paper can be dated to about 8.1.1918 from remarks in a letter Lawrence sent his parents on that day. See *HL* p. 347; *MB* p.137.

The front of this *Supplementary Paper* carries the note: 'N.B. – Recipients of these Papers should exercise the utmost discretion in communicating their contents to any other person, and, in any case, should not show them, or mention their existence, to any but British Officials holding posts of high responsibility.' The word 'British' is a clear indication that this series of papers was not intended for French eyes.

23. *Ibid.* pp. 2-3.

24. *Ibid.* pp. 4-5. The strong anti-Sherifian feeling among many Syrian exiles must have become clear to Lawrence during his visit to Cairo in December 1917. The city contained a sizeable community of Syrians, and some of their leaders were in close touch with the Arab Bureau. Clayton was well aware of their feelings and had written to Sykes in late November: 'There is . . . a very real fear amongst Syrians of finding themselves under a Government in which the patriarchalism of Mecca is predominant. They realize that the reactionary principles from which the Sherif of Mecca cannot break loose are incompatible with progress on modern lines. Increased touch between Syrian intellectuals . . . and Mecca accentuates rather than diminishes this feeling, by disclosing the ineptitude and inertia of Sherifian Government.' (Transmitted in Sir F. R. Wingate to Foreign Office London, telegram 1281, 28.11.1917. Sykes papers, St Antony's College, Oxford.) Lawrence clearly wrote his paper to dissuade British officials from paying too much attention to these Syrians.

25. T. E. Lawrence to G. F. Clayton 22.1.1918. WO 158/634. Partly omitted from *MB* p. 139. FO 882/7.

26. *Ibid.* Omitted from *MB* p. 139.

27. T. E. Lawrence, *SP* chs. LXXXV-LXXVI pp. 476 and 482. For his contemporary report on the battle see T. E. Lawrence to G. F. Clayton, 26.1.1918 *DG* pp. 240-43. WO 158/634. In *Seven Pillars* Lawrence described the report as 'meanly written for effect . . . a near-proof parody of regulation use' (ch. LXXXVI p. 483). The comment seems to imply that in this official account he presented the battle as a more organised and considered affair than it had really been.

28. Lawrence had written to the British at Beersheba appealing for extra funds on 22.1.1918. Four days later he again stressed the financial problem in a letter to Clayton, adding: 'There was a mistake about money, which I will explain next time I see you.' (T. E. Lawrence to G. F. Clayton 26.1.1918. WO 158/634.)

29. T. E. Lawrence to G. F. Clayton 26.1.1918. WO 158/634.
30. T. E. Lawrence, SP(O) ch. 101. Dawnay rarely took an active role in the campaign. He spoke no Arabic and suffered from bad health.
31. A. G. C. Dawnay to Chief of the General Staff, General Headquarters EEF, 15.2.1918. WO 158/616.
32. *Ibid.*
33. *Ibid.*
34. Comment by T. E. Lawrence on the typescript of *Lawrence and the Arabs* by R. R. Graves, 1927 *B:RG* p. 98.
35. A. G. C. Dawnay to Chief of the General Staff, GHQ, EEF, 15.2.1918. FO 141/668/4322.
36. T. E. Lawrence to G. F. Clayton 12.2.1918. *MB* p. 141. FO 882/7 fo. 267.
37. *Ibid* fo. 267v.-268 *MB* p. 142.
38. *Ibid* fo. 267v *MB* p. 141.
39. T. E. Lawrence, *SP*(O) ch. 99. Lawrence here gives a much more detailed account of this reconnaissance than he does in the final text.
40. T. E. Lawrence, *SP*(O) ch. 99. In the published version of *Seven Pillars* (ch. XC) Lawrence obscured the fact that Zeid was lying to him about the money having been spent. When he made the popular abridgement *Revolt in the Desert* he was even more circumspect, writing merely: 'an accidental circumstance constrained me to leave [Zeid] and return to Palestine for urgent consultation with Allenby' (p. 299). Later the same year, when Robert Graves was working on his biography, Lawrence explained this reticence: 'Zeid did admirably afterwards . . . and I don't want him reflected on. Please take this seriously. I've avoided all the trouble in the *Revolt* version.'

By 1933 he evidently felt he could be more explicit. In an early draft of his biography of Lawrence, Liddell Hart left the impression that Zeid had indeed spent the money on tribal wages: Lawrence noted against this 'a pretence' (*B:LH* p. 106). Liddell Hart altered his text accordingly.

Contemporary documents leave little doubt that the money Zeid appropriated was the special grant made available to Lawrence, at his own request, for an offensive east of the Dead Sea.

Soon after arriving in Tafileh, Lawrence had sent an Arab called Jeddua el Safi across to the British lines at Beersheba with an urgent request for additional funds. His message read in part: 'I am really sending in Jeddua for money. The figures of tribal wages given Zeid at Guweira prove rather inadequate (i.e. the Sakhur get £22,000, and not £6,000) and we are going to be out of funds perhaps before we take Kerak, even. Can you send me, via Jeddua, £30,000 special grant? This will be quicker than fetching from Akaba, even if there was the money at Akaba.' He added that the £30,000 would be particularly neccessary if Kerak did not rise of its own accord, and had to be taken by force. (T. E. Lawrence to G. F. Clayton, 22.1.1917 *MB* p. 139. WO 158/634.

Lawrence also enclosed a message for A. J. Nayton, the Commandant at Beersheba, expressing his hope that the money would be sent up from Cairo as soon as possible, and that Jeddua would be trusted to bring it across to Tafileh himself (T. E. Lawrence to Commandant Beersheba, 22.1.1918, Bodleian R).

In the event, these suggestions were not followed. Nayton wrote many years later: 'I did not consider Jeddua to be a safe enough messenger and informed T. E.

accordingly' (A. J. Nayton to A. W. Lawrence, 9.1.1946. Bodleian R). Lawrence seems to have been told that the £30,000 he had asked for would be routed via Akaba, rather than Beersheba.

Subsequently, having travelled to Guweira to fetch the money himself, he wrote to Clayton: 'The gold had already reached there when I got there, and is on the way up [to Tafileh]'. (T. E. Lawrence to G. F. Clayton 12.2.1918 *MB* p. 140. FO 882/7 fo. 267). Other remarks in this letter make it clear that the gold in question was the £30,000 he had previously requested for action against Kerak and Madeba. Against Lawrence's account of his plans in this region Clayton later added the note: 'Cancelled owing to Zeid' (fo. 260).

The matter is slightly confused by a telegram from Hogarth, who met Lawrence in Palestine immediately after this incident. Hogarth wired to Cairo: 'Last night Lawrence arrived . . . after a row with Zeid who in his absence had appropriated the balance of the special fund reserved for the purchase of camels . . . [Zeid] remains rooted at Tafila and is unwilling to advance to Kerak.' (Message from D. G. Hogarth, Arsec [Arab Section] GHQ to Arbur, telegram AS015, 23.2.1918. WO158/634.)

If this statement were correct, it would imply that the missing funds had not been those earmarked for the Dead Sea campaign, but those for the purchase of riding camels for the Maan operation later that spring. Lawrence had been entrusted with supplying these animals (see p. 479). However, in his letter to Clayton of 12.2.1918 Lawrence stated clearly that the £30,000 he had brought up from Guweira was meant solely for the northern tribes (quoted on p. 480: reference given above). He had only just been told of the camel-buying scheme, so it cannot be the case that any of the scant funds already in Tafileh were designated for this purpose.

The likeliest explanation for this confusion is that Hogarth had not properly grasped the details of Lawrence's explanation. At the time of their meeting Lawrence was in a distressed and exhausted state.

41. *Ibid.* In his book *T. E. Lawrence, An Arab View* (London, OUP, 1966, pp 150-1) S. Mousa disputes Lawrence's statement that he intended to resign. His argument is based on a passage in Alec Kirkbride's book *A Crackle of Thorns* (London, John Murray, 1956) recounting a conversation with Lawrence in February 1918. Mousa assumes that this exchange took place during Lawrence's ride to Beersheba on February 19th-22nd. This is incorrect: Kirkbride could not have accompanied Lawrence on that journey as he had left Tafileh on February 14th, some days before the row with Zeid erupted. Lawrence accompanied Kirkbride for part of an *earlier* journey (see p. 480), and that was the context for the conversation cited by Mousa.

Lawrence's intention of resigning is not alluded to in any contemporary document, but this is hardly surprising. Only three or four people knew anything about it, and circumstances forced him to change his mind at once. D. G. Hogarth was among those who read *Seven Pillars* before publication, and he would surely have protested if the account of the matter given there was untrue.

42. *Ibid.* The remark about Feisal's 'full knowledge' of the fraudulent basis of the Revolt was omitted from the published text.

43. Note by T. E. Lawrence on the typescript of LH:*TEL*, 1933 *B:LH* p. 106.

Chapter 23. A False Start

February – May 1918

1. T. E. Lawrence, comment on the typescript of *Lawrence and the Arabs* by R. R. Graves *B:RG* p. 98.

   For Smuts' mission to Egypt and Palestine see the printed report in WO 106/1545. Jericho was captured by the British on February 22nd 1918.

2. T. E. Lawrence to his family 8.3.1918 *HL* p. 348; *MB* p. 144.

3. T. E. Lawrence, *SP*(O) ch. 100.

4. A. B. Robertson to the Deputy Quarter-Master General 24.2.1918. WO 158/616.

5. T. E. Lawrence, *SP*(O) ch. 100.

6. W. G. A. Ormsby-Gore, 'The Future of Palestine, Syria and Arabia', report for Sir T. B. M. Sykes 30.1.1918. FO 371/3399 fos. 412-13. Ormsby-Gore was at that time an assistant secretary to the Cabinet, working with Sykes. A few weeks later he would be appointed British liaison officer to the Zionist Mission sent out to Palestine under Chaim Weizmann (see pp. 512-4). He had been a member of the Arab Bureau during 1916-17.

7. R. H. A. Storrs to G. F. Clayton (CPO Adv HQ) 15.1.1918. FO 371/3389 fos. 42-3.

8. *Ibid.* Storrs was on good terms with the Franciscan Fathers. They ran the only English-language printing press in Jerusalem and printed, among other things, an edition of the *Occasional Poems of Henry Cust*. Their edition of *O.E.T.A. Standing Orders and General Instructions for the Information of Officers* (Jerusalem, October 1918) displays a sense of humour: at the end of a section on policing (after paragraphs headed 'Register of persons wanted', 'Register of stolen property', etc.) there is a delicately printed rose.

9. G. G. Butler to Department of Information London, August 1917, quoted in a letter from an unidentified official at the Foreign Office to J. L. Fisher (War Office) 13.12.1917. FO 395/86.

10. L. J. Thomas to J. Buchan, 10.12.1917. FO 395/86 no. 23678.

11. Sir T. B. M. Sykes to G. F. Clayton, telegram 32, 2.3.1918. FO 371/3383. In his book *The Independent Arab* (London, John Murray, 1933) p. 163 Hubert Young stated that Lowell Thomas's visit to Akaba had been arranged with Lawrence beforehand. On the typescipt of the book Lawrence wrote: 'This is all wrong. He had seen me in Jerusalem, and had prevailed upon Allenby to allow him to come to Akaba – where nobody wanted him' (Bodleian R, transcript). This is borne out by Thomas's own statements: see *With Lawrence in Arabia* (London, Hutchinson, 1925) p. 97.

12. T. E. Lawrence, *SP* ch. XCII p. 507.

13. T. E. Lawrence, *SP*(O) ch. 100.

14. T. E. Lawrence to his family 8.3.1918 *HL* p. 348; *MB* p. 145.

15. H. W. Young, *op. cit.* note 11 above, p. 143.

16. T. E. Lawrence, comment on the typescript of *Lawrence and the Arabs* by R. R. Graves, 1927 *B:RG* p. 93.

17. Sir E. H. H. Allenby (C-in-C EEF) to the War Office, telegram GS1001, 9.3.1918. WO 95/4415.

18. Lawrence told Liddell Hart that he made this recommendation 'At dinner, to Allenby'(*B:LH* p. 127. See also *B:RG* p. 97.) He later repeated the joke by claiming a Distinguished Flying Cross 'for presence of mind in not shooting down two

Bristol Fighters, which were attempting to air-machine gun my party'(*B:RG* p. 101. See also *B:LH* p. 127). This incident occurred during his reconnaissance trip in early June 1918; it is referred to in *SP*(O) ch. 109.

19. T. E. Lawrence, *SP* ch. XCII p. 508. Their real names are given in Lawrence's war notebook.

20. For Thomas's more extravagant claims see *Asia*, the journal of the American Asiatic Association, September, October, and December 1919. See also p. 624.

21. T. E. Lawrence to E. M. Forster 17.6.1925. King's College, Cambridge. Thomas used this visit to Petra as the basis for a highly-coloured account of a battle (between Maulud's Arabs and the Turks) that took place there in October 1917. In this account he states, incorrectly, that Lawrence was present and directing the Arab operations. (L. J. Thomas, *op. cit.* note 11 above, pp. 165-6, 180-7.)

22. War Diary, Hejaz Operations 30.3.1918, 'Summary of Arab Operations during March 1918.' WO 95/4415. I have found no contemporary evidence that gives the precise date for Thomas's visit to Akaba. However, all accounts agree that he met Lawrence there, and that shortly afterwards Lawrence set off on a mission inland. This narrows down the possible dates to a small number of occasions in the spring and summer of 1918. H. W. Young (*op. cit.* note 11 above) places Thomas's visit before the beginning of the Maan operations in April. Lawrence made detailed notes on a proof of Young's book, and would probably have commented if this date were inacurrate. Assuming that Young is correct, Thomas must have arrived in Akaba between March 21st and 30th, when Lawrence was also there.

23. L. J. Thomas, *op. cit.* note 11 above, Foreword pp. vi-vii.

24. T. E. Lawrence to E. M. Forster 17.6.1925. King's College, Cambridge.

25. T. E. Lawrence, *SP*(O) ch. 102.

26. T. E. Lawrence, written answer to a question from B. H. Liddell Hart, September 1933 *B:LH* p. 166. Lawrence added that his own party and the captured Turks 'were fellow-guests of the Arabs, and very sympathetic towards one another'. See also the discussion of the timing of these operations, *ibid* p. 108.

27. T. E. Lawrence, *SP* ch. XCIII pp. 516-7.

28. These disagreements, and the modified plan which emerged, are described in A. G. C. Dawnay, report to Chief of the General Staff, General Headquarters EEF, 1.5.1918. FO882/7 fos 277-86. See also War Diary, Hejaz Operations, entry for 6.4.1918, WO 95/4415. In *Seven Pillars* (ch. XCII) Lawrence gives the impression that the argument started some time before the heated conferences described by Dawnay. This may well be the case.

29. For an outline of these operations see 'Summary of Arab Operations during April 1918, Northern Hejaz' (Hejaz Operations war diary. WO 95/4415.)

30. T. E. Lawrence, *SP*(O) ch. 104. Dawnay's report on these operations stated: 'The British officers present (Lt Col Lawrence and Major Maynard) speak in terms of high praise of the behaviour of all ranks of the Arab regular army, who, throughout the operations, despite heavy casualties, fought with great gallantry and determination.' A. G. C. Dawnay to Chief of the General Staff, General Headquarters EEF, 1.5.1918. FO 882/7 fo. 282.

31. T. E. Lawrence, comment on the typescript of *Lawrence and the Arabs* by R. R. Graves, 1927, *B:RG* p. 100.

32. A. G. C. Dawnay to Chief of the General Staff, General Headquarters EEF, 1.5.1918. FO 882/7 fo. 283.

33. T. E. Lawrence, comment on the typescript of LH:*TEL*, 1933, *B:LH* p. 110.
34. T. E. Lawrence, comment on the typescript of *Lawrence and the Arabs* by R. R. Graves, 1927, *B:RG* p. 100.
35. *AB* No. 87, 30.4.1918 p. 141. See also *AB* No. 92, 11.6.1918 p. 186.
36. T. E. Lawrence, comment on the typescript of LH:*TEL*, 1933, *B:LH* p. 112.
37. A. G. C. Dawnay to Chief of the General Staff, General Headquarters EEF, 1.5.1918. FO 882/7 fo.286.
38. T. E. Lawrence, comment on the typescript of LH:*TEL*, 1933, *B:LH* p. 110.
39. *Ibid.* For a detailed account of these events see A. J. Hill, *Chauvel of the Light Horse* (Melbourne University Press, 1978) pp. 145-52. Lawrence's account of the débâcle in *Seven Pillars* (ch. XCV p. 525) is not quite accurate. He implies that the offer of Arab help had come from a minor sheikh, Fahad, who controlled only a small number of men. In fact it came from a much more important figure, Mirzuk el Tikhemi, who had remained in the Amman area when Lawrence returned south in April. This is evident from a contemporary account by Young, who was with Mirzuk at the time ('1,000 miles on a camel', undated but *c.* late April 1918. Young papers, Young 2, KCL).
40. T. E. Lawrence, *SP*(O) ch. 106. The damage which the first Amman failure had done to Feisal's morale is clear from a report by Dawnay, who had to break the news to him at a meeting on April 6th. According to Dawnay, the news 'was received by him with the utmost concern, the Emir being evidently convinced that our retirement could only have been under pressure of a severe reverse, the reaction of which upon the tribes he obviously looked to with the gravest apprehension.' Dawnay argued that the British retreat was only a minor and temporary setback, but Feisal was not easily convinced. Dawnay reported: 'Outwardly Sherif Feisal expressed his satisfaction with this explanation, but it was evident that inwardly he continued to view our withdrawal with bitter disappointment.' A. G. C. Dawnay to Chief of the General Staff, General Headquarters EEF, 1.5.1918. FO 882/7 fo. 277-8
41. Jemal Pasha to Sherif Feisal, translation enclosed with P. C. Joyce to General Staff, Hejaz Operations 5.6.1918. WO 158/634. The translation is dated '2.6.1918' but this appears to be a typing error. Intelligence notes sent in with the translation state that: 'On 3rd May an aeroplane arrived at Maan from Kutrani, bringing a post, and shortly afterwards a small party, bearing a white flag, arrived at Simna with a letter from Jemal Pasha to Sherif Faisal. A copy of this letter, which is obviously very secret, is attached. I recommended Sherif Faisal to return the party to Maan without a reply of any sort, and this course was probably followed.' Joyce's confidence on this last point was almost certainly mistaken: see pp. 511-12 above.
42. T. E. Lawrence, *SP*(O) ch. 106.
43. *Ibid.*

Chapter 24. Going it Alone

May – June 1918

1. T. E. Lawrence, *SP*(O) ch. 110.
2. T. E. Lawrence, comment on the typescript of LH:*TEL*, 1933, *B:LH* pp.113-4.
3. The German forces launched a major offensive on the Western front on 21st March 1918 and, within four months, recovered all the territory that the Allies had gained since 1915.

4. T. E. Lawrence, *SP* ch. XCV p.527.

5. T. E. Lawrence, memorandum, undated but *c.* 16.5.1918. At the time of writing, the copy of this document in WO 158/640A is incomplete: only the second page remains in the file. The passage from the missing first page quoted here is taken from *LAA* p. 235. The date of the memorandum can be deduced from *SP(O)* ch. 107. Here Lawrence states that during his visit to GHQ in mid-May 1918 he offered to replace the Egyptian Transport personnel at Akaba with Arabs. There is a reference to this matter in the memorandum.

6. *Ibid.* WO 158/640A.

7. T. E. Lawrence, *SP* ch. CI p. 554. See also *B:LH* p. 114.

8. T. E. Lawrence, memorandum, undated but *c.* 16.5.1918, WO 158/640A.

9. T. E. Lawrence, comment on the typescript of LH:*TEL*, 1933, *B:LH* p. 113. Lawrence had always considered Damascus a feasible goal if the Hauran peasantry were brought out: see pp. 450, 462 above. In proposing this new scheme, Lawrence realised that he was in effect 'reviving the plan of the Hauran rising rejected by me out of nervousness in October, 1917' (*SP(O)* ch. 110). The risks would be at least as great in 1918.

10. *Ibid.* p.167.

11. See p. 536 above. Documents show that by this time Feisal was ready to bargain seriously with the Turks (some references are given in note 28 below). Note also a remark in a telegram by G. F. Clayton: 'Sherif Feisal . . . has already expressed to Major Lawrence that as soon as the Arabs have secured their aim in Arab territories it will be necessary for them to make terms with the Turks.' (telegram I.B. 1055, 2.4.1918, PRO 30/30/10). Clayton assumed, too readily it seems, that this meant *after* the military defeat of Turkey.

12. P. C. Joyce, broadcast talk on his service with Lawrence, 30.4.1939. Akaba Archive, Akaba II 18, KCL.

13. T. E. Lawrence to his family 15.7.1918 *HL* p. 351; *MB* p. 152. Bodleian MS Res. C13.

14. A. G. C. Dawnay to P. C. Joyce 27.5.1918. Akaba Archive M20, KCL.

15. In the draft *Seven Pillars* Lawrence wrote: 'This offensive would be really ours, in the sense that Allenby would now be the junior partner, and it was my opinion that we must strengthen the Arab regulars numerically before we engaged ourselves in so great a hazard. I suggested [to Feisal] that we ask his father to transfer to Akaba the regular units at present working with the Emirs Ali and Abdulla in front of Medina. Their reinforcement, and the yield of our recruiting from Palestine and elsewhere, would raise us to ten thousand strong in uniformed men' (*SP(O)* ch. 110).

16. T. E. Lawrence, *SP(O)* ch. 110. A few weeks later Lawrence revised and added to the plan, and it is this modified version which appears in both texts of *Seven Pillars*. However, contemporary documents show that he had worked out the main elements of the scheme, including the idea of bringing regulars from the Hejaz, by the end of May.

17. T. E. Lawrence, *SP* ch. XCV p. 527.

18. T. E. Lawrence, *SP(O)* ch. 110. Lawrence's statements about the likely success of his plan are inconsistent, and he seems to have felt very uncertain. When communicating with GHQ he emphasised his doubts; conversely, Joyce's later testimony (see p. 506) and *Seven Pillars* suggest that he put on a display of

optimism for the benefit of the Arabs. In truth, the venture was a complete gamble: dramatic success and serious failure were both quite possible.

19. T. E. Lawrence, comment on the typescript of LH:*TEL*, 1933, *B:LH* p. 112.
20. P. C. Joyce to A. G. C. Dawnay (General Staff, Hejaz Operations) 31.5.1918. WO 158/634.
21. T. E. Lawrence, *SP*(O) ch. 106. In the draft of LH:*TEL* Liddel Hart described how the RAF rendered 'definite help' to Feisal in the early summer of 1918. Lawrence commented on this: 'Not strong enough. They were invaluable now' (*B:LH* p.111).
22. T. E. Lawrence, comment on the typescript of LH:*TEL*, 1933, *B:LH* p. 112.
23. T. E. Lawrence, *SP*(O) ch. 109. Lawrence later described this 'testament' as: 'A queer statement, denying the divinity of Christ; which no Christian could make and no Moslem would make. The sort of tactless remark a nervous man might blurt out' (*B:RG* p. 100).
    This reconnaissance journey is omitted from the final text of *Seven Pillars*, although it is described at length in the draft. In *Lawrence and the Arabs* (London, Jonathan Cape, 1927) Graves mentions the journey and also this incident, but misdates them July 1918.
24. T. E. Lawrence, comment on the typescript of LH:*TEL*, 1933, *B:LH* p. 113.
25. T. E. Lawrence, 'Sidelights on the Arab War', unsigned article in *The Times* (London) 4.9.1919.
26. B. H. Liddell Hart, notes on a conversation with Lawrence, 1.8.1933 *B:LH* p. 142. Lawrence later told an American acquaintance that 'Feisal and Jemal were carrying on quite serious peace negotiations all 1918. I saw both sides' letters unbeknownst: I should have been morally indignant with Feisal, only England was secretly negotiating with the Talaat [one of the ruling Turkish triumvirate], also to my unofficial knowledge, all 1918 too. All is fair in love, war and alliances.' T. E. Lawrence to W. Yale, 22.10.1929 *DG* p. 672.
27. D. G. Hogarth, memorandum enclosed with report to Sir R. W. Graham 9.8.1918. FO 371/3381 fo. 113.
28. Paraphrase of an unsigned undated letter from Sherif Feisal to Jemal Pasha, early June 1918. Commenting on a translation of the message, Hogarth wrote: 'It is not certain that it is Feisal's, but it could hardly have been sent . . . without his cognisance. It bears internal evidence of having been influenced or dictated by the Syrian officers in his entourage.' FO 371/3381 fo. 113.
    The documents show that Feisal had been prepared to offer similar terms for some weeks. See Sir F. R. Wingate to Foreign Office London, telegram 541, 23.3.1918, FO 371/3403 fo. 359, and Sir F. R. Wingate to Foreign Office London, telegram 655, 8.4.1918, FO 371/3403 fos. 372-3.
29. Foreign Office London to Sir F. R. Wingate, *c.* 9.1.1918. CAB 27/23.
30. G. F. Clayton to Sir T. B. M. Sykes, 4.2.1918. FO 371/3398 fo. 620.
31. T. E. Lawrence to G. F. Clayton, 12.2.1918. FO 882/7 fo. 268.
32. GHQ to Commandant Akaba, dispatch 2300, 24.5.1918. WO 95/4370.
33. P. C. Joyce, 'Interview between Dr. Weizmann and Sherif Feisal' 5.6.1918. FO 882/14 fos. 364-5. Lawrence's absence from this meeting is confirmed by *AB* No. 93, 18.6.1918, p. 208. Weizmann later implied that Lawrence had been present (see *Trial and Error*, London, Hamish Hamilton, 1949, p. 292, and also a confused account in *Friends*, pp. 219-20. In both places Weizmann claims to have met Lawrence in June at or near Akaba).

34. T. E. Lawrence, quoted in G. S. Symes, *Tour of Duty* (London, Collins, 1946) pp. 31-2. These notes were dictated by Lawrence, at Symes's request, while he was waiting for an aeroplane at Aboukir aerodrome. Symes does not give a date, but it cannot be earlier than mid-June 1918, when Lawrence seems to have had his first serious talks with Weizmann. Clayton wrote on June 18th: 'Weizmann . . . has done very well with Faisal and at least has established excellent personal relations. He has also had long discussions with Lawrence, and they seem quite agreed on main principles' (G. F. Clayton to G. A. Lloyd 18.6.1918. Lloyd papers GLLD 9/3, Churchill College, Cambridge). Lawrence's pocket diaries show that the date must be either June 15th or July 9th 1918.

35. *Ibid.* p.32.

36. T. E. Lawrence, 'Tribal Politics in Feisal's Area' printed in *Arab Bulletin Supplementary Paper* No. 5, 24.6.1918, pp. 1-5. FO 882/13. For the bedouin's 'malignant prejudice' against the wearing of hats, see Appendix IV, article 17, p. 963.

37. P. C. Joyce, Intelligence notes enclosed with a letter to General Staff, Hejaz Operations, 5.6.1918. WO 158/634.

Chapter 25. Third Time Lucky
June – September 1918

1. See 'Address presented by Seven Syrians to H.C. Cairo on the 7th May 1918', translation enclosed in Sir F. R. Wingate to A. J. Balfour, dispatch 90, 7.5.1918. FO 371/3380 fos. 561-7.

   A statement of British War Aims was made by Lloyd George in a speech to the Trade Unions on 5th January 1918 (the text is published as Appendix 2 to chapter LXX of the *War Memoirs of David Lloyd George*). President Wilson's 'Fourteen Points' were contained in a speech made three days later (January 8th) to a joint session of the two Houses of Congress (see *President Wilson's Foreign Policy: Messages, Addresses, Papers*, edited by J. B. Scott, New York, OUP, 1918, pp. 354-73). In Point I, Wilson asked for: 'Open covenants of peace, openly arrived at, after which there shall be no private international understandings of any kind but diplomacy shall proceed always frankly and in the public view.' Point V required 'A free, open-minded, and absolutely impartial adjustment of all colonial claims, based upon a strict observance of the principle that in determining all such questions of sovereignty the interests of the populations concerned must have equal weight with the equitable claims of the government whose title is to be determined.' Point XII argued that 'The Turkish portions of the present Ottoman Empire should be assured a secure sovereignty, but the other nationalities which are now under Turkish rule should be assured an undoubted security of life and an absolutely unmolested opportunity of autonomous development'.

2. Sir F. R. Wingate to A. J. Balfour, dispatch 90, 7.5.1918. FO 371/3380 fos. 558-9. Wingate also commented: 'It seems to me not improbable that the submission of this address at the present juncture, when the Allied military situation appears unfavourable and enemy propaganda against our aims in the Arab districts is active, has a special significance'.

3. Foreign Office London to Sir F. R. Wingate, telegram 753, 11.6.1918. FO 371/3381 fo. 27.

4. *Ibid.* fos. 27-8. British officials could argue that the promises relating to areas in the second category ('areas emancipated . . . by the action of the Arabs themselves during the present war') did not apply to Syria and Lebanon, as at the time the declaration was issued these territories clearly came into the *fourth* category ('areas still under Turkish control'). Hence the phrase 'during the present war' could only mean 'during the war up to the issue of the declaration'.

   The early draft of this document in FO 371/3380 (fos. 571-2) suggests that this ambiguity was deliberate, and not the result of incompetence.

5. Sir F. R. Wingate to Foreign Office, telegram 948, 16.6.1918. FO 371/3381 fos. 7-8. Wingate's proposed reply was discussed at a meeting of the Eastern Committee on 18.6.1918. The chairman, Lord Curzon, thought that 'what they wished to tell the King was that the old Agreement no longer applied; but before definitely stating so we should have to consult the French.' Sykes suggested that Hussein could be told at once that 'so far as we were concerned' the Agreement was dead, 'subject to the concurrence of the French.' (Minutes of the Eastern Committee, 18.6.1918, CAB 27/24 p.2.) For the Foreign Office reply to Wingate on this matter see telegram 797, 21.6.1918, FO 371/3381.

6. See Sir F. R. Wingate to A. J. Balfour, dispatch 127, 25.6.1918. The paraphrase of Hogarth's remarks given in this dispatch suggests that when presenting the declaration to the Syrians he avoided the ambiguous phrase about areas liberated by the Arabs 'during the present war'. He may have felt it wise to use a more cautious (and less deceptive) form of words because of the Foreign Office telegram of 21.6.1918 to Wingate (see note 5 above). This told Wingate that the Sykes-Picot Agreement could not be regarded as truly dead unless and until the French concurred.

   If, however, Hogarth did adjust the phrasing of the declaration, this does not seem to have had any effect on the sense in which it was understood by the Arabs or the majority of British officials who knew about it (see for example Allenby's interpretation, quoted on p. 570).

7. Sir F. R. Wingate to Foreign Office London, telegram 1055, 9.7.1918, citing information sent to him by C. E. Wilson.

8. *AB* No. 95, 2.7.1918, p. 229. In *Seven Pillars* (ch. XCVII p. 534) Lawrence makes no allusion to the ibn Saud problem, and implies that Hussein's refusal to send troops north was merely capricious. His own report to the Arab Bureau (reference in note 11 below) shows that he understood the true situation.

9. T. E. Lawrence to Sherif Hussein 25.6.1918 (translation) *MB* pp. 147-8, Bodleian R. The original document is the only known example of a letter in Arabic written by Lawrence.

10. *Ibid MB* pp. 148-9. Lawrence's letter concludes: 'I beg you, Sir, to burn this letter after reading it, because I am writing to you about matters which I should have disclosed orally.'

11. See *AB* No. 96, 9.7.1918, pp. 245-6.

12. Lawrence seems to have formed the impression that the Allied and Turkish forces were approximately equal in strength. See, for example, *Seven Pillars*, introduction to Book IX, p. 536. This was incorrect: at this time the Turks were far inferior in numbers and badly demoralised. See A. P. Wavell, *The Palestine Campaigns* (London, Constable, 1928) p. 193, 195: 'General Allenby . . . had a superiority of about two to one in total forces.'

13. T. E. Lawrence, *SP*(O) ch. 111.
14. T. E. Lawrence to his family 15.7.1918 *HL* p. 350; MB p.152. Bodleian MS Res C13.
15. T. E. Lawrence to his family 24.9.1917, *HL* p. 341; MB p. 123. Bodleian MS Res C13.
16. T. E. Lawrence to V. W. Richards 15.7.1918 *DG* pp. 244-6; *MB* p. 149-51.
17. A. G. C. Dawnay to P. C. Joyce 15.7.1918. Akaba Archive, Akaba/I M29, KCL.
18. W. H. Bartholomew to Sir E. H. H. Allenby 15.7.1918. WO 158/639B. A corrected version of Dawnay's memorandum on the Camel Corps plan was sent to GHQ on 17.7.1918. This was filed in place of the original manuscript copy, submitted a few days earlier, which was apparently destroyed. See A. G. C. Dawnay to General Staff, General Headquarters, 17.7.1918 and enclosure dated 16.7.1918.
19. T. E. Lawrence, *SP* ch. XCVIII p. 539.
20. A. G. C. Dawnay to P. C. Joyce, 3.7.1918. Akaba Archive, Akaba I M12, KCL.
21. A. G. C. Dawnay to P. C. Joyce, 12.6.1918. Akaba Archive, Akaba/I M/26, KCL. In his book *The Independent Arab* (London, John Murray, 1933, p. 195), Young gives the impression that this new role was his own idea.
22. *Ibid.*
23. See H. W. Young, *op. cit.* note 21 above, pp. 195-7.
24. A. G. C. Dawnay to P. C. Joyce, 3.7.1918. Akaba Archive, Akaba I M/28, KCL. A covering letter for the orders of the same date, to be found in Akaba Archive, Akaba I M12.

    For Stirling's views on Young see *Safety Last* (London, Hollis & Carter, 1961, p. 80): 'He was a strong man, clever in an intellectual sense and practically able but terribly touchy. For many months I was the only person in the force with whom he did not quarrel'.

    Although Lawrence frequently disagreed with Young about military strategy and tactics in Syria, he admired his ability. Years later, when Liddell Hart suggested that Young was mediocre, Lawrence firmly denied it (see *B:LH* p. 149).
25. P. C. Joyce to A. G. C. Dawnay 20.6.1918. Akaba Archive, Akaba I H/82, KCL.
26. A. G. C. Dawnay to P. C. Joyce 3.7.1918. Akaba Archive, Akaba I M/28, KCL.
27. A. G. C. Dawnay to P. C. Joyce 15.7.1918. Akaba Archive, Akaba I M/29, KCL.
28. *Ibid.*
29. See *B:LH* p. 115: 'we did not use W/T for "operation" messages. Allenby every morning for breakfast had the log of Turkish signals over the preceding 24 hours: we read their every message – and I presumed they read all of ours. To keep our moves secret we used air-mail or word of mouth. To keep the Turks' public, one of my cares was to distribute wire-cutters over their rear, and cut their telegraph at least daily.'
30. H. W. Young: *op. cit.* n. 21 above. For the final version of Young's detailed transport plans see P. C. Joyce (Lt-Col O.C. Northern Hejaz Troops) to General Staff, Hejaz Operations 23.7.1918. Young papers 6/1, KCL. The plan was submitted to Cairo in this form, but it seems there had also been an earlier version which Lawrence refers to in *Seven Pillars* (ch. XCVIII p. 539). Lawrence and Dawnay had set aside this earlier scheme when drawing up the new Deraa plan in Egypt.
31. P. C. Joyce (Commandant Akaba) to A. G. C. Dawnay (Hedgehog Cairo), telegram 29301, 1.8.1918. Young papers 14, KCL.
32. T. E. Lawrence, *SP* ch XCV p. 529. Comments made by Lawrence in *Seven Pillars*

and by Young in *The Independent Arab* (*op. cit.* note 21 above) have led many people to suppose that they did not like one another. This is untrue: Lawrence brought Young into the Colonial Office in 1921, and they subsequently corresponded on friendly terms until Lawrence's death. Young sent a page proof of *The Independent Arab* to Lawrence, and adopted many of Lawrence's corrections and suggestions, even though it must have been very costly to make changes at such a late stage in the book's production.

33. Sir T. B. M. Sykes, memorandum, 3.7.1918. FO 371/3381 fo. 21.
34. *Ibid.*
35. 'Paper B' enclosed with the above. FO 371/3381 fo. 26.
36. F. Georges-Picot, note for Sir T. B. M. Sykes 30.6.1918 (author's translation). FO 371/3383 fo. 477.
37. Sir H. H. Wilson to Sir E. H. H. Allenby, draft telegram dated 21.7.1918, FO 371/3383 fo. 433.
38. Sir E. H. H. Allenby to Sir H. H. Wilson 26.7.1918. FO 882/17 fo. 105.
39. See Minutes of a Meeting of the Eastern Committee, 8.8.1918. FO 371/3381 fo. 45 and Appendix fo. 46v. The idea of an Anglo-French declaration originated in the drafts which Sykes presented to Georges-Picot in late June 1918 (see p. 532). The content and wording of the declaration were discussed on various occasions during the summer and autumn of 1918. For Hogarth's views see his letter to Lord Robert Cecil of 18.8.1918, and the draft enclosed (FO371/3381 fos. 99-100. Note, however, that the alterations to the draft here are not in Hogarth's handwriting). The French Ambassador agreed to the idea of a declaration at a meeting chaired by Cecil on 30.9.18, the day an Arab Government was declared in Damascus. For the text of the declaration finally issued on November 9th 1918 see chapter 27 p. 581.
40. *Ibid* fo. 45.
41. *Ibid.*
42. *Ibid.*
43. R. V. Buxton to an unidentified recipient, letter in the form of a diary, entry dated 4.8.1918. Typescript copy in author's possession.
44. T. E. Lawrence, *SP(O)* ch. 113.
45. T. E. Lawrence, comment on the typescript of *Lawrence and the Arabs* by R. R. Graves, 1927, *B:RG* p.103.
46. T. E. Lawrence, *SP* ch. XCIX p. 545.
47. *Ibid.* p. 546.
48. *Ibid.* ch. CI, p. 555.
49. *Ibid.* p. 553-4.
50. T. E. Lawrence, *SP(O)* ch. 115.
51. Thirty-five Turks were killed and 120 captured. See Buxton's brief report in Akaba to Hedgehog, telegram, 8.8.1918. The casualty figures Lawrence gives in *SP* ch. CI p. 553 are incorrect.
52. R. V. Buxton to an unidentified recipient, letter in the form of a diary, entry dated 16.8.1918. Typescript copy in the author's possession.
53. *Ibid.*
54. See *SP* ch. CIII. Lawrence does not mention that he was ill at the time.
55. R. V. Buxton to an unidentified recipient, letter in the form of a diary, dated 23.8.1918. Typescript copy in author's possession.
56. *Ibid*, entry dated 24.8.1918.

57. A translation of the *Qibla* statement is given in *AB* No. 104, 24.9.1918, p.333.
58. T. E. Lawrence, *SP*(O) ch 121.
59. R. V. Buxton to an unidentified recipient, letter in the form of a diary, entry dated 26.8.1918 (but these sentences clearly written a few days later). Typescript copy in author's possession.
60. Message from T. E. Lawrence forwarded in Commandant Akaba to Hedgehog Cairo, telegram 518, 30.8.1918. FO 882/13 fo. 121.
61. T. E. Lawrence *SP*(O) ch. 121.
62. P. C. Joyce (Akaba) to J. R. Bassett (Jeddah), telegram 74, 3.9.1918. FO 686/52.
63. T. E. Lawrence, *SP* ch. CV1 p. 579. The message in question is probably the one translated in J. R. Bassett to Arbur, telegram W737, 4.9.1918. FO 686/52. This begins with a curious 'apology' which was presumably meant to be sarcastic: 'I declare . . . that the fault and crime are mine, because I have given certain orders to my son which he has not thought proper, and perhaps my orders to him were such as I had no right to give or . . . contrary to the general interest.' However, Hussein then went on to state his desire to 'purify the post of Chief Command from appearing to be a fraud in the eyes of the Govt. and the world, owing to Jaafar arrogating to himself the title of C.-in-C.'
64. Message from P. C. Joyce in Commandant Akaba to Hedghog Cairo, 7.9.1918. WO 157/738.

Chapter 26. A Hollow Triumph

September – October 1918

1. T. E. Lawrence, *SP*(O) ch. 122.
2. T. E. Lawrence, 'The Destruction of the 4th Army', undated but published in *AB* No. 106, 22.10.1918. FO 882/7 fo. 352.
3. T. E. Lawrence, *SP* ch. CVII, p. 586.
4. T. E. Lawrence, *SP*, epilogue.
5. T. E. Lawrence, *SP*, first stanza of the dedicatory poem.
6. T. E. Lawrence to G. J. Kidston, undated but 1919. *MB* p. 169. Bodleian R (transcript).
7. *Ibid.*
8. T. E. Lawrence, written answer to a question by B. H. Liddell Hart, 3.9.1933 *B:LH* p. 169. See also *B:LH* p. 156.
9. T. E. Lawrence to F. el Akle 3.1.1921. Bodleian R (photocopy of original).
10. Hogarth was in London for much of the late summer of 1918. If he visited the British Museum to discuss the Carchemish site he may have learned of Dahoum's death then.
11. T. E. Lawrence to C. F. Shaw 17.6.1928. BL Add. MS 45904.
12. T. E. Lawrence, *SP*, final stanza of the dedicatory poem.
13. A. G. C. Dawnay to General Staff GHQ (BGGS) 1.9.1918. WO 157/738.
14. T. E. Lawrence, *op. cit.* note 2 above, fo. 353. Lawrence later described the 'very careful and elaborate' measures used to deceive the Turks at this time in a written note for Liddell Hart (see *B:LH* pp. 119-20). The bluff had an immediate effect: in early September the Turks began to concentrate forces at Hesa and sent two columns into the Tafileh region. Lawrence was delighted by this news, as any activity in this area would detract from the Turkish strength farther north.

15. T. E. Lawrence, *op. cit.* note 2 above, fo. 352.
16. For details, see 'War Diary of Hejaz Armoured Car Battery on Operations, Sept 9th to Oct 30th 1918', entry for 14.9.1918. WO 95/4415.
17. T. E. Lawrence, *op. cit.* note 2 above, fo. 354.

    In *Seven Pillars* (ch. CVIII) Lawrence wrongly states that this action took place on 15.9.1918 (the last book of *SP* contains several small errors of this kind). For the correct dates see 'War Diary of Hejaz Armoured Car Battery on Operations, Sept 9th to Oct 30th 1918'. WO 95/4415; also W. F. Stirling 'Outline of Operations, Northern Hedjaz Army' *c.* 19.9.1918. WO 157/738.
18. T. E. Lawrence, *SP* ch. CIX p. 593.
19. 'War Diary of the Hejaz Armoured Car Battery on Operations, Sept 9th to Oct 30th' notes under the date 17.9.1918: 'During these operations, the only offensive the enemy could take was through the air, which he did vigorously, having no less than nine bombing planes in the air at the same time during the greater part of the day. Casualties, however, were few' (WO 95/4415).

    Of the two fighter aircraft allocated to the Arab operations, one had already been damaged and declared unfit for further service. The other, piloted by Lieutenant Junor, managed to dispel much of the immediate air threat by engaging the Turkish planes in a series of spectacular dogfights. See 'Summary of Operations W/E 21.9.1918', AIR 1/1167/204/100/8 and *SP* ch. CIX.
20. T. E. Lawrence, *op. cit.* note 2 above, fo. 356. In *SP* ch. CX, Lawrence incorrectly dates this action 16.9.1918: see note 17 above.

    The 'tulip' was a special technique for demolishing railway sleepers, devised by Lawrence and Peake. Lawrence explained the method in the *Arab Bulletin*: 'Dig a hole midway between the tracks under a mid-rail sleeper, and work out the ballast from the hollow section of the sleeper. Put in two slabs of guncotton, return the ballast to the hole, and light . . . The gas expansion arches the sleeper eighteen inches above the rail, draws the metals six inches towards one another, humps them three inches above the horizontal, and twists the web from the bottom inwards . . . This three-dimensional distortion of the rails is impossible to straighten and they have to be cut or scrapped' (*AB* no. 106, 22.10..1918, p. 344n.) Elsewhere, he wrote: 'The appearance of a piece of rail treated by this method is most beautiful, for the sleepers rise up in all manner of varied forms, like the early buds of tulips.' (*ETEL* p. 211.)
21. 'War Diary of Hejaz Armoured Car Battery on Operations, Sept 9th to Oct 30th 1918', entry for 19.9.1918. WO 95/4415.
22. T. E. Lawrence, *SP*(O) ch. 130.
23. 'Message from General Allenby to Emir Feisal' 20.9.1918. Young papers 19, KCL. The Arab contribution, useful as it had been, is obviously exaggerated here. Dawnay added a handwritten note for Joyce: 'Please deliver this in suitably fruity language to Feisal.'

    The RAF 'Summary of Operations Week Ending 28.9.1918' confirms that the plane from Palestine arrived on September 21st, not September 20th as stated by Lawrence in *Seven Pillars* (AIR 1/1667/204/100/8). As the sole purpose of this flight was to bring the latest news of EEF operations, there is every reason to suppose that the documents quoted on pp. 548-50 were on board. In his book *The Independent Arab* (London, John Murray, 1933, pp. 238-9), H. W. Young states that Lawrence brought these messages with him when he returned from Palestine on

September 22nd. If so, the most likely explanation is that they had remained in his possession since the 21st, when the aeroplane brought them to Azrak. Young, who had not been at Azrak on that date, would have seen the letters for the first time when Lawrence returned with them.

24. A. G. C. Dawnay to P. C. Joyce, undated but 20.9.1918. Akaba Archive M11, KCL.
25. *Ibid.*
26. *Ibid.*
27. W. H. Bartholomew (Major-General, Chief of the General Staff, Egyptian Expeditionary Force) to P. C. Joyce 21.9.1918. WO 157/738.
28. T. E. Lawrence, *Revolt in the Desert* (London, Jonathan Cape, 1927) pp. 392-3. In his account of this incident, written specially for the 1927 abridgement, Lawrence confused Wadi Fara with another valley some forty miles farther north.
29. T. E. Lawrence, *SP* ch. CXIII p. 615.
30. Minutes of a meeting of the War Cabinet held on 20.9.1918. CAB 23/7 fo. 118.
31. *Evening Standard*, London, 25.9.1918.
32. Censorship and Press Committee Notice 26.9.1918. IWM. See also minutes of a meeting of the War Cabinet held on 25.9.1918. CAB 23/7, fo. 125.
33. A. J. Balfour to Lord Derby [British Ambassador in Paris], telegram 805, 23.9.1918. FO 371/3383 fo. 482.
34. A. J. Balfour, statement handed to P. Cambon on 23.9.1918. Repeated in the telegram cited in note 33 above.
35. Foreign Office London to Lord Derby [British Ambassador in Paris], telegram 2015, 25.9.1918. FO 371/3383 fo. 489. Repeated in Sir H. H. Wilson (CIGS) to Sir E. H. H. Allenby (GOC-in-C Egypt), undated but probably 25.9.1918. FO 371/3383 fo. 498.
36. T. E. Lawrence to General Staff, GHQ, 24.9.1918. WO 157/738. Both this telegram and the one quoted on pp. 554-5 suggest that the Arab move to Sheikh Saad was designed to prevent the Turks leaving Deraa before the British cavalry arrived. However, in statements after the event Lawrence claimed that he was hoping for a more dramatic outcome. In a report written a few weeks later he stated: 'It seemed to us . . . that we might now venture to put ourselves between Deraa and Damascus . . . so as to force the immediate evacuation of the former' (T. E. Lawrence, *op. cit.* note 2 above, fo. 358). The same motive is given in *Seven Pillars*: 'Our new endeavour should be to force the quick evacuation of Deraa, in order to prevent the Turks there reforming the fugitives into a rearguard.' (*SP* ch. CXV p. 622).

There are two possible explanations for the discrepancy. One is that Lawrence's later statements were politically motivated. As the move against the railway led, in the event, to a Turkish evacuation of Deraa, he may have decided to represent this as part of a deliberate plan. In this way, the Arab contribution to the advance on Damascus might appear enhanced. Alternatively, it is possible that Lawrence was indeed hoping to bring about an evacuation, but neglected to mention this to GHQ. Allenby and his staff had warned against independent action by the Arabs, and had they known of the real intention behind Lawrence's move they might have ordered him to wait.

In reality, the discrepancy between these stated objectives – containing Deraa or provoking a panic evacuation – is not so great as at first appears. The real aim of the Arab move to Sheikh Saad was a negative one: to prevent the Turks from making an orderly evacuation by rail. Lawrence's plan would certainly have this effect, but he could not tell which of the alternative courses the Turks would choose. He must have known that a complete evacuation by road was one possibility, but he could hardly have counted on this result.

37. T. E. Lawrence to A. G. C. Dawnay 25.9.1918. WO 157/738. The move to Sheikh Saad was strongly opposed by Young. He argued that the Arabs had done everything Allenby had asked, and this new move into the path of the enemy's retreat might be extremely dangerous for the regulars: 'our tiny force would be in the position of the hunter who stands in the only line of escape of the driven lion, instead of waiting on a flank to shoot him as he dashes by.' (H. W. Young *op. cit.* note 23 above, p. 245). Lawrence's experience of irregular warfare led him to reject this conventional military argument. He knew that it would always be possible to fall back into the hill country if things became too dangerous.

He was also aware of political factors, about which Young knew nothing. In the draft *Seven Pillars* he wrote: 'if we withdrew to Jebel Druse, we ended our active service before the game was won, leaving the last brunt to Allenby. To be sure, he had given us the Fourth Army, and our formal "duty" was completed, but I had always been shy of this word "duty". . . . To my mind we owed no duty to anyone, though we served Allenby to the best of our ability because there lay our interest to win the war. Yet I was very jealous for the Arab honour, and for them I would go forward at all costs. They had joined the war to win their freedom, and, while, winning it was easy, the abiding resolve to keep it could be sealed only by their blood and effort . . . By thrusting behind Deraa into Sheikh Saad we . . . would forbid the Turks fighting again this side of Damascus . . . even if we all lost our lives in the business . . . such a cost would be cheap payment. By it we as good as took Damascus' (*SP*(O) ch. 132. In the published text Young is given the pseudonym 'Sabin').

Years later, Lawrence told Liddell Hart that he had rejected Young's argument because 'it threw away the chance to consolidate the terrain for which the Arabs had been fighting two years. Remember the Cairo promise, "The Arabs shall keep what they take" [i.e. the declaration to the Seven Syrians]' (*B:LH* p. 149).

38. Sir E. H. H. Allenby (Commander-in-Chief) to Sherif Feisal, transmitted in L. J. Bols to T. E. Lawrence 25.9.1918. WO 157/738.

39. Sir E. H. H. Allenby (GOC in C Egypt) to Sir H. H. Wilson (CIGS), telegram EA 1707, 30.9.1918. FO 371/3383 fo. 528.

40. 'Special Instructions' issued by General Staff Australian Mounted Division (signed by Major A. Chisholm), 29.9.1918. WO 95/4551. These instructions to troops were evidently based on orders received from Allenby some days earlier. In a subsequent report, General Chauvel, the Commander of the Desert Mounted Corps, stated that he had been given his 'final instructions for the capture of Damascus' on 26th September. ('Report by Lieutenant-General Sir H. G. Chauvel . . . on the Capture of Damascus and the arrangements made for the Civil Administration thereof' 2.10.1918. WO 95/4371.)

The last sentence quoted from the 'Special Instructions' reads in full: 'Damascus will be left under the present civil administration and no national flags will be flown.' Chauvel's subsequent actions, and his various statements, show that he took his orders to mean that he should recognise the existing Turkish administration. This is curious, since Allenby's decision to allow Feisal into Damascus, and his other statements at the time (see pp. 555-6), make his intentions clear.

Allenby's instructions to Chauvel have not been found, but events suggest that they were not explicit on the question of recognising Arab as opposed to other forms of government. Allenby and his advisers may have felt that direct orders to this effect could not be given until further guidance came from London. As it happened, a letter telling Allenby to recognise Arab governments wherever possible had already been drafted at the Foreign Office, but had not been sent because of the need to consult the French (see note 74 below).

In the circumstances, it seems likely that the instructions issued to Chauvel on 26.9.1918 were limited to a general statement that he should recognise whatever arrangements he found in being. Having given Feisal permission to advance to Damascus and taken steps to prevent Allied forces entering the city before him, Allenby could safely assume that the result would be an Arab administration.

In this connection note also remarks in *Seven Pillars* about General Barrow, who was also at the corps commanders' meeting of 26.9.1918. Lawrence wrote: 'he had no orders at all to the status of the Arabs. Clayton did us this service, thinking we should deserve what we should assert' (*SP* ch. CXVII p. 636).

41. See T. E. Lawrence, *op. cit.* note 2 above, fo. 358.
42. *Ibid* fos. 359-60.
43. *Ibid* fo. 361.
44. Lord Birdwood, *Nuri as-Said* (London, Cassell, 1959) p. 85.
45. W. J. Childs to S. Gaselee 20.4.1926. FO 370/215 fo. 185. It might be argued that Lawrence was here referring obliquely to his knowledge of Feisal's secret correspondence with Kemal, and not to an actual meeting. However, Lawrence's account of his discussions with Kemal refers in some detail to matters which were unlikely to have arisen in the letters. One might doubt that such a meeting occurred *if* the movements of the two men made it seem improbable: but this is not the case. It is significant that Childs's letter should refer specifically to 'September 1918', the one period when they could easily have met.
46. *Ibid* fo. 185v. The account ends: 'Mustapha Kemal . . . told Colonel Lawrence that at the beginning of 1918 he had become the leading spirit of those Pan-Turks who put pressure on Enver Pasha and required that Turkish interests must come before German. By this time Mustapha Kemal's following had grown so powerful that the party was able to dictate the broad lines of Turkish military policy. It insisted that immediate steps should be taken to realize Pan-Turkish aspirations in the East. Mustapha Kemal asserted that at this stage it was plain to him and his supporters that Germany would lose the war: they demanded therefore that Turkey's remaining military resources should be devoted to exploiting Pan-Turkish aims. They required the concentration of 100,000 Turkish troops in Trans-Caucasia and North Western Persia. Mustapha Pasha told Colonel Lawrence that he had declared at the time that if 100,000 Turkish troops were in the Caspian regions when Germany collapsed the exhausted Entente Powers would find it impossible to eject them. The Powers might hold Turkey in Europe and Constantinople and the Straits, but they could not in practice overrun Anatolia nor maintain themselves there. With 100,000 Turkish troops in Trans-Caucasia the Turks would speedily reach Trans-Caspia and once they were in Central Asia he saw no limits to the possibilities which would offer. A Turkish army could appear on the frontier of Afghanistan; it could reach Eastern Turkestan and Mongolia if desired. In Mustapha Kemal's opinion a Turkish army at large in Central Asia would have everything its own way, and secure for Turkey

territorial gains far outweighing any losses which might occur in the West.

'This plan, Mustapha Kemal explained, Enver Pasha had at last been compelled to adopt and put into execution, in spite of German opposition. But the Turkish troops concentrated for the purpose had never reached the numbers required, nor was the policy adopted in time' (fos. 186-7).

47. See H. E. Wortham, *Mustapha Kemal of Turkey* (London, The Holme Press, 1930) p. 67.

48. T. E. Lawrence, *SP* ch. CXVII p. 634.

49. T. E. Lawrence, comment on the typescript of LH:*TEL*, 1933, *B:LH* p. 152.

50. Sir G. de S. Barrow, *The Fire of Life* (London, Hutchinson, n.d. but 1941) p. 211. In *Seven Pillars* (ch. CXVII) Lawrence accused Barrow of treating the Arabs as 'a conquered people', and wanting to impose order in a heavy-handed manner. Barrow's account of the station incident, and of the Deraa situation generally, is plainly a riposte to these accusations. The former he described as 'a revolting scene . . . far exceeding in its savagery anything that has been known in the conflicts between nations during the past 120 years and happily rare even in earlier times.' According to Barrow, Lawrence refused to intervene on the grounds that this was the Arab 'idea of war'.

Although no one else who was there at the time has mentioned the incident, a contemporary document bears out some of the details in Barrow's account. A War Diary entry for Sept 28th records: 'Deraa was evacuated during the night by the enemy, who had burned most of the railway buildings and some portion of the material and rolling stock. Deraa was found to be in a state of great confusion, numbers of enemy wounded and exhausted men were lying in the station and in railway trucks. Regular Sherifian forces in small numbers and a considerable number of irregulars and bedouins were in the town and railway junction.' (War Diary, General Staff 4th Cavalry Division, Volume III. WO 95/4510.)

Barrow was clearly galled by Lawrence's jeering account of their meetings in *Seven Pillars*. In his own book he denies that these conversations took place in any form at all (see pp. 209, 210-11, 214-5) and accuses Lawrence of wholesale invention. However, two of the meetings he denies are recorded by another witness, Frank Stirling, in terms similar to Lawrence's (see W. F. Stirling, *Safety Last*; London, Hollis and Carter, 1953; p. 92).

On one point Barrow was definitely entitled to protest at Lawrence's account. *Seven Pillars* (ch. CXVII p. 635) complains that Barrow and his troops delayed unnecessarily at Remthe on the way to Deraa. Contemporary war diaries show that this charge is without foundation.

51. T. E. Lawrence, *SP*(O) ch. 135.

52. T. E. Lawrence to W. F. Stirling 15.10.1924 *MB* p. 275. See also *B:LH* p. 153.

53. War Diary, General Staff 4th Cavalry Division, Volume IV, 1.10.1918. WO 95/4510.

54. T. E. Lawrence, *op. cit.* note 2 above, fo. 363. Lawrence's remarks show that he did not realise that one column had in fact escaped from the Arabs.

55. T. E. Lawrence, *SP* ch. CXIX p. 643.

56. T. E. Lawrence, *SP*(O) ch. 136. This acknowledgement that the Australians had been ordered to stay outside Damascus does not appear in the final text. In his essay 'The Capture of Damascus, 1 October 1918' (*The Chatham House Version*, London, Weidenfeld and Nicolson, 1970), E. Kedourie makes much of the decision

to prevent the Australians from entering the city first, implying that this invalidates the whole idea that Damascus was the climax of the Arab campaign. He does not mention the fact that on 20.9.1918 the Arabs had been ordered not to go to Damascus (for political and military reasons) when they were certainly in a position to do so. In essence, the later order to the Australians was a compensation for this. Although Kedourie's essay is sometimes described as 'definitive', it was written before most of the Government papers became available.

57. W. F. Stirling, *op. cit.* note 50 above, p. 94.
58. T. E. Lawrence to General Staff, GHQ, 1.10.1918 *MB* pp. 154-5. WO 157/738.
59. See T. E. Lawrence, *op. cit.* note 2 above, fo. 364. Lawrence had met Ali Riza on his ride to Damascus in June 1917.
60. In 1919 Lawrence wrote a report on the Algerian brothers which makes it clear why he acted as he did: 'These brothers . . . were judged insane in 1911, but escaped detention in asylums by free use of their wealth. Mohammed Said holds a world's record for three successive fatal pistol accidents. He accompanied the [German] propaganda mission of Frobenius to the Red Sea for the Sudan in 1915, but turned back . . . as Frobenius did not treat him with sufficient dignity. He was then removed to Brusa with his brothers, and kept under loose surveillance. The Ottoman Government soon decided that they might be useful, and Abd el Kadir offered to run a counter Sherifian propaganda . . . against the British in Egypt. He was accordingly released from Brusa and sent down to Damascus. Thence he made a sham escape to Feisal'.

After describing Abd el Kader's treacherous role in the Yarmuk expedition, Lawrence continued with a history of the brothers' activities in 1918. In the spring of that year, 'Mohhammed Said . . . came across to Feisal with false friendly letters from Jemal in answer to some Feisal had sent to him with my approval. Just before he came Ali Riza [Rikabi] sent a note to Feisal to say that Mohhammed Said was coming to make anti-Arab propaganda among the officers of the Arab army. So we isolated him, and in disgust he only stayed two days in the camp.

'Abd el Kadir now became Jemal's confidential adviser on Arab questions and raised volunteers for him. These fought the British on the first and second Amman raids, and did well for the Turks.

'When . . . Feisal's flying column attacked the Deraa district, Abd el Kadir at once transferred his volunteers to the Hauran, and garrisoned the railway against us. We captured a lot of them [at Ezraa on September 26th], and they told us of all his efforts against us. When the Turkish débâcle came, Abd el Kadir ran away quickly to Damascus, and, as soon as the Turks had gone, took forcible control of the local government, in virtue of the remains of his Algerian volunteers . . . If ever two people deserved hanging or shooting in Syria, they were these two brothers' (T. E. Lawrence to W. F. Stirling [DCPO] 28.6.1919 *MB* pp. 165-6).

61. T. E. Lawrence, *op. cit.* note 2 above, fos. 363-4.
62. T. E. Lawrence to W. F. Stirling (Deputy Chief Political Officer) 28.6.1918 *MB* p. 166.
63. 'Report by Lieutenant-General Sir H. G. Chauvel . . . on the Capture of Damascus, and the arrangements made for the Civil Administration thereof' 2.10.1918. WO 95/4371.
64. T. E. Lawrence to General Staff, GHQ, 1.10.1918 *MB* p. 155. WO 157/738.
65. Australian war diaries show that the 3rd Light Horse Brigade passed through the

north of Damascus at about 6 a.m. on October 1st (WO 95/4551). The senior officer present dismounted at the Town Hall and took what he understood to be the 'surrender' of Damascus from Mohamed Said. This took place an hour or two before Sherif Nasir made his formal entry.

When Lawrence discovered what had happened, he must have been very annoyed. These events might be used by political opponents to undermine Arab claims to self-government in Damascus. In the draft *Seven Pillars* he wrote: 'These sporting Australians saw the campaign as a point-to-point with Damascus as the post which the best horse would pass first. We saw it as a serious military operation, in which any unordered priority would be a meaningless or discreditable distinction. We were all under Allenby, and Damascus was the fruit of his genius'(*SP*(O) ch. 136). Irritation over this matter helps to explain his bad relationship with Chauvel and his disparaging treatment of the Australians in *Seven Pillars*.

Lawrence did not mention in *Seven Pillars* that Australian troops were in Damascus before the Arabs made their triumphal entry (or that, by arrangement with Allenby, they were supposed to give the Arabs precedence). He admitted to Robert Graves: 'I was on thin ice when I wrote the Damascus chapter . . . *S.P.* is full of half-truth, here' (*B:RG* p. 104). This was almost certainly a tactical error: on the basis of these omissions, detractors such as E. Kedourie have claimed that his whole account is discredited.

66. Until he met Lawrence for the second time Chauvel regarded Damascus as an enemy city which had surrendered to his men: this is surely the real significance of the misunderstandings about the 'vali'. He now learned that, by the time his troops went in, all Turkish officials had left and had been replaced by a form of Arab administration. This would seem to have invalidated the 'surrender' accepted by his forces from Mohammed Said. He also learned that at least some Arab irregulars had entered the city the night before his own men did (though Lawrence's figure of four thousand, in *SP* ch. CXIX, p. 644 may be exaggerated). The entry of these Arabs is apparent from Lawrence's report of 1st October, which Chauvel now read for the first time. (i.e. T. E. Lawrence to General Staff, GHQ, 1.10.1918. WO 157/738 *MB* p. 155.)

Chauvel cared passionately about the honour of being 'first in' to Damascus. The day after meeting Lawrence, he submitted a report stating that his troops had entered the city on the 'evening' of September 30th – i.e. before any Arab irregulars had gone in. ('Report by Lieutenant-General Sir H. G. Chauvel . . . on the Capture of Damascus, and the arrangements made for the Civil Administration thereof' 2.10.1918. WO 95/4371). This claim is not borne out by the war diaries. When the *Palestine News* of 10.10.1918 published an unsigned article by Lawrence stating that Arab troops had been first into Damascus, Chauvel protested vehemently: 'In order to avoid the risk of any such misrepresentation being handed down to history, I, as General Officer Commanding the troops that captured Damascus from the Turko-German forces, hereby definitely state that no Arab troops entered the city of Damascus until after Australian, British and Indian troops had moved right through it and all organised enemy forces had either been killed captured or dispersed.' (Sir H. G. Chauvel to CGS, General Headquarters, EEF 23.10.1918. WO 95/4371.)

Chauvel's post-war accounts continue to harp on this point, and on the claim that Damascus was 'definitely *surrendered*' to his troops. He must have been deeply resentful of the popular impression, created by Lowell Thomas, that Damascus had been captured by Lawrence. As commander of the disastrous second trans-Jordan raid (see p. 499-500) he had particular reason to regard the Arabs as undeserving.

67. T. E. Lawrence, *SP*(O) ch. 137.

68. T. E. Lawrence to General Staff, GHQ, 1.10.1918 *MB* p. 155. WO 157/738.

69. T. E. Lawrence *SP* ch. CXX p. 651.

70. G. F. Clayton to Foreign Office London, telegram C1, 8.10.1918. Wingate papers 150/2/8, Durham.

71. Although there had been sporadic looting since the early morning of October 1st, the situation appears to have become more serious that afternoon. According to EEF war diaries, Colonel Bourchier, the officer in charge of the remaining Allied troops in Damascus 'was forced, in the interests of discipline, and on account of the extraordinary noise and apparent unrest in Damascus to place guards on many of the public institutions, consulates, hospitals, etc.' (WO 95/4351).

It seems that the Algerian brothers hoped to turn the escalating public disorder to political ends. This is the aspect of the situation which Lawrence emphasised in his accounts. Some days after the event he wrote that in the evening of October 1st: 'Abd el-Kadir called together his friends and some leading Druses, and made them an impassioned speech, denouncing the Sherif as a British puppet, and calling on them to strike a blow for the Faith in Damascus. By morning this had degenerated into pure looting, and we called out the Arab troops, put Hotchkiss round the central square, and imposed peace in three hours, after inflicting about twenty casualties.

'The part played by the Druses was an ignoble one . . . They hung round behind our horse, never entering the fight, and waited till Damascus was taken. They then paraded before the Sherif [Nasir], and began to loot the inhabitants . . . the Arabs checked them at this and drove them out of the town' (T. E. Lawrence, *op. cit.* note 2 above, fo. 364. See also G. F. Clayton to Foreign Office London, telegram C1, 8.10.1918, Wingate papers 150/2/8-9, Durham.)

In *Seven Pillars* Lawrence wrote: 'When things began I had called up Chauvel, who at once offered his troops. I thanked him, and asked that a second company of horse be drafted to the Turkish barracks [Bourchier's headquarters] . . . to stand by against call: but the fighting was too petty for that call.' (*SP* ch. CXXI p. 653) Entries in the war diaries of Bourchier's force for October 2nd suggest that this is correct. The following day Allenby wrote to his wife: 'The town is quiet now, but there was a little pillaging and shooting . . . quickly repressed by Lawrence' (to Lady Allenby, 3.10.1918, wrongly dated 3.9.1918. Allenby papers, St Antony's College Oxford.)

72. G. F. Clayton to Foreign Office London, telegram 80, 7.10.1918. FO 371/3383 fo. 608.

73. T. E. Lawrence, *SP* ch. CXXII p. 658.

74. War Office to General Headquarters, Egypt, telegram 67558, 1.10.1918. WO 37/960. This repeats a message from the Foreign Office to the Director of Military Intelligence dated 24.9.1918 (FO 371/3383). French approval had to be sought before these instructions could be passed on to Allenby.

75. *Ibid.*

76. *Ibid.*

77. T. E. Lawrence, *SP* ch. CXXII p. 660.

78. I have quoted the version of Chauvel's account given to the Director of the Australian War memorial in 1936. His statement exists in several slightly different

forms, the earliest of which seems to date from 1923 (see A. J. Hill, *Chauvel of the Light Horse*, Melbourne University Press, 1978, pp. 242-3). Although Chauvel stated that his later accounts were 'copies' of notes he made at the time, these notes have apparently not been found. It is therefore misleading for Hill to hold up 'Chauvel's unadorned contemporary recital of the events' as a corrective to *Seven Pillars* (p. 185). In reality, the 1922 text of *Seven Pillars* (*SP*(O)) was written earlier than the first of Chauvel's known accounts.

For some of the problems of Chauvel's account see notes 79 and 81 below.

79. Sir H. G. Chauvel, statement given to the Director of the Australian War Memorial, 1936. Chauvel's account of the meeting concludes: 'Lawrence told the Chief that he would not work with a French Liaison Officer and that he . . . had better . . . go off to England. The Chief said: "Yes! I think you had!", and Lawrence left the room.

'I thought the Chief had been a little hard on Lawrence and told him so. He said, "Very well, send him down to my Headquarters and tell him I will write to Clive Wigram [Assistant Private Secretary to George V] about him, asking him to arrange for an audience with the King. I will also give him a letter to the Foreign Office in order that he might explain the Arab point of view." General Allenby then left by car for Tiberias.'

Chauvel implies that Lawrence left Damascus in a fit of pique because he failed to get his way at this interview. In reality, Lawrence had expressed a wish to leave Damascus two days earlier (see p. 564). Liddell Hart later recorded Lawrence's emphatic denial that there had been any unpleasantness with Allenby at the meeting: 'Definitely no. Had the greatest difficulty in persuading Allenby to let him go – wanted him to go on to Aleppo – "nice as pie".' (*B:LH* p. 128.) No letters from Allenby of the kind Chauvel describes have been found, either in Foreign Office papers or the Royal Archives at Windsor.

80. If Allenby did ask Lawrence the questions Chauvel reports (see p. 567), then they *were* presumably intended to find out what Lawrence had told Feisal about Sykes-Picot. Lawrence may have sidestepped this difficult topic by answering as though the questions referred only to the latest administrative arrangements, of which he knew nothing.

81. The final pages of Chauvel's statement (not quoted here) show that his account of the 3rd October meeting was written in the light of difficulties which arose over the Lebanon shortly afterwards (see pp. 569-71). His statement makes it clear that he held Feisal and Lawrence responsible for these events, and this belief may well have affected the words he ascribes to them here.

According to Chauvel, the meeting ended when 'the Chief told Feisal that . . . he must accept the situation until the whole matter was settled at the conclusion of the war. Feisal accepted this decision and left with his entourage'. This actually seems to refer to the agreement over the Lebanon reached some weeks later (see p. 571).

Chapter 27. The View from Europe

October 1918 – January 1919

1. T. E. Lawrence to W. Yale 22.10.1929 *DG* pp. 670-1.
2. E. H. H. Allenby (GOC-in-C) to War Office, London, telegram P695, 6.10.1918. FO 371/3383 fo 557.

3. G. F. Clayton to Foreign Office, London, telegram 80, 7.10.1918. FO 371/3383 fos. 607-8.
4. This press release was transmitted to London in G. F. Clayton to Foreign Office London, telegram 98, 8.10.1918. FO 371/3383 fos. 567-74.
5. G. F. Clayton to Sir F. R. Wingate 11.10.1918. Wingate papers W150/2/80-81, Durham.
6. G. F. Clayton to Foreign Office, London, telegram 115, 12.10.1918. FO 371/3384 fo. 27.
7. E. H. H. Allenby (GOC-in-C) to War Office, London, telegram EA1777, 13.10.1918. FO 371/3384 fo. 221.
8. The circumstances under which Lawrence acquired this rug are discussed in J. M. Wilson, *T. E. Lawrence* (London, National Portrait Gallery, 1988) p. 96.
9. T. E. Lawrence to R. H. Scott 14.10.1918 *DG* p. 258.
10. T. E. Lawrence to W. Yale 22.10.1929 *DG* p. 670.
11. T. E. Lawrence, written reply to a question from B. H. Liddell Hart, September 1933. *B:LH* p. 165.
12. Wingate wrote to Allenby on October 15th: 'Lawrence . . . intends to talk plainly when he gets to London – they should welcome the views of such an expert as he is, though I expect our French Allies will find them not exactly palatable' Wingate papers W150/3, Durham.
13. Lord Winterton to Lord Robert Cecil 16.10.1918. Cecil papers, BL Add. MS 51094.
14. T. E. Lawrence, note on the draft of *Lawrence and the Arabs*, 1927, *B:RG* p. 93.
15. T. E. Lawrence, written answer to a questionnaire from B. H. Liddell Hart, September 1933. *B:LH* p. 165.
16. Lord Robert Cecil: 'Memorandum', 28.10.1918. FO 371/3384 fo. 424.
17. *Ibid.*
18. Sir G. M. W. Macdonogh: 'Note on policy in the Middle East', 28.10.1918. CAB 27/35 fo. 183. At a meeting of the Eastern Committee on December 5th, Macdonogh confirmed that he had consulted Lawrence before drawing up this memorandum.
19. *Ibid*
20. T. E. Lawrence, note on the draft of *Lawrence and the Arabs*, 1927, *B:RG* p. 108.
21. Minutes of the 37th meeting of the Eastern Committee of the War Cabinet, 29.10.1918. CAB 27/24 fo. 150.
22. *Ibid*
23. *Ibid.*
24. *Ibid.* fo. 151.
25. *Ibid.*
26. T. E. Lawrence to his family 5.9.1918 *HL* p. 340. Bodleian MS Res C13.
27. Sir A. J. Stamfordham to T. E. Lawrence 17.1.1928 *LTEL* p. 186.
28. B. H. Liddell Hart, transcript of an interview with T. E. Lawrence, omitted from *B:LH*. Bodleian R (transcript).
29. *Ibid.*
30. *Ibid.*
31. See, for example, the comments by W. S. Churchill in *Friends* pp. 193-4.
32. T. E. Lawrence: 'The Reconstruction of Arabia', memorandum to the Eastern Committee of the War Cabinet *DG* pp. 268-9.
33. E. T. Leeds in *L-L* p. 116.
34. F. Georges-Picot, telegram, 14.11.1918, quoted in *HGM* p. 308 (author's

translation).

35. T. E. Lawrence to F. R. Wingate for transmission to Sherif Hussein, telegram 1340, 8.11.1918. FO 371/3384 fo. 569.

36. Anglo-French Declaration, released on 9.11.1918. Text in D. Hunter Miller, *My Diaries of the Conference of Paris* (New York, Appeal Printing, 1924) Vol. 15 pp. 507-8.

37. D. G. Hogarth: 'Memorandum on Certain Considerations of Settlement of Western Asia' 15.11.1918. CAB 27/36 fo. 142.

38. *Ibid.*

39. G. F. Clayton to Foreign Office, London, telegram 190, 18.11.1918. FO 371/3385 fos 174-5.

40. *Ibid.* fos 176-7.

41. Note [to the Foreign Office] communicated by P. Cambon 18.11.1918. FO 371/3385 fo. 163.

42. *Ibid.*

43. Sir A. Hirtzel: 'Policy in Arabia', 20.11.1918. CAB 27/37 fo. 75.

44. *Ibid.*

45. *Ibid.* fo. 76.

46. Lord Robert Cecil, minutes of the 38th meeting of the Eastern Committee of the War Cabinet, 21.11.1918. CAB 27/24 fo. 158.

47. Lord Derby, Paris, to Foreign Office London, telegram 1576, 22.11.1918. FO 371/3385 fo. 275.

48. Forwarded in E. Vicars (British Consul General Lyons) to Foreign Secretary London, telegram 25, 29.11.1918. FO 371/3418 fos. 431-2.

49. E. Vicars (British Consul General Lyons) to Foreign Secretary London, 1.12.1918. FO 371/3418 fo. 412.

50. For accounts of this episode, see *HGM* pp. 310-18, M. J-M. Larès, *T. E. Lawrence, la France et les Français* (Paris, Imprimerie Nationale, 1980) pp. 162-3 and *Annexe* 14 to the earlier edition (Lille, Service de Réproduction des Thèses, 1978) pp. 406-8, where Bertrand's report is printed in full. See also *B:LH* p. 168.

51. Report by M. Bertrand 1.12.1918, M. J-M. Larès *op. cit.* note 50 above (Lille edition) p. 408 (author's translation).

52. For information about this conversation see S. Roskill, *Hankey, Man of Secrets*, Vol. II (London, Collins, 1972) pp. 28-9 and *DBFP* I/4 pp. 340-1.

53. Lord Robert Cecil to D. Lloyd George 2.12.1918. Lloyd George papers F/6/5/52, House of Lords.

54. Eastern Committee Meetings held to establish British policy at the Peace Conference were: No. 39, 27.11.1918 (Mesopotamia); No. 40, 2.12.1918 (Caucasus and Armenia); No. 41, 5.12.1918 (Syria and Palestine); No. 42, 9.12.1918 (Syria and Palestine). These topics were also discussed at subsequent meetings.

55. Verbatim transcript of 41st meeting of the Eastern Committee of the War Cabinet, 5.12.1918. CAB 27/44 fo. 186.

56. *Ibid.* fos. 187-8.

57. Sir E. Crowe, minute, 5.12.1918. FO 371/3418 fos 406-7.

58. Lord Hardinge, undated minute, FO 371/3418 fo. 407.

59. Note from the French Embassy, London, to the Foreign Office, dated 9.12.1918 but delivered 11.12.1918. FO 371/3418 fos. 436-7.

60. A. J. Balfour, 'Memorandum', 11.12.1918. FO 406/40 p. 7.

61. C. Weizmann: 'Dr. Weizmann's interview with Emir Feisal at the Carlton Hotel, December 11th 1918. Colonel Lawrence acting as interpreter.' FO 371/3420.

62. *Ibid.* There were further contacts between Feisal and Weizmann in London, and on January 3rd 1919 they signed an 'Agreement between the King of the Hedjaz and the Zionists', The text is reprinted in D. Hunter Miller, *op. cit.* note 36 above, Vol. 3 pp. 188-9.

63. See *B:LH* p. 157. Romancers have often claimed that Lawrence wore full Arab dress in London and Paris, this being a better story than the truth, which was that he wore khaki with an Arab head-dress when with Feisal (as did other members of the Hedjaz delegation).

64. For Lawrence's account of this episode, see D. Hunter Miller *op. cit.* note 36 above, Vol. 1 p. 74. The story evidently circulated at the Peace Conference, and it has even been suggested that the incident took place there. In view of the number of officials present who had some command of Arabic, this seems extremely improbable, and Miller's account is much more plausible.

65. T. E. Lawrence to G. Dawson 15.12.1918. Bodleian R (transcript).

66. *Ibid.*

67. T. E. Lawrence to C. M. Doughty 25.12.1918. Gonville and Caius College, Cambridge.

68. 'Interview with Sherif Feisal' (minutes) 27.12.1918. FO 371/4162.

69. *Ibid.*

70. 'Memorandum by the Emir Feisal'. FO 608/80 fo. 122. Lawrence's surviving manuscript (a slightly earlier draft) is Houghton MS Eng 1252 (341).

Chapter 28. The Peace Conference

January – September 1919

1. T. E. Lawrence to C. F. Shaw 18.10.1927. BL Add. MS 45903.

2. This can only be an approximate calculation: Lawrence wrote seven of the eleven Books which make up *Seven Pillars* while he was in Paris, and he said that the whole text, if completed, would have run to about 250,000 words (see *SP* p. 21).

3. Lawrence's letters confirm that Meinertzhagen saw the first draft of *Seven Pillars*. Many years later Meinertzhagen alleged that while in Paris Lawrence had lowered the manuscript to him on a string from the hotel room immediately overhead (*Middle East Diary* London, Cresset Press, 1959, p. 51). This story seems almost as improbable as the personal confessions which Meinertzhagen claimed Lawrence made to him during the Peace Conference. Meinertzhagen's diaries are demonstrably incorrect on many points, and it seems to me that much of the content is pure fantasy.

4. Notes of this conversation, in Lawrence's hand, are in FO 608/97 fos. 445-7. However, Lawrence was not present at the meeting and this account probably comes from an Arab source. A series of further discussions took place between Feisal and Gout during the conference. They were mostly in a similar vein.

5. Sir A. Hirtzel, 'The French Claims in Syria' 14.2.1919. PRO 30/30/10 pp. 6-7. See FO 608/107 fo. 393 for British Delegation comments on this paper.

6. In a letter of 16.3.1919 Gertrude Bell stated that she was spending most of her time with Lawrence (see *The Letters of Gertrude Bell* ed. Lady Bell, London, Ernest Benn, 1927, Vol. 2, p. 468).

7. G. F. Clayton, memorandum, 11.3.1919. Lloyd George papers F/205/3/9. House of Lords.

8. *Ibid.*

9. *Ibid.*

10. *Ibid.*

11. 'English translation of the French draft of a proposed new Anglo-French Agreement on Syria' PRO 30/30/10. The draft was circulated on February 6th (see M. J-M. Larès, *T. E. Lawrence, la France et les Français*, Paris, Imprimerie Nationale, 1980, p. 175).

12. *Ibid.*

13. See 'French plans for organisation of Syria in event of its becoming a French Sphere' 3.2.1919. FO 608/105.

14. Minutes on the French proposals for a new Anglo-French Agreement, PRO 30/30/10.

15. Much of the propaganda put out by French pressure groups seems to have been intended to persuade their own Government, and, as is often the case with such campaigns, its effect on foreigners was counter-productive. Other attempts to put the French message across were badly mishandled. See for example J. T. Shottwell's comments on the effect of an interminable speech given by Shukri Ghanem (a Syrian who had lived in France for many years) at a meeting of the Council of Ten on February 13th (J. T. Shottwell, *At the Paris Peace Conference,* New York, Macmillan, 1937, p. 178).

16. For examples of these accusations and British replies see S. Pichon to A. J. Balfour, 'Note upon the British aims in Asia Minor', 31.1 1919. PRO 30/30/10; S. Pichon to the British Ambassador in Paris, note, 6.2.1919. FO 406/41 pp. 16-19; Lord Curzon to P. Cambon, 19.3.1919 FO 406/41 pp. 42-4.

17. See M. J-M. Larès, *op. cit.* note 11 above, p. 169.

18. J. T. Shottwell, *op. cit.* note 15 above, p. 129.

19. *Ibid.*

20. See M. J-M. Larès, *op. cit.* note 11 above, p. 170.

21. Sir A. Hirtzel, 'The French claims in Syria' 14.2.1919. PRO 30/30/10.

22. Experienced Zionist politicians were aware that opposition to their programme might easily be aroused by tactless demands. However, the Peace Conference provided a public forum for extremists of many different persuasions, and their outpourings in the press and elsewhere undid much skilful diplomacy. The Zionist movement was by no means the only political pressure group to suffer from this problem.

23. S. Bonsal, *Suitors and Suppliants, the Little Nations at Versailles'* (New York, Prentice-Hall, 1946) p. 56.

24. T. E. Lawrence, minute, 10.3.1919. FO 608/105. The subject of the minute was a letter from King Hussein to the Syrian Union Party, in which he took violent exception to the treatment of Syria as a unit outside his proposed Pan-Arab union. A. J. Toynbee had minuted, for Lawrence's attention: 'King Hussein seems very much at sea over the possible relations between Hejaz and Syria, and letters like this from him may do harm. Can Feisal do anything?.' The passage quoted is from Lawrence's reply.

25. T. E. Lawrence, comment on the typescript of LH:*TEL*, 1933, *B:LH* p. 101.

26. 'Un Diplomate "Le Colonel Lawrence" ' *Paris Midi* 7.3.1919 (author's translation).

27. Lord Riddell, *Intimate Diary of the Peace Conference and After, 1918-1923'* (London, Victor Gollancz, 1933) p. 25.

28. For a 'Memorandum on Syria' circulated after this meeting see D. Hunter Miller, *My Diaries of the Conference of Paris* (New York, Appeal Printing, 1924) Vol. 7, pp. 169-70. The memorandum records that, 'Upon being urged to explain his views of a Syrian settlement, Colonel Lawrence admitted that the proposal to send a Commission to Syria had been prompted by the failure of the French authorities to approach the Emir Feisal in a conciliatory way and that it would undoubtedly be far better if the Commission could sit in Paris and come to an agreement upon general principles before going to Syria in order to clear up by investigations on the spot any details of procedure and local organisation.' Note the word 'admitted', which suggests that this was a view imposed upon Lawrence by the meeting rather than his own opinion.

29. From Feisal's diary, sold at Sothebys, London, on 28.3.1983.

30. T. E. Lawrence, minute, 3.5.1919. FO 608/93 fo. 197.

31. Quoted in Lord Derby [British Ambassador in Paris] to Foreign Office, telegram 639, 18.4.1919. PRO 30/30/10.

32. T. E. Lawrence, minute on the above, 1.5.1919. FO 608/93 fo. 195.

33. L. du P. Mallett, minute, late June 1919. FO 608/97 fo. 149. See also minutes dated 4.7.1919 on Lawrence's movements, FO 371/4146 fo. 356.

34. Sir R. Rodd to Foreign Office London, telegram 346, 18.5.1919. FO 371/3809.

35. R. Cooper [British air attaché in Rome] to Deputy Director of Air Intelligence, Air Ministry, London. Report AA4. 20.5.1919. AIR 1/10102/204/5/1319.

36. Sir R. Rodd to A. J. Balfour, telegram, 21.5.1919. FO 608/97 fo. 143.

37. Foreign Office London to High Commissioner Cairo, telegram 694 'personal', 5.6.1919. FO 141/453/6347.

38. For the circumstances under which Philby was chosen for this role, see E. Monroe *Philby of Arabia* (London, Faber and Faber, 1973) pp. 99-100.

39. Sir A. Hirtzel to Lord Curzon 19.6.1919. FO 371/4149 fo. 149A.

40. G. K. Kidston, minute, 20.6.1919. FO 371/4181 fos. 159-60.

41. T. E. Lawrence to Feisal, forwarded in A. J. Balfour to Lord Allenby, telegram 66, 15.7.1919. FO 608/106 fo. 163.

42. P. H. Kerr to D. Lloyd George 16.7.1919. Lloyd George papers 6/89/3/4, House of Lords.

43. T. E. Lawrence, minute, undated but late July 1919. FO 608/92 fo. 354.

44. Quoted in F. W. Pember to T. E. Lawrence 18.6.1919. Bodleian R (transcript).

45. Unsigned carbon copy of a letter from the War Office to the Foreign Office, 5.8.1919. FO 608/97 fo. 157.

46. R. G. Vansittart, for A. J. Balfour, to Lord Curzon, 13.8.1919. FO 608/97 fo. 159.

47. A. J. Clark-Kerr (for Lord Curzon) to R. G. Vansittart, 21.8.1919 *DBFP* 1/4 pp. 354-5.

48. R. G. Vansittart, minute on the above, 25.8.1919. FO 608/97.

49. T. E. Lawrence, letter to the editor of *The Times* (London), 8.9.1919, published 11.9.1919.

50. G. K. Kidston, minute, 12.9.1919. FO 371/4182 fo. 436.

51. See for example Sir G. Graham (Paris) to Lord Curzon 13.9.1919. FO 608/81, reporting on an article by 'Pertinax' in the *Echo de Paris* of the same date: 'The arguments of English "colonials" which fill London newspapers are not reassuring.

They amount to saying that England has made engagements with France and with the Arabs and cannot treat with France without the approval of the Arabs, not to speak of the League of Nations so neglected in other quarters. France cannot admit this interpretation of the Grey–Cambon [Sykes-Picot] agreements of 1916. When they were concluded the Foreign Office did not reveal agreements with the Sherif of Mecca [this accusation was incorrect]. France only promised the Sherif independence from Turkey.' Similar comments were made in other French papers, all of which dubbed Lawrence a British imperialist.

52. 'Aide-mémoire in regard to the Occupation of Syria, Palestine, and Mesopotamia pending the decision in regard to Mandates' 13.9.1919. FO 608/106.
53. T. E. Lawrence, memorandum to C. B. Harmsworth [Under-Secretary of State for Foreign Affairs] undated, but not later than 15.9.1919 (the date of the FO filing stamp; this date was often two or three days later than the date a document was written). FO 371/4236.
54. G. K. Kidston, minute, 17.9.1919. FO 371/4236.
55. T. E. Lawrence, draft letter to D. Lloyd George, dated 'Thursday 9.19', and therefore almost certainly written on 18.9.1919. In his edition of Lawrence's letters, D. Garnett mistakenly associated this letter with what he termed the 'Yale Plan' for a Middle East settlement. This was a plan which Professor William Yale told Garnett he had promoted as a private individual, and had almost succeeded in bringing to fruition. However, the documents show that Yale had a greatly exaggerated idea of the importance attached by British and French officials to his private initiative and, as a result, Garnett's editorial account of the plan (*DG* pp. 282-7) has little bearing on the diplomatic events that were taking place. There is no mention of Yale's scheme in British Foreign Office or Cabinet documents (on this point see *DBFP* I/4 p. 422 n.2).

Chapter 29. In the Wings
September 1919 – December 1920

1. T. E. Lawrence to Lord Curzon 25.9.19 *DG* p. 291 (where the letter is wrongly dated 27.9.1919).
2. See the statement by J. M. Keynes printed in *DG* (p. 261), which reads, in part, 'When I knew him in the spring of 1919, I should have said that he was a man fully in control of his nerves and quite as normal as most of us in his reactions to the world'.
3. D. Garnett, citing Lawrence's mother, *DG* p.294.
4. T. E. Lawrence to C. F. Shaw 14.4.27 *MB* p. 325. BL Add. MS 45903.
5. Quoted in J. E. Wrench, *Struggle 1914-1920* (London, Ivor Nicholson & Watson, 1935) pp. 363-4.
6. P. Burton, *Adventures Among Immortals* (London, Hutchinson, n.d.) p. 204.
7. *Daily Telegraph*, London, 2.10.1919.
8. T. E. Lawrence to E. M. Forster 17.6.1925 *MB* p. 283. King's College, Cambridge.
9. *Strand Magazine* (London) Vol. LIX, January 1920, p. 44. This is the earliest record of a statement by Lawrence showing knowledge of his father's true identity.
10. See L. J. Thomas in *Friends* p. 213.
11. *Op. cit.* note 9 above.

12. T. E. Lawrence to Sir A. J. Murray 10.1.20 *MB* pp. 171-2. Houghton bMS Eng 1252 (156).
13. *Ibid. MB* p. 173.
14. 'Interview with Col. Lawrence: Sidelights on the Joys of Desert Warfare' in *The Globe* (London) 12.12.1918.
15. T. E. Lawrence to P. Burton, quoted in Burton, *op. cit.* note 6 above, p. 207, where no date is given.
16. R. R. Graves in *B:RG* p. 10.
17. For information relating to this loss see for example *B:LH* p. 145; Sir D. Brownrigg, *Unexpected, a Book of Memories* (London, Hutchinson, n.d.) p. 58, and contemporary press reports (one is reproduced in J. M. Wilson, *T. E. Lawrence*, London, National Portrait Gallery, 1988, p. 150). There is no evidence whatsoever to support the theories advanced by some writers that Lawrence either did not lose the manuscript, or lost it deliberately.

    Reports of this incident vary considerably in detail, particularly with regard to the station at which the manuscript was lost and the train journey Lawrence was making at the time. The account given here is probably correct, as it corresponds both to Lawrence's own statements and to Alan Dawnay's version as told by Brownrigg.
18. Sir D. Brownrigg, *op. cit.* note 17 above, p. 58.
19. T. E. Lawrence, *Some Notes on the Writing of the Seven Pillars of Wisdom* (privately printed, 1927, reprinted in *SP* p. 21).
20. T. E. Lawrence to F. Manning 15.5.30 *DG* p. 692.
21. T. E. Lawrence to E. Garnett 26.8.22 *DG* p. 360.
22. Comment on the draft of *Lawrence and the Arabs* by R. R. Graves, 1927, *BRG* p. 117.
23. T. E. Lawrence, passage written for R. R. Graves, 1927. Houghton bMS Eng 1252 (66). Compare R. R. Graves, *Lawrence and the Arabs* (London, Jonathan Cape, 1927) pp. 413-17.
24. In choosing to present the Arab case in this way, Lawrence played into the hands of critics such as E. Kedourie, who have attacked his account because it places so little emphasis on the British contribution. Had he admitted that there was a large measure of interdependence between British and Arab forces, his case would have withstood such criticism much better.
25. T. E. Lawrence to W. Yale 22.10.1929 *DG* p. 671.
26. T. E. Lawrence to C. B. Harmsworth *c.* 15.9.19. FO 371/4236.
27. T. E. Lawrence to Lord Winterton 22.4.20 *DG* pp. 302-3.
28. T. E. Lawrence to H. St.J. B. Philby 21.5.1920 *MB* p. 179. Philby papers, St Antony's College, Oxford (photocopy of original).
29. See Lord Winterton, *Orders of the Day* pp. 91-2 and p. 100.
30. *Daily Express* (London) 28.5.1920.
31. *Ibid.*
32. *Sunday Times* (London) 30.5.1920.
33. *Ibid.*
34. T. E. Lawrence to R. D. Blumenfeld 11.7.1920 *DG* p. 306.
35. T. E. Lawrence to W. F. Stirling 26.7.1920. Bodleian R (transcript).
36. T. E. Lawrence to F. N. Doubleday 30.6.1920. Bodleian R (transcript).
37. T. E. Lawrence to V. W. Richards, undated, but probably June or July 1920.

Bodleian R (transcript).

38. T. E. Lawrence to F. N. Doubleday 21.7.1920. Bodleian R (transcript).
39. T. E. Lawrence to F. N. Doubleday 20.3.1920 *DG* pp. 300-301.
40. This figure is based on the sum paid by the City of Birmingham Art Gallery at this period for a second oil portrait of Feisal by John.
41. T. E. Lawrence to D. G. Hogarth 27.6.1923. For a possible explanation of Lawrence's willingness to give away such a large sum see the final paragraph on p. 944.
42. T. E. Lawrence to F. N. Doubleday 29.3.1920 *MB* p. 176. Bodleian R (transcript).
43. T. E. Lawrence, letter to the editor of *The Times* (London) 22.7.1920 *DG* pp. 307-8.
44. T. E. Lawrence, 'France, Britain, and the Arabs' in the *Observer* (London) 8.8.1920 *DG* p. 312.
45. T. E. Lawrence, 'Mesopotamia' in the *Sunday Times* (London) 22.8.1920 *DG* p. 315. The particular target of this article was Colonel A. T. Wilson, Acting Civil Commissioner in Baghdad.
46. 'English King for Arabs? Colonel Lawrence on Mesopotamia: Simple Solution: Blunders of British Administration' (article based on an interview with Lawrence) Daily News (London) 25.8.1920.
47. T. E. Lawrence to F. N. Doubleday 14.5.1920 *DG* p. 305.

Chapter 30. Adviser to Churchill

January 1921 – August 1922

1. T. E. Lawrence to F. el Akle 3.1.1921 omitted from *MB* p. 183. Bodleian R (photocopy of original).
2. T. E. Lawrence to E. H. Marsh 17.1.1921 *WSC* Docs IV/2 p. 1314.
3. T. E. Lawrence to C. M. Doughty 28.1.1921 *DG* p. 324. Gonville and Caius College, Cambridge.
4. Foreign Office London to High Commissioner for Egypt, telegram 100, 12.2.1921. FO 141/453/6347.
5. T. E. Lawrence, note on the typescript of *Lawrence and the Arabs* by Robert Graves, July 1927, *B:RG* p. 110.
6. For Young's post-war career in the Foreign Office see his *The Independent Arab* (London, John Murray, 1933, chs XI-XII). For Lawrence's statement to Liddell Hart that he selected Young and R. Meinertzhagen as his assistants see *B:LH* p. 143.

    Lawrence surely recognised that Young's flair for thinking out precise detail was complementary to his own slightly disorganised political insight. As a team they were formidable, and such arguments as they had were about procedure rather than objectives.

    I have not used Meinertzhagen's *Middle East Diary* (London, Cresset Press, 1959) or his other works as source materials for this book. It is clear from the internal evidence that these diaries were very extensively 'written up' for publication, years after the events concerned. As the original diaries seem to have been destroyed, it would be a waste of time trying to guess which parts of the text we now have are contemporary.

7. Sir J. E. Masterton-Smith to W. S. Churchill *WSC* Docs 4/2 pp. 1348-9. Masterton-Smith had just been appointed Permanent Under-Secretary of State at the Colonial Office.

8. W. S. Churchill to his wife 16.2.1921 *WSC* Docs 4/2 p. 1355.
9. T. E. Lawrence, undated note, *c.* 17.2.1921. CO 732/3 fo. 402.
10. *Ibid.*
11. The draft agenda, handwritten by Lawrence and Young, is in CO 732/4.
12. Note by B. H. Liddell Hart of a conversation with Lawrence 1.8.1933 *B:LH* p. 143.
13. T. E. Lawrence to R. R. Graves 'Saturday' [19.2.1921] *B:RG* p. 10.
14. *Ibid.* p. 11.
15. They were published in *The World's Work* (Garden City, N.Y.) Vol. XLII Nos. 3-6, July-October 1921. For some reason when Graves offered these articles he put a very modest price on them, considerably below the amount Lawrence knew from his literary agent that an American journal would be prepared to pay. In *B:RG* p. 14 Graves appears to imply that Lawrence had over-valued the articles, whereas in reality it was he who had asked too little for them.
16. T. E. Lawrence to W. S. Blunt 2.3.1921 *MB* p. 184. Fitzwilliam Museum, Cambridge.
17. W. S. Churchill to D. Lloyd-George 14.3.1921 *WSC* Docs 4/2 p. 1389.
18. T. E. Lawrence to R. R. Graves, 1927 *B:RG* p. 112.
19. W. S. Churchill to D. Lloyd-George, telegram, 18.3.1921. Lloyd-George papers F/9/3/13, House of Lords.
20. T. E. Lawrence to his mother 20.3.1921 *HL* pp. 35-3; *MB* p. 185. Bodleian MS Res C13.
21. T. E. Lawrence to Feisal, transmitted as a postscript addressed to E. H. Marsh in W. S. Churchill to D. Lloyd-George, telegram, 23.3.1921, part V. Lloyd George papers F/9/3/21, House of Lords.
22. T. E. Lawrence to Sir J. E. Shuckburgh, telegram L1, 1.4.1921 (forwarded to the Secretary of State for the Colonies by the High Commissioner for Palestine, 4.4.1921). FO 371/6372 fo. 13.
23. T. E. Lawrence to his mother 12.4.1921 *HL* p. 353; *MB* pp. 185-6. Bodleian MS Res C13.
24. T. E. Lawrence to W. S. Churchill, telegram L4, *c.* 9.4 1921, forwarded to the Secretary of State for the Colonies by the High Commissioner of Palestine, telegram 72, 10.4.1921. FO 371/6372 fo. 33.
25. T. E. Lawrence to his mother 12.4.1921 *HL* p. 353; *MB* p. 186. Bodleian MS Res C 13.
26. T. E. Lawrence to W. S. Churchill 15.4.1921, forwarded in Viscount Allenby to Lord Curzon, telegram 240, 15.4.1921. FO 406/46 pp. 133-4.
27. T. E. Lawrence to W. S. Churchill, telegram, 22.4.1921 FO 406/46 p. 157. On 30.4.1921 Churchill approved Lawrence's return.
28. T. E. Lawrence to R. R. Graves, 1927 *B:RG* p. 114.
29. T. E. Lawrence to R. R. Graves, 1927 *B:RG* p. 112. For publication, Lawrence altered this to read: 'I take to myself credit for some of Mr. Churchill's pacification of the Middle East for while he was carrying it out he had the help of such knowledge and energy as I possess' (*ibid.*) He also told Graves: 'Winston was my very friendly and kindly chief, and has still his career to make. So we must give him credit for all he can carry' (*B:RG* p. 127).
30. T. E. Lawrence to R. R. Graves, 1927, *B:RG* p. 80.
31. T. E. Lawrence to R. R. Graves 21.5.1921 *B:RG* p. 15.
32. C. E. S. Palmer to Lord Curzon 30.4.1921 CO 730/9 fo. 437. Lawrence minuted:

'Maulud is a very honest, blunt, and slashing old patriot who has dared more and suffered more for Arab independence than any one I know. He is a leader of the extremists in Mesopotamia and is respected by them in spite of his stupidity, because of his courage. I wish he was in Baghdad now.' (Minute, 25.5.1921. CO 730/9. Maulud's bravery during the Arab campaign is described in *SP*. He was later to become President of the Chamber of Deputies in Iraq.

33. L. C. Jane to S. Roberts 1.6.1921. National Library of Wales.
34. T. E. Lawrence, preface to the catalogue of an exhibition of Arab portraits by Eric Kennington held at the Leicester Galleries, 1921 *OA* p. 153.
35. T. E. Lawrence to E. H. Kennington 12.6.1921 *DG* p. 330.
36. T. E. Lawrence to Mr. Murray [a member of the Foreign Office staff] 4.7.1921. FO 371/7714 fo. 105.
37. T. E. Lawrence to Mr. Murray 7.7.1921. FO 371/7714 fo. 105.
38. L. Oliphant to Messrs Hutchinson & Co., 15.7.1921 FO 371/7714 fo. 100.
39. It was not until the autumn of 1923 that Lawrence heard of further moves to have Thomas's book published. He wrote to Hogarth on August 23rd: 'Lowell Thomas still lurks in the background, and if his book is the fulsome thing I expect, he will force the truth out of me ' (*DG* p. 429). A month later, he said to Cape: 'I am sorry Lowell Thomas returns to the charge with his book. The Foreign Office quashed it once for me: but have no status now I have left them. So I suppose it must be endured.' (25.9.1923. Bodleian R, transcript). The book was published in America in 1924, and in England in 1925.
40. Minute by T. E. Lawrence on a telegram dated 6.7.1921 from Sir P. Z. Cox (High Commissioner for Mesopotamia) to W. S. Churchill (Secretary of State for the Colonies). CO 737/822.

Lawrence had been forewarned of Philby's attitude in a private letter from Joyce, who had gone to help create an Arab army in Baghdad. There was considerable opposition to Feisal among the Anglo-Indian administrators who were still serving in Mesopotamia. For details of the sequence of events which led to Philby's dismissal see E. Monroe, *Philby of Arabia* (London, Faber & Faber, 1973) pp. 107 *et seq.* Despite Philby's known opposition to Feisal, and his efforts for his own preferred candidate, Saiyid Taleb, he had been sent by Cox to welcome Feisal to Iraq. This had proved to be an error of judgment, and Cox telegraphed on July 6th: 'I hoped that Philby would manage to come to a satisfactory understanding with Feisal but I regret to say that this was not the case. Philby started back with Feisal but got fever and remained at Hillah until July 3rd. Feisal meanwhile arrived and was very bitter as to Philby's attitude. Philby said that he had thought it best to be quite frank with Feisal: while Feisal complained that Philby had made it abundantly clear that he was hostile to Feisal's cause and that it was common talk of all up the line that Philby was strongly in favour of a republic.

'Philby had also told Feisal that he had disapproved of action I had taken in regard to Saiyid Talib and complained of me not having consulted him. This I consider highly improper. Philby as Adviser in charge of the Ministry of the Interior was obviously in a position in which his pronounced personal view must inevitably exercise some influence over Arab and British officials serving under him and thus even influence our elections. Therefore I consider it incompatible with the interests of His Majesty's Government that he should retain his post and I instructed him to hand over his duties to Mr. J. S. Thomson . . .

'Philby has done very good administrative work: is a very capable officer: and I am for many reasons very sorry to lose his services but he is of a fanatical nature which is his weak point and is apt to allow his personal bias to outweigh his duty to his Government. Therefore I saw no alternative but to take the above action' (Sir P. Z. Cox [High Commissioner for Mesopotamia] to W. S. Churchill [Secretary of State for the Colonies], telegram, 6.7.1921. CO 537/822).

E. Monroe (*op. cit.* above, p. 116) states that there is no evidence in Colonial Office files that Lawrence was responsible for Philby's posting to Trans-Jordan, even though Philby himself always said that he had owed the job to Lawrence. It seems that she must have overlooked the minute Lawrence wrote on July 6th. Although the idea of sending Philby to Trans-Jordan was not wholly new, if no one in an influential position had spoken up for him at this moment he would have had little chance of such an appointment, in the wake of his dismissal by Cox.

41. Lord Curzon to T. E. Lawrence 7.7.1921 FO 406/47 p. 74.
42. On July 7th Lawrence wrote to W. S. Blunt: 'I go straight to Jidda, to see King Hussein, and then perhaps to Yemen: return probably in two months.' (*MB* p. 187. Fitzwilliam Museum, Cambridge). In the event, he did not return until Christmas.
43. W. S. Churchill (Secretary of State for the Colonies) to H. L. Samuel (High Commissioner for Palestine) telegram 188, 11.7.1921. FO 371/6372 fo 142.
44. During his stay in Egypt, Lawrence found time to send Churchill information about the activities of Arab nationalists in Cairo, some of whom were vehemently opposed to his mission. See FO 371/6396 fos 179-80.
45. T. E. Lawrence to Lord Curzon (Prodrome London), telegram L5, 2.8.1921 *MB* p. 188. FO 686/93.
46. T. E. Lawrence to Lord Curzon (Prodrome London), telegram L6, 4.8.1921 *MB* p. 189. FO 686/93.
47. T. E. Lawrence to Lord Curzon (Prodrome London), telegram L7, 7.8.1921. FO 686/93.
48. T. E. Lawrence to Lord Curzon (Prodrome London), telegram L8, 7.8.1921. FO 406/47 pp. 93-4.
49. Resident Aden to W. S. Churchill (Secretary of State for the Colonies) 22.8.1921, telegram CO21. CO 725/1.
50. T. E. Lawrence to Sir J. E. Shuckburgh 20.4.1922. CO 725/4. Lawrence's predictions about the future of Perim proved to be incorrect.
51. T. E. Lawrence to E. H. Kennington 25.8.1921 *MB* p. 190. Bodleian R (transcript). This was the covering letter for Lawrence's preface to the catalogue of Kennington's forthcoming exhibition of Arab portraits, to be held at the Leicester Galleries. In the same letter he wrote: 'I hope to be back [in London] soon: with Abdulla' [he was expecting to accompany Abdullah to England].
52. T. E. Lawrence to Lord Curzon (Prodrome London), telegram L15, 7.9.1921 *MB* pp. 190-1. FO 686/93.
53. T. E. Lawrence to Lord Curzon (Prodrome London), telegram L25, 22.9.1921 *MB* p. 191. FO 686/93.
54. Undated, unnumbered message from Lawrence, contained in Jidda to High Commissioner for Egypt, telegram 253, 25.9.1921. This message had evidently been delayed, as Lawrence had left Jidda for Egypt three days earlier.
55. T. E. Lawrence to E. H. Kennington 1.10.1921 *DG* p. 334; partially omitted from *MB* p. 192.

56. *Ibid. DG* p. 333, partially omitted from *MB* p. 192.
57. H. L. Samuel (High Commissioner for Palestine) to W. S. Churchill (Secretary of State for the Colonies), telegram 436, 24.10.1921. CO 733/7 fos. 65-6.

    For an impression of Lawrence during these weeks in Trans-Jordan see H. St.J. B. Philby, *Forty Years in the Wilderness* (London, Robert Hale, 1957) pp. 93-108. The text includes references to Lawrence from Philby's diaries.
58. H. L. Samuel to W. S. Churchill, dispatch 2241/Pol., 24.11.1921. CO 733/7 fo. 436.
59. T. E. Lawrence to W. S. Churchill (Secretary of State for the Colonies), telegram, 28.11.1921. FO 406/48 p. 160.

Chapter 31. The Decision

January – August 1922

1. T. E. Lawrence to Sir H. M. Trenchard early January 1922 *MB* pp. 192-3. It is clear that this letter began with a page or pages referring to other matters. This first section, which probably carried a date, has become separated from the sheet containing Lawrence's request to join the RAF. Trenchard replied on January 11th.
2. T. E. Lawrence to E. H. Kennington 16.2.1922. Bodleian R (transcript).
3. T. E. Lawrence to C. H. St.J. Hornby 14.2.1922. Bodleian R (transcript).
4. T. E. Lawrence to G. F. Clayton 15.8.1922 *MB* p. 198. Clayton Papers 693/11, Durham (photocopy of original).
5. T. E. Lawrence to R. R. Graves 12.11.1922 *DG* p. 379; *B:RG* p. 23. Houghton bMS Eng 152 (41).
6. T. E. Lawrence to V. W. Richards 15.7.1918 *DG* p. 244 (for a longer extract from this letter see pp. 524-5).
7. T. E. Lawrence to D. G. Hogarth 13.6.1923 *DG* p. 424.
8. When Woolley tried to restart the Carchemish excavations after the war, he wrote telling Lawrence about the situation there (letters on this subject are at All Souls College, Oxford). Correspondence in the archives of the British Museum confirms that Lawrence had expressed a wish to join Woolley. However, this became impossible once Syria was under French control.
9. T. E. Lawrence to H. G. Andrews *c.* 15.3.1934. Bodleian R (transcript).
10. When writing to Graves about his reasons for enlisting, Lawrence did not mention this project. His reticence seems to have had something to do with his relationship with Graves: the surviving correspondence shows that while Lawrence was keen to discuss and criticise Graves's work, he preferred to show his own writing to other critics, notably Edward Garnett and (later) E. M. Forster.
11. T. E. Lawrence, note on the typescript of *Lawrence and the Arabs* by R. R. Graves, July 1927 *B:RG* p. 91.
12. T. E. Lawrence to Sir H. Baker 6.11.1928. Most of Lawrence's armoured car and flying experience was gained after the move to Akaba in the summer of 1917. However, he made an armoured car expedition lasting several days in April-May of that year (when he went to recover parts from an RFC aeroplane that had crash-landed in Wadi Hamdh, see p. 401. The episode is not described in *Seven Pillars*).

    Lawrence also wrote: 'It was a course I had decided on in 1919: and had suggested to Air Marshal Sir Geoffrey Salmond before the Armistice: but not till Winston had given the Arabs a fair deal was I free to please myself. That accounted for the delay till 1922.' (T. E. Lawrence, note on the typescript of *Lawrence and the Arabs* by Robert Graves, *c* June 1927 *B:RG* p. 77).

It is possible that Lawrence's choice of the RAF was influenced by his contact with RAF flying crews during his prolonged journey by air from Paris to Cairo in 1919 (see pp. 611-13). A reminiscence of this flight by one of the pilots is printed in *DG* pp. 276-9; it ends with a reported remark by Lawrence that he was thinking of joining the Air Force. However, I have found nothing in Lawrence's own writings to confirm that he was influenced by his experiences during this journey. Moreover, the reminiscence in *DG* was written about twenty years after the events described, and contemporary documents show that it contains a number of factual inaccuracies.

According to a note by Liddell Hart made after a conversation with Lawrence on May 12th 1929, Lawrence claimed to have flown two thousand hours during the war. This figure is clearly absurd: even if he had flown eight hours a day, it would still have taken him 250 days to reach this total. It is possible that Liddell Hart was responsible for the error, jotting down two thousand where Lawrence had said two hundred. On the other hand, Lawrence was often inaccurate, as many people are, when quoting figures casually. Also, he may have tended to exaggerate his flying experience, in view of his subsequent RAF service. He had, of course, made many flights during the war and may well have clocked up two hundred hours.

13. See note 12 above.
14. There are comments by Liddell Hart bearing on this in the Liddell Hart papers, KCL.
15. T. E. Lawrence, *SP*(O) ch. 118.
16. R. R. Graves, *B:RG* p. 15.
17. These nightmares are referred to by A. E. Chambers in *Friends* p. 340, and also in Lawrence's letters.
18. T. E. Lawrence to R. R. Graves, undated, *B:RG* p. 31.
19. T. E. Lawrence: *SP*(O) ch. 87.
20. T. E. Lawrence: *SP*(O) ch. 136 and Epilogue.
21. T. E. Lawrence: *SP*(O) ch. 118.
22. *Ibid.* The coaling episode seems to have taken place in 1909, when Lawrence was short of funds on his way back from Syria. It cannot have lasted as long as a fortnight (see ch. 3 note 22)
23. *Ibid.*
24. T. E. Lawrence to R. R. Graves 18.1.1923 *B:RG* p. 24.
25. Sir H. M. Trenchard to T. E. Lawrence 11.1.1922. Bodleian R (transcript).
26. T. E. Lawrence to his mother 15.2.1922 *HL* pp. 354-5. The statement that Lawrence did not wish to govern anything again is symptomatic of the refusal to take responsibility which marked his later life. This feeling, undoubtedly a reaction against his wartime experiences, seems to have become stronger over the years. While it already affected his views about the future, it was only much later that he cited it as one of his reasons for *remaining* in the ranks. It is doubtful that it played a great part in the original decision to enlist for a relatively short period. Biographers have not been sufficiently careful to distinguish between the motives that led to this original enlistment in 1922 and those that made life in the ranks of the RAF so attractive to him after he had experienced it.
27. T. E. Lawrence to V. W. Richards 22.2.1922. Bodleian R (transcript).

28. T. E. Lawrence to E. H. Kennington 10.4.1922 *DG* p. 340.
29. T. E. Lawrence to S. F. Newcombe *c.* 16.4.1922. Bodleian R (transcript)
30. Note by Lawrence on the flyleaf of his copy of *The Singing Caravan*, by R. Vansittart. Bodleian R (transcript).
31. T. E. Lawrence, *Seven Pillars of Wisdom* manuscript, 1922, Bodleian.
32. T. E. Lawrence to R. L. Binyon, draft, Bodleian R (transcript).
33. T. E. Lawrence to W. S. Blunt 23.7.1922 *MB* p. 197. Fitzwilliam Museum, Cambridge.
34. Correspondence sent for publication to the *Morning Post* (London). It appeared on 20.7.1922. Lawrence's letter is dated 4.7.1922; Churchill's reply 17.7.1922.
35. T. E. Lawrence to E. H. Kennington, dated 'Monday', *c.* 10.7.1922.
36. T. E. Lawrence to G. F. Clayton 15.8.1922 *MB* p. 198. Clayton papers 693/11, Durham (photocopy of original).
37. T. E. Lawrence to P. Nash 3.8.1922. Dartmouth College Library, New Hampshire.
38. T. E. Lawrence to E. Garnett 22.8.1922 *DG* pp. 358-9; *MB* pp. 201-2.
39. T. E. Lawrence to E. Garnett 23.8.1922. Bodleian R (photocopy).
40. T. E. Lawrence to E. Garnett 26.8.1922 *DG* pp. 360-1.
41. Sir O. Swann to T. E. Lawrence 16.8.1922 *LTEL* pp. 187-8.
42. T. E. Lawrence to R. R. Graves 12.11.1922 *DG* p. 379; *B:RG* p. 23. Houghton bMS Eng 1252 (41).

Chapter 32. Aircraftman Ross

September 1922 – January 1923

1. *Daily Mail* (London) 4.9.1922.
2. T. E. Lawrence to Sir Oliver Swann 1.9.1922 *DG* p. 364; *MB* pp. 208-9.
3. T. E. Lawrence to E. M. Forster 6.8.1928 *DG* p. 619. King's College, Cambridge.
4. T. E. Lawrence, *The Mint*, Part 1 chapter 25, p. 90.

It has been said that Lawrence's remarks about discipline in the ranks are petulant and misconceived; that it was his decision to enlist, and he should have been prepared to accept the consequences. Yet if his various statements about discipline are taken together, they suggest a different interpretation. The philosophy of military discipline by which he judged Uxbridge was based on his earlier experience during the Arab Revolt. His failing was not petulance, but an unwillingness to rethink his opinions in relation to the requirements of the RAF. This unwillingness reflects an aspect of Lawrence's temperament: he had little taste for analytical thought. Moreover, the philosophical passages in his writing often express quite simple arguments in a very laborious manner. In 1927 he wrote to David Garnett: 'Forster, like you, hates the gummy passages where the words stick together, in mimicry of my thinking, but that's how I think – inch by inch, circumspectly and agglutinatively' (30.11.1927 Bodleian R, transcript). For whatever reason, the logic behind Lawrence's arguments is quite often confused.

The discipline of the recruits' course provoked some of his most bitter writing: 'This learning to be sterile, to bring forth nothing of our own, has been the greater half of our training and the more painful half. Obedience, the active quality, is easy. We came in wanting to be very obedient and we are pathetically grateful to Taffy for ordering us about from dawn till dark . . . It's quite another thing to learn to flop, passively, when the last order's completed: hard to wait supinely for the next.

Fellows want to forestall orders out of self-respect. Self-respect is one of the things troops have to jettison, as a tacit rebelliousness of spirit, a subjective standard. We must have no standards of our own . . . After a while of this régime troops' intellects and wills go back to God, who made them' (*The Mint* Part 2 ch. 21, p. 159). Lawrence watched this change taking place in the other men's attitudes, but he refused to accept it for himself; resisting stubbornly while recording what he saw in his notes.

He had already expressed the convictions which underlie such criticisms two years before he went to Uxbridge. In 1920 he had written an article for the *Army Quarterly* in which he set out various conclusions about the desert campaign. The essay stated that a lack of formal discipline had been an important limitation to the Arab forces, a factor which had made the Revolt quite different from conventional warfare. He drew this contrast in the following passage: 'we could not hope for any *esprit de corps* to reinforce our motives. Soldiers are made a caste either by being given great pay and rewards in money, uniform, or political privileges; or, as in England, by being made outcasts, cut off from their fellows by contempt. We could not knit man to man, for our tribesmen were in arms willingly, by conviction . . . Any of the Arabs could go home whenever the conviction failed him. Our only contract was honour.

'Consequently we had no discipline, in the sense in which it is restrictive, submergent of individuality, the lowest common denominator of men. In regular armies in peace it means the limit of energy attainable by everybody present: it is the hunt not of an average, but of an absolute, a 100-per-cent. standard, in which the ninety-nine stronger men are played down to the level of the worst. The aim is to render the unit a unit, and the man a type, in order that their effort shall be calculable, their collective output even in grain and in bulk. The deeper the discipline, the lower the individual efficiency, and the more sure the performance. It is a deliberate sacrifice of capacity in order to reduce the uncertain element, the bionomic factor, in enlisted humanity, and its accompaniment is *compound* or social war, that form in which the man in the fighting line has to be the product of the multiplied exertions of the long hierarchy, from workshop to supply unit, which maintains him in the field. The Arab war was *simple* and individual'. ('The Evolution of a Revolt', in the *Army Quarterly* (London) Vol. I, No. 1, October 1920, pp. 66-7).

Regular officers might well have questioned these sweeping generalisations about the role of discipline in a conventional army; but Lawrence's remarks in this article were tangential to its main purpose, and drew no response. Probably those readers who felt critical thought that he had little direct knowledge of conventional military discipline. Lawrence told Wavell in 1923 that most people found the article 'either recondite, or too smart' (23.5.1923. Bodleian R, transcript).

He had enlisted in the Air Force knowing that the new service was entirely dependent on engineering technology. He did not therefore expect its discipline to be like that of a traditional military organisation. In the nineteenth century, a naval or army officer had been able to perform the tasks of every man under his command, and he was head of a simple hierarchy. In the RAF, technology had changed this position (as it did later in the other Services). The officer-pilot now needed the support of technical craftsmen whose expertise he would never master, and the organisation of military units had changed from a simple hierarchy to a team.

Lawrence thought that a skilled technician working in such a team had a special status unlike that of the conventional soldier. Traditional subordination could not apply, because the aircraftman would have to take intelligent decisions within his own special field, for which his superior officer would not necessarily be qualified: 'Let the militarists have their way to its *n*th degree of futility. Time played into our hands. If the technical men held together, and, ruefully smiling, offered both cheeks and the conduct of their handicrafts to discipline, why in no time the whole freedom of the future would be forced on them, by the discovery that the soldier and the mechanic were mutually destructive ideals. As the art of flying grew richer, the trade must deepen in mystery, or go under – and there could be no failure for the R.A.F. ... The officers might delay progress for a few years: no more. Even now the airmen called the tune, in work-hours' (*The Mint*, Part 3, ch. 13, p. 193).

Lawrence therefore believed that individual technicians in the Air Force should have initiative and take pride in their work. Yet the traditional discipline instilled at Uxbridge seemed bent on destroying all trace of such individuality. His superiors would have argued that the new style of team-work called for an even stronger (if less obvious) discipline than that in a simple hierarchy. Conflicts of interest and opinion within a team are inevitable; but in an efficient military unit the leader's decisions must never be challenged.

One flaw in Lawrence's thinking, therefore, was a failure to distinguish between discipline (as a fixed and absolute concept) and the changing pattern of military organisation. Organisation affects the way in which discipline is applied, but it cannot change the nature of discipline itself, and the object of the recruits' course was to instil the basic principle of authority.

Lawrence's confused thinking opened the way to the romantic doctrine of leadership by consent, which had worked, after a fashion, during the Arab Revolt. Between the wars, few people would have advocated this form of discipline for the ranks of the British armed services, but Lawrence did so in a letter written to a Labour MP in 1929: 'A possible modification of the enlistment regulations *might* be brought in by some progressive government: to allow service men to give notice (a month, three months, six months: even a year . . .) and leave the service in peace time. At present to buy yourself out is difficult. The application is usually refused. Anyway the permission is an act of grace: whereas it should be a right. I think the knowledge that their men could leave the service would effect a revolution in the attitude of officers and N.C.Os towards us. It would modify discipline profoundly, for the good, by making it voluntary: something we could help, if we wished. We would become responsible, then, for our behaviour. At present we are like parcels in the post. It is the peace-army and navy and air force which is the concern of parliament. War is madness, for which no legislation will suffice. If you damage the efficiency of war, by act of Parliament, then when the madness comes Parliament will first of all repeal its damaging acts' (T. E. Lawrence to E. Thurtle 1.4.1929 *DG* p. 648). The argument is patently invalid, since at that time it would have been folly to teach regular soldiers a philosophy of discipline which might impair their military efficiency in war.

In Lawrence's case, both the 'team' argument and the concept of voluntary discipline embodied an unstated assumption: that principles which would have worked in his own case could be applied with equal success to everyone in the ranks of the RAF. In his determination to become like the other men, he seems to have overlooked the enormous differences between his own values and theirs. By upbringing and experience he was a member of the ruling élite which had been trained to administer the British Empire. Since childhood, he had been taught to revere concepts such as honour, patriotism, duty and responsibility. During the Great War these values had inspired a whole generation of young officers to perform voluntary acts of extraordinary courage and self-sacrifice. But there was an immense difference between the education of this ruling élite and that of the working classes. Few people at that time would have assumed that men in the ranks would show the same degree of self-sacrifice without the impetus of discipline.

The truth therefore was that Lawrence's views about discipline in the RAF were not properly thought out, and that this reflects the distaste for theoretical thinking to which he often referred: 'being so English as I am, gives one a distrust for systems of any kind, and I don't believe I could think out anything worth while. When I try to think, it lasts about five minutes, and then digresses along some pathway of a dream. And if I try to understand any reputable philosopher, I find myself either lost or yawning in half an hour' (to H. Williamson 2.4.1928. Exeter University Library).

5. T. E. Lawrence, *The Mint* Part 1 ch. 18, p. 67.
6. T. E. Lawrence to W. Rothenstein 25.9.1922. Houghton bMS Eng 1148 (859).
7. T. E. Lawrence to E. H. Kennington 15.10.1922. Bodleian R (transcript).
8. T. E. Lawrence to W. Roberts 17.9.1922. Bodleian R (transcript).
9. T. E. Lawrence to W. Roberts 6.9.1922. Bodleian R (transcript).
10. T. E. Lawrence to W. Roberts 21.10.1922. Bodleian R (transcript).
11. T. E. Lawrence to R. V. Buxton 28.8.1922. Jesus College, Oxford.
12. T. E. Lawrence to R. V. Buxton 27.10.1922. Jesus College, Oxford.
13. T. E. Lawrence to W. Roberts 28.11.1922. Bodleian R (transcript).
14. T. E. Lawrence to W. Roberts 16.2.1923. Bodleian R (transcript).
15. T. E. Lawrence to S. C. Cockerell 15.10.1924 *DG* pp. 468-9.
16. T. E. Lawrence to E. Garnett 7.9.1922 *DG* p. 366.
17. Edward Garnett's son David, who edited Lawrence's letters for publication, claimed that 'Lawrence could not face the idea of publishing the whole book, and asked Edward Garnett to make an abridgement of it.' (*DG* p. 353). The contemporary correspondence shows that this is incorrect: Lawrence mentioned that he had had an offer for an abridgement, which he did not intend to accept. Garnett seized upon this and proposed that he himself should abridge the text.
18. T. E. Lawrence to E. Garnett 7.9.1922 *DG* pp. 366-7.
19. E. Garnett to T. E. Lawrence 9.9.1922 *LTEL* p. 88. The Royal [Army] Flying Corps (RAFC) had become part of the new Royal Air Force in 1917.
20. T. E. Lawrence to E. Garnett September 1922 *DG* p. 367.
21. V. W. Richards to T. E. Lawrence 24.9.1922. Bodleian R (transcript).
22. T. E. Lawrence to V. W. Richards n.d. (replies to 24.9.1922) *MB* pp. 223-6 (where it is tentatively dated early 1923). Bodleian R (transcript).
23. T. E. Lawrence to D. G. Hogarth 29.10.1922 *DG* p. 374. Bodleian R (transcript).
24. T. E. Lawrence, *The Mint*, Part 2 ch. 21, p. 159.
25. T. E. Lawrence to E. Garnett 6.11.1922 *DG* p. 377.
26. T. E. Lawrence to E. Garnett 12.11.1922 *DG* p. 380.
27. *Ibid.*
28. T. E. Lawrence to C. M. Doughty 6.11.1922 *DG* p. 375. Gonville and Caius College, Cambridge. Lloyd George's coalition had fallen on October 19th, and the

'present Ministry' referred to was the new Conservative cabinet formed by Bonar Law.

29. *Daily Telegraph* (London) 15.11.1922.

30. T. E. Lawrence to E. Marsh 18.11.1922. Berg Collection, New York Public Library.

31. T. E. Lawrence, draft preface to *The War in the Desert* 18.11.1922 *DG* pp. 345-6. Houghton.

32. T. E. Lawrence to Sir Oliver Swann 19.11.1922 *DG* pp. 381-2.

33. T. E. Lawrence to R. D. Blumenfeld 11.11.1922 *MB* pp. 211-12. Bodleian R (transcript).

34. T. E. Lawrence to E. Garnett 20.11.1922 *DG* p. 383. Bodleian R (transcript).

35. T. E. Lawrence to W. Roberts 28.11.1922. Bodleian R (transcript).

36. E. Garnett to T. E. Lawrence 23.11.1922 *LTEL* p. 93.

37. *Ibid.*

38. T. E. Lawrence to R. D. Blumenfeld 24.11.1922 *MB* pp. 213-14. Bodleian R (transcript). The apparent inconsistency in Lawrence's statements about the number of his scars is accounted for in a letter to John Buchan: 'The *Seven Pillars* doesn't perhaps bring out clearly enough that I was wounded in nine different scraps (sometimes two or three damages at once: I have about fifty scars tallied on me)' (20.6.1927. Queen's University Archives, Kingston, Ontario).

39. T. E. Lawrence to W. Roberts 28.11.1922. Bodleian R (transcript).

40. C. Findlay, 'The amazing A.C.2.' in *The Listener* (London) Vol. LIX, No. 1523, 5.6.1958, p. 938.

41. T. E. Lawrence to Sir Hugh Trenchard 28.3.1923 *DG* pp. 405-6. Bodleian R (transcript).

42. C. Findlay, *op. cit.* note 40 above, pp. 937-8.

43. T. E. Lawrence to G. B. Shaw 30.11.1922 *MB* pp. 214-15 (where 'rot' is printed 'not'). Jesus College, Oxford.

44. T. E. Lawrence to E. Garnett [1.12.1922] *DG* p. 385.

45. G. B. Shaw to T. E. Lawrence 1.12.1922 *LTEL* p. 161-2.

46. T. E. Lawrence to G. B. Shaw 7.12.1922 *DG* p. 388. BL Add. MS 50540.

47. *Ibid.*

48. T. E. Lawrence to E. Garnett 7.12.1922 *DG* p. 386.

49. *Ibid.*

50. T. E. Lawrence to H. J. Cape 14.12.1922. Bodleian R (transcript).

51. W. Guilfoyle to Sir Oliver Swann 16.12.1922 *SIR* pp. 71-2. Curiously, a letter exists from Lawrence to William Roberts, clearly dated '11.xii.22', which contains the remark: 'It looks as though they may throw me out of the R.A.F. at once. I'll write in a day or two, and say.' If this letter is correctly dated, it might suggest that Lawrence already knew of the press enquiries at Farnborough referred to by Guilfoyle. It is also possible, however, that the letter to Roberts is misdated, and was written on 11.1.1923 when Lawrence's continuation in the RAF hung in the balance. I have found no collateral evidence to confirm either date (the letter to Roberts was sold at Sotheby's, New York, on 11.12.1984, lot 253).

52. G. B. Shaw to T. E. Lawrence 17.12.1922 *LTEL* pp. 164-5.

53. *Ibid.* p. 166.

54. T. E. Lawrence to H. J. Cape 21.12.1922. Bodleian R (transcript).

55. T. E. Lawrence to R.V. Buxton 21.12.1922 *DG* pp. 388-9. Jesus College, Oxford.

56. T. E. Lawrence to H. Baker 25.12.1922 *DG* p. 389.

57. *Daily Express* (London) 27.12.1922.

58. *Ibid.*

59. *Daily Express* (London) 28.12.1922.

60. R. D. Blumenfeld, *R.D.B's Procession* (London, Ivor Nicholson & Watson, 1935) p. 116. Blumenfeld implied in this account that he first knew of the enlistment when Lawrence called on him at the *Daily Express* office in RAF uniform. This visit probably took place at a later date, because Lawrence first mentioned his enlistment to Blumenfeld in a letter of 11.11.1922.

61. T. E. Lawrence to G. B. Shaw 27.12.1922 *DG* pp. 390-1; omitted from *MB* p. 216. BL Add. MS 50540.

62. G. B. Shaw to T. E. Lawrence 28.12.1922 *LTEL* pp. 167-8. A clipping from the *Daily News* of the same date was attached to this letter.

63. *Ibid.*

64. For example, *Revolt in the Desert* was published before *Seven Pillars* in the following countries (with respective dates): Britain and America (1927, 1935); France (1927, 1936); Germany (1927, 1936); Italy (1930, 1949); Sweden (1927, 1939); Denmark (1928, 1936).

65. C. F. Shaw to T. E. Lawrence 31.12.1922. BL Add. MS 45903.

66. G. B. Shaw to T. E. Lawrence 4.1.1923 *LTEL* pp. 168-70.

67. T. E. Lawrence to H. J. Cape 7.1.1923 *DG* p. 393.

68. *Ibid.*

69. T. E. Lawrence to R. Savage 7.1.1923 *MB* p. 218. Bodleian R (transcript).

70. T. E. Lawrence to C. F. Shaw 8.1.1923 *MB* p. 219. BL Add. MS 45903.

71. T. E. Lawrence to R. Savage 7.1.1923 *MB* p. 218. Bodleian R (transcript).

72. T. E. Lawrence to C. F. Shaw 8.1.1923 *MB* p. 2129. BL Add. MS 45903.

73. T. E. Lawrence to R. R. Graves 18.1.1923 *B:RG* p. 24; *MB* p. 221. Houghton bMS Eng 1252 (43).

74. T. E. Lawrence to C. F. Shaw 31.8.1924 *MB* p. 273. BL Add. MS 45903.

75. T. E. Lawrence to E. H. Kennington 22.2.1923. Bodleian R (transcript).

76. J. E. Mack, *A Prince of our Disorder* (Boston, Little, Brown, 1976) p. 323.

77. Interview with A. E. Chambers 18.2.1968.

78. D. Stewart, *T. E. Lawrence* (London, Hamish Hamilton, 1977) p. 276.

79. Most of T. E. Lawrence's letters to R. A. M. Guy are in the Houghton Library. They show that Guy wrote repeatedly about his various difficulties, asking Lawrence for financial help. A number of Lawrence's contemporaries in the ranks have told me that some individuals took advantage of his generosity, and it is difficult to avoid the conclusion that Guy was one of these 'spongers'.

80. T. E. Lawrence to R. A. M. Guy 25.12.1923 *MB* p. 253. Houghton bMS Eng 1252 (233).

81. One can discount such obviously leading remarks as Stewart's comment: 'Guy visited the cottage which became the focus of Lawrence's private life' (*op. cit.* note 78 above, p. 276). Countless friends visited Lawrence at Clouds Hill.

82. Stewart made great play of the fact that Lawrence had bought Guy a suit and overcoat in the spring of 1923, whereas this was typical of Lawrence's generosity towards friends who were short of money.

83. T. E. Lawrence to R. A. M. Guy 30.3.1923. Houghton bMS Eng 1252 (246).

84. T. E. Lawrence, *The Mint*, Part 2 ch. 2, pp. 109-10.

85. T. E. Lawrence to E. H. Kennington 15.9.1927. Bodleian R (transcript).

86. T. E. Lawrence to G. B. Shaw 30.1.1923 *DG* p. 397.
87. T. E. Lawrence to R. R. Graves 18.1.1923 *B:RG* p.24; *MB* p. 221. Houghton bMS Eng 1252 (43).
88. Viscount Templewood, *Empire of the Air* (London, Collins, 1957) p. 255.
89. L. J. Thomas, in *Friends* p. 215.

Chapter 33. Tank Corps Private

January – December 1923

1. Lawrence tried both directly and indirectly to discover the true reason for his dismissal. He was told repeatedly that his presence in the ranks was an embarrassment to junior officers.
2. T. E. Lawrence to B. E. Leeson 4.2.1923 *DG* p. 398.
3. *The Leo Amery Diaries*, Vol. I, ed. J. Barnes and D. Nicholson (London, Hutchinson, 1980) p. 319.
4. T. E. Lawrence to T. B. Marson, Trenchard's personal assistant, 28.1.1923 *DG* pp. 394-5.
5. *Ibid.*
6. Sir Hugh Trenchard to T. E. Lawrence 30.1.1923 *LTEL* p. 197.
7. *Op. cit.* note 3 above, p. 319.
8. T. E. Lawrence to E. Garnett 30.1.1923 *DG* p. 396. See also T. E. Lawrence to G. B. Shaw 30.1.1923 *DG* pp. 396-7.
9. T. E. Lawrence to Lady Scott 5.2.1923 *DG* p. 399. Cambridge University Library. On April 13th 1923, two months after this letter, Shaw admitted to S. C. Cockerell that he had 'still about forty pages to read' (see *The Best of Friends* ed. V. Meynell, London, Rupert Hart-Davis, 1956, p. 29).
10. T. E. Lawrence to C. E. Wilson 6.2.1923. Bodleian R (transcript).
11. T. E. Lawrence to W. Roberts 7.2.1923. Bodleian R (transcript).
12. T. E. Lawrence to P. Nash 7.2.1923. Dartmouth College Library, Dartmouth, New Hampshire.
13. T. E. Lawrence to W. Roberts 16.2.1923. Bodleian R (transcript).
14. T. E. Lawrence to C. E. Wilson 16.2.1923. Bodleian R (transcript).
15. Sir P. W. Chetwode to T. E. Lawrence 17.2.1923. Bodleian R.
16. T. E. Lawrence to R. Isham 22.11.1927 *DG* p. 545. The story that Lawrence chose this pseudonym because of his friendship with Bernard Shaw has no logical basis. Lawrence hardly knew the Shaws at this date; their close friendship developed later. Doubtless when he chanced on the name, Lawrence found the coincidence amusing.
17. T. E. Lawrence to S. C. Cockerell 22.10.1923 *DG* pp. 437-8.
18. T. E. Lawrence to A. E. Chambers 21.3.1923 *DG* p. 403; *MB* p. 230. Bodleian.
19. T. E. Lawrence, *The Mint*, Part 1 ch. 22, pp. 82-3.
20. T. E. Lawrence to L. G. Curtis 19.3.1923 *DG* pp. 410-11; *MB* p. 227. All Souls College, Oxford.
21. *Ibid. DG* p. 412; *MB* p. 228.
22. T. E. Lawrence to L. G. Curtis 27.3.1923 *DG* pp. 412-13; *MB* p. 232. All Souls College, Oxford.
23. *Ibid.*
24. *Ibid. DG* p. 414; *MB* p. 233.

25. T. E. Lawrence, *The Mint*, Part 2 ch. 18, p. 149. The first four words of the Creed are: 'I believe in God'.
26. T. E. Lawrence, *SP* ch. CVII p. 586.
27. The doctrine of the 'progress of mankind', in its arrogant Victorian form, persisted well into the twentieth century. It was finally shattered, for most people, by events in Nazi Germany.
28. A. Dixon, *Tinned Soldier* (London, Jonathan Cape, 1941) pp. 296-7.
29. T. E. Lawrence to F. E. Hardy 25.3.1923 *MB* p. 231. Bodleian R (transcript).
30. T. E. Lawrence to H. J. Cape 30.3.1923. Bodleian R (transcript).
31. T. E. Lawrence to E. Garnett 12.4.1923 *DG* p. 409.
32. Lawrence often redrafted important and 'literary' letters. In a letter home from Carchemish he had written 'I have had little time to compose anything worth writing. And even this is the first copy, which I must send you for lack of time to revise.' (8.10.1912 *HL* p. 236. Bodleian MS Res C13). Drafts of letters to Lord Curzon and the Anglican Bishop of Jerusalem survive, among others (see for instance *DG* pp. 342-4). On the other hand he once told Charlotte Shaw that the best letters were those sent in their first draft.
33. T. E. Lawrence: 'A Sea-Trip'. The text given here is taken from a printed facsimile of the manuscript, which came to me as a clipping from an unidentified journal or catalogue. The diplomat was Philby, see p. 613.
34. A. Dixon, *op. cit.* note 28 above, pp. 294-5.
35. T. E. Lawrence to R. V. Buxton 15.8.1923. Jesus College, Oxford. Buxton had commanded the Imperial Camel Corps expedition in Syria, and was therefore well-qualified to criticise relevant sections of *Seven Pillars*.
36. T. E. Lawrence to R. V. Buxton 22.9.1923 *DG* p. 432; *MB* p. 245. Jesus College, Oxford.
37. T. E. Lawrence to A. P. Wavell 11.5.1923 *MB* pp. 234-5. Bodleian R (transcript).
38. T. E. Lawrence to R.V. Buxton 11.5.1923. Jesus College, Oxford.
39. T. E. Lawrence to A. R. D. Fairburn 12.5.1923. Alexander Turnbull Library, Wellington, New Zealand.
40. T. E. Lawrence to L. G. Curtis 14.5.1923 *DG* pp. 416-17; *MB* p. 237. All Souls College, Oxford.
41. T. E. Lawrence to H. J. Cape 4.6.1923. Lawrence was of course aware of the parallel with Richard Burton, another famous 'Arabian' who had translated the *Thousand and One Nights*. He thought Burton 'wrote so difficult an English style as to be unreadable. Also he was pretentious and vulgar' (*B:RG* p. 67). Lawrence had given his set of Burton's translation away to a friend in the Colonial Office.
42. T. E. Lawrence to H. J. Cape 12.6.1923. Bodleian R (transcript).
43. T. E. Lawrence to H. J. Cape 8.7.1923. Bodleian R (transcript).
44. T. E. Lawrence to H. J. Cape 11.8.1923. Bodleian R (transcript).
45. *Ibid.*
46. T. E. Lawrence to F. E. Hardy 15.8.1923 *DG* p. 427. Dorset County Museum, Dorchester.
47. T. E. Lawrence to E. H. Kennington 15.8.1923. Bodleian R (transcript).
48. T. E. Lawrence to G. L. Bell 18.8.1923 *DG* pp. 427-8. Newcastle University Library.
49. T. E. Lawrence to H. J. Cape 19.8.1923. Bodleian R (transcript). Cape did not send him Garnett's abridgement.

50. T. E. Lawrence to D. G. Hogarth 23.8.1923 *DG* pp. 428-9. Bodleian R (transcript).
51. T. E. Lawrence to R. R. Graves 8.9.1923 *DG* pp. 429-31; *B:RG* pp. 26-7. Houghton bMS Eng 1252 (46).
52. T. E. Lawrence to his mother 22.11.1923 *HL* p. 356. Bodleian MS Res C13.
53. F. E. Hardy to S. C. Cockerell 25.11.1923 in *Friends of a Lifetime* ed. V. Meynell (London, Jonathan Cape, 1940) p. 310.
54. T. E. Lawrence to H. J. Cape 13.9.1923. Bodleian R (transcript).
55. T. E. Lawrence to R. A. M. Guy 17.9.1923 *MB* p. 244. Houghton bMS Eng 1252 (248).
56. T. E. Lawrence to R. V. Buxton 4.10.1923 *DG* pp. 434-5. Jesus College, Oxford.
57. T. E. Lawrence, dust-jacket blurb for *Sturly*, *DG* pp. 438-9.
58. T. E. Lawrence to H. J. Cape 25.9.1923. Bodleian R (transcript).
59. T. E. Lawrence to E. Garnett 26.9.1923. Bodleian R (transcript).
60. T. E. Lawrence to L. G. Curtis 25.9.1923. All Souls College, Oxford.
61. T. E. Lawrence to E. Garnett 4.10.1923 *DG* pp. 433-4.
62. T. E. Lawrence to L. G. Curtis 4.10.1923. All Souls College, Oxford.
63. *Ibid.*
64. T. E. Lawrence to H. J. Cape 11.10.1923. Bodleian R (transcript).
65. T. E. Lawrence to A. E. Chambers 5.11.1923 *MB* pp. 249-50. Bodleian.
66. T. E. Lawrence to S. C. Cockerell 22.10.1923 *DG* p. 437.
67. *Ibid. DG* p. 438.
68. T. E. Lawrence to S. C. Cockerell 27.10.1923 *op. cit.* note 53 above, pp. 359-60.
69. T. E. Lawrence to R. V. Buxton 5.11.1923. Jesus College, Oxford.
70. T. E. Lawrence to H. Flecker 5.11.1923 *MB* p. 249. Flecker papers.
71. T. E. Lawrence to D. G. Hogarth 14.11.1923 *DG* p. 440. Bodleian R (transcript).
72. *Ibid.*
73. S. Sassoon to T. E. Lawrence 26.11.1923 *LTEL* p. 154 (where the last paragraph quoted is omitted). Bodleian R (transcript). Sassoon's admiration for *Seven Pillars* was genuine. See for example his letters of 24.11.1923, 30.12.1923 and 3.1.1924 to S. C. Cockerell (printed in *op. cit.* note 9 above, pp. 32-5.
74. T. E. Lawrence to E. H. Kennington 4.12.1923. Bodleian R (transcript).
75. T. E. Lawrence to D. G. Hogarth 6.12.1923. Bodleian R (transcript).

Chapter 34. Tribulations of a Publisher

December 1923 – December 1924

1. T. E. Lawrence to E. H. Kennington 13.12.1923 *MB* p. 251. Bodleian R (transcript).
2. *Ibid. MB* p. 252.
3. T. E. Lawrence to R. V. Buxton 13.12.1923 *DG* pp. 442-3. Jesus College, Oxford.
4. T. E. Lawrence to G. B. Shaw 13.12.1923. BL Add. MS 50540.
5. G. B. Shaw to T. E. Lawrence, December 1923. Bodleian R (transcript).
6. D. G. Hogarth to G. B. Shaw 4.6.1923. Bodleian R (transcript).
7. For Shaw's efforts to secure a pension for Lawrence see *Collected Letters of Bernard Shaw* Vol III, ed. D. H. Laurence (London, Max Reinhardt, 1985) pp. 828-32, 852-4; see also G. B. Shaw to Lawrence 11.1.1924 *LTEL* pp. 172-3; T. E. Lawrence to G. B. Shaw 14.1.1924 *DG* p. 451.
8. T. E. Lawrence to G. B. Shaw 20.12.1923 *DG* p. 447. BL Add. MS 50540.
9. D. G. Hogarth to G. G. Dawson 3.2.1924. Bodleian.

10. T. E. Lawrence to R. V. Buxton 23.12.1923. Jesus College, Oxford.

11. *Ibid.*

12. Lord Grey of Fallodon to T. E. Lawrence 30.12.1923. Bodleian R (transcript).

13. T. E. Lawrence to D. G. Hogarth 21.1.1924 *DG* p. 451. Bodleian R (transcript).

14. T. E. Lawrence to A. P. Wavell 27.12.1923 *DG* p. 449. The allusion to 'the old army' may refer to Lawrence's pre-war service in the RGA.

15. T. E. Lawrence to A. P. Wavell 23.1.1924. Bodleian R (transcript).

16. Lawrence's introduction was published in R. Garnett, *The Twilight of the Gods and other Tales*, illustrated by H. Keen (London, John Lane the Bodley Head, 1924).

17. T. E. Lawrence to H. J. Cape 23.1.1924. Bodleian R (transcript).

18. T. E. Lawrence to H. J. Cape 30.1.1924. Bodleian R (transcript). Pierre Custot's *Sturly* was translated by Richard Aldington and published by Cape in 1924. Cape used the unsigned dust-jacket blurb by Lawrence (see *DG* pp. 438-9).

19. T. E. Lawrence to H. Williamson 2.4.1928. Exeter University Library. In this letter Lawrence gives the date of his re-reading *Seven Pillars* as 1923, in which case he could be referring to reading the text while working on Edward Garnett's abridgement. However, this would not be consistent with the phrase 'after forgetting it for two years'. It seems much more likely that he is referring to his first detailed reading of the text with a view to revision, which probably began in late December 1923. Lawrence made similar remarks about his disappointment on re-reading *Seven Pillars* to several other people.

20. T. E. Lawrence to H. G. Granville-Barker 7.2.1924 *DG* pp. 452-3. Houghton bMS Eng 1020.

21. E. M. Forster to T. E. Lawrence mid-February 1924 *LTEL* p. 58. Siegfried Sassoon had sent *Seven Pillars* to Forster, with Lawrence's permission.

22. See *LTEL* p. 63 note 3. This passage was omitted from the final text of *Seven Pillars*.

23. E. M. Forster to T. E. Lawrence mid-February 1924 *LTEL* pp. 60-2.

24. *Ibid.* p. 60.

25. T. E. Lawrence to E. M. Forster 20.2.1924 *DG* p. 455; *MB* p. 256. King's College, Cambridge. In a footnote on this letter David Garnett remarked: 'Edward Garnett alone had been writing about *Seven Pillars of Wisdom* for months' (*DG* p. 455 note 3). The implication that Lawrence was lying is unjust: David Garnett's loyalty to his father seems to have blinded him to the fact that there was a radical difference between the general praise which had been heaped on *Seven Pillars* by Edward Garnett and others, and the very detailed criticisms now made by Forster (David Garnett's error is repeated in *MB* p. 256).

26. *Ibid.* pp. 455-6; *MB* pp. 256-7.

27. T. E. Lawrence to G. W. M. Dunn 11.3.1931 *DG* pp. 715-16. Bodleian R (transcript).

28. T. E. Lawrence to J. Hanley 28.12.1931 *DG* p. 738. Bodleian R (transcript).

29. E. M. Forster to T. E. Lawrence 22.2.1924 *LTEL* p. 64.

30. E. M. Forster to A. C. Forster 23.3.1924 *Selected Letters of E. M. Forster* Vol. II, ed. M. Lago and P. N. Furbank (London, Collins, 1985) p. 50. P. N. Furbank gives the first contact between Lawrence and Forster as 22.2.1921, when Forster and Lawrence were both present at a social function in London. It seems that Forster wrote to Lawrence after this, but received no reply (see P. N. Furbank, *E. M. Forster, a Life*, Vol. II, London, Secker & Warburg, 1978, p. 119 footnote 1. See also *Friends* p. 282)..

31. 'Colonel Lawrence: Tank Corps Private' in the *Daily Express* (London) 27.2.1924.
32. T. E. Lawrence to Sir Hugh Trenchard 1.3.1924 *MB* p. 258. Bodleian R (transcript).
33. *Ibid.*
34. T. E. Lawrence to C. F. Shaw 16.4.1928. HRHRC Texas (photocopy). At that time Bumpus Ltd. was bookseller to the King. J. G. Wilson, the manager, was related neither to A. T. Wilson nor to C. E. Wilson (nor to the present author).
35. T. E. Lawrence to C. F. Shaw 26.3.1924 *MB* p. 262. BL Add. MS 45903.
36. *Ibid. MB* pp. 261.
37. *Ibid. MB* pp. 261-2.
38. For an account of Lawrence's taste in music see W. W. James in *Friends* (1937 edition, pp. 513-22), and the list of gramophone records found at Clouds Hill after Lawrence's death (*ibid.* pp. 523-9).
39. T. E. Lawrence to F. E. Hardy 31.1.1924 *MB* p. 255. Bodleian R (transcript).
40. T. E. Lawrence to C. F. Shaw 30.4.1924. BL Add. MS 45903.
41. E. M. Forster, 'The Life to Come', published in a revised form in the *Abinger Edition* of Forster's works: *The Life to Come, and other Stories* ed. O. Stallybrass (London, Arnold, 1972) pp. 65-82.
42. T. E. Lawrence to E. M. Forster 30.4.1924 partially published in *Selected Letters of E. M. Forster* Vol. II, ed. M. Lago and P. N. Furbank (London, Collins, 1985) p. 56, note 1. King's College, Cambridge.
43. *Ibid.*
44. E. M. Forster to T. E. Lawrence 3.5.1924 *op. cit.* note 42 above, p. 55. King's College, Cambridge.
45. *Ibid.*
46. *The War in the Air*, Vol. I by Sir Walter Raleigh (Oxford, Clarendon Press, 1922); Vol. II by H. A. Jones (Oxford, Clarendon Press, 1928). Trenchard's biographer, Andrew Boyle, wrote that after Raleigh died in 1923: 'The short-list of candidates to complete the work soon grew shorter under the terms imposed by the Cabinet Office at Trenchard's instigation until the best were eliminated altogether. Finally, the task went by default to an industrious civil servant, H. A. Jones, who had assisted Raleigh in his researches and who laboured for a decade to produce five more volumes of painstaking fact dressed in the drabbest of prose. The raw material of perhaps the most romantic chapter in our military history since the first Elizabethan age was dutifully stirred to the consistency of a suet pudding, partly through Trenchard's refusal to permit the necessary licence to writers of Raleigh's brilliance.' A. Boyle, *Trenchard* (London, Collins, 1962) p. 514.
47. T. E. Lawrence to D. G. Hogarth 9.5.1924 *DG* pp. 459-60 *MB* pp. 266-7.
48. *Ibid. MB* p. 277.
49. T. E. Lawrence to R. R. Graves 9.5.1924 *B:RG* p. 28. Houghton bMS Eng 1252 (47).
50. This property belonged to another branch of the Chapman family and was never inherited by Thomas Chapman, Lawrence's father, whose younger sister Caroline married her cousin Sir Montagu Richard Chapman of Killua, the 5th Baronet. The title but not the Killua property passed to Thomas Chapman in 1914. See Appendix I.
51. T. E. Lawrence to F. E. Hardy 27.1.1924. Bodleian R (transcript).
52. T. E. Lawrence to his mother 18.5.1924 omitted from *HL* p. 358.
53. T. E. Lawrence to H. G. Granville-Barker 9.5.1924 *MB* p. 266. Houghton bMS Eng

1020. Lawrence's belief that he might have been given the surname 'Chapman' at birth was a genuine misapprehension.

54. T. E. Lawrence to A. E. Chambers 3.8.1924. Bodleian.

55. For example he wrote to Lady Sandwich: 'Shaw or Lawrence, as you please. Both are assumed names, and I like the shorter, because it's short.' 18.8.1924. Bodleian R (transcript).

56. T. E. Lawrence to E. Garnett [18.5.1924]. Bodleian R (transcript).

57. T. E. Lawrence to H. G. Granville-Barker 18.5.1924. Houghton bMS Eng 1020.

58. T. E. Lawrence to C. F. Shaw 3.6.1924. BL Add. MS 45903.

59. T. E. Lawrence to C. F. Shaw 10.7.1924. BL Add. MS 45903.

60. T. E. Lawrence to C. F. Shaw 17.8.1924. BL Add. MS 45903.

61. T. E. Lawrence to his mother 18.8.1924 *HL* p. 359. Bodleian MS Res C13.

62. T. E. Lawrence to C. F. Shaw 31.8.1924 *MB* p. 271. BL Add. MS 45903.

63. T. E. Lawrence to E. Garnett 16.9.1924 omitted from *DG* p. 466. Bodleian R (transcript).

64. T. E. Lawrence to C. St.J. Hornby 27.9.1924. Bodleian R (transcript).

65. T. E. Lawrence to S. C. Cockerell 27.9.1924. Bodleian R (transcript).

66. T. E. Lawrence to C. F. Shaw 27.9.1924. BL Add. MS 45903.

67. C. F. Shaw to T. E. Lawrence undated, but *c.* 6.10.1924. HRHRC Texas.

68. G. B. Shaw to T. E. Lawrence 7.10.1924 *Collected Letters of Bernard Shaw* Vol. III, ed. D. H. Laurence (London, Max Reinhardt, 1985) pp. 884-6. Private collection.

69. Bound page proof of Chapters I-VIII of *Seven Pillars* 1924, pp. 1-2. Published in *OA* pp. 140-1 (also in English and Penguin editions of *Seven Pillars* since 1940). The omission of this important statement at the beginning of the 1926 and 1935 editions of *Seven Pillars* led some people to allege that Lawrence had exaggerated his own role in a misleading way.

70. T. E. Lawrence to C. F. Shaw 13.10.1924. BL Add. MS 45903. The list of officers was incorporated in the acknowledgements that preface *SP* (p. 6), but Lawrence's remarks about his own role did not appear in British editions until the suppressed introductory chapter was restored in 1940. They are still omitted from most editions published overseas. Lawrence included a reference to the semi-colons in his *SP* acknowledgements, p. 6.

71. *Ibid.*

72. T. E. Lawrence to C. St.J. Hornby 17.10.1924. Bodleian R (transcript).

73. T. E. Lawrence to R. V. Buxton 7.10.1924. Jesus College, Oxford.

74. T. E. Lawrence to R. V. Buxton 25.11.1924 *DG* pp. 470-1. Jesus College, Oxford.

75. T. E. Lawrence to H. G. Granville-Barker 5.12.1924. Houghton bMS Eng 1020.

76. T. E. Lawrence to L. G. Curtis 5.12.1924. All Souls College, Oxford.

77. T. E. Lawrence to L. G. Curtis 2.1.1925. All Souls College, Oxford.

78. When I wrote to Bruce on 15.4.1969 pointing out certain historical problems in the material quoted by the *Sunday Times*, he replied on May 1st that my letter contained serious allegations against the newspaper, and had been forwarded to them for attention. His letter ended with a crudely expressed threat that I should restrict my enquiries since otherwise I would get my fingers badly burned.

As a result of Bruce's action I was invited to meet Phillip Knightley of the *Sunday Times*, and we discussed my findings as well as Knightley's own conclusions about parts of the Bruce document (such as the India section) which had been omitted from the *Sunday Times* article. The outcome was that the subsequent book, *The Secret Lives of Lawrence of Arabia* (by P. G. Knightley and C. Simpson, London, Nelson, 1969), presented the Bruce story with considerably strengthened reservations. My own conclusion was, and still is, that no self-respecting historian could accept anything in Bruce's account without confirmation from a reliable independent source.

79. J. E. Mack, *A Prince of our Disorder* (Boston, Little, Brown, 1976) p. 446.

Chapter 35: Escape from the Tank Corps
January – August 1925

1. T. E. Lawrence to Sir Hugh Trenchard 6.2.1925 partially quoted *MB* pp. 276-7 (where 'discreet' is transcribed 'decent'); *SIR* pp. 105-6.
2. T. E. Lawrence to R. V. Buxton 18.2.1925. Jesus College, Oxford.
3. *Ibid.*
4. T. E. Lawrence to M. Pike 23.2.1925. Bodleian R (transcript).
5. T. E. Lawrence to E. H. Kennington 7.3.1925. Bodleian R (transcript).
6. T. E. Lawrence to R. V. Buxton 26.3.1925 *DG* p. 472. Jesus College, Oxford.
7. *Ibid.*
8. T. E. Lawrence to C. F. Shaw 26.3.1925 *MB* p. 277. BL Add. MS 45903.
9. T. E. Lawrence to H. J. Cape 21.4.1925 *DG* pp. 474-5.
10. G. B. Shaw to S. Baldwin 28.4.1925 in *Collected Letters of Bernard Shaw*, Vol. III, ed. D. H. Laurence (London, Max Reinhardt, 1985) pp. 909-10.
11. T. E. Lawrence to C. St.J. Hornby 10.5.1925. Bodleian R (transcript).
12. T. E. Lawrence to C. F. Shaw 16.5.1925 *MB* pp. 279-80. BL Add. MS 45903.
13. T. E. Lawrence to R. V. Buxton 16.5.1925. Jesus College, Oxford.
14. T. E. Lawrence to L. G. Curtis, undated, but May 1925. All Souls College, Oxford.
15. T. E. Lawrence to J. Buchan 19.5.1925 *DG* pp. 475-6; *MB* p. 280-1. Queen's University Archives, Kingston, Ontario.
16. S. Baldwin to J. Buchan 10.6.1925. Queen's University Archives, Kingston, Ontario.
17. This was Hodgson's first work for a private press; afterwards he was to be pressman for many years at the Gregynog Press.
18. T. E. Lawrence to P. Wyndham Lewis 8.6.1925. Cornell University Libraries.
19. T. E. Lawrence to E. Garnett 13.6.1925 *DG* pp. 476-7; partially omitted from *MB* p. 281.
20. T. E. Lawrence to E. M. Forster 17.6.1925 *MB* pp. 282-4. King's College, Cambridge.
21. T. E. Lawrence to R. V. Buxton 20.6.1925 *DG* p. 478. Jesus College, Oxford.
22. T. E. Lawrence to C. F. Shaw 28.6.1925. BL Add. MS 45903.
23. T. E. Lawrence to E. Garnett 21.6.1925. Bodleian R (transcript).
24. T. E. Lawrence to C. F. Shaw 4.7.1925 omitted from *MB* p. 285. BL Add. MS 45903.
25. *Ibid. MB* p. 285.
26. T. E. Lawrence to J. Buchan 5.7.1925 *DG* p. 478; *MB* p. 286. Queen's University Archives, Kingston, Ontario.
27. T. E. Lawrence to E. Garnett 17.7.1925 *DG* p.479. Lawrence may by this time have heard from Charlotte Shaw about the part played by Garnett.

28. T. E. Lawrence to E. Garnett 27.7.1925 *DG* pp. 479-80.

Chapter 36. Ambition fulfilled

August 1925 – December 1926

1. T. E. Lawrence to R. V. Buxton 15.8.1925. Jesus College, Oxford.
2. T. E. Lawrence to E. Palmer 7.9.1925 *DG* p. 485. The Tank Corps had become the Royal Tank Corps in October 1923.
3. T. E. Lawrence to C. F. Shaw 28.9.1925 *MB* pp. 289-91. BL Add. MS 45903.
4. T. E. Lawrence to E. Garnett 3.11.1925. Bodleian R (transcript).
5. T. E. Lawrence to E. Candler 22.9.1925. KCL (transcript).
6. T. E. Lawrence to C. F. Shaw 17.11.1925. BL Add. MS 45903.
7. T. E. Lawrence to W. Roberts 10.12.1925. Bodleian R (transcript).
8. T. E. Lawrence to S. C. Cockerell 29.12.1925 *DG* p. 488.
9. T. E. Lawrence to R. V. Buxton 4.1.1926. Jesus College, Oxford. Lawrence nevertheless kept exact details of the number of copies and the subscribers' names. These records can now be found at HRHRC Texas and the Houghton Library.
10. T. E. Lawrence to H. J. Cape 28.1.1926. Bodleian R (transcript).
11. T. E. Lawrence to A. N. H. M. Herbert February or March 1923, quoted in *The Man who was Greenmantle* by M. Fitzherbert (London, John Murray, 1983) p. 243.
12. T. E. Lawrence to F. E. Hardy 13.2.1926. Bodleian R (transcript).
13. T. E. Lawrence to H. J. Cape 22.2.1926. Bodleian R (transcript). Lawrence may by this time have known that a biography of Doughty was to be written by D. G. Hogarth.
14. T. E. Lawrence to Whittingham & Griggs 15.3.1926. Bodleian R (transcript).
15. T. E. Lawrence to H. J. Cape 25.5.1927 *DG* p. 518.
16. T. E. Lawrence to H. H. Banbury 25.5.1926. Bodleian R (transcript).
17. T. E. Lawrence to F. E. Hardy 21.6.1926 *DG* pp. 498-9.
18. T. E. Lawrence to C. F. Shaw 22.8.1926 *MB* pp. 304-5. BL Add. MS 45903.
19. T. E. Lawrence to C. F. Shaw 24.8.1926 omitted from *MB* p. 305. BL Add. MS 45903.
20. T. E. Lawrence to D. Knowles 18.10.1926. Bodleian R (transcript).
21. T. E. Lawrence to M. Pike 18.10.1926. Bodleian R (transcript).
22. T. E. Lawrence to J. G. Wilson 25.5.1926 *DG* p. 497. Sir J. W. Fortescue was Librarian at Windsor Castle, 1905-26.
23. Sir H. Trenchard to T. E. Lawrence 22.11.1926 *LTEL* p. 198.
24. T. E. Lawrence to C. F. Shaw 2.12.1926. BL Add. MS 45903.
25. T. E. Lawrence to G. Brough 27.9.1926 *DG* p. 499. Bodleian R (transcript). It is often thought that Lawrence chose Brough Superior motorcycles because he liked riding very fast. In December 1927 he wrote: 'The point of glory in a Brough was that lazy touring speed, maintained, you felt, without effort on the engine's part, for all day' (to D. Knowles 30.12.1927 *DG* p. 562).
26. T. E. Lawrence to D. G. Hogarth 19.5.1927. Bodleian R (transcript).
27. E. Bishop, *The Debt we owe: the Royal Air Force Benevolent Fund 1919-1969* (London, Longmans, 1969) p. 121.
28. T. E. Lawrence to D. G. Hogarth 1.6.1927. Bodleian R (transcript).
29. T. E. Lawrence to his mother 1.12.1926 *HL* pp. 362-3. Bodleian Ms Res. C13. Lawrence's original estimate for printing the subscribers' *Seven Pillars* had been

£3,000. The final figure of £13,000 given here almost certainly included about £3,000 he had spent on portraits before work on the subscribers' edition began. Excluding this, the subscribers' copies, which sold for thirty guineas, had in reality cost over ninety guineas each to produce. However, both these figures ignore the production cost of the many copies Lawrence gave away free. If he had sold all the two hundred copies printed at thirty guineas, the revenue would have been £6,000, leaving a loss of about £4,000 on the edition (excluding the cost of the portraits).

Chapter 37. A Fresh Start

January – June 1927

1. T. E. Lawrence to J. S. Hollings 11.1.1927. Bodleian.
2. T. E. Lawrence to E. H. Marsh 22.2.1927 *DG* p. 505. New York Public Library.
3. T. E. Lawrence to his mother 11.1.1927 *HL* p. 364; *MB* p. 315. Bodleian MS Res C13.
4. T. E. Lawrence to C. F. Shaw 28.1.1927 *MB* p. 316. BL Add MS 45903.
5. T. E. Lawrence to C. F. Shaw 15.3.1927. BL Add. MS 45903.
6. *Ibid.*
7. T. E. Lawrence to L. G. Curtis 1.3.1927. All Souls College, Oxford.
8. T. E. Lawrence to F. el Akle 28.1.1927 *MB* p. 316. Bodleian R (photocopy). A few months later, in a letter to Edward Garnett about Herbert Read's review of *Revolt*, Lawrence wrote: 'I entirely repudiate his suggestion that one race is better than another. This is the purest jingoism and Morning Postliness. They apply it to the Irish, and so to myself.' (1.12.1927 *DG* p. 550).
9. T. E. Lawrence to L. G. Curtis 1.3.1927. All Souls College, Oxford.
10. T. E. Lawrence to D. Knowles 30.12.1927 *DG* p. 562.
11. T. E. Lawrence to his mother 11.1.1927 omitted from *HL* p. 364 *MB* p. 315. Bodleian MS Res C13.
12. T. E. Lawrence to C. F. Shaw 28.1.1927 omitted from *MB* pp. 316-17. BL Add. MS 45903. When Charlotte Shaw asked what he was reading, he replied on 16.3.1927: 'My Greek Books? Certainly. I have never forgotten it: so I began with Xenophon's *Anabasis* . . . Till now I've only read forty or fifty pages. After Xenophon, who will last me for many weeks, I'll tackle Herodotus, and then the *Odyssey*, spending only a little time daily on them, using a dictionary for the doubtful words. Greek literature is so good, that it is almost the best second language for a reader.' BL Add. MS 45903.
13. Viscount Allenby to T. E. Lawrence 22.1.1927. Bodleian R (transcript).
14. T. E. Lawrence to C. F. Shaw 4.3.1927 *MB* pp. 319-20. BL Add. MS 45903. Lowell Thomas's lectures had been re-titled *With Allenby in Palestine and Lawrence in Arabia*.
15. T. E. Lawrence to E. H. Kennington 15.2.1927 *DG* p. 507.
16. The highest price recorded for a copy of the subscribers' *Seven Pillars* during Lawrence's lifetime was £570 obtained at a London auction in November 1927.
17. G. B. Shaw, preface to *Catalogue of an Exhibition of Paintings, Pastels, Drawings and Woodcuts illustrating Col. T. E. Lawrence's book "Seven Pillars of Wisdom"* (London, The Leicester Galleries, 1927, Exhibition No. 427) pp. 9-10.
18. T. E. Lawrence to E. H. Kennington 15.2.1927 *DG* p. 509.

19. T. E. Lawrence to C. F. Shaw 15.2.1927. BL Add. MS 45903.

20. T. E. Lawrence to E. Garnett 1.8.1927 *DG* p. 533; omitted from *MB* pp. 341-2.

21. T. E. Lawrence to C. F. Shaw 24.2.1927 omitted from *MB* pp. 317-8. BL Add. MS 45903. D. G. Hogarth had written an article: 'Lawrence of Arabia, the story of his book' in *The Times*, 13.12.1926. There had also been a mischievous article on *Seven Pillars* which had considerably embarrassed Lawrence: 'Outspoken book by Lawrence of Arabia' (*Evening Standard*, London, 19.10.1926). This consisted mainly of character sketches taken from *Seven Pillars*.

22. T. E. Lawrence to R. V. Buxton (quoting Buxton) 4.3.1927 *MB* p. 319. Jesus College, Oxford.

23. *Ibid.*

24. Full-page advertisement in *The World's Work* (Garden City, N.Y.) Vol. LIII, No. 6, April 1927.

25. There had been problems with both English and American serialisations of *Revolt*. Serial rights were initially offered to the *Daily Telegraph* and the American *Asia* magazine. After some negotiations *Asia* declined, and *Revolt* was serialised in *The World's Work*, a Doubleday publication. The London *Daily Telegraph* had accepted the serialisation, but the Managing Proprietor Lord Burnham changed his mind just before Lawrence sailed for India. After further discussions, Burnham decided to go ahead after all. His wavering irritated Lawrence since a large sum of money was involved: 'If I'd been in Savage's place [Burnham would] have paid £500 extra for the liberty of changing his silly little mind twice – 'pears he's noted for that'. (T. E. Lawrence to R. V. Buxton 16.2.1927. Jesus College, Oxford).

26. Jonathan Cape Ltd. press advertisement, March 1927.

27. T. E. Lawrence to C. F. Shaw 7.4.1927. BL Add. MS 45903.

28. T. E. Lawrence to C. F. Shaw 14.4.1927 *MB* pp. 323-4. BL Add. MS 45903.

29. T. E. Lawrence to C. F. Shaw 21.4.1927. BL Add. MS 45903.

30. Leonard Woolf, 'The Epic of the Modern Man' [review of *Revolt in the Desert*], in *The Nation and Athenaeum* (London) 19.3.1927, p. 857.

31. T. E. Lawrence to C. F. Shaw 4.5.1927. BL Add. MS 45903.

32. W. L. S. Churchill to T. E. Lawrence 16.5.1927 *LTEL* p. 24. Lawrence had written in the front of Churchill's copy of *Seven Pillars*: 'Winston Churchill who made a happy ending to this show. T.E.S. 1.12.1926.' In 1932 he was to add: 'And eleven years after we set our hands to making an honest settlement, all our work still stands: the countries having gone forward, out interests having been saved, and nobody killed, either on our side or the other. To have planned for eleven years is statesmanship. I ought to have given you *two* copies of this work!' (Reproduced in facsimile in Churchill's *Great Contemporaries* (London, Thornton Butterworth, 1937) p. 163.

33. Full-page advertisement in *The World's Work* (Garden City, N.Y.) Vol. LIII, No. 5, March 1927.

34. T. E. Lawrence to C. F. Shaw 4.3.1927 omitted from *MB* pp. 319-20. BL Add. MS 45903.

35. T. E. Lawrence to E. M. Forster 27.4.1927. King's College, Cambridge.

36. T. E. Lawrence to C. F. Shaw 16.6.1927. BL Add. MS 45903.

37. T. E. Lawrence to C. F. Shaw 24.11.1927. BL Add. MS 45903. Lawrence's regular letters to Charlotte Shaw are of considerable interest because they provide a record of his life which spans several years.

38. Lawrence's gifts and indefinite loans to Charlotte Shaw included the following:
    One of the five bound and corrected copies of the 'Oxford' Seven Pillars (loaned in 1922, now in the British Library).

    One of the 1919 portrait drawings by Augustus John (given in 1926; now in the National Portrait Gallery, London).

    A copy of the subscribers' *Seven Pillars* (given in 1926, now in the New York Public Library).

    The manuscript verse anthology *Minorities* (given in 1927, now in the Bodleian Library).

    The penultimate corrected typescript draft of *The Mint* (given in 1927-8, now in the British Library).

    A typed fair copy of *The Mint* (now in the British Library).

    The final manuscript of his translation of the *Odyssey* (given in 1932, now in the British Library).

39. T. E. Lawrence to A. W. Lawrence 5.5.1927 *HL* p. 365.
40. T. E. Lawrence to H. J. Cape 15.5.1927. Bodleian R (transcript).
41. T. E. Lawrence to E. Eliot 16.6.1927 *MB* pp. 333-4. Messrs. Tweedie & Prideaux, Solrs. Another passage in this letter suggests that Lawrence might have thought that the Killua property would have been inherited by his father: 'My father was a younger son of an Irish family called Chapman, of Killua, in Co. Meath. His own place was called South Hill, also in Meath. His widow, Lady Chapman, and her daughters still live there: but Killua has been sold.' Lawrence refers repeatedly to Debrett in letters about the Chapman family. He had probably been misled by the edition of *Debrett's Illustrated Baronetage* current in 1919. This did not make it clear that the Killua property belonged to a different branch of the Chapman family, and would not have passed to his father.
42. T. E. Lawrence to R. T. R. P. Butler 15.3.1927. Bodleian R (photocopy).

Chapter 38. Life at Karachi

June – December 1927

1. T. E. Lawrence to R. V. Buxton 12.5.1927. Jesus College, Oxford.
2. T. E. Lawrence to C. F. Shaw 23.6.1927. BL Add. MS 45903.
3. T. E. Lawrence to C. F. Shaw 7.7.1927. BM Add. MS 45903.
4. G. H. Doran, *Chronicles of Barabbas* (N.Y., Harcourt, Brace, 1935) p. 395.
5. *Ibid.* p. 396. There seems to be a surprising contrast between Doran's enthusiastic promotion of *Revolt* in 1927 and his retrospective cynicism. It may be that his attitude was influenced by the fact that Lawrence was friendly with F. N. Doubleday, whose publishing firm merged with Doran's in 1927. Doran found himself unable to work with Doubleday, and sold his interest in the company.
6. English-speaking critics of Lawrence's writing have generally overlooked the fact that it has been so successful in translation. First *Revolt*, then, after Lawrence's death, *Seven Pillars of Wisdom* became classics of their kind in several languages. Since the idiosyncrasies of Lawrence's style cannot be passed on in these translations, the attraction of *Seven Pillars* must lie in other qualities which appeal to readers from a wide range of cultural backgrounds.
7. T. E. Lawrence to C. F. Shaw 29.9.1927. BL Add. MS 45903.

8. On 9th November 1926 Robert Graves had written to Lawrence asking for £150-£250 (then a very considerable sum) to be used for work on a building to accommodate himself, his wife Nancy, and Laura Riding (Bodleian R, transcript).

9. T. E. Lawrence to D. G. Hogarth 1.6.1927. Bodleian R (transcript).

10. T. E. Lawrence to C. F. Shaw 1.6.1927 *MB* p. 331. BL Add. MS 45903.

11. *Ibid. MB* p. 330.

12. T. E. Lawrence to E. H. Marsh 10.6.1927 *DG* pp. 521-2. Berg Collection, New York Public Library.

13. T. E. Lawrence to C. F. Shaw 1.6.1927 *MB* pp. 330-1. BL Add. MS 45903.

14. R. R. Graves to T. E. Lawrence 3.6.1927. Bodleian R (transcript).

15. T. E. Lawrence to R. R. Graves 9.6.1927 *B:RG* p. 45.

16. R. R. Graves to T. E. Lawrence *c.* 3.6.1927. Bodleian R (transcript).

17. R. R. Graves in *B:RG* p. 44. Graves's account of the origins of the project is inaccurate.

18. R. R. Graves to S. Sassoon 5.6.1927, *In broken Images, Selected Letters of Robert Graves 1914-1946* ed. P. O'Prey (London, Hutchinson, 1982) p. 175.

19. G. B. Shaw to T. E. Lawrence 12.4.1928 *LTEL* p. 177.

20. T. E. Lawrence to R. R. Graves 28.6.1927 omitted from *B:RG* p. 48. Houghton fMS Eng. 1252 (347)

21. *Ibid.* partially quoted, in a modified form, in *B:RG* pp. 113-14.

22. T. E. Lawrence to L. G. Curtis 14.7.1927 *DG* p. 530. All Souls College, Oxford.

23. T. E. Lawrence to C. F. Shaw 29.9.1927. BL Add. MS 45903.

24. T. E. Lawrence to R. R. Graves 28.6.1927 *B:RG* p. 54. Houghton fMS Eng 1252 (347). Lawrence had written to R. V. Buxton on 16.2.1927: 'the eighteen Kennington pastels I bought for £720 and £1200 which Winston paid me in 1921, when I was still solvent.' (Jesus College, Oxford).

25. *Ibid. B:RG* p. 56.

26. Lawrence was still corresponding with Fareedeh el Akle in 1927. Her letters expressed a profound admiration and affection towards him, strongly coloured by her Christian faith and belief in Arab nationalism. There was no doubt a risk that this unsophisticated devotion would be misinterpreted by Graves.

27. T. E. Lawrence to R. R. Graves 9.6.1927 *B:RG* p. 45. Houghton bMS Eng 1252 (56).

28. Cf. Robert Graves's claim (*B:RG* p. 47) that two-thirds of the book was derived from *Seven Pillars*. Graves's text runs to 424 pages, of which 328 are on the war period and contain little material from sources other than *Seven Pillars*.

    George H. Doran, the American publisher of both *Revolt* and Graves's book, did not share Cape's motivation about the biography, since he was still able to print *Revolt*. As is usual in such cases, it was Cape who took editorial responsibility for Graves's book.

29. T. E. Lawrence to J. E. L. Wrench 5.5.1927 *MB* p. 327. BL Add. MS 59543.

30. T. E. Lawrence to F. Yeats-Brown 8.7.1927 *MB* p. 340 BL Add. MS 59548.

31. *Ibid.*

32. Lawrence's *Spectator* reviews are listed in Appendix 5, p. 972.

33. T. E. Lawrence to C. F. Shaw 15.9.1927. BL Add. MS 45903.

34. T. E. Lawrence to F. N. Doubleday 16.6.1927. Princeton University Library. It is interesting that Lawrence should have approached Doubleday rather than Cape for translating work. In part this may have been because he had let Cape down over

Sturly in 1924, but it is also clear that Lawrence felt qualms of conscience towards Doubleday, to whom he had promised American rights of the abortive *Seven Pillars* abridgement in 1920 (see chapter 29), whereas Savage and Cape had sold American rights of *Revolt* to George H. Doran.

When Doubleday's American business merged with Doran's in 1927, Doubleday became publisher of *Revolt*. Lawrence wrote to him: 'It has always secretly hurt my feelings that anyone else should print *Revolt in the Desert* in your country . . . please understand that I'm most happy and delighted to know that you are now my American owner.'(7.12.1927. Princeton University Library).

35. T. E. Lawrence to E. Garnett 10.6.1927 omitted from *DG* p. 520. Bodleian R (transcript).

36. E. Garnett to T. E. Lawrence 18.7.1927 *LTEL* pp. 94-5. The Syrian journey referred to is Lawrence's secret ride to Damascus in June 1917.

37. T. E. Lawrence to E. Garnett 1.8.1927 *DG* p. 532; *MB* pp. 341-2. Bodleian R (transcript).

38. *Ibid. MB* p. 342.

39. T. E. Lawrence to C. F. Shaw 14.7.1927. BL Add. MS 45903.

40. R. R. Graves to C. F. Shaw, undated, BL Add. MS 45903. The diaries referred to are now in the British Library.

41. C. F. Shaw to R. R. Graves 27.7.1927. Bodleian R.

42. C. F. Shaw to R. R. Graves 8.8.1927. Bodleian R.

43. *Ibid.* Such was Charlotte Shaw's jealousy of her relationship with Lawrence that she later refused to collaborate with David Garnett's posthumous edition of Lawrence's letters. When this was published she was evidently upset (see her letter to Dorothy Walker 6.3.1939, in *Mrs G.B.S.*, by J. Dunbar, London, Harrap, 1963, p. 300). She was probably very hurt to discover that Lawrence had been close friends with so many other people, and had told them things she had previously believed he had confided exclusively to her.

44. T. E. Lawrence to C. F. Shaw 18.8.1927 partly omitted from *MB* pp. 344-5. BL Add. MS 45903. There had been no ambiguity whatsoever in Lawrence's suggestion that Graves should contact Charlotte Shaw about letters!

45. T. E. Lawrence to R. R. Graves 30.7.1927 *B:RG* p. 91. Houghton bMS Eng 1252 (58)

46. Note by T. E. Lawrence on the typescript of *Lawrence and the Arabs*, *B:RG* p. 92.

47. T. E. Lawrence to R. R. Graves 3.8.1927 *B:RG* p. 95. Houghton bMS Eng 1252 (59).

48. T. E. Lawrence to C. F. Shaw 4.8.1927. BL Add. MS 45903.

49. T. E. Lawrence to R. R. Graves 17.8.1927 *B:RG* p 133.

50. T. E. Lawrence to C. F. Shaw 18.8.1927 omitted from *MB* pp. 344-5. BL Add. MS 45903.

51. T. E. Lawrence to R. R. Graves 1.10.1927 *B:RG* pp. 136-7.

52. T. E. Lawrence to C. F. Shaw 8.12.1927. BL Add. MS 45903.

53. T. E. Lawrence to R. R. Graves 24.12.1927 *B:RG* pp. 141-2. Houghton bMS Eng 1252 (63).

54. W. M. M. Hurley (adjutant, RAF Karachi), *Friends* p. 401.

55. T. E. Lawrence to F. N. Doubleday 25.8.1927 omitted from *MB* p. 345. Princeton University Library.

56. T. E. Lawrence to E. Garnett 22.9.1927 *DG* p. 541.

57. T. E. Lawrence to E. Garnett 1.8.1927 *DG* p. 532; *MB* p. 342.
58. T. E. Lawrence to C. F. Shaw 27.10.1927. BL Add. MS 45903.
59. *Ibid.*
60. Lawrence's article was published, probably in its original form, under the title 'Ramping', in the *Journal of the Royal Air Force College, Cranwell*, Vol. XI, No. 1, Spring 1931. It was signed pseudonymously with the initials 'J.C.' It may be a coincidence that these were the initials of his parents' family names, Junner (or Jenner) and Chapman.
61. T. E. Lawrence to E. Garnett 15.11.1927. Bodleian R (transcript).
62. T. E. Lawrence to D. Knowles 30.12.1927 *DG* pp. 560-1.
63. T. E. Lawrence to C. F. Shaw 8.12.1927. BL Add. MS 45903.
64. T. E. Lawrence to C. F. Shaw 8.5.1928. BL Add. MS 45904.
65. *The Letters of Gertrude Bell* ed. Lady Bell, 2 vols. (London, Ernest Benn, 1927).
66. T. E. Lawrence to C. F. Shaw 18.10.1927 *MB* pp. 348-50. BL Add. MS 45903.
67. T. E. Lawrence to R. V. Buxton 10.6.1927. Jesus College, Oxford.
68. R. Isham to T. E. Lawrence 29.6.1927. Bodleian R (transcript).
69. R. Isham to T. E. Lawrence 7.7.1927. Bodleian R (transcript).
70. *Ibid.*
71. T. E. Lawrence to R. Isham 10.8.1927 *MB* p. 344. Bodleian R (transcript).
72. Review of *Revolt in the Desert* by T. E. Lawrence and *With Lawrence in Arabia* by Sir A. T. Wilson in *Journal of the Central Asian Society*, Vol. 14, 1927, pp. 282-5.
73. T. E. Lawrence to C. F. Shaw 27.10.1927. BL Add. MS 45903.
74. T. E. Lawrence to E. H. Kennington 15.9.1927. Bodleian R (transcript).
75. T. E. Lawrence to C. F. Shaw 8.9.1927. BL Add. MS 45903.
76. T. E. Lawrence to R. V. Buxton 11.11.1927. Jesus College, Oxford. J. E. Mack states: 'his letters reveal an increasing nihilism and self-disparagement during the Karachi period, which the news of Hogarth's death in November only served to deepen.' (*A Prince of our Disorder*, Boston, Little, Brown, 1976, p. 368) In my opinion this conclusion is wrong, and the quotations Mack uses to support it are not representative. Viewed as a whole, Lawrence's letters from Karachi show an increasingly high morale, especially after the reviews of *Revolt in the Desert*. Hogarth's death was a severe but temporary setback.
77. T. E. Lawrence to C. F. Shaw 10.11.1927 *MB* pp. 353-4. BL Add. MS 45903.
78. T. E. Lawrence to R. Isham 22.11.1927 *DG* p. 544.
79. T. E. Lawrence to E. Garnett 30.11.1927 *MB* pp. 357-8. Bodleian R (transcript).
80. T. E. Lawrence to Sir H. M. Trenchard 17.3.1928 *MB* p. 369. Bodleian R (transcript).
81. T. E. Lawrence to Sir H. M. Trenchard 22.12.1927. Bodleian R (transcript).
82. T. E. Lawrence to T. B. Marson 20.1.1928 *DG* p. 570. Bodleian R (transcript).
83. T. E. Lawrence to A. P. Wavell 9.2.1928 omitted from *DG* p. 576. Bodleian R (transcript).
84. See T. E. Lawrence to H. H. Banbury 25.1.1928. Bodleian R (transcript). Referring to this incident, H. Montgomery Hyde named the CO at Karachi as W/C Reginald Bone (*Solitary in the Ranks*, London, Constable, 1977, p. 142). However, Bone's distinguished RAF career does not match the information contained in Lawrence's letters about the officer involved. Moreover, Bone was still serving in India when Lawrence returned to England in January 1929; he visited Lawrence on board the S.S. *Rajputana* before she sailed from Karachi.

85. T. E. Lawrence to C. F. Shaw 12.5.1927 omitted from *MB* p. 328. BL Add. MS 45903.
86. T. E. Lawrence to C. F. Shaw 27.12.1927. BL Add. MS 45903.
87. T. E. Lawrence to C. F. Shaw 4.1.1928. BL Add. MS 45903.
88. *Ibid.*
89. *Ibid.* •

Chapter 39. New Projects and Old
January – May 1928

1. B. Rogers to T. E. Lawrence 4.3.1928. Bodleian R.
2. *Ibid.*
3. R. Isham to T. E. Lawrence 6.12.1927. Bodleian R (transcript).
4. T. E. Lawrence to R. Isham 2.1.1928. Bodleian R (transcript).
5. *Ibid.*
6. *Ibid.*
7. T. E. Lawrence to C. F. Shaw 2.1.1928. BL Add. MS 45916.
8. *Ibid.*
9. T. E. Lawrence to S. C. Cockerell 2.2.1928 *Friends of a Lifetime*, ed. V. Meynell (London, Jonathan Cape, 1940) p. 367.
10. T. E. Lawrence to C. F. Shaw 2.2.1928. BL Add. MS 45903.
11. *Ibid.*
12. L. V. Hogarth to T. E. Lawrence 14.3.1928. Bodleian R (transcript). No biography of Hogarth has yet been published, although a considerable amount of relevant material survives. To judge by the many documents I have seen, a properly researched study would totally dispel the sensational allegations that Hogarth's pre-war archaeological work was a disguise for British Intelligence activity.
13. T. E. Lawrence to F. E. Hardy 11.1.1927 *DG* p. 503.
14. F. E. Hardy: *The Later Years of Thomas Hardy* (London, Macmillan, 1930) p. 434.
15. T. E. Lawrence to H. S. Ede 20.1.1928 *DG* p. 566. University of East Anglia, Norwich.
16. C. F. Shaw to T. E. Lawrence 16.1.1928. BL Add. MS 45922.
17. T. E. Lawrence to C. F. Shaw 2.2.1928. BL Add. MS 45903.
18. T. E. Lawrence to C. F. Shaw 25.2.1928. BL Add. MS 45903.
19. T. E. Lawrence to C. F. Shaw 1.3.1928. BL Add. MS 45903.
20. T. E. Lawrence to C. F. Shaw 16.3.1928. BL Add. MS 45903.
21. *Ibid.* Lawrence was referring to press statements, at the time of his discharge from Farnborough in the winter of 1922-3, that he had been working on an RAF book.
22. T. E. Lawrence to Sir Hugh Trenchard 17.3.1928 *MB* pp. 369-70. Bodleian R (transcript).
23. *Ibid.*
24. T. E. Lawrence to E. Garnett 15.3.1928 *DG* pp. 579-80. Lawrence burned the original notes and the rough pencil draft of *The Mint* at Karachi, so that only Charlotte Shaw's corrected typescript and Garnett's fair copy survived. He had, however, already sent Garnett a single sheet of the original notes in their pasted-up form (reproduced in *DG*, plate facing p. 619, and now at HRHRC Texas). Lawrence had also sent a page of the rough pencil draft to Charlotte Shaw, which she preserved with his letters (BL Add. MS 45903). Lawrence told Garnett on

22.3.1928 that Charlotte Shaw had seen a draft of *The Mint*.

25. *Ibid.*

26. Literary dedications to T. E. Lawrence include the following (listed in chronological order):

1. 'The Pier Glass' (poem) by R. R. Graves, dedicated 'To T. E. Lawrence, who helped me with it'. Published in *The Pier Glass* (London, Secker, 1921).

2. *On English Poetry*, by R. R. Graves (London, Heinemann, 1922). Dedication: 'To T. E. Lawrence of Arabia and All Souls College, Oxford and to W. H. R. Rivers of the Solomon Islands and St. John's College, Cambridge, my gratitude for valuable critical help, and the dedication of this book'.

3. 'The Clipped Stater' (poem) by R. R. Graves, dedicated 'To Thomas Edward Shaw', published in *Welchman's Hose* (London, The Fleuron Press, 1925).

4. *My Head! My Head!*, by R. R. Graves (London, Secker, 1925). Dedicated 'To T. E. Lawrence'.

5. *The Eternal Moment*, by E. M. Forster (London, Sidgwick & Jackson, 1928). Dedicated 'To T.E. in the absence of anything else'.

6. *Cécile* by F. L. Lucas (London, Chatto & Windus, 1930). Dedicated 'To the author of "The Seven Pillars of Wisdom" '.

7. 'Apologia Dei' (essay) by F. Manning, dedicated 'To T. E. Shaw'. Published in *Scenes and Portraits* by F. Manning (revised and enlarged edition, London, Peter Davies, 1930).

8. *Julius Caesar* by John Buchan (London, Peter Davies, 1932). Dedicated 'To my friend Aircraftsman T. E. Shaw'.

9. *The Ghost of Napoleon* by B. H. Liddell Hart (London, Faber & Faber, 1933). Dedicated 'To "T. E." who trod this road before 1914'.

10. *Salar the Salmon* by Henry Williamson, London, Faber & Faber, 1935. Dedicated 'To T. E. Lawrence of *Seven Pillars of Wisdom* and V. M. Yeates of *Winged Victory*'.

27. T. E. Lawrence to C. F. Shaw 11.1.1928. BL Add. MS 45903.

28. Lawrence's letter to Edward Garnett about *Tarka the Otter* is published in T. E. Lawrence: *Men in Print* ed A. W. Lawrence (London, The Golden Cockerel Press, 1940) pp. 41-54. As a result of Lawrence's criticisms, Williamson made a number of changes to the text. These were first included in the fourth edition of *Tarka* (London, Putnams', June 1928); the imprint reads: 'slightly revised, following suggestions of "T.E.L." '

29. A. P. Wavell to T. E. Lawrence 8.1.1928 *LTEL* p. 209.

30. Sir H. L. Samuel to T. E. Lawrence 11.3.1928. Bodleian R (transcript).

31. Sir H. M. Trenchard to T. E. Lawrence 10.4.1928 *LTEL* p. 200.

32. G. B. Shaw to T. E. Lawrence 12.4.1928 *LTEL* pp. 175-6.

33. When Charlotte Shaw died, she bequeathed her letters from Lawrence to the British Museum Library. Bernard Shaw afterwards added the *Mint* draft to this collection, but urged that there should be no publicity about the gift: 'If a word about *The Mint* gets into the press there will be the devil to pay. You will be inundated with journalists wanting to see it and to have a story about Lawrence and my late wife. I remember the horror of Ronald Storrs when he learned that Lawrence had given a copy to a lady, and that she had perhaps actually read it (which, by the way, I greatly doubt that she ever did, though she may have sampled it as I did myself)'. G. B. Shaw to the Department of Manuscripts, 17.4.1944. BL Add. MS 45916.

34. E. Garnett to T. E. Lawrence 22.4.1928 *LTEL* pp. 96-8.

35. T. E. Lawrence to E. Garnett 23.4.1928 *DG* pp. 596-8.

36. T. E. Lawrence to Sir H. M. Trenchard 1.5.1928 omitted from *DG* p. 600. Bodleian R (transcript).

37. Lawrence later wrote to Charlotte Shaw: 'The cause of my move was a statement in conversation to a friend of mine of the C.O. at Karachi, which made me see I was living within reach of hurt' (11.6.1928. BL Add. MS 45904).

38. T. E. Lawrence to E. Garnett 23.4.1928 *DG* pp. 595-6.

39. T. E. Lawrence to C. F. Shaw 17.5.1928 *MB* p. 374. BL Add. MS 45904. E. M. Dowson died aged 33; D. G. Rossetti died aged 54.

Chapter 40. The Edge of the World

May 1928 – January 1929

1. T. E. Lawrence to H. S. Ede 30.6.1928 *DG* pp. 614-5. University of East Anglia, Norwich. Lawrence gave Miranshah and Miramshah as alternative spellings, but habitually used the former.

2. T. E. Lawrence to Sir H. M. Trenchard 22.12.1927. Bodleian R (transcript).

3. T. E. Lawrence to C. F. Shaw 4.6.1928. BL Add. MS 45904.

4. T. E. Lawrence to C. F. Shaw 15.6.1928. BL Add. MS 45904.

5. T. E. Lawrence to R. Isham 30.6.1928. Bodleian R (transcript).

6. T. E. Lawrence to C. F. Shaw 17.7.1928. BL Add. MS 45904.

7. T. E. Lawrence to C. F. Shaw 18.8.1928. BL Add. MS 45904.

8. T. E. Lawrence to Sir H. M. Trenchard 5.8.1928. Bodleian R (transcript).

9. R. Isham to T. E. Lawrence 11.8.1928. Bodleian R (transcript).

10. *New York Sun*, late July 1928. An article along similar lines had been submitted on July 23rd 1928 to the *New York World*, who had rejected it (see *DG* pp. 631-2).

11. B. Rogers to T. E. Lawrence 3.9.1928. Bodleian R.

12. *Ibid.*

13. T. E. Lawrence to Sir E. Walker and W. Merton 10.10.1928. Houghton bMS Eng 1252 (218).

14. *Ibid.*

15. T. E. Lawrence to B. Rogers 10.10.1928. Houghton bMS Eng 1252 (161).

16. *Evening News* (London) 26.9.1928. This appears to have been the first article in a British newspaper alleging that Lawrence was involved in secret activities in India. David Garnett's praise for the *New York World* (*DG* p. 631) was misplaced: it reprinted this absurd piece on September 27th.

17. Letter from C. M. J. Barrington, an Army Reserve officer, to the editor of the *Sunday Express* (London) quoted in the issue of 30.9.1928.

18. *Sunday Express* (London) 30.9.1928. This was the first article in a British newspaper to claim specifically that Lawrence was in Afghanistan.

19. G. Agar-Robartes, India Office, minute dated 2.10.1928. L/P&S/11/293/5310.

20. Sir F. H. Humphrys to the India Office, telegram, 2.10.1928. FO 371/13283, fo. 218.

21. F.O. minute, 10.10.1928. FO 371/13283, fo. 211.

22. E. M. B. Ingram, Foreign Office, minute, 10.10.1928, FO 371/13283, fos. 211-2.

23. L. Oliphant, Foreign Office, minute to the Secretary of State, 10.10.1928. FO 371/13283, fos. 213-4.

24. L. B. Wakely to Sir F. H. Humphrys 25.10.1928. FO 371/13283, fo. 216.
25. T. E. Lawrence to C. F. Shaw 25.6.1928. BL Add. MS 45904.
26. T. E. Lawrence to C. F. Shaw 30.10.1928. BL Add. MS 45904.
27. T. E. Lawrence to E. M. Forster 12.12.1928 *DG* pp. 625-6. King's College, Cambridge.
28. T. E. Lawrence to E. Garnett 11.12.1928. Bodleian R (transcript). The works referred to are *Sigurd the Volsung* by William Morris and *Marmion* by Sir Walter Scott. Morris wrote *Sigurd* in an 'archaic' metre of his own invention, used again in his translation of the *Odyssey*.
29. T. E. Lawrence to C. F. Shaw 18.12.1928. BL Add. MS 45904.
30. T. E. Lawrence to C. F. Shaw 18.9.1928. BL Add. MS 45904.
31. N. C. Manhood to E. Garnett 29.10.1928. Bodleian R (transcript).
32. T. E. Lawrence to E. Garnett 4.12.1928. Bodleian R (transcript).
33. Sir H. M. Trenchard to T. E. Lawrence 30.11.1928 *LTEL* p. 206.
34. T. E. Lawrence to Sir H. M. Trenchard 27.12.1928. Bodleian R (transcript).
35. *Daily News* (London) 5.12.1928.
36. Quoted in the *Sunday Times* (London) 9.12.1928.
37. P. J. Patrick, minute, 12.12.1928. L/P&S/11/293/5310.
38. Sir C. W. Jacob, comment added to the above.
39. Sir F. H. Humphrys, telegram to Delhi and F.O., London 13.12.1928. L/P&S/10/1203.
40. *Empire News* (Manchester) 16.12.1928. A retraction of this article was later published: 'Although the source from which these articles came appeared to be reliable, the *Empire News* is now in possession of further facts which make it clear that they were not written by anyone possessing the authority claimed. Moreover, the statements regarding the alleged presence in Afghanistan of Colonel Lawrence and Trebitsch Lincoln were in every material respect, contrary to fact'. (*Empire News* 14.4.1929).
41. *Free Press Mail Service* 27.12.1928. FO 371/13992.
42. T. E. Lawrence to E. Walker 25.12.1928. Houghton bMS Eng 1252 (220)
43. Sir F. H. Humphrys to Delhi and London, telegram, 3.1.1929. FO 371/13988.
44. Sir H. M. Trenchard to Sir W. G. H. Salmond, 5.1.1929 (copy sent by Trenchard to the India Office) L/P&S/11/293/5310. The message was cabled to Salmond in a paraphrased version as AM 25A/5/1.
45. Sir H. M. Trenchard to Sir A. Hirtzel, 5.1.1929. L/P&S/11/293/5310.
46. *The Times* (London) 6.1.1929.

Chapter 41. Plymouth

January – September 1929

1. T. E. Lawrence to 'Walters' 31.3.1929. Bodleian R (transcript).
2. *Army and Navy Gazette* 24.1.1929.
3. Sir H. M. Trenchard to T. E. Lawrence, quoted in *SIR* p. 182.
4. Sir H. M. Trenchard to T. E. Lawrence, quoted in *DG* p. 324.
5. *Manchester Guardian* 4.2.1929. The interview referred to appeared in the *Illustrated Sunday Graphic* (London) on 3.2.1929. On arrival in London, Lawrence had been taken to a flat in Cromwell Road which belonged to Sydney Smith's

sister-in-law, Patty Edelston, see C. S. Smith, *The Golden Reign* (London, Cassell, 1940) pp. 26-31.

6. T. E. Lawrence to Sir H. M. Trenchard 5.2.1929 *MB* p. 400. Trenchard papers.

7. T. E. Lawrence to E. Thurtle 9.2.1929 *DG* p. 641; *MB* p. 401.

8. *Ibid. MB* p. 402.

9. T. E. Lawrence to E. M. Forster 5.2.1929 *DG* p. 641. King's College, Cambridge.

10. C. F. Shaw to L. G. Curtis 5.2.1929. Bodleian MS Curtis 96.

11. *Ibid.*

12. R. V. Buxton to L. G. Curtis 6.2.1929. Bodleian MS Curtis 96.

13. After Lawrence's death, George Brough vehemently denied that he had ever given Lawrence discounts, although Lawrence himself had told Liddell Hart that these were given in exchange for use of his name in advertising. Such arrangements between manufacturers and famous consumers are relatively common, but are always officially denied, since otherwise the product endorsement would seem worthless. Brough later gave discounts to Lawrence by exchanging his old machine for a new model on very generous trade-in terms.

14. T. E. Lawrence to S. F. Newcombe 22.2.1929 *MB* p. 403. Bodleian R (transcript).

15. B. Rogers to H. Watson Kent, in *Printing and Graphic Arts* (Lunenberg, Vermont) Vol. 3, No. 3, September 1955, p. 68.

16. C. Bigham (Viscount Mersey), *A Picture of Life* (London, John Murray, 1946) p. 342.

17. T. E. Lawrence to A. G. C. Dawnay 28.2.1929 *MB* p. 404 (with transcription errors). Bodleian R (transcript).

18. T. E. Lawrence to Sir H. Baker 8.3.1929. Bodleian R (transcript).

19. T. E. Lawrence to his mother 19.3.1929 *HL* p. 376. Bodleian MS Res C13.

20. T. E. Lawrence to H. S. Ede 20.3.1929 *DG* pp. 644-5. Bodleian R (transcript).

21. T. E. Lawrence to J. W. Easton 1.4.1929 partly quoted in *MB* p. 410. Private collection.

22. Sydney Smith's files on the 1929 Schneider Trophy contest are now at Houghton, fMS Eng 1252 (334). They include many documents drafted or annotated by Lawrence.

23. *John Bull* (London) 13.4.1929.

24. T. E. Lawrence to H. A. Ford 18.4.1929 *DG* p. 650-1; *MB* pp. 416-7.

25. T. E. Lawrence to B. Rogers 1.5.1929 *MB* p. 420. Houghton bMS Eng 1252 (163).

26. B. Rogers to T. E. Lawrence, undated retained copy or draft. Houghton bMS Eng 1252 (279). This letter reached Lawrence on 15.5.1929.

27. *Ibid.*

28. *Ibid.*

29. T. E. Lawrence to C. F. Shaw 16.5.1929. BL Add. MS 45904.

30. T. E. Lawrence to B. Rogers 23.5.1929. Houghton bMS Eng 1252 (164).

31. T. E. Lawrence to C. F. Shaw 27.4.1929 *MB* p. 418. BL Add. MS 45904.

32. T. E. Lawrence to C. F. Shaw 1.5.1929 omitted from *MB* p. 421. BL Add. MS 45904.

33. T. E. Lawrence to C. F. Shaw 12.8.1927. BL Add. MS 45903.

34. T. E. Lawrence, inscription in a copy of his translation of the *Odyssey* given to the Sydney Smiths, reproduced in C. S. Smith, *The Golden Reign* (London, Cassell, 1940) p. 6.

35. T. E. Lawrence to Sir H. M. Trenchard 12.7.1929 *DG* pp. 662-3.

36. Lord Thomson to G. B. Shaw 24.7.1929. Bodleian R (transcript).

37. T. E. Lawrence to B. Rogers 30.7.1929. Houghton bMS Eng 1252 (167).

38. *Ibid.*

39. For further information about this portrait see J. M. Wilson, *T. E. Lawrence* (London, National Portrait Gallery, 1988) p. 212.

40. A. E. John to T. E. Lawrence 3.9.1929. Bodleian R (transcript).

41. T. E. Lawrence to A. G. C. Dawnay 17.9.1929. Bodleian R (transcript).

42. See C. S. Smith: *op. cit.* note 5 above, p. 62. J. Jarché, who did photograph Lawrence at Calshot, contrary to official instructions, claimed in his memoirs *People I have Shot* (London, Methuen, 1934) pp. 227-8 that many photographers had done so, and that their pictures of him had appeared all over the world. No photographs of Lawrence at Calshot have been found in a search through the major British papers at the time (including Jarché's own).

43. Sir H. M. Trenchard to T. E. Lawrence 16.9.1929. Trenchard papers.

Chapter 42. Odyssey and the Biscuit

October 1929 – March 1931

1. Jonathan Cape Ltd. to B. H. Liddell Hart October 1929 *B:LH* p. 36.

2. T. E. Lawrence to B. H. Liddell Hart 28.10.1929 *B:LH* p. 38.

3. *Ibid.*

4. T. E. Lawrence to C. F. Shaw 26.10.1929 *MB* p. 430. BL Add. MS 45904.

5. T. E. Lawrence to C. F. Shaw 19.11.1929. BL Add. MS 45904.

6. *Ibid.*

7. T. E. Lawrence to C. F. Shaw 4.12.1929. BL Add. MS 45904.

8. T. E. Lawrence to C. F. Shaw 15.12.1929. BL Add. MS 45904.

9. *Ibid.*

10. T. E. Lawrence to Sir H. M. Trenchard 18.12.1928. Bodleian R (transcript)

11. T. E. Lawrence to R. R. Graves 30.12.1929 *B:RG* p. 162.

12. T. E. Lawrence to C. F. Shaw 2.1.1930. BL Add. MS 45904.

13. T. E. Lawrence to C. F. Shaw 19.1.1930 *MB* p. 436. BL Add. MS 45904.

14. E. M. Forster to T. E. Lawrence 16.12.1929 *LTEL* pp. pp. 72-3.

15. T. E. Lawrence to E. M. Forster 23.1.1930. Kings College, Cambridge.

16. T. E. Lawrence to H. Williamson 3.5.1930. University of Exeter.

17. T. E. Lawrence to C. F. Shaw 25.2.1930 omitted from *MB* p. 439. BL Add. MS 45904.

18. T. E. Lawrence to D. Garnett 10.2.1930. Bodleian R (transcript)

19. T. E. Lawrence to C. F. Shaw 6.2.1930 *MB* pp. 436-7. BL Add. MS 45904.

20. This pamphlet, titled *Colonel Lawrence and Others on "Her Privates We"*, gave an account of an alleged telephone call from Lawrence to Peter Davies.

21. T. E. Lawrence to A. L. Snagge 4.3.1930 *DG* pp. 683-4.

22. T. E. Lawrence to H. J. Cape 21.2.1930. Bodleian R (transcript).

23. J. M. Barrie to T. E. Lawrence 20.3.1930. Bodleian R (transcript).

24. T. E. Lawrence to J. Buchan 21.3.1930 *DG* p. 686.

25. T. E. Lawrence to E. Thurtle 8.3.1930 *DG* p. 684.

26. T. E. Lawrence to E. Thurtle 13.3.1930 *DG* p. 685.

27. T. E. Lawrence to C. F. Shaw 27.3.1930 omitted from *MB* p. 440. BL Add. MS 45904.

28. T. E. Lawrence to G. W. M. Dunn 27.3.1930. Bodleian R (transcript).
29. T. E. Lawrence to C. F. Shaw 19.4.1930. BL Add. MS 45904.
30. T. E. Lawrence to L. G. Curtis 22.4.1930. All Souls College, Oxford.
31. T. E. Lawrence to F. Manning 15.5.1930 *DG* p. 692.
32. T. E. Lawrence to E. Garnett 27.5.1930. Bodleian R (transcript).
33. *Ibid.*
34. T. E. Lawrence to H. S. Ede 15.7.1930. Bodleian R (transcript).
35. T. E. Lawrence to F. N. Doubleday 2.7.1930. Bodleian R (transcript).
36. T. E. Lawrence to B. Rogers 3.8.1930. Houghton bMS Eng 1252 (183).
37. T. E. Lawrence to F. Manning 7.8.1930. Bodleian R (transcript).
38. T. E. Lawrence to C. F. Shaw 15.8.1930 *MB* p. 441. BL Add. MS 45904. Coward subsequently amused Lawrence by beginning a letter of July 25th: 'Dear 338171 (may I call you 338?)' (*LTEL* p. 27).
39. *The Times* (London) 14.8.1930.
40. Minute, 18.8.1930. Foreign Office file 14524/80, 1930.
41. T. E. Lawrence to E. Garnett 29.6.1930. Bodleian R (transcript).
42. T. E. Lawrence to H. S. Ede 30.8.1930. Bodleian R (transcript).
43. T. E. Lawrence to H. Williamson 6.9.1930 partly in *MB* p. 442. University of Exeter.
44. R. R. Graves in *B:RG* p. 165.
45. At one point in this complicated relationship Laura Riding had attempted to commit suicide by jumping out of a window. Graves had jumped after her (see M. Seymour-Smith, *Robert Graves*, London, Hutchinson, 1982, pp. 166-7).
46. T. E. Lawrence to D. Garnett 4.5.1929 omitted from *DG* p. 658. Bodleian R (transcript).
47. T. E. Lawrence to R. V. Buxton 10.9.1930. Jesus College, Oxford.
48. T. E. Lawrence to F. N. Doubleday 18.9.1930 *DG* pp. 698-701; *MB* pp. 444-6.
49. T. E. Lawrence to C. F. Shaw 5.10.1930. BL Add. MS 45904.
50. Ironically, when Lawrence had suggested that one of the new airships should cross the Empty Quarter of Arabia, Thomson had considered including him in the crew.
51. T. E. Lawrence to R. V. Buxton 5.10.1930. Jesus College, Oxford.
52. T. E. Lawrence to F. E. Hardy 24.10.1930. Bodleian R (transcript).
53. T. E. Lawrence to B. Rogers 1.11.1930. Houghton bMS Eng 1252 (184)
54. T. E. Lawrence to C. F. Shaw 26.11.1930. BL Add. MS 45904.
55. T. E. Lawrence to B. Rogers 2.12.1930. Houghton bMS Eng 1252 (187).
56. T. E. Lawrence to E. Thurtle 28.11.1930 *DG* p. 707.
57. *Hansard*, House of Commons, Vol. 246, Col 308, 10.12.1930.
58. T. E. Lawrence to B. H. Liddell Hart 11.12.1930 *B:LH* p. 42.
59. T. E. Lawrence to C. F. Shaw 5.12.1930 *MB* p. 447. BL Add. MS 45904.
60. T. E. Lawrence to Sir E. Walker 29.12.1930. Bodleian R (transcript).
61. T. E. Lawrence to H. S. Ede 26.1.1931. Bodleian R (transcript).
62. From the manuscript notes known as 'Leaves in the Wind'. BL Add. MS 46355.
63. T. E. Lawrence to C. F. Shaw 6.2.1931 *MB* p. 449. BL Add. MS 45904.
64. *Ibid.*
65. Inquest of the Iris Flying Boat crash, 18.2.1931. Press cutting from an unidentified newspaper, 19.2.1931.
66. T. E. Lawrence to B. Rogers 25.2.1931. Houghton bMSEng 1252 (190).

Chapter 43. A Taste of Freedom
February 1931 – March 1933

1. Scott-Paine had been managing director of the Supermarine aircraft company in Southampton during the First World War, when the company manufactured seaplanes. He had left Supermarine in 1923 and founded the British Power Boat Company in 1931. He had also run a commercial flying-boat service, and was on the board of Imperial Airways.
2. Scott-Paine was by this time building planing hulls of the hard-chine type, a very light and economical method of construction.
3. *The Times* (London) 12.3.1931.
4. T. E. Lawrence to C. F. Shaw 26.3.1931. BL Add. MS 45905.
5. Report drafted by T. E. Lawrence (signed K. B. Lloyd, Squadron Leader, Mount Batten) 2.3.1931, printed in G. G. Pilborough, *The History of the Royal Air Force Marine Craft 1918-1986* Appendix 1b, *The 200 Class Seaplane Tender* (London, Canimpex, 1986) p. 126.
6. T. E. Lawrence to D. Knowles 19.4.1931 *DG* pp. 720-1.
7. T. E. Lawrence to C. F. Shaw 26.4.1931. BL Add. MS 45905.
8. *Ibid.*
9. T. E. Lawrence to Bruce Rogers 16.4.1931. Houghton bMS Eng 1252 (191)
10. T. E. Lawrence, draft notes on the *Odyssey*. Houghton bMS Eng 1252 (333). The text differs slightly from the final version, which was printed as a 'Translator's Note' in the published version of his *Odyssey*. The beginning only has been quoted here.
11. B. Rogers to H. W. Kent 24.4.1931 *Printing and Graphic Arts* (Lunenberg, Vermont) Vol. 4 No. 2, May 1956, p. 49.
12. T. E. Lawrence, note on an imaginary autogiro, *B:RG* pp. 168-9. The book for which this was written was *No Decency Left* by Barbara Rich [pseud. of R. R. Graves and L. Riding] (London, Jonathan Cape, 1932)
13. W. E. G. Beauforte-Greenwood to S. Smith 13.5.1931, published in *The Golden Reign* by C. S. Smith: (London, Cassell, 1940) pp. 144-5.
14. T. E. Lawrence to W. E. G. Beauforte-Greenwood 7.6.1931. Bodleian R (transcript).
15. W. E. G. Beauforte-Greenwood to C. H. Scott-Paine 9.6.1931. Bodleian R (transcript).
16. T. E. Lawrence to W. E. G. Beauforte-Greenwood 18.6.1931 *DG* p. 726.
17. T. E. Lawrence to W. E. G. Beauforte-Greenwood 14.7.1931 *DG* pp. 729-30.
18. T. E. Lawrence: final manuscript page of his *Odyssey* translation 15.8.1931. HRHRC Texas (now separated from the manuscript, which is BL Add. MS 45930).
19. T. E. Lawrence to C. F. Shaw 14.10.1931 *MB* p. 458. BL Add. MS 45904.
20. *Ibid.*
21. T. E. Lawrence to W. E. G. Beauforte-Greenwood 29.10.1931. Bodleian R (transcript).
22. T. E. Lawrence to W. E. G. Beauforte-Greenwood 6.11.1931. Bodleian R (transcript).
23. T. E. Lawrence to C. F. Shaw 28.11.1931. BL Add. MS 45904.
24. T. E. Lawrence to F. Manning 2.1.1932. Bodleian R (transcript).
25. *News Chronicle* (London) 8.1.1932.

26. T. E. Lawrence to W. E. G. Beauforte-Greenwood 11.1.1932. Bodleian R (transcript).
27. *Ibid.*
28. T. E. Lawrence to W. E. G. Beauforte-Greenwood 20.1.1932. Bodleian R (transcript).
29. *Ibid.*
30. T. E. Lawrence to G. Brough 7.2.1932. Bodleian R (transcript).
31. T. E. Lawrence to G. Brough 5.3.1932 *DG* p. 739.
32. T. E. Lawrence to C. S. Smith 6.3.1932, C. S. Smith (*op. cit.* note 13 above) pp. 182-3.
33. *Ibid.*
34. See *The Times* (London) 31.3.1932, 'Motor-Boats for the R.A.F.' and 16.4.1932, 'Voyage of an R.A.F. Motor-Boat'. A letter from Lawrence to G. Dawson of 21.4.1932 indicates that these articles were written by the aeronautical correspondent, whose name was Shepherd. However, the very detailed factual content can only have come from Lawrence, who commented to Dawson, somewhat tongue-in-cheek: 'I wonder just how Shepherd did his writing, because he seemed to take no notes, just looked calmly at [the boats] and listened easily – yet all the stuff came out in print, admirably expressed and arranged. It struck me as a little better than most reporting I've met' (Bodleian R, transcript).
35. 'Notes by Captain Beauforte-Greenwood on the introduction to the Royal Air Force of high-speed craft'. AIR 5/1372 fo. 121.
36. T. E. Lawrence to C. F. Shaw, *c.* 18.4.1932. BL Add. MS 45904.
37. T. E. Lawrence, report Air Ministry (S.5) 4.6.1932. Houghton bMS Eng 1252 (105).
38. T. E. Lawrence to C. F. Shaw 14.6.1932. BL Add. MS 45904.
39. T. E. Lawrence to C. F. Shaw 20.8.1932. BL Add. MS 45904.
40. *Ibid.*
41. J. C. Walton to C. W. Orde 19.8.1932. FO 371/16188 fo. 89.
42. *The Writers' and Artists' Year Book 1930* (London, A & C Black, 1930) p. 86.
43. *Sunday Chronicle* (London) 28.8.1932. It has been stated, incorrectly, that press articles at this time had connected Lawrence with the armoured boats. This publicity did not occur until the end of 1933 (see *B:LH* pp. 198-200)
44. T. E. Lawrence to W. S. Burch 6.9.1932 quoted in E. Bishop, *The Debt We Owe* (London, Longmans, 1969) p. 17.
45. T. E. Lawrence to C. F. Shaw 11.10.1932. BL Add. MS 45904.
46. T. E. Lawrence to W. B. Yeats 12.10.1932 *DG* p. 744.
47. T. E. Lawrence to W. Merton 22.10.1932. Houghton bMS Eng 1232 (141).
48. T. E. Lawrence to L. B. Namier 18.10.1932. Bodleian R (transcript).
49. T. E. Lawrence to W. Rothenstein 20.10.1932 *DG* p. 749.
50. T. E. Lawrence to R. White 17.10.1932. Bodleian R (transcript).
51. T. E. Lawrence to C. F. Shaw 21.10.1932. BL Add. MS 45904.
52. T. E. Lawrence to R. A. M. Guy 18.10.1932. Bodleian R (transcript).
53. T. E. Lawrence to C. F. Shaw 24.11.1932. BL Add. MS 45904.
54. T. E. Lawrence to H. J. Cape 26.11.1932. Bodleian R (transcript). HRHRC Texas.
55. T. E. Lawrence to H. J. Cape 16.12.1932. Bodleian R (transcript). HRHRC Texas.
56. T. E. Lawrence to C. S. Smith 16.12.1932, in C. S. Smith (*op. cit.* note 13 above) p. 198.
57. T. E. Lawrence to C. F. Shaw 11.1.1933. BL Add. MS 45904.

58. T. E. Lawrence to Sir P. A. G. D. Sassoon 12.1.1933. Bodleian R (transcript).
59. T. E. Lawrence to B. Rogers 19.12.1932. Houghton bMS Eng 1252 (199).
60. T. E. Lawrence to R. V. Buxton 16.2.1932. Jesus College, Oxford.
61. T. E. Lawrence to G. W. M. Dunn 28.2.1933. Bodleian R (transcript)
62. T. E. Lawrence: application for discharge from the RAF *DG* pp. 762-3.

Chapter 44. Last RAF Duties

March 1933 – February 1935

1. T. E. Lawrence to C. F. Shaw 6.3.1933. BL Add. MS 45904.
2. Sir W. G. H. Salmond to T. E. Lawrence 17.3.1933. Bodleian R (transcript).
3. T. E. Lawrence to Sir P. A. G. D. Sassoon 30.3.1933 *DG* pp. 764-5.
4. T. E. Lawrence to C. S. Smith 3.4.1933, quoted in C. S. Smith, *The Golden Reign* (London, Cassell, 1940) p.207.
5. Extract from Lawrence's RAF personal file. Bodleian R (transcript).
6. T. E. Lawrence to C. F. Shaw 24.4.1933. BL Add. MS 45904.
7. Eventually, however, the job was given to Corporal Bradbury, on Lawrence's recommendation.
8. Published as *Garroot, the Adventures of a Clydeside Apprentice* by Ian McKinnon [pseudonym of Ian Tyre] (London, Jonathan Cape, 1933).
9. T. E. Lawrence to K. W. Marshall 19.8.1933. Bodleian R (transcript).
10. T. E. Lawrence to Viscountess Astor 1.6.1933. Reading University Library.
11. T. E. Lawrence to C. F. Shaw 3.10.1933. BL Add. MS 45904.
12. T. E. Lawrence to C. F. Shaw 31.8.1933 *MB* p. 476. BL Add. MS 45904.
13. T. E. Lawrence to his mother 27.9.1933 *HL* pp. 381-2. Bodleian MS Res C13.
14. Much of this information was later published in *B:LH*.
15. T. E. Lawrence to C. F. Shaw 16.6.1933. BL Add. MS 45904.
16. T. E. Lawrence to C. F. Shaw 25.6.1933. BL Add. MS 45904.
17. T. E. Lawrence to C. F. Shaw 29.6.1933. BL Add. MS 45904.
18. B. H. Liddell Hart to T. E. Lawrence 13.7.1933. Bodleian R (transcript).
19. T. E. Lawrence to B. H. Liddell Hart 26.7.1933 *B:LH* p. 75.
20. T. E. Lawrence to C. F. Shaw 23.8.1933. BL Add. MS 45904.
21. T. E. Lawrence to C. F. Shaw 3.10.1933. BL Add. MS 45904.
22. T. E. Lawrence to his mother 17.4.1934 *HL* p. 392. Bodleian MS Res C13.
23. B. H. Liddell Hart to T. E. Lawrence 13.7.1933. Bodleian R. (transcript).
24. T. E. Lawrence to E. M. Forster 7.10.1933. King's College, Cambridge.
25. A. L. Snagge to T. E. Lawrence 21.6.1933. Bodleian R (transcript).
26. T. E. Lawrence to A. L. Snagge 5.7.1933 *DG* p. 770. See also K. Scott (Lady Kennett), *Self-Portrait of an Artist* (London, John Murray, 1949) pp. 295-6, where her diary entry for 7.7.1933 is quoted. That day she met Feisal who told her that he had lunched the previous day with Lawrence and other wartime comrades. References in the press suggest that Lawrence may have seen Feisal several times during Feisal's stay in London.
27. T. E. Lawrence to David Garnett 3.11.1933. Bodleian R (transcript).
28. T. E. Lawrence to K. W. Marshall 17.11.1933. Bodleian R (transcript).
29. Undated press cutting from an unidentified newspaper, late November or early December 1933. Author's collection.
30. T. E. Lawrence to B. H. Liddell Hart, early December 1933 *B:LH* p. 199.

31. T. E. Lawrence to C. F. Shaw 9.12.1933 *MB* p. 478. BL Add. MS 45904. The quotation cited by Lawrence is from Samuel Taylor Coleridge, and refers to the stars: 'And everywhere the blue sky belongs to them, and is their appointed rest and their native country and their natural homes, which they enter unannounced, as lords that are certainly expected, and yet there is a silent joy at their arrival' ('The Rime of the Ancient Mariner'). Lawrence frequently alluded to this passage when writing about man's conquest of the air, but he had liked it for a long time: it is echoed in a letter to V. W. Richards of 15.7.1918 (*DG* p. 245).

32. T. E. Lawrence to A. S. Frere-Reeves 25.9.1933. RAF Museum, Hendon.

33. T. E. Lawrence to G. W. Howard 20.12.1933. Bodleian R (transcript).

34. *Ibid.*

35. T. E. Lawrence to Viscountess Astor 31.12.1933 *DG* p. 788; *MB* p. 481. Reading University Library.

36. T. E. Lawrence to H. S. Ede 31.12.1933. Bodleian R (transcript).

37. *Ibid.*

38. T. E. Lawrence to K. W. Marshall 20.3.1934. Bodleian R (transcript).

39. T. E. Lawrence to his mother 21.3.1934 *HL* p. 387. Bodleian MS Res C13.

40. T. E. Lawrence to his mother 6.4.1934 *HL* pp. 388-9. Bodleian MS Res C13.

41. 'Aircraftman Shaw : Help in preparing Ship for Far East Trip', *Daily Mail* (London) 29.3.1934.

42. T. E. Lawrence to B. H. Liddell Hart 7.4.1934 *B:LH* p. 212.

43. *Daily Express* (London) 5.3.1934.

44. T. E. Lawrence to W. Fontana 2.5.1934. Bodleian R (transcript).

45. T. E. Lawrence to W. Fontana 17.5.1934. Bodleian R (transcript).

46. T. E. Lawrence to C. F. Shaw 18.5.1934 *MB* p. 489. BL Add. MS 45904.

47. T. E. Lawrence to 'Captain L.-J.' 12.5.1934. Photocopy in author's possession.

48. T. E. Lawrence to 'Captain L.-J.' 17.5.1934. Photocopy in author's possession.

49. S. F. Carter to B. H. Liddell Hart 26.11.1934. Liddell Hart papers 9/13/69 KCL.

50. B. H. Liddell Hart to S. F. Carter 10.12.1934. Liddell Hart papers 9/13/69 KCL.

51. Sir O. E. Mosley, *My Life* (London, Nelson, 1968) p. 226.

52. See T. E. Lawrence to F. Rodd 23.11.1934 *DG* p. 830. For an account of this extraordinary proposal see A. Boyle, *Montagu Norman* (London, Cassell, 1967) pp. 296-7.

53. T. E. Lawrence to an unidentified recipient 16.11.1934. Houghton bMS Eng 1252 (267).

54. T. E. Lawrence to H. Williamson 20.12.1934. Exeter University Library.

55. T. E. Lawrence to Viscount Carlow 14.9.1934 *DG* p. 819.

56. T. E. Lawrence to C. F. Shaw 31.12.1934 *MB* p. 510. BL Add. MS 45904.

57. T. E. Lawrence to B. H. Liddell Hart 12.9.1934 *B:LH* p. 225.

58. T. E. Lawrence to H. J. Cape 6.8.1934. Bodleian R (transcript).

59. T. E. Lawrence to H. J. Cape 3.5.1934. Bodleian R (transcript).

60. T. E. Lawrence to C. F. Shaw 16.11.1934 *MB* p. 498. BL Add. MS 45904.

61. T. E. Lawrence to F. Manning 16.11.1934 *MB* p. 499. Bodleian R (transcript).

62. T. E. Lawrence to R. A. M. Guy 31.1.1935. Houghton bMS Eng 1252 (117).

63. T. E. Lawrence to E. Spurr 31.1.1935. Bodleian R (transcript). Many years later it was claimed that Lawrence had been closely involved in Edward Spurr's schemes to build a new kind of high-speed boat (see H. F. King 'Another Lawrence' in *Flight International*, London, February 1966). I have found no contemporary evidence

whatsoever to support the extraordinary statements made in this article and in subsequent references to the subject elsewhere. While there is no doubt that Lawrence knew Spurr, their first encounter seems to have taken place very late in Lawrence's service career and it is impossible that Lawrence met him on many occasions. The close working partnership that has been alleged cannot in reality have taken place, either before or after Lawrence left the RAF. Moreover, none of Lawrence's enthusiastic letters about the design of high-speed marine craft refer to the design principles used in the prototype Spurr built, three years after Lawrence's death. The most probable explanation of the Spurr-Lawrence association is that Spurr felt encouraged by some conversations he had had with Lawrence at a very early stage in his thinking about the new design. The Spurr prototype was not very successful, and it is difficult to see how its design could have been used in applications other than speed record attempts (a boat built on this principle could not easily turn at speed). Some writers have described Spurr's design as a hovercraft, but this is incorrect. Spurr's patents refer to the aerodynamic lift of aerofoil hull sections, but do not (despite H. F. King's claims) even appear to envisage the principle known as a ram wing (which creates lift by trapping air in a wedge-shaped slot between the hull and the water surface when the boat is travelling at speed). Talk of Lawrence's involvement in forerunners of surface effect ships or hovercraft is fantasy.

64. T. E. Lawrence to C. F. Shaw 26.1.1935 *MB* pp. 515-6. BL Add. MS 45904.
65. *Ibid. MB* p. 516.
66. T. E. Lawrence to R. R. Graves 4.2.1935 *DG* pp. 851-3; *MB* pp. 520-2; *B:RG* pp. 181-3.
67. T. E. Lawrence to E. Garnett 23.12.1927. Bodleian R (transcript).
68. *Sunday Express* (London) 17.2.1935. Lawrence's letter to T. W. Beaumont of 31.1.1935 is printed in *MB* p. 517.
69. T. E. Lawrence to W. Merton 24.2.1935. Bodleian R (transcript).
70. T. E. Lawrence to P. Knowles 20.2.1935 *DG* p. 857.

Chapter 45. Clouds Hill

March – May 1935

1. T. E. Lawrence to T. W. Beaumont 25.2.1935. Bodleian R (transcript).
2. *Evening Standard*, London, 2.3.1935.
3. T. E. Lawrence to P. Davies 28.2.1935 *DG* p. 859; *MB* pp. 525-6.
4. T. E. Lawrence to S. C. Cockerell 6.3.1935. Bodleian R (transcript).
5. T. E. Lawrence to T. B. Marson 6.3.1935. Bodleian R (transcript).
6. T. E. Lawrence to P. Knowles 19.3.1935 *DG* p. 862.
7. T. E. Lawrence to W. S. Churchill 19.3.1935 *Winston Churchill* Vol. V, Companion Part 2, Documents, (London, Heinemann, 1981) pp. 1120-1; *MB* p. 528.
8. T. E. Lawrence to the Hon. E. Harmsworth, undated draft, *DG* pp. 860-1.
9. T. E. Lawrence to Sir J. E. L. Wrench 1.4.1935 *MB* p. 530. Bodleian R (transcript).
10. J. Buchan to T. E. Lawrence 12.3.1935 *LTEL* pp. 21-2.
11. T. E. Lawrence to J. Buchan 1.4.1935 *DG* pp. 862-3.
12. T. E. Lawrence to G. Brough *DG* p. 867; *MB* p. 530.
13. T. E. Lawrence to H. S. Ede 5.4.1935 *DG* pp. 865-6.
14. T. E. Lawrence to E. Plamer 5.4.1935. Bodleian R (transcript).

15. T. E. Lawrence to T. E. Willis. Bodleian R (transcript).
16. T. E. Lawrence to T. B. Marson 6.4.1935. Bodleian R (transcript).
17. T. E. Lawrence to R. V. Buxton 13.4.1935 partially omitted from *MB* pp. 531-2. Jesus College, Oxford.
18. T. E. Lawrence to Bruce Rogers 6.5.1935 *MB* p. 536. Houghton bMS Eng 1252 (210).
19. T. E. Lawrence to E. M. Forster 7.5.1935 *DG* p. 871. King's College, Cambridge.
20. Viscountess Astor to T. E. Lawrence 7.5.1935. Bodleian R (transcript, misdated 7.4.1934).
21. T. E. Lawrence to Viscountess Astor 8.5.1935 *DG* p. 972; *MB* p. 537. Reading University Library.
22. T. E. Lawrence to K. T. Parker 12.5.1935 *MB* p. 540. Bodleian R (transcript)
23. T. E. Lawrence to H. Williamson, telegram, 13.5.1935 *DG* p. 872. In 1937, Henry Williamson claimed that this telegram had been sent in response to a letter suggesting that Lawrence should meet Hitler (*Friends* p. 455). This claim is now known to have been completely fictitious. The letter to which Lawrence was replying contained no mention of Hitler. Moreover, Williamson himself did not become closely involved with fascism until two years after Lawrence's death.

Envoi

Page 937

T. E. Lawrence to F. Manning 15.5.1930 *DG* p. 693. The statement that Lawrence did not believe finally in the Arab movement must refer to his rejection of the ambition held by Hussein and others for a united Arab state embracing Syria, Mesopotamia, and the Arabian Peninsula.

Page 938

Sir A. T. Wilson, *Thoughts and Talks, 1935-7* (London, Right Book Club, 1938) p. 33.

J. Buchan, *Memory Hold the Door* (London, Hodder & Stoughton, 1940) p. 229.

C. F. Shaw, quoted in J. Dunbar, *Mrs G.B.S., A Biographical Portrait of Charlotte Shaw* (London, George G. Harrap, 1963) p. 300.

Appendix I

1. The Latin reads '*Crescit sub pondere virtus*'.
2. Lawrence's paternal grandmother was Louisa Vansittart; Robert Vansittart was descended from her father, Arthur Vansittart (1775-1829). On this side of his father's family Lawrence was very well connected. For example, he was descended from the statesman and diplomat William Eden (Baron Auckland, 1744-1814), whose wife, Eleanor Elliott, was a sister of the first Earl of Minto. Had he been able to admit to these family relationships, he would have held a social position that he could never have acquired as 'Lawrence'.
3. Curiously, on Lawrence's birth certificate his mother's family name is given as 'Maden', a name that is mentioned on no other occasion. It has been suggested to me that this probably arose from a misunderstanding. Tremadoc is still, today, in a part of Wales where a large proportion of people speak Welsh. At the time of Lawrence's birth, English would have been little used there and spoken with a strong accent. Lawrence's father spoke with an educated Irish accent, his mother

with a Scots accent. It therefore seems quite likely that when the registrar asked in English for the 'Maiden name' the answer was misunderstood, and the name 'Maden' is simply a corruption of 'Maiden'. Ivor Wynne Jones, who made this suggestion, has told me that such errors were not uncommon.

4. T. R. Lawrence to T. E. Lawrence, draft, 8.3.1916. Bodleian R (transcript).

5. LH:*TEL* p. 14.

Appendix II

1. See p. 115. Source: US National Archives and Records, RG59, Department of State Decimal File, 1910-1929. Several of the place-names in this document have been silently corrected, as the versions in the original typescript were misspelt in a manner which was misleading (e.g. Hauran for Harran).

2. For an account of Ibrahim Pasha's death see C. L. Woolley, *Dead Towns and Living Men* (London, OUP, 1920) p. 186.

3. Lawrence had visited the Sheikh of Harran on 17th-19th July 1911, see 'Diary of a Journey Across the Euphrates' in *OA* pp. 12-20.

Appendix III

1. See p. 277. Source: Typed copy sent by G. F. Clayton to Sir F. R. Wingate, Wingate papers 137/7/4-23, Durham. It is presumed that this typed copy is the 'censored' version of the report.

Appendix IV

1 See p. 435. Source: Lawrence's manuscript, FO 882/7 fos. 93-97.

Acknowledgements

I offer my heartfelt gratitude to the many individuals and institutions who have helped me. I have valued not only their assistance, but also their courtesy and interest which have been a constant source of encouragement.

My thanks go first of all to A. W. Lawrence, who entrusted me with this biography. His support helped to smooth my path on countless occasions, and he has dealt meticulously with my queries.

This book would not have been completed, even now, without the years of work contributed by Dr Lilith Friedman. She has patiently and painstakingly followed up thousands of queries and has remained cheerful even when the search proved fruitless.

I am also greatly indebted to St John Armitage, who found answers to even the most obscure questions about the Arab world and helped in many other ways. His criticisms of the draft were invaluable.

During the final stages of research and writing I was joined by a succession of short-term postgraduate assistants: Ian Wood, John Vice, Jonathan Newell, Maria White, Jonathan Law, Vincent Landon, and Martin Rowe. Two of them, Ian Wood and Jonathan Law, stayed for more than a year, and their contributions have been proportionately greater. All, however, brought a lively enthusiasm, good humour, and a great deal of effort. I am indebted to Miss Sally Hirst of the Oxford University Appointments Committee and to Brian Holden Reid of Kings College, London, for help in recruiting them.

Special thanks go to my editors at Heinemann, Dan Franklin and Jane Carr, for their encouragement and constructive criticism. I hope that this book will be some reward for their skill and exemplary patience. I am also grateful to several people who read and commented on the draft, notably Jonathan Law, Hilary Hockman, my father, Professor Clifford Wilson, Lawrie Hooley, and Peter and Barbara Metcalfe. In addition, sections of the book have been seen by A. W. Lawrence, Maurice Larès, Allen Mandelbaum, Jonathan Mandelbaum, John Randle, and several specialists in the history of the Middle East. In many instances I have been able to adopt their suggestions, to the reader's benefit.

I could not have attempted to index a story as complex as this one. I am therefore extremely grateful to Hazel Bell, who tackled the job with impressive skill. I owe her not merely thanks but an immense apology, having halted her work for several months while I rewrote fifteen chapters in the middle of the book. I am also grateful to Neil Hyslop, who provided exactly the maps I had hoped for.

Special acknowledgement is due to Imogen Parker and Rachel Calder of Curtis Brown, who made it possible for me to write this book in the way I wished. Finally, I owe an incalculable debt to my wife and children for their encouragement, help, and understanding.

The following people and institutions have contributed in one way or another to this project, and I offer each of them my sincere thanks: J. B. Acres; The Rev. Dennis Ackroyd; the Air Historical Branch; J. G. Simmons of All Souls College, Oxford; The Ashmolean Museum, Oxford; Earl Baldwin of Bewdley; Patrick Bannerman; Nicolas Barker; R. D. Barnett; Robert Barrett; Caroline Barron; Miriam Benkovitz; Jean Béraud Villars; Nicholas Birnie; Dave Blunden; Denis Boak; many members of the staff of the Bodleian Library but especially D. S. Porter; René Boudet; T. F. Brenchley; the staff of the British Library; the staff of the Department of Western Asiatic Antiquities at the British Museum; Janet Wallace, archivist at the British Museum; C. L. Brook; Cambridge University Library; M. V. Carey, one of the Trustees of the *Seven Pillars of Wisdom* Trust; A. E. Chambers; the staff of the Churchill Archives Centre, Churchill College, Cambridge; the Comptroller and City Solicitor of the City of London; the *Daily Express*; Dartmouth College Library, New Hampshire; Lord Deedes; R. N. R. Peers of the Dorset Natural History and Archaeological Society; Christopher Dowling; John Dreyfus; H. S. Ede; Malcolm Escombe; Anne Fisher; the Fitzwilliam Museum, Cambridge; Jack and Anne Flavell; J. D. Fleeman; R. Forbes-Morgan; Peter Fowler; P. N. Furbank; the librarian, Gonville and Caius College, Cambridge; Graham C. Greene; Dee Gue; Les Gunnell; David Gunston; Rosemary Hallsmith; D. B. Harden; Rodney G. Dennis and other members of staff at the Houghton Library, Harvard; W. Heffer and Sons; George Hilton; H. J. Hodgson; G. W. Holderness; Michael Holroyd; Peter and Kath Hopkirk; the staff of the Library of the House of Lords; Guyla Houston; Major E. S. Humphreys and his son Lt. Col D. M. Humphreys; the Imperial War Museum; Israel State Archives; Peter Janson Smith; the staff of the Liddell Hart centre for Military Archives, King's College, London; Crispin Jameson; D. A. Rees of Jesus College, Oxford; Christopher Kennington; Lord Kennet; John Kerr; King's College, Cambridge; Phillip Knightley; Mary M. Lago; Stanhope Landick; Maurice Larès; F. C. Lay; Hugh Leach; Julian Leeds; Lewis Leeds; Cole

Lesley; Lady Liddell Hart; Adrian Liddell Hart; John E. Mack; Magdalen College, Oxford; Edward Maggs; Jonathan Mandelbaum; Peter Metcalfe; Elizabeth Monroe; H. Montgomery Hyde; James Moran; P. R. S. Moorey; Konrad Morsey; Suleiman Mousa; Oscar Muscarella; the National Army Museum; the National Library of Scotland; the National Library of Wales; the National Maritime Museum; Robin Gibson and Honor Clerk of the National Portrait Gallery; The National Trust; Rodney Needham; Desmond Neill; the New York Public Library; The State University of New York at Buffalo; Newcastle University Library; Sir Michael Newton; G. W. Nichols; Philip M. O'Brien; Oxford City Library; the Oxford School; the Oxford Union; Oxford University Archives; Oxford University Local Examinations Board; Gladys Page; Rupert Chapman and other staff of the Palestine Exploration Fund; Robert Payne; Bob Pearson; Penguin Books; Brian D. Price; Princeton University Library; Denys Pringle; the staff of the Public Record Office, London; Purdue University Libraries; Douglas Library, Queen's University, Kingston, Ontario; Reading University Library; Lord Rennell; The Rev J. S. Reynolds; Rhodes House, Oxford; Adrian Rance; Arabella Rivington; Ruth M. Robbins; Anthony Rota; Rona Roy; the Royal Agricultural College, Cirencester; RAF Mount Batten; the Commanding Officer, RAF Uxbridge; the RAF Museum, Hendon; the Royal Archives, Windsor Castle; the Royal Armouries; the Royal Artillery Institution; the Royal Society for Asian Affairs; the Royal Tank Corps Museum, Bovington, the Royal United Services Institute; the library and archives staff at the Middle East Centre, St Antony's College, Oxford; C. Morgenstern of St John's College, Oxford; Frances Say; Peter T. Scott; Basil E. Sebley; John Sherwood; John Sims; G. Stott; the Society of Authors; Sotheby & Co.; Ian Taylor; Sue Thatcher-Brown; Valerie Thompson; *The Times*; Lesley Forbes and other members of staff at the library of the University of Durham; the staff of London University Library; the Museum of the History of Science, University of Oxford; the staff of the Harry Ransom Humanities Research Center, University of Texas at Austin; the Victoria and Albert Museum; the Weizmann Archives; Hugh Williamson; Richard Windsor and his staff; Ivor Wynne Jones; Worcester College, Oxford; the Beinecke Rare Book and Manuscript Library, Yale University; A. J. Young, and Geoffrey Young. I fear that this list may be incomplete, and offer both thanks and apologies to anyone I have overlooked. Moreover, I am no less grateful to those who took the trouble to reply to my enquiries even though they were unable to help.

For the use of copyright material and papers from particular collections I gratefully acknowledge the kind permission of the following: The Literary Executors of Lady Astor; Samuel French Ltd and the Literary Estate of J. M. Barrie (unpublished letter Copyright © the Literary Estate of J. M. Barrie 1989); General Sir Hugh Beach (for W. H. Beach); The Trustees of the British Museum (for material from various British Museum archives); Curtis Brown Ltd, London, and the Estate of Sir Winston Churchill (for the letter from Winston Churchill to T. E. Lawrenc, the extract from Churchill's speech to the Oxford High School, and the extract from Churchill's *Life of Lord Randolph Churchill*). The Controller of Her Majesty's Stationery Office (for Crown Copyright material in the Public Record Office and elsewhere); Lord Deedes (for W. H. Deedes); Gonville and Caius College, Cambridge (for C. M. Doughty); John Sherwood (for James Elroy Flecker); King's College, Cambridge, Executor of the E. M. Forster Estate (for E. M. Forster); The Literary Estate of Edward Garnett; A. P. Watt Limited for the Estate of Robert Graves; extracts from unpublished letters Copyright © The Estate of Robert Graves 1989; The Estate of Aubrey Herbert (for material from the Aubrey Herbert papers); Dr Caroline Barron (for D. G. Hogarth and L. V. Hogarth); The India Office Library and Records (for Crown Copyright papers in the India Office Library); The Fellows of Jesus College, Oxford (for material from the Jesus College Archives); Jonathan Cape Ltd and the *Seven Pillars of Wisdom* Trust (for passages from Lawrence's letters and the 1922 draft of *Seven Pillars of Wisdom* by T. E. Lawrence, unpublished text Copyright © the *Seven Pillars of Wisdom* Trust 1989, and also from *T. E. Lawrence to his Biographers Robert Graves and Liddell Hart*, copyright 1938, renewed © 1965, and from *T. E. Lawrence by his Friends*); Professor A. W. Lawrence, Jonathan Cape Ltd., Doubleday, and the *Seven Pillars of Wisdom* Trust for passages from *The Mint*, Copyright © 1936, 1955 by Doubleday, a division of Bantam Doubleday Dell Publishing Group, Inc. Doubleday, for passages from *Seven Pillars of Wisdom* by T. E. Lawrence, Copyright 1926, 1935 by Doubleday, a division of Bantam Doubleday Dell Publishing Group, Inc.; The Bodleian Library, Oxford, and the Houghton Library, Harvard (for papers from their respective T. E. Lawrence collections); The Trustees of the Liddell Hart Centre for Military Archives, King's College, London (for material from the Liddell Hart papers, the Akaba Archive, and the H. W. Young papers); Lady Lloyd and Churchill College, Cambridge (for material from the Lord Lloyd papers); The Palestine Exploration Fund (for archive material); The Trustees of the Will of Mrs Bernard Shaw (for Charlotte Shaw); The Society of Authors on behalf of the Bernard Shaw Estate (for Bernard Shaw); unpublished Shaw letter Copyright © The Bernard Shaw Estate 1989. Durham University Library (for material from the Sudan Archive and from the Clayton Papers); The Royal Air Force Museum, Hendon (for the papers of Lord Trenchard); Viscount Samuel (for Herbert Samuel); The Estate of Lord Wester Wemyss and Churchill College, Cambridge (for material from the Wemyss papers); United States National Archives and Records (for the report by F. Willoughby Smith). At the time of writing I have been unable to trace the executors of S. F. Carter, H. A. Manhood, and A. L. Snagge, and I apologise to them and to any other copyright owners I have inadvertently overlooked. If they will contact me I will do my best to make amends. Brief quotations from published works are not listed separately above, and I gratefully acknowledge the owners of these copy- rights. The source of material from all published works is stated in the references and has not been repeated here.

The illustrations have been reproduced by kind permission of the following: The Bodleian Library, Oxford (for photographs from the T. E. Lawrence papers); The Trustees of the British Museum (for photographs and drawings from Carchemish, and of Hypnos); Dr. Maurice Larès; The Trustees of the Liddell Hart Centre for Military Archives (for the photograph of Lawrence, Churchill, and Gertrude Bell at Cairo); The Hulton Picture Company (for the Cairo Conference group); Magdalen College, Oxford (for Lawrence's sketch for *Crusader Castles*); the family of Janet Laurie; Merton College, Oxford (for the OTC group); The Ashmolean Museum, Oxford (for Lawrence and Hogarth by A. John; Lawrence by W. Roberts); B. D. Thompson (for Dahoum by Dodd); The Imperial War Museum (for photographs from their T. E. Lawrence collection and the last radio message from Kut); The National Portrait Gallery (for Lawrence by A. John; Lawrence by H. Coster; Lord Allenby by E. Kennington; Lord Trenchard; Doughty by A. John); John Sims for the photograph of T. E. Lawrence by Wing Commander R. G. Sims; Rolls-Royce Motor Cars Ltd. (for Lawrence entering Damascus); Associated Press (for Mrs Shaw); The National Trust (for plans of Clouds Hill); a private collector for the head-and-shoulders sketch of Lawrence in uniform by A. John. The Fitzwilliam Museum Cambridge (for Thomas Hardy by A. John); other illustrations are from the author's collection.

Index